New Perspectives on

Microsoft®
Visual Basic® 5.0
for Windows®

COMPREHENSIVE

The New Perspectives Series

The New Perspectives Series consists of texts and technology that teach computer concepts and microcomputer applications (listed below). You can order these New Perspectives texts in many different lengths, software releases, custom-bound combinations, CourseKits™ and Custom Editions®. Contact your Course Technology sales representative or customer service representative for the most up-to-date details.

The New Perspectives Series

Computer Concepts

Borland® dBASE®

Borland® Paradox®

Corel® Presentations™

Corel® Quattro Pro®

Corel® WordPerfect®

DOS

HTML

Lotus® 1-2-3®

Microsoft® Access

Microsoft® Excel

Microsoft® Internet Explorer

Microsoft® Office Professional

Microsoft® PowerPoint®

Microsoft® Visual Basic® 4.0

Microsoft® Visual Basic® 5.0

Microsoft® Windows® 3.1

Microsoft® Windows® 95

Microsoft® Windows NT® Server 4.0

Microsoft® Windows NT® Workstation 4.0

Microsoft® Word

Microsoft® Works

Netscape Navigator™

Netscape Navigator™ Gold

New Perspectives on
Microsoft®
Visual Basic® 5.0
for Windows®

Michael V. Ekedahl

William A. Newman
University of Nevada—Las Vegas

COURSE TECHNOLOGY

ONE MAIN STREET, CAMBRIDGE, MA 02142

an International Thomson Publishing company I(T)P®

Cambridge • Albany • Bonn • Boston • Cincinnati • London • Madrid • Melbourne • Mexico City
New York • Paris • San Francisco • Singapore • Tokyo • Toronto • Washington

New Perspectives on Microsoft Visual Basic 5.0 for Windows®—Comprehensive is published by Course Technology.

Associate Publisher	Mac Mendelsohn
Series Consulting Editor	Susan Solomon
Product Manager	Cindy Johnson
Developmental Editor	Kathleen Habib
Production Editor	Jean Bermingham
Text and Cover Designer	Ella Hanna
Cover Illustrator	Douglas Goodman

© 1998 by Course Technology—I(T)P®

For more information contact:

Course Technology
One Main Street
Cambridge, MA 02142

ITP Europe
Berkshire House 168-173
High Holborn
London WCIV 7AA
England

Nelson ITP, Australia
102 Dodds Street
South Melbourne, 3205
Victoria, Australia

ITP Nelson Canada
1120 Birchmount Road
Scarborough, Ontario
Canada M1K 5G4

International Thomson Editores
Seneca, 53
Colonia Polanco
11560 Mexico D.F. Mexico

ITP GmbH
Königswinterer Strasse 418
53227 Bonn
Germany

ITP Asia
60 Albert Street, #15-01
Albert Complex
Singapore 189969

ITP Japan
Hirakawacho Kyowa Building, 3F
2-2-1 Hirakawacho
Chiyoda-ku, Tokyo 102
Japan

Trademarks
Course Technology and the Open Book logo are registered trademarks and CourseKits is a trademark of Course Technology. Custom Editions is a registered trademark of International Thomson Publishing.

I(T)P® The ITP logo is a registered trademark of International Thomson Publishing.

Microsoft, Visual Basic, and Windows are registered trademarks of Microsoft Corporation in the United States and/or other countries. Course Technology is an independent entity from Microsoft Corporation, and not affiliated with Microsoft in any manner.

Some of the product names and company names used in this book have been used for identification purposes only and may be trademarks or registered trademarks of their respective manufacturers and sellers.

Disclaimer
Course Technology reserves the right to revise this publication and make changes from time to time in its content without notice.

ISBN 0-7600-4668-9

Printed in the United States of America

1 2 3 4 5 6 7 8 9   01 00 99 98 97

At Course Technology we have one foot in education and the other in technology. We believe that technology is transforming the way people teach and learn, and we are excited about providing instructors and students with materials that use technology to teach about technology.

Our development process is unparalleled in the higher education publishing industry. Every product we create goes through an exacting process of design, development, review, and testing.

Reviewers give us direction and insight that shape our manuscripts and bring them up to the latest standards. Every manuscript is quality tested. Students whose backgrounds match the intended audience work through every keystroke, carefully checking for clarity and pointing out errors in logic and sequence. Together with our own technical reviewers, these testers help us ensure that everything that carries our name is error-free and easy to use.

We show both how and why technology is critical to solving problems in college and in whatever field you choose to teach or pursue. Our time-tested, step-by-step instructions provide unparalleled clarity. Examples and applications are chosen and crafted to motivate students.

As the New Perspectives Series team at Course Technology, our goal is to produce the most timely, accurate, creative, and technologically sound product in the entire college publishing industry. We strive for consistent high quality. This takes a lot of communication, coordination, and hard work. But we love what we do. We are determined to be the best. Write us and let us know what you think. You can also e-mail us at **NewPerspectives@course.com**.

The New Perspectives Series Team

Joseph J. Adamski	Jessica Evans	Mac Mendelsohn
Judy Adamski	Marilyn Freedman	William Newman
Roy Ageloff	Kathy Finnegan	Dan Oja
Tim Ashe	Robin Geller	David Paradice
David Auer	Donna Gridley	June Parsons
Daphne Barbas	Kate Habib	Harry Phillips
Dirk Baldwin	Roger Hayen	Sandra Poindexter
Jean Bermingham	Charles Hommel	Mark Reimold
Rachel Bunin	Cindy Johnson	Ann Shaffer
Joan Carey	Janice Jutras	Karen Shortill
Patrick Carey	Chris Kelly	Susan Solomon
Sharon Caswell	Mary Kemper	Susanne Walker
Barbara Clemens	Stacy Klein	John Zeanchock
Rachel Crapser	Terry Ann Kremer	Beverly Zimmerman
Kim Crowley	John Leschke	Scott Zimmerman
Michael Ekedahl		

Preface The New Perspectives Series

What is the New Perspectives Series?

Course Technology's **New Perspectives Series** is an integrated system of instruction that combines text and technology products to teach computer concepts and microcomputer applications. Users consistently praise this series for innovative pedagogy, creativity, supportive and engaging style, accuracy, and use of interactive technology. The first New Perspectives text was published in January of 1993. Since then, the series has grown to more than 100 titles and has become the best-selling series on computer concepts and microcomputer applications. Others have imitated the New Perspectives features, design, and technologies, but none have replicated its quality and its ability to consistently anticipate and meet the needs of instructors and students.

What is the Integrated System of Instruction?

New Perspectives textbooks are part of a truly Integrated System of Instruction: text, graphics, video, sound, animation, and simulations that are linked and that provide a flexible, unified, and interactive system to help you teach and help your students learn. Specifically, the *New Perspectives Integrated System of Instruction* includes a Course Technology textbook in addition to some or all of the following items: Course Labs, Course Test Manager, Online Companions, and Course Presenter. These components— shown in the graphic on the back cover of this book—have been developed to work together to provide a complete, integrative teaching and learning experience.

How is the New Perspectives Series different from other microcomputer concepts and applications series?

The **New Perspectives Series** distinguishes itself from other series in at least four substantial ways: sound instructional design, consistent quality, innovative technology, and proven pedagogy. The applications texts in this series consist of two or more tutorials, which are based on sound instructional design. Each tutorial is motivated by a realistic case that is meaningful to students. Rather than learn a laundry list of features, students learn the features in the context of solving a problem. This process motivates all concepts and skills by demonstrating to students *why* they would want to know them.

Instructors and students have come to rely on the high quality of the **New Perspectives Series** and to consistently praise its accuracy. This accuracy is a result of Course Technology's unique multi-step quality assurance process that incorporates student testing at at least two stages of development, using hardware and software configurations appropriate to the product. All solutions, test questions, and other supplements are tested using similar procedures. Instructors who adopt this series report that students can work through the tutorials independently with minimum intervention or "damage control" by instructors or staff. This consistent quality has meant that if instructors are pleased with one product from the series, they can rely on the same quality with any other New Perspectives product.

The **New Perspectives Series** also distinguishes itself by its innovative technology. This series innovated Course Labs, truly *interactive* learning applications. These have set the standard for interactive learning.

How do I know that the New Perspectives Series will work?

Some instructors who use this series report a significant difference between how much their students learn and retain with this series as compared to other series. With other series, instructors often find that students can work through the book and do well on homework and tests, but still not demonstrate competency when asked to perform particular tasks outside the context of the text's sample case or project. With the **New Perspectives Series**, however, instructors report that students have a complete, integrative learning experience that stays with them. They credit this high retention and competency to the fact that this series incorporates critical thinking and problem-solving with computer skills mastery.

How does this book I'm holding fit into the New Perspectives Series?

New Perspectives applications books are available in the following categories:

Brief books are typically about 150 pages long, contain two to four tutorials, and are intended to teach the basics of an application.

Introductory books are typically about 300 pages long and consist of four to seven tutorials that go beyond the basics. These books often build out of the Brief editions by providing two or three additional tutorials.

Comprehensive books are typically about 600 pages long and consist of all of the tutorials in the Introductory books, plus a few more tutorials covering higher-level topics. Comprehensive books typically also include two Windows tutorials and three or four Additional Cases. The book you are holding is a Comprehensive book.

Advanced books cover topics similar to those in the Comprehensive books, but go into more depth. Advanced books present the most high-level coverage in the series.

Custom Books The New Perspectives Series offers you two ways to customize a New Perspectives text to fit your course exactly: *CourseKits*™, two or more texts packaged together in a box, and *Custom Editions*®, your choice of books bound together. Custom Editions offer you unparalleled flexibility in designing your concepts and applications courses. You can build your own book by ordering a combination of titles bound together to cover only the topics you want. Your students save because they buy only the materials they need. There is no minimum order, and books are spiral bound. Both CourseKits and Custom Editions offer significant price discounts. Contact your Course Technology sales representative for more information.

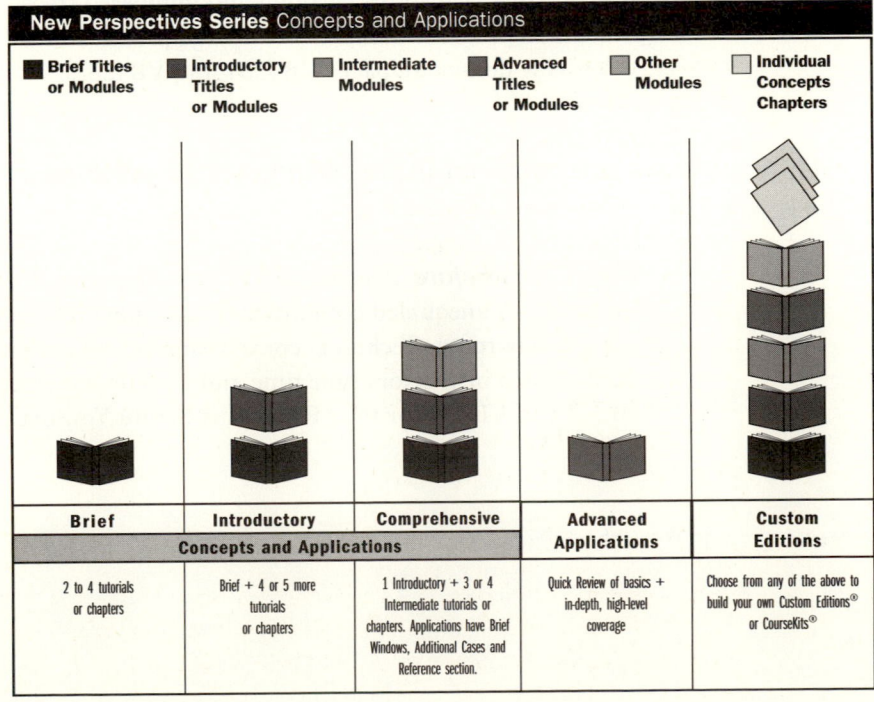

New Perspectives Series Concepts and Applications

Brief Titles or Modules	Introductory Titles or Modules	Intermediate Modules	Advanced Titles or Modules	Other Modules	Individual Concepts Chapters
Brief	**Introductory**	**Comprehensive**	**Advanced Applications**		**Custom Editions**
Concepts and Applications					
2 to 4 tutorials or chapters	Brief + 4 or 5 more tutorials or chapters	1 Introductory + 3 or 4 Intermediate tutorials or chapters. Applications have Brief Windows, Additional Cases and Reference section.	Quick Review of basics + in-depth, high-level coverage		Choose from any of the above to build your own Custom Editions® or CourseKits®

In what kind of course could I use this book?

This book can be used in any course in which you want students to learn all the most important topics of Visual Basic 5.0 for Windows, including working with data from another file or database. Students learn how to plan, program, and debug the Visual Basic applications using modern programming techniques and practicing good graphical user interface. It is particularly recommended for a full-semester course on Visual Basic. This book assumes that students have learned basic Windows 95 navigation and file management skills from Course Technology's *New Perspectives on Microsoft Windows 95—Brief* or an *equivalent* book.

How do the Windows 95 editions differ from the Windows 3.1 editions?

Sessions We've divided the tutorials into sessions. Each session is designed to be completed in about 45 minutes to an hour (depending, of course, upon student needs and the speed of your lab equipment). With sessions, learning is broken up into more easily-assimilated portions. You can more accurately allocate time in your syllabus, and students can better manage the available lab time. Each session begins with a "session box," which quickly describes the skills students will learn in the session. Furthermore, each session is numbered, which makes it easier for you and your students to navigate and communicate about the tutorial. Look on page VB 1.5 for the session box that opens Session 1.1.

Quick Checks Each session concludes with meaningful, conceptual Quick Check questions that test students' understanding of what they learned in the session. Answers to the Quick Check questions in this book are provided on pages VB 6.45 through VB 6.52 and VB 12.49 through VB 12.55.

New Design We have retained the best of the old design to help students differentiate between what they are to *do* and what they are to *read*. The steps are clearly identified by their shaded background and numbered steps. Furthermore, this new design presents steps and screen shots in a larger, easier to read format. Some good examples of our new design are pages VB 2.31 and VB 2.32.

What features are retained in the Windows 95 editions of the New Perspectives Series?

"Read This Before You Begin" Pages These pages are consistent with Course Technology's unequaled commitment to helping instructors introduce technology into the classroom. Technical considerations and assumptions about software are listed to help instructors save time and eliminate unnecessary aggravation. See pages VB 1.2 and VB 7.2 for the "Read This Before You Begin" pages in this book.

Tutorial Case   Each tutorial begins with a problem presented in a case that is meaningful to students. The problem turns the task of learning how to use an application into a problem-solving process. The problems increase in complexity with each tutorial. These cases touch on multicultural, international, and ethical issues—so important to today's business curriculum. See page VB 1.3 for the case that begins Tutorial 1.

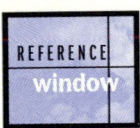

Step-by-Step Methodology   This unique Course Technology methodology keeps students on track. They enter data, click buttons, or press keys always within the context of solving the problem posed in the tutorial case. The text constantly guides students, letting them know where they are in the course of solving the problem. In addition, the numerous screen shots include labels that direct students' attention to what they should look at on the screen. On almost every page in this book, you can find an example of how steps, screen shots, and labels work together.

TROUBLE?

TROUBLE? *Paragraphs*   These paragraphs anticipate the mistakes or problems that students are likely to have and help them recover and continue with the tutorial. By putting these paragraphs in the book, rather than in the Instructor's Manual, we facilitate independent learning and free the instructor to focus on substantive conceptual issues rather than on common procedural errors. Some representative examples of TROUBLE? paragraphs appear on pages VB 1.17 and VB 2.19.

REFERENCE window

Reference Windows   Reference Windows appear throughout the text. They are succinct summaries of the most important tasks covered in the tutorials. Reference Windows are specially designed and written so students can refer to them when doing the Tutorial Assignments and Case Problems, and after completing the course. Page VB 1.28 contains the Reference Window for setting the size and position of a form.

Task Reference   The Task Reference contains a summary of how to perform common tasks using the most efficient method, as well as references to pages where the task is discussed in more detail. It appears as a table at the end of the book.

Tutorial Assignments, Case Problems, and Lab Assignments   Each tutorial concludes with Tutorial Assignments, which provide students with additional hands-on practice of the skills they learned in the tutorial. See page VB 1.44 for examples of Tutorial Assignments. The Tutorial Assignments are followed by four Case Problems that have approximately the same scope as the tutorial case. In the Windows 95 applications texts, the last Case Problem of each tutorial typically requires students to solve the problem independently, either "from scratch" or with minimum guidance. See page VB 1.45 for examples of Case Problems. Finally, if a Course Lab accompanies a tutorial, Lab Assignments are included after the Case Problems. See page VB 1.49 for examples of Lab Assignments.

Additional Cases   Three interactive cases help students incorporate all their knowledge of Microsoft Visual Basic in new, real-life settings.

Exploration Exercises   The Windows environment allows students to learn by exploring and discovering what they can do. Exploration Exercises can be Tutorial Assignments or Case Problems that challenge students, encourage them to explore the capabilities of the program they are using, and extend their knowledge using the Help facility and other reference materials. Page VB 1.45 contains Exploration Exercises for Tutorial 1.

What supplements are available with this textbook?

Student Developer's Kit Students can discover more about Visual Basic's capabilities with the New Perspectives *Student Developer's Kit* CD-ROM. The disc contains a sampling of hundreds of additional controls produced by third party vendors that can be used in Visual Basic programs. Students can also print a complete listing of the standard Visual Basic object naming conventions and access design documentation templates for use in planning their programs. The *Student Developer's Kit* CD-ROM also includes the Visual Basic Control Creation Edition. The Visual Basic Control Creation Edition is a complete standalone edition of Visual Basic that allows students to create different types of ActiveX controls that can be used by other programs and are ready for use on the Internet. See the page facing the back cover for more about the *Student Developer's Kit* CD-ROM.

Course Labs: Now, Concepts Come to Life Computer skills and concepts come to life with the New Perspectives Course Labs—highly interactive tutorials that combine illustrations, animation, digital images, and simulations. The Labs guide students step-by-step, present them with Quick Check questions, let them explore on their own, test their comprehension, and provide printed feedback. Lab icons at the beginning of the tutorial and in the tutorial margins indicate when a topic has a corresponding Lab. Lab Assignments are included at the end of each relevant tutorial. The Lab available with this book and the tutorial in which it appears is:

Visual Programming
Tutorial 1

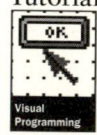

Course Test Manager: This cutting-edge Windows-based testing software helps instructors design and administer tests and pre-tests. The full-featured online program permits students to take tests at the computer where their grades are computed immediately following the completion of the exam. Automatic statistics collection, student study guides customized to the students' performance, and printed tests are only a few of the features.

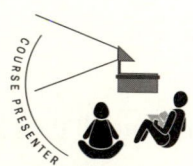

Course Presenter: This lecture presentation tool allows instructors to create electronic slide shows or traditional overhead transparencies using the figure files from the book. Instructors can customize, edit, save, and display figures from the text in order to illustrate key topics or concepts in class.

Online Companions: Dedicated to Keeping You and Your Students Up-To-Date When you use a New Perspectives product, you can access Course Technology's faculty sites and student sites on the World Wide Web. You can browse the password-protected Faculty Online Companions to obtain online Instructor's Manuals, Solution Files, Student Files, and more. Please see your Instructor's Manual or call your Course Technology customer service representative for more information. Student and Faculty Online Companions are accessible by clicking the appropriate links on the Course Technology home page at **http://www.course.com**.

Instructor's Manual New Perspectives Series Instructor's Manuals contain instructor's notes and printed solutions for each tutorial. Instructor's notes provide tutorial overviews and outlines, technical notes, lecture notes, and extra Case Problems. Printed solutions include solutions to Tutorial Assignments, Case Problems, Additional Cases, and Lab Assignments.

Student Files Student Files contain all of the data that students will use to complete the tutorials, Tutorial Assignments, Case Problems, and Additional Cases. A Readme file includes technical tips for lab management. See the inside covers of this book and the "Read This Before You Begin" pages for more information on Student Files.

Solution Files Solution Files contain every file students are asked to create or modify in the tutorials, Tutorial Assignments, Case Problems, and Additional Cases.

The following supplements are included in the Instructor's Resource Kit that accompanies this textbook:

- Instructor's Manual
- Solution Files
- Student Files
- Visual Programming Course Lab
- Course Test Manager Release 1.1 Test Bank
- Course Test Manager Release 1.1 Engine
- Course Presenter

Some of the supplements listed above are also available over the World Wide Web through Course Technology's password-protected Faculty Online Companions. Please see your Instructor's Manual or call your Course Technology customer service representative for more information.

Acknowledgments

Our appreciation goes to each of the reviewers whose suggestions and comments helped to create this book. We would also like to thank Mac Mendelsohn for giving us flexibility in creating this book. We would like to thank all the members of the New Perspectives team who helped guide the book's development and production. We would also like to thank the staff at GEX for their fine work.

Special thanks to Kate Habib for her valuable suggestions and efforts as developmental editor, and to Cindy Johnson for her efforts. We would also like to thank the members of the New Perspectives Team for their help in making the book possible. We would like to thank Mitchell Harhay for his development of the test bank.

Michael V. Ekedahl thanks his wife Katrina for her patience while he completed his work. He would also like to thank his dogs Rio and KC for their constant companionship.

William A. Newman thanks his wife Anthea, mother Irene, and mother-in-law Annette Karnas for their encouragement and support. Special thanks to his two dogs Sasha and Sabrina for their companionship.

Michael V. Ekedahl
William A. Newman

Table of Contents

NEW PERSPECTIVES SERIES

Microsoft®
Visual Basic® 5.0
for Windows®

LEVEL I

TUTORIALS

Read This **Before You Begin**

Getting Started with Visual Basic

Creating and Running a Program for Southern Properties Group

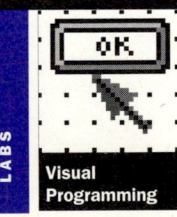

LABS
Visual Programming

OBJECTIVES

In this tutorial you will:

- Start and exit Visual Basic

- Create a Visual Basic program using a tool called a Wizard

- Identify the components of the Visual Basic environment

- Access Visual Basic Help

- Run a Visual Basic program

- Create a new Visual Basic program without a Wizard

- Draw controls on a form

- Write Visual Basic statements that will execute when a user clicks items on a menu

- Save the components of a Visual Basic program

CASE

Southern Properties Group

Southern Properties Group, located in Boca Raton, Florida, has been leasing and selling commercial real estate in southern Florida for more than five years. The company was started by Gerrold Campbell, who retired from a large real estate firm in New York City. This year he decided to computerize many of the company's operations so Southern Properties Group could be more responsive to the needs of its clients.

Mark Fisk is the chief computer programmer/analyst for Southern Properties Group. Based on Mark's recommendations, the company is beginning to use Visual Basic 5 for Windows 95 as its standard programming language. Mark believes that Southern Properties Group should use Visual Basic for its programs for several reasons:

- The company uses many other Windows 95 programs, and Visual Basic programs can include buttons, menus, and other Windows 95 features that users are accustomed to already.

- Visual Basic has an Integrated Development Environment (IDE). That is, you write your Visual Basic statements and test your programs in the same windows the user sees when the program is running.

- Programs can be written quickly in Visual Basic because of the many other tools available to the programmer.

- Visual Basic can work effectively with business data because it can interact with databases like Microsoft Access.

The first program Gerrold asked Mark to create was one that will display pictures of the various pieces of real estate that Southern Properties Group has available for sale or lease. Before you create this program, Mark suggests you create a sample program so you can identify the different Visual Basic windows and how they are used to create, run, and save a program. This way you can become familiar with the Visual Basic user interface and the different parts of a program. In this tutorial, you will create a sample program and then create another program that will allow sales agents to view and show clients the pictures.

Using the Tutorials Effectively

These tutorials will help you learn about Visual Basic 5 for Windows 95. The tutorials are designed to be used at a computer. Each tutorial is divided into sessions. Watch for the session headings, such as Session 1.1 and Session 1.2. Each session is designed to be completed in about 45 minutes, but take as much time as you need. It's also a good idea to take a break between sessions.

Before you begin, read the following questions and answers. They are designed to help you use the tutorials effectively.

Where do I start?

Each tutorial begins with a case, which sets the scene for the tutorial and provides background information to help you understand what you will be doing in the tutorial. Read the case before you go to the lab. In the lab, begin with the first session of a tutorial.

How do I know what to do on the computer?

Each session contains steps that you will perform on the computer to learn how to use Visual Basic 5 for Windows 95. Read the text that introduces each series of steps. The steps you need to do at a computer are numbered and set against a colored background. Read each step carefully and completely before you try it.

How do I know if I did the step correctly?

As you work, compare your computer screen with the corresponding figure in the tutorial. Don't worry if your screen display is somewhat different from the figure. The important parts of the screen display are labeled in each figure. Check to make sure these parts are on your screen.

What if I make a mistake?

Don't worry about making mistakes—they are part of the learning process. Paragraphs labeled "TROUBLE?" identify common problems and explain how to get back on track. Follow the steps in a TROUBLE? paragraph *only* if you are having the problem described. If you run into other problems:

- Carefully consider the current state of your system, the position of the pointer, and any messages on the screen.

- Complete the sentence, "Now I want to…" Be specific, because you are identifying your goal.

- Develop a plan for accomplishing your goal, and put your plan into action.

How do I use the Reference Windows?

Reference Windows summarize the procedures you learn in the tutorial steps. Do not complete the actions in the Reference Windows when you are working through the tutorial. Instead, refer to the Reference Windows while you are working on the assignments at the end of the tutorial.

How can I test my understanding of the material I learned in the tutorial?

At the end of each session, you can answer the Quick Check questions. The answers for the Quick Checks are at the end of the book.

After you have completed the entire tutorial, you should complete the Tutorial Assignments and Case Problems. They are structured carefully so you will review what you have learned and then apply your knowledge to new situations.

What if I can't remember how to do something?

You should refer to the Task Reference at the end of the book; it summarizes how to accomplish tasks using the most efficient method. The Notes column includes shortcuts or additional information.

Before you begin the tutorials, you should know how to use the menus, dialog boxes, Help system, and My Computer in Windows 95. Course Technology publishes two excellent texts for learning Windows 95: *New Perspectives on Microsoft Windows 95—Brief* and *New Perspectives on Microsoft Windows 95—Introductory*.

Now that you have seen how to use the tutorials effectively, you are ready to begin.

SESSION

1.1

In this session you will learn about the different windows and components of the Visual Basic system, and how to use them. You will learn how to start Visual Basic, use the online Help, create and save a Visual Basic project, run and stop a program, and exit Visual Basic.

What Is Visual Basic?

Visual Basic is a computer programming language. **Computer programming** is the process of writing a set of organized statements that accomplish a specific task using a programming language. A **programming language**, like the English language, uses words with a specific meaning, connected together in a specific order, to form a statement. A **statement** is much like a sentence in English. Just like English, the spelling of words and rules about how those words are connected together to form statements are clearly defined. A reader usually can understand the meaning of a sentence written in English even when words are misspelled or punctuation is not correct. When programming a computer, however, the statements you type must be exactly correct. The rules describing the valid statements of a programming language are known as **syntax**. When you assemble several statements together to accomplish a task, you create a program. A **program** is a set of statements written in a computer language to accomplish a specific task. Some tasks may be simple, like adding a list of numbers together. Other tasks may be extremely complex, like navigating a satellite. In this tutorial you will use the Visual Basic programming language to create a program that will display different graphical images on the screen as selected by the sales agents. The program will contain words used to form statements. All the statements together form the computer program. In this book you will learn how to use the Visual Basic 5 programming language.

When you write a computer program in Visual Basic, you use various tools to design the user interface. The **user interface** is what a user of the program sees on the screen and how the user interacts with the program. The screen that the user sees is called a form. A **form** is a window just like any other window you see in Windows 95. It can contain tools like buttons, and boxes that contain text. These buttons also are considered windows. A **window** is any rectangular area on the screen and can exist inside another window.

Visual Basic also has a user interface, just as programs like Microsoft Word and Excel have a user interface. When you create programs with Visual Basic, you use an **Integrated Development Environment (IDE)**. That is, all of the tools necessary to create and run a program have been combined into a single user interface, rather than operating as separate programs. In other words you can create the user interface for your program, write the necessary statements and run your program inside of the IDE.

Visual Basic is an **event-driven** programming language, which means that different pictures, boxes, and buttons on the screen can respond to events. An **event** is an action that occurs as a result of some user activity. One event is generated when the user clicks a button while a different event is generated when the user types characters into a text box or places the cursor in the text box. These events result in the program's statements being executed to perform a specified task.

Visual Basic also is an **object-oriented** programming language. That is, you use objects like buttons to perform tasks. Think of an **object** as a real-world item that you use every day. A telephone, for example, can be thought of as an object. As such, you can clearly define the actions a telephone can perform. When you pick up a telephone, it responds to the event by providing a dial tone. As numbers are dialed on the phone, it responds to different events by sending audible tones to the telephone system to dial the number. A telephone also has certain behaviors or settings. That is, it can be off the hook or on the hook. Also, it can be connected to another phone or not. The actions performed by an object and the behavior of an object are similar to the nouns and verbs of a sentence. Each object has a predefined set of behaviors called **properties** (nouns), and can perform a predefined set of actions called **methods** (verbs).

You use different tools to create objects on a form, such as buttons the user can click and boxes that can display text or pictures. Some tools are designed to reflect how you might fill out a paper form. For example, there are tools that allow the user to check a box or choose one item from a list of items.

In Visual Basic, these tools are called **controls**. Each kind of control has a different appearance (properties), responds to events which can vary for different controls, and can perform a unique set of actions (methods). In this tutorial you will learn how to use four different controls.

- A **Label** control consists of a box that displays text to describe the purpose of another control.

- A user will enter characters into a **TextBox** control to specify the name of a picture stored on the disk.

- The **Image** control consists of a box that can display pictures saved in certain graphic formats. The Image control in your program will display the file typed by the user into the text box.

- The **CommandButton** control allows the user to click a command button to display the picture specified by the file name, which is stored in the text box, into the Image control.

You add a control to a form by drawing a copy of the control on the form. Each control you place on a form is considered an object. Figure 1-1 shows a sample of Visual Basic controls drawn on a form, and their purpose.

Figure 1-1 ◀
Sample of Visual Basic controls

enter letters and numbers into a TextBox control

display a graphical image into an Image control

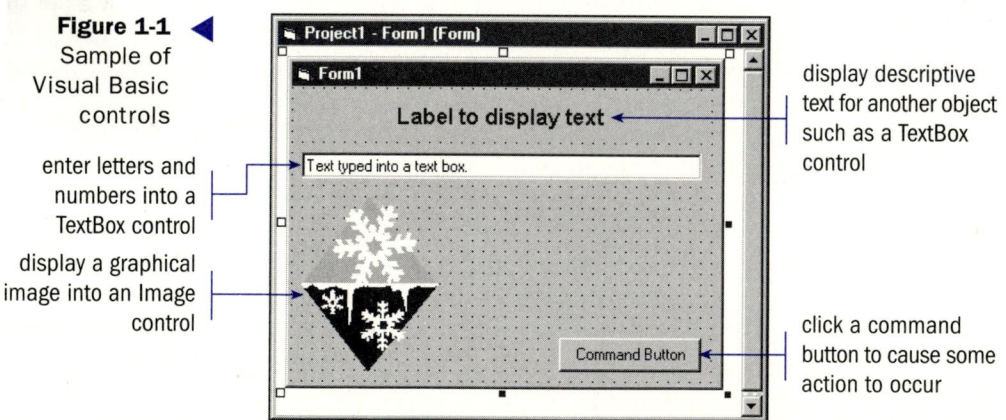

display descriptive text for another object such as a TextBox control

click a command button to cause some action to occur

A control is considered a class. A **class** is just a template for an object that defines the supported properties, methods, and events. When you draw a control on a form, you are creating an object, or an **instance** of a class.

Each form is stored as a separate file on the disk. In Visual Basic, the specifications for all the forms used by a program are stored in another file called a project file. A **project file** lists each file used in the program along with information about the controls used. It acts as a container for all the program components. Each part of your program stored as a file on the disk is called a **module**. A **standard module** contains Visual Basic statements that can be used by several forms. Each program has a single project file that lists the components of the program. One of these components is the form module. The **form module** contains all the objects on the form and all the code for those objects. **Code** is the statements written for a program to perform a specific action. The sample project you are creating for Mark will contain two forms and one standard module. The project manages all the different components of your program. Figure 1-2 shows the relationship between a project file, its forms, and standard modules.

Figure 1-2 ◀
Visual Basic
files

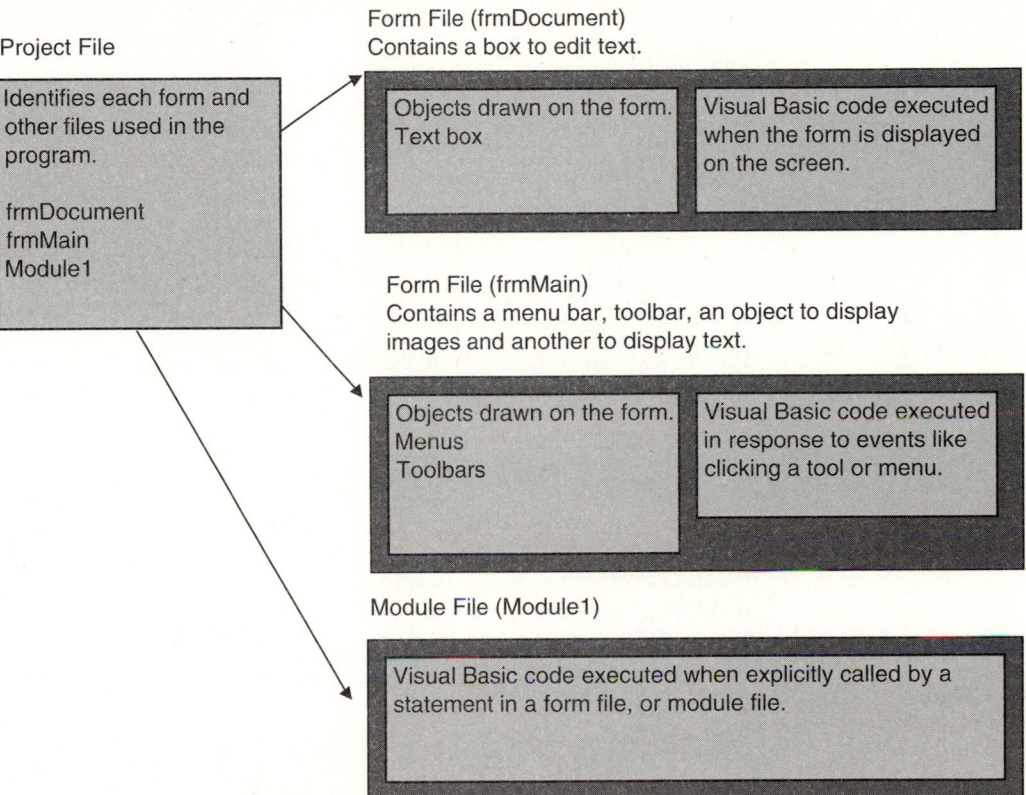

With Visual Basic, programming is a three-step process. First, you create the user interface, then you write the statements to perform each of the tasks required by the program. The third step is a loop; you test the program, correct any errors, and test the program again. Figure 1-3 shows the steps you take to write a program.

Figure 1-3 ◀
Steps for
writing a
program

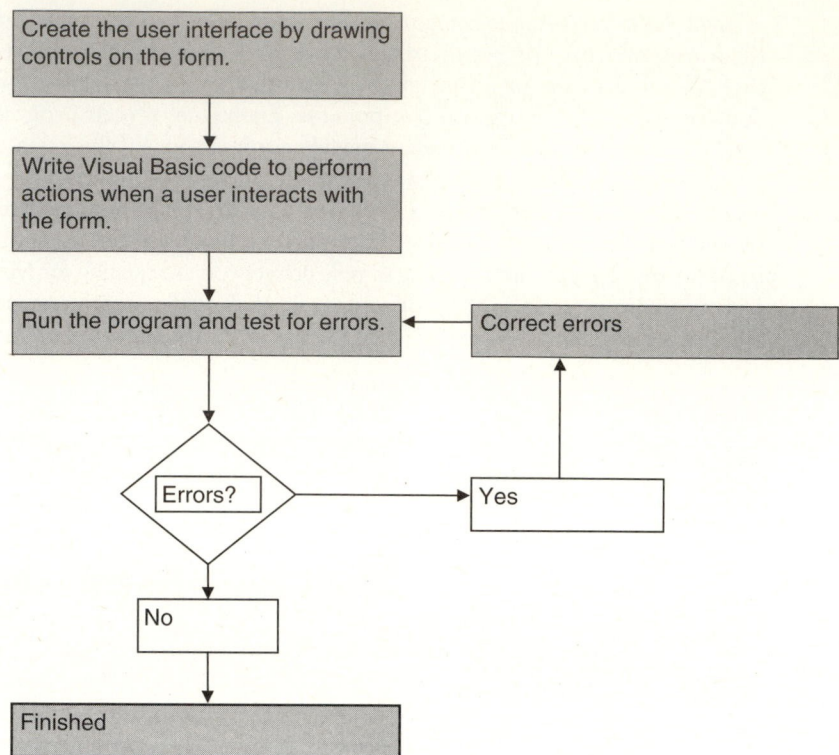

After drawing the boxes, buttons, and other objects on the form, you need to write the Visual Basic statements that are executed when a user enters text or clicks a button. These statements will perform the tasks needed to solve the problem. For example, Southern Properties Group needs a program to display graphical images stored as individual files on the computer's disk. Therefore, you will write a program that contains statements to display an image when a user types a file name into a text box, and clicks a command button to display the picture. As you write code to accomplish specific tasks, you will want to test the code to make sure it works correctly.

Starting Visual Basic

To create the program for Mark, you first need to start Visual Basic. You can start Visual Basic using the Start button on the taskbar or a shortcut icon on the Windows 95 desktop, if an icon has been defined for Visual Basic on the computer you are using. Your instructor will tell you how to start Visual Basic in your particular environment.

To start Visual Basic using the Start button:

1. Make sure your computer is on and the Windows 95 desktop is displayed on your screen.

2. Find the Start button, which usually is located at the bottom-left corner of the screen on the taskbar.

3. Click the **Start** button to display the Start menu, then point to the **Programs** command.

 When the Programs command is highlighted, a submenu appears listing the programs available on your computer.

4. Move the mouse pointer to the item labeled **Microsoft Visual Basic 5.0**. Another submenu appears, listing the options available in the Visual Basic system. See Figure 1-4.

Figure 1-4 ◀
Starting Visual
Basic

Visual Basic 5.0

Windows 95 Start
button

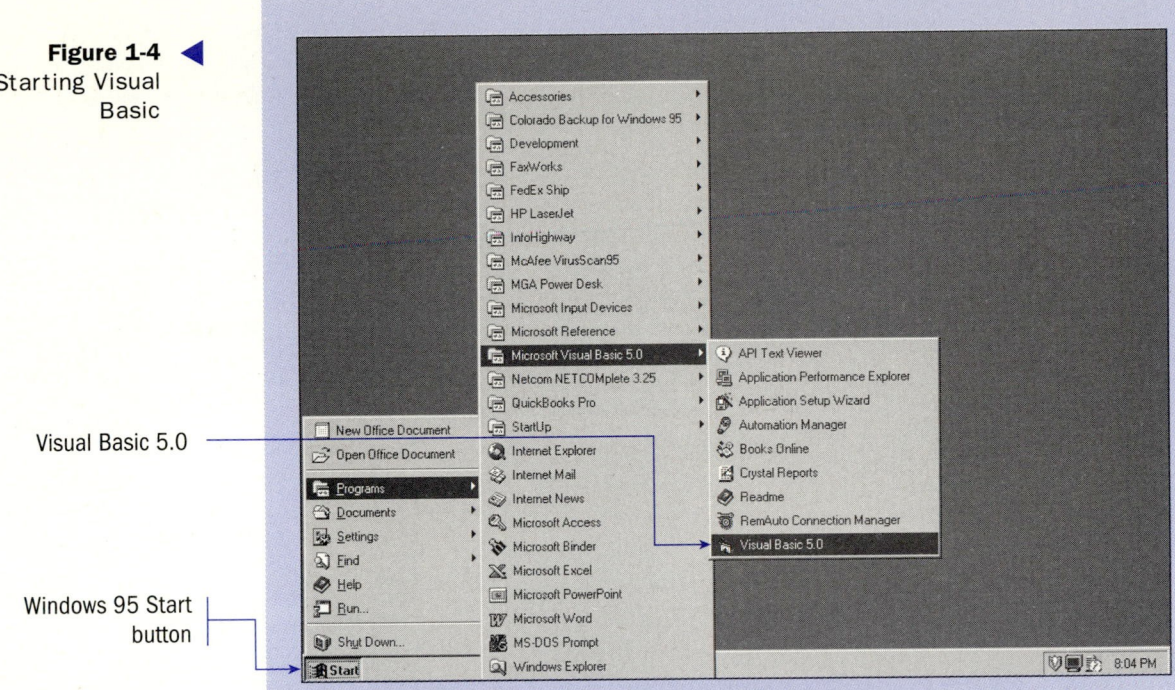

The Start menu options on your screen might be different from those in Figure 1-4, depending on the software you have on your computer.

TROUBLE? If the Microsoft Visual Basic 5.0 option is not listed on your Programs menu, check to see if a shortcut icon for Visual Basic appears on the desktop, then double-click the icon to start Visual Basic. If you cannot locate Visual Basic anywhere on your computer, ask your instructor or lab staff for assistance.

5. Click **Visual Basic 5.0**.

The introductory Visual Basic screen appears while the rest of the Visual Basic system is loaded into the computer's memory. This introductory screen commonly is called a splash screen. It provides a visual clue to the user that the desired program is being loaded. Once Visual Basic is loaded, the New Project window will appear and your screen should look similar to Figure 1-5.

Figure 1-5 ◀
New Project
window

click Open

click here so the New
Project window will
not open each time
you start Visual Basic

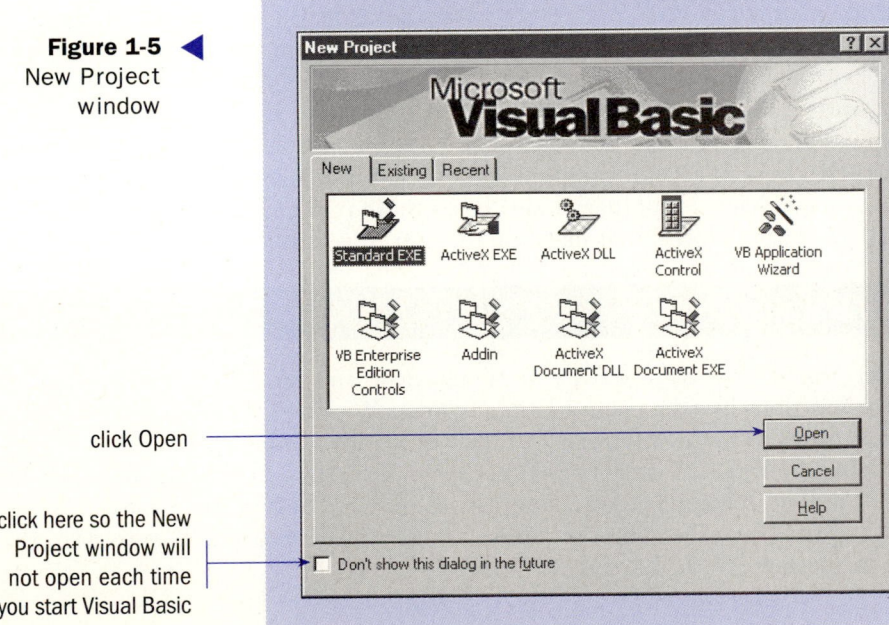

TROUBLE? If the New Project window shown in Figure 1-5 does not appear, your computer may be configured differently. Depending on how you or the lab manager set up your computer, some windows might be open or closed initially, or might be a different size. Skip Step 6.

6. Click the **Don't show this dialog in the future** check box to prevent the New Project window from opening every time Visual Basic is started. Click the **Open** button. When you start Visual Basic from now on, your screen will look similar to Figure 1-6, and Visual Basic will create a default project for you.

Figure 1-6
Visual Basic windows

menu bar
toolbar
toolbox
Project window
Properties window

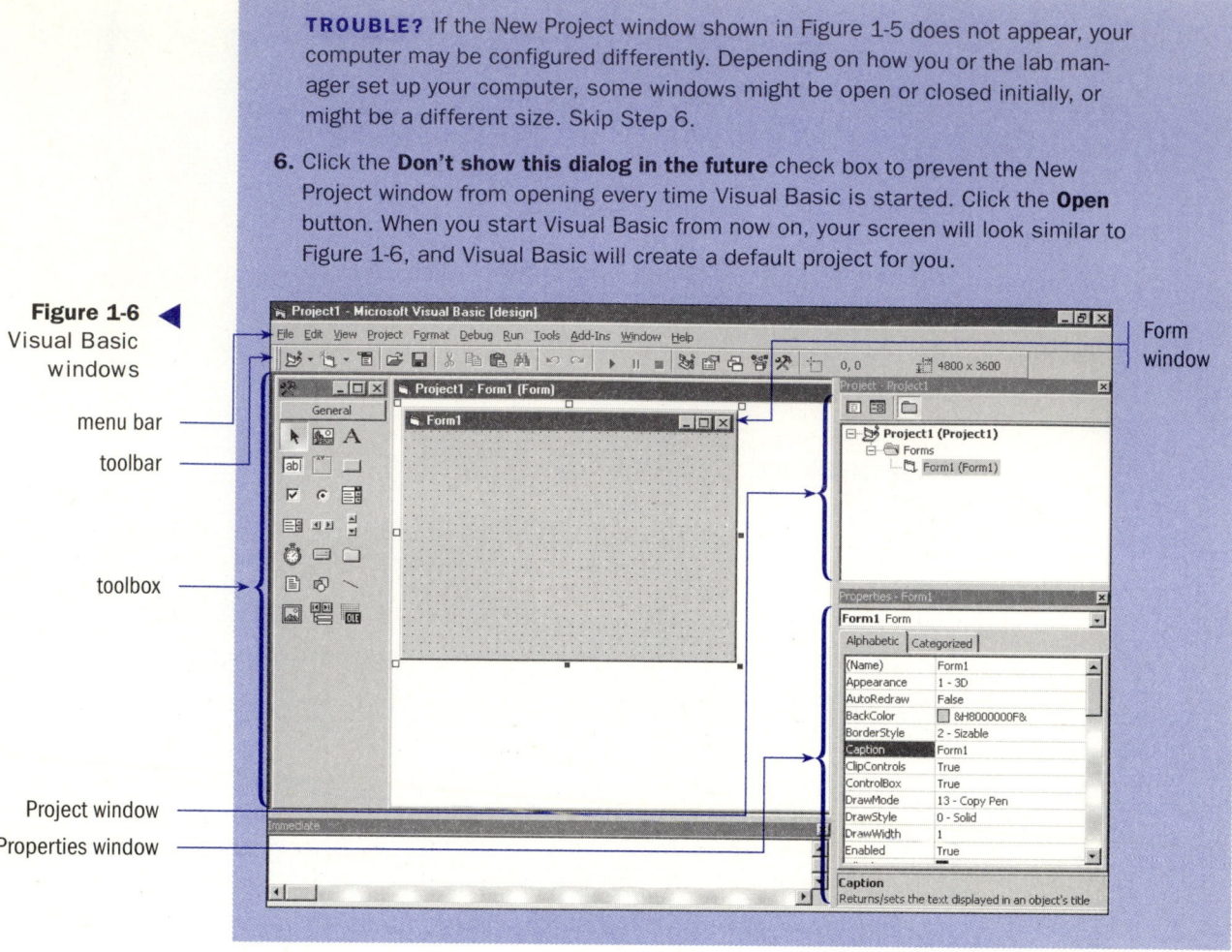

When you start Visual Basic and open different project files, the size and location of the windows on the screen will vary. You can change the size and position of most Visual Basic windows to suit your own preferences, just as you can resize or move other windows in Windows 95. Some of the windows in Figure 1-6 may not be visible on your screen, depending on the current settings of your application.

When you start Visual Basic, be sure the Visual Basic startup screen contains the text Visual Basic Learning Edition 5.0, Visual Basic Professional Edition 5.0, or Visual Basic Enterprise Edition 5.0. There are several operating differences between Version 5.0 and older versions. You must be using Version 5.0 of Visual Basic to complete these tutorials.

Notice the IDE contains several components common to many other Windows 95 programs. It has a menu bar and toolbar. It also has a toolbox that allows you to create the buttons and other visual objects that make up the user interface.

The Menu Bar and Toolbar

The menu bar provides the commands you use to create and run Visual Basic programs. The menu bar functions like the menu bar in any other Windows 95 program.

The toolbar provides buttons for many of the commands available from the menu bar. Clicking a toolbar button is a faster way of choosing a command than using the menu bar. As in other Windows 95 applications, you can display a ToolTip for a button on the Visual Basic toolbar by positioning the mouse pointer on the button. The ToolTip that appears shows the name of the button.

To practice displaying a ToolTip for a toolbar button:

1. Position the mouse pointer over the **Add Standard EXE Project** button 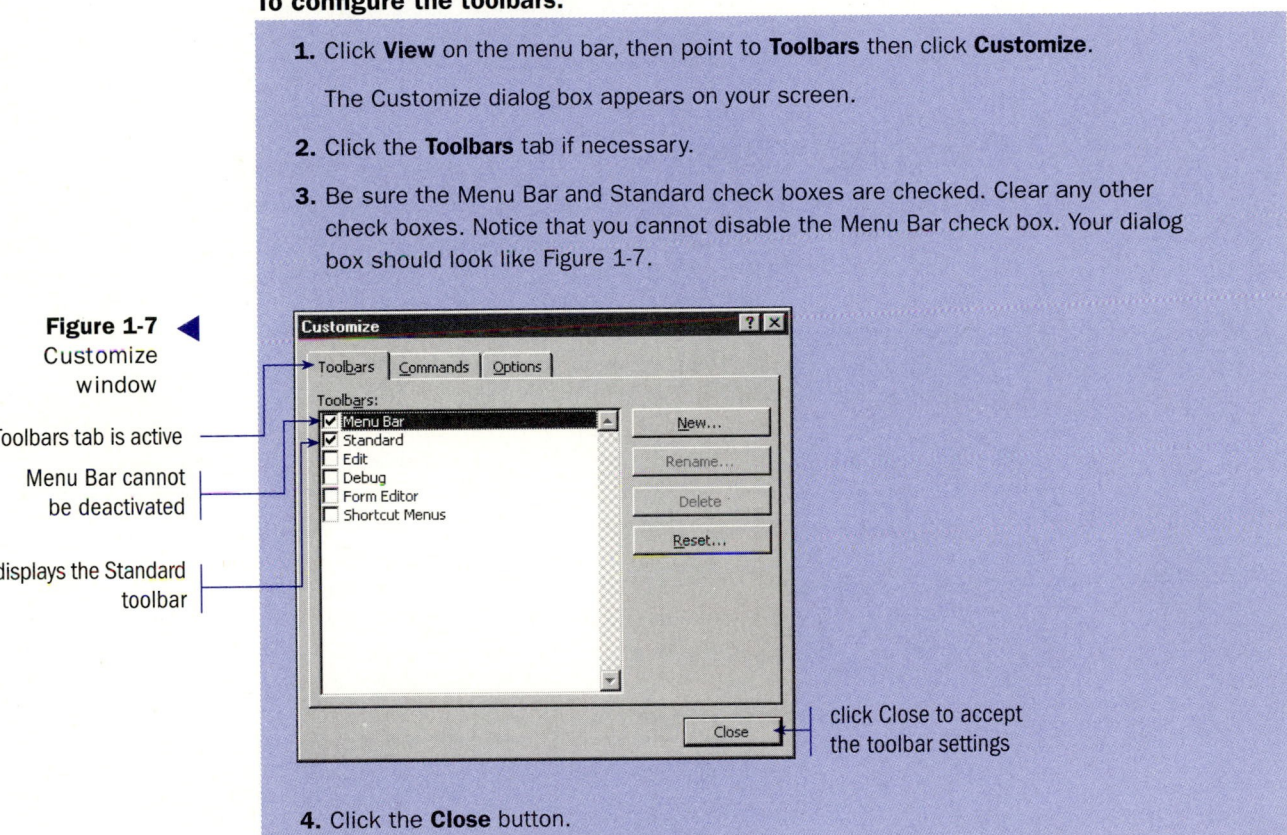 at the far left of the toolbar.

After a few seconds, the ToolTip appears and displays the button name, Add Standard EXE Project.

2. Move the mouse pointer off the button. The ToolTip disappears.

The Visual Basic toolbars can be customized depending on your personal preferences or the specific actions you are performing. This is accomplished by adding or removing different groups of tools from the toolbar. Mark suggests you verify that only the Standard toolbar is showing.

To configure the toolbars:

1. Click **View** on the menu bar, then point to **Toolbars** then click **Customize**.

The Customize dialog box appears on your screen.

2. Click the **Toolbars** tab if necessary.

3. Be sure the Menu Bar and Standard check boxes are checked. Clear any other check boxes. Notice that you cannot disable the Menu Bar check box. Your dialog box should look like Figure 1-7.

Figure 1-7 ◀
Customize
window

Toolbars tab is active ⎯⎯

Menu Bar cannot
be deactivated

displays the Standard
toolbar

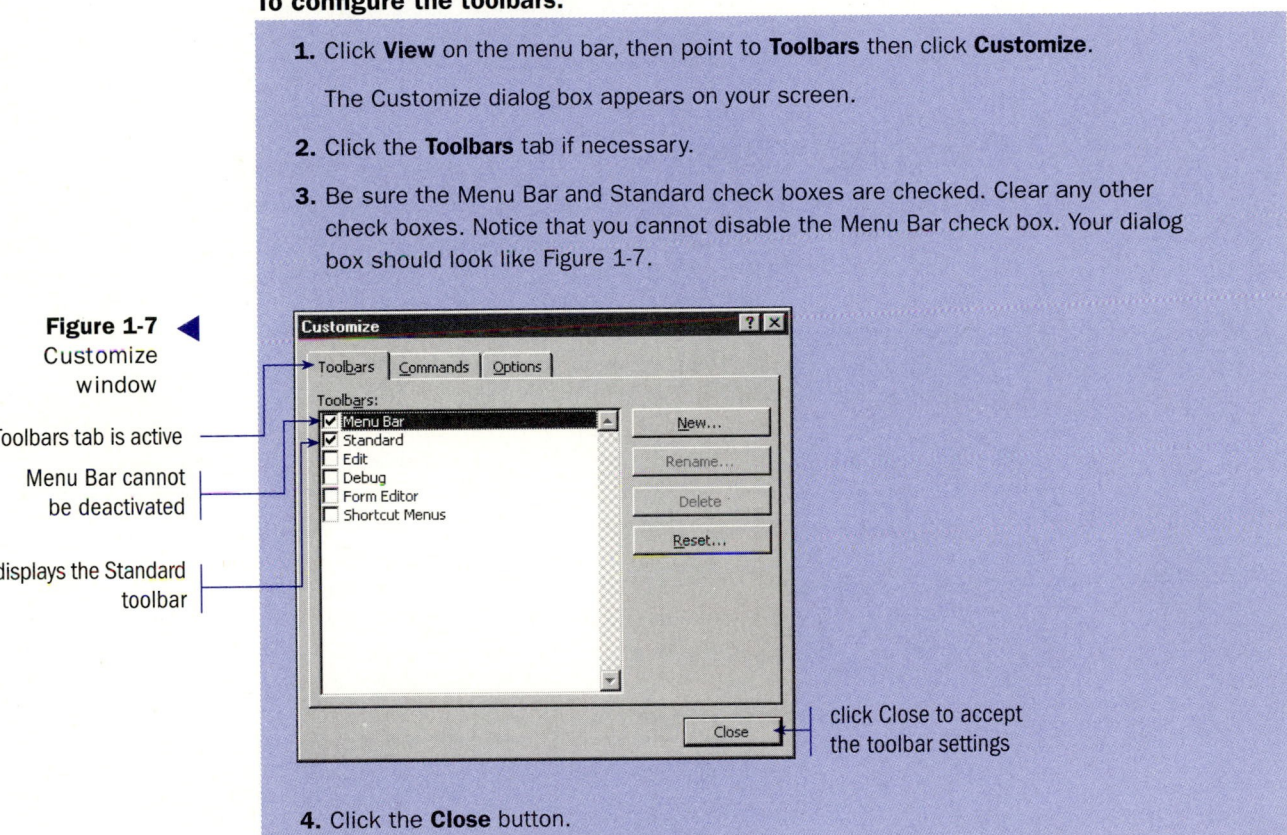

click Close to accept
the toolbar settings

4. Click the **Close** button.

Planning a Program

You always should consider carefully the problem you are trying to solve and the best solution to the problem before you begin writing the program. Part of planning a program consists of deciding on the placement and purpose of the buttons, boxes, and other components seen by the user. You should consider carefully the layout and organization of the different visual elements, and the specific tasks they will perform, before sitting down and creating the program on the computer. This will make the programming process easier and less error prone. Mark has created the main form's screen layout as shown in Figure 1-8. It lists the controls on the form and their placement.

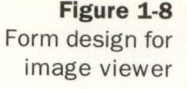

Figure 1-8
Form design for
image viewer

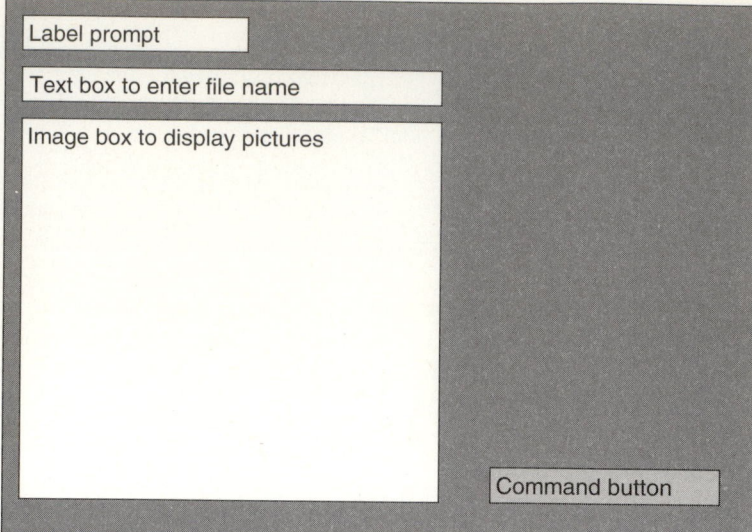

Label prompt

Text box to enter file name

Image box to display pictures

Command button

Creating a Project

When you want to create a Visual Basic program, you begin by either creating an empty project file with no visible objects or statements, or using a Wizard to create a project for you. A Wizard can help you create a template for the different parts of the project, which you can then expand on to make the program perform the specific tasks you desire.

The **Application Wizard** creates a project that is a template for a completed program. That is, it will create the forms, menus, toolbars, and other items for you to perform tasks like opening and closing files. You as the programmer must modify this template to accomplish specific tasks like displaying the graphical files you open. The Application Wizard only can create new programs. It is not possible to use the Application Wizard to modify programs that already have been created.

Creating a project in Visual Basic with the Application Wizard is much like creating a document in Microsoft Word using a template. You select an item from the Visual Basic menu bar or toolbar to create a new project, then specify the characteristics of the project. Mark suggests you create a new project file using the Application Wizard to identify the different parts of a Visual Basic program.

To start the Application Wizard:

1. Click **File** then **New Project** on the menu bar. The New Project window appears as shown in Figure 1-9.

Figure 1-9
Creating a new
project

click VB Application
Wizard

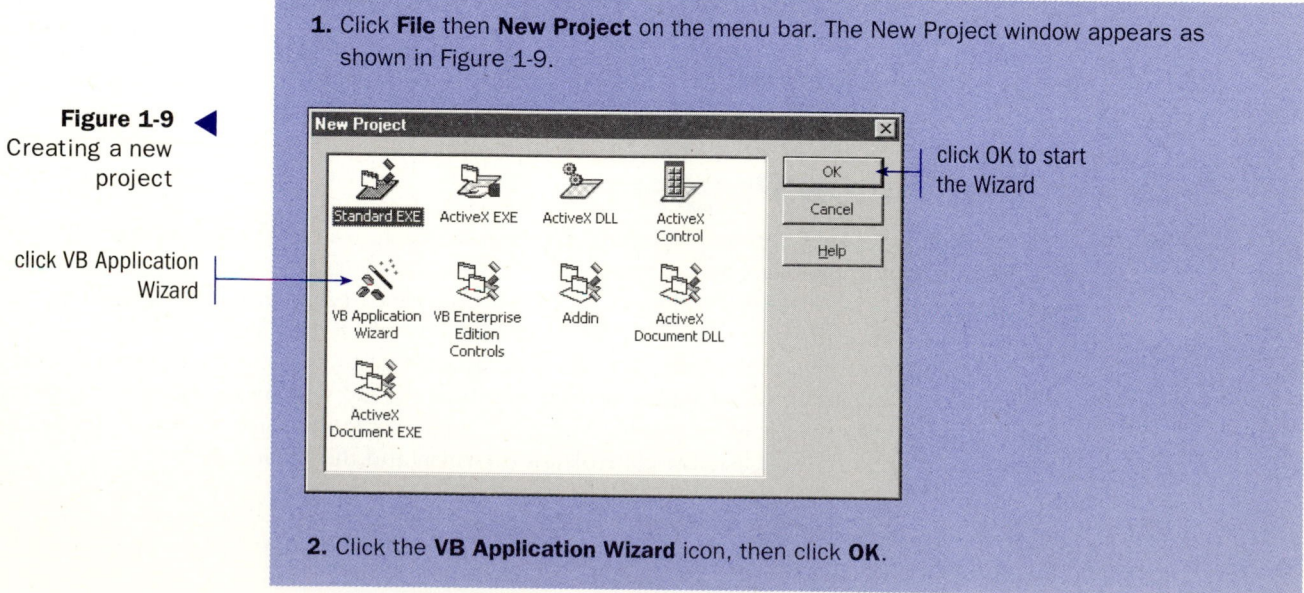

click OK to start
the Wizard

2. Click the **VB Application Wizard** icon, then click **OK**.

3. The Application Wizard - Introduction dialog box opens as shown in Figure 1-10.

Figure 1-10
Using the
Application
Wizard

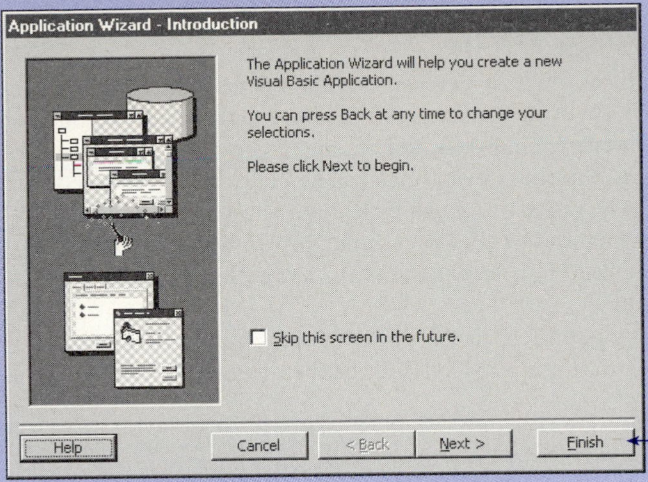

click Finish to
create the project

TROUBLE? If you do not see this dialog box, but see a dialog box titled Application Wizard - Interface Type, do not worry. Click the Finish button on the dialog box and the Application Wizard will create the same application.

4. Click **Finish**.

When clicked, Visual Basic will begin to create the program template for you. You will see several windows opening and closing as Visual Basic creates each of the different parts of the program. The template contains the foundation for a more complete Visual Basic program.

5. If you see the dialog box shown in Figure 1-11, click **OK**.

Figure 1-11
Application
Created dialog
box

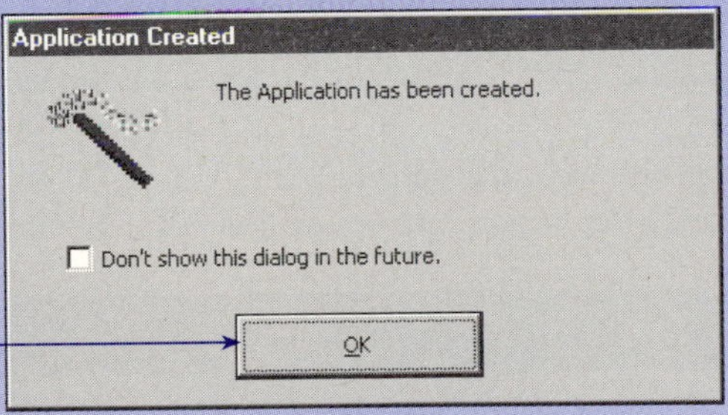

click OK to close
the dialog box

6. If you see the dialog box shown in Figure 1-12, click **Close**.

Figure 1-12
Application
Wizard
Summary
Report

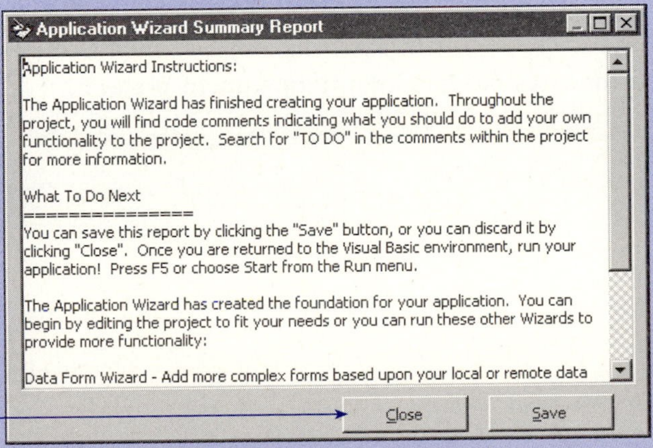

click Close to close
the report

Now that you have created your first project, Mark suggests you look at the Help system about projects so you can begin to understand the system's components and how they work.

Getting Help

Visual Basic has an extensive Help system that provides on-screen information about Visual Basic components, features, commands, and so on. For example, you can look up how to write Visual Basic statements or how to use any of the financial and mathematical functions built into Visual Basic. The Help system is based on the idea of hypertext, which means that you can navigate through the Help system by looking at definitions of terms you do not understand or related topics without having to search for the information. Most of the Help screens contain examples you can copy and paste into actual Visual Basic code.

You can get help at any time by pressing the F1 key or by selecting an option from the Help menu. Figure 1-13 describes the options available on the Help menu.

Figure 1-13 ◀
Help menu
options

Microsoft Visual Basic Help Topics	Displays the Help window that provides a list of available Help Topics on the Contents tab or searches for a particular topic from the Index tab.
Books Online	Activates Visual Basic Books Online containing complete reference information about Visual Basic. Depending on your system configuration, the CD-ROM containing the Visual Basic software must be inserted into the CD-ROM drive.
Obtaining Technical Support	Displays the Contents tab of the Help window where you can search for different ways to get support for Visual Basic.
Microsoft on the Web	Allows you to access the Internet, if your computer is set up correctly, for information about Visual Basic
About Microsoft Visual Basic	Displays a dialog box telling you the version number, a copyright notice, and the amount of available memory.

Depending on whether you are running the Visual Basic Learning, Professional, or Enterprise edition, your Help menu options might differ from those shown in Figure 1-13.

Using the Index Tab

The Index tab of the Help window displays an alphabetical list of topics, just like a typical index in the back of a book. You either can scroll through the list and select a topic or type a topic to find information about it.

Mark suggests you use the Index tab to find Help information about projects.

To use the Index tab to find information about projects:

1. Click **Help** on the menu bar, then click **Microsoft Visual Basic Help Topics**.

2. Make sure the Index tab is selected in the Help window, as shown in Figure 1-14.

Figure 1-14 ◀
Index tab of the
Help window

Index tab selected

type text into this
text box

matching entries
are displayed in
this list box

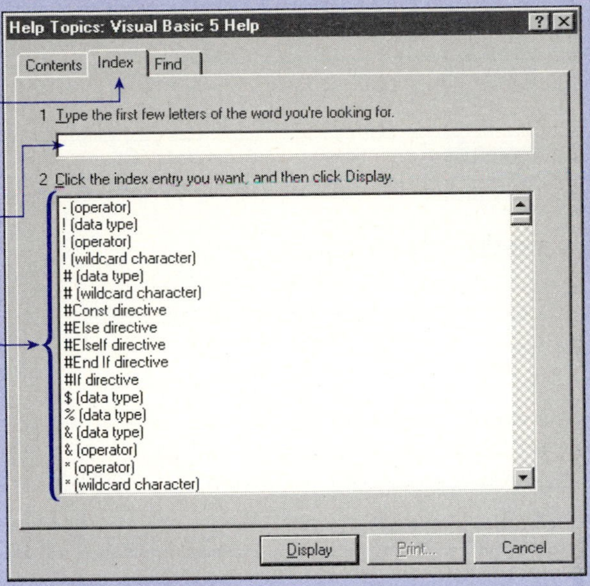

Notice that a flashing cursor appears in the text box at the top of the window. In this text box, you type the word or words for which you want Help information.

3. In the text box, type **projects**. As you type, the box listing available Help topics changes to match the text you are typing.

4. In the list box, make sure the topic **projects** (with subentries) is highlighted, then click the **Display** button. The Topics Found dialog box opens. See Figure 1-15.

Figure 1-15 ◀
Topics Found
dialog box

click this topic

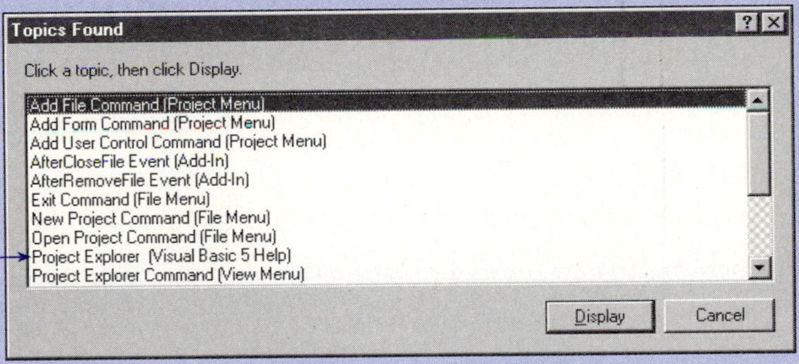

5. Click the topic **Project Explorer (Visual Basic 5 Help)**, then click the **Display** button. The Help system displays information about the Project Explorer. See Figure 1-16.

Figure 1-16 ◀
Help
information
about the
Project
Explorer

scroll up arrow

scroll box

scroll down arrow

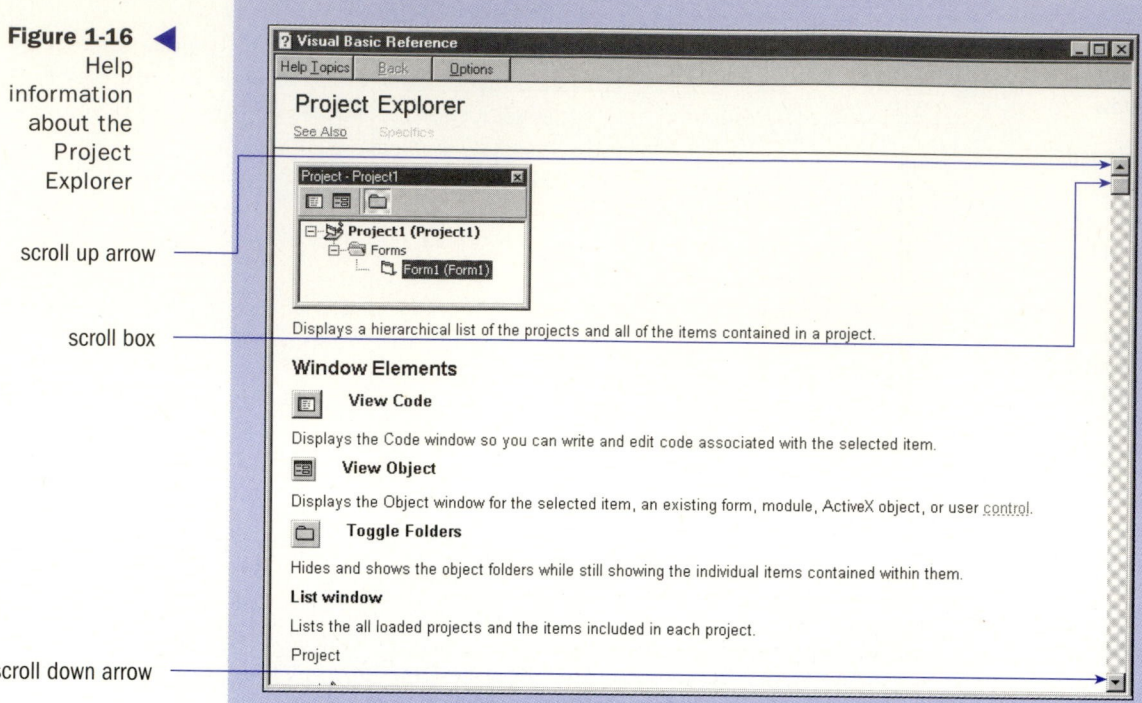

Depending on the settings of your system, the size and shape of your Help window might differ from the window in Figure 1-16. Just like most windows, you can move the mouse pointer over a window's border and drag the border to increase or decrease its size depending on your personal preference.

6. Read the displayed information, using the up and down scroll arrows or the scroll box to move through the screen.

7. When you are finished reading the information, scroll to the top of the screen. Note that some terms are displayed in a different color and underlined with dashes. You can click these terms to display additional Help information.

8. Click the highlighted text **Forms**, read the displayed definition of this term, then click anywhere on the screen to close the definition window. You may need to scroll down through the Help screen to locate the highlighted text depending on the size of the Help window and the resolution of your computer's monitor.

Note the text "See Also" at the top of the screen. You can click this text to display a list of related Help topics.

9. Click **See Also**, look at the displayed list of related topics, then click the **Cancel** button on the Topics Found window to close it.

10. Click the **Close** button ☒ on the Help window title bar to close the window and exit the Help system.

Now that you have learned how to use the Help system and viewed information on a project, you are ready to work on the project for Mark. Before you look at the different parts of a project, you should save your work to your Student Disk. As you make changes to a program, they are not saved to your Student Disk until you explicitly do so. Saving your work frequently will prevent accidental loss due to a power outage, or other computer malfunction.

Saving the Project

You now need to use the Save File As and Save Project As dialog boxes to save the different files that make up the project. When a project is saved for the first time, each of the form files is saved first, then the project file is saved. Thus, you will be asked to save the two form files, the standard module file, and the project itself.

As you create and work on programs, it is a good idea to save your work to the Student Disk regularly so it will not be lost as a result of a power outage or system failure. Although the forms and the project are stored in separate files, you can save them using one Visual Basic command.

Mark would like you to save this project using the default name "Project1", and the form files also with the default names. Visual Basic creates standardized names for each form it created, so you do not need to change any of the form names. The standardized names for forms begin with the prefix "frm" followed by descriptive words for the form.

To save the Southern Properties Group project:

1. Place your Student Disk in drive A.

   TROUBLE? If you don't have a Student Disk, you need to get one before you can proceed. Your instructor either will give you one or ask you to make your own.

   If your floppy disk drive is not drive A, substitute the appropriate name of your floppy disk drive throughout these tutorials.

2. Click **File** on the menu bar, then click **Save Project** to activate the Save File As dialog box as shown in Figure 1-17. Because you have not yet saved any of the files associated with the project, Visual Basic first will ask you to save each of the files that make up the project, then save the project file itself.

Figure 1-17 ◀
Saving the form

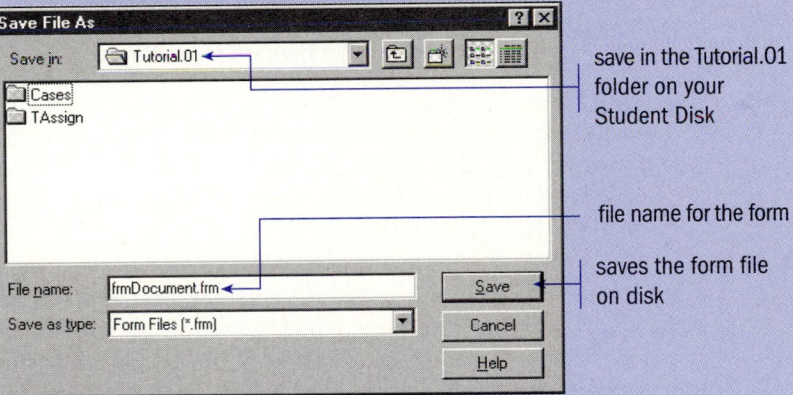

save in the Tutorial.01 folder on your Student Disk

file name for the form

saves the form file on disk

3. Click the Save in list arrow, click **3½ Floppy (A:)**, then double-click the folder named **Tutorial.01**

4. Because you will use the default file name supplied by Visual Basic, you do not need to type in the file name. Click the **Save** button in the dialog box to save the first form.

5. The Save File As dialog box will appear again asking you to save the form named **frmMain**. Click **Save** to save the form. Because you already specified the folder in the previous step, you do not need to change the Save in list box entry.

6. The Save File As dialog box appears again asking you to save the basic module named Module1. Click **Save** again to save the module named **Module1** using the default name.

7. Finally the Save Project As dialog box appears as shown in Figure 1-18. Click **Save** to save the project file.

Figure 1-18 ◀
Saving the
project

file name for the
project

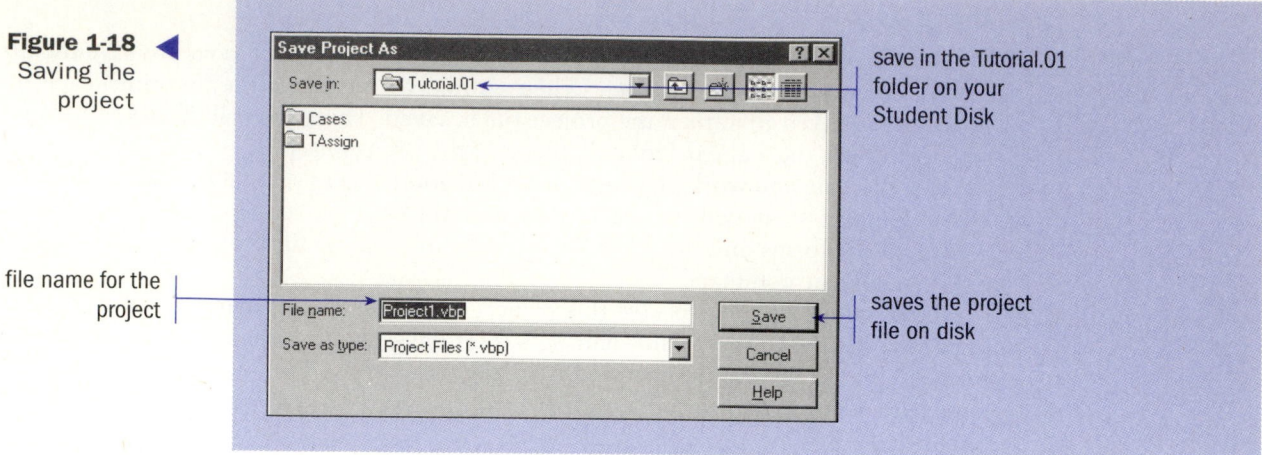

Now that you have saved the project, you can open it at any time using the Open Project command on the File menu. The project file then will locate all the forms and other Visual Basic components and load them.

The Visual Basic Environment

The Visual Basic Integrated Development Environment (IDE) can be used in two modes. You can select the mode by clicking Tools then Options on the menu bar to open the Options dialog box. The Advanced tab contains a check box named SDI Development Environment. If this box is checked, Visual Basic will operate in SDI mode. Otherwise it will operate in MDI mode.

- Using the single document interface (SDI) mode, the different windows used by Visual Basic can appear anywhere on the screen.

- Using the multiple document interface (MDI) mode, the region of each Visual Basic window appears inside another window called an **MDI parent window**. This is much like working with multiple documents in Microsoft Word or multiple spreadsheets and charts in Microsoft Excel. Each Word document or Excel spreadsheet appears inside the region of another window.

Which mode to use is a matter of personal preference but this book will use the MDI mode so it is easy to determine which windows are applicable to Visual Basic. The main Visual Basic screen (MDI parent window) contains common Windows 95 components, such as the menu bar and toolbar, plus application-specific components such as the Project Explorer, Form window, Properties window, and toolbox. Together, these windows allow you to design, create, edit, run, and test programs. Which windows are open and their position on the screen also is a matter of personal preference.

Another feature of the Visual Basic IDE is called docking. When docking is turned on, different windows can be displayed and moved relative to the other windows and the edge of the MDI parent window. When turned off, windows are positioned anywhere inside the MDI parent window. In this tutorial you will not use docking. Mark suggests you begin by verifying that Visual Basic is running in MDI mode and that docking is turned off.

To do this you will use the Options dialog box. This dialog box is used to configure Visual Basic's user interface to fit your particular needs.

To configure the Visual Basic environment:

1. Click **Tools** then **Options** on the menu bar to open the Options dialog box.

2. Click the **Advanced** tab in the dialog box.

3. Be sure the **SDI Development Environment** check box is not checked.

4. Click the **Docking** tab in the dialog box.

5. Be sure only the **Toolbox** check box is checked.

6. Click **OK** to close the Options dialog box.

As you develop the programs throughout this book, you should open, close, and resize the windows as you see fit. There is neither a right number of windows to keep open or closed nor a proper size for those windows. Mark suggests you now look at the different windows that make up the IDE so you can develop your own program in the next session.

Interactive Development Environment Windows

In addition to the toolbar and menu bar, Visual Basic uses several windows in which you design the user interface, the appearance of the objects you create, and write Visual Basic statements.

Project Explorer

The **Project Explorer** shows all the program components. You use the Project Explorer to manage the program components. (The project is the same as the program.) A project usually consists of at least one form, which is referred to as a form module. Other types of modules, including standard modules and class modules, also can be a part of a project. Visual Basic also can work with several projects at a time.

To open the Project Explorer:

1. Click the **Project Explorer** button on the toolbar if necessary to activate the Project Explorer as shown in Figure 1-19.

Figure 1-19 ◀
Project
Explorer

Toggle Folders button

View Code button

View Object button

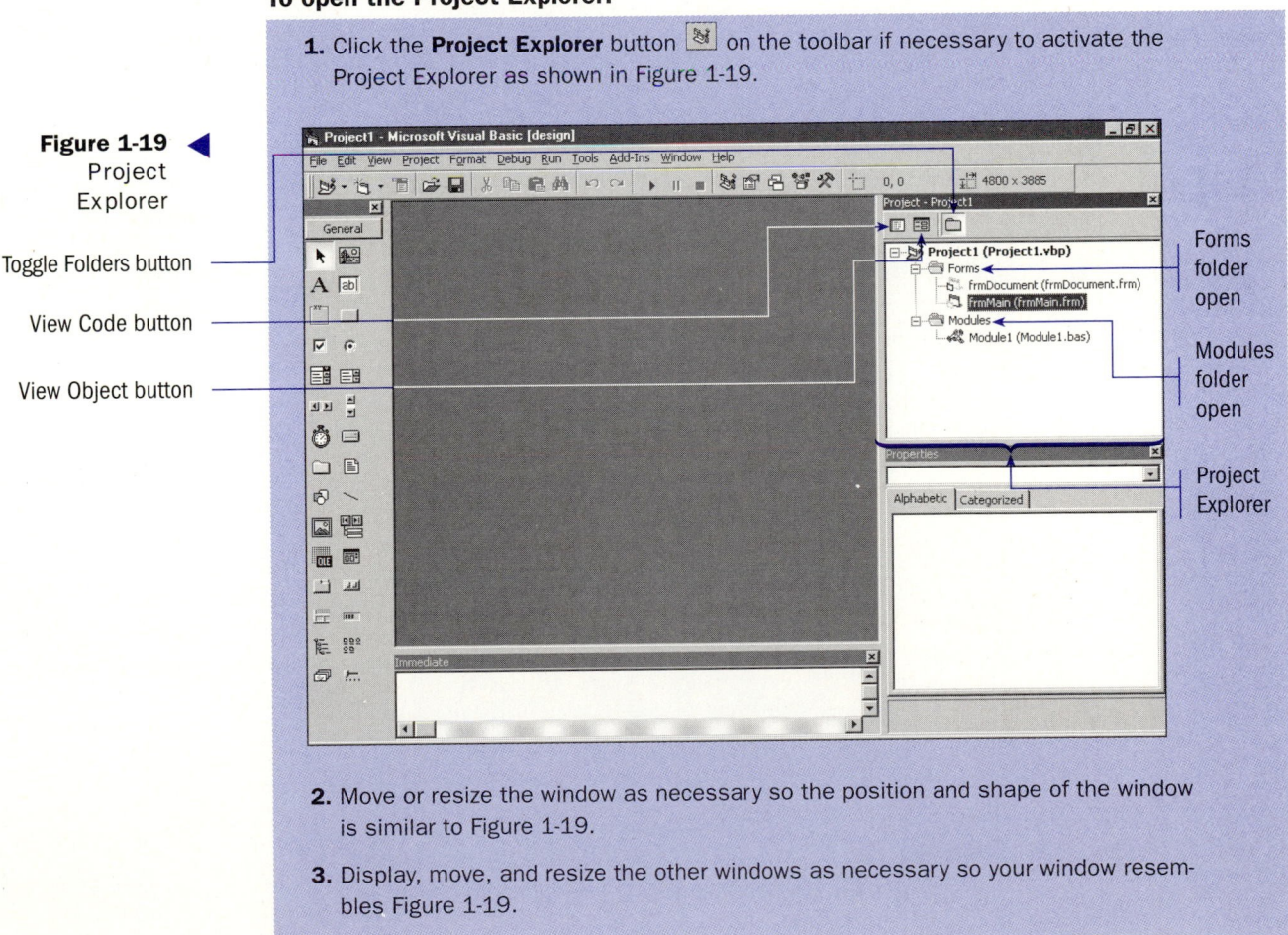

Forms
folder
open

Modules
folder
open

Project
Explorer

2. Move or resize the window as necessary so the position and shape of the window is similar to Figure 1-19.

3. Display, move, and resize the other windows as necessary so your window resembles Figure 1-19.

The Project Explorer displays a hierarchical list of all the forms and modules used in a project. Forms and modules appear in different folders much like they do in the Windows Explorer program. Each line in the Project Explorer has the following components.

■ A box containing a plus or a minus sign. Clicking the plus sign will open the folder and display its contents. Clicking the minus sign will close the folder such that its contents will not be displayed.

■ An icon describing the type of object or file.

■ The name of the object used inside of Visual Basic.

■ The file name of the object saved on the disk.

The Project Explorer also contains three buttons.

■ The **View Code** button opens a window to display the Visual Basic statements that apply to the selected module.

■ The **View Object** button displays a form or other object in a window called the Object window.

■ The **Toggle Folders** buttons is used to hide and show the object folders.

Mark suggests you list the complete hierarchy so you can identify all the files used in the project, then look at the main form created by the Application Wizard.

To identify the project components and view a form:

1. If any of the folders are closed, click the **plus** button ⊞ next to the folder in the Project Explorer to open the folder.

2. Click the form named **frmMain**.

   TROUBLE? If you cannot see frmMain in the Project Explorer, the Forms folder may be closed. Click the "+" sign next to Forms to open it. Then repeat Step 2.

3. Click the **View Object** button in the Project Explorer to display the Form window. Your screen should look like Figure 1-20.

Figure 1-20 ◄
Displaying
a form

form's menu bar

form's toolbar

frmMain displayed

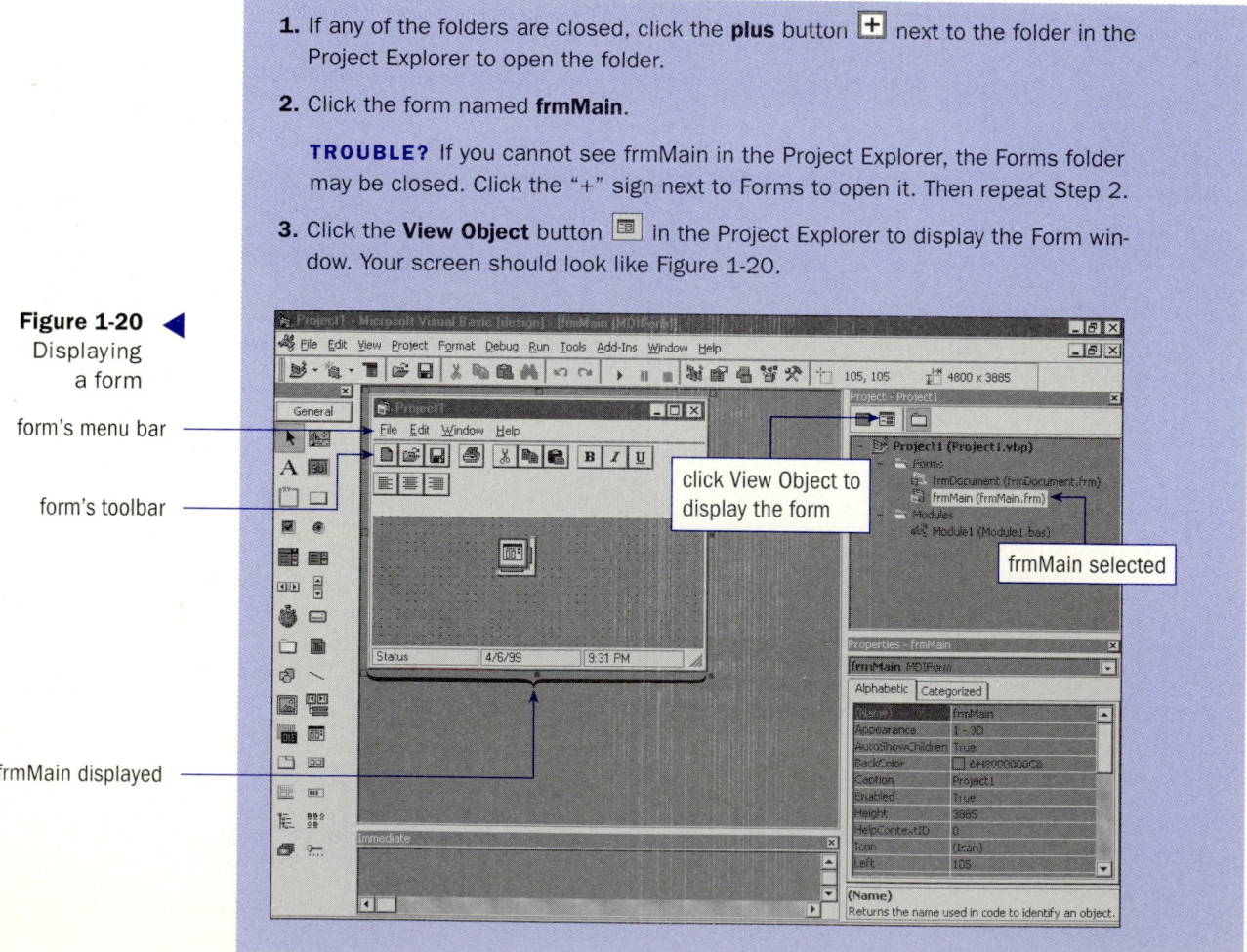

The Form Window

The **Form window** is the window in which you design the user interface for the program. When a user runs the program, the user communicates with the program by clicking buttons or typing characters into the objects on the form. As shown in Figure 1-20, the Form window shows the main form that was created by the Application Wizard. The Wizard created several objects on the form. It created a menu bar and toolbar to execute commands. It also set the caption of the form on the title bar.

Properties Window

The **Properties window** provides options you use to manage the appearance of each object on a form. A **property** is a characteristic of an object, such as the object's color, caption, screen location, or size.

To display the Properties window for the form:

1. Click the **Properties Window** button 🖼 on the toolbar to activate the Properties window if necessary.

2. Use the scroll bar to locate the Caption property. Note that the value for this property is the same as the caption shown on the form. By setting properties in this way, you can change the appearance of the form or other object. See Figure 1-21.

Figure 1-21 ◀
Properties
window
components

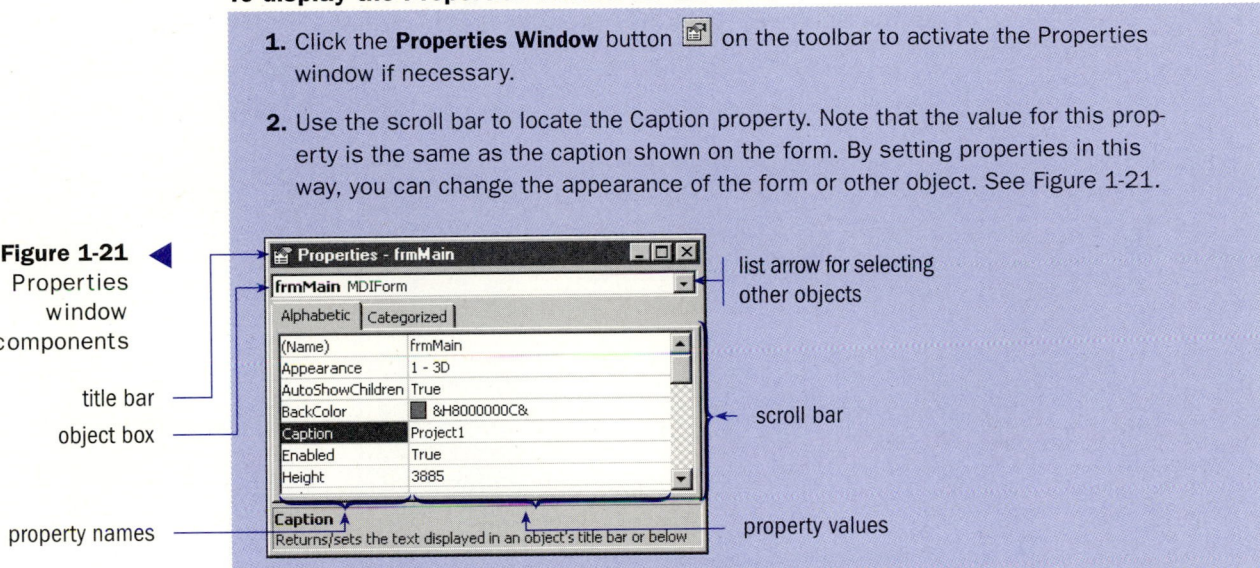

You will use the Properties window in the next session when you create the program to display graphical images.

Toolbox

The **toolbox** contains all the visual tools necessary to create a program. You use the icons in the toolbox to place controls on a form. As noted earlier, a control is a class, such as a box, button, or label. When you draw an instance of a control on a form it becomes an object. You can create objects that users interact with, and objects to enhance the visual appeal of a form.

Mark suggests you run the program to see the different objects he created. To help you identify the different controls in the toolbox, a ToolTip is displayed whenever the mouse is positioned over a control for about one second.

Running a Program

Now you can run the program and begin to interact with its objects. By using some of the different Visual Basic controls, you will begin to see how they function before creating the program for Mark to display images.

Operating Modes

Visual Basic always operates in either run mode, design mode, or break mode. The title bar at the top of the Visual Basic menu bar indicates the current mode. When you are in the process of running a program, the Visual Basic title bar contains the text "run," meaning that your program is being executed, or is in **run mode**. In another mode called **design mode** you perform activities like creating and saving projects, designing forms, setting properties, and writing code. You will learn more about design time in Session 1.2 when you create the program to display graphical images. **Break mode** is similar to run time, but your program temporarily is suspended allowing you to examine the program statements as they are being executed. You will learn more about break mode in later tutorials.

When you run a program, Visual Basic loads the startup, or first form, and displays all the objects drawn on the form. The Application Wizard sets the main form as the startup form for you. After the main form is displayed, the document form is displayed inside the region of the main form. Then the program waits for you to interact with it. When you click an item on the menu or a toolbar button, you generate an event, and Visual Basic executes the code written in response to the event.

Mark suggests you test the program to see how a Visual Basic program looks when it runs.

To run the Southern Properties Group project:

1. Click the **Start** button ▶ on the toolbar. A document form appears inside of the main form, and the Visual Basic title bar displays [run]. Figure 1-22 shows the running form.

Figure 1-22 ◀
Running a
program

title bar

menu bar

toolbar

document form
(frmDocument)

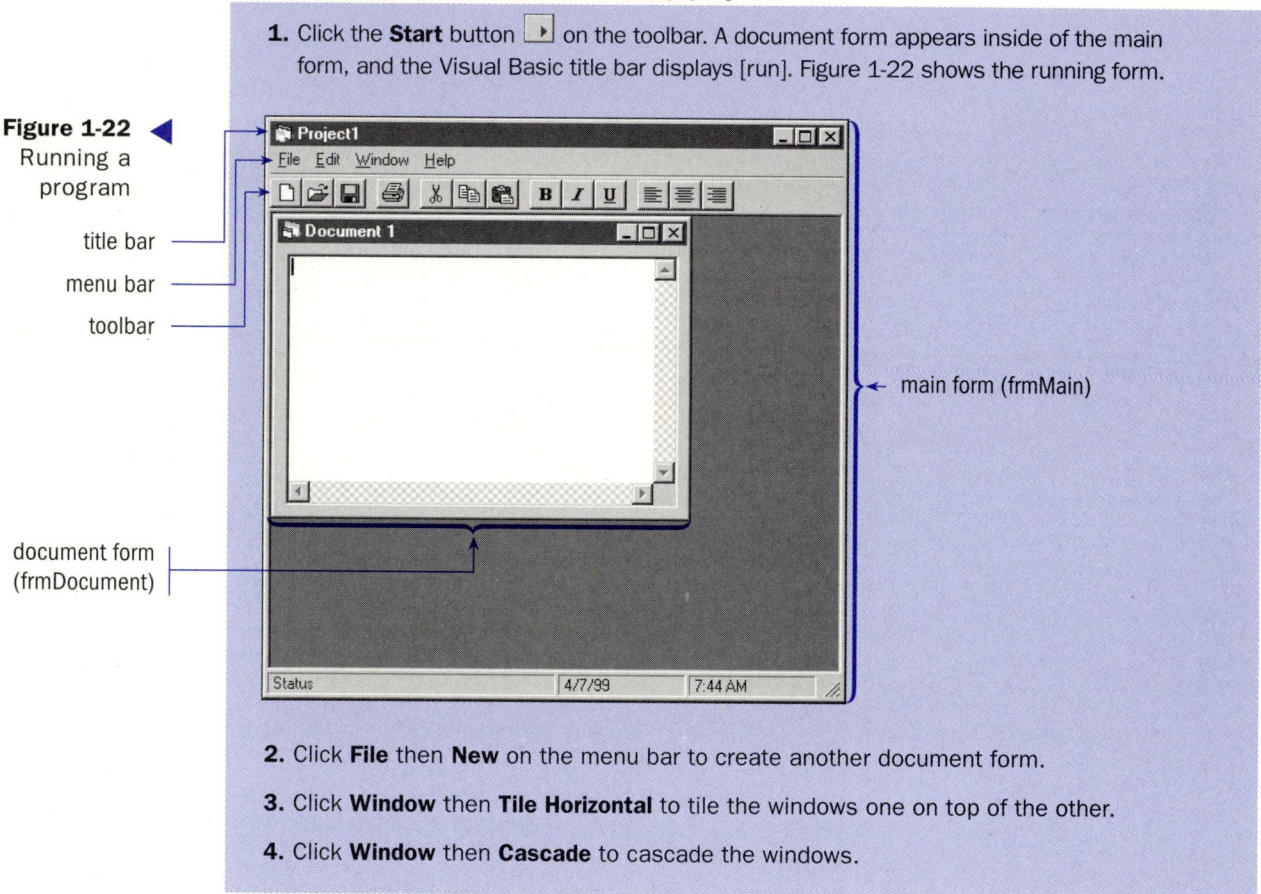

main form (frmMain)

2. Click **File** then **New** on the menu bar to create another document form.

3. Click **Window** then **Tile Horizontal** to tile the windows one on top of the other.

4. Click **Window** then **Cascade** to cascade the windows.

The Application Wizard wrote the necessary statements to manage the windows for you and to create new windows. It did not, however, complete all the code. For example, most of the buttons will display a message indicating that the code goes here, telling you that the procedure is not complete. The next step is to stop running the program.

Stopping a Program

You have finished looking at the Southern Properties Group program, so you now can stop running it. When you stop a program from running, you change the operating mode from run mode to design mode. There are two ways to stop running a program—using the End button on the toolbar or the End command on the Run menu.

To stop running the Southern Properties program:

1. Click the **End** button ▪ on the toolbar. Visual Basic stops running the program and returns to design mode. Note that the form no longer contains information and the title bar displays the text "[design]".

Exiting Visual Basic

Now that you have created the Southern Properties Group demo program, and saved the project and other files, you can exit Visual Basic. Because you have not made any changes to the program since last saving it, you do not have to save it again before exiting.

You can exit Visual Basic either by clicking the Close button on the Visual Basic title bar or choosing the Exit command from the File menu. When you exit Visual Basic, it checks to see if you have made any changes to your program that need to be saved. If there are unsaved changes to the project or any of the forms, Visual Basic displays a message asking if you want to save the file that was changed. Before exiting, Visual Basic closes all open forms and the project file.

To exit Visual Basic:

1. Click the **Close** button ☒ on the Visual Basic title bar.

TROUBLE? If you resized the form or made any other changes to it, Visual Basic will ask if you want to save the changes to the files that have been modified. Click the No button.

Visual Basic closes any open forms, then closes the project file and exits Visual Basic.

Quick Check

1. Describe the steps to create a program.

2. What is the Application Wizard?

3. What is a project?

4. What is a form?

5. What is the difference between using the Index tab and the Contents tab on the Help window to locate specific information?

6. How do you run and stop a program?

SESSION 1.2

In this session, you will learn how to create a new project without a Wizard, how to create instances of controls on a form, and how to set properties for the form and its objects. You will add Visual Basic statements to the program so it can open and display graphical images. Finally, you will test the completed program.

Creating a New Project

The project you created in Session 1.1 contained the structure of a program so you could identify the parts of a Visual Basic program and how to run it. Mark now would like you to create a new project without a Wizard, and then create the user interface so the new program can display graphical images. When you start Visual Basic, it automatically will create a new project for you.

To create the new project for Southern Properties Group:

1. Start Visual Basic if you have not already done so. Visual Basic creates a new project with a single form for you as shown in Figure 1-23.

Figure 1-23 ◀
New project created by Visual Basic

toolbox contains controls for project

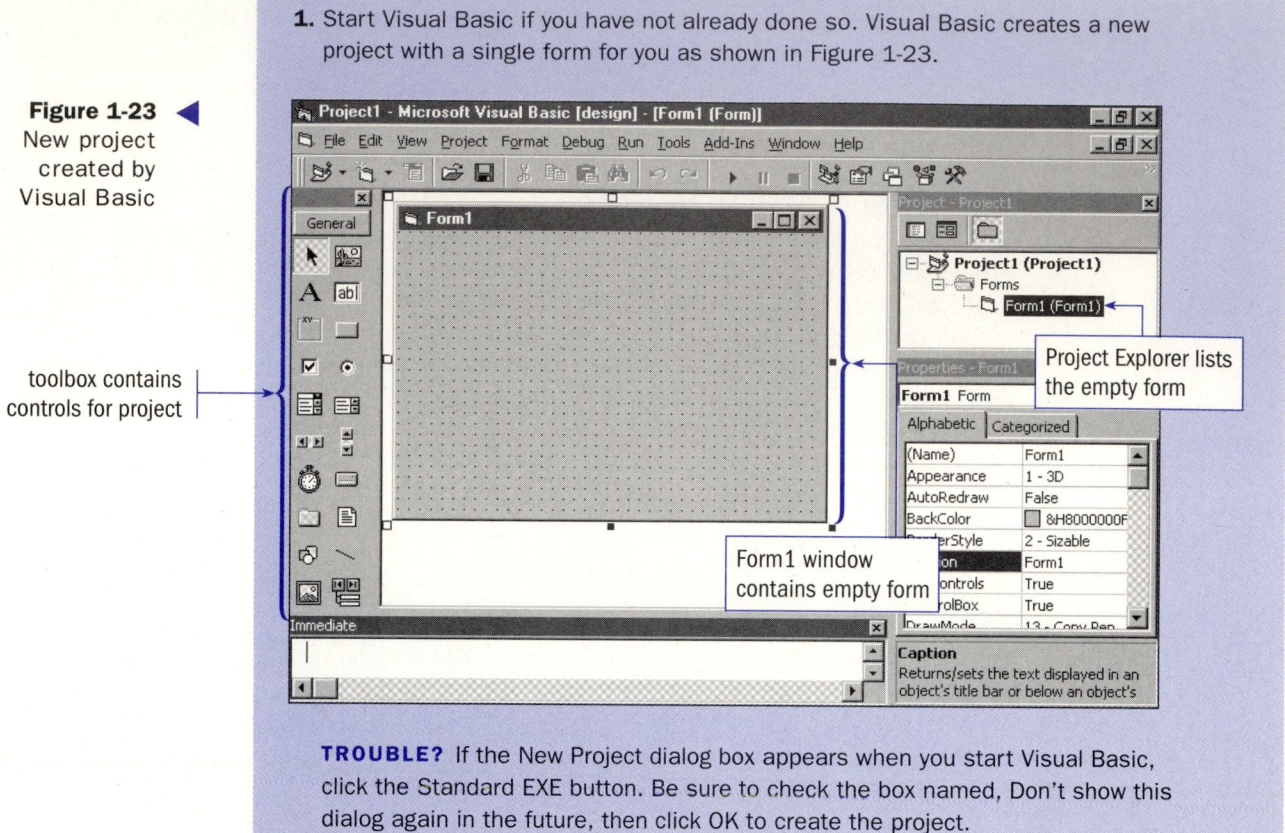

TROUBLE? If the New Project dialog box appears when you start Visual Basic, click the Standard EXE button. Be sure to check the box named, Don't show this dialog again in the future, then click OK to create the project.

As shown in Figure 1-23, the new project contains a single form named Form1. Also, the toolbox contains the different controls that you can use to create objects on the form. Finally, both the Project Explorer and Properties window contain information about the current project and object, respectively.

You need to create four objects on the form. You need an Image object that will display the pictures Southern Properties Group has stored on the computer. A text box needs to be created in which the user can type a file name to display. A command button needs to be created that, when clicked, will cause the image to be displayed. Finally, a label needs to be created that will describe the purpose of the text box. Mark suggests you use the Help system to learn more about the specific controls you will be adding to your form. The fastest way to get help on a control is to open a window called the toolbox that contains all the available controls, activate the control by clicking it, then press the F1 key to display the Help window.

To learn more about the Label control:

1. Click the **Toolbox** button ⚒ on the toolbar to open the toolbox if necessary.

2. Click the **Label** control **A** on the toolbox. Remember, if you leave the mouse over a control for a few seconds the ToolTip will appear.

3. Press the **F1** key to display Help information about the control.

   The Visual Basic Help window opens to the page describing the Label control.

Because you will be using both the Label and CommandButton controls when you create your program, you will print a copy of the Help Topic for reference later on. Like most programs, Visual Basic supports shortcut menus. A **shortcut menu** is a menu that appears when the right mouse button is clicked. The list of menu items depends on the active window or active control. Shortcut menus provide a quick way to execute frequently used commands.

To print the Help Topics for the Label and CommandButton controls:

1. Read the text in the displayed Help window, using the scroll arrows and scroll box to move through the text.

2. Click the **right mouse** button while the cursor is positioned in the Help window to activate the shortcut menu, then click **Print Topic** on the shortcut menu.

   The Print dialog box will appear on your screen.

3. Click the **OK** button in the Print dialog box.

4. Click the **Help Topics** button at the upper-left corner of the Help window.

5. Click the **Index** tab if necessary.

6. Enter the text **CommandButton control** in the text box, then click **Display**.

7. Click the **right mouse** button while the cursor is positioned in the Help window to activate the shortcut menu, then click **Print Topic** on the shortcut menu.

   The Print dialog box will appear on your screen.

8. Click the **OK** button in the Print dialog box.

In addition to the Label and CommandButton controls, your program also will include an Image control. So, you also will display and print Help information about this control.

Using the Table of Contents

The Contents tab of the Help system displays a set of books, each of which contains a particular category of information. You click a book icon to open it and display the topics in that category; then you can choose a particular topic to view. You will use the Contents tab to view information about the Image control.

To use the Contents tab to find information about the Image control:

1. Click the **Help Topics** button in the upper-left corner of the Help window.

   Your screen should look like Figure 1-24. If necessary, click the Contents tab to make it the active tab.

Figure 1-24 ◀
Contents
tab of the
Help window

Contents tab active ——

open this book icon ——

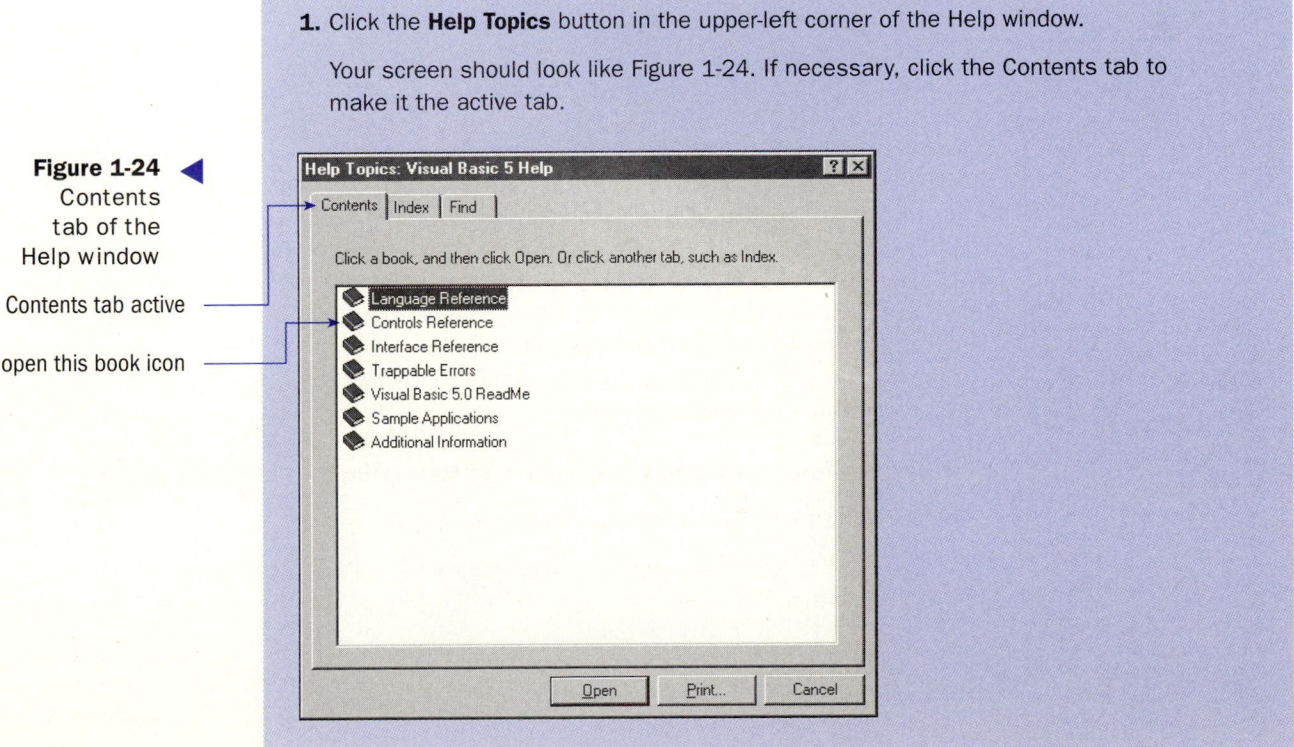

Depending on whether you are running the Visual Basic Learning, Professional, or Enterprise edition, the items listed in the Contents tab might differ from those shown in Figure 1-24.

2. Click the book icon labeled **Controls Reference**, then click the **Open** button. The icon changes from a closed book to an open book and several other options appear.

3. Click the book icon labeled **Intrinsic Controls,** then click **Open** again, as shown in Figure 1-25.

Figure 1-25 ◀
Contents tab
with an
open book

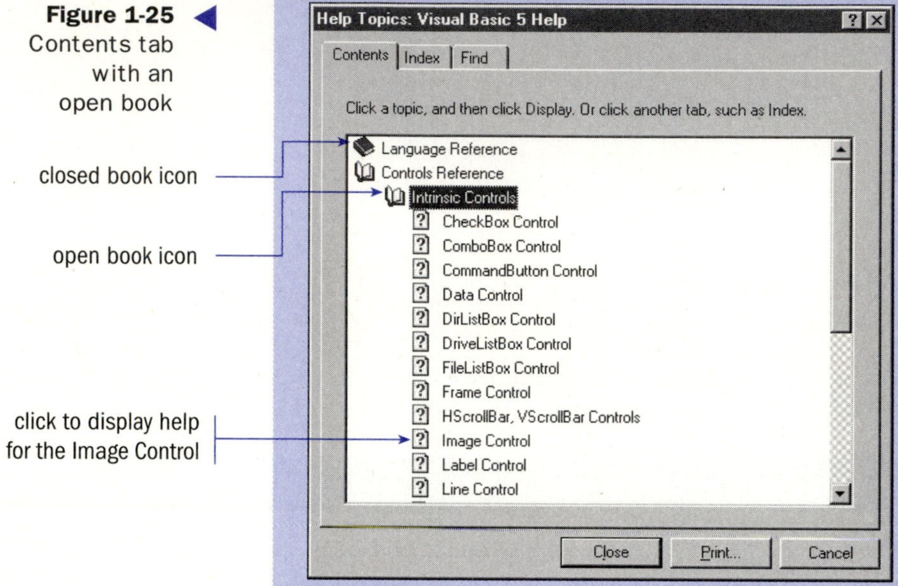

closed book icon

open book icon

click to display help
for the Image Control

4. Click the **Image control** Help Topic, then click the **Display** button to open it. Read the text in the Help Topic that explains the Image control.

5. Use the shortcut menu to print the Help Topic.

6. Click the **Close** button ☒ on the Help window title bar to close the window and exit the Help system.

Now you are ready to begin creating the buttons and boxes on the blank form. First, you need to set the properties of the form itself and then you can create the necessary control instances. When Visual Basic was started, a new project was created with a single form. Now you are ready to modify the form so it is useful to Southern Properties Group. In this case, you need to change the size of the main form so the images Mark wants to display will fit inside the region of the form, and set the form's Caption property to display a more meaningful title in the form's title bar.

To set or change any property, you first need to display the Properties window for the selected object (in this case, the form).

To display the Properties window for the main form using the shortcut menu:

1. Click **Form1 (Form 1)** in the Project Explorer.

   TROUBLE? If necessary, open the Project Explorer by clicking the Project Explorer button.

   If the forms are not displayed under the Forms folder click the "+" sign to display them.

2. Click the **View Object** button ⊞ at the top of the Project Explorer. The Form1 window becomes the active window.

3. Click the **right mouse** button while the cursor is positioned over the Form1 window to activate the shortcut menu.

4. Click **Properties** to activate the Properties window, then click the **Categorized** tab if necessary. See Figure 1-26.

Figure 1-26
Properties
window
components

title bar

object box

Height property

property names

property values

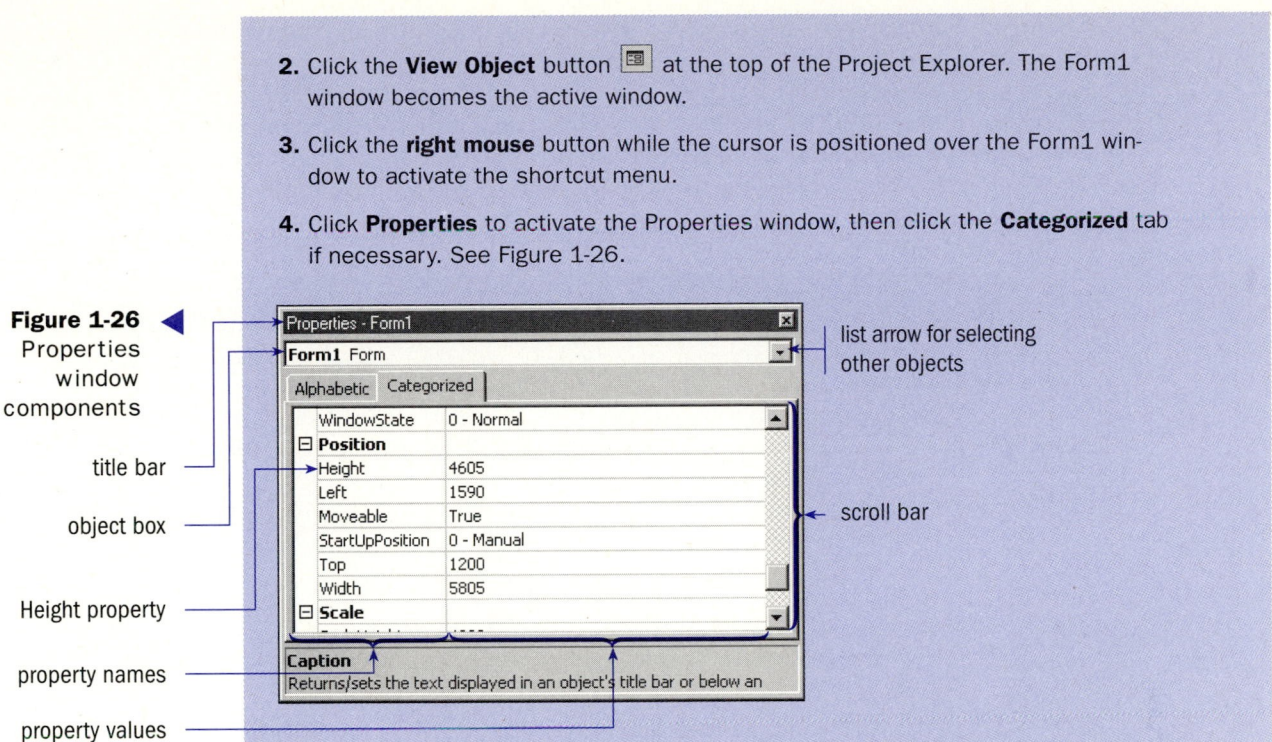

list arrow for selecting other objects

scroll bar

The Properties window title bar identifies the current object, in this case Form1, which is the value of the Name property assigned to the form. The object box identifies the selected object, which also is Form1, followed by the type of the object, which is a form. The list arrow at the right side of the object box allows you to select another object and display its properties. The left column in the window lists the properties available for the selected object, and the right column lists the current value for each property. If all the properties will not fit in the window, you can use the displayed scroll bar to scroll through the Properties window. Note that properties either can be displayed in alphabetical order or in a categorized order by clicking the Alphabetic or Categorized tab. The Categorized tab divides properties into categories based on their purpose. For example, the Position category lists the properties that control the size and position of the form on the screen.

To view properties in the Properties window:

1. Use the scroll bar to move through the list of properties to see which properties you can set for a form.

2. Click the **Categorized** tab in the Properties window to view the properties applicable to a form organized by category.

You now can use the Properties window to set properties for the form.

Setting the Size and Position of a Form

The needs of a particular program determine the size of each form. The program you are creating will display a 3-by-3-inch picture or smaller. In addition, you will be adding a Label object to the form that will display the name of the currently loaded file. This information will occupy the top 1 inch of the form. Thus, the form should be about 4 inches tall and 4½ inches wide. The dimensions of a form are set using the Height and Width properties. All Visual Basic dimensions are measured in twips. A **twip** is a unit of screen measurement specifying about 1440 twips per inch. So, to create a 4-by-4½-inch form, you would set the Height and Width properties to 4335 and 5025 twips, respectively. The size indicator on the far right of the toolbar tells you the height and width in twips of the current object.

You also can specify where on the screen the form should be displayed by setting the Left and Top properties. If you set both the Left and Top properties of a form to zero (0), the form would be displayed in the upper-left corner of the screen. The position indicator on the right of the toolbar tells you the position of the current object. If the object is a form, the position is relative to the upper-left corner of the screen. If the object is an instance of a control you drew on the form, the position is relative to the upper-left corner of the form.

REFERENCE window

SETTING THE SIZE AND POSITION OF A FORM

- If the Properties window is not displayed, place the pointer in an empty area of the form, click the right mouse button to display the shortcut menu, then click Properties.
- Click the value for the Height property, then type in the new value for the height.
- Click the value for the Width property, then type the new value for the width.
- Click the values for the Left and Top properties, then type the new value for each.

To change the size and location of the form relative to the screen, you need to change four properties: Height, Width, Left, and Top. Mark has asked that you create a 4-by-4½-inch form, located about 1 inch from the upper-left corner of the screen. Remember that 1 inch equals approximately 1440 twips, so the height of the form will be 4335, the width of the form will be 5025, and the left and top dimensions will be 1440 each.

To set the size and position of the form:

1. Be sure the Properties window is active and set to the form named **Form1**. Click the **Categorized** tab.

2. Scroll down the Properties window to locate the **Position** section.

3. Locate the **Height** property, then highlight its default property value. The text you type next will replace the highlighted default value.

4. Type **4335**.

5. Press the **Enter** key.

   The form changes size on your screen.

6. Locate the **Width** property, highlight the property value, then type **5025**.

7. Locate the **Left** property, highlight the property value, then type **1440**.

   The size and location of the form changes as you enter each value.

8. Locate the **Top** property, highlight the property value, then type **1440**.

   The form repositions itself to the new Top property value on your screen.

Setting the Caption for a Form

Like any window in Windows 95, a Visual Basic form contains text in the title bar to identify the purpose of the form. You specify this text by setting the form's Caption property. Unlike a name, a caption can include spaces and punctuation characters. Although the caption can contain any number of characters, it should fit in the title bar of the form.

Mark suggests you use the caption "Southern Properties Group - Image Viewer" for the form you are editing. This will communicate the purpose of the form to the user.

To set the caption for the form:

1. Locate the **Caption** property in the Appearance section of the Properties window, then highlight its property value **Form1**.

2. Type **Southern Properties Group - Image Viewer**. The caption in the form's title bar changes to the new value. See Figure 1-27.

Figure 1-27 ◀
Setting the
form's caption

caption in the
form's title bar

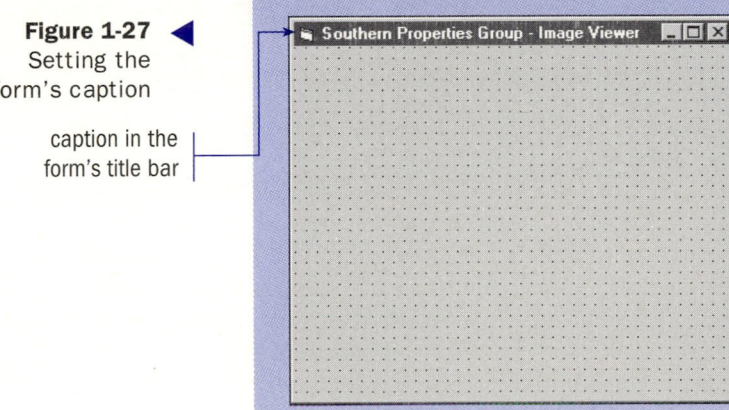

Southern Properties Group - Image Viewer

Now that you have set the properties for the form, you are ready to create instances of the necessary controls on the form. Then you can set the properties for each control.

Setting the Name of the Form

In addition to the Caption property, each object you create has an associated name, which is stored in the Name property of the object. When Visual Basic created the form for you, it assigned a default name (Form1) for the form. Mark suggests, however, you assign a more meaningful name to the form. Note that the Caption and Name properties are different. You use the Caption property to display informational text inside the title bar of the form; and you use the Name property to identify the object and to refer to it when writing Visual Basic statements. You should set the Name property for most objects so the code in your program is easier to understand. There are several rules for naming objects like forms:

- The first character of the name must be a letter.

- The following characters can be letters, numbers, or the underscore character.

- The name must be fewer than 255 characters in length.

- A name cannot include special characters such as symbols or spaces.

- A name should begin with a standard prefix describing the type of the object.

Mark suggests you set the name of the form so the name describes its purpose. Because the standard prefix of the form is frm and the program is an image viewer for Southern Properties Group, he suggests you use the name frmSouthernImageViewer.

To set the name for the form:

1. Locate the **Name** property in the Misc section of the Properties window, then highlight its property value **Form1**.

2. Enter the name **frmSouthernImageViewer**.

Before continuing to create the objects on the form, Mark suggests you first save both the form and the project. If you make a mistake, you will be able to open the files you already saved and continue.

To save the form and project files:

1. Be sure your Student Disk is in the drive then click **File** on the menu bar, then click **Save Project** to activate the Save File As dialog box. Remember that any unsaved forms are saved, then the project is saved.

2. Click the **Save in** list arrow, click **3½ Floppy (A:)**, then click the folder named **Tutorial.01**.

3. Accept the default file name **frmSouthernImageViewer.frm,** then click **Save**.

4. After saving the form, the Save Project As dialog box will appear. Enter the project name **Southern Image Viewer.vbp**, then click **Save**.

You now have saved the form and project files to your Student Disk. If you make a mistake, you can start by loading the project file named Southern Image Viewer.vbp and begin again from this point. By saving your work frequently, you will be able to start again from that point and continue. Mark suggests you continue by creating the necessary objects on the form to display pictures of the properties they sell.

Adding Controls to a Form

When you place a control on a form, you are creating an instance of the control that also is known as an object. The form itself also is an object. You can have multiple occurrences or instances of the same type of object on a form. That is, you can have three buttons on the same form that perform different actions like an OK button, a Cancel button, and a Help button. The controls available on the toolbox depend on both the version of Visual Basic you are using and whether or not any third-party add-in controls have been added to the toolbox. A **third-party add-in control** is a control created by another vendor and sold for use with the standard Visual Basic controls. Such add-in controls can provide added functionality, such as spell checking, or they might simply provide ways to make your programs more visually appealing.

In this session you need to use four different controls to create the program as shown in Figure 1-28; a text box for the user to type in the name of a file, a label to describe the purpose of the text box, an image to display the picture stored in the file, and a command button that, when clicked, will cause the picture to be displayed.

Figure 1-28 ◀
Controls
created on
the form

label

text box

image

command button

You will begin by adding a Label control that will describe to the user the purpose of the text box in which they will enter a file name. You then will create the text box. Remember, you use the controls on the toolbox to add objects to a form. After you place an object on the form, you can manipulate it; for example, you can reposition, resize, or delete any object you create.

Adding a Label Control

The Label control allows you to display text on your form. For example, you might want a label to include text that identifies another object. Another use of the label is to display the results of some computation. For example, you might have a program that adds sales numbers and displays a number representing total sales. You can display such a value in a label. Remember, labels are for display purposes only; a user cannot interact with a label. Like a form, labels too have properties. In addition to having Caption, Height, Left, Top, and Width properties, a label has properties that describe the font and color of the foreground and background.

REFERENCE window	**ADDING A LABEL CONTROL TO A FORM**
	■ Click the Label control on the toolbox.
	■ Click and drag the mouse to draw and position a label on the form.
	■ Set the Caption property to the desired text.
	■ Set the Height, Left, Top, and Width properties to change the label's position on the form.

In this case, the label you will add to your form will display a prompt that will describe the purpose of the control it identifies, the text box. The prompt will not change while the program is running. (You will create the TextBox control later in this session.)

To add the Label control to your form:

1. Click the **Label** control 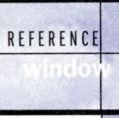 on the toolbox.

   Move the pointer to the left side of the Form window, which is where you want the upper-left corner of the Label object to be located. See Figure 1-28 for the location of the Label control. The pointer changes to $+$.

2. Click and hold down the **left mouse** button, then drag the pointer down and to the right to create an outline of the Label object.

   Notice that while you are in design time the form includes a grid of dots. When you draw objects on the form, the object is aligned with the dots on the grid.

3. When the size of the object is similar to the size of the Label object shown in Figure 1-29, release the left mouse button. The object appears on the form.

Figure 1-29 ◀
Creating a label

default caption
for object

sizing handles

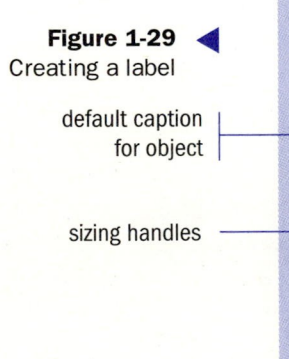

TROUBLE? Do not worry if the Label object on your screen is not exactly in the same location or is not the same size as the object shown in the figure. You will reposition and resize objects later.

Note that Visual Basic assigns a name to the object; in this case, Label1. Each object on a form must have a unique name. Therefore, if you place a second instance of the Label control on the form without changing the name of the first label, Visual Basic would assign the name Label2 to the second Label object. Also, notice the eight small, colored boxes that appear around the border of the label. These boxes are called **sizing handles** and they identify the active object. You can use the handles to resize the object, as you will learn later in this session. Because the label is the active object, the Properties window shows the properties for this object.

Setting a Label's Properties

Just as a form has properties, each object on a form has properties. The properties of an object can determine the appearance of the object (for example, its color), the font of the object's text (if any), the position of the object on the screen, and whether or not the object is visible on the screen. Some properties, such as color and screen location, are common to most types of objects. Other properties are unique, however, and define the specific attributes of a particular object type. As an analogy, consider two objects—an automobile and an airplane. Both an automobile and an airplane have similar properties, such as color, weight, and engine size. This does not necessarily mean that they have the same color, just that each has a color. Some properties, however, are meaningful only to the airplane; for example, only an airplane has a wing size. Visual Basic objects are similar. For example, both a label and an image have properties like Left and Top that determine where the object appears on the form. Because the label is used to display text, however, it has a Caption property to describe text, while the image has a Picture property to describe the picture to be displayed.

Next, you need to set the properties for the Label object. Although you can set properties at any time while you are developing the program, it is best to set them immediately after creating the object so you do not forget to set the necessary properties. Here you need to set the Caption property for the label to describe the purpose of the text box you will create in a moment.

Naming the Label Object

The initial name of the Label object you created is Label1, just as the initial name of the form object was Form1. Like the form, you should change the name to a more meaningful one by setting the Name property.

The label you just created contains a prompt to describe the contents of the text box you will create in a moment so lblPrompt is an appropriate name.

To set the Caption and Name properties of the Label object:

1. Make sure the Label object still is selected (that is, handles appear on the object).

2. Click the **Alphabetic** tab in the Properties window if necessary, then highlight the default **Caption** property value **Label1**.

3. Enter **Enter file name:** as the caption.

4. Highlight the default value for the **Name** property. Enter the text **lblPrompt** for the property's value. The Label object now contains the text you just entered. See Figure 1-30.

Figure 1-30 ◄
Setting
the label's
properties

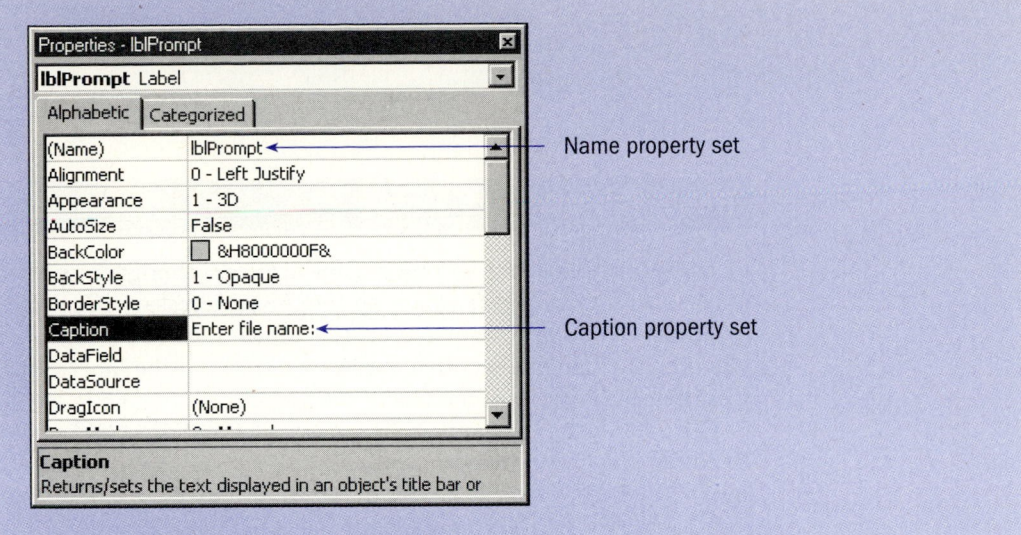

Name property set

Caption property set

Moving an Object

When you create an object on the form, you often will need to change the location of the object—perhaps because a design specification has changed or because the objects on the form are not visually balanced. You can move any object on a form by first clicking the object to select it then using the pointer to drag the object to a new location. You will practice moving the Label object on your form.

To move the Label object:

1. Make sure the Label object still is selected. (The sizing handles should be visible.)

2. Place the pointer anywhere within the Label object, but not on a handle.

3. Click and hold down the **left mouse** button, then move the mouse to drag the object to a different location. An outline of the object appears on the form and moves to show the new object position as you move the mouse. See Figure 1-31.

Figure 1-31 ◄
Moving the
label

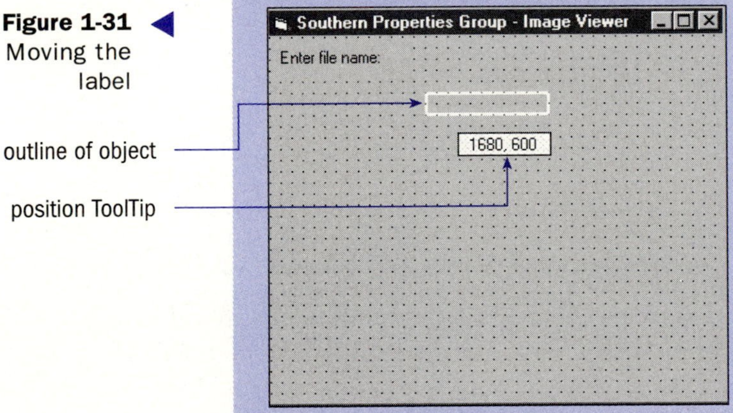

outline of object ————

position ToolTip ————

> Southern Properties Group - Image Viewer

Enter file name:

1680, 600

Note that the position indicator ToolTip shows the position of the active object, the label.

4. Release the left mouse button when the object is in the location you want.

5. Use the mouse to move the Label object back to the original location shown in Figure 1-31.

6. To deselect the Label object, click anywhere in a blank area of the Form window. The form now becomes the selected object, and its properties are displayed in the Properties window.

Resizing an Object

In addition to moving an object, you also can change an object's size by modifying the object's width or height. Again, this might be necessary because of changes in design specifications or to improve or correct the appearance of objects on the form. For example, if you create a Label object that is too small to hold the label's Caption property value, you would need to increase the size of the object.

To resize the Label object:

1. Click the Label object to select it and display the sizing handles.

TROUBLE? If you accidentally double-click the object, the Code window will be activated. (You will learn more about the Code window later in this session.) Click the Close button ☒ on the Code window title bar to close the window, then repeat Step 1.

2. Position the pointer on the handle in the lower-right corner of the object. The pointer changes to ↘. When you use one of the four corner sizing handles to resize an object, the object will be resized both horizontally and vertically. When you use one of the center sizing handles, the object will be resized in one direction only, depending on the handle you are using.

3. Click and hold down the **left mouse** button, then move the pointer down and to the right to increase the size of the object, as shown in Figure 1-32.

Figure 1-32 ◄
Resizing
the label

outline shows the
resized object

ToolTip shows new
width and height

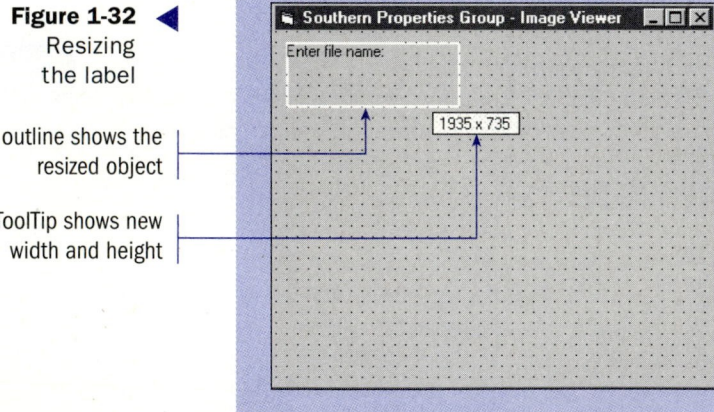

Note that the ToolTip reflects the width and height of the active object, the label.

4. Release the left mouse button when the object is the size you want.

Just as you set the size and position of the form by setting the Height, Left, Top, and Width properties of the form, you can set the properties of an object in the same way. The only difference is that the Left and Top properties of an object are relative to the form, not the entire screen.

To set the size and position of the label using the Properties window:

1. Click the label to activate it. The Properties window displays the properties for the Label object.

2. Set the following properties for the Label object in the Properties window: Height = **255**; Left = **120**; Top = **120**; Width = **1215**.

Deleting an Object

Occasionally, you will need to delete an object from a form, perhaps because you created the object by mistake or the object is no longer used in the program. To delete an object you simply click the object then press the Delete key. Because you will be using the Label object in your program, there is no need to delete it.

Now that you have created the label and set its properties, you can create the next object on the form—the TextBox object.

Adding a TextBox Control to a Form

There is another control similar to a label that works with text called a TextBox control. In addition to just displaying textual information, however, the user can enter text into a text box. Like the label, it has a Name property. It also has the same properties as the label to describe the position of the label on the form. The information displayed in a text box, however, is controlled by the Text property rather than the Caption property. A text box also has a three-character prefix like a label. The standard three-character prefix for a text box is "txt".

Because the text box you are creating will be used to get the file name of a picture from the user, Mark suggests you set the Name property for the object to txtFileName. Also, because the user will enter the text into this object when the program is running, the Text property should be blank when the program starts.

To create the text box:

1. Click the **TextBox** control [ab] on the toolbox.

2. Move the pointer to the left side of the Form window just below the label you created, which is where you want the upper-left corner of the TextBox object to be located. See Figure 1-33 for the location of the TextBox control.

Figure 1-33 ◀
Creating the
text box

new TextBox object ──

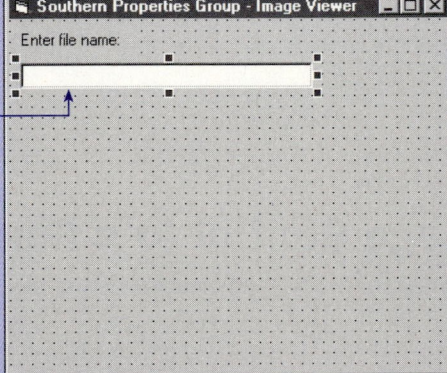

3. Click and hold down the **left mouse** button, then drag the pointer down and to the right to create an outline of the TextBox object.

   Notice that while you are in design time the form includes a grid of dots. When you draw objects on the form, the object is aligned with the dots on the grid.

4. Set the Name property to **txtFileName.**

5. Remove the text from the Text property.

6. Set the Height property to **285**, the Left to **120**, the Top to **480**, and the Width to **3255**.

Adding a CommandButton Control to a Form

After the user enters the file name containing a picture into the text box, you need a way to tell the program that it should use the file name to display the picture in an image. There is a control called a command button that when clicked will perform some type of action, like displaying a picture. You probably have used command buttons before, as they are used throughout most Windows 95 programs. When you used the Options dialog box in the first session to customize Visual Basic settings, the dialog box had three command buttons across the bottom of the form with the captions OK, Cancel, and Help. In this session you need to create a command button that, when clicked, will display a picture in an Image object. You will create the Image object later in the session.

Like the Label and TextBox objects you just created, the command button uses the same properties to define the size of the button and its position on the form. Inside a command button you usually create a descriptive prompt to describe the button's purpose. The prompt, like the label, is stored in the Caption property. Like the other objects you have created, you should set the name of a command button using a standard prefix followed by a name that describes the button's purpose. The standard prefix for a command button is "cmd". Because the command button will be used to display an image, you will name the button cmdDisplayImage.

Mark suggests you now create the command button and set the necessary properties.

To create the command button and set its properties:

1. Click the **CommandButton** control 🔲 on the toolbox.

2. Draw a command button on the form.

3. In the Properties window, click the **value** column for the Name property.

4. Enter the name **cmdDisplayImage**.

5. Click the **Caption** property. You may need to use the scroll bars to locate the property.

6. Enter the caption **Display Image**. Note that as you edit the value of the Caption property, the caption in the command button changes.

7. Set the Height property to **375**, the Left to **3480**, the Top to **3480**, and the Width to **1335**.

Adding an Image Control to a Form

The program you are creating for Southern Properties Group must display different graphical images as selected by the user. You also can include graphic images or pictures on a form to add visual interest to your program. Graphic images are stored in many different formats. In this case the images Southern Properties Group is using are Windows bitmap files. Bitmap files have the extension .bmp.

The Image control allows you to display graphic images on a form. If you display too many large images in your program at the same time, the program may run slowly.

By default, the picture you insert into an Image object has a fixed size and may differ from the size and shape of the Image object. So, if you create a 1-by-1-inch Image object on your form and insert a 2-by-2-inch picture, the picture will appear cropped. Setting the Image object's Stretch property to True causes the picture to be the size of the Image object.

Whether or not you should set the Stretch property to True depends on the particular picture you are placing on the form. For example, if the shape of the picture is significantly different from the shape of the Image object and the Stretch property is set to True, the picture will be scaled to fill the Image object and could appear distorted. Like the Label control, the Image control should have a standard prefix for the Name property so you can identify the type of object easily as you write Visual Basic code. The standard prefix for an Image object is "img".

REFERENCE window

ADDING AN IMAGE CONTROL TO A FORM

- Click the Image button on the toolbox.
- Click and drag the mouse to draw the Image object on the form.
- Set the Name property to the prefix img followed by a meaningful description.
- Set the Stretch property to True to cause the picture to be stretched to fill the Image object, or leave it set to False to include the picture in your form at its original size.
- Set any other necessary properties for the selected Image object in the Properties window.

Mark suggests you create the Image object now and set its properties so it can display different images when the program is running. Because all the images will be of the same size, you do not need to set the Stretch property to True.

To create the Image object:

1. Click the **Image** control 🖼 on the toolbox.

2. Position the pointer in the upper-left corner of the form.

3. Hold down the **left mouse** button and move the mouse down and to the right. An outline of the Image object is displayed.

4. In the Properties window, set the Height property to **2895**, the Left property to **120**, the Top property to **960**, and the Width property to **3255**.

5. Set the Name property to **imgCurrent**. Your form should look like Figure 1-34.

Figure 1-34 ◄
Creating the
Image object

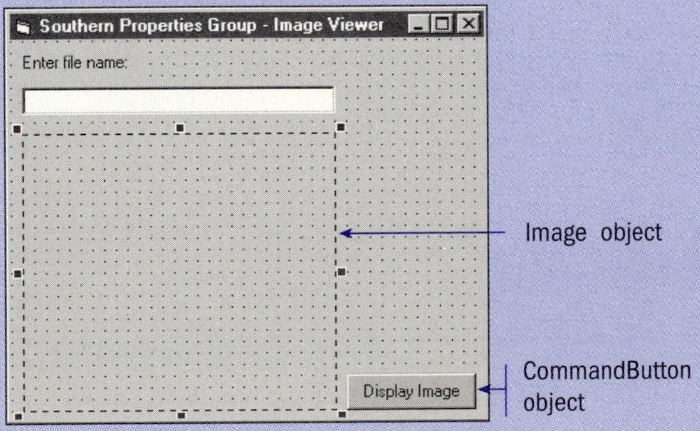

Image object

CommandButton object

You have created the necessary objects to display the file name and an image. The next step in the program's development is to write the necessary statements to accomplish these tasks.

The Code Window

To create the Visual Basic code that will display a graphical image, and its corresponding file name, you must define the actions taken when the event (clicking an item on the menu) occurs. These actions consist of Visual Basic code contained in event procedures. An **event procedure** is a set of Visual Basic statements that are executed when a user performs an action on an object, such as clicking a command button. An object can have several different event procedures. For example, some objects can execute one series of statements when the user clicks the mouse button and another series of statements when the user double-clicks the mouse button. This is because these are two different events, and an object can execute different event procedures in response to different events.

You write all Visual Basic statements using a text editor called the **Code window**. After you type a line of code and press the Enter key, Visual Basic will format the line and check the syntax of the statement to make sure it is correct. If you enter a statement that Visual Basic cannot understand, it will display a dialog box describing the error.

The code you write will perform one task. It will load a picture into the Image object you created. This code needs to be executed when the user clicks the command button on the form.

Entering the Code for the Command Button

To create the code for the command button, you need to open the Code window and enter the necessary statement. Before you can write the code for the cmdDisplayImage object's Click event procedure, you need to learn how to use the Code window to select an object and the appropriate event procedure.

The Code window contains two list boxes. The Object list box shows all the objects in your program, which consist of the form itself and all the different controls you have drawn on the form. The Procedure list box lists all the different events to which the object can respond. Each object can respond to events like a command button being clicked. The events shown in the Procedure list box depend on the type of object you selected, because different objects respond to different events.

There are two ways to locate a specific event procedure for an object. If you double-click an object like a command button, the Code window will be opened to the most frequently used event for the object. In the case of the command button, this is the Click event. You also can select an event procedure manually by first selecting the desired object using the Object list arrow, then selecting the desired event procedure using the Procedure list arrow.

To select the object and event in the Code window:

1. Be sure the Form window is the active object.

2. Click the **right mouse** button while the cursor is positioned inside of the Form window to activate the shortcut menu.

3. Click **View Code** on the shortcut menu. The Code window opens.

4. Click the **Object** list arrow, then click **cmdDisplayImage**, as shown in Figure 1-35.

Figure 1-35 ◄
The Code window

Object list box

Object list arrow

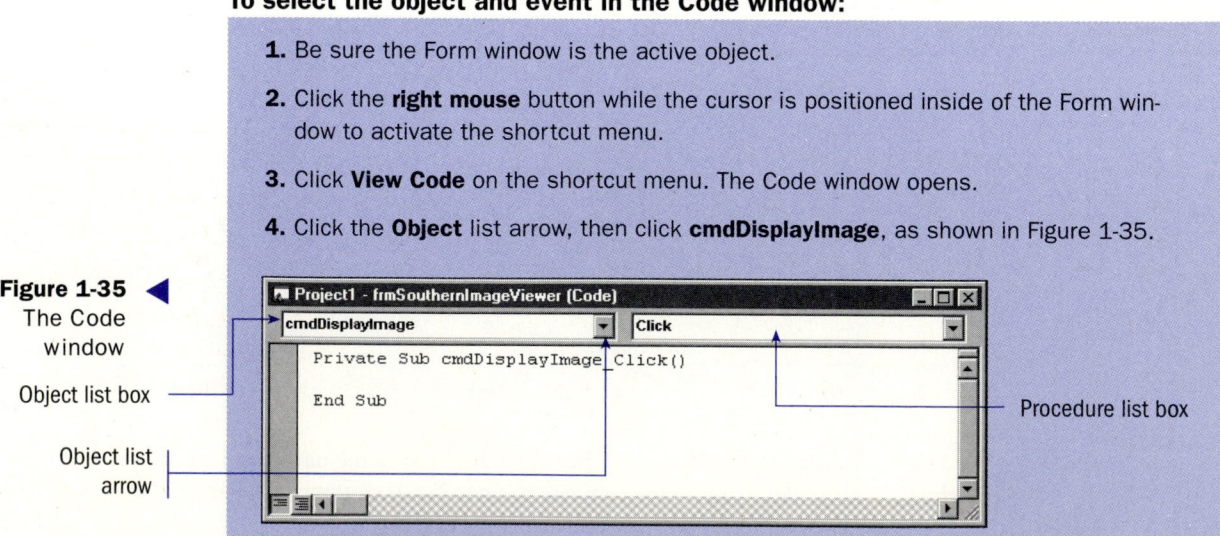

Procedure list box

```
Private Sub cmdDisplayImage_Click()

End Sub
```

TROUBLE? The size and shape of the Code window might differ from the window in Figure 1-35. You can resize the Code window to suit your preferences. The initial entries in the Object and Procedure list boxes also might differ from those in the figure, depending on the object selected when the Code window opened.

You need to write the code to display the file in the Image object and the file name in the Label object. Now that you have selected the object and the event procedure, you can complete the code necessary to open a graphical image and display it in an Image object. You need to type the statements shown in bold:

```
Private Sub cmdDisplayImage_Click( )
    'Load the image using the file name stored in
    'the TextBox control.
    imgCurrent.Picture = LoadPicture(txtFileName.Text)
End Sub
```

Before you enter the code in the Code window, take a moment to first examine each statement separately and see what it does.

```
Private Sub cmdDisplayImage_Click( )
```

The line begins with the words Private Sub. The Private and Sub keywords tell Visual Basic that this is the beginning of an event procedure that can contain Visual Basic code. The word Private tells Visual Basic that this event procedure only can be used inside this form. The word Sub tells Visual Basic that the procedure will not send information back to other procedures. Visual Basic created the Private Sub statement automatically.

```
End Sub
```

The End Sub statement tells Visual Basic where the event procedure stops. When this statement is reached, the program will stop executing the event procedure and wait for the user to do something that causes another event. Visual Basic created the End Sub statement automatically.

The procedure named cmdDisplayImage_Click( ) will be executed when a user clicks the Display Image command button. Notice that the name of the event procedure consists of the name of the object (stored in the Name property) followed by an underscore, followed by the name of the event. It is by using this procedure name that Visual Basic can determine which event procedure to execute. If you accidentally change the name of the procedure, Visual Basic will not be able to locate the event procedure and execute the code it contains in response to an event.

```
'Load the image using the file name stored in
    'the TextBox control.
```

These two statements are known as program comments. You include **program comments** in code to explain the purpose of the program and describe what it accomplishes. A program comment always begins with the apostrophe character ('). Visual Basic ignores all program comments and does not execute them.

```
imgCurrent.Picture = LoadPicture(txtFileName.Text)
```

This line in the program contains a statement that is executed by Visual Basic. This statement is made up of two parts; a leftmost side and a rightmost side separated by an equal sign (=). This is called an **assignment statement**. In other words, the task on the rightmost side is performed and assigned to the leftmost side. The rightmost side contains a **function** named LoadPicture. A function is a way of executing a set of statements that perform a common task. Visual Basic supplies you with several **intrinsic functions** to perform mathematical tasks like computing the square root of a number or loading a graphical image into an Image object. To send information to a function, you use arguments. **Arguments** contain information like numbers, in the case of the function to compute a square root, or a string of characters representing a file name, in the case of the LoadPicture function. When you use a function in a Visual Basic statement, you call the function. When you call a function, the code in the function is executed using the supplied arguments. After the code has been executed, intrinsic functions return a value like the square root of a number, or an object like a graphical image.

This statement also sets a property a run time. Until now, you have set an object's properties by changing values in the Properties window when you created the objects. You also can write Visual Basic statements that allow you to view and change properties while a program is running. You can perform many tasks, such as changing the font of text in a text box for emphasis while a user is entering text.

As you have seen, you can use the Properties window to set the Caption property of a label. You also can set many properties at run time using Visual Basic code. When to set properties depends on the needs of your program. Properties that do not change, or the initial value for a property, such as a label's caption, should be set at design time using the Properties window. When the appearance of an object needs to change while the program is running, you must change the property by writing Visual Basic code. In fact, you cannot use the Properties window while the program is running. For example, you might set the initial font and type style of a label using the Properties window. Then, when the object is active while the program is running, the font can change to emphasize the object to the user.

To set the properties of an object while the program is running, you use the following syntax for the code you enter in the Code window:

ObjectName.PropertyName = value

- *ObjectName* is the name you assigned to the object's Name property when you created it. Remember, Visual Basic always assigns a name to an object. You should set the Name property to change the name to something meaningful to your program.

- *PropertyName* is the name of the object's property you want to change while the program is running.

- The *value* is the new value for the property. You must be careful to assign only valid values to properties. For example, properties such as Caption can contain any text value, whereas properties such as Picture, which you use to control the graphical image displayed in an Image object, can contain only pictures.

The LoadPicture function is used to load a graphical image into the Picture property of an Image object at run time. The LoadPicture function accepts one argument—a string of characters containing the name of the file to be loaded into the picture—and returns the picture that can be stored in the Picture property of an Image object.

This statement is shown indented in the code. Statements between the Private Sub and End Sub statements usually are indented so the start and end of a procedure can be recognized easily. Indenting statements is solely for the benefit of the programmer. Visual Basic ignores all leading spaces and tab characters that you use to indent statements.

Now that you understand the code you need to write, you're ready to enter the code in the Code window.

To enter the code for the Display Image command button:

1. Enter the code as shown in Figure 1-36.

Figure 1-36 ◀
Entering
statements in
the Code
window

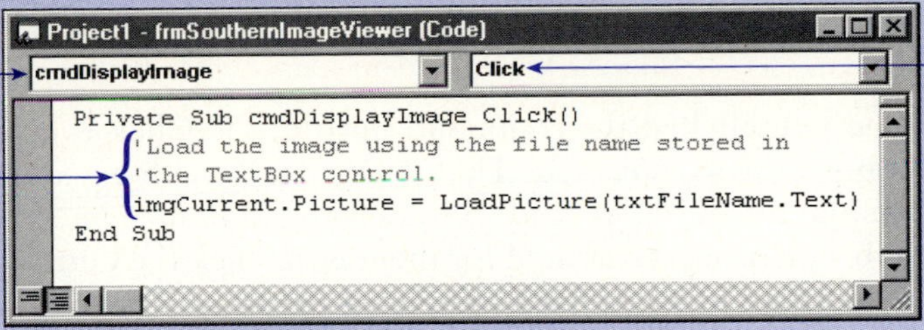

cmdDisplayImage
object selected

enter these three
statements

```
Project1 - frmSouthernImageViewer (Code)                    _ □ ×
cmdDisplayImage              ▼   Click ◀                    ▼        ◀— Click event selected
    Private Sub cmdDisplayImage_Click()                           ▲
        'Load the image using the file name stored in
        'the TextBox control.
        imgCurrent.Picture = LoadPicture(txtFileName.Text)
    End Sub                                                       ▼
```

2. Click the **Close** button ⊠ on the Code window title bar to close the window.

   Now that your program is complete, Mark suggests you run it, verify it is working correctly, and save the form and project files.

Running the Completed Program

To run a program, you simply click the Start button on the toolbar. Remember, any time you run a program, Visual Basic switches from design mode to run mode, activates the startup form, and waits for user input. You can stop a program at any time by clicking the End button on the toolbar.

To run and test the program:

1. Click the **Save Project** button 🖫 on the toolbar to save your work.

2. Click the **Start** button ▶ on the toolbar.

   Your form appears on the screen; Visual Basic has loaded all the form's objects and their associated code.

3. Test the program by entering the file named **A:\Tutorial.01\Item1.bmp**.

4. Click the **Display Image** command button to load the image stored in the file named **Item1.bmp**.

5. The graphical image and file name should appear in the main form as shown in Figure 1-37.

Figure 1-37 ◀
Running the
completed
program

image displayed

Southern Properties Group - Image Viewer

Enter file name:
A:\Tutorial.01\Item1.bmp ◀— enter the file name to display

Display Image — click the command button to display the image

6. Click the **End** button ▪ on the toolbar.

7. Click the **File** menu, then click **Exit** to exit Visual Basic.

When you clicked the command button, the Click event procedure corresponding to the button was executed. That is, Visual Basic located the event procedure named cmdDisplayImage_Click and executed the statement you wrote. Then it located the End Sub statement and waited for the user to click the button again.

Congratulations, you have completed the task of writing your first Visual Basic program. Mark is pleased with the results and is certain you are ready to create more challenging programs.

Quick Check

1. What is the Properties window used for?

2. What is the purpose of the Label and TextBox controls?

3. How do you resize, move, and delete objects?

4. What is the purpose of the Image control?

5. What is the purpose of the Code window?

Figure 1-38 lists and defines the new terms presented in this tutorial.

Figure 1-38 ◀
New terms

Term	Definition
Application Wizard	The Application Wizard is a tool that creates a template for a program that you then can modify to perform the different tasks you desire.
Arguments	An argument is how information is passed to a function. Arguments contain information like numbers or text.
Assignment statements	An assignment statement is a type statement containing a leftmost side, an equal sign, and a rightmost side. The value of the leftmost side is stored in the rightmost side.
Basic module	A type of module containing statements that can be used by other modules.
Break mode	Break mode is an operating mode of Visual Basic where the execution of the program temporarily is suspended.
Class	A class is a template for an object that defines the supported properties, methods, and events.
Code	A Visual Basic statement or statements to accomplish a particular task.
Code window	The Code window is a text editor where you enter Visual Basic statements. You can select an object and event procedure, then type statements into the window.
Computer programming	Computer programming is the process of writing a set of organized statements that accomplish a specific task.
Control	A control is a tool used to perform some task in Visual Basic. Every control has a set of characteristics known as properties. A control can recognize different events, such as a mouse click or a keystroke.
Design time	Design time is an operating mode of Visual Basic where you create an object on the form, and write the Visual Basic statements to perform the tasks in your program.

Figure 1-38 ◀
New terms
(continued)

Term	Definition
Event	An event is an action that occurs because of some user or program activity. A program can respond to events, such as clicking a mouse button or typing a keystroke.
Event-driven	An event-driven program is a program that performs actions in response to some user activity like clicking a button.
Event procedure	A set of Visual Basic statements that are executed in response to a user action like clicking the mouse.
Form	When a user runs a program, the user communicates with the program using the objects on the form. Forms are stored on the disk with the extension .frm. Form names are stored in the program's project file.
Form module	A form module contains all the objects on the form, and the code for those objects
Form window	A form window is a window in which you design a user interface.
Function	A function is a way of executing a set of statements to perform a common task.
Instance	An instance is a control drawn on a form. An instance of a control also is considered an object.
Integrated Development Environment (IDE)	The Integrated Development Environment (IDE) contains all the tools necessary to create, run, and test a Visual Basic computer program.
Intrinsic functions	An intrinsic function is a function supplied by Visual Basic to perform a common task like loading a picture.
MDI parent window	An MDI parent window is a window that contains other windows. The Visual Basic IDE has an MDI parent window that displays all the other Visual Basic windows.
Method	A method describes the different actions you can perform on an object. For example, many objects support a Move method that allows you to reposition the object on the form while the program is running.
Module	A module is a part of your program stored as a file on the disk. All the parts of a form are stored in a single file, which is called a form module.
Object	An object is an instance (occurrence) of a control drawn on a form. An object might be a label or an image.
Object-oriented	An object-oriented programming language uses objects like buttons and boxes to perform tasks.
Program	A program is a set of statements written in a computer language to accomplish a specific task. The task may be as simple as adding two numbers together or as complex as computing the payroll for a large corporation.
Programming language	A programming language uses words with a specific meaning connected together in a specific order to form statements. All the different words with a specific meaning make up a programming language.
Program comments	A program comment is a line that begins with the apostrophe character ('). These comments are used to describe the task that is being performed. Visual Basic ignores program comments and does not execute them.
Project Explorer	The Project Explorer shows all the program components. It is used to manage the program components.
Project file	A project file is the collection of files that make up a Visual Basic program. A project file is stored on the disk with the extension .vbp. A project file contains a list of the forms and other parts of a program.

Figure 1-38 ◀
New terms
(continued)

Term	Definition
Properties window	The Properties window provides options you use to manage the appearance of each object on a form.
Property	A property is a characteristic of an object, such as the object's color, caption, screen location, or size. Properties also determine whether an object is visible or not.
Run time	Run time is one of the operating modes of Visual Basic. When in run time, the user can interact with the objects on the form.
Sizing handles	Sizing handles are boxes that surround the active object. You can use the handles to resize the object by clicking and dragging the mouse over the handle.
Shortcut menu	A shortcut menu is a menu that appears when the right mouse button is clicked. A shortcut menu provides a quick way to execute frequently used commands.
Statements	A statement is like a sentence in English. It is made up of different words entered in a defined order to accomplish a specific task.
Syntax	Syntax is the rules describing the valid statements for a programming language.
Third-party add-in control	A third-partyadd-incontrol is a control that is not part of Visual Basic. Instead, it is written by another software vendor for use in Visual Basic. The control adds additional functionality to Visual Basic.
Toolbox	The toolbox is a window containing all the different controls available for use in your program.
Twip	A twip is a device, independent unit of measurement used to position objects on the screen. There are about 1440 twips per inch.
User interface	The user interface is what the user of the program sees on the screen and how the user interacts with the program.
Window	A window is any rectangular area on the screen.

Tutorial Assignments

Amy DuBrava, an account manager at Southern Properties Group, reviewed the program you created that displayed graphical images. Amy would like you to create another program to display a stop light that can be green, yellow, or red, depending on which command button is clicked. To do this you will need to create an Image object to display three similar pictures. You also will need three command buttons that, when clicked, will display the correct image. Each object should have an appropriate name and caption. When you finish creating the program, you will run and test it. When complete, your form should look like Figure 1-39.

Figure 1-39 ◀

1. Make sure your Student Disk is in the appropriate disk drive, then start Visual Basic.

2. Set the appropriate property so the title bar of the form contains the text **Southern Properties Group - Stop Sign**.

3. Set the Name property of the form to **frmSouthernStopSign**.

4. Resize the form so it is similar to Figure 1-39.

5. Draw an Image control on the form. Refer to Figure 1-39 for placement and sizing.

6. Set the name of the image to **imgStopSign**.

7. Set the Stretch property so the picture will fill in the region of the Image object.

8. Create three command buttons. Set the Caption property of the buttons to **Stop**, **Caution**, and **Go.** Set the Name property for each command button using the correct prefix and be sure the name conveys the purpose of the object.

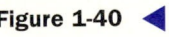

9. The images are stored in three different files, **Stop.ico**, **Caution.ico**, and **Go.ico**. When the command button is clicked, you need to display the image corresponding to the button. In addition to using the Text property of a text box as an argument in the LoadPicture function, you can specify a file name explicitly by enclosing the file name in quotes. Thus, to display the image named **Stop.ico** stored in the folder named **A:\Tutorial.01\TAssign** into the object name **imgStopSign**, you would use the following statement.

```
imgStopSign.Picture = LoadPicture("A:\Tutorial.01\TAssign\StopSign.ico")
```

10. Write the necessary statements in the Click event procedure for each command button to display the corresponding bitmap file into the image object. Add a program comment to the event procedure to describe its purpose.

11. Save the form and project in the **TAssign** folder of the **Tutorial.01** folder on your Student Disk. Use the form name **frmSouthernStopSign** and the project name **Southern Stop Sign.vbp**.

12. Run the program.

13. Click each of the command buttons to be sure that a stop sign appears with the green, yellow, and red light appearing.

14. Correct any mistakes you have made and save your work again if necessary.

15. Exit Visual Basic.

Case Problems

1. Advance Computer Graphics Advance Computer Graphics uses a large number of graphic images in the Visual Basic programs created throughout the company. The owners of Advanced Computer Graphics know that Windows 95 contains a large number of bitmap (bmp) graphics files and they would like to use the Image control to display them on their forms. But they are unsure about how the Stretch property works. You will create a program with a text box for the user to enter the name of a bitmap image and a command button that when clicked will display the selected bitmaps into two Image objects. One of these Image objects will have the Stretch property set to True, and one will have the Stretch property set to False. This will illustrate to the owners how the Stretch property controls the size of Image objects. When complete, your screen should look like Figure 1-40.

Figure 1-40 ◄

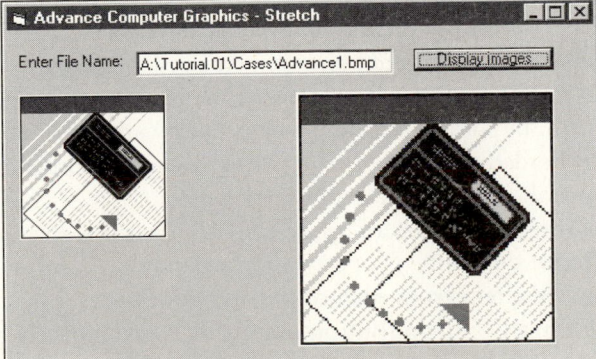

1. Make sure your Student Disk is in the appropriate disk drive, then start Visual Basic.
2. Resize the form as shown in Figure 1-40.
3. Set the form name to **frmAdvanceImage**.
4. Set the title bar on the form so it contains the text **Advance Computer Graphics - Stretch**.
5. Draw a text box on the form and set the Name property using the correct prefix.
6. Remove the initial text from the text box.
7. Draw a label to describe the purpose of the text box. The text in the label should read **Enter File Name:**.
8. Draw two Image objects on the form, one on the right side of the form and one on the left. Make both objects fairly large, but leave room for the CommandButton object.

9. Change the Stretch property of the right Image object to **True** so the bitmap will fill in the region of the object.
10. Create a command button and set the caption as shown in Figure 1-40.
11. Set the Name of the command button to **cmdDisplayImages**.
12. Write two statements that will execute when the button is clicked; one to display the selected bitmap into the first image object, and the second statement to load the selected bitmap into the other image.
13. Save the form and project using the names **frmAdvanceImage.frm** and **Advance Image.vbp**. Be sure to save the project in the folder named **Tutorial.01\Cases** on your Student Disk.
14. Run the program using the bitmap images named **Advance1.bmp** and **Advance2.wmf**. These files are stored in the **Cases** folder of the **Tutorial.01** folder on your Student Disk.
15. Correct any mistakes you have made and save your work again if necessary.
16. Exit Visual Basic.

2. Atlantic Beverages Atlantic Beverages is a wholesale supplier of soft drinks specializing in the hotel industry. The delivery manager, Sam Levinson, would like a program to produce a list that will be used by the company's drivers. The program you create will move a variety of standard text items to different parts of the completed shipping document. You'll create a sample form to demonstrate how text can be moved to different parts of the form. The form you need to create will include three labels and three command buttons. Figure 1-41 shows the completed form.

Figure 1-41 ◀
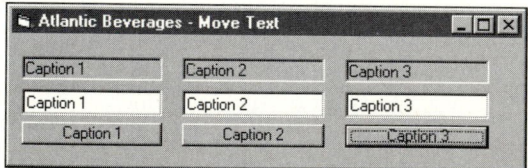

1. Make sure your Student Disk is in the appropriate disk drive, then start Visual Basic.
2. Set the name of the form to **frmAtlanticMoveText**.
3. Set the title bar so it contains the text shown in Figure 1-41.
4. Draw three Label objects of approximately the same size in the upper half of the form. Be sure to set the Name property appropriately.

5. Set the BorderStyle property to **1 - Fixed Single** so a border appears around the labels.
6. Remove the text from each of the labels.
7. Draw three text boxes of approximately the same size just below the labels. Be sure to set the Name property appropriately.
8. Remove the text from each of the text boxes.
9. Draw three CommandButton objects of approximately the same size in the lower half of the form. Set the caption of each command button to **Caption 1**, **Caption 2**, and **Caption 3**, respectively, and set the Name property appropriately.

10. Open the Code window for the first command button's Click event.
11. Write the two statements that will display the command button's caption in the corresponding label and text box.
12. Save the form and project in the **Cases** folder of the **Tutorial.01** folder on your Student Disk. Use the names **frmAtlanticMoveText.frm** and **Atlantic Move Text.vbp**.
13. Run the program and click each command button. The caption of the command button should appear in the corresponding label and text box as shown in Figure 1-41.
14. Correct any mistakes you have made and save your work again if necessary.
15. Exit Visual Basic.

3. Kate's Printing Kate's Printing prints unique greeting cards for the general public. When customers come into the shop they typically see a variety of fonts, styles, colors, etc. to help them choose their cards. Kate Liu, the owner of the shop, wants to know if a Visual Basic program could be used to demonstrate the various printing options to customers by changing different properties of a label, command button, line, and image. You will look at a number of properties for each of these controls. Consult the Visual Basic Help system for additional information about the different properties.

1. Start Visual Basic.
2. Starting from the top middle of the form and working down, draw a Label object, a TextBox object, and a CommandButton object.
3. Select the Label object, then select at least five properties that you have not seen before and use them to modify the characteristics of the Label object. Make sure the Properties window does not obscure the Label object. In particular, change the various Font properties, and observe the results. Write down what occurs when you change each property. The following is a list of some commonly used label properties:

   BackColor (choose a variety of colors from the palette)

   BorderStyle (cycle through the options)

   ForeColor (choose a variety of colors from the palette)

   Font (choose a variety of sizes and types)

   Height (choose various sizes)

   Left (choose various sizes)

   Width (choose various sizes)

4. Repeat Step 3 for each of the other objects. If you do not see an obvious change to make to the object, consult the Help system for that property.
5. Save the form and project using the names **frmKateFonts.frm** and **Kate Fonts.vbp**. Be sure to save the projects in the **Cases** folder of the **Tutorial.01** folder on your Student Disk.
6. Exit Visual Basic.

4. Mountaintop College Mountaintop College is a small, private two-year college in the Sierra Nevada. The chairperson of the computer department, Mary Gorden, would like an organization chart of the department, but she does not have a computer application specifically designed for drawing organization charts. You will use Visual Basic to create the organization chart. The top box of the chart will contain the name of the department chairperson (Mary Gorden). Two middle-level boxes will contain the names of the two computer instructors, Judie Kindschi and Tom Galvez. One bottom-level box will contain your name. You will use labels as the boxes that hold the names. After the form for the organization chart is created, it will look like Figure 1-42. You will run the program to test it.

Figure 1-42 ◀

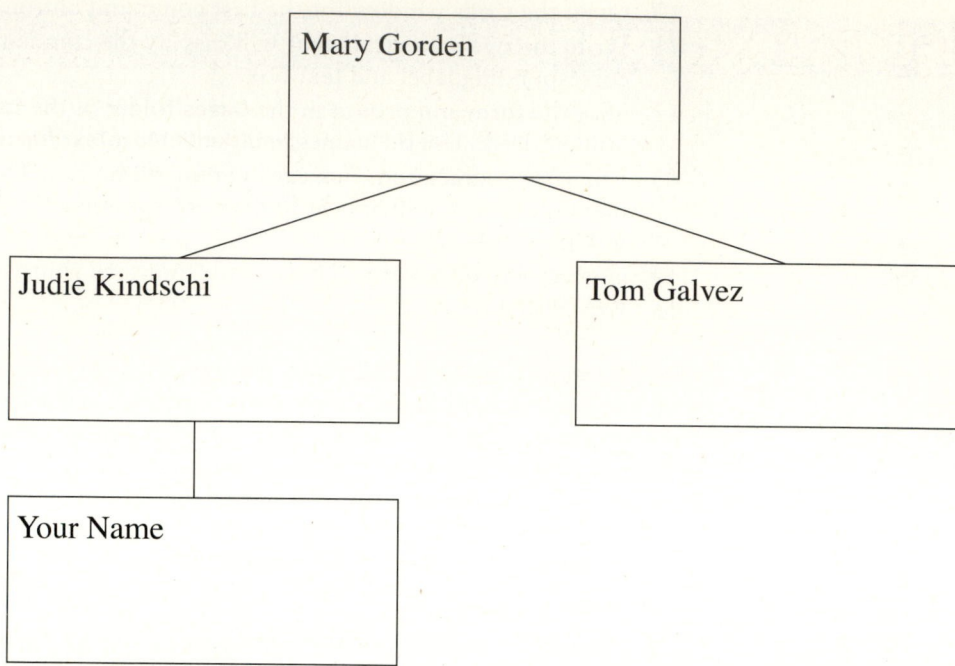

1. Start Visual Basic.
2. Starting from the top and working down, draw four labels that resemble the boxes shown in Figure 1-42.

3. Change the BorderStyle property of all four labels to **1 - Fixed Single**.
4. Look up "Line control" in online Help and read the Help information. Then, using the Line control, draw lines showing the departmental relationship between the labels.
5. Draw a CommandButton object on the bottom-right side of the form.
6. Specify the caption **Click Here To Insert Names** for the CommandButton object. If the entire caption does not fit in the command button, increase the size of the button.
7. Open the Code window for the CommandButton object and type the following program comment as the first two lines of code:

   ```
   'This code will place each department member's name in the
   'appropriate label.
   ```

8. Type the following lines of Visual Basic code between the Private Sub and End Sub lines. Substitute your name for the reference Your Name.

   ```
   Label1.Caption = "Mary Gorden"
   Label2.Caption = "Judie Kindschi"
   Label3.Caption = "Tom Galvez"
   Label4.Caption = "Your Name"
   ```

9. Close the Code window.
10. Run the program.
11. Click the command button to insert the names. Your screen looks like Figure 1-42. If any names do not fit correctly in the label, click the End button on the toolbar and resize the label. Repeat this step as necessary until all names are fully displayed in the labels.
12. End the program.
13. Save the form and project using the names **frmMountaintopOrgChart.frm** and **Mountaintop Org Chart.vbp**. Be sure to save the projects in the **Cases** folder of the **Tutorial.01** folder on your Student Disk.
14. Exit Visual Basic.

Visual Programming Lab

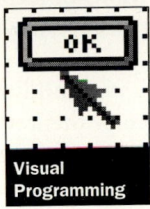

Visual Programming

This Lab Assignment is designed to accompany the interactive Course Lab called Visual Programming. To start the Visual Programming Lab, click the Start button on the Windows 95 taskbar, point to Programs, point to Course Labs, point to New Perspectives Applications, and click Visual Programming. If you do not see Course Labs on your Programs menu, see your instructor or lab manager.

In the Visual Programming Lab, you use an event-driven, object-oriented programming environment to create simple programs. This lab provides a "taste" of what it would be like to program in a visual language such as Visual Basic.

1. Click the Steps button to learn how to create a graphical user interface containing buttons, labels, and text boxes. As you work through the steps, answer all the Quick Check questions. After you complete the steps, you will see a Summary Report of your answers. Follow the directions on the screen to print this report.

2. In Explore, create a program to calculate the total cost of carpeting a room. Test your program, then print it showing the cost of $12.99/square yard carpeting for a 10 x 14-foot room.

   Assume the room is rectangular. The known information is the length and width of the room, and the price of a square yard of carpet. You must calculate:

   ■ the square feet of carpet needed (length * width of room)

   ■ the square yard of carpet needed (square feet/9)

   ■ the total price of carpet (price per square yard * the square yards needed)

   Your user interface should look like Figure 1-43.

Figure 1-43 ◀

```
┌──────────────────────────────────────────────────────────────┐
│ ▬         Visual Programming - EDIT                    ▼ ▲ │
│ File   Run   Help                                             │
│ ┌────┐  ┌──────┐  ┌──────┐   Current Program   🗑  Please dispose of │
│ │    │  │  AB  │  │ abl  │      SOL2.VPG            objects properly! │
│ └────┘  └──────┘  └──────┘                                    │
│  Button    Label    Text Box                                  │
│──────────────────────────────────────────────────────────────│
│ Carpeting Calculator                                          │
│                                                               │
│ This program calculates the cost of                           │
│ carpeting a rectangular room.                                 │
│                                                Length:  ┌──────┐│
│ Instructions: Enter the dimensions of the      Width:   ┌──────┐│
│ room and the price per square yard of                          │
│ the carpet, then click the Calculate Cost   Price Per Yard: ┌──────┐│
│ button.                                                        │
│                                              ┌──────────────┐  │
│                                              │ Calculate Cost│  │
│                                              └──────────────┘  │
│                                                               │
│              The square footage of the room is  ┌──────┐      │
│                 Yards of carpet needed is       ┌──────┐      │
│           The total price of carpeting will be $ ┌──────┐     │
│                                                               │
└──────────────────────────────────────────────────────────────┘
```

3. Suppose you like to shop from catalogs. Your favorite catalog is having a sale—selected merchandise is discounted 10%, 20%, 30%, or 40%. You want to know how much you'll save if you buy some of the merchandise you want. In Explore, create a program to calculate savings. Test your program, then print it showing the savings for an $863 item at a 30% discount.

Assume the items you purchase will be discounted, and there is no additional charge for shipping. The known information is the original price of the item and its discount—10%, 20%, 30%, or 40%. Calculate how much you will save. (For example, for a 10% discount, multiply the original cost by .10.) Your user interface should look like Figure 1-44.

Figure 1-44 ◄

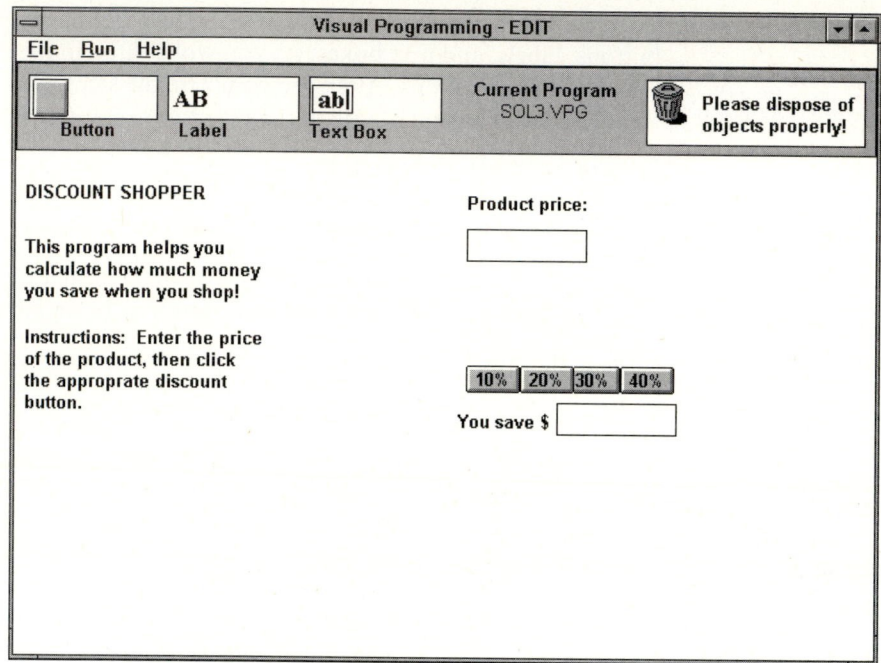

4. In your recording studio, studio musicians are paid by the hour, but your sound technicians are salaried. You started to make a program to calculate weekly paychecks, but it doesn't seem to work. Your assumption is that some employees are salaried and some are hourly. You know the salaries for the salaried employees. You know the hourly wage and the hours worked each pay period for the hourly employees. You want to calculate the weekly pay for salaried employees (wages/52) and the weekly pay for hourly employees (wages * hours).

In Explore, open the program **pay.vpg** and test it.

Enter **32240** in the Wages box, then click the Salaried button. The output should be 620. Next enter **8** in the Wages box and **40** in the Hours box. Click the Hourly button. The output should be 320. Find what's wrong with this program and correct it. Print your solution.

Understanding Code and Variables

Designing and Writing a Financial Calculator Program
for the Island Financial Company

OBJECTIVES

In this tutorial you will:

- Become familiar with the elements of program design

- Create multiple instances of labels, text boxes, and command buttons

- Use properties to change font sizes, font color, and the alignment of characters

- Modify the tab order of objects on a form

- Use graphical objects on a form to create a visually appealing user interface

- Declare and use variables to store information

- Create expressions to perform computations like multiplication and division

- Write code inside a form module to compute the future value of an investment and format the results

- Use Visual Basic functions to convert data, format data, and compute financial values

- Identify syntax and run-time errors

Island Financial Company

CASE

The Island Financial Company maintains its headquarters in Honolulu, Hawaii, and has branch offices on each of the neighboring Hawaiian Islands. The company has been managing the investments of the wealthy retired population of the Hawaiian Islands for over five years. Island Financial was started by Kaiopo Iniki and his wife, Selena. Selena has a background in computer programming and experience in Visual Basic.

As part of the Island Financial Company's everyday business practices, analysts forecast their clients' investment growth over time. The analysts use this information to estimate cash flow and income, and to prepare the necessary financial statements. Often, clients use these statements to consider the effects of different interest rates on their income. To streamline the forecasting process, Kaiopo and Selena have asked you to help Selena create a Visual Basic program that will compute the necessary information.

Before creating the program, Selena spent time designing it so it would meet the needs of the financial analysts using it. Once her design was complete, she began to create many of the objects on the form. She still needs to create the remaining objects, write the statements to compute the future value of an investment, and then run and test the program to make sure it works properly. After reviewing Selena's design specifications, you will help her complete the program to calculate the future value of investments made by Island Financial's clients.

SESSION

2.1

In this session you will learn the basic elements of good design and how to design a form for a program, create multiple instances of objects that make up the user interface and set their properties, and set the tab order of objects on a form.

Designing a Computer Program

Selena has been a programmer for many years, and she realizes that creating programs involves more than simply sitting down at a computer, designing the interface, and writing the code. In fact, to ensure a quality product, Selena has established strict guidelines specifying that an adequate amount of time be spent understanding the problem and finding the best solution before writing the actual program. You would not think of starting to build a house without a set of plans and some thought given to the materials and time involved. The same is true for programming. A little time spent in planning will save you many hours of work debugging a program or correcting design flaws. Computer programs look and work better with some forethought to the final product and where that product will fit into other programs. The company has a standard set of steps, known as a **methodology**, for designing programs. The methodology requires that each step be completed in sequence before moving on to the next step. The steps in designing a computer program are as follows:

1. Completely understand the problem and what data you need to solve it.

2. Analyze and break down the problem into simple, nontechnical terms using English sentences.

3. Sketch a picture of the user interface design for each computer screen in the program.

4. Identify the tasks that are to be performed and where those tasks will be performed.

After these steps are accomplished, you can begin creating the actual user interface and writing program code. Selena uses a methodology or design tool called the Newman-Ekedahl Application Development Tool (**NEADT**). For complete information about this design tool refer to the Design Appendix. Selena already completed the design specifications and the user interface for the program.

To view and print the NEADT chart for the calculator program:

1. Using Microsoft Word, open the file named **Island.doc** that is located in the Tutorial.02 folder on your Student Disk. If you do not have Word, open the file named **Island.txt** using WordPad.

2. Print the file.

3. Exit the word processing program.

The five forms that make up the NEADT chart describe what the program should do and how it will do it. The first form simply defines the general goal of the program in English terms called **pseudocode**. The second form shows the design of the user interface.

Moving from the general to the specific, the third form (level 3) provides the detail about the specific tasks that need to be performed, and where and when. For the calculator program, certain tasks need to be performed when the user clicks one of the two buttons, and as each text box gets and loses focus. Figure 2-1 shows the user interface design (level 2).

Figure 2-1 ◀
User interface design for the calculator program

input section

output section

descriptive labels

command button to clear input and output objects

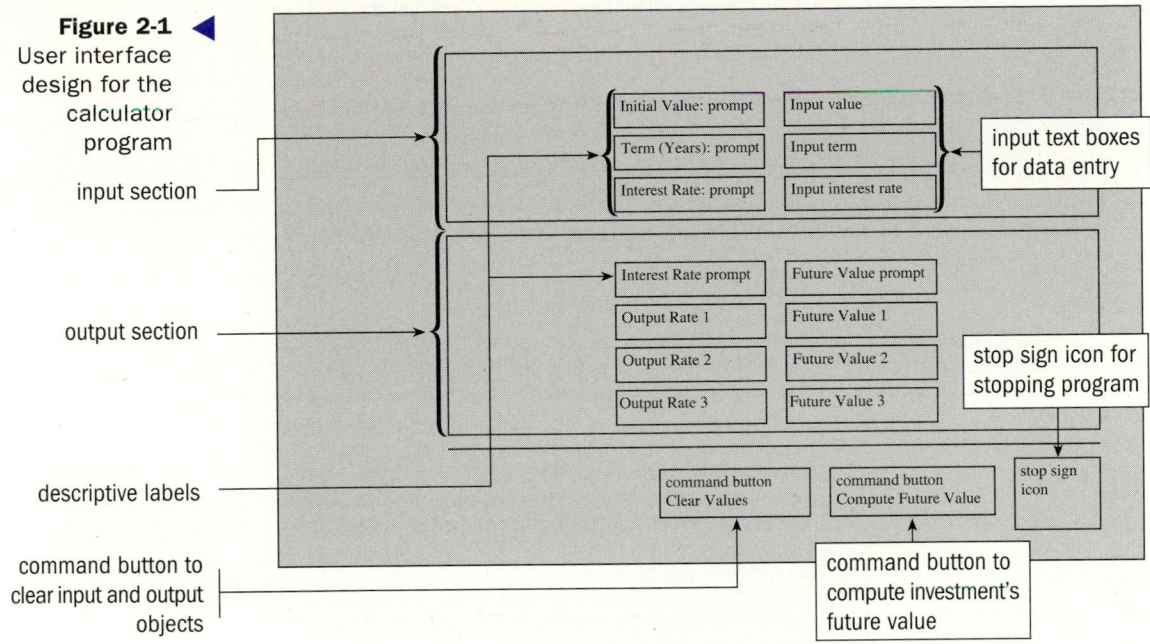

As shown in Figure 2-1, the interface will provide three text boxes for the user to input the necessary data—the initial value of the investment, the term, and the interest rate. Note that the design includes descriptive labels (prompts) to the left of these three text boxes so that the user will know what data to enter in them. The interface also contains labels for the three different interest rates and the corresponding future values of the investment. The form also will include two command buttons—one to compute the future values of an investment using the three interest rates, and the other to clear both the input and output values in preparation for another calculation. Finally, a stop sign image will be used to stop the program. Level 4 contains a more detailed breakdown of where the tasks are performed and the properties that are set.

Designing a user interface requires a bit of an artistic eye and adherence to several design principles. Figure 2-2 describes the principles that will help you create a good user interface.

Figure 2-2 ◀
Principles
of a good
user inter-
face

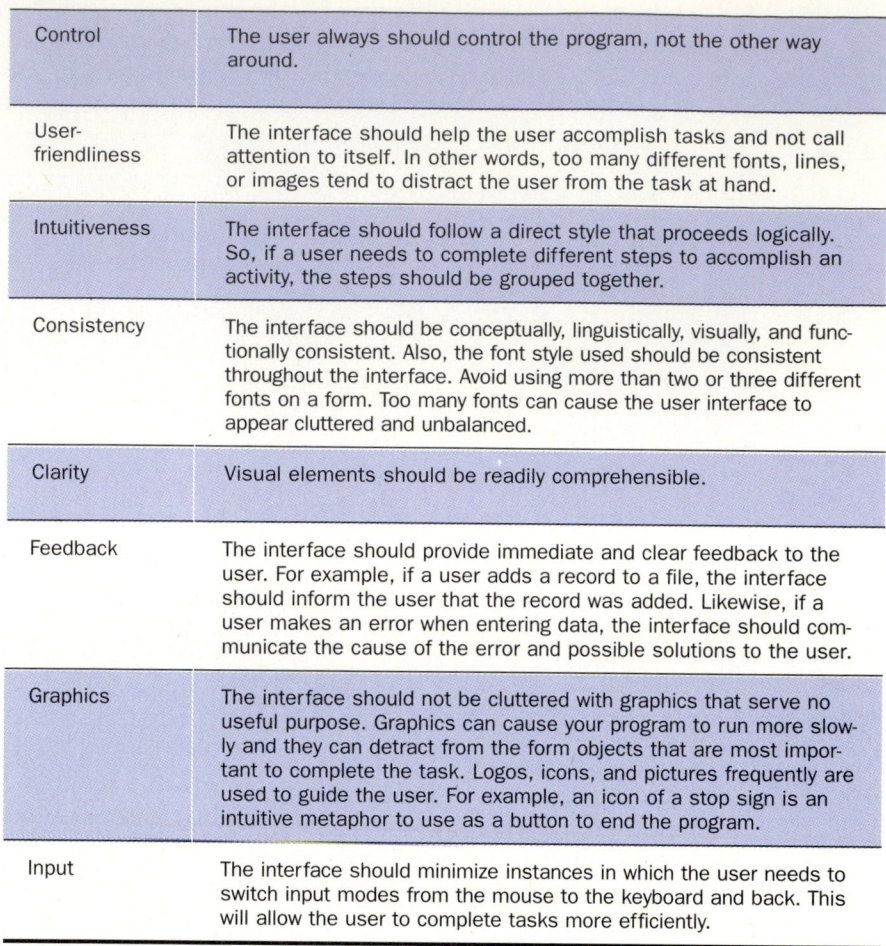

Control	The user always should control the program, not the other way around.
User-friendliness	The interface should help the user accomplish tasks and not call attention to itself. In other words, too many different fonts, lines, or images tend to distract the user from the task at hand.
Intuitiveness	The interface should follow a direct style that proceeds logically. So, if a user needs to complete different steps to accomplish an activity, the steps should be grouped together.
Consistency	The interface should be conceptually, linguistically, visually, and functionally consistent. Also, the font style used should be consistent throughout the interface. Avoid using more than two or three different fonts on a form. Too many fonts can cause the user interface to appear cluttered and unbalanced.
Clarity	Visual elements should be readily comprehensible.
Feedback	The interface should provide immediate and clear feedback to the user. For example, if a user adds a record to a file, the interface should inform the user that the record was added. Likewise, if a user makes an error when entering data, the interface should communicate the cause of the error and possible solutions to the user.
Graphics	The interface should not be cluttered with graphics that serve no useful purpose. Graphics can cause your program to run more slowly and they can detract from the form objects that are most important to complete the task. Logos, icons, and pictures frequently are used to guide the user. For example, an icon of a stop sign is an intuitive metaphor to use as a button to end the program.
Input	The interface should minimize instances in which the user needs to switch input modes from the mouse to the keyboard and back. This will allow the user to complete tasks more efficiently.

Creating the Calculator Program

According to Selena's design specifications for the calculator program, a user will supply input values representing an initial value, term, and beginning interest rate. When the user clicks the Compute Future Value button, the program will process and display the three future value results along with the interest rates, based on the input values. The finished form for the calculator program will look like Figure 2-3.

Figure 2-3 ◀
Completed
calculator
form

labels identifying
input

labels identifying
output

line

command button
to clear input
and output

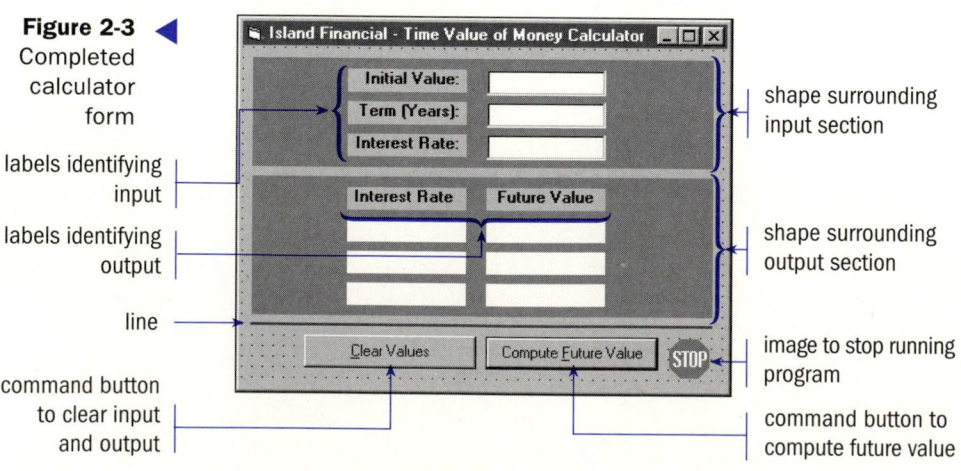

shape surrounding
input section

shape surrounding
output section

image to stop running
program

command button to
compute future value

You will begin by opening the project file that contains the partially completed calculator form and saving it with a different name. Saving files to a new name will keep the original files intact, allowing you to start over if you make a serious mistake.

To start Visual Basic and open the project file containing the calculator form:

1. Be sure your Student Disk is in the appropriate disk drive.

2. Start Visual Basic then open the project file named **Island.vbp** located in the Tutorial.02 folder on your Student Disk.

   Selena already created the form for the program and added some objects to it.

3. Highlight **frmIslandCalculator** in the Project Explorer if the form does not appear on the screen.

   TROUBLE? If the Project Explorer is not open on your screen, click the Project Explorer button on the toolbar to open the window.

4. Click the **View Object** button 🔳 in the Project Explorer, if necessary. The Form window opens and displays the partially completed form. See Figure 2-4.

Figure 2-4 ◀
Calculator form with some objects created

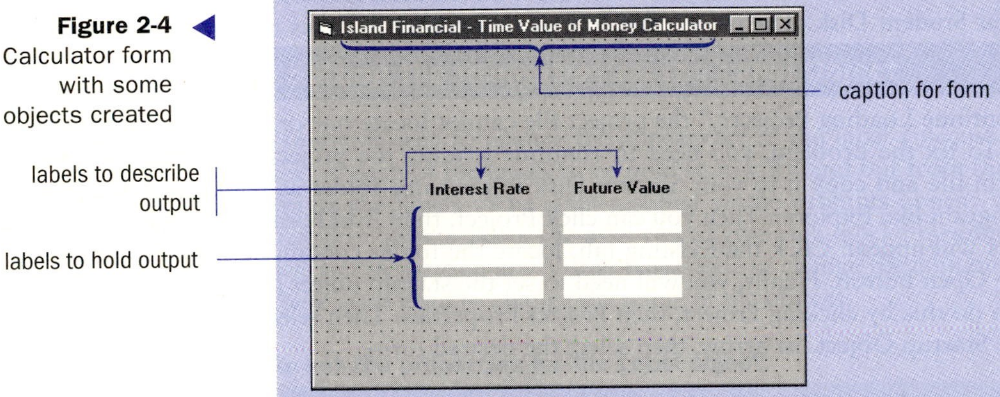

labels to describe output

labels to hold output

caption for form

Before working on the form, you will save it with a different name, then save the project file with a different name. Doing so will keep the original files intact, allowing you to start over if you make a serious mistake.

5. Click **File** on the menu bar, then click **Save frmIsland.frm As**.

6. Select the **Tutorial.02** folder on your Student Disk, change the entry in the File name text box to **frmIslandCalculator.frm**, then click the **Save** button to save the form with the new name.

7. Click **File** on the menu bar, then click **Save Project As**.

8. Select the **Tutorial.02** folder on your Student Disk, change the entry in the File name text box to **Island Calculator.vbp**, then click the **Save** button to save the project file with the new name.

As you perform the steps to write the program, you frequently will save your work. If you make an error you cannot correct, you can load the most recently saved copies of the form and project files and continue your work from that point.

Note the objects that Selena already has created. The two labels containing the text, Interest Rate and Future Value, identify the output areas for the program. The labels below the two prompts display the output data after the program processes it. Finally, Selena set the form's Caption property to "Island Financial - Time Value of Money Calculator" that appears in the title bar of the form.

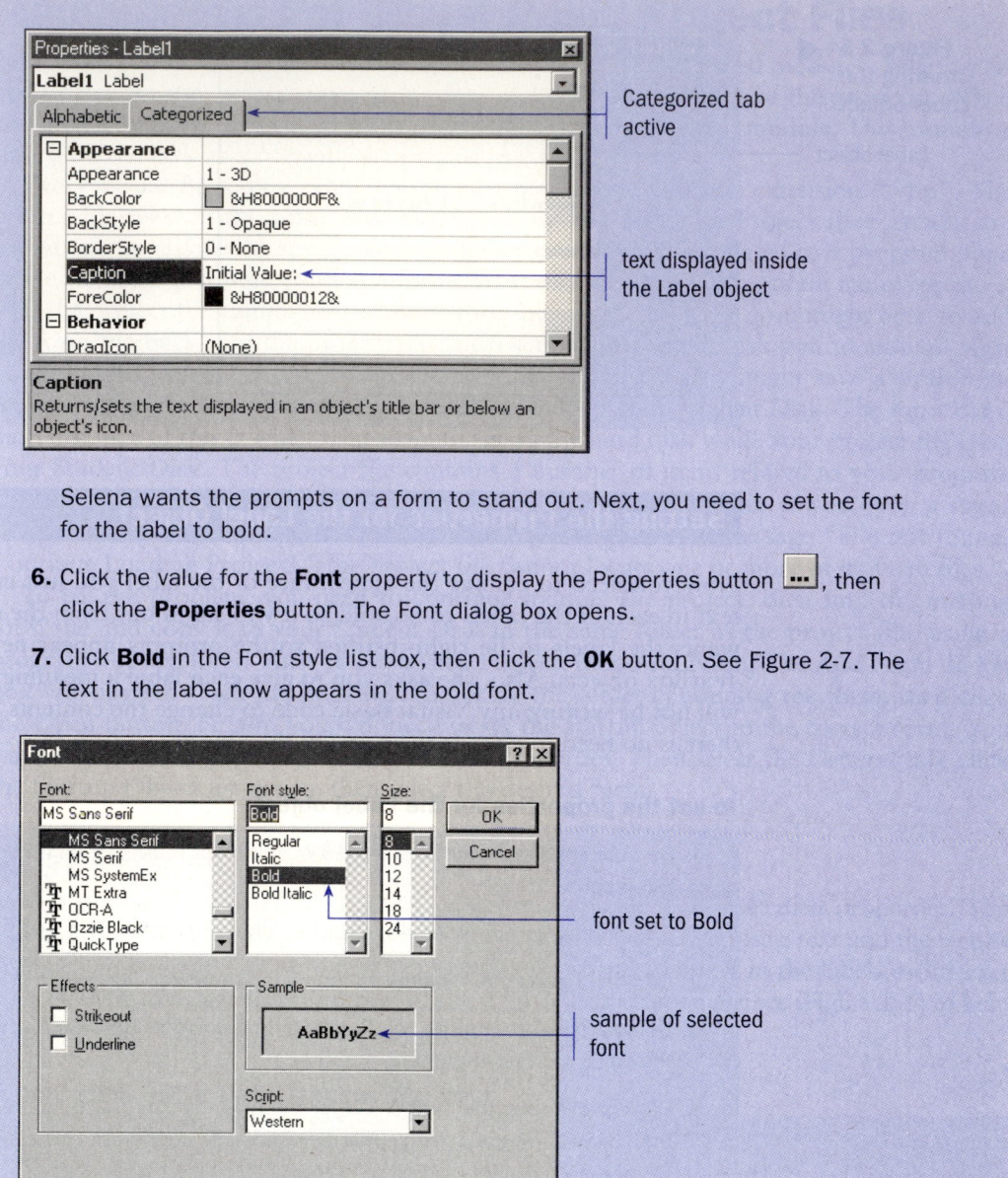

Categorized tab
active

text displayed inside
the Label object

Selena wants the prompts on a form to stand out. Next, you need to set the font
for the label to bold.

6. Click the value for the **Font** property to display the Properties button ⬛, then
click the **Properties** button. The Font dialog box opens.

7. Click **Bold** in the Font style list box, then click the **OK** button. See Figure 2-7. The
text in the label now appears in the bold font.

Figure 2-7 ◀
Font dialog box

font set to Bold

sample of selected
font

Creating Multiple Instances of Objects

So far, you have created only one instance of an object on your form. You could create
additional instances of the Label object by following the same steps you just completed.
Each new object you create, however, would assume the default (standard) properties of
the control, and you would have to change each individually. To save time and effort,
Selena suggests you use the copy and paste features to make copies of the Label object
already on the form and preserve the properties you set in the Initial Value object.

As you create additional instances of an object, Visual Basic assigns them unique
names. For example, if you create two labels, they will be named Label1 and Label2,
respectively.

Tip: When you will be writing statements that set the properties of an object, you should change the name so it conforms to the Naming Conventions Appendix. This will make your program more readable. When an object like a label is being used as a prompt, however, there is no need to change the object name because you will never write statements to operate on the object.

You now are ready to create the labels to prompt the user for the term of the investment in years and the interest rate.

To create the additional Label objects:

1. If necessary, click the **Initial Value:** label to select it.

2. Click the **Copy** button 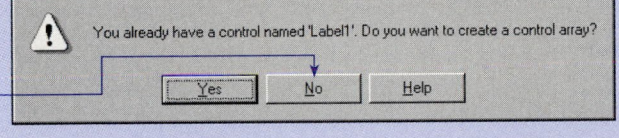 on the toolbar to copy the object on the Windows Clipboard.

3. Click the **Paste** button on the toolbar to paste a copy of the object from the Clipboard onto the form.

   Visual Basic displays a message box asking if you want to create a control array. See Figure 2-8. Control arrays are used to manipulate objects as a group and are discussed in later tutorials. For now, you do not want to create a control array.

Figure 2-8 ◀
Control array
message box

click No ──

Microsoft Visual Basic

⚠ You already have a control named 'Label1'. Do you want to create a control array?

    Yes   No   Help

4. Click the **No** button to close the message box. The copy of the Label object appears in the upper-left corner of the form.

   TROUBLE? If you clicked the Yes button by mistake, a control array was created. To delete the control array, delete both the object you just pasted and the original object you copied on the Clipboard. Then re-create the original label, set its properties, and repeat Steps 1 through 4.

5. Click and hold the mouse button on the object, then move the object by dragging it below the first label you created. Your screen should look like Figure 2-9.

Figure 2-9 ◀
Copying and
pasting the
Label object

original label ──

copied label ──

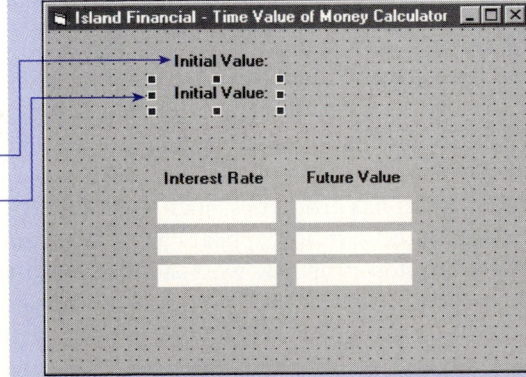

Island Financial - Time Value of Money Calculator

Initial Value:
Initial Value:

Interest Rate   Future Value

Note that the copied label already has the correct property values for right-justified alignment and bold font. The only property you need to set is the Caption property.

6. Set the Caption property in the Appearance section for the copied label to **Term (Years):**.

7. Activate the Form window by clicking its title bar, click the **Paste** button 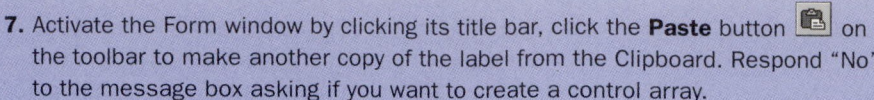 on the toolbar to make another copy of the label from the Clipboard. Respond "No" to the message box asking if you want to create a control array.

TROUBLE? If a new copy of the object did not appear in the upper-left corner of the form, either the Form window was not active or the contents of the Clipboard were cleared. Make sure the Form window is active; if it is, then the Clipboard was cleared. Click one of the labels you created, click the Copy button on the toolbar. Then repeat Step 7.

8. Move the new label below the second label you created.

9. Set the Caption property for the third label to **Interest Rate:**. Your form should look like Figure 2-10.

Figure 2-10 ◀
Descriptive
labels on the
form

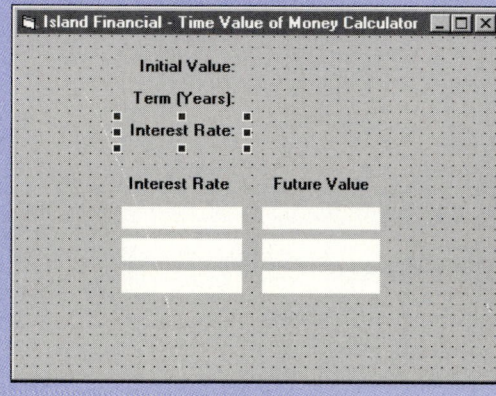

Next, you need to create text boxes for user input to the right of each label prompt. Unlike the labels you just created, you will need to write Visual Basic code that will use the information in these objects to compute the future value of an investment. Thus, you will set the Name property of each object to make the program more readable.

Creating a TextBox Object

A **TextBox** object displays textual information and allows a user to type in values so those values can be used in the program. A text box is similar to a label. Only Visual Basic code, however, can change the contents of a label while the program is running; a user cannot type information into it.

> *Tip:* Use the Label control for text that will not change, like prompts,
> or when only output will be displayed. Use the TextBox control
> when the object must both receive input and display output.

Like a label, a TextBox object has properties, such as Alignment and Font, that you can set so the text a user enters in the text box appears as you desire. The text displayed in a label is controlled by the Caption property, whereas the text displayed in a text box is controlled by the Text property. The text box has some properties that allow it to behave differently than a label. If you want the text to appear on multiple lines you can set the MultiLine property to True. Sometimes, the text may not fit in the region of the text box. If the MultiLine property is set to True, you can set the ScrollBars property to True, allowing the user to scroll through the contents that are not visible on the screen.

CREATING A TEXTBOX OBJECT

- Click the TextBox control on the toolbox, then use the mouse to draw a TextBox object on the form.
- Set the necessary properties for the TextBox object, such as Alignment, BorderStyle, and Font, in the Properties window.
- If you want the text to appear on multiple lines, set the MultiLine property to True.
- If you want scroll bars to appear, set the ScrollBars property to True. The ScrollBars property is meaningful only if the MultiLine property is set to True.
- If you want the text to be right-justified, then set the Alignment property to 1 - Right Justify. You also must set the MultiLine property to True.
- If you want the text box to appear blank when the program is first started, delete the default Text property.
- If you want to set the Text property to blank with Visual Basic code, use the statement *TextBoxName*.Text = "".
- Set the prefix for the Name property to "txt", followed by a descriptive name.

Now you will create the three text boxes in which a user will enter the necessary input data for the initial value, term, and interest rate. These boxes will appear to the right of the labels that you created to identify the text boxes. The first text box is used to enter the initial value for the investment. Because the prefix for a TextBox object is "txt", Selena suggests you name the object txtInitialValue.

To create the first TextBox object for the calculator program:

1. Click the **TextBox** control 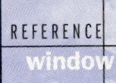 on the toolbox, then use the mouse to draw a text box on the form to the right of the Initial Value: label.

2. The text box should be the same size as the adjacent label, and aligned to the right of it. In the Position section, set the Height property of the label to **285**, the Left property to **2760**, the Top property to **240**, and the Width property to **1335**.

3. For the text box, set the Name property in the Misc section to **txtInitialValue**.

   Next, you need to set the Text property, which determines what text, if any, is initially displayed in the text box when a user runs the program. Selena wants the text boxes to be empty so a user can immediately type the input data into them. So, you need to delete the default Text property value.

4. Select the default value **Text1** for the Text property in the Misc section, then press the **Delete** key.

You now can create the remaining TextBox objects by copying and pasting the text box you just created.

To copy and paste the other two TextBox objects:

1. Make sure the text box you just created is selected and the Form window is active.

2. Click the **Copy** button on the toolbar. A copy of the TextBox object is placed on the Clipboard, overwriting the current contents of the Clipboard, if any.

3. Click the **Paste** button 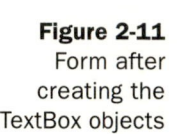 on the toolbar. When the message box appears for creating a control array, click the **No** button. A copy of the text box is pasted on the form.

4. Move the new text box to the right of the Term (Years): label.

5. For the new text box, set the Name property in the Misc section to **txtTermYears**.

6. Activate the Form window, then click the **Paste** button 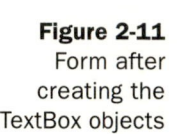 on the toolbar to paste another copy of the text box on the form. Be sure not to create a control array.

7. Move the new text box to the right of the Interest Rate: label.

8. For the new text box, set the Name property in the Misc section to **txtInterestRate**. Your form should look like Figure 2-11.

Figure 2-11 ◄
Form after
creating the
TextBox objects

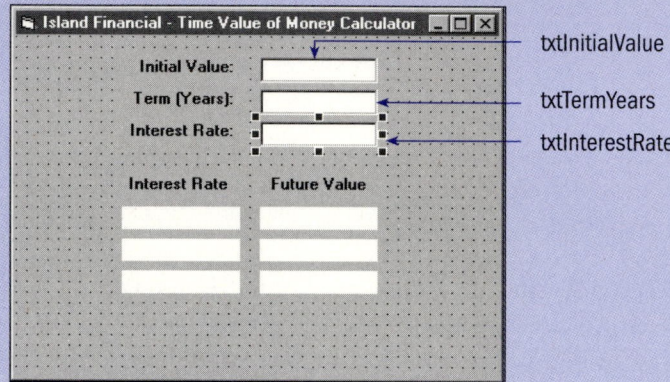

txtInitialValue

txtTermYears

txtInterestRate

TROUBLE? If the position or the size of any label or text box is not correct, click and drag the object to reposition it, or use the sizing handles to resize the object as necessary.

Next, you need to create the two CommandButton objects on the form. The first command button allows a user to click a button to calculate the future values for the three different interest rates. The second command button allows a user to clear the values in preparation for another calculation.

Creating a CommandButton Object

The **CommandButton** control on the toolbox allows you to create a button that a user clicks to carry out an action. This is much like the buttons you have used in dialog boxes; buttons like OK and Print. When a user clicks a command button, Visual Basic executes the code written for the button's Click event. You will write these statements in the next session. A command button usually appears as a three-dimensional raised object. Inside the object you can place text to describe the button's function or display a picture to metaphorically describe the button's purpose. In this session you will learn how to display text in the command button. Because most physical buttons are raised off of some surface, command buttons almost always should appear raised.

> *Tip:* Most windows, like the Print and Options dialog boxes in Visual Basic, place all the buttons horizontally across the bottom of the form or vertically along the rightmost side. Notice that the buttons are of the same size and positioned the same distance from each other. You should include these design standards in the programs you create to present the most consistent and easy-to-use user interface.

Like a label, a command button has a Caption property and a Name property. It has additional properties, however, to control its appearance.

- You can create your own ToolTips by setting the **ToolTipText** property. Whenever the mouse pointer is positioned over the button for about one second, the message stored in this property will appear just below the button.

- The CommandButton control has a **Default** property that, when set to True, allows a user to press the Enter key as an alternative to clicking the button to activate the button's Click event procedure. Only one CommandButton object on a form can be the default object, that is, have its Default property set to True. It would not make sense to try to have two default objects that would both try to respond to the Enter key being pressed.

- You also can create a hot key for a command button. A **hot key** is a set of keystrokes like Alt+C that, when typed, will act just like clicking the command button. You create a hot key by inserting an ampersand character (&) in the Caption property just before the character you want to act as the hot key. Each hot key on a form must be unique.

- Like other objects, you should use a standard prefix for the name. The standard prefix for the command button is "cmd".

Setting the Default property of a command button can improve the form's user interface, because it allows the user to press the Enter key to execute the most commonly used button rather than having to move their hand from the keyboard to the mouse and back. It is important to minimize the transitions between the keyboard and mouse whenever possible in the user interface. Using hot keys also allows the user a quick way to click a command button.

REFERENCE window	**CREATING A COMMANDBUTTON OBJECT**
	- Click the CommandButton control on the toolbox, then use the mouse to draw a CommandButton object on the form.
	- Set the Caption property to describe the purpose of the button. If you want to include a hot key, precede the hot key character by an ampersand.
	- Set the Default property to True to allow the user to press the Enter key rather than clicking the button. Only one button per form may have the Default property set to True.
	- Set the ToolTipText property to display a message that will be helpful to the user.
	- Set the prefix for the Name property to "cmd", followed by a descriptive name.

Now you need to create the command buttons for the calculator program. When a user runs the calculator program and clicks the Compute Future Value command button, the program will calculate the different future values based on information the user has entered. When the Clear Values button is clicked, the contents of the input text boxes and output labels will be cleared.

According to Selena's design, each button will include a meaningful caption to identify its function and a ToolTip to assist the user. Like the other objects you just created, the command button should have a descriptive name identifying the purpose of the object. Because the prefix of a command button is "cmd", and the button's purpose is to compute a future value, Selena suggests you name the first object "cmdComputeFutureValue".

To create the CommandButton object and set its properties:

1. Click the **Save Project** button 🖫 to save the form and project.

2. Click the **CommandButton** control ▢ on the toolbox, then use the mouse to draw the CommandButton object on the form, below the rightmost column at the bottom of the form.

3. Set the Height property of the button to **375**, the Left property to **2760**, the Top property to **3240**, and the Width property to **1935**.

4. Set the Caption property of the command button to **Compute &Future Value**. Alt+F is the hot key combination for the command button.

5. Set the Name property of the command button to **cmdComputeFutureValue**.

   Next, you need to set the Default property for the command button to True so that a user can press the **Enter** key to activate the button. This will make it easier for a user to complete the form by typing the input data, then pressing the **Enter** key to calculate the results.

6. Click the value for the **Default** property, click the **Properties** button ⏷ then click **True**. See Figure 2-12. With this setting, a user either can press the **Enter** key or click the command button to activate it.

Figure 2-12 ◀
Setting the command button properties

Alphabetic tab shown

Default property set to True

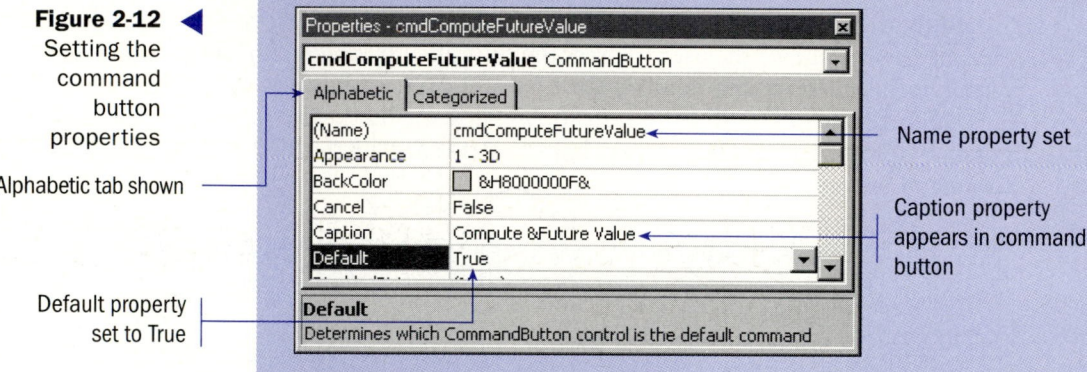

Name property set

Caption property appears in command button

7. Click the value for the **ToolTipText** property, then type **Click to compute the investment's future value.**

Next, you need to create the command button to clear the values of the input text boxes and the output labels. Like the command button you just created, this button also will have a meaningful caption, a hot key, and a ToolTip.

To create the Clear Values command button:

1. Click the **Compute Future Value** command button to activate it.

2. Click the **Copy** button 🖺 on the toolbar. A copy of the CommandButton object is placed on the Clipboard, overwriting the current contents of the Clipboard, if any.

3. Click the **Paste** button 🖺 on the toolbar. When the message box appears for creating a control array, click the **No** button. A copy of the command button is pasted on the form.

4. Move the object to the left of the Compute Future Value button and set the Caption property to **&Clear Values**, the Name property to **cmdClearValues**, and the ToolTipText property to **Reset the calculator.**

Because you copied and pasted the object, the new command button inherited the properties of the original, including the Default property. This is not the desired default button.

5. Activate the Properties window for the **cmdComputeFutureValue** command button and reset the Default property to **True**.

The next object you need to create is an Image object that will contain a stop sign icon. Selena wants a user to be able to click the icon to stop the program from running.

Creating an Image Object

In Tutorial 1 you used the Image control to create an Image object that contained different graphical images. You also can create an Image object that will respond to an event when clicked. Because the standard prefix for an Image object is "img", and most menus use the word Exit to exit a program, a good name for the object is imgExit. As you saw in Tutorial 1, part of creating an image is to load a picture into the Image object by setting its Picture property. The image chosen by Selena is a stop sign that is stored as an icon file on your Student Disk. Icons and images can significantly improve the user interface of your program by providing a metaphorical clue to the button or object's purpose. In addition, icons add interest to your program. Because the size of the Image object is the same size as the image file stored on the disk, you do not need to set the Stretch property.

To create the Image object and set its properties:

1. Click the **Image** control 🖾 on the toolbox, then use the mouse to draw the Image object to the right of the command button on the form.

2. Set the Height property to **480**, the Left property to **4800**, the Top property to **3240**, and the Width property to **480**.

3. Click the value for the **Picture** property to display the **Properties** button 🔽 , then click it. The Load Picture dialog box opens.

4. Make sure Tutorial.02 is the displayed folder, click **Stop.ico**, then click the **Open** button. The stop sign icon appears in the Image object. See Figure 2-13.

Figure 2-13 ◀
Creating the
Image object

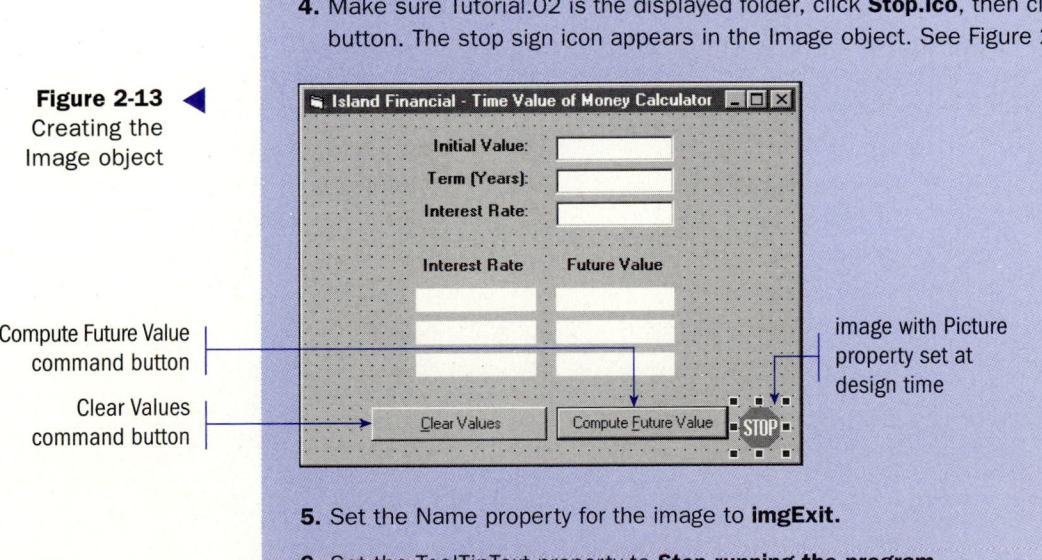

Compute Future Value
command button

Clear Values
command button

image with Picture
property set at
design time

5. Set the Name property for the image to **imgExit**.

6. Set the ToolTipText property to **Stop running the program.**

Setting the Tab Order

Every form has only one active object at a time. When you type text into a TextBox object, for example, you are using the active object that is said to have the **focus**. When using a program, you generally change the focus between one object and another by pressing the Tab key or clicking an object.

The TabIndex property for an object determines the order in which the object receives the focus when a user presses the Tab key. This order, called the **tab order**, is determined initially by the order in which you created objects on the form, but you can change the tab order by changing the value of the TabIndex property. When you change the TabIndex property of an object, the TabIndex properties of the other objects are adjusted accordingly. The TabIndex property begins by counting from 0 and incrementing each object by 1. So, the first object has a TabIndex property of 0, the second a TabIndex property of 1, the third a TabIndex property of 2, and so on. You do not have to set the tab order for objects such as labels, because they never receive the focus.

> *Tip:* Setting the tab order logically for the objects on the form is important; you want to make sure it follows a vertical or horizontal sequence each time the user presses the Tab key. When a user types information into the objects on a form, the information should be completed from top to bottom or left to right, depending on the program.

The analysts at Island Financial will type information into the three text boxes you created on the form. The objects are arranged in a column, so the tab order should move from top to bottom. Initially, the tab order will be the order in which the objects were created on the form. The order should be set so the first text box in the column (txtInitialValue) receives the focus first, then the next text box, and so on. So, the first text box needs a TabIndex property setting of 0, the second a TabIndex property setting of 1, and the third a TabIndex property setting of 2. After typing information in all the TextBox objects the user usually will want to activate the Compute Future Value button, so its TabIndex property setting will be 3. After calculating the present value, it is likely that the user will want to clear the values to prepare for another calculation, so the Clear Values button will have a TabIndex property setting of 4.

To set the TabIndex property of the objects used for input:

1. Click the **TextBox** object to the right of the Initial Value: label to select it.

2. Change the TabIndex property value for the text box to **0**. A TabIndex property of 0 indicates that this object will be the active object (first object to receive the focus) when a user runs the program.

3. Click the **TextBox** object to the right of the Term(Years): label, then set its TabIndex property to **1**.

   When a user presses the **Tab** key after entering the initial value of the investment, this text box will receive the focus and the user can enter the term.

4. Click the **TextBox** object to the right of the Interest Rate: label, then set its TabIndex property to **2**.

   After a user enters the term and presses the **Tab** key, the text box for Interest Rate will have the focus and the user can enter the interest rate.

5. Click the **Compute Future Value** command button, then set its TabIndex property to **3**.

   After a user enters the interest rate and presses the **Tab** key, the command button will have the focus.

6. Click the **Clear Values** command button, then set its TabIndex property to **4**.

You only need to set the tab order for those objects that can receive focus, like command buttons and text boxes, so you do not have to change the TabIndex property for any other objects on the form. Even though an image can respond to a Click event, it cannot actually receive focus so that TabIndex property is not applicable.

Next, you need to add the visual objects to the form—a line to separate the command button and stop sign image from the rest of the form, and two dark gray areas to identify the input and output sections.

Improving the User Interface with Graphical Controls

You have seen that the organization and position of different controls can have an effect on the user interface, and the consistency between these visual elements will improve the user interface. Sometimes you want the user to perceive several controls as belonging to a group. For example, the calculator can be viewed as three sections: a section for input, a section to display the output, and a section containing the buttons to perform processing. To communicate this to the user, you can change the shading of these sections by using another control called the **Shape** control. In addition to drawing shapes on a form, you also can draw lines to separate groups of objects.

Color also is an important part of the user interface. When selecting colors for your program, keep them simple and consistent. While different applications may have different color requirements, the following guidelines should help you with color selection.

- Use bright colors like red, orange, and yellow to attract the user's attention to something important or extraordinary. As such, use of these colors should be restricted to unusual conditions.

- For the objects the user regularly interacts with, choose neutral soft colors. Generally, form backgrounds should be light gray, for example.

- Similar objects should have similar colors. That is, all the labels on a form describing text boxes should have the same color and font.

- Make sure there is adequate contrast between foreground and background colors. Text boxes, for example, should have a white background and a dark-colored or black text foreground.

- Remember, the user of your program may be color-blind.

Adding a Shape Object to the Form

Selena suggests that you separate the input and output sections of the program by enclosing them in a dark gray region. To do this, you need to learn how to use the Shape object.

The Shape object will identify visually the input and output sections of the form.

A Shape object has several properties to define its size, pattern, color, border, and shape.

- The **BackColor** and **BackStyle** properties work together to define the shape's background. When the BackStyle property is set to its default, 0-Transparent, the BackColor setting is ignored.

- The **BorderStyle** property defines the appearance of the border surrounding the shape. This property can assume any of the values listed in the Properties window for the shape or on the BorderStyle property Help screen.

- The thickness of the shape's border is set using the **BorderWidth** property. A BorderWidth setting of 0 indicates that no border will be drawn around the shape.

- The **FillColor** property works with the FillStyle property to set the color of the shape. When the FillStyle property is set to its default, 1-Transparent, the FillColor setting is ignored.

- The **FillStyle** property lets you draw a pattern on the shape's background. You can identify the valid values for the different patterns in the Properties window for the shape.

- The appearance of the Shape control is set using the **Shape** property (not to be confused with the Shape control). This is the Shape property of the Shape control. The valid values for the Shape property are Rectangle, Square, Oval, Circle, Rounded Rectangle, and Rounded Square.

- The **Visible** property of a shape can be set to True or False. A shape can be seen at run time only when its Visible property is set to True.

For more information about the properties for a Shape object, or how to set them by writing code that will be executed at run time, look at online Help for the specific property.

The calculator program will include a rectangular shape drawn around the input and output sections of the program to visually identify the two sections to the user.

REFERENCE window	**ADDING A SHAPE OBJECT TO A FORM**
	- Click the Shape control on the toolbox.
	- Click and drag the mouse to draw a shape on the form.
	- Set the BackColor and BackStyle properties to define the shape's background appearance.
	- Set the BorderStyle property to create a solid, dashed, or dotted border.
	- Set the BorderWidth property to increase or decrease the thickness of the border. To remove the border set the BorderStyle to 0 - Transparent.
	- Set the Shape property to make the object a rectangle, oval, circle, or other shape.
	- The standard prefix for a Shape object is "shp".

Selena suggests that you now create the Shape object for both the input and output sections of the form and change their appearance so they appear dark gray with a solid black border. Because you will not write any code to reference properties of the shapes, there is no need to change the Name property.

To add the Shape objects to the calculator program:

1. Click the **Shape** control 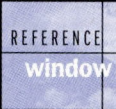 on the toolbox.

2. Move the pointer to the form and draw an outline of the shape so it looks like the shape shown in Figure 2-14. By default, the Shape control draws a rectangle.

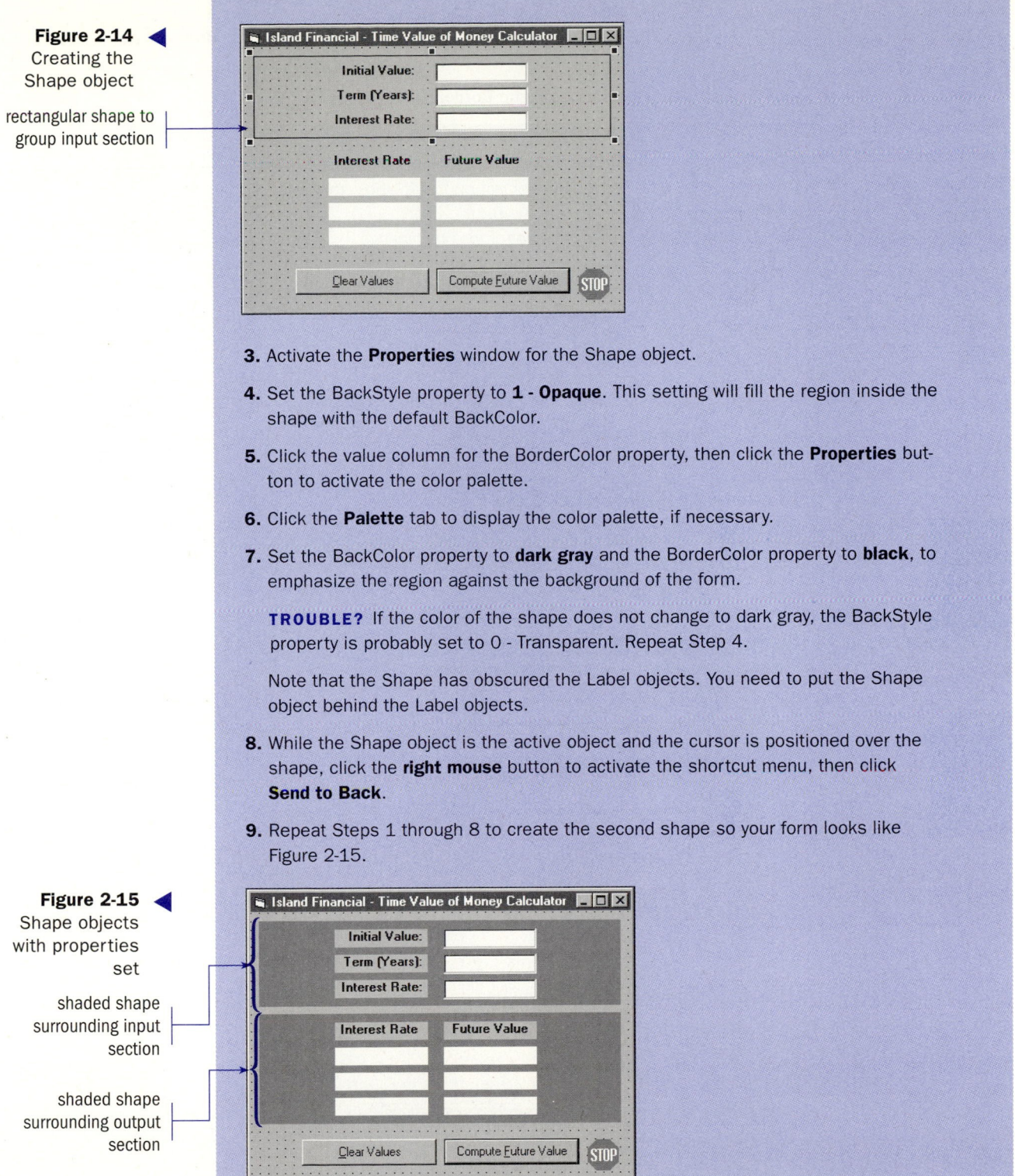

Figure 2-14
Creating the
Shape object

rectangular shape to
group input section

3. Activate the **Properties** window for the Shape object.

4. Set the BackStyle property to **1 - Opaque**. This setting will fill the region inside the shape with the default BackColor.

5. Click the value column for the BorderColor property, then click the **Properties** button to activate the color palette.

6. Click the **Palette** tab to display the color palette, if necessary.

7. Set the BackColor property to **dark gray** and the BorderColor property to **black**, to emphasize the region against the background of the form.

> **TROUBLE?** If the color of the shape does not change to dark gray, the BackStyle property is probably set to 0 - Transparent. Repeat Step 4.

Note that the Shape has obscured the Label objects. You need to put the Shape object behind the Label objects.

8. While the Shape object is the active object and the cursor is positioned over the shape, click the **right mouse** button to activate the shortcut menu, then click **Send to Back**.

9. Repeat Steps 1 through 8 to create the second shape so your form looks like Figure 2-15.

Figure 2-15
Shape objects
with properties
set

shaded shape
surrounding input
section

shaded shape
surrounding output
section

Creating a Line Object

You also can draw lines to identify different sections of the form or to draw attention to a particular form area by using the Line control on the toolbox. You can draw lines in any direction and choose different thicknesses and colors for lines.

- The color of the line can be changed by setting the **BorderColor** property.

- You also can create dashed and dotted lines by setting the **BorderStyle** property.

- The thickness is set using the **BorderWidth** property.

REFERENCE
window

CREATING A LINE OBJECT

- Click the Line control on the toolbox, then use the mouse to draw a line on the form.
- To define the color of the line, change the BorderColor property.
- To change the type of line, set the BorderStyle property. For example, the style could be dashed or solid.
- To change the thickness of the line, set the BorderWidth property.
- The standard prefix for a Line object is "lin".

In the calculator program, Selena suggests you draw a horizontal line to separate the input and output sections from the buttons.

To create a horizontal line on the form:

1. Click the **Line** control ⬚ on the toolbox, then use the mouse to draw a horizontal line between the output section (labels and text boxes) and the processing section (command buttons and stop sign). Release the mouse button when the line is the same width as the shape above it. See Figure 2-16.

Figure 2-16 ◄
Creating the
Line object

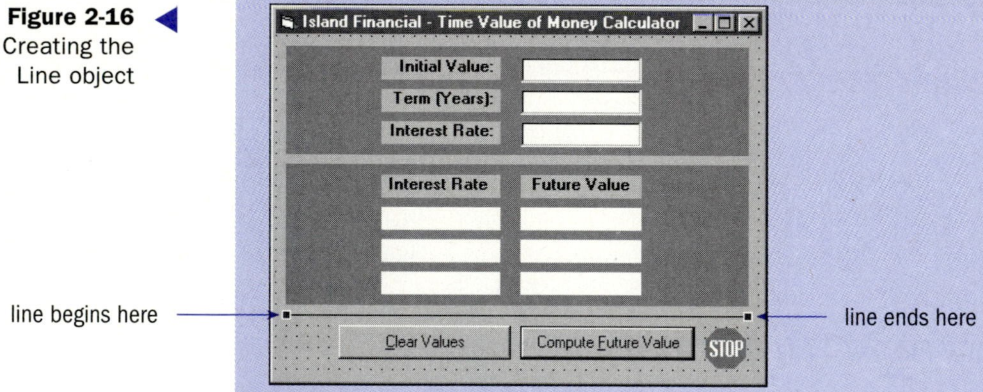

line begins here →

line ends here

2. Set the BorderWidth property to **2**.

3. Click the value column of the BorderColor property.

4. Click the **Properties** button ▼ to open the color palette. Set the BorderColor property to **light blue**.

   Your line should look like the one shown in Figure 2-17.

Figure 2-17 ◄
Setting the
line's color and
thickness

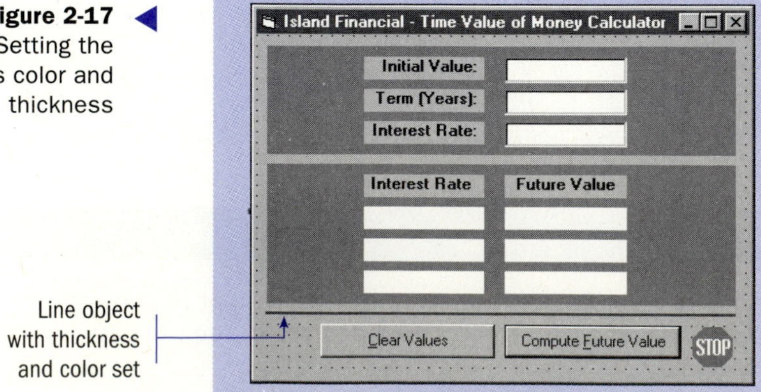

Line object
with thickness
and color set →

> **TROUBLE?** If the line is in the wrong place or is not horizontal, click the object to select it. Use the mouse to reposition the line, or use the mouse on one of the sizing handles to resize the line, as necessary.

The form now contains all the necessary objects as shown in Selena's plan. This is a good time to save the form and project files.

To save the form and project files:

1. Make sure the Form window is active.

2. Click the **Save Project** button 🖫 on the toolbar.

Quick Check

1. Describe the differences between a Label control and a TextBox control.

2. How do you change the font of a text box's or label's contents?

3. What is the benefit of using the Windows Clipboard to create new instances of a control?

4. What is the purpose of the CommandButton control?

5. What is focus and how do you change the order in which objects receive focus?

6. What is the purpose of the Shape and Line controls?

7. Describe the effects of using different colors in a user interface.

Now that you have completed Session 2.1, you can exit Visual Basic or you can continue to the next session.

SESSION

2.2

In this session, you will set properties using Visual Basic code, declare form-level and local variables, use the Val, Format, and Future Value functions. You also will understand the types of errors that can prevent your program from running correctly.

Setting Properties Using Visual Basic Code

To improve the user interface, Selena wants to emphasize the active text box by displaying the text in blue bold while the user is entering the text (has focus). When the user presses the Tab key to move to a different object, the text in the newly selected object should appear in a blue bold type and the text in the previously selected object should no longer be bold. To accomplish this task, you need to learn about two events applicable to the text box.

As you have seen, objects can respond to events like being clicked. Different objects can respond to different events. A TextBox object can respond to several events, including GotFocus and LostFocus.

- The **GotFocus** event occurs when a text box receives the focus.

- The **LostFocus** event occurs when a text box loses focus.

You can write code for these events to provide visual help to the user, such as displaying a message in a status bar, changing the type style of text, or performing other tasks. In your program, you need to use the GotFocus and LostFocus events to change the type style of text in the active object to bold and change the color of the text.

Before you can write the code for the GotFocus and LostFocus events, you need to learn how to use the Code window to select an object and the appropriate event procedure. The Code window contains two list boxes. The Object list box shows all the objects on the form. After you select an object, you can select an event procedure from the Procedure list box. The events shown in the Procedure list box depend on the type of object you selected, because different objects respond to different events. When you select an object, Visual Basic sets the Procedure list box to the most commonly used event for that object. The Code window can display a single procedure or multiple procedures depending on which view (located at the lower-left corner of the Code window) is selected. If the Procedure View button is active, the Code window will display one procedure at a time, as shown in Figure 2-18. If the Full Module View button to the right of it is active, multiple procedures are displayed separated by a horizontal line.

You will begin by opening the Code window to the first object you need to program, txtInitialValue.

To select the Code window for frmIslandCalculator:

1. Click the **Project Explorer** button 🔳 on the toolbar, if necessary, to open the Project Explorer.

2. Highlight the form named **frmIslandCalculator,** then display the form.

   TROUBLE? If frmIslandCalculator is not visible, the Forms folder probably is not open; click the Open Folder button 🔳 next to the Forms folder.

3. Double-click the object named txtInitialValue to activate it and open the Code window. The Code window opens as shown in Figure 2-18.

Figure 2-18 ◀
Selecting an object in the Code window

view one procedure (active)

view many procedures

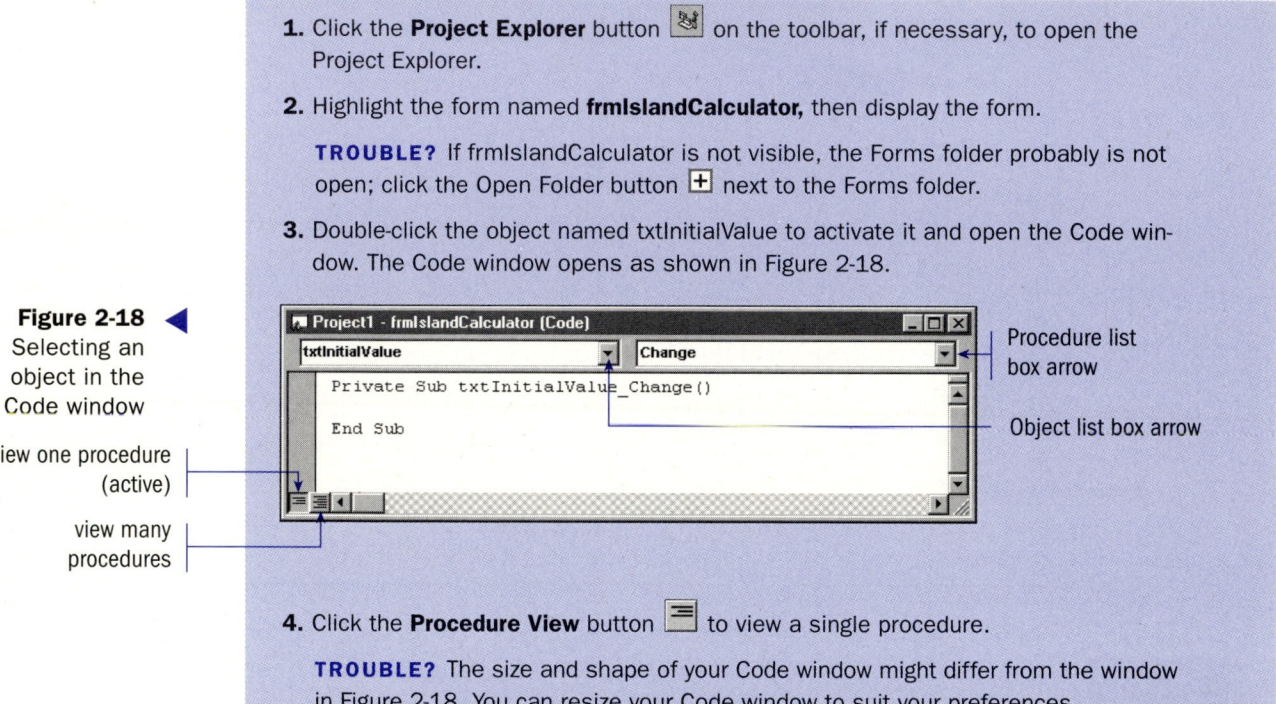

Procedure list box arrow

Object list box arrow

4. Click the **Procedure View** button 🔳 to view a single procedure.

   TROUBLE? The size and shape of your Code window might differ from the window in Figure 2-18. You can resize your Code window to suit your preferences.

Well-Written Comments

While a few small programs are self-explanatory, most are not. Comprehensive standardized program comments will help you and other programmers understand what your program is doing and how. Comments should be written as you develop a program. As you modify what a program does, the comments should be changed to reflect the program's new behavior.

All procedures you write should begin with a comment block if the procedure is not self-explanatory. This comment block should contain the following elements.

- The purpose of the procedure.
- Information that the procedure needs (inputs) to operate properly. These usually are variables that are declared outside the procedure or variables in other forms.
- A description of what the procedure produces (outputs).

These guidelines are a foundation for good comments. As you develop more and larger programs, you may find it useful to add more information like a history of revisions. This is especially important when multiple programmers develop and modify a program. Comments in many programs may comprise 50 percent or more of the program's statements. Increasing the number of comments will not affect the speed of your program, because when you create an executable file of your program, all the comments are removed. They are used only by the developers as they look at the code.

You must observe the following syntax rules when writing comments:

- Any line beginning with an apostrophe is considered a comment line and is ignored by Visual Basic.

- Any characters following an apostrophe after a statement on one line are considered a comment and are ignored by Visual Basic.

You will continue to work on Selena's program by selecting the first text box, txtInitialValue, and its GotFocus event.

To select the GotFocus event procedure for the txtInitialValue object in the Code window:

1. Click the **Procedure View** button ▤, if necessary.

   Next, you need to specify the correct desired object and event procedure. Selena wants the text typed into the text boxes to be bold and dark blue when each TextBox object has the focus. So, you need to select the GotFocus event for the first text box named txtInitialValue.

2. Click the **Object** list arrow, then click **txtInitialValue**, if necessary.

3. Click the **Procedure** list arrow, then click **GotFocus**. The code you will enter for the event will be executed when the TextBox object gets the focus. See Figure 2-19.

Figure 2-19 ◀
Select an object and event procedure

Procedure list box arrow

click the GotFocus event

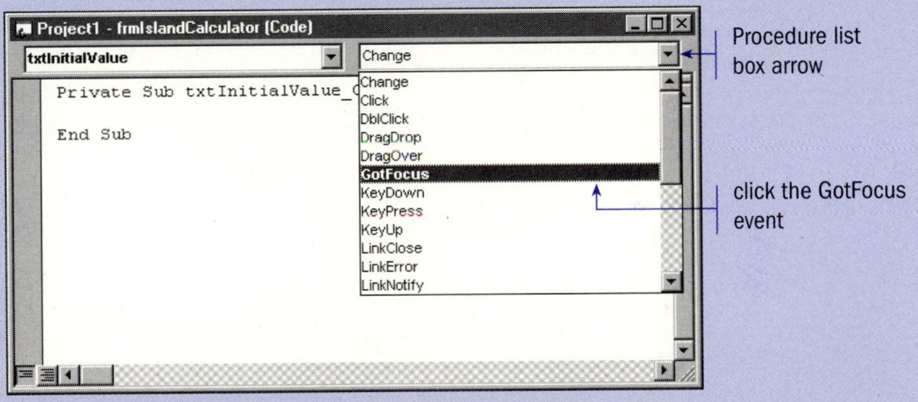

   TROUBLE? If the object or event procedure does not appear in the list box, use the scroll bars to search for them.

The TextBox object supports 23 different events. In addition to getting and losing focus, a Change event occurs each time the contents of a text box change. This is useful if you want to verify that the user entered valid information in the text box. Each time a user types a character into a text box, a KeyPress event also is generated, allowing you to find out exactly what key the user typed into the box. Even though Visual Basic generates these events while your program is running, you do not need to write code to respond to them. Thus, if you do not want to validate keystrokes, you would not write any code for the KeyPress event. Understanding the different events supported by an object and when they occur is an important part of Visual Basic programming. You will learn more about events in the next tutorial.

Visual Basic makes the process of writing code easier by helping you complete statements. This feature, called automatic code completion, displays list boxes with applicable properties and their values as you write statements.

Now that you have selected the object and the event procedure, you can write the code for the event so that text typed in the object will be bold and dark blue while the user is typing it. The FontBold property, when set to True, causes the text to appear in bold type.

To change the font when the text box receives focus:

1. First enter the comment as shown in Figure 2-20.

2. In the blank line between the beginning and ending lines of code, enter the code shown in Figure 2-20. Note that when the period (.) is typed, Visual Basic displays a list of the applicable properties that you can set.

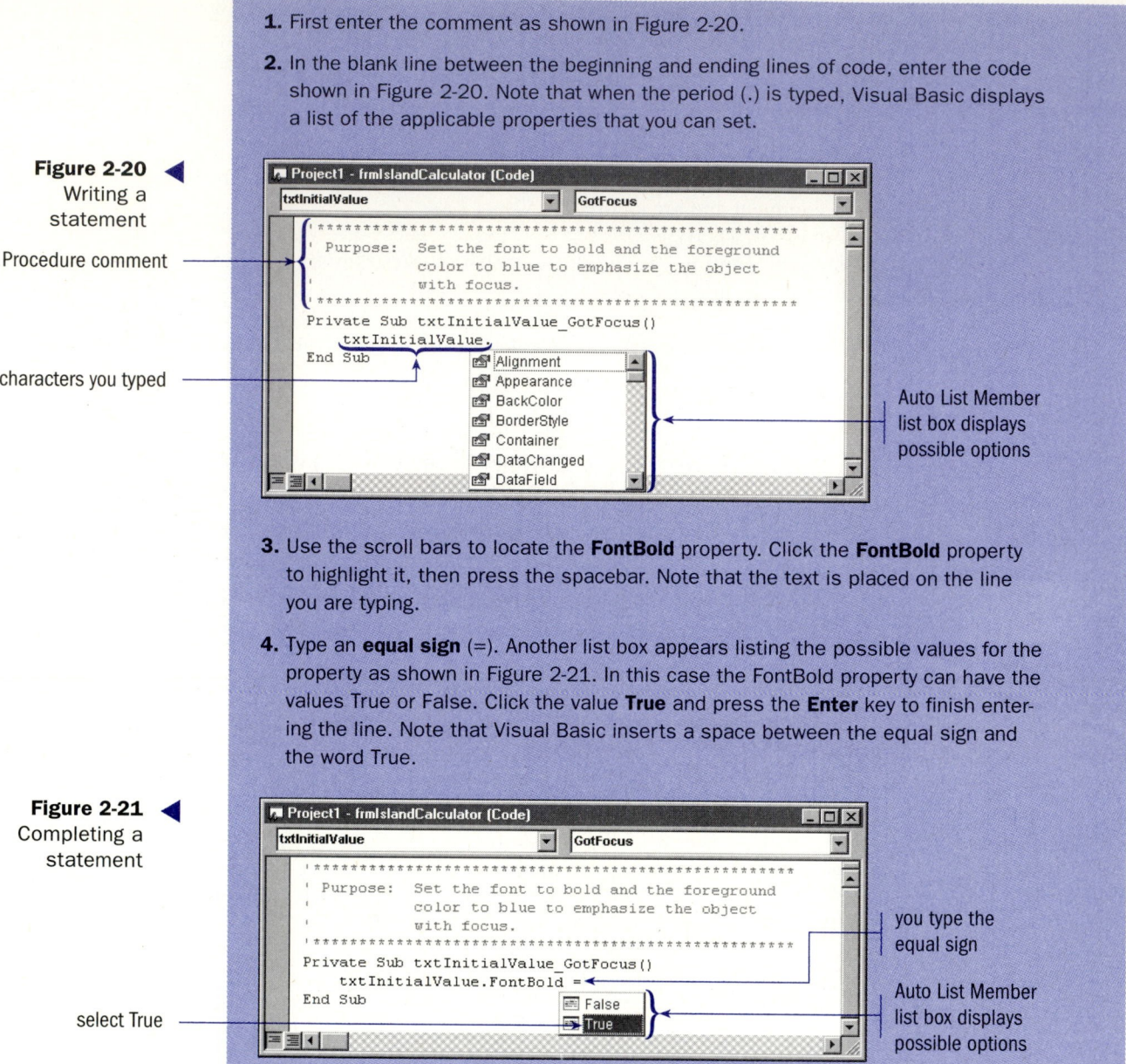

Figure 2-20 ◀
Writing a statement

Procedure comment

characters you typed

Auto List Member list box displays possible options

3. Use the scroll bars to locate the **FontBold** property. Click the **FontBold** property to highlight it, then press the spacebar. Note that the text is placed on the line you are typing.

4. Type an **equal sign** (=). Another list box appears listing the possible values for the property as shown in Figure 2-21. In this case the FontBold property can have the values True or False. Click the value **True** and press the **Enter** key to finish entering the line. Note that Visual Basic inserts a space between the equal sign and the word True.

Figure 2-21 ◀
Completing a statement

select True

you type the equal sign

Auto List Member list box displays possible options

Now you need to write the code to change the color of the text when the object receives focus. As with other properties, the color of an object can be set at design time using the Properties window or at run time using Visual Basic code. The easiest way to specify a color at run time is to use a constant.

Looking Up Intrinsic Constants with the Object Browser

Constants have values that do not change while the program is running. There are two types of constants: intrinsic constants and user-defined constants. **Intrinsic constants** are defined by Visual Basic. **User-defined constants** are defined by you, the programmer, with a Visual Basic statement. You will learn about user-defined constants in later tutorials.

Using a Visual Basic tool called the Object Browser, you will see how to express color values as intrinsic constants. Visual Basic has defined several intrinsic constants you can use in a program to make it more readable and intuitive.

The **Object Browser**, which is available only at design time, allows you to look at the intrinsic constants defined by Visual Basic that relate to the properties of all the objects you create, as well as the modules and procedures you have defined for your project. Many of these constants also are listed in the Help system.

To make your program more readable, you will use intrinsic constants to change the color of the foreground text in each text box when it has focus. Before you can use these constants, you need to find out their names. You can look up intrinsic constants using the Object Browser. The names of all Visual Basic intrinsic constants begin with the prefix "vb".

To use the Object Browser to examine the intrinsic constants applicable color:

1. Click the **Object Browser** button 📷 on the toolbar. The Object Browser dialog box opens.

2. Click **ColorConstants** in the Classes section of the Object Browser dialog box. Use the scroll bars if needed to locate the correct list item.

   The Members of 'ColorConstants' section of the dialog box contains the different color constants, as shown in Figure 2-22.

Figure 2-22 ◀
Object Browser
dialog box

vbBlack will return the
color to its original
setting

Click vbBlue to view
its value

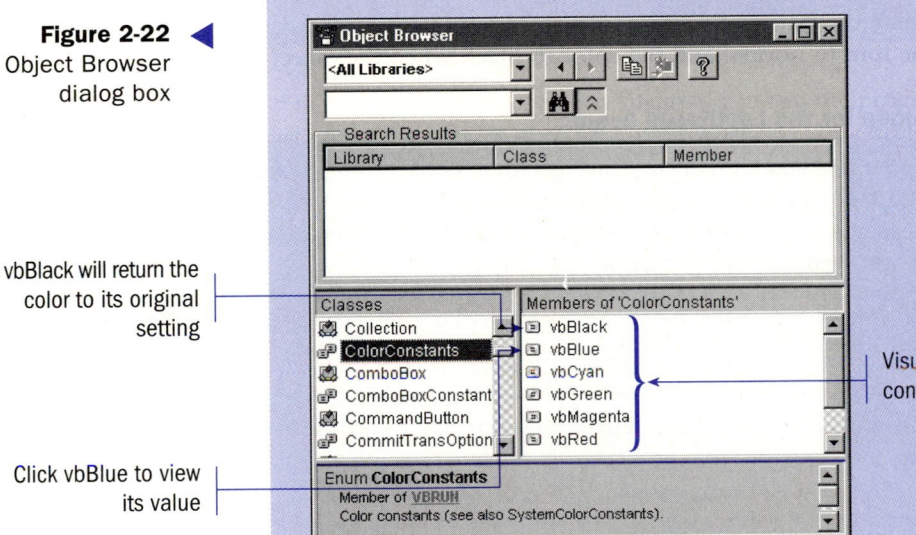

Visual Basic color
constants

3. Click **vbBlue**. Notice that the value of the constant, 16711680, is displayed at the bottom of the dialog box. You could use either the number 16711680 or the constant vbBlue to set the color. As you can see, the constant name is much more meaningful when you are programming or reading code.

4. Click the **Close** button ☒ on the Object Browser title bar to close the Object Browser.

When you use intrinsic constant names in a program, Visual Basic converts the names into their respective values when the program is run, which makes the program more readable and reliable. For example, if you needed to set the ForeColor property to blue, the following two statements would accomplish this; however, the statement containing the constant makes it easier for the programmer to understand that the foreground color is set to blue:

```
txtInitialValue.ForeColor = 16711680
txtInitialValue.ForeColor = vbBlue
```

You will use intrinsic constants to write the code to change the foreground color of the text box to blue.

When you want to stop running a program, you always can click the End button on the toolbar, as you did in the preceding steps. Most programs, however, are saved as "exe" files and are run outside of the Visual Basic environment. Thus, the user will not see the End button on the toolbar. Therefore, the program should include a button or image that the user can click to stop the program from running. This button or image should respond to the Click event that executes the End statement, which works in the same way as the End button on the toolbar. To include the End statement in a procedure, you simply type the word "End" before the End Sub statement in the Code window.

In your program, Selena wants a user to be able to click the stop sign image to stop the program from running. So, you need to write the code for the Image object's Click event procedure.

To write the code for the Image object:

1. Open the Code window and select the **imgExit** object.

2. Click the **Procedure** list arrow, and select the **Click** event, if necessary.

3. Type the word **End** on the line above the End Sub statement. Because this procedure is very intuitive, there is no need to include a comment.

4. Click the **Close** button ⊠ on the Code window title bar to close the window.

Variables

In addition to receiving user input with text boxes and displaying information with labels, a program generally needs to perform computations on the input to produce the output. The calculator program you are writing for Selena needs to compute two interest rates based on the annual interest rate entered into the Interest Rate text box. The program then must compute the future value of an investment based on the different interest rates. To store the results of the computations while the program is running, you use variables. A **variable** is a programming element used to store a value in the program. Like an object, every variable you create has a name. A variable is much like a box where you can store and retrieve information.

Every variable also has a data type that determines the kind of output the variable can store. A variable can store either textual information or numbers, but not both. There are specific data types to store whole numbers, numbers containing decimal points, and dates. Other data types store values like True or False. Unlike objects, a variable does not have properties nor does it respond to events. It simply stores information while the program is running.

Just like object names, variable names should adhere to certain standards. Figure 2-24 presents some basic requirements and recommendations for naming variables. When you create a variable, you should assign it a name that adheres to the naming conventions in the Naming Conventions Appendix.

Figure 2-24 ◄
Variable
naming
conventions

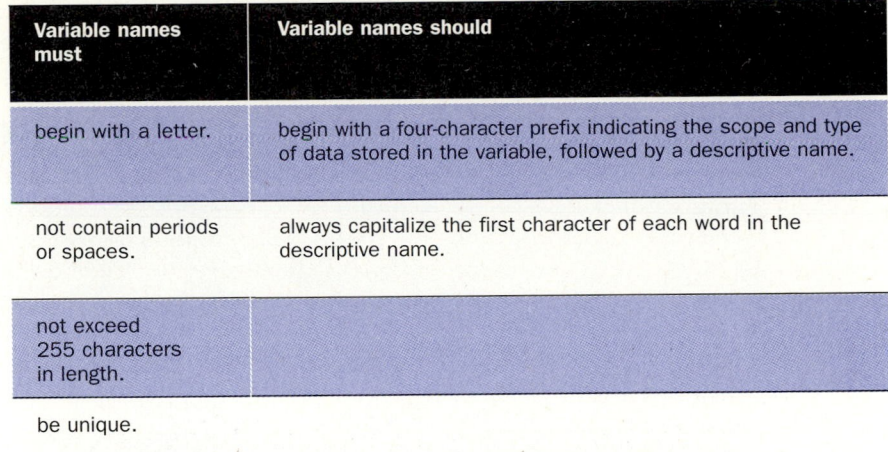

Variable names must	Variable names should
begin with a letter.	begin with a four-character prefix indicating the scope and type of data stored in the variable, followed by a descriptive name.
not contain periods or spaces.	always capitalize the first character of each word in the descriptive name.
not exceed 255 characters in length.	
be unique.	

Figure 2-25 contains examples of valid and invalid variable names.

Figure 2-25 ◄
Variable
names

Valid Variable Name	Invalid Variable Name
strValidStringName	1InvalidStringName
intValid_Integer	intInvalid.Integer

Declaring a Variable

The process of creating a variable is known as declaring a variable. To declare a variable, you use either the Visual Basic **Private** statement or **Dim** statement, which have the following syntax:

[**Private**|**Dim**] *Varname* **As** *Type*

- The **Private** keyword causes the variable to be created. The variable can be used only in the form in which it is declared, but by all the procedures in the form. Another keyword, **Public**, is used to create variables that can be used by different forms and modules and is discussed in later tutorials.

- The **Dim** keyword, depending on where it is used, creates variables that can be used only in the procedure in which they are declared or may be used by other procedures.

- *Varname* is the name you want to assign to the variable.

- *Type* is the data type of the variable. The data type can be any valid Visual Basic data types. Figure 2-26 lists the data types you will use in this tutorial. A programmer can create additional data types as well.

Every declared variable consumes physical space in computer memory. Variables of different types consume a different amount of space and store different kinds of values. Also, variables should have a prefix that identifies the data type of the variable.

Figure 2-26 lists some of the Visual Basic data types, their storage sizes in bytes, standard prefixes, and some possible values for each type. You will learn about other Visual Basic data types in other tutorials.

Figure 2-26 ◀
Partial
list of
Visual Basic
data types

Data Type	Storage Size	Prefix	Possible Values
Integer	2 bytes	int	Positive and negative whole numbers between -32768 and 32767. A number such as 84 or -1715 can be stored as an integer.
Single	4 bytes	sng	A number with a decimal point, such as 3.14, -10034.388, or 0.113.
String	1 byte per character	str	You can store up to about 2 billion characters for variable-length strings. Text entries such as "John Doe" or "Pacific Ocean" are stored as strings.

Choosing the correct data type for a variable is important. For example, if a variable will contain only whole numbers (numbers without a decimal point), you should choose the Integer data type instead of Single. Although a program usually works with either data type, operations on floating point values (numbers with a decimal point) take considerably longer to perform. Also the Single type variable consumes more memory than an Integer type variable. Although you will not declare any String variables in this program, the information stored in the Text property of a TextBox object always is considered a String in Visual Basic. When you want to perform a calculation on a String, you must convert it to a number.

When you use the Private or Dim statement to declare a variable, you are *explicitly* declaring the variable, but there is another way to create variables. If you use a variable name in any Visual Basic statement without first explicitly declaring the variable with the Private or Dim statement, Visual Basic will create the variable for you. This is referred to as implicit declaration, and is strongly discouraged. For example, if you intended to use a variable named InterestRate in a statement but you made a typographical error, Visual Basic would assume you wanted to create a new variable. Although the program would run, the variable would not contain the correct information. So, the results would be wrong when you use the variable in a computation.

You can prohibit Visual Basic from implicitly creating variables by using the Option Explicit statement, which has the following syntax:

Option Explicit

- This statement forces variable names to be explicitly defined with the Dim or Private statement. If you try to use a variable that was not declared with the Dim or Private statement, Visual Basic will display a dialog box telling you the variable is not defined. The Option Explicit statement also helps you identify incorrectly spelled variables that would create other errors, called logic errors, which are more difficult to detect. All programs you create in this book will contain the Option Explicit statement.

- The Option Explicit statement should be the first statement in the general declarations section of the form.

Tip: To include the Option Explicit statement in all your programs click Tools then Options on the menu bar. Be sure the Require Variable Declarations check box on the Editor tab is checked. Any new project or module then will include the Option Explicit statement.

Local and Form-Level Variables

Now that you know how to declare variables, you need to know where to declare them. If you declare variables inside a procedure (between the Private Sub and End Sub statements), you can use the variable inside that procedure only. A variable declared inside a procedure exists only while the procedure is running, and is called a **local variable**. If you declare a variable outside a procedure, the variable can be used by all the different procedures in your form. The variable and its value exist whenever the program is running; this type of variable is called a **form-level variable.**

If (General) is displayed in the Object list box and (Declarations) is displayed in the Procedure list box, this is known as the general declarations section, and you use it to declare form-level variables.

Now you need to open the Code window and select the general declarations section so that you can enter the form-level variables for your program.

To open the general declarations section of the Code window:

1. Click the **View Code** button ▣ in the Project Explorer to open the Code window.

2. Click the **Object** list arrow then click **(General)**.

3. Click the **Procedure** list arrow then click **(Declarations)**, if necessary.

In the general declarations section of each form, you should include a series of comments called a comment block containing a brief description of the form's purpose. This description should describe what the form does.

Declaring Form-Level Variables

Some of the variables in the calculator program need to be used by different event procedures, so you must declare them as form-level variables. In addition to a prefix to identify the type of a variable, you should precede form-level variables with the character "m" to indicate that they can be used by the entire form module. Selena suggests you use msngMonthRate1, msngMonthRate2, and msngMonthRate3 as the names for the three variables to hold the monthly interest rates. Also, because interest rates are expressed with a decimal point (i.e., 7% is expressed as 0.07), you will use the Single data type for the variables.

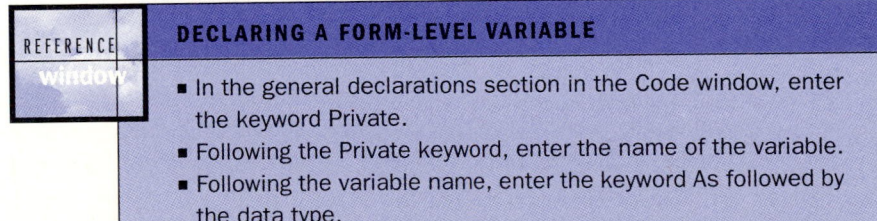

REFERENCE window

DECLARING A FORM-LEVEL VARIABLE

- In the general declarations section in the Code window, enter the keyword Private.
- Following the Private keyword, enter the name of the variable.
- Following the variable name, enter the keyword As followed by the data type.

Now you are ready to declare the three form-level variables for your program.

To declare the variables for the three monthly interest rates:

1. Make sure the Code window shows **(General)** as the selected object and **(Declarations)** as the selected procedure.

2. Enter the comments and variable declarations as shown in Figure 2-27. As you write the statements notice that the automatic code completion feature of Visual Basic will open list boxes containing possible options.

Figure 2-27 ◀
Declaring form-
level variables

each comment
line starts with
the ' character

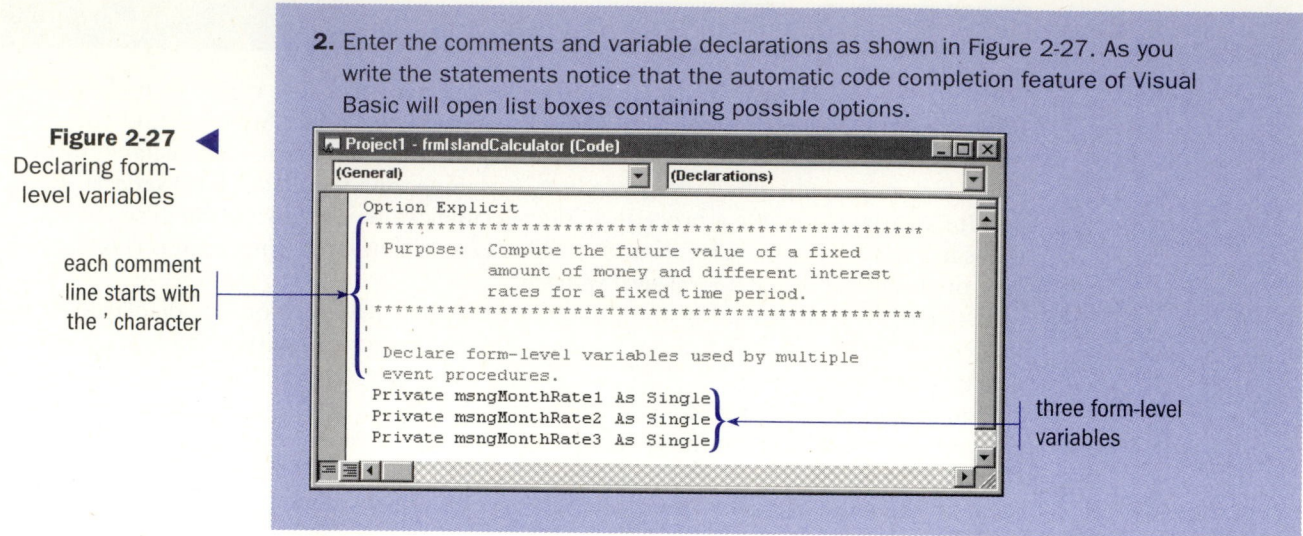

```
Option Explicit
'*********************************************************
' Purpose:  Compute the future value of a fixed
'           amount of money and different interest
'           rates for a fixed time period.
'*********************************************************
'
' Declare form-level variables used by multiple
' event procedures.
Private msngMonthRate1 As Single
Private msngMonthRate2 As Single
Private msngMonthRate3 As Single
```

three form-level
variables

The first statement (Option Explicit) tells Visual Basic you must declare all variables in the module before using them. The next lines are comment lines, so they each must start with the apostrophe (') character.

> *Tip:* You can include blank lines between comments or statements, known as whitespace, which is ignored by Visual Basic. Inserting whitespace in your code between the declaration of groups of related variables or between other related statements can improve the readability of the code. Including the apostrophe on a blank line is optional.

The last three lines declare three different form-level variables of the Single data type to store the three monthly interest rates. Because they are form-level variables of the Single data type their names begin with the prefix "msng".

When you type the statements into the Code window, Visual Basic automatically capitalizes the first character of all reserved words, even if you type in lowercase letters. **Reserved words** are words that are part of the Visual Basic language. Option Explicit, Private, Dim, As, and Single are all reserved words.

Declaring Local Variables

In addition to declaring form-level variables, you need to declare local variables that will be used only inside the Click event procedure for the Compute Future Value command button. These variables will hold the three future values of the investment and the input data entered by the user. There is a significant difference between local variables, declared inside a procedure, and form-level variables, declared in the general declarations section. The storage space in computer memory is allocated for form-level variables when the program starts and remains allocated whenever the form is open. Storage space for local variables is allocated only when a procedure is executed, and the space is deallocated when the procedure finishes. So, by declaring local variables you can reduce the total amount of memory used by variables. By decreasing the amount of memory your program uses, it generally will run faster and leave more memory for other Windows 95 programs to run.

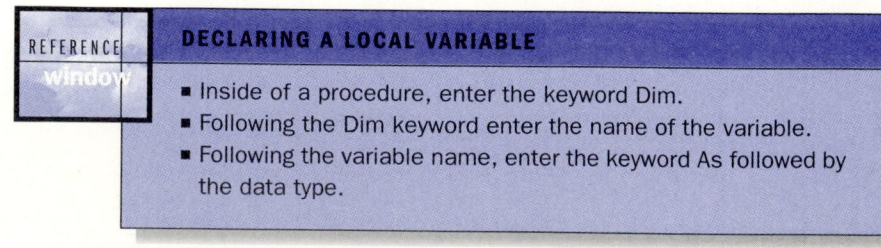

REFERENCE
window

DECLARING A LOCAL VARIABLE

- Inside of a procedure, enter the keyword Dim.
- Following the Dim keyword enter the name of the variable.
- Following the variable name, enter the keyword As followed by the data type.

You now can declare the variables that will hold the results of the future value computations and the variables that will hold the input data entered by the user. These local variables will exist only while the Compute Future Value command button's Click event procedure is running.

To declare the local variables for the Compute Future Value command button's Click event:

1. Make sure the **Code** window is active.

2. Click the **Object** list arrow, then click **cmdComputeFutureValue**.

3. Be sure that the **Procedure** list box is set to the **Click** event.

4. Enter the comments and variable declarations shown in Figure 2-28.

Figure 2-28 ◀
Declaring local variables for the command button

Comment block to describe procedure's purpose

statements indented to improve readability

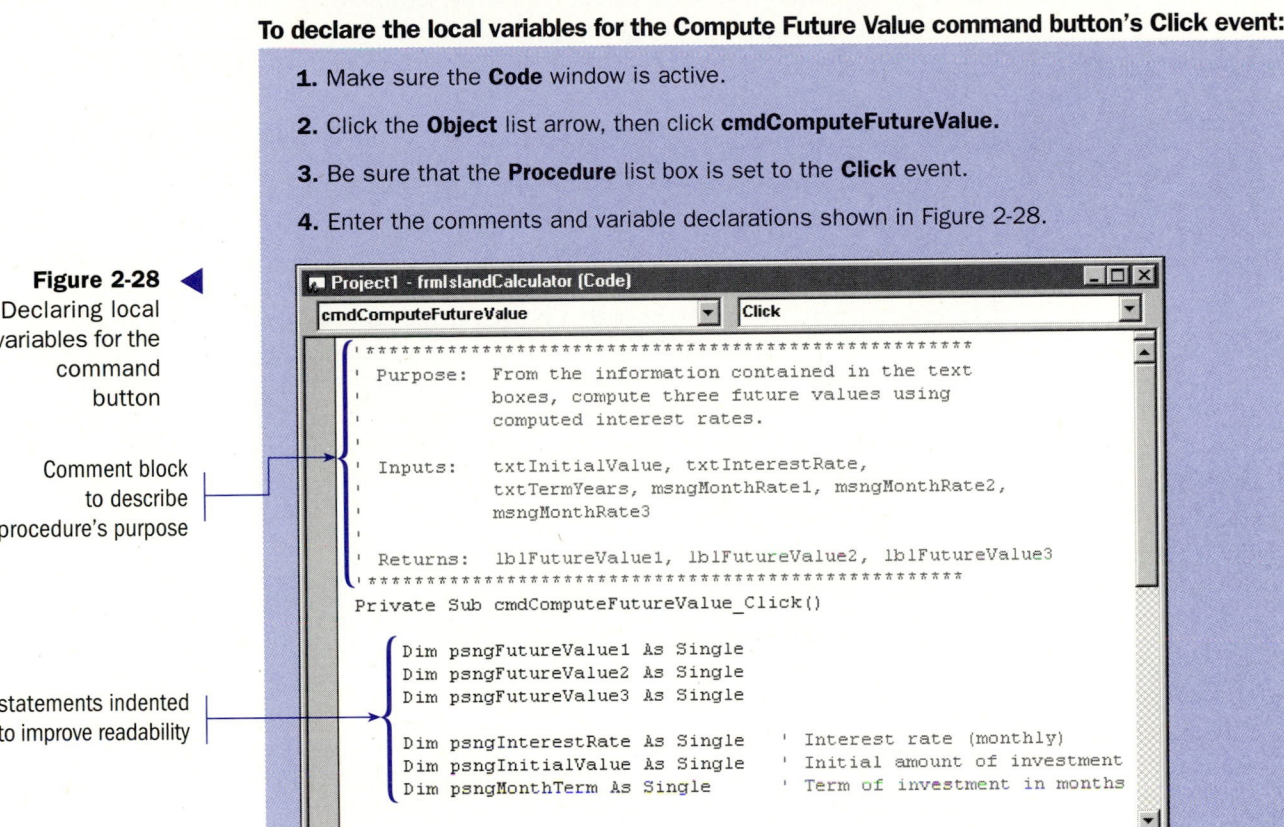

```
Project1 - frmIslandCalculator (Code)                          _ □ ×
cmdComputeFutureValue            ▼    Click                      ▼
'******************************************************
'  Purpose:   From the information contained in the text
'             boxes, compute three future values using
'             computed interest rates.
'
'  Inputs:    txtInitialValue, txtInterestRate,
'             txtTermYears, msngMonthRate1, msngMonthRate2,
'             msngMonthRate3
'
'  Returns:   lblFutureValue1, lblFutureValue2, lblFutureValue3
'******************************************************
Private Sub cmdComputeFutureValue_Click()

    Dim psngFutureValue1 As Single
    Dim psngFutureValue2 As Single
    Dim psngFutureValue3 As Single

    Dim psngInterestRate As Single   ' Interest rate (monthly)
    Dim psngInitialValue As Single   ' Initial amount of investment
    Dim psngMonthTerm As Single      ' Term of investment in months
```

Notice the comment block at the beginning of the event procedure. It contains a brief description of the procedure's purpose, the inputs, and the outputs. The variable names psngFutureValue1, psngFutureValue2, and psngFutureValue3 indicate that the Single data type variables will be used to store the results of the three future value computations while the procedure is executing. When the procedure finishes (the End Sub statement is reached), these variables no longer exist and thus cannot be used by other procedures in the program. Because they are local variables, the "m" prefix is replaced with the prefix "p" indicating a procedure level (local) variable. When you perform arithmetic computations on variables that contain a decimal point, you must use a numeric data type like Single.

All the statements inside a procedure should be indented evenly so the beginning and end of the procedure are clearly identifiable. Four spaces (a tab) is considered the standard. Notice that the comment describing the three future value variables is indented the same number of spaces as the statements the comment describes. Proper indentation will be especially important as your procedures become large enough that they cannot be completely displayed in the Code window.

Using Expressions and Operators to Manipulate Variables

Now that all the variables for your program have been declared, you can store information in them and use them to compute the output for your program. For example, you need to take the annual interest rate entered by the user and divide it by 12 to get the monthly interest rate. The result of this computation will be stored in the form-level variable msngMonthRate1, which you declared earlier.

You use **expressions**, which consist of variables, **operators** (+, − , and so on), and constants, in statements to perform calculations and store the results in other variables. Operators fall into three categories: arithmetic, comparison, and logical. The simple expressions in Figure 2-30 through Figure 2-32 later in this section use the addition (arithmetic) operator and the division (arithmetic) operator to perform computations and store the results in other variables.

When you write expressions using operators and variables, you need to understand the concept of precedence. **Precedence** is a term used to explain the standard order of execution in which arithmetic operations are performed with operators like + − / ^ and *. The concept of precedence was formulated to allow an expression to be written as one continuous statement to a computer. To do this, the computer scans the formula from left to right, looking for an operation that has the highest level of precedence. The highest level of precedence is to raise a number to a power. If the computer does not find any operations at that level, it goes to the beginning of the expression and starts at the next level, multiplication and division, and looks for those operations. If the computer finds an operator at the proper level, the computer executes that operation. If the computer finds more than one operator at the same level, it performs the leftmost operation first.

Figure 2-29 lists the Visual Basic operators that work with numeric data in the order of their precedence and gives an example of each.

Figure 2-29 ◀
Arithmetic
operators

Operators in Order of Precedence	Description	Example
^	Raises a number to the power of an exponent	2 ^ 3 is equal to 8
*, /	Multiplication and division	2 * 3 is equal to 6 8 / 4 is equal to 2
\	Integer division	10 \ 3 is equal to 3 5 \ 2 is equal to 2
Mod	Modulo Arithmetic; returns the integer remainder of a division operation	10 mod 3 is equal to 1
+, −	Addition and subtraction	2 + 3 is equal to 5 2 − 3 is equal to −1

Often, you need to change the standard order of operations to ensure that the correct sequence of operations is performed. You can do so by using one or more matched pairs of parentheses. By enclosing an operation within parentheses, that operation takes precedence over the levels in the standard order. For example, in the formula (Var1 + Var2) ^{Var3}, the addition would take place first rather than the exponentiation, because the addition operator is enclosed in parentheses. In the formula ((Var1 + Var2) − (Var3 + Var4)) ^{Var5}, the parentheses are **nested**, which means that the innermost and leftmost operation Var1 + Var2 would occur first, (Var3 + Var4) would occur second, the result of ((Var1 + Var2) − (Var3 + Var4)) would occur next, and finally the result would be raised to the power Var5. Consider the formula shown in Figure 2-30.

Figure 2-30 ◀
Algebraic
formula

$$\left(\frac{Var1+Var2}{Var3+Var4}\right) * Var5^{Var6}$$

In Figure 2-30, the order of operations clearly is shown by the way the formula is presented. If you transformed this formula directly into a computer-readable expression, it would look like the formula in Figure 2-31.

Figure 2-31 ◀
Computer-
readable
expression

Var1 + Var2 / Var3 - Var4 * Var5 ^ Var6

Without using parentheses, the order of operations would follow the standard order of evaluation, but adding parentheses will change the results. Figure 2-32 shows the different order evaluation with and without parentheses.

Figure 2-32 ◀
Evaluating
expressions

Standard order of evaluation

Var1 + Var2 / Var3 - Var4 * Var5 ^ Var6

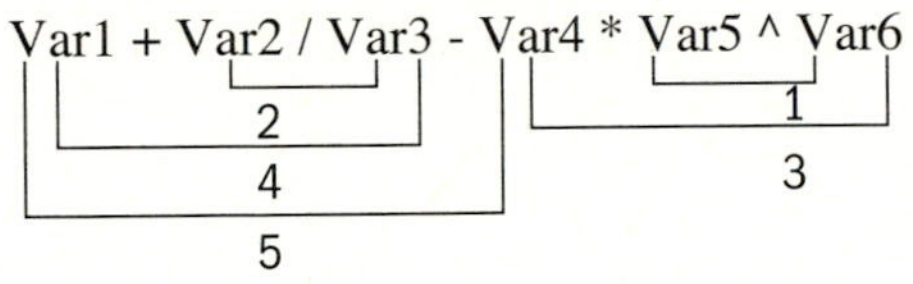

Order of evaluation with parentheses

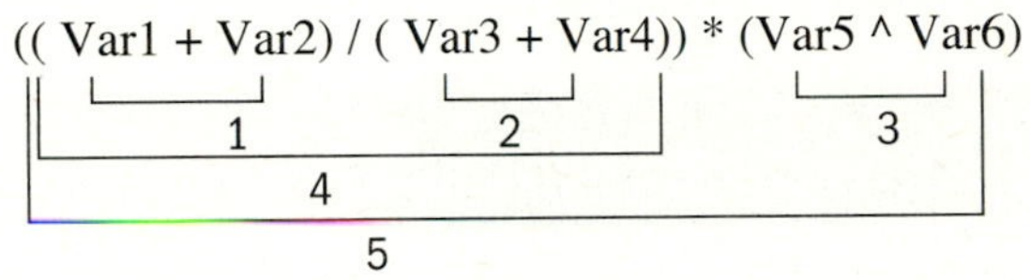

((Var1 + Var2) / (Var3 + Var4)) * (Var5 ^ Var6)

Additional parentheses also can improve the readability of your program, so you should use them liberally. Including parentheses around the sub-expression (Var5 ^{Var6}) in Figure 2-32 does not change the order of the expression, but it does enhance the readability by clarifying the order in which you want the computer to evaluate the expression.

In addition to writing expressions containing arithmetic operators, you also can write expressions that use operators to perform comparisons. Comparisons are useful to evaluate such situations as whether or not two numbers are equal or two text strings are the same. Furthermore, you also can use logical operators to connect expressions together. You will learn about comparison and logical operators later in this text.

Using Visual Basic Functions

Visual Basic includes financial and mathematical functions, which are **intrinsic functions** built into the programming language. Functions are procedures that have been written by the language designers. Like an event procedure, a function procedure contains one or more Visual Basic statements that are executed when a user performs an action. Function procedures differ from event procedures in that you have to explicitly write a Visual Basic statement to call them. Function procedures also return a value like a number string or other data type that you can store into a variable or a compatible object property. This is referred to as calling a function. In your program, you will use three intrinsic function procedures: the Val function, the Format function, and the Future Value (FV) function. You can look up how to use other intrinsic functions in Visual Basic online Help.

Converting Data Using the Val Function

Although the values entered by the user in the three TextBox objects will contain only digits (0 - 9) and possibly a decimal point, Visual Basic stores each of these values in a text box as a string of characters rather than a number. Visual Basic does not know how you intend to use the information stored in a TextBox object, so it always stores the value as a string of characters. When the program tries to perform an arithmetic operation on the text in the text box, Visual Basic tries to convert the value from a string of characters to a number. If the user entered a letter instead of a number in one of the TextBox objects, however, Visual Basic cannot properly convert the value into a number, and a run-time error will occur. You will learn about run-time errors later in this session.

The **Val** function converts a string of characters (a value assigned the String data type) to a number, which is necessary if you want the data to be used in a calculation. To use a number in a calculation, you need to convert the information into a numeric value and store the result in a variable specifically created as a numeric value. The Val function performs this task automatically. If the string contains letters, the Val function stops scanning the string and returns the value of the digits already scanned. When you use a function like Val, you provide information to it using an **argument**. Variables in your program, constants, or literal values can be used as arguments.

You use the following syntax for the Val function:

result = **Val**(*string*)

- The Val function accepts one argument, a *string*, and attempts to convert the string into a numeric value. The converted value is stored in *result*, a variable or object property.

- If *string* contains no digits, the value 0 is stored in *result*.

Figure 2-33 shows how the Val function would convert several different strings.

Figure 2-33 ◀
Results
of the Val
function

Expression	Result
Val(123.4a)	123.4
Val("")	0
Val(aaa)	0
Val(23aa34)	23

Notice the string named "" in Figure 2-33. This is known as an empty string or **Null string**. If you want to delete the text from the Caption property of a label or the Text property of a text box, you must assign an empty string to the property.

The next step in creating your program is to write the code for the event procedure to update the three labels containing interest rate values whenever the interest rate text box looses focus. Just as you wrote code to change the type style when an object became active (GotFocus) or became inactive (LostFocus), you now need to add code to display the different interest rates in the output section, whenever the value of the Interest Rate text box loses focus.

The future value of the investment should compound interest monthly, so you need to compute the value of the variables for the three monthly interest rates. The future value is computed using the variables msngMonthRate1, msngMonthRate2, and msngMonthRate3 when the user clicks the Compute Future Value command button.

To write the code for the Interest Rate TextBox object's LostFocus event:

1. Select the **txtInterestRate** object and the **LostFocus** procedure in the Code window.

2. Enter the code shown in bold at the beginning of the event procedure:

```
Private Sub txtInterestRate_LostFocus()
    Dim psngInterestRate As Single     'Interest rate (monthly)
    psngInterestRate = Val(txtInterestRate.Text)
    msngMonthRate1 = psngInterestRate / 12
    msngMonthRate2 = (psngInterestRate + 0.01) / 12
    msngMonthRate3 = (psngInterestRate + 0.02) / 12
End Sub
```

Before you proceed, you need to examine the code in more detail. First, notice that the procedure is named "txtInterestRate_LostFocus( )." This name indicates that the program will respond to a LostFocus event generated by the object named txtInterestRate. Whenever a user changes the focus from txtInterestRate to another object, the statements in this LostFocus event procedure will be executed.

```
Dim psngInterestRate As Single     'Interest rate (monthly)
```

This statement creates a local variable named psngInterestRate. The variable is local because you declared it inside the event procedure txtInterestRate_LostFocus and, therefore, it can be used inside this procedure only. This variable will store the numeric representation of the annual interest rate contained in the TextBox object named txtInterestRate.

```
psngInterestRate = Val(txtInterestRate.Text)
```

This statement uses the Val function to convert the text a user enters (stored in the Text property of the txtInterestRate text box), into a numeric value and stores the result in the variable psngInterestRate so it can be used in the subsequent calculations. Even though a user will enter a number into this text box, Visual Basic will store the entry as a string of characters rather than a numeric value.

```
msngMonthRate1 = psngInterestRate / 12
msngMonthRate2 = (psngInterestRate + 0.01) / 12
msngMonthRate3 = (psngInterestRate + 0.02) / 12
```

Recall that you declared the variables msngMonthRate1, msngMonthRate2, and msngMonthRate3 in the general declarations section, so they are form-level variables and can be used by this or any procedure in the form module. The user will enter an annual interest rate value. Because the interest on an investment is compounded every month, however, these statements divide the annual rate by 12; the number of months in a year. Then the statements compute different interest rates by adding 1% to the annual rate. Note that parentheses are needed to override the default precedence rules, so that the addition is completed before the division.

Formatting a Numeric Value

The code you just wrote computes the monthly interest rate for the three form-level variables. These variables will be used in the Click event procedure for the command button to compute the future value of the investment. So, now you have all the information needed to display the three interest rates in the output labels. Remember from Tutorial 1 that you displayed text in a label by setting its Caption property. You will use the Caption property again to display information. This time, however, you will display numbers instead of text. Selena wants interest rate values to appear with a leading zero (0) and two decimal places. You can change the way numbers are displayed using the Format function, which has the following syntax:

Format(*expression*[,*format*])

- The **Format** function reads the numeric value contained in the *expression* and converts it to a string. The function allows you to control the appearance of the string by placing information in the *format* argument. Unlike the Val function, the Format function requires two arguments.

- You can specify an optional *format* argument in one of two ways. You can select from a list of named formats that already have been defined for you, or you can use special symbols to control, in more detail, the appearance of the text. One of the more common named formats, the **Fixed** format, displays information with two decimal places and a leading zero (0) if the value is less than one (1). Another format, **Currency**, displays information with a leading dollar sign and two decimal places. Use Help on the Format function to look at all the options for named formats.

When you use the Format function, or write other more complicated statements, the statement might not fit on a single line in the Code window. You can break up a line using the underscore (_) character at the end of a line to tell Visual Basic that the next line is a continuation of the statement on the current line. When used in this way, the underscore character is called a **continuation character**. You always must precede the continuation character with a space. You cannot put a trailing comment at the end of a line with a continuation character. You can insert a continuation character only between words, but you cannot break up a word. You can break up an expression into multiple lines but you cannot split a variable name over multiple lines. If a statement still will not fit within the displayed region of the Code window, you should include the continuation character at the end of the multiple lines. Generally you indent **continuation lines** — lines that follow the continuation character in a statement — so they stand out in the code.

Next, you will enter the statements that format the different interest rates; these statements are split over two lines to improve the readability of the code.

To display the formatted values in the interest rate Label objects:

1. Add the following code to the end of the LostFocus event procedure for the Interest Rate text box so the different rates will be formatted correctly whenever the user moves the cursor to another object. Be sure to enter the code just after the statements you just wrote to calculate the monthly interest rates. Note that after the word Format is typed, Visual Basic will display a ToolTip to help you fill in the arguments.

```
lblInterestRate1.Caption = Format(psngInterestRate, _
    "Fixed")
lblInterestRate2.Caption = Format(psngInterestRate + _
    0.01, "Fixed")
lblInterestRate3.Caption = Format(psngInterestRate + _
    0.02, "Fixed")
```

The statements appear after the variable declarations and calculations, and place the results in the label captions with the Format function, so each numeric value will appear with a leading zero (0) and two decimal places, as specified by the named format, Fixed.

There are many different formats supported by the Format function. For more information start Help and select Format function.

Next, you need to write the code for the CommandButton object that will compute the future value of the initial investment at different interest rates.

Using the Future Value Function

The **Future Value (FV)** function returns the future value of a fixed amount of money based on a constant interest rate. The FV function has the following syntax:

FV (*rate*,*periods*,*payment*[,*present-value*][,*type*]])

- The *rate* represents the interest rate per period, and *periods* represents the number of time periods.

- If regular payments are made, they are identified in *payment*. So, if you are computing the future value of a fixed amount, which does not involve regular payments, the value of *payment* would be 0. You can think of a regular payment as making a deposit into the investment account each period.

- The next two arguments are optional, which is why they are enclosed in brackets. When computing the future value of an amount, the *present* or (*current*) *value* of the sum is listed. The *type* argument is used to describe when payments are made. If payments are made at the end of the period, the value for *type* is 0. If payments are made at the beginning of a period, the value for *type* is 1.

Your program will use the FV function to compute the three future values of an investment made by an Island Financial client. Because the statements containing the FV function are too long to fit on a line, you will use the continuation character to break the statement across two lines.

To create the code necessary to compute the future values:

1. Select the **cmdComputeFutureValue** object and the **Click** event procedure in the Code window.

2. Enter the following code after the Dim statements, which you entered earlier:

```
psngMonthTerm = Val(txtTermYears.Text) * 12
psngInitialValue = Val(txtInitialValue.Text)

psngFutureValue1 = FV(msngMonthRate1, psngMonthTerm, 0, _
    -psngInitialValue)
psngFutureValue2 = FV(msngMonthRate2, psngMonthTerm, 0, _
    -psngInitialValue)
psngFutureValue3 = FV(msngMonthRate3, psngMonthTerm, 0, _
    -psngInitialValue)

lblFutureValue1.Caption = Format(psngFutureValue1, _
    "Currency")
lblFutureValue2.Caption = Format(psngFutureValue2, _
    "Currency")
lblFutureValue3.Caption = Format(psngFutureValue3, _
    "Currency")
```

Before proceeding, take a minute to examine in more detail the code you just entered.

```
psngMonthTerm = Val(txtTermYears.Text) * 12
```

Earlier, when writing the LostFocus event procedure for the txtInterestRate object, you set the variables for the three monthly interest rates, which you will use to compute the future value of the investment. But, you need to compute the term of the investment expressed in months. To do so, this statement multiplies the term of the investment expressed in years by 12 and stores the result in the variable psngMonthTerm. Because the information in the text box is a string of characters, the statement includes the Val function to convert the string to a number before performing the multiplication.

```
psngInitialValue = Val(txtInitialValue.Text)
```

This statement calls the Val function to convert the initial value of the investment, which is stored as a string of characters in the Initial Value text box, into a numeric value.

```
psngFutureValue1 = FV(msngMonthRate1, psngMonthTerm, 0, _
    -psngInitialValue)
psngFutureValue2 = FV(msngMonthRate2, psngMonthTerm, 0, _
    -psngInitialValue)
psngFutureValue3 = FV(msngMonthRate3, psngMonthTerm, 0, _
    -psngInitialValue)
```

These three statements call the FV function to compute the future value of the investment using three different interest rates. You already set the value for the first argument, msngMonthRate1, when you defined the LostFocus event procedure for the txtInterestRate object. Remember the three monthly rate variables are form-level variables declared in the general declarations section, so they can be used by any procedure in your program. The second argument, psngMonthTerm, is the term of the investment, which you defined at the beginning of this event procedure. Both the rate and term are expressed in months. Because there are no additional deposits for the investment, the third argument representing the payment is 0. Because the statements were too long to fit on a line, you use the continuation character. Also the continuation line was indented for readability.

For all arguments, payments are represented by negative numbers. Because the variable psngInitialValue represents the initial payment, the number should be negative.

```
lblFutureValue1.Caption = Format(psngFutureValue1, _
    "Currency")
lblFutureValue2.Caption = Format(psngFutureValue2, _
    "Currency")
lblFutureValue3.Caption = Format(psngFutureValue3, _
    "Currency")
```

These three statements display the results in the appropriate Label objects by storing the formatted number in the Caption property of the appropriate label. The statements use the Currency format so numbers will be displayed with a leading dollar sign and two decimal places. Again, this will improve the appearance of the information for the user.

You now have completed all the code to compute the future values of the investment, format the future values with a leading dollar sign, and display the output in the appropriate labels. You now are ready to test your program and run the code you just have written. Selena suggests you use an initial investment amount of $1500.00, an interest rate of .05, and a term of 10 years.

To run the program and enter the test values:

1. Close the **Code** window.

2. Click the **Save Project** button 🖫 on the toolbar to save your work.

3. Click the **Start** button ▶ on the toolbar to run the program. Your form should look like Figure 2-34.

Figure 2-34 ◀
Running the
completed
calculator
program

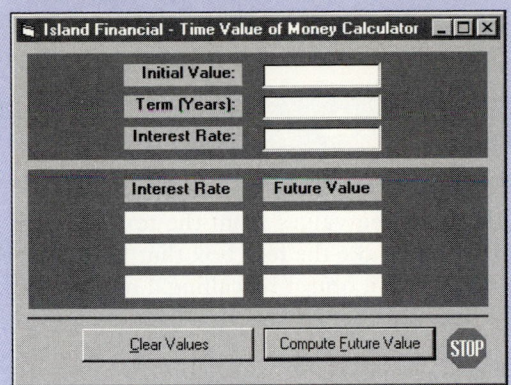

4. Enter the values shown in the text boxes in Figure 2-35, pressing the **Tab** key to move from one text box to the next.

5. Press the **Tab** key to move to the Compute Future Value button.

Because you set the Default property of the command button to True, you can press the **Enter** key to activate the command button, and execute its Click event procedure.

6. Press the **Enter** key to activate the Compute Future Value button. The program calculates the results for the three interest rates and the corresponding future values. See Figure 2-35.

Figure 2-35 ◀
Testing the
calculator
program

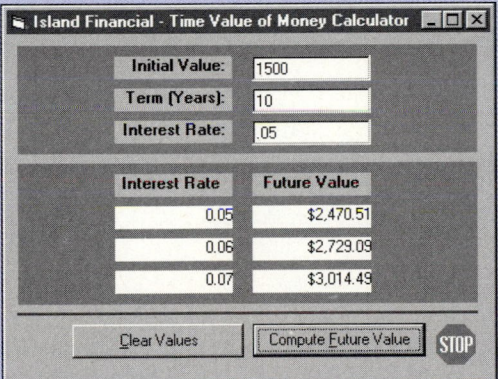

TROUBLE? If your results differ from those in Figure 2-35, there is probably an error in the code for either the cmdComputeFutureValue object's Click event procedure or the txtInterestRate object's LostFocus event procedure. Stop the program then check the event procedures in your program first for code accuracy against the code shown in the tutorial figures. Also, refer to the next section, "Handling Errors," for help in identifying and correcting errors. Make any necessary corrections, then repeat Steps 2 through 6.

7. Click the **stop sign** image to stop the program from running.

Pressing the Enter key to activate the Click event for the Compute Future Value command button causes the code you wrote to multiply the annual term of the investment by 12 to derive the term expressed in months. The monthly interest rates were computed in the LostFocus event procedure for the txtInterestRate object. This information was supplied as arguments to the FV function to compute the future value. You did not have to worry about exactly how Visual Basic computed the future value. The intrinsic function did this for you. The output then was displayed according to the settings specified by the Format function.

Explicitly Setting the Focus

The final step in the program is to program the Clear Values command button. This button when clicked must clear the values from the text boxes used for input, the label to hold the output, then finally make the text box that holds the initial value get focus. You can explicitly set the focus to an object by calling a method called set focus. Methods are like procedures built into an object. The following statement will set the focus to the object named txtInitialValue.

```
txtInitialValue.SetFocus
```

You now can write the code for the Clear Values command button.

To program the Clear Values command button:

1. Activate the Code window to the **Click** event procedure for the object named **cmdClearValues.**

2. Enter the following statements, shown in bold, into the Code window.

```
Private Sub cmdClearValues_Click()
    txtInitialValue.Text = ""
    txtTermYears.Text = ""
    txtInterestRate.Text = ""
    lblInterestRate1.Caption = ""
    lblInterestRate2.Caption = ""
    lblInterestRate3.Caption = ""
    lblFutureValue1.Caption = ""
    lblFutureValue2.Caption = ""
    lblFutureValue3.Caption = ""
    txtInitialValue.SetFocus
End Sub
```

These statements clear the text from the object on the form and set the focus to the text box named txtIntialValue. You now should test to be sure the code for the button is working correctly.

To test the Clear Values command button:

1. Save the program.

2. Start the program.

3. Enter the values shown in Figure 2-35 and click the **Compute Future Value** button.

4. Click the **Clear Values** button. The values in the text boxes, the output interest rates, and the output future values should be blank, and the cursor should be located in the Initial Value text box.

5. End the program.

You now have written all the code for the calculator. If you made mistakes writing statements, or entered invalid data in any of the text boxes, however, you may have received an error. There are several causes for errors and types of errors.

Handling Errors

Errors are divided into three types: syntax errors, run-time errors, and logic errors. **Syntax errors** occur when a statement you have written violates the rules of the Visual Basic language. Typographical errors, mismatched parentheses, omitting the comment character as the first character on a comment line, are all examples of syntax errors. Visual Basic identifies some syntax errors while you are writing code in the Code window. After you type each line, Visual Basic scans the line for correctness.

Many errors are not discovered until you run a program. These are **run-time errors**, and they occur when you enter a valid statement that is impossible to carry out for some reason.

Logic errors occur when your program contains a design problem that causes the program to produce incorrect results. For example, you might have added two variables together rather than multiplied them. Logic errors are not found by Visual Basic; you must identify and correct them.

Fixing Syntax Errors

When a syntax error occurs, Visual Basic displays a message box like the one shown in Figure 2-36.

Figure 2-36 ◄
Syntax error
message box

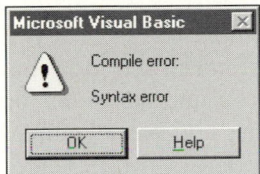

To correct a syntax error, click the OK button in the message box. Visual Basic activates the Code window and highlights the statement containing the error. Analyze the statement and make the necessary corrections. Continue running the program by clicking the Start button on the toolbar.

Fixing Run-time Errors

A common run-time error occurs when the program tries to store too large a number in a variable. This is called **numeric overflow**. For example, if you try to enter too large a number in your calculator program's text boxes, a numeric overflow error will occur. Run-time errors also occur when you try to store the wrong kind of information in a variable, and when you try to perform arithmetic operations, such as multiplication, on variables that do not contain numbers. The latter is called a **type mismatch** error, because when you perform the arithmetic operation, Visual Basic expects the variables to contain numbers, not text.

To practice fixing a run-time error, you purposely will generate an error by entering values that are too large for the text boxes in the input section.

To purposely generate a run-time error:

1. Click the **Start** button ▶ on the toolbar to run the program.

2. Enter the value **1000000** for the Initial Value, **100000** for the Term (Years), and **100000** for the Interest Rate, then press the **Enter** key to activate the Compute Future Value button. Remember to use the **Tab** key to move around in the form. Visual Basic displays the run-time error message box indicating numeric overflow. See Figure 2-37.

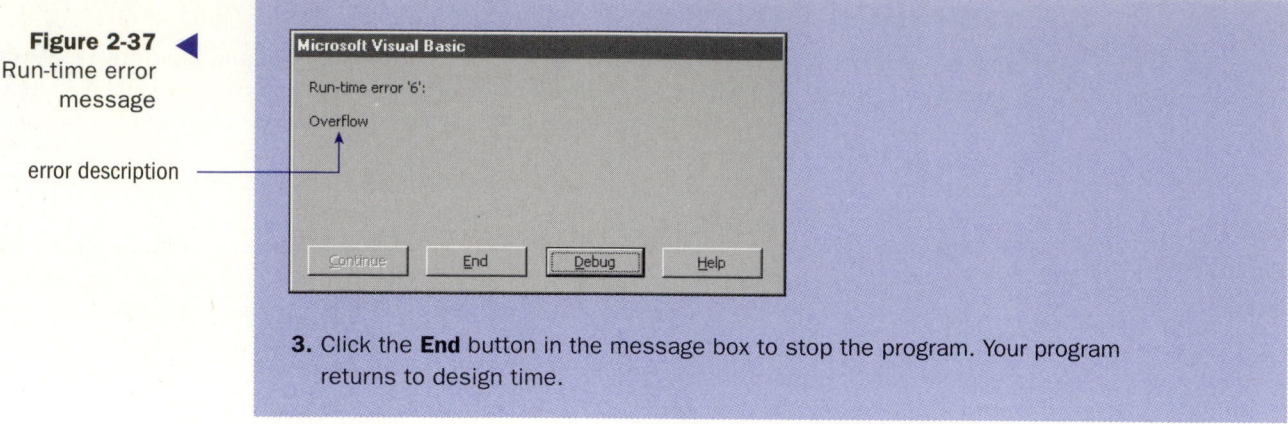

Figure 2-37 ◀
Run-time error
message

error description

3. Click the **End** button in the message box to stop the program. Your program returns to design time.

Locating and correcting errors in your program is an important part of the programming process. For more information about locating and correcting errors refer to the Debugging Appendix. After you have corrected any errors you have made, it is a good idea to print the program code.

Printing Your Program

As you develop a program, it often is helpful to print the code you have written, the object properties you changed using the Properties window, or an Image of the form itself. Furthermore, as your programs become larger and more complex, it is helpful to have a printed copy of all the code available for reference.

Now that your program is complete, Selena asks you to print the entire program so she can keep it for later reference.

To print the elements of the calculator program:

1. Click **File** on the menu bar, then click **Print**. The Print dialog box opens. See Figure 2-38.

Figure 2-38 ◀
Print dialog box

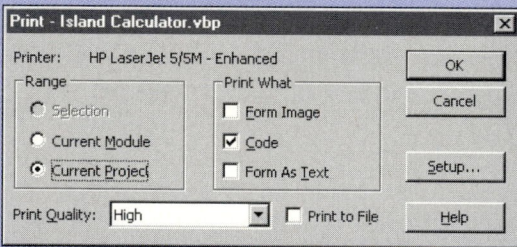

2. Click the **Current Module** option in the Range section of the Print dialog box, because there is only one module in your program.

3. Select the **Form Image**, **Code**, and **Form As Text** options in the Print What section of the dialog box, then click the **OK** button.

   Visual Basic will print the Code for your Island Calculator project first, the Form As Text next, and finally the Form Image.

4. Exit Visual Basic.

The Code option prints the contents of the general declarations section and then each of the procedures you have written for the form. The Form As Text option prints all the objects you created on the form and the properties you changed. For each object, all the properties you set using the Properties window are displayed. If you did not change a property, it will not be printed. As you learned in Tutorial 1, the Form Image option prints an Image of the form as it appears on the screen.

Now examine the information you just printed. The Code contains all the code in your program. First, the statements in the general declarations section are printed. Then each of the event procedures is printed in alphabetical order of the object's name.

Look at the selected output from the Form As Text section, the second part you printed.

```
VERSION 5.00
```

The first line lists the version of Visual Basic.

```
Begin VB.Form frmIslandCalculator
BackColor     = &H00C0C0C0&
Caption       = "Island Financial - Time Value of Money
                 Calculator"
ClientHeight = 3840
ClientLeft   = 3330
ClientTop    = 2970
...
```

These lines define the form itself, identifying the name of the form and the properties set for the form, including all the nondefault values on the form, such as the background color. Remember, the Caption property was set for you already. The ClientHeight, ClientLeft, and ClientTop properties determine the form's position on the screen. You did not set these properties explicitly—Visual Basic set them when you created the form. Depending on the location of your form on your screen, these property values might differ from those in your printout.

```
Begin VB.CommandButton cmdComputeFutureValue
Caption      = "Compute Future Value"
Default      = -1  'True
Height       = 375
Left         = 2760
TabIndex     = 3
ToolTipText  = "Click to compute the investment's future value."
Top          = 3360
Width        = 1935
End
```

These lines identify the properties you set for the CommandButton object. As with the form, the Caption and position of the object are defined, but two new properties—Default and TabIndex—also are listed. You set the Default property so the Click event occurs when a user presses the Enter key. You also set the TabIndex property, which determines the order in which objects are selected when a user presses the Tab key. Finally, the definition is terminated by the End statement.

The output includes a final End statement that signifies the end of the form definition.

Your calculator now is complete. Selena plans on showing the analysts how to use the program so they can begin testing it. After they are confident that it is producing correct results, Selena plans on making the program available to the analysts so they can use it to forecast investments.

Quick Check

1. What is the purpose of the Dim and Private statements?

2. Describe the difference between the GotFocus, LostFocus, and Click events and when they occur.

3. Put the following operators in their correct order of precedence: MOD, +, −, \ , ^, *, /.

4. What is the difference between syntax errors, run-time errors, and logic errors?

5. List the three options for printing a program and describe the output that each option produces.

Figure 2-39 lists and defines the new terms presented in this tutorial.

Figure 2-39 ◄
New terms

Term	Definition
Argument	An argument is the way you send information to a function. Arguments can be variables, literal values, constants, object properties, or expressions.
Continuation character	The continuation character (an underscore in Visual Basic) allows you to write a statement that spans multiple lines.
Continuation lines	Lines that follow the continuation character in a statement.
Expression	An expression consists of operators that perform tasks, such as addition, on operands, which are variables, constants, or literal numbers.
Focus	Only one object on a form is active at one time. For example, if a TextBox object is active, the user can type information into it. The active object is said to have the focus.
Form-level variables	Form-level variables are declared in the general declarations section of a form with the Private keyword. They exist whenever the form is loaded and can be used by all the procedures in the form.
Hot key	A set of keystrokes that when typed will act just like clicking the command button (i.e., Alt+C).
Intrinsic constants	Constants defined by Visual Basic to make a program more readable.
Intrinsic function	Intrinsic functions perform many mathematical, financial, or other operations using code already written and built into the Visual Basic system.
Local variable	A variable declared with the Dim statement that only exists while the procedure is executing. Local variables can be referenced only inside the procedure in which they were declared.
Logic error	A logic error occurs whey your program contains a design problem that causes the program to produce incorrect results. For example, you might have added two variables together, rather than multiplying them
Methodology	A well-defined standardized set of steps to design a computer program.
NEADT	A design methodology that helps you identify the components of your program and break them down.
Nested	Parentheses are used to change the order of operations (performed according to precedence within the parentheses). Parentheses also enhance the readability by clarifying the order of evaluation.
Null string	A Null string is a string that contains no data. In other words the string is empty.
Numeric overflow	A common run-time error that occurs when the program tries to store too large a number in a variable.
Object Browser	Available only at design time. Allows you to look at the intrinsic constants defined by Visual Basic that relate to the properties of all the objects you create, as well as the modules and procedures you defined for your project.
Operators	Operators are used in expressions to perform computations and comparisons. Examples of operators are +,–,*, /, and ^.
Precedence	Precedence is the predetermined order in which arithmetic operators are evaluated.

Figure 2-39 ◀
New terms
(continued)

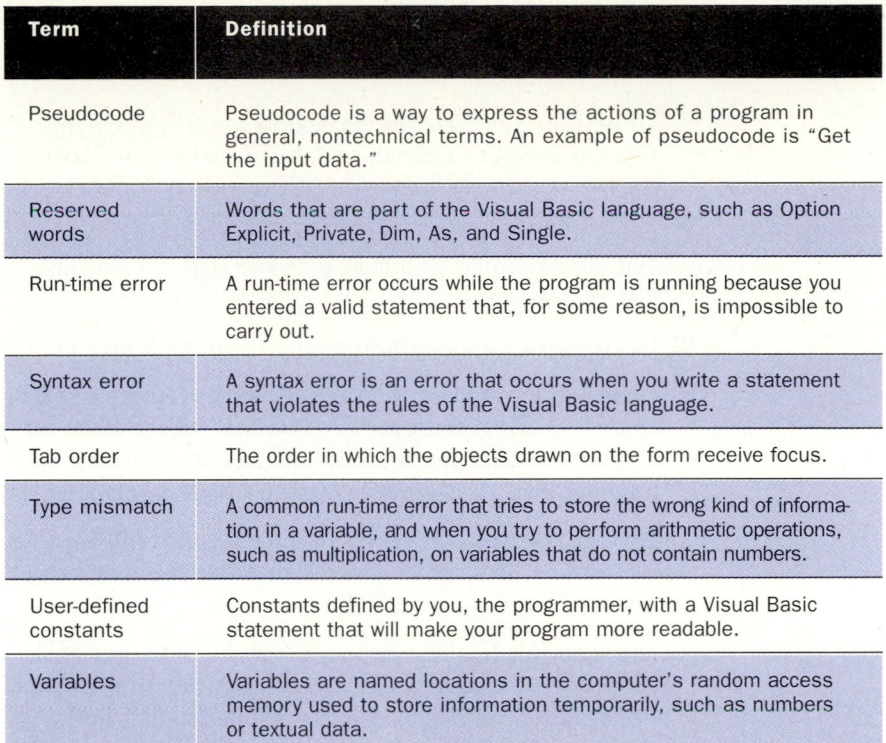

Term	Definition
Pseudocode	Pseudocode is a way to express the actions of a program in general, nontechnical terms. An example of pseudocode is "Get the input data."
Reserved words	Words that are part of the Visual Basic language, such as Option Explicit, Private, Dim, As, and Single.
Run-time error	A run-time error occurs while the program is running because you entered a valid statement that, for some reason, is impossible to carry out.
Syntax error	A syntax error is an error that occurs when you write a statement that violates the rules of the Visual Basic language.
Tab order	The order in which the objects drawn on the form receive focus.
Type mismatch	A common run-time error that tries to store the wrong kind of information in a variable, and when you try to perform arithmetic operations, such as multiplication, on variables that do not contain numbers.
User-defined constants	Constants defined by you, the programmer, with a Visual Basic statement that will make your program more readable.
Variables	Variables are named locations in the computer's random access memory used to store information temporarily, such as numbers or textual data.

Tutorial Assignments

In addition to investment services, the Island Financial Group provides tax preparation services for its clients. Selena has asked you to create a program that will compute the straight-line depreciation of an asset for a period. The program should provide an interface that allows the user to input the initial cost of an asset, the value of an asset at the end of its useful life, and the life of the asset. Because the program has a similar function as the future value calculator you just created, its user interface should be very similar. To create the program, you will use the SLN function, which is an intrinsic financial function like the FV function. When complete, your user interface should look like Figure 2-40.

Figure 2-40 ◀

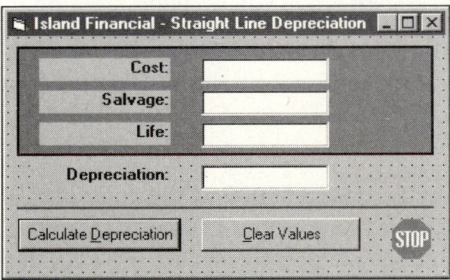

1. Make sure your Student Disk is in the appropriate disk drive, then start Visual Basic.

2. Create a new project if necessary.

3. Change the Caption property of the form to **Island Financial - Straight Line Depreciation**. Change the Name property to **frmIslandDepreciation**.

4. Draw four Label objects in a column on the form.

5. Change the Caption property of these labels to **Cost:**, **Salvage:**, **Life:**, and **Depreciation:** starting from the top label.

6. Check the Font and Alignment property values for the Island Calculator project. Change the Font and Alignment properties of the labels to use the same settings as the Island Calculator.

7. Draw four TextBox objects next to the labels. Change the Name property of the text boxes to **txtCost**, **txtSalvage**, **txtLife**, and **txtDepreciation**, starting from the top text box. Change the Text property for each text box to blank.

8. Draw a Shape object behind the Cost:, Salvage:, and Life: labels and text boxes. The shape should be a dark gray rectangle to resemble the shapes in the Island Calculator project.

9. Draw two CommandButton objects on the bottom of the form.

10. Change the Name property of the leftmost button to **cmdCalculateDepreciation**; change its Caption property to **Calculate Depreciation**. Set it as the default button and use the character **D** as the hot key. Adjust the width of the command button to accommodate its caption as needed. Create a ToolTip for the command button.

11. Change the Name property of the rightmost button to **cmdClearValues**; change its Caption property to **Clear Values**. Use the character **C** as the hot key. Create a ToolTip for the command button.

12. Draw an Image object in the bottom-right corner of the form. Change its Name property to **imgExit**. Set its Picture property to the **stop.ico** file in the **TAssign** folder of the **Tutorial.02** folder on your Student Disk.

13. Draw a Line object between the Depreciation: label and text box and the command buttons. The line should be light blue to resemble the line in the Island Calculator project.

14. Open the Code window for the imgExit object's Click event procedure, then enter the code that will end the running program when this button is clicked. Remember to include comments about what the procedure does in all your code.

15. Open the Code window for the cmdClearValues object's Click event procedure and enter code that will set to blank the Text property of the four TextBox objects and set the focus to the text box named txtCost.

16. Use the Index tab in the Help window to consult Visual Basic online Help for information on financial functions. Open the Help window for the SLN function. Print the Help topic to guide you through creating the rest of this program.

17. Open the Code window for the cmdCalculateDepreciation object's Click event procedure. Type the code that will set the txtDepreciation object's Text property to the straight-line depreciation of txtCost, txtSalvage, and txtLife. Format the result as Currency. Enter a comment to describe what this procedure does.

18. Test your program by entering **100000** as the asset cost, **50000** as the salvage value, and **5** for the asset life in years. Click the Calculate Depreciation button to cause the depreciation function to execute. The result should be $10,000.00 as the depreciation amount for each year.

19. Test the Clear Values button.

20. Continue to run and test the program with numbers of your choice in the Cost, Salvage, and Life text boxes.

21. Test the stop sign.

22. Print the form image.

23. Save the project as **Island Depreciation.vbp** in the **TAssign** folder of the **Tutorial.02** folder on your Student Disk. Accept the default form name, **frmIslandDepreciation.frm**.

24. Exit Visual Basic.

Case Problems

1. Perfect Printing Perfect Printing is a business that specializes in unique printing products for industrial applications. The owner, Roger Kringle, would like to have a program that can display a variety of fonts, sizes, and colors on a computer screen after a user types in some text. Roger asks you to write a program for Perfect Printing that tests different fonts in an output label using a text box for input. Your finished form should look similar to Figure 2-41.

Figure 2-41 ◄

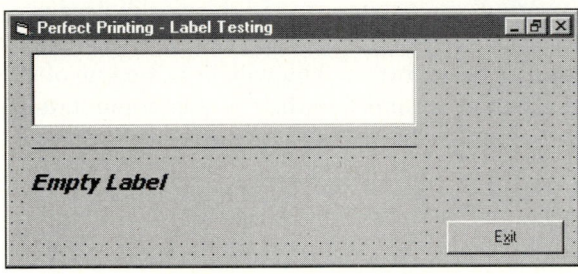

1. Make sure your Student Disk is in the appropriate disk drive, then start Visual Basic.

2. Create a new project if necessary.

3. Change the Name property of the form to **frmPerfectLabelTesting**. Change the Caption property of the form to **Perfect Printing - Label Testing**.

4. Draw a TextBox object on the form. Change its Name property to **txtInput**. Delete the value of the Text property to clear it.

5. Draw a Label object on the form below the TextBox object. It should be about the same size as the text box. Change its Name property to **lblOutput**. Change its Caption property to **Empty Label.** Change the formatting of the label so that it resembles Figure 2-41.

6. Draw a line that separates the text box from the label.

7. Draw a CommandButton object on the form. Change its Name property to **cmdExit**. Change its Caption property to **Exit**. Use the character **x** as the hot key for the button.

8. Create a ToolTip for the command button.

9. Open the Code window for the cmdExit object's Click event procedure, then type the code that will exit the running program when this button is clicked. Remember to include a comment that describes what this procedure does.

10. Open the Code window for the txtInput object and select its Change event procedure. Type the code that will set the Caption property of the lblOutput object to anything typed in the text box (that is, the Text property of the text box). Consult Visual Basic online Help for more information on the Label object's Caption property and the TextBox object's Change event and Text property. Remember to include a comment that describes what this procedure does.

11. Run the program.

12. Type anything you want in the text box, and note the results displayed in the label.

13. Test the Exit button.

14. Open the Properties window for the lblOutput object and change the Font, Font Style, and Size properties to any setting you choose. Change the BackColor and ForeColor to any combination that you think looks the best.

15. Run and test the program.

16. Repeat Steps 12 and 13, changing the properties until you are satisfied with the results.

17. Change the MultiLine property of the text box to **True.** Then run the program again and type multiple lines in the text box. How does the label react?

18. Print the form image and code.

19. Save the project as **Perfect Label Testing.vbp** in the **Cases** folder of the **Tutorial.02** folder on your Student Disk. Accept the default form name, **frmPerfectLabelTesting.frm.**

20. Exit Visual Basic.

2. Timberline Ltd. Timberline Ltd. is an engineering firm that constructs planning models in Visual Basic of various ecosystems around the world. Because so much of the work at Timberline Ltd. is based on using proper formulas in their calculations, it is important for the model formulas to be correct. You will work on one of these models to test your ability to convert algebraic formulas to their proper computational form. Specifically, you will build a program to convert and test the formulas shown in Figure 2-42:

Figure 2-42 ◄

$$1 \quad \frac{(mintVar1 + mintVar2)}{(mintVar3)}$$

$$2 \quad \frac{(mintVar1)^{mintVar5}}{(mintVar2)(mintVar4)}$$

$$3 \quad \frac{(mintVar1 - mintVar2)^{mintVar3}}{(mintVar4)}$$

$$4 \quad \frac{(mintVar4 - mintVar2)(mintVar3)}{(mintVar5)^{mintVar2}}$$

$$5 \quad \left(\frac{\frac{mintVar2}{mintVar1}}{\frac{mintVar4}{mintVar5}} \right)^{mintVar2}$$

$$6 \quad \frac{\left(\frac{mintVar1}{mintVar2} \right)\left(\frac{mintVar3}{mintVar4} \right)}{(mintVar5)^{mintVar1}}$$

When complete, your form should look like Figure 2-43.

Figure 2-43 ◄

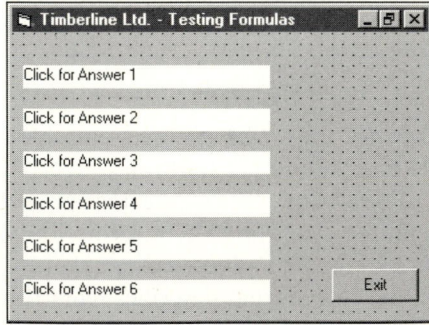

1. Make sure your Student Disk is in the appropriate disk drive, then start Visual Basic.

2. Create a new project if necessary.

3. Change the Name property of the form to **frmTimberlineTesting.** Change the Caption property of the form to **Timberline Ltd. – Testing Formulas.**

4. Open the general declarations section in the Code window and type the code that requires variables to be declared in the program and declare five Integer type variables—**mintVar1, mintVar2, mintVar3, mintVar4,** and **mintVar5.** Consult Visual Basic online Help for more information on declaring Integer-type variables.

5. In the Code window for the frmTimberlineFormulas object's Load event procedure, assign numerical values to each of the variables as follows: **mintVar1 = 1**, **mintVar2 = 2**, **mintVar3 = 3**, **mintVar4 = 4**, and **mintVar5 = 5**. Consult the Visual Basic online Help for more information on assigning a value to a variable. Close the Code window for the form.

6. Draw a CommandButton object on the lower-right corner of the form. Change its Caption property to **Exit.** Change its Name property to **cmdExit.**

7. Open the Code window for the cmdExit object's Click event procedure, then type the code that will exit the running program when this button is clicked.

8. Draw six Label objects in one column on the form. Change the Name property for the objects to **lblAnswer1, lblAnswer2, lblAnswer3, lblAnswer4, lblAnswer5,** and **lblAnswer6**, starting from the top label. Set the background color to white so the labels stand out from the rest of the form. Change the Caption property for the Label objects to **Click for Answer 1, Click for Answer 2**, etc.

   Hint: The Copy and Paste commands also work within the Properties window.

9. Open the Code window for the lblAnswer1 object's Click event procedure, then enter the expression that will set the caption of lblAnswer1 to the converted algebraic form of Formula 1 in Figure 2-42. Consult Visual Basic online Help for more information on setting the Caption property of the label with Visual Basic code.

10. Create a ToolTip for each of the labels and the command button.

11. In the remaining five Label objects, enter the proper formula conversion for the formulas 2 through 6 in Figure 2-42. Close the Code window.

12. Save the project as **Timberline Testing Formulas.vbp** in the **Cases** folder of the **Tutorial.02** folder on your Student Disk and accept the default form name, **frmTimberlineTesting.frm**.

13. Run the program and test each label. The following answers should be displayed in the labels:

    lblAnswer1.Caption = 1

    lblAnswer2.Caption = 0.125

    lblAnswer3.Caption = –0.25

    lblAnswer4.Caption = 0.24

    lblAnswer5.Caption = 6.25

    lblAnswer6.Caption = 0.075

If any of your answers do not match the answers shown, you have made a mistake converting a formula. Click the Exit button. Fix each incorrect expression by changing the code in the Code window for the appropriate label. Repeat this step until your answers are correct.

14. Test the Exit button.

15. Print the Form Image and the Code.

16. Save the project again if you made any corrections after you last saved, then exit Visual Basic.

3. Summit Bank Summit Bank has asked you to modify some of its customer reports. The bank purchased a set of add-on financial controls from a vendor and installed them in your copy of Visual Basic. These controls have no errors but they all seem to require that data, having the type Single, be formatted differently. Refer to Visual Basic online Help for more information about the Format function.

When finished, your user interface should look like Figure 2-44.

Figure 2-44 ◀

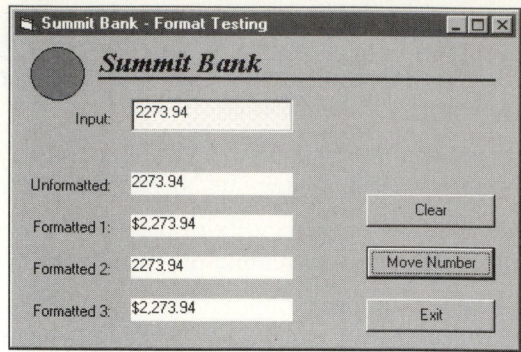

1. Create the NEADT documentation and a test program according to Steps 2 through 12.

2. Start Visual Basic and create a new project.

3. Set the Name property of the form to **frmSummitFormatTesting**.

4. Draw the shape, line, and title label, and set the properties as shown in Figure 2-44.

5. Draw the top text box. Name the text box with a valid name. Clear the Text property. Change its background color and font if you like.

6. Draw four empty labels. Name the labels with valid names of your choice. Clear their captions. Change their background colors and fonts if you like.

7. Draw a working Exit command button.

8. Draw a command button with a valid name and the caption **Move Number**.

9. Create a ToolTip for each of the command buttons.

10. Declare a Single data type variable in the general declarations section in the Code window with a valid name.

11. Write a statement in the Move Number command button's Click event procedure to move: the Text property value of the top text box to the Single data type variable you declared using the Val function; and the Single data type variable to the first label with no formatting, to the second label formatted as Currency, to the third label formatted as Fixed, and to the fourth label formatted as $#,###,###.##. Refer to Visual Basic online Help for more information about the Format function. Draw descriptive labels for the text box and output labels and set the appropriate properties.

12. Save the project as **Summit Format Testing.vbp** in the **Cases** folder of the **Tutorial.02** folder on your Student Disk. Accept the default form name.

13. Test your program with a variety of numbers, both integer and decimal. Use the text box to enter a number, and then click the Move Number button.

    Hint: Do not use any special characters such as dollar signs or commas when you type the number or the Val function will not be able to perform the conversion operation.

14. When you are finished, save the form and project again, if you have made any changes since your last save.

15. Print the Form Image, the Code, and the Form As Text.

16. Exit Visual Basic.

4. Ms. Phillips Grading Program One of your former instructors at school, Ms. Phillips, would like you to design and build a Visual Basic program that will take the name of a student and the student's three test grades for the term, then compute the average for the tests and display a letter grade. To build a good program for Ms. Phillips, you first need to start with a good design. Refer to the Design Appendix, then create the necessary NEADT documentation for the grading program.

Objects and the Events They Generate

Developing an Event-Driven Cash Register Program for Master Burger

In this tutorial you will:

- Create instances of several new controls including scroll bars, check boxes, frames, and option buttons

- Create a control array

- Write code for event procedures that will generate other events

- Execute code conditionally using the If and Select Case statements

- Create Function and Sub procedures

- Display a message box by calling the MsgBox function

- Perform operations on text strings

CASE

Master Burger Company

Master Burger Company is a fast-food franchise business with headquarters in Lemming, California. Currently, it operates more than 270 stores in the United States and Europe, and is planning to expand into New Zealand and Australia. The company's mission always has been to provide fresh food and exceptionally fast service, so it maintains a very simple menu of food items to avoid any spoiled or stale food. Gill Clark, the information services manager, wants you to use Visual Basic to develop a prototype for a point-of-sale cash register program to be used in each Master Burger restaurant. Ultimately, the company will use this cash register program to perform additional tasks, such as tracking inventory and using a touch screen for input.

For the prototype program, the mouse will be the only input device. The program will eventually be used, however, on a computer with a touch screen for all user input. So, the program must only use Visual Basic controls that do not require keyboard input. You can use a box for each menu item that, when checked, indicates the item has been ordered. The program will use scroll bars to change the quantity ordered for each menu item. Each store delivers orders and charges for delivery based on distance. To simplify the delivery charges, they divide the delivery area into three zones and charge a different amount for each zone.

When an item is selected or the quantity ordered for an item changes, the program must compute the extended price of the item (unit price $\times$ quantity ordered), the sales tax for the order, any delivery charges, and the order total.

Master Burger has been experimenting recently with 24-hour operation. To attract more business during these hours, they offer a 10% discount for purchases made between 1 A.M. and 8 A.M. The cash register must be able to compute this discount and deduct it from the order total.

SESSION

3.1

In this session you will learn how to use the ScrollBar, CheckBox, Frame, and OptionButton controls to create the user interface for a cash register program that will receive input only from a mouse. You also will create event procedures that change the values of other objects, which in turn will generate other events.

Designing the Program

The program you will create is a prototype of the complete cash register program that Gill will show to senior management before putting the final program in the company's 270 stores. The following are some of the significant design criteria for the program:

- The clerk must be able to select menu items and specify the quantity ordered for each menu item by clicking objects. No keyboard input can be used.

- The program must update extended prices (unit price $\times$ quantity ordered) for each item when the quantity ordered changes.

- Whenever the extended price for an item changes, the sales tax and order total must be recomputed and displayed.

- The delivery amount, if any, must be computed and displayed when one of the delivery buttons is clicked. The order total also must be recomputed and displayed.

- The discount, if any, must be calculated depending on the time the order is placed. The order total also must be recomputed and displayed.

Gill already has completed the NEADT documentation for the program. You can look at this design documentation to help you create the program.

To view and print the NEADT charts for the cash register program:

1. Using Microsoft Word, open the file **Master.doc,** which is located in the **Tutorial.03** folder of your Student Disk. If you do not have Word, open the file **Master.txt** using WordPad.

2. Print the file and then exit the word processing program.

It is helpful to keep the NEADT charts next to you as you create the program. Gill already has designed the user interface screen, as shown in Figure 3-1.

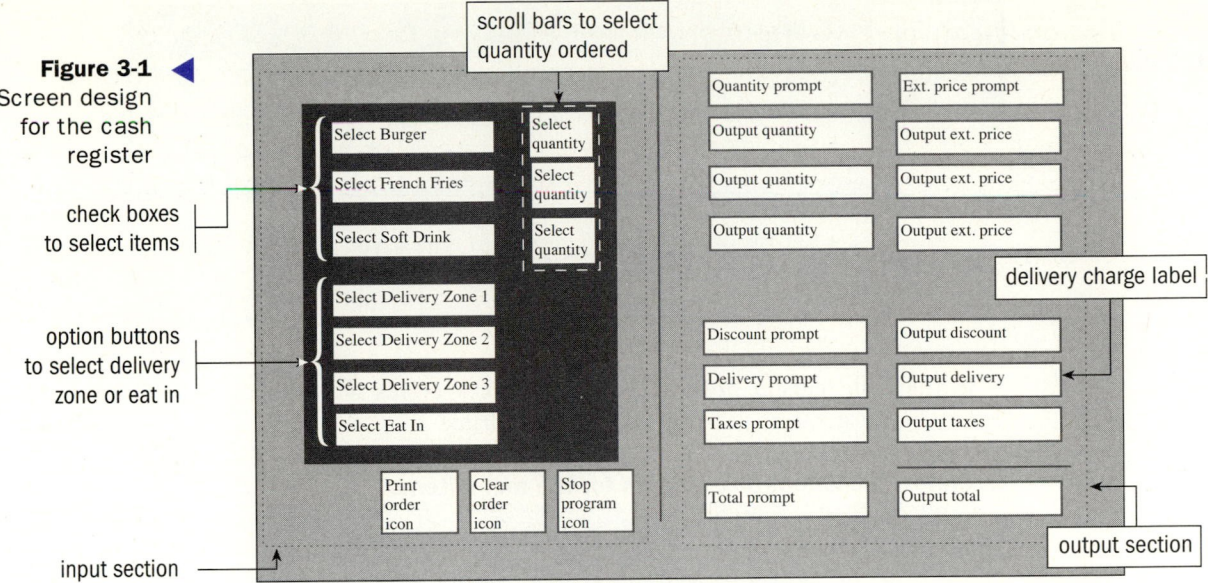

Figure 3-1 ◄
Screen design
for the cash
register

check boxes
to select items

option buttons
to select delivery
zone or eat in

input section

The user interface design visually identifies the objects used for input by enclosing them in a different colored box. These input objects will be used to select a menu item and the quantity ordered. The Stop program icon will be used to exit the program. The output section contains several Label objects that display and describe the output.

Adding a CheckBox Object to the Form

The cash register program needs three objects to represent the menu items for a burger, french fries, and soft drink, so a clerk can click the items as the customer orders them. Visual Basic provides several ways to indicate an item has been ordered. You could add a TextBox object and have the clerk type in a number, but that would require input from the keyboard, which would violate the design specifications. In this case a **CheckBox** control is the best control for the task, because a clerk can click a check box to mark an item that has been ordered.

To create the order menu check list, you will create multiple instances of the CheckBox control—one for each menu item. This is the task object on the NEADT chart—to create three check boxes representing the three different products sold by Master Burger.

A check box, like a command button, can respond to the Click event. When a check box becomes checked or cleared in this cash register, you want to execute code that will perform one action or another action if the check box is cleared. A CheckBox object has three valid values. If it is not checked (default) the Value property is 0 - Unchecked. When a check box is checked, the Value property is 1 - Checked. Finally, if a check box is dimmed, the Value property is 2 - Grayed. A CheckBox object that is dimmed has a gray check mark in it; it neither is checked nor unchecked. If you click a dimmed check box once, it becomes unchecked; if you click it twice, it becomes checked. You can use a dimmed check box so the user can tell that the box neither is checked nor unchecked and that input needs to be provided. When the user clicks the check box, Visual Basic sets the Value property for the check box and generates a Click event. Like many other controls, the check box supports the Caption property to describe the object's purpose. The standard prefix for a check box is "chk".

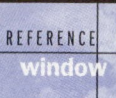

> REFERENCE
> **window**
>
> **ADDING A CHECKBOX CONTROL TO A FORM**
>
> - Click the CheckBox control on the toolbox.
> - Click and drag the mouse to draw a check box on the form.
> - Set the Caption property to describe the object's purpose.
> - Set the Name property to a prefix of "chk" followed by a descriptive name.
> - Set the Value property at design time if you want the initial value to be different from the default (unchecked).

In the cash register program, different check boxes will indicate whether a customer ordered a burger, french fries, and/or a soft drink.

To create the CheckBox objects for the menu items:

1. Make sure your Student Disk is in the appropriate disk drive and start Visual Basic.

2. Open the project file named **Master.vbp** in the **Tutorial.03** folder on your Student Disk.

3. View the form named **frmMaster**. Your form should look like Figure 3-2.

Figure 3-2 ◄
Initial cash
register form

shape to contain
input objects

Print command button

Clear
command buton

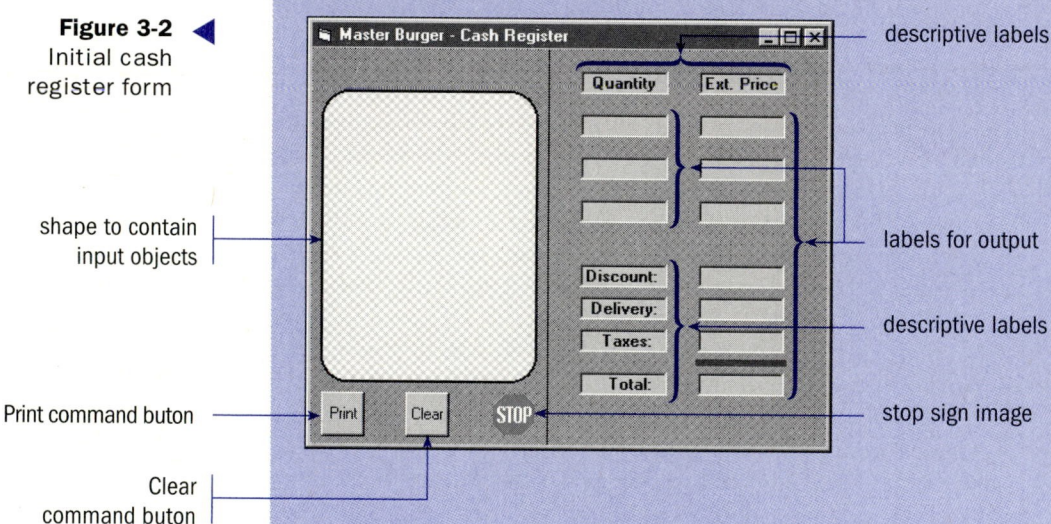

descriptive labels

labels for output

descriptive labels

stop sign image

Gill already has created the shape to hold the input objects, the stop sign icon to exit the program, and all the output labels. Before adding objects to the form, you will save it and the project file with different names to keep the original files intact in case you make a serious mistake and need to restart.

4. Be sure the form is active then save the form as **frmMasterCashRegister.frm**, and save the project as **Master Cash Register.vbp.**

5. Click the **CheckBox** control on the toolbox.

6. Draw a check box inside the Shape object, as shown in Figure 3-3. Use the ToolTip to make the object 1335 x 255.

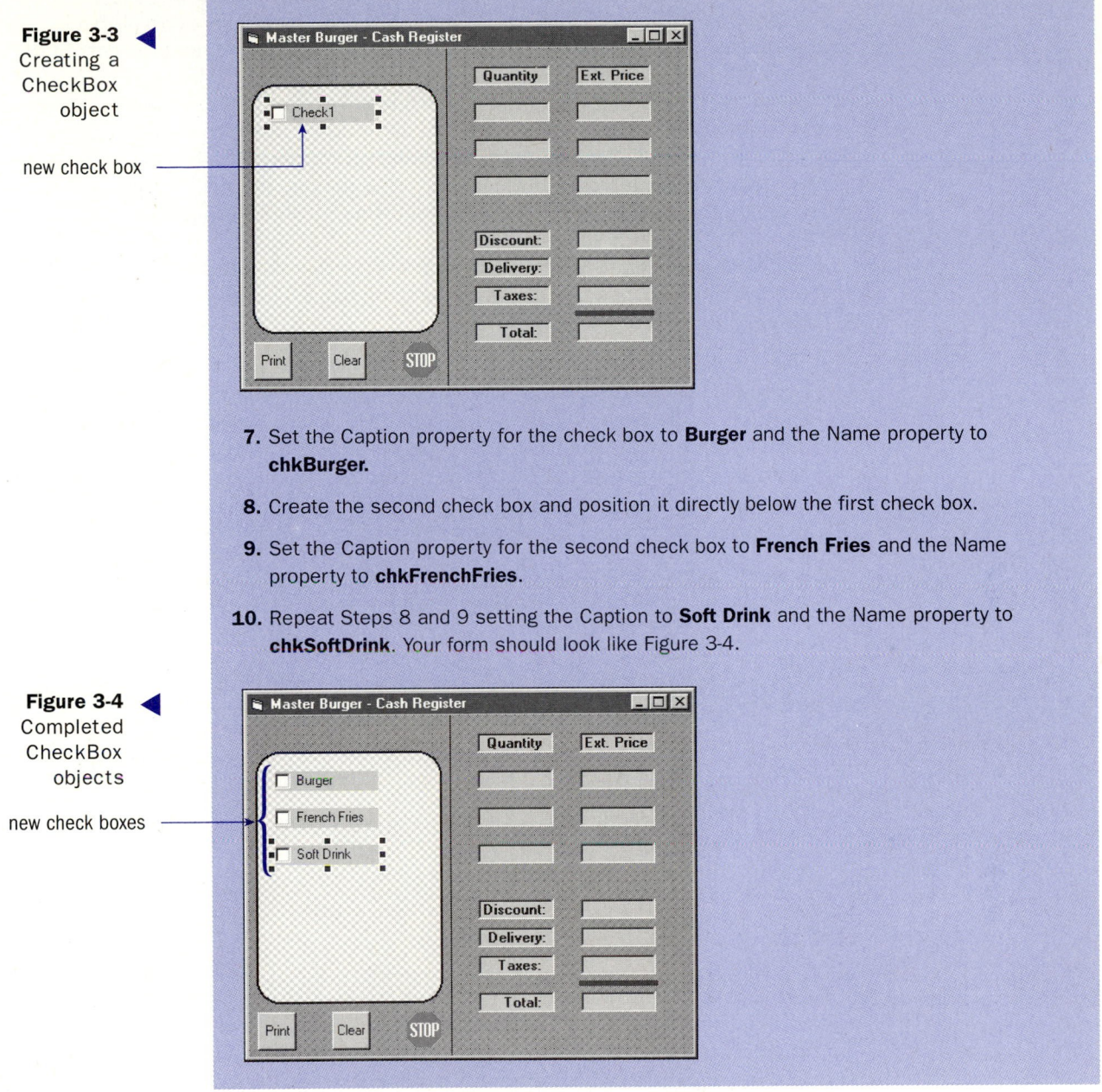

Figure 3-3 ◄
Creating a
CheckBox
object

new check box ──

7. Set the Caption property for the check box to **Burger** and the Name property to **chkBurger.**

8. Create the second check box and position it directly below the first check box.

9. Set the Caption property for the second check box to **French Fries** and the Name property to **chkFrenchFries**.

10. Repeat Steps 8 and 9 setting the Caption to **Soft Drink** and the Name property to **chkSoftDrink**. Your form should look like Figure 3-4.

Figure 3-4 ◄
Completed
CheckBox
objects

new check boxes ──

Now you can create the objects that will specify the order quantity of a specific item.

Adding Scroll Bars to the Form

The user interface for the cash register program must permit a clerk to use only a mouse or touch screen to enter the quantity. For example, if a customer orders three burgers, the clerk will click the Burger check box to indicate the item has been ordered, but the clerk also needs to indicate that the customer wants three burgers. Because the mouse or touch screen is the only means of input, the clerk cannot type in the number of burgers ordered using a control such as a text box.

You could create two command buttons for each item—one that would contain the code to increment a variable representing the quantity ordered, and one that would contain the code to decrement the variable. Although this approach would work, you would have to write several lines of code, so it is not the most efficient or easiest solution. Visual Basic supports a **ScrollBar** control that will increment and decrement the quantity ordered of an item without requiring you to write any code. Determining the correct control for a particular task makes the programming job more efficient and the program easier to use.

Visual Basic provides vertical and horizontal scroll bars, which work in the same way as the scroll bars in most Windows 95 programs. The two types of scroll bars share the same properties. The choice of which one to use depends on the requirements of the user interface. Horizontal scroll bars are well-suited for measures of distance, such as inches, because the metaphor of a ruler on a map tends to be a left-to-right sliding scale. Because you would think of an order quantity going up or down rather than left to right, the vertical scroll bar is the better choice for the cash register program. In circumstances where the type of scroll bar is irrelevant, consider using the one that will balance the layout of the screen. In this session you will use the following ScrollBar properties:

- The **Value** property of a scroll bar is an integer that contains the current value of the scroll bar. When a user clicks on the scroll bar, a Change event is generated and Visual Basic sets the Value property.

- The range of valid values is controlled by the **Max** and **Min** properties. A scroll bar is divided into two regions. When a user clicks the arrows, the Value property increases or decreases by the value contained in the **SmallChange** property. The default value of the SmallChange property is 1. When a user clicks the region between the arrows, the Value property changes by the value of the **LargeChange** property. The default value of the LargeChange property is 1. Figure 3-5 shows the two regions of a vertical scroll bar.

- The prefix for a vertical scroll bar (VScrollBar) control is "vsb" and the prefix for a horizontal scroll bar (HScrollBar) control is "hsb".

Figure 3-5 ◀
Changing
the value
of a vertical
scroll bar

click here to change
Value property
by LargeChange

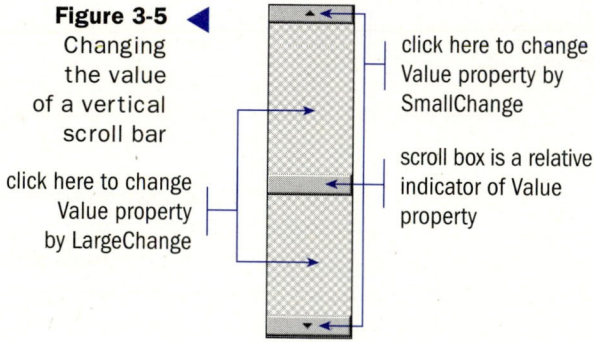

click here to change
Value property by
SmallChange

scroll box is a relative
indicator of Value
property

By default, the value of a vertical scroll bar grows as the bar moves downward. If you set the Min property to 0 and the Max property to 25, clicking the up arrow would cause the value to decrease, and clicking the down arrow would cause the value to increase. Think of using a scroll bar to scroll down through a document; the down arrow moves you from line 1 of the document to the next line. The line number continues to grow as you move down the document, as illustrated in Figure 3-6.

Figure 3-6 ◀
Setting the
Max and Min
properties

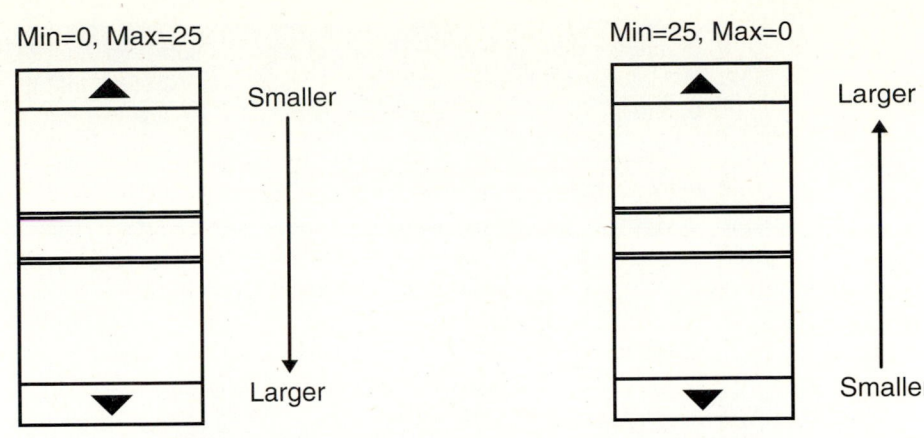

ADDING A SCROLLBAR CONTROL TO A FORM

- Click the VScrollBar or HScrollBar control on the toolbox.
- Click and drag the mouse to draw a scroll bar on the form.
- In the Properties window set the LargeChange property for the scroll bar to the value by which the scroll bar will change when any gray area of the scroll bar is clicked. Set the SmallChange property for the scroll bar to the value by which the scroll bar will change when either arrow is clicked.
- Set the Min and Max property values for the scroll bar to define the range for the scroll bar.
- Set the Name property to a prefix of "vsb" or "hsb" followed by a descriptive name.

For the cash register program, you will create three vertical scroll bars that can be used to specify the quantity ordered for each of the three products on the menu. This is the second task in the NEADT chart—to change the quantity of each menu item using a scroll bar. When a clerk clicks the vertical scroll bar's up arrow, the order quantity for the specific item must increase by 1. When a clerk clicks the scroll bar's down arrow, the order quantity must decrease by 1.

By setting the Max property to 0 and the Min property to the expected value of the largest order, the value of a scroll bar will increase when its up arrow is clicked. Gill thinks it is reasonable to set 25 as the expected value of the largest order.

To create the vertical scroll bars on the form and set their Min and Max properties:

1. Click the **VScrollBar** control ▭ on the toolbox.

2. Draw a scroll bar between the Burger check box and its quantity ordered label. Refer to Figure 3-7 for the placement of the scroll bars.

3. Activate the **Properties** window for the scroll bar and set its Name property to **vsbBurger.**

4. Set the value of the Max property to **0** and the Min property to **25**.

5. Create a second vertical scroll bar between the French Fries check box and its quantity ordered label. Set its Name property to **vsbFrenchFries**, its Max property to **0**, and its Min property to **25**. Remember if you copy and paste the scroll bar, the Max and Min properties are copied from the original scroll bar as well.

6. Create the third vertical scroll bar between the Soft Drink check box and its quantity ordered label. Set its Name property to **vsbSoftDrink,** its Max property to **0**, and its Min property to **25**. Your screen should look like Figure 3-7.

Figure 3-7 ◀
Completed
ScrollBar
objects

new scroll bars

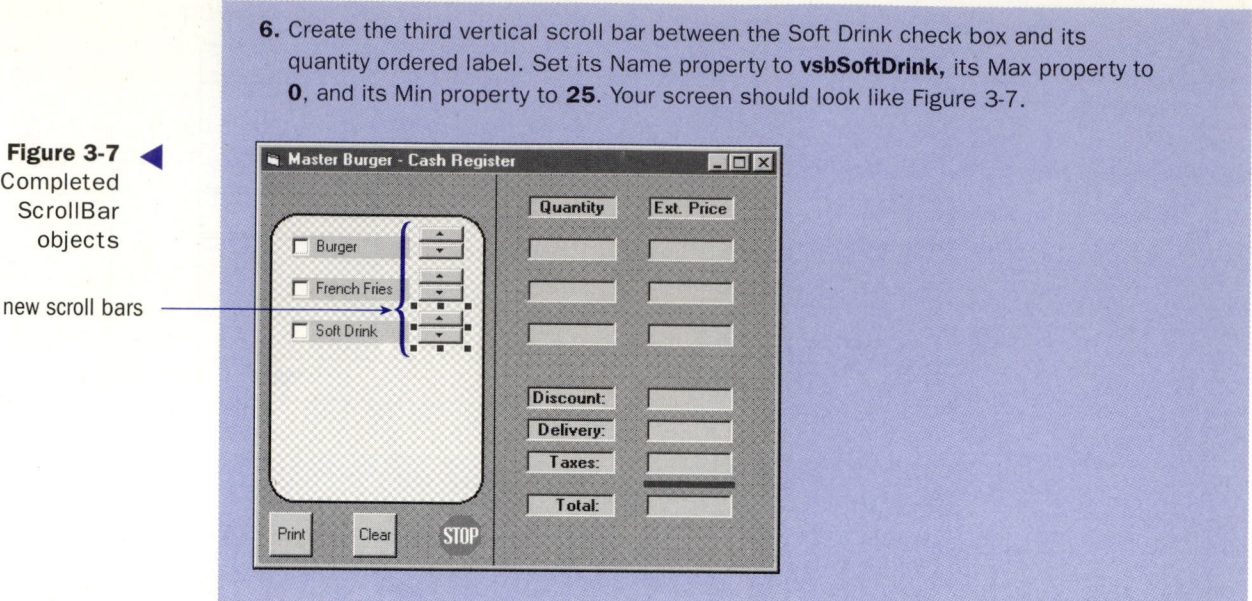

You have completed setting the necessary properties for the scroll bars. Note that you did not need to change the SmallChange or LargeChange properties from their default values (1), because you want the quantity ordered to increase or decrease by 1 when any part of the scroll bar is clicked. You now are ready to create the next part of the user interface: the buttons to select the delivery zone.

Using Option Buttons

You now will learn how to use another control, the OptionButton control, to allow a clerk to select the correct delivery zone or to specify that the order would be eaten in the restaurant. For Master Burger the delivery cost is relative to the delivery address, so different rates are charged based on the delivery distance. Each store breaks the delivery area into three zones. While you could use a check box to select a delivery area, the CheckBox control would not ensure that the clerk marked only one delivery area in the group, so it would not be appropriate. Also, because the mouse must be the only means of input, a TextBox control is not a possibility either. The **OptionButton** control allows you to create a group of items from which a user can select only one item at a time. Option buttons often are called **radio buttons,** referring to buttons in car radios that allow you to press a button to select a station.

> *Tip:* Option buttons consume a large amount of space on the screen. Use option buttons only when the number of choices is fewer than 5; when the number of choices exceeds 5, consider using a list box or combo box, which will be discussed in Tutorial 6.

OptionButton objects usually are positioned and operate as a group inside another object known as a frame. When you draw a **Frame** object on a form and place option buttons inside the frame, the option buttons form an **option group**. Only one of the OptionButton objects in an option group can be selected at a time.

To implement Gill's design, you need to specify whether an order is delivered and if so, to which zone. To do so, you will add a frame and four option buttons to the form. When a clerk clicks one of the four option buttons, the other three option buttons in the group will be unselected automatically.

When you create a frame that will be used to group other controls like option buttons, you must draw the frame first, then draw the controls inside the frame. If you do not draw the controls inside the frame, the buttons will not belong to the same option group. Thus, it will be possible to click more than one button. If you draw an object outside a frame and then try to move the object inside the frame, it will appear on top of the frame but the buttons will not function as an option group. Finally, if you use the Clipboard to copy and paste buttons, you must make the frame the active object before pasting the button.

Creating a Frame

You create a Frame object in the same way that you created a Shape object in Tutorial 2. The size of the frame you draw must be large enough to hold the option buttons. Like other objects, a frame can be resized as needed. The standard prefix for a Frame object is "fra". If you do not write code to operate directly with the Frame object, you do not need to change the Name property. The Frame object also supports the Caption property; typically, the frame's caption provides the user with a descriptive message about the purpose of the option buttons it holds. To customize a frame's appearance you can set the BackColor, BorderStyle, and ForeColor properties. These properties have the same effect as the shape's properties.

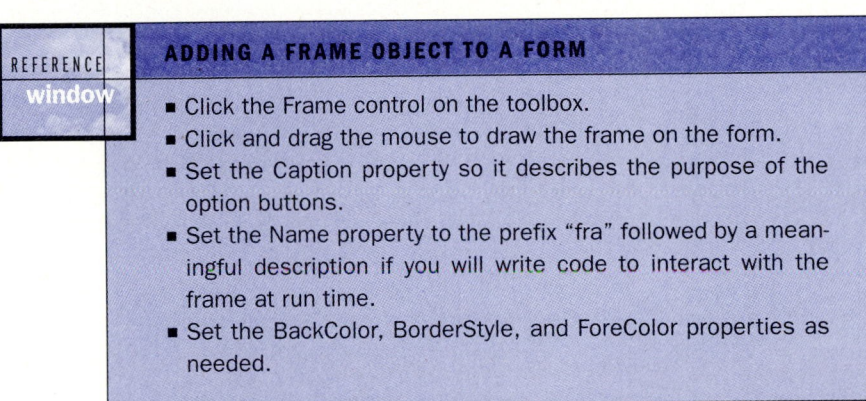

REFERENCE window	**ADDING A FRAME OBJECT TO A FORM**
	■ Click the Frame control on the toolbox.
	■ Click and drag the mouse to draw the frame on the form.
	■ Set the Caption property so it describes the purpose of the option buttons.
	■ Set the Name property to the prefix "fra" followed by a meaningful description if you will write code to interact with the frame at run time.
	■ Set the BackColor, BorderStyle, and ForeColor properties as needed.

You will create a Frame object, named fraDelivery that will contain four option buttons indicating the correct delivery zone.

To add the Frame object to the form:

1. Click the **Frame** control 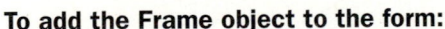 on the toolbox, then draw a rectangular frame on the form below the CheckBox objects.

2. Set the Caption property of the frame to **Delivery**. Because you will not write any code for this object, there is no need to set the Name property. See Figure 3-8.

Figure 3-8 ◀
Creating a
Frame object

caption

new Frame object

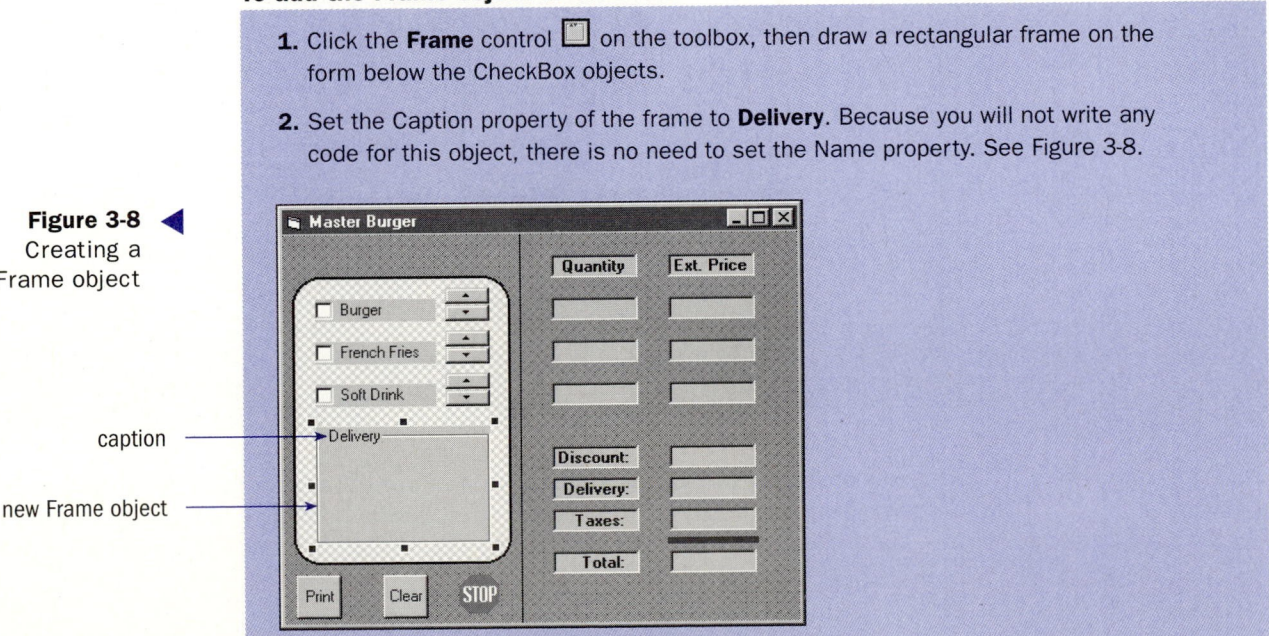

Creating Option Buttons

When you create OptionButton objects, you are interested in finding out which single button is clicked from a group of buttons inside a frame. The OptionButton object supports the Caption property and has the standard naming prefix of "opt".

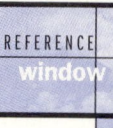

REFERENCE window	ADDING AN OPTIONBUTTON OBJECT TO A FRAME
	▪ Click the frame that will contain the option button. ▪ Click the OptionButton control on the toolbox. ▪ Click and drag the mouse inside the frame to draw an option button in the frame. ▪ Set the Caption property to describe the object to the user. ▪ Set the Name property to a prefix of "opt" followed by a descriptive name.

You will create four option buttons (one for each delivery zone and one for an order eaten in the restaurant) inside the frame. These option buttons will make up an option group. Visual Basic will allow you to create multiple option groups by creating multiple frames and inserting option buttons in them. You will name the option button optDelivery, because it indicates the delivery location of the order; its caption, however, will be Zone 1.

To add the first option button to the Frame object:

1. Make sure the Frame object is active.

2. Click the **OptionButton** control ⊙ on the toolbox.

3. Draw an option button inside the frame. Set the option button's Name property to **optDelivery** and its Caption property to **Zone 1**. Your form should look like Figure 3-9.

Figure 3-9 ◀
Creating an
OptionButton
object

new OptionButton
object

You still need to create the remaining option buttons but before you do, you must learn about a way to create objects so that instead of each responding to a unique Click event procedure, they will all respond to a Click event by executing the same Click event procedure.

Creating Objects with the Same Name

The next step in developing the program is to create the other three option buttons. Until now, each object you have created on a form has had a unique name and unique event procedures. That is, two different command buttons will execute different Click event procedures. It is possible to group objects together, using a control array, so they all share the same name and event procedures. This process is particularly well-suited to working with the option buttons inside an option group, because you typically want to manipulate option buttons as a unit. A **control array** is a group of controls of the same type (like an option button) that share the same name and event procedures. Control arrays improve a program's efficiency. When you add an object, such as another option button, to a control array of option buttons, the new object shares the properties and event procedures with the other option buttons. Because the objects share event procedures, system memory is conserved. Control arrays also provide a way to overcome the programming limitations of Visual Basic controls. You can specify up to 256 different control names on a form. Even this small cash register program contains 33 instances of various controls. If you need more than 256 controls on a form, you can use control arrays. Each control array can contain a maximum of 32,767 objects.

Creating a Control Array

Depending on which option button is clicked, the program must apply the correct delivery charge or no charge if the order is eaten in the restaurant. You will use a control array for the option buttons so you only need to write one event procedure.

When you create objects in a control array, the objects share the same name; that is, they have the same value for the Name property. The **Index** property is an integer that Visual Basic uses in conjunction with the Name property to uniquely identify each object in a control array. The Index property starts at zero (0) for the first object and increments by one (1) for each subsequent object in the control array. Event procedures for control arrays receive an argument named Index, that contains the value of the Index property for the selected object. You can use the Index property to determine which option button is selected from an option group.

The easiest way to create a control array of option buttons is to copy and paste one object to create multiple instances of the object.

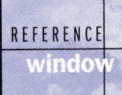

REFERENCE window

CREATING A CONTROL ARRAY OF OPTION BUTTONS

- Create an instance of an option button on the form, then activate the option button.
- Copy the option button to the Windows Clipboard by pressing Ctrl+C.
- Click the Frame object to activate it.
- Paste the copied option button into the frame by pressing Ctrl+V.
- Be sure the option button appears at the top of the frame, not at the top of the form.
- Click the Yes button in the message box that asks if you want to create a control array.
- Move the new option button to the appropriate location.
- Paste and move each option button you want to add to the control array.

You will copy the first option button and paste it into the Delivery frame three times to create the option buttons for delivery to Zone 2, Zone 3, and Eat In.

To create the remaining objects of the control array:

1. Click the **Zone 1** option button to select it.

2. Press **Ctrl+C** to copy the OptionButton object to the Windows Clipboard.

3. Click the **Delivery** frame to select it. The handles should appear around the frame.

4. Press **Ctrl+V** to paste the copied option button into the frame.

   A message box opens and asks if you want to create a control array.

5. Click the **Yes** button. The copy of the option button appears in the upper-left corner of the frame.

   TROUBLE? If the option button appears in the upper-left corner of the form rather than the frame, the option button is considered to be on the form rather than on the frame. For the buttons to work correctly, delete the option button, then repeat Steps 3 and 4.

6. Drag the new option button below the **Zone 1** option button, then set the Caption property of the new option button to **Zone 2**. Note that the value of the Index property is 1 and the name has not changed from optDelivery.

   Most controls have an Index property, which contains an integer number that you use with a control array to uniquely identify each member of the control array. You will use the Index property to identify which of the four option buttons on your form currently is selected.

7. Repeat Steps 3, 4, and 6 to create the third and fourth option buttons, and set the Caption properties to **Zone 3** and **Eat In**, respectively. Because the object you are pasting is now a member of a control array, you are not asked again if you want to create a control array.

Figure 3-10 ◀
Creating a
control array of
option buttons

option buttons
in control array

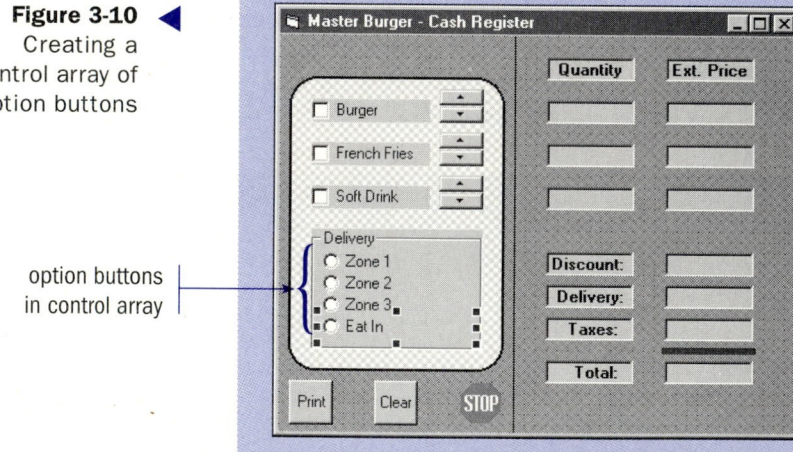

Gill suggests you run the program to verify that the option buttons are working correctly; that is, that only one button at a time can be selected.

To test the option buttons:

1. Save the project then start the program.

2. Click each of the option buttons. Only one button should be selected at a time.

3. End the program.

All the visible form objects are now in place. Next, you need to begin to write the Visual Basic code to compute and display the output in the different labels already drawn on the screen.

Using Boolean Values

To help a Master Burger clerk visually identify when an item has been ordered, Gill wants each scroll bar, its corresponding quantity ordered, and extended price labels to be visible only when the item's check box has been clicked. The scroll bar and labels should be invisible when an item's check box has not been clicked. You can accomplish this by setting the Visible property of the scroll bar and labels to True or False.

True and False are the valid Boolean values. A **Boolean variable** operates like an on/off switch; True signifies on and False signifies off. If you assign any value other than True or False to a Boolean variable, the value will be converted to True or False. If the value is 0, then it is converted to False. All other values are converted to True. Many properties accept Boolean values like True and False. Just as you can declare variables as Integer and Single, you can declare variables as the Boolean data type. The following list describes some of the more common properties that accept the Boolean values, True and False.

- The **Visible** property for an object determines whether or not the object appears on the screen when the program is running. As with other properties, you can set the Visible property for an object at design time using the Properties window, or by writing code in an event or general procedure that will be called at run time.

- The **Enabled** property for an object determines whether or not the object will respond to events. If you set the Enabled property of an object to False, clicking it will not generate a Click event.

- Option buttons support a **Value** property like a check box or scroll bar. But the value contains a Boolean value. If True, the option button in the option group is clicked and the others are not. When you explicitly set the Value of an option button to True with Visual Basic code, the button that was selected previously is no longer selected, and a Click event is generated. If you set the value of the selected option button to False, then none of the option buttons will be selected.

When the program first starts, Gill would like the most common option, an order being eaten in the restaurant, to be selected. To do this, you need to set the Eat In option button to True. This is the option button with the Index value of 3 named optDelivery.

To set the default option button to Eat In:

1. Open the Code window for the Form_Load event procedure and enter the following code shown in bold:

```
Private Sub Form_Load()
    optDelivery(3).Value = True
End Sub
```

This statement causes the Eat In option button to be selected when the form is first loaded. Notice the syntax of the statement. Like other controls you have used, you reference a specific property by typing the object's name, the object's Index value in parentheses, followed by a period (.), followed by the name of the property. The Index value specifies which specific option button in the array you want to set.

When the cash register program starts, no scroll bars or labels should appear on the form until a clerk clicks the corresponding check box. You could set the Visible property for each object individually, but this would be time consuming. Visual Basic allows you to select different types of objects and display only the properties common to all of the objects in the Properties window. You then can set any of the common properties all at once. In this case you need to change the Visible property for two different types of objects: scroll bars and labels. To select more than one object, you click the first object to display its handles; then you press and hold down the Shift key and click the additional objects. When you select and work with multiple objects, the Properties window does not display an object name.

To set the Visible property for the scroll bars and labels:

1. Make the Form window active. Press and hold down the **Shift** key as you click each scroll bar and each label for quantity ordered and extended price. As you activate an object, it is marked with blue handles and the other selected objects appear with dimmed handles. See Figure 3-11.

Figure 3-11 ◀
Selecting
multiple
objects

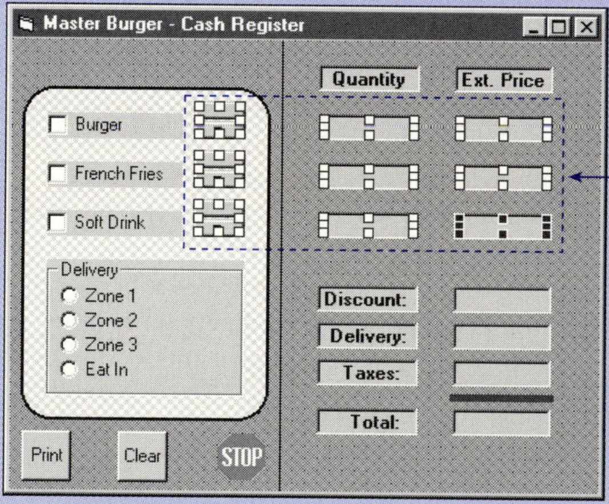

marked objects
appear with handles

As shown in Figure 3-12, the Properties window displays only those properties that are common to both a label and a vertical scroll bar. Note that the object in the title bar may be different depending upon the last item selected.

Figure 3-12 ◀
Properties
window for
multiple
selected
objects

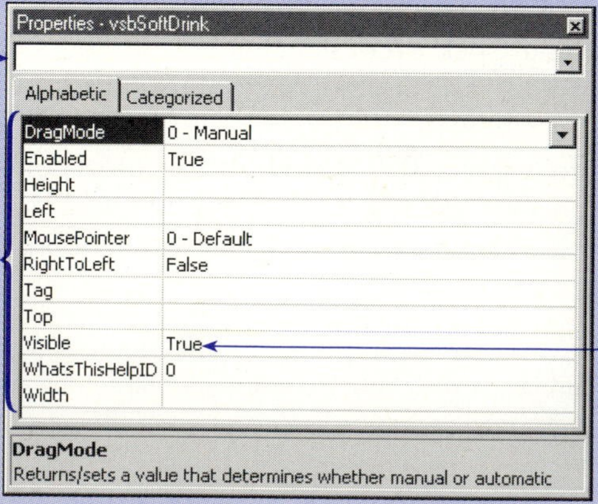

no object
name displayed

only properties
common to a label
and vertical scroll
bar are displayed

set this property
to False

2. Set the Visible property for the selected objects to **False**.

The objects still are visible. The Visible property is applied at run time, so the objects will not disappear from the screen until the program is run.

3. Save the project and then start the program to test that the objects are not visible in run time. Your form should look like Figure 3-13.

Figure 3-13 ◄
Invisible
objects

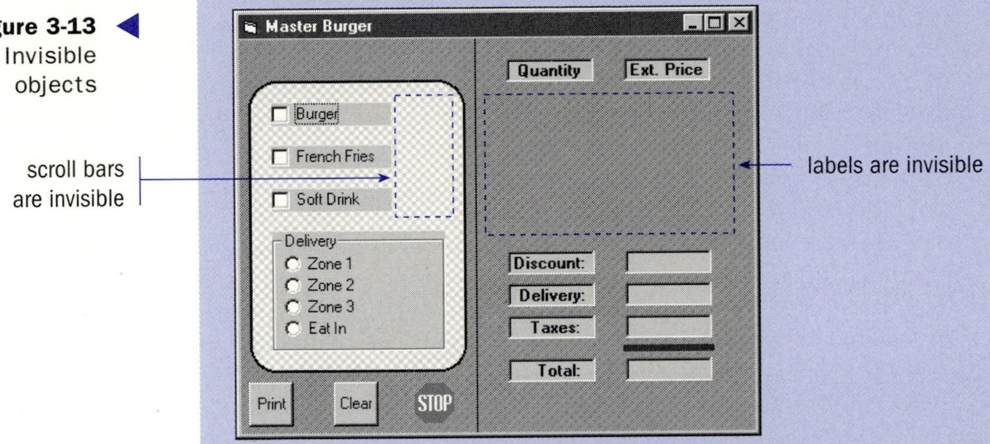

scroll bars
are invisible

labels are invisible

Notice the form at run time does not display the scroll bars or corresponding labels.

4. End the program.

You now need to write the code to make the scroll bar, quantity ordered, and extended price labels visible when a clerk clicks the corresponding check box.

Writing Statements with Conditions

Now that your program starts running with the scroll bars and labels invisible, you need to write the code that will cause these objects to become visible if a corresponding check box is checked. You want the scroll bars and labels to remain invisible, or become invisible again, if the corresponding check box is not checked. Thus, you will set the Visible property of each object to a Boolean value of True or False. You also want the Initial value of the scroll bar to be set to 1.

The programs you have developed until now have all executed statements sequentially in the order they appear in the procedure, until the procedure reaches the End Sub statement. This is fine for simple tasks, but most programs need the capability to execute one set of statements in certain circumstances and another set of statements in different circumstances. Visual Basic allows you to write statements to address different conditions. For example, you can write a statement such as, "If a menu item check box is checked, then make its corresponding scroll bar and labels visible; otherwise, make these objects invisible." The following pseudocode shows the statement in generic form.

```
If some expression is True Then
    execute one group of statements.
Otherwise
    execute a different group of statements.
End of If statement
```

Using Comparison Operators

To determine which set of statements to execute, you use a conditional statement. A **conditional statement** allows you to execute one series of statements when a condition is True and another set of statements when a condition is False. When you write a conditional statement, you use comparison operators on two values or expressions. The values can be compared in many ways using **comparison operators**. The comparison operators used by Visual Basic are equal to (=), not equal to (<>), less than (<), greater than (>), less than or equal to (<=), greater than or equal to (>=), or contains the string (Like). The result of a conditional operation always must be either True or False and, therefore, produces a Boolean value. Comparison operators all have the same precedence. When used with arithmetic operators, however, the arithmetic operations are performed first then the comparison operations are performed.

To determine which statements to execute in your program, you will use the comparison operator equal to (=) with an If statement to determine if one value is the same as another. Comparison operators seldom are used by themselves. Rather, they are included as part of some statement. The simplest form of an If statement, which will execute a set of statements only if a specific condition is True, has the following syntax:

If *condition* **Then**

  statement(s)

End If

- The *condition* part of an If statement must evaluate to a Boolean value of True or False.

- The *statement(s)* part can be any valid Visual Basic statement(s), which is(are) executed when the condition is True.

- If the *condition* is False, the *statement(s)* before the **End If** is(are) not executed, and execution of the program continues at the statement following the End If.

The following pseudocode describes a simple If statement that will execute statements if the French Fries check box is checked.

```
If the French Fries check box is checked Then
  Make the corresponding scroll bar visible
  Make the corresponding label visible
  Set the value of the scroll bar to 1
End of If statement
```

This statement is useful, but it does not account for situations in which a different activity needs to be executed when a condition is False. The cash register program must make the scroll bar visible when a menu item is selected and invisible when the item is not selected. This type of If statement, often called an If...Then...Else statement, has the following syntax:

If *condition* **Then**

  statements executed when the condition is True

Else

  statements executed when the condition is False

End If

■ If the *condition* is True, then the *statement(s)* before the **Else** statement is(are) executed, then execution continues at the *statement* following the End If statement.

■ If the *condition* is False, the statements after the Else statement are executed.

This If...Then...Else statement is represented with the following pseudocode:

```
If the French Fries check box is checked Then
    Make the corresponding scroll bar visible
    Make the corresponding label invisible
    Set the value of the scroll bar to 1
Otherwise execute the following statements
    Make the corresponding scroll bar invisible
    Make the corresponding label invisible
    Set the value of the scroll bar to 0
End of If statement
```

You will write an If...Then...Else statement to make visible or invisible the scroll bars and the quantity ordered and extended price labels for each menu item when its corresponding check box is checked. For example, when the chkBurger object is checked, the Visible property for the vsbBurger, the lblQtyBurger and lblExtBurger output labels should be set to True; otherwise they should be set to False.

To make the user interface as intuitive and easy to use as possible, Gill wants the program to set the value of the corresponding scroll bar and quantity ordered label when the value of the check box changes. When the box first is checked, the quantity ordered scroll bar must be set to 1, the most likely quantity that will be ordered. You can do this by setting the Value property of the scroll bar to 1 when you set its Visible property to True. You will set the Caption of the label in a moment.

Occasionally, a customer will decide not to order a product that already has been checked. When a check box is unchecked, the scroll bar and the labels for quantity ordered and extended price need to be set to 0 and become invisible again.

Using Object Browser, you will see which intrinsic constants to use to express one of three valid check box values: 0 - Unchecked, 1 - Checked, or 2 - Grayed.

To use the Object Browser to examine the intrinsic constants applicable to a check box:

1. Open the **Object Browser**.

2. Click **CheckBoxConstants** in the Classes section of the Object Browser dialog box.

   The Members of 'CheckBoxConstants' section displays three constants—vbChecked, vbGrayed, and vbUnchecked, as shown in Figure 3-14.

Figure 3-14 ◀
Object Browser
dialog box

intrinsic constants
supported by
CheckBox object

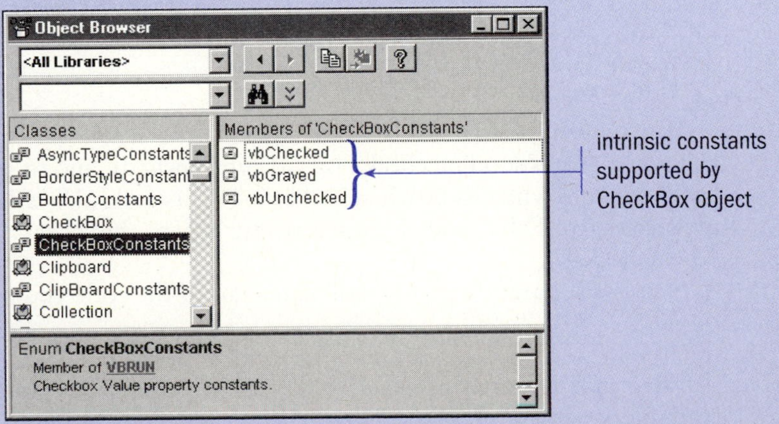

3. Click **vbChecked**. Notice the value of the constant (1) is displayed at the bottom of the dialog box.

4. Click **vbGrayed** and notice the value of the constant is 2.

5. Click **vbUnchecked** and notice the value of the constant is 0.

6. Close the **Object Browser**.

When you use intrinsic constant names in a program, Visual Basic converts the names into their respective values when the program is run, which makes the program more readable and reliable. For example, if you needed to set the Value property to Unchecked, the following two statements would accomplish this; however, the statement containing the constant makes it clearer that you want the value to be Unchecked:

```
chkBurger.Value = 0
chkBurger.Value = vbUnchecked
```

You will use intrinsic constants to write the code to make the scroll bars and labels visible when a clerk checks a check box.

To set the Visible property for the scroll bars and labels based on the check box values:

1. Open the Code window for the chkBurger_Click event procedure and enter the following code (shown in bold):

```
Private Sub chkBurger_Click()
    If (chkBurger.Value = vbChecked) Then
        vsbBurger.Visible = True
        vsbBurger.Value = 1
        lblQtyBurger.Visible = True
        lblExtBurger.Visible = True
    Else
        vsbBurger.Visible = False
        vsbBurger.Value = 0
        lblQtyBurger.Visible = False
        lblExtBurger.Visible = False
    End If
End Sub
```

2. Repeat Step 1 for the chkFrenchFries_Click event procedure. Be sure you use the object names **vsbFrenchFries**, **lblQtyFrenchFries**, and **lblExtFrenchFries**. Remember, you can select the code you just wrote and use the copy and paste operations.

3. Repeat Step 1 for the chkSoftDrink_Click event procedure. Be sure you use the object names **vsbSoftDrink**, **lblQtySoftDrink**, and **lblExtSoftDrink**.

You now have written the code to make the scroll bars and labels visible when the value of a corresponding check box is 1 (vbChecked), and to set the Value property of the scroll bar to 1 when its box first is checked. This code also will reset the Visible and Value properties to False and 0, respectively, when the check box Value property is 0 (vbUnchecked).

Notice the parentheses in the If statement of the code you just wrote.

```
If (chkBurger.Value = vbChecked) Then
```

While not required to evaluate the statement correctly, parentheses can improve the readability of your program. They make it clear that chkBurger.Value is compared against the constant vbChecked first. If True, the statements before the Else are executed. If False, then the statements after the Else are executed.

Tip: Use parentheses liberally in your programs to improve readability and reduce logic errors caused by misunderstanding precedence. Note that adding parentheses will not slow down the execution of your program.

Now that the event code for each check box is complete, you have reached a milestone in your program. It is a good time to save your work, test your program, and correct any errors.

To test the check boxes:

1. Save the project and then start the program.

2. Click the **Burger** check box. The corresponding scroll bar, vsbBurger, and the labels, lblQtyBurger and lblExtBurger, become visible.

3. Click the **Burger** check box again. The objects are invisible again.

4. Repeat Steps 2 and 3 for the **French Fries** and **Soft Drink** check boxes.

    TROUBLE? If the visibility of an object does not change in response to a click in the corresponding check box, end the program, then open the Code window for the CheckBox object's Click event procedure and verify that your code is identical to the code shown in the previous tutorial steps. Make any necessary corrections, then repeat Steps 1 through 4.

5. End the program.

The cash register screen now displays the corresponding scroll bars and quantity ordered fields when a check box is checked and makes those objects invisible when the corresponding check box is not checked. You are ready to begin programming the scroll bar objects so that when the user moves the scroll bars, the corresponding quantity ordered label is updated.

In this program, you need to know when the numeric value of a scroll bar changes, so the program can update the quantity ordered and extended price of an item and display the information in the corresponding Label objects. Whenever a clerk clicks part of a scroll bar and changes its value, a Change event is generated. You use a Change event with the Value property of the scroll bar in a computation to update the captions of the necessary labels. Figure 3-15 shows how each event causes the next event. Whenever the clerk clicks the check box representing a menu item, the scroll bar is set to 1; this also causes a Change event to be generated for the scroll bar.

Figure 3-15 ◀
Relationship between events (1)

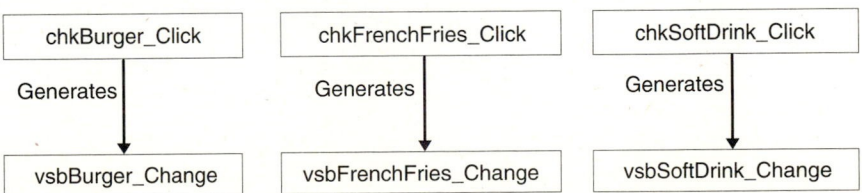

Now you need to write the code to program the Change event that will update the caption in the quantity ordered label whenever the value of the scroll bar changes.

To write the code that will place the value of a scroll bar into its quantity ordered label:

1. Open the Code window for the vsbBurger_Change event and enter the following code (shown in bold):

```
Private Sub vsbBurger_Change()
    lblQtyBurger.Caption = vsbBurger.Value
End Sub
```

When one of the scroll arrows is clicked, the program generates a Change event for the vsbBurger object. The code in this Change event procedure copies the Value property of vsbBurger to the Caption property of lblQtyBurger.

You now need to create the same code for the scroll bars for the French Fries and Soft Drink items.

2. Repeat Step 1 for the vsbFrenchFries_Change event, using the names **lblQtyFrenchFries** and **vsbFrenchFries**.

3. Repeat Step 1 for the vsbSoftDrink_Change event, using the names **lblQtySoftDrink** and **vsbSoftDrink**.

Whenever a clerk clicks a scroll bar, the caption of the corresponding label will display the quantity ordered for the item, as indicated by the value of the scroll bar.

Gill suggests that you test the program to see whether or not the quantity ordered labels are updated correctly when a scroll bar is clicked. Testing the program also will give you an opportunity to see how the Change event works for a scroll bar. Because you have set the Max and Min properties, you cannot set the Value property outside the specified range.

To test the scroll bars and their corresponding quantity ordered labels:

1. Save the project and then start the program.

2. Click the **Burger** check box. The corresponding label displays the value 1.

3. Click the Burger scroll bar's **up arrow**. The corresponding label displays the value 2.

4. Click the Burger scroll bar's **down arrow**. The label displays the value 1. Because you did not change the SmallChange property from the default value of 1, the value of the scroll bar changes by 1 each time you click one of its arrows.

5. Repeat Steps 2 through 4 to test the French Fries and Soft Drink scroll bars and display labels.

TROUBLE? If any quantity ordered label did not change, end the program, and open the Code window for the corresponding scroll bar. Check the code and make sure the Caption property is set for the correct Label object.

If the value of an item incremented or decremented incorrectly, check the Min and Max properties of the corresponding scroll bar; Min should be 25 and Max should be 0. Make any necessary corrections, then repeat Steps 1 through 4.

6. End the program by clicking the **End** button ■ on the toolbar. You cannot use the stop sign icon because the code has not been written yet.

Note that when you click one of the scroll arrows for a menu item, the value of its scroll bar changes. This means that a Change event is generated for the scroll bar. This process is illustrated in Figure 3-16.

Figure 3-16 ◄
Relationship
between
events (2)

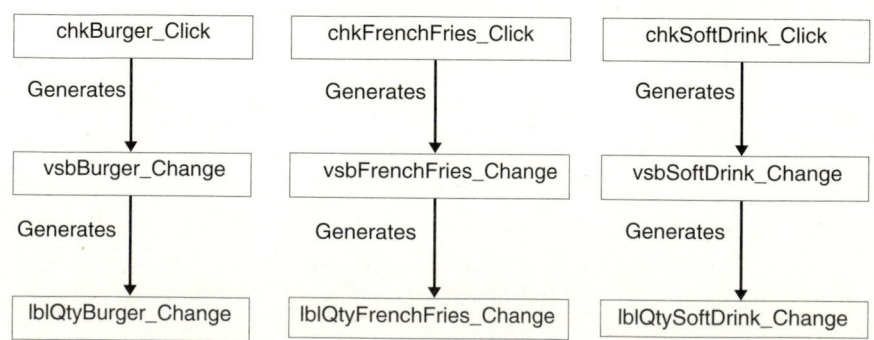

chkBurger_Click	chkFrenchFries_Click	chkSoftDrink_Click
Generates	Generates	Generates
vsbBurger_Change	vsbFrenchFries_Change	vsbSoftDrink_Change
Generates	Generates	Generates
lblQtyBurger_Change	lblQtyFrenchFries_Change	lblQtySoftDrink_Change

Creating User-Defined Constants

You still must create the code to compute and display the labels for the extended prices (unit price × quantity ordered), as described in the pseudocode Gill wrote for the program. Before you can compute the extended price, you need to include the price of each item in the program. You could declare variables for the prices and assign values to them as you did in Tutorial 2, or just use numbers in the computations. In this case, however, the price of an item will not change while the program is running, so a constant is more suitable for storing the prices. You used an intrinsic constant in the If statement you wrote to determine if a check box is checked. You also can create user-defined constants by using the **Const** (constant) statement. The syntax for a user-defined constant is:

[**Public | Private**] **Const** *constantname* [**As** *type*] = *expression*

- The **Public** keyword is used at the form level to declare constants that can be used by all procedures in all forms and other modules. You need this keyword only if you have more than one form in your project. The **Private** keyword is used at the form level to declare a constant that can be used only by procedures in the form where the constant is declared. Constants are Private if you omit the Public or Private keyword. You should use explicitly the Private keyword, however, to declare form-level constants and improve your program's clarity.

- You can declare constants in the general declarations section of a Form module or inside a procedure. Constants declared in the general declarations section are visible to the module in which they are declared when the Private keyword is used, and visible to the other modules in a project when the Public keyword is used. Constants declared inside a procedure are only visible to the procedure in which they are declared.

- The *constantname* assigned to a user-defined constant should follow the naming conventions for variables. That is, it begins with a three-letter prefix describing its data type, followed by a descriptive name. The entire constant name should be prefixed with the letter "c" indicating a constant.

- Constants can represent any of the Visual Basic data types by using the optional **As** *type* clause. If you don't explicitly declare the constant type using the **As** *type* clause, the constant has the data type that is most appropriate for the expression. Explicitly supplying the desired data type, however, will create more readable code and prevent possible type conversion errors.

- The *expression* represents a valid Visual Basic expression that becomes the value of the constant. The expression often is a simple value, such as a price, but it also can consist of other constants and operators. See the Visual Basic online Help for more information on the Const statement.

Because your program has only one form, the constants need to be visible only to the form in which they are declared, so you will declare them as Private. Each constant will be declared as a Single data type, because the prices contain a decimal point. The price constants will be used in various expressions throughout the program to compute the extended prices of products ordered.

> *Tip:* Creating user-defined constants makes a program more readable and easier to maintain, because when the value of a constant changes, you only need to change the value once in the statement where the constant is created. For the cash register program, when the price of an item changes, you only need to change the constant once rather than searching for each occurrence of the price used in the program.

> **TROUBLE?** If an extended price is not computed correctly, end the program, and activate the Code window for the Change event procedure of the corresponding quantity ordered Label object. Be sure that the code is the same as the code shown in the previous set of steps. Make any necessary corrections, then repeat Steps 1 and 2.
>
> If an extended price is not formatted as currency, check that you wrote the correct Format statement for the correct corresponding extended price label. Repeat Steps 1 and 2.

3. End the program.

You have completed the cash register programming for this session. The user of the program can select items and specify the corresponding quantity ordered. Whenever the quantity ordered changes, the extended price of the item will be recomputed. Notice you took advantage of the Change event to determine when the extended price needs to be recomputed instead of forcing the user to explicitly click a command button to complete the extended price. In the next session you will learn how to compute the totals, the delivery charges, and the discount.

Quick Check

1. What is the function of a check box?

2. What values can a check box contain?

3. Define the following scroll bar properties: Min, Max, LargeChange, SmallChange, and Value.

4. What is a Boolean value?

5. Write the code for the following pseudocode statements:

   If the Visible property of lblTaxes is equal to True, Then set the caption to 33.

   If the Visible property of lblTaxes is not equal to False, Then set the value to 0.

   If the January sales (lblJan) are greater than the February sales (lblFeb), Then add 1 to the value of the caption of January sales.

   If yesterday is less than today, Then end the program.

6. Describe the difference between a Change event and a Click event.

7. Describe how one event can generate another event.

Now that you have completed Session 3.1, you can exit Visual Basic or you can continue to the next session.

SESSION

3.2

In this session you will learn how to write more complex If statements and learn about a new statement called the Select Case statement. You also will create your own procedures, called general procedures, which are activated explicitly by your program rather than as a response to an event. You also will learn how to perform operations on String variables and display a message box to confirm an action.

Select Case Statements and Option Buttons

The option buttons on the cash register program should trigger a delivery charge only if the order will be delivered. For Zone 1 the delivery amount is $1.50, for Zone 2, $2.50, and for Zone 3, $3.50.

Earlier you used an If statement to test a condition and execute one set of the statements when the condition was True and another set when the condition was False. Sometimes the decision to be made has more than two possible outcomes. For example, the delivery decision has four outcomes—the order was eaten in the restaurant, or delivered to one of three different zones. The most efficient method in situations requiring three or more choices is to use one of two different statements: an If statement or a Select Case statement.

The If statement with more than two outcomes has the following syntax:

If *condition1* **Then**

   statement-block1

ElseIf *condition2* **Then**

   statement-block2

[ElseIf *condition-n* **Then**

   statement-block-n]

[Else

   [*statements*]]

End If

- If *condition1* is True, the statements contained in *statement-block1* up to the ElseIf clause are executed, then the entire If statement exits whether or not any of the other *conditions* are True and execution continues at the statement following the End If.

- If *condition1* is False and *condition2* is True, the statements contained in *statement-block2* up to the next ElseIf clause are executed. The entire If statement exits whether or not any of the remaining *conditions* are True and execution continues at the statement following the End If.

- The statement block following each successive ElseIf clause is executed if the previous conditions were False and it is True. The entire If statement exits whether or not any of the remaining *conditions* are True and execution continues at the statement following the End If.

- If none of the conditions is True, the statements inside the Else clause are executed if one exists, then the If statement exits. The Else clause is optional. If there is no Else clause, the If statement exits and execution continues at the statement following the End If.

Figure 3-18 illustrates how this type of If statement works by examining where an order will be eaten.

Figure 3-18 ◄
Analyzing the
If statement

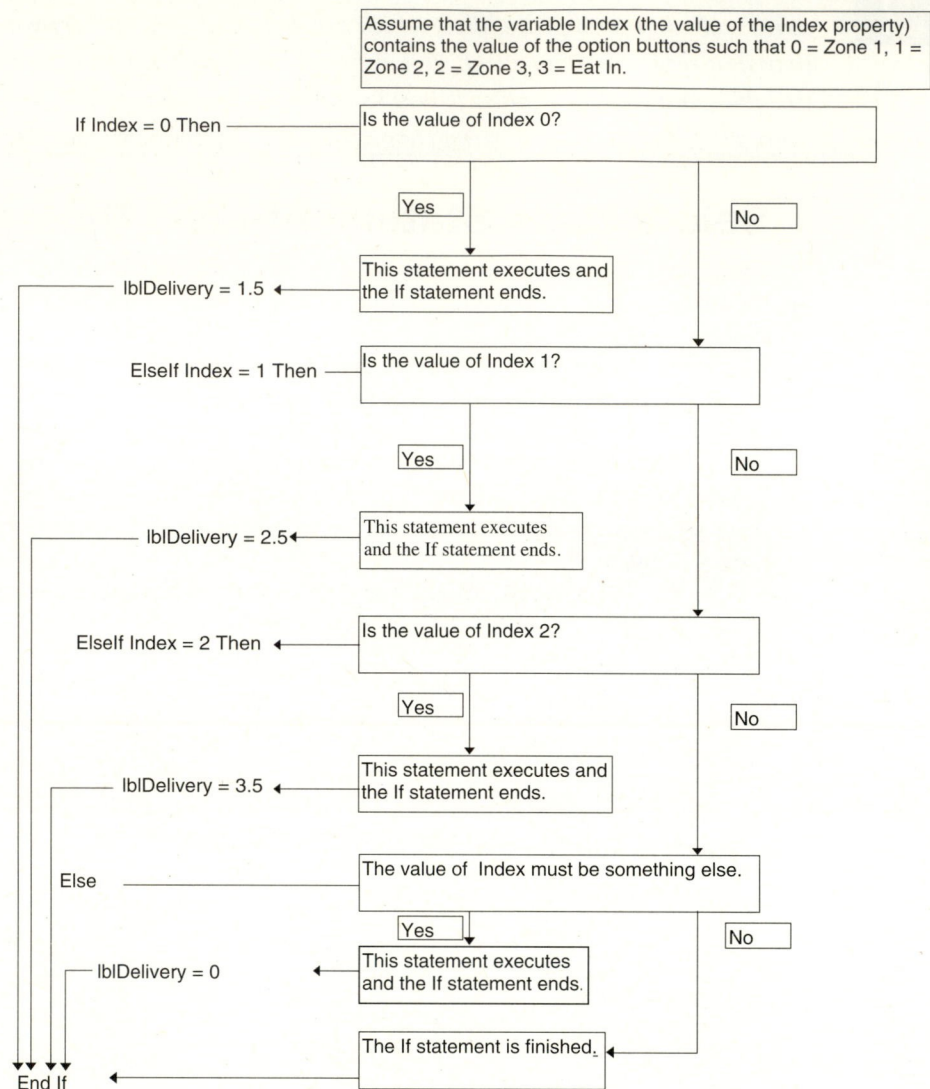

In circumstances where an ElseIf condition in an If statement uses the same expression and compares it to a different value, the Select Case decision structure can both simplify program logic and make a program more readable. **Select Case** statements are like If statements, but instead of testing multiple expressions, the Select Case statement tests only one expression and executes different statements based on the results of the expression. The following is the syntax of a Select Case statement:

Select Case *testexpression*

   Case *expressionlist1*

      statement-block1

   Case *expressionlist2*

      statement-block2

   Case *expressionlist-n*

      statement-block-n

   [Case Else

      [*statements*]]

End Select

- Visual Basic executes the Select Case statement by evaluating the *testexpression* once when the Select Case statement first starts. It then compares the *expressionlist1* with the *testexpression*. If they are the same, the statements in *statement-block1* are executed, then the entire Select Case statement exits. If they are not the same, the *expressionlist2* is compared with the *testexpression*. This process is repeated until there are no more expressions to be tested.

- If no expression matches the *testexpression*, the statements in the optional Case Else clause are executed. If no expression matched the *testexpression* and the Case Else statement is omitted, then no statement block will be executed.

- If more than one *expressionlist* is the same as the *testexpression*, only the statements in the first matching Case are executed.

- The *expressionlist* can be a list of values—such as 6,7,8—separated by commas. It also can be a range of values separated by the word To, as in 5 To 10. Refer to Visual Basic online Help for more information on the Select Case statement.

Figure 3-19 shows the If statement from Figure 3-18 written as a Select Case statement.

Figure 3-19 ◄
Analyzing the
Select Case
statement

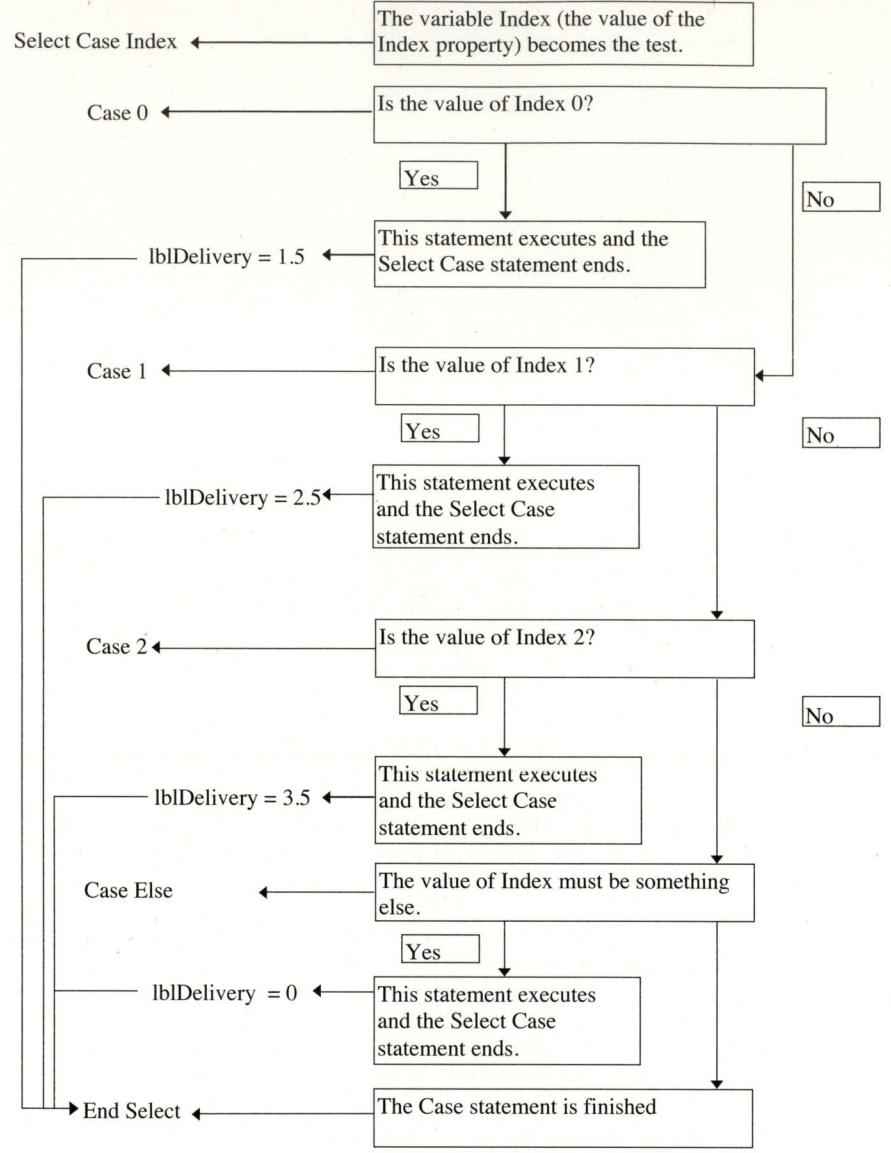

Tip: The code in Figure 3-19 will execute more quickly than the code in
Figure 3-18 because Visual Basic only needs to check the Index
once in the first line of the Select Case statement, rather than for
each If and ElseIf. In addition, this Select Case statement will
make your program easier to read than the longer If statement.

Using the Select Case Statement with a Control Array

You now need a way to check which Delivery option button is clicked and write a Select
Case statement to update the delivery charges and order total accordingly. In the control
array of option buttons, a specific option button is identified by its Index property. Visual
Basic uses the Index property as an argument in the option buttons' Click event procedure
to indicate which object in the control array caused the Click event to occur. When you
call a procedure you send arguments to the procedure by enclosing the argument in parentheses, just like you did when you called functions like Val and FV. These procedures then
receive the arguments and perform operations on them. Your Click event procedure will
receive an argument, just as the Val procedure receives and processes arguments.

Like variables, an argument has a name and a data type, which are shown in the declaration
for the argument. Figure 3-20 shows the argument for the optDelivery_Click event procedure.

Figure 3-20 ◄
Argument in
the event
procedure

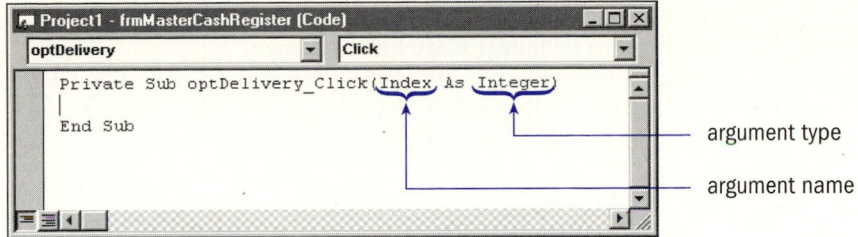

Notice that the syntax of the argument looks like any other declaration statement except that the keyword, Dim or Private, is omitted. It contains a variable name, Index, and an As clause followed by the data type, Integer. Visual Basic stores the Index of the active option button as a local variable so you can use it in the event procedure. If you have more than one control array of option buttons on a form, each control array of option buttons uses a local variable of the name, Index. Like other local variables, this variable only exists while the procedure is running. This is the method of communicating information from one procedure to another or, in this situation, having the system communicate information to your event procedure. If the Zone 1 option button is clicked, Visual Basic will set the Index property to 0; if the Zone 2 option button is clicked, Visual Basic will set the Index property to 1; if the Zone 3 option button is clicked, Visual Basic will set the Index property to 2; and if the Eat In option button is clicked, Visual Basic will set the Index property to 3. This is how Visual Basic keeps track of, and shares code among, the control array's objects.

You will use this information to determine the delivery charge, if any, by writing the necessary Select Case statement in the Code window for the control array's Click event.

To write the Select Case statement to assign the necessary delivery charge:

1. Start Visual Basic, if necessary.

2. Open the project named **Master Cash Register.vbp** that you created in Session 3.1 and view the form, if necessary.

3. Activate the Code window for the **optDelivery_Click** event procedure and enter the following code (shown in bold):

```
Private Sub optDelivery_Click(Index As Integer)
    Select Case Index
        'Zone 1
        Case 0
            msngDelivery = 1.5
        'Zone 2
        Case 1
            msngDelivery = 2.5
        'Zone 3
        Case 2
            msngDelivery = 3.5
        'Eat In
        Case 3
            msngDelivery = 0
    End Select

    lblDelivery.Caption = Format(msngDelivery, "Currency")
End Sub
```

This sequence of statements is executed when any of the four option buttons is clicked. You determine which option button is clicked by looking at the value stored in the Index property. The Select Case statement works by first evaluating the value of Index, and then executing the statements for the respective case. The delivery charge then is formatted and displayed by setting the caption of lblDelivery. Because there is no other possibility, you did not need to include a Case Else statement.

The cash register program now computes a delivery charge if appropriate. You have reached another milestone in your program. You now should check that the Delivery option buttons and Delivery label work correctly.

To test the Delivery option buttons and Delivery label:

1. Save the project and then start the program.

2. Click each of the **option buttons** in the Delivery control array.

   The Delivery label changes with each option button clicked.

   TROUBLE? If the Delivery label does not reflect the changes when each option button is clicked, end the program. Check that the code in the option buttons' Click event matches the code in the previous set of steps, then repeat Steps 1 and 2.

3. End the program.

Creating a General Procedure

According to the program specifications written by Gill, the cash register program must compute the taxes and order total automatically whenever the extended price of a menu item changes. To accomplish this, you can use the same code for all three event procedures, lblExtBurger_Change, lblExtFrenchFries_Change, and lblExtSoftDrink_Change. Instead of writing the same lines of code in each of the three event procedures, you can create a procedure called a general procedure, and then call the general procedure with one line of code in the individual event procedures. A **general procedure** is like an event procedure, but you must explicitly call a general procedure because it does not respond to an event. One of the keys to writing successful programs is to divide tasks into logical components, such as general procedures, which then can be reused within the same program or in one or more different programs.

There are two types of general procedures: **Function procedures** (functions), and **Sub procedures** (subroutines). The difference between functions and subroutines is how they communicate their results to the procedure from which they were called. Functions return a result of a specific data type that you generally assign to a variable or appropriate property. Subroutines do not return a value.

When you create a general procedure like the one to compute the taxes and order total, you must specify the procedure name, type, and scope. Visual Basic will help you by creating a template for the procedure from information you supply in the Add Procedure dialog box.

To open the Add Procedure dialog box for the form:

1. Be sure the Code window is active then click the **Tools** menu, then click **Add Procedure**. The Add Procedure dialog box opens. See Figure 3-21.

Figure 3-21 ◀
Add Procedure
dialog box

Type section

Scope section

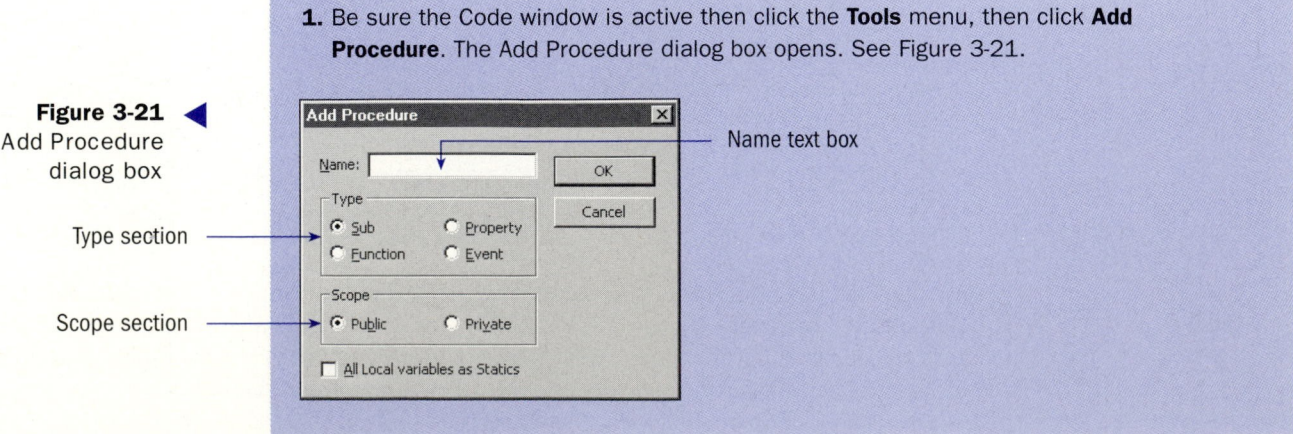

Name text box

TROUBLE? If the Add Procedure command is dimmed on the Tools menu, be sure the Visual Basic title bar displays [design], and that the Code window is the active window.

The Add Procedure dialog box consists of three sections—Name, Type, and Scope.

- In the **Name** text box you type a name for the general procedure. The requirements for procedure names are the same as for variables. You do not need to supply, however, the four-character prefix indicating the procedure's scope and type.

- The **Type** identifies whether the procedure is a Sub (subroutine) procedure, Function procedure, Property procedure, or Event procedure. **Sub** procedures communicate information to other parts of the program by setting form-level variables, but do not return values to the procedures from which they were called. **Function** procedures return values to the procedures from which they were called. **Property** procedures are used in a different type of module, called a class module, to create properties for the objects in a class module. **Event** procedures are used to create user-defined events.

- Public and Private are the keywords that describe the **Scope** of the procedure. If a procedure is **Private**, it can be called only from the form in which it is declared. If it is **Public**, the procedure can be called from anywhere in the project. Public procedures are useful only when a program contains more than one Form module or other modules.

You will use the Add Procedure dialog box to create the general procedure that will calculate the taxes and order total when any extended price changes. Because you do not need any value to be returned to the calling procedure, you will create a Sub procedure. Also, you will declare the general procedure as Private, because all the code for your program is contained in the same form.

To write the general procedure to compute the taxes and order total:

1. Type **ComputeTotals** in the Name text box.

2. In the Type section, click the **Sub** option button.

3. In the Scope section, click the **Private** option button.

4. Click the **OK** button.

   The Code window will become active; "(General)" will appear in the Object list box and "ComputeTotals" will appear in the Procedures list box. This indicates that the ComputeTotals procedure is not executed when an event occurs to a specific object, but is general to the Form module and can be called explicitly by any event or general procedure. Because the procedure is Private, it only can be called from event or general procedures in this form.

5. Enter the following code into the procedure:

```
Private Sub ComputeTotals()
    Dim psngSubtotal As Single
    Dim psngTaxes As Single

    psngSubtotal = msngExtBurger + msngExtFrenchFries + _
        msngExtSoftDrink

    psngTaxes = csngPercentTax * psngSubtotal
    lblTaxes.Caption = Format(psngTaxes, "Currency")
    lblTotal.Caption = Format(psngSubtotal + psngTaxes _
        + msngDelivery, "Currency")
End Sub
```

Now you can examine each line of the code in more detail.

```
Dim psngSubtotal As Single
Dim psngTaxes As Single
```

The variables psngSubtotal and psngTaxes are declared inside the ComputeTotals general procedure because you only need these variables when this procedure is running. These variables are considered local to the procedure, and other event or general procedures are not able to reference them. Furthermore, the memory for the variables exists only while the procedure is executing; it is allocated only when the procedure is called, and then it is released when the procedure terminates.

```
psngSubtotal = msngExtBurger + msngExtFrenchFries + _
    msngExtSoftDrink
```

This statement computes a subtotal by adding together the extended prices for each item. Remember that you declared the variables msngExtBurger, msngExtFrenchFries, and msngExtSoftDrink in the general declarations section of the Form module. These values were set by the Change event procedure of the corresponding quantity ordered label. Because the statements are too long to fit on a line, you needed to use the statement continuation character, as you did in Tutorial 2.

```
psngTaxes = csngPercentTax * psngSubtotal
```

Using the subtotal from the previous statement and the form-level constant representing the sales tax rate, this statement computes the sales tax.

```
lblTaxes.Caption = Format(psngTaxes, "Currency")
```

Because all the results representing a dollar amount need to be displayed with a leading dollar sign and two decimal places, this statement formats the sales tax and displays the formatted result in the label.

```
lblTotal.Caption = Format(psngSubtotal + psngTaxes _
    + msngDelivery, "Currency")
```

This statement computes the total using the local subtotal and sales tax variables, and the form-level delivery variable. Notice that rather than storing the order total in a separate variable, the computation was performed inside the first argument of the Format statement. This can be done because the value of lblTotal will never be used in another calculation, and because Visual Basic lets you embed expressions inside arguments. First psngSubtotal, psngTaxes, and msngDelivery are added together. Then the Format statement is called with the result and the second argument of Currency.

While the Add Procedure dialog box created a procedure template for you, it is not the only way to create a new Sub procedure in a module. You also can create a Sub procedure by typing the Private Sub and End Sub statements, if you desire.

Calling the General Procedure

Once you have created a general procedure, you need to call it from either a general or event procedure. Gill's design for the cash register program specifies that when the extended price of an item changes, the taxes and order total must recompute automatically. So, the ComputeTotals general procedure should be called in the Change event procedure for each extended price label. You need to call the ComputeTotals general procedure by typing its name in the appropriate event procedure. You also will format each extended price label as Currency.

To call the general procedure to compute the taxes and order total:

1. Activate the Code window for the **lblExtBurger_Change** event procedure. Be sure it is the Change event, not the Click event. Enter the following code:

```
Private Sub lblExtBurger_Change()
    ComputeTotals
End Sub
```

Calling the ComputeTotals general procedure in the Change event for this extended price label ensures that when the extended price changes, the taxes and order total will be updated.

2. Repeat Step 1 for the lblExtFrenchFries_Change event procedure. Be sure you select the object named **lblExtFrenchFries** instead of lblExtBurger.

3. Repeat Step 1 for the lblExtSoftDrink_Change event procedure. Be sure you select the object named **lblExtSoftDrink** instead of lblExtBurger.

Now that you have written all the code for the ComputeTotals general procedure and called the procedure whenever an extended price changes, you should examine the relationship between the events in the program. Figure 3-22 illustrates these relationships.

Figure 3-22 ◄
Event diagram for the cash register program

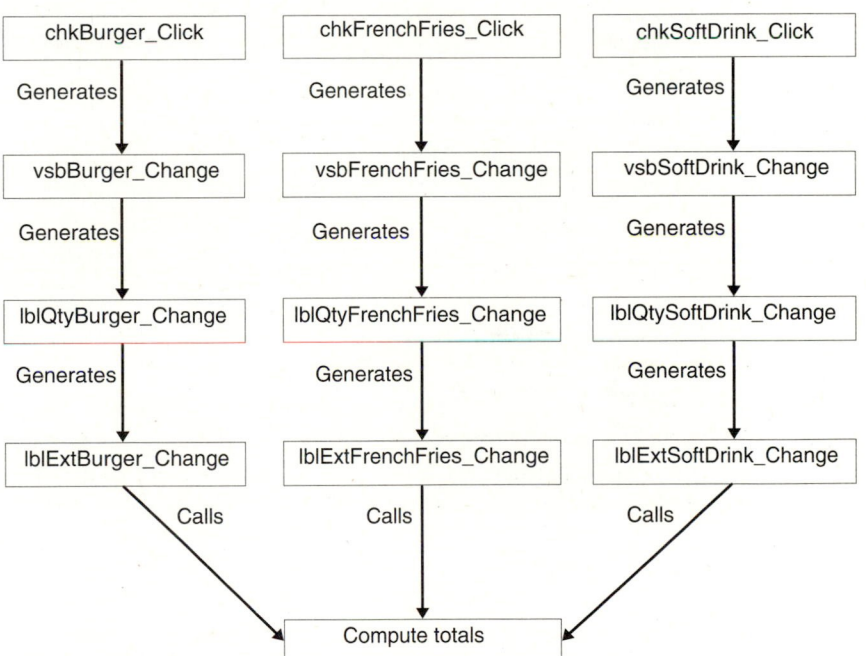

When a clerk clicks one of the check boxes, the value of the corresponding scroll bar is changed by the code in the Click event procedure causing a Change event to be generated for the scroll bar. The code for the scroll bar's Change event then updates the quantity ordered, generating another Change event. The Change event for the quantity ordered, in turn, updates the extended price. The Change event for each extended price label calls the ComputeTotals general procedure, which updates the taxes and order total labels. Understanding the relationship between multiple objects and the different events that occur is critical to writing Visual Basic programs. Now you will run the program and test it to verify that the order total is being computed correctly and being recomputed when necessary.

To test the general procedure to compute the taxes and order total:

1. Save the project and then start the program.

2. Enter an order and make sure the taxes and order total are computed correctly.

   TROUBLE? If the taxes and total do not change, be sure that each extended price object is calling the ComputeTotals general procedure.

3. Click the **Zone 1** option button.

   Notice that the order total does not change because you have not yet written the code to add the delivery charges to the order total.

4. End the program.

According to Gill's design specifications, the order total must be updated when the value of lblDelivery changes. Recall that the ComputeTotals general procedure adds together the subtotal, taxes, and delivery charges to get a total each time any extended price changes. To update the total when the delivery charge changes, the lblDelivery_Change event also must call the ComputeTotals general procedure.

To compute the total when the Delivery label changes:

1. Type the following code in the Code window for the **lblDelivery_Change** event procedure:

   ```
   Private Sub lblDelivery_Change()
       ComputeTotals
   End Sub
   ```

2. Save the project then start the program.

3. Enter an order, including a delivery zone. Make sure the total updates when you click the appropriate Delivery option button.

4. Test each of the option buttons.

   TROUBLE? If lblTotal does not update correctly when you click one of the option buttons, end the program. Make sure you have called the ComputeTotals general procedure from the lblDelivery_Change event procedure. Repeat Steps 2 through 4.

Now ComputeTotals updates the order total whenever the delivery charge changes.

As indicated in Gill's design specifications, Master Burger has been experimenting with keeping some stores open 24 hours a day. To increase sales volume between the hours of 1 A.M. and 8 A.M. Master Burger offers a 10% discount on the entire order. The discount, however, does not apply to the delivery charge. To accomplish this task you need to create another general procedure that will compute a discount. This time you will create a Function procedure, however, because the procedure will return a value—the amount of the discount. The Function procedure also will take an argument — the current subtotal of the order. The function will determine whether or not the order should be discounted, and apply the discount to the subtotal depending on the time of day. It then will return the amount of the discount. When a procedure returns a single value like this, writing a function reduces the number of variables you need to declare and improves the readability of the program.

To create a Function procedure to determine and compute the discount:

1. Open the **Add Procedure** dialog box. Remember the Code window must be active.

2. Set the Name to **ComputeDiscount**, the Type to **Function,** and the Scope to **Private.**

3. Click the **OK** button to close the Add Procedure dialog box.

Just as when you created a Sub procedure, Visual Basic creates a template for the procedure and activates the Code window. The procedure is declared as a Function, however. The Function statement, while similar to the Sub statement, has parts to define the data type of the value that will be returned to the calling procedure. The Function statement has the following syntax:

[Public | Private] Function *Name* [(*argumentlist*)] [**As** *type*]

   [*statementsName = expression*]

End Function

- The optional **Public** keyword indicates that the function can be used by the other forms in the program. The optional **Private** keyword indicates that the function is accessible only to the procedures in the form where it is declared.

- The required *Name* argument contains the name of the procedure and must be unique. The requirements for a Function procedure's name are the same as for a Sub procedure.

- The optional *argumentlist* describes the names and data types of the arguments passed to the function.

- The optional **As** *type* clause determines the data type of the value returned by the function.

- By assigning the *Name* of the function to an *expression*, the return value of the function is set.

- The **End Function** statement causes the function to terminate.

You now are ready to complete the code for the argument list, the return data type of the function, and the local variables. The ComputeDiscount function uses one argument —the order subtotal—to compute the discount. This is the value returned by the function. The argument is a Single data type and the function returns a Single data type because both numbers can contain a decimal point.

To declare the function's arguments:

1. Enter the code shown in Figure 3-23.

Figure 3-23 ◀
Creating
a function

argument name

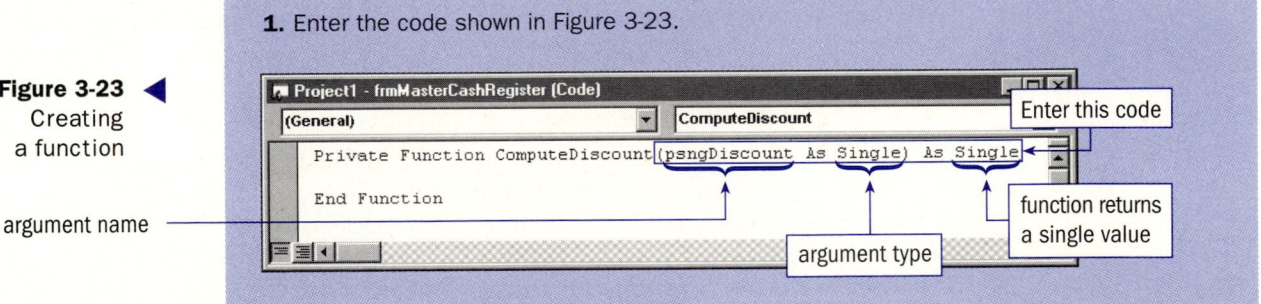

The local variable psngDiscount is the function's argument name. The first "As Single" sets the data type of psngDiscount to Single; the second "As Single" sets the data type of ComputeDiscount to Single. In other words, the function ComputeDiscount will return a Single. Figure 3-23 shows the argument name, type, and return value.

To complete the procedure, you need to write the If statement that will determine whether or not the hour is between 1 A.M. and 8 A.M.

To accomplish this task you first must learn how to get the time of day from the computer's system. Visual Basic has several intrinsic functions that help you work with dates and times. When you work with dates, you generally use the Date data type. The information in a Date data type is stored as a number that can hold dates between January 1, 1000 and December 31, 9999. When you display a Date variable in a label, however, you see a string like:

`12/12/99 3:33 PM`

> *Tip:* For years between 1000 and 1999, Visual Basic only displays the last two digits of the year. For years 2000 or greater, Visual Basic displays all four digits of the year. Some older programs stored only the last two digits of the year. This problem, known as the millennium problem, will affect many programs when the year 2000 arrives.

There are three different functions that retrieve the date from the system. Each returns a Date and takes no arguments.

- The **Now** function returns the current date and time.
- The **Date** function returns the current date.
- The **Time** function returns the current time.

Figure 3-24 illustrates the functions that look at the different parts of a Date variable.

Figure 3-24 ◀
Date Functions

Function name	Description	Example
Day(*date*)	Return an integer between 1 and 31 representing the date of the month.	`pintVar = Day(Now())`
Month(*date*)	Returns an integer between 1 and 12 representing the month of the year.	`pintVar = Month(Now())`
Year(*date*)	Returns an integer representing the year; the full year is returned (that is, 1999, not 99).	`pintVar = Year(Now())`
Hour(*date*)	Returns an integer representing the hour of the day between 0 and 23.	`pintVar = Hour(Now())`
Minute(*date*)	Returns an integer between 0 and 59 representing the minute.	`pintVar = Minute(Now())`
Second(*date*)	Returns an integer between 0 and 59 representing the second.	`pintVar = Second(Now())`

For the cash register program, you are interested in the hour of the day so you need to use the Now function to first obtain the time of day. This can be accomplished by calling the Now function and using that result as the argument to the Hour function. Notice these functions are nested. That is, the Now function appears as an argument to the Hour function. When a function appears as an argument to another function, the function in the innermost parentheses is executed first.

To determine the hour of the day:

1. Enter the following code into the ComputeDiscount general procedure:

```
Dim pintHour As Integer
pintHour = Hour(Now())
```

This statement creates a local variable, pintHour. The current hour is computed by first calling the Now function, then calling the Hour function with one argument—the value returned by the Now function.

Creating an If Statement with Logical Operators

To create the If statement that will check the time of day you need to learn how to use a new kind of operator called a logical operator. **Logical operators** define the relationship between different expressions, much like conjunctions define the relationship between the parts of a sentence in English. The sentence, "If the hour of the day is earlier than 8 A.M. and equal to or later then 1 A.M., then compute a discount.", uses the conjunction and logical operator **And**. Thus, the statements on the leftmost and rightmost sides of the conjunction both must be True for the sentence to be True. If either or both of the statements are False, then the sentence is False. Figure 3-25 shows the more common logical operators.

Figure 3-25 ◄
Logical
operators

Logical Operator	Definition	Example	Result

And	If both expressions evaluate to True, result is True. If either expression evaluates to False, result is False.	`If 2 > 1 And 3 > 1,Then`
		`    statements`
		`End If`
		`If 1 > 2 And 3 > 1,Then`
		`    statements`
		`End If`
			True
			
			False

Or	If either or both expressions evaluate to True, result is True.	`If 2 > 1 Or 3 > 1, Then`
		`    statements`
		`End If`
		`If 1 > 2 Or 3 > 1,Then`
		`    statements`
		`End If`
		`If 1 > 2 Or 1 > 3,Then`
		`    statements`
		`End If`
			True
			
			True
			
			False

Xor	If one, and only one, of the expressions evaluates to True, result is True. If either expression is Null, however, result also is Null.	`If 2 > 1 Xor 3 > 1,Then`
		`    statements`
		`End If`
		`If 1 > 2 Xor 3 > 1,Then`
		`    statements`
		`End If`
		`If 1 > 2 Xor 1 > 3,Then`
		`    statements`
		`End If`
			False
			
			True
			
			False

Not	If expression is True, then result is False. If expression is False, then result is True. If expression is Null, then result is Null.	`If Not 1 > 2,Then`
		`    statements`
		`End If`
		`If Not 2 > 1,Then`
		`    statements`
		`End If`
			True
			
			False

Like arithmetic operators, logical operators have an associated precedence. All operations involving arithmetic operators and comparison operators are performed first. Then the logical operations are performed in the following order: Not, And, Or, Xor.

You now can convert the sentence, "If the hour of the day is earlier than 8 A.M. and equal to or later then 1 A.M., then compute a discount.", and write the statement in the general procedure.

To compute the order discount:

1. Enter the following code into the ComputeDiscount general procedure after the declaration and assignment statements.

```
If (pintHour >= 1) And (pintHour < 8) Then
    ComputeDiscount = psngDiscount * 0.1
Else
    ComputeDiscount = 0
End If
```

The If statement you just wrote first determines if the variable pintHour is greater than or equal to 1. This result is either True or False. Then the variable pintHour is tested to see if it is less than 8. While not necessary, the parentheses help show that these operations are performed first. This result is either True or False. Finally, the two intermediate results are evaluated with the And. Thus, if both are True, then the If statement is True and the discount will be applied. Notice you set the amount of the discount to the name of the function. Thus, the discount amount will be returned to the calling procedure.

You have completed the code so the ComputeDiscount general procedure will determine whether the hour is between 1 A.M. and 8 A.M., and then calculate the discount accordingly. Now you need to call the function in the ComputeTotals general procedure so this discount will be subtracted from the total, if applicable.

To modify the ComputeTotals procedure to compute the discount and subtract it from the order total:

1. Open the Code window for the **ComputeTotals** general procedure and modify the following statements shown in bold.

```
Private Sub ComputeTotals ( )
    Dim psngSubtotal As Single
    Dim psngTaxes As Single
    Dim psngDiscount As Single

    psngSubtotal = msngExtBurger + msngExtFrenchFries + _
        msngExtSoftDrink
    psngDiscount = ComputeDiscount(psngSubtotal)

    psngTaxes = csngPercentTax * psngSubtotal
    lblTaxes.Caption = Format(psngTaxes, "Currency")
    lblDiscount.Caption = Format(psngDiscount * -1, _
        "Currency")
    lblTotal.Caption = Format(psngSubtotal + psngTaxes _
        + msngDelivery - psngDiscount, "Currency")
End Sub
```

The first new statement declares a local variable to hold the discount amount.

The second new statement calls the ComputeDiscount function and stores the result in the local variable psngDiscount. Remember that you declared the function to accept one argument, a Single, and returns a Single. Thus you used a variable containing the order subtotal as the function's argument and stored the result in the Single variable you just declared.

The next statement formats the variable and places it in the Label object's caption. The value is multiplied by -1 so it will be displayed as a negative number.

The addition to the final statement subtracts the discount amount from the order total.

You now should test the program to be sure the program is working correctly. Note that depending on the time of day, you may need to modify temporarily your If statement to a different time.

To test the discount:

1. Save the project.

2. Start the program and enter order values.

TROUBLE? If the discount does not appear surrounded by brackets indicating a negative number, end the program and be sure that the code that places the discount in lblDiscount's caption multiplies the discount amount by –1, then repeat Step 2.

TROUBLE? If the discount amount is not being subtracted from the order total, end the program and be sure that you added "- psngDiscount" to the statement that places the order total in lblTotal's caption.

> **TROUBLE?** If the discount does not appear, the current time of day probably is not included within the hours 1 A.M. and 8 A.M.; temporarily modify your If statement so it includes the current time of day.
>
> **3.** End the program.

Now that you have written the statements to compute the order discount, if applicable, you can proceed to program the Print and Clear command buttons.

Printing a Form Image

As part of the design specifications, the cash register program must be able to print each order to the default printer. To do this, you need to call a method of the Form object called **PrintForm**. The PrintForm method has the following syntax:

formname.**PrintForm**

- The **PrintForm** method prints an image of a form, as it appears on the screen.
- If *formname* is omitted, the current form is printed. If *formname* is specified, that form is printed.

Before calling this method, you must write the code for the Print command button that, when clicked, will print the form.

Creating a Command Button with Graphical Images

Gill would like to continue to use graphical pictures in all the buttons so the program has a consistent visual appearance. The CommandButton control will let you display a picture like the Image control. The command button, however, will let you display different pictures depending on the state of the control. To display pictures in a command button, you must learn about some new properties:

- The **DisabledPicture** property defines the picture displayed while the button is disabled and the Enabled property is False.
- The **DownPicture** property defines the picture displayed while the button is being clicked.
- The **Picture** property displays the bitmap or other picture when the button is enabled but not depressed.
- The **Style** property has two settings. When set to **0 - Standard**, the control displays the text stored in the Caption property as you have done before. When set to **1 - Graphical**, the control displays different graphical pictures depending on the state of the control. If a caption exists, it will be displayed in the command button along with the appropriate picture.

You now are ready to set the properties for the cmdPrint command button so it will display an image of a printer.

To display a picture in the cmdPrint command button:

1. Remove the text from the **Caption** property and set the Style property to **1 - Graphical**.

2. Set the Picture property to **A:\Tutorial.03\ImgPrint.bmp**; the name of the bitmap image on your Student Disk. Notice that the image will appear in the command button.

> **3.** Open the Code window to the cmdPrint object's Click event then enter the following statement in the **Code** window:
>
> **frmMasterCashRegister.PrintForm**

This statement prints the form named frmMasterCashRegister to the printer. Because this is the current form, the statement could have been written as:

```
PrintForm
```

In addition to the cmdPrint command button, Gill created a button to set up the cash register for a new order. This button, when clicked, must uncheck each check box, then set the quantity ordered (stored in the Value property of each scroll bar) to 0. Finally, you need to set the option button corresponding to the Eat In delivery status to True so that appears selected.

To program the cmdClearOrder command button:

> **1.** Remove the text from the **Caption** property and set the Style property to **1 - Graphical**.
>
> **2.** Set the Picture property to **A:\Tutorial.03\ImgClear.bmp**; the name of the bitmap image on your Student Disk. Notice that the image will appear in the command button.
>
> **3.** Enter the following statements into the **Click** event procedure for the command button named cmdClearOrder:
>
> ```
> chkBurger.Value = vbUnchecked
> chkFrenchFries.Value = vbUnchecked
> chkSoftDrink.Value = vbUnchecked
> optDelivery(3).Value = True
> ```

The first three statements uncheck each of the check boxes. Remember the code you wrote for each check box's Click event to change the value of the scroll bars and make the scroll bars and corresponding labels invisible.

Because a Click event occurs whenever the value of a scroll bar changes, or the object is clicked explicitly, you do not have to clear explicitly the scroll bars to anything else. The code to respond to the different events already performs all the necessary tasks for you.

Because the option button corresponding to the Eat In delivery status has an Index value of 3, you set the Value property of this option button to True. This will cause this button to be selected. You have completed programming the Print and Clear command buttons. You now should test that these buttons are working properly.

To test the Print and Clear command buttons:

> **1.** Save the project and then start the program.
>
> **2.** Enter an order.
>
> **3.** Click the **Print** button on the form. The form should be printed on the default printer.
>
> **4.** Click the **Clear** button on the form. The order total, taxes, and discount should be set to 0 (zero), the labels and scroll bars should be invisible, and the Eat-In option button should be selected.

The final step in the cash register program is to program the stop program icon. When clicked, a message should be displayed asking the user if they actually want to exit the program or continue processing.

Creating a String Variable

In this session you need to display a message to verify that the clerk intended to exit the cash register program. Until now, you have not created a variable to contain text. The data type for a variable that contains text is String. You declare **String variables** using the Dim and Private statements just like Single and Integer numbers. There are two types of strings: fixed-length strings, which always store the same number of characters, and variable-length strings, which can store strings of different sizes. In this session you will store text strings of different lengths into String variables and the number of characters in the String variable will change at run time. Thus you will use variable-length strings.

When you assign text to the string, you surround the text in quotation marks. Just as you can perform operations on numbers, you also can perform operations on text strings. For example, you can append the contents of one string to another. This process is called **concatenation.** You concatenate strings together using the ampersand (&) operator. The following statement will concatenate two strings and store the result in the variable pstrPrompt2. Notice that a space character is stored between Gill and Clark.

```
pstrPrompt2 = "Gill" & " " & "Clark"
```

The variable pstrPrompt2 contains the string "Gill Clark". Every character in a string can be represented by a number between 0 and 255 or by a Visual Basic key code constant. The first 128 characters conform to a standard set of characters known as ASCII and represent all the standard characters on a keyboard. The other 128 characters are used for special characters and symbols. For example, a space is represented by the number 32 or by the constant, vbKeySpace. The KeyCodeConstants class in the Object Browser lists each of these constants. You also can refer to the Naming Appendix on your Student Disk for a chart of all ASCII characters and the corresponding KeyCodeConstants.

To use the numbers or constants as characters in a string, you must use the String function called Chr, which has the following syntax:

Chr(*charcode*)

- The function **Chr** converts a number or a key code constant into a character in a string.

- The charcode argument is a long integer between 0 and 255 or any valid Visual Basic constant defined by KeyCodeConstants.

Part of the ASCII character or key code constant set contains codes for characters that are not displayed on the screen. There are characters that perform special actions like starting a new line or inserting a tab. For example, a line feed character, represented by the number 13 causes the cursor to advance to the first column of the next line. You can use the return character to display a descriptive message on multiple lines. For example, the following statement will store the following sentences on two lines by embedding a return character between the two strings:

```
pstrPrompt = "You are about to exit the cash register." & _
    Chr(vbKeyReturn) & _
    "Are you sure you want to do this?"
```

The sentence enclosed in the first set of quotation marks will appear first in the variable, then the concatenation character, &, adds the return character, Chr(vbKeyReturn), to the string of text. The text within the second set of quotation marks will appear on a new line of text; this text also is joined by the concatenation operator. The following code would perform the same operation using the ASCII character code in place of the key code constants.

```
pstrPrompt = "You are about to exit the cash register." & _
    Chr(13) & _
    "Are you sure you want to do this?"
```

Displaying a Multiline Message in a Message Box

To prevent the program from exiting if a clerk accidentally clicks the stop sign image, Gill wants the program to display a message in a dialog box asking the clerk to confirm exiting the program. The dialog box will include a Yes button for exiting the program and a No button for not exiting it. Visual Basic supports a standard dialog box called a **message box** that will display a message, an icon to identify the importance of the message, and a standard set of buttons, like a Yes button and No Button or an OK button.

Based on the value returned, the program will use an If statement to determine whether or not the clerk wants to continue using the cash register program or exit it. The MsgBox function accepts arguments to control the message displayed in the box (prompt), any icons that can be displayed (buttons), and the caption for the message box (title). The MsgBox function has the following syntax:

MsgBox(*prompt*[, *attributes*][, *title*])

- The **MsgBox** function displays a message box.

- The *prompt* is a string expression that controls the text displayed in the message box. This text is sent to the MsgBox function as an argument. The maximum number of characters allowed in a prompt is 1024. You can create the arguments for the text using String variables.

- The *attributes* argument is an expression containing intrinsic constants that define the behavior of the message box. The vbMsgBoxStyle class in the Object Browser lists each of these constants.

- You can include a *title* for the message box, which appears in the title bar of the message box in the same way as the form's Caption property.

Gill suggests that you use the online Help system to learn more about the MsgBox function.

To view information about the MsgBox function using Help:

1. Start the online Help system and use the **Index** tab to search for **MsgBox function**.

2. Print a copy of the Help page and close Help.

The first group of constants, those with the values 0 through 5, determines the buttons that appear in the message box. Notice that the constant to display a message box with Yes and No buttons can be represented either by the constant vbYesNo or the value 4. Inside the message box, you can include one of several different icons to help communicate the importance of the message. The second group of constants, those with the values 16 through 64, identifies the corresponding icons.

Tip: You should carefully consider which icon to display in a message box. If you are asking a question, display a Warning Query icon using the vbQuestion constant. Use the Critical Message icon (vbCritical) to indicate only very serious problems or consequences. Use the Warning Message icon (vbExclamation) for less critical problems. Use the Information Message icon (vbInformation) when you are explaining something.

You can use one of three constants from the third group to define which button is the default. Pressing the Enter key as an alternative to clicking the button can activate the button assigned as the default. These constants are named vbDefaultButton1, vbDefaultButton2, vbDefaultButton3, and vbDefaultButton4. They correspond to the first, second, third, and fourth buttons in the message box. Assigning a default button is optional; if a default button does not make sense in your program, do not set a default value.

One constant from each group is added together to make up the attributes argument. If you do not want to select an item from a group, just omit the constant. Now you are ready to write the code for the message box that will appear when a clerk clicks the stop sign to exit the cash register program. The Warning Query message box will ask the clerk to confirm exiting the program. You will set No as the default button to minimize the possibility of accidentally exiting the cash register program.

To add a message box to the cash register program:

1. Open the Code window for the **imgStop_Click** event procedure and enter the following code:

```
Private Sub imgStop_Click()
    'Create arguments for MsgBox function.
    Dim pintAnswer As Integer
    Dim pstrPrompt As String
    Dim pintAttributes As Integer
    Dim pstrTitle As String

    'Set the values for the arguments.
    pstrPrompt = _
        "You are about to exit the cash register." & _
        Chr(vbKeyReturn) & _
        "Are you sure you want to do this?"
    pintAttributes = vbYesNo + vbQuestion + _
        vbDefaultButton2
    pstrTitle = "Cash Register"

    'Call the MsgBox function.
    pintAnswer = MsgBox(pstrPrompt, pintAttributes, _
        pstrTitle)

    'Test which button the user clicked.
    If pintAnswer = vbYes Then
        End
    End If
End Sub
```

The local variables will contain the returned value and arguments in preparation for calling the MsgBox function.

The attributes argument pintAttributes creates a message box with a Yes button and a No button and a Warning Query icon, and sets the No button as the default.

The Title statement sets the title of the message box to Cash Register. Finally, the MsgBox function is called and the returned value is tested to find out which button the clerk clicked.

Gill asks you to test the program again to make sure the message box works properly and the program is ending normally.

To test the message box function:

1. Save the project and then start the program.

2. End the program by clicking the **stop sign** image. The message box in Figure 3-26 opens.

Figure 3-26 ◀
Message box

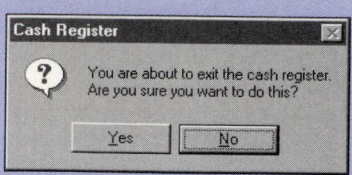

3. Click the **No** button to continue running the cash register program.

4. Continue to test that the **Yes** button ends the program.

TROUBLE? If the message box does not open, end the program, and compare the code for the imgStop object with the code in the previous steps. Make the necessary corrections, then repeat Steps 1 through 4.

5. Exit Visual Basic.

You now have completed the cash register program. It takes advantage of several different events to keep the extended price of items and the order totals up to date without making the user click a command button to recompute these values. Also, it satisfies the design requirements of using only controls that can operate without keyboard input. Gill is pleased with the prototype cash register and presents it to senior management.

1. What is a frame?

2. What is the relationship between a frame and a group of option buttons?

3. Write a statement to concatenate two strings "Do you want to" and "continue" displayed on separate lines. Store the result in a String variable named pstrPrompt.

4. Describe the difference between an If statement and a Select Case statement.

5. What is a control array?

6. What is the difference between a Function procedure and a Sub procedure?

7. Describe how message boxes are used in a program.

8. What is the purpose of logical operators?

Figure 3-27 lists and defines the new terms presented in this tutorial.

Figure 3-27 ◀
New terms

Term	Definition
Boolean variable	A Boolean variable is a variable that can have the value True or False. A Boolean variable operates like an on/off switch; True signifies on and False signifies off.
Comparison operators	Comparison operators are used to test whether or not a conditional statement is True or False. They are made up of equal to (=), not equal to (<>), less than (<), greater than (>), less than or equal to (<=), greater than or equal to (>=), or contains the string (Like).
Concatenation	Concatenation is the process of appending one string to another using the ampersand (&) operator.
Conditional statement	A conditional statement is a statement that is used to execute one series of statement when a condition is True and another statement when a condition is False. The If statement is an example of a conditional statement.
Control array	A control array is a term used to describe multiple objects that have the same name and event procedure. You reference the members of a control array using the object's name and its Index property.
Function procedure	A function procedure is a type of general procedure that performs a task using arguments supplied to the function, then processes those arguments. When complete, it returns a value to the calling procedure. The value returned by the function procedure is always of the same data type. Function procedures commonly are referred to as functions.
General procedure	A general procedure, like an event procedure, contains Visual Basic statements to perform some task. Unlike an event procedure, however, a general procedure is not called by the system in response to an event. Rather, you must explicitly call a general procedure.
Logical operators	Logical operators connect expressions together much like conjunctions connect sentences together in English. Logical operators consist of And, Or, Xor and Not.
Message box	A message box is used to open a pop-up message window. The user can click one of several buttons. A message box is displayed on the screen when the MsgBox function is called.
Option group	An option group is a way of creating option buttons so that only one button of the group may be selected at a time. This is accomplished by creating a frame, then creating each option button in the frame.
Radio button	A radio button is a common name for the option buttons contained in an option group. The name comes from the notion of the buttons on a car radio; only one button can be selected at a time.
String variable	A string variable is a data type that stores one or more characters.
Sub procedure	A Sub procedure is a type of general procedure that performs a task using arguments supplied to the function, then processes those arguments. It does not return a value when complete. Sub procedures commonly are referred to as subroutines.

Tutorial Assignments

Each Master Burger franchise has eight tables available for customers. In these Tutorial Assignments, you will create a program that clerks will use to determine if a table is occupied or needs cleaning, and what, if any, condiments are needed at the table. This information and the time of day needs to be recorded in the text boxes that represent each table.

When placing an eat-in order, the clerk assigns an available table to the customer and sets the table status to "Occupied". When the customer leaves, the table status is changed to "Needs cleaning". After it has been cleaned, the table status is "Clean". The clerk also can designate any condiments that are running low at a table. At Master Burger, table settings include the following condiments: catsup, mustard, salt, and pepper.

In the seating chart program, each table will have a table number from 1 to 8 and will be part of a TextBox control array that can display multiple scrollable lines. Table numbers will be selected with a vertical scroll bar. The status will be written to the current table's text box with the current date and time when a status change occurs. Because more than one condiment can be needed at the same time, the clerk will click one or more check boxes indicating the condiments needed, then click the Write table needs button to write a line containing the date and time. The program also will include a stop sign image that will exit the program. Figure 3-28 shows the completed user interface for the seating chart program.

Figure 3-28 ◀

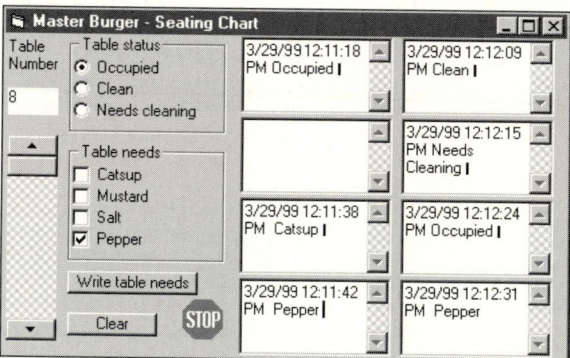

1. Make sure your Student Disk is in the appropriate disk drive, then start Visual Basic.

2. Change the form's caption to **Master Burger - Seating Chart** and change its name to **frmMasterSeatingChart**.

3. Draw the first of eight text boxes for the Tables control array, then remove the initial text and set the name to **txtTable**. The text box should be able to display multiple lines of text and contain vertical scroll bars.

4. Copy and paste seven more text boxes for the control array on the form. Be sure that you answer **Yes** in the message box asking if you want to create a control array.

5. Draw two frames on the form to hold the option buttons and check boxes. Set the caption for each frame as shown in Figure 3-28. Because you will not write code to reference the Frame objects, you do not need to set the Name property.

6. Draw the first option button of the control array in the frame, then set its name to **optTableStatus** and its caption to **Occupied**. Copy and paste the option button to create the remaining two option buttons in the control array and set the captions as shown in Figure 3-28. Remember to select the frame before you paste, or the object will be contained by the form rather than the frame, and to answer **Yes** in the message box asking if you want to create a control array.

7. Create a control array of four check boxes named **chkTableNeeds** inside the second frame. Be sure to set the captions as shown in Figure 3-28.

8. Draw a vertical scroll bar to the left of the frames and set the name to **vsbTableNumber**. The range of valid values should be between **1** and **8**. As the scroll bar is moved upward, the value should increase.

9. Draw a label to display the table number, then set its Name property to **lblTableNumber**. Change the background color to white. Clear the caption; the caption will be set at run time by the scroll bar.

10. Draw a label above lblTableNumber and set its Caption property to **Table Number**.

11. Draw two command buttons on the form as shown in Figure 3-28. Set the names to **cmdWriteTableNeeds** and **cmdClear**, respectively, and set the captions for each command button. Be sure also to create a ToolTip.

12. Draw an image on the form that holds the **stop.ico** file in the **TAssign** folder in the **Tutorial.03** folder on your Student Disk. Name the image **imgExit**, then write the code for a typical program exit. Set the Stretch property so the file will be sized to the image you drew on the form.

13. In the general declarations section in the Form Module, require that all variables be declared explicitly.

14. Create a Sub procedure named WriteTableNeeds that will accept two arguments named **pintTable** (the current table number displayed in the Table Number label) and **pstrTableNeeds** (the condiments checked in the Table needs frame). This Sub procedure will be used to display the message in a corresponding text box.

15. Enter code into the procedure that will:

   ■ Use pintTable as the Index argument for the txtTable control array. This will allow you to reference the current table.

   ■ Set the Text property of txtTable to a text string that includes: the current date and time with the Now function, then a space, then the pstrTableNeeds variable, then another space, then the current Text property of txtTable. This will cause the most current entry to appear at the beginning of the text box.

16. Open the Code window for the optTableStatus_Click event and declare a variable named **pstrTableStatus**. You will use this string to hold a text string identifying the current status of the table.

17. Write a Select Case statement that will set the variable **pstrTableStatus** to the text **Occupied**, **Clean**, or **Needs cleaning**, depending on which option button is checked.

18. Add the following statement to call the WriteTableNeeds function, with the current table number as the first argument and the message as the second argument, after computing pstrTableStatus. Note that you need to subtract one (1) from the value of the scroll bar because the scroll bar begins numbering at one (1) while the function you just wrote loads a control array of text boxes indexed from zero (0).

```
WriteTableStatus (vsbTableNumber.Value -1), _
    pstrTableStatus
```

19. Activate the cmdWriteTableNeeds_Click event procedure, then create the following If statement to call the WriteTableNeeds function using the current table number and the catsup condiment as arguments.

```
If chkTableNeeds(0) = vbChecked Then
    WriteTableNeeds (vsbTableNumber.Value - 1), _
    "Catsup"
End If
```

20. Write the necessary If statements to write a message for the other three check boxes. Be sure to change the check box's argument to the correct index and the text string to the correct condiment each time.

21. Write the necessary statements to clear the active option button and uncheck each of the check boxes. *Hint:* You need to set the Value property.

22. Set the caption of lblTableNumber so it holds the value of the scroll bar each time the scroll bar value changes.

23. Save the form as **frmSeatingChart.frm** in the **TAssign** folder in the **Tutorial.03** folder on your Student Disk. Save the project as **Master Seating Chart.vbp** in the same folder.

24. Test the program by selecting a table number, a table status, and table needs and clicking the Write table needs command button. Be sure to test different tables, different boxes, and different option buttons. Click the Clear command button to verify that the check boxes and option buttons are cleared. Exit the program using the stop sign.

25. The table number does not initially appear when you run the program. Why is this? Modify the program to display an initial value of 1 in the lblTableNumber object's caption. When you have corrected any errors and are satisfied that the program works correctly, click the stop sign to exit the program. *Hint:* When does the code move the table number to the Label object's caption?

26. Examine the code in WriteTableNeeds general procedure. On a piece of paper, write down the purpose of each block of code and describe how it performs its function.

27. Save the form and project again. Print the form and the code. Exit Visual Basic.

Case Problems

1. Easy Carpet Emporium Easy Carpet Emporium stores specialize in low-cost home carpeting. The company would like a carpet selecting program that its customers can use to select the color, fabric, and pile of carpeting after looking through the samples in the store. This system will allow Easy Carpet to have only one salesperson on the floor to process the order after it has been entered into the computer by the customer.

In response to the customer clicking the Select button, the carpet selector program will clear any existing text from the text box, examine the option buttons the customer has checked, and then build a text string describing the carpet in a text box.

The NEADT chart for the carpet selector program is stored on your Student Disk in the **Cases** folder in the **Tutorial.03** folder. First you will print the design specifications and then create a sample program for Easy Carpet to use as a prototype in one of their stores. When you are finished, the program's user interface should look like Figure 3-29.

Figure 3-29 ◀

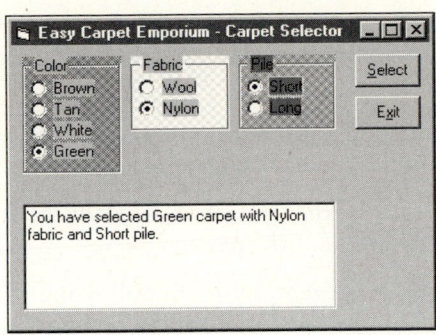

1. Make sure your Student Disk is in the appropriate disk drive. Using Microsoft Word open and print the NEADT chart stored in the file **Easy.doc**, in the **Cases** folder in the **Tutorial.03** folder on your Student Disk. If you do not have Word, use WordPad to print the file **Easy.txt**. Close the word processing program.

2. Start Visual Basic and begin a new project, if necessary. Set the form's Name property to **frmEasyCarpetSelector** and its Caption property to **Easy Carpet Emporium - Carpet Selector**.

3. Create a frame for the Color options, then set the caption to **Color**, and the background color to **light blue**.

4. Create a control array of four option buttons in the Color frame. Name the option buttons **optColor**, change the background color to **light blue**, and set the Caption property of the option buttons to **Brown, Tan, White**, and **Green**, respectively. Make sure that you select the frame after you copy the first option button and before you paste each subsequent option button; otherwise the option group will not work correctly.

5. Create a frame for the Fabric options, then set the caption to **Fabric**, and the background color to **light yellow**.

6. Create a control array of two option buttons in the Fabric frame. Name the option buttons **optFabric**, change the background color to **light yellow**, and set the Caption property of the option buttons to **Wool** and **Nylon**, respectively.

7. Create a frame for the Pile options, then set the caption to **Pile**, and the background color to **orange**.

8. In the Pile frame, create a control array of two option buttons. Name the option buttons **optPile**, change the background color to **orange**, and set the Caption property to **Short** and **Long**, respectively.

9. Create a text box to display the customer's selection, then set the name to **txtCarpet**. The text box should display multiple lines of text. Clear the initial text.

10. Create a command button at the right of the form named **cmdSelect** and set the caption as shown in Figure 3-29. Use **S** as the hot key for the Select command button.

11. Draw an Exit command button below the Select command button, then write the code for a typical program exit. Use **X** as the hot key for the Exit command button.

12. In the general declarations section in the Form module, declare the variables **mintIndexColor**, **mintIndexFabric**, and **mintIndexPile** that will preserve the local variable Index that is passed to each of the option button's procedures for use in the text box. Require that all variables be declared before they can be used in code.

13. Open the Code window for the optColor_Click event and type the statement that will assign the local optColor variable Index as a form-level variable mintIndexColor.

14. Repeat Step 13 for the other two option buttons' Click events, using the variable names defined in the general declarations section.

15. Open the Code window for the cmdSelect_Click event and write the statement to remove the contents of the text box.

16. Still in the cmdSelect_Click event, write the following If statement to verify that one button from each in the optColor option group is selected. Note that when the Exit Sub statement is reached, the procedure exits and no more statements in the procedure will executed.

```
If mintIndexColor = -1 Then
    MsgBox ("Select a color")
Exit Sub
End If
```

17. Write If statements to check that selections were made for the other two option groups and display an applicable message.

18. Create a string that will store the carpet selection information in a string like the following:

> You have selected *optColor(mintIndexColor).Caption*
> carpet with *optFabric(mintIndexFabric).Caption* fabric and
> *optPile(mintIndexPile).Caption* pile.

Hint: Remember to use the concatenation character to combine text strings you enclose in quotation marks and the option button captions. Figure 3-29 shows a sample string.

19. Store the contents of the variable pstrOutput into the text box.

20. Clear the Color option buttons by setting the Index variables back to -1 (no option button selected) using the following code:

```
optColor(mintIndexColor).Value = False
mintIndexColor = -1
```

21. Repeat the statements for the other two option groups.

22. Save the form as **frmCarpetSelector.frm** and save the project as **Easy Carpet Selector.vbp** in the **Cases** folder in the **Tutorial.03** folder on your Student Disk.

23. Test the program. When you have corrected any errors and are satisfied that the program works correctly, click the Exit button.

24. Print the Code and Form Image. Exit Visual Basic.

2. Nutrition Foods Nutrition Foods is a national chain of health food stores. They specialize in pesticide-free and artificial-fertilizer-free fruits and vegetables.

Nutrition Foods franchises allow one group manager to be in charge of up to four franchises. Each group manager receives a commission based on the overall sales of the franchises to which the manager is assigned. Nutrition Foods would like a calculator program to compute automatically the commission for each group manager.

The calculator program will include labels to identify and display the sales for each region, the commission, the total commission, and the total sales; scroll bars to enter the sales amounts in $100 increments; and a command button to exit the program.

The labels identifying and displaying the sales for each region will be a control array, as will the scroll bars for entering the sales amounts.

Each time a scroll bar's Change event occurs, the program will recalculate automatically the total commission and the total sales amounts in the appropriate labels. The manager's commission is paid at the following rates:

- For Sales < $5000, Commission = 0

- For Sales >= $5,000 and <= $50,000, Commission = 1% of Sales

- For Sales > $50,000 and < $250,000, Commission = 2% of Sales

- For Sales >= $250,000, Commission = 3% of Sales

Figure 3-30 shows the completed user interface.

Figure 3-30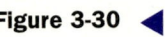

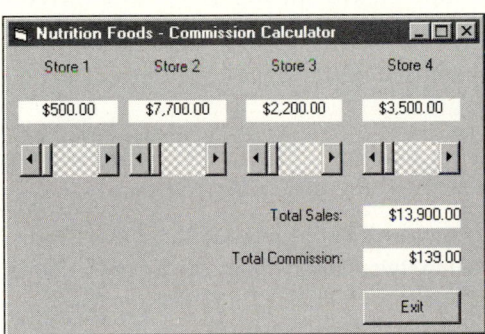

1. Make sure your Student Disk is in the appropriate disk drive. Start Visual Basic and begin a new project, if necessary.

2. Set the form's name to **frmNutritionCommissionCalculator** and its caption to **Nutrition Foods - Commission Calculator.**

3. Create four labels across the top of the form and set their captions to **Store 1, Store 2, Store 3**, and **Store 4**, respectively. Align the text in the center of the labels.

4. Create a control array of four labels below the store number labels, and set the name to **lblRegionSales**, set the background color to **white**, and remove the text from the caption.

5. Create a control array of four horizontal scroll bars below the Label control array such that the smallest value, 0, is at the left of the scroll bar, and the largest value, 10000, is at the right. Name the object **hsbRegionSales**. Recall that you were asked that the sales be entered in $100 increments; later, you will multiply the scroll bar value by 100.

6. Create two identifying labels below the Store 3 column and set the captions to **Total Sales** and **Total Commission**, respectively.

7. Create two output labels below the Store 4 column, and set their properties to **lblTotalSales** and **lblTotalCommission**, respectively; set the background color to **white**; and remove the text from the caption.

8. Create an Exit command button with the appropriate code to end the program, in the lower-right corner of the form.

9. Open the Code window for the hsbRegionSales control array's Change event and declare the following variables: **plngSubtotal** will hold the subtotal of the sales for each region, and **psngCommissionPercent** will calculate and hold the percentage of sales the group manager has earned.

10. Open the Code window for the hsbRegionSales control array's Change event. Type the code that will set each lblRegionSales object's Caption property to the value of its corresponding scroll bar multiplied by 100 and format it as Currency. *Hint*: You need to use the Index argument to reference the correct label and scroll bar.

11. After you have set the caption of the lblRegionSales object, calculate plngSubtotal by adding together the value of each scroll bar and multiplying the sum by 100. *Hint*: You need to use the index of each scroll bar in the control array and the Value property.

12. Write an If statement to calculate the commission. Using the variable plngSubtotal, which you computed in Step 11, test the amount against the sales amount to determine the commission rate. Store the commission rate in the variable psngCommissionPercent.

13. Write the statement that will format plngSubtotal as currency and place it in the caption of lblTotalSales.

14. Write the statement that will calculate the commission and store the result in the Caption property of lblTotalCommission.

15. Save the form as **frmNutritionCommissionCalculator1.frm** and the project as **Nutrition Commission Calculator1.vbp** in the **Cases** folder in the **Tutorial.03** folder on your Student Disk.

16. Test the program by clicking each ScrollBar object and observing the results in the Total Commission and Total Sales labels. Verify with a calculator that the commission rules are being applied correctly. When you are satisfied that the program works correctly, click the Exit button.

17. Print the Form Image and the Code.

18. Change the If statement in the hsbRegionSales code to a Select Case statement and test the program.

19. Save the form as **frmCommissionCalculator2.frm** and the project as **Nutrition Commission Calculator 2.vbp** in the **Cases** folder in the **Tutorial.03** folder on your Student Disk. Print the Form Image and the Code. Exit Visual Basic.

3. Williams Lumber Company   Williams Lumber Company sells a variety of lumber products to contractors in Dallas Texas. Most lumber, like 2 × 4's, 2 × 6's, and 2 × 8's are sold in fixed lengths, like 8', 10', 12', and 14', but are priced by the foot. The company would like you to create a program to determine the total feet and total cost for each type of lumber. Your form should be divided into an input and output section using two shapes. The input area needs a label for the customer name and a corresponding text box. You need to create three check boxes for the different types of lumber— 2 × 4, 2 × 6, and 2 × 8. Each product is sold in four lengths—8', 10', 12', and 14'. You need to create a check box for each length of each product. The programming process will be easier if you use a control array for each procedure length. Thus, you will have a control array of check boxes for the lengths of 2 × 4's, another for 2 × 6's, and another for 2 × 8's. Each check box needs to have a corresponding text box to specify quantity desired. These also should be created as control arrays. All the orders are delivered to one of four areas. The charge for delivery is based on the number of feet delivered and the delivery zone as follows:

- 1 to 499 feet = $10.00

- 500 to 999 feet = $20.00

- 1000 to 2000 feet = $30.00

- more than 2000 feet = $40.00

Add to these charges $10.00 for Delivery Area 1, $20.00 for Delivery Area 2, $30.00 for Delivery Area 3, and $40.00 for Delivery Area 4.

In the output section of the form, create labels to hold the number of feet of each product and the total cost. You will need another label to hold the delivery charge and the order total.

The charge for lumber is based on the number of feet ordered as follows:

- 2 × 4 = $0.16/foot

- 2 × 6 = $0.22/foot

- 2 × 8 = $0.31/foot

You should use constants for these values.

Your program needs three command buttons. One to compute the order total based on the input, another to clear each of the input and output fields in preparation for a new order, and an Exit button. Figure 3-31 shows the completed user interface for the program.

Figure 3-31 ◄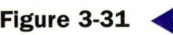

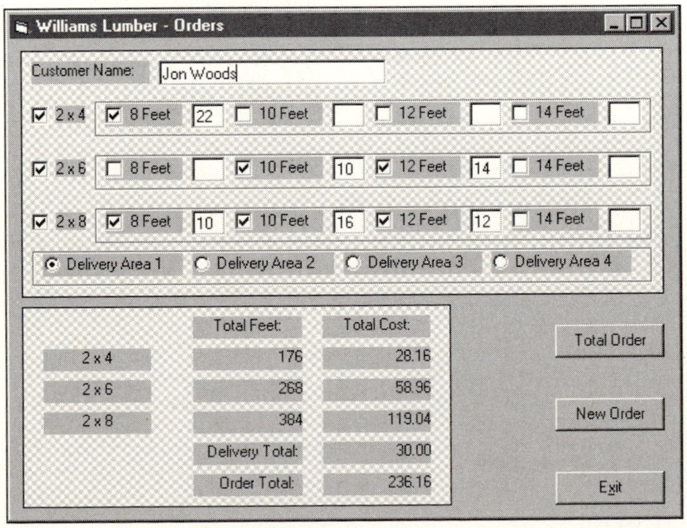

4. Ms. Phillips Grading Calculator This case problem is an extension of Case Problem 4 of Tutorial 2. One of your former teachers, Ms. Phillips, wants a program that will take in the name of a student and the student's three test scores from the term. The program then will calculate the average score and assign a letter grade based on the following ranges: A >= 90, B = 79 to 89, C = 69 to 78, D = 59 to 68, F < 59. Create the calculator program using the Select Case statement to assign a letter grade based on the average. Display the result in a label in response to the Click event for a Calculate command button. Also include a Clear button to clear the text and captions of all the necessary objects before the input of data for another student, set the focus back to the student's name, and code an Exit button. The code for the Exit button should display a message box asking Ms. Phillips if she wants to exit the program. Check to ensure that your input objects have the correct tab order. Print the Form Image and the Code. Save the form as **frmPhillipsGradingCalculator** and the project as **Phillips Grading Calculator.vbp** in the Cases folder in the **Tutorial.03** folder on your Student Disk.

Creating a Program to Manage Data

Developing a Contact Management System for Atlantic Marketing

OBJECTIVES

In this tutorial you will:

- Add a menu system to a program

- Connect to a database with a Data control

- Set properties of controls to interact with a database

- Write Visual Basic code to locate, add, change, and delete information in a database

- Locate records in a database using a search string

- Validate user input

- Write Visual Basic code to detect errors that occur while a program is running

CASE

Atlantic Marketing

Atlantic Marketing, headquartered in Egan, Minnesota, has been providing marketing services to companies in the greater Minneapolis/St. Paul area since 1978. The sales staff of Atlantic Marketing currently use a paper-based contact management system to keep track of a clients' name, telephone number, estimated sales, and notes describing the interaction between each client and the sales force. Each client also is assigned a unique client ID number. The current contact management system consists of a paper form for each client. Each salesperson keeps these forms in a binder, sorted by the client's last name; notes describing each interaction with the client are also written on the form. Because Atlantic Marketing now has more than 1,000 clients and approximately 2,500 prospective clients, the current paper-based system has become slow and burdensome.

Nina Valenza, a programmer for Atlantic Marketing, was asked to develop a program to automate the contact management system. Nina decided to use Visual Basic together with a Microsoft Access database to manage the information. A database makes any program that needs to manage large quantities of data much simpler to write. The contact management system must be able to store each client's name, ID number, telephone number, the date added, estimated sales, and client notes—all sorted by the client's last name. The system must operate with infinite clients and simplify client retrieval. A salesperson must be able to add, change, and remove clients from the database. Nina already has created the Access database, test data, and a form containing the necessary objects. You will help her complete the contact management system.

SESSION

4.1

In this session you will create a menu system containing items that will allow users to add, change, and delete records from a database file, locate different records in the database, and exit the program. You also will learn how to write code that will execute when a menu item is clicked.

Viewing the Program Documentation

Nina planned the contact management system based on the current paper form, which is shown in Figure 4-1.

Figure 4-1 ◀
Paper contact
management
form

> **Atlantic Marketing**
> **Contact Management Form**
>
> **Last Name:**   Allen   **Telephone Number:** (208) 555-7986
>
> **First Name:**   Mary   **Date Added**:   3/22/99
>
> **Client ID**   3   **Estimated Annual Sales:** $4200.00
>
> Notes:
>
> 3/22/99 Referred by John Alexander. Client sells sporting equipment to the upscale buyer. Looking for a comprehensive marketing program to increase sales to the midrange buyer.
>
> 4/7/99 First meeting with Mary. She wants a preliminary plan and proposal by 5/15.
>
> 5/13/99 Delivered and presented proposal. Will convene with senior management.

The paper form contains a client's name and ID number, telephone number, date added, and estimated annual sales revenue. There are several lines on the form to allow a salesperson to record notes. Nina has completed the NEADT charts for the contact management system. She suggests you review the design specifications so you can familiarize yourself with the project. The NEADT charts are stored in the file AM_CMS.doc on your Student Disk.

To view and print the NEADT charts for the contact management system:

1. Make sure your Student Disk is in the appropriate disk drive. Using Microsoft Word, open the file named **AM_CMS.doc** located in the Tutorial.04 folder on your Student Disk. Otherwise open the file **AM_CMS.txt** using WordPad.

2. Print the file then exit the word processing program.

Look at the NEADT charts for the program. Notice you will create a program to add, change, delete, and locate client information in an Access database using commands located on a menu bar. Keep the NEADT charts on hand for reference as you complete the program. You will begin by opening the project file named AM_CMS.vbp stored on your Student Disk.

To open the project file for the contact management system:

1. Start Visual Basic and open the project file named **AM_CMS.vbp** in the Tutorial.04 folder on your Student Disk. Activate the form named **frmAtlanticContact**.

2. Save the form as **frmAtlanticContact.frm**.

3. Save the project as **Atlantic Contact.vbp**.

As you look at the form, you can see that Nina created all the labels and text boxes needed to display the information contained in the database. The form is shown in Figure 4-2.

Figure 4-2 ◀
Initial contact
management
system form

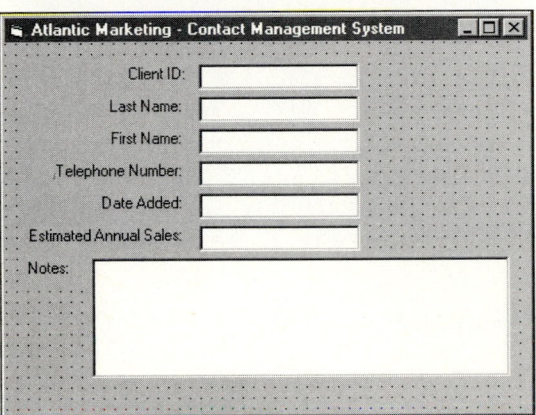

Adding Menus to a Program

Although you could use command buttons to perform the tasks in this program—printing the form; exiting the program; adding, updating, deleting, and locating client information—you will find that as programs become larger, the number of command buttons can become excessive. In fact, a form with eight or ten command buttons would cause the form to appear cluttered and disorganized. Menus can be an integral part of the user interface of a Visual Basic program and provide users with another way to complete tasks. Menus also organize user tasks. For example, the File menu includes the Print and Exit commands. The Edit menu includes the commands to add, change, and delete data in the underlying database. The Find menu will be used to locate client information. If each of these menu items were command buttons, you would need to search through several buttons to locate the correct one. Menus you create in Visual Basic function in the same way as menus in any Windows 95 program. The menus you create will allow the user to: print a copy of the form; exit the program; add, update, and delete client information; and locate different clients.

The menus you create consist of several parts. Figure 4-3 shows the anatomy of a menu.

Figure 4-3 ◀
Anatomy
of a menu

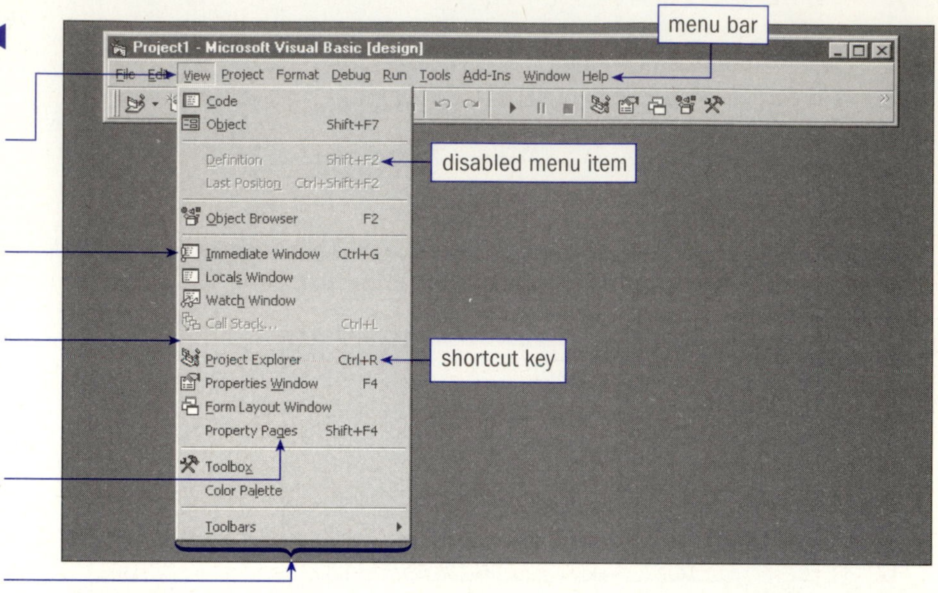

menu title

menu item

separator bar

hot key

menu

You will use the **Menu Editor** in Visual Basic to create the menu bar and menu items, as Nina requested. Each menu item has a name and caption, and can respond to a Click event procedure.

Windows 95 and Visual Basic menus support shortcut keys and hot keys (or access keys). A **shortcut key** is a function key (such as F5) or a key combination (such as Ctrl+A or Ctrl+X) that executes a command. Command buttons and menu items support shortcut keys; you cannot create a shortcut key for a menu title. A **hot key** is a key you press while holding down the Alt key to open a menu or carry out a command. For example, Alt+F opens the File menu in most Windows 95 applications.

Creating the Menu Titles for the Contact Management System

The first step in creating a menu is to create the menu titles that appear on the menu bar. Each menu title has a Caption property that contains the text the user sees on the screen. The first letter of a menu caption should be capitalized. You can create a hot key for a menu title by inserting the ampersand character (&) in the caption immediately to the left of the character you want to use as the hot key. Be careful not to specify the same hot key for two items on a menu. If you do, only the hot key for the first menu item will be recognized. Menu titles are objects and, as such, you should use the standard prefix "mnu" for the Name property followed by a descriptive name. The descriptive name should be the same as the menu's caption with any spaces removed. The program you are creating will have a single form. Because menus are bound to forms, each form in your program can have a unique menu associated with it.

CREATING A MENU SYSTEM

- Click Tools on the menu bar, then click Menu Editor to activate the Menu Editor or click the Menu Editor button on the toolbar.
- In the Caption text box, type the title for the menu or the caption of the menu item. If you want to create a hot key for the menu or menu item, place the ampersand (&) character to the left of the character to be used as the hot key.
- In the Name text box, type the name for the menu title or menu item. Each menu name must be unique and should begin with the prefix "mnu".
- If you want to create a shortcut key for the menu item, select a shortcut key from the available keys displayed in the Shortcut list box.
- Indent the menu items below their appropriate menu titles by clicking the right arrow key.
- To enter another menu title or menu item, press the Enter key or click the Next button.
- To insert a new menu title or menu item between existing entries, click the appropriate existing entry, and then click the Insert button. The new menu item will be inserted before the active entry.
- To exit the Menu Editor, click the OK button.

Nina wants you to create the menu items necessary to add, update, delete, and select different clients. The menu titles for the contact management program are File, Edit, and Find. You will write the code for all of the menus in Sessions 4.2 and 4.3.

To create the menu titles for the program:

1. Make sure the form is displayed on your screen, and is active.

2. Click the **Menu Editor** button 📄 on the toolbar to open the Menu Editor. See Figure 4-4.

Figure 4-4 ◀
Menu Editor
components

menu item properties →

menu list box →

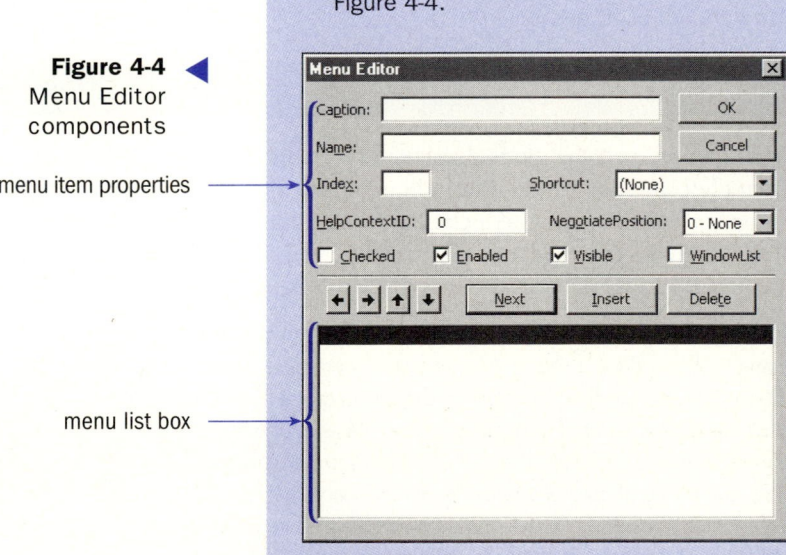

TROUBLE? If the Menu Editor button is disabled, make sure the form is the active window and then repeat Step 2. Because menus are bound to a form, the form must be active before you can open the Menu Editor. Also, the Menu Editor is available only at design time; make sure the Visual Basic title bar says [design].

3. In the Caption text box, type **&File**. The & character to the left of the letter "F" identifies Alt+F as the hot key combination for the File menu.

4. In the Name text box, type **mnuFile**. Your screen should look like Figure 4-5.

Figure 4-5 ◀
Creating the
File menu title

menu title caption —

menu title name —

menu title appears
in menu list box —

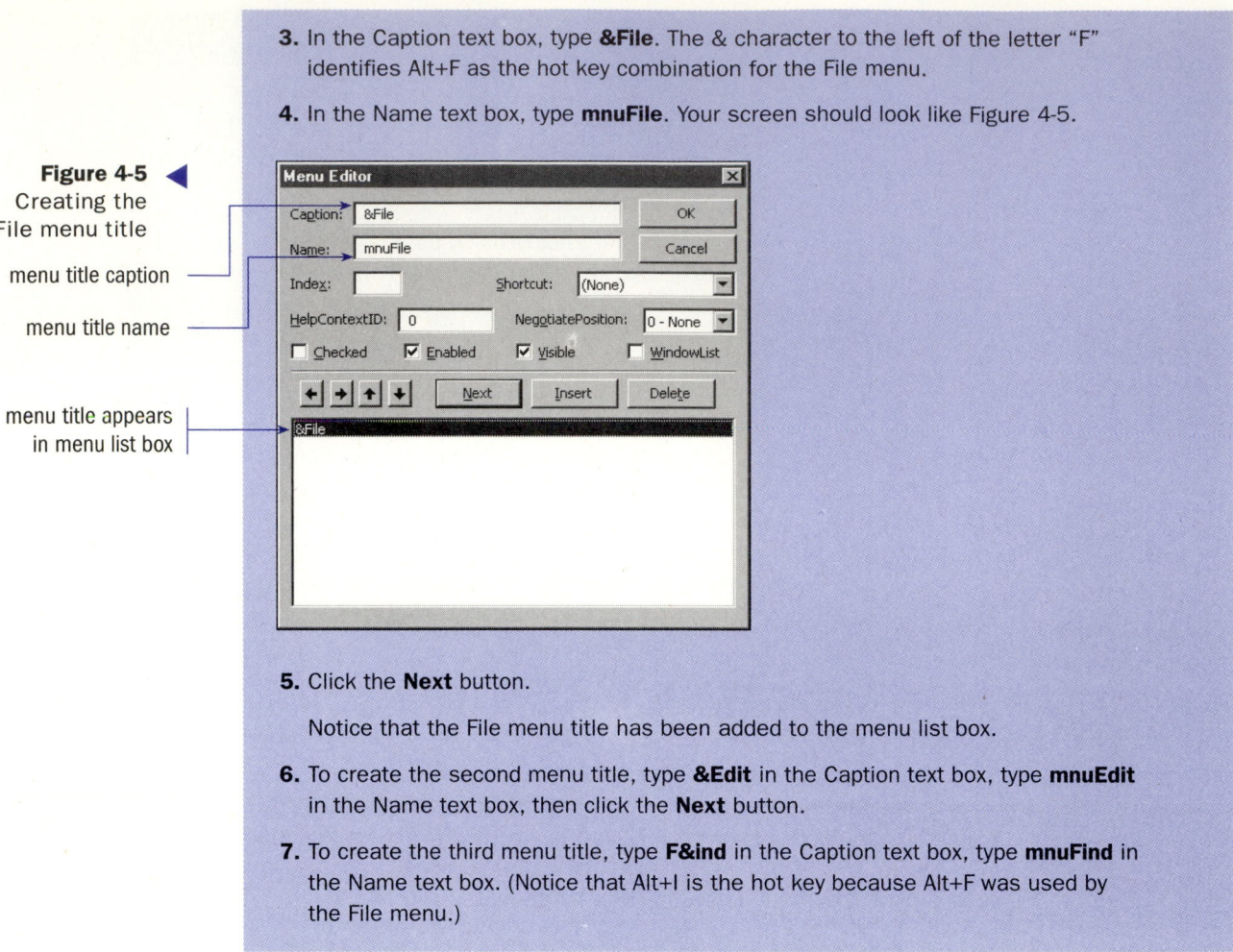

5. Click the **Next** button.

Notice that the File menu title has been added to the menu list box.

6. To create the second menu title, type **&Edit** in the Caption text box, type **mnuEdit** in the Name text box, then click the **Next** button.

7. To create the third menu title, type **F&ind** in the Caption text box, type **mnuFind** in the Name text box. (Notice that Alt+I is the hot key because Alt+F was used by the File menu.)

You have created the three menu titles for the contact management program. Your next task is to add the menu items to each menu.

Creating Menu Items

Now you must create the menus, and the items displayed on them when the user clicks on the menu title bar. When clicked, each menu item will generate a Click event and call the corresponding event procedure. This is just like clicking a command button to generate a Click event. Although the menu titles generate a Click event, you do not have to write any code to activate the menu when a menu title is clicked; Visual Basic does this for you.

> *Tip:* Several style guidelines will help you create menus that have a similar look and feel to menus in other Windows 95 programs. A menu item's caption should be short enough to appear on one line, but it can contain multiple words to convey its purpose. When menu items contain multiple words, the first letter of each word should be capitalized and each word should be separated by a space. The first letter of a menu item's caption always should be capitalized. If a menu item displays a dialog box or requires the user to complete other information, the item's name should be followed by an ellipsis (…).

You can create a hot key for a menu item with the & character, as you did for the menu titles. The name of a menu item also should begin with the prefix "mnu" and include the title of the menu on which it appears, for example, the Print menu item on the File menu will have the name "mnuFilePrint". Now you will create the Print and Exit menu items for the File menu and the menu items for the Edit menu.

To create the menu items for the File and Edit menu titles:

1. In the menu list box, click &Edit to select the Edit menu, then click the **Insert** button to insert a blank line before the Edit menu.

2. Type **&Print** in the Caption text box, then type **mnuFilePrint** in the Name text box. This sets the hot key combination to Alt+P for the Print menu item.

3. Click the **right arrow** button ◰ to change the indent level of the menu item. This causes the Print menu item to be an item on the File menu. Notice when a menu item is indented, it appears with four leading dots (....). See Figure 4-6.

Figure 4-6 ◀
Adding a
menu item

Print menu item on
File menu (indented)

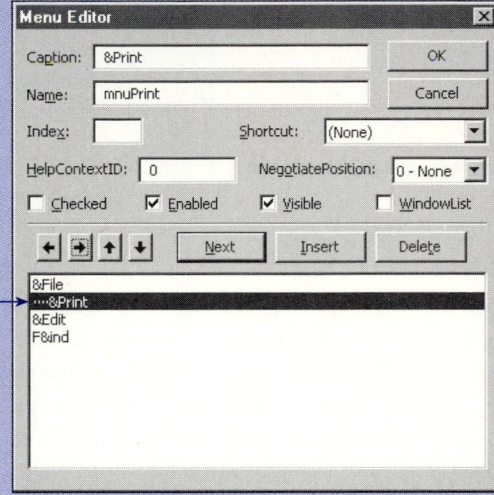

4. Click the **Next** button then click the **Insert** button to insert a new menu item. Repeat Steps 2 and 3 using the caption **E&xit** and the name **mnuFileExit.** Note that Alt+X is the hot key for the Exit menu item rather then Alt+E. Windows 95 programs use this letter rather than the first character.

5. Click the **Next** button until the Find menu is highlighted, then click the **Insert** button to insert a new menu item before the Find menu.

6. Repeat Steps 2 and 3 using the following captions and names:

Caption	Name
&Add	**mnuEditAdd**
&Edit Record	**mnuEditRecord**
&Update	**mnuEditUpdate**
&Delete	**mnuEditDelete**
&Refresh	**mnuEditRefresh**

The Menu Editor looks like Figure 4-7.

Figure 4-7 ◀
File and Edit
menus
completed

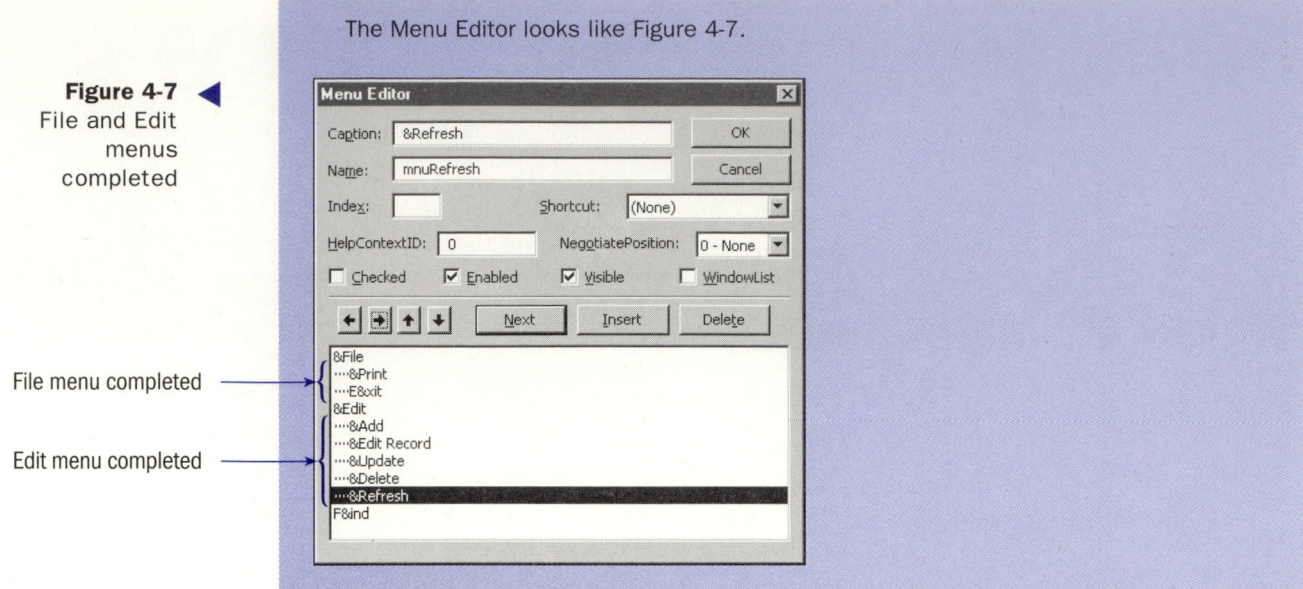

File menu completed →

Edit menu completed →

Notice that the name mnuEditRecord violates the rule of using the Caption for the name. If you followed the rule, however, the name would be mnuEditEditRecord, which may seem confusing. In cases where the menu's caption may cause the name to be misleading or too long, change the name or abbreviate as necessary.

Menus have other characteristics to improve their appearance and make them more efficient for the user. For example, you can draw separator bars, and create shortcut keys.

Creating Submenus with Shortcut Keys and Separator Bars

Windows 95 programs also can separate menu items with a separator bar. A **separator bar** is a horizontal line that visually groups related menu items together to make the interface easier to use. Like all components of a menu, a separator bar must have a unique name or be a member of a control array. You create a separator bar by setting a menu item's Caption property to a hyphen (-).

Also, menu items can have submenus. A **submenu** is a menu item that displays another menu, rather than executing code in an event procedure. You can make a menu item display on a submenu by indenting it another level. Nina wants the Find menu to include the submenu Navigate, which will contain the items First, Last, Previous, and Next. The Find menu also needs to contain a menu item to search for last name. Nina would like the Navigate and Last Name items to be separated by a separator bar. The Last Name item should include a shortcut key definition so users can choose the item using both the keyboard and the mouse. A shortcut key is appropriate because the user then will enter the last name, which can eliminate the transition from the mouse to the keyboard. Also, searching for a last name is expected to be a commonly executed command. You specify the shortcut key for a menu item by selecting it from the Shortcut list box in the Menu Editor. You cannot create shortcut keys that are not listed in the Shortcut list box. For command buttons, you create shortcut keys by placing the ampersand character (&) in the button's caption immediately to the left of the character you want to designate as the shortcut; for example, the caption E&xit would set the shortcut key for the Exit button to Alt+X.

> *Tip:* Create shortcut keys for the more frequently used menu items. This will minimize the number of keystrokes needed to activate a menu item. By allowing both mouse and keyboard input for the menus, the interface will appeal to the broadest number of users. When selecting characters for a shortcut key, use characters that are the same as those used in other common programs. For example, many programs use Ctrl+P as the shortcut key for printing. Using the first character of the menu caption also is common.

To create the menu items for the Find menu:

1. In the menu list box, click the blank line below the Find menu option.

2. Type **&Navigate** in the Caption text box, then type **mnuFindNavigate** in the Name text box.

3. Click the **right arrow** button 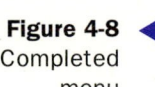 to indent the Navigate menu item.

4. Click the **Next** button. Notice that the next line in the menu list box automatically is indented and will place the next entry on the Find menu.

5. Create the separator by setting the caption to a hyphen (-) and the name to **mnuFindSep**.

6. Click the **Next** button.

7. Type **&Last Name...** in the Caption text box, then type **mnuFindLastName**.

8. Click the Shortcut list arrow, then select Ctrl+A. Notice that the menu list box for the Last Name item now contains the shortcut key for the last name.

The final step in creating the menus is to create the menu items that will be displayed when the Navigate submenu is selected. These items need to appear under the Navigate submenu item in the menu list box, so they will be indented with eight dots.

To create the items on the Navigate submenu:

1. Enter the following menu items such that they appear below the Navigate menu item and be sure you click the **right arrow** button to indent each item.

Caption	Name	Shortcut
&First	mnuFindNavigateFirst	Ctrl+F
&Last	mnuFindNavigateLast	Ctrl+L
&Previous	mnuFindNavigatePrevious	Ctrl+P
&Next	mnuFindNavigateNext	Ctrl+N

Your screen should look like Figure 4-8.

Figure 4-8
Completed
menu

shortcut keys

The Find menu is complete. Later, you will write the code for these items in the appropriate event procedures. Nina asks you to check the accuracy of the menus. If you forgot to indent a menu item, it might appear on the menu bar rather than within the menu title. You also need to verify that the hot keys and shortcut keys appear. You can view all the menu items, hot keys, and shortcut keys at design time, so there is no need to run the program.

To view the menus:

1. Click the **OK** button to close the Menu Editor.

TROUBLE? If you receive an error message indicating that a menu item must have a name, you may have neglected to assign a menu name. Click the OK button to close the message box. The menu item in question will be highlighted. Enter a valid name in the Name text box. If you receive the error message "Menu control array must have an index" you have assigned the same name to two menu items. Like other objects you have created, menu items can be created as a control array, each sharing the same event procedure. You need to assign an index to the menu using the Index text box or assign a unique name to each item. Visual Basic will not create a control array of menu items for you.

2. Save the project.

3. Click the **File** menu on your form. The menu items are displayed. See Figure 4-9.

Figure 4-9 ◀
File menu
displayed

File menu

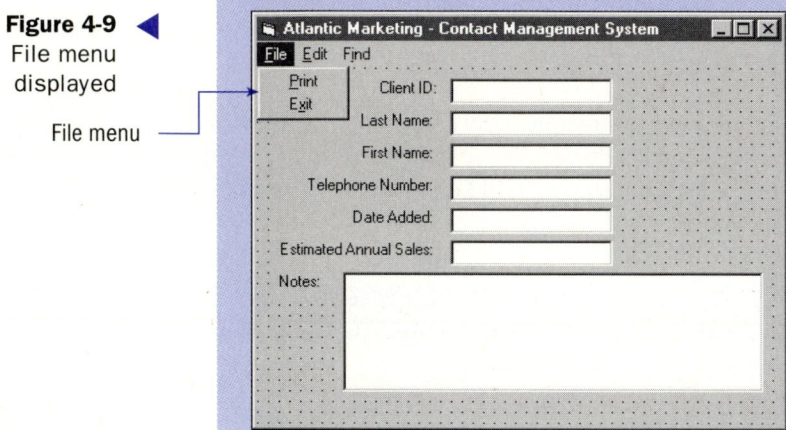

4. Click the **Edit** menu on your form. The menu items are displayed. See Figure 4-10.

Figure 4-10 ◀
Edit menu
displayed

Edit menu

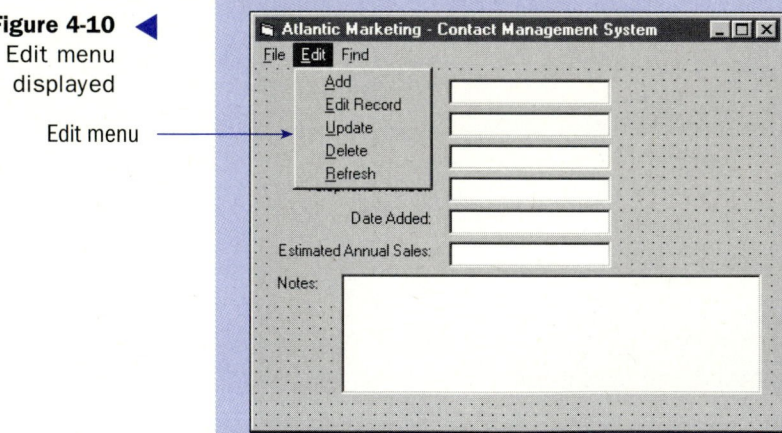

5. Click the **Find** menu on your form, then click the **Navigate** submenu to display its menu items. The menu items are displayed. See Figure 4-11.

Figure 4-11 ◀
Find menu
displayed

separator bar

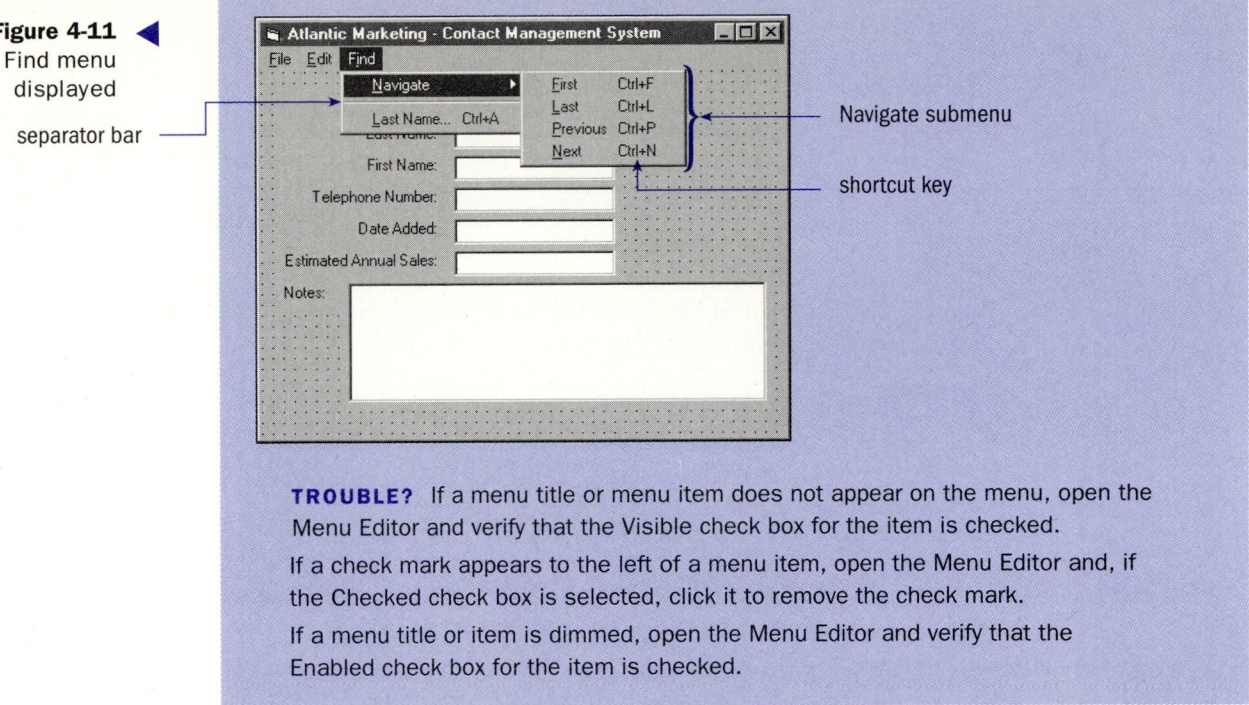

Navigate submenu

shortcut key

TROUBLE? If a menu title or menu item does not appear on the menu, open the Menu Editor and verify that the Visible check box for the item is checked.

If a check mark appears to the left of a menu item, open the Menu Editor and, if the Checked check box is selected, click it to remove the check mark.

If a menu title or item is dimmed, open the Menu Editor and verify that the Enabled check box for the item is checked.

Creating an Event Procedure for a Menu Item

The first menu item you need to program is the Exit menu item on the File menu. The mnuFileExit object's Click event should end the program. You write the code for a menu's Click event procedure in the same way as you would for a command button. That is, you can locate the object and event procedure in the Code window.

> *Tip:* You can open quickly the Code window to a menu item's Click event procedure by clicking the menu title then clicking on the desired menu item rather than locating the event procedures in the Code window.

To write the code for the Exit menu item:

1. Click the **File** menu on your form. The menu items are displayed.

2. Click the **Exit** menu item. The Code window displays the mnuFileExit_Click event procedure.

3. Enter the **End** statement into the event procedure.

The Exit menu item is operational. Now you can proceed to write the code to print the form. You need to use the PrintForm method, like you did in Tutorial 3, to print the form.

To write the code for the PrintForm method:

1. In the Code window, display the **mnuFilePrint_Click** event procedure.

   Enter the **PrintForm** statement into the event procedure.

2. Close the Code window.

3. Save the project.

You have completed the user interface for the contact management system. Nina suggests you run the program and test the Print and Exit menu items.

To test the PrintForm and Exit menu items:

1. Click **File** then **Print** to print an image of the form on the printer.

2. Click **File** then **Exit** to stop the program.

The menu system, and the code for each item on the File menu, are complete. The menu is a better interface than creating 12 command buttons, which would make the screen appear confusing and cluttered.

Quick Check

1. Describe the design criteria for menu item names.

2. What is the difference between a menu title and a menu item?

3. What are hot keys and shortcut keys?

4. What is a separator bar?

5. What is a submenu? How do you create a submenu?

The menu system is now complete. As you complete the different components of the program, you will add the necessary code to the proper event procedures. You have completed this session. You can now take a break or continue to Session 4.2.

SESSION

4.2

In this session you will create an instance of the Data control to communicate with an Access database. You will learn how to set additional properties of TextBox objects so they can display information contained in the database and store information in the database. You also will learn how to locate information in a database using the Data control, and how to add, update, and delete that information.

Understanding How Visual Basic Uses a Database

Before you can complete the program, you need to understand what a database is, and how Visual Basic objects interact with a database. A **database** is a set of information related to a particular topic or purpose. Information is stored in a database within a table. Most databases contain several tables. A **table** consists of rows and columns. The column defines a name for, and characteristics of, the stored information. The columns in a table are called **fields**. In the Atlantic Marketing database Nina created seven fields to hold the information. Client ID, Last Name, First Name, Telephone Number, Date Added, Estimated Sales, and Notes are the fields in the tblContact table. The actual information in the table is stored in the rows. The rows in a table are called **records**. Figure 4-12 shows the six rows (records) and column names (fields) in the table. As you can see, field names have the prefix "fld". So she could test the program, Nina entered six records as test data.

Figure 4-12 ◄
Database
table fields
and records

six records

seven columns

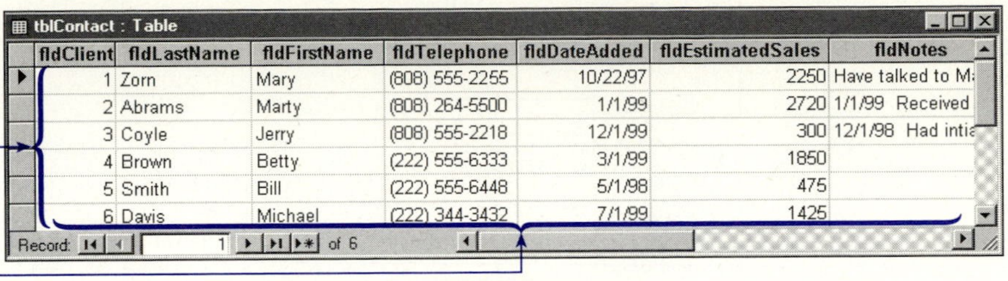

fldClient	fldLastName	fldFirstName	fldTelephone	fldDateAdded	fldEstimatedSales	fldNotes
1	Zorn	Mary	(808) 555-2255	10/22/97	2250	Have talked to M:
2	Abrams	Marty	(808) 264-5500	1/1/99	2720	1/1/99 Received
3	Coyle	Jerry	(808) 555-2218	12/1/99	300	12/1/98 Had inti:
4	Brown	Betty	(222) 555-6333	3/1/99	1850	
5	Smith	Bill	(222) 555-6448	5/1/98	475	
6	Davis	Michael	(222) 344-3432	7/1/99	1425	

In a modern database, or database management system (DBMS), multiple users can access the information contained in the database at the same time. If two users add records at the same time, the DBMS keeps track of each request without causing an error or losing either user's information. When you are working in Visual Basic and Windows 95, the **Microsoft Jet database engine** is the DBMS that retrieves data from, and stores data in, an Access database. A database can organize and store information so it can be viewed and retrieved based on the needs of a particular user. For example, the contact management system represents only part of the data that Atlantic Marketing needs to manage. Another component of the company's data is its sales system. If information about sales accounts could be accessed by the contact management system, a salesperson could view sales history before talking with an existing client.

Most databases in use today are **relational**; that is, information is contained in several tables that can be related together in different ways. In other words, billing transactions could be stored in one table, and client information in another. A relational database management system (RDBMS) allows you to define the relationships between these different pieces of information. For example, in the Atlantic Marketing database, information in the tblContact table is related to the information in the tblSales table using a query. A **query** is an instruction to a database to return a set of records from one or more tables in a specific order. The use of an RDBMS to manage large volumes of data has become increasingly popular as the software technology has evolved and the computer hardware has become fast enough to run this complex software effectively. Refer to the Database Appendix for more information.

Using the Data Control to Open a Database

Before you can communicate with the database Nina created, you need to connect your program to the database. There are two ways to interact with a database from a program. One way is to write Visual Basic statements that will access a database; the other is to use the **Data control** in the toolbox. The Data control enables you to move from record to record and to display information inside other controls on the form. By setting the properties of the Data control you can use its buttons to locate different database records without writing any code at all. You cannot use the Data control to create new databases, only to connect to existing ones. You can create your own databases using Microsoft Access.

You need to create a Data control to establish communication with the database Nina created. The standard prefix for a Data control is "dat". Like a label, the Data control supports the Caption property. This controls the text displayed inside the Data control.

To create the Data control:

1. Start Visual Basic, if necessary, and open the project named **Atlantic Contact.vbp** from Session 4.1.

2. Click the **Data** control 🖼 on the toolbox and draw an instance of the Data control across the bottom of the form. See Figure 4-13.

Figure 4-13 ◄
Creating the
Data control

caption

Previous
Record button

First Record button

draw Data
control here

Next Record button

Last Record button

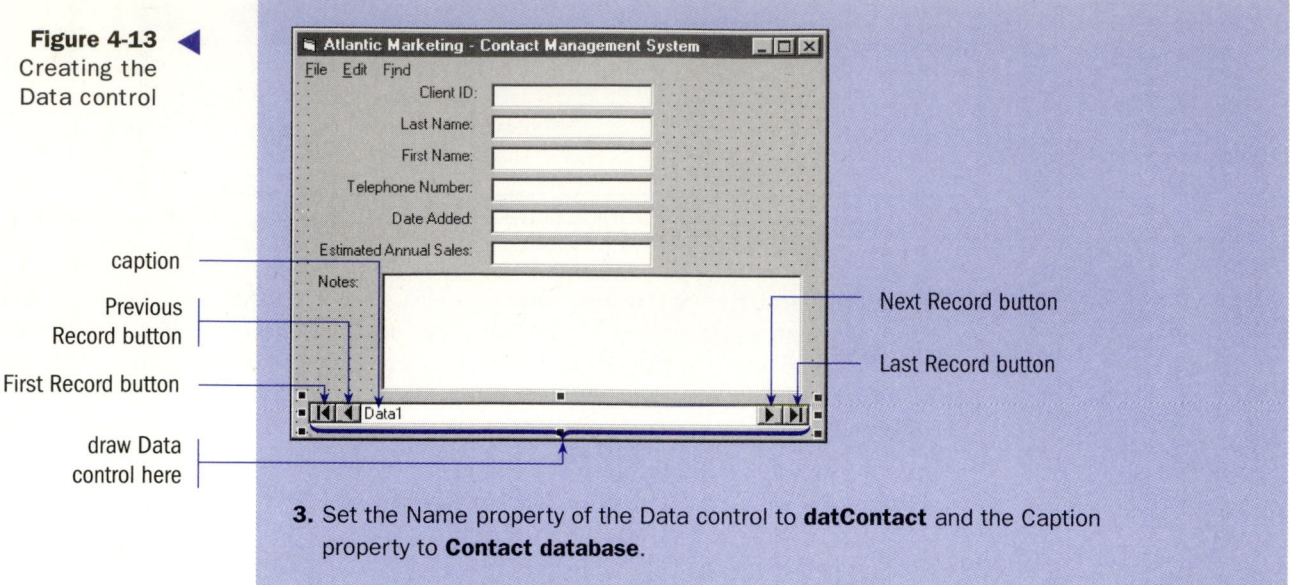

3. Set the Name property of the Data control to **datContact** and the Caption
property to **Contact database**.

The database Nina created contains the tables and other information you need to complete your program. Although the form now contains an instance of the Data control, it cannot store or display the information in the existing database until you set the necessary properties to connect the Data control to the database.

The properties of the Data control that allow you to communicate with the database are the Connect, DatabaseName, RecordSource, and RecordsetType properties.

■ The **Connect** property provides the information about the kind of database. The Data control can operate with Access, dBASE, FoxPro, and Paradox databases using the Connect property. The Connect property is set to Access by default.

■ The **DatabaseName** property identifies the name and location (folder) of the database file. Note that Microsoft Access database files have the extension ".mdb".

■ The **RecordSource** property identifies the table or query in the database that you want to use.

■ The **RecordsetType** property determines what operations can be performed on the table or query you identified when you set the RecordSource property. By default, the RecordsetType property is set to 1 - Dynaset.

When you set these properties, the Data control creates the necessary objects to access a table in the database at run time.

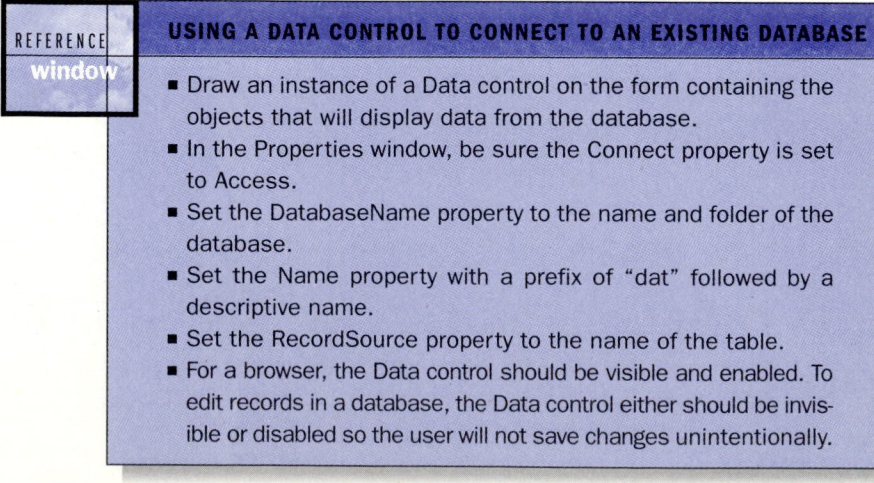

REFERENCE
window

USING A DATA CONTROL TO CONNECT TO AN EXISTING DATABASE

■ Draw an instance of a Data control on the form containing the objects that will display data from the database.
■ In the Properties window, be sure the Connect property is set to Access.
■ Set the DatabaseName property to the name and folder of the database.
■ Set the Name property with a prefix of "dat" followed by a descriptive name.
■ Set the RecordSource property to the name of the table.
■ For a browser, the Data control should be visible and enabled. To edit records in a database, the Data control either should be invisible or disabled so the user will not save changes unintentionally.

The order in which you set the Data control properties is important. You should select the database (DatabaseName property) before you select the table (RecordSource property). Then, when you set the RecordSource property, Visual Basic connects to the database and shows you a list of its available tables. The file that contains the contact management test database is named AM_CMS.mdb and is stored in the Tutorial.04 folder on your Student Disk.

To connect the Data control to the contact management database:

1. In the Properties window for the Data control you just created, make sure the value of the Connect property is **Access**.

2. Click the value column of the **DatabaseName** property.

3. Click the **Properties** button [...] and choose the file **AM_CMS.mdb** in the Tutorial.04 folder on your Student Disk.

4. The Properties window should look like Figure 4-14.

Figure 4-14 ◀
Setting the
DatabaseName
property

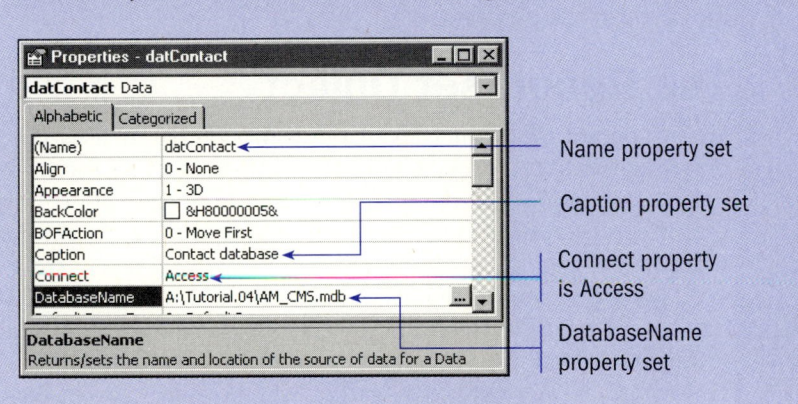

You have identified the database you want to use so the Data control can establish a connection with the database for the contact management system. Now you need to identify the database table or query you want. To do so, you set the RecordSource property to a table or query that exists in the database. The Properties window will display a list of available tables or queries in the database from which you can select. The standard prefix for a table object is "tbl". The query for the contact management system is named qryContact. The standard prefix for a query is "qry".

To view the tables in the AM_CMS database and set the RecordSource property:

1. Click the value column of the **RecordSource** property, then click the **Properties** button [▼] to display the list of tables. Your Properties window should look like Figure 4-15.

Figure 4-15 ◀
Setting the
RecordSource
property

set the Record
Source property
to qryContact

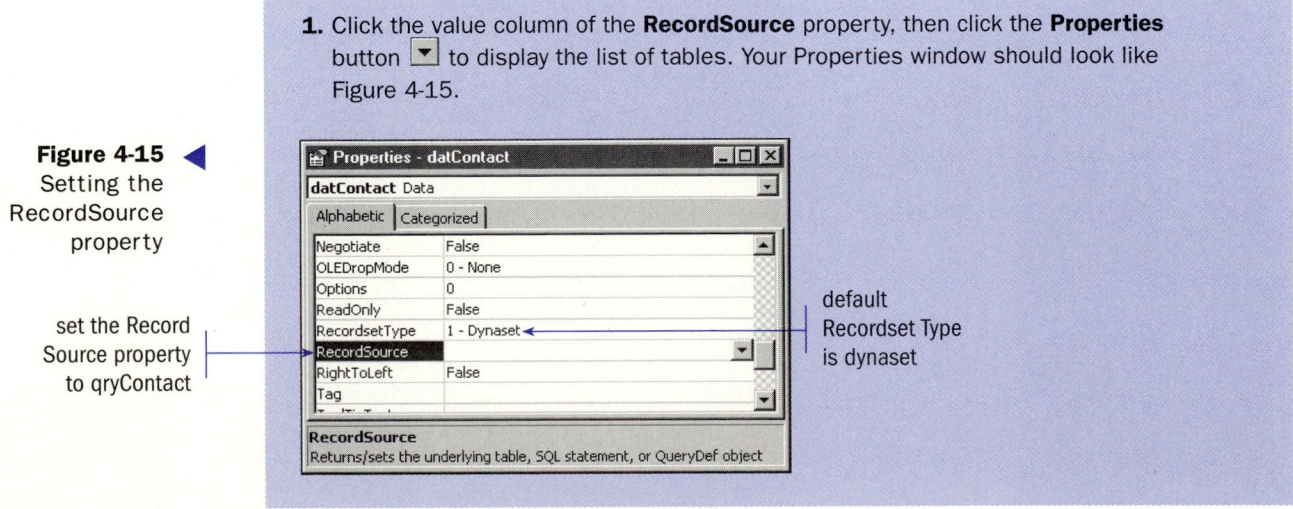

TROUBLE? If no information appears when you click the Properties button ▼ for the RecordSource property, then the database is not selected properly. Verify that the DatabaseName property is set to the correct path and filename, A:\Tutorial.04\AM_CMS.mdb, and that the file exists on your Student Disk. Then repeat Step 1.

2. Click **qryContact** to select the table. Check that the RecordsetType property is set to **1 - Dynaset**, the default setting.

3. Click the **Properties** button ▼ for the RecordsetType property to see the other options for this property.

Note the default setting of 1 - Dynaset for the RecordsetType property. A **dynaset** is a dynamic view of the information contained in a database table or query. You can create dynasets to view and change the contents of rows from one or more tables, depending on the needs of the program.

The Recordset Object

When you set the properties of the Data control, it uses that information to create an object called a recordset. A reference to this object is stored in the Recordset property of the Data control when the program is run. The Data control is set indirectly at run time, thus does not appear in the Properties window. You use the Recordset object at run time to locate different records and to add, change, and delete records.

A **Recordset object** is a view of the data stored in the database. When you look at records stored in the Recordset object, only one record can be active at a time. The **current record pointer** indicates the active record in a Recordset object. You do not access the current record pointer explicitly. Rather, you move the current record pointer indirectly using the Recordset object's methods.

You can find out if the current record pointer is at the beginning or end of the recordset using the BOF and EOF properties of the Recordset object.

- When the current record pointer is positioned just before the first record, **BOF** is True, and the recordset is at the beginning of file. Otherwise, BOF is False.

- When the pointer is positioned just after the last record, **EOF** is True, and the recordset is at the end of file. Otherwise, EOF is False.

The buttons on the Data control call different procedures that act on the Recordset object. A procedure that acts on an object is called a **method**. Figure 4-16 illustrates how a Recordset object is created by the Data control and shows some of its properties and methods.

Figure 4-16 ◀
The Recordset
object

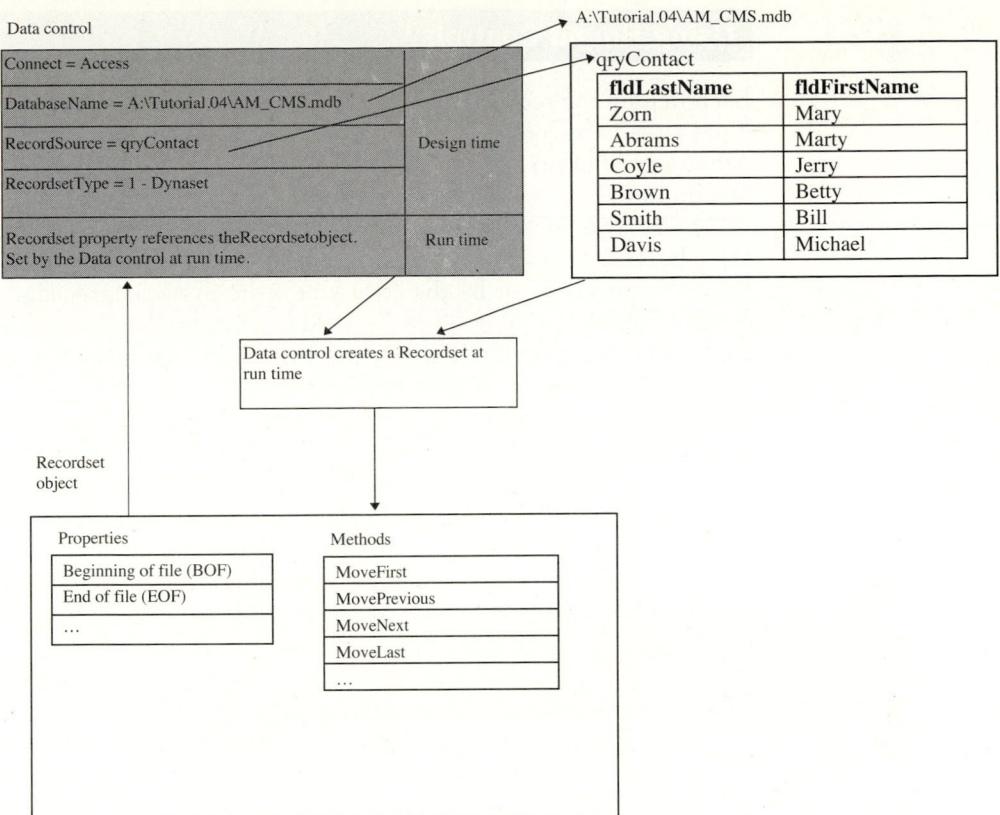

By setting the Connect, DatabaseName, RecordSource, and RecordsetType properties at design time, the Data control will be able to retrieve information from the query named qryContact at run time. It does this by creating a Recordset object and storing the object in the Recordset property of the Data control. Once the Recordset object is created by the Data control you can locate records and perform other operations.

Objects and Their Methods

An object is made up of properties, events, and methods. The methods of an object contain code that is built inside the object to accomplish a task. Consider a television's remote control as an object. The remote control is capable of a specific number of methods, or actions, such as changing a channel or adjusting the volume. You could use the ChannelUp and ChannelDown methods to set the CurrentChannel property. Likewise there are methods that apply to the Recordset object. Methods supply functionality to an object.

The Data control simplifies the process of working with a Recordset object by providing buttons that navigate through the records in the Recordset object without explicitly calling methods. There are limitations to the Data control, however. For example, it does not support a method to remove a record from a Recordset object. To do this you need to call the methods of the underlying Recordset object (stored in the Recordset property of the Data control).

So you can learn more about the methods applicable to the Recordset object, Nina suggests you look at the Help system. Using the Index tab, find information on recordsets, then Recordset Object, Recordsets Collection Summary (DAO). Print the information for future reference.

A Recordset object is considered a **Data Access Object**. Data Access Objects (DAO) enable you to use a programming language to access and manipulate data in databases, and to manage databases, their objects, and their structure.

The Data control allows you to click buttons located on the control to navigate through records without writing any code. In essence, it calls methods for you. Nina wants the user to be able to use the menu items you created in the first session to move forward and backward through the client list. This requires the fields to be connected to the text boxes.

Using Bound Controls

Each field in the recordset needs to be displayed in the corresponding TextBox object that Nina already has created on the form. No code needs to be written to accomplish the task. All you need to do is set some new properties for each TextBox object and it will display information from the database table.

The TextBox objects on your form are the same as those you created in previous tutorials. The Text property of these TextBox objects, however, will not be explicitly set in the Properties window or by the code you write in event procedures. Rather, each TextBox control will be bound to a specific field in a Recordset object. A **bound control** displays the changes in the current record of the Recordset object on the form. When a text box is bound to a Recordset object, changes in the current record of the Recordset object are reflected in the TextBox object. Each bound TextBox object corresponds to a field in the Recordset object. Bound controls often are referred to as **data aware** controls. Many different controls that can hold text (such as the Label or ListBox control) and graphics (such as the ImageBox or PictureBox control) can be bound to a field in a Recordset object.

The process of binding an object to a Recordset object requires setting properties you have not used yet. These properties are common to all bound controls. When you create a bound control such as a text box, these properties initially are blank; you must set them explicitly.

- The **DataField** property is set to a field inside the table or query. When you select a field with the Properties button, Visual Basic looks in the database table or query, which you specified with the DataSource property to see the list of available fields. By using the standard prefix "fld", you can immediately determine the type of object you are working with.

- The **DataSource** property of a bound control is set to an instance of a Data control drawn on the same form. To see the list of available choices for this property, you click its Properties button. In the contact management program, this property will be set to datContact (the name you assigned to the Data control). If a form will interact with multiple tables or queries, you can create multiple Data controls, then select the desired Data control.

Tip: When you create instances of bound controls and set their properties at design time, it is important that you set the properties of the Data control first. If the Data control does not reference an existing table or query in a database, the bound TextBox objects will not display the table names and field names. Set the DataSource property before setting the DataField property when creating a bound text box. If you try to set the DataField first, Visual Basic cannot look into a table and show the list of available fields.

REFERENCE window

BINDING A CONTROL TO A DATABASE FIELD

- Create an instance of a valid control (text box, label, etc.) on the form.
- In the Properties window for that object, set the DataSource property to the name of the Data control.
- Set the DataField property to the corresponding field in the database table.
- For a browser, the bound control either should be invisible or disabled so the user will not unintentionally make changes. To edit records in a database, the bound control should be both visible and enabled.

Figure 4-17 shows the properties used to bind controls to interact with fields in a Recordset object.

Figure 4-17 ◀
Bound controls

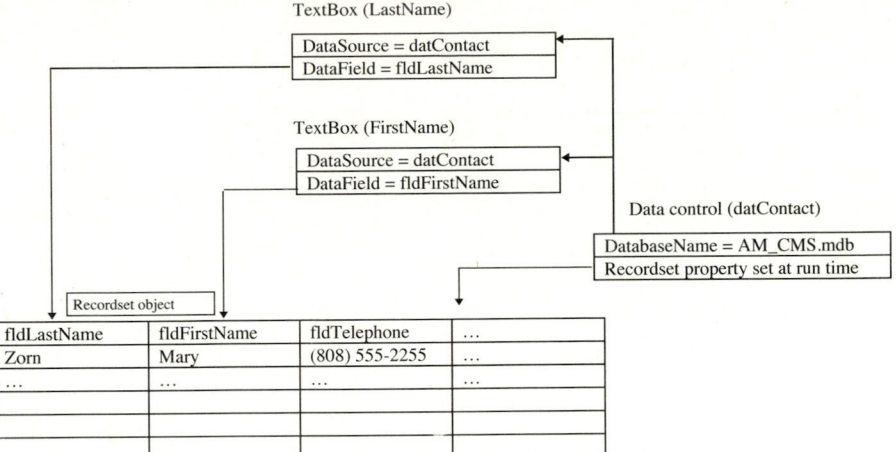

You will set the DataSource property for all the TextBox objects on your form as a group, because they all must be set to datContact, the only Data control on the form. Then you will set the DataField property for each TextBox object to its corresponding field in the database table. At run time, each object will interact with a field in the Recordset object created by the Data control.

To set the properties for the TextBox objects:

1. Press and hold down the **Shift** key and click all seven **TextBox** objects to select them. Your form should look like Figure 4-18.

Figure 4-18 ◀
Selecting
multiple
text boxes

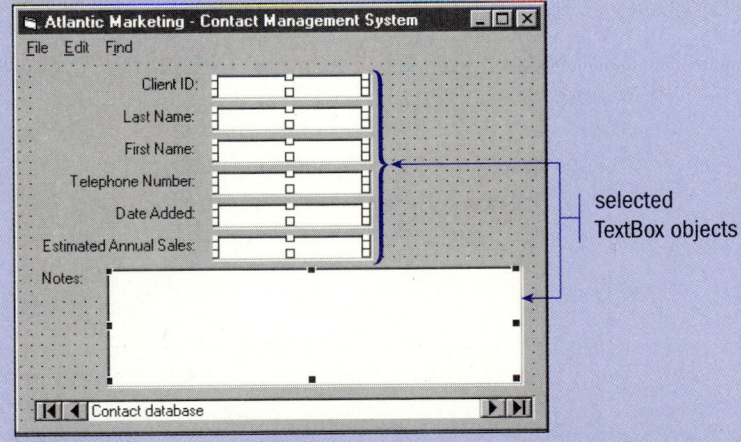

2. In the Properties window, set the DataSource property to **datContact**, the name of the Data control. This is the only available option because there is only one Data control on the form. The Properties window should look like Figure 4-19.

Figure 4-19 ◀
Setting the
DataSource
property

no object displays
in Object list
box
when multiple
objects are selected

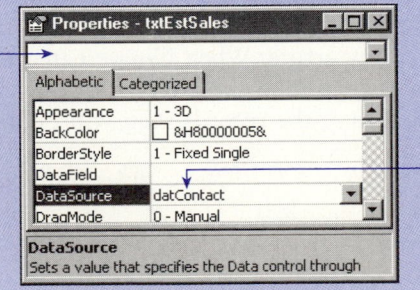

3. Click any blank area of the form to deactivate the selected objects.

4. Click the text box for **Client ID**.

5. Click the Properties button ▼ for the DataField property. Your Properties window should look like Figure 4-20.

Figure 4-20 ◀
Setting the
DataField
property

available fields
shown in list box

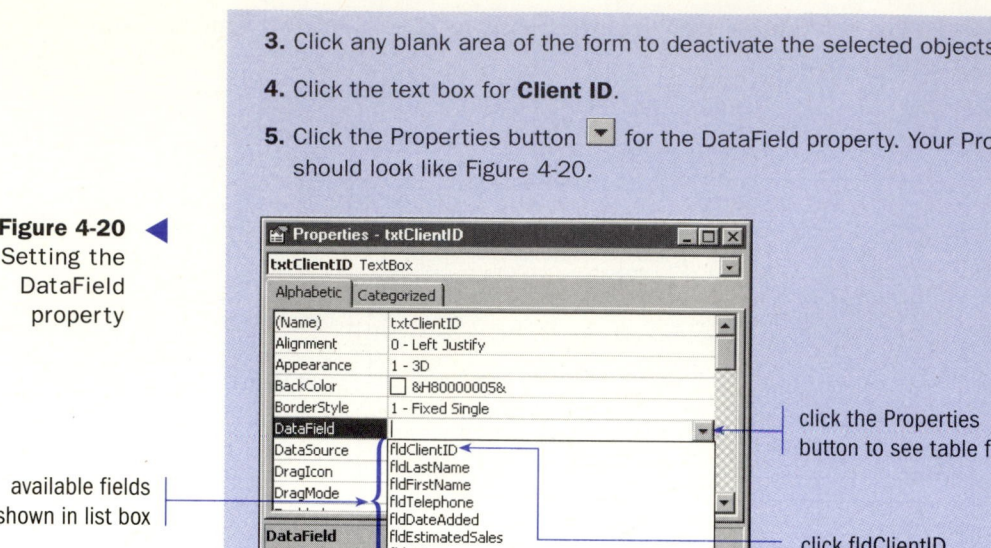

click the Properties
button to see table fields

click fldClientID

TROUBLE? If clicking the Properties button does not display the fields in the database or you get an error message, the DataSource property is not set correctly. Be sure the DataSource property is set to datContact. Also, check that the DatabaseName property of the Data control is set to the file AM_CMS.mdb in the Tutorial.04 folder on your Student Disk, and that the database exists there.

6. In the displayed list of fields, click **fldClientID**.

The text box txtClientID now is bound to the field fldClientID in the table tblContact. When you run your program, the information contained in this record will be displayed in the text box.

7. Repeat Steps 4 through 6, setting the DataField property as follows:

Object	Property
txtLastName	**fldLastName**
txtFirstName	**fldFirstName**
txtTelephoneNumber	**fldTelephoneNumber**
txtDateAdded	**fldDateAdded**
txtEstimatedSales	**fldEstimatedSales**

Nina also created a text box for notes. The table includes a Notes field, which contains notes the salesperson writes about interactions with the client. You need to modify the properties for the txtNotes object so that it will display several lines of text from the Notes field of the database.

8. For the **txtNotes** object, set the MultiLine property to **True**, the ScrollBars property to **2 - Vertical**, and the DataField property to **fldNotes**.

The program now will display the appropriate information from a database record in the text boxes when you run the program, and you can move from record to record using the buttons on the Data control. This is a good time to save the project, check that the program works, then correct any errors. When Nina created the database and the table containing the clients, she designed it so the table records would appear sorted by last name. When you run the program, the records then will be displayed alphabetically by last name.

To run and test the program:

1. Save the form and project files.

2. Start the program. The first record in the Recordset object is displayed. See Figure 4-21.

Figure 4-21 ◀
Form with multiline text box

information from Notes field displayed in text box →

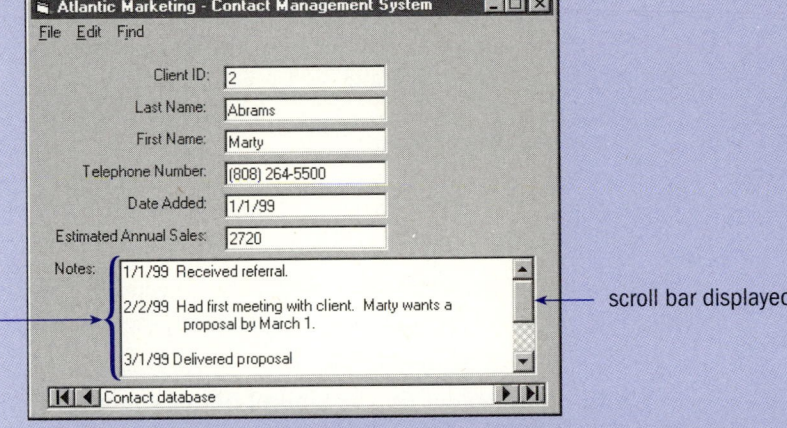

← scroll bar displayed

The record for Marty Abrams is displayed because Abrams is the first last name alphabetically in the database.

3. Drag the scroll box in the Notes text box to the bottom of the scroll bar. The rest of the information from the Notes field is displayed.

   TROUBLE? If you cannot scroll through the Notes field information, you probably neglected to set the MultiLine property to True. Stop the program, set the MultiLine property for the Notes text box to True, and then repeat Steps 1 and 2.

4. Click the **Next Record** button ▶ in the Data control. The form now displays the information for Betty Brown.

5. Click the **Previous Record** button ◀ in the Data control. The form displays the information for Marty Abrams again.

6. Click the **Last Record** button ▶| in the Data control. The form displays the information for Mary Zorn.

7. Click the **First Record** button |◀ in the Data control. The form displays the information for Marty Abrams again.

8. End the program.

The text boxes now connect to the database table using the Data control and display the client ID, name, telephone number, date added, estimated annual sales information, and notes from the Recordset object in the text boxes.

In addition to using the buttons on the Data control, you can call the methods of the Recordset object explicitly. The methods of the Recordset object operate on data in the database table or query. For example, you can locate records in the table using the following four methods:

- The **MoveFirst** method locates the first record in the Recordset object.

- The **MoveLast** method locates the last record in the Recordset object.

- The **MoveNext** method locates the next record in the Recordset object.

- The **MovePrevious** method locates the previous record in the Recordset object.

These four methods are not supported explicitly by the Data control. Rather, they are supported by the Recordset object, which is stored in the Recordset property of the Data control at run time. Thus, you could use the following statement to find the next client stored in the Recordset object created by the Data control named datContact. When you call an object's methods, you include a period (.) between the object and method names.

```
datContact.Recordset.MoveNext
```

This statement calls the MoveNext method on the Data control's (datContact's) Recordset property, which is the Recordset object. While this statement is valid, you can save a considerable amount of typing by creating an object variable to store a Recordset object. The three-character prefix for a Recordset object is "rst". To create an object variable you use the following syntax:

Private *varname* **As [New]** *Object*

- The name of the object variable is specified with *varname* and must follow the standard naming conventions for variables.

- The **New** keyword is used to create new objects. In this session you will use the object variable to reference an existing object, the Recordset object, so you will not use the New keyword.

- *Object* is a placeholder for the kind of object you want to reference.

After you create an object variable, the variable must be set to point to an existing object or to create a new instance of an object. You accomplish this using the Set statement, which has the following syntax:

Set *varname* = [[**New**] *objectexpression* | **Nothing**]

- The *varname* can be any valid object variable name.

- The **New** keyword creates a new instance of the object.

- The *objectexpression* can be any existing instance of an object, such as a recordset, a form, or an instance of a control, when the New keyword is not used.

- The **Nothing** keyword is used to disassociate an object variable from an actual object. When you assign Nothing to an object variable, the variable will no longer refer to an actual object. If there are multiple object variables that reference the same object, setting all of them to Nothing will free the memory and system resources used by the object.

Thus, you could use the following statements to declare an object variable, then set that variable to a valid instance of a recordset:

```
Private mrstContact as Recordset
Set mrstContact = datContact.Recordset
```

The first statement creates a Recordset object variable named mrstContact. Like other variables you have created, it contains nothing until you store information in it.

The second statement stores information in the object variable using the Set statement. Then you could call the MoveNext method on the mrstContact recordset.

You now can create an object variable and assign it to the existing Recordset object. Because you will use this variable in many different event procedures, it should be declared in the general declarations section of the Form module.

To create an object variable:

1. Enter the following statement in the general declarations section of the Form module after the Option Explicit statement.

```
Private mrstContact As Recordset
```

Now that you have created a variable to hold the Recordset object, you must assign it to a valid recordset instance before it can be used. Normally you would assign a value like this once, when the form was loaded. There is an event, however, called the Reposition event that occurs each time you locate a different record in a recordset and occurs before the Load event for the form. You will need to write code for this event that will reference the recordset before the form is loaded, so you must assign the variable in this event procedure.

While you could set the value of the object each time the recordset is repositioned, it only needs to be done once. Thus you need to create a variable and an If statement to test the variable to determine whether or not it is the first time the event has occurred. You cannot use a local variable because its value is lost each time the procedure exits. A form-level variable would work but there is another way of creating the variable that is better suited to this purpose. The **Static** statement works much like the Private and Dim statements. It creates variables that, like form-level variables, retain their value whenever the form is running. Like variables declared inside a procedure using the Dim statement, however, the variable only can be referenced by that procedure. The **Static** keyword has the following syntax:

Static *varname* [**As** *type*]

- *Varname* can be any valid variable name.

- *Type* can be any valid data type or object type.

> *Tip:* When the value of a variable must be retained whenever a module is running, declare it as a Static variable inside the appropriate event or general procedure. As programs get larger, form-level variables may be used by several procedures. It becomes difficult to keep track of each procedure that is manipulating the variable, and logic errors easily can happen. Using a Static variable, no other procedure can reference it and any possible side effects are eliminated.

Nina suggests that you write the If statement that will determine if the Reposition event is occurring for the first time.

To set the object variable to a recordset instance:

1. Enter the following statements in the Reposition event for datContact:

```
Static pblnFirst As Boolean
    If pblnFirst = False Then
        Set mrstContact = datContact.Recordset
        pblnFirst = True
    End If
```

The Static statement declares the variable pblnFirst as a Boolean variable. While only visible from this general procedure, the value of the variable remains while the program is running. The first time the procedure is executed, the value of the variable is False, so the statements inside the If block are executed. The next time the procedure is executed, the value of the variable is True so the statements in the If block are not executed.

Now that the object variable is assigned to the active recordset, you can proceed to call the methods to locate different records from the menu item's event procedures.

To write the code for the items on the Find menu:

1. Open the Code window for the menu named **mnuFindNavigateFirst** and select the **Click** event procedure. Remember you can click **Find**, **Navigate**, **First** to select the Click event procedure for this menu item.

2. Enter the following code in the window:

```
Private Sub mnuFindNavigateFirst_Click()
    mrstContact.MoveFirst
End Sub
```

3. Enter the following statements into the respective event procedures:

for the mnuFindNavigateLast object's Click event,

```
mrstContact.MoveLast
```

for the mnuFindNavigatePrevious object's Click event,

```
mrstContact.MovePrevious
```

for the mnuFindNavigateNext object's Click event,

```
mrstContact.MoveNext
```

4. Save the project then run the program.

5. Test the items on the Navigate submenu to be sure they are locating different records in the database.

6. End the program.

While the buttons on the Data control allow the user to browse through the data in the database, there is a side effect. If a user makes changes to a record and then locates a different record using the Data control's buttons, those changes will be saved to the database table or query. If you want to let the user abandon changes to a record, you can use properties supported by the recordset. Therefore, Nina would like the commands on the menu bar to be used for all database navigation and updating. There are two ways to prevent the user from interacting with the Data control. You could disable the Data control, to prevent it from responding to user activity, or you can make it invisible. Nina suggests that you make the Data control invisible. Although the user cannot see the Data control, your program can continue to set properties and call methods at run time.

To make the Data control invisible at run time:

1. Set the Visible property of the Data control to **False**.

Sometimes the decision to make an object invisible, or to disable it, is subjective. As a general rule, if the visible object provides no information to the user, make it invisible; otherwise, disable it.

Understanding the Beginning and End of File

Nina would like to disable the Previous Record menu item when the recordset is at the beginning of the file and the Next Record menu item when the recordset is at the end of the file. That is, the menu items should appear gray and not respond to the Click event. This will give the user a visual clue that these operations cannot be performed.

Nina also would like the Next and Previous items on the Navigate submenu to be disabled when the BOF or EOF properties are True, respectively. Any visible object, like a command button, text box, or menu item can be disabled at run time by setting its Enabled property to False. The objects you have used always have been enabled (the Enabled property is set to True). When disabled, a control cannot receive focus although it does remain visible. That is, a command button or menu item will do nothing (not cause an event to occur) when clicked. The object also will appear with a gray foreground. Nina would like you to write the necessary statements to enable and disable the menu items.

To accomplish this task, you need to know when the position of the current record pointer changes. The Reposition event for the Data control occurs whenever the current record pointer is moved. Thus, you can write the statements in this event procedure to determine if the BOF or EOF properties of the recordset are True, and disable the corresponding menu items.

To disable and enable a visible object:

1. Open the Code window for the **datContact** object's **Reposition** event procedure and enter the following code into the window after the existing code:

```
If mrstContact.BOF = True Then
    mnuFindNavigatePrevious.Enabled = False
Else
    mnuFindNavigatePrevious.Enabled = True
End If

If mrstContact.EOF = True Then
    mnuFindNavigateNext.Enabled = False
Else
    mnuFindNavigateNext.Enabled = True
End If
```

The first If statement determines if the current record pointer is at the beginning of file and enables or disables the Previous menu item accordingly. The second If statement determines if end of file has been reached and enables or disables the Next menu item accordingly. Nina would like you to test this code you have just written.

To test the menu items:

1. Save the project and run the program.

2. Click the **Find** menu then click **Navigate** then **Last**.

3. Click the **Find** menu then click **Navigate** then **Next**. The current record pointer is now at the end of file.

4. Click **Find**, then **Navigate** again to verify the Next menu item is disabled.

5. End the program.

If you disable the Data control rather than making it invisible, you can enable and disable its buttons. This depends on the value of two properties that determine what happens when you try to locate the previous record when the first record is current, or try to locate the next record when the last record is current. The **BOFAction** property defines the behavior of the Data control when the user tries to locate the beginning of file (BOF) and can have one of two values:

- When set to **0 - Move First**, clicking the Previous Record button when the first record is the current record, will cause the first record to remain the current record.

- When set to **1 - BOF**, the current record will be set to the beginning of file (there is no current record) and the Data control's Previous Record button will be disabled. The BOF property of the recordset also will become True.

The **EOFAction** property works similarly and controls the action taken when the Next Record button on the Data control is clicked when the current record is the last record in the recordset.

- When set to **0 - MoveLast**, clicking the Next Record button when the last record is current will cause the last record to remain the current record.

- When set to **1 - EOF** the current record will be set to the end of file (there is no current record) and the Data control's Next Record button will be disabled. The EOF property of the recordset will become True.

- When set to **2 - Add New**, a new record will be added. (This is just like calling the recordset's AddNew method.)

Now that you have programmed the menu items to navigate through the database records, Nina suggests you proceed to write the code to modify the contents of the database.

Adding, Updating, and Deleting Database Records

By creating objects on a form and setting the necessary properties, you have created a Visual Basic program that will operate with a database. So far you only can navigate through the records in a Recordset object. Now that your program and its objects are communicating with the database, you can proceed to the next phase of the program's development: providing add, update, and delete capabilities to the user. You need to write the necessary Visual Basic statements for each menu item's Click event procedure to add, update, and delete records in the Recordset object.

Adding New Database Records

The Recordset object has a method that allows you to add records to a database. When the AddNew method is called, a new blank record is created, which you then can edit. After entering the information for the new record, you need to call the Update method to store the new record in the database. The syntax for the Recordset object's AddNew method is:

Object.**AddNew**

- *Object* must be a valid instance of a recordset.

- The **AddNew** method acts on a Recordset object and will create an empty database record to be edited.

The RecordsetType property of your Data control is set to 1 - Dynaset; therefore, all new records will be inserted at the end of the Recordset object, even if it was sorted. You need to write the code to add a new blank record to your database when the Add menu item is clicked.

To write the code to add new database records:

1. Open the Code window for the object named **mnuEditAdd** and select the **Click** event procedure.

2. Enter the following code in the window:

```
Private Sub mnuEditAdd_Click()
    mrstContact.AddNew
End Sub
```

The AddNew method operates on a Recordset object. When the program calls the AddNew method, a new blank record is created. A user then can enter data into each of the bound text boxes to identify the new client for Atlantic Marketing.

Updating Existing Database Records

When you want to change information in an existing record, you first must make the current record editable using the Edit method of the Recordset object. This places the information in the current record into a temporary storage area in the computer's memory called the copy buffer. The **copy buffer** stores the current record and any changes made to it before those changes actually are written to the underlying database table or query. By storing the changes in the copy buffer, you can choose not to update the database if you made an error. After making changes, you can save them explicitly, using the Update method of the Recordset object. When you move from one record to another by explicitly calling the methods of the Recordset object, such as MovePrevious or MoveNext, or if you close the Recordset object without calling the Update method, your changes will be lost. Sometimes this is what you want to do. For example, if you make changes to the data and notice a mistake, you can leave the record without saving the changes. The syntax for the Edit and Update methods are:

Object.**Edit**

Object.**Update**

- *Object* must be a valid instance of a recordset.
- The **Edit** method must be called to edit an existing record before the Update method, to allow editing on the record.
- The **Update** method acts on the recordset and writes the changes of a record created by the AddNew method or an edited record to the database.

To put a new record in sorted order, you also need to use the Requery method of the Recordset object. If you do not call the Requery method, newly added records always will appear at the end of the Recordset object until the program is run again, causing the Recordset object to be refreshed. The syntax of the Requery method is:

Object.**Requery**

- *Object* must be a valid instance of a recordset.
- The **Requery** method reloads the contents of the underlying table or query into the recordset. When the Requery method is called, the query is run again and any changes made by you, or another user, will be reflected in the recordset. So that any bound text boxes will display information from the new recordset, you should call a method like MoveFirst after calling the Requery method.

You now can proceed to write code for the Edit Record, Update, and Refresh menu items.

To write the code to edit, update, and sort the database records:

1. Activate the Code window for the **mnuEditRecord_Click** event procedure and enter the following code:

```
Private Sub mnuEditRecord_Click()
    mrstContact.Edit
End Sub
```

2. Activate the Code window for the **mnuEditUpdate_Click** event procedure and enter the following code:

```
Private Sub mnuEditUpdate_Click()
    mrstContact.Update
End Sub
```

3. Activate the Code window for the **mnuEditRefresh_Click** event procedure and enter the following code in the window:

```
Private Sub mnuEditRefresh_Click()
    mrstContact.Requery
    mrstContact.MoveFirst
End Sub
```

Examine the code you wrote to update the database any time a user adds or changes a record.

```
mrstContact.Edit
```

The Edit method operates on a Recordset object. When the program calls the Edit method, the current contents of the record are stored in the copy buffer. Any changes made by the user will be reflected in the contents of the copy buffer but not in the table saved on the disk until the Update method is called.

```
mrstContact.Update
```

When the Update menu item is clicked, the contents of the copy buffer are written to the Recordset object and therefore saved to the underlying table in the database. In other words, they become permanent. This menu item needs to be called after adding a new record or editing an existing record.

```
mrstContact.Requery
mrstContact.MoveFirst
```

The Requery method causes the Recordset object to be reinitialized so it will continue to be in sorted order. The MoveFirst method repositions the current record to the first record in the database, giving the user a visual clue that the recordset has been resorted. If you wanted to resort the recordset if a name was changed, or a new contact was added, you could have called the Requery and MoveFirst methods in the Add and Update menu item event procedures.

As you add and edit records, a property is set that contains the status of the current record. The **EditMode** property is supported by the Recordset object and can assume one of three values.

- The constant **dbEditNone** indicates that no editing operation is in progress.

- The constant **dbEditInProgress** indicates that the Edit method has been called and the current record is in the copy buffer.

- The constant **dbEditAdd** indicates the AddNew method has been called, and the current record in the copy buffer is a new record that has not been saved to the database table or query.

Nina wants you to use the Add, Edit Record, and Update menus to add a new record to the test database to make sure the program is working correctly.

To use the Add and Update menu items on your form to add a record to the database:

1. Save the project then start the program.

2. Click the **Edit** menu on your form, then click **Add** to create a new blank record.

3. Enter the information shown in Figure 4-22.

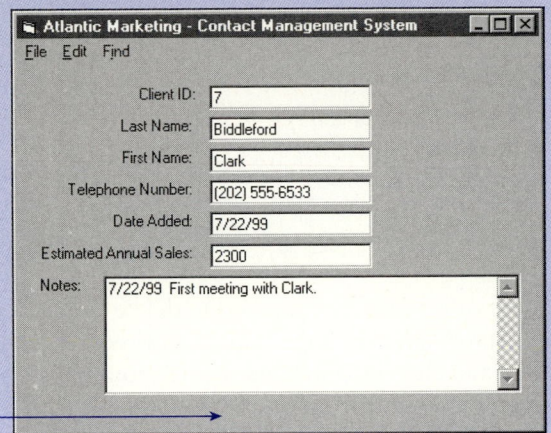

Figure 4-22 ◀
Adding
a record to
Contact table

Data control
is invisible

4. Click **Update** on the Edit menu on your form to save the new record to the database. The form displays the information for Marty Abrams again and the record you just added is stored at the end of the recordset.

   TROUBLE? If you receive a run-time error, you probably tried to update the database without completing all the fields. End the program and then repeat Steps 1 through 4.

5. Type **Ctrl+L** to locate the last record. Because you have not run the Requery method, Clark Biddleford appears at the end of the recordset.

6. Click the **Edit** menu then **Refresh** to reload the recordset in sorted order.

7. Locate the record for Clark Biddleford.

   The new record was added between the records for Marty Abrams and Betty Brown.

8. End the program.

When the program calls the Update method, the changes are stored immediately in the underlying table in the database. If the power goes out or the computer crashes, none of the changes made will be lost. When you start the program again, Clark Biddleford's record will remain.

You now are ready to program the Delete menu item that will allow salespeople to remove obsolete records from the database.

Deleting Database Records

You need to write the necessary statement for the Click event procedure to delete an existing record from the database. To do this, you will use the Delete method of the Recordset object. The syntax for the Delete method is:

Object.**Delete**

- *Object* must be a valid instance of a recordset.

- The **Delete** method is used to delete the current record from a Recordset object, which removes the corresponding row from the underlying database table. When the program calls the Delete method on a Recordset object, the information from the deleted record still appears in the text boxes on the form.

After the Delete method removes the current record, you explicitly should move the current record pointer to another record with the MoveNext or MoveFirst methods of the Recordset object. Now you will write the code for the Delete menu item's Click event procedure.

To write the code to delete database records:

1. Open the Code window for the **mnuEditDelete** menu's Click event procedure.

2. Enter the following code in the window:

```
Private Sub mnuEditDelete_Click()
    mrstContact.Delete
    mrstContact.MoveNext
End Sub
```

The first statement calls the Delete method to delete the current record of the Recordset object. The second statement positions the current record pointer on the next record of the Recordset object and clears the deleted record from the screen.

You now can manipulate information in the database with Visual Basic in addition to navigating through the existing information. A user can add, update, and delete information with a simple click of a menu. You have reached another milestone in the development of your program, so this is a good time to save your completed work, and test the code you have written for the Delete menu item.

To test the code for the Delete menu item:

1. Save the project then start the program.

2. Click **Find** then **Navigate** then **Next** to locate the record for Clark Biddleford.

3. Click **Edit** then **Delete** to delete the record. After deleting the record, notice the form displays the record for Betty Brown, the next record in the Recordset object.

   TROUBLE? If you receive a run-time error, you might have tried to delete a record when no record was displayed in the form. End the program and then repeat Steps 1 through 3.

4. End the program.

Your program now can locate, add, change, and delete records. These functions are common to nearly every program you will ever create to manage data in a database.

Quick Check

1 What properties does the Data control use to communicate with an existing Access database?

2 What is a bound control and what are the properties used to bind a control to data? What is a Recordset object?

3 What are the properties and the settings for those property values needed to create a text box in which you can display and navigate through multiple lines of text?

4 List and describe the methods to add, update, and delete information in a database.

5 What is the difference between the Enabled and Visible properties?

Now that you have completed Session 4.2, you can exit Visual Basic or you can continue to the next session.

In this session you will learn how to locate records using a search string, how to validate user input, and how to prevent user errors from crashing a program when a run-time error occurs.

Searching for Records

Nina knows that moving from record to record using the Navigate submenu is sufficient only when working with a small number of records. But the contact management system will ultimately contain about 3,500 client records. The salespeople need to locate a specific record quickly, without scrolling through 3,500 records.

You can use the FindFirst method, which acts on a Recordset object, to locate a specific record easily. The method will be familiar because the current paper-based system is organized by last name. The syntax for the FindFirst method is:

*Object.***FindFirst** *criteria*

- The *Object* can be any valid Recordset object.

- The **FindFirst** method locates the first record in a recordset that satisfies the criteria. The current record pointer is moved to that record.

- The *criteria* defines which records in the database will be located. If several records match the criteria, the first record found will become the active record.

- You can use the **FindNext** method after the FindFirst method to locate subsequent occurrences of records matching the criteria. The FindNext method has the same syntax as the FindFirst method. See the Help system for more information on the FindFirst and FindNext methods.

Locating a Record Using an Input Box

Nina wants the form to include a dialog box in which the user can enter a last name, and a corresponding command button that, when clicked, will locate and display the record with the specified last name. You can do this without placing any other objects on the form by using a window that will appear only when called. This approach is consistent with the Windows 95 user interface. When a user wants to locate a specific record, the user will click the Find menu item and a temporary window, called an input box, will appear. An **input box** is similar to a message box; however, an input box sends a text string back to your program. Thus, the user can enter the last name of the client to search for and click a button in the input box. The input box will close and then, using the string returned by the input box function, the FindFirst method is called and the client's record will be displayed on the screen, if it exists.

To display an input box, you call the InputBox function, which has the following syntax:

string = **InputBox**(*prompt*[,*title*][,*default*])

- When the **InputBox** function is called it displays a prompt, a text box to enter input, and two command buttons—OK and Cancel. The InputBox function always returns a value. If the user clicks the OK button, the contents of the input box are returned to the program and stored in a variable. If the user clicks the Cancel button, the InputBox function returns a *string* with no characters in it. This is known as a zero-length string. You can use an input box for any task that must prompt the user to enter a text string.

- The *prompt* argument contains descriptive text that will appear inside the input box.

To test the code for the Last Name menu item:

1. Save the project then start the program.

2. Click the **Find** menu on your form then click **Last Name**. The Find input box appears.

3. Enter the last name **Zorn** in the Find input box as shown in Figure 4-24.

Figure 4-24 ◀
Find input box

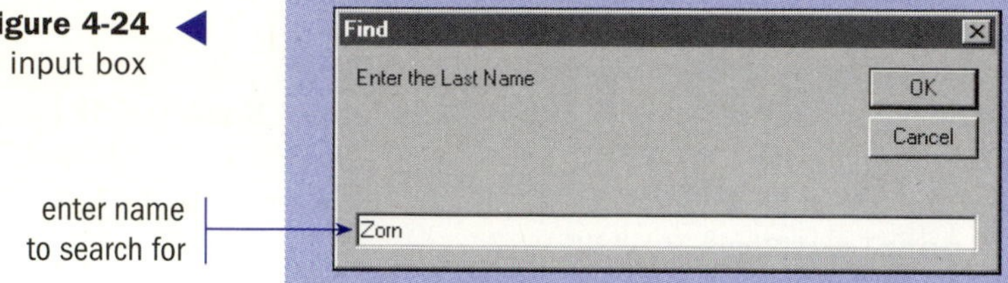

enter name
to search for ┤

Find	☒
Enter the Last Name	OK
	Cancel
Zorn	

4. Click the **OK** button. The form now displays the information for Mary Zorn.

5. Repeat Steps 2 through 4 to search for the last name **Zidmo**. The message box appears telling you that the last name Zidmo is not in the database.

6. End the program.

Verifying the Correctness of Data with the Validate Event

In addition to notifying the user when the beginning and end of file have been reached, Nina would like to make sure the user enters valid data. For example, before a record is changed in the database, she wants to make sure that both a first and last name were entered, that the value entered for the date is in the correct format, and that a valid number was entered for the estimated annual sales. Visual Basic supports several classification functions that determine the characteristics of a variable or object property like the Text property of a text box. A **classification function** is a function that determines the data type of a variable.

You can use the IsDate function to determine if a date value is a date or can be converted to a valid date, and the IsNumeric function to determine if a number value is valid (that is, it contains only numbers and an optional decimal point). The IsDate and IsNumeric functions use the following syntax:

IsDate(*string*)

IsNumeric(*string*)

- Each of these functions takes one argument, *string*.

- Each of these functions returns a Boolean value. If *string* is a valid date or number, **IsDate** and **IsNumeric** return True, respectively. If *string* is not a valid date or number the respective function returns False.

You can use the IsDate and IsNumeric functions in an If statement in the contact management system to determine if input is valid. While you could place these If statements in the LostFocus events for each text box, the Data control supports an event called the Validate event that is well-suited for this purpose. The Validate event uses the following syntax:

Private Sub *Object*_**Validate** ([*index* **As Integer**,] *action* **As Integer**, *save* **As Integer**)

    statements

End Sub

- *Object* is any instance of a Data control.

- Several different actions cause a **Validate** event to occur. Whenever the current record is repositioned, a record is updated, or a record is deleted, the argument is passed to the Validate event using an argument named *action*.

- The optional *index* argument identifies the Data control, if it is a member of a control array.

- The *action* argument is an integer that indicates the operation causing this event to occur. Each of these actions can be expressed as a constant. The *statements* in the Validate event procedure determine to which constant the *action* argument should be set. Valid constants for the *action* argument are: vbDataActionCancel, vbDataActionMoveFirst, vbDataActionMovePrevious, vbDataActionMoveNext, vbDataActionMoveLast, vbDataActionAddNew, vbDataActionUpdate, vbDataActionDelete, vbDataActionFind, vbDataActionBookmark, vbDataActionClose, and vbDataActionUnload. Refer to the Help system for more information about these constants.

- The *save* argument is a Boolean expression specifying whether bound data has changed.

In this session, you will need to cancel the current action, like updating a record, whenever invalid data is detected. If the input is valid, then the update will proceed. If not, you can display a message box to the user describing the nature of the problem and then cancel the update. To do this you set the action argument to the constant vbDataActionCancel when invalid data is detected. When the end of the event procedure is reached, the Update method that caused the Validate event will be canceled.

Nina would like you to program the Validate event for the Data control to make sure that both the First Name and Last Name text boxes contain text, that the Date Added text box contains a valid date, and that the Estimated Annual Sales text box contains a valid number. You first will declare variables that only will be used within the Validate procedure: pstrMessage will hold the message the user sees if there is invalid data and pintReturn will hold the return value of the MsgBox function. Because these variables only are used by this procedure, they are declared as local variables.

To validate the user input and display a message if necessary:

1. Open the Code window for the **datContact** object's **Validate** event procedure.

2. Enter the following code in the window:

```
Dim pstrMessage As String
Dim pintReturn As Integer
If Action = vbDataActionUpdate Then
    If txtLastName.Text = "" Or txtFirstName.Text = _
        "" Then
        pstrMessage = _
            "You must enter both a first and last name"
        Action = vbDataActionCancel
    End If
    If IsDate(txtDateAdded.Text) = False Then
        pstrMessage = pstrMessage & Chr(vbKeyReturn) & _
            "The date " & txtDateAdded.Text & _
            " is not a date"
        Action = vbDataActionCancel
    End If
```

```
     If IsNumeric(txtEstimatedSales.Text) = False Then
         pstrMessage = pstrMessage & Chr(vbKeyReturn) & _
             "The estimated sales " & _
             txtEstimatedSales.Text & " is not a number"
         Action = vbDataActionCancel
     End If
     If Action = vbDataActionCancel Then
         pintReturn = _
             MsgBox(pstrMessage, vbOKOnly, "Input error")
     End If
 End If
```

These statements test the value of each user input field. Notice the MsgBox function is called only once. You could have called it each time you detected invalid input, but that could confuse the user with several message boxes appearing one after another.

```
If Action = vbDataActionUpdate Then
```

The statement to test for valid input only needs to be executed when the user is trying to update a record. If a record is repositioned, or is being deleted, there is no need to verify these changes. In other words, when the Update method is called, the Action argument is set to vbDataActionUpdate and the Validate event occurs. Thus, you checked this argument to determine whether or not to validate the input.

```
If txtLastName.Text = "" Or txtFirstName.Text = _
    "" Then
    pstrMessage = _
        "You must enter both a first and last name"
    Action = vbDataActionCancel
End If
```

The If statement determines if either txtLastName or txtFirstName contains no text. If either of these conditions is True, then the string pstrMessage changes accordingly. By setting the variable Action to the constant vbDataActionCancel, the Update method that causes this event will be canceled when the event procedure ends.

```
If IsDate(txtDateAdded.Text) = False Then
    pstrMessage = pstrMessage & Chr(vbKeyReturn) & _
        "The date " & txtDateAdded.Text & _
        " is not a date"
    Action = vbDataActionCancel
End If
```

This If statement calls the IsDate function to determine whether or not the date added contains a valid date value. If it does not (that is, IsDate is False), then additional information is appended to the existing contents of the message, and the Update action will be canceled. The next If statement behaves identically but uses the IsNumeric function to check that the Estimated Annual Sales text box contains a valid number.

```
If Action = vbDataActionCancel Then
    pintReturn = _
        MsgBox(pstrMessage, vbOKOnly, "Input error")
End If
```

Finally, the contents of the argument Action are checked to see if the pending method that caused this Validate event needs to be canceled. If so, the message box is displayed.

Nina suggests you test the code for the Validate event.

To test the code for the Validate event:

1. Save the project then start the program.

2. Click **Edit** then **Add.**

3. Enter **10** as the client ID. Leave the first and last names blank. Enter **1/1/1/3** as the date. Enter **22.3.3** as the estimated annual sales amount.

4. Click **Edit** then **Update** to attempt to save your changes.

5. A message box should appear describing the input errors, as shown in Figure 4-25.

Figure 4-25 ◀
Input error
message box

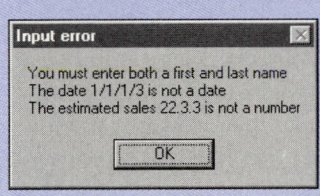

Developing an Error Handler

Because this program will be used by the entire sales force of Atlantic Marketing, Nina does not want the program to generate a run-time error if a user tries to perform an impossible action. The three most likely offenses a user will commit in the contact management system are trying to update a record that has not been edited, trying to delete a nonexistent record, and entering incorrect data in the name fields. Nina created the database such that each record must have a first name and a last name. Nina has asked you to find a way to avert these problems.

These problems can be solved by writing a set of Visual Basic statements that will execute when a run-time error occurs. This set of statements is referred collectively to as an error handler. An **error handler** is made up of a set of statements inside a procedure that executes when a run-time error occurs. An error handler in a procedure is said to be enabled when an error handler is included in that procedure. When a run-time error occurs, the error handler becomes active; that is, it begins to execute the statements that make up the error handler. Figure 4-26 illustrates the processing that takes place by a procedure's error handler.

Figure 4-26 ◀
Control flow of
an error handler

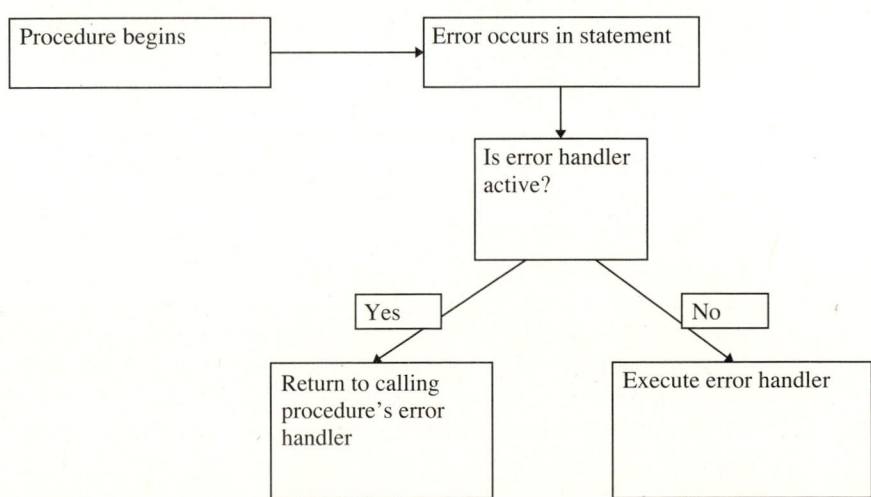

If the error handler is enabled but not active, then the statements in the calling procedure's error handler are executed. If another run-time error occurs while the error handler is executing, control returns to the calling procedure. This process continues until an enabled but inactive error handler is found.

The code in an error handler is not a separate Function or Sub procedure but rather a set of statements inside a procedure. Depending on the cause and severity of the error, your error handler may display a message box describing the cause of the error to the user or it may reset the variables. The error handler then can continue execution of the program.

Trapping Errors Resulting from an Update Statement

One of the problems that can occur when working with a database is when a user tries to update a record when no current record exists or when duplicate records would violate rules contained in the database. Trying to update a record before making it available for editing also will cause an error. Entering invalid data for a field also will cause a run-time error but you already have solved that problem by checking the input in the Data control's Validate event. You need to create a means by which errors will not stop the program from running. Nina wants the program to tell the user what is wrong and allow the user to continue.

You can use the On Error statement to identify errors and optionally a Resume Next statement to tell the program where to continue processing. The On Error statement creates an enabled error handler for the procedure. The Resume Next statement, when executed, will cause execution to continue at the statement following the statement that caused the error. If the Resume Next statement is omitted, then statements will continue to be executed until an End Sub or Exit Sub is reached. The On Error statement has the following syntax:

On Error GoTo *ErrorHandler*

  statements

Exit Sub

ErrorHandler:

  statements

[Resume Next]

- The **On Error** statement tells Visual Basic that when a run-time error occurs in this procedure, the *ErrorHandler* will be called. You do not explicitly call the error handler. Rather, Visual Basic calls it when an error occurs. If an error occurs, Visual Basic uses the **GoTo** statement to determine the code that will be executed in response to the error.

- The name *ErrorHandler* is called a line label. The line label is used to define a location in your program. It identifies a single line of code. Line labels must begin in the first column, must start with a letter, and end with a colon (:). In this case, when the error handler is called, the next statement that will be executed is the statement following the line:

  ```
  ErrorHandler:
  ```

- After the statements in the error handler have executed, the optional **Resume Next** statement tells Visual Basic to continue execution at the statement immediately following the statement that caused the error. Otherwise, execution continues in the error handler until an End Sub or Exit Sub statement is reached.

- Usually, a procedure exits when the last line of the procedure (End Sub) is reached, which means Visual Basic would continue execution of the procedure, causing the statements in the error handler to be executed even if there was no error. The **Exit Sub** statement can occur anywhere in a procedure and does not have to be part of an error handler. When the Exit Sub statement is reached, the procedure will exit. Because the error handler usually appears at the end of a procedure, the Exit Sub statement is necessary to exit a procedure when no error occurs. Otherwise, the error handler would execute every time the procedure was called.

When an error occurs in the contact management system, Nina wants the program to execute code in response to the error and display a message in a message box that explains the cause of the error to the user.

When an error occurs, a numeric code and description of the error is stored in a predefined object called the **Err object**. A predefined object works just like other objects you have used. You do not create an instance of the Err object, however. It is created by Visual Basic for you. This information is stored in the Err object's properties as follows:

- The **Description** property contains a short description of the error.

- The **Number** property contains a numeric value representing the error.

- The **Source** property contains the name of the object or program that originally generated the error.

The error handler you create will display a general message for run-time errors that occur in the mnuEditUpdate object's Click event procedure. The message will tell the user the number and the description of the error encountered.

To display a message when a run-time error occurs and continue program execution:

1. Open the Code window for the **mnuEditUpdate** object's **Click** event procedure.

2. Enter the following code in the window (shown in bold):

```
Private Sub mnuEditUpdate_Click()
    Dim pstrMessage As String
    On Error GoTo mnuEditUpdate_Error
    mrstContact.Update
    Exit Sub

mnuEditUpdate_Error:
    pstrMessage = "Cannot perform operation" & _
        Chr(vbKeyReturn) & "Error #" & _
        Err.Number & ":" & Err.Description
    MsgBox pstrMessage, vbExclamation, _
        "Atlantic Contact - Database Error"
End Sub
```

Examine the code you just wrote. The code will be executed whenever clicking the Update menu item causes a run-time error. This will happen if a user tries to update a record when no current record exists, a duplicate client ID is found, or the record has not been made available for editing.

```
On Error GoTo mnuEditUpdate_Error
```

The first line of code identifies the line label for the error handler (mnuEditUpdate_Error) in the procedure. When an error occurs, the statement following the line label named mnuEditUpdate_Error: will be executed. Remember that run-time errors still occur, but the program is dealing with the errors. This also is known as error trapping. **Error trapping** is a programming concept that you use to prevent run-time errors from ending a program.

```
Exit Sub
```

Notice the location of the Exit Sub statement. This causes the procedure to exit and return to the calling procedure or, in this case, wait for more events. Without this statement, Visual Basic would continue execution of the procedure. This would cause the statements in the error handler to be executed, even if there was no error.

```
mnuEditUpdate_Error:
```

2. Enter the following code in the window:

```
Private Sub mnuEditRecord_Click()
    Dim pstrMessage As String
    On Error GoTo mnuEditRecord_Error
    mrstContact.Edit
    Exit Sub

mnuEditRecord_Error:
    pstrMessage = "Cannot perform operation #" _
        & Err.Number & ":" & Err.Description
    MsgBox pstrMessage, vbExclamation, _
        "Atlantic Contact - Database Error"
End Sub
```

3. Save the project.

4. Run the program.

5. Test the handler by typing **Ctrl+L** to locate the last record. Type **Ctrl+N** to locate the end of file.

6. Click **Edit** then **Edit Record** to try to edit the nonexistent record. The message box should appear.

7. End the program.

The contact management system now is complete. Nina is certain various objects on the form—Data control, text boxes, menu—will make it easy for the Atlantic Marketing salespeople to enter, locate, and maintain information about clients. The error handlers will help users correct errors while running the program. Nina knows the contact management system is a great improvement over the paper-based system, and is confident it will be well received by the salespeople.

Quick Check

1 What is the purpose of the FindFirst method of the Recordset object, and how would you use it in a Visual Basic statement?

2 What is the purpose of an input box?

3 What is the purpose of an error handler and what Visual Basic statements are used to create an error handler?

4 What is the purpose of data validation?

5 What is the Resume Next statement used for?

6 What is the difference between the End Sub and Exit Sub statements?

Figure 4-29 lists and defines the new terms presented in this tutorial.

Figure 4-29 ◀
New terms

Term	Definition
Bound control	A bound control displays the changes in the current record of the Recordset object on the form. A bound control can provide access to a specific field in a database through a Data control by setting the DataSource and DataField properties. Also called data aware controls.
Classification functions	Classification functions determine the characteristics of a variable or object property, such as the IsDate and IsNumeric functions.
Copy buffer	The copy buffer stores the current record and any changes made to it before those changes actually are written to the underlying database table or query.
Current record pointer	The current record pointer indicates the active record in a Recordset object. You do not access the current record pointer explicitly. Rather, you move the current record pointer indirectly using the Recordset object's methods.
Data Access Objects	Data Access Objects (DAO) enable you to use a programming language to access and manipulate data in a database, and to manage tables, their objects, and their structure.
Data aware controls	Also called bound controls. A data aware control displays the changes in the current record of the Recordset object on the form. A data aware control can provide access to a specific field in a database through a Data control by setting the DataSource and DataField properties.
Data control	The Data control is a control that is used to bind the data in a Microsoft Access database to other controls in your Visual Basic program.
Database	A database is a collection of related information organized in tables.
Dynaset	A dynaset is a dynamic view of the information contained in a database table or query.
Error handler	An error handler is made up of a set of statements inside a procedure that executes when a run-time error occurs.
Error trapping	Error trapping is a programming concept that you use to prevent run-time errors from ending a program.
Field	A field is a column of data stored in a table.
Hot key	Also called access key. The underlined character of a menu title or menu item that allows the title or item to be activated by pressing the Alt key and the hot key at the same time.
Input box	An input box is like a message box. An input box returns a string that can be used by your program.
Menu Editor	The Menu Editor is a dialog box that allows you to create a menu system for your program.
Method	A method is a procedure that acts on an object. It contains code that is built inside the object to accomplish a task.
Microsoft Jet database engine	The Microsoft Jet database engine is the DBMS that retrieves data from, and stores data in, an Access database.
Query	A query is an instruction to a database to return a set of records from one or more tables in a specific order.
Record	A record is a row of data stored in a table.
Recordset object	Recordset objects are created at run time by the Recordset property of the Data control. They are a view of the data stored in the database.
Relational database	A relational database stores information in several tables that can be related together in different ways.
Separator bar	A separator bar is a horizontal line that visually groups related menu items together to make the interface easier to use.

Figure 4-29 ◀
New terms
(continued)

Term	Definition
Shortcut key	A shortcut key, is a function key (such as F5) or a key combination (such as Ctrl+A or Ctrl+X) that executes a command.
Submenu	A submenu is a menu item that displays another menu, rather than executing code in an event procedure.
Table	A table consists of rows and columns. The column defines a name for, and characteristics of, the stored information.

Tutorial Assignments

Nina has asked you to design a program for Atlantic Marketing that can be used by each salesperson and the sales manager to look at the sales records of each client. Each client may have one or more sales records. The program needs to be able to locate a specific client using an input box. After a client is located, the user needs to be able to continue to look at the sales records for the selected client. You will need to create command buttons to accomplish this. The first will display the input box and locate the first record if it is found. The second should locate the next record given the selected criteria. The information is stored in a query based on the contact table and the sales table. The query is named qryContactSales. Users will locate records in the query using the command buttons, so the Data control should be invisible. Figure 4-30 shows the completed form for the program.

Figure 4-30 ◀

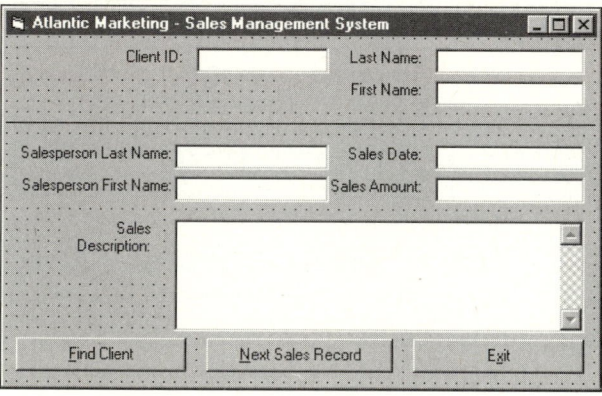

1. Make sure your Student Disk is in the appropriate disk drive, then start Visual Basic.

2. Create a new project and save the form with the name **frmAtlanticSales.frm** and the project with the name **Atlantic Sales.vbp** in the **TAssign** folder in the **Tutorial.04** folder on your Student Disk.

3. Change the form name to **frmAtlanticSales**, and its caption to **Atlantic Marketing - Sales Management System**.

4. Draw a Data control on the form. Set the Visible property so that the Data control will not be visible when the program is run. Set the properties of the Data control so it will connect to the table named **qryContactSales** in the Access database named **AM_CMS.mdb** in the **TAssign** folder in the **Tutorial.04** folder on your Student Disk. The Recordset object created should be a **Dynaset** type recordset. Name the Data control **datContactSales**. *Note:* Because it will be invisible when the program runs, it does not matter where you draw the Data control; you will just use its functionality to connect to the database.

5. Draw eight text boxes and their corresponding labels so your form looks like Figure 4-30. The Sales Description text box must be able to display multiple lines and should contain vertical scroll bars. Set the name for each text box as follows:
   txtClientID
   txtLastName
   txtFirstName
   txtSalesLastName
   txtSalesFirstName
   txtSalesDate
   txtSalesAmount
   txtSalesDescription

6. Set the necessary properties for each text box so it can communicate with the Data control you created in Step 5. The corresponding field names in the table are as follows:
   fldClientID
   fldLastName
   fldFirstName
   fldSalesLastName
   fldSalesFirstName
   fldSalesDate
   fldSalesAmount
   fldSalesDescription

7. Create three command buttons on the form to find a client, find the next sales record, and exit the program as shown in Figure 4-30. Be sure each command button has a hot key as shown in Figure 4-30. The command buttons should be named, **cmdFindClient**, **cmdNextSalesRecord**, and **cmdExit**.

8. Declare a String variable named **mstrLastName** such that it can be used by all the event procedures in the program. This variable will be used to build a search string for record retrieval from the database. Require that all variables be declared explicitly.

9. Activate the Code window for the cmdExit object's Click event procedure. Write the code to end the program.

10. Activate the Code window for the cmdFindClient object's Click event procedure. Write the statement to display an input box that will ask the user what last name to find. The return value of the input box should be the last name the user is searching for, stored in the string named mstrLastName. Include a descriptive prompt and title for the input box.

11. In the same event procedure in the Code window write the statement that will create the search string. You will use this string when you call the FindFirst method in the next step.

12. Write the statement to locate the first record in the recordset having the specified criteria. To do this you will need to call the FindFirst method of the recordset.

13. Activate the Code window for the cmdNextSalesRecord object's Click event and write the statement to locate the next record in the recordset having the specified criteria. To do this you will need to call the FindNext method of the recordset.

14. Save the project.

15. Test the program by clicking the **Find Client** button and entering the name **Zorn**. Click the **Find Next Sales Record** button to locate the other records for the client Zorn.

16. Repeat Step 15 for the client named **Cantor**.

17. Exit the program by using the **Exit** command button.

18. Print the Form Image and Code.

19. Exit Visual Basic.

Case Problems

1. Neptune Warehouse Neptune Warehouse stores a variety of goods for the auto parts industry. Lou Ortiz is in charge of creating a simple system that will allow the company to manage its inventory. She has asked you to create the menu system for the program. Later, the code will be written for each of the menu items you create. She has designed the appearance of the menus on paper as shown in Figure 4-31, and wants you to use the Menu Editor to create the actual menu items.

Figure 4-31 ◀

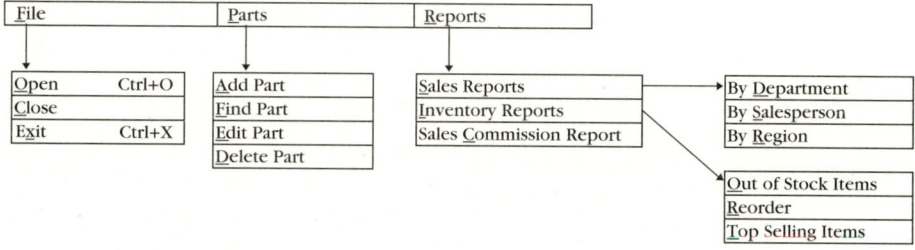

1. Make sure your Student Disk is in the appropriate disk drive, then start Visual Basic.

2. Create a new project and change the form name to **frmNeptuneInventory**, and its caption to **Neptune Warehouse - Inventory**.

3. Save the form with the name **frmNeptuneInventory.frm** and the project with the name **Neptune Inventory.vbp** in the **Cases** folder in the **Tutorial.04** folder on your Student Disk.

 EXPLORE

4. Create the menus according to the specifications in Figure 4-31. Be sure to choose appropriate names for each menu item and set the shortcut and hot keys as described.

5. After you have created the menus, be sure to check that each menu item is in the correct place.

6. Save the form and project.

7. Exit Visual Basic.

2. Henderson Music Henderson Music is a small music store in a college town. Valerie Henderson, the store's owner, wants a program to display items from its music collection database. The music collection database was created using Microsoft Access. The three items to be displayed are **Music Category, Recording Artist Name**, and **Recording Title**. Valerie has asked you to create a test program with the title, **Henderson Music**. She wants the program to contain three text boxes and three Data controls. Each text box will be bound to one of the three Data controls so when a user clicks a Data control, one of the categories will be displayed in the matching bound text box. You do not have to write any code for the Data controls to access the database in this program, but you should provide descriptive labels for the objects. Each data control also should contain a caption that describes the table in the database. You will write only one line of code for the working **Exit** button. Make sure you use valid names for the objects on the form. Each of the three Data objects will connect to **Music.mdb**, which is located in the **Cases** folder in the **Tutorial.04** folder on your Student Disk. The RecordSource for each Data control should be set to **tblMusicCategory**, **tblRecordingArtistName**, and **tblRecordingTitle**, respectively. The DataSource and DataField properties for the bound text boxes should be set to the name of the appropriate Data control, as follows:

tblMusicCategory	**tblRecordingArtist**	**tblRecordingTitle**
fldMusicCategory	**fldRecordingArtistName**	**fldRecordingTitle**
	fldRecordingLabel	
	fldFormat	
	fldNumberofTracks	

When your form and code are complete, test the program, and save the form as frmHendersonMusic and the project as Henderson Music in the Cases folder in the Tutorial.04 folder on your Student Disk. Print the Form Image and the Form as text.

3. Galaxy Personnel Galaxy Personnel is a payroll and personnel services company in Denver, Colorado. Each day hundreds of weekly time sheets need to be entered into a database. Because the volume of data entry in payroll is so large, and accuracy is so important, they need a form that will validate all user input before adding records. Also, to minimize the number of keystrokes, or mouse buttons, the user needs to type to add a time sheet, the program needs to validate automatically when the last data entry field loses focus. If correct, the program should add the record to the database, then clear the text boxes of their contents in preparation for the next record, and set the focus to the first data entry field. If there are any errors in the input, then the program should display a message box, cancel the update, and set the focus back to the first input field. The program will operate in two modes. While in Browse mode, the user should be able to click the buttons on the data control to locate different records but not change the contents of the text boxes. When in Add mode, the data control should be invisible, and the text boxes enabled so the user can add records. When the program is first started, the form should be in Browse mode. The following table shows the names of the fields, their valid values, and a brief description of the field.

Figure 4-32 ◀
Field names
and valid
values

Field name	Description	Valid values
fldEmployeeID	Employee identification number	Between 100 and 1000
fldHoursWorked	Number of hours worked	Must be greater than 0 and less than 60
fldPayRate	Rate of employee pay	Between 4.25 and 32.5
fldPayDate	Date paid	Must be a valid date value

When complete your form should look like Figure 4-33.

Figure 4-33 ◀

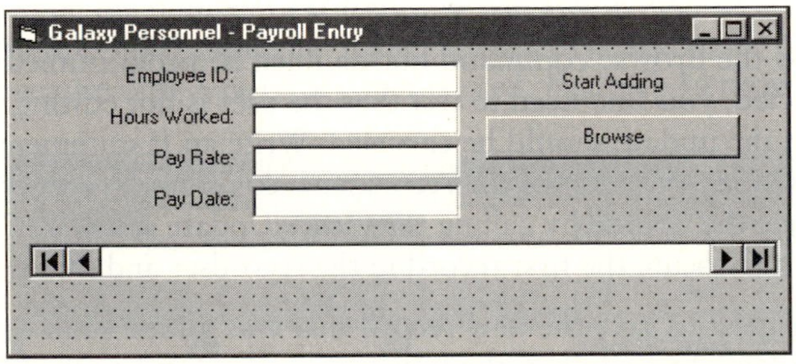

1. Make sure your Student Disk is in the appropriate disk drive and start Visual Basic.

of the form elements you have created in the past—a title bar, a border, or any input objects—because the user will not need to do anything to the form.

A Form object has properties that allow you to control the appearance of a form. The **BorderStyle** property of the Form object works differently from the BorderStyle property of the Shape object in that it is read-only at run time. You can change the settings of the BorderStyle property to modify the behavior of forms.

- When set to **0 - None**, the form will not display a border or title bar at run time.

- When set to **1 - Fixed Single**, the form only can be resized using the Maximize or Minimize buttons on the form's title bar.

- When set to **2 - Sizable** (the default setting) the form displays a border and a title bar, allowing the user to resize the form while the program is running.

- When set to **3 - Fixed Dialog**, the form cannot be resized and no Maximize and Minimize buttons are displayed on the form's title bar.

In addition to changing the form's border, you can set the form's position on the screen. While you could set the Left and Top properties of the form, the Form object supports another property called the **StartUpPosition** property.

- When set to **0 - Manual**, the form appears as defined by the Left and Top properties.

- When set to **2 - CenterScreen**, the form is centered on the whole screen.

- When set to **3 - WindowsDefault**, the window appears on the upper-left corner of the screen.

There are other BorderStyle and StartUpPosition property settings you can use in your program. Look at the Help screens for the BorderStyle property and the StartUpPosition property of the Form object for further information.

Mary suggests you now set the splash screen properties so it appears in the center of the screen with no border at run time. Because you now have two forms in your program, you must be careful to set the properties for the correct form and object. Only one Properties window can be active at a time. The Properties window sets the property values for an active form. Thus, you can click on a form to activate it, then change the properties as necessary.

To remove the form's borders and set the startup position:

1. Activate the Properties window for the object named **frmSplash**. Be sure the title bar of the Properties window says "frmSplash" or you will set the properties for the wrong object.

2. Set the BorderStyle property to **0 - None**. Note that the form has no caption. Because the title bar will not appear at run time, the caption is not relevant.

3. Set the StartUpPosition property to **2 - CenterScreen**.

Although the splash screen has been added to your program, it will not appear on the screen when the program first is started, because the project still will load its default startup form, frmMain. You now need to learn how to control the startup object that is displayed when a program is started. When a program is started, Visual Basic can display any form in the project or call a Sub procedure with the name Main.

The procedure Sub Main is not contained inside a Form module like the other procedures you have seen. Rather it is contained in a different kind of module called a standard module. A **standard module** is like a Form module but contains only general procedures and variable declarations commonly accessed by other modules within a program. Standard modules also are called bas modules. You can write general procedures in standard modules that are used by different forms in your program. It also is in a standard module that you write the procedure Sub Main. Before you can write the Sub Main procedure, you must create the new standard module.

To add a standard module to your program:

1. Click **Project** then **Add Module** on the menu bar. The Add Module dialog box will appear as shown in Figure 5-3.

Figure 5-3 ◀
Adding a standard module to the project

New tab is active

click Module to add a bas module

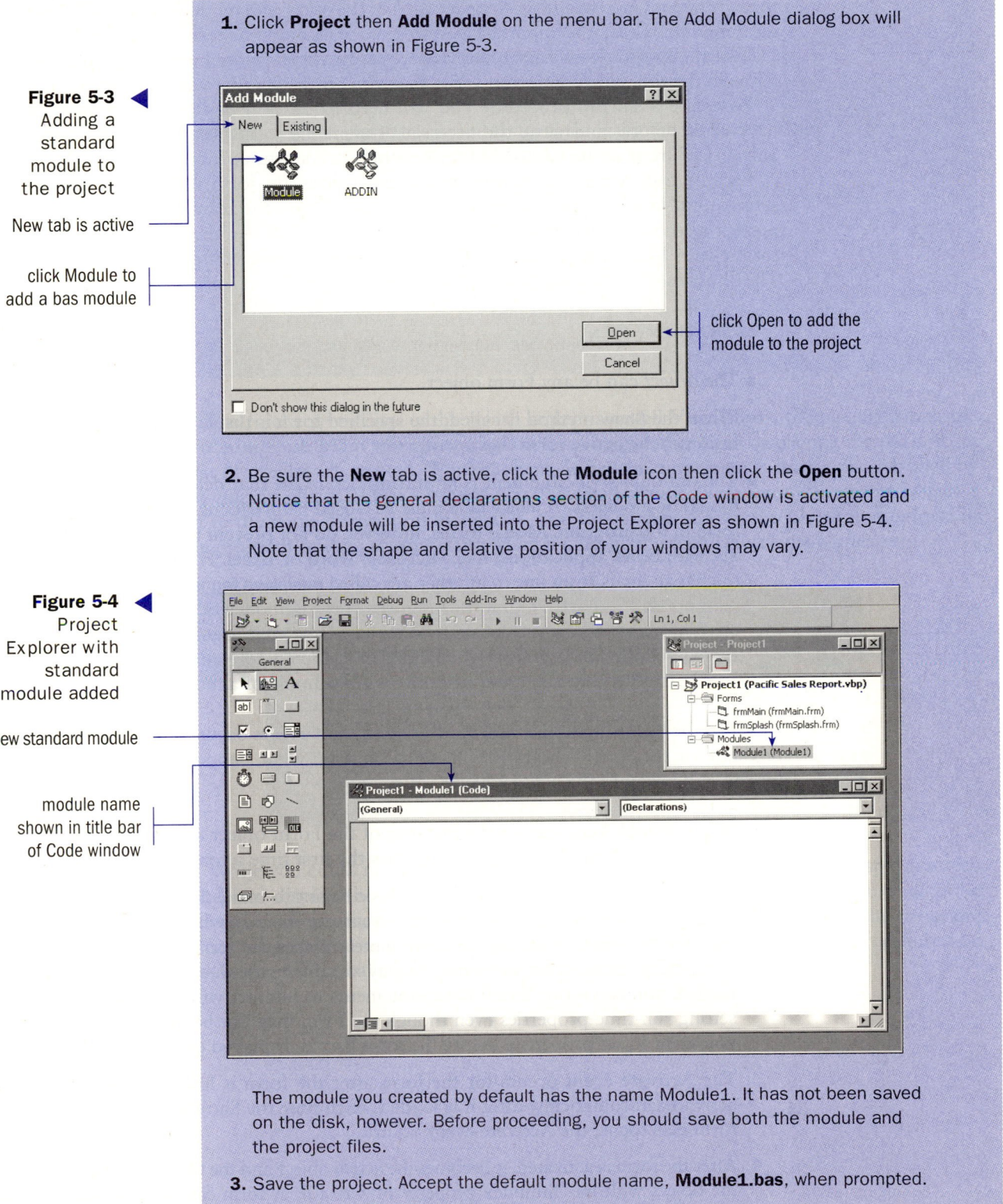

click Open to add the module to the project

2. Be sure the **New** tab is active, click the **Module** icon then click the **Open** button. Notice that the general declarations section of the Code window is activated and a new module will be inserted into the Project Explorer as shown in Figure 5-4. Note that the shape and relative position of your windows may vary.

Figure 5-4 ◀
Project Explorer with standard module added

new standard module

module name shown in title bar of Code window

The module you created by default has the name Module1. It has not been saved on the disk, however. Before proceeding, you should save both the module and the project files.

3. Save the project. Accept the default module name, **Module1.bas**, when prompted.

Now that the new standard module and project have been saved, Mary would like you to insert the procedure to display the splash screen when the program is started.

To change the startup object:

1. Click **Project** then **Project1 Properties** on the menu bar to open the Project Properties dialog box as shown in Figure 5-5.

Figure 5-5
Setting the startup object

General tab is active

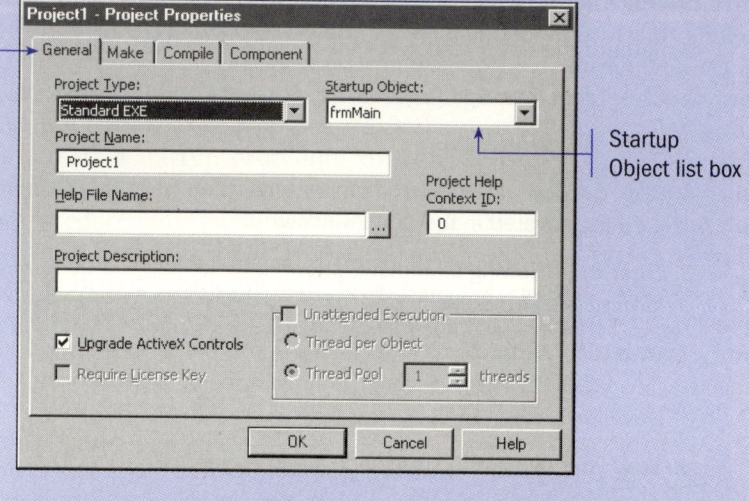

Startup Object list box

2. Be sure the **General** tab is active, then click the **Startup Object** list arrow.

   Notice there are three objects listed in the Startup Object list box corresponding to each module in the project.

3. Select **Sub Main** then click the **OK** button.

4. Save the project.

You now have completed the necessary steps to display the splash screen when the program is started rather than displaying the Main form. Mary suggests you test your work to be sure the splash screen is being displayed.

To test that the splash screen is being displayed:

1. Start the program. The splash screen shown in Figure 5-6 should be displayed in the center of the screen.

Figure 5-6
Splash screen at run time

TROUBLE? If the splash screen does not appear, you may have set the wrong project properties or written the statements in the wrong module. End the program and be sure you have set the startup object to Sub Main and the statement to call the Show method for the object named frmSplash in the Sub Main procedure. Repeat Step 1.

> **TROUBLE?** If the form did not appear in the center of the screen, you did not set the form's properties correctly. End the program and set the frmSplash object's StartUpPosition property to 2 - CenterScreen. Repeat Step 1.
>
> Notice the splash screen has no title bar or border because you set the BorderStyle property to 0 - None.

> **2.** End the program.

Your program now uses the Sub Main general procedure to display the splash screen and then the Main form. You now are ready to insert and display the other forms needed by the program.

Inserting a Form from a Template

When the program starts, after the splash screen is displayed, Mary would like another form to be displayed. This second form, called a login form, will ask the user to enter a name and employee ID. This user information will be displayed on the printed reports, and ultimately will be recorded to database tables when changes are made.

While you could create the login form by adding a blank form to the project and creating the necessary labels, text boxes, and command buttons, Visual Basic supplies several templates of common forms that you can add to your project and modify slightly to perform a specific task. This makes the program development process much easier. A **template** is an existing form that provides a way for you to reuse components, like forms, and add them to projects. One template that Visual Basic provides is a login form template. This form is used to obtain a user name and password from the user before continuing to execute the program.

REFERENCE window	**ADDING A TEMPLATE FORM TO YOUR PROJECT**
	■ Click Project then Add Form on the menu bar to display the Add Form dialog box.
	■ Click the New tab, if necessary.
	■ Click the desired form template to add an About Dialog, Log In Dialog, Options Dialog, or Splash Screen.
	■ Click Open to add the template to your project.

You now need to add the login template form to your program, and modify it to get the employee ID and employee name.

To add a login template to your project:

> **1.** Click **Project** then **Add Form** on the menu bar to open the Add Form dialog box.

> **2.** Click the **New** tab, if necessary.

removed from the screen and the computer's memory with the Unload statement. If you had used the Hide method, the splash screen would continue to take up memory. Because the splash screen will not be used again, there is no need for it to remain in memory. Finally, the login form is displayed as a modal form using the Show method with the vbModal argument.

You now have completed the statements to display the splash screen, load the forms into memory, then display the login form. Mary suggests you now run the program to see that the login form is being displayed after the splash screen and that the splash screen is being removed from the screen.

To test that the login form is being displayed:

1. Start the program. The splash screen appears for a moment then disappears. After the splash screen is unloaded, the login form appears.

   TROUBLE? If the login form does not appear, make sure you called the Show method on the frmLogin object in the Sub Main procedure.

   TROUBLE? If the splash screen still is visible, be sure you called the Unload statement on the frmSplash object in the Sub Main procedure.

2. End the program.

Now that the login form appears in your program, you must modify the labels and statements to make sure the user enters the correct information. First, you need to change the contents of the labels and the names of the text boxes.

To modify the properties of the login form's objects:

1. Be sure the **login form** is the active window.

2. Change the Caption property of the first label from User Name: to **Employee ID**.

3. Change the Caption property of the second label from Password: to **Employee Name**.

   TROUBLE? If your new captions do not fit, you may need to resize the form, labels, and/or text boxes. Use the sizing handles to size the objects so the new captions will fit.

4. Change the Name property of the first text box from txtUserName to **txtEmployeeID.**

5. Change the Name property of the second text box from txtPassword to **txtEmployeeName**.

   The PasswordChar property is used to prevent the characters typed by the user from being displayed on the screen. If a character is placed in this property, that character will be displayed in the text box for each character typed by the user.

6. Delete the **asterisk** (*) from the PasswordChar property of the txtEmployeeName text box.

7. Save the project.

Next you need to write the code to hide the login form. Before you can write this code you need to learn to reference the current form. The **Me** keyword allows you to reference the current form without retyping the form name over and over. Thus, if you wanted to call the Hide method on the current form, you could write the following statement:

```
Me.Hide
```

This statement gives you a way to hide the current form after the information is entered. Remember the login form either must be hidden or unloaded before the user can interact with the rest of the program because it was displayed as a modal form. You need a way to check whether the user clicked the OK button or the Cancel button on the form. You can accomplish this by storing the value True or False in a Boolean variable declared in the login form, and then checking the value of that variable in the Sub Main procedure.

In the past, your programs have had only one form. When a variable needed to be used by more than one event or general procedure on a form, you have declared the variable in the general declarations section of the Form module using the Private keyword. Variables declared with the Private keyword, however, cannot be used by other forms or standard modules. To accomplish this, you must use the **Public** keyword. To declare a Public variable, you use the same syntax as you have used to declare Private variables. Thus, to declare a Public variable named LoginSucceeded that has a data type of Boolean you would use the following statement:

```
Public LoginSucceeded As Boolean
```

Public variables behave differently depending on whether they are declared in a Form module or a standard module. If they are declared in a Form module, they are referenced just like the properties of an object. Thus, when you want to reference the Public variable named LoginSucceeded in the Form module named frmLogin you will use the following statement:

```
frmLogin.LoginSucceeded
```

If a Public variable is declared inside a standard module, it can be referenced by any module in your program and is not considered a property. Rather it is called a global variable. A **global variable** is a variable that can be referenced by any module in a program and whose value exists while the program is running. It is referenced like the Private variable you already have used.

Because the Public variable is declared in a Form module and is treated as a property, you did not use the standard prefix for the variable. Rather, you used a name that looks like a property. Property names generally use complete words with the first letter of each word capitalized.

The Public variable was declared in the login form by the template, so you now are ready to write the statements to check that the user entered both an employee ID and a name when the OK button is clicked. If the information was entered, you need to set the variable LoginSucceeded to True. If not, you need to display a message box asking the user to enter the information. If the Cancel button is clicked, you need to set the variable LoginSucceeded to False. The login form template has code in it to validate the user name and password. This code needs to be modified to verify that the user entered a value in both of the text boxes when the OK button is clicked.

To modify the statements to validate the user input:

1. Activate the Code window for the **cmdOK_Click** event procedure in the login form. Remember your program has multiple forms, so be sure you are entering the code into the correct form.

2. Remove the existing code and replace it with the following statements:

```
Private Sub cmdOK_Click( )
    If txtEmployeeID.Text <> "" _
        And txtEmployeeName.Text <> "" Then
        LoginSucceeded = True
        Me.Hide
    Else
        MsgBox ("Enter your employee ID and name")
    End If
End Sub
```

The code for the cmdCancel button's Click event already has been written.

3. Activate the **cmdCancel_Click** event procedure and note that the statements set the variable LoginSucceeded to False and then call the Hide method.

4. Save the project.

This If statement tests that both of the text boxes contain data. If they do, then the variable LoginSucceeded is set to True. Otherwise a message box is displayed telling the user to enter his or her employee ID and name.

Now that you have programmed the OK button on the login form, you must write the necessary statements to determine whether the OK or Cancel button was clicked. This code needs to be written in the Sub Main procedure. After the user has filled in the information in the login form, the code will test the value of the variable LoginSucceeded and display the Main form in the program if it is True and end the program if it is False.

You now are ready to write the statements to determine whether or not the login was successful. Otherwise the program should exit. Remember, because this is a Public variable in a Form module it is treated just like any other form property. You will hide the form rather than unloading it because you will need to reference the LoginSucceeded property in the Sub Main procedure to determine if the login was successful and later when the report is printed. Remember, when a form is unloaded, its objects and variables are removed from the computer's memory and can no longer be used.

To add the statements to test that the login was successful:

1. Append the following statements to the end of the Sub Main procedure just before the End Sub statement:

```
If frmLogin.LoginSucceeded = False Then
    End
Else
    frmMain.Show
    frmLogin.Hide
End If
```

2. Save the project.

The If statement tests to determine the value of the Public variable named LoginSucceeded in the frmLogin form. Because this variable is considered a property of the form, you specify the object name (frmLogin) followed by a period (.), followed by the property name (LoginSucceeded). If the value of this variable is False, then the program will end. If it is True, then the Main form (frmMain) will be displayed. Even though the frmLogin form no longer appears on the screen, the form and its objects still exist. Because the information in the text boxes in frmLogin will be used when you print the reports in the next session, you hide the form rather then unloading it so the objects still exist.

You now have completed all the code to display the splash screen, the login form, and then the Main form. Mary suggests you run the program to test that each form is being displayed.

To test the program:

1. Start the program. The splash screen is displayed briefly while the other forms are loaded, then disappears and the login form is displayed. The login form appears as shown in Figure 5-9.

Figure 5-9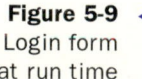
Login form
at run time

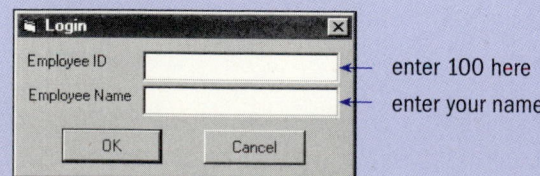

2. Enter **100** as the employee ID, then your name, then click the OK button to continue to display the Main form.

3. End the program.

Mary would like you to create two additional forms—one will display inventory data, and the other sales data. These forms each will use a Data control to establish a connection with a database table and bound text boxes to display that data just like the form you created in Tutorial 4. Instead of creating a new form, however, and then all the necessary objects, you can use a wizard. A **wizard** is a tool that leads a user step-by-step through an unusually long, difficult, or complex programming task. The wizard you will use to create the form for you is called the Data Form Wizard. The Data Form Wizard works by asking you to complete a series of questions in several dialog boxes that tell the wizard the database, table, and fields you want to use. After you have answered the questions, the wizard will create the form for you. It will not only create the Data control and bound text boxes, but also can create and write code for command buttons to insert, update, and delete records.

Mary suggests you now use the Data Form Wizard to create a form that will display data from the inventory table.

To use the Data Form Wizard to create a form:

1. Click **Project** then **Add Form** to display the Add Form dialog box.

TROUBLE? If you get an introductory Add Form dialog box, click the Don't show this dialog in the future check box and click OK.

TROUBLE? If you are using Visual Basic 5.0 Learning Edition, there are no Wizards. You will have to create a form that resembles Figure 5-16 on your own and connect it to the appropriate fields in the database Pacific.mdb in the Tutorial.05 folder on your Student Disk.

2. Click the **New** tab, if necessary, then double-click **VB Data Form Wizard**. When the Data Form Wizard – Introduction dialog box displays, click the Next button. The Database Type dialog box will appear as shown in Figure 5-10.

Figure 5-10 ◄
Database Type
dialog box

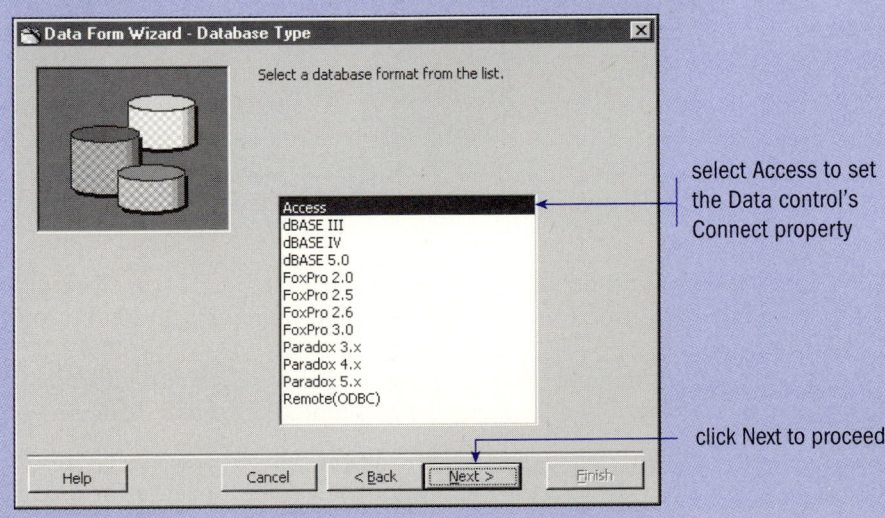

select Access to set
the Data control's
Connect property

click Next to proceed

3. Select **Access**. This sets the Connect property for your Data control. Click the **Next** button. The Database dialog box shown in Figure 5-11 appears on your screen.

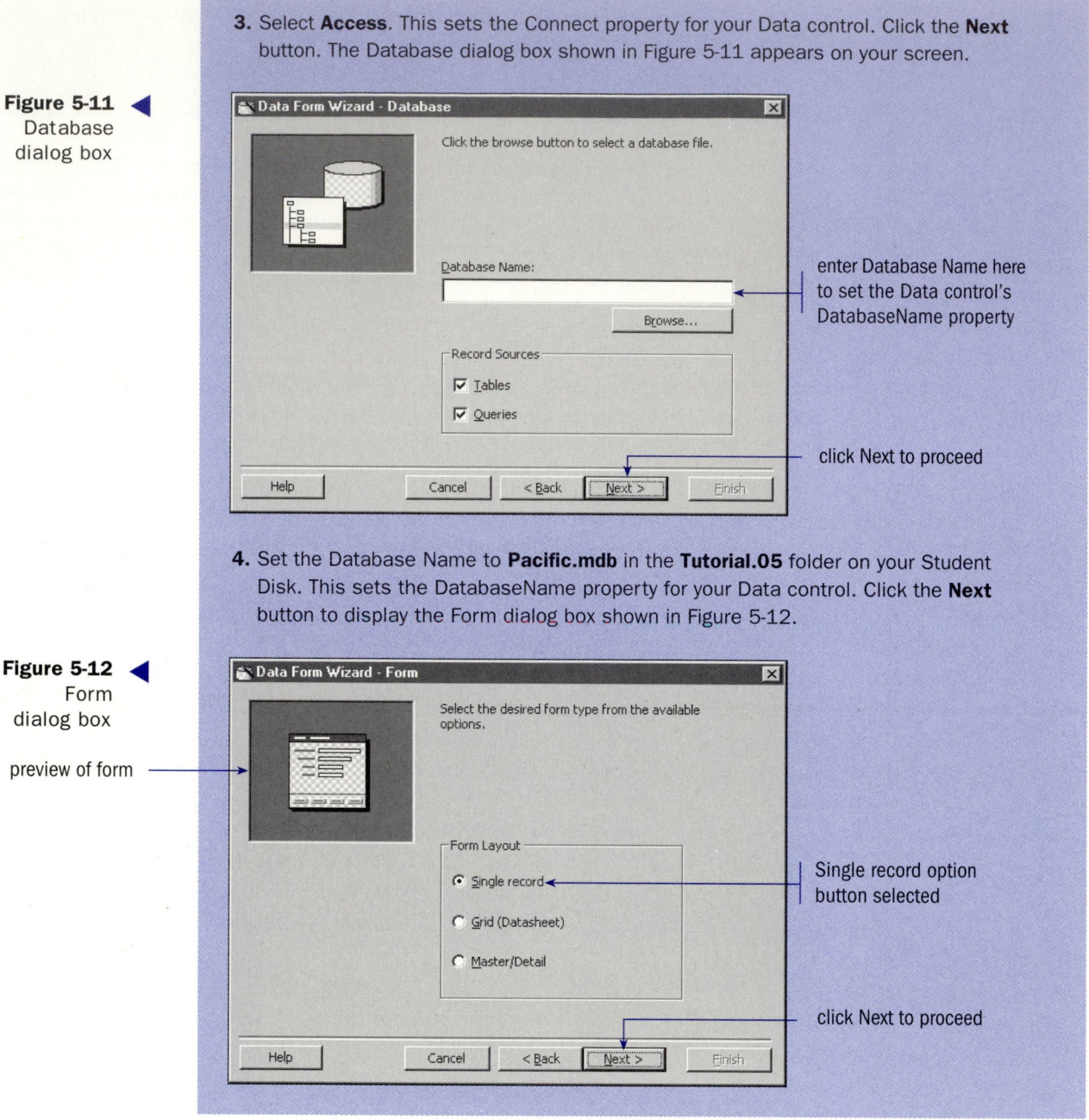

Figure 5-11 ◄
Database
dialog box

enter Database Name here
to set the Data control's
DatabaseName property

click Next to proceed

4. Set the Database Name to **Pacific.mdb** in the **Tutorial.05** folder on your Student Disk. This sets the DatabaseName property for your Data control. Click the **Next** button to display the Form dialog box shown in Figure 5-12.

Figure 5-12 ◄
Form
dialog box

preview of form

Single record option
button selected

click Next to proceed

The Form dialog box is used to tell the Data Form Wizard how the data should appear on the form. You can select from three different option buttons:

- If the Single record option button is selected, the form will be created so only one record will be displayed at a time. This is like the form you created in Tutorial 4.

- If the Grid (Datasheet) option button is selected, the form will display several records at a time in a grid. Each record will appear on a single line and each field will appear in a column.

- If the Master/Detail option button is selected, the form will operate with two tables.

Mary would like a single record to appear on the form at a time so you will select the Single record option button.

To create a form that will display a single record:

1. Click each of the option buttons and observe the display preview.

2. Click the **Single record** option button, then click the **Next** button to display the Record Source dialog box shown in Figure 5-13.

Figure 5-13 ◀
Record Source
dialog box

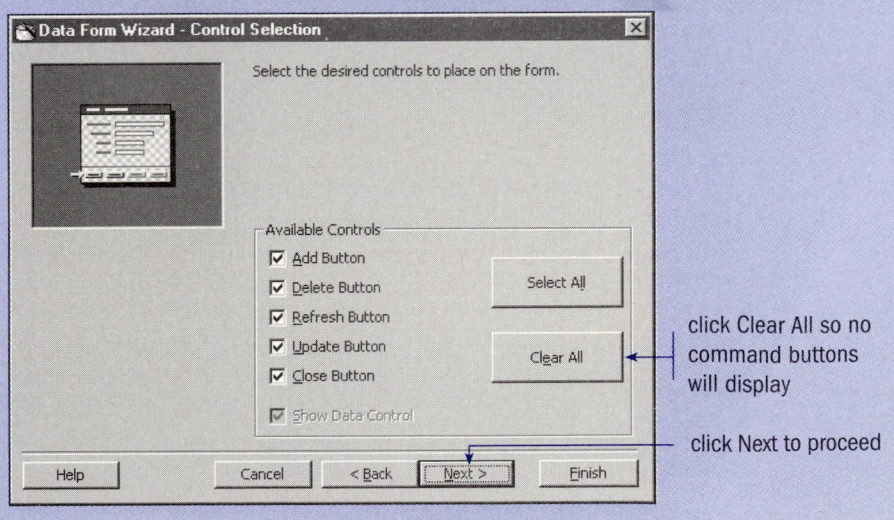

Move All Fields to the
Right button

Available Fields
list box

select table named
tblProduct to set the
Data control's
RecordSource property

Selected Fields
list box

click Next
to proceed

3. Click the **Record Source** list arrow to display a list of available tables in the database.

4. Select the table named **tblProduct**. This sets the RecordSource property of your Data control. The names of the fields are displayed in the Available Fields list box.

5. Click the **Move All Fields to the Right** button 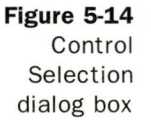. All the field names move from the Available Fields list box to the Selected Fields list box. This sets the properties that will bind the objects on your new form to the fields in the table.

6. Click the **Column to Sort By** list arrow and select the field named **fldProduct ID**. At run time, the records will be sorted by the Product ID field.

7. Click the **Next** button to display the Control Selection dialog box shown in Figure 5-14.

Figure 5-14 ◀
Control
Selection
dialog box

click Clear All so no
command buttons
will display

click Next to proceed

The Control Selection dialog box defines the form's buttons. For example, if you only wanted the user to see the navigation buttons on the Data control, you would not check any of the boxes. Mary wants the salespeople only to look at product information, so you will not add any command buttons to the form.

To specify the buttons that will be created on the form:

1. Click the **Clear All** button so all the Available Controls check boxes are not checked, then click the **Next** button to display the Finished! dialog box shown in Figure 5-15.

Figure 5-15 ◄
Finished
dialog box

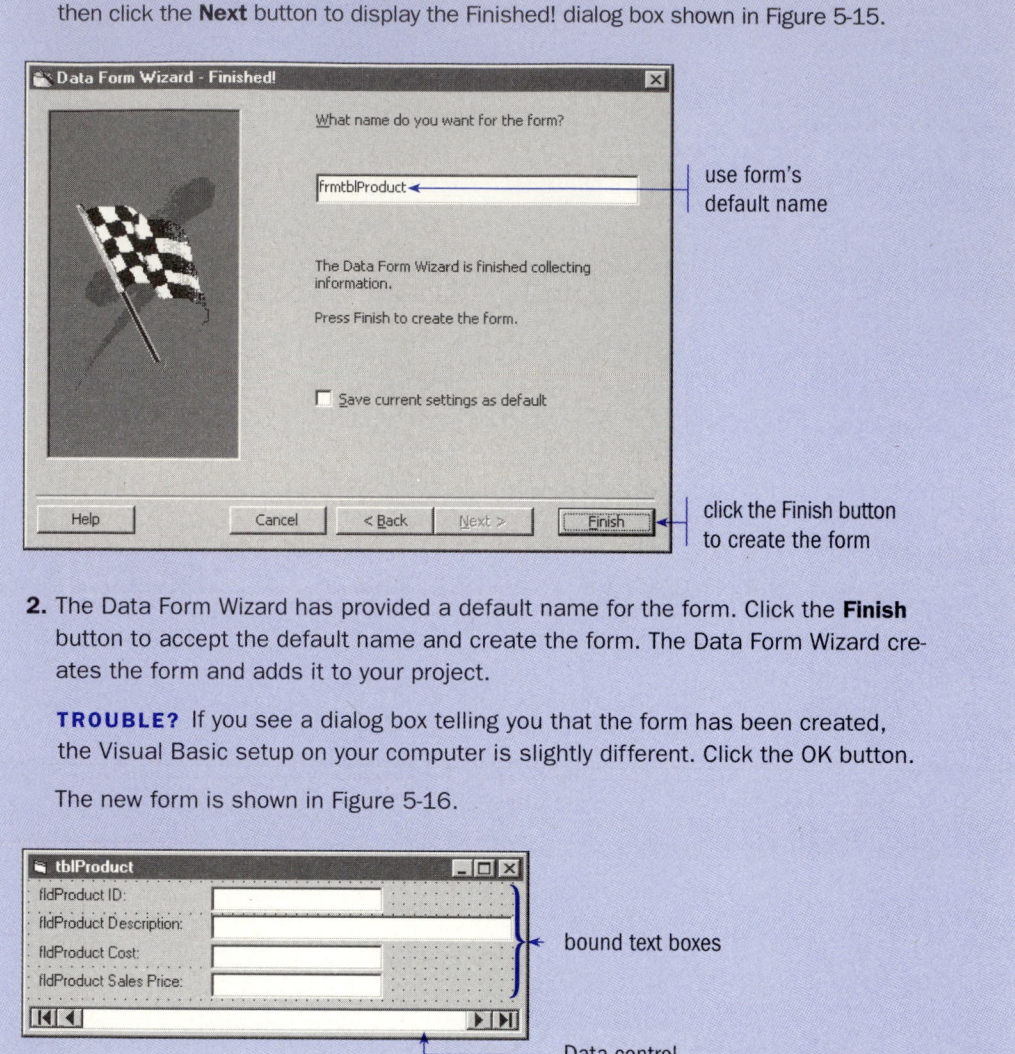

use form's
default name

click the Finish button
to create the form

2. The Data Form Wizard has provided a default name for the form. Click the **Finish** button to accept the default name and create the form. The Data Form Wizard creates the form and adds it to your project.

   TROUBLE? If you see a dialog box telling you that the form has been created, the Visual Basic setup on your computer is slightly different. Click the OK button.

   The new form is shown in Figure 5-16.

Figure 5-16 ◄
Completed
form

tblProduct	_ □ ×
fldProduct ID:	
fldProduct Description:	
fldProduct Cost:	
fldProduct Sales Price:	

bound text boxes

Data control

3. Save the form and the project. Accept the default form name when prompted.

The Data Form Wizard has created the Data control to communicate with a table in the database. Also, four bound text boxes have been created, corresponding to each of the fields in the table, and labels were created based on the field names. You now should change the title of the form and the caption of each label to improve the appearance of the form.

To change the form's title and the captions of each label:

1. Change the form's caption from tblProduct to **Pacific Electronics - Product Table**.

2. Remove the 'fld' prefix from each label's caption.

Although the form has been created, the Data Form Wizard has not written the code to display the form on the screen. Mary would like the form to be loaded with the other forms when the program is started and displayed when the user clicks the product item on the Main form's View menu. Therefore you need to call the Show method in the mnuViewProduct object's Click event procedure. The form should be loaded in the Sub Main procedure. While this form could be displayed as a modal form, Mary would like the user to be able to interact with the Main form and this form at the same time, so you will not display it as a modal form.

To write the code to load and display the Product form:

1. Activate the Code window for the **mnuViewProduct_Click** event procedure on the form named frmMain.

2. Enter the following statement, shown in bold, into the event procedure:

```
Private Sub mnuViewProduct_Click( )
    frmtblProduct.Show
End Sub
```

3. Activate the Code window for the **Sub Main** procedure in Module1.

4. Add the following statement to the Sub Main procedure immediately after the statement to load the Main form.

```
Load frmtblProduct
```

5. Save the project.

Now that you have created the form to display the list of products and wrote the code to open the form, Mary suggests you test the program to be sure it is working properly.

To test the View Product menu item and the Product form:

1. Start the project.

2. Enter **100** as the employee ID, then your name into the login form, then click the **OK** button. The Main form appears.

3. Click **View** then **Product** on the Main form's menu bar. The Product Table form appears as shown in Figure 5-17.

Figure 5-17 ◀
Completed
form at
run time

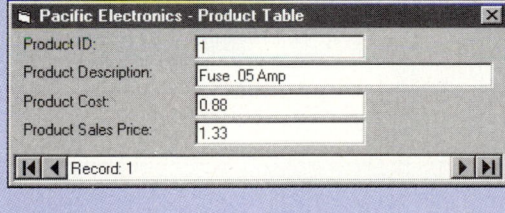

4. End the program.

The program for Pacific Electronics now displays the splash screen and login form. After the login form is displayed, and the user enters an employee ID and name, the Main form is displayed. The user can click the menu items to display the other forms as necessary.

Quick Check

1. What is the purpose of the startup object?

2. What is the purpose of a splash screen?

3. Describe the events that occur when the Show method is called?

4. What is the difference between the Hide method and the Unload statement?

5. What is a modal form?

6. What is the Data Form Wizard used for?

You have completed this session; you can take a break or continue on to Session 5.2.

SESSION 5.2

In this session you will design a sales report of sales records contained in a database. You will connect to the database using a Data control on the Main form, write code to print each record by enclosing the statements in a loop, write code to interact directly with the fields in the Recordset object, and use a counter and an accumulator to compute total orders and sales totals.

Specifying the Information for the Sales Report

In Session 4.2 you used the Data control to create a Recordset object based on the information you specified for the DatabaseName and RecordSource properties. In Session 5.1 you also used the Data control but it was created for you by the Data Form Wizard. In this session you again will use the Data control to create a Recordset object at run time. This Recordset object, however, will be based on information from two tables instead of one.

You can combine information from two or more tables by creating a query. Mary already has created the query using Access. Refer to the Database Appendix for more information on creating a query. Figure 5-18 shows the records and fields in the query.

Figure 5-18 ◀
Pacific
Electronics
sales query

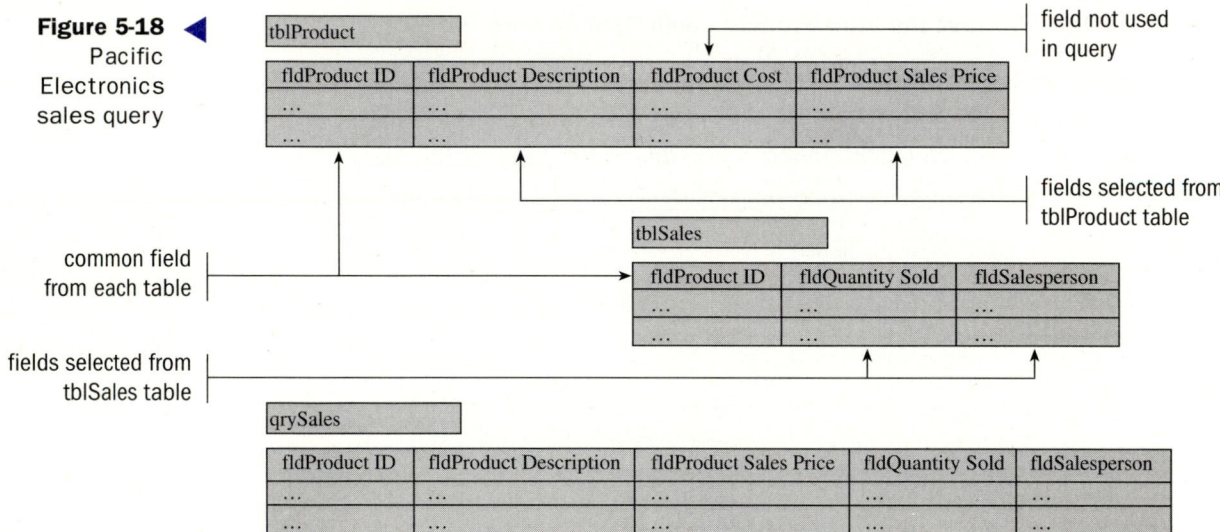

The query contains information from the tables named tblProduct and tblSales. The tblProduct table contains the Product Description, Product Cost, and Product Sales Price fields. The tblSales table contains the Quantity Sold and Salesperson fields. The Product ID is contained in both tables and is used to join them together in the query.

Before you can print any sales reports, you must connect the Main form to the database, Pacific.mdb, in the Tutorial.05 folder on your Student Disk. The user will not use this form to view the records in the database, only to print a report.

To connect the Main form to the sales query:

1. Start Visual Basic and open the project file named **Pacific Sales Report.vbp** in the Tutorial.05 folder on your Student Disk. If necessary, display the Main form.

2. Click the **Data** control 🖾 on the toolbox and draw an instance of the Data control across the bottom of the form. See Figure 5-19.

3. Set the DatabaseName property of the Data control to **Pacific.mdb** in the **Tutorial.05** folder on your Student Disk, and set the RecordSource property to **qrySales**.

4. Set the Caption property to **datSales** and the Name property of the Data control to **datSales**.

5. Set the Visible property to **False**. Because Mary does not want the user to use the buttons on the Data control, it should not be visible at run time. Your form looks like Figure 5-19.

Figure 5-19 ◀
Creating the
Data control on
the Main form

Data control

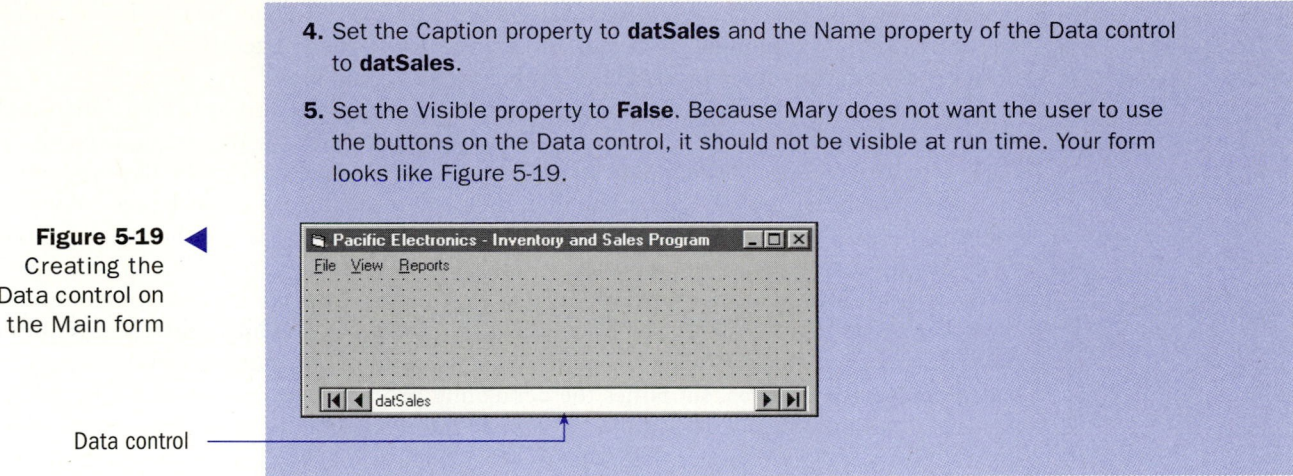

You can use the Recordset object created with the Data control to access the information in the sales database. In the form you opened, Mary already has created menu items to print the sales report. Now you can begin to design and create the sales report based on the information in the sales database.

Designing a Report

Just as a well-designed form makes the user interface of a program easy to use, a well-designed report makes the report easy to read and understand. In general, a report should have a page title that describes the report. Reports often are organized into columns. Each column should have a title that describes the information contained in the column, and the columns should be spaced evenly on the page. That is, the left and right margins should be the same, the spacing between the columns should be uniform, and numeric data should be aligned such that the decimal points are aligned under each other. Figure 5-20 illustrates the sales report you will create in this session.

Figure 5-20 ◀
Sales Report
layout

page title

column titles

report totals

detail lines

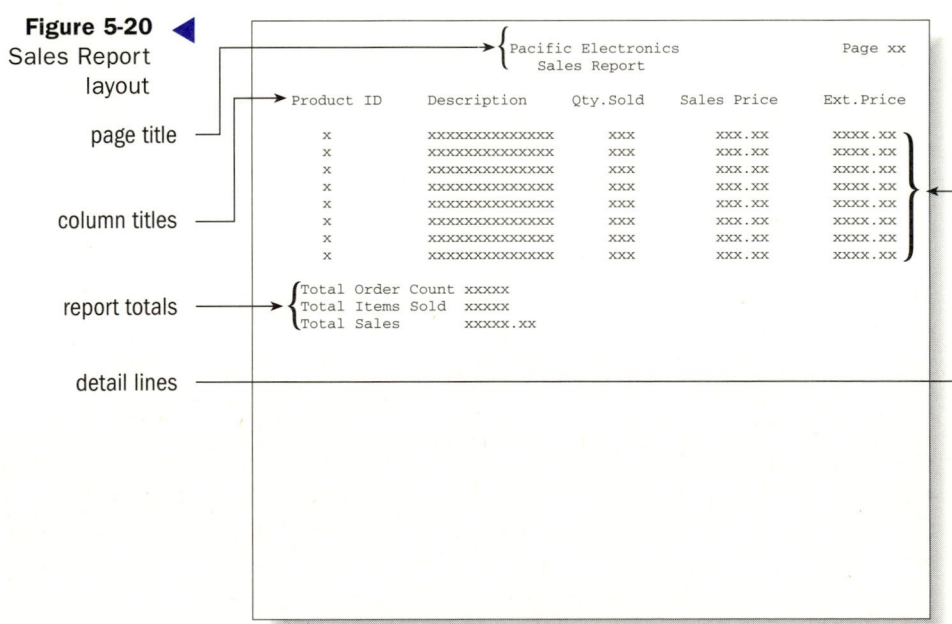

In addition to the page title and column titles, the report includes detail lines. When you print the detail lines of your report, you print a line for each record in the recordset. To do this, you execute the same statements repeatedly for each record printed in the report. When you print the detail records, you use variables to count the number of orders and accumulate the number of items ordered and total sales. After all the records have been processed, the report prints the totals below the detail lines.

Refer to your NEADT charts. The page and column titles need to print first. Then each detail line needs to print. After each record has been processed, the report totals print. All these activities will occur when the user clicks the Sales Report item on the Reports menu.

Some reports are more complicated than the one you will create, but the basic logic of printing a report is useful for beginning nearly every report you print. Although you could write all the code to print the report in a single event procedure, you instead will divide the code into different general procedures, as you did in Tutorial 3 when you computed the order totals in the cash register program. This process of dividing a task into multiple subtasks is called **modularization**. Dividing your programs into multiple procedures, also called **component modules**, simplifies the debugging process, because you can identify the procedure containing an error and focus on only those few lines of code. As your program grows, you can use component modules in other sections of the program or in other programs. This will save time in the development process. The program you will complete for Mary will include one general procedure to print the titles, one to print the detail lines, and one to print the report totals.

Printing a Report with the Printer Object

There are several ways of printing text and graphics in Visual Basic. In this session you will learn how to print using the **Printer** object, which initially is set to the default system printer from the Printers collection. A **collection** is an object that contains similar objects. It is simply a way of grouping like objects together. Although you have not worked with them explicitly, the Controls collection lists all the controls on a form and the Recordsets collection identifies the open Recordset objects in a database. The Printers collection contains each of the printers defined on your system. Visual Basic sets the Printer object to the default printer on your system. Just as the Recordset object supports several methods to manipulate data in a database table or query, the Printer object supports different methods to control how your output will be printed on the page. In this tutorial you will use the Font property, and EndDoc, NewPage, and Print methods of the Printer object.

The Font property sets the font for the printer. Depending on the type of printer attached to your computer, different fonts may be available. You can use the Windows 95 Control Panel to view the different fonts on your printer. The Font property has the following syntax:

object.**Font** = "*font name*"

- The *object* can be a Form, Printer, or any other object that supports the **Font** property.

- The *font name*, enclosed in quotation marks, can be any valid font installed on your computer. Note that the screen fonts that apply to a Form object and the printer fonts that apply to the Printer object may differ.

Many fonts are proportional. That is, the space used by a character depends on the size of the character. Thus, the letter "I" will take up less space than the letter "W". When printing reports, this is not always desirable because it is difficult to align a decimal point exactly when printing columns of numbers. Monospace fonts can be used in this situation. A monospace font uses the same amount of space for each character. One of the most common monospace fonts is named Courier New, and is available on nearly every computer and printer. Mary suggests you set the font in the Form_Load event procedure so all printing in this program will use this font.

To set the printer font:

1. Activate the Code window for the form named **frmMain**.

2. Enter the following statement, shown in bold, into the Form_Load event procedure:

```
Private Sub Form_Load( )
    Printer.Font = "Courier New"
End Sub
```

One method supported by the Printer object is the Print method. You will use the Print method of the Printer object more than any other method. The Print method has the following syntax:

[*object.*]**Print** *outputlist*

- The **Print** method prints text to the *object*—a form, printer, or the Immediate window. If you call the Print method without an object, the text will be printed to the form from which it is called. The Print method accepts optional arguments that define the text to be printed and the format of the text. If an object is specified, the object and Print method are separated by a period.

- The *outputlist* describes the text to be printed, and how that text is formatted. It has the following syntax:

[**Spc**(*number*) | **Tab**(*number*)] *expression* [*character-position*]

  - The *expression* represents the data to print. It can be a text string enclosed in quotation marks, a variable, or a reference to a property of an object.

  - If the optional **Spc** argument is included, space characters will be inserted in the output before the *expression* is printed. The space characters are inserted after the previously printed characters. The number of space characters inserted is specified by the *number* argument. The **Spc** argument is useful for inserting a fixed number of spaces between the column titles in a report.

  - If the optional **Tab** argument is included, the *expression* will be inserted at the absolute column number specified by the *number* argument. The **Tab** argument is useful for aligning all the detail lines to the correct column. Using **Spc** or **Tab** is often a matter of personal preference.

  - The optional *character-position* argument specifies the insertion point for the next *expression*. If you place a semicolon here, the insertion point of the next *expression* immediately follows the last character displayed. The default *character-position* is the first absolute column on a new line.

The NewPage method ends the current page and advances to the next page on the printer. The NewPage method has the following syntax:

Printer.NewPage

- The **NewPage** method advances to the next printer page and resets the print position to the upper-left corner of the new page. If you have printed only a partial page when the NewPage method is called, the partial page is printed and any other text you send with the Print method appears on the next page.

- The **Printer** object also supports a **Page** property that keeps track of the current page number. The Page property initially is set to one (1). Each time the **NewPage** method is called, it increases the Printer object's Page property by one (1). Also, if a page becomes full, and a new page is started, the Page property will be incremented by one (1).

The EndDoc method ends a print operation sent to the Printer object. The EndDoc method has the following syntax:

Printer.EndDoc

- When the **EndDoc** method is called, any unprinted text sent to the **Printer** object with the Print method is printed. If you have printed only a partial page when the EndDoc method is called, the partial page is printed.

- After the **EndDoc** method is called, the Page property of the **Printer** object is set to one (1) again.

Each time you call the Print method, the information is not immediately sent to the printer. Rather the information is stored in the printer buffer. The **printer buffer** is an area of the computer's memory that holds printed output before it is sent to the printer. When this buffer is full, or the EndDoc method is called, the information is sent to the printer. You will use the EndDoc method to send any information remaining in the printer buffer to the printer after the titles, detail lines, and report totals have been printed.

Printing a Page Title on a Report

The first step in printing the report is to print the page title across the top of the page and then the column titles spaced evenly across the page. You will create a general procedure to do this. Remember, you should name a general procedure so you can recognize easily what it does. In this case, Mary suggests you name this general procedure PrintTitles. As with any general procedure, it must be called explicitly from a general or event procedure. Mary suggests you place these procedures in the Main form containing the Sales Report menu item because they only will be used by this form. You could create a standard module for the general procedures, and then the module could be used by more than one program easily.

You need to print the report titles in the PrintTitles general procedure, as shown in Figure 5-21. Notice the page titles are positioned using the Tab( ) argument and the column titles are positioned relative to each other using the Spc( ) argument.

Figure 5-21 ◀
Sales report
headings

15 spaces; Spc(15)

column 31; Tab(31)

column 34; Tab(34)

5 spaces; Spc(5)

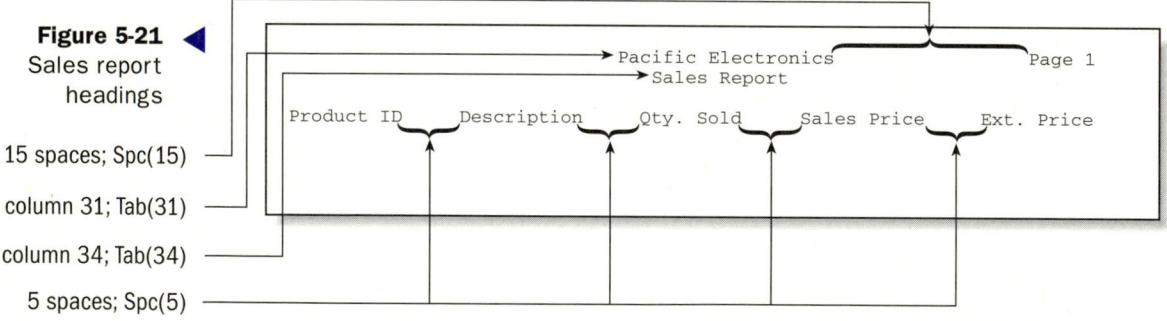

To print the page and column titles on the Sales Report:

1. Activate the Code window for the form named **frmMain**.

2. Click **Tools** on the menu bar, then click **Add Procedure**. The Add Procedure dialog box opens.

3. In the Name text box, type **PrintTitles**. Click the **Sub** and **Public** option buttons, then click the **OK** button. The new procedure is activated in the Code window.

4. Enter the following code into the procedure (shown in bold):

```
Private Sub PrintTitles( )
    Printer.Print Tab(31); "Pacific Electronics";
    Printer.Print Spc(15); "Page ", Printer.Page
    Printer.Print Tab(34); "Sales Report"
    Printer.Print ""
    Printer.Print Tab(6); "Product ID";
    Printer.Print Spc(5); "Description";
    Printer.Print Spc(5); "Qty. Sold";
    Printer.Print Spc(5); "Sales Price";
    Printer.Print Spc(5); "Ext. Price"
    Printer.Print ""
End Sub
```

When the statements in the PrintTitles general procedure are executed, they will print the page and column titles shown in Figure 5-21 to the printer. Remember, nothing actually may be sent to the printer until the Printer.EndDoc method is called. Information only is sent to the printer when the printer buffer becomes full or the EndDoc method is called.

The first three statements use the Print method of the Printer object to print a title on the report containing the company name (Pacific Electronics), page number, and report name (Sales Report), respectively. The Tab argument is used to position the text on the lines; the first line is indented 31 characters and the second line is indented 34 characters so the page title will be centered on the lines. Notice that each Tab argument is followed by a semicolon so the next argument (the company name or report name) will print on the same line, immediately following this argument. If a semicolon (;) does not appear, the Printer object moves to the leftmost column of the next line. The page number is printed at the right margin. The fourth statement uses the Print method of the Printer object with a null string so the page title will be separated visually from the column titles by a blank line.

The next five statements print the column titles. You could have called the Print method once to print the line of column titles; however, if you placed all these titles on the same line of code, it would not fit in one screen and would be difficult to read. Breaking the task down into several statements that call the Print method improves the readability of your program. In these statements, the Spc argument prints five spaces between each of the columns. The first four lines end with semicolons because you want to print each of the five column titles on the same line. After printing the last column title (Ext. Price), the Printer object moves to the next line. The final statement prints a blank line to separate the column titles from the detail records that will be printed.

Printing the Detail Lines on a Report

Now that you have written the code to print the page and column titles in the sales report, you must write the code to print each of the sales records. You will use an object variable to set the Recordset object to access the sales data contained in the database Mary created.

Creating an Object Variable

As in Tutorial 4, you will create an object variable to reference the Recordset object. You will declare a Private object variable in the general declarations section of the Form module for the form named frmMain, because the variable will be used by several procedures in this form but will not be used by any other forms. Using this variable will save typing, because you will be able to use a short variable name in place of datSales.Recordset each time you reference the recordset. The mnuReportsSalesReport_Click event procedure needs to perform all the tasks to print the sales report. One of these tasks is initializing the object variable. Therefore, you will set the value of the object variable to the current recordset in this event procedure.

The first step is to declare the object variable that will reference the Recordset object created by the Data control at run time.

To create an object variable that points to the datSales.Recordset object:

1. Activate the general declarations section of the Form module for the form named **frmMain**.

2. Append the following statement to the general declarations after the Option Explicit statement:

   ```
   Private mrstSales as Recordset
   ```

3. Activate the Code window for the **mnuReportsSalesReport** object's **Click** event procedure.

4. Enter the following code in the window:

   ```
   Set mrstSales = datSales.Recordset
   ```

The statement in the general declarations section creates a new Recordset object variable named mrstSales, which can be used wherever you would use datSales.Recordset. The prefix "m" indicates that this is a module-level variable, and "rst" indicates that the variable references a Recordset object. This will help reduce typing and make your program easier to read. The Private statement you wrote only creates an object variable.

The Set statement you wrote in the mnuReportsSalesReport_Click event points the variable mrstSales to an existing Recordset object, which is created for you by the Data control at run time. This Recordset object variable can be used by all the procedures in this form because you declared it as a Private variable in the general declarations section of the Form module.

Now that you have created the mrstSales object variable and set it to the Recordset property of the Data control, mrstSales references a valid instance of a Recordset object at run time. You can use this variable to reference the contents of the current record and send the different fields of the record to the printer buffer. To do this, you need to use this object variable in a set of statements that will print each record of the database in turn.

Creating a Do Loop

Because the program must examine, compute totals for, and print each record from the sales query, you need a way to execute the same statements repeatedly. A **Do loop** repeats a block of statements while a condition is True or until a condition becomes True. The Do loop has the following syntax:

Do [While|Until] *condition*

   statements

Loop

- The **Do** statement evaluates the *condition* before any of the statements are executed.

- If you use the **While** keyword, the *statements* are executed while the *condition* is True, the *condition* is tested again and, if it still is True, the *statements* are executed again. Whenever the *condition* becomes False, the loop exits, and the statement after the **Loop** statement is executed.

- If you use the **Until** keyword, the *statements* are executed until the *condition* is True. Then the loop exits and the statement after the **Loop** statement is executed.

You will use a Do loop to move one by one through each sales record in the new Recordset object you created, until there are no more records in the recordset. When there are no more records in the Recordset object, the end of the recordset has been reached. Every Recordset object has an **EOF** (End Of File) property that is False whenever there are more records in the Recordset object and True when the end of the file has been reached. You will use the EOF property of the mrstSales object variable to determine when there are no more sales records to process. You also will use the MoveNext method of the Recordset object like you did in Tutorial 4 to move one by one through each sales record in a Do Until loop. The Do loop you will use has the following format:

```
Do Until mrstSales.EOF = True
    statements
    mrstSales.MoveNext
Loop
```

This syntax shows only a prototype for moving through the Recordset object. You will insert statements to print each of the sales records contained in the current Recordset object.

You will test the Do loop and Print method statements for the detail lines of your report as you develop them. This way, you can locate and correct errors by looking at small pieces of code rather than having to debug a large procedure. First, you will test the loop structure by printing a test string to the Immediate window. (For more information on the Immediate window and the Debug.Print method refer to Appendix A.) The menu item must initialize the object variable before it does anything else, so you will add the Do loop after the Set statement in the Sales Report menu item's Click event procedure.

To create the Do loop structure for the sales report:

1. Activate the Code window for the **mnuReportsSalesReport** object's **Click** event procedure in the form named frmMain.

2. Append the following statements to the end of the procedure, just before the End Sub line:

```
Do Until mrstSales.EOF = True
    Debug.Print "RecordFound"
    mrstSales.MoveNext
Loop
```

3. Save the project.

This loop first checks the EOF property of the Recordset object. If the EOF property is not True, it executes the statements and tests the condition again.

```
Do Until mrstSales.EOF = True
```

The Do Until statement looks at the EOF property of the Recordset object. If the end of file has not been reached (EOF = False), the statements inside the loop are executed. If the end of file has been reached (EOF = True), there are no more records in the Recordset object and the loop exits.

```
Debug.Print "RecordFound"
```

The Debug.Print statement uses the Print method of the Debug object. You can print information in the Immediate window by using the Print method of the Debug object. The Print method of the Debug object works just like the Print method of the Printer object, except that you do not need to call the EndDoc method to send the text to the Immediate window. The Print method of the Debug object can be called only at run time. Refer to the Debugging Appendix for more information about the Debug.Print statement.

The text string RecordFound is the argument to the Debug.Print statement. It will be printed in the Immediate window every time the loop executes. In addition to text strings, you can print variables and object properties to the Immediate window at run time. If your program is not working properly, you can include Debug.Print statements inside any general or event procedure to trace the execution of the program and look at the values of variables and objects.

```
    mrstSales.MoveNext
Loop
```

After the text string is printed to the Immediate window, the MoveNext method positions the current record pointer at the next sales record in the Recordset object. When the Loop keyword is reached, the Do Until statement is executed again and the EOF property of the Recordset object variable is tested to determine if there are more records to process.

You have written enough code at this point to test the program and determine if the loop is accessing each of the records in the Recordset object and terminating correctly.

To test that the Do Until loop is working properly:

1. Click **View** then **Immediate window** on the menu bar to open the Immediate window.

2. Start the program, then run it.

3. Position and size the Immediate window so you can see it and the form named frmMain at the same time.

4. Enter **100** as the employee ID entry, then your name into the login form. Click the **OK** button.

5. Click **Reports** then **Sales Report** on the Main form's menu bar.

   The text "RecordFound" prints in the Immediate window seven times, once for each sales record.

   TROUBLE? If your program displays the line of text without stopping after the seventh time, you have created an error called an infinite loop. This is a common problem with Do loops. In this case, it would happen if the Recordset object never reached the end of file. End the program by pressing Ctrl+Break and make sure that the Do loop matches the code in the previous steps and that the MoveNext method is being called inside the Do loop. Save the project and repeat Steps 2 through 5.

6. End the program.

Mary is satisfied that the Do loop works correctly and finds each record. Because the Do loop and the Debug.Print statement work, you can continue to develop the program. You will replace the Debug.Print statement with the statements that will print the detail lines for the report. The statements to print each record in the Recordset object will be enclosed in a general procedure, just as the titles were. The Click event procedure for the Sales Report command button will call this general procedure once for each record to print the report. Therefore, the code in the Click event procedure will be much shorter and simpler to comprehend.

Printing the Detail Lines

The general procedure you will create will print each record in the Sales Report each time the loop is executed. For each record, you need to print the Product ID, Product Description, and other fields in columns so each field appears under its corresponding column title. To align each field to the exact position of its column title, you will use the Tab( ) argument of the Print method. The information you need to print will come from the fields of the Recordset object.

Before you can print a field inside a Recordset object, you need to learn how to write the syntax to reference the field in Visual Basic. The fields that make up the Recordset object are considered members of the Fields collection of the Recordset object. Referencing a collection member is similar to referencing the different properties of an object. When you refer to an object's properties, you use the following syntax:

ObjectName.PropertyName

When you reference a particular object in a collection, you use an exclamation point (!) instead of a period (.). So, to reference a specific member (field) in a Recordset object, you use the following syntax:

RecordsetName!FieldName

Unlike Visual Basic variable and object names, field names in Access databases can contain spaces. So that the Microsoft Jet database engine knows you are using a field with an embedded space, you must put the field name in brackets. When field names do not contain spaces, the brackets are optional.

> *Tip:* Using brackets will help the reader of your program know that
> you are referring to a field name.

To reference the Product ID field in the Recordset object mrstSales, you would use the following statement:

```
mrstSales![Product ID]
```

Before you can write the procedure, you need to know the different fields in the Recordset object. Figure 5-22 shows the fields you need to print in the Sales Report.

Figure 5-22 ◀
Fields in the
Recordset
object

Field name	Description
fldProduct ID	Product identification number
fldProduct Description	Description of product
fldQuantity Sold	Quantity sold of product
fldProduct Sales Price	Sales price of product

The extended price is not a field stored in the database. Rather, you will compute this value by multiplying the quantity sold by the product sales price.

You will create a general procedure to print the current record's fields. In this general procedure you will use a variable to calculate and hold the temporary value of the extended price. Again, this general procedure should be Private because it only will be used by this module. It also should be declared as a Sub procedure because it does not return any information to the calling procedure.

Because the product sales price and extended price fields contain currency information, each column should be formatted such that the decimal points are aligned. This will give the report a professional appearance. To do this you need to learn about a new statement and how to use a fixed-length string. Until now each string you have created has been a variable-length string; that is, the size of the string depended on the number of characters stored in the string. You now need a way, however, to allocate a fixed number of characters to hold the product sales price and extended price and align the information into the rightmost characters of the string.

To declare a fixed-length string, you use the following syntax.

Dim *varname* **As String** * *size*

- The *varname* can be any valid variable name.
- The *size* argument represents the exact size of the string. For example, to declare a string that will store three characters you would set *size* to 3.

For example, the statement:

```
Dim pstrQuantitySold As String * 3
```

always will store three characters in the pstrQuantitySold variable. If the quantity sold is 4, pstrQuantitySold will store two placeholder characters in addition to the "4". You also need a way to store characters in the string so they are stored in the rightmost characters. By default, when you store characters in a fixed-length string, they are stored in the string from left to right. If there are not enough characters to fill the string, spaces are stored in the remaining characters. This can be accomplished using the RSet statement. The **RSet** statement has the following syntax:

RSet *stringvar* = *string*

- The **RSet** statement takes two arguments.
- The *string* argument contains the source string or input string.
- The *string* then is stored in *stringvar* such that the rightmost characters are filled first. Spaces are stored in any remaining characters in a fixed-length string.

For example, the statement:

```
RSet pstrQuantitySold = Str(mrstSales![fldQuantitySold])
```

will send to the printer the quantity sold fixed string such that the rightmost characters are filled first, that is, "4" on the far right, then the two spaces to the left.

You now will add the statements that will print and format the detail lines for your report.

To write the statements to print the current record's fields:

1. Activate the Code window for **frmMain**.

2. Click **Tools** on the menu bar, then click **Add Procedure** to open the Add Procedure dialog box.

3. In the Add Procedure dialog box, create a form-level Sub procedure named **PrintDetail**.

   The Code window activates the procedure you just created.

4. Enter the following code into the procedure (shown in bold):

```
Private Sub PrintDetail( )
    Dim pcurExtPrice As Currency
    Dim pstrQuantitySold As String * 3
    Dim pstrSalesPrice As String * 6
    Dim pstrExtPrice As String * 7

    pcurExtPrice = mrstSales![fldQuantity Sold] * _
        mrstSales![fldProduct Sales Price]

    Printer.Print Tab(5); mrstSales![fldProduct ID];
    Printer.Print Tab(21); _
        mrstSales![fldProduct Description];
    RSet pstrQuantitySold =
        Str(mrstSales![fldQuantity Sold])
```

```
            Printer.Print Tab(39); pstrQuantitySold;
            RSet pstrSalesPrice = _
                Format(mrstSales![fldProduct Sales Price], "Fixed")

            Printer.Print Tab(53);
            Printer.Print pstrSalesPrice;
            RSet pstrExtPrice = Format(pcurExtPrice, "Fixed")
            Printer.Print Tab(68); pstrExtPrice
        End Sub
```

5. Save the project.

When the statements in the PrintDetail general procedure are executed, they will print the contents of each field in the current record to the printer buffer. Remember, nothing actually may be sent to the printer until the Printer.EndDoc method is called. You want the page and column titles, the detail lines, and the totals to be printed together, so you will not call the EndDoc method until you have printed all the information by calling the general procedures.

```
    Dim pcurExtPrice As Currency
    Dim pstrQuantitySold As String * 3
    Dim pstrSalesPrice As String * 6
    Dim pstrExtPrice As String * 7
```

These statements declare the variables. The variable pcurExtPrice will hold the value of the extended price for the current record. The Currency data type is used to store variables representing dollars and cents. The variables pstrQuantitySold, pstrSalesPrice, and pstrExtPrice are the fixed-length strings that will be used to display the output.

```
    pcurExtPrice = mrstSales![fldQuantity Sold] * _
        mrstSales![fldProduct Sales Price]
```

This statement computes the total sales amount for an item (the extended price) by multiplying the quantity sold by the product sales price and storing the result in the local variable pcurExtPrice.

```
    Printer.Print Tab(5); mrstSales![fldProduct ID];
    Printer.Print Tab(21); _
        mrstSales![fldProduct Description];
    RSet pstrQuantitySold = Str(mrstSales![fldQuantity Sold])

    Printer.Print Tab(39); pstrQuantitySold;
    RSet pstrSalesPrice = _
        Format(mrstSales![fldProduct Sales Price], "Fixed")

    Printer.Print Tab(53);
    Printer.Print pstrSalesPrice;
    RSet pstrExtPrice = Format(pcurExtPrice, "Fixed")
    Printer.Print Tab(68); pstrExtPrice
```

These Printer.Print statements look similar to the statements you wrote to create the page title. Instead of simply printing text strings enclosed in quotation marks, however, these statements print information from the mrstSales object. Each Printer.Print statement moves to the appropriate column, as specified by the Tab function, and prints the contents of the fixed-length string the current record. The Product Sales Price value will be formatted with two decimal places using the Fixed argument and then stored in the fixed-length string right-justified. Because the Tab and field name arguments end with a semicolon, each argument is printed on the same line. The final Printer.Print statement moves to the final column, prints the value of the temporary variable, formatted with two decimal places, and moves to the first column of the next line.

Now you can modify the Sales Report menu item's Click event procedure to print the report. All you need to do is call the general procedure PrintTitles to print the report titles and the general procedure PrintDetail, where the Debug.Print statement currently is called to print the detail lines when the menu item is clicked.

To modify the Click event procedure to call the print procedures:

1. Activate the Code window for the **mnuReportsSalesReport** object's **Click** event procedure.

2. Change the contents of the event procedure as shown in bold:

```
Private Sub mnuReportsSalesReport_Click( )
    Set mrstSales = datSales.Recordset
    'Print the report title and column titles
    PrintTitles
    Do Until mrstSales.EOF = True
        'Print a detail line on the report
        PrintDetail
        mrstSales.MoveNext
    Loop
    'Send the contents of the printer buffer to the
    'printer
    Printer.EndDoc
End Sub
```

3. Save the project.

The first statement you added calls the PrintTitles general procedure. It is called only once, because the titles should appear only once on the report. Therefore, this statement is outside the Do loop.

Next, the Do loop prints the contents of each record by calling the PrintDetail general procedure, and steps through each record in the Recordset object by calling the MoveNext method. The MoveNext method must be called after the PrintDetail general procedure is called. If the program called the MoveNext method first, it would skip over the first record in the Recordset object before printing, and the first record would never be printed.

```
Printer.EndDoc
```

This statement calls the EndDoc method. All the information stored in the printer buffer is sent to the Printer object—your default printer.

Mary suggests you test the program at this point to verify that the Sales Report is working properly.

To test the Sales Report:

1. Start the program, then complete the information in the login form.

2. Click **Reports** then **Sales Report** on the Main form's menu bar. Your Sales Report looks like Figure 5-23.

Figure 5-23 ◀
Sales Report
with detail lines

Product ID	Description	Qty. Sold	Sales Price	Ext. Price
		Pacific Electronics	Page	1
		Sales Report		
1	Fuse .05 Amp	1	1.33	1.33
1	Fuse .05 Amp	3	1.33	3.99
2	Fuse .10 Amp	1	1.45	1.45
3	Power Supply 150w	10	64.51	645.10
4	Power Supply 200w	4	83.27	333.08
5	Chip UART	13	30.00	390.00
6	Resistor 3332	9	13.34	120.06

Notice that the Product ID number 1 is printed twice. This is because there were two sales records for the item.

TROUBLE? If the detail lines on the report are not formatted correctly, check the PrintDetail general procedure.

TROUBLE? If the alignment is not correct, verify that the tab positions are correct.

TROUBLE? If you receive a run-time error telling you that an item is not found in the collection, make sure the field names are spelled correctly.

3. End the program.

Mary viewed the report and is satisfied it will print the page title, the column titles, and the detail lines for each record in the Recordset object. Now she would like you to print the order count, number of items sold, and total sales below the detail lines. Just below these lines, she would like the employee name and employee ID printed.

Computing Totals with Counters and Accumulators

To compute the order count, number of items sold, and total sales, you will create variables to hold these three values. Each time a record is printed, the program must add one (1) to the order count and then update the items sold and total sales by the value of the respective field in the current record. You can do this using variables that work as counters and accumulators.

A **counter** is a variable that increases by one (1) each time some activity occurs, such as a record being printed. You first initialize the value of the counter to zero (0). Then the counter describing the number of records is increased, or incremented, by one (1). Incrementing a program counter has the following syntax:

MyCounter = MyCounter + 1

- Each time the program executes this statement, the existing value of *MyCounter* is replaced by its previous value plus one (1).

An **accumulator** is like a counter but instead of increasing the variable by one (1), accumulators are used to tally values. Updating an accumulator has the following syntax:

MyAccumulator = MyAccumulator + value

- Each time the program executes this statement, the existing value of *MyAccumulator* is replaced by its previous value plus *value*.

- In your program, each time a sales record is printed the following should occur:

  - The counter representing the total orders should increase by one (1).

  - The accumulator representing the total items sold will increase by the quantity of items in the current record.

  - The accumulator representing the total sales will increase by the dollar value of the current record.

Figure 5-24 shows how the counter and accumulators will work in your program.

Figure 5-24 ◀
Counters and
accumulators

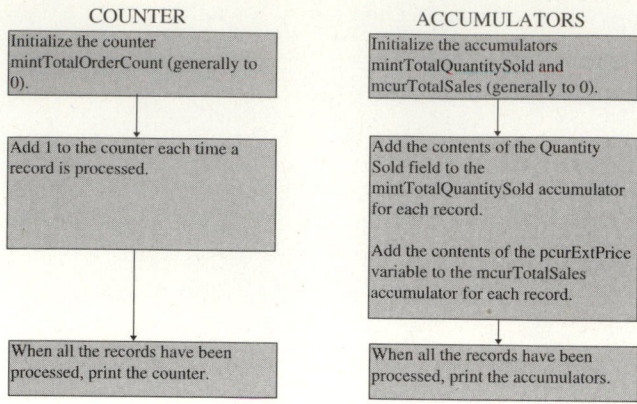

You need to create the counter, mintTotalOrderCount, and the first accumulator, mintTotalQuantitySold, as Integer data types. The second accumulator, mcurTotalSales, will be a Currency variable to hold the two decimal places needed for dollar amounts. Because the counter and accumulators will be used by multiple procedures in your program, you need to declare them as form-level variables. Counters and accumulators often are initialized when the form loads. If you initialized these values in the Form_Load event procedure, however, the report would be correct the first time it was printed. But, if you printed the report again without reloading the form, the values would not reset, and the report totals would be incorrect.

To declare and initialize the counters and accumulators:

1. Activate the general declarations section of the Form module for the form named **frmMain** and append the following declarations to the end of the existing declarations:

```
Private mintTotalOrderCount As Integer
Private mintTotalQuantitySold As Integer
Private mcurTotalSales As Currency
```

2. Activate the Code window for the **mnuReportsSalesReport** object's **Click** event procedure.

3. Enter the following code immediately below the Set statement:

```
mintTotalOrderCount = 0
mintTotalQuantitySold = 0
mcurTotalSales = 0
```

The first three statements create the form-level variables. After processing each of the sales records and updating the counter and accumulators, the program needs to print the contents of these variables.

Whenever a user clicks the Sales Report menu item at run time, the second three statements will set the value of the counter and accumulators to zero (0). You initialize these values in the menu item's Click event procedure so they will be reset and the report will produce the correct values every time it is printed.

Now you can write the statements to update the counter and accumulators each time a detail line is printed. Because the incrementing must take place each time a record is printed, it makes sense to place this code inside the PrintDetail procedure you already wrote.

To update the PrintDetail procedure to increment the values of the counter and accumulators:

1. Activate the Code window for the **PrintDetail** general procedure in frmMain.

2. Insert the following lines to update the counter and accumulators to the PrintDetail general procedure just before the End Sub statement:

```
mintTotalOrderCount = mintTotalOrderCount + 1
mintTotalQuantitySold = mintTotalQuantitySold + _
    mrstSales![fldQuantity Sold]
mcurTotalSales = mcurTotalSales + pcurExtPrice
```

3. Save the project.

Each time a detail record is printed, the total order count is incremented by one (1). The value of the total items sold accumulator increases by the contents of the Quantity Sold field of the current record, and the value of the total sales accumulator increases by the contents of the pcurExtPrice variable for the current record.

You now need to print the totals after all the sales records have been processed. You can place the statements for printing the counter and accumulators in a general procedure and then call them with one simple statement in the command button's Click event procedure. This will keep the Click event procedure small and easy to read.

To create the procedure to print the counter and accumulators:

1. Be sure the Code window for the form named frmMain is active.

2. Click **Tools** on the menu bar, then click **Add Procedure** to open the Add Procedure dialog box.

3. In the Add Procedure dialog box, create a form-level Sub procedure named **PrintTotals**.

   The Code window activates the procedure you just created.

4. Enter the following code into the procedure (shown in bold):

```
Private Sub PrintTotals( )
    Printer.Print ""
    Printer.Print " Total Order Count "; Tab(20); _
        mintTotalOrderCount
    Printer.Print " Total Items Sold "; Tab(20); _
        mintTotalQuantitySold
    Printer.Print " Total Sales "; Tab(20); mcurTotalSales
End Sub
```

5. Save the project.

As with any other general procedures, you need to call explicitly the PrintTotals procedure. When called, it first will print a blank line as specified by the double quotation marks, to visually separate the totals from the detail lines. Then the procedure will print the total order count prompt and value. The Printer object then will move to a new line, print the total items sold prompt and value, move to a new line, and print the Total Sales prompt and value.

In addition to printing the totals, you also need to print the employee name and ID of the person printing the report. Remember, this information is stored in the text boxes of the login form that is loaded but not visible. Whenever you reference an object in a different form, you must precede the object name with the form name separated by a period. This is the same as referencing a Public variable in a different form. Thus, to reference the Text property of the object name txtEmployeeName in the form named frmLogin you use the following syntax:

```
frmLogin.txtEmployeeName.Text
```

You now can write the statements to print the totals, employee name, and employee ID to the sales report. Because these lines should appear once on the report after the totals are printed, the code should appear after the PrintTotals procedure is called. If you placed these statements in the PrintTotals procedure the program would have produced the same results. Because the procedure, name PrintTotals implies that totals are being printed on a report, however, the statements were placed here. Deciding how to organize the procedures in your program and what each of them does can be subjective at times.

To call the PrintTotals general procedure and print the employee name and ID on the Sales Report:

1. Activate the Code window for the **mnuReportsSalesReport** object's **Click** event procedure.

2. Append the following statements to the event procedure, just before the Printer.EndDoc statement:

```
PrintTotals
Printer.Print ""
Printer.Print " Employee name: "; _
    frmLogin.txtEmployeeName.Text
Printer.Print " Employee ID: "; _
    Tab(17); frmLogin.txtEmployeeID.Text
```

3. Save the project.

The first statement you added calls the PrintTotals procedure and sends the totals to the printer after all the records have been read. The next three statements print a blank line then a line containing the employee name then a line containing the employee ID, each aligned and preceded by a descriptive message.

You now have completed all the components of the Sales Report for Pacific Electronics. Because you divided the tasks of printing the report into several different general procedures, Mary can make changes to the report titles, the formatting of the detail lines, or the report totals without having to look at unrelated code. Now Mary asks you to test the completed program to see if the report prints correctly. You already have tested the code to print the report titles and detail lines, so any problems that might exist would be due to errors in the code for the counter and accumulators.

To test the completed Sales Report:

1. Start the program then complete the login form.

2. Click the **Reports** menu on the Main form then click **Sales Report** to print the Sales Report. Your report should look like Figure 5-25.

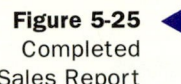

Figure 5-25 ◀
Completed
Sales Report

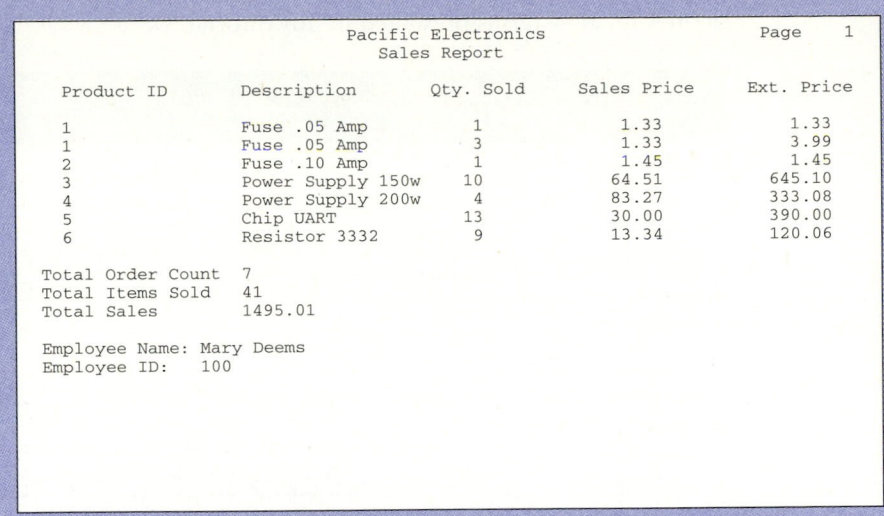

```
                              Pacific Electronics                    Page    1
                                Sales Report

    Product ID        Description        Qty. Sold     Sales Price      Ext. Price

    1                 Fuse .05 Amp            1            1.33            1.33
    1                 Fuse .05 Amp            3            1.33            3.99
    2                 Fuse .10 Amp            1            1.45            1.45
    3                 Power Supply 150w      10           64.51          645.10
    4                 Power Supply 200w       4           83.27          333.08
    5                 Chip UART              13           30.00          390.00
    6                 Resistor 3332           9           13.34          120.06

    Total Order Count  7
    Total Items Sold   41
    Total Sales        1495.01

    Employee Name: Mary Deems
    Employee ID:   100
```

TROUBLE? If the counter and accumulators do not appear on the report, be sure the program calls the PrintTotals procedure in the mnuSalesReport_Click event procedure before the EndDoc method is called.

TROUBLE? If the values of the counter or accumulators are not correct, be sure they are being updated correctly in the PrintDetail general procedure.

TROUBLE? If the output is not formatted correctly, verify that the PrintTotals general procedure is correct.

3. Then save any changes and repeat Steps 1 and 2.

4. End the program.

The Pacific Electronics Sales Report now is complete. Salespeople can click the Sales Report command button to print a report based on the underlying database. The report contains the page title required by Pacific Electronics, which includes the company name and the report title. It also includes the Product ID, Description, Quantity Sold, Sales Price, and Extended Price value for each record in the Recordset object. Finally, the report counts the number of orders and accumulates the total items sold and the total sales.

Mary will distribute the sales reporting program to the sales managers for testing so they can verify that the information in the Sales Report is correct and is organized and formatted in a way that is most useful to them.

Quick Check

1. Describe the purpose of the NewPage and EndDoc methods of the Printer object.

2. What is the difference between the Tab and Spc arguments of the Print method?

3. What is the difference between a Do Until and a Do While loop?

4. Write the Visual Basic statements for the following pseudocode:

    Execute the following two statements while there are more records in the Recordset object named rstPacific:

    Print the field named fldProductID to the Immediate window

    Move to the next record

5. What are the purposes of a counter and an accumulator?

Now that you have completed Session 5.2, you can exit Visual Basic. Figure 5-26 lists and defines the new terms presented in this tutorial.

Figure 5-26 ◀
New terms

Term	Definition
Accumulator	An accumulator is like a counter but instead of increasing *the variable* by *one (1)*, accumulators are used to tally values.
Collection	A collection is an object that contains similar objects. It is simply a way of grouping like objects together.
Component modules	Component modules are the multiple general procedures used to accomplish a specific task.
Counter	A counter is a variable that increases by one (1) each time some activity occurs, such as a record being printed. You first initialize the value of the counter to zero (0). Then the counter describing the number of records is increased, or incremented, by one (1).
Do loop	A set of statements including a Do While and Do Until statement that will be executed until or while a condition is True.
Global variable	A global variable is a variable that can be referenced by any module in a program and whose value exists while the program is running.
Modal form	A modal form is a form that must be closed (hidden or unloaded) before another form in the program can receive focus.
Modeless form	A modeless form is a form that can lose focus without being closed.
Modularization	Modularization is the process of dividing a large task into multiple subtasks.
Printer buffer	The printer buffer is an area of the computer's memory that holds printed output before it is sent to the printer. When this buffer is full, or the EndDoc method is called, the information is sent to the printer.
Splash screen	The splash screen is the initial screen that appears on your computer when a program first is started. It provides the user with a brief description of the program and its purpose.
Standard module	A standard module is like a Form module but contains only general procedures and variable declarations commonly accessed by other modules within a program. Standard modules commonly are called bas modules.
Startup object	The startup object can be a single form or general procedure that is executed when the program is run.
Template	A template is an existing form that provides a way for you to reuse components, like forms, and add them to projects.
Wizard	A wizard is a tool that leads a user step-by-step through an unusually long, difficult, or complex programming task.

Tutorial Assignments

Pacific Electronics requires a product report describing the items it sells, the cost to Pacific, and what Pacific charges for it. The report must contain the Product ID, the Product Description, the Product Cost, and the Product Price for each item. The report also must total the number of items sold and allow the user to specify whether the report will be printed to the screen or printed on the printer. The report will contain a final line stating that you tested the program.

This report is a prototype for a more complex report, so the underlying database does not have a large number of items. Therefore, you do not have to consider page or screen breaks.

You need to create a menu item to generate the report. You will enter your name into the program using a login form. The finished Main form will look like Figure 5-27 while the report is printed on the screen, and the login form like Figure 5-28.

Figure 5-27 ◀

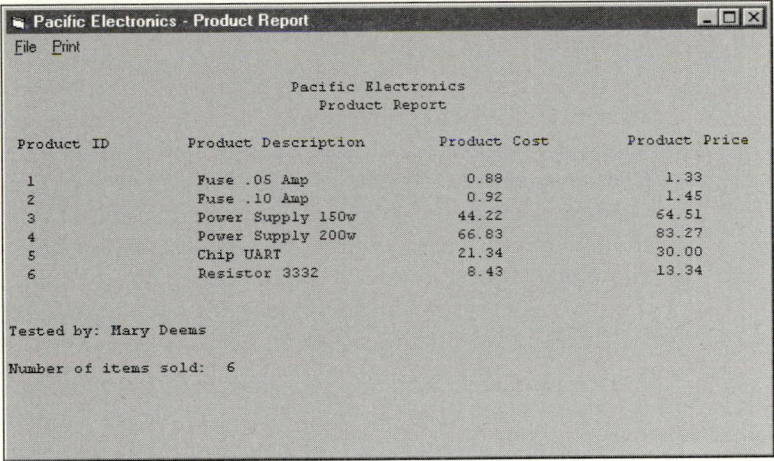

Figure 5-28 ◀

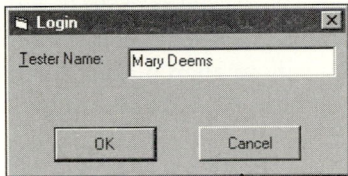

1. Make sure your Student Disk is in the appropriate disk drive, then start Visual Basic.

2. Create a new project named **Pacific Product Report.vbp** in the **TAssign** folder in the **Tutorial.05** folder on your Student Disk.

3. Write the statements in the Form_Load event procedure for the Main form that will set the Font property for both the Printer object and the Main form to a proportional spaced font.

4. Change the form's caption to **Pacific Electronics - Product Report** and its name to **frmMain,** then save the form. Accept the default name.

5. Draw a Data control named datProduct on the form and set the necessary properties to connect to the database named **Pacific.mdb** in the **TAssign** folder in the **Tutorial.05** folder on your Student Disk. Connect to the table named **tblProduct**. Because the user only will be using the Data control to print the product report, it should be invisible at run time.

6. Create a Recordset object variable named **mrstProduct** that will be used by all the procedures in the form. Create a form-level Integer variable named **mintItemCount** that will be used to tally the number of items sold. Require that all variables be declared explicitly.

 7. Add a login form to the project. Modify the login form and its boilerplate code so that it requires the tester to type in his or her name. If the user clicks the OK button on the form, set a Public variable LoginSucceeded to True if a name was entered and display a message box asking for the tester name if none was entered. If the user clicked the Cancel button, set the value of LoginSucceeded to False. You will use another procedure to test the value of LoginSucceeded. Save the form. Accept the default name.

8. Add a standard module to the project. Save the standard module as **Module1.bas** in the **TAssign** folder in the **Tutorial.05** folder on your Student Disk.

9. In the standard module, create a general Sub procedure named **Main**. Add the statements to display and repaint the login form, then test the LoginSucceeded variable and either go on to the Main form or end the program. Set the startup object to the Sub Main procedure. *Hint:* You will need to access the tester name that is typed into the login form's text box when you print the report, so do not unload the login form entirely.

10. Create a form-level general Sub procedure named **PrintTitles** on the Main form. This procedure will print the page title. The first line of the page title should be blank. The second line of the page title should contain the text **Pacific Electronics** centered on the page. The third line should contain the text **Product Report** centered on the page. The fourth line should be blank. The fifth line should contain four column heads: **Product ID, Product Description, Product Cost,** and **Product Price**. Format the columns so that the space between the columns is the same, and the left and right margins are equal. Refer to Visual Basic Help for the Print method, if necessary.

11. Create another general Sub procedure named **PrintDetail** to print the detail lines for the report. The information for each line is stored in a field in the Recordset object named **mrstProduct**. The names of the fields are **fldProduct ID, fldProduct Description, fldProduct Cost,** and **fldProduct Sales Price**, respectively. The detail lines should appear under the corresponding column titles. Write the statement to increment the counter variable, **mintItemCount**, containing the number of different items on the report. Be sure to align output for the fields **fldProduct Cost** and **fldProduct Sales Price** so each is formatted with two decimal places and the decimal point is aligned.

12. Create another general procedure named **PrintFooter**. Write the necessary statements to print two blank lines, then the text **Tested by:** followed by the name of the program tester from the login form. The PrintFooter procedure then should print the text **Total items sold:** followed by the value of the variable **mintItemCount**.

13. Using the Menu Editor, create a menu with two titles, **File** and **Print**. Create an **Exit** menu item under the File menu title that will end the program. The Print menu title should have two menu items, **Print to Printer** and **Print to Screen**. Be sure to use appropriate names, captions, shortcuts, and access keys for each menu.

14. In the Click event procedure for the Print to Printer menu item, write the statement that will assign the Recordset object variable **mrstProduct** to the existing Recordset object, stored in the current Data control named datProduct.

15. In the same event procedure, call the general procedures to print the headings.

16. In the same event procedure, create a Do loop in which you call the general procedure to print the detail lines and increment the counter, then write the statement to move to the next record, until the end of file is reached.

17. In the same event procedure, call the general procedure to print the report footer so that appears one time, after all the detail lines have been printed.

18. Call the EndDoc method to empty the contents of the printer buffer.

19. Write the code for the Print to Screen menu item to print the same report you just created to the form instead of the printer. *Hint:* If you call the Print method without an object, the arguments of the Print method will print to the form.

20. In the Code window for the mnuExitItem_Click event, add the code that will end the program.

21. Save the form and the project.

22. Run the program. Execute the **Print to Screen** menu item and verify that the report is correct. If the report contains any errors, correct them. If necessary, change the width and position of the form on the screen. Repeat Steps 17 and 18.

23. When the report prints correctly to the screen, execute the **Print to Printer** menu item and verify that the report is correct. If the report contains any errors, correct them, and repeat Steps 17 and 19.

24. Click the **Exit** menu item to end the program.

25. Exit Visual Basic.

Case Problems

1. Helping Hand Incorporated Helping Hand Incorporated organizes and solicits contributions for various charities in the northern United States and Canada. As part of their business activities, Helping Hand staff members often write letters to possible donors. The same letter is written and then sent to a large number of donors, and Helping Hand would like to have a program to speed up this process. The program will allow staff members to compose a letter and add a closing on one form, and use another form to capture the donor name and address information. You can print the letter or exit the program from either form. Because many people receive the same letter, the program should clear the address fields after the letter is printed, but contents of the letter should remain the same in preparation for the next letter. The volunteer's name will be added to the letter from the information gathered on the login form. You will create the program for Helping Hand.

Figure 5-29 shows the completed form for composing the letter and Figure 5-30 shows the form for entering the address.

Figure 5-29 ◀

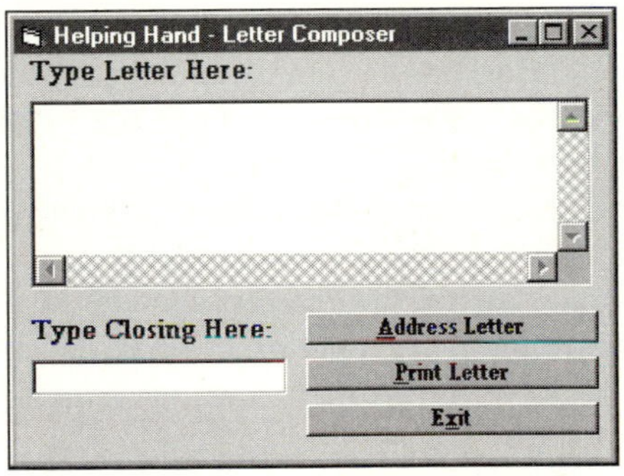

Helping Hand - Letter Composer
Type Letter Here:

Type Closing Here: Address Letter
                       Print Letter
                       Exit

Figure 5-30 ◀

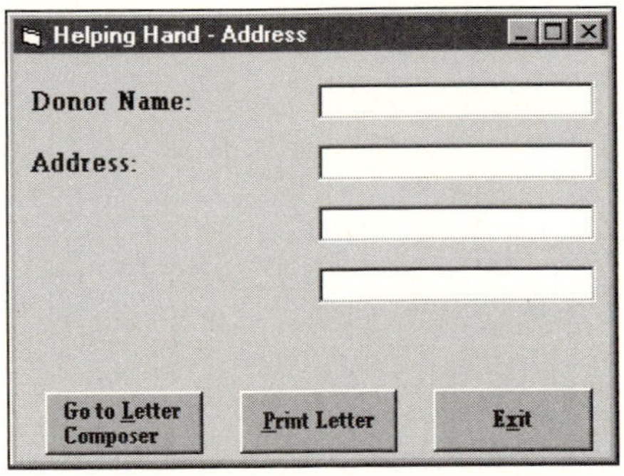

Helping Hand - Address

Donor Name:
Address:

Go to Letter Composer   Print Letter   Exit

1. Make sure your Student Disk is in the appropriate disk drive, then start Visual Basic and create a new project.

2. Change the form name to **frmHelpingLetter** and change its caption to **Helping Hand - Letter Composer**.

3. Save the form using the default name in the **Cases** folder in the **Tutorial.05** folder on your Student Disk. Save the project using the name **Helping Hand Letter Generator.vbp**.

4. Draw a large multiline text box with both vertical and horizontal scroll bars in the middle of the form to hold the text of the letter. Name the text box **txtLetter**. Remove the initial text from the object. Draw an identifying label with the caption **Type Letter Here:**.

5. Draw a text box in the lower-left corner of the form; the text box will be used to add a standard closing to a letter. Remove the initial text from the text box and change the name to **txtClosing**. Draw an identifying label with the caption **Type Closing Here:**.

6. Draw three command buttons in the lower-right corner of the form as shown in Figure 5-29 with the captions **Address Letter**, **Print Letter**, and **Exit**, respectively. Give the buttons appropriate names and hot keys. Add the appropriate code for the Exit button.

7. Open the Code window for the Address Letter button's Click event and add code to hide the frmHelpingLetter object and show the frmHelpingAddress object.

8. Create a second form with the name **frmHelpingAddress** and the caption **Helping Hand - Address**. Save the form using the default name in the **Cases** folder in the **Tutorial.05** folder on the Student Disk.

9. Draw two identifying labels on the leftmost side of the form with the captions **Donor Name:** and **Address:**, respectively.

10. Draw four blank text boxes down the rightmost side of the form. Change the Name property to **txtDonor**, **txtAddress1**, **txtAddress2**, and **txtAddress3**, respectively.

11. Draw three command buttons along the bottom of the form (refer to Figure 5-30). Change their captions to **Go to Letter Composer**, **Print Letter**, and **Exit**, respectively. Give the buttons appropriate names and hot keys. Add the appropriate code for the Exit button.

12. Open the Code window for the Go to Letter Composer button's Click event and type the code that will show the frmHelpingLetter object and hide the frmHelpingAddress.

13. Use the Add Module dialog box to add a standard module to the project. Save the module as **Helping.bas** in the **Cases** folder in the **Tutorial.05** folder on the Student Disk. Save the project.

14. Create a general procedure named **PrintLetter**. Type the code that will print a letter to the printer with the layout show in Figure 5-31. *Hint:* Remember to reference the form name for the text boxes when you call the Print method. Remember, you can use the Date function to print the current date on the letter.

Figure 5-31 ◀

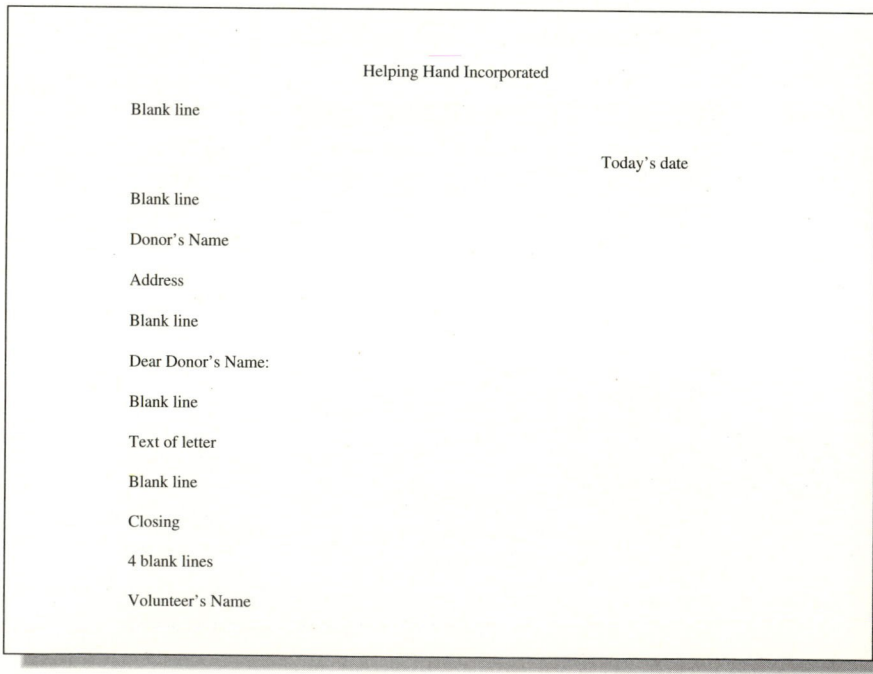

Helping Hand Incorporated

Blank line

Today's date

Blank line

Donor's Name

Address

Blank line

Dear Donor's Name:

Blank line

Text of letter

Blank line

Closing

4 blank lines

Volunteer's Name

15. Open the Code window for the Click event procedure for the Print Letter command button. Write the code to call the PrintLetter general procedure.

16. Add the necessary statements to clear the contents of the input text boxes on the frmHelpingAddress form just after the letter is printed.

17. Write the statements to print the letter from the Print Letter command button on the form named frmHelpingLetter.

18. Use the Add Form dialog box to add a splash screen to the project. In a label that fills the form, type the title **Helping Hand Incorporated**. Change the font and colors to a style you like. Save the form as **frmHelpingSplash.frm** in the **Cases** folder in the **Tutorial.05** folder on the Student Disk.

19. Use the Add Form dialog box to add a login form. Change the form and its boiler-plate code to require the user to type a volunteer name in the txtVolunteerName text box. The identifying label for the text box should have the caption **Volunteer Name:**. Write the code that will display the frmHelpingLetter object after the volunteer types a name in the text box and clicks the OK button, and that will end the program if the volunteer clicks the Cancel button. Save the form as **frmHelpingLogin.frm** in the **Cases** folder in the **Tutorial.05** folder on the Student Disk.

20. Use the Add Procedure dialog box to add a project-level Sub procedure named **Main**. Add code to the Sub Main procedure to display and repaint the splash screen, load all the forms in the program, then display the login form and hide the splash screen.

21. Set the project properties so Sub Main is the startup object.

22. Save the project.

23. Run the program. The first form displayed is the splash screen, then the login form. Type your name in the Volunteer Name: text box and click the OK button.

24. The Letter Composer form appears. Type a thank you letter in the letter text box, then add a closing. Click the Address Letter command button.

25. Type information of your choice in the Donor Name and Address text boxes. Click the Print Letter button. Check that all the fields correctly print what you entered in each form.

26. Enter another address and generate another letter, then go back to the first form and change the letter you already wrote. Test the Print Letter button on the Letter Composer form.

27. When you have finished testing the program, exit it by clicking the Exit button.

28. Print the Form Image and Code for all the forms. Save any changes to the project.

29. Exit Visual Basic.

2. Toys, Toys, Toys, and More Toys Toys, Toys, Toys, and More Toys is a toy manufacturer operating in western Europe. The company has decided to begin work on a comprehensive stock control application. The anticipated system will use an Access database to store information about the toys currently being manufactured, how many toys of each type are in stock, and delivery estimates for toy orders currently in production. Because this is a new application, you will design the startup screen, create a second screen, and then test the links between the two screens. You will use a Data control to retrieve the toy names from a test database.

Figure 5-32 shows the completed startup splash screen for the program.

Figure 5-32 ◀

1. Make sure your Student Disk is in the appropriate disk drive, then start Visual Basic. Create a new project.

2. Use the Add Form dialog box to add a splash screen to the project file. (Use the splash screen template.) Change the properties of the labels and remove the extra labels so the splash screen looks like Figure 5-32. Add a Line object to the splash screen. Set the Name property to **frmToysSplash** and save the form with the default name in the **Cases** folder in the **Tutorial.05** folder on your Student Disk.

3. Save the project using the name **Toys Stock Control.vbp**.

4. Remove the code from the Form_Load event procedure on the splash screen.

5. Using the Data Form Wizard, create a form based on the table **tblToyProducts** in the database named **Toys.mdb** in the **Cases** folder in the **Tutorial.05** folder on your Student Disk. Use all the fields in the table and sort the information using the field **fldProductName**. The form should have Add, Delete, Refresh, and Update buttons. Change the caption of this form to **Toys, Toys, Toys, and More Toys - Stock Control**. Change the caption of the labels so they are more meaningful to the user.

6. Create a command button on the form named **cmdExit** and write the code to end the program. If necessary, move the existing command buttons so they all appear on the same line.

7. Save the form using the default name in the **Cases** folder in the **Tutorial.05** folder on your Student Disk.

8. Use the Add Module dialog box to add a new standard module to the project.

9. Save the standard module using the name **Toys.bas** in the **Cases** folder in the **Tutorial.05** folder on your Student Disk.

10. Use the Add Procedure dialog box to insert a project-level Sub procedure named **Main** to the module.

11. In the Code window for the **Sub Main** procedure, write the necessary statements to display and repaint the splash screen, then display the frmtblToyProducts object and unload the splash screen.

12. Change the startup object to Sub Main.

13. Save the project.

14. Run the program. The splash screen appears, then the Stock Control form appears. Click the Data control arrows to view the stock information.

15. Click the Exit button to end the program.

16. Print the Form Image and Code for both forms. Exit Visual Basic.

3. Jill Jones Distribution Jill Jones is a marketing representative for a distributor of kitchen supplies. Her sales territory consists of the southwestern United States although she sometimes services clients outside that region. She presently has a database listing customer names, telephone numbers, and information. She spends much of her time traveling to customer's sites to sell products. Just before she leaves on a trip, she looks at a list of the clients in a particular city, and makes notes about the client to optimize her itinerary and make sure she does not forget to contact a client. She would like a program that would facilitate this review for her by allowing her to select a city, then display all the clients in that city. She needs to be able to edit the information and then print the report. To do this, you will need to connect a form to her database using the Data control. Then locate all the records in a particular city. If a customer record is in that city, then you will need to add a line containing the customer's name and telephone number to a multiline text box. Otherwise, you should ignore the record. She also would like the option of displaying all the customer records, regardless of city. When complete, the form for this program should look like Figure 5-33.

Figure 5-33 ◀

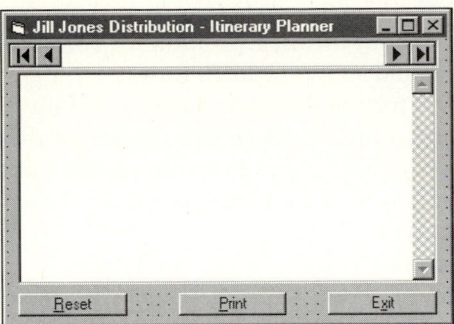

1. Start Visual Basic and create a new project.
2. Set the form name to **frmJillJones** and the caption to **Jill Jones Distribution - Itinerary Planner**. Save the form file using the default name to the **Cases** folder in the **Tutorial.05** folder on your Student Disk.
3. Save the project using the name **Jill Jones Itinerary.vbp** in the **Cases** folder in the **Tutorial.05** folder on your Student Disk. Remember to save your work frequently in case you make a mistake.
4. Create a multiline text box with a vertical scroll bar. Name the text box **txtNames**.
5. Create three command buttons at the bottom of the form. Be sure to assign meaningful names and hot keys to each of the buttons as illustrated in Figure 5-33.
6. Create a Data control that will access the table named **tblCustomers** in the database named **dbJill.mdb** in the **Cases** folder in the **Tutorial.05** folder on your Student Disk. Because Jill will not interact with the Data control at run time, make it invisible. Name the Data control **datCustomers**.

7. Use the Add Form dialog box to add a login form to the project.
8. Change the object on the form so there is one label and a text box for Jill to enter the desired city. The text box should be named **txtCity**. Remove the Cancel button. Create a frame with two option buttons in a control array named **optSelect**. The captions for the option buttons should be **One City** and **All Cities**, respectively.
9. Change the caption of the OK button to **Lookup Names**.

10. Change the code for the Lookup Names command button form so it requires Jill either to click the One City option button and enter the city's name in the text box or click the All Cities button to continue. If the correct information is entered, hide the form and set the value of the global variable LoginSucceeded to True.

11. Create a standard module named **JillJones.bas**. Create a general Sub procedure named Main and change the project properties so this is the startup object. The procedure should display the login form as a modal form. Then write another statement in this procedure to display the other form. Because the login form must be hidden before control can revert to another form and the form will not be hidden until correct information is entered into the login form, there is no need to check in the Main procedure that the correct information was entered.

12. You need to write an If statement to determine which option button is selected, locate the customers from one city or all cities, then display the selected records in the text box you created each time the Main form is activated. Display the fields named **fldFirstName**, **fldLastName**, and **fldTelephone** for the matching items in the Main form's text boxes. *Hint:* If Jill selected a single city you will need to use the FindFirst method to locate the first record matching the selected city. Then, in a loop, use the FindNext method to locate additional matching records. Remember, the NoMatch property is set to True when the FindNext method cannot locate another record. If Jill is selecting all of the customers, then you need to set the current record pointer to the first record in the recordset, then write a loop to locate each record in the table. Remember to use the concatenation characters, space constant characters, and carriage return line feed constant characters to format the output and move to a new line every time you add a name.

13. Write the code for the Click event for the Reset button on the Main form to clear the contents of both forms, reposition the recordset to the first record, hide the Main form and show the login form.
14. Write the statements for the Print button on the Main form to use the Print method of the Printer object to print the contents of the txtNames object. Be sure to call the EndDoc method to flush the printer buffer.
15. Write the statements so the Exit button will unload the form and exit the program when it is clicked.
16. Save the project before testing.
17. Test the program by selecting all cities, then click the Reset button to clear the information. Select the city **Las Vegas** and click the Lookup Names button again. You see a list of six names and telephone numbers.
18. Correct any errors, save the project, and print both forms as text and code. Exit Visual Basic.

4. Mort Enterprises Mort Enterprises is a small auto loan company in Central California. Their customers frequently request loan amortization schedules. A loan amortization schedule displays the payment amount of a loan. Then for each payment made, a line is printed on a report that displays the beginning balance of the loan, the interest charged for the period, the amount of the payment applied to the principal of the loan, and the new balance. Thus, a line needs to be printed for each payment to be made. After the last payment is made, the balance on the loan is zero. Thus, for each payment, you need to compute the amount of interest. This can be computed by multiplying the beginning balance of the loan by the interest rate. Then you can compute the principal by subtracting the interest amount from the payment. The new balance is computed by subtracting the amount of the payment applied to the principal from the beginning balance. You need to perform these computations for each payment using the new beginning balance. You can perform these computations inside a loop that will execute once for each payment.

You need to create a program with two forms. The startup form is shown in Figure 5-34. It contains three labels and corresponding text boxes. There is an Exit command button and a button to compute the amortization schedule. When this button is clicked, the current form should be hidden and the output form displayed. Using the information from the text boxes on the other form, you need to display the output. This output should include the payment amount, and column titles for the month, beginning balance, interest, principal, and ending balance.

Figure 5-34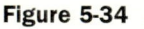

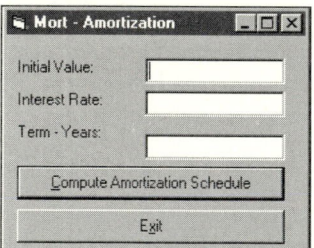

Reading and Writing Text Files into List Boxes and Arrays

Creating a Quotation System for Star Plant Supply

CASE

Star Plant Supply

Rose Blain is the owner of Star Plant Supply, a company that has been supplying plants to landscaping firms in Naples, Florida, since 1986. Currently Rose employs nine people. Eight of the staff members perform deliveries, unload shipments, and track inventory. Rose also has an assistant to help her manage the business.

Before Rose's customers place an order, they require a verbal or written price estimate, or quotation. Her customers want to make sure they are getting the best price for each item they buy, so they shop around. They also need to meet deadlines for their landscaping projects, so they must obtain quotations quickly. Rose currently maintains a price list and uses a quotation form and calculator to write customer quotations. Her business is growing so rapidly that she often cannot write all the requested quotations. This means she loses the sale. Also, because Rose needs to look up the price of each item by hand when she writes quotations, the current system is prone to errors. Furthermore, she has noticed she makes occasional errors when computing and adding extended prices. Rose wants a computerized system that will 1) help her keep up with the volume of quotations she has to write and, 2) compute the pricing information for her automatically.

Rose's friend, Mack Woolard, has been helping her to develop the quotation system in Visual Basic. Mack has been creating a program for her, but he does not have time to complete it, so they have asked you to finish it. Rose is not very familiar with computers and she is a poor typist, so she wants to be able to select an item from a list of the products she carries, enter the quantity requested, then have the program compute the extended price of the item. Most customers want a running total of the items they have requested, so she also wants the program to add together the extended prices of all the items and compute a quotation total each time an item is added to the quotation.

Rose's assistant, Joan Grayson, used WordPad to create a price list of all Star Plant Supply's products. Each product is listed on a separate line followed by the corresponding price for the item. Joan updates this file when the prices change or new items are added. Mack explains that the quotation program can read this text file and use the information to produce the quotations for the customers after some modifications have been made to the text file.

SESSION 6.1

In this session you will read information from a text file into a series of variables stored as one unit called an array. You also will insert items into a list box and combo box using code, and access the items of a list box using the List and ListIndex properties. Also, you will write a For loop to step through the items in a list box.

Analyzing the Program

Mack already has written the NEADT charts, and designed the screen for the quotation program. Also, he has created a form with most of the objects he plans to use. He has not written any code yet or set many of the properties for the objects he created. Before you begin working on the program, you should review the design specifications.

To view and print the NEADT charts for the quotation program:

1. Make sure your Student Disk is in the appropriate disk drive. Using Microsoft Word, open the **Star.doc** file in the **Tutorial.06** folder on your Student Disk. If you do not have Word, open the **Star.txt** file using WordPad.

2. Print the file then exit the word processing program.

Examine the NEADT charts. All the product descriptions will be stored in a list that Rose can use to choose products. Rose will be able to add a product to the quotation by clicking the product in the list, typing the quantity requested, and then clicking a button to add the item to the output section of the price quotation. The program also includes a Remove Item command button, which will delete a product from the output lists and recompute the quotation total whenever an item is deleted. The Write Quotation command button will allow Rose to print the quotation to a text file. Then Rose can use the text file in her word processing program to format and print quotations for customers. The New Quotation command button will clear the contents of all the output list boxes and quotation total so Rose can enter a new quotation. The program will include four list boxes for output: Product Description, Quantity, Price Each, and Extended Price. Keep the printed NEADT charts next to you while you complete the program. So that Rose can give customers immediate feedback about the quotation total, the extended price of an item and the quotation total will be computed each time an item is added to the quotation. Mack has completed the screen design for the program, as shown in Figure 6-1.

Figure 6-1 ◀
Screen design
of the quotation
form

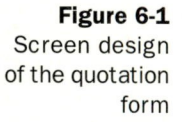

Product prompt			Add Item command button	
Product combo box			Remove Item command button	
Quantity prompt			Write Quotation command button	
Quantity text box			New Quotation command button	
Discount check box			Quit Program command button	

Product Description prompt	Quantity prompt	Price Each prompt	Extended Price prompt	Picture prompt
Product Description list box	Quantity list box	Price Each list box	Extended Price list box	Picture

| Quotation Total prompt | Quotation Total text box |

Following good user-interface design principles, Mack divided the screen into two sections—the upper section for input and the lower section for output. Each section is bordered by a frame for visual identification. In this case, the frames are not being used to group together option buttons. Rather, they are used only to visually separate the input and output sections of the program.

When Rose clicks the Add Item command button, the program will look up the price of the selected item, and then multiply it by the quantity requested in order to compute the extended price. Then, the item, quantity ordered, price, and extended price will be displayed in the output section of the form. Finally, the quotation total will be computed and displayed in the output section of the form.

You will begin by opening the project file that Mack already created.

To open the partially completed quotation program:

1. Start Visual Basic and open the project file named **Star.vbp** in the **Tutorial.06** folder on your Student Disk. Activate the form named **frmStar.frm**. Your form should look like Figure 6-2.

Figure 6-2 ◀
Initial quotation
screen

input section ──▶

output section ──▶

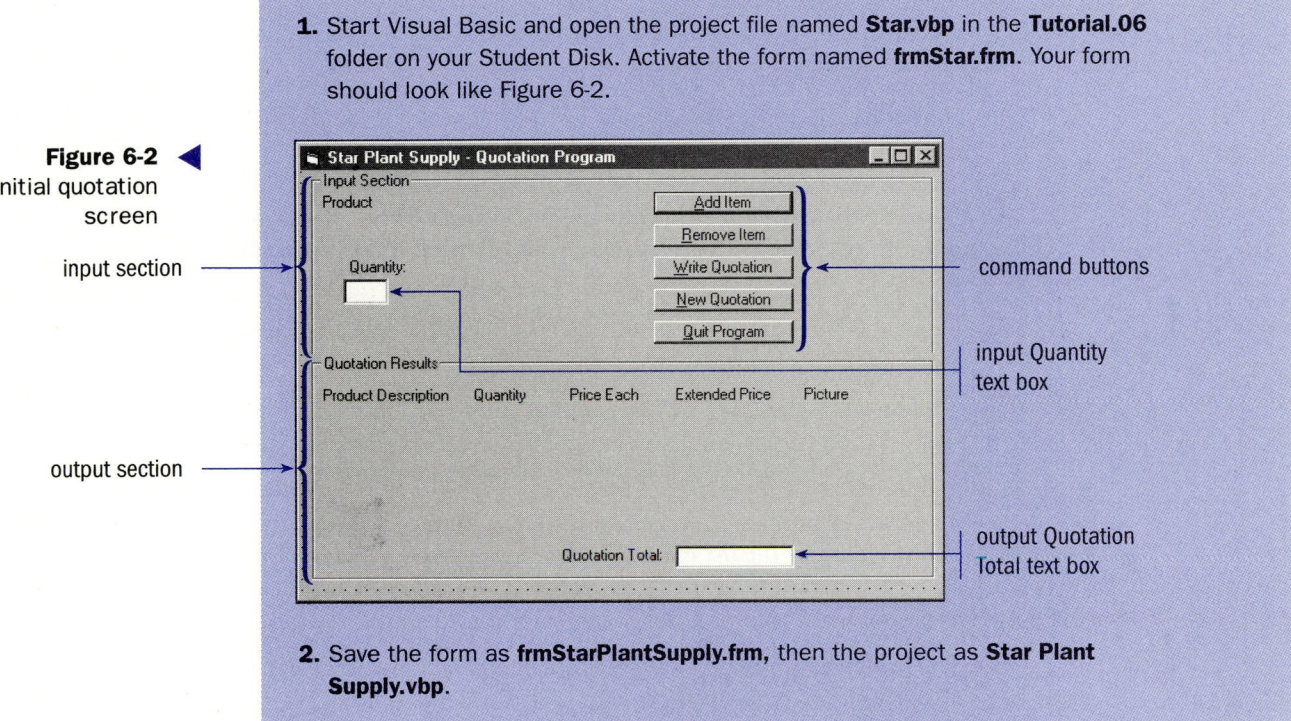

command buttons

input Quantity
text box

output Quotation
Total text box

2. Save the form as **frmStarPlantSupply.frm**, then the project as **Star Plant Supply.vbp**.

Mack suggests you begin by creating the remaining controls on the form.

Displaying a List of Items in a Combo Box

Remember, Rose wants to select a product from a list of items she has in inventory. She does not want to have to type the name of each item every time she prepares a bid. The solution to this problem is to use a combo box. A **ComboBox** control can display a list of items from which the user can select one item. There are three styles of combo boxes you can use by setting the object's **Style** property:

- Setting the Style property to **0 - Dropdown Combo** allows a user either to select an item from a dropdown list of suggested choices or type in a new item. No options appear until the user clicks the list arrow at the right of the combo box.

- Setting the Style property to **1 - Simple Combo** displays a text box and a list, which does not drop down. All the choices appear in the list at all times. Whenever the list will not fit inside the region of the object, a scroll bar is displayed. The user can specify a value for the combo box that is not in the list of suggested choices.

- Setting the Style property to **2 - Dropdown List** only allows a user to select an item from a preset dropdown list of choices. As in a dropdown combo box, no options appear until the user clicks the list arrow at the right of the combo box.

Figure 6-3 shows how the different combo boxes will appear on a form.

Figure 6-3 ◀
Types of
ComboBox
objects

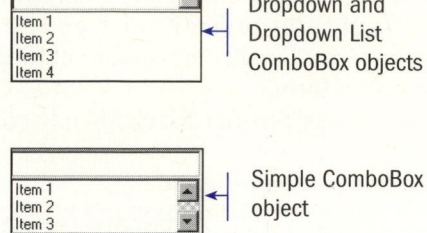

In addition to the Style property, there are other properties that determine contents of the combo box and how those contents appear to the user.

- The **List** property specifies the items stored in the combo box. It is used to add items to the combo box at design time. If you want to add items at run time, you do not need to use the Properties window to set the List property.

- The **Sorted** property, when set to True, causes the items to be displayed in alphabetical order even if the items were not added in alphabetical order.

- The combo box can be used as a bound control; that is, it can reference a record in a Recordset object by setting its **DataSource** and **DataField** properties. This is identical to the process you used to bind the TextBox object to a database.

- The **ItemData** property is a list of long integer values with the same number of items as the control's List property. You can use the numbers associated with each item to identify the list items. The most common use of the ItemData property is as an index into another array. When you insert an item with the AddItem method, an item also is inserted into the ItemData array.

- The **NewIndex** property works with the ItemData property. If you are adding items to a list that is sorted, each new item is added to the list in alphabetical order. To determine where an item was inserted, you use the NewIndex property. The NewIndex property returns the item most recently added to a combo box or list box.

- The **ListIndex** property is an integer value that identifies the currently selected item in a list box. The first item in the list has a ListIndex property value of zero (0), the second item has a value of one (1), and so on. If no item has been selected, the ListIndex property has a value of minus one (-1).

- The **ListCount** property is an integer value that returns the number of items in a list. If the list is empty, the ListCount is zero (0); otherwise, the value of ListCount is the number of items in the list.

In your program you will add the items to the combo box when the program is run so you do not need to set the List property in the Properties window at design time. Also, because the quotation program will not interact with a database, there is no need to set the DataSource and DataField properties. Because the items will appear in the list in the same order as they appear in the input file, you will not set the Sorted property or use the ItemData property. Because Rose only will select items from the list rather than adding new items, and because there is not room on the form to display each item in the list, you will use a dropdown combo box. The standard prefix for a combo box is "cbo".

To create the ComboBox object for your program:

1. Click the **ComboBox** control on the toolbox and draw an instance of a combo box as shown in Figure 6-4.

Figure 6-4
Creating the
ComboBox
object

new ComboBox
object

list arrow

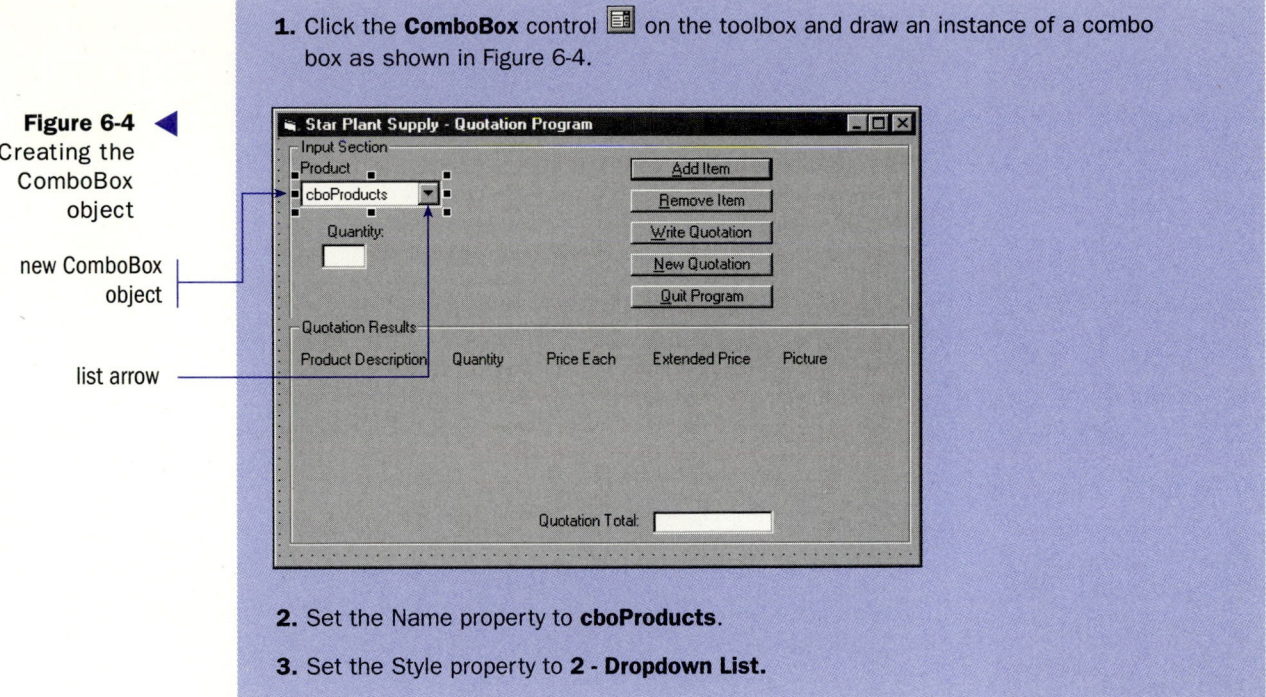

2. Set the Name property to **cboProducts**.

3. Set the Style property to **2 - Dropdown List.**

You will add the items to the combo box when the program is run from information contained in the price list Joan created.

The ListBox Control

After Rose selects a product from the combo box, she wants the item, quantity ordered, price, and extended prices to be displayed in the output section of the program. Because there will be several items in any given quotation, the control must be able to display several items. There is another control that is similar to a combo box called the **ListBox** control. They share almost the same properties. The user cannot enter new items into a list box by typing in information, however. Rather items must be added either at design time by setting the List property or at run time by calling a method of the list box. You now will create the list boxes that will be used to display the quotation information. The standard prefix for a list box is "lst". Because you are creating list boxes to store the products that are quoted, quantity selected, price, and extended price, you will name the objects lstQuotedProduct, lstQuotedQty, lstQuotedPrice, and lstQuotedExtPrice.

To create the ListBox objects that will display the items in a quotation:

1. Click the **ListBox** control ⊞ on the toolbox and draw an instance of a list box as shown in Figure 6-5. Set the Name property to **lstQuotedProduct**.

Figure 6-5 ◀
Creating the
ListBox objects

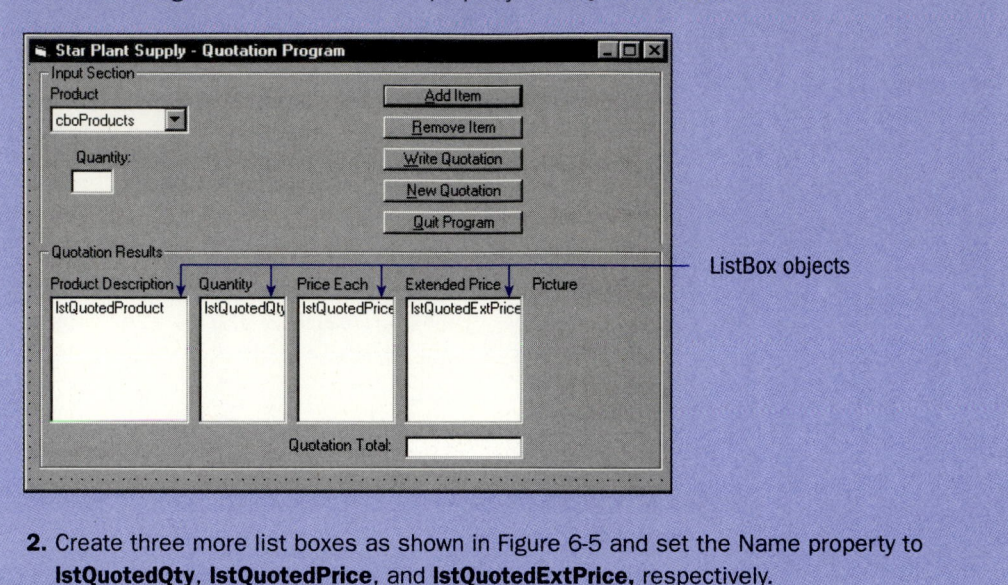

ListBox objects

2. Create three more list boxes as shown in Figure 6-5 and set the Name property to **lstQuotedQty**, **lstQuotedPrice**, and **lstQuotedExtPrice**, respectively.

The price list, which Joan created in WordPad, lists each of Star Plant Supply's products on a separate line followed by the corresponding price for each product. Joan updates this list when the prices change or new items are added to the inventory. Figure 6-6 shows the first nine items of the text file.

Figure 6-6 ◀
Price list for
Star Plant
Supply

Flower - Iris	4.37
Flower - Lilac	5.22
Herb - Mint	1.88
Shrub - Juniper	4.18
Shrub - Boxwood	9.22
Tree - Ash	43.80
Tree - Pine	28.60
Tree - Oak	33.84
Tree - Olive	19.20

The quotation program you are creating can read and use this text file. Joan needs to make some changes to the formatting, however, so Visual Basic can read the file. To use the text file with Visual Basic, Joan must remove the tabs and enter commas with no spaces, to separate the products from the prices. Also, the product names must be enclosed in quotation marks because they contain text rather than numbers.

Loading a Text File into a Program

When the quotation program starts, the first thing it must do is load all the products into the Product combo box. There are three options available for loading the product and price list. First, you could store the product information in a database and use a Data control and its Recordset property with a Do loop to add each item. Second, you could load the product and pricing information into the computer's memory from a text file when the program first starts. Third, you could set the List property at design time to load the items.

The decision to use a text file or a database to store the data is based on several factors. When the number of items to be used is relatively small, they can be read effectively from a text file and stored in the computer's memory using list boxes and combo boxes without slowing down your system. Reading the information from a database each time a product is accessed would take longer than finding the information in a list or a variable. The information in your input list is read-only; that is, once the information is loaded into the program, it will not be changed. So, there is no need to write individual records back to a database. Also, Rose wants to continue using the text file containing the price list. In this way if the computer is not available because of a disk failure, or if she is preparing a quotation outside the office, she can refer to a printout of the price list to prepare quotations manually. Your program will read the product information from the text file that Joan created.

In Tutorials 4 and 5 you accessed a table in a database by creating an instance of a Data control and using the methods of the Data control and the Recordset object to navigate through the records. Unlike a database, a text file is not an object. Instead of calling the methods of an object like a recordset, you use a Visual Basic statement to open a text file. Once a text file is open, you can read the file from beginning to end. This way of accessing a text file is called **sequential access**. A program cannot explicitly locate a specific line in a text file without reading all the lines preceding it. Also, it is not possible to move backward through a file when reading it sequentially.

Opening a Text File

When you open a text file, you must open explicitly the file and tell Visual Basic what operations you want to perform on it. You open a text file with the **Open** statement, which has the following syntax:

Open "*pathname***" For [Input | Output | Append] As #***filenumber*

- The *pathname* contains a string describing the name and location of the file you want to open. It must be enclosed in quotation marks if you enter text, but the quotation marks should be omitted if you use a variable.

- One of three options—Input, Output, or Append—must be included in the Open statement or Visual Basic will generate a syntax error.

- If the file is opened **For Input**, it already must exist. You can read information contained in the file but you cannot write to the file when it is opened For Input. This is the method you will use to read the file for the Star Plant Supply quotation program.

- If the file is opened **For Output**, you can write to the file but you cannot read it. If the file does not exist, Visual Basic will create it for you. If the file does exist, the existing contents will be deleted. The user will not be asked to confirm the deletion. You can create a message box to ask for confirmation from the user with the MsgBox function. The **For Output** option is useful if you want to rewrite an existing file entirely.

- If the file is opened **For Append**, information you write to the file will be appended to the end of the file, but you cannot read from it. If the file does not exist, Visual Basic will create it for you. Unlike opening a file For Output, the existing contents of a file opened **For Append** will not be deleted.

- The *filenumber* is an arbitrary integer number you assign as a reference to the file while it is open. The *filenumber* must be preceded by the **#** character. If you do not specify a *filenumber*, Visual Basic will generate a syntax error.

- If you want to read a file opened For Output or For Append, or write a file opened For Input, you must close the file and open it again using the desired option.

> Tip: Although you can use any integer number, starting the filenumber at #1 for the first open file and #2 for the second open file will make your program more understandable. Although you can have several files open at once, you cannot open an infinite number of files. Windows 95 determines how many total files you can have open at once, which varies from system to system. It is a good practice to close a file once you are done reading it or writing to it.

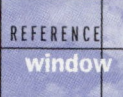

OPENING A TEXT FILE

- To open a file for reading, type the Open statement followed by the filename and the For Input clause after the filename in quotation marks.
- To assign a filenumber to the file, type As #*n* at the end of the Open statement, where *n* is an integer number not already assigned to an open file. To make your programs more readable, the first file you open should have a filenumber of 1.

Because the information contained in the text file must be loaded before Rose can begin preparing any quotations, the program should read the text file and place the information into the combo box in the form input section in the Form_Load event procedure.

To write the code to open the text file:

1. Open the Code window for the **Form_Load** event procedure.

2. Enter the following code in the window (shown in bold):

```
Private Sub Form_Load( )
     Open "A:\Tutorial.06\Product.txt" For Input As #1
End Sub
```

This statement opens the price list file, Product.txt, in the Tutorial.06 folder on your Student Disk. Because you will be reading information into the program, you opened the file For Input. It is the first open file, so its filenumber is #1.

Reading a Text File

After opening the file For Input, the program can read each of the products from the file into the Product combo box. You could enter all the items at design time by setting the combo box's List property, but if you did so, any changes to the list of products would have to be made by changing the properties using the Properties window. Because Rose and Joan are not very familiar with computers, they do not want to have to modify the program. Reading the products from a file is the best solution, because Joan can update the text file in WordPad when products are added and removed or the prices change. As long as Joan keeps the price list current, every time Rose runs the program it will read the current information from the text file.

> *Tip:* If the contents of a combo or list box are likely to change, you should read the items at run time from a text file or database table. If the contents will not change, set the List property at design time.

The **Input #** statement is used when each line of the file contains information separated by commas, and any text strings in the file are enclosed in quotation marks. The Input # statement has the following syntax:

Input #*filenumber, varlist*

- The **Input #** statement reads a line of text from an open file. When an input file has information separated by commas, each item of information can be thought of as a field, like in a database. Each field of information in the text file must be separated by a comma and any text strings in the file must be enclosed in quotation marks.

- The *filenumber* can be any valid filenumber assigned by the Open statement, preceded by the **#** character.

- The *varlist* is a list of variables, separated by commas, which are assigned values read from the file. The data type of each variable should correspond to the data type in the respective field.

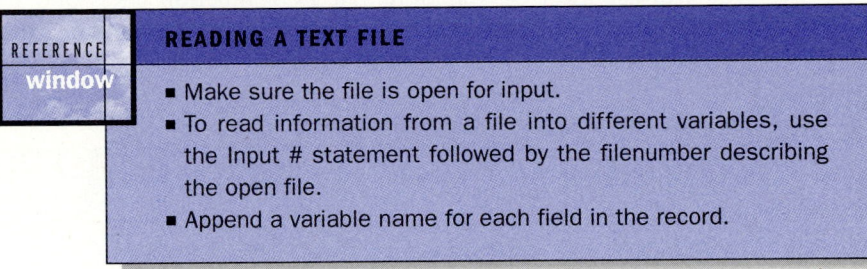

REFERENCE window

READING A TEXT FILE

- Make sure the file is open for input.
- To read information from a file into different variables, use the Input # statement followed by the filenumber describing the open file.
- Append a variable name for each field in the record.

Visual Basic can read text files using an Input # statement when each field in a line is separated, or delimited, by a comma, and string information is enclosed in quotation marks. This type of file is called an **ASCII-delimited file** and is supported by most word processing, spreadsheet, and database programs. Joan has converted the WordPad text file into a form suitable for reading by your Visual Basic program. Figure 6-7 shows part of the ASCII-delimited file for the quotation program.

Figure 6-7 ◀
ASCII-delimited file with two fields

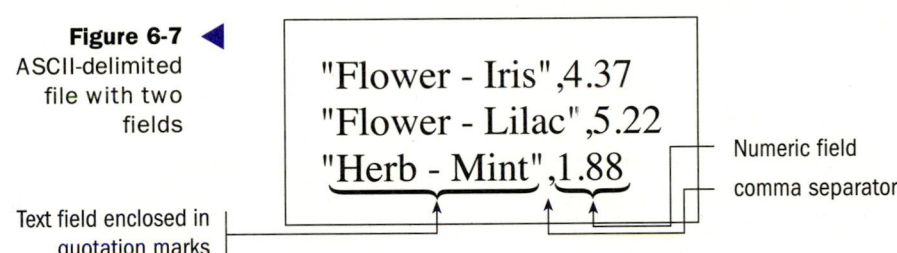

```
"Flower - Iris",4.37
"Flower - Lilac",5.22
"Herb - Mint",1.88
```

Numeric field

comma separator

Text field enclosed in quotation marks

As shown in Figure 6-7, the input file contains two items of information separated by a comma. Each of these items can be thought of as a field. The first field contains text enclosed in quotation marks. The second field is numeric; it is not enclosed in quotations. Each line in the file can be thought of as a record. In Figure 6-7 there are three records.

When you create an ASCII-delimited file, you need to be sure that each record contains the correct number of fields. If there is no information for the field, a blank entry should be created with two commas next to each other. Each line must end with a carriage return, including the last line. Typically, if the input file is not correct, your program will generate a run-time error indicating that you tried to read past the end of file.

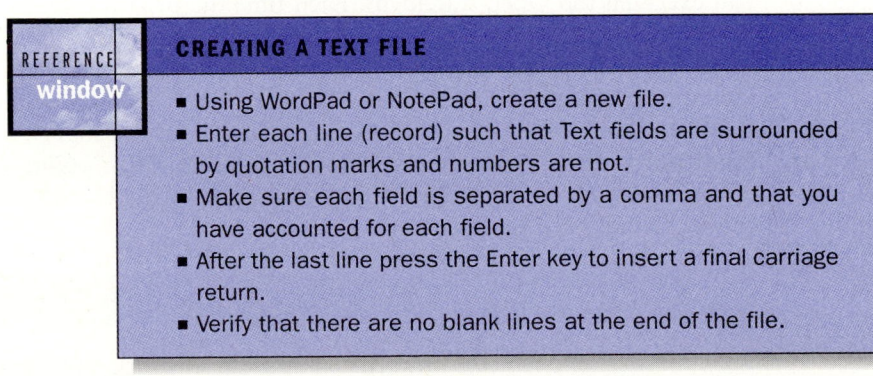

REFERENCE window

CREATING A TEXT FILE

- Using WordPad or NotePad, create a new file.
- Enter each line (record) such that Text fields are surrounded by quotation marks and numbers are not.
- Make sure each field is separated by a comma and that you have accounted for each field.
- After the last line press the Enter key to insert a final carriage return.
- Verify that there are no blank lines at the end of the file.

Generally you want the text to be read just after the file is opened, so the program should read the file immediately after opening it in the Form_Load event procedure. To do this, you will create a variable that will store temporarily the information before adding it to the Product combo box.

To read the text file, you will create a Do loop that calls the Input# statement repeatedly until the end of file has been reached. To determine when the end of file has been reached, you will use the EOF function. The EOF function takes one argument—the filenumber assigned to the file. The function returns the value True when the end of the input file has been reached; otherwise, it returns the value False.

To read the text file into the variables:

1. Make sure the Code window for the **Form_Load** event procedure still is active.

2. Enter the following code in the window (shown in bold):

```
Dim pstrProduct As String
Dim psngPrice As Single
Open "A:\Tutorial.06\Product.txt" For Input As #1
Do Until EOF(1) = True
    Input #1, pstrProduct, psngPrice
Loop
```

These statements read the input from the text file and load the items into the variables named pstrProduct and psngPrice.

```
Dim pstrProduct As String
Dim psngPrice As Single
```

The Dim statements declare two variables. The variable pstrProduct will store the name of each product. The variable psngPrice will store the price of each product, which you will be using later in the session. You must include the Dim statements before the Open statement because all variables must be declared before they are used.

```
Do Until EOF(1) = True
    Input #1, pstrProduct, psngPrice
Loop
```

The EOF function works with a text file in the same way that the EOF property works with a Recordset object. The EOF function determines when the end of file is reached. This is used to exit the Do loop. The EOF function returns the value False unless the end of file has been reached; then it returns the value True. The argument 1 is the filenumber corresponding to the open file.

In the Input statement, the filenumber #1 is associated with the file you opened when you executed the Open statement. Each time the program reads a line from the file, the values read are stored in the variables pstrProduct and psngPrice. If the input file included more than two fields on a line, you would have stored the fields in additional variables separated by commas. Because the number of variables in the Input statement must correspond to the number of fields in the file, the variable psngPrice must be included here, even though the program is not using this variable at this point.

The Loop statement sends the program back to the Do statement to determine if the end of file has been reached.

The AddItem Method

The text file has been read into the computer's memory, but the items need to appear in the combo box. The AddItem method acts on both ComboBox and ListBox objects and is used to add an item to the list of choices for each at run time. The AddItem method has the following syntax:

object.**AddItem** *text*

- *object* represents any valid combo box or list box.

- The **AddItem** method adds an item to the list of choices at run time.

- The *text* represents the item to be added to the list, which will appear in the combo box or list box when the program is running. So, if you wanted to add five different items to a list you would call the AddItem method five times with different text strings.

You now can write the statement to call the AddItem method that will store the contents of the variable pstrProduct into the combo box. This statement needs to be executed each time a record is read from the input file, so it should be inside the Do loop.

To add each product to the combo box:

1. Make sure the Code window for the **Form_Load** event procedure still is active.

2. Enter the following code into the event procedure just after the Input # statement and before the Loop statement:

```
cboProducts.AddItem pstrProduct
```

Whenever a program finishes using a file, the program should close the file. Because Windows 95 limits the number of files you can have open at one time, closing files that are not being used will ensure there are adequate filenumbers remaining. Also, each open file consumes some memory. So, too many open files can slow down your computer, depending on the amount of memory it has.

Closing the File

When the program finishes reading a file, the program should close the file explicitly using the Close statement. The **Close** statement has the following syntax:

Close [[#]1][,[#]2]...

- The **Close** statement is used to close explicitly one or more files.

- The arguments can be one or more filenumbers separated by commas. So, to close file #1 and #2 you would write the following statement:

```
Close #1, #2
```

- If you do not specify a *filenumberlist*, any files opened with the Open statement are closed. If you are working with several files, including such a Close statement just before the program exits will guarantee that all files have been closed.

> *Tip:* Whenever you are finished processing a file, use the Close statement to close explicitly the file. This will prevent corruption of a file in the event of a power failure or a program being terminated improperly.

You currently have one file open, Product.txt, which is associated with the filenumber #1. You now need to write the code to close this file.

To close the open text file:

1. Open the Code window for the **Form_Load** event procedure.

2. Enter the following line of code, just before the End Sub statement:

```
Close #1
```

When the running program reaches this statement, the program will close the Product.txt file. The filenumber #1 will no longer be associated with the file. If a program needs to read the file again, the program must open the file again with the Open statement.

You now should test the Do loop to see if the products in the text file are being read into the Product combo box.

To test the Do loop:

1. Save the project then start the program.

2. Click the list arrow on the rightmost side of the combo box. Your screen should look like Figure 6-8.

Figure 6-8 ◄
Combo box
with products

products from text file
stored in combo box

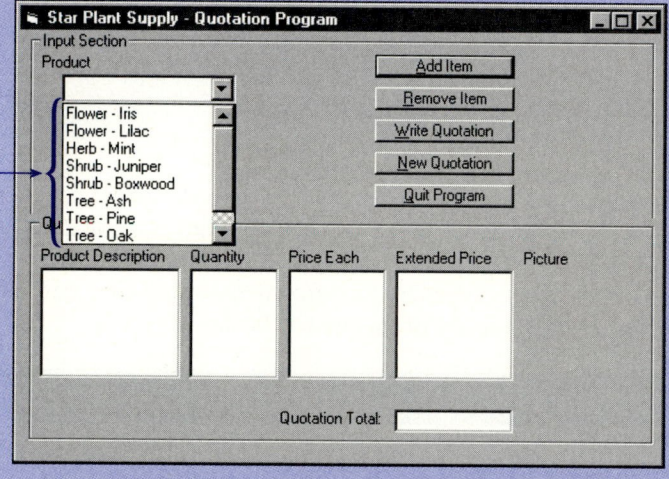

Notice the Product combo box now contains the products that Rose sells. Because all the products will not fit into the combo box, scroll bars appear so she can scroll through the list.

TROUBLE? If the products are not being loaded in the combo box, make sure the code you wrote matches the code in the previous steps. If incorrect information is being loaded, make sure both variables are listed in the Input # statement. Make any necessary corrections, then repeat Steps 1 and 2.

3. Test the **Quit Program** button to end the program.

Now, every time you run the program, the information in the first field of the Product.txt file will be stored in the Product combo box.

Creating an Array to Store Information

In each program you have written until this point, you have declared variables that can store only a single item of information, such as a price. In the quotation program, you need to store the prices for each product sold by Star Plant Supply. When Rose selects an item from the combo box containing the products, the program needs to look up the corresponding price. The company sells many different products, so you would need many different variables to store the information. Although creating different variables does not present a problem in this case, consider a company that sells 500 or 5,000 products. The problem becomes more complicated when you need to add new products, because you would need to create new variables.

You have seen how several objects of the same type can be grouped together in a control array. Each object in a control array has the same name and is referenced with its Index property value, which is unique. You can group variables together in the same way using an array. An **array** is a variable that contains a list of several items of the same data type. Each item in an array is called an **element**. Each individual element is referenced by a unique index number, called a **subscript**. When you want to access an individual element in an array, you use the array name and the subscript to reference the element.

You can create an array to store the prices of each item in one variable, just as you can store many items in one combo or list box. Figure 6-9 shows the relationship between the information stored in the array and the combo box.

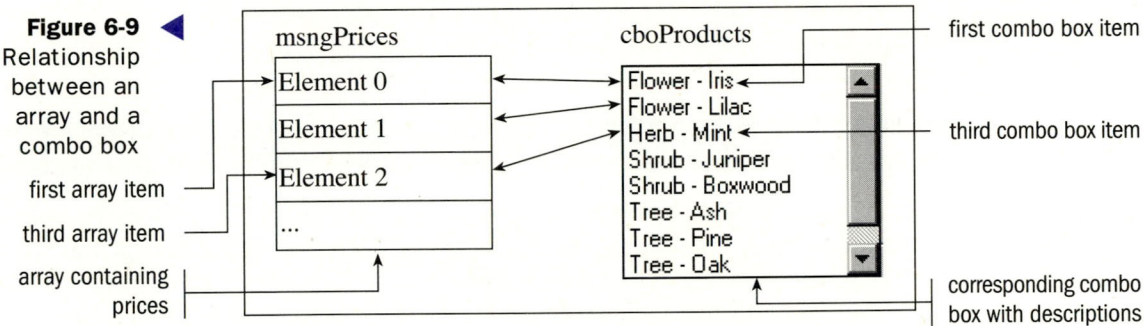

Figure 6-9 ◄
Relationship between an array and a combo box

first array item

third array item

array containing prices

In Figure 6-9 the array msngPrices contains three elements, numbered 0 through 2, that correspond to the product descriptions stored in the cboProducts combo box. Thus, the price for the first product, Flower - Iris, is stored in the first element of msngPrices, which is element 0.

When you create an array, you use the Dim, Private, and Public statements, just as you do when you declare any variable. An array is simply a variable that contains many elements of the same data type.

To declare an array that can be used in a single module, you use a Private statement in the general declarations section of the Form module with the following syntax:

Private *array-name*([*lower-bound* **To**]*upper-bound*) **As** *datatype*

- The *array-name* can be any valid variable name.

- The *lower-bound* defines the first element of the array. If you do not specify a lower-bound, it will be set to 0 by default. The keyword **To** specifies the range of the array.

- The *upper-bound* defines the last element of the array.

- The array can be declared as any valid *datatype* using the keyword **As**.

You need to create an array to store the price for each of the products loaded into the Product combo box. Like any variable, an array declared in the general declarations section of the Form module is available to all procedures in the module if the Private keyword is used, and all procedures in all modules if the Public keyword is used. If you declare an array inside a procedure using the Dim statement, the array is considered local to the procedure and can be referenced inside that procedure only. Because the array you create will be used by many procedures on the form, you must declare the array in the general declarations section. Because there is only one form, the array should be Private.

Like variables, arrays consume memory. If you make an array too large, memory will be wasted because Visual Basic allocates memory for each element in the array whether or not the program stores values in each element. So, you should try to estimate accurately the number of elements in the array. Rose estimates she will sell at most 100 different products, so the array should be declared to hold 100 items. You do not need to store a value in each element of an array right away. You can add values later. Running the program with some empty array elements will not cause an error. Because the array is a form-level array that will hold prices, you will use the Single data type and the name msngPrices.

To declare an array to contain the prices of the products:

1. Activate the general declarations section of the Code window for the Form module.

2. Enter the following statement in the Code window after the Option Explicit statement:

```
Private msngPrices(0 To 99) As Single
```

The array msngPrices contains 100 elements. The first element is 0 and the last element is 99. Each element in the array is defined as a Single data type, which is the appropriate data type because the prices will contain a decimal point.

Storing Information in an Array

Once the array has been declared, you need to store information in it. This information will consist of the price for each item. Each price will correspond to an item in the Product combo box, as shown in Figure 6-9, but the array will include 100 elements instead of three.

When you store information in an array and retrieve information from an array, you are interested in a specific element rather than the contents of the entire array. In this case, the array stores the price for each product in the inventory. When you need to look up a price in the array, you are looking for the price of a particular item, rather than all the prices.

Next, you need to load the prices into the array. The price of each product must be stored in the array such that the first item in the Product combo box will correspond to the price contained in the first element of the array.

The procedure for loading the prices into the array is similar to the procedure you used to load the products into the combo box. Because all the products and corresponding prices must be loaded into the computer's memory before Rose can begin writing a quotation, the array should be loaded at the same time that the products are loaded into the combo box. So, you can modify the existing Form_Load event procedure to add the necessary statements for loading prices into the array. In fact, you can expand the Do loop that reads the products into the Product combo box so it also loads the prices into the array. So you can keep track of the current array element, you need to create a variable to be used as a subscript. Because a subscript always contains a whole number, you will declare it as an integer. Each time through the Do loop, the subscript must be incremented by one (1) much like a counter.

To write the code for loading the prices into the array:

1. Activate the Code window for the **Form_Load** event procedure.

2. Add the following statements to the event procedure (shown in bold):

```
Dim pintCurrentItem As Integer
pintCurrentItem = 0
Open "A:\Tutorial.06\Product.txt" For Input As #1
Do Until EOF(1)
    Input #1, pstrProduct, psngPrice
    cboProducts.AddItem pstrProduct
    msngPrices(pintCurrentItem) = psngPrice
    pintCurrentItem = pintCurrentItem + 1
Loop
```

The code you just entered will load the prices from the text file into the array.

```
Dim pintCurrentItem As Integer
pintCurrentItem = 0
```

The variable pintCurrentItem is used as an array subscript, which is always a whole number. Because you want the program to load the first line of the text file into the first element of the array, you initialized the pintCurrentItem variable to one (0).

```
msngPrices(pintCurrentItem) = psngPrice
pintCurrentItem = pintCurrentItem + 1
```

Each time a line is read from the file, the variable used in the Input # statement, psngPrice, is assigned to the element in msngPrices corresponding to the product contained in the Product combo box. Whenever you reference an array, you use the subscript to identify the element of the array you are referring to. Because the variable pintCurrentItem was initialized to zero (0), the first value of psngPrice will be stored at element position 0. This is the lower bound, or first element, of the array. Next, pintCurrentItem is incremented explicitly by one (1) so the next time through the loop, the value of psngPrice will be stored in the next element.

All the products and prices will be loaded into the program when it starts. When Rose clicks a product in the combo box, the program must determine which item she selected so it can find the corresponding price from msngPrices. The program also needs to copy this information into the ListBox objects used for output when the Add Item command button is clicked. The ListIndex property of the ComboBox object solves this problem.

The **ListIndex** property is an integer value that identifies the currently selected item in a list or combo box. The expression List1.ListIndex returns the integer index for the currently selected item in the ListBox object named List1. This is similar to the way you reference an element in an array with a subscript, but with an array you are not using a property. You can assign a value to the ListIndex property for a list or combo box. When you do, you set the active item for the list. For example, if you wanted to make the currently selected item the first item of a list box, you would set its ListIndex property to zero (0). If you wanted to deselect all items in the list, you would set the ListIndex property to minus one (-1).

Adding an item to the quotation is the most common event that Rose will trigger in this program. To allow Rose to press the Enter key to add an item to the quotation, Mack set the Default property of the Add Item command button to True in the Properties window. You now need to program the Add Item command button to look up the price for the selected product and store the product and price information in the output list boxes. The selected product is stored in the Text property of the cboProducts combo box. This must be added to the Product Description output list box. You also need to add the item's price to the Price Each output list box. This information should be formatted with two decimal places so you will use the Format statement with the Fixed argument.

To program the Add Item command button to look up prices and add both product and price information to the output ListBox objects:

1. Activate the Code window for the **cmdAdd_Click** event procedure.

2. Enter the following code in the window (shown in bold):

```
Private Sub cmdAdd_Click( )
    lstQuotedProduct.AddItem cboProducts.Text
    lstQuotedPrice.AddItem _
        Format(msngPrices(cboProducts.ListIndex), "Fixed")
    cboProducts.ListIndex = -1
End Sub
```

Each time Rose clicks a product in the Product combo box and then clicks the Add Item command button, the code you just wrote will add the information into the Product Description and Price Each output list boxes.

```
lstQuotedProduct.AddItem cboProducts.Text
```

This statement adds the text of the currently selected item in the Products combo box to the output list box lstQuotedProduct.

```
lstQuotedPrice.AddItem _
    Format(msngPrices(cboProducts.ListIndex), "Fixed")
```

This statement uses the array you created to locate the price for the selected product. To do this, the value of the ListIndex property of the currently selected product in the Products combo box is referenced, and that value becomes the subscript referenced in the msngPrices. Figure 6-10 shows how this process works. To display the prices with two decimal places, you used the Format function with the Fixed argument.

Figure 6-10 ◀
Adding the product and price to the output lists

third item (Herb - Mint) is selected; this is cboProducts.text

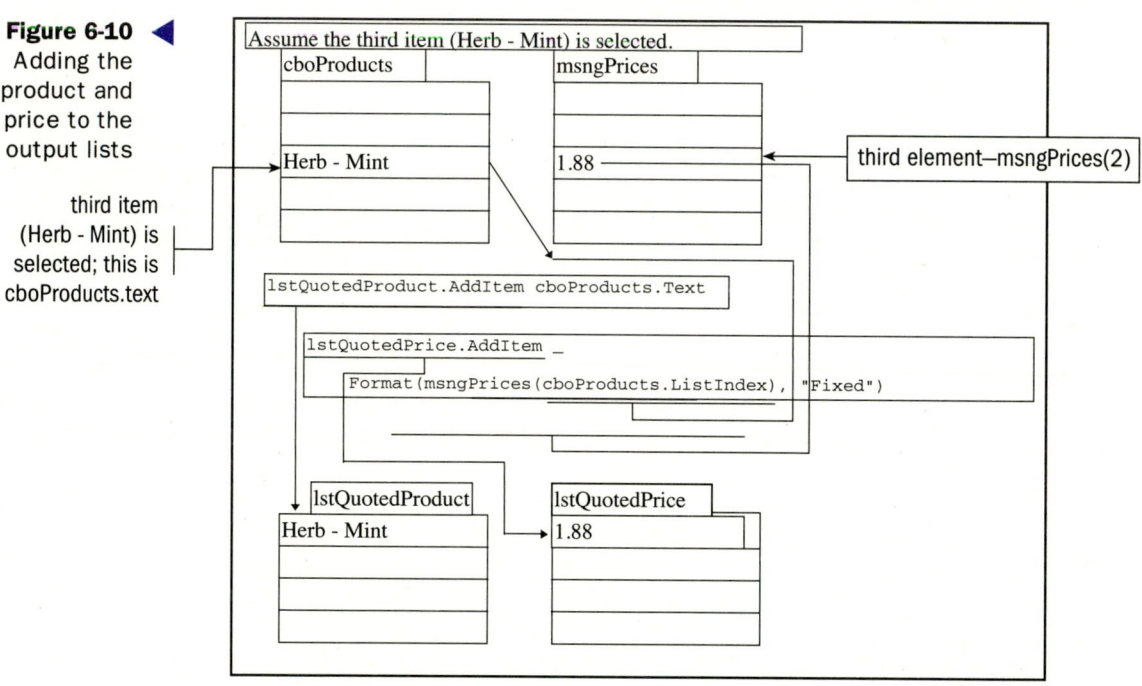

```
cboProducts.ListIndex = -1
```

This statement sets the ListIndex property of the combo box to -1, which deselects the item in the Product combo box so it is clear for the next product selection.

You now should test the program to determine if the Add Item command button is working properly. When clicked, this button should add the selected product and its corresponding price to the quotation, and then deselect the active item in the Product combo box.

To test the Add Item command button:

1. Save the project then start the program.

2. Click the list arrow in the Product combo box, then click the product **Herb - Mint**.

3. Click the **Add Item** command button. Your screen should look like Figure 6-11.

Figure 6-11
Testing the Add
Item command
button

no active item after
clicking Add Item
command button

output product
description

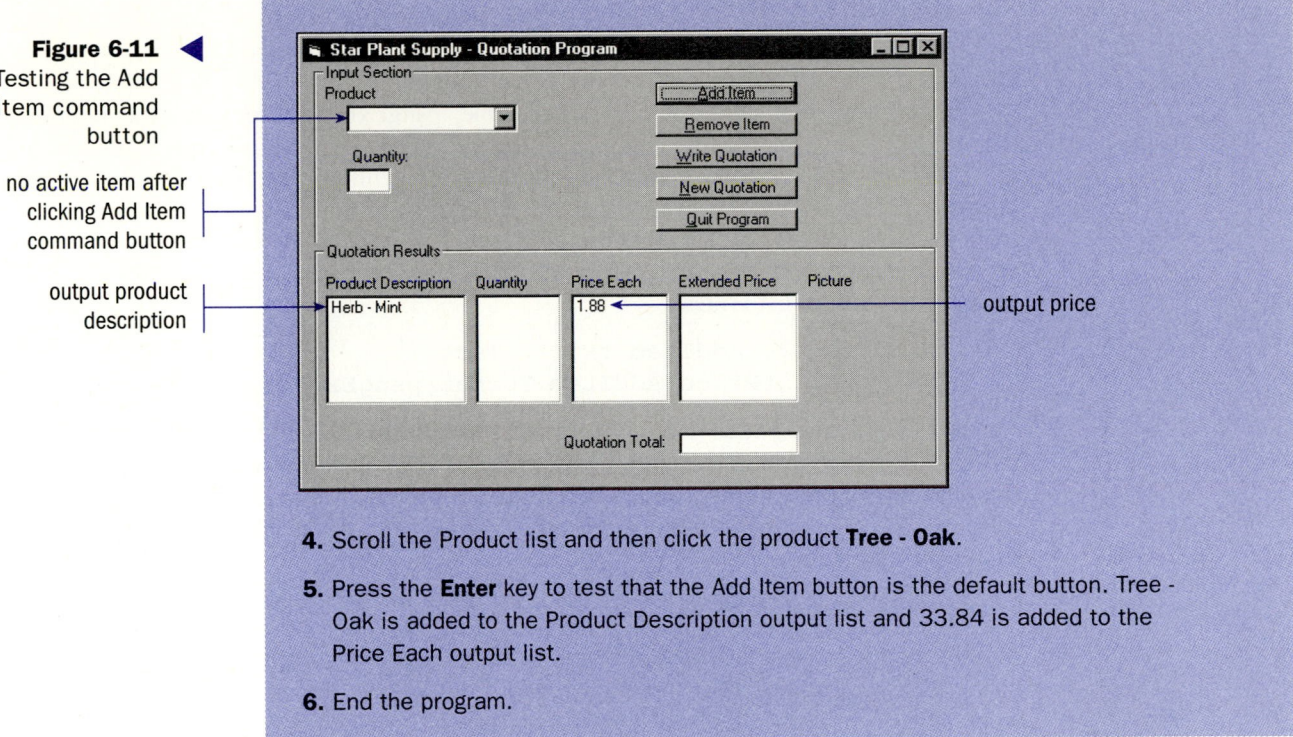

output price

4. Scroll the Product list and then click the product **Tree - Oak**.

5. Press the **Enter** key to test that the Add Item button is the default button. Tree - Oak is added to the Product Description output list and 33.84 is added to the Price Each output list.

6. End the program.

Now you are ready to add the quantity ordered and the extended prices to the corresponding output list boxes. This also needs to occur when the Add Item command button is clicked. The quantity ordered will be typed in the text box and must be added to the Quantity output list box. The extended price needs to be stored in a local variable. Because the variable only is used by this procedure, it is declared as a local variable. Because the variable will store prices, it must be declared as a Single data type. The variable will be named psngExtPrice. The extended price is computed by looking up the correct price in the msngPrices array, and multiplying that value by the quantity ordered. The output should be displayed with two decimal places, so you will use the Format statement with the Fixed argument. The result then is displayed in the Extended Price output list box.

To write the code for the Quantity Ordered and Extended Price output list boxes:

1. Activate the Code window for the **cmdAdd** object's **Click** event procedure.

2. Add the following statements to the event procedure (shown in bold):

```
Dim psngExtPrice As Single
lstQuotedProduct.AddItem cboProducts.Text
psngExtPrice = (txtQty.Text * _
    msngPrices(cboProducts.ListIndex))
lstQuotedPrice.AddItem _
    Format(msngPrices(cboProducts.ListIndex), "Fixed")
lstQuotedQty.AddItem txtQty.Text
lstQuotedExtPrice.AddItem Format(psngExtPrice, "Fixed")
cboProducts.ListIndex = -1
txtQty.Text = ""
```

The code you added will copy the quantity from the Quantity text box in the input section to the Quantity list box in the output section. It also will compute the extended price and place it in the Extended Price list box in the output section.

```
Dim psngExtPrice As Single
psngExtPrice = (txtQty.Text * _
    msngPrices(cboProducts.ListIndex))
```

The first statement creates a local variable, psngExtPrice, to store the temporary extended price used in this procedure. The local variable you declared then is used to store the extended price of the product. To produce the extended price, you use the ListIndex property of the Product combo box as the subscript of the array, and multiply the value stored in each element of the array by the quantity ordered value stored in the Text property of the txtQty object. After computing the extended price, the program can add the items to the output list boxes.

```
lstQuotedQty.AddItem txtQty.Text
lstQuotedExtPrice.AddItem Format(psngExtPrice, "Fixed")
```

The first statement adds the quantity of the specific item (stored in the Text property of the Quantity text box) to the lstQuotedQty list box. The second statement adds the computed extended price to the lstQuotedExtPrice list box by calling the AddItem method. To display the extended price with two decimal places, you called the Format function with the Fixed argument.

```
txtQty.Text = ""
```

This statement sets the Text property of the txtQty text box to a blank value, which clears the Quantity text box and makes the form ready for the next product and quantity to be added.

Now you should test the program to verify that the output is being added to the correct ListBox objects, that the extended prices are being computed properly, and that the input combo and text boxes are being reset.

To test the extended price and quantity output:

1. Save the project and start the program.

2. Enter the products and quantities shown in Figure 6-12.

Figure 6-12 ◀
Completed
output list
boxes

input section cleared
for next selection

output list boxes
completed

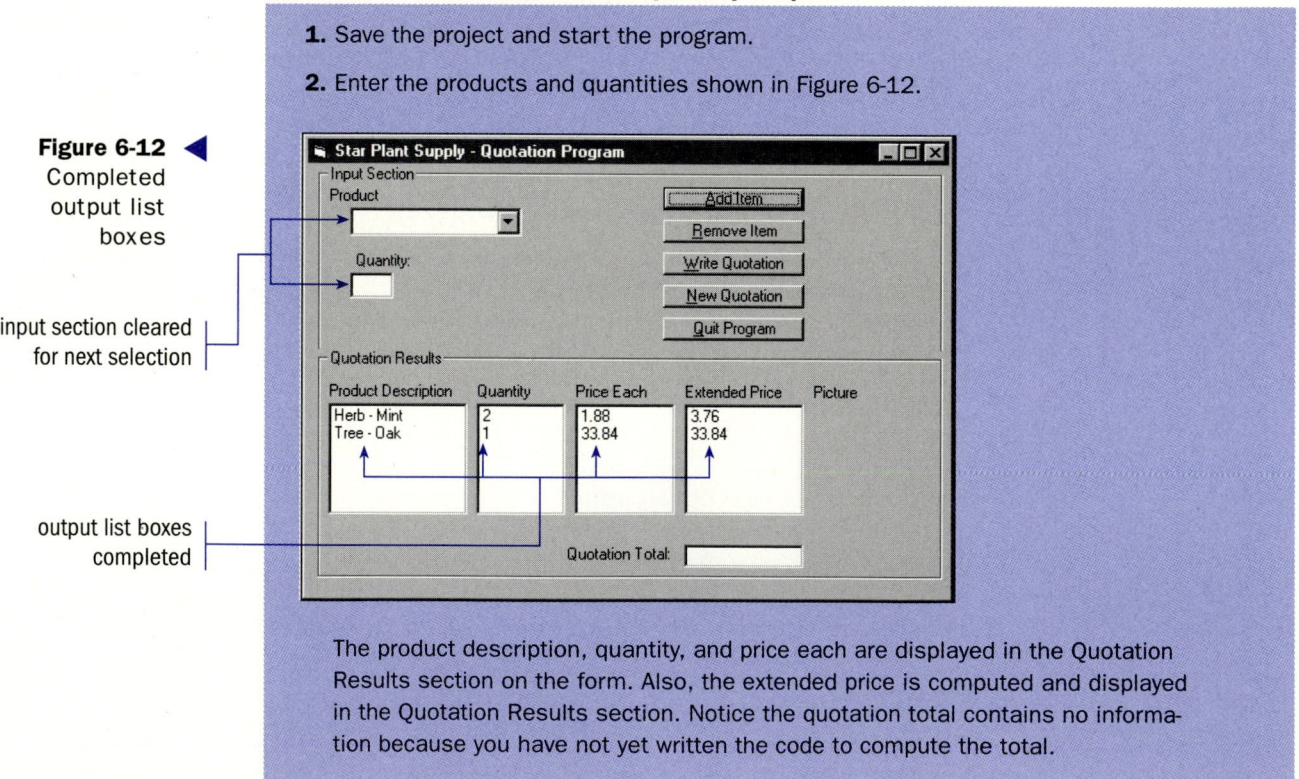

The product description, quantity, and price each are displayed in the Quotation Results section on the form. Also, the extended price is computed and displayed in the Quotation Results section. Notice the quotation total contains no information because you have not yet written the code to compute the total.

TROUBLE? If you do not enter a valid number in the Quantity text box, the program will generate a run-time error when it tries to multiply the quantity requested by the price. End the program and then repeat Steps 1 and 2, making sure you enter the number "2" in the Quantity text box.

3. End the program.

You have completed the statements to store the product description, quantity, price each, and extended price in the output list boxes. Your next task is to update the quotation total each time an item is added.

Looping Through the Items in a List Box

In previous tutorials you used the Change or LostFocus event of an object to call a general procedure that calculates totals each time the value of the object changed or the focus moved to a different object. In this case, unlike a TextBox object, the ListBox object does not support the Change event. So, the program must update the total when the Add Item command button is clicked.

You have seen how to use a Do loop with the EOF function to examine each line of a text file repetitively until the end-of-file condition is reached. In that situation the program does not know how many lines are in the text file. Rather, the loop terminates when the end-of-file condition is true.

You still could use a Do loop to step through each item in the Extended Price list box as well, by creating a variable used as an index. Another ListBox property, the ListCount property, is an integer that contains the number of items in a list. If the list or combo box is empty, the ListCount is zero (0); otherwise, the value of ListCount is the number of items in the list.

Your Do loop would use a variable to represent the ListIndex property. It would contain a statement to increment the variable each time through the loop. Before executing the loop again, the condition in the Do loop would test that the variable representing the current ListIndex property is less than the number of items in the list box (represented by the ListCount property), and exit the loop when it has examined all of the items.

Visual Basic provides another kind of looping structure that works like a counter. Each time the statements in the loop are executed, a counter is incremented until the counter is the same as some value you assign. This type of looping structure is called a **For loop** and it uses the For statement.

You can use a For statement when you know in advance how many times the statements in the loop need to be executed. Because your program includes items in a list box, the number of items (represented by the ListCount property) are known at any given time. So, a For loop is appropriate for stepping through each item in the list box. When you use a For loop, you do not have to write any statements to increment the variable you are using as a counter. Instead, the For statement does this for you. The For loop has the following syntax:

For *counter* = *start* **To** *end* [**Step** *increment*]

    [*statement-block*]

    [**Exit For**]

    [*statement-block*]

Next [*counter*]

Consider the For loop as a structure that works with counters, as illustrated in Figure 6-13.

Figure 6-13 ◀
The For loop

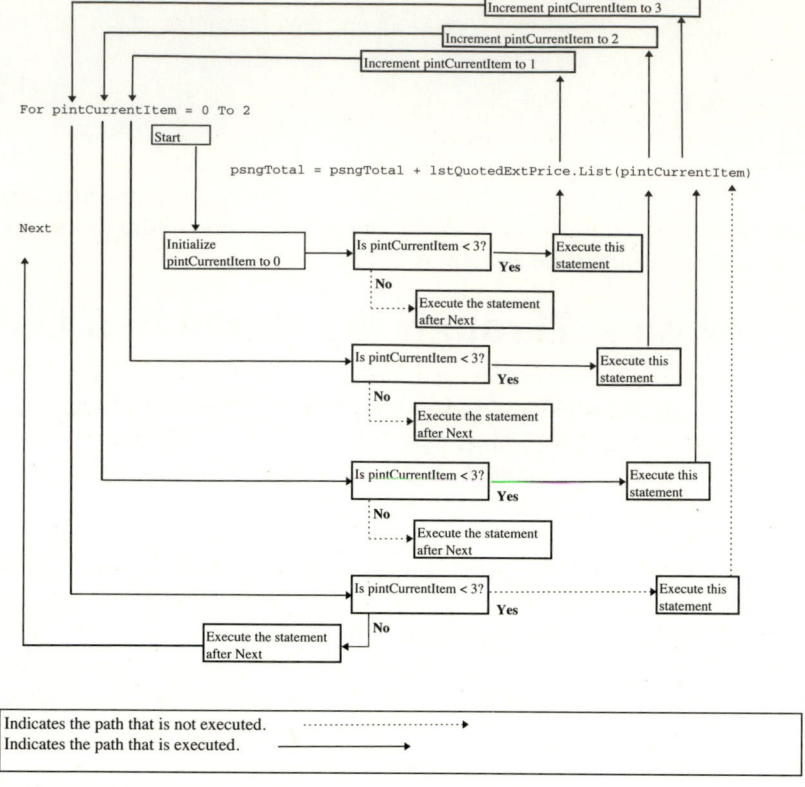

When you execute a For loop, the following happens:

1. The *counter* is initialized to the value of *start* the first time the For loop is executed. The counter is a variable of the Integer data type that you already declared using a Dim, Private, or Public statement. To look at the first item in a list box, *start* should have a value of zero (0), the lower bound of the list box.

2. Every time through the loop, the value of the counter is increased by the *increment*. If the increment is not specified, the default value is one (1). So, after the statements in the loop are executed, the counter must be incremented by one (1) to look at every item in the list box.

3. When the value of the counter is greater than *end*, the For loop exits and the *statement-block* in the loop is not executed again. This will happen after all the items in the list box have been examined.

4. If the counter is less than *end*, the first *statement-block* is executed; *end* would be the number of items in the list box.

5. If an Exit For statement is reached, usually enclosed in an If statement as the result of an abnormal condition, the For loop will exit. Otherwise the next *statement-block* is executed. A For loop does not require an Exit For statement. For example, if you are adding to the contents of the list boxes and wanted to make sure each list box contained a number, you could use an Exit For statement to stop the loop if one of the list boxes contained invalid data. Because the prices are taken from a text file and the extended prices are computed by the program, rather than entered by the user, you do not need to check for valid data. So, an Exit For statement is not necessary.

6. When the Next statement is reached, the *counter* is incremented and the For loop is tested again.

The List property of the ListBox and ComboBox objects, used with an index, acts like an array. The List property has the following syntax:

object.**List**(*index*)

- The **List** property references the text in each item of the list or combo box.

- You use the List property with an *index* of the item just as you use the subscript for an array. The first list item has an index of zero (0). If you wanted to reference the text of the second item (remember, its ListIndex property is one (1)) to the list box named lstMyList, you would use the following statement:

```
lstMyList.List(1)
```

For the quotation program, you want to create a loop that will step through all the items in the Extended Price list box so the program can compute the quotation total. The first item in the list box has an index of zero (0). The ListCount property tells you how many items are in the list. You can compute the index value of the last item in the list by subtracting one (1) from the ListCount property. You now have the information for the start and end conditions of the For loop. You can use the List property with the index to reference the item you want the program to look at. This index should be the *counter* from the For loop. The index of the first item in a list box is always zero (0), so the For loop should start at zero (0) and end when all the items have been examined (ListCount - 1).

Using a For loop and the properties of the list box, you can compute the quotation total by adding together each extended price in the Extended Price list box. You need to declare a variable to be used as an accumulator that will store the quotation total. This variable will be named psngTotal. Because the variable only will be used by the procedure, it will be declared as a local variable. Each time through the loop, the program must add the extended price to the accumulator. When the loop is complete (each item has been examined), the result should be formatted with two decimal places and a leading dollar sign and displayed in the lblTotal label. Thus, you will use the Format statement and store the result in the Caption property of lblTotal.

Because the program also must compute the quotation total when products are removed, you can write the necessary code once in a general procedure and call the general procedure whenever the total needs to be recomputed. You will name the procedure ComputeTotal to communicate its purpose. Because the program consists of a single form and the general procedure will be used by multiple procedures, you will declare the procedure as Private. You need to use the Insert Procedure dialog box to create this procedure before writing the code.

To compute the quotation total using a For loop:

1. Make sure the Code window is active. Because you are going to create a new general procedure, it does not matter which object and event procedure currently are active in the Code window.

2. Click **Tools** on the menu bar, then click **Add Procedure** to open the Add Procedure dialog box.

3. In the Name text box, type **ComputeTotal**.

    You will create a Sub procedure because it will not return a value.

4. In the Type section, click the **Sub** option button.

    You will declare the procedure as Private because it only will be used by this form.

5. In the Scope section, click the **Private** option button.

6. Click the **OK** button.

7. Enter the following statements in the Code window (shown in bold):

```
Private Sub ComputeTotal( )
    Dim psngTotal As Single
    Dim pintCurrentItem As Integer
    psngTotal = 0
    For pintCurrentItem = 0 To _
        lstQuotedExtPrice.ListCount - 1
        psngTotal = psngTotal + _
            lstQuotedExtPrice.List(pintCurrentItem)
    Next
    lblTotal.Caption = Format(psngTotal, "Currency")
End Sub
```

With the For loop, these statements use a counter (pintCurrentItem) to look at each value in the Extended Price list box and add the value to an accumulator (psngTotal).

```
Dim psngTotal As Single
Dim pintCurrentItem As Integer
psngTotal = 0
```

These statements declare two local variables, which exist only while the procedure is running. The variable psngTotal is used as an accumulator. Each time the program steps through an item in the Extended Price list box, it adds the extended price to psngTotal. The variable pintCurrentItem is used as the counter in the For loop. You initialize the variable by setting the value of psngTotal to zero (0). The For loop initializes the value of the counter pintCurrentItem.

```
For pintCurrentItem = 0 To _
    lstQuotedExtPrice.ListCount - 1
    psngTotal = psngTotal + _
        lstQuotedExtPrice.List(pintCurrentItem)
Next
```

> *Tip:* It is a good practice to initialize variables explicitly before the program begins processing. This gives the reader of your program a clear indication of what the value of the variable should be when the procedure starts.

The For loop steps through each item in the lstQuotedExtPrice list box by starting at item zero (0). This is the start value of the For loop. You could use a similar For loop to go through all of the elements in an array, because you know the number of elements (represented by the array subscript).

The List property of the list box retrieves the contents of the list box, in this case the extended prices, and adds them to the variable for the total. Remember, the List property is like an array; it requires an index of the element. In this case, the index is the loop's counter, pintCurrentItem.

When the Next statement is reached, the value of the counter pintCurrentItem is incremented by one (1). If the new value of the counter is less than or equal to ListCount - 1, then the statements in the loop are executed again. This process continues until there are no more items in the list box, which means that the counter has reached the end value, ListCount, and the For loop will exit. Recall that no Exit statements are needed to exit a For loop—it exits automatically when the end value of the counter is reached.

```
lblTotal.Caption = Format(psngTotal, "Currency")
```

This statement formats the quotation total with two decimal places and a leading dollar sign.

Now that you have written the ComputeTotal general procedure, you need to call it explicitly. The cmdAdd_Click procedure controls what occurs when a product is added to the quotation. If you want the quotation total to be updated whenever a product is added to the quotation, you need to call the general procedure from the cmdAdd_Click event procedure.

To call the ComputeTotal general procedure:

1. Activate the Code window for the **cmdAdd_Click** event procedure.

2. Add the following statement to the procedure, just before the End Sub statement:

```
ComputeTotal
```

You should run the program to verify that the quotation total is being computed correctly.

To test the quotation total:

1. Save the project then start the program.

2. Enter the products and quantities shown in Figure 6-14.

Figure 6-14 ◄
Testing the
quotation total

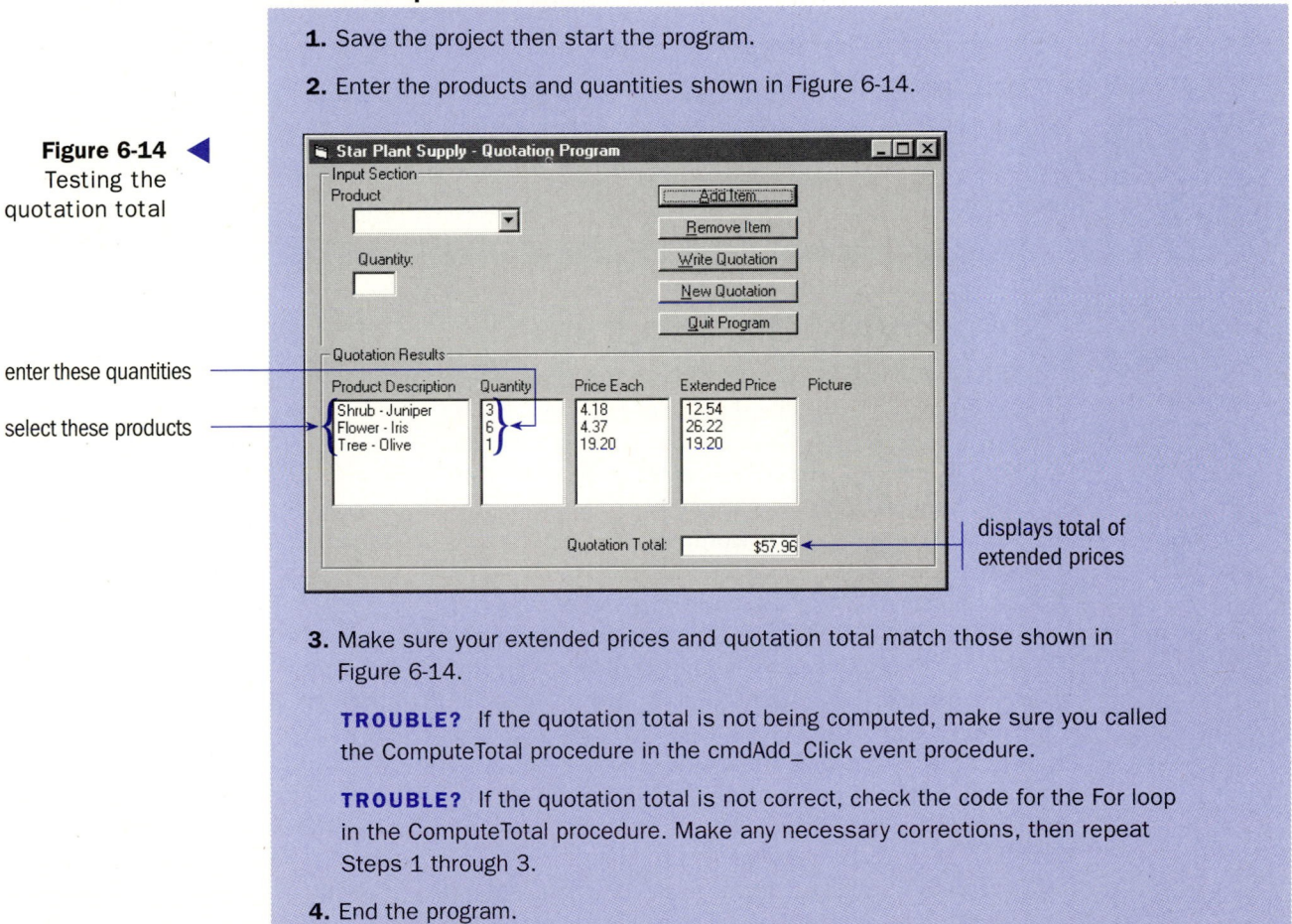

enter these quantities

select these products

displays total of
extended prices

3. Make sure your extended prices and quotation total match those shown in Figure 6-14.

TROUBLE? If the quotation total is not being computed, make sure you called the ComputeTotal procedure in the cmdAdd_Click event procedure.

TROUBLE? If the quotation total is not correct, check the code for the For loop in the ComputeTotal procedure. Make any necessary corrections, then repeat Steps 1 through 3.

4. End the program.

You have completed the first phase of the quotation program. Rose now can add products, quantities, and prices to a quotation and see the new total of the quotation each time she adds a product. Rose also can create her quotations electronically, with a minimal amount of typing. By preserving the contents of the text file containing the product and price information, she still can print a copy of the file when she needs to use a hard copy.

 **Quick Check**

1. Describe the difference between using a database and sequential access for processing. Describe the advantages and disadvantages of each method.

2. What is the purpose of the Open statement, the Input # statement, and the Close statement?

3. What is the EOF function used for?

4. Declare an array named Prices with 20 elements and a lower bound of 1.

5. Describe the purpose of the List, ListCount, and ListIndex properties of a list box.

6. Write a For loop that will count from 20 to 100 and print the value of the counter.

7. What is the purpose of the Exit For statement?

SESSION

6.2

In this session you will learn how to remove one specific item from a list box and how to remove all the items in a list box at once. You also will create a two-dimensional array, use the Variant data type for storing multiple kinds of data, display pictures at run time in a PictureBox control, and write program results to a text file.

Modifying the Program

Rose spent some time reviewing and testing your program with Mack. Rose still needs to be able to clear all the output list boxes so she can prepare a new quotation. Also, when she is preparing a quotation, she needs the capability to delete specific products from the quotation if the customer decides to omit items to maintain the budget for a project. For this, Mack included a Remove Item button that needs the code to delete a quoted product from the output and recompute the total whenever an item is removed. Finally, Rose wants a way to write the quotation results to a file she can format and then print the quotation using her word processing program.

Rose and Mack also have some suggestions to improve the program so it more closely models Rose's business activities. Rose often gives customers a discount depending on their annual purchasing volume, so she wants the program to be able to apply the discount. You will add a new Apply Discount check box that will enable Rose to apply a discount to the prices she charges, when appropriate. She also would like to display pictures of the different products on the form for those times when the customer is in the office. In this way customers can see the products they are ordering. Mack suggests you complete the development of the program. Next to the output list boxes, you will need to include a picture box, which will display pictures of the different products. You need to complete the programming for the Remove Item, Write Quotation, and New Quotation buttons, and the new check box and picture box.

Clearing the Contents of a List Box

After Rose completes a quotation, she needs to reset all the output list boxes and the quotation total to begin a new quotation for another customer. The New Quotation command button Mack created will be used to reset the list boxes used for output in preparation for another quotation. You needed to delete all the items from the ListBox objects and set the quotation total to zero (0) again. You can delete all the items from the list boxes using the Clear method for each of the four ListBox objects. The Clear method has the following syntax:

object.**Clear**

- The *object* can be any valid ListBox or ComboBox object.

- The **Clear** method removes all items from the object.

You now can write the code for the New Quotation command button. You will call the Clear method for each of the list boxes and reset the total to zero (0).

To program the New Quotation command button:

1. Open the project file named **Star Plant Supply.vbp** in the **Tutorial.06** folder on your Student Disk, if necessary.

2. Open the Code window for the **cmdNewQuotation_ Click** event procedure.

3. Enter the following code in the window (shown in bold):

```
Private Sub cmdNewQuotation_Click( )
    lstQuotedProduct.Clear
    lstQuotedQty.Clear
    lstQuotedPrice.Clear
    lstQuotedExtPrice.Clear
    lblTotal.Caption = ""
    txtQty.Text = ""
    cboProducts.ListIndex = -1
End Sub
```

These statements clear the input and output objects in preparation for another quotation.

```
lstQuotedProduct.Clear
lstQuotedQty.Clear
lstQuotedPrice.Clear
lstQuotedExtPrice.Clear
```

The Clear method deletes all the items in a list box, and is called in these four statements for each of the four output list boxes.

```
lblTotal.Caption = ""
txtQty.Text = ""
cboProducts.ListIndex = -1
```

These statements erase the value of the Caption property of the Label object used for the quotation total, clear the contents of the Quantity text box, and deselect the active item in the Product combo box. You need to clear the Quantity text box and the Product combo box because if Rose selects a new product or enters a new quantity, but does not click the Add Item button to add those selections to the output and clear these objects, they still would be selected.

Now you should run and test the program to be sure the code for the New Quotation command button is working properly.

To test the New Quotation command button:

1. Save the project then start the program.

2. Enter the products and quantities shown in Figure 6-15.

Figure 6-15 ◄
Testing the
New Quotation
command
button

objects will be blank
after clicking New
Quotation button

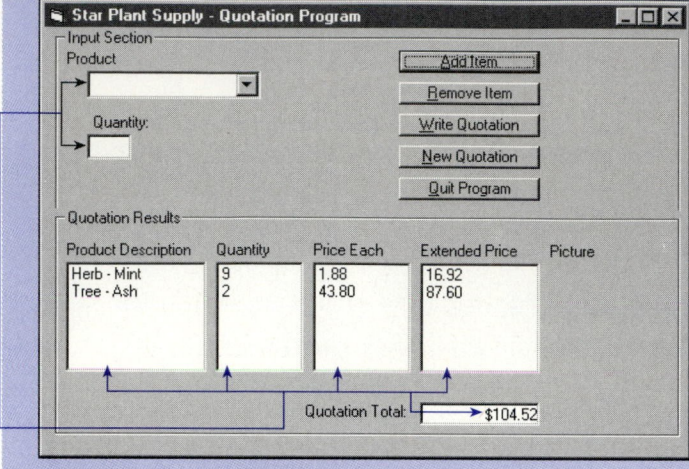

3. Click the **New Quotation** command button. Each line in the output list boxes is erased. The Quotation Total label is blank and no product is selected in the Product combo box.

> **TROUBLE?** If the output lists and quotation total did not clear, check the code for the New Quotation command button and make sure you called the Clear method for each of the output ListBox objects and set the text box's Text property to an empty string. Make any necessary corrections, then repeat Steps 1 through 3.

4. End the program.

Now that you have used the Clear method to remove all the items from a list box, you can proceed to write the statements that will allow Rose to remove an individual item from one of the output list boxes.

Removing a Specific Item from a List Box

Just as you used the AddItem method to add an item to a list box, you can use the **RemoveItem** method to delete an item from a list box. The RemoveItem method has the following syntax:

object.**RemoveItem** *index*

- The *object* is any valid list or combo box.

- The **RemoveItem** method takes one argument—the *index* of the item you want to delete. If you want to remove the first item, the index is zero (0); if you want to remove the second item, the index is one (1), and so on.

The program needs to call the RemoveItem method for each output list box when the Remove Item command button is clicked. You will use a temporary procedure-level Integer variable representing the ListIndex property as the index argument for each call to the RemoveItem method. Whenever an item is removed from the quotation, you need to recompute the total, so you will call the ComputeTotal general procedure you wrote earlier.

To write the code to delete an item from the output list boxes:

1. Activate the Code window for the **cmdRemove_Click** event procedure.

2. Enter the following code in the window (shown in bold):

```
Private Sub cmdRemove_Click( )
    Dim pintIndex As Integer
    pintIndex = lstQuotedProduct.ListIndex
    If pintIndex > -1 Then
        lstQuotedProduct.RemoveItem pintIndex
        lstQuotedQty.RemoveItem pintIndex
        lstQuotedPrice.RemoveItem pintIndex
        lstQuotedExtPrice.RemoveItem pintIndex
        ComputeTotal
    End If
End Sub
```

These statements remove a selected item from the output ListBox objects and recompute the quotation total.

```
Dim pintIndex As Integer
pintIndex = lstQuotedProduct.ListIndex
```

These two statements declare the variable pintIndex and store the index of the currently selected item into that variable. When the program calls the RemoveItem method on the active item in the list, the ListIndex property is set to minus one (-1) because the active item no longer exists. If you try to use the ListIndex property, rather than the temporary variable, as the argument to the RemoveItem method when its value is -1, the program would generate a run-time error because you would be attempting to remove a nonexistent item.

```
If pintIndex > -1 Then
    lstQuotedProduct.RemoveItem pintIndex
    lstQuotedQty.RemoveItem pintIndex
    lstQuotedPrice.RemoveItem pintIndex
    lstQuotedExtPrice.RemoveItem pintIndex
    ComputeTotal
End If
```

This code uses an If statement to determine if an item is selected in the lstQuotedProduct list box. If no item is selected, the value of the ListIndex property and of pintIndex is minus one (-1), so no attempt will be made to remove an item when none has been selected. Next, the RemoveItem method is called for each of the four output list boxes. Then, because the program removed an item, it computes the quotation total again by calling the ComputeTotal general procedure.

You now should test your program to determine if the cmdRemove_Click event works properly.

To test the Remove Item command button:

1. Save the project then start the program.

2. Enter the products and corresponding quantities into the quotation, as shown in Figure 6-16.

Figure 6-16 ◀
Testing the
Remove Item
command
button

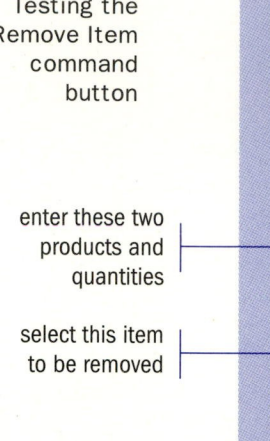

enter these two
products and
quantities

select this item
to be removed

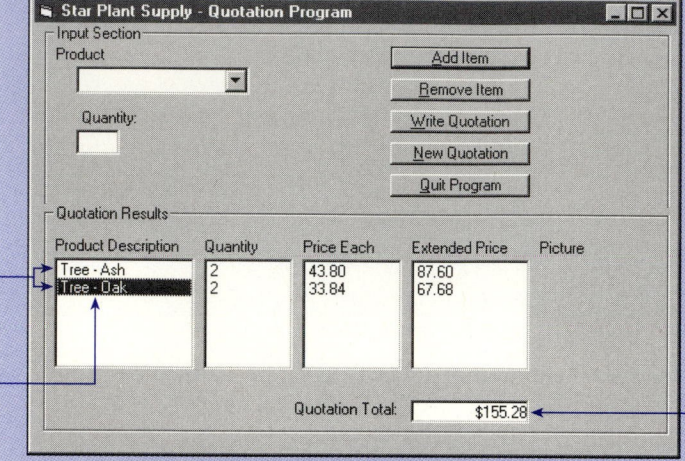

total will update
after clicking Remove
Item button

3. Click the product **Tree - Oak** in the output list box, as shown in Figure 6-16.

4. Click the **Remove Item** command button. The program removes the item Tree - Oak from the output lists and recomputes the quotation total.

   TROUBLE? If you receive a run-time error or if the item Tree - Oak was not deleted from the list and the quotation total was not recalculated, make sure your code for the cmdRemove_Click event procedure is the same as the code in the previous steps. Make any necessary corrections, then repeat Steps 1 through 4.

5. Make sure no product is selected in the Product Description list box.

6. Click the **Remove Item** command button. No item is removed from the lists and no error is generated because the If statement tested that nothing was selected.

7. End the program.

Rose has looked at the program and thinks it is very easy to use. She quickly can look up each product she sells and see a quotation without worrying about looking up the wrong price or making a computational error. And, with the Remove Item command button, she can delete items from the quotation without starting over. She also would like the program to compute a discount for customers with a large annual sales volume. To do this, you need to create a check box to indicate whether or not a discount needs to be applied and an array that can hold both the regular and discounted prices.

Creating a Two-dimensional Array

One way to tell the program when to use the regular price and when to use the discounted price is to include a second price list array that contains the discounted prices. But you also can create an array with two columns for each product. One column will contain the regular price and the other column will contain the discounted price.

The array you need to create, with one column for the regular prices and another for the discounted prices, is called a **two-dimensional array**. Two-dimensional refers to rows and columns. The one-column array you created in the previous session to contain the prices for the products is a one-dimensional array because it contains only rows. In the two-dimensional array for regular and discounted prices, one dimension, the rows, will hold the information for each element in the array, and the other dimension, the columns, will hold the regular prices in one column and the discounted prices in the second column. Figure 6-17 shows part of the two-dimensional array for the regular and discounted prices.

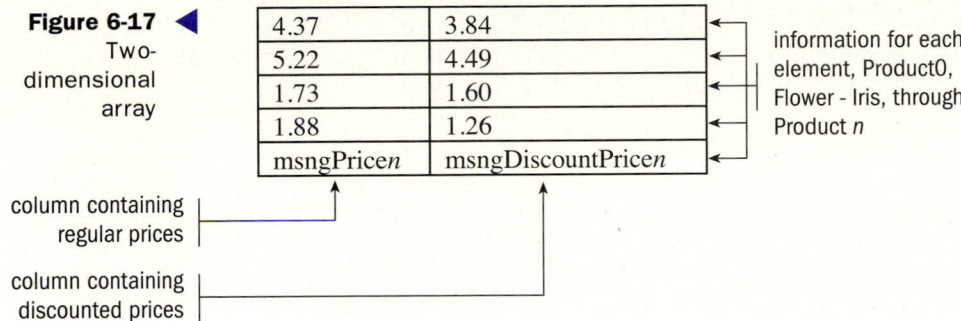

Figure 6-17 ◄
Two-
dimensional
array

column containing
regular prices

column containing
discounted prices

4.37	3.84
5.22	4.49
1.73	1.60
1.88	1.26
msngPrice*n*	msngDiscountPrice*n*

information for each
element, Product0,
Flower - Iris, through
Product *n*

Like the one-dimensional array you created in the first session, a two-dimensional array is not an object. Rather it is a variable that contains elements. In a two-dimensional array, you make a reference to an individual element using a subscript, just as you do with a one-dimensional array. You must supply, however, a subscript for each dimension of the array. So, a two-dimensional array has two subscripts. One subscript identifies the row number and the other identifies the column number. The syntax to create a two-dimensional array is similar to the syntax to create a one-dimensional array:

Private *array-name*([*lower-bound* **To**] *upper-bound*, [*lower-bound* **To**] _
upper-bound) **As** *datatype*

- This statement declares a form-level array with the name *array-name*, which can be any valid variable name.

- The first subscript is the range of rows and the second is the range of columns. The first *lower-bound* defines the element in the first row of the array. The second *lower-bound* defines the element in the first column of the array. If you do not specify a lower-bound, it will be set to zero (0) by default.

- The first *upper-bound* defines the element in the last row of the array. The second *upper-bound* defines the element in the last column of the array.

- The *datatype* can be any valid Visual Basic data type.

You need to change the price array msngPrices so it has two columns. The first column will store the regular prices and the second column will store the discounted prices.

To declare the two-dimensional array:

1. Activate the general declarations section of the Code window for the Form module.

2. Change the declaration of the msngPrices in the window (shown in bold):

```
Dim msngPrices(0 To 99,0 To 1) As Single
```

This statement declares a two-dimensional array made up of 100 rows and two columns. There are 100 products that can be stored in the rows for each of the two different prices.

Now you need to write the statements to load the array. Joan already has changed the contents of the text file to contain the discounted prices separated by commas. You need to create a variable named psngDiscountPrice, which is needed to store the discounted prices, and modify the Input # statement in the Form_Load event procedure so it reads all the contents of the new file. The first subscript refers to the rows, as in the original array. The second subscript refers to the columns. The first column can be referenced using a subscript of zero (0). The second column has a subscript of one (1).

To declare the discounted price variable, modify the Input # statement, and load the discounted prices into the array:

1. Activate the Code window for the **Form_Load** event procedure.

2. Change the Open statement so it reads the file named **Product2.txt** rather than Product.txt.

3. Enter the following variable declarations into the **Form_Load** event procedure just after the other variable declarations:

```
Dim psngDiscountPrice As Single
Dim pstrPicture As String
```

Note that you will use the variable pstrPicture later in the session to store the file-names containing pictures of the products Rose sells. Because it is in the text file, you have to read it now.

4. Modify the Input # statement as follows (shown in bold):

```
Input #1, pstrProduct, psngPrice, _
    psngDiscountPrice, pstrPicture
```

5. Change the existing msngPrices statement in the event procedure, and add the new msngPrices statement to match the following code (shown in bold):

```
msngPrices(pintCurrentItem, 0) = psngPrice
msngPrices(pintCurrentItem, 1) = psngDiscountPrice
```

The changes you just made to the Form_Load event procedure will load the price information into a two-dimensional array.

```
msngPrices(pintCurrentItem, 0) = psngPrice
msngPrices(pintCurrentItem, 1) = psngDiscountPrice
```

These statements store the values of the variables into each column of the msngPrices. The first statement stores the regular prices into the first column (column 0), and the second statement stores the discounted prices into the second column (column 1). The row is defined by the variable pintCurrentItem and is set by the For loop.

Now you can create the Apply Discount check box and make the necessary modifications to the Add Item command button so the correct price will be used depending on whether or not the Apply Discount check box is checked. To do so, you need to write an If statement to determine the value of the check box. You will use this information to determine whether to use the regular or discounted price.

To add the discount check box and code the Add Item command button to assign the appropriate price:

1. Create a check box as shown in Figure 6-18.

2. Set the Caption property to **Apply Discount** and the Name property to **chkDiscount**.

Figure 6-18 ◀
Creating the
discount check
box

Apply Discount
check box

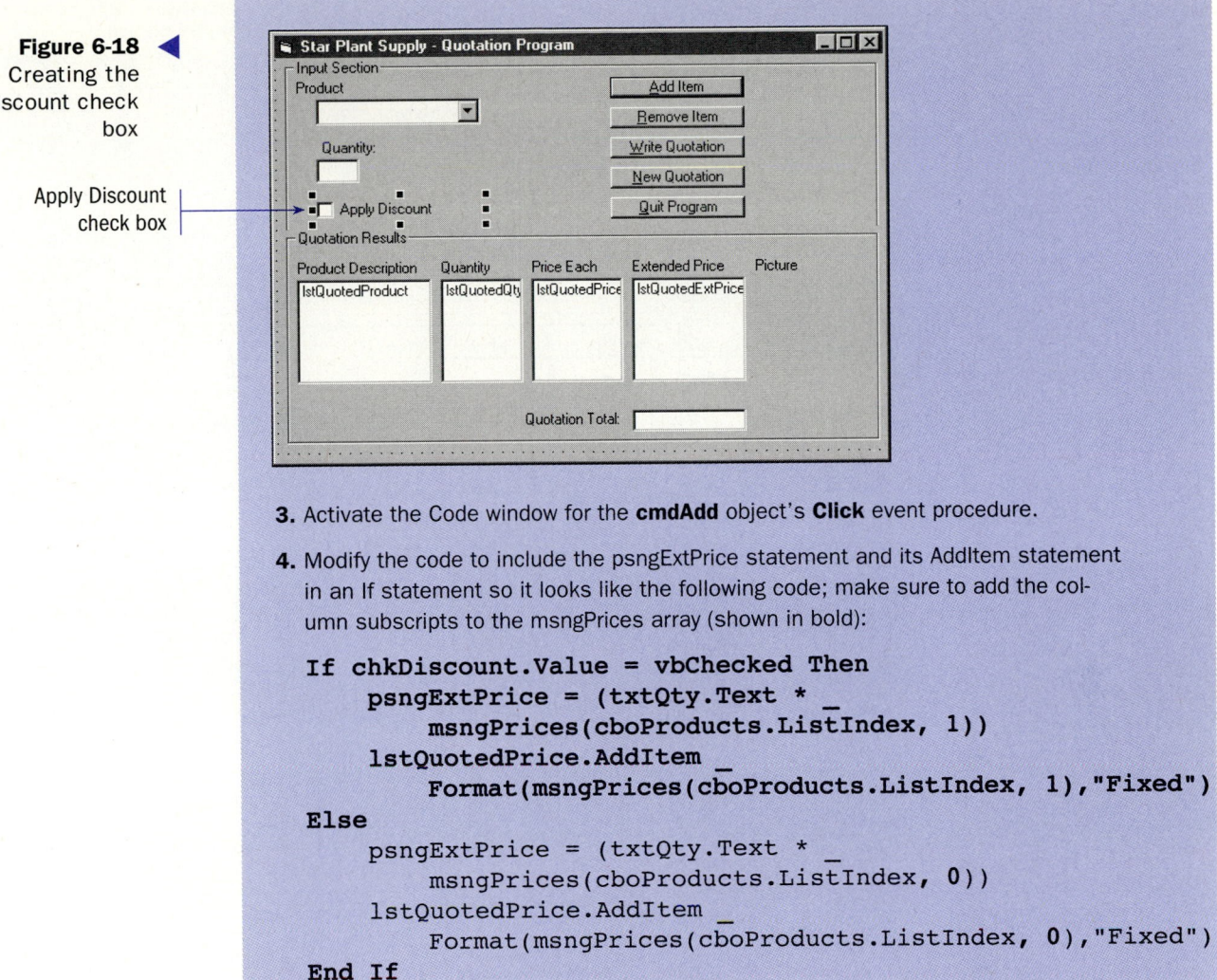

3. Activate the Code window for the **cmdAdd** object's **Click** event procedure.

4. Modify the code to include the psngExtPrice statement and its AddItem statement in an If statement so it looks like the following code; make sure to add the column subscripts to the msngPrices array (shown in bold):

```
If chkDiscount.Value = vbChecked Then
    psngExtPrice = (txtQty.Text * _
        msngPrices(cboProducts.ListIndex, 1))
    lstQuotedPrice.AddItem _
        Format(msngPrices(cboProducts.ListIndex, 1),"Fixed")
Else
    psngExtPrice = (txtQty.Text * _
        msngPrices(cboProducts.ListIndex, 0))
    lstQuotedPrice.AddItem _
        Format(msngPrices(cboProducts.ListIndex, 0),"Fixed")
End If
```

This code uses an If statement to apply a discount if the Apply Discount CheckBox object is checked. If the object is not checked, the regular prices are used. You now can test the program to determine if the regular and discounted prices are being computed correctly.

To test the discounted prices:

1. Save the project then start the program.

2. Click the **Apply Discount** check box to select it.

3. Enter the products and corresponding quantities into the quotation, as shown in Figure 6-19.

Figure 6-19 ◄
Testing the
discount prices

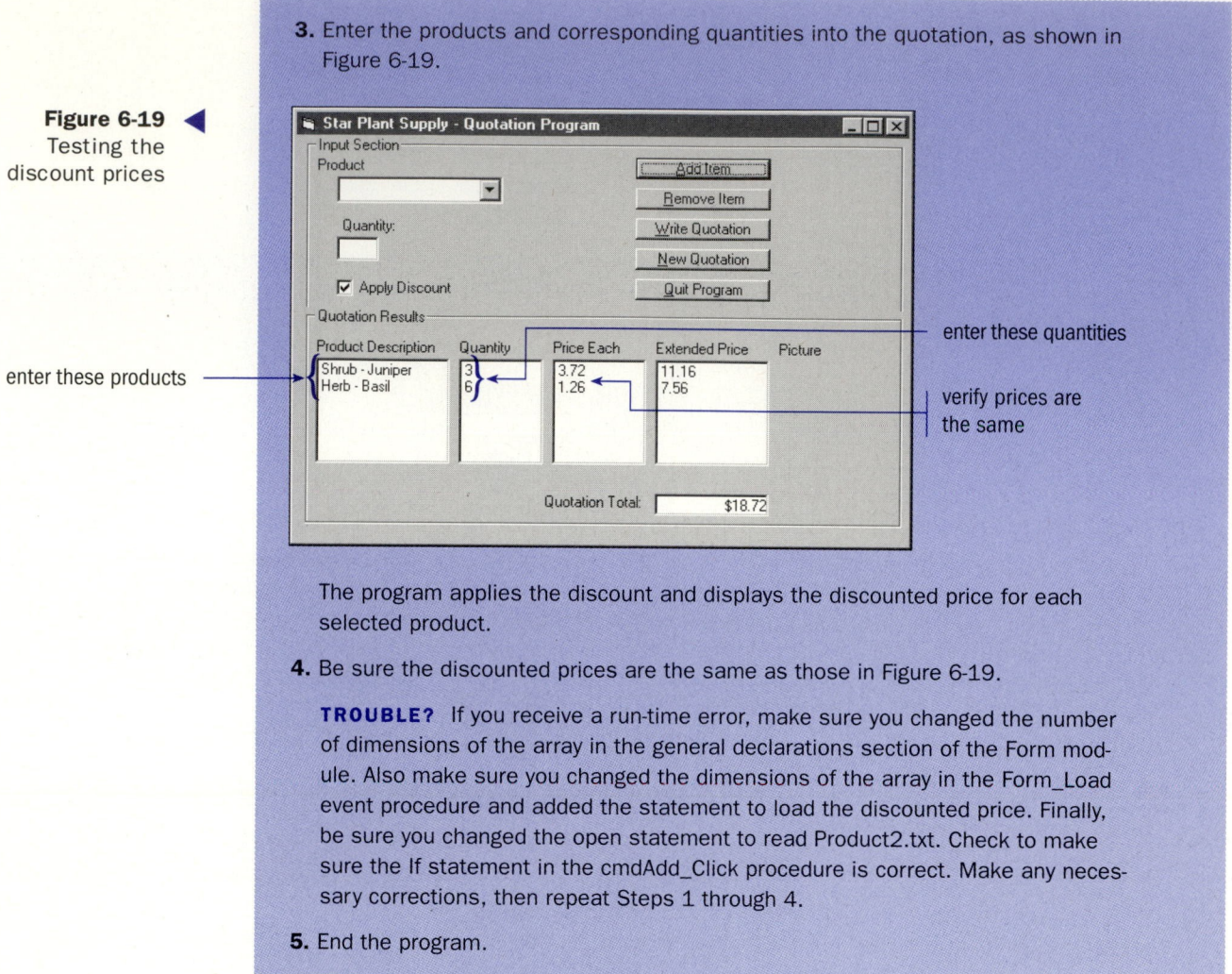

enter these products

enter these quantities

verify prices are
the same

The program applies the discount and displays the discounted price for each selected product.

4. Be sure the discounted prices are the same as those in Figure 6-19.

TROUBLE? If you receive a run-time error, make sure you changed the number of dimensions of the array in the general declarations section of the Form module. Also make sure you changed the dimensions of the array in the Form_Load event procedure and added the statement to load the discounted price. Finally, be sure you changed the open statement to read Product2.txt. Check to make sure the If statement in the cmdAdd_Click procedure is correct. Make any necessary corrections, then repeat Steps 1 through 4.

5. End the program.

Now the program can calculate the quotations at the regular price or at the discounted price. Rose also would like to display pictures of the products to her customers when they are in the office as she prepares their quotations. At some point, she will have pictures of all the products, but currently she has only a few images that were supplied as samples by different vendors.

Adding Pictures to a Form

You can use either a PictureBox object or an Image object to display pictures on a form. The **PictureBox** object supports more events and properties than the Image object. For example, a picture box can respond to a Change event in addition to a Click event.

Unlike the Image control, the PictureBox control cannot resize pictures with the Stretch property. The pictures Rose intends to use will all be the same size, so you can create a PictureBox control that is the same size as the pictures.

As with the Image control, you could assign the pictures to the picture box by setting the Picture property in the Properties window at design time. But then your program would contain only one picture. You want the picture displayed to depend on the active product; therefore, you should set the Picture property with code, rather than in the Properties window.

Joan has changed the price list file, Product2.txt, so it includes a field containing the filename of the picture. The program must be able to load the file containing the picture when an item in the Product combo box is selected. You could create another array of the String data type. When you load the price, you could write another statement to load the filename of the picture using the filename contained in the other array. In this case the other array would be a one-dimensional array.

You have learned that all the elements in an array must be of the same data type. You want to store numbers with a decimal point—regular prices in one column and discounted prices in another—and strings (picture filenames), in the third column. On the surface, this seems to break the Visual Basic "rule" of using variables of the same data type. Another option, however, will allow you to include prices and filenames in the same array.

Arrays of Variant Data Type

Visual Basic supports a data type called **Variant**, which can store all the different data types such as Integer, Single, and String. However, the Variant data type cannot store Fixed length strings or user-defined types. For example, Var1 declared as a Variant data type could contain the values 1, 1.05, TRUE, "Hello", or "c:\windows\waves.bmp". Visual Basic accomplishes this by storing the data type of the variable in the variable itself. If you store an integer into a variant array or variable, the variable is an Integer Variant data type. If you later store a string in the variant, the variable becomes a String Variant data type. Variant variables, and members of variant arrays, can change their data type while a program is running.

So, to hold both the prices and the picture filenames, you can create a two-dimensional variant array and use the first and second columns as Single Variant data types for the regular prices and discounted prices, and the third column as a String Variant data type for the picture filenames.

To declare an array of the Variant data type you use the Private, Public, or Dim statements, as you have done before.

> *Tip:* Because Visual Basic stores the data type of a variable inside the variable, and must determine the type of data stored in a Variant variable whenever it is referenced, operations on Variant variables are much slower than operations on Integer or Single variables. Thus, you should use Variant variables only when necessary.

To develop the code to work with the pictures as well as the prices, you need to change the two-dimensional array msngPrices, which contains prices (Single data type), to a two-dimensional array of variants (Single and String data types). You also need to specify a third column to hold the picture filenames from the text file.

To change the msngPrices to a Variant array:

1. Open the general declarations section of the Code window for the Form module.

2. Change the declaration for msngPrices in the window (shown in bold):

```
Dim msngPrices(0 To 99,0 To 2) As Variant
```

Now that you have declared the three-column array of a Variant data type, you can write the code to load the picture filenames into the third column of the array. The specific picture should be loaded when Rose clicks a product so a customer in the office can see the product being quoted. To do this, you need to modify the Form_Load event procedure. In your array the first subscript still represents the rows, and the second subscript represents the columns. The regular prices are represented by the column subscript zero (0); the discounted prices are represented by the column subscript one (1); and the picture filenames are represented by the column subscript two (2).

To load the filenames into the Variant array:

1. Create a PictureBox object as shown in Figure 6-20.

Figure 6-20
Creating the
PictureBox
object

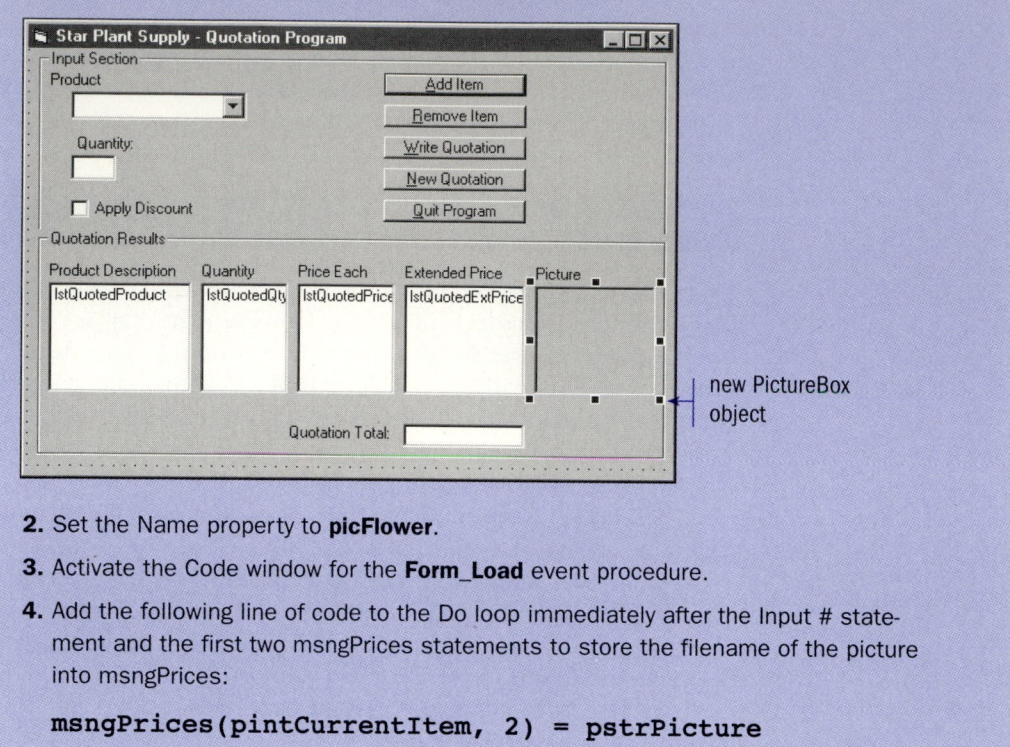

new PictureBox
object

2. Set the Name property to **picFlower**.

3. Activate the Code window for the **Form_Load** event procedure.

4. Add the following line of code to the Do loop immediately after the Input # statement and the first two msngPrices statements to store the filename of the picture into msngPrices:

```
msngPrices(pintCurrentItem, 2) = pstrPicture
```

This statement stores the picture filenames into the third column of the array. Now you can write the code for displaying a picture in the picture box when an item in the Product combo box is clicked. When Rose clicks a product in the Product combo box, the program must load the corresponding picture using its filename. You can do this by calling the **LoadPicture** function at run time. The LoadPicture function supports one argument, the filename of a picture, and has the following syntax:

object.**Picture** = **LoadPicture**(*filename*)

- The **Picture** property of any valid *object* can be set using the **LoadPicture** function.

- The *filename* can be any filename containing a picture.

The third column of the array contains the filenames of the pictures you want to show in the quotation program. You will use the ListIndex property of the cboProducts ComboBox object as a subscript of the array to look up the correct filename.

To load the pictures into the picture box:

1. Activate the Code window for the **cboProducts_Click** event procedure.

2. Enter the following code in the window:

```
Private Sub cboProducts_Click( )
    If cboProducts.ListIndex > -1 Then
        picFlower.Picture = _
            LoadPicture(msngPrices _
            (cboProducts.ListIndex, 2))
    End If
End Sub
```

When an item in the Product combo box is clicked, the code you just wrote will display the corresponding picture in the picture box. The first statement determines if an item is selected in the Product combo box. The subsequent statements are called only if an item is selected (ListIndex > -1). The second statement calls the LoadPicture function with one argument—the filename of the picture to load. The filenames are stored in the third column of the msngPrices. The current row is determined by using the current index (ListIndex property) of cboProducts.

Now you should test the new picture box and the code you added to the cboProducts_Click event procedure.

To test the picture box:

1. Save the project then start the program.

2. Click **Flower - Iris** in the Product combo box. The picture of the selected product appears in the PictureBox object, as shown in Figure 6-21.

Figure 6-21 ◄
Testing the picture box

selected product

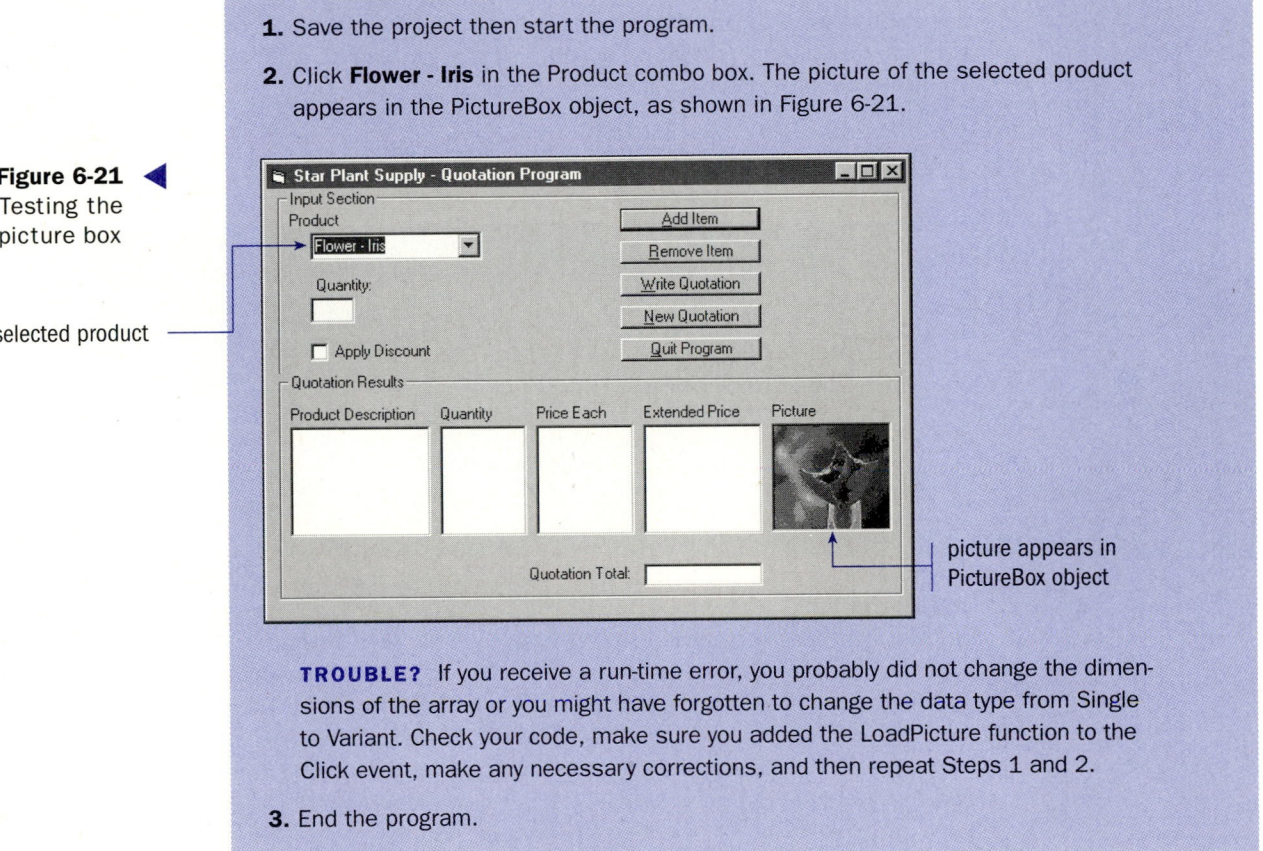

picture appears in PictureBox object

TROUBLE? If you receive a run-time error, you probably did not change the dimensions of the array or you might have forgotten to change the data type from Single to Variant. Check your code, make sure you added the LoadPicture function to the Click event, make any necessary corrections, and then repeat Steps 1 and 2.

3. End the program.

Your program now will display pictures for those items that have pictures available by setting the Picture property of the PictureBox object at run time.

Writing a Text File

Some of Rose's customers want a printed copy of a quotation. Rose currently uses a word processing application to format the information. She likes the layout she has created and sometimes customizes the printout for an individual customer's needs. She wants to use the information produced by this quotation program in her word processing documents.

Visual Basic supports a **Write #** statement that will write text to ASCII-delimited files, which then can be read by most word processing, spreadsheet, and database programs. This is the same type of file you used to read text into the quotation program when you called the Input # statement.

When you write a text file, just as when you read one, you first must open the file using the Open statement. You used the Open statement For Input in the previous session to read the text file containing the product and price information. This time you need to use the Open statement with the For Output argument so you can write a file. Then, you can use the Write # statement to write information from the program to the text file. Remember, if the file already exists when you open it For Output, it will be overwritten.

As with other files you open, you must close a text file when you are finished writing to it. The syntax of the Write # statement is:

Write #*filenumber*, [*outputlist*]

- The **Write #** statement writes to a file that already has been opened For Output or For Append. It also inserts commas between each item in the *outputlist* and places quotation marks around strings as they are written to the file. Numeric data always is written using the period (.) as the decimal separator. Files written with the Write # statement can be read easily with the Input # statement.

- The *filenumber* is a valid filenumber created by an Open statement.

- Each item in the *outputlist* is usually a variable or object property in your program separated by a comma. The *outputlist* is similar to the *inputlist* of the Input # statement.

- In the file, Visual Basic will insert commas between the fields and surround String variables with quotation marks.

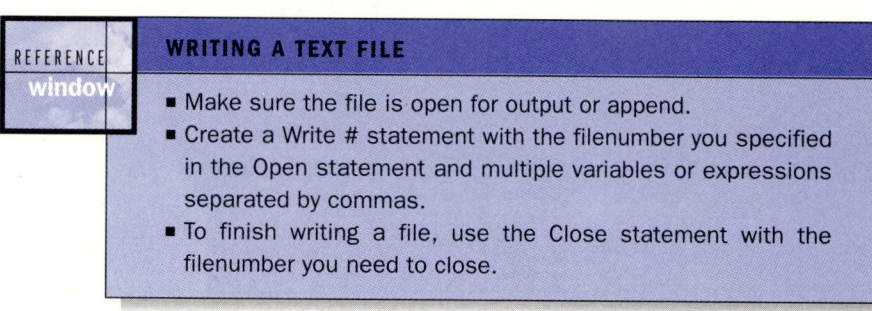

REFERENCE window

WRITING A TEXT FILE

- Make sure the file is open for output or append.
- Create a Write # statement with the filenumber you specified in the Open statement and multiple variables or expressions separated by commas.
- To finish writing a file, use the Close statement with the filenumber you need to close.

You need to add the statements to the Write Quotation command button so clicking this button will create a text file of the quotation output. Rose then will be able to read the file into her word processing program so she can format it. To do this you need to open the file For Output and create a For loop to examine every item in the output list boxes, just as you did to include every item in the ComputeTotal general procedure. Inside the For loop, you need to use the Write # statement to write the contents of each output list box—Product Description, Quantity, Price Each, and Extended Price—to the text file. Because you have no open files, you can reuse filenumber 1.

To write the code to create a text file of the current quotation output:

1. Open the Code window for the **cmdWriteQuotation_Click** event procedure.

2. Enter the following code in the window:

```
Private Sub cmdWriteQuotation_Click( )
    Dim pintCurrentItem As Integer
    Dim pstrFileName As String
    pstrFileName = _
        InputBox("Enter the filename", "Write File")
    If pstrFileName <> "" Then
        Open pstrFileName For Output As #1
        For pintCurrentItem = 0 To _
            lstQuotedExtPrice.ListCount - 1
            Write #1, _
                lstQuotedProduct.List(pintCurrentItem), _
                Val(lstQuotedQty.List(pintCurrentItem)), _
                Val(lstQuotedPrice.List(pintCurrentItem)), _
                Val(lstQuotedExtPrice.List(pintCurrentItem))
        Next
```

```
        Close #1
    End If
End Sub
```

The code to write an ASCII-delimited file is similar to the code to read one. You open the file, using a loop to write each line in the file, and close the file once all the lines have been written. So Rose can specify the folder and filename she wants to use, you call the InputBox function to get a string that will be used as a filename.

```
pstrFileName = _
    InputBox("Enter the filename", "Write File")
If pstrFileName <> "" Then
    Open pstrFileName For Output As #1
```

This statement opens the file using the Open statement if a filename was specified and assigns the active filenumber. Instead of opening the file For Input (reading the file) you need to open the file For Output (writing the file). When opened For Output, the contents of the file are overwritten if the file already exists. If you want to append information to a file, you use the For Append option.

```
For pintCurrentItem = 0 To _
    lstQuotedExtPrice.ListCount - 1
    Write #1, _
        lstQuotedProduct.List(pintCurrentItem), _
        Val(lstQuotedQty.List(pintCurrentItem)), _
        Val(lstQuotedPrice.List(pintCurrentItem)), _
        Val(lstQuotedExtPrice.List(pintCurrentItem))
Next
```

The For loop steps through each item in the output list box lstQuotedExtPrice, starting at zero (0) and ending at the end of the list (ListCount -1). A line is written for each of the items quoted. Each line written contains the four items from the output list boxes. Visual Basic will insert a comma between each item. Because the items in a list box are treated as strings, these statements call the Val function on the quantity, price, and extended price fields so they are converted to numbers and written without quotation marks.

Now you need to test the program one more time to make sure the Write Quotation command button works correctly.

To test the Write Quotation command button:

1. Save the project then start the program.

2. Enter the products and corresponding quantities, as shown in Figure 6-22.

Figure 6-22 ◀
Testing the
Write Quotation
command
button

enter these products
and quantities

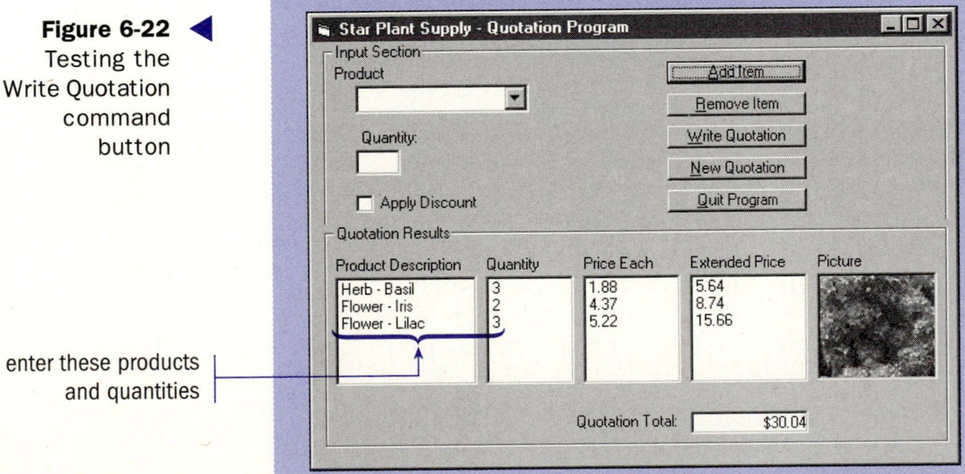

3. Click the **Write Quotation** command button.

4. Enter the filename **A:\Tutorial.06\Quote.txt,** then click the OK button.

The program output is written to the file Quote.txt in the Tutorial.06 folder on your Student Disk.

The file Quote.txt contains the information shown in Figure 6-23. You can open it in WordPad or any word processing program.

Figure 6-23 ◄
Contents of
text file

```
"Herb - Basil",3,1.88,5.64
"Flower - Iris",2,4.37,8.74
"Flower - Lilac",3,5.22,15.66
```

5. End the program then exit Visual Basic.

6. Open Quote.txt in your word processing program and compare it to Figure 6-23. Exit your word processing program.

The quotation program now is complete. When Rose starts the program, the text file containing the price list will be loaded into the computer's memory. When she selects a product in the Product combo box, a picture of the product (if one exists) will be displayed in the picture box. Rose can enter a quantity and click the Add Item command button to display the product description, the quantity, the price per product, and the extended price in the output section of the form. The price per product either can be the regular or the discounted price, based on the customer's volume of sales. All Rose needs to do to determine which price to use is click the Apply Discount check box. Rose can clear one or all products from the output section of the quotation program. The quotation total will be updated with every change to the output section of the form. Finally, Rose can write the quotation to a text file, which she can use to format the quotation in her word processing program and print a copy for the customer.

Quick Check

1 What is the purpose of the RemoveItem method and the Clear method of the ListBox and ComboBox objects?

2 What is the difference between a one-dimensional and a two-dimensional array?

3 How does the procedure to open a file for writing differ from the procedure to open a file for reading?

4 What is the Variant data type?

5 What is the purpose of the Write # statement?

Figure 6-24 lists and defines the new terms presented in this tutorial.

Figure 6-24
New terms

Term	Definition
Array	An array is a variable that contains a list of several items having the same data type. You create an array using the Dim, Public, or Private statements. The number of items in an array is defined by the array's lower and upper bounds.
ASCII-delimited file	An ASCII-delimited file is a text file that contains one or more fields separated by commas. Text fields are enclosed in double quotation marks. The period (.) is used as the decimal point in numbers containing a fractional part.
Element	An element is a specific item in an array.
For loop	A For loop is a statement that works with a counter variable that increments each time the loop is executed. When the counter does not meet some condition, the For loop exits. The loop will increment the counter for you.
Sequential access	Sequential access is the process of reading a text file from beginning to end using the Open, Input #, and Close statements.
Subscript	A subscript is an integer value that is used to reference a specific element in an array.
Two-dimensional array	A two-dimensional array is an array made up of rows and columns. Two-dimensional arrays use two subscripts to reference an element. One subscript defines the row; the other defines the column.
Variant	The Variant data type is a data type that can contain any of the other Visual Basic data types. The type of data contained in a Variant variable can be changed at run time.

Tutorial Assignments

One of Star Plant Supply's customers, Maria Cepada, works for a large software company. She suggested that Rose provide an information display computer in her store so customers could use it to find out about the many varieties of flowers and plants that Star Plant Supply carries. Rose is somewhat hesitant to purchase such a computer, and she asks you to create a sample program that initially will show pictures of three types of roses and supply both background and planting information to the customer. Rose will evaluate the sample program to determine if she wants to provide an information display computer.

Figure 6-25 shows the completed form design for the program. Eventually, this program could be expanded to include hundreds of graphic and text files for Star Plant Supply, which Rose hopes will attract a large number of new customers. The program will use a PictureBox object to display the pictures of the roses, a frame containing option buttons to select the flower types, and a multiline text box to display a description of the flowers.

Figure 6-25

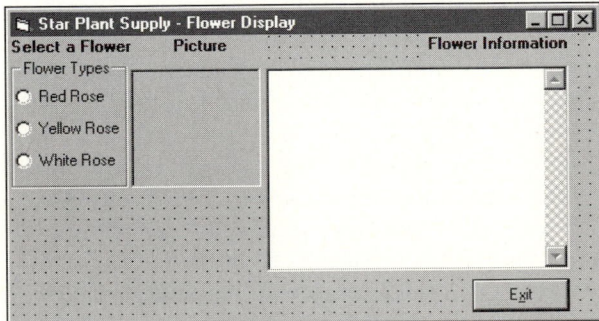

1. Make sure your Student Disk is in the appropriate disk drive, and then start Visual Basic.
2. Change the Caption property to **Star Plant Supply - Flower Display** and the Name property to **frmStarFlowerDisplay**.
3. Create a frame on the form with the caption Flower Types. See Figure 6-25 for object positions and sizes.

4. Create a control array of three OptionButton objects named **optFlowers** in the frame. Set the caption of the three option buttons to **Red Rose**, **Yellow Rose**, and **White Rose**, respectively.

5. Create a working Exit command button with Alt+X as the hot key.

6. Draw a PictureBox object on the form and set its name to **picFlowers**. Adjust the size of the form as needed to add the objects.

7. Draw a multiline text box with vertical scroll bars to hold the flower information on the form. Set the Name property to **txtInfo**, then clear the Text property.

8. Draw three identifying labels above the three objects you just created, and set the Alignment property of the labels to **2 - Center**. From left to right, set the captions of the labels to **Select a Flower**, **Picture**, and **Flower Information**.

9. Open the general declarations section of the Code window for the form module and create a one-dimensional array of the String data type with three elements named **mstrFlowerInfo**. Create two other String variables named **mstrRoseInfo** and **mstrOutInfo**; these will be used to load the values into the array. Require that all variables be declared explicitly.

10. To load the names of the three different roses into the mstrFlowerInfo array when the form is loaded, write the necessary code in the Form_Load event procedure. Store the filename **A:\Tutorial.06\TAssign\RedR.bmp** into the first element of the array, **A:\Tutorial.06\TAssign\YellowR.bmp** into the second element, and **A:\Tutorial.06\TAssign\WhiteR.bmp** into the third element. The file path names must be in quotation marks.

11. When the form is loaded, the program must load the description of the flowers into the Flower Information text box. This information is stored in the file **Rose.txt** in the **TAssign** folder in the **Tutorial.06** folder on your Student Disk. Add to the end of the Form_Load procedure the statement to open the file for input. Because this is the only file open, use filenumber 1.

12. Now you can read the records into the string mstrOutInfo. You need to append a carriage return character and a new line character to the end of each line so the message box will display the text correctly. Remember you can use the constant **vbCrLf** to accomplish this. Write a Do loop to input filenumber 1 into the variable named mstrRoseInfo. Write another statement to concatenate to the existing contents of the variable mstrOutInfo, a carriage return and line feed and the contents of mstrRoseInfo.

13. The String variable mstrOutInfo now contains the text describing the flowers and planting instructions. You now need to store this text in the Text property of the txtInfo text box. Write this statement after the loop you just created.

14. Write the statement to close filenumber 1.

15. Now you can write the code to load the pictures of the different roses. A picture will be loaded into the picture box when a user clicks one of the option buttons. So, the code should be executed when an option button is clicked. Because the option buttons belong to a control array, the same code will execute when any one of the option buttons is clicked. You need to call the LoadPicture function. The argument should be stored in the array mstrFlowerInfo(*subscript*) where *subscript* is 0, 1, or 2—the same as the index of the control array. You should store the result in picFlowers.Picture.

16. Write the statements to clear the value of the option button when the program starts. This will cause no picture to be loaded until an option button is selected.

17. Save the project as **Star Flower Display** in the **TAssign** folder in the **Tutorial.06** folder on your Student Disk.

18. Run your program. Click any option button to see the corresponding picture of the rose that was copied using the Copy function of the Microsoft Encarta software package and the Paste and Cut functions of Paint. Note that the picture display would be much faster if the .bmp files were stored on the hard disk. Scroll through the Flower Information text box to read the roses text that was loaded from Microsoft Encarta as a text file. Click the Exit command button to exit the program.

19. Print the Form Image and Code, then exit Visual Basic.

Case Problems

1. Valley Computer Supply Valley Computer Supply carries a wide variety of computers and computer accessories. Joe Kent, the business manager, keeps a list of all the different computers and accessories in a sequential file, with each computer listed on a separate line. This file is used for a variety of reports and to answer customer questions about what vendors Valley Computer Supply does business with. Joe would like to use this file for a report, but the list is not sorted alphabetically by product name, as the report requires. You will write a program to sort the list using the Sort property of an invisible list box. Figure 6-26 shows the completed form.

Figure 6-26 ◀

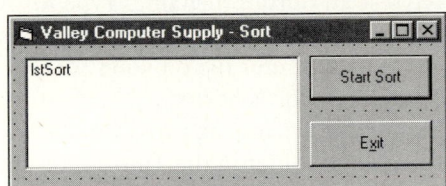

1. Start WordPad or any word processing program and examine the file **Computer.txt** in the **Cases** folder in the **Tutorial.06** folder on your Student Disk. This file contains the unsorted list of computer names. Exit WordPad or the word processing program without saving the file.
2. Start Visual Basic.
3. Change the form's caption to **Valley Computer Supply - Sort** and change its name to **frmValleySort**.
4. Draw a command button, with the caption **Start Sort** and the name **cmdStartSort**. Make this the default button for the form. Position and size all objects as shown in Figure 6-26.
5. Create a working Exit command button with Alt+X as the hot key.

6. Draw a list box on the form. Set its name to **lstSort**. Set its properties so the list box will be sorted and invisible at run time.
7. All the processing will occur when the cmdStartSort button is clicked, so you need to write all your code and declare all your variables in its Click event procedure. Open the Code window for the cmdStartSort_Click event and declare three local String variables: **pstrComputerName** will hold the computer name as it is placed into the list box, **pstrInputFileName** will hold the name of the input file, **pstrOutputFileName** will hold the name of the output file. Declare a local Integer variable named **pintCount** that will be used within a For loop that writes to the output file.
8. Using the InputBox function with the prompt: **"Enter Input Filename"**, store the user's response in the variable called **pstrInputFileName**.
9. Using the InputBox function with the prompt: **"Enter Output Filename"**, store the user's response in the variable called **pstrOutputFileName**.
10. Open **pstrInputFileName** for input using the results of the InputBox function. Remember to assign the file a valid filenumber.

11. Create a Do loop to read each computer name and add it to the list box you already created. Because there is one computer name on a line, the Input # statement should store the field in the variable **pstrComputerName**. To store the computer names in the list box, you need another statement that will add an item to the lstSort list box. The text of the item you want to add is in the variable **pstrComputerName**.
12. Open **pstrOutputFileName** for output using the results of the InputBox function.

13. Write a For loop that will loop through all the items in the list box and write the items to the output file. Remember, the first item in a list box is 0. You can use the ListCount property to find out how many items are in the list box. Inside the For loop, create a Write # statement that will write the correct item to the output file. Remember, you can use the List property with the pintCount variable as its argument, which is set by the For loop to indicate the correct item.

14. Close all the files.

15. Change the caption of the Start Sort command button to contain the number of records sorted followed by a space and the string **Records Sorted**. You will need to concatenate the two strings to do this. Remember, the ListCount property of the lstSort object contains the number of items in the list box. This is the number of items sorted.

16. Save the project as **Valley Computer Sort** in the Cases folder in the Tutorial.06 folder on your Student Disk.

17. Run the program. Click the **Start Sort** command button. The program will request an input filename. Type **A:\Tutorial.06\Cases\Computer.txt** in the input box.

18. The program will request an output filename. Type **A:\Tutorial.06\Cases\Sorted Computer.txt** in the second input box. The program will sort the Computer text file and create the Sorted Computer file on your Student Disk. The Start Sort button now should say 11 Records Sorted.

19. Open WordPad or any word processing program and look at the **Sorted Computer.txt** file in the Cases folder in the Tutorial.06 folder on your Student Disk. Note that the names of the computers have been sorted by the invisible list box's Sort property.

20. Print the list, then close the word processing program and return to Visual Basic. Print the Code and Form Image, then exit Visual Basic.

2. Sundown Hospital Sundown Hospital is a small regional hospital that serves as a primary care center. Sundown Hospital admits approximately 20 individuals per day and would like a method of storing and recalling admitted patient information. The program will display previous patient information and accept new patient information. The program also will store the information in a sequential file for later use and be able to call up the information quickly for an admitted patient at any time by storing the sequential file as a two-dimensional array. Occasionally the hospital loses power to the admitting station. The staff would like to be able to start the program and recover all the admitted patient data. Therefore, after each new patient is added, the program will append that information to the sequential file and close the file so it cannot be corrupted. The admitting interface form already has been completed. You now have to add the code that will perform the tasks. Figure 6-27 shows the completed form.

Figure 6-27 ◀

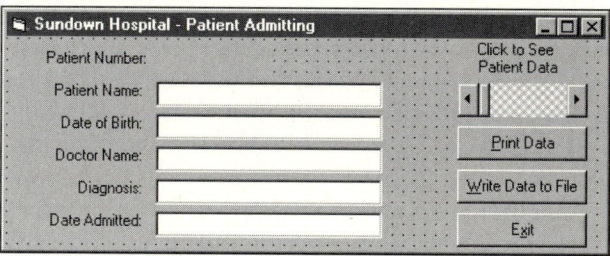

1. Make sure your Student Disk is in the appropriate disk drive, then start Visual Basic.

2. Click **Project** then click **Remove Form1** to clear the default Form1. Click **Project** then **Add File**. Load the form **frmSunDN.frm** in the **Cases** folder in the **Tutorial.06** folder on your Student Disk, then change the startup form to this new form.

3. Save the form as **frmSundownHospital** and the project as **Sundown Hospital – Patient Admitting** in the **Cases** folder in the **Tutorial.06** folder on your Student Disk.

4. Open the general declarations section of the Code window for the Form module. Declare a two-dimensional string array of 50 rows and 6 columns named **mstrPatients**. The first element of the array should be (1,1), not (0,0).

5. Open the Code window for the Form_Load event procedure and open the **A:\Tutorial.06\Cases\Patient.txt** file for input using filenumber 1. Write a Do loop to load the information in the file into the two-dimensional array mstrPatients you just created. Use the variable **pintRow** as a counter that will be incremented by one (1) each time through the loop. The Do loop should end when the end of file is reached.

6. Inside the Do loop, write an Input # statement to read the file into the different rows and columns of the array mstrPatients. The file **Patient.txt** has six fields, so there will be six arguments to the Input # statement. The first argument will be **mstrPatients(mpintRow,1)**. Remember, the lower bound of the array is 1,1, not 0,0. Increment the counter before the Loop statement.

7. Write the code to close the text file.

8. Create a general procedure to display the current patient. Use the Value property of the scroll bar hsbPNumber as the array subscript to store the patient information into the corresponding text boxes and labels on the form. The names of the objects correspond to the columns, as follows:

lblPatientNumber	Value of the scroll bar hsbPNumber or Column 1
txtPatientName	Column 2
txtDOB	Column 3
txtDoctorName	Column 4
txtDiagnosis	Column 5
txtDateAdmitted	Time when patient was admitted or Column 6

As the final part of the Form_Load event procedure, call the general procedure you just wrote to display the first patient.

9. Write the code for the Write Data to File command button so when it is clicked it appends the information for the patient shown on the screen to the file **A:\Tutorial.06\Cases\Patient.txt**. *Hint*: Open the file For Append. Write the contents of the six objects to the fields in the file you just opened. Make sure you write them in the same order.

10. Write the code to close the file.

11. Write the code for the scroll bar so when the user changes the value of the scroll bar the current patient information (stored in the two-dimensional array) will be displayed in the text boxes and labels. All you need to do is call the general procedure you already wrote.

12. Program the Exit button.

13. Set the initial focus to **txtPatientName**. Save your form and project.

14. Run the program. The sequential file Patient.txt already includes some sample patient data. Click the scroll bar to advance through the existing patient data to a blank screen. Type in patient data of your choice for five patients. After you type in the information for each patient, click the **Write Data to File** command button. Review the patient data by clicking the scroll bar. Exit the program.

15. Run the program again and observe that by clicking the scroll bar, the data you entered has been appended to the file and loaded into the data array in the program for use by Sundown Hospital's admitting staff.

16. Add a command button to the form with **&Print Data** as the caption. Name the button **cmdPrint**. In the cmdPrint_Click event write a nested For loop using the Print method that will print the two-dimensional patient array to the printer. The external part of the nested For loop first will use an If statement to test for a null string in the first column of the next row of the array.

17. Next, write the external part of the nested For loop that will vary the row of the array from one (1) to the number of records you have in the file (check using the scroll bar if you do not remember how many records you have).

18. Write the internal part of the For loop that will vary the column from one (1) to six (6) and call the Print method of the Printer object to print each element in the array's current row. The Print statement in the nested For Next statement will take the form of **Printer.Print PatientTbl(Row, Column);**. The ";" turns off automatic line feeds.

19. Write a Printer.EndDoc statement after the last Next statement that will send the output to the printer.

20. Run the program. Click the **Print Data** command button and examine your output. There is no line feed after each patient's six fields are printed. Add a line containing the **Printer.Print** statement between the two Next statements, click the command button again, and observe the results.

21. Save the changes. Print the Form Image and Code. Exit Visual Basic.

3. Super Office Super Office sells small office supplies to the general public. Manny Garcia, customer service manager for Super Office would like a program that will read a sequential data file containing item names and prices. Place the item names in a list box and the prices in a one-dimensional array that can contain up to 10 Single data type items. The program should load a ListBox with the item name (sorted alphabetically) and the matching ItemData property of the ListBox object with an integer subscript that references where in the one-dimensional array the price is stored. Allow the clerk to click a ListBox item, enter the quantity, and calculate the extended price by using the ItemData property as a subscript to retrieve the price from the array. When the Add Purchase button is clicked, copy the name of the selected product from the input list box to the output list box. Copy the quantity ordered to the output list box, and compute the extended price and sales tax. Assume the sales tax rate is 5%. Each time an item is added compute the total. When the Reset button is clicked, clear each of the output list boxes, the total, and input quantity requested. Also make sure that no item is selected. When the Remove Item command button is clicked, check to see that a product in the output list box is selected. If so, delete the product, quantity, price, extended price, and tax from the output list boxes and recompute the order total.

Create a PictureBox object to display a logo using a graphic file of your choice. Use WordPad or any word processing program to create a sequential data file with at least five items and prices, and save the file as **Office.txt** in the **Cases** folder in the **Tutorial.06** folder on your Student Disk. Look at any of the sequential files used in this tutorial to see how records and fields are stored. Run the program and correct any errors. Save the form as **frmSuperOffice** and the project as **Super Office - Prices** in the **Cases** folder in the **Tutorial.06** folder on your Student Disk. Print the Form Image, Form As Text, and Code. Figure 6-28 shows the completed form.

Figure 6-28 ◄

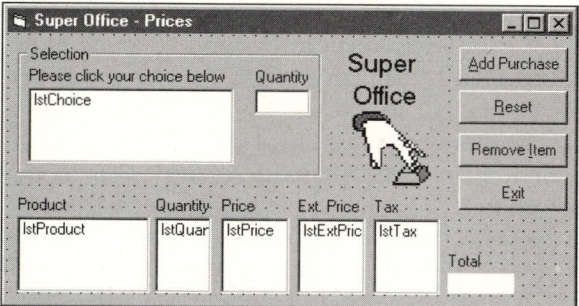

4. Consumers Catalog Sales Consumers Catalog Sales sells specialty items directly to its customers around the world. The company would like to have a program that both displays customer address data (Customer Name, Address 1, Address 2, City, State or Province, Zip Code or Postal Code, and Country) and allows for adding new customer data to the file. The data is stored in a sequential file and is read into a two-dimensional array with 50 rows and 7 columns. The existing customer names should be loaded into a combo box so they can be selected by the user. The ItemData property of the ComboBox object will be used to store the row location of the customer information stored in the array. This is necessary because the combo box will sort the names in the box, and the sorted combo box list will not reflect the sequence of the array information. Your program should have four command buttons. The first should clear the contents of the text boxes and deselect the current item from the combo box. The second command button should add new data to the ASCII-delimited file. Each time a new record is added, it is written to both the array and the sequential file. *Hint:* Use the ListIndex property of the ComboBox object with the ItemData property to directly reference information in the array. Additionally, the program should provide a command button to print out a mailing label for the customer displayed on the screen. The last command button should end the program.

Create the sequential data file with at least five records using addresses of your choice in WordPad or any word processing program. Make sure you have seven fields in each record, separated by the comma-delimiter, and that you press the Enter key after each line. Save the file as **Consumer.txt** in the **Cases** folder in the **Tutorial.06** folder on your Student Disk. Run the program and correct any errors. When finished, save the form as **frmConsumersMailing** and the project as **Consumers Mailing** in the **Cases** folder in the **Tutorial.06** folder on your Student Disk. Print the Form Image, Form As Text, and Code.

Answers to Quick Check Questions

SESSION 1.1

1. Creating a program can be divided into three steps. First you create the interface by drawing the controls on the form. Then you write the necessary Visual Basic statements to accomplish the tasks the program needs to perform. The third and final step is a loop — test the program, correct any errors, and test the program again.

2. The Application Wizard creates a project that is a template for a completed program. That is, it will create the forms, menus, toolbars, and other items for you to perform tasks like opening and closing files. You as the programmer must modify this template to accomplish specific tasks like displaying the graphical files you open. The Application Wizard only can create new programs. It is not possible to use the Application Wizard to modify programs that already have been created.

3. A project contains all the information about the files that make up a Visual Basic program. This information includes the forms used in the program, and other files containing Visual Basic statements. You can change the files used by a project by using the Project window.

4. A form is an object that contains other objects that allow the user to interact with the program. For example, the user can interact with text boxes and see descriptive information in labels on a form. A form has several properties that describe its appearance. These properties include the BackColor and BorderStyle. Just like other objects, a form can respond to events.

5. The Index tab is used to search for information directly using keywords. As you type characters, the subjects matching your characters will display in a window. You can click the desired topic to display help for that item. Using the Contents tab is much like looking through a table of contents.

6. Run the current project. This has the effect of switching Visual Basic from design mode to run mode. End the current project. This has the effect of switching Visual Basic from run mode to design mode. Open an existing project.

SESSION 1.2

1. The Properties window is used to change the properties of the active object while Visual Basic is in design mode. Each object, including forms and controls created from the toolbox, has a fixed set of properties you can set by using the Properties window. Different objects have different properties.

2. The Label control is used to display output from your program. This output is controlled by the Caption property. The property can be set using the Properties window while in design mode or using Visual Basic code while in run mode. A text box allows a user to enter information during run time. It also can be used to display information for the user during run time.

3. You can move an object by clicking the object and holding down the left mouse button while moving the mouse on the screen. An outline of the object will be displayed while it is being moved. To position the object, release the mouse button. To resize an object, click the object. Then, hold down the left mouse button on one of the sizing handles. Move the mouse until the object is of the desired size and release the mouse button. To delete an object, click the object and press the Delete key.

4 The Image control is used to display a picture inside the region of the object. The picture that is displayed is controlled by the Picture property. You can cause the picture to be resized to fill the region of the Image by setting the Stretch property to True.

5 You write all Visual Basic statements in a window called the Code window. It allows you to select the object and procedure for which you want to write statements.

SESSION 2.1

1 The Label control only can display information; it cannot allow a user to enter information into it. While the Label control and the TextBox control have common properties such as font size and font type, only the TextBox control allows the user input during run time.

2 During design time, select a text box to make it the active object, then open the Properties window. Select the Font property to activate the Font dialog box. The Font dialog box allows the programmer to select from a list of available fonts, sizes, and styles for the text box.

3 By using the Windows Clipboard you are able to copy not only the current object, but the properties that you have set for that object. For example, if you create a text box with the font changed to Arial 35 point, then copy that control to the Clipboard and paste it on the form, you will not have to set the font size again because the FontSize property of 35 was copied along with the text box. It is a way to simplify redundant tasks.

4 A command button is used to execute code when the user clicks the button. This event is called the Click event. The user can write statements to perform a specific task in response to a Click event.

5 There is only one control on a form at a time that can be active. This control then is said to have the focus. To change the order in which controls receive focus, use the TabIndex property. Begin with a zero (0) for the first object, a one (1) for the second object, and so forth.

6 The Shape control will allow you to create a shape on a form. This is an easy way to visually group related objects. It makes it easier for the user to understand where objects are and how they relate to one another if they are grouped together. The Line control puts a line on the form. This line can be used to divide the form into logical regions. The top of the form can have input areas while a line will separate the bottom where the output area is.

7 Most visible objects on a form, and the form itself, support different colors. While there are times different colors should be used, remember that strong colors can become distracting. Very bright or unusual colors should be used when you are trying to convey a message such as a warning signal, not when you simply are entering data.

SESSION 2.2

1 The Dim statement is used to declare variables explicitly. Variables have a data type that describes the kind of information the variable can store. If the Dim statement is used inside a procedure, the procedure variable is local and cannot be used by any other procedure in the program. The Private statement is used to declare a variable in the general declarations section of the Form module. Private variables exist while the Form module is activated and can be used by any procedure in the Form module.

2 When a user clicks an object it receives focus. At this time, the GotFocus event occurs for the object. When the user clicks or presses the Tab key to move to another object, the LostFocus event occurs. The Click event occurs when the user clicks an object. This happens after the GotFocus event occurs for an object.

3 Exponentiation (^) is performed first
Multiplication (*) and division (/) are performed next in the order of their appearance in the expression.
Integer division is performed next (\).
Modulo arithmetic is performed next (Mod).
Addition (+) and subtraction (-) are performed in the order of their appearance in the expression.

4 Syntax errors are caused when you incorrectly use Visual Basic statements or write other statements that have no meaning to Visual Basic. The Visual Basic Code window will detect syntax errors for you as you write your program. Run-time errors occur while your program is running and are the result of an error that could not be detected when the code was being written. Run-time errors can be caused by trying to perform arithmetic operations on variables that do not contain numbers or by calling intrinsic functions with incorrect arguments. Logic errors occur when you write Visual Basic statements that are correct, but the statements do not correctly solve the problem.

5 Clicking the Print command on the File menu will activate the Print dialog box. You can print the code in your program using the Code option. If you want to print the different objects created on the form, the properties, and their settings, use the Form As Text option. Finally, the Form As Image option will print an image of the form to the printer.

SESSION 3.1

1 A check box is a control that allows the user to place a check mark in the object.

2 A check box can have three values. It can be checked, unchecked, or dimmed. You can find out the status of a check box by looking at the Value property at run time. If a check box is dimmed, the object neither is checked nor unchecked.

3 The Min and Max properties describe the valid range of values for a scroll bar. The value must be between Min and Max. The LargeChange and SmallChange properties describe how much the value of the scroll bar will be changed. When you click the scroll arrows, the value will be increased or decreased by the value of the SmallChange property. When you click in the region of the scroll bar, the value of the scroll bar will be changed by the value of the LargeChange property. The Value property is an integer that defines the current value of the scroll bar.

4 Boolean values are a Visual Basic data type that only can contain the values of True or False. You cannot store any other value in a Boolean variable.

5
```
If lblTaxes.Visible = True Then
    lblTaxes.Caption = 33
End If

If lblTaxes.Visible <> False Then
    lblTaxes.Caption = 0
End If
```

```
If lblJan.Caption > lblFeb.Caption Then
    lblJan.Caption = Val(lblJan.Caption) + 1
End If

If yesterday < today Then
    End
End If
```

6   The Change event occurs when the contents of an object changes. The Change event applies to scroll bars and text boxes. The Click event occurs when the user clicks the mouse on an object. The Click event is useful with the CommandButton and Image objects.

7   When an event procedure for an object changes the value of another object, a change event will occur for that object. If the changed object changes the value of another object, a Change event will occur for that object.

SESSION 3.2

1   A frame is used to contain other objects, like option buttons, so they will operate as a group. A frame also can be used to visually identify parts of a form.

2   When you create option buttons inside a frame, they are said to be contained by the frame. Thus, only one option button in the frame can be active at any one time. You can create several frames on a form.

3
```
Dim pstrPrompt As String
pstrPrompt = "Do you want to " & vbCrLf & "Continue"
```

4   Both an If statement and Select Case statement are conditional statements. An If statement can test several different conditions, however, while a Select Case statement tests the value of one expression. Then depending on the value of the expression, different statements are executed.

5   A control array allows you to create several objects that have the same name and share the same event procedures. You reference individual elements (objects) in a control array using the Index property in parentheses, followed by the object name.

6   Functions return a value with a specific data type. The value returned by a function usually is assigned to a variable name or a property of an object. Subroutines do not return values. Both functions and subroutines can accept arguments to communicate information to the function or subroutine.

7   Message boxes are useful to confirm a user action like exiting the program. Message boxes are displayed by calling the MsgBox function. A Message Box will be displayed when the MsgBox function is called. The window has a title bar, descriptive text, and buttons the user can click. You can take different actions depending on which button the user clicked.

8   Logical operators define the relationship between different expressions, much like conjunctions define the relationship between the parts of a sentence in English. Logical operators include And, Or, Xor, and Not.

SESSION 4.1

1 Several style guidelines will help you create menus that have a similar look and feel to menus in other Windows 95 programs. A menu item's caption should be short enough to appear on one line, but it can contain multiple words to convey its purpose. When menu items contain multiple words, the first letter of each word should be capitalized and each word should be separated by a space. The first letter of a menu item's caption always should be capitalized. If a menu item displays a dialog box or requires the user to complete other information, the item's name should be followed by an ellipsis (...).

2 A menu title displays a menu item. Menu items in turn execute statements contained in their Click event procedure.

3 A shortcut key is a function key (such as F5) or a key combination (such as Ctrl+A or Ctrl+X) that executes a command. Command buttons and menu items support shortcut keys; you cannot create a shortcut key for a menu title. A hot key is a key you press while holding down the Alt key to open a menu or carry out a command.

4 A separator bar is a horizontal line that visually groups related menu items together to make the interface easier to use. Like all components of a menu, a separator bar must have a unique name or be a member of a control array. You create a separator bar by setting a menu item's Caption property to a hyphen (-).

5 A submenu is a menu item that displays another menu, rather than executing code in an event procedure. You can make a menu item display on a submenu by indenting it another level.

SESSION 4.2

1 The Data control uses the Connect property to determine the type of database to be used. By default, the value of this property is Access. The DatabaseName property is used to identify the actual database that is used. After setting the database name, the RecordSource property is used to specify the individual table that the Data Control will reference. Finally, the RecordsetType property determines the kind of Recordset that will be created by the Data control at run time.

2 When a control is used to display data from a database or save data to a database, it is referred to as a bound control. You can bind controls to a database by setting the DataSource property to the name of an existing Data control and the DataField property to a field in the table identified by the Data control. You always should set these properties after creating and setting the properties for the Data control.

3 A text box that can display multiple lines of text is called a multiline text box. To create a multiline text box you need to set the MultiLine property to True. If the text will not fit in the region of the text box, you should set the ScrollBars property to 1 - Horizontal to display a horizontal scroll bar across the bottom of the text box, or 2 - Vertical to display a vertical scroll bar across the rightmost side of the text box. If you want both horizontal and vertical scroll bars to appear, set the ScrollBars property to 3 - Both.

4 AddNew is a method of the Recordset object. When executed, it will create a new record ready for editing. Update also is a method of the Recordset object. Once a record has been changed, all changes are stored in the copy buffer until the Update method is called. Delete is a method of the Recordset object that will remove the current record from the Recordset. It is important to remember that the record still will be visible until you move to another record, even after it has been deleted. To change an existing record, you need to call the Edit method of the Recordset then make any changes to the record, and then call the Update method.

5 The Enabled property, when set to True, will allow the object to interact with the user at run time. If the Enabled Property is set to False, then the user will not be able to interact with the control. When the Visible property is set to True, the control is visible to the user; if it is set to False the user will not be able to see the control.

SESSION 4.3

1 The FindFirst method of the Recordset object will locate the first record in a Recordset that satisfies some criteria. If a record matching the criteria is located, the current record pointer is positioned to the first record in the Recordset satisfying the criteria. If the Recordset contains more than one record that satisfies the criteria, the FindFirst method locates the first occurrence. The following statement would locate the first occurrence of the name "Smith" in the fldLastName field:

```
datContact.Recordset.FindFirst "fldLastName = " & "'" & _
    "Smith" & "'"
```

2 An input box is a window that is opened when the InputBox function is called. It is used to obtain a text string from the user. An input box has two buttons. If the user clicks the OK button, the text string will be returned from the function. If the user clicks the Cancel button, the text string will be empty.

3 An error handler is used so your program will not end as a result of a run-time error. The On Error statement is used to set up an error handler in a procedure. Usually the statement is followed by a GoTo statement. When an error occurs, the statement after the label will be executed. The Resume Next statement is used inside the error handler to execute the statement following the one that caused the error.

4 Data validation is used when a user enters information that will be used late in the program, because you must be sure the data entered has the appropriate data type, and is within an acceptable range.

5 The Resume Next statement specifies that when a run-time error occurs, the next statement to be executed is the statement following the statement where the error occurred.

6 The Exit Sub statement stops the procedure wherever it is placed. If used in a procedure with an error handler, it will allow the user to exit the procedure, if an error is not detected, without activating the code for an error.

SESSION 5.1

1 The startup object is the first object executed when the program is started. The startup object can be a form of a procedure named Sub Main contained in a standard module.

2 A splash screen is a form that requires no interaction from the user and is displayed at the beginning of an application while the rest of a program is being loaded. It shows information describing the program name and version.

3 When Visual Basic creates the instance of the Form object at run time, the Initialize event occurs first. This event only occurs the first time a form is loaded. The Load event occurs next as Visual Basic begins to make the form the active object. The Activate event occurs for the form after the form is loaded. A startup form is activated automatically after it is loaded. Each time the Show method is called or the form gets focus, the Activate event occurs. After the form is activated, it becomes the active object and the

GotFocus event occurs for the object with the TabIndex property of zero (0). A form can become active by user action, such as clicking the form, or by using the Show or SetFocus methods in code.

4 The Hide method will remove the form from the screen, but it will remain loaded. The Unload statement will remove the form from the screen and the computer's memory. If you hide a form you may still manipulate its controls but you cannot do so if it is unloaded.

5 When a form is displayed as a modal form, the user must close or hide the form before another object in the program can receive focus. The user can interact with other programs, however.

6 The Data Form Wizard is used to generate a form with the Add, Update, and Delete controls already on the form and ready to access a table or query in the database. It reduces time in creating code, and once created, the form can be adjusted to be custom fit to the user's specific needs.

SESSION 5.2

1 The NewPage method advances the paper in the printer to the next page and resets the position of the printer to the upper-left corner of the page. The EndDoc method sends any text remaining in the printer buffer to the printer, and then resets the Page property.

2 The Spc argument is used to print blank spaces counting from where the output begins to print. This will allow the user to line up columns. The Tab argument will insert spaces starting from the left margin. Both are ways to line up data on a report.

3 A Do Until loop executes statements until some condition is True. A Do While loop executes while some condition is True.

4
```
Do While rstPacific.EOF = False
    Debug.Print rstPacific![fldProductID]
    rstPacific.MoveNext
Loop
```

5 An accumulator or a counter most commonly is used in a loop. An accumulator is used to tally values like totals sales while a counter is used to count the number of occurrences of an activity. That is, a counter can be used to count the number of records in a Recordset. An accumulator can be used to tally the sales amount stored in each record, and will store the result in a variable. This then can be used to know how many objects, records, or items there are. This is especially useful when the exact number of objects is not known or can change often.

SESSION 6.1

1 When you are reading and writing information that needs to be kept sorted, or you are working with a large amount of data, you should consider using a database. When the amount of data you are reading is quite small, however, you often can use a text file. While you use the methods of the Recordset object to read, write, and locate records in a Recordset, you use the Visual Basic statements (Open, Close, Input, and Write) to read and write text files. You cannot locate a specific record in a text file without reading all the records before it.

2 The Open statement is used to Open text files. If the For Input clause is used, the file will be opened for reading. If the For Output clause is used, the file will be opened for writing, and any existing contents will be deleted from the file. If the For Append clause is used, data written to the file will be appended to any existing contents. The Input statement is used to read a file. When you are finished reading or writing a file, it should be closed explicitly using the Close statement.

3 The EOF function is used to determine the end of a text file. It returns True when the end of file has been reached and False otherwise.

4 `Dim Prices(1 to 20) As Single`

5 Each of these properties applies to a ListBox object. The List property takes one argument — an Integer index. It will return the text contained in the corresponding list item. The ListCount property is an Integer value that defines how many items are in a list. The ListIndex property is an Integer value that defines the active item in a list. If the value is -1, then no item is selected.

6
```
For pintCount = 20 to 100
    Print pintCount
Next
```

7 The Exit For statement is used to exit a For loop before the counter no longer meets the specified condition. It is useful to exit the loop as a result of some error condition like invalid data.

SESSION 6.2

1 The RemoveItem method takes one argument — the index of the item to remove. When called with a ListBox object, the specified item will be removed. The Clear method is used to Remove all the items from a list box at once. It takes no arguments. Both methods set the ListIndex property to -1 after they are called because there is no longer an active item.

2 A one-dimensional array consists of rows whereas a two-dimensional array is made up of rows and columns. You use one subscript with a one-dimensional array and two subscripts with a two-dimensional array.

3 When you open a file for reading, you use the For Input clause on the Open statement. When you open it for writing, you use the For Output or For Append clause. You use the Input statement to read a file and the Write statement to write a file.

4 The Variant data type can contain data from any of the other Visual Basic data types. In addition to storing the variable, Visual Basic stores the current data type of a variable.

5 The Write # statement is used to create, or append to, an ASCII-delimited file. Files created or appended with the Write # statement can be read with the Input # statement.

Microsoft®
Visual Basic® 5.0
for Windows®

LEVEL 2

TUTORIALS

Read This **Before You Begin**

STUDENT DISKS

To complete the tutorials and end-of-tutorial assignments in this book, you need three Student Disks. Your instructor will either provide you with Student Disks or ask you to make your own.

If you are asked to make your own Student Disks, you will need three blank, formatted high-density disks. You will need to copy a set of folders from a file server or the *Student Developer's Kit* CD-ROM onto your disks. Your instructor will tell you which computer, drive letter, and folders contain the files you need. The following table shows you which folders go on each of your disks, so that you will have enough disk space to complete all the tutorials, Tutorial Assignments, and Case Problems.

Student Disk	Write this on the disk label	Put these folders on the disk
1	Intermediate Tutorials 7–8	Tutorial.07, Tutorial.08
2	Intermediate Tutorials 9–10	Tutorial.09, Tutorial.10
3	Intermediate Tutorials 11 & 12, Additional Cases	Tutorial.11, Tutorial.12, AdditionalCases

When you begin each tutorial, be sure you are using the correct Student Disk. See the inside front or inside back cover of this book for more information on Student Disk files, or ask your instructor or technical support person for assistance.

USING YOUR OWN COMPUTER

If you are going to work through this book using your own computer, you need:

■ **Computer System** Microsoft Windows 95 or Microsoft Windows NT 4.0 (or later), and either Microsoft Visual Basic 5.0 Enterprise Edition, Microsoft Visual Basic 5.0 Professional Edition, Microsoft Visual Basic 5.0 Learning Edition, or Microsoft Visual Basic 5.0 Control Creation Edition must be installed on your computer. This book assumes a complete installation of Microsoft Visual Basic. The screens captured for this text show Microsoft Visual Basic 5.0 Professional Edition.

■ **Student Disks** You can make student disks from the files on the *Student Developer's Kit* CD-ROM. You will not be able to complete the tutorials or end-of-tutorial assignments in this book using your own computer until you have Student Disks. The Student Disk files may also be obtained electronically over the Internet or from your instructor. See the inside front or inside back cover of this book for more details.

VISIT OUR WORLD WIDE WEB SITE

Additional materials designed especially for you are available on the World Wide Web. Go to **http://www.course.com**.

To complete the tutorials in this book, your students must use a set of student files on three Student Disks. These files are included in the Instructor's Resource Kit and the *Student Developer's Kit* CD-ROM. They may also be obtained electronically over the Internet. See the inside front or inside back cover of this book for more details. Follow the instructions in the Readme file to copy the files to your server or standalone computer. You can view the Readme file using WordPad.

Once the files are copied, you can make Student Disks for the students yourself, or tell students where to find the files so they can make their own Student Disks. Make sure the files get correctly copied onto the Student Disks by following the instructions in the Student Disks section above, which will ensure that students have enough disk space to complete all the tutorials and end-of-tutorial assignments.

COURSE TECHNOLOGY STUDENT FILES

You are granted a license to copy the Student Disk files to any computer or computer network used by students who have purchased this book.

Examining Database Objects and Structured Query Language (SQL)

Creating a Payroll Program for Paymaster

OBJECTIVES

In this tutorial you will:

- Learn about the collections and objects that make up a database and how to work with them in programs

- Use the properties and methods of a collection

- Write a type of For loop, called a For Each loop, that operates on a collection

- Learn a different way to insert, update, and delete data in a database using a language called SQL

CASE

Paymaster Payroll Services

Paymaster Payroll Services, located in Kansas City, Missouri, provides payroll services to more than 150 U.S. companies who find it more cost effective and efficient to outsource their payroll processing. Virgil Meeks is the information systems department manager for Paymaster. He is responsible for all the computer applications needed to compute the payroll for each client, print the necessary reports, and paychecks. Virgil has assigned you the task of creating several parts of a new payroll program in Visual Basic to replace their existing software.

Virgil wants you to complete the following tasks:

- Print a report of each table in the database; for each table, print the name of each field along with its data type and size.

- Read an ASCII file containing an employee ID and the number of hours worked into a database table. Using that data, the program must compute the gross pay, payroll taxes, and net pay, for each employee having a record in the ASCII file.

- Write the statements to select different records from the database and display them into a multiline text box based on information specified by a user.

SESSION

7.1

In this session you will write statements to connect to a database, and print out the tables and fields in the database without using the Data control. You also will learn how to use the properties and methods of a collection.

Analyzing the Program

Virgil already has defined the structure of the database and created all the tables. This information is saved in the Tutorial.07 folder on your Student Disk. He also has created the NEADT charts for the program. He suggests you review the design documentation and refer to it as you develop the program.

To look at the design specifications for the event registration database:

1. Start **Microsoft Word** and load the file named **Pay.doc** located in the **Tutorial.07** folder on your Student Disk.

2. Print the NEADT charts and exit your word processing program.

Connecting to a Database with Code

Unlike the programs you have written previously, you will not use a Data control to interact with a database. Rather, you will write statements to open a database and perform operations on the data in the database. You have used objects like a recordset to navigate through the records of a table. The Recordset object, however, is only one object supported by the Microsoft Jet database engine. The Microsoft Jet database engine supports several different objects having properties and methods. Every table, field, query, and recordset in a database is stored as an object in the database. Each object, like a table in a database, has properties to define its name, when the table was created, the last time it was updated, and methods like OpenRecordset to create a Recordset object.

If a database has four tables, then there are four objects; one to represent each table. These objects are grouped together into collections; just as each printer on the system is stored as a Printer object in the Printers collection, each table in a database is stored in a collection. These objects and collections make up a hierarchy of objects called the Data Access Objects (DAO) hierarchy.

The **Data Access Objects (DAO) hierarchy** is made up of collections, which contain zero, one, or many objects of the same type. Some objects contain other collections, which in turn, contain other objects. DAO is referred to as a hierarchy because the collections and objects are related together such that they form an inverted tree structure.

> *Tip:* A collection object's name is plural and each object's name in the collection is singular. This notation is standard for each collection and its objects, so you can distinguish easily the collection from the objects stored in the collection. For example, the Databases collection stores each Database object. There is one Database object for each database you open.

Before you can reference DAO objects in code, you must make the corresponding object library available to your program. An **object library** provides information to Visual Basic about a set of objects like DAO. Object library files have the extension ".olb". You can create a reference to the object library using the References dialog box.

To make the DAO object library available to your program:

1. Open the project named **Paymast.vbp** in the **Tutorial.07** folder on your Student Disk. View the form named **Paymast.frm**. The form should look like Figure 7-1.

Figure 7-1 ◀
Paymaster–
Main Payroll
Form

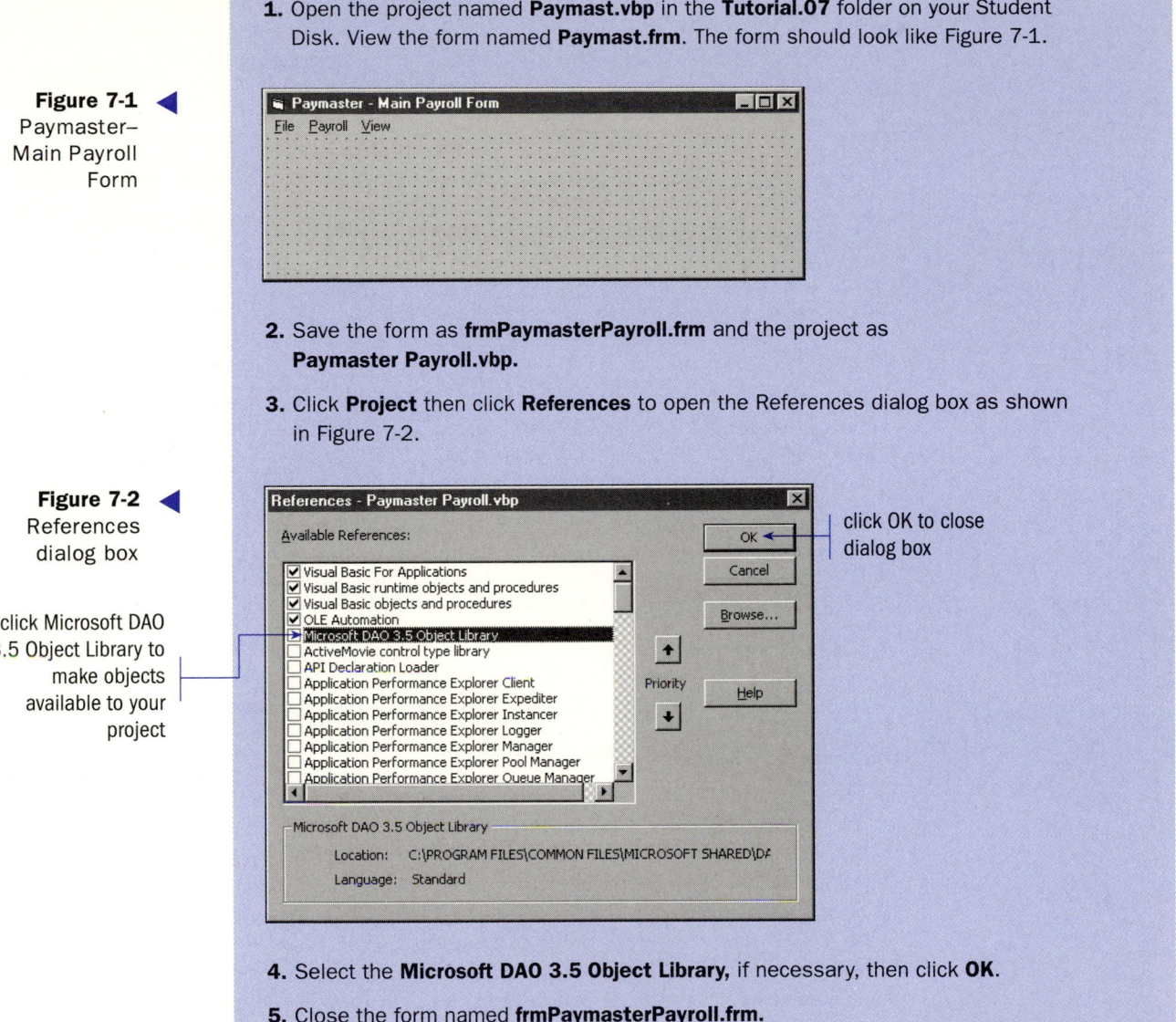

2. Save the form as **frmPaymasterPayroll.frm** and the project as **Paymaster Payroll.vbp**.

3. Click **Project** then click **References** to open the References dialog box as shown in Figure 7-2.

Figure 7-2 ◀
References
dialog box

click Microsoft DAO
3.5 Object Library to
make objects
available to your
project

click OK to close
dialog box

4. Select the **Microsoft DAO 3.5 Object Library**, if necessary, then click **OK**.

5. Close the form named **frmPaymasterPayroll.frm**.

Once a reference to the DAO object library has been created, the object library will appear in the Object Browser and you can reference the DAO objects in code.

At the top of the DAO hierarchy is the DBEngine object. The DBEngine object contains all the objects in the DAO hierarchy and is the interface you use to work with the Microsoft Jet database engine. You do not create an instance of the DBEngine object; rather, it is predefined. This is a rare instance where you do not declare an object variable before using it.

When the Microsoft Jet database engine first is accessed, a session is created, and the session is destroyed when the Microsoft Jet database engine is closed. A **session** contains all the open databases for a user. In DAO, a session is implemented as a Workspaces collection containing one or more Workspace objects. When the DBEngine object is created for you, the Workspaces collection also is created and a single Workspace object is created in the Workspaces collection. This is known as the Default Workspace. The **Default Workspace** is a Workspace object, created automatically when you connect to the Microsoft Jet database engine. Usually, only one session is necessary for a user, hence one

Workspace object in the Workspaces collection. It is possible to create multiple sessions, thus creating multiple Workspace objects. Unlike the Printers collection, you do not reference the Workspaces collection directly. Rather, the DBEngine object contains the Workspaces collection. Figure 7-3 shows the relationship between the DBEngine object and the Workspaces collection.

Figure 7-3 ◀
Relationship
between
DBEngine and
Workspaces

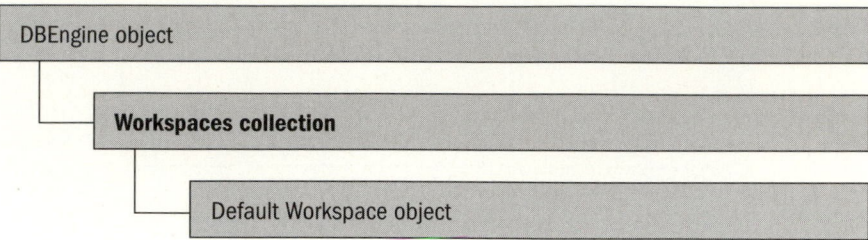

To reference a collection that is contained by another object, you use the same syntax as you use to reference an object's properties or methods. The collection has the following syntax:

objectname.collectionname

- The *objectname* can be any object, like the DBEngine object, that contains a collection. An object may contain more than one different collection.

- The *collectionname* can be any collection contained by an object.

To reference the Workspaces collection you would write the following statement fragment:

```
DBEngine.Workspaces
```

Although you now can reference the Workspaces collection, you need a way to reference an individual Workspace object stored in the collection. Most collections allow you to access an individual object in a collection in two ways.

- You always can use a numeric index to reference an individual object in a collection. The numeric index is a number starting at zero or one, and incremented by one for each object in the collection. That is, every collection either is a **zero-based** or **one-based collection**, depending on the collection. Whenever you use a collection, check the Help page for the collection to determine whether the first item in the collection is zero or one. This discrepancy is historical—older collections are numbered starting at zero. At some point, it generally was agreed upon that collections numbered starting at one were more intuitive. Thus, most new collections begin numbering at one.

- Most collections allow you to reference an object using a string key. A **string key** is a string that uniquely identifies an object in the collection. A string key provides a more intuitive way to reference each object in the collection.

To reference an individual object contained in a collection using an index, or string key, you use the Item method of the collection with an index. The Item method has the following syntax:

objectname = [*parentobjectname*].*collectionname*.**Item**(*index*)

- The **Item** method takes one argument—an *index* or *string key*—and returns the specified object from the collection.

- The *parentobjectname* is the name of an object containing the collection.

- The *objectname* is an object of the same type as the object stored in the collection.

- The *collectionname* can be any valid collection.

- The *index* can be an Integer number representing the object in the collection. If the collection supports a string key, *index* can contain a text string enclosed in quotes or a String variable.

Because the Workspaces collection is zero-based, the Default Workspace (the first item in the collection) has an index of zero (0). The string key for the Default Workspace is #Default Workspace#. To reference the Default Workspace (the Workspace created by the Microsoft Jet database engine), you could write the following equivalent statements:

```
Set wsCurrent = DBEngine.Workspaces.Item(0)
Set wsCurrent = DBEngine.Workspaces.Item _
    ("#Default Workspace#")
```

This statement returns the first Workspace object in the Workspaces collection, which is the Default Workspace.

Default Methods and Properties

Most objects have a default method or a default property. **Default methods** and **default properties** allow you to call a method or reference a property of an object without specifying the name of the method or property. There are two reasons to use default methods and properties in a program.

- Default methods and properties can reduce the amount of typing.

- When you use a default method or property, different code in the object is executed than when you specify the default property explicitly. Statements that use default properties or methods are executed approximately 25 percent faster.

The Item method is the default method of the Workspaces collection. So the following statements will produce the same results as the previous two statements to reference the Default Workspace:

```
Set wsCurrent = DBEngine.Workspaces(0)
Set wsCurrent = DBEngine.Workspaces("#Default Workspace#")
```

In the previous two statements the Item method was omitted because it is the default method. Notice that the period (.) that separates the object from the method name is removed.

Each Workspace object contains a collection called the Databases collection. This collection is empty until a database is opened. When a database is opened, a Database object is created and added to the Databases collection. If there is one open database, then the Databases collection contains one Database object. If there are two open databases, then the Databases collection contains two Database objects. Figure 7-4 shows the relationship between the Workspaces and Databases collections and the objects that they contain.

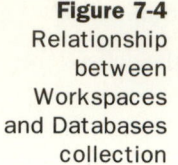

Figure 7-4
Relationship
between
Workspaces
and Databases
collection

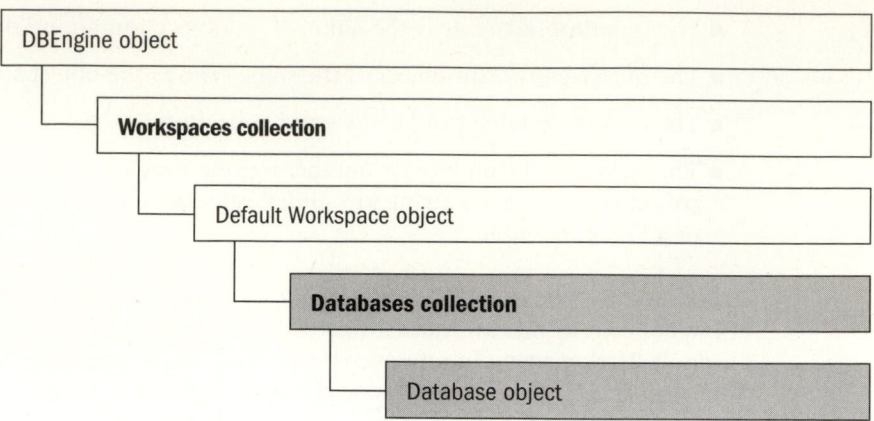

While the programs you have written have opened only one database at a time, it is possible for a program to open several databases.

Opening a Database Programmatically

Each program you have written so far has used the Data control to open a database and create a Recordset object. You also can open a database by writing a Visual Basic statement that calls a method of the Workspace object.

Now that you can reference the Default Workspace, you can use one of its methods to open a database. As you have seen, each object supports a fixed set of methods and properties, and the Workspace object is no exception. It supports a method named OpenDatabase, which is used to open an existing database. The OpenDatabase method has the following syntax:

Set *database* = *workspace*.**OpenDatabase** (*dbname, options, read-only, connect*)

- When the **OpenDatabase** method is called, a database is opened, a new Database object is created in the Databases collection, and a reference to a Database object is stored in the variable *database*.

- The variable *database* must be declared as a Database object variable.

- The *dbname* must contain either a text string, or variable, representing the folder and filename of the database to be opened.

- The *options* argument either can be True or False. If True, then the database is opened in exclusive mode meaning that no other user can open the database until the session has ended. If False, the database is opened in shared mode meaning it can be accessed by multiple users. If you do not specify *options,* multiple users can access the database.

- The optional *read-only* argument can be True or False. If True, then you can read data in the database but you cannot make any changes. If False, the default, data both can be read and written.

- The optional *connect* argument is used to specify information like passwords.

Like other object variables, DAO objects have standard prefixes indicating the object's type. The Database object uses the "db" standard prefix. Thus, the following statements could be used to open the database named Paymast.mdb in the Tutorial.07 folder on your Student Disk:

```
Public dbPaymaster as Database
    Set dbPaymaster = DBEngine.Workspaces(0). _
        OpenDatabase("A:\Tutorial.07\Paymast.mdb")
```

In addition to having a default method or property, many objects and methods have a default collection or object. For example, the OpenDatabase method will refer to the Default Workspace if no workspace is specified. Thus, the previous Set statement can be abbreviated to the following statement:

```
Set dbPaymaster = _
    OpenDatabase("A:\Tutorial.07\ Paymast.mdb")
```

Because the OpenDatabase method by default applies to the Default Workspace object stored in the Workspaces collection, you can use this syntax. This has the effect of adding the newly opened database object to the Databases collection.

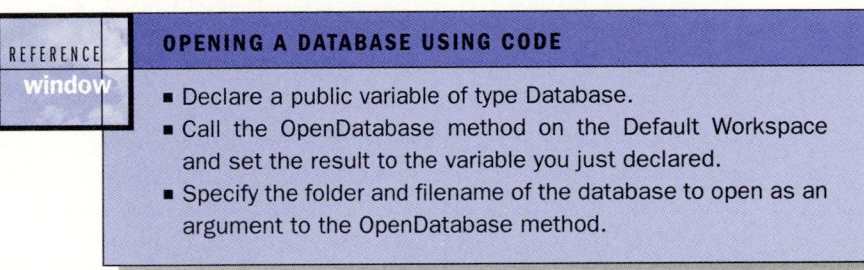

REFERENCE window

OPENING A DATABASE USING CODE

- Declare a public variable of type Database.
- Call the OpenDatabase method on the Default Workspace and set the result to the variable you just declared.
- Specify the folder and filename of the database to open as an argument to the OpenDatabase method.

The object variable representing the Database object will be used by several procedures in multiple forms, so it must be declared as a public variable in the general declarations section of the standard module. Because the database will be used while the program is running, it should be opened when the startup form is loaded.

To open the database for Paymaster:

1. Enter the following statement in the general declarations section of the standard module named **basGeneral**:

   ```
   Public dbPaymaster As Database
   ```

2. Enter the following statement on the form_Load event procedure for the form named **frmPaymasterPayroll**:

   ```
   Set dbPaymaster = _
       OpenDatabase("A:\Tutorial.07\Paymast.mdb")
   ```

The variable dbPaymaster was declared as a Database type object in the first statement. The second statement you wrote opens the database and sets the Database object variable to the open database.

Programming the Database Object

Each Workspace object contains a collection called the Databases collection. The Databases collection in turn contains zero or more Database objects such that there is one Database object for each open database. Thus, you can open several databases at the same time. In this session, you will open only one database, so there will be only one Database object in the Databases collection. Like any other object, the Database object supports several properties:

- The **Name** property contains the full path and filename of the database.

- The **Version** property of a Database object corresponds to a version of the Microsoft Jet database engine.

On the report documenting the database, Virgil wants the database name and the database version printed on the top of the report. You can accomplish this by printing the Name and Version properties of the Database object in the Immediate window. Virgil suggests you print all the components of the report in the Immediate window. He will change all the statements to print to the printer after the program is tested and working correctly.

To print the database name and version on the report:

1. Activate the Code window to the **Click** event for the menu item named **mnuFilePrintObjects** on the form named **frmPaymasterPayroll**.

2. Enter the following statements into the Click event procedure:

```
Debug.Print "Database Name: "; dbPaymaster.Name
Debug.Print "Database Version: "; dbPaymaster.Version
```

3. Save the program then run it.

4. Click **File** then **Print Objects** on the menu bar to test the code you just wrote, then activate the Immediate window to verify the program is connected to the database and both the properties printed. The Immediate window should look like Figure 7-5.

Figure 7-5 ◀
Database
object
properties

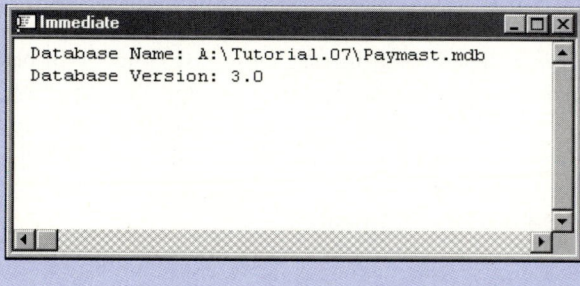

5. End the program.

These statements use the Name and Version properties of the Database object named dbPaymaster. The properties are printed in the Immediate window with a brief description.

Programming the TableDef Object

Each Database object contains several other collections. For example, each Database object contains a collection named TableDefs. This collection contains zero (0) or more TableDef objects representing the different tables in your database. There is one TableDef object for each table in the database. Figure 7-6 shows the relationship between the TableDefs collection and TableDef object to the other objects in the DAO hierarchy.

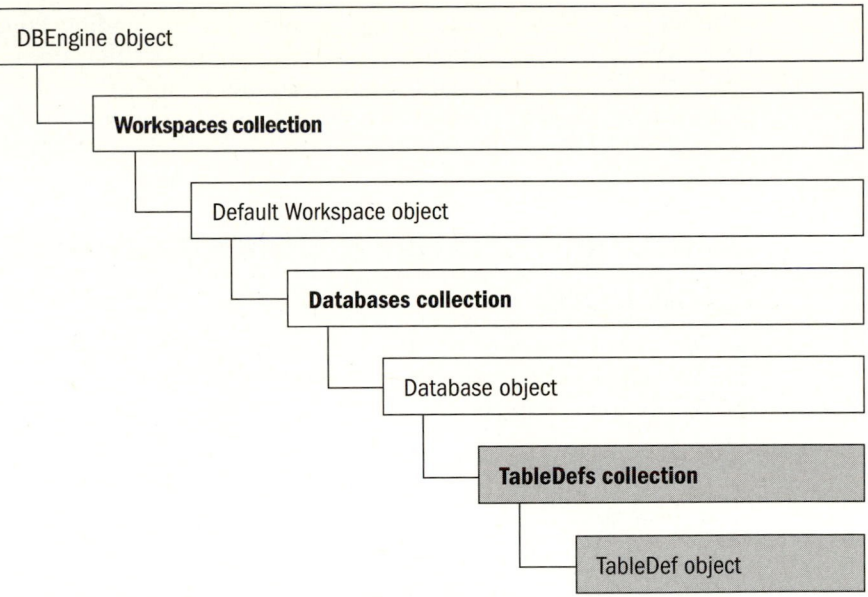

Each TableDef object supports several properties as shown in the following list:

- The **Name** property indicates the name of the table. This is the same name used to specify a table name to the Data control.

- The **RecordCount** property indicates the number of records in the table.

- The **DateCreated** property returns the date and time that the TableDef object was created.

- The **LastUpdated** property returns the date and time of the most recent change made to the TableDef object.

Once a database is opened, you can access the various tables contained in the Database object through the TableDefs collection. Because the TableDefs collection is contained in a Database object, you can reference the collection, assuming the object variable dbPaymaster is a valid database instance, with the following statement fragment:

```
dbPaymaster.TableDefs
```

However, you are not interested in the TableDefs collection but rather the individual TableDef objects stored in the collection. Like the Workspaces collection, you can reference an individual element by supplying the element number inside parentheses. Note that the TableDefs collection is zero-based. Thus, to reference the first TableDef object in the TableDefs collection, you could use the following statement:

```
Set tdfCurrent = dbPaymaster.TableDefs(0)
```

Even though this statement will reference the first TableDef object, you do not know how many TableDef objects there are in the TableDefs collection. That is, you do not know how many tables there are in the database. Every collection supports a property called Count. The **Count** property of a collection contains the number of objects in a specific collection. You can use the Count property in a For loop to look at each object in the collection. For example, to print the name of each TableDef object in the TableDefs collection, you would write the following For loop:

```
Dim pintCount as Integer
For pintCount = 0 To dbPaymaster.TableDefs.Count - 1
    Debug.Print dbPaymaster.TableDefs(pintCount).Name
Next
```

This For loop uses pintCount as a counter to examine each TableDef object in the TableDefs collection. Because the collection is numbered from zero (0), you need to subtract one (1) from the Count property as the ending condition in the For loop. Otherwise, you would attempt to reference an object that does not exist. The statement inside the For loop used pintCount as an index into the TableDefs collection. Thus, the argument of the Print statement, dbPaymaster.TableDefs(pintCount), refers to a single table (a TableDef object) from the TableDefs collection. By adding the Name property to the end of the argument, you are referencing the name of the table.

Iterating Through a Collection with a For Each Loop

While this For loop works, there is a variation of the For loop, called the For Each loop, that is used to iterate through each object in a collection. Its syntax is nearly identical to the For loop you have been using:

For Each *element* **In** *group*

   [*statements*]

[**Exit For**]

   [*statements*]

Next [*element*]

- The *element* must be an object variable of the same type as the objects in the collection, a general object, or a Variant. That is, if you wanted to examine each TableDef object in the TableDefs collection, *element* must be declared as a TableDef object type, a Variant data type, or an Object data type.

- The *group* defines the collection you want to examine.

- The *statements* work the same as in the For loops you already have used.

You can replace the previous For loop with the For Each loop shown below. This loop requires that you declare a TableDef object as the element in the loop. The first time through the loop, tdfCurrent will reference the first TableDef object. The second time through the loop, the second TableDef object is referenced. The For Each loop continues until there are no more TableDef objects in the collection. Like other object variables, a TableDef object has a standard prefix. The standard prefix for a TableDef object is "tdf".

```
Dim tdfCurrent as TableDef
For Each tdfCurrent In dbPaymaster.TableDefs
    Debug.Print tdfCurrent.Name
Next
```

In this For Each loop, dbPaymaster.TableDefs represents the group. You used this syntax because the TableDefs collection is contained by the Database object. The element is tdfCurrent. Each time through the loop you used the Name property of the individual TableDef object to print the name of the table in the Immediate window.

REFERENCE window	ITERATING THROUGH THE OBJECTS IN A COLLECTION WITH A FOR EACH LOOP
	■ Declare a variable of the same type as the object in the collection.
	■ Create a For Each loop using the object you just declared as the member part of the loop.
	■ Write statements as necessary inside the loop to operate on each object in the collection.

In addition to declaring an object variable as the same type as the objects in a collection, you can use two other data types:

- In addition to storing data types like Integer and Single, the Variant data type can be used to store an object. The Variant data type only should be used when the variable will be used to reference different types of objects, or an object's type is not known, because operations on Variant data is slow.

- The Object data type can store any kind of object. At run time, the type of the object is bound to the Object type variable. Like a Variant data type, use of the Object data type will decrease performance.

> *Tip:* When you use a For Each loop, use an object variable that is the same type as the objects in the collection. Although you can use a Variant or Object data type as the element name in the For Each loop, the loop will run significantly slower. Use a For Each loop instead of a For loop to iterate through the objects in a collection to improve readability and performance.

You already have printed the database name and version on the report. Next, you need to list each of the tables in the database. Virgil will use this report to document the database so other programmers working on the project can determine easily the name of each table. Figure 7-7 shows the different tables in the database as they are stored in the DAO hierarchy.

Figure 7-7 ◀
Tables in
Paymaster
database

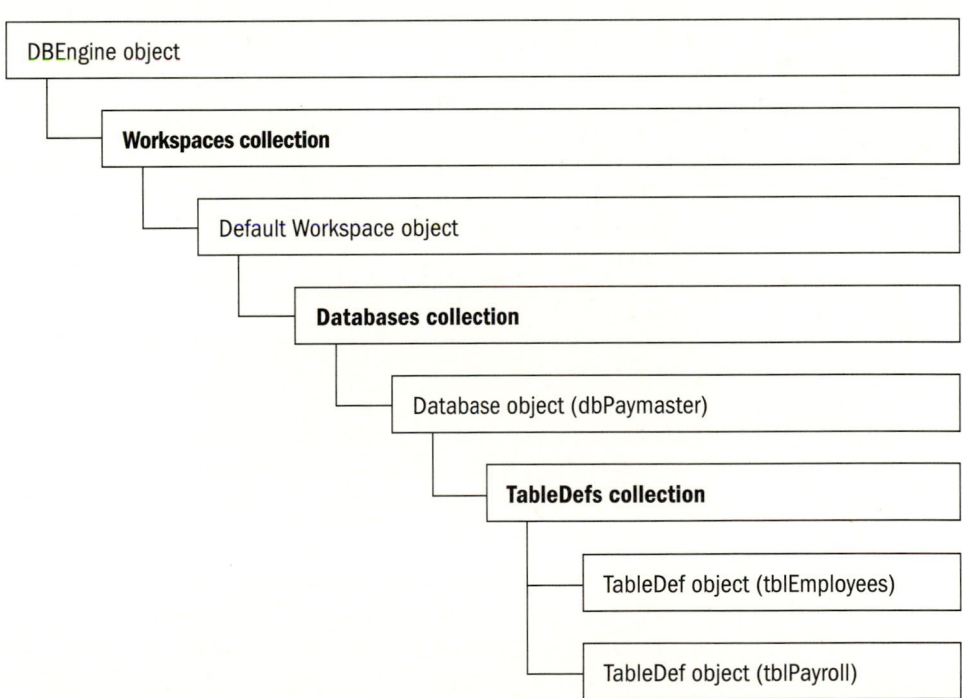

You can step through each table in the TableDefs collection by writing a For Each loop. For each TableDef, you need to print selected properties on the database documentation report. Thus, you need to declare a local object variable to store a reference to an individual TableDef object and use that as the member in the For Each loop.

To print the table name, number of records, and last access time of each TableDef object:

1. Activate the Code window to the Click event for the menu item named **mnuFilePrintObjects** on the form named **frmPaymasterPayroll**.

2. Enter the following statement into the event procedure just before the Debug.Print statements you just wrote:

```
Dim tdfCurrent As TableDef
```

3. Enter the following statements into the menu's **Click** event procedure just after the Debug.Print statements:

```
For Each tdfCurrent In dbPaymaster.TableDefs
    Debug.Print " "
    Debug.Print "Name: "; tdfCurrent.Name
    Debug.Print "Record count: "; _
        tdfCurrent.RecordCount
    Debug.Print "Date created: "; _
        tdfCurrent.DateCreated; " ";
    Debug.Print "Last updated: "; _
        tdfCurrent.LastUpdated
    Debug.Print " "
Next
```

This For Each loop examines each TableDef object in the TableDefs collection and prints out several properties.

```
For Each tdfCurrent In dbPaymaster.TableDefs
```

This statement uses the TableDef object variable named tdfCurrent as the element in the loop. The first time through the loop, tdfCurrent references the first table. The second time through the loop, tdfCurrent references the second table. The loop continues until all the tables have been examined.

```
Debug.Print " "
Debug.Print "Name: "; tdfCurrent.Name
Debug.Print "Record count: "; _
    tdfCurrent.RecordCount
Debug.Print "Date created: "; _
    tdfCurrent.DateCreated; " ";
Debug.Print "Last updated: "; _
    tdfCurrent.LastUpdated
```

The Name, RecordCount, DateCreated, and LastUpdated properties all apply to a TableDef object. Each of these properties is printed in the Immediate window with a prompt describing the property. You now should test the menu item to be sure it is working correctly.

To verify each TableDef object is being printed:

1. Save the program then start it.

2. Click **File** then click **Print Objects.**

3. Open the **Immediate window** and be sure the last few lines of your output looks like Figure 7-8.

Figure 7-8
Tables in
Paymaster
database

system table

user tables

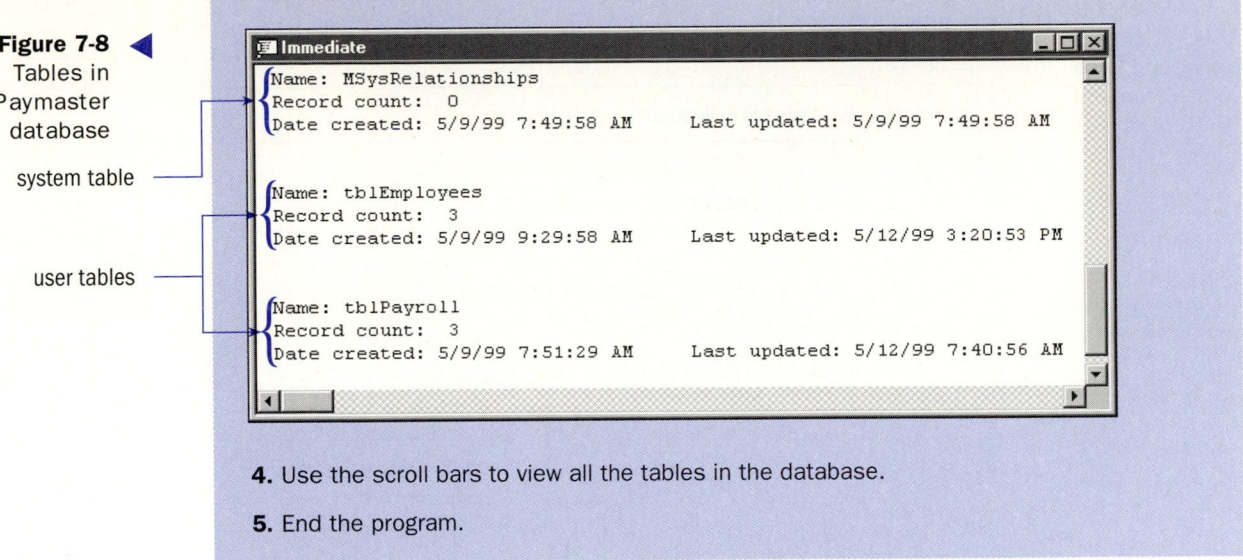

4. Use the scroll bars to view all the tables in the database.

5. End the program.

Note that the database contains eight TableDef objects. The first six objects begin with the prefix "MSys". The Microsoft Jet database engine created these tables when the database was created and they are called system tables. **System tables** are tables used by the Microsoft Jet database engine to manage the other tables, fields, queries, and other objects created by the user. You, as a programmer, should never attempt to modify the data contained in these tables or delete the tables. If you do, the database will no longer work. The remaining two tables named tblEmployees and tblPayroll were created by Virgil for use with the payroll program. These tables in turn contain fields to store data.

Programming the Field Object

Just as each Database object has one TableDefs collection containing one TableDef object for each table, each TableDef object has a Fields collection. The Fields collection contains all the fields in a table. Each field is stored as a Field object in the Fields collection. Field objects have the "fld" prefix. Like a TableDef object, a Field object has properties. These properties define the name of the field, its data type, size, and other related attributes. The following list describes some properties of the Field object:

- The **Name** property indicates the name of the field. This is the same name used to select a field name in a bound control like a text box. Unlike in a text box, the Name property is not set using the Properties window.

- The **Type** property is used to set or return the data type of an object. Each data type can be represented by an intrinsic constant. For a listing of those constants, see Help on the Type property for a Field object.

- The **Size** property sets or returns the maximum number of bytes for a Field object. For numeric fields, the size is set automatically when the Type property is set. For the Text data type, the Size property defines the maximum number of characters that can be stored in the field.

- The **Required** property is True if a Field object must contain a value, and False otherwise.

The Fields collection and the Field objects contained in the collection are stored in the DAO hierarchy, such that a TableDef object contains the Fields collection as shown in Figure 7-9.

Figure 7-9 ◀
Relationship
between Fields
collection and
Field object

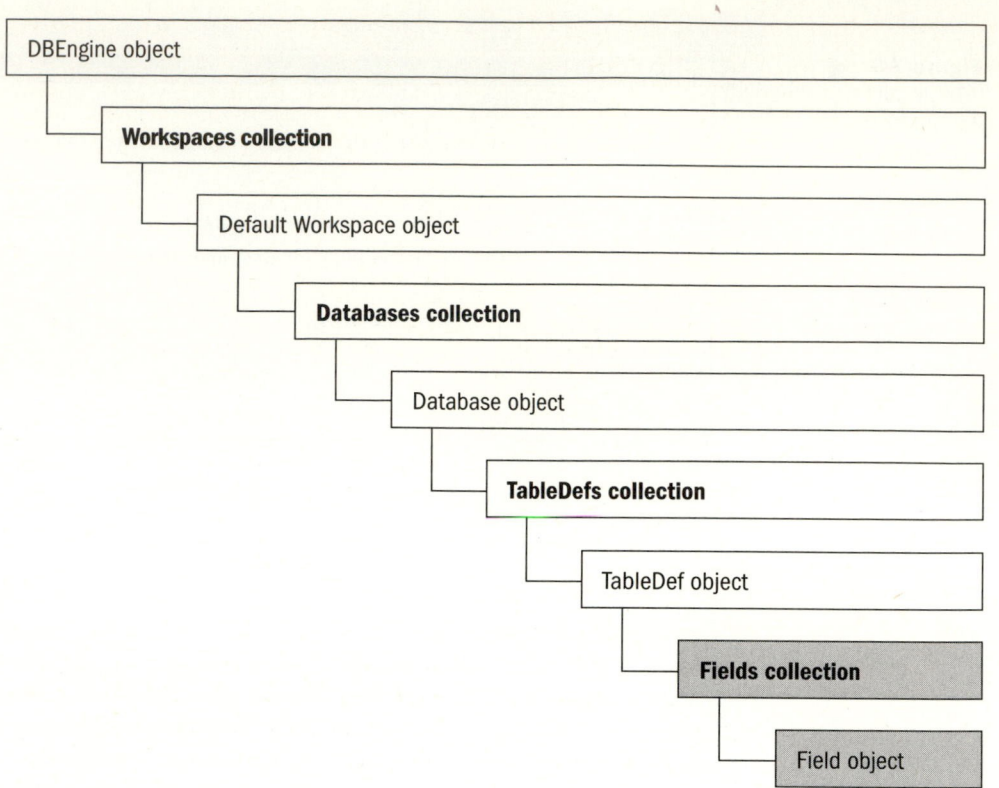

You can use the same type of For Each loop to look at each of the fields in a table. The member of this loop should be a Field object and the loop needs to examine the Fields collection. Thus, you will need to declare another local variable to store the Field object. Because you want this loop to execute for each TableDef object, it needs to be located inside the For Each loop you just wrote.

To print the Name, Type, Size, and Required properties of each Field object in a Fields collection:

1. Activate the Code window to the Click event for the menu item named **mnuFilePrintObjects** on the form named **frmPaymasterPayroll.**

2. Append the following variable declaration to the event procedure just after the Dim statement declaring tdfCurrent:

```
Dim tdfCurrent As TableDef
Dim fldCurrent As Field
```

3. Append the following statements, shown in bold, to the event procedure:

```
For Each tdfCurrent In dbPaymaster.TableDefs
    . . .
    Debug.Print "Last updated: "; tdfCurrent.LastUpdated
    For Each fldCurrent In tdfCurrent.Fields
        Debug.Print "    Name: "; fldCurrent.Name;
        Debug.Print "    Type: "; fldCurrent.Type;
        Debug.Print "    Field size: "; _
            fldCurrent.Size
        Debug.Print "    Required: "; fldCurrent.Required
    Next
    Debug.Print " "
Next
```

This For Each loop executes for each TableDef object and prints the pertinent information for each field. This information is stored in the properties of the Field object. Note that the structure of the loop is identical to the loop you just wrote.

```
For Each fldCurrent In tdfCurrent.Fields
```

This For Each statement examines each field in the Fields collection. This collection can be referenced using the current TableDef object stored in the variable named tdfCurrent. Thus, you used the syntax tdfCurrent.Fields. Note that each TableDef object contains one Fields collection.

```
Debug.Print "    Name: "; fldCurrent.Name;
Debug.Print "    Type: "; fldCurrent.Type;
Debug.Print "    Field size: "; _
    fldCurrent.Size
Debug.Print "    Required: "; fldCurrent.Required
```

Using the variable fldCurrent as the member in the For Each loop, these statements print the values of four different properties. Because these properties apply to the field object, you used the syntax fldCurrent.*propertyname*.

Now that you have written the code to examine each field in each table, you should test your program to be sure it is working correctly.

To verify that each field is being printed:

1. Save the program then start it.

2. Click **File** then **Print Objects** on the form.

3. Open the **Immediate window** and be sure the last few lines of output look like Figure 7-10.

Figure 7-10 ◀
Printing Field
objects

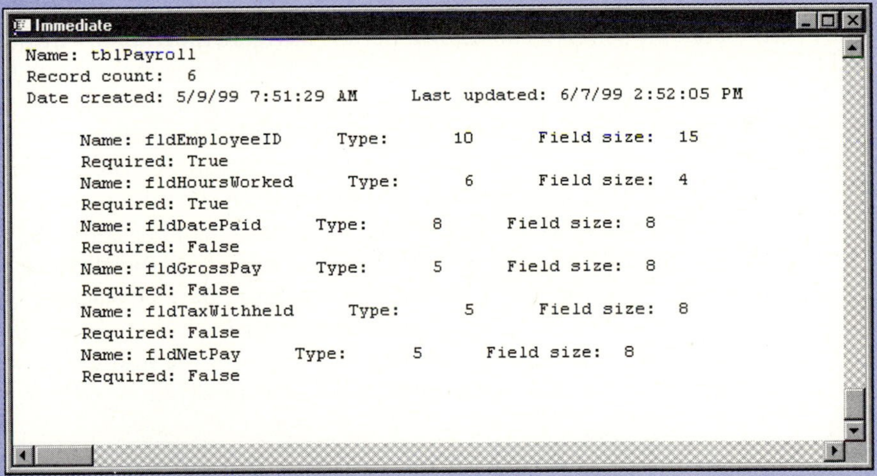

```
Immediate                                                    _ □ X
Name: tblPayroll
Record count:  6
Date created: 5/9/99 7:51:29 AM      Last updated: 6/7/99 2:52:05 PM

    Name: fldEmployeeID      Type:      10      Field size:   15
    Required: True
    Name: fldHoursWorked      Type:       6      Field size:   4
    Required: True
    Name: fldDatePaid      Type:     8      Field size:   8
    Required: False
    Name: fldGrossPay      Type:     5      Field size:   8
    Required: False
    Name: fldTaxWithheld      Type:       5      Field size:   8
    Required: False
    Name: fldNetPay      Type:     5      Field size:   8
    Required: False
```

4. End the program.

The program now prints each of the tables and forms in the Immediate window. Virgil will change the Debug.Print statements to Printer.Print statements to print the report to the default printer.

Quick Check

1. Describe two ways to reference an individual object in a collection.

2. What is the difference between a zero-based and a one-based collection?

3 What is the meaning of a default property or method? Why are they important?

4 What is the relationship between a Database, TableDef, and Field object?

5 What is the difference between a For loop and a For Each loop?

You have completed this session. You now may quit Visual Basic or proceed to the next session.

SESSION

7.2

In this session you will learn how to add, change, and delete data in a table and query using the Structured Query Language rather than the Data control.

Writing SQL Statements

Most database management systems provide two models to manipulate data in a database. In previous tutorials you have used the navigational model. Using the **navigational model** you move forward and backward directionally through records or locate records directly using a method like FindFirst. The Microsoft Jet database engine supports another method of access that uses the relational model. The **relational model** allows a single statement to perform an action on several records at once and is implemented using the Structured Query Language (SQL).

Structured Query Language (SQL) is a language defined by the American National Standards Institute (ANSI) and is used widely in database applications. It is made up of a set of statements that allow you to add, change, and delete database data. When you execute an SQL statement, you do not navigate individually through the records in a recordset. Rather, you execute a statement that will operate on one or more rows of data at the same time.

Most implementations of the SQL language contain extensions. That is, each vendor supplying a version of SQL adds enhancements they believe improve their product. Despite this, most parts of the language are consistent from one database to another.

SQL consists of three Data Definition Language (DDL) statements and four Data Manipulation Language (DML) statements. **Data Definition Language (DDL)** statements are used to change the structure of a database. **Data Manipulation Language (DML)** statements are used to add, change, and delete records in a database table or query. In this session you will learn how to use the basic forms of the four DML statements. Figure 7-11 lists the different DML statements and a brief description of their purposes.

Figure 7-11 ◀
DML
statements

Statement	Description
SELECT	Retrieves one or more rows from a database table or query
INSERT	Inserts rows into a database table
UPDATE	Changes the contents of one or more existing column(s)
DELETE	Removes one or more rows from a database table

Notice the DML statements all appear in uppercase letters. It is a standard naming convention to use capital letters for all SQL keywords like **INSERT** and **UPDATE**. One of two actions can occur when one of the four DML statements is executed. The actions are as follows:

- One type of statement returns records from a database and stores them into a Recordset object as a result of a **SELECT** statement. This is referred to as a **select query**.

- The other type of statement performs an action on a database table or query but does not return any records. These actions include adding, updating, and removing records. Action statements do not return a recordset. This is referred to as an **action query.**

Virgil usually receives the payroll information as ASCII-delimited files. The first step in computing the payroll is to read the ASCII file in the database table containing the time sheets. This file has the format shown in Figure 7-12.

Figure 7-12 ◀
Fields in
ASCII file

Employee ID	Hours Worked
"A23448"	40
"A44228"	30
"A55433"	30.5

In the previous tutorial you learned how to write a program to read a sequential file in list and combo boxes. This time, the information needs to be stored in a database table so the payroll can be computed. Thus, you need to write a Do loop to read each record from the sequential file. You also, however, need a way to insert a record in the database. Instead of calling the methods of a recordset, you can use the INSERT statement. The INSERT statement will be called for each record in the text file.

Inserting Database Records with the INSERT Statement

There are two forms of the INSERT statement. The first is used to append a single record to a table, while the second is used to append multiple records. The syntax for the first form is:

INSERT INTO *target* [(*field1*[, *field2* [, ...]])]

   VALUES (*value1*[, *value2*[, ...])

- The *target* is the name of the table or query where the records will be appended.

- For each *field* in the target, the **INSERT INTO** statement will store data in the field.

- The values stored in the fields are specified using the **VALUES** clause and *value1*, *value2*, and so on. Each value is inserted such that *value1* corresponds to *field1*, *value2* corresponds to *field2*, and so on. The number of fields and values must be the same. Commas must separate each value. Text data must be enclosed by quotation marks but numeric data should not. A pound sign (#) must enclose Date fields. If you need to embed a single quotation mark into a string, you can use chr(34)—the code for the single quotation mark character.

If you do not specify a field and a corresponding value for a table, then a Null value is inserted for the missing columns. If the number of fields does not correspond to the number of values, then a run-time error will occur. If you want to insert a row into the table named tblPayroll that has the fields fldEmployeeID, fldHoursWorked, and fldDatePaid, you could use the following syntax:

```
INSERT INTO tblPayroll _
    (fldEmployeeID,fldHoursWorked,fldDatePaid) _
    Values ('A32147',40,#2/23/99#)
```

Many tables require a unique index. For example, the file containing an employee ID and name may require the Employee ID be unique. If you execute an SQL statement that would violate the rules of the database, a run-time error will occur. You can write an error handler to trap this error and advise the user of the condition.

When you want to execute an SQL statement that performs an action like an INSERT statement, you do not open a recordset like you have done in the past. Rather, you call a method, called Execute, that applies to a Database object. The **Execute** method executes an SQL statement that runs an action query. If the statement returns rows from a database table or query (a select query), you instead open a recordset using the OpenRecordset method of the Database object. The Execute method has the following syntax:

*object.***Execute** *source*, *options*

- The *object* must be a Database object. The Database object usually is created using the OpenDatabase method.

- The *source* is a string containing the SQL statement or the Name property value of a QueryDef object.

- The optional *options* argument contains one or more constants to determine characteristics of the statement. For more information about these constants, see the Help page for the Execute method.

Virgil suggests you first write the structure of the Do loop to read the input, test the loop, then write the INSERT statement to insert each record into the appropriate database table. You will need to declare two local variables to hold the two fields from the ASCII file. The input file is stored in the file named Paymast.txt in the Tutorial.07 folder on your Student Disk.

To write the structure of the Do loop to read the ASCII-delimited input file:

1. Activate the Code window to the Click event procedure for the menu item named **mnuPayrollReadASCIIFile** on the form named **frmPaymasterPayroll**.

2. Enter the following statements, shown in bold, into the Code window:
```
Private Sub mnuPayrollReadASCIIFile_Click( )
    Dim pstrEmployeeID As String
    Dim psngHoursWorked As Single
    Open "A:\Tutorial.07\Paymast.txt" For Input As #1
    Do Until EOF(1)
        Input #1, pstrEmployeeID, psngHoursWorked
    Loop
    Close #1
End Sub
```

Because the input file contains the two fields (Employee ID and Hours Worked), you declared two variables to hold the information. Employee ID is a string and the Hours Worked is a number that may contain a decimal point. The Do loop reads the input file into the two variables until the end-of-file is reached. The next step in the process is to write the necessary code to create the INSERT statement. When you create an INSERT statement in Visual Basic, you first must store the INSERT statement into a String variable then use that variable as an argument to the Execute method. Storing the INSERT statement into the String variable requires that you concatenate each part of the INSERT statement together until the string is built.

For this INSERT statement, you are inserting three fields into the table named tblPayroll. The first field, fldEmployeeID, is a string. The second field, fldHoursWorked, is a Single data type. The third field, fldDatePaid, is a Date data type. Remember that when you use an INSERT statement to insert a string, the string must be enclosed in single quotation marks. When you insert a date, the date must be enclosed in pound signs. The following code segment shows how to create the string to insert a record into the table named tblPayroll:

```
pstrSQL = "INSERT INTO tblPayroll " & _
    "(fldEmployeeID,fldHoursWorked,fldDatePaid)" & _
    " VALUES ('" & pstrEmployeeID & "'" & "," & _
    psngHoursWorked & "," & "#" & pdatDatePaid & "#" & ")"
```

Notice that the local variable is named pstrSQL. The word SQL in all capital letters may seem to violate the standard naming conventions of capitalizing the first character of each word. SQL keywords, however, always appear in capital letters so this convention is used in variable names.

The most difficult part of executing an SQL statement from Visual Basic is creating the String variable to hold the SQL statement to be executed. Because the string can become quite long, you either must use continuation lines so each line will fit into the Code window, or use several assignment statements to build the string. Which to use is a matter of personal choice. When the number of continuation lines exceeds four or five, however, consider using multiple assignment statements to improve readability. The first line contains the INSERT statement followed by the required table name (tblPayroll). The next line contains the field names in the table. Note that the field names are enclosed in parentheses. The next three lines require careful examination. Because the field, pstrEmployeeID, is a text string, the value must be enclosed in single quotation marks. These characters must be inserted manually into the string. If the value of pstrEmployeeID had the value A12345, then the following code segment—

```
" VALUES ('" & pstrEmployeeID & "'"
```

—will produce the following string:

```
VALUES ('A12345'
```

The next line concatenates to the string the value of psngHoursWorked. Because this is a number, it must not be surrounded by quotation marks. This is true for all types of numbers.

The final line builds the part of the text string to store the date paid. Because the data type of this field is a Date, pound signs must enclose the value. If the value of the variable pdatDatePaid were 2/23/99, then the following code segment—

```
"#" & pdatDatePaid & "#"
```

—will produce the following string:

```
#2/23/99#
```

Thus, if the value of pstrEmployeeID was A12345, the value of psngHoursWorked was 30, and the value of pdatDatePaid was 2/23/99, the value of the String variable pstrSQL would be:

```
INSERT INTO tblPayroll _
    (fldEmployeeID,fldHoursWorked,fldDatePaid)_
    VALUES ('A12345',30,#2/23/99#)
```

Note that this string was formatted on multiple lines but is stored as a continuous string of characters in the String variable.

REFERENCE window

CREATING AN INSERT STATEMENT

- Declare a String variable to hold the INSERT statement.
- Store in the variable the INSERT INTO keyword, followed by the table name, followed by the field names enclosed in parentheses, and separated by commas.
- Append the VALUES clause followed by the values enclosed in parentheses. For the Text data type, enclose the string in single quotation marks. For numeric data, omit the single quotation marks. For the Date data type, enclose the value in pound signs.
- Call the Execute method of a Database object with one argument—the String variable containing the INSERT statement.

Now that you know how to create the String variable containing the INSERT statement, you can enter the code in the Do loop you already wrote. After creating the String variable, you need to call the Execute method of the Database object to execute the INSERT statement. The INSERT statement will create a new record with three fields— Employee ID, Hours Worked, and Date Paid. The Employee ID and Hours Worked fields are stored in the variables used in the Input # statement. Virgil wants the Date Paid field to be specified by the user using an input box.

To write the statements to build the INSERT statement and call the Execute method:

1. Activate the Code window to the Click event procedure for the menu item named **mnuPayrollReadASCIIFile** on the form named **frmPaymasterPayroll**.

2. Enter the following statements, shown in bold, in the Code window:

```
Dim pstrEmployeeID As String
Dim psngHoursWorked As Single
Dim pdatDatePaid As String
Dim pstrSQL As String
pdatDatePaid = InputBox("Enter date paid", _
    "Paymaster", Date)
Open "A:\Tutorial.07\Paymast.txt" For Input As #1
Do Until EOF(1)
    Input #1, pstrEmployeeID, psngHoursWorked
    pstrSQL = "INSERT INTO tblPayroll " & _
        "(fldEmployeeID,fldHoursWorked,fldDatePaid)" & _
        " VALUES ('" & pstrEmployeeID & "'" & "," & _
        psngHoursWorked & "," & _
        "#" & pdatDatePaid & "#" & ")"
    dbPaymaster.Execute pstrSQL
Loop
```

Each time a record is read from the text input file named Paymast.txt and stored in the two variables, the string pstrSQL is built containing the correct INSERT statement. Once the statement is built, the Execute method is called using the Execute method on the open database. The Execute method requires one argument—a string containing the statement to be executed.

You now should verify that the records in the text file were read correctly. Virgil created a form using the Data Form Wizard to view records in the table, tblPayroll. You should use that form to verify that each record was read correctly.

To verify that the file Payroll.txt was read correctly:

1. Save the project then run it.

2. Click **Payroll** then click **Read ASCII File** on the main form's menu bar.

3. When the input box appears, click **OK**. Note that the current date should be in the input box.

4. On the main form click **View** then **Payroll Form** on the menu bar to open the payroll form. Scroll through the records and be sure that records appear having the current date.

5. End the program.

Now that you have inserted the Employee ID, Hours Worked, and Date Paid fields into the Payroll table, you need to compute the gross pay, payroll taxes, and net pay from the information you just read. This can be accomplished using the UPDATE statement.

Updating Database Records with the UPDATE Statement

The UPDATE statement is used to change one or more rows from one or more columns in a table or query. Consider a situation where you need to change the contents of several records in a table. You could create a Recordset object and a corresponding Do loop to examine each record in the recordset. Each time you wanted to change the contents of a field, you would need to call the Edit method of a recordset, set the field contents, and call the Update method on the Recordset object.

While this method will work, there is another way using the relational model. You can write an SQL UPDATE statement that will update many rows using the same statement. The UPDATE statement has the following syntax:

UPDATE *tablename*

    SET *fieldname* = *newvalue*[, *fieldname* = *newvalue*] ...

- The *tablename* is the name of an existing table or query.

- The *fieldname* is a field from the table or query specified by *tablename*.

- The *newvalue* can be a literal value or expression.

The expression in an UPDATE statement looks like an assignment statement. That is, it has a left-hand side and a right-hand side. The left-hand side contains the name of a field in the table or query. The right-hand side is a combination of field names, properties, literal values, or variables that evaluate to a single value. Figure 7-13 shows examples of valid expressions given the fields fldGrossPay (a number), fldEmployeeID (a string), and fldDatePaid (a date).

Figure 7-13 ◀
Expressions in
an UPDATE
statement

Expression	Description
fldEmployeeID = 'A1234'	Sets the value of the field named fldEmployeeID to the string "A1234".
fldEmployeeID = 'A' & '1234'	Produces the same result as the last expression using string concatenation.
fldTaxWithheld = 24.23	Sets the value of the field fldTaxWithheld to the value 24.23.
fldTaxWithheld = fldGrossPay * .20	Sets the value of the field fldTaxWithheld to the value of the field fldGrossPay * the constant value .20.
fldTaxWithheld = fldGrossPay * fldTaxRate	Sets the value of the field fldTaxWithheld to the value of the field fldGrossPay * the value stored in the field fldTaxRate.
fldDatePaid = #7/22/99#	Sets the value of the field fldDatePaid to the date value 7/22/99.

The first step to compute the payroll was to load the information from the text file. Now you need to use that information to compute the gross pay, taxes withheld, and the net pay. To compute the gross pay, you need to multiply the hourly rate by the hours worked. To compute the tax withheld, you need to multiply the gross pay by the tax rate. Finally, to compute the net pay, you need to subtract the taxes withheld from the gross pay. These fields are not all in the same table, however, so Virgil already has created a query. Figure 7-14 shows the tables used in the query.

Figure 7-14 ◀
Paymaster
query

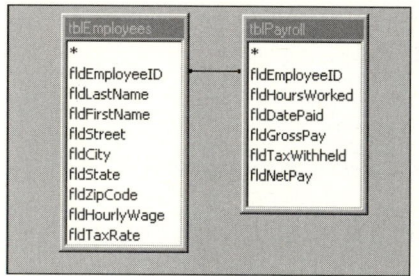

For more information about queries refer to the Database Appendix. The UPDATE statement works much like the INSERT statement you just used. First, the UPDATE statement performs an action query. That is, it updates fields in a table rather than selecting rows from a table and returning them as a Recordset object. But the UPDATE statement operates on many rows rather than on a single row. When you used a recordset, you performed operations inside a Do loop once for each record in a recordset. When you use an UPDATE statement, it selects all the rows to update and then performs the specified operation on each row selected. Figure 7-15 shows how the UPDATE statement works.

Figure 7-15 ◀
How the
UPDATE
statement
works

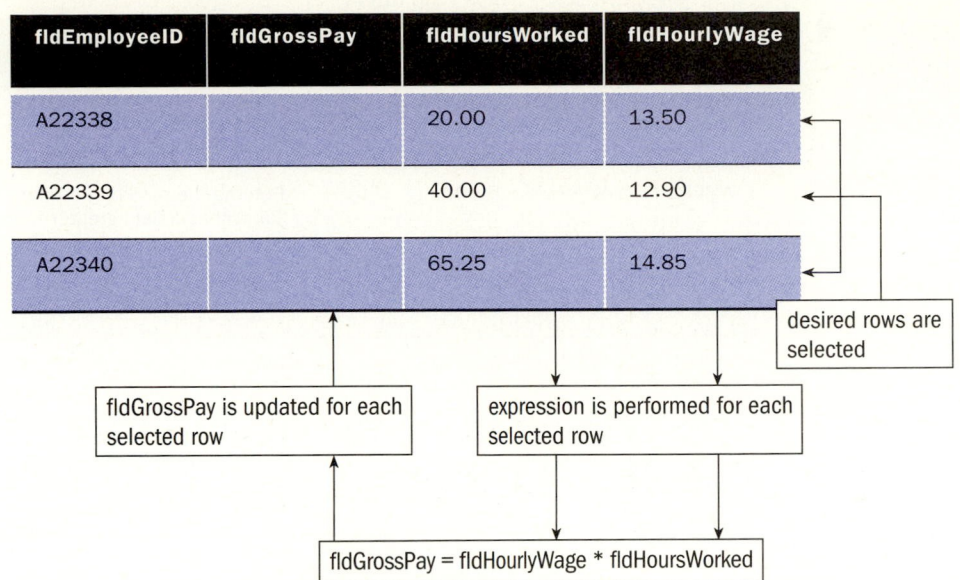

You use the UPDATE statement by creating a string, then using that string as an argument to the Execute method. The following code segment shows the statement to build the string that will update the field named fldGrossPay by multiplying fldHourlyWage by fldHoursWorked for every record in the query named qryEmployeesPayroll.

```
Dim pstrSQL As String
pstrSQL = "UPDATE qryEmployeesPayroll " & _
    "SET fldGrossPay = fldHourlyWage * fldHoursWorked"
```

The first argument of the UPDATE statement represents the table or query to be updated. The expression after the SET statement is the *value* part of the UPDATE statement, which is an expression. The expression multiplies the fldHourlyWage by fldHoursWorked and stores the result in fldGrossPay. This action is performed for every row in qryEmployeesPayroll rather than on a single row. You want to compute the payroll only for the records you just added, however. Remember that each record in tblPayroll has a Date Paid field. You need to use this field in the UPDATE statement to restrict the rows that are updated to a specific date. You can accomplish this task using a WHERE clause. A WHERE clause contains an expression much like the expression in an IF statement. That is, the expression evaluates to True or False. A WHERE clause has the syntax:

WHERE *conditionlist*

■ The *conditionlist* has the syntax:

fieldname operator value

- ■ The *fieldname* is the name of a field from the table or query used in the SELECT statement.

- ■ The *operator* works like the operator in an If statement's condition.

- ■ The *value* can be a variable, property, or literal value. If the value is a date, then the value must be enclosed in pound signs (#). If the value is a string, then it must be enclosed in single quotation marks (').

- ■ Multiple conditions can be concatenated together using the **And** and **Or** statements.

When used in an UPDATE statement, the expression is tested for every row in the table or query. If the expression is True, then the record is updated as described by the SET part of the UPDATE statement. If the expression is False then the record is ignored. Figure 7-16 shows samples of different WHERE clauses.

Figure 7-16 ◀
Expressions in
a WHERE
clause

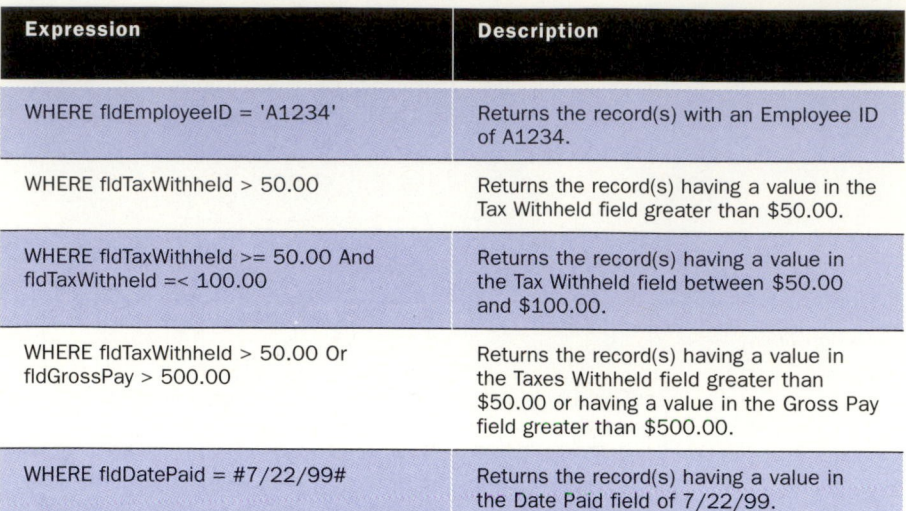

Expression	Description
WHERE fldEmployeeID = 'A1234'	Returns the record(s) with an Employee ID of A1234.
WHERE fldTaxWithheld > 50.00	Returns the record(s) having a value in the Tax Withheld field greater than $50.00.
WHERE fldTaxWithheld >= 50.00 And fldTaxWithheld =< 100.00	Returns the record(s) having a value in the Tax Withheld field between $50.00 and $100.00.
WHERE fldTaxWithheld > 50.00 Or fldGrossPay > 500.00	Returns the record(s) having a value in the Taxes Withheld field greater than $50.00 or having a value in the Gross Pay field greater than $500.00.
WHERE fldDatePaid = #7/22/99#	Returns the record(s) having a value in the Date Paid field of 7/22/99.

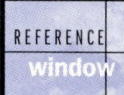

REFERENCE
window

CREATING AN UPDATE STATEMENT

- Declare a String variable to hold the UPDATE statement.
- Store in the variable the UPDATE keyword, followed by the table name, followed by the SET keyword.
- Append an expression to the SET keyword.
- Append a WHERE clause, if necessary.
- Call the Execute method of a Database object with one argument—the String variable containing the UPDATE statement.

Virgil suggests you create the UPDATE statement to update the gross pay for each payroll record you just read when you executed the INSERT statement. To accomplish this, you need to create a variable containing the correct UPDATE statement with a WHERE clause to restrict the rows updated to those rows that were just loaded.

To write the UPDATE statement to compute the gross pay:

1. Activate the Code window to the Click event procedure for the menu item named **mnuPayrollComputePayroll** for the form named **frmPaymasterPayroll**.

2. Enter the following statements, shown in bold, in the Code window:

```
Dim pstrSQL As String
Dim pstrDatePaid As String
pstrDatePaid = InputBox("Enter date paid", _
    "Paymaster", Date)

pstrSQL = "UPDATE qryEmployeesPayroll " & _
    "SET fldGrossPay = " & _
    "fldHourlyWage * fldHoursWorked " & _
    " WHERE fldDatePaid = " & "#" & _
    pstrDatePaid & "#"
dbPaymaster.Execute pstrSQL
```

These statements declare the String variable used as the argument to the Execute method and another String variable to hold the date paid. After the string representing the SQL statement is completed, the Execute method is called.

```
pstrSQL = "UPDATE qryEmployeesPayroll " & _
    "SET fldGrossPay = " & _
    "fldHourlyWage * fldHoursWorked" & _
    " WHERE fldDatePaid = " & "#" & _
    pstrDatePaid & "#"
```

This UPDATE statement updates the column fldGrossPay in the query qryEmployeesPayroll by multiplying the column fldHourlyWage by the column fldHoursWorked. Only those records having a date paid matching the value specified will be updated. Virgil suggests you now verify that the UPDATE statement worked correctly.

To verify that the UPDATE statement updated the proper values:

1. Save the program then start it.

2. Click **Payroll** then click **Compute Payroll** on the main form's menu bar.

3. Click **OK** in the input box to use the current date.

4. Click **View** then **Payroll Form** on the menu bar. Scroll through the records on the form and be sure that the gross pay has been computed for each of the three employees.

5. End the program.

The UPDATE statement you just wrote updates the Gross Pay field, but the Taxes Withheld and Net Pay fields also need to be computed. To accomplish this, you need to write two more UPDATE statements in the same event procedure to change the contents of these fields.

The taxes withheld are computed by multiplying the gross pay (computed in the last step) by the tax rate. The net pay is computed by subtracting the taxes withheld from the gross pay. Virgil suggests that you write these statements now.

To write the UPDATE statement to compute the taxes withheld and the net pay:

1. Activate the Code window to the Click event procedure for the menu item named **mnuPayrollComputePayroll** in the form named **frmPaymasterPayroll**.

2. Append the following statements, shown in bold, to the event procedure just before the End Sub statement:

```
pstrSQL = "UPDATE qryEmployeesPayroll " & _
    " SET fldTaxWithheld = " & _
    "fldGrossPay * fldTaxRate" & _
    " WHERE fldDatePaid = " & "#" & _
    pstrDatePaid & "#"
dbPaymaster.Execute pstrSQL

pstrSQL = "UPDATE qryEmployeesPayroll " & _
    " SET fldNetPay = fldGrossPay - fldTaxWithheld" & _
    " WHERE fldDatePaid = " & "#" & _
    pstrDatePaid & "#"
dbPaymaster.Execute pstrSQL
```

These UPDATE statements update the fields fldTaxWithheld and fldNetPay for those records having the same date paid as specified by the user.

```
pstrSQL = "UPDATE qryEmployeesPayroll " & _
    " SET fldTaxWithheld = " & _
    "fldGrossPay * fldTaxRate" & _
    " WHERE fldDatePaid = " & "#" & _
    pstrDatePaid & "#"
dbPaymaster.Execute pstrSQL
```

This UPDATE statement multiplies fldGrossPay by fldTaxRate and stores the result in the field fldTaxWithheld. Only those records where the value of the field fldDatePaid is the same as the variable pstrDatePaid are updated. Because the field fldDatePaid is a Date data type, the value of the variable pstrDatePaid must be enclosed by pound signs (#). Once the UPDATE statement is built and stored in the string pstrSQL, the Execute method is called and the records in the database query are updated.

The second UPDATE statement is identical to the first but fldTaxWithheld is subtracted from fldGrossPay to compute fldNetPay. Virgil suggests you now run the program again to test the two new UPDATE statements.

To verify the UPDATE statement updated the proper values:

1. Save the program then start it.

2. Click **Payroll** then **Compute Payroll** on the main form.

3. Click **OK** in the input box to use the current date.

4. Click **View** then **Payroll Form** on the menu bar to open the form displaying the payroll records. Scroll through the records on the form and be sure the Tax Withheld and Net Pay fields have been computed for each of the employees.

5. End the program.

In addition to updating records in a table or query using an SQL statement, you also can delete records.

Removing Database Records with the DELETE Statement

The DELETE statement allows you to remove one or more rows from a table. Again, you could create a recordset and call the Delete method for each record you want to delete, but you can call the DELETE statement once to remove several records just like you can call the UPDATE statement once to update several records. The syntax of the DELETE statement is:

DELETE *

    FROM *tableexpression*

    WHERE *criteria*

- The *tableexpression* is the name of the table from which records are deleted.

- The *criteria* is an expression that determines which records to delete and has the same format as the WHERE clause in the UPDATE statement. That is, the expression contained in criteria must evaluate to True or False. If True, then the record is deleted. If False, the record is ignored.

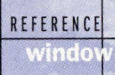

REFERENCE window	**CREATING A DELETE STATEMENT**
	▪ Declare a String variable to hold the DELETE statement. ▪ Store in the variable the DELETE keyword, followed by an asterisk (*), followed by the FROM keyword. ▪ Append the table name to the statement. ▪ Append a WHERE clause, if necessary. ▪ Call the Execute method of a Database object with one argument—the String variable containing the DELETE statement.

The length of time Paymaster maintains payroll information in the database depends on the customer. Each month, they back up the database, then they delete obsolete payroll records from the table named tblPayroll. Virgil would like you to write the necessary DELETE statement to remove those payroll records that were entered on the same date specified by the user in an input box. To accomplish this, you will write a DELETE statement in a String variable. Because the DELETE statement performs an action query rather than returning rows in a recordset, you will call the Execute method of the Database object like you did for the UPDATE and INSERT statements.

To delete obsolete payroll records from the database:

1. Activate the Code window to the Click event procedure for the menu item named **mnuPayrollDeleteOldPayroll** on the form named **frmPaymasterPayroll**.

2. Enter the following statements, shown in bold, to the event procedure:

```
Dim pstrSQL As String
Dim pstrDatePaid As String

pstrDatePaid = InputBox("Enter date paid", _
    "Paymaster", Date)
pstrSQL = "DELETE * FROM tblPayroll " & _
    " WHERE fldDatePaid = " & _
    "#" & pstrDatePaid & "#"
dbPaymaster.Execute pstrSQL
```

After declaring local variables to hold the SQL string containing the DELETE statement and the date paid entered by the user, you called the InputBox function to get the correct date from the user. Then, you built the string containing the DELETE statement. This statement will delete all the records from the table tblPayroll where the value of the field named fldDatePaid is less than or equal to the date paid value entered by the user. Virgil suggests you now test these statements to be sure the DELETE statement is working correctly.

To test the DELETE statement:

1. Save the program then start it.

2. Click **Payroll** then **Delete Old Payroll** on the menu bar.

3. Click **OK** in the input box to select the current date.

4. All the payroll records you created in the previous steps should have been deleted. Click **View** then click **Payroll Form** to verify this has happened.

5. End the program.

Your program now performs all tasks necessary to insert records into a table from an ASCII file. The program then uses an UPDATE statement to compute the gross pay, withholding taxes, and the net pay. It also has a feature to delete old payroll records.

Quick Check

1. What is the difference between DDL and DML?

2. What two actions can occur as a result of a DML statement?

3. Write an INSERT statement to INSERT the fields fldID, fldLastName, and fldDateAdded into the table named tblNames. Use the values 1, "Ike Smith", and 8/12/99 as the value for each field, respectively.

4. What is the purpose of the Execute method of the Database object?

5. Write an UPDATE statement to update the field fldHoursWorked to the value 40 in the table tblPayroll where the field fldID is equal to 123.

6. What is the purpose of a WHERE clause?

7. Write a DELETE statement to delete the records from the table named tblPeople where the field fldDateChanged is less than March 23, 1999.

You have completed this session. You may now quit Visual Basic or proceed to the next session.

SESSION 7.3

In this session you will learn how to use an SQL statement that returns a recordset rather than performing an action.

The SELECT Statement

The SELECT statement is used to retrieve a set of records from a database and can be used to retrieve records from multiple tables or queries. When you use a SELECT statement with a database like Microsoft Access, you can type the statement into one window and view the results of those statements into another window. When you use the SELECT statement with Visual Basic, however, the SELECT statement is used as an argument to the OpenRecordset method. When the OpenRecordset method is called, the SELECT statement is executed and the resultant rows are retrieved and stored in a Recordset object. This is the same type of object that the Data control has been creating for you. You can scroll through the records and make changes to a recordset by calling the recordset's methods as you have done in the past.

The SELECT statement has several different parts. Rather than examining the entire syntax of the statement, you will learn how to use it in its simplest form, then write more complex SELECT statements using the different options. The basic syntax for the SELECT statement is:

SELECT *

    FROM *tableexpression*

- The * indicates that every field from the table should be selected.

- The *tableexpression* can be an existing table or query name.

This form of the SELECT statement will retrieve all the records from a table or query using all the fields in the table or query. To use a SELECT statement in Visual Basic, you enclose the statement in a String variable. Then, you use that String variable as an argument to the OpenRecordset method instead of an existing table or query name. This process is just like the one you used to create INSERT, UPDATE, and DELETE statements. The first step is to create the actual SELECT statement and store it in a String variable. If you wanted to select all the rows from the query named qryEmployeesPayroll, you would write the SELECT statement and store it in a variable using the following syntax:

```
pstrSQL = "SELECT * FROM qryEmployeesPayroll"
```

Because the SELECT statement you will write in this session will consist of many different clauses, Virgil suggests you write the statement so each individual clause is stored in a separate String variable. Once all the different clauses are created, you can concatenate them into the String variable containing the entire SELECT statement.

You will need a variable to store the completed SELECT statement, another to store the FROM clause, and another to hold the individual fields selected by the user. You also need a local variable to store the recordset that will be opened when the OpenRecordset method is called. You have used the OpenRecordset method with one argument—a table name—to open a recordset. Instead of using an existing table or query name as an argument, however, you use a String variable containing the SELECT statement. Each Recordset object has a place in the DAO hierarchy. Each Database object contains a Recordsets collection. For each open recordset, there is an object in the Recordsets collection. Figure 7-17 shows the relationship between the Recordsets collection and the Recordset object in the DAO hierarchy.

Figure 7-17 ◀
Relationship between Recordsets collection and Recordset object

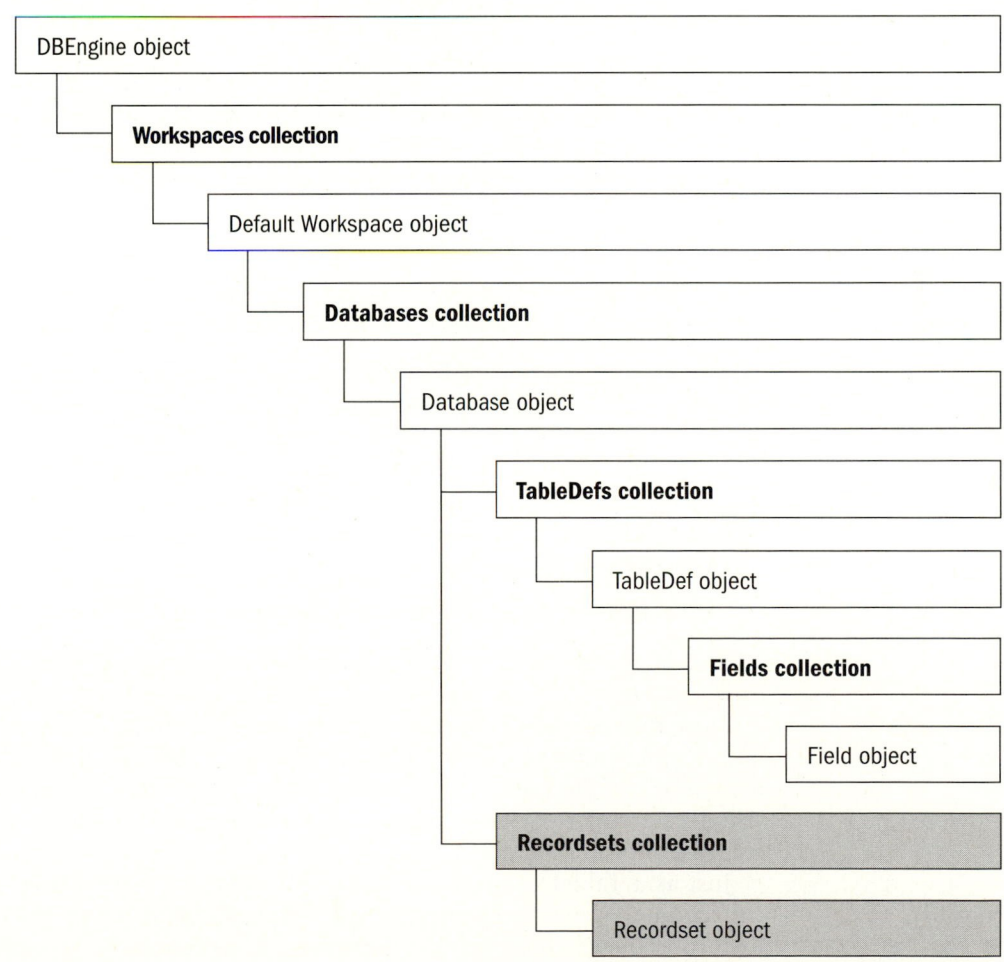

Your first step will be to develop a simple version of the SELECT statement to select all the fields from the query named qryEmployeesPayroll.

To create a Recordset object using an SQL statement:

1. Open the Code window to the **cmdSelect_Click** event procedure on the form named **frmPaymasterSelect**, then enter the following statements, shown in bold.

```
Private Sub cmdSelect_Click( )
    Dim pstrSQL As String
    Dim pstrFROM As String
    Dim pstrFields As String
    Dim prstCurrent As Recordset

    pstrFields = " *"
    pstrFROM = " FROM qryEmployeesPayroll"

    pstrSQL = "SELECT" & pstrFields & pstrFROM
    Set prstCurrent = dbPaymaster.OpenRecordset(pstrSQL)
End Sub
```

These statements declare the String variables to store the SELECT statement and the necessary information in the variables for each clause, then open a recordset.

```
Dim pstrSQL As String
Dim pstrFROM As String
Dim pstrFields As String
Dim prstCurrent As Recordset
```

The first statement declares the variable pstrSQL to hold the completed string for the SELECT statement. The variable pstrFROM will hold the FROM clause and pstrFields will hold the fields selected by the user. The object variable prstCurrent will be used to reference the open recordset.

```
pstrFields = " *"
pstrFROM = " FROM qryEmployeesPayroll"
pstrSQL = "SELECT" & pstrFields & pstrFROM
```

These three statements build the SELECT statement. For the first version, you are selecting all the fields from the query so you used the asterisk (*) character instead of specifying individual fields. Notice the character is preceded by a space. This is necessary to insert a space between the SELECT statement and the fields. The next statement builds the FROM clause. You are selecting records from the query named qryEmployeesPayroll. The next statement concatenates the SELECT statement to the fields to the FROM clause. The variable pstrSQL contains the text:

```
SELECT * FROM qryEmployeesPayroll
```

The final statement opens the recordset and stores a reference to it in the variable prstCurrent.

Once the recordset is opened, each record needs to be displayed into the multiline text box. Virgil wants the information arranged in columns so the data in each field is easy to read. Because the user will be able to select a different combination of fields to display, you need a way to determine both the number of fields and the name of each field in the recordset at run time.

Just as a TableDef object has a Fields collection, a Recordset object also has a Fields collection that works the same way. That is, there is one Fields collection for each Recordset object. That Fields collection contains zero (0) or more Field objects identifying the field name, its size, and its data type. Figure 7-18 shows the relationship between the Fields collection and Field object, and their relationship to the DAO hierarchy.

Figure 7-18 ◀
Relationship
between Fields
collection and
Field object

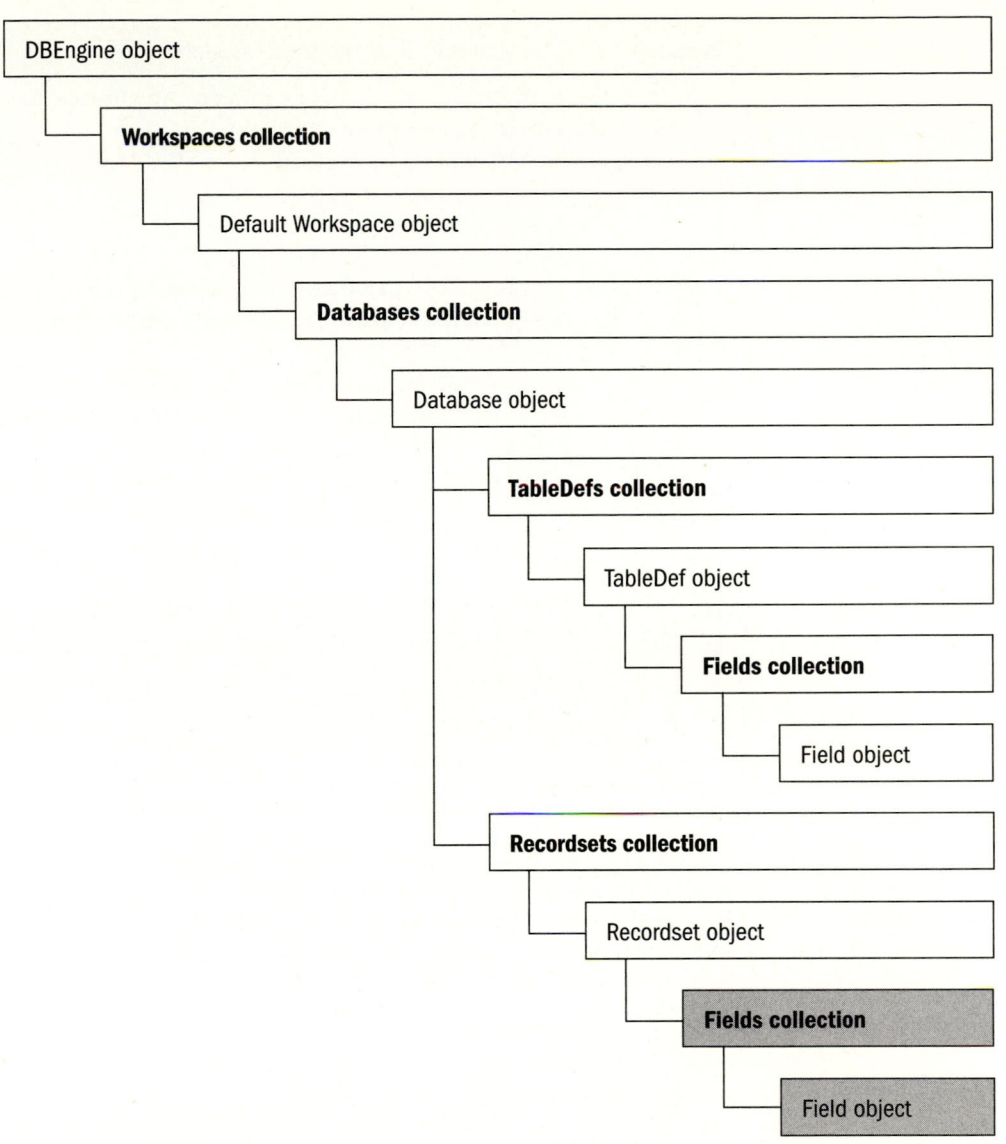

For fields containing textual data, Virgil wants the width of a column to be the same as the size of the field (stored in the Size property of the Field object). For numeric fields, the column width should be 15 spaces. Fifteen spaces will be adequate to display the field names and the data.

Virgil wants the first line of the text box to display the field names selected by the user. Under the field names each record will be displayed. The first step is to examine the Fields collection of the Recordset object. For each field, you need to print the field name in a column. Because you are examining each item in a collection, you can write a For Each loop. To make the program as modular as possible, and to minimize the size of the event procedure for the Select Records command button, you will create a general procedure to print the titles. The procedure will take one argument—the active recordset whose fields you want to print.

To print the column titles:

1. Be sure the Code window is active for the form named **frmPaymasterSelect.**

2. Click **Tools** then **Add Procedure**. Set the procedure name to **PrintFields,** the type to **Sub,** and the Scope to **Private**. Click **OK** to close the dialog box.

3. Enter the following statements into the procedure:

```
Private Sub PrintFields(prstArg As Recordset)
    Dim pfldCurrent As Field
    Dim pstrLine As String
    Dim pintSpaces As Integer
    Dim pintCounter As Integer

    For Each pfldCurrent In prstArg.Fields
        pstrLine = pstrLine & pfldCurrent.Name

        If pfldCurrent.Type <> dbText Then
            pintSpaces = 15 - Len(pfldCurrent.Name)
        Else
            pintSpaces = pfldCurrent.Size - _
                Len(pfldCurrent.Name)
        End If

        For pintCounter = 0 To pintSpaces
            pstrLine = pstrLine + " "
        Next
    Next
    txtSQLOutput = pstrLine & vbCrLf
End Sub
```

These statements examine each field in the Fields collection of the Recordset object passed as an argument to the Sub procedure. For each Field object in the collection, the data type is determined. If the data type is Text, the width of the column is set to the number of characters in the string. Otherwise, it is set exactly to 15 characters.

```
Dim pfldCurrent As Field
Dim pstrLine As String
Dim pintSpaces As Integer
Dim pintCounter As Integer
```

The variable pfldCurrent is declared as a field object used to reference each field in the Fields collection. The variable pstrLine will contain the line for the column names displayed in the multiline text box. Variables pintSpaces and pintCounter will be used in a For loop to insert the correct number of spaces in the column.

```
For Each pfldCurrent In prstArg.Fields
```

The For Each loop steps through each Field object in the recordset's Fields collection. Each time through the loop the variable pfldCurrent is set to the current Field object. When there are no more fields in the Fields collection, the loop will terminate.

```
pstrLine = pstrLine & pfldCurrent.Name
```

Inside the For Each loop, the name of the current field, stored in the Name property of the Field object named pfldCurrent, is appended to the string containing the line. Thus, the field name will appear as a title for the column.

```
If pfldCurrent.Type <> dbText Then
    pintSpaces = 15 - Len(pfldCurrent.Name)
Else
    pintSpaces = pfldCurrent.Size - _
        Len(pfldCurrent.Name)
End If
```

Then, the type of the field is determined using an If statement. The field's type is stored in the Type property of the Field object. This value is compared against the intrinsic constant dbText. If the field's type is not Text then the variable pintSpaces is set to 15 minus the length of the column name. These spaces will be appended to the column name so the column uses exactly 15 characters. If the field contains text, then the size of the field is used as the column width. The length of the field is subtracted from the size of the fields to determine the number of spaces to append to the column to make it the correct width.

```
For pintCounter = 0 To pintSpaces
        pstrLine = pstrLine & " "
    Next
Next
```

Once the number of spaces to append to the column has been determined, the correct number of spaces must be appended to the line containing the column names. This was accomplished using a For loop to count the number of spaces then appending them to the line.

```
txtSQLOutput = pstrLine & vbCrLf
```

The final statement in the procedure stores the line containing the column names into the text box txtSQLOutput. The default property for a text box is Text, so the property name does not need to be specified.

> *Tip:* The default property for a text box is Text. Use the default property
> to reduce typing and improve the performance of the statement.

It is important to note that instead of using the variable pstrLine to create the line, you could have stored each string into the text box individually. It is considerably faster to store values in variables than properties, however.

> *Tip:* When you are using the value of a property frequently, create a
> variable of the proper type and read or write data to the property
> only when necessary to improve performance.

Now that the Sub procedure is written to print the column headings, you need to call the procedure when the Select Records command button is clicked and test the program.

To call the Sub procedure to print the column titles:

1. Open the Code window to the **cmdSelect_Click** event procedure then enter the following statements, shown in bold, just before the End Sub statement:

```
PrintFields prstCurrent
```

2. Save the project then start it.

3. Click **View** then **Select Records Form** on the main form's menu bar.

4. Click the **Select Records** command button on the form to select all the payroll records. The column titles should appear as shown in Figure 7-19.

Figure 7-19 ◄
Printing
field titles

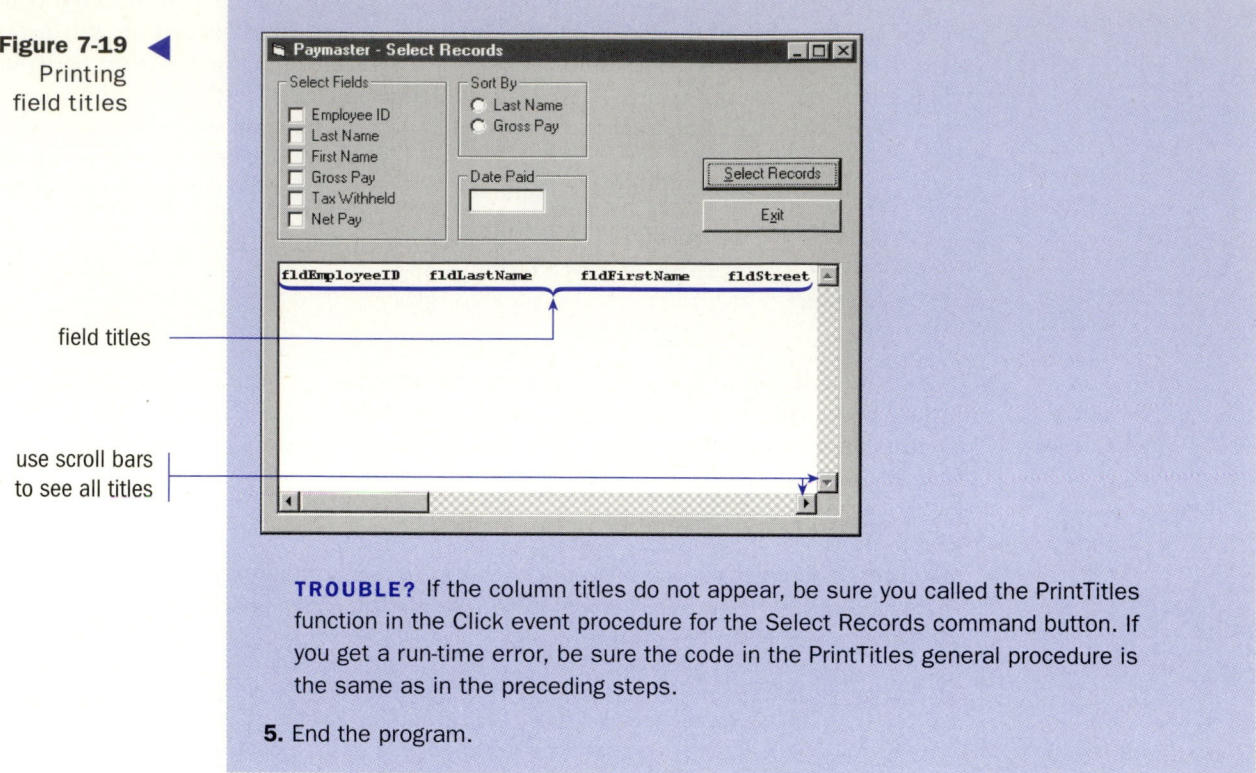

field titles ──────

use scroll bars
to see all titles ──

TROUBLE? If the column titles do not appear, be sure you called the PrintTitles function in the Click event procedure for the Select Records command button. If you get a run-time error, be sure the code in the PrintTitles general procedure is the same as in the preceding steps.

5. End the program.

Now that the columns are displayed in the text box, you need to create another loop to print each of the records in the recordset. To do this, you need to create a Do loop to look at each record. For each record, each field in the recordset's Fields collection must be printed. This loop will be very similar to the one you just created. To keep the Click event procedure for the Select Records command button small, you will create another general procedure to print this information.

To print the column titles:

1. Be sure the Code window is active for the form named **frmPaymasterSelect**.

2. Click **Tools** then **Add Procedure**. Set the procedure name to **PrintRecords**, the type to **Sub**, and the Scope to **Private**. Click **OK** to close the dialog box.

3. Enter the following statements into the procedure:

```
Private Sub PrintRecords(prstArg As Recordset)

    Dim pfldCurrent As Field
    Dim pstrLine As String
    Dim pintSpaces As Integer
    Dim pintCounter As Integer

    Do Until prstArg.EOF

        For Each pfldCurrent In prstArg.Fields
            pstrLine = pstrLine & pfldCurrent
```

```
                        If pfldCurrent.Type <> dbText Then
                            pintSpaces = 15 - Len(pfldCurrent)
                        Else
                            pintSpaces = pfldCurrent.Size - _
                                Len(pfldCurrent)
                        End If

                        For pintCounter = 0 To pintSpaces
                            pstrLine = pstrLine & " "
                        Next
                    Next
                    txtSQLOutput = txtSQLOutput & pstrLine & vbCrLf
                    pstrLine = ""

                    prstArg.MoveNext
                Loop
            End Sub
```

4. Enter the following statement into the **cmdSelect_Click** event procedure just before the End Sub statement:

```
PrintRecords prstCurrent
```

Like the For Each loop you just wrote, this loop steps through each field in the current recordset and prints the contents of the field. This is done for each record in the recordset. The variables used in this general procedure are the same as for the general procedure you just wrote.

```
Do Until prstArg.EOF
```

This Do loop is the main loop for the procedure. The variable prstArg represents the recordset created by the OpenRecordset method and the SELECT statement. This recordset is passed as an argument to the procedure. The loop will examine each record in the recordset.

```
For Each pfldCurrent In prstArg.Fields
```

Each Recordset object has a Fields collection. This For Each loop examines each Field object in the Fields collection (stored as a collection in the Recordset object). The Field object is stored in the variable pfldCurrent.

```
pstrLine = pstrLine & pfldCurrent
```

The variable pstrLine is the string containing the line that will be displayed in the text box. This statement appends to the line the contents of the current field. The default property of the Field object is the Value property or the contents of the field. You could use the syntax pfldCurrent.Value, but using the default property will make the program run faster and reduce typing.

```
If pfldCurrent.Type <> dbText Then
    pintSpaces = 15 - Len(pfldCurrent)
Else
    pintSpaces = pfldCurrent.Size - _
        Len(pfldCurrent)
End If
```

This If statement is used to determine a column's width. If the data type of the column is Text, represented by the constant dbText, then the width of the column is the same as the width of the underlying data. If the data type is not Text, then the width of the column is 15. For each type of field, the variable pintSpaces contains the number of spaces that need to be appended to make the column widths the same.

```
For pintCounter = 0 To pintSpaces
    pstrLine = pstrLine & " "
Next
```

This For loop, using the variable pintSpaces as the counter, appends to the output line the necessary number of spaces to align the next column.

```
txtSQLOutput = txtSQLOutput & pstrLine & vbCrLf
pstrLine = " "
prstArg.MoveNext
```

These last three statements display the line stored in the variable pstrLine in the text box. Note that the line is appended to the existing text box contents, and that the line ends with a carriage return. Then, the current line (pstrLine) is reinitialized. Finally, the last statement in the loop calls the MoveNext method to locate the next record in the recordset.

Virgil again suggests you save your work and test that the recordset is locating each field, and each field is being printed.

To test that the fields are being displayed under the appropriate field titles:

1. Save the project then start it.

2. Click **View** then **Select Records Form** on the main form's menu bar.

3. Click the **Select Records** command button on the form to select all the payroll records. The column titles should appear as shown in Figure 7-20.

Figure 7-20 ◀
Printing fields

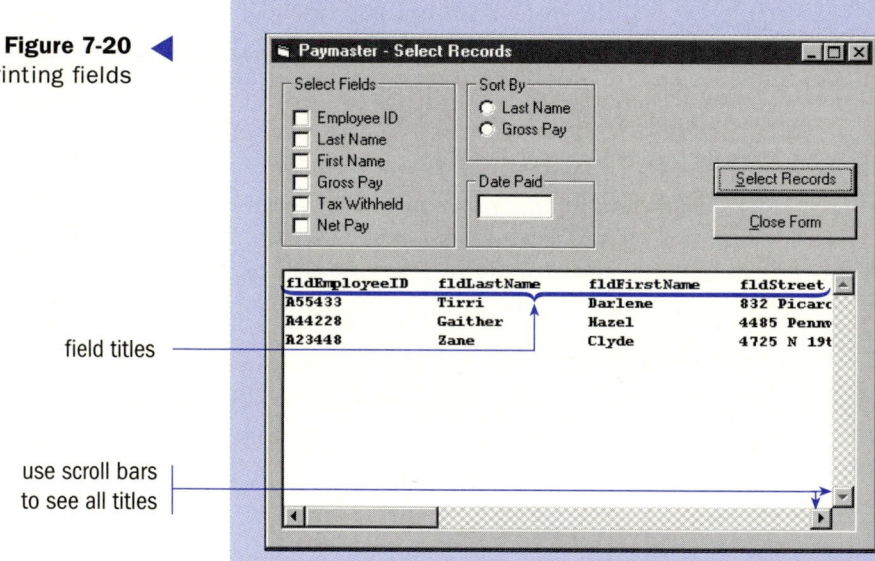

field titles

use scroll bars
to see all titles

4. End the program.

> **TROUBLE?** If the field names do not appear under the column titles, be sure that you called the PrintFields function in the Click event procedure for the Select Records command button. If you get a run-time error, be sure the code in the PrintFields general procedure is the same as in the preceding steps.

In addition to printing all the rows, Virgil wants to be able to restrict the rows displayed to a specific date paid. To accomplish this, you need to know how to use a WHERE clause with a SELECT statement.

Using the WHERE Clause with a SELECT Statement

Often, you want to limit the number of records that should be retrieved. In this case Virgil wants to give the user the ability to select only records for a specific pay period, or all the records depending on whether or not there is a value in the Date Paid text box. You can accomplish this by selecting only those records with a specific date stored in the fldDatePaid. To write this form of a SELECT statement, you need to use one of the clauses supported by the SELECT statement, known as a WHERE clause. The WHERE clause has the same syntax as it does in the UPDATE and DELETE statements. This form of the SELECT statement has the following syntax:

SELECT * **FROM** *tableexpression* [**WHERE** *conditionlist*]

- This form of the SELECT statement is identical to the last one, but with the WHERE clause added. The optional WHERE clause requires one argument—*conditionlist*. The *conditionlist* is used to restrict the number of rows returned by the SELECT statement. The *conditionlist* and WHERE clause have the same syntax as they do in the UPDATE and DELETE statements.

You now need to create a WHERE clause and append it to the SELECT statement so the user can select records for a specific date paid. Because the data in the Date field is stored as a Date data type rather than a string or number, you will need to enclose the date inside the # characters. For example, to select all the records with a date paid of 2/2/99, you would use the following syntax:

```
SELECT * FROM qryEmployeesPayroll WHERE fldDatePaid =
#2/2/99#
```

The condition looks much like the If statement you would use if you were selecting these records from an existing recordset. Instead of having to write the code to step through each record to determine if the date is correct, the SELECT statement examines each of the records for you and returns only those where the condition in the WHERE clause is True.

The SELECT statement, as it is presently written, has a limitation. While it would retrieve the records having a date paid value of 2/2/99, the user cannot select another date. The solution is to build the parts of the SELECT statement at run time, then create the recordset. Concatenating a string, like you have done in the past, does this.

To create the WHERE clause to select a specific date paid:

1. Open the Code window to the **cmdSelect_Click** event procedure then enter the following statement, shown in bold, just after the declaration for the variable pstrFROM:

   Dim pstrWHERE As String

2. Enter the following statements, shown in bold, just after the line that builds the FROM clause:

   ```
   pstrFROM = " FROM qryEmployeesPayroll"
   If txtDatePaid = "" Then
       pstrWHERE = ""
   Else
       pstrWHERE = " WHERE fldDatePaid = " & "#" & _
           txtDatePaid & "#"
   ```

```
End If
pstrSQL = "SELECT" & pstrFields & pstrFROM & _
     pstrWHERE
```

3. Save the program then start it.

4. Click **View** then **Select Records Form** on the main form's menu bar.

5. Enter **3/24/99** as the date, then click **Select Records**. Your form should look like Figure 7-21.

Figure 7-21 ◄
Printing
selected
records

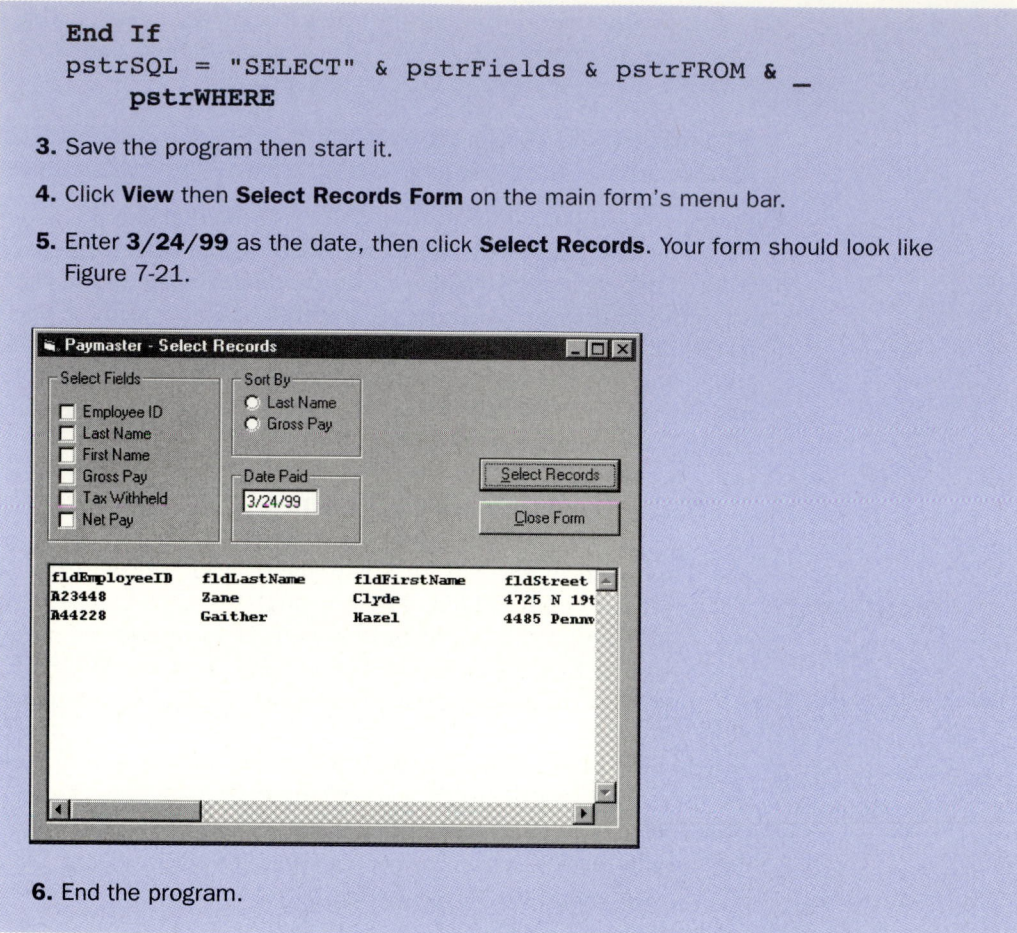

6. End the program.

The If statement determines whether or not there is a value in the text box named txtDatePaid. If there is, then the WHERE clause is created to select only records with a specific date paid. Otherwise, all records are selected. Note the WHERE clause is stored in the string pstrWHERE and appended to the statement to create the pstrSQL variable.

Creating an ORDER BY Clause to Sort Records

In addition to determining which records are returned to the recordset, you also can specify how those records are sorted. The ORDER BY clause is usually the last clause specified in the SELECT statement. The ORDER BY clause is followed by one or more field names followed by the optional keywords, ASC or DESC. If ASC is used then the records are returned in ascending sequence. If DESC is used then they are returned in descending sequence. If neither is used then ASC is assumed. If multiple field names are used then commas must separate each field. This form of the SELECT statement has the following syntax:

SELECT * **FROM** *tableexpression*

   [**WHERE** *conditionlist*]

     [**ORDER BY**] *field1* [**ASC** | **DESC**][, *field2* [**ASC** | **DESC**][, ...]]

- The ORDER BY clause accepts one or more *fields* separated by commas. Each *field* can be sorted in ascending or descending order depending on whether or not the optional **ASC** or **DESC** keywords are used. If omitted then the **ASC** option is assumed.

- If multiple fields are specified, the first field is sorted. If there are duplicate values, then the values in the second field will appear sorted.

Virgil wants the users to be able to sort the selected records, either by last name, or by the amount of gross pay for the period. To accomplish this, you need to add an ORDER BY clause to the SELECT statement you already have created. Virgil has created two option buttons on the form in the control array named optOrderBy. If the first option button is selected, you need to sort the records by the Last Name field. If the second option button is selected, you need to sort the records by the Gross Pay field.

To sort the selected records:

1. Open the Code window to the **cmdSelect_Click** event procedure, then enter the following statement, shown in bold, just after the declaration for the variable pstrWHERE.

```
Dim pstrORDERBY As String
```

2. Enter the following statement just after the If statement you just wrote and modify the statement that stores the value in the variable pstrSQL:

```
If optOrderBy(0) = True Then
    pstrORDERBY = " ORDER BY fldLastName"
Else
    pstrORDERBY = " ORDER BY fldGrossPay"
End If
pstrSQL = "SELECT" & pstrFields & pstrFROM & _
    pstrWHERE & pstrORDERBY
```

These statements cause the records returned by the SELECT statement to be in sorted order, either by last name, or by gross pay.

```
If optOrderBy(0) = True Then
    pstrORDERBY = " ORDER BY fldLastName"
Else
    pstrORDERBY = " ORDER BY fldGrossPay"
End If
```

The option group optOrderBy contains two option buttons. If the first option button is active, then the records are sorted by last name. Otherwise, they will be sorted by gross pay. The ORDER BY clause is stored in the variable pstrORDERBY and will be used in the SELECT statement.

```
pstrSQL = "SELECT" & pstrFields & pstrFROM &
    pstrWHERE _ & pstrORDERBY
```

You modified the SELECT statement to incorporate the ORDER BY clause before calling the OpenRecordset method.

Selecting Specific Fields from a Table or Query

All the SELECT statements you have written so far have retrieved all the fields from a single table. It is possible, however, to select individual fields from a table using the following version of the SELECT statement:

SELECT [*table.*]*field1* [**AS** *alias1*][, [*table.*]*field2* [**AS** *alias2*] [, ...]]

    FROM *tableexpression*

      [**WHERE...**]

- The names of the fields are specified using *field1*, *field2*, ... Each field is separated by a comma. If you include more than one field, the fields are retrieved in the order listed.

- If you want the names of the column headers to be different than the original field names, specify the AS *alias* clause.

Virgil wants you to use the check boxes he created on the form to allow the users to select all or some of the fields from the underlying query. To do this, you will need to write If statements to determine which check boxes are checked, then build a string containing a list of fields accordingly. You also will need to remove the line that stores the * character in the string strFields.

To write the statement to select specific fields from the query:

1. Open the Code window to the cmdSelect_Click event procedure.

2. Remove the following statement:

```
pstrFields = " *"
```

3. Enter the following statements, shown in bold, in place of the statement you just deleted:

```
pstrFields = " fldEmployeeID"
If chkLastName = vbChecked Then
    pstrFields = pstrFields & ",fldLastName"
End If
If chkFirstName = vbChecked Then
    pstrFields = pstrFields & ",fldFirstName"
End If
If chkGrossPay = vbChecked Then
    pstrFields = pstrFields & ",fldGrossPay"
End If
If chkTaxWithheld = vbChecked Then
    pstrFields = pstrFields & ",fldTaxWithheld"
End If
If chkNetPay = vbChecked Then
    pstrFields = pstrFields & ",fldNetPay"
End If
```

4. Save the program then start it.

5. Click **View** then **Select Records Form**.

6. Check the boxes shown in Figure 7-22, then enter the current date. Click the **Select Records** button. Your output should look like Figure 7-22.

Figure 7-22
Printing
selected fields

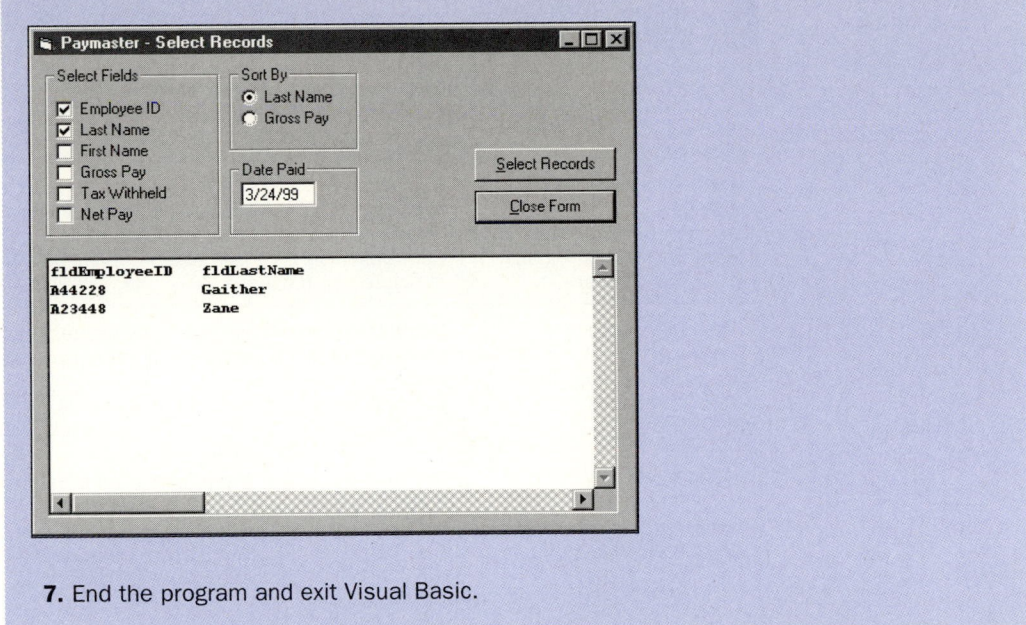

7. End the program and exit Visual Basic.

You have completed the program for Virgil. He now can perform many of the functions to compute the payroll. It now is possible to read data from a text file and insert records into the database. It also is possible to compute the payroll and delete obsolete records. Finally, the users will have extensive flexibility in selecting records from the database.

1. What is the purpose of an ORDER BY clause?

2. What is stored in the Recordsets collection and Recordset object?

3. What information is stored in the Fields collection of a Recordset object?

4. How do you select individual fields from a table or query?

Figure 7-23 lists and defines the new terms presented in this tutorial.

Figure 7-23 ◄
New terms

Term	Definition
Action query	This type of statement performs an action on a database table or query but does not return any records. These actions include adding, updating, and removing records. Action statements do not return a recordset.
Data Access Objects (DAO)	Data Access Objects (DAO) consist of all the objects and collections used to interact with the Microsoft Jet database engine programmatically.
Data Definition Language (DDL)	Data Definition Language (DDL) statements are used to change the structure of a database.
Data Manipulation Language (DML)	Data Manipulation Language (DML) statements are used to add, change, and delete records in a database table or query.
Default method	A default method is the method called when no method name is specified explicitly.
Default property	A default property is the property set or returned by a statement when a property name is not specified explicitly.
Default Workspace	The Default Workspace is a Workspace object created for you by the Microsoft Jet database engine when you first access the Microsoft Jet database engine.
Navigational model	Using the navigational model you move forward and backward directionally through records or locate records directly using a method like FindFirst.
Object library	An object library provides information to Visual Basic about a set of objects like DAO.
One-based collection	A one-based collection is a collection having an index value of one (1) for the first item, and is incremented by one (1) for each object in the collection.
Relational model	The relational model allows a single statement to perform an action on several records at once and is implemented using the Structured Query Language (SQL).
Select query	This type of statement returns records from a database and stores them into a Recordset object as a result of a SELECT statement.
Session	A session contains all the open databases for a user and is implemented as a Workspaces collection containing one or more Workspace objects.
String key	A string key is a string that uniquely identifies the object in the collection. A string key provides a more intuitive way to reference each object in the collection.
Structured Query Language (SQL)	SQL is a language defined by the American National Standards Institute (ANSI), and is used widely in database applications. It is made up of a set of statements that allow you to add, change, and delete database data.
System tables	System tables are tables used by the Microsoft Jet database engine to manage the other tables, fields, queries, and other objects created by the user.
Zero-based collection	A zero-based collection is a collection having an index value of zero (0) for the first item, and is incremented by one (1) for each object in the collection.

Tutorial Assignments

In addition to computing payroll information, Virgil needs to be able to update information about each employee. Specifically, he needs a program with a command button that will update the hourly wage of all employees by some percentage specified by the user. He also needs another command button that will delete all the records pertaining to a specific employee from both of the tables containing the payroll and the employees. When complete, your form should look like Figure 7-24.

Figure 7-24 ◀

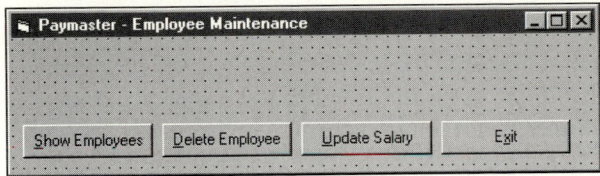

1. Make sure your Student Disk is in the appropriate disk drive, then start Visual Basic.

2. Set the appropriate property so the title bar of the form contains the text **Paymaster – Employee Maintenance**.

3. Set the Name property of the form to **frmPaymasterEmployee**.

4. Save the form as **frmPaymasterEmployee.frm** and the project as **Paymaster Employee.vbp** in the **TAssign** folder of the **Tutorial.07** folder on your Student Disk.

5. In the general declarations section of the Form module, create a variable named **dbCurrent** so it can store a Database object.

6. Write the statement to open the database named **A:\Tutorial.07\TAssign\Paymast.mdb** when the form is loaded.

7. Create a command button to exit the program.

8. Create a command button named **cmdUpdateSalary** and set the caption as necessary. Create a tooltip for the button.

9. In the Click event procedure for the command button you just created, declare the necessary local variables to display an input box. The input box should get a number representing the percentage of the salary increase to give all employees.

10. Using the value returned by the input box, create an SQL UPDATE statement to increase the value of the field named fldHourlyWage by the percentage specified by the user.

11. Execute the UPDATE statement.

12. Create a second command button named **cmdDeleteEmployee** and set the caption and tooltip as necessary.

13. In the Click event procedure for the command button you just created, declare the necessary variables and write the statement to display an input box. The input box should get an Employee ID number (a text string).

14. Using the value returned by the input box, create two DELETE statements. The first should remove all the records from the table named **tblPayroll** where the field named **fldEmployeeID** matches the Employee ID specified by the user. The second should remove the record from the table named **tblEmployees**, where the field named **fldEmployeeID** matches the Employee ID specified by the user.

15. Execute each of the DELETE statements.

16. Using the Data Form Wizard, create a form based on the table named **tblEmployees**. Select all the fields. Because the form will be used only to verify the success or failure of the UPDATE and DELETE statements, the form only should have a Refresh button. Change the captions for the form and labels as necessary. Save the form using the name **frmtblEmployees**.

17. Create a final command button named **cmdShowEmployees**. Set the caption and tooltip as necessary. Write the statement to show the form you just created as a modal form.

18. Test the program by looking at the hourly wage for each employee on the form created by the Data Form Wizard. Close this form then click the Update Salary command button. Enter **.10** into the input box to give each employee a 10 percent raise. Open the other form again to verify the salaries were updated.

19. Test the Delete Employee command button by deleting one of the employees from the database. Use the second form to verify the employee was deleted.

20. Save your work, print the Form as Text and Code.

21. Exit Visual Basic.

Case Problems

1. Steel Fabricators Steel Fabricators purchases raw steel to fabricate beams and other parts used in large buildings. They purchase their steel from many overseas sources. Due to currency fluctuations in the countries where the steel is purchased, the price must be updated for each item from a particular country. Prices can be changed upward or downward depending on the country of origin. Steel Fabricators needs a program to update the prices and view the price list. When complete, your screen should look like Figure 7-25.

Figure 7-25 ◀

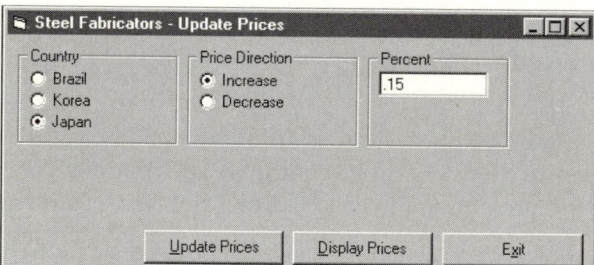

1. Make sure your Student Disk is in the appropriate disk drive, then start Visual Basic.

2. Set the form name to **frmSteelPrices** and the caption to **Steel Fabricators – Update Prices**.

3. Save the form as **frmSteelPrices.frm** and the project as **Steel Prices.vbp** in the **Cases** folder of the **Tutorial.07** folder on your Student Disk.

4. In the general declarations section of the Form module, create a variable named **dbCurrent** so it can store a Database object.

5. Open the database named **A:\Tutorial.07\Cases\Steel.mdb** when the form is loaded.

6. Create a command button to exit the program.

7. Create a Frame object and set the caption to **Country.**

8. Create a control array of three option buttons named **optCountry**. Set the caption of the option buttons to **Brazil, Korea**, and **Japan**.

9. Create a second Frame object with the caption **Price Direction**.

10. Create a control array of two option buttons named **optDirection** in the frame. Set the caption of the option buttons to **Increase** and **Decrease**.

11. Create a Frame with the caption **Percent** and a text box inside the frame named **txtPercent**.

12. Create two command buttons. One to update prices and another to display a form containing the price list. Set the name and captions as necessary.

13. In the command button to update prices, write the statements in the Click event procedure to determine which option button is selected and store the selected country name into a String variable.

14. Write the statements to store the price change percentage into a Single variable. If the price is increasing, the number should be positive. If the price is decreasing, multiply the number by –1 to make it negative.

15. Store in a local String variable an UPDATE statement that will update the field named **fldItemPrice** in the table named **tblPriceList** where the field named **fldCountry** is the same as the selected country. The price stored in fldItemPrice should be increased or decreased by the percentage amount specified by the user.

16. Using the Data Form Wizard, create a form based on the table named **tblPriceList**. Save the form using the default name.

17. Program the second command button to display this form as a modal form.

18. Test the program by displaying the original price list, then increasing and decreasing the prices by different percentages.

19. Save the forms and project again.

20. Print each Form as Text and Code.

2. Kismet Real Estate Sales Kismet Real Estate Sales is a residential real estate brokerage firm in Kissimmee, Florida. Each month, they receive all the sales transactions in the area for the past year in an ASCII file. When the ASCII file is received, rather than replacing existing records in the database, they remove all the records, then read the ASCII file into a table. The sales agents use the data to perform comparative price analyses. Figure 7-26 shows the completed form.

Figure 7-26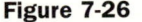

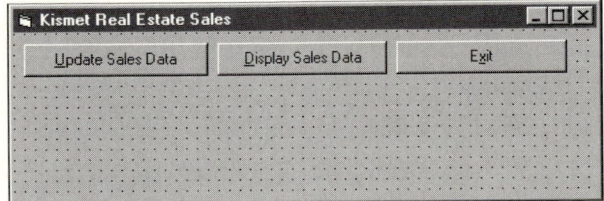

1. Make sure your Student Disk is in the appropriate disk drive, then start Visual Basic.

2. Set the name of the form to **frmKismet** and set the form's caption. Save the form as **frmKismet.frm** and the project as **Kismet.vbp**.

3. In the general declarations section of the Form module, create a variable named **dbCurrent** so it can store a Database object, then using that variable, open the database named **A:\Tutorial.07\Cases\Kismet.mdb** when the form is loaded.

4. Create two command buttons on the form. The first will delete the existing records from the sales table, then read the ASCII file containing the new data into the same table. The second will open another form to display the sales data.

5. Create a command button to exit the program.

6. In the Click event procedure for the first command button, create the necessary variables and write the statements to delete all the records from the database table named **tblSales**.

7. Inside the same event procedure, open the file **Kismet.txt** for input and create a Do loop to read each record in the file. Inside the Do loop write the statement to read the fields in each record into a local variable. The input file contains five fields that correspond to the fields in the table tblSales. These fields are named **fldArea, fldAddress, fldDateSold, fldSalesAmount**, and **fldSquareFeet**. They are stored in the input file in that order.

8. Create a local String variable to hold an SQL statement. Store in the variable an INSERT statement that will insert each of the five fields into the table named **tblSales**. Note fldArea and fldAddress are String variables, fldDateSold is a Date data type; fldSalesAmount is a Single data type, and fldSquareFeet is an Integer data type. This task needs to be performed inside the Do loop.

9. Execute the INSERT statement.

10. Using the Data Form Wizard, create a form based on the table named **tblSales**. Save the form using the default name.

11. Test the program by running the program, then clicking the **Display Sales Data** command button. Look at the second form to see that the records on the form match the records in the text file.

12. Exit Visual Basic.

 **3. AquaTech** Aquatech manufactures water purification equipment for national distribution. Bill and Sara Grimes have purchased the business recently and are working on the computer system. They have located a database file on the computer and want to find out the tables and fields in the database. The database is named **AquaTech.mdb** and is stored in the **Cases** folder of the **Tutorial.07** folder on your Student Disk. They would like you to prepare a report listing each table and its properties. For each table, each field in the table should be listed. For each field, print the field's name, size, and data type. The report should be printed to the default printer.

 **4. Lester International** Lester International manufactures and sells household products. They need a program to identify all the tables and fields in the database. Do not print any of the system tables. They also want menu items that will load data into each table from an ASCII file. They also receive an ASCII file of products to be deleted. Using this file, you will need to read a record, then delete the corresponding record from each table. Using the information you gathered when you printed the tables and fields, create an ASCII file for each table to test the program.

The ASCII files are named **Master.txt** and **Details.txt** and the database is named **Lester.mdb**. All three files are stored in the **Cases** folder of the **Tutorial.07** folder on your Student Disk.

Using Custom Controls to Open Files and to Interact with a Database

Creating an Event Registration System for Starlight Events

OBJECTIVES

In this tutorial you will:

- Understand the different types of controls used by Visual Basic

- Add ActiveX controls to a project

- Load multiple records from a recordset into the DBCombo control

- Load multiple records from a recordset into the DBGrid control that will display the rows and columns of a database

- Use the CommonDialog control to specify a database to be opened and the font and font attributes displayed in a visible control

CASE

Starlight Events

Katrina Voors is the owner of Starlight Events that provides event registration and meeting planning services to the various conventions and trade shows in Phoenix, Arizona. Her clients include trade associations and other groups, who hold conventions in Phoenix. The primary function of Starlight Events is to manage both mail-in and telephone reservations for the meetings, banquets, and other functions that occur at these events.

Gus Black has worked for Starlight Events as their computer programmer for several years and is in the process of converting the existing Event Registration system from a DOS-based program to a program that will operate with Windows 95.

Gus decided to maintain a separate database for each client so he could back up each database to tape when an event was finished to make the disk space available for the next upcoming client and its convention. Because many clients who use the services of Starlight Events do so only once, or on a very infrequent basis, this method of backing up to tape will make the Event Registration system very efficient. Gus already has created the database and has hired you to assist in the process of completing the user interface and the necessary code to interact with the database.

SESSION 8.1

In this session you will learn about ActiveX controls and how to use two ActiveX controls—the DBCombo and DBGrid controls—to interact with the data in a database table.

Analyzing the Program

Gus already has defined the structure of the database and created all the tables. This information is saved in the Tutorial.08 folder on your Student Disk. He also has created the NEADT charts for the program. He suggests you review the design documentation and refer to it as you develop the program.

To look at the design specifications for the event registration database:

1. Make sure your Student Disk is in the appropriate disk drive. Using Microsoft Word, open the file named **Slight.doc** located in the **Tutorial.08** folder on your Student Disk. Otherwise, open the file **Slight.txt** using WordPad.

2. Print the file then exit the word processing program.

The database contains three different tables. The table named tblEvents contains a unique event ID number, a description, and the date of the event. Another table, called tblPeople, contains the names and addresses of each convention participant. The third table, tblRegistration, contains each of the event registrations. The tables are designed so a person can register for multiple events. Each event ID in the table tblEvents must be unique. Each member ID in the table tblPeople also must be unique.

Figure 8-1 shows each of the database tables and the relationships between the tables.

Figure 8-1 ◄
Tables and relationships in Starlight Events database

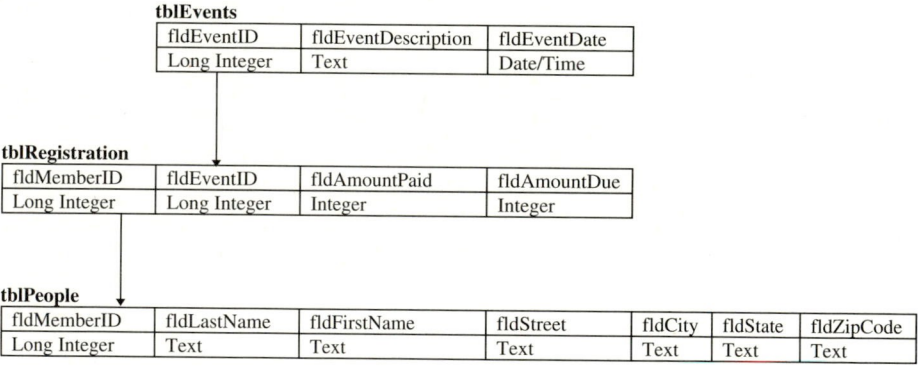

tblEvents

fldEventID	fldEventDescription	fldEventDate
Long Integer	Text	Date/Time

tblRegistration

fldMemberID	fldEventID	fldAmountPaid	fldAmountDue
Long Integer	Long Integer	Integer	Integer

tblPeople

fldMemberID	fldLastName	fldFirstName	fldStreet	fldCity	fldState	fldZipCode
Long Integer	Text	Text	Text	Text	Text	Text

The program you are about to write will allow the user to display all the different event descriptions in a type of combo box. Once an event description is selected, you will display all the different event registrations applicable to the selected event. The user then will be able to add, change, and delete the individual registrations. Gus already has created the menu system for the project. He wants you to add the necessary controls to the form and program each menu item.

To open the partially completed event registration program:

1. Start **Visual Basic** and open the project **Slight.vbp** in the **Tutorial.08** folder on your Student Disk.

2. Open the **Project Explorer**, if necessary, and view the form named **frmStarlightEvents**. The form should look like Figure 8-2.

Figure 8-2
Initial form for
Starlight
Events

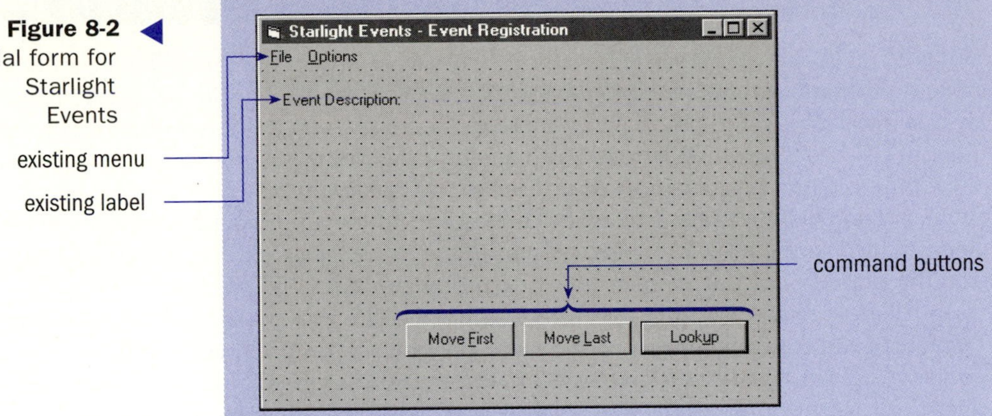

existing menu

existing label

command buttons

3. Save a copy of the form and project using the names **frmStarlightEvents.frm** and **Starlight Events.vbp,** respectively.

Gus already has created the menu system for the program. You need to create the remaining objects, then write the code for the event registration program.

Types of Controls

Throughout this book, you have been using controls on the toolbox to create a program's user interface. These controls, however, make up only one of three types of controls you can use with Visual Basic.

- All the controls you have used so far are intrinsic controls. **Intrinsic controls**, like intrinsic functions, are part of Visual Basic itself and are included in the executable files Visual Basic produces.

- Many controls you will want to use as you develop more complex applications are called ActiveX controls. **ActiveX controls** work like the other controls you have used but they are not actually part of Visual Basic. Rather they are built using a standard technology called component object modules (COM). **Component object modules (COM)** technology allows you to use a control or object with different programming languages including Visual Basic. These controls are stored as separate files on the disk with the extension ".OCX, .DLL, or .EXE". Programming languages other than Visual Basic, like Visual C++, also can use ActiveX controls. Additionally, you can use Visual Basic to create your own ActiveX controls.

- The third type of control is an insertable object. **Insertable objects** allow you to program another application's objects, like a Microsoft Excel Worksheet object or a Microsoft Word Document object. These objects can be added to the toolbox as controls or referenced programmatically as objects.

One of Visual Basic's strengths is that you can extend the functionality of the programming language by using and creating different ActiveX controls. There are several ActiveX controls that are supplied with the Professional and Enterprise Editions of Visual Basic. Additionally, software vendors sell different controls to perform specific tasks like sending faxes or generating bar codes. ActiveX controls frequently are referred to as custom controls.

Making an ActiveX Control Available to a Project

When Visual Basic first is started, intrinsic controls like text boxes, scroll bars, and combo boxes automatically are added to the toolbox for you. If you want to use an ActiveX control, in addition to the standard controls supplied by Visual Basic, you first must add the control to your project. When you add an ActiveX control to your project, you can use the Components dialog box to select the controls you want to use. After you have added the new controls, they will appear in the toolbox. When you add a control to a project, a line is added to the project file indicating the control is being used, so you do not need to add the ActiveX control to the toolbox each time you load the project.

In this tutorial you will use three different ActiveX controls. One is called the **CommonDialog** control and is used for tasks like opening and saving files. When you open and save files in Windows 95, you may have noticed that the dialog boxes look very similar for different applications like Microsoft Word, Excel, and even Visual Basic. This is because they all rely on a standard dialog to perform these tasks.

The other controls you will use are called the **DBCombo** and **DBGrid** controls. The programs you have created up to this point all have displayed a single record at a time. The DBGrid control, like other bound controls you have used, can be bound to an instance of the Data control just like a text box, but instead of displaying a single row, it displays several rows of data at the same time. Also, the DBGrid control does not display a single field like a bound text box. Rather it can display all the fields or selected fields in a table or query. The DBCombo control works like the intrinsic ComboBox control but it can read and write data from a database table.

REFERENCE window	**MAKING ACTIVEX CONTROLS AVAILABLE TO A PROJECT**
	■ Click Project then click Components on the menu bar.
	■ Use the Components dialog box to select the check box to the left of each ActiveX control you want to make available to your project. Remember, ActiveX controls are stored as separate files on your computer. Thus, the file containing the control must exist on the computer where the program is being developed and where the program will be running.
	■ Use the Controls tab of the Components dialog box to add specific controls to a project. When you select a control, the filename is displayed in the Location frame.
	■ If an ActiveX control is not listed in the Components dialog box, you can look for the control by clicking the Browse button.

For this project, you need to add the CommonDialog, DBList, DBCombo, and DBGrid controls. Gus suggests you add these controls to the project so you can create instances of the controls on the form.

To add ActiveX controls to your project:

1. Click **Project** then **Components** on the menu bar. The Components dialog box appears as shown in Figure 8-3. Note that the Controls tab may contain different controls depending on the configuration of your system.

Figure 8-3 ◀
Components
dialog box

Controls tab is active

click these three
check boxes to
include controls in
project

system controls are
displayed in controls
list box

click Browse to look
for other controls

filename and path of
highlighted control

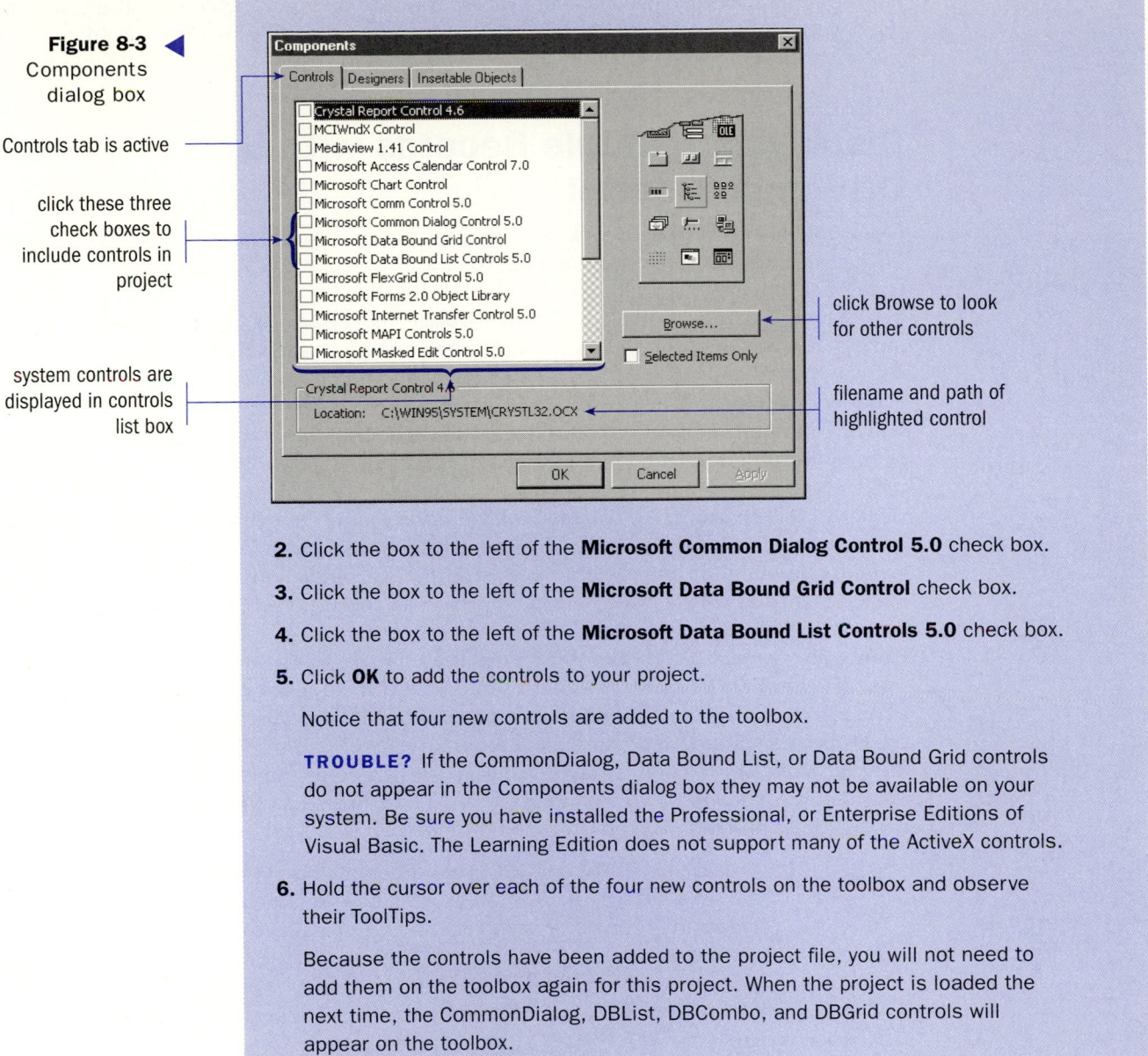

2. Click the box to the left of the **Microsoft Common Dialog Control 5.0** check box.

3. Click the box to the left of the **Microsoft Data Bound Grid Control** check box.

4. Click the box to the left of the **Microsoft Data Bound List Controls 5.0** check box.

5. Click **OK** to add the controls to your project.

Notice that four new controls are added to the toolbox.

TROUBLE? If the CommonDialog, Data Bound List, or Data Bound Grid controls do not appear in the Components dialog box they may not be available on your system. Be sure you have installed the Professional, or Enterprise Editions of Visual Basic. The Learning Edition does not support many of the ActiveX controls.

6. Hold the cursor over each of the four new controls on the toolbox and observe their ToolTips.

Because the controls have been added to the project file, you will not need to add them on the toolbox again for this project. When the project is loaded the next time, the CommonDialog, DBList, DBCombo, and DBGrid controls will appear on the toolbox.

Once an ActiveX control is displayed on the toolbox, you can create an instance of it by clicking the control and positioning it on the form. After creating an instance of the control, you can set its properties at design time, or run time, depending on the needs of your program.

> *Tip:* When creating programs with several controls, you should consider limiting the number and quantity of ActiveX controls. For each type of ActiveX control you use, Visual Basic must load the ActiveX control when the form is loaded. This causes your program to take longer to load. Also, your program will consume more memory. If your system has inadequate memory, or the program is very large, your program may run more slowly.

Unlike other controls you have used, most ActiveX controls have an additional dialog box called Property Pages. **Property Pages** are used to set design time properties that may not be available using the Properties window. Property Pages consist of multiple tabs. Each tab is called a **Property Page**. The Property Pages are different for each custom control you use. You can access the Property Pages for an ActiveX control as you would its Properties window, by activating the desired control instance and clicking the right mouse button on the control, then clicking Properties on the shortcut menu. You also can click the Properties button on the line labeled Custom in the control's Properties window.

Note that some properties only may be set in the Properties window while other properties only may be set using the Property Pages.

Displaying Multiple Records with the DBCombo Control

Gus would like to be able to look at all the registrations for a given event. Before viewing the registrations, however, he would like to be able to select which event he wants to view from a list of the different events in the table tblEvents.

The two ActiveX controls, called the **DBList** and **DBCombo** controls, work like the intrinsic ListBox and ComboBox controls but they support several other properties allowing you to read and write data in a database table. Both are bound controls, which like a list or combo box, will display multiple items from the database.

The DBList and DBCombo controls work the same way with two exceptions. The DBList control displays information like a list box does. That is, multiple lines always are visible on the screen. If the size of the object, as it is drawn on the form, cannot display all the lines, then scroll bars will appear. The DBCombo control works like a combo box in that the DBCombo box supports a drop-down combo box from which the user can select an item.

Like other bound controls you have used, the DBCombo control can obtain its information from a Recordset object created by the Data control. Thus, you set the RowSource property of the DBCombo control to a valid instance of a Data control. Like the ComboBox control, the DBCombo control is used to display a single column of information. The ListField property is used to specify which field in the recordset should be displayed in the DBList or DBCombo box at run time. This property only can be set using the Properties window at design time. Like other ActiveX controls, the DBCombo control must be added on the toolbox before you can use it in your program. Like other controls, these ActiveX controls have a standard prefix. The standard prefix for the DBList control is "dls" and the standard prefix for the DBCombox box is "dbc".

> *Tip:* Because the DBList and DBCombo controls are so similar, they are stored as a single OCX file. As such, they are added on the toolbox as one unit. In fact, both controls share much of the same code.

The following list describes some of the properties supported by the DBList and DBCombo controls:

- The **RowSource** property is the name of a Data control, and identifies the source table or query.

- The **ListField** property is a field in the table or query identified by the Data control. The field specified in the ListField property will be displayed in the DBList or DBCombo control.

- The **Text** property is set to the value identified by the ListField property. When an item in the list is selected, it is stored in the Text property. The Text property is the default property for the DBCombo and DBList controls.

- The **MatchEntry** property controls how the DBCombo or DBList controls perform searches based on user input. The MatchEntry property can store two different constants. If set to **dblBasicMatching**, the control searches for the next match containing the character entered using the first letter of entries in the list, repeatedly typing the same letter cycles through all the entries in the list beginning with that letter. If set to **dblExtendedMatching**, the control searches for an entry matching all characters entered. The search is done as characters are being typed, further refining the search. When the MatchEntry property is set to dblExtendedMatching and the user enters a backspace or waits more than a few seconds, the matching string is reset.

■ The **Style** property can be set to one of three values. If set to **0 - Dropdown Combo** or **1 - Simple Combo**, the user either can select from the list of choices or enter a new item. The 0 - Dropdown Combo setting saves space on the form because the list portion closes when the user selects an item. If set to **2 - Dropdown List**, the user must select a choice from the existing list of choices.

Gus would like you to create a DBCombo box that will display information from the table named tblEvents. To do this, you first need to create a Data control, set its properties to connect to the database, then create the DBCombo box and set its properties. Because Katrina wants to see the event descriptions for each event in the table, you will set the ListField property to the fldDescription field in the table tblEvents. Because the DBCombo box will not be used to add new events, you will set the Style property to 2 - Dropdown List.

To add the Data control and DBCombo control to the form:

1. Create an instance of the Data control at the bottom of the form as shown in Figure 8-4. Set the Name property to **datEvents**, the DatabaseName property to **A:\Tutorial.08\Slight.mdb**, and the RecordSource property to **tblEvents**. Because the user will not interact with the Data control at run time, set the Visible property to **False**.

2. Create an instance of the DBCombo control on the form as shown in Figure 8-4.

Figure 8-4 ◀
Creating an instance of the DBCombo control

new DBCombo object ─→

new Data control ─→

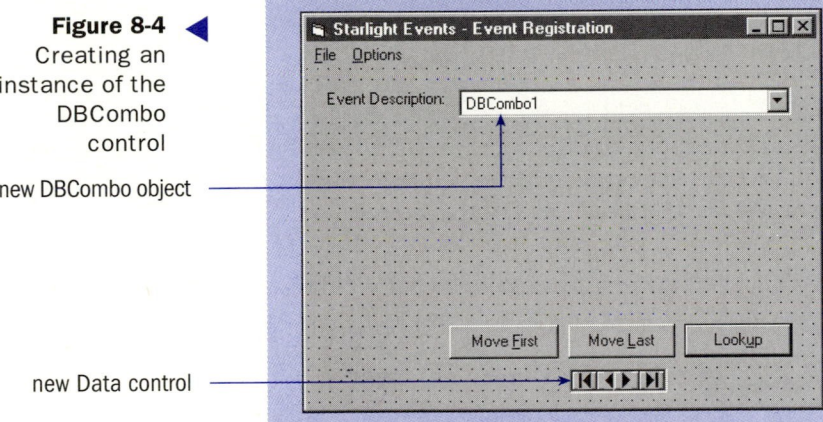

3. Set the Name property to **dbcEvents**.

4. Set the RowSource property to **datEvents**, the ListField property to **fldEventDescription**, and the MatchEntry property to **1 - dblExtendedMatching**.

5. Set the Style property to **2 - dbcDropdown List** to prevent the user from trying to add a new event.

6. Set the TabIndex property to **0** so this will be the first object to receive focus when the program is run.

7. Remove the text from the **Text** property.

These are the only steps necessary to cause the rows contained in the field fldEventDescription to be displayed in the DBCombo object at run time. You now can test your program to verify the records are being loaded correctly.

To test the DBCombo Control:

1. Save the project then start it.

2. Click the **list arrow** in the combo box to display the records. Your screen should look like Figure 8-5.

Figure 8-5 ◄
Testing
DBCombo
object

click list arrow to
display table records

event descriptions
displayed

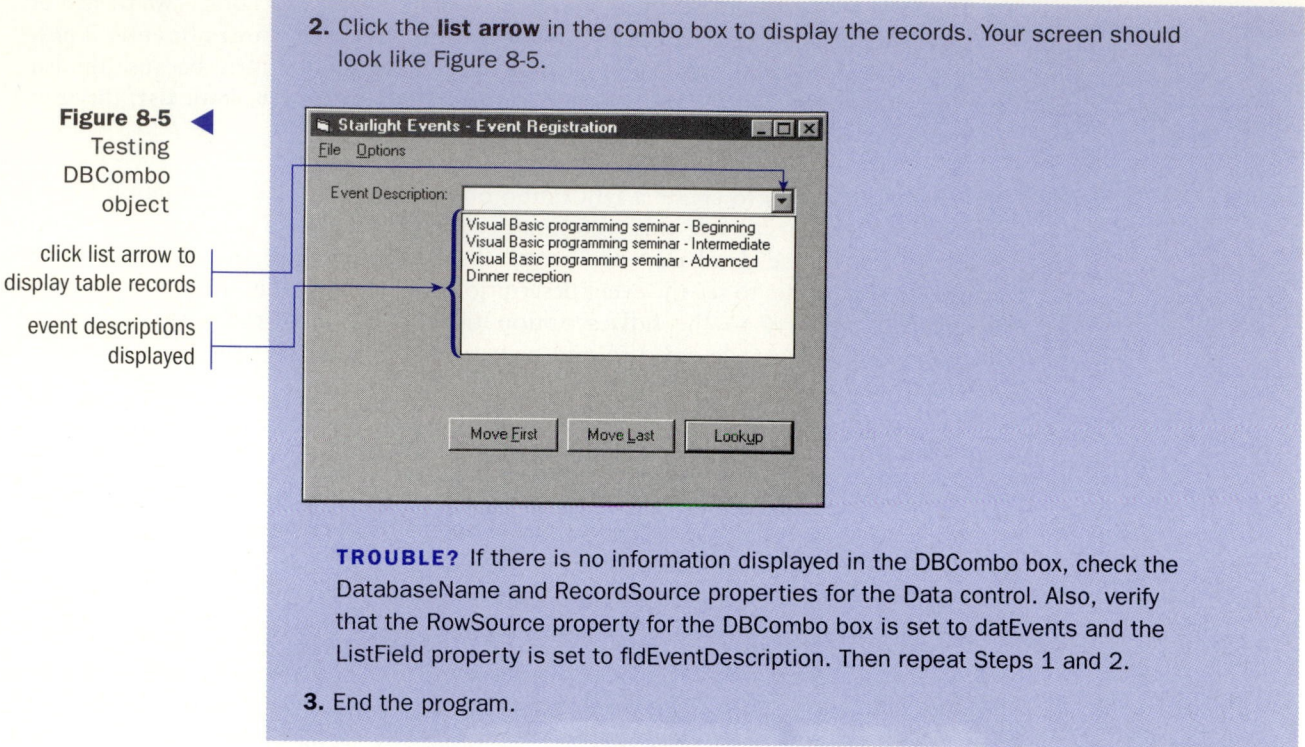

TROUBLE? If there is no information displayed in the DBCombo box, check the DatabaseName and RecordSource properties for the Data control. Also, verify that the RowSource property for the DBCombo box is set to datEvents and the ListField property is set to fldEventDescription. Then repeat Steps 1 and 2.

3. End the program.

In addition to reading data from a Data control, the DBCombo and DBList controls can store the value of another field for the selected record in a property. For example, even though the event description is displayed in the DBCombo box, you can store the value of the event ID in another property of the control. This process uses two different properties that work like the ListField and Text properties.

- The **BoundColumn** property specifies a column in the source Data control.

- The **BoundText** property contains the value identified by the bound column. When a record is selected, the value stored in the corresponding BoundColumn is stored in the BoundText property.

When a user selects an item from the DBCombo list, the value of the BoundText property is set based on which column is the BoundColumn. Figure 8-6 illustrates the relationship between the ListField, Text, BoundColumn, and BoundText properties.

Figure 8-6 ◄
Relationships
between
ListField, Text,
BoundColumn,
and BoundText
properties

selected row

value of Text property

value of BoundText
property

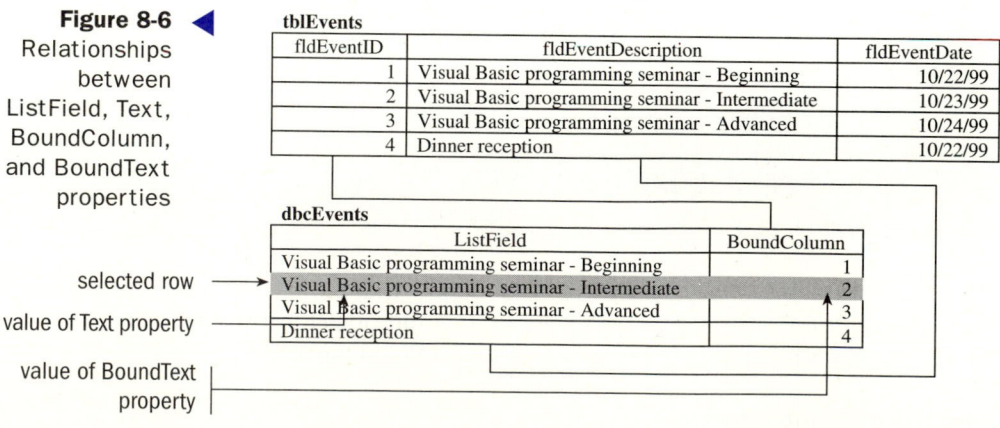

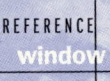

USING A DBLIST OR DBCOMBO OBJECT TO DISPLAY INFORMATION FROM A DATABASE

- Make sure the DBList and DBCombo controls appear on the toolbox.
- Draw an instance of a DBList or DBCombo control on the form.
- Set the RowSource property to the name of an existing Data control.
- Set the ListField property to the field to be displayed in the object.
- Set the MatchEntry property as desired to control how an item will be selected.
- If you need to use information from the same row but a different column than the one specified by the ListField property, set the BoundColumn property to the desired column. When an item is selected, the contents of the BoundColumn will be stored in the BoundText property of the DBList or DBCombo box.

When Katrina selects an event description from the DBCombo box, she wants to display all the event registrations having a corresponding event ID. The event registrations are stored in the table named tblRegistration. In that table the event ID for the registration is stored, but the event description is not. Thus, at run time you need to allow Katrina to select an event description, then store the corresponding event ID in the BoundText property of the DBCombo box. You will use this property later in the session to select all corresponding event ID's from the registration table.

To store the event ID when an event description is selected:

1. Activate the **Properties window** for the DBCombo box dbcEvents. Note you must use the Properties window rather than the Property Pages because the BoundColumn property cannot be set on the Property Pages.

2. Set the BoundColumn property to **fldEventID**.

When an event description is selected at run time, the BoundText property will be set to the corresponding event ID. Katrina wants to be able to display all the event registrations corresponding to a specific event ID. She would like to be able to see several registrations, however, rather than having to scroll through each one individually. The DBGrid control displays data like a spreadsheet. Each field appears in a column and several records can be displayed at the same time.

Displaying Multiple Rows and Columns with the DBGrid Control

Like other bound controls you have used, the DBGrid control displays information from a database based on a Recordset object created by a Data control. The DBGrid control displays all the rows and selected columns at the same time. It also either can display field names as column headers or you can specify your own column headers. An instance of the DBGrid control has a fixed number of columns and any number of rows. The DBGrid control can store about 1700 columns. The number of rows varies based on the configuration of your system. The intersection of a row and column in a DBGrid control is called a **cell**. Like other controls, the DBGrid control uses a standard prefix "dbg". The rows and columns appearing in the DBGrid can be loaded automatically at run time by connecting the DBGrid to a Data control and setting the DataSource property:

■ The **DataSource** property is set to the name of an existing Data control. All the rows and columns in the recordset created by the Data control will be displayed in the DBGrid control.

Because Katrina wants to view all the registrations at the same time, you will display them in a DBGrid. You now need to create a second Data control on the form to refer to the table tblRegistration rather than the table tblEvents and the DBGrid control itself. At run time, there will be two active Recordset objects instead of just one. In DAO terms there will be two Recordset objects in the Recordsets collection. Once the second Data control is created, and its properties set to connect to the table named tblRegistration, you can create the DBGrid control and set its DataSource so the DBGrid control can display the records in the recordset. Unlike the other bound controls you have used, the DBGrid control displays information for multiple fields. Therefore, there is no DataField property to specify a specific field.

As with other bound controls, the underlying Data control for a DBGrid control either can be visible or invisible at run time. When the Data control is visible, clicking the buttons on the Data control will cause the current record pointer to be updated. When the current record pointer is updated, the current record indicator in the DBGrid control will be updated accordingly.

To create an instance of the DBGrid control:

1. Create an instance of the Data control at the bottom of the form as shown in Figure 8-7 and set the Name property to **datRegistration**, the DatabaseName property to **A:\Tutorial.08\Slight.mdb**, and the RecordSource property to **tblRegistration**. Because the user will not interact with the Data control at run time, set the Visible property to **False**.

2. Click the **DBGrid** control ▦ on the toolbox and draw an instance of the control on the form as shown in Figure 8-7.

Figure 8-7 ◄
DBGrid object

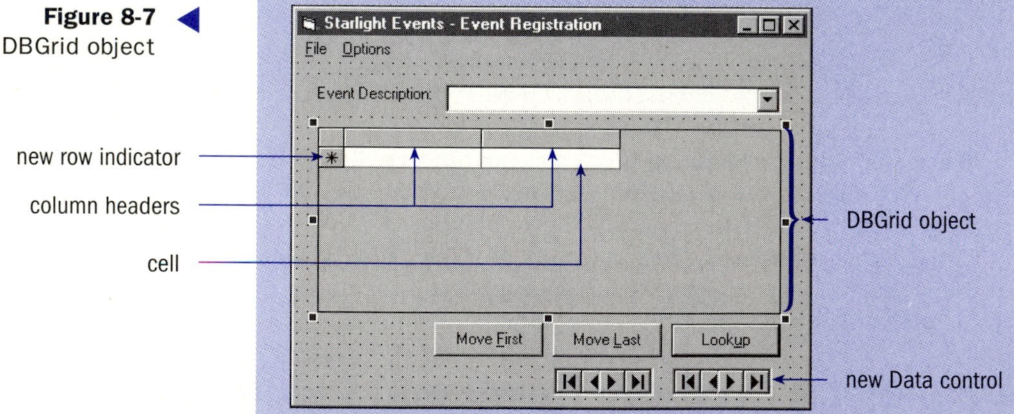

new row indicator ——
column headers ——
cell ——

DBGrid object

new Data control

3. Activate the Properties window and set the Name property to **dbgRegistration**.

4. Set the DataSource property to **datRegistration**—the name of the Data control you just created.

When the DBGrid control is created, by default it displays two rows and two columns at design time. Each column has an empty column header. Inside the column header, you can display a prompt describing the column. When the program is run, the DBGrid control will connect to the recordset created by the Data control and display all the columns and rows. The titles for each column will be the same as the name of the field in the table.

To the left of the first row, status information is displayed. At design time, an asterisk (*) appears in the status column. This is the symbol for a new row.

Just as other controls you have used can receive focus and become the active object, each cell in the DBGrid control can become the active cell. The active cell is identified by two DBGrid control properties as follows:

- The **Row** property identifies the active row. The first active row is zero (0), the second is one (1), and so on.

- The **Column** property identifies the active column. The first active column is zero (0), the second is one (1), and so on.

At run time, you use different keys to navigate through the rows and columns displayed on the screen. You can change the active cell to the previous or next row using the Up and Down arrow keys. The Left and Right arrow keys allow you to change the active cell to the previous and next column. The Home key will change the active cell to the first column in the current row. To view rows not displayed on the screen, you can use the scroll bars or press the Page Up or Page Down keys. By default, you cannot use the Tab key to move from cell to cell. Pressing the Tab key will cause the DBGrid to lose focus and the next control to receive focus. You also can click the mouse in a cell to activate it.

To test the DBGrid control:

1. Save the project then start it. Your screen should look like Figure 8-8.

Figure 8-8 ◀
Testing DBGrid
object

current record
indicator

column headers

cells

scroll bar to
locate records

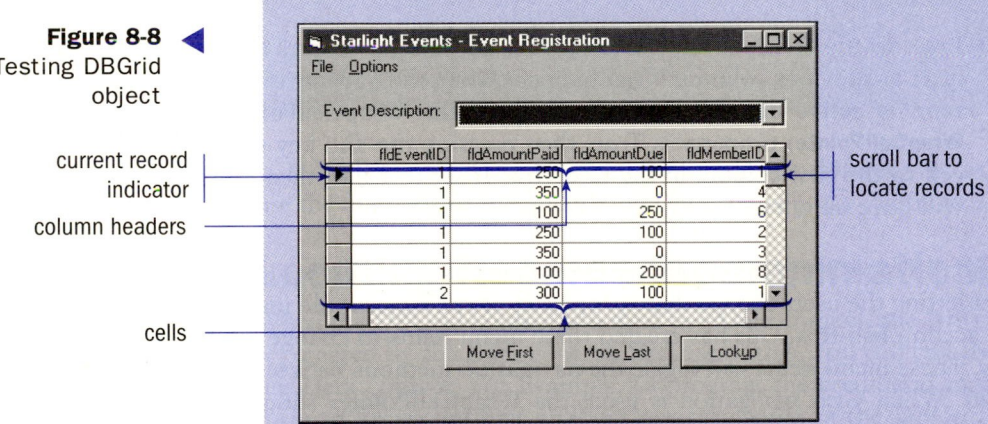

Notice the columns and rows are displayed in the DBGrid object. By default, the DBGrid displays the field names in the column header and the current record indicator is positioned on the first row when the object is first activated.

TROUBLE? If no information is displayed in the DBGrid control at run time, be sure the DatabaseName and RecordSource properties of the second Data control, datRegistration, are correct, and the DataSource property for the DBGrid control is set to the name of the correct Data control.

2. Click the DBGrid control to make it the active object.

3. Use the arrow keys to locate different cells. Note that pressing the Left arrow key in the first column or the Right arrow key in the last column has no effect.

4. Use the scroll bar to locate rows not visible in the control.

5. Press the **Tab** key. Notice the control loses focus.

6. End the program.

These statements operate on the underlying Recordset object created by the Data control and will locate the first and last record in the recordset. You now should test the program to verify the Move First and Move Last command buttons are working correctly.

To test the command buttons:

1. Save the project then start it.

2. Click the **Move First** and **Move Last** command buttons to verify the current record is being repositioned.

3. End the program.

You can call the other methods of the Recordset object just as you have done in the previous tutorials. For example, you can call the AddNew, Update, and Delete methods.

When you run the program, notice the information in the control is formatted poorly. First, the numeric columns are not aligned properly, and the names of the columns are not descriptive names but rather the names of the actual fields.

Formatting Columns in the DBGrid Control

The DBGrid control gives you considerable flexibility in formatting the object's contents. Gus suggests you change the names of the columns from the names of the fields to names that are more meaningful to the user. He also wants a caption added above the columns. To change this formatting, you need to activate the Property Pages for the DBGrid control. By default, the DBGrid control does not display the different fields in the table in the column headers until the program is run. To format each column, you must retrieve explicitly the field names from the underlying table or query. Once this is done, the columns can be formatted.

To select and format the columns in the DBGrid:

1. Activate the **DBGrid** control and click the right mouse button, then click **Retrieve Fields** on the shortcut menu to load the fields in the DBGrid. The DBGrid control will look up the fields in the underlying database table. Notice that the field names are displayed in the column headers of the DBGrid as shown in Figure 8-9.

Figure 8-9 ◀
Displaying
fields in DBGrid

column names
displayed in column
headers after
retrieving fields

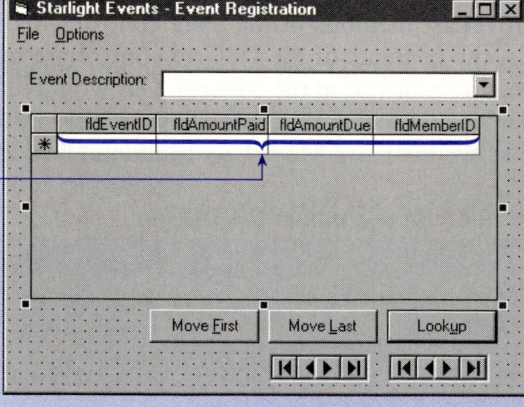

2. Click the right mouse button over the **DBGrid** control, then click **Properties** on the shortcut menu to activate the Property Pages for the DBGrid control. Figure 8-10 shows the Property Pages for the DBGrid control.

Figure 8-10
Property Pages
for DBGrid

General tab active
(General tab on
Property Pages)

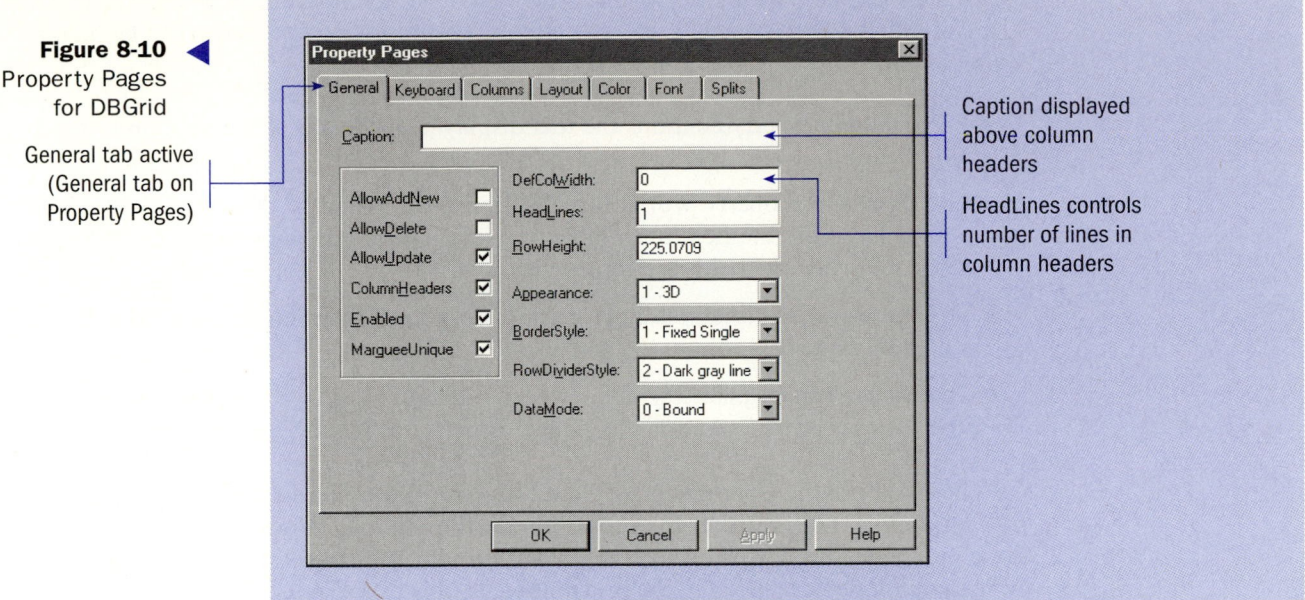

Caption displayed
above column
headers

HeadLines controls
number of lines in
column headers

The Property Pages for the DBGrid control defines both the general appearance of the object on the form and the appearance of each column. The General tab on the Property Pages defines properties that apply to all the columns in the DBGrid. Some of these properties include:

- The **Caption** property will cause a caption to be displayed in the DBGrid on its own line just above the column headers.

- The **HeadLines** property is a value between 0 and 10 and identifies the number of lines displayed in the column headers.

- The **BorderStyle** property, if set to **1 - Fixed Single**, draws a border around the region of the DBGrid control. If set to **0 - None**, a border is not drawn.

- The **RowDividerStyle** describes the characteristics of the line separating each row and column. For a description of the valid settings, see the Help topic RowDividerStyle property.

Gus wants a caption displayed in the control and one line in each of the column headers.

To set the general properties for the DBGrid control:

1. Be sure the **General** tab on the Property Pages is active.

2. Set the Caption property to **Event Registrations**.

   Note that the HeadLines property is 1, which is the default.

3. Click the **Apply** button.

   The caption appears in the DBGrid control.

Now that you have performed the general formatting of the DBGrid control, you need to format the individual columns. The Columns tab on the Property Pages defines the behavior of each column in the DBGrid. In fact the Columns property is a Columns collection used to store Column objects. The Columns collection is a zero-based collection, containing one Column object for each column in the DBGrid object. Each Column object in the Columns collection supports the properties that pertain to an individual column like the column's caption, the field in a table or query to be displayed, a default value if any, and the format of the data displayed in the column. The Columns tab on the Property

Pages is used to define the title, format, and field of each column displayed in the DBGrid. The Column list box is used to select a column. The following properties can be set on the Columns tab:

- The **Caption** property contains the text displayed at the top of the column (the column header).

- The **DataField** property works like the DataField property that applies to a text box. It identifies the field for a table or query. The DataField property is set automatically when the fields are retrieved.

- The **DefaultValue** property is a placeholder for you to program an event that will set a default value of a column.

- The **NumberFormat** property defines how numeric data in a column is displayed. The formats are the same as the named formats used in the Format statement.

When you use the Columns tab on the Property Pages, you first select a column using the Column list box, then set the properties for the column. You now can format each of the columns in the DBGrid. Note that you will not need to set the DataField property. When you loaded the fields in the previous steps, this property was set for you automatically by the DBGrid control itself. Gus suggests you now set the caption for each column and specify a Currency format for the Amount Due and Amount Paid columns because they represent monetary values.

To format the columns in the DBGrid:

1. Be sure the **Property Pages** for the DBGrid object is open. Click the **Columns** tab to activate it. The first column, fldEventID, is active by default.

2. Set the Caption property for the column fldEventID to **Event ID**.

3. For the columns **fldAmountPaid** and **fldAmountDue**, set the NumberFormat property to **Currency** and the Caption property to **Amount Paid** and **Amount Due**, respectively.

4. For the column **fldMemberID**, set the Caption property to **Member ID**.

5. Click **OK** to close the Property Pages. Your form should look like Figure 8-11.

Figure 8-11 ◀
Changing DBGrid's column headers

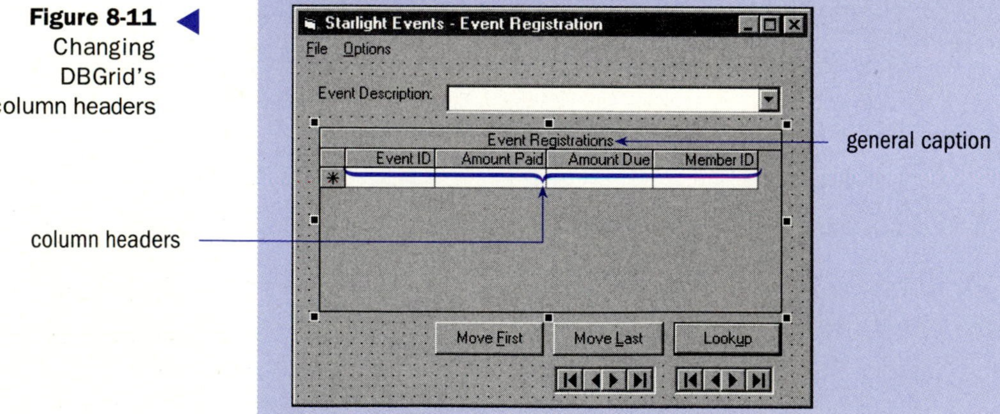

general caption

column headers

The Layout tab on the Property Pages works like the Columns tab in that you use the Column list box to select a column, then set the properties that define the layout of the column.

- The **Split** object is used to split the region of the DBGrid into multiple panes much like you can split a spreadsheet in Microsoft Excel.

- If the **AllowSizing** property is set to True, the mouse pointer changes to a double-headed arrow when positioned over the row divider. The user can resize the rows by dragging them at run time.

- The **Alignment**, **Visible,** and **Width** properties work like properties of the same names for the other controls you have used.

Katrina would like the numeric data right-justified so the decimal points are aligned. Because you set the NumberFormat property to Currency, the columns can be aligned using the Alignment property on the Layout tab on the Property Pages. In addition, the DBGrid control currently displays the Event ID field in the registration table. Because Katrina always enters registration information for the event selected in the DBCombo box, the value of this field will be the same as the event ID stored in the BoundText property of the currently selected item from the DBCombo box. To improve the user interface, Gus suggests you do not display this column. When a column is not visible in the DBGrid control, it still can be referenced using Visual Basic code even though the user cannot interact with the column.

In addition to making the Event ID column invisible, Gus wants each of the numeric columns to be right-justified. The DBGrid control sets the alignment based on the data type of the field and the Numeric format selected on the Columns tab. Gus wants to verify the alignment is correct for each of the Numeric fields.

To align the numeric data and make the Event ID column invisible:

1. Open the **Property Pages** for the object named **dbgRegistration**.

2. Click the **Layout** tab as shown in Figure 8-12.

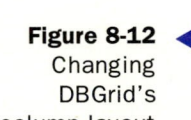
Figure 8-12
Changing
DBGrid's
column layout

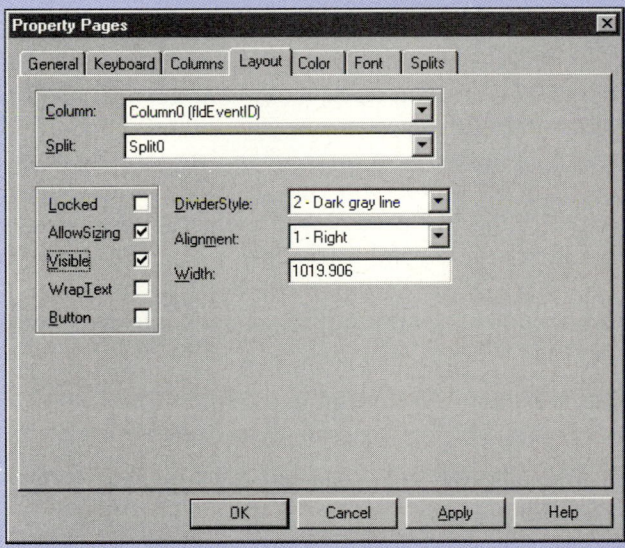

3. Use the Column list box to select the column named **Column0 (fldEventID)**.

4. Click the **Visible** check box to remove the check and make the column invisible.

5. Click the **Apply** button.

6. Use the Column list box to select the column named **Column3 (fldMemberID)** and verify the Alignment property is set to **1 - Right**.

7. For the fields **fldAmountPaid** and **fldAmountDue**, verify the Alignment property is set to **1 - Right**.

8. Click **OK** to close the Property Pages.

Gus suggests you now test the program to determine that the formatting of the columns is correct. The Event ID column should not be visible and the Amount Paid and Amount Due columns should be formatted with two decimal places and aligned at the decimal point.

To test the formatting of the DBGrid control:

1. Save the project then start it.

The information in the DBGrid control should look like Figure 8-13.

Figure 8-13 ◀
Testing
DBGrid's
column layout

numeric columns
right-justified

Currency format

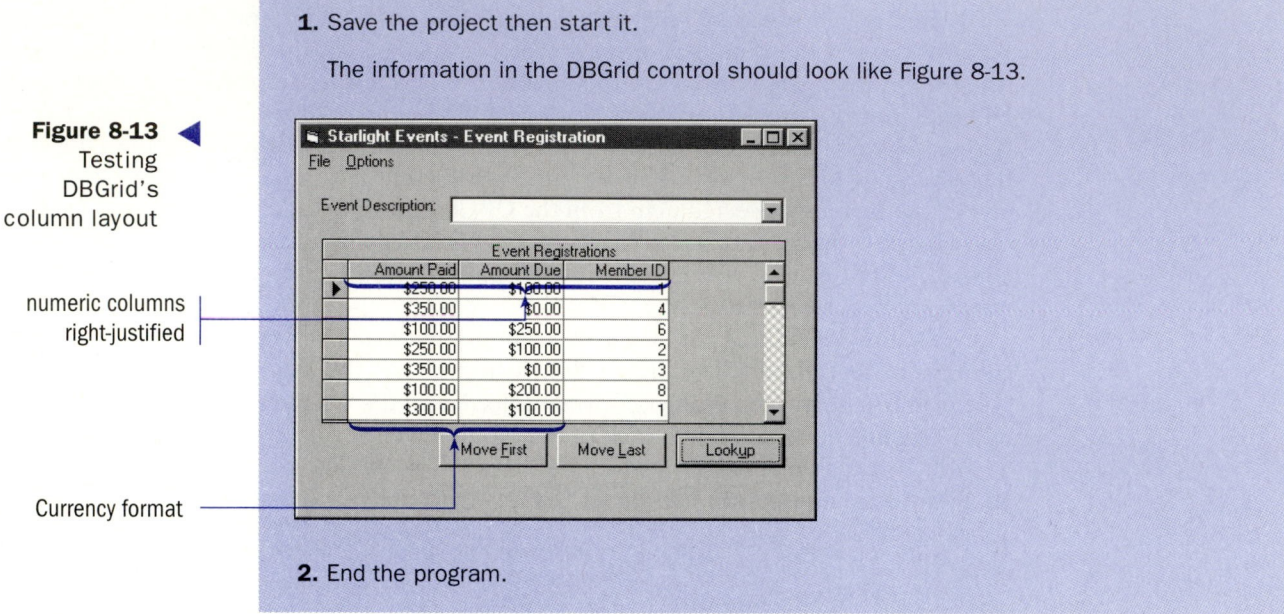

2. End the program.

The next step in the process is to resize the columns. To resize the columns, you could set the Width property by specifying a number for the Width on the Layout tab on the Property Pages. You also can resize the columns by making the control User Interface (UI) active. **User Interface (UI) active** means you can insert, move, delete, and resize the individual columns by dragging them rather than using the Property Pages to set the values. To make the control UI active, you click the right mouse button to activate the shortcut menu, then click Edit. The control will remain UI active until the control is no longer the active object. Once the control is UI active, you can perform the following tasks:

■ Remove columns by activating a column, clicking the right mouse button, then clicking Cut.

■ Insert new columns by activating a column, clicking the right mouse button, then clicking Insert. The new column is inserted to the left of the active column.

■ Add a column to the end of the list of columns by clicking the right mouse button, then clicking Append.

■ Resize a column by positioning the cursor over the column dividers, holding down the left mouse button, then dragging the column to increase or decrease the width.

■ Resize the height of a row by positioning the cursor over a row divider, then dragging the row up or down to decrease or increase the height of the row.

Gus now would like you to practice changing the size of the rows and columns.

To reformat the row and column sizes:

1. Activate the **DBGrid** control, click the right mouse button, then click **Edit** to make the control UI active.

2. Move the cursor to the first column separator. See Figure 8-14. Notice the cursor will appear as a ✛.

3. Hold down the left mouse button, then drag the column to the left to decrease its size.

4. Move the cursor to the column divider between each of the column separators. Increase and decrease the size of the columns to familiarize yourself with the process.

5. Resize the object until it is the same size as shown in Figure 8-14.

Figure 8-14 ◀
Resizing
DBGrid's
columns

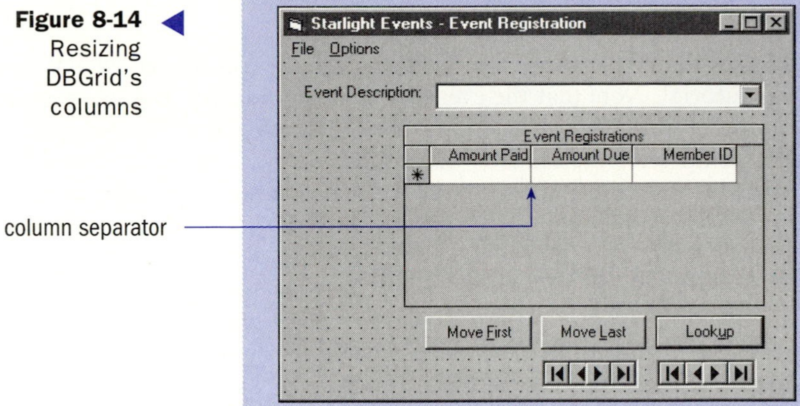

column separator ——

Now that the properties are set, you need to write the code that will synchronize the current selection in the DBCombo box with the records displayed in the DBGrid. Currently the DBGrid displays all the records in the recordset. Gus only wants to see the registrations for the currently selected event, however.

Because the information displayed in the DBGrid is based on the Recordset object created by the datRegistration Data control, you need to change the records in this recordset whenever the user selects an event. In the past you have set the RecordSource property of the Data control to a table or query. It also is possible to set the RecordSource property at run time, then call the Refresh method of the Data control. When the Refresh method is called, the Data control uses the value of the DatabaseName and RecordSource properties to create a new Recordset object and store a reference to it in the Recordset property of the Data control. In addition to specifying a table or query name, you can create a SELECT statement of the same form as you used in the previous tutorial, then set the RecordSource property to the SELECT statement. When the Refresh method is called, the SELECT statement is executed and a new recordset created.

Gus set the Lookup command button as the default button so Katrina could select an event description from the DBCombo object, then press the Enter key. Thus, you need to write the statement to refresh the recordset in the Click event procedure for this command button.

To select only event registrations for the current event:

1. Activate the Code window for the **Click** event for the **cmdLookup** object.

2. Enter the following statements into the procedure:

```
Private Sub cmdLookup_Click( )
    Dim pstrSQL As String

    If dbcEvents.Text <> "" Then
        pstrSQL = "SELECT * FROM tblRegistration " & _
            " WHERE fldEventID = " & dbcEvents.BoundText & _
            " ORDER BY fldMemberID "
        datRegistration.RecordSource = pstrSQL
        datRegistration.Refresh
        dbgRegistration.Visible = True
    End If
End Sub
```

These statements create the SQL statement and store it in the variable pstrSQL. Then, by setting the RecordSource property and calling the Data control's Refresh method, a new recordset is created by the Data control. Notice all the statements are enclosed in an If statement. The If statement verifies that an item is selected from the DBCombo object.

```
pstrSQL = "SELECT * FROM tblRegistration " & _
    " WHERE fldEventID = " & dbcEvents.BoundText & _
    " ORDER BY fldMemberID "
```

This statement creates the SQL statement in the same way as you created an SQL statement in the previous tutorial. Note that the event ID corresponding to the selected event description is stored in the BoundText property of the DBCombo box. This value is used to create the WHERE clause for the SELECT statement. Because Starlight Events keeps their paper records sorted by member ID, the records appear in the same order because of the ORDER BY clause.

```
datRegistration.RecordSource = pstrSQL
datRegistration.Refresh
```

The first statement assigns the SELECT statement stored in the variable pstrSQL to the RecordSource property of the Data control corresponding to the DBGrid control. The second statement causes the SELECT statement to be executed. When the recordset is refreshed, the selected records automatically will be displayed in the DBGrid.

Whenever Katrina selects an event description in the DBCombo box object, these statements will execute and only the registrations for the event ID corresponding to the event description are selected in the new recordset. Those records then are displayed in the DBGrid control. Gus suggests you test the program to be sure the code you just wrote is working correctly.

To test the Lookup command button:

1. Save the project then start it.

2. Click the **list arrow** in the Event Description combo box to display the records and select the description **Visual Basic programming seminar - Beginning**.

3. Press the **Enter** key to execute the code you just wrote in the Lookup button's Click event. Because the command button is the default object, you can press Enter to execute the Click event for the command button. Your form should look like Figure 8-15. Note that only six records are displayed in the DBGrid control.

Figure 8-15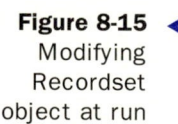
Modifying
Recordset
object at run
time

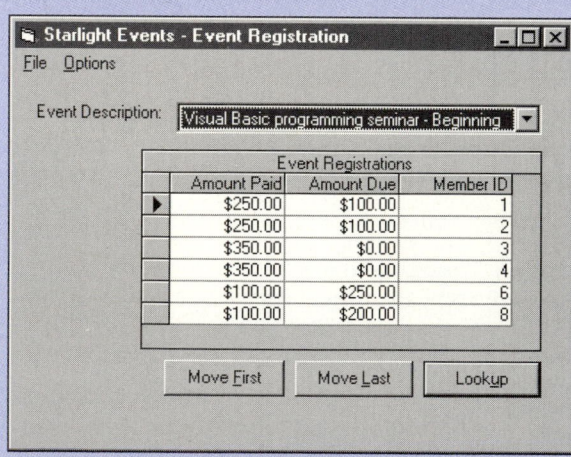

TROUBLE? If all the records continue to be selected, check the code you just wrote and make sure it matched the code in the preceding steps and repeat Steps 1 through 3.

4. End the program.

After selecting an event from the DBCombo object, the corresponding event registrations are displayed in the DBGrid control. In addition, the user interface was improved by formatting the numeric columns, and modifying the captions. Because you programmed the menu items to change the behavior of the Tab key while the DBGrid control is active, the user can customize the behavior of the control for their personal preference.

Quick Check

1 What is the difference between an intrinsic control, an ActiveX control, and a component object module?

2 What is the purpose of the Components dialog box?

3 Describe the purpose of the following properties as they pertain to the DBCombo and DBList controls: ListField, Text, BoundColumn, and BoundText.

4 How do you change the behavior of the Tab key while the DBGrid object has focus?

5 What are the Columns collection and Column object as they pertain to the DBGrid control?

6 What is the relationship between the DBGrid control and the corresponding Data control?

You have completed this session. You either may exit Visual Basic or continue to the next session.

SESSION

8.2

In this session, you will learn how to add, change, and delete records using the DBGrid control. You will write code to open a database explicitly and change fonts using the CommonDialog control. Finally, you will learn how to use the Controls collection.

Modifying Data with the DBGrid Control

The DBGrid control allows the user to add, change, and delete records. For the user to add a new record to the DBGrid and the underlying recordset, the AllowAddNew property must be set to True either at run time or at design time using the General tab on the Property Pages. Just as the Data control responds to events like Reposition and Validate allowing you to verify input before writing data to a table in the database, the DBGrid control supports several events that occur when the user moves from field to field or from one row to another. Some of these events occur for actions involving the record or row in the DBGrid. Other events occur for actions involving a specific column. The DBGrid control has a copy buffer much like the Data control. Changes made to the current record are stored in the DBGrid's copy buffer. When the user locates a different record, the fields in the DBGrid control's copy buffer are written to the Data control. In fact, events for the Data control can be generated by the DBGrid control. For example, when changes are made in a record, or a new record is located, a Validate event and/or Reposition event occurs on the underlying Data control. You can write code to respond to these events as necessary. There are three properties that determine whether or not a user can add, change, and delete records. The three properties are as follows:

- The **AllowAddNew** property can be set to True or False. If set to True, the user can add new records to the recordset, and the last row displayed in the DBGrid control is blank to permit users to enter new records. If set to False, new records cannot be added, and no blank line is displayed. If the underlying recordset is not updatable, new records cannot be added even when the AllowAddNew property is True.

- The **AllowUpdate** property can be set to True or False. If set to True, the user can modify data in the DBGrid, otherwise data cannot be modified. Note that the Recordset object may not enable updates even if AllowUpdate is True for the DBGrid control. In this case a trappable error occurs when the user tries to change the record.

- The **AllowDelete** property can be set to True or False. If set to True, records can be deleted from the DBGrid, otherwise records cannot be deleted. Again, if the underlying recordset is not updatable, then records cannot be deleted and a trappable error occurs when the user tries to change the record.

Katrina wants to be able to add, change, and delete records directly from the DBGrid control, so you need to set the AllowAddNew, AllowUpdate, and AllowDelete properties to True.

To set the properties to add, change, and delete records:

1. Be sure the DBGrid control is the active object.

2. Click the right mouse button, then click **Properties** to activate the Property Pages for the object.

3. Be sure the General tab on the Property Pages is active.

4. Be sure the **AllowAddNew**, **AllowUpdate**, **AllowDelete**, and **Enabled** check boxes are checked.

5. Click the **Apply** button.

6. Close the Property Pages.

By checking these check boxes, you will be able to add, change, and delete records. Before modifying data in the underlying table, however, you first should validate any user input to make sure it is correct.

Adding Records with the DBGrid Control

When the user wants to add a new record to the DBGrid control, they click a column in the last row of the DBGrid. This row is marked with an asterisk (*) and only is displayed if the AllowAddNew property is True. As the user enters information into each of the columns, several events occur. Some of these events pertain to the entire record while other events pertain to the individual cells. You can respond to these events and validate user input. The following list describes the events pertaining to an entire record, and the order in which they occur when a record is added:

1. The **BeforeInsert** event occurs when the user enters the first character in a new row in the DBGrid.

2. After entering data in each field and moving to a different row or different object on the form, the **BeforeUpdate** event occurs. You can use this event to validate input. If a field contains invalid data, you can set the Cancel argument to True to cancel the update. Setting the Cancel argument to True for the BeforeUpdate event has the same effect as setting it to True in the Validate event for the Data control.

3. After the record is written to the underlying database table, the **AfterUpdate** event occurs. If the BeforeInsert or BeforeUpdate events were canceled, this event will not occur.

4. Finally, the **AfterInsert** event occurs. If the BeforeInsert or BeforeUpdate events were canceled, this event will not occur.

When adding a new record, the Amount Due and Amount Paid fields must be validated to make sure they contain numeric data. Also, the Member ID field must be validated to be sure that the member ID exists in the table named tblPeople. Finally, the event ID must be stored in the Event ID column even though the column is not visible on the screen. Remember, this information is stored in the BoundText property of the DBCombo box. Remember also, that the DBGrid control contains a Columns collection, which in turn contains Column objects. Just as you used other collections in the previous tutorial, you can use the Columns collection to store a value in any column at run time. You can reference the zero-based collection by index or use a string key. The string key has the same value as the field name. There is one Column object for each column in the DBGrid control whether or not the column is visible. The Column object supports a Value property, which contains the value displayed in the column. The **Value** property is the default property. If the column named fldEventID were the first column in the Columns collection, the following three statements would be equivalent:

```
dbgRegistration.Columns(0).Value = 100
dbgRegistration.Columns(0) = 100
dbgRegistration.Columns("fldEventID") = 100
```

> *Tip:* The Value property of the Column object is the default property. Using the default property will save typing and improve program performance. Using the string key will improve readability.

When Katrina tries to add a record, the event ID from the DBCombo box must be stored in the first column of the active row in the DBGrid control. You can use the Columns collection with an index of zero (0) or the string key "fldEventID" to specify the column. Gus suggests you write the necessary assignment statement to accomplish this task.

To store the current event ID into the current column:

1. Activate the Code window for the **BeforeUpdate** event for the **dbgRegistration** object.

2. Enter the following statement into the Code window:

```
Private Sub dbgRegistration_BeforeUpdate(Cancel As Integer)
    dbgRegistration.Columns("fldEventID") = _
        dbcEvents.BoundText
End Sub
```

This statement assigns the current event ID, stored in the BoundText property of the DBCombo box, in the Event ID column in the DBGrid. You used the Columns collection with the string key fldEventID to specify the column. You also could have used the index zero (0).

Validating Data with the DBGrid Control

When the Amount Paid or Amount Due fields are changed, which also will occur when a user is filling in information in a new record, Katrina would like the program to make sure that the data entered is a valid positive number. Also, when a record is deleted, she wants a message box to be displayed requesting confirmation from the user before the record actually is deleted.

In addition to writing statements in response to events that occur to an entire row, there are several events that validate the information contained in a cell. The process of validating data with the DBGrid control is similar to the process you used when you programmed the Data control's Validate event. That is, you checked the value of a field. If there was an error you set the Cancel argument to True to stop the update from taking place.

The following list summarizes some of the events supported by the DBGrid control applicable to a cell:

- The **BeforeColUpdate** event occurs when a cell loses focus, and before the changed data is copied to the DBGrid's copy buffer. This gives you an opportunity to validate changes made to the column and advise the user if there are any errors. If there is an error, you can display a message box, and set the Cancel property to True to prevent the update.

- The **BeforeColInsert** and **AfterColInsert** events work like the BeforeUpdate and AfterUpdate events and can be canceled. For more information, see the DBGrid control Help topic.

When a user changes the contents of the Amount Paid or Amount Due fields, the input needs to be validated to be sure each field contains a numeric value. To do this, you can write code to respond to the BeforeColUpdate event. The BeforeColUpdate event has three arguments:

- The **ColIndex** argument is an Integer value identifying the column. The ColIndex of the first column is zero (0), the second is one (1), and so on. Thus, you use the ColIndex argument to find the currently selected column. The ColIndex has the same value as the corresponding index in the Columns collection.

- The **OldValue** argument contains the value of the cell before it was changed.

- The **Cancel** argument, when set to True, will cause the update to be canceled. The contents of the cell are restored to the old value and focus is restored to the cell in the control.

After changes are made to a cell, and just before another cell becomes active, the BeforeColUpdate event occurs, and the ColIndex argument contains the index of the column that is about to become inactive. You can write a Select Case statement to determine the column and validate the fields as necessary. You now are ready to write the statements to validate that any changes made to the Amount Paid and Amount Due fields are valid.

To write the code to validate changes to the Amount Paid and Amount Due fields:

1. Activate the Code window for the **dbgRegistration** object's **BeforeColUpdate** event procedure.

2. Enter the following statements in the Code window:

```
Select Case ColIndex
    Case 1
        If Not (IsNumeric _
            (dbgRegistration.Columns(ColIndex).Value)) Then
            MsgBox ("Cannot Update Amount Paid.")
            Cancel = True
        End If
    Case 2
        If Not (IsNumeric _
            (dbgRegistration.Columns(ColIndex).Value)) Then
            MsgBox ("Cannot Update Amount Due.")
            Cancel = True
        End If
End Select
```

These statements verify that the Amount Paid and Amount Due columns contain valid numbers. The event procedure is called whenever the user changes the contents of a cell and moves to another cell. So you can determine the current column, the ColIndex is passed as an argument to the procedure. The first column has a ColIndex value of zero (0), the second has a value of one (1) and so on.

```
Select Case ColIndex
    Case 1
        If Not (IsNumeric _
            (dbgRegistration.Columns(ColIndex).Value)) Then
            MsgBox ("Cannot Update Amount Paid.")
            Cancel = True
        End If
```

These statements execute when the argument ColIndex has a value of one (1), representing the Amount Paid column. To obtain the current value of this column, you selected the current column from the Columns collection of the DBGrid object. By specifying the Value property, you obtained the value stored in the current column. If the Value property did not contain a valid number, then you displayed a message box and set the value of Cancel to True. This has the effect of canceling the update operation. The old value is restored in the contents of the cell and focus is returned to the column.

```
    Case 2
        If Not (IsNumeric _
            (dbgRegistration.Columns(ColIndex).Value)) Then
            MsgBox ("Cannot Update Amount Due.")
            Cancel = True
        End If
```

These statements have the same affect as the preceding statements. The third column, however, is used rather than the second column. Thus, the message was changed appropriately. You now are ready to test the code you just wrote to verify the Amount Due and Amount Paid fields are being properly validated.

To verify the code for the BeforeColUpdate event:

1. Save the project then start it.

2. Locate the event named **Visual Basic programming seminar - Intermediate**.

3. Click the **Lookup** button to locate the corresponding event registrations.

4. Change the Amount Paid field in one of the rows to **32.33.3** and move the cursor to another cell. The message box should appear.

5. Click **OK** in the message box. The previous value in the Amount Paid field should be restored and focus should be restored to the Amount Paid cell.

6. Change the Amount Due field to **32JK** and move the cursor to another cell. The message box should appear.

7. Click **OK** in the message box. The previous value in the Amount Due field should be restored and focus should be restored.

8. End the program.

Now that you can validate changes to the Amount Due and Amount Paid fields, you need to write the code to validate the Member ID field to be sure it contains a valid member. That is, for every event registration, there must be a corresponding Member ID number in the table named tblPeople. To accomplish this, you can add statements to the Select Case statement you just wrote to look up, in the table tblPeople, the member ID typed by the user. These statements need to create a SELECT statement, then open a recordset. If there is a record in the recordset, then the member is on file, and the record can be added or updated. If the recordset is empty, then no member exists in the table tblPeople, and the update needs to be canceled. You now can proceed to write the statements to validate the Member ID field.

To verify a member exists in the table tblPeople:

1. Activate the Code window for the **dbgRegistration** object's **BeforeColUpdate** event procedure.

2. Enter the following statement to declare a recordset as the first statement in the event procedure:

```
Dim pstrSQL As String
Dim prstCurrent As Recordset
```

3. Append the following statements in the Code window just before the End Select statement:

```
Case 3
    pstrSQL = "SELECT * FROM tblPeople " & _
        " WHERE fldMemberID = " & _
        dbgRegistration.Columns(ColIndex).Value
    Set prstCurrent = _
        DBEngine.Workspaces(0).Databases(0). _
        OpenRecordset(pstrSQL)
    If prstCurrent.RecordCount = 0 Then
        MsgBox ("Member ID Not Found.")
        Cancel = True
    End If
    Set prstCurrent = Nothing
```

These statements execute when the user changes the value of the Member ID field. First, they create a SELECT statement to try to find a record in the table named tblPeople with a matching member ID. If a record is found, the update continues. Otherwise, a message box is displayed and the update is canceled.

```
pstrSQL = "SELECT * FROM tblPeople " & _
    " WHERE fldMemberID = " & _
    dbgRegistration.Columns(ColIndex).Value
```

This statement creates the SELECT statement to select any records from the table tblPeople, where the member ID is the same as the member ID in the current cell. This value is stored in the third column of the DBGrid.

```
Set prstCurrent = _
    DBEngine.Workspaces(0).Databases(0). _
    OpenRecordset(pstrSQL)
```

This statement creates the recordset. In the previous tutorial you used the OpenRecordset with a Database object. This statement does the same thing but uses a different syntax. Because you have not created explicitly a Database object variable, you have no object with which to call the OpenDatabase method. But there is an open database created by the Data control; you can use the first database in the Databases collection. The first Database object is stored in the Default Workspace, which is the first Workspace object in the Workspaces collection. The Workspaces collection is a member of the DBEngine object.

```
If prstCurrent.RecordCount = 0 Then
    MsgBox ("Member ID Not Found.")
    Cancel = True
End If
```

When the recordset is created, the RecordCount property contains the number of records in the recordset. If it is zero (0), then there are no records, so the message box is displayed and the update will be canceled.

```
Set prstCurrent = Nothing
```

Because the recordset will not be used again, it is destroyed explicitly by setting the value of the object to Nothing. Gus suggests you test the code you have written and attempt to add a new record.

To add a new event registration and test the member ID validation statements:

1. Save the project then start it.

2. Using the combo box, select the event named **Visual Basic programming seminar – Beginning**, then click **Lookup**.

3. Create a new record by clicking the first column in the last row with the asterisk (*) in the column indicator. Enter **100.00** for the amount paid. Enter **200.00** for the amount due. Enter the value **10222** for the member ID. The form should look like Figure 8-16.

Figure 8-16 ◄
Adding a new record to DBGrid

current record indicator indicates record is being edited

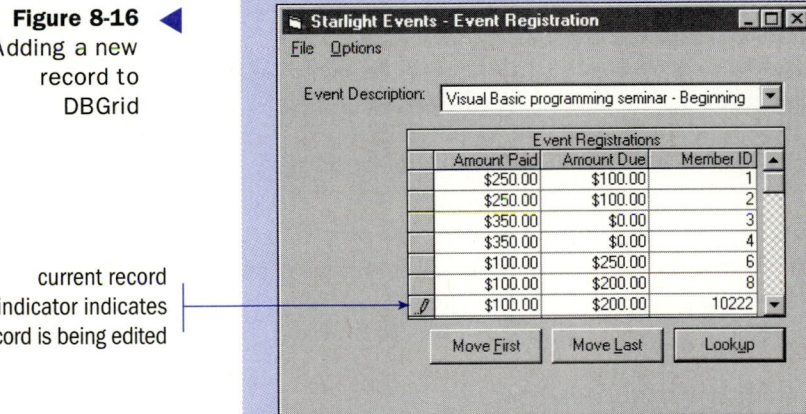

4. Use an appropriate cursor key to move the current record indicator to another record, causing the BeforeUpdate event to occur.

5. Because this member is not on file, the message box should appear explaining the cause of the error. Click **OK** in the message box. Note the value 10222 is removed from the Member ID field and the focus returns to that cell.

6. Enter the value **9** for the member ID and locate a different record. The record you just entered will be added.

7. End the program.

The program now adds and updates registration information. If invalid data is entered in a cell, then an appropriate message box is displayed. You now need to write the code to display a message box and confirm the deletion before proceeding.

Deleting Records with the DBGrid Control

By setting the AllowDelete property to True on the General tab on the Property Pages, the DBGrid control will allow the user to delete records by clicking a record in the record indicator column, then pressing the Delete key. So the user does not delete a record accidentally, Gus wants a message box to be displayed just before the record is actually deleted from the underlying recordset.

The DBGrid control supports two events pertaining to record deletion:

- The **BeforeDelete** event occurs just before removing a selected record from the Database. If the Cancel argument is set to True, the deletion will be canceled and the AfterDelete event will not occur.

- The **AfterDelete** event occurs immediately after the record is deleted.

To write the statements to confirm deletion:

1. Activate the Code window for the **dbgRegistration** object's **BeforeDelete** event procedure.

2. Enter the following statements into the Code window:

```
Private Sub dbgRegistration_BeforeDelete(Cancel As Integer)
    Dim pintAnswer As Integer
    pintAnswer = MsgBox _
        ("Are you sure you want to delete this record?", _
        vbYesNo)
    If pintAnswer <> vbYes Then
        Cancel = True
    End If
End Sub
```

These statements display a message box asking the user to confirm the deletion of the currently selected record. If the user clicks the Yes button, the current record will be deleted. Otherwise, the Cancel argument is set to True and the record will not be deleted. Gus suggests you now test the code you just wrote to ask for confirmation before a record is deleted.

To test the statement to confirm deletion:

1. Save the project then start it.

2. For the record you just added, click the record selector column as shown in Figure 8-17. Note that the entire record should appear highlighted.

Figure 8-17 ◀
Deleting a
record from
DBGrid

click here to select
record

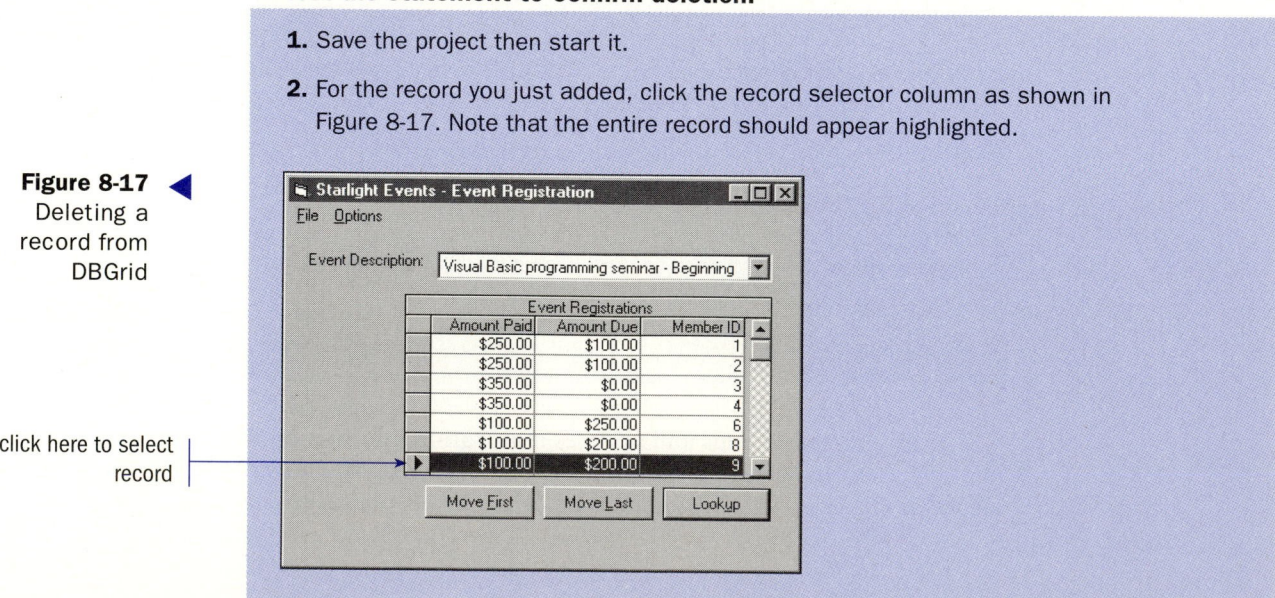

> **3.** Press the **Delete** key. The message box should appear requesting you to confirm the deletion.
>
> **4.** Click **Yes**. The message box closes and the record is removed from the DBGrid control and the underlying recordset.
>
> **5.** End the program.

Although the program you have written for Starlight Events works well for a single client, the user cannot select a specific database. Because there is one database for every client, Gus wants the program to allow the user to select a specific database in any folder on any drive, then be able to modify the event registrations for that database.

Creating an Instance of the CommonDialog Control

There is an ActiveX control, called the **CommonDialog** control, that can be used to display six standard dialog boxes. Each dialog box performs a specific function as shown in Figure 8-18.

Figure 8-18 ◀
Standard
dialog boxes

Dialog box	Description
Open	Allows you to select a file to be opened by specifying the drive, directory, filename extension, and filename.
Save As	Allows you to select a file to be saved by specifying the drive, directory, filename extension, and filename.
Color	Allows the user either to select a color from a color palette, or to create and select a custom color.
Font	Allows the user to select a font by specifying a font size, color, and style.
Print	Allows the user to specify how output should be printed.
Help	Starts the Windows Help Engine (Winhlp32.exe) and displays a Help file.

Like the other controls you have used, you must create an instance of the CommonDialog control on a form before you can use it in your program. Once an instance is created, you can call the object's methods using Visual Basic code. You can also set properties at design time using the Properties window and Property Pages, or at run time by writing Visual Basic code.

Unlike other controls you have used, the CommonDialog control is not displayed at run time so its position on the form is not important. It appears only at design time to remind you that there is a valid instance of the control and so you can click it to activate the Properties window and Properties Pages.

> *Tip:* Generally a program only needs one instance of the CommonDialog control. You can set its properties such that at run time, it will perform different tasks like opening or saving files, sending data to the printer, or setting fonts and colors. Using only one instance of the CommonDialog control will cause your program to consume less memory and improve performance.

Creating an Open Dialog Box Using the CommonDialog Control

Gus does not want a specific database to be opened or displayed on the form when the Event Registration system is first started. Rather, he wants the user to be able to select the database corresponding to a particular client by selecting a menu item, then choosing a database in a dialog box. The CommonDialog control allows you to use standard dialog boxes to open, save, and print files, and set colors and fonts. Remember, because the CommonDialog control is an ActiveX control it needs to be added on the toolbox, which you did at the beginning of the tutorial. The CommonDialog control uses the standard prefix "dlg".

To create an instance of the CommonDialog control:

1. Click the **CommonDialog** control ▦ on the toolbox, and draw an instance of the control on the form.

   Because the control will not be displayed at run time, the exact position of the control is not important. You should create it, however, so it does not obscure another control. Also, the size of the control is not relevant. No matter the region you define for the instance of the CommonDialog control, it will appear as a small square about the same size as the control on the toolbox.

2. Open the Properties window and set the Name property to **dlgOne.**

3. Click the **Value** column of the Custom property, then click the **Properties** button ⊡ to open the Property Pages for the CommonDialog control, as shown in Figure 8-19.

Figure 8-19 ◀
CommonDialog
control
Property Pages

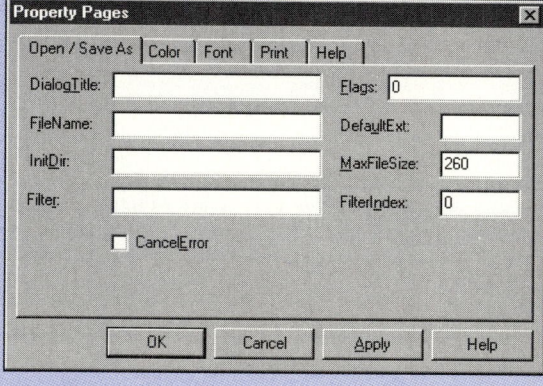

Remember, the CommonDialog control supports six different dialog boxes to perform six different common tasks. The CommonDialog control's Property Pages support different tabs to organize the properties that apply to each of the different dialog boxes. At this time, you need to set the properties that will describe the characteristics of the Open dialog box so the user can select a specific file to open. Before setting these properties, you first must understand the purpose of each. The following list describes the effect of setting each of the different properties for the Open and Save As dialog boxes:

- The **DialogTitle** text box is used to specify the title that appears on the Open and Save As dialog boxes.

- If you want a default filename to appear in the **FileName** text box when the CommonDialog control appears at run time, set the **FileName** property to the name of the file.

- The **InitDir** text box defines the initial directory that will be scanned for files.

- To select only files with a specific filename extension, you can use the **Filter** property. The Filter property is used to provide a list of options in the Files of type list box. The user then can click one of these options to display files of a particular type. The Filter property has the following syntax:

object.**Filter** [= *description1|filter1|description2|filter2...*]

  - The *object* must be a valid instance of a CommonDialog object.

  - Each filter is made up of a description and a corresponding filter. The *description* appears in the list box. The *filter* should be a three-character file extension. Files having that extension will be displayed in the Look in list box. A vertical bar separates each filter and description. Do not put spaces between the vertical bars as they will appear in the description or be used in the filter. The description should be a brief description of the file type followed by the name of the file extension in parentheses.

    The following statement will set the Filter property of an object named dlgOne to look for Microsoft Access databases:

```
dlgOne.Filter = "Access Database (*.mdb)|*.mdb|All Files|*.*"
```

- The **FilterIndex** property works with the Filter property. It is useful to specify a default filter when there are multiple filters. Each filter has a unique index beginning with zero (0). Thus, to set the second filter to the default filter you should set the FilterIndex property to zero (0).

- The **CancelError** property is used so you can determine if the user clicked the OK button or the Cancel button. If set to True, a run-time error will be generated when the user clicks the Cancel button. You then can write an error handler to perform the appropriate processing.

The **Flags** property is used to further control the behavior of the different dialog boxes. Depending on the application, you may want the user to be able to select multiple files or allow a new file to be created. For more information on the Flags property, see the CommonDialog Control Constants Help topic. The following list describes some of the valid flags:

- The flag **cdlOFNCreatePrompt** specifies that the dialog box will prompt the user to create a new file that does not exist currently.

- The flag **cdlOFNFileMustExist** indicates that the user only can select files that already exist. If the user specifies a file that does not exist, a warning message is displayed.

- The flag **cdlOFNNoChangeDir** indicates that the user cannot change directories.

- The flag **cdlOFNPathMustExist** indicates that the path already must exist.

> *Tip:* Generally your program will open files of a specific type. In this session you are opening files that have the extension ".mdb" (Microsoft Access database). Thus, you only want files to appear in the list box that have the extension ".mdb" by default. A user may have changed the extension of a file, however, so you also must provide the user with the opportunity to look at all files.

Now you are ready to set the properties of the CommonDialog control so it will open files with the ".mdb" extension and look in Tutorial.08 folder on your Student Disk by default. Gus suggests that you set the caption of the dialog box to Open Database. If the user clicks the Cancel button then no database should be opened.

To set the design time properties of the CommonDialog control:

1. Make sure the Property Pages dialog box for the CommonDialog control still is open, and that the **Open / Save As** tab is active.

2. Type **Open Database** in the DialogTitle text box.

3. Type **A:\Tutorial.08** in the InitDir text box.

4. Type **Microsoft Access database (*.mdb)|*.mdb|All Files|*.*** in the Filter text box.

5. Make sure the value for the FilterIndex property is **0**, its default setting.

6. Click the **CancelError** check box to select it.

7. Click **OK** to close the Property Pages dialog box and apply the properties to the CommonDialog control.

Now that you have set the properties for the CommonDialog control, you need to call a method to display the appropriate dialog box. Remember, the user does not interact with the CommonDialog control by clicking it at run time.

Displaying the Open Dialog Box on the Screen

The next step is to write the code that will display the Open dialog box when the File Open menu item is clicked. Which of the standard dialog boxes displays, depends on which of several methods is called.

When the CommonDialog's ShowOpen method is called, a dialog box similar to the one shown in Figure 8-20 will be displayed on the screen.

Figure 8-20
Open dialog box

DialogTitle property value displayed in title bar

no default filename selected

Filter property determines Files of type

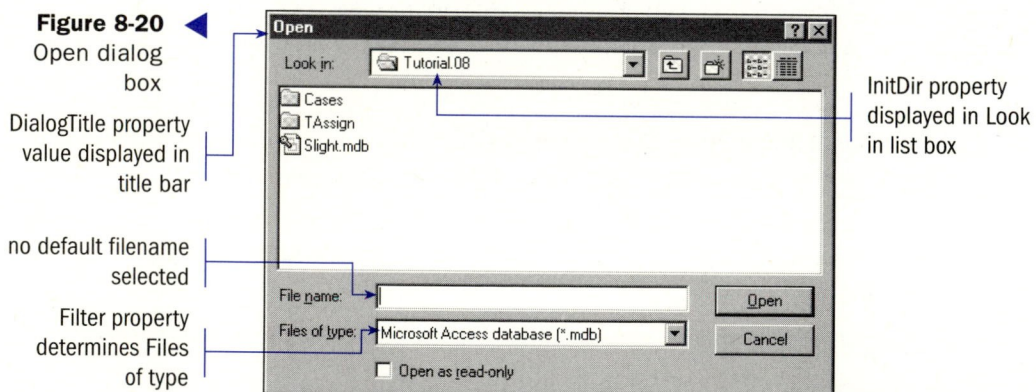

InitDir property displayed in Look in list box

Unlike other controls you have used, the user does not interact with the instance of the CommonDialog control you created on the form. Instead, the dialog box is opened when you call one of the methods applicable to the control. The CommonDialog control supports six methods. Each method will display a different dialog box when it is called. Figure 8-21 describes these different methods.

Figure 8-21 ◀
Methods of
CommonDialog
control

Method	Description
ShowColor	Displays the CommonDialog control's Color dialog box.
ShowFont	Displays the CommonDialog control's Font dialog box.
ShowHelp	Runs Winhlp32.exe and displays the Help file specified.
ShowOpen	Displays the CommonDialog control's Open dialog box.
ShowPrinter	Displays the CommonDialog control's Print dialog box.
ShowSave	Displays the CommonDialog control's Save As dialog box.

REFERENCE
window

CREATING AN OPEN COMMONDIALOG CONTROL

- Make sure the CommonDialog control has been added on the toolbox. Draw an instance of the CommonDialog control on a form.
- Set the InitDir property to the initial directory to be scanned for files.
- Set the DialogTitle property to control the caption displayed in the dialog box at run time.
- If a default filename should appear in the File name text box, set the FileName property.
- Set the Filter property to the desired file extensions.
- To determine if the user clicked the Cancel button, set the CancelError property to True, then create an error handler in the procedure where the ShowOpen method is called.
- After setting all the properties, call the ShowOpen method to display the dialog box.
- After calling the ShowOpen method, the selected path and filename are stored in the FileName property.

In this session you are using the CommonDialog control to open an existing database. Thus, you need to call the ShowOpen method. When the method is called, the Open dialog box will appear on the screen. The CommonDialog control is modal, like a message box or input box. That is, you either must select a file to open or click the Cancel button before interacting with the other forms in the program. Because you set the CancelError property to True, a run-time error will occur if the user clicks the Cancel button in the CommonDialog control. Thus, you need to write an error handler. If a filename was specified, the database should be opened, and all the controls on the form should be made visible. Otherwise, they should remain invisible.

To call the ShowOpen method:

1. Activate the Code window for the **mnuFileOpen_Click** event. (Remember, you can click Open on the File menu while in design mode to activate the Code window for this event procedure.)

2. Enter the following statements in the Code window:

```
Private Sub mnuFileOpen_Click( )
      On Error GoTo ErrorHandler
      dlgOne.ShowOpen
      Exit Sub
ErrorHandler:
End Sub
```

When the ShowOpen method is called, Visual Basic will display the Open dialog box created by the CommonDialog control so the user can select the desired filename. The Open dialog box is closed when the user clicks the OK button or the Cancel button.

The CommonDialog control does not actually open a file for you. Rather, it provides a way for the user to specify a filename to be opened. You still must connect the program to the database. You can accomplish this by setting the DatabaseName and RecordSource properties of each Data control at run time, then call the Refresh method to create the recordset.

When the user selects a filename using the CommonDialog control, the filename selected is stored in the FileName property of the CommonDialog control. You can use this value to set the DatabaseName property of each Data control. Once the DatabaseName property is set, you need to call the Refresh method for the information to be loaded correctly into the recordset.

To open a database at run time:

1. Make sure the Code window for the **mnuFileOpen_Click** event procedure still is active.

2. Enter the following statements, shown in bold, in the event procedure:

```
      On Error GoTo ErrorHandler
      dlgOne.ShowOpen
      datEvents.DatabaseName = dlgOne.filename
      datEvents.Refresh
      datRegistration.DatabaseName = dlgOne.filename
      Exit Sub
ErrorHandler:
End Sub
```

These statements set the current database to the filename specified by the user. If no filename is selected (i.e., the user clicked the Cancel button), a run-time error will occur and no file will be opened.

```
datEvents.DatabaseName = dlgOne.filename
datEvents.Refresh
```

The first statement uses the filename, stored in the FileName property of the CommonDialog control and stores that filename in the DatabaseName property of the first Data control. The second statement calls the Refresh method of the Data control. This causes the recordset to be refreshed. Thus, the records in the database table are loaded into the recordset.

```
datRegistration.DatabaseName = dlgOne.filename
```

This statement selects the database for the DBGrid control. The recordset for this control will be refreshed when the user selects an event description from the DBList control.

Using the Controls Collection

As the program presently exists, the controls are visible, even though the user has not selected a database to open. Gus wants the visible controls to remain hidden until the user successfully opens a database. Then, the controls should become visible. One way to do this would be to set the Visible property to True for each control individually after the database is loaded. There is, however, another collection, called the Controls collection, that contains one Control object for each object on the screen. Even though this form only has a few visible objects, the following steps will illustrate the use of the Controls collection.

The Controls collection works like other collections you have used. It is a zero-based collection containing Control objects. For each control drawn on a form, there exists one Control object in the Controls collection. The Controls collection has one property, Count, which specifies the number of Control objects in the collection. You use the following syntax to reference a control in the Controls collection:

object.**Controls**(*index*)

- The *object* can be any form in your program. There is one Controls collection for each form. If the object is omitted, the current form is assumed.

- The *index* can be a numeric index, starting at zero (0), or a string key. The string key for a control is the same as the Name property of the control.

Instead of writing several statements to make each control on a form visible or invisible, you can use a For Each loop to examine each control in the Controls collection.

Before writing this loop, you need a way to determine the type of control. Because each menu item is a Control object in the Controls collection, if you set the Visible property to False for all the controls, the menus also would become invisible. There is a Visual Basic keyword, called TypeOf, which allows you to determine the type of any object. This keyword is used in an If statement and has the following syntax:

If TypeOf *objectname* **Is** *objecttype* **Then**

    [*statements*]

EndIf

- The *objectname* can be any object reference. For example, the *objectname* could be an instance of a control drawn on the form or an object variable.

- The *objecttype* is any valid type of object including objects you draw on a form or other objects like DAO objects. The type of a menu title or menu item is "menu", and the type of a command button is "CommandButton".

Gus suggests you make all the objects, except for the menu items, invisible when the program is started. When a database is opened, the objects should become visible. This will improve the user interface because the user will not be able to try to select an event or work with event registrations until the database has been opened.

You could write a For Each loop in the Form_Load event procedure to make the controls invisible and another in the mnuFileOpen event procedure to make the controls visible when the database is opened. But, because these loops are identical, it will take less code to create a general procedure that accepts one argument: a Boolean value to determine if the controls are being made visible or invisible.

To write the general procedure to make the controls visible or invisible:

1. Make sure the Code window is active.

2. Click **Tools** then **Add Procedure** to open the Add Procedure dialog box. Set the name to **SetVisible**, the scope to **Private**, and the type to **Sub**.

3. Enter the following statements into the general procedure:

```
Private Sub SetVisible(pblnArg As Boolean)
    Dim pctlCurrent As Control
    For Each pctlCurrent In Controls
        If Not (TypeOf pctlCurrent Is Data _
            Or TypeOf pctlCurrent Is CommonDialog _
            Or TypeOf pctlCurrent Is Menu) Then
            pctlCurrent.Visible = pblnArg
        End If
    Next
End Sub
```

This Sub procedure sets the Visible property of each control in the Controls collection to True or False depending on the value of the argument pblnArg.

```
Dim pctlCurrent As Control
For Each pctlCurrent In Controls
```

The first statement creates a local variable of type Control for use as the member in the For Each loop. The For Each loop examines each control in the Controls collection. Each time through the loop, a reference to the current Control object is stored in the variable pctlCurrent. You can reference pctlCurrent just like any other control drawn on the form. That is, you can set or read its properties and call its methods.

```
If Not (TypeOf pctlCurrent Is Data _
    Or TypeOf pctlCurrent Is CommonDialog _
    Or TypeOf pctlCurrent Is Menu) Then
        pctlCurrent.Visible = pblnArg
End If
```

The If statement uses the TypeOf keyword to determine the type of control stored in the variable pctlCurrent. There are three types of controls that always should be invisible—the Data controls, the Menu objects, and the CommonDialog control. Thus, you wrote an If statement to test if the type of the control is one of the above. The Not keyword causes the Visible property to be set if the type of control is one of these types. You should note that the CommonDialog control does not support the Visible property. If you try to set the Visible property, a run-time error will occur. You now need to write the statements to call this general procedure when the form is loaded so the objects will be invisible. To do this, you need to call the general procedure you just wrote with the argument False, when the form is loaded, and again with the argument True, when a database is opened successfully.

To make the objects invisible when the form is loaded and visible when a database is opened:

1. Activate the Code window for the **Form_Load** event procedure and enter the following statement:

```
SetVisible False
```

2. Activate the Code window for the **mnuFileOpen_Click** event procedure and enter the following statement just after the ShowOpen method is called:

```
SetVisible True
```

These statements make the controls invisible when the form first is loaded and visible after a database is opened. Gus suggests you test the program again to make sure it is working properly.

To verify the controls are visible and invisible at the proper time:

1. Save the project then start it. Note that the menus are the only objects visible on the form.

2. Click **File** then **Open** on the form's menu bar.

3. Select the filename **Slight.mdb** in the **Tutorial.08** folder on your Student Disk. The bound Data controls, command buttons, and labels should be visible.

4. End the program.

To further improve the user interface, Gus would like the user to be able to customize the font and font size for the DBCombo and DBGrid objects.

Understanding the Screen and Printer Fonts

Fonts are divided into screen and printer fonts. While there are common fonts installed on nearly all computers, some computers have unique fonts that may not always be available. The printer fonts installed on a system depend on the type of printer and the fonts installed on the printer. Be aware that the supported screen and printer fonts on a system may differ.

Determining the fonts available on your system can be accomplished by looking at the following two objects:

- The **Screen** object allows you to manipulate the forms and controls on the screen.

- The **Printer** object represents the default printer on the system.

Each object supports the following two properties to allow you to determine the fonts applicable to each object:

- The **FontCount** property returns the number of fonts available for the screen or active printer.

- The **Fonts** property returns a list that works much like a zero-based collection. You reference a specific font name by supplying a numeric index from 0 to FontCount - 1.

Thus, if you wanted to print all the screen fonts on the system, you could use the following For loop:

```
Dim pintCount As Integer
For pintCount = 0 To Screen.FontCount - 1
    Debug.Print Screen.Fonts(pintCount)
Next
```

The For loop steps through each of the screen fonts and prints the name of the font to the Immediate window.

Tip: The Fonts property is not a collection of Font objects. It merely returns a list of the fonts installed. Therefore, you cannot use a For Each loop to iterate through the collection.

Gus would like to give each user the opportunity of changing the font displayed in both the DBCombo and DBGrid controls. Both controls support the Font object, which in turn, has the following properties:

- The **Bold** property can be True or False. If True the font is bold. Otherwise, it is not.

- The **Italic** property can be True or False. If True the font is italic. Otherwise, it is not.

- The **Name** property identifies the name of the font. The list of available fonts can vary from computer to computer.

- The **Size** property identifies the size of the font in points.

- The **StrikeThrough** property can be True or False. If True a line is drawn through the font. If False no line is drawn.

- The **Underline** property can be True or False. If True the font is underlined. If False the font is not underlined.

Using the Font object and these properties, you can change the current font and attributes of the DBCombo box. The following statement will set the size of the font in the DBCombo box named dbcEvents to 10 points:

```
dbcEvents.Font.Size = 10
```

Note the syntax of this statement. You are referencing the Font object pertaining to the object dbcEvents. The Font object in turn supports the Size property.

At run time, Gus would like the user to select a menu item to display the CommonDialog control applicable to fonts. When the user selects a font or its attributes, the font displays in both the DBGrid and DBList controls. You can accomplish this task by calling the ShowFont method of the CommonDialog control. After the ShowFont method is called, the following CommonDialog properties are set. You can use the following properties to set the font for other visible objects on the form.

- The **FontBold** property can be True or False, indicating the font should appear in a bold or standard typeface.

- The **FontItalic** property can be True or False, indicating the font should appear italicized or normal.

- The **FontStrikethru** property can be True or False, indicating the font should appear with a line through each character or not.

- The **FontUnderline** property can be True or False, indicating the font should be underlined or not.

- The **FontName** property identifies the name of the font.

- The **FontSize** property identifies the size of the font in points.

When you use the CommonDialog control with the ShowFont method, you first need to set the Flags property of the control to tell the CommonDialog control whether you want to display screen or printer fonts, or both. These values can be represented by the following constants:

- If set to **cdlCFScreenFonts**, only the screen fonts will be listed in the Font dialog box.

- If set to **cdlCFPrinterFonts**, only the printer fonts will be listed in the Font dialog box.

- If set to **cdlCFBoth**, then both printer and screen fonts will be listed in the Font dialog box.

Before calling the ShowFont method, you must set the Flags property to one of these values or a run-time error will occur when the method is called. In addition to these values, there are several other flags that can be set to control the font's appearance in the CommonDialog control. For more information, see Help on the Flags property for the Font Dialog.

After you set the Flags property for the CommonDialog control and call the ShowOpen method, you need to use the relevant properties of the CommonDialog control to set the font characteristics of both the DBCombo box and DBGrid. Because you are working with several properties, you will need to write an assignment statement for each property. That is, you will need to write the following statements to set the properties for the DBCombo box:

```
dbcEvents.Font.Bold = dlgOne.FontBold
dbcEvents.Font.Italic = dlgOne.FontItalic
dbcEvents.Font.Name = dlgOne.FontName
dbcEvents.Font.Size = dlgOne.FontSize
```

There is a statement called the With statement, however, that gives you a way to select an object and apply the object to many statements.

Using the With Statement

The With statement allows you to perform a series of statements on a specific object without specifying the name of the object. The With statement has the following syntax:

With *object*

  [*statements*]

End With

- The *object* can be the name of any object.

- There can be one or more *statements* executed on the object.

- Between the With and End With statements, you can nest With statements.

Using a With statement, the preceding statements can be replaced with the following With block:

```
With dbcEvents
    .Font.Bold = dlgOne.FontBold
    .Font.Italic = dlgOne.FontItalic
    . . .
End With
```

Because each statement uses the Font object, you can modify the With statement as follows to reduce typing:

```
With dbcEvents.Font
    .Bold = dlgOne.FontBold
    .Italic = dlgOne.FontItalic
    . . .
End With
```

Gus suggests you now write the statements to change the font for both the DBCombo and DBGrid controls using the ShowFont method for the CommonDialog control and a With statement.

To change the font of the visible objects:

1. Activate the Code window for the **mnuOptionsFonts_Click** event procedure.

2. Enter the following statements into the event procedure:

```
Private Sub mnuOptionsFonts_Click( )
     dlgOne.Flags = cdlCFScreenFonts
     dlgOne.ShowFont
     With dbcEvents.Font
          .Bold = dlgOne.FontBold
          .Italic = dlgOne.FontItalic
          .Name = dlgOne.FontName
          .Size = dlgOne.FontSize
     End With
     With dbgRegistration.Font
          .Bold = dlgOne.FontBold
          .Italic = dlgOne.FontItalic
          .Name = dlgOne.FontName
          .Size = dlgOne.FontSize
     End With
End Sub
```

Now that you have written the statements to change the font and font characteristics of the two visible objects, you can test the program to be sure the font is working properly.

To verify the user can change the font of the visible objects:

1. Save the project then start it.

2. Click **File** then **Open**, and select the database named **Slight.mdb** in the Open dialog box. Click **OK**.

3. Click **Options** then **Fonts** on the form's menu bar to open the Font dialog box.

4. Select a font, style, and size, then click **OK**. The font should appear in both the DBCombo and DBGrid controls.

5. End the program and exit Visual Basic.

You now have completed the program for Starlight Events. The user can add, change, and delete records in the DBGrid control. In addition the user can select any database to open using the CommonDialog control. Finally, the user can customize the interface by changing the fonts.

Quick Check

1. What are a Control object and Controls collection?

2. What is the purpose of the TypeOf keyword and where is it used?

3. What are the methods of the CommonDialog control, and what is the purpose of each?

4. What is the difference between screen and printer fonts? What objects do you use to reference screen and printer fonts?

Figure 8-22 lists and defines the new terms presented in this tutorial.

Figure 8-22 ◀
New terms

Term	Definition
ActiveX controls	ActiveX controls are not part of Visual Basic. Rather, they are built using a standard technology called component object modules (COM). ActiveX controls are stored as separate files on the disk with the extensions ".OCX, .DLL, or .EXE".
Cell	A cell is defined by the intersection of a row and column in the DBGrid control.
Component object modules (COM)	Component object modules (COM) technology allows objects to be shared among many different applications written with different programming languages.
Insertable objects	Insertable objects allow you to program another application's objects, such as a Microsoft Excel Worksheet object or a Microsoft Word Document object.
Intrinsic controls	Intrinsic controls are part of Visual Basic itself and are included in the executable files Visual Basic produces.
Property Pages	A tabbed dialog box used to set design time properties for an ActiveX control that may not be available using the Properties window. Each tab is called a Property Page.
User Interface (UI) active	The term User Interface (UI) active applies to the DBGrid control. UI active means you can insert, move, delete, and resize the individual columns by dragging them rather than using the Property Pages to set the values.

Tutorial Assignments

In addition to entering event registrations, the employees of Starlight Events need to look up all the event registrations for a particular client. Because the member ID is the unique key for a particular person, Gus would like a staff member to be able to select a member ID. After selecting a member ID, the program should look up all the event registrations for that person. This way, when a person who will be attending a conference calls, it is possible to look up their event registration. Gus has decided, however, that the program you just wrote will be used to add, change, and delete event registration. This new program only will be used to display existing registrations. When complete, the form should look like Figure 8-23.

Figure 8-23 ◀

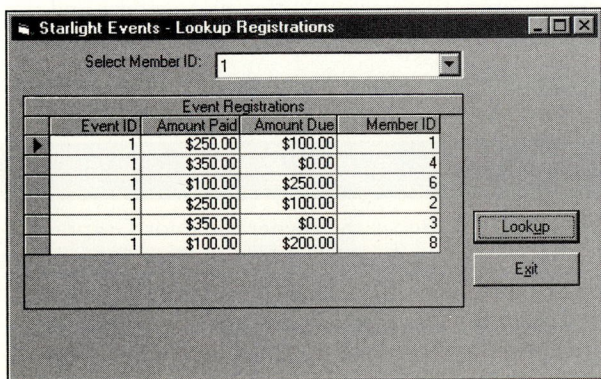

1. Make sure your Student Disk is in the appropriate disk drive, then start Visual Basic.

2. You will need to use the DBCombo and DBGrid control. Because these are ActiveX controls, use the Components dialog box to add them to your project.

3. Set the form's caption as shown in Figure 8-23. Set the name of the form to **frmStarlightLookup**. Save the form in the **TAssign** folder in the **Tutorial.08** folder on your Student Disk using the default name and save the project using the filename **Starlight Lookup.vbp**.

4. Create two Data controls on the form such that they are not visible at run time. Set the name of one Data control to **datPeople**. Set the necessary properties so it will connect to the database named **Slight.mdb** in the **TAssign** folder in the **Tutorial.08** folder on your Student Disk. Select the table named **tblPeople**. Set the name of the second Data control to **datRegistration**, connect it to the table named **tblRegistration** in the database named **Slight.mdb** in the **TAssign** folder in the **Tutorial.08** folder on your Student Disk.

5. Create a DBCombo box such that the field displayed is the field named **fldMemberID** in the table named **datPeople**.

6. Set the name of the DBCombo to **dbcPeople** and remove the initial text from the object.

7. Create a descriptive label for the DBCombo as shown in Figure 8-23.

8. Create a DBGrid control that will display information from the table **datRegistration**. Set the name to **dbgRegistration.**

9. Change the General tab on the Property Pages so that the user cannot add, change, or delete records.

10. Set the necessary properties so the column headers look like those shown in Figure 8-23.

11. Create a command button named **cmdLookup** that will display in the DBGrid control all the event registration records for the selected person. Set the Caption and Default properties as shown in Figure 8-23.

12. Declare the necessary variables and write the SELECT statement to select all the fields from the table tblRegistration where the current member ID stored in the DBCombo is the same. Make sure the records are ordered by event ID.

13. Assign the SELECT statement you just wrote to the RecordSource property of the DBGrid control and refresh the underlying recordset so that only the correct records are displayed in the DBGrid control.

14. Create a working **Exit** command button.

15. Save the form and project.

16. Test the program by selecting different members and verifying that the corresponding event registrations appear in the DBGrid object.

17. Print the Form as Text and Code, then exit Visual Basic.

Case Problems

1. Color Graphics Ellen Natchez is the owner of Color Graphics. Color Graphics is a graphic arts company in Santa Fe, New Mexico. They have several different computers and printers in the office. Each of these computers has different screen and printer fonts available. Ellen would like you to write a program to display in list boxes each of the available screen and printer fonts on a specific computer. When complete, your form should look like Figure 8-24.

Figure 8-24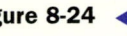

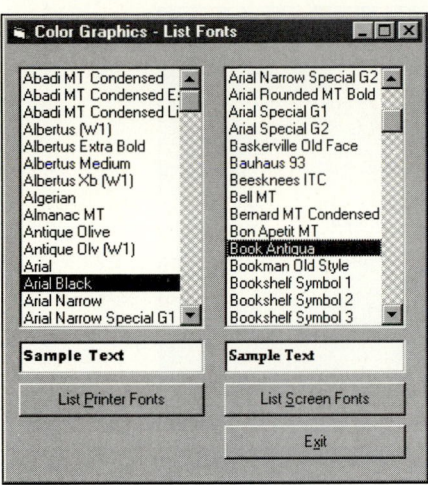

1. Make sure your Student Disk is in the appropriate disk drive, then start Visual Basic.

2. Set the caption of the form to **Color Graphics - List Fonts,** and set the name of the form to **frmColorGraphicsListFonts**.

3. Save the form using the default name and the project using the name **Color Graphics List Fonts.vbp** in the **Cases** folder in the **Tutorial.08** folder on your Student Disk.

4. Create three command buttons on the form as shown in Figure 8-24. Set the caption of the first command button to **List Printer Fonts** and the caption of the second command button to **List Screen Fonts**. Set the name of each command button as appropriate. Create a working **Exit** command button.

5. Create two list boxes named **lstPrinterFonts** and **lstScreenFonts**. The contents of each list box should appear in sorted order.

6. Create two text boxes as shown in Figure 8-24.

7. In the Click event procedure for the List Printer Fonts command button, write a For loop to display each printer font in the List Printer Fonts list box. Remember, you use the AddItem method to add an item to a list box at run time. The printer fonts are stored in the Fonts property of the Printer object. The Fonts property is used with an index from 0 to FontCount - 1.

8. In the Click event procedure for the List Screen Fonts command button, write a For loop to display each screen font in the corresponding list box. The fonts are listed in the Fonts property of the Screen object.

9. Write the necessary code for each list box's Click event procedure so that when a font is selected, the string **Sample text** appears in the corresponding text box in the selected font.

10. Save the project then exit Visual Basic.

2. Data Helpers Data Helpers is a consulting company that helps different businesses to better manage their data. One of the first tasks they perform is to look at the tables in an existing database, then the contents of those tables. They want you to write a program that will allow the user to select a database to open. When a database is selected, the program should display each of the tables in the database. When a table is selected, each of the rows and columns needs to be displayed in a DBGrid. When complete, your screen should look like Figure 8-25.

Figure 8-25 ◀

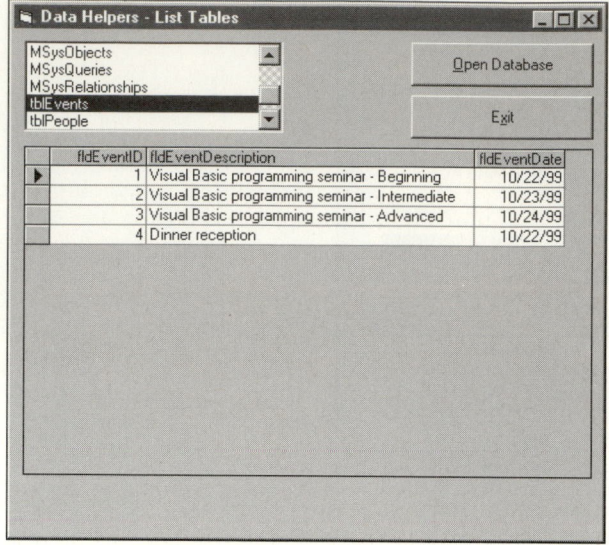

1. Make sure your Student Disk is in the appropriate disk drive, then start Visual Basic.

2. Set the form name to **frmDataHelpers**, and change the form's caption as shown in Figure 8-25.

3. Save the form using the default name and use the project name **Data Helpers.vbp** in the **Cases** folder in the **Tutorial.08** folder on your Student Disk.

4. Add the CommonDialog and DBGrid controls on the toolbox.

5. Create an instance of the CommonDialog control on the form and set the name of the object to **dlgOne**.

6. Using the correct Property Pages for the Open dialog box, set the caption to **Open Database**, the initial directory to **A:\Tutorial.08** and the Filter such that only files with the extension ".mdb" are located. If the Cancel button is clicked, the program should generate a run-time error.

7. Create a Data control on the form and set the Name to **datAny**. Make the Data control invisible at run time.

8. Create a DBGrid control on the form and set the name to **dbgAny**. Connect this DBGrid to the Data control you just created.

9. Create a list box on the form named **lstTables**.

10. Create two command buttons. One button will open the database and one will exit the program. Set the captions as shown in Figure 8-25.

11. Write the necessary code to call the ShowOpen method of the CommonDialog control. Because you set the properties such that clicking the Cancel button will cause a run-time error, you need to write an error handler for this procedure. If the user did not select a file, exit the procedure. If there is not a run-time error, write the necessary statement to open the database specified by the user. You need to call the OpenDatabase method on the filename returned by the CommonDialog control. Then write a For Each loop to examine each table in the TableDefs collection of the database. For each table, add the name of the table to the list box. To do this you can use the Name property of the current TableDef object.

12. Create two form-level variables named **mdbCurrent** as type Database and **mdbTableDef** as type TableDef.

13. When the user clicks a table in the list box, the contents of the table need to be displayed in the DBGrid control. You need to set the necessary properties of the Data control to connect to the selected database and a table in the database, then refresh the recordset. Because the DBGrid control already is set up to connect to the Data control, all the records in the selected table should be displayed.

14. Test the program by opening a database. For testing, use the database named **Slight.mdb** in the **TAssign** folder in the **Tutorial.08** folder on your Student Disk. The tables should be displayed in the list box. Click a table in the list box. The contents of the table should be displayed in the DBGrid control.

15. Save your work then print the form as Text and Code.

16. Exit Visual Basic.

3. Intex Electronics Intex Electronics is an electronics manufacturer in San Jose, California. They make memory and other chips for sale in personal and other computers. They want you to create a prototype for a form to look at pending orders and enter new orders. This form will interact eventually with their database. This prototype will not, however. The completed form is shown in Figure 8-26.

Figure 8-26 ◀

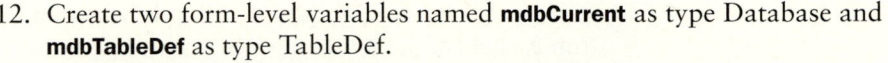

The form will operate in two modes as follows:

■ In browse mode, all the option buttons, text boxes, and check boxes should be disabled because they are used to add, change, and delete records only.

■ In edit mode, the buttons and boxes should be enabled.

1. Make sure your Student Disk is in the appropriate disk drive, then start Visual Basic.

2. Set the form name to **frmIntexElectronics**, and change the form's caption as shown in Figure 8-26.

3. Save the form using the default name and use the project name **Intex Electronics.vbp** in the **Cases** folder in the **Tutorial.08** folder on your Student Disk.

4. Create the labels, text boxes, command buttons, and option buttons as shown in Figure 8-26. Be sure the options buttons are members of a control array.

5. Create the necessary modules and call them so when the Browse command button is clicked, the following will occur: If the type of the control is an option button, check box, or text box, disable the button, but if the type of the control is a label, change the font from bold to normal. When the Edit button is clicked, enable each option button, check box, and text box. Change the font of the label from normal to bold.

6. Save the form and project.

7. Run the program, enter a test date to check that the code for the two command buttons is working correctly.

8. Print the form Code.

9. Exit Visual Basic.

4. Leopard Foods Leopard Foods is a wholesale food distributor in Boise, Idaho. They would like you to create a form to help manage their inventory. Leopard Foods buys products directly from the manufacturers. Thus, there is a table tblManufacturer in the database called Leopard.mdb in the Cases folder in the Tutorial.08 folder on your Student Disk. Leopard.mdb represents the manufacturers. Each manufacturer has several products stored in the table tblProducts. These two tables are linked with the common field fldManufacturerID. They want you to create a new form with two parts. The first part of the form should contain several bound text boxes to display information pertinent to the manufacturer. You need to use the Data control to navigate through each manufacturer. Because this information will not be changed, disable the text boxes. Whenever a manufacturer is selected using a button on the Data control, the corresponding products should be displayed in the DBGrid control on the form. The user should be able to add, change, and delete records in the DBGrid. When records are added or changed, be sure to validate each input field. When records are deleted, display a message box to confirm the deletion. The completed form is shown in Figure 8-27.

Figure 8-27 ◀

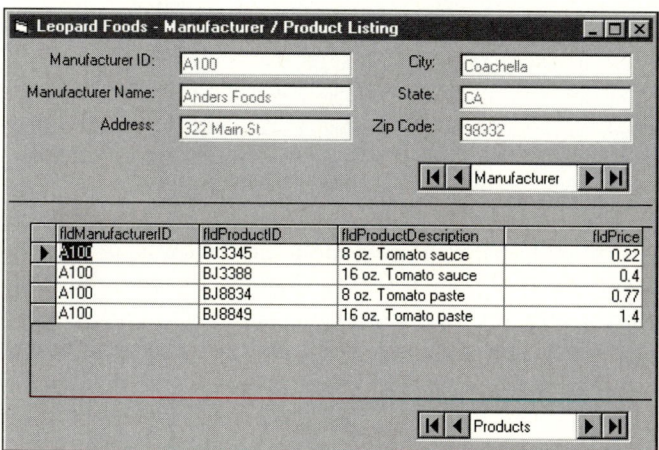

Toolbars and Advanced Reports

Creating a Part-Management System for Power Parts

CASE

Power Parts

Power Parts manufactures and distributes electrical parts for commercial power plants from its main office in Cleveland, Ohio. Since 1928 they have been manufacturing very specialized electrical parts that are complex to install. So the installation procedures are shipped with each part to guide the installer through the task. This helps to avoid installation errors that could cause the part to fail or harm other parts.

Ted MacDonald is the information systems manager for Power Parts. He has assigned you the task of developing a program that will allow the user to select a part from a database. Once a part is selected, the installation procedure needs to be displayed and printed. The user also must be able to change the installation procedure, and add and change formatting to the installation procedure like setting the text to bold, italic, and underline.

To accomplish these tasks, Ted would like to supply a toolbar for the program to execute common functions in addition to the menu bar. This toolbar will work like other Windows toolbars. The user clicks a button on the toolbar to execute a task. Ted would like the user to call the common formatting functions like changing the typeface to bold, underline, or italic.

In addition they need two reports. One report will print a list of part numbers and the gross annual sales. The other will print the total value of the inventory. Ted would like two of the buttons to print the reports. You will create the reports in Session 9.2 of this tutorial.

SESSION 9.1

In this session you will learn how to create a toolbar for a program using the Toolbar and ImageList controls, and use ActiveX controls to format text.

Reviewing the Program Design

Ted already has completed the NEADT charts that describe the processing required by the program. He suggests you now review this documentation to become more familiar with the project.

To view and print the NEADT charts for the inventory and sales program:

1. Make sure your Student Disk is in the appropriate disk drive. Using Microsoft Word, open the file **Power.doc** in the **Tutorial.09** folder on your Student Disk. Otherwise, open the file **Power.txt** using WordPad.

2. Print the NEADT charts and close the word processing program.

The NEADT charts contain objects to display a part number and part category. Also, there is an object to display the corresponding installation procedure. The user can print reports, and format the installation procedure using a menu bar or corresponding buttons on a toolbar. There are several general procedures to perform these tasks. These procedures are called when either a menu item is selected or a corresponding toolbar button is clicked.

Creating a Toolbar

In addition to allowing the user to click command buttons and menus to perform actions, you can enhance a program's user interface by adding a toolbar. You can create toolbars that work like other toolbars in Windows 95 programs. Each button on a toolbar should correspond to a menu item. When a menu item is used frequently, creating a corresponding toolbar button will improve the user interface. Figure 9-1 shows the completed form with a toolbar.

Figure 9-1 ◀
Completed form

toolbar with buttons

formatted installation procedure

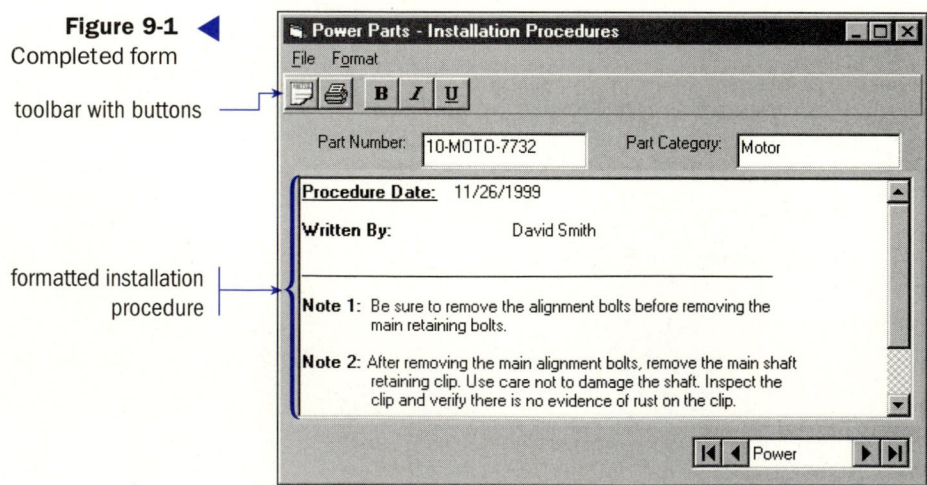

As shown in Figure 9-1, the toolbar contains several buttons with graphical images displayed inside of them. Buttons on a toolbar work somewhat like command buttons. That is, when the button is clicked an event occurs. But instead of generating a different Click event for each button, a ButtonClick event is generated for the toolbar. The code you write for this event procedure first must determine which button was clicked and then perform the corresponding action depending on which button was clicked. Buttons on a toolbar can work in one of three ways:

- The default behavior is for a button to display unpressed, and when pressed, it displays recessed while the ButtonClick event procedure is running. When the event procedure is finished, the button displays unpressed again. This type of button is suitable for tasks like opening and saving files.

- A button can work like a toggle switch. That is, a button can display unpressed or pressed depending on the status of a button. Pressed generally indicates On; unpressed generally indicates Off. A toggle button is suitable for describing the status of an object, like a font being bold or normal.

- A button can be part of a group of buttons. Conceptually, this is similar to an option group. Only one button from a group of buttons can display recessed. This is useful for describing a mutually exclusive list. For example, when aligning text in a paragraph, the paragraph can be left-aligned, right-aligned, or centered. But only one option is valid at a time.

It also is possible to display other controls like list boxes in a toolbar. When you create a toolbar in Visual Basic, you use two different controls:

- The **ImageList** control stores a collection of bitmap or icon images. The ImageList control should be created before the Toolbar control. Like the CommonDialog control, the ImageList control is not visible at run time. The icons stored in the ImageList control are displayed inside the Toolbar control at run time. The ImageList control has the standard prefix of "ils".

- The **Toolbar** control contains a collection of buttons. Each button on the toolbar represents a Button object. The icon displayed in a button comes from a corresponding ImageList. The Toolbar control has the standard prefix of "tbr".

The Toolbar and ImageList controls are ActiveX controls. Thus, they must be added to the project file before they can be used. Like the DBList and DBCombo controls, the Toolbar and ImageList controls are stored with several other controls in a single file and are two of the Microsoft Windows Common Controls. The Microsoft Windows Common Controls include the TabStrip, Toolbar, StatusBar, ProgressBar, TreeView, ListView, ImageList, and Slider controls. Like any ActiveX control, you must add a reference to the control to the project file before it displays in the toolbox and is available for use. In this session you will need to use several ActiveX controls. Ted suggests you add them to the project file all at once to save time.

To add the Microsoft Windows Common Controls to the project:

1. Start Visual Basic and open the project **Power.vbp** in the **Tutorial.09** folder on your Student Disk.

2. Save the form with the name **frmPowerProcedure** and the project with the name **Power Procedure.vbp**.

3. Click **Project** then **Components** to open the Components dialog box. Be sure the **Controls** tab is selected.

4. Use the scroll bars to locate the **Microsoft Windows Common Controls 5.0** and click the check box.

5. Click the check boxes for the **Microsoft Rich Textbox Control 5.0**, the **Microsoft Masked Edit Control 5.0**, and the **Crystal Report Control 4.6**.

6. Click **OK** to add the controls to the toolbar, and close the Components dialog box.

Tip: The Microsoft Windows Common Controls are available only with the Professional and Enterprise editions of Visual Basic. The file comctl32.ocx must exist on the computer to develop or run programs using the Microsoft Windows Common Controls. The files richtx32.ocx and msmask32.ocx must be present to use the RichTextBox and MaskEdBox controls, respectively.

Now that you have added the necessary controls to the project, you can begin to create the toolbar. The first step to create a toolbar is to create an instance of the ImageList control and set its properties.

Using the ImageList Control

A toolbar usually displays an image in each button on the toolbar. The images are not stored in the toolbar itself. Rather the images are stored in another control called the ImageList control. The **ImageList** control stores a collection of bitmap or icon images. It supports a property called ListImages. The **ListImages** property stores a collection of ListImage objects. The ListImages collection is a one-based collection that works like other collections you have used. You can reference each individual **ListImage** object in the collection using a numeric index or a string key. Each **ListImage** object in the collection can contain a bitmap or icon of any size. Like other ActiveX controls, you set the properties for the ImageList control using either the Properties window or the control's Property Pages. Figure 9-2 shows the relationship between the ImageList control, the ListImages property, and the ListImage objects in the collection.

Figure 9-2 ◄
Relationship
between
ListImages
collection and
ListImage
object

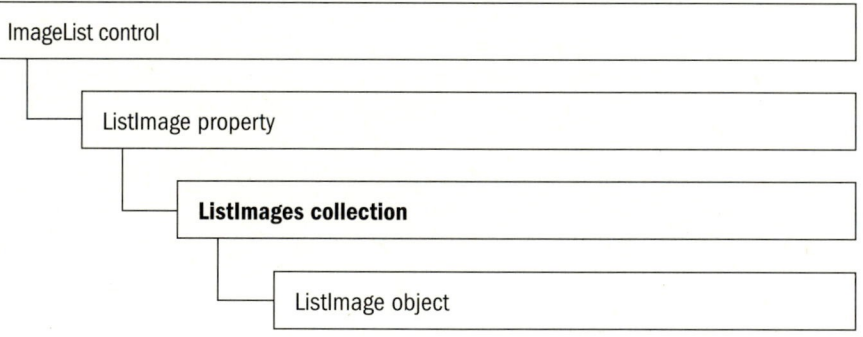

Ted suggests you now create the ImageList control, set its name, and display the Property Pages dialog box.

To create the ImageList control and display the Property Pages:

1. Click the **ImageList** control 🖻 and draw an instance of the control on the form. Note the ImageList control is not visible at run time so it does not matter where the control is placed.

2. Using the Properties window set the Name property to **ilsPower**.

3. Click the right-mouse button on the control then select **Properties** on the shortcut menu. The Property Pages dialog box is displayed as shown in Figure 9-3.

Figure 9-3
ImageList
control
Property Pages
dialog box

button sizes

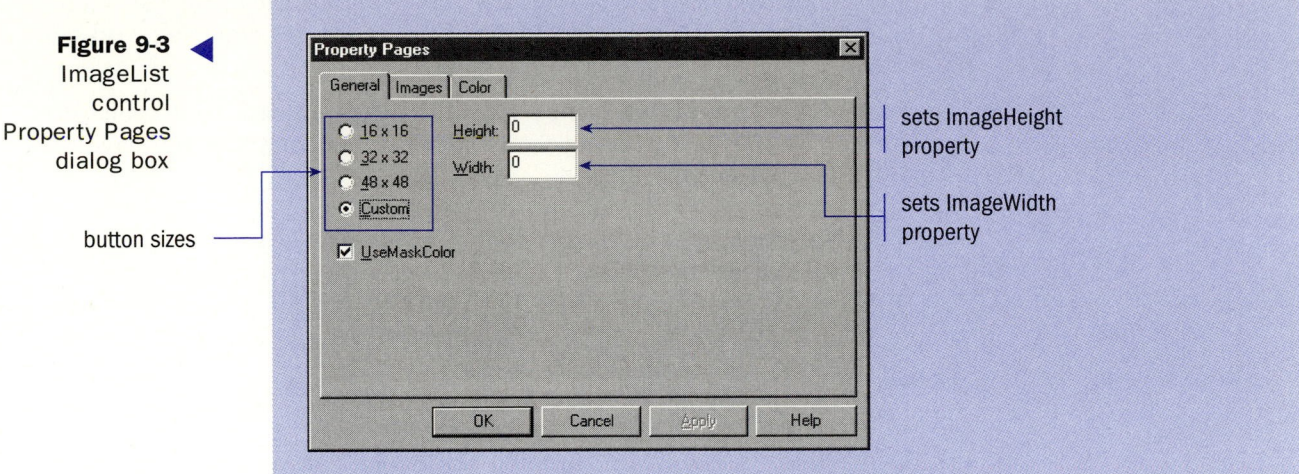

The first step in using the ImageList control is to define the height and width of each image. Each image must be the same size. The General tab in the Property Pages dialog box contains the properties that apply to all the images stored in the control.

- The **ImageHeight** and **ImageWidth** properties define the height and width of the image, respectively. The value of these properties is measured in pixels. These properties must be set before adding any images to the ImageList control. If you try to set either of these properties after adding an image, an error will occur. Note that all images in the ImageList must be of the same size. Typically, most icons either are 16 x 16 pixels or 32 x 32 pixels. The General tab in the Property Pages dialog box will let you use one of these default sizes or to select a different size icon.

Ted suggests you use the standard 16 x 16 pixel button size. This will provide a small button the same size as the buttons found in Microsoft Word and Excel, and many other programs.

To set the general properties for the ImageList:

1. Click the **16 x 16** button on the General tab in the Property Pages dialog box.

2. Click the **Apply** command button in the Property Pages dialog box to record the changes.

Once the general properties have been set, you can add each image to the ImageList object and set the properties pertaining to each individual image. Adding the images and setting their properties either can be done at design time using the Property Pages or at run time using code. When you use the Property Pages, each ListImage object is added automatically to the ListImages collection. If you perform this task at run time, you must call the Add method on the ListImages collection, then set the properties of each individual object. This method works much like the Add method for other collections and has the following syntax:

object.**Add**([*index*,][*key*,]*picture*)

- The required *object* is the name of a ListImages collection.

- The **Add** method is called on the ListImages collection for each image you want to add to the collection.

- The optional *index* argument is an integer specifying the position of the image in the collection. If omitted, the image is appended to the end of the collection.

- The optional *key* argument is a unique string that identifies the ListImage object. If you try to specify a duplicate key, an error will occur. The key argument works just like a string key for other collections you have used.

- The required *picture* argument is the name of the picture to add to the collection. A picture typically is loaded using the LoadPicture function like you have used with a PictureBox control.

Given an ImageList named ilsPower, you could add two images to the ListImages collection with the following statements:

```
ilsPower.ListImages.Add _
    ("Print",LoadPicture("A:\Tutorial.09\Print.bmp"))
ilsPower.ListImages.Add _
    ("Bold",LoadPicture("A:\Tutorial.09\Bold.bmp"))
```

Using the Property Pages to set the properties at design time, you can insert images to and remove images from the underlying ListImages collection. As shown in Figure 9-4, the Images tab in the Property Pages dialog box contains two command buttons to accomplish this.

Figure 9-4 ◀
Images tab in
Property Pages
dialog box

remove an image
from ListImages
collection

insert an image to
ListImages collection

selected images are
displayed in Images
list box

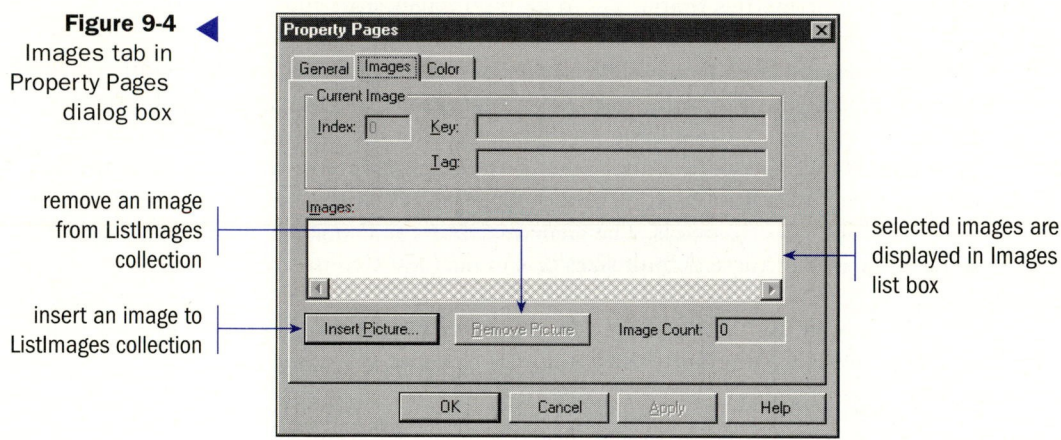

You can add an image by clicking the Insert Picture command button and selecting a bitmap or icon file in a dialog box to add to the collection. Each image added to the collection is displayed in the Images list box. As you add images to the Images list, you can set the key to the string key you want to use to reference the individual ListImage objects in the collection. Like with any collection, each string key in the collection must be unique. The numeric index is set for you when you add an image. Even though you can type a value into the Index text box on the Images tab in the Property Pages dialog box, changes you make will not be recorded. Rather the Property Pages dialog box sets the index value for you.

You can use the Remove Picture command button to remove ListImage objects from the collection.

> *Tip:* Add the images in the same order as they will display on the toolbar. This way, the numeric index values will be organized in the same order as the buttons will display. This will make the program more readable. Also, use a string key that describes the purpose of the image. This also will improve the program's readability. String key values are case-sensitive. Be sure you use uppercase and lowercase characters as desired.

CREATING AN IMAGELIST OBJECT AND ADDING IMAGES

- Draw an ImageList object on the form. Note the control is not visible at run time.
- Set the Name property to ils, followed by a meaningful name.
- Activate the General tab in the Property Pages dialog box, and set the image size as desired. If using the Custom image size, set the height and width manually.
- Activate the Images tab in the Property Pages dialog box for the desired ImageList object.
- Click the Insert Picture command button.
- Select the image.
- Set the Key property to a unique value that identifies the purpose of the image.
- Insert as many images as will be needed for the toolbar.

You now need to add each of the images to the ImageList control. Ted has identified five common tasks that the user should be able to execute from the toolbar so you need to create five images. These images will correspond to printing an installation procedure, printing an inventory report and changing the formatting of the procedure by setting the font to bold, italic, and underline. These activities correspond to menu items that Ted already created.

To add the ListImage objects to the ImageList:

1. Click the **Images** tab in the Property Pages dialog box to activate it.

2. Click the **Insert Picture** command button to open the Select picture dialog box.

3. Select the image named **Procedure.ico** in the **Tutorial.09** Folder on your Student Disk.

4. Click the **Open** button to display the image.

5. Set the Key property to **Procedure**.

6. Repeat Steps 2 through 5 to insert the images named **Print.bmp**, **Bold.bmp**, **Italic.bmp**, and **Underln.bmp** with the Key property of each image set to **Print**, **Bold**, **Italic**, and **Underline**, respectively. Note the Key property is case-sensitive. Your screen should look like Figure 9-5.

Figure 9-5 ◀
Adding Images
to ListImage
control

five images displayed —

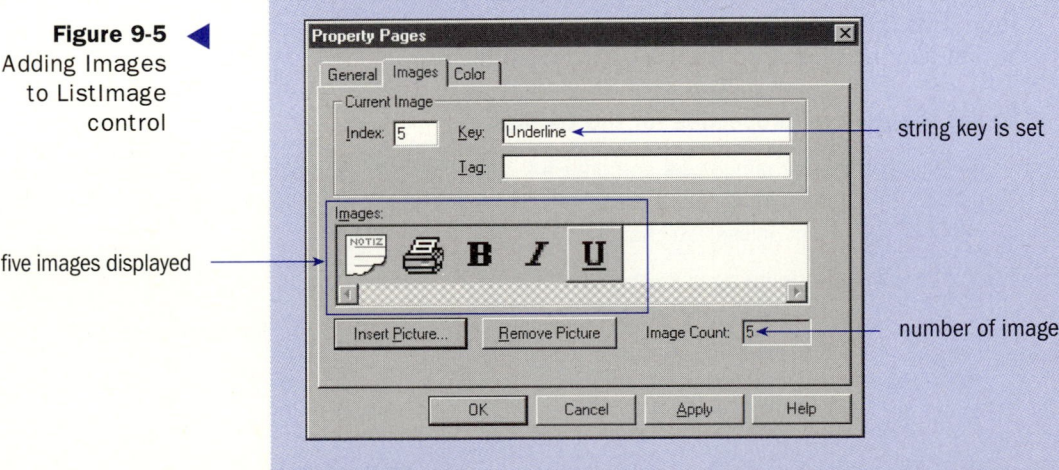

string key is set

number of images

7. Click the **OK** command button to close the Property Pages dialog box.

After adding the images to the ImageList control, you can create the toolbar, add buttons to the toolbar, then in each button, store a reference to the image in the ImageList control.

Using the Toolbar Control

When you create a toolbar on a form, it usually occupies the entire width of the form and displays just under the menu, if a menu exists. Like the ImageList control, the Toolbar control has Property Pages to set design-time properties. The General tab in the Property Pages dialog box contains the properties applicable to the entire toolbar and the Buttons tab is used to set properties that are applicable to each individual button.

The following general properties apply to the toolbar:

- The **Align** property defines where a toolbar displays on the form. If set to the constant vbAlignTop, the toolbar displays at the top of the form, just below the menu. The width of the toolbar will be the same as the form. You can change the Align property to cause the toolbar to display at the bottom, left, or right of the form, or any user defined position. Refer to the Align Property Help topic for more information.

- The **Appearance** property can be set to 0 - ccFlat or 1 - cc3D. By default it is set to 3D, and the toolbar displays raised off the surface of the form. Otherwise, it is not raised off the form's surface. Note the BorderStyle property must be set to 1 - ccFixedSingle for the toolbar to display raised.

- The **BorderStyle** property can be set to 0 - ccNone or 1 - ccFixedSingle. If set to None, the default, no border displays around the toolbar. If set to Fixed Single, a border is displayed.

- The **ButtonHeight** and **ButtonWidth** properties set the height and width of each individual button on the toolbar. Each button must be of the same height and width.

- The **Height** and **Width** properties are read-only properties describing the height and width of the Toolbar object.

- The **ImageList** property should be set to the name of an ImageList object already drawn on the form.

- The **ShowTips** property defines whether or not a ToolTip is displayed for each toolbar button.

Ted suggests you now create the toolbar and set the properties that pertain to the toolbar itself. The toolbar should display across the top of the form. The height of the toolbar should be the same size as the buttons you just stored in the ImageList control. Also, Ted would like the toolbar to display raised from the form.

To set the general properties for the toolbar:

1. Click the **Toolbar** button ⬚ and draw a toolbar across the top of the screen. Note that the toolbar will display across the top of the screen automatically. You cannot move the object unless you change the alignment property.

2. Set the Name property to **tbrPower** using the Properties window.

3. Activate the General tab in the Property Pages dialog box for the Toolbar object.

4. Set the ImageList property to **ilsPower**.

5. Set the BorderStyle property to **1 - cc FixedSingle**.

6. Make sure the Appearance property is set to **1 - cc3D**. Click **Apply** to record the changes. Your toolbar should look like Figure 9-6.

Figure 9-6 ◀
ToolBar object

ToolBar object ─────→

ImageList object ─────→

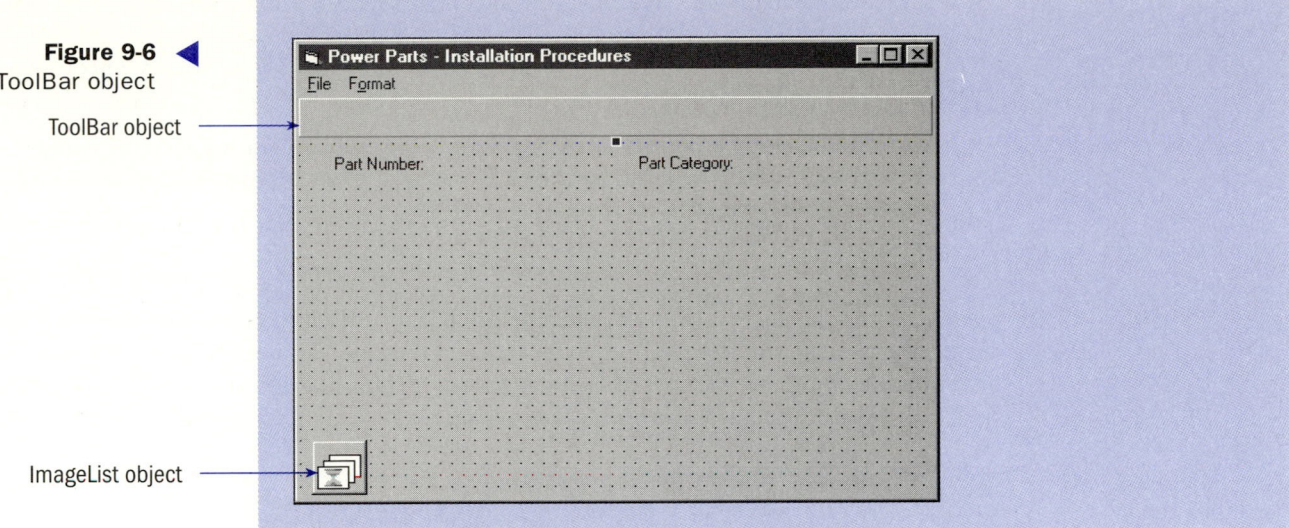

Each toolbar can have zero or more buttons. The Buttons property of the Toolbar object references a **Buttons** collection. Each **Button** object in the Buttons collection represents a button on the toolbar. The Buttons collection is a one-based collection that can be referenced by an Integer number or a string key. The following list describes the properties pertaining to a Button object:

- If the button should contain text, set the **Caption** property. Usually, buttons do not have a caption. Rather they store icons or bitmaps.

- The **Image** property holds either the numeric index or string key of the corresponding image stored in the ListImages property of the ImageList control. A toolbar must be associated with an ImageList control before the Image property can be set.

- The **ToolTipText** property accepts a string and returns or sets a ToolTip for the button.

- The **Value** property has two possible values. If set to 0 - tbrUnpressed, the button is not pressed, and if set to 1 - tbrPressed, the button is pressed. You can read and write this property at run time to determine or change the status of a button.

- The **Visible** and **Enabled** properties can make the toolbar invisible or disabled, respectively.

- The **Style** property of the toolbar controls the appearance of a button and how a button interacts with other buttons on the toolbar.

Once you have bound a toolbar to an ImageList by setting the ImageList property of the toolbar, you cannot change the images in the ImageList control. To change the images in the ImageList, you must set the ImageList property of the toolbar to None, then you can change the images in the ImageList.

The Style property can be set to one of five constants as defined in the following list:

- If set to **tbrDefault,** the button is not dependent on any other buttons. That is, it is not part of a group. When the ButtonClick event procedure corresponding to the button is running, it displays recessed. When the procedure is finished, the button returns to its normal appearance.

- If set to **tbrCheck,** the button works like a toggle switch. When clicked, the button displays recessed. When clicked again, the button returns to its normal appearance. When clicked, the button has a value of **tbrPressed**, and the value of **tbrUnpressed** when not clicked.

- If set to **tbrButtonGroup**, only one button can be selected from a group of buttons. When a button in a group is clicked, the button displays recessed. All other buttons in the group are no longer recessed. It is possible for no button in a group to display recessed.

- If set to **tbrSeparator** a button is created eight pixels wide. It is used to visually separate buttons and has the same purpose as a separator bar between two menu items.

- If set to **tbrPlaceholder,** a blank space is created in the toolbar for other controls to be displayed.

After setting the general properties for the toolbar, you need to create the individual buttons on the toolbar, and set the properties for each button. You need to create five buttons corresponding to the five pictures in the ImageList control. To add the buttons on the toolbar, you use the Buttons tab in the Property Pages dialog box. Figure 9-7 shows the Buttons tab.

Figure 9-7 ◀
Buttons tab in
Property Pages
dialog box

string key for button

string key or index of
image stored in
ImageList object

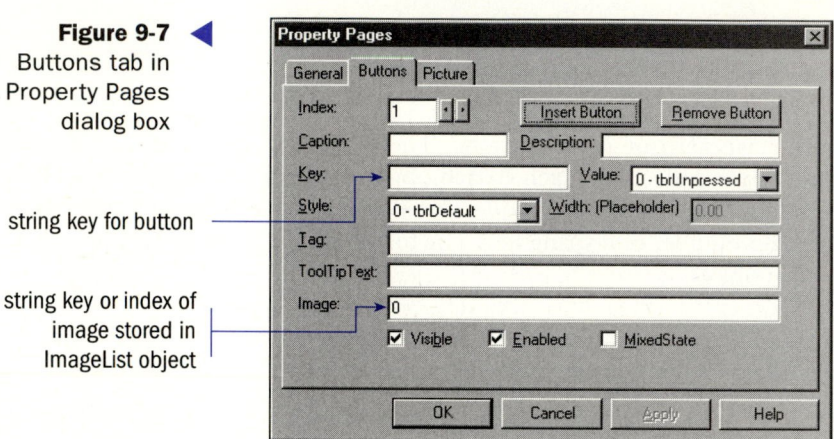

To add a button on the toolbar, you click the Insert Button command button on the Buttons tab in the Property Pages dialog box. To delete a button from the toolbar, you select the index of the button to be deleted, then click the Remove Button command button. Each button on the toolbar has associated Index and Key values. These values allow you to uniquely identify a Button object in the Buttons collection. Note that the Buttons collection is a separate collection from the ListImages collection. The Buttons collection contains information about the button and the key or index of the buttons' images stored in the ListImages collection. Figure 9-8 shows this relationship.

Figure 9-8 ◀
Relationship
between
Buttons
collection and
Button object

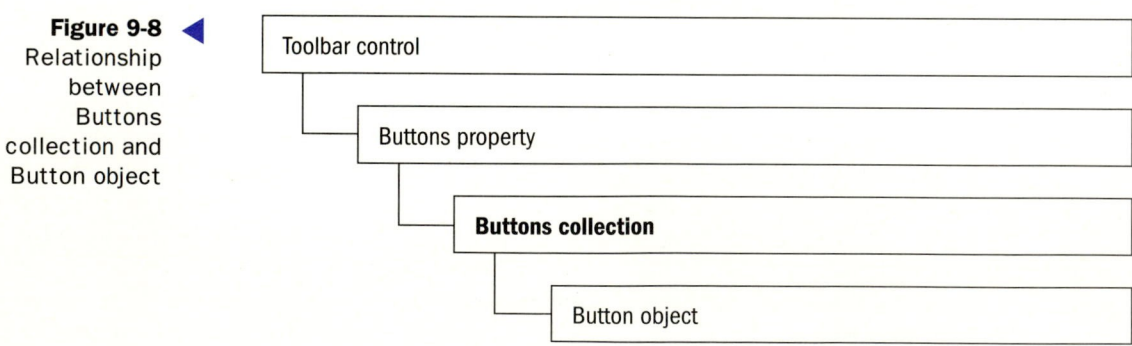

> **REFERENCE window**
>
> ## CREATING A TOOLBAR
>
> - Draw an instance of the Toolbar control on the form.
> - Set the ImageList property to the name of an existing ImageList object on the form.
> - For each button you want to create on the toolbar, click Insert Button then specify the image, the key, and the ToolTip, if any.

Ted suggests you now add the buttons on the toolbar to print the procedure and to print the report you will create in the next session. After these two buttons, a separator button should be created to visually separate the print buttons and the formatting buttons. You also need to set the properties so each button will display the correct image.

To add the buttons to the toolbar:

1. Click the **Insert Button** command button on the Buttons tab in the Property Pages dialog box.

2. Make sure the Index is set to **1**.

3. Set the Key to **Procedure**, then the ToolTipText to **Print Procedure**.

4. Set the Image to **Procedure**.

   TROUBLE? If you receive a message box with the message "Element not found," be sure the Image property is correct. If it is, open the Property Pages dialog box for the ImageList control, and make sure you set the Key property correctly for the image.

   TROUBLE? The Key values for these collections are case-sensitive. If you get an error message trying to set the Image property, make sure the case is the same as the key you specified when you created the ImageList control.

5. Click **Apply**.

6. Repeat Steps 1, 3, 4, and 5 setting the Key to **Print**, the ToolTipText to **Print Report** and the Image to **Print**. The Index for this button should be set to **2**. Note that as you add each button, it will display on the toolbar.

7. Click the **Insert Button** command button to insert a button with an Index set to **3**.

8. Set the Style to **3 - tbrSeparator**.

9. Click **Apply**.

The buttons to change the formatting of text should work like toggle switches. When clicked, the text should be formatted appropriately. That is, when the Bold button is pressed, text should be formatted in a bold typeface and the button should display recessed indicating the typeface. When clicked again, the bold formatting should be removed, and the button should no longer display recessed. To accomplish this you need to set the Style property of these buttons to tbrCheck.

To create the Bold, Italic, and Underline buttons:

1. Make sure the Buttons tab in the Property Pages dialog box is active.

2. Click the **Insert Button** command button. The Index of the new button should be set to **4**.

3. Set the Key to **Bold**, the Style to **1 - tbrCheck**, the ToolTipText to **Bold**, and the Image to **Bold**. Click **Apply**.

4. Click the **Insert Button** command button again. The Index of the new button should be set to **5**.

5. Set the Key to **Italic**, the Style to **1 - tbrCheck**, the ToolTipText to **Italic**, and the Image to **Italic**. Click **Apply**.

6. Click the **Insert Button** command button. The Index of the new button should be set to **6**.

7. Set the Key to **Underline**, the Style to **1 - tbrCheck**, the ToolTipText to **Underline**, and the Image to **Underline**. Click **Apply**.

8. Click **OK** to apply the changes and close the Property Pages dialog box. The toolbar should look like Figure 9-9.

Figure 9-9 ◀
Completed
toolbar

separator

printing buttons

formatting buttons

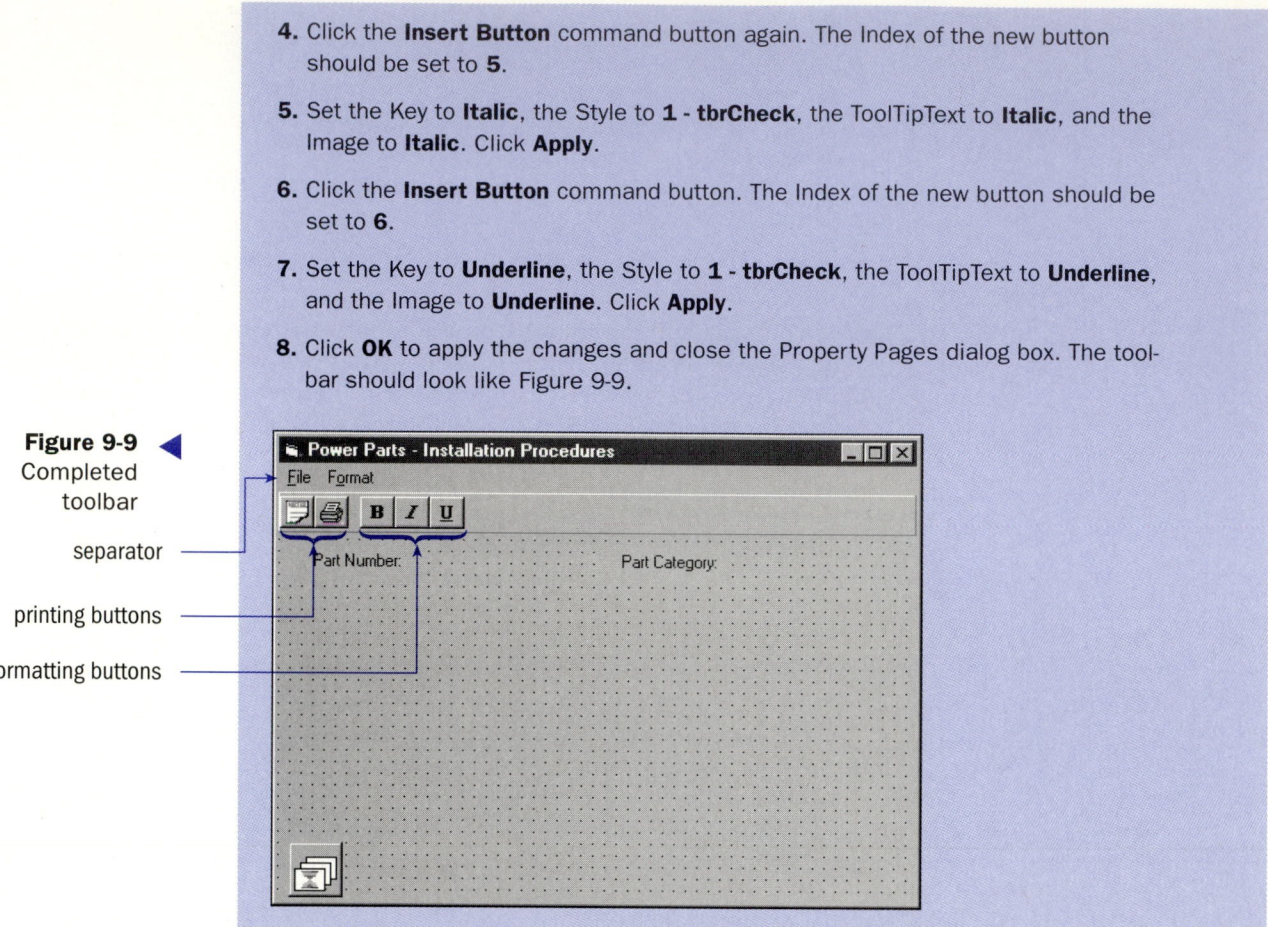

Now that you have created the toolbar, you need to create the other objects on the form to display inventory items and their corresponding installation procedures. To do this, you will use different controls that work much like the TextBox control you have been using.

Using the MaskEdBox Control

The MaskEdBox control is similar to a text box. That is, the user can enter text into the control, and it also can display text. Many text strings require formatting when the user types input. For example, dates often are formatted such that the month, day, and year are separated by a forward slash (/). Telephone numbers often are formatted with the area code in parentheses and the parts of a telephone number separated by dashes (-). You can use the MaskEdBox control to perform this formatting and validate user input.

The MaskEdBox control is a bound control. You can set the DataField and DataSource properties to display a field from a Data control, just like you have done with a text box. To use a mask, you can set two different properties. One property controls the input, and the other controls the formatted output. The MaskEdBox control works by applying a format mask to textual data. The process works much like formatting data with a Format statement. When you use a mask, you define the characteristics of each character displayed in the control. Mask characters are of two types:

- Some characters are placeholders to define the valid characters that can be stored at a specific character position.

- Other characters are treated as literal characters. Literal characters can be used to give a clue about the data, or perform formatting like surrounding the area code of a telephone number by parentheses. Figure 9-10 lists the different mask characters and their purpose.

Figure 9-10 ◀
Mask characters

Mask Character	Purpose
#	Digit placeholder
.	Decimal separator (appears as a literal character)
,	Thousands separator (appears as a literal character)
:	Time separator (appears as a literal character)
/	Date separator (appears as a literal character)
\	Causes the next character to be treated as a literal; allows you to use '#', 'A', and '&' characters in the mask
&	Character placeholder
>	Converts all the characters that follow the symbol to uppercase
<	Converts all the characters that follow the symbol to lowercase
A	Alphanumeric character placeholder; valid values are a–z, A–Z, or 0–9
9	Digit placeholder
C	Character placeholder
?	Letter placeholder; valid values are a–z and A–Z

You can use these characters to create input masks. Figure 9-11 shows several common input masks and the corresponding purpose.

Figure 9-11 ◀
Mask samples

Sample	Description
(###) ###-####	Telephone number
#####-####	Zip plus four
###-##-####	Social Security number
##/##/##	Date
##:##:##	Time
cccccccccc	10-character text field

When a user types a character in a position that violates the rules for the input mask, the ValidationError event occurs and the character will not be displayed in the MaskEdBox control. The MaskEdBox control supports several properties in addition to those found in a standard text box. The properties are as follows:

- The **Mask** property is used to define an input mask for input validation. The Mask property does not check for content. That is, no error will occur if a date or time value is outside of the valid range.

- The **Format** property is used to control the output format. The Format property works much like the Format function. Refer to the Format property Help topic for more information.

The **PromptChar** property is used to display a prompt to the user. Those character positions where the user can enter data will display this character. By default the value is an underscore (_). A common use of the PromptChar property is to include asterisks (*) when you type a password, so no one can read the password on your screen over your shoulder.

The MaskEdBox control has a standard prefix of "med".

Power Parts uses a standard format for all their part numbers. Figure 9-12 describes the format for a part number.

Figure 9-12 ◀
Part number
format

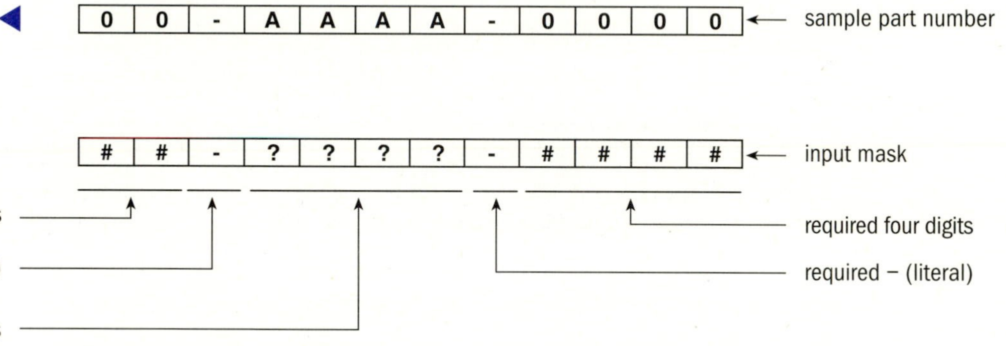

| 0 | 0 | - | A | A | A | A | - | 0 | 0 | 0 | 0 | ◀— sample part number |

| # | # | - | ? | ? | ? | ? | - | # | # | # | # | ◀— input mask |

required two digits
required – (literal)
required four letters

required four digits
required – (literal)

Part numbers read and written to the database always should be displayed using this standard format so you will need to use a dash (-) as a literal character. Also, the first two characters, and the last four, must contain digits, so you will use the digit placeholder (#). The middle four characters must be letters so you need to use the (?) placeholder for those characters. Because the MaskEdBox control will interact with a database, you also need to create a Data control and set the necessary properties.

To create the Data and MaskEdBox controls and set their properties:

1. Create a **Data** control on the form as shown in Figure 9-13. Set the Caption to **Power,** the Name to **datPower**, the DatabaseName to **A:\Tutorial.09\Power.mdb,** and the RecordSource to **tblParts**.

2. Click the **MaskEdBox control** button ##| and draw an instance of the control as shown in Figure 9-13. Set the Name to **medPartNumber**. Using the Properties window, set the DataSource property to **datPower** and the DataField property to **fldPartNumber**.

3. Create a second **MaskEdBox control**. Set the Name to **medPartCategory**, the DataSource property to **datPower**, and the DataField to **fldPartCategory**.

Figure 9-13 ◄
New
MaskEdBox
controls

medPartNumber

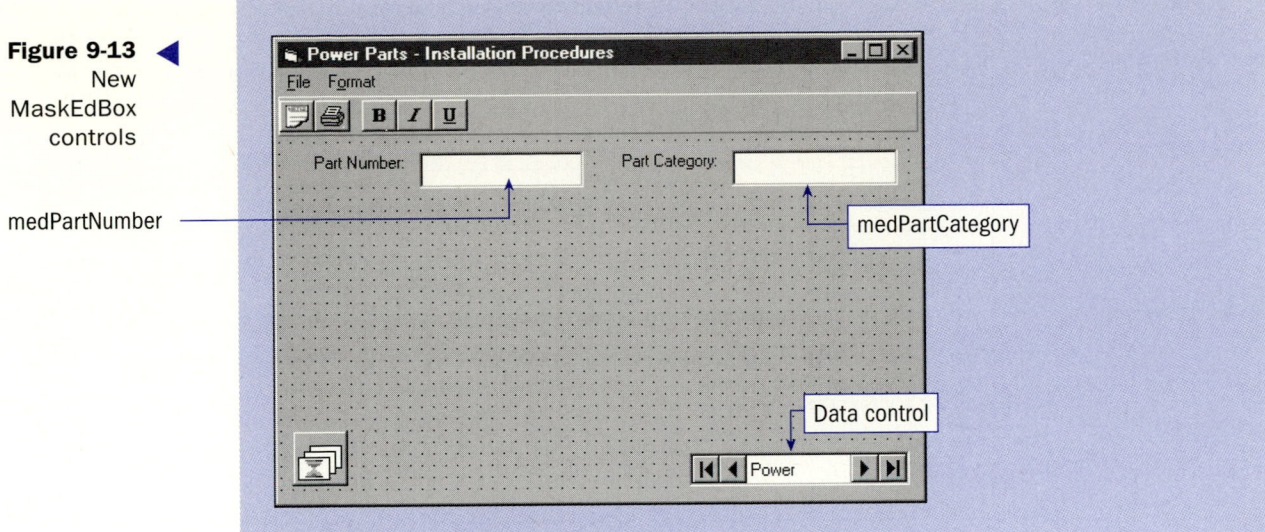

At this time, the MaskEdBox control will function just like an ordinary bound text box because you have not defined an input mask. You now need to set the input mask so any data entered or changed by the user will be in the proper format for the part number.

To change the input mask for the part number:

1. Activate the Property Pages dialog box for the MaskEdBox control named **medPartNumber**.

2. Set the Mask property to **##-????-####**.

3. Click **OK** to close the Property Pages dialog box.

Now that the mask is set, you can run the program to display different part numbers.

To test the MaskEdBox controls:

1. Save the project then start it.

2. The part number **10-MOTO-7732** should be displayed in the Part Number text box.

3. End the program.

The next step in the program is to create the necessary object to display the installation procedure corresponding to a part number. Each procedure is stored inside a field in the table tblPower. You need to display the procedure in a type of text box called a rich text box to preserve the formatting of the text.

Using the RichTextBox Control

There is another type of text box control called the RichTextBox control. The **RichTextBox** control works much like the TextBox control you have used except it can display data in Rich Text Format. **Rich Text Format (RTF)** is a standardized file format that is compatible with many other word processing programs. Rich Text Format files support different fonts and formatting of characters. The standard prefix for a RichTextBox control is "rtf". The RichTextBox control also can read and write ASCII files. Figure 9-14 shows a segment of a Rich Text Format file.

Figure 9-14 ◀
Rich Text
Format file

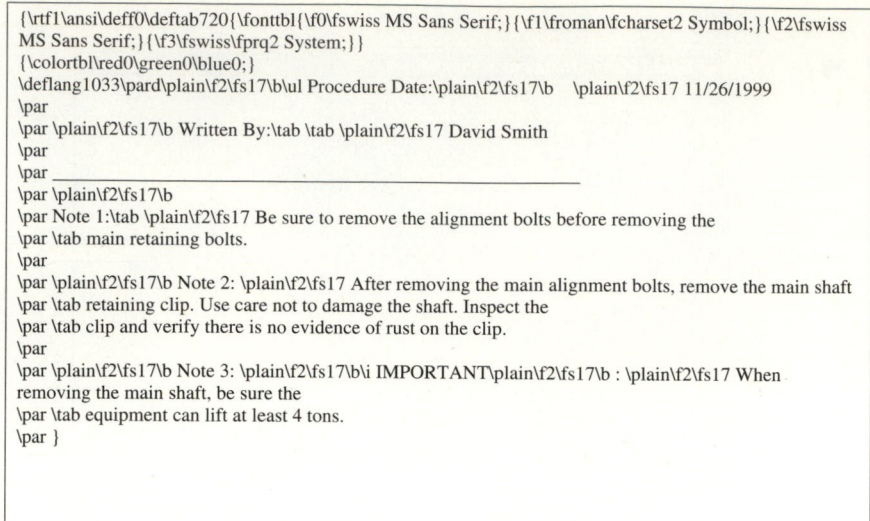

```
{\rtf1\ansi\deff0\deftab720{\fonttbl{\f0\fswiss MS Sans Serif;}{\f1\froman\fcharset2 Symbol;}{\f2\fswiss
MS Sans Serif;}{\f3\fswiss\fprq2 System;}}
{\colortbl\red0\green0\blue0;}
\deflang1033\pard\plain\f2\fs17\b\ul Procedure Date:\plain\f2\fs17\b   \plain\f2\fs17 11/26/1999
\par
\par \plain\f2\fs17\b Written By:\tab \tab \plain\f2\fs17 David Smith
\par
\par _____
\par \plain\f2\fs17\b
\par Note 1:\tab \plain\f2\fs17 Be sure to remove the alignment bolts before removing the
\par \tab main retaining bolts.
\par
\par \plain\f2\fs17\b Note 2: \plain\f2\fs17 After removing the main alignment bolts, remove the main shaft
\par \tab retaining clip. Use care not to damage the shaft. Inspect the
\par \tab clip and verify there is no evidence of rust on the clip.
\par
\par \plain\f2\fs17\b Note 3: \plain\f2\fs17\b\i IMPORTANT\plain\f2\fs17\b : \plain\f2\fs17 When
removing the main shaft, be sure the
\par \tab equipment can lift at least 4 tons.
\par }
```

As you can see from Figure 9-14, special characters are embedded into the file to describe the formatting of the characters. The RichTextBox control will interpret these characters and display the formatted output inside the region of the rich text box.

Like a text box, the RichTextBox control can be used as a bound control. That is, it can interact with a field in a database by setting the DataSource and DataField properties. You also can set the MultiLine and ScrollBars properties just like a text box. The rich text box also can be used in an unbound mode.

The RichTextBox control has methods to read and write RTF files without the aid of a database. You can open and close files using two methods. The **LoadFile** method will read a file from the disk into a rich text box. The **SaveFile** method will write the text in a rich text box to a file on the disk. The SaveFile and LoadFile methods have the same arguments.

*object.***LoadFile|SaveFile** *pathname, filetype*

- The *object* is any valid instance of a RichTextBox control.

- The **LoadFile** or **SaveFile** methods are called on the RichTextBox control.

- The required *pathname* argument must contain the folder and filename of the file to load in the control.

- The optional *filetype* argument must be an Integer constant specifying the type of file to be loaded. It can have one of two values. If set to **0 - rtfRTF**, the default, the file is assumed to be a valid RTF file. If set to **1 - rtfText**, a text file is loaded.

Ted suggests you now create the rich text box, and set its properties to display the RTF data from the field fldPartProcedure in the table tblPower. To accomplish this, you set the DataField and DataSource properties as you have done previously.

To create the RichTextBox control:

1. Click the **RichTextBox control** button ⊞. Draw an instance of the RichTextBox control using Figure 9-15 as a reference.

2. Using the Properties window, set the Name property to **rtfPartProcedure**, the DataSource property to **datPower**, and the DataField property to **fldPartProcedure**.

3. Set the MultiLine property to **True** and set the ScrollBars property to **3 - rtfBoth**.

4. Save the project then start it. The procedure for the first record should be displayed as shown in Figure 9-15.

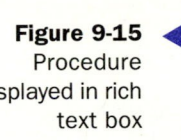

Figure 9-15 ◀
Procedure
displayed in rich
text box

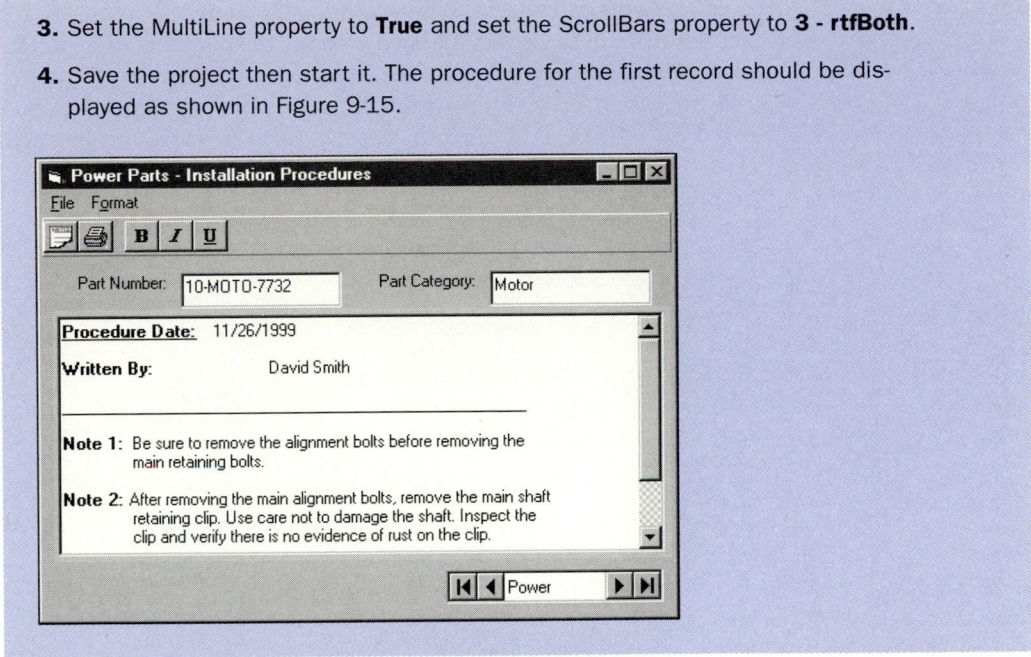

Note that the text in Figure 9-15 is formatted such that text displays in bold, italic, and underlined font styles. The next step in the program is to write the necessary code to change the formatting of the information by clicking buttons on the toolbar or selecting an item on the menu.

Printing an RTF File

You can print the contents of the rich text box by calling the SelPrint method on the rich text box. The SelPrint method has the following syntax:

object.**SelPrint**(*hDC*)

- The *object* must be the name of a RichTextBox control.

- The **SelPrint** method prints the selected contents of the rich text box. If there is no selected text, then all contents of the rich text box are printed. If there is selected text, only the selected text is printed. If you use the Printer object as the destination of the text from the RichTextBox control, you first must initialize the device context of the Printer object by printing something like a zero-length string.

- The required *hDC* argument is the device context of the device you want to use. This is stored in the hDC property of the Printer object. A device context is a link between a Windows application, a device driver, and a device like a printer.

Thus, to print the contents of the rtfPartProcedure object you would use the following statements:

```
Printer.Print ""
rtfPartProcedure.SelPrint(Printer.hDC)
```

When you call the SelPrint method, the contents of the rich text box are sent to the default printer. Because you need to print the contents of a rich text box on either a menu item or toolbar button, you need to create a general procedure to perform the task, then call the general procedure when either the menu item or the button is clicked. You now can create the general procedure, then call it from the proper menu item.

To print the RTF file:

1. Insert a Private general procedure named **PrintProcedure**. Set the Type to **Sub** and the Scope to **Private**.

2. Insert the following statement in the procedure:

```
Private Sub PrintProcedure( )
    rtfPartProcedure.SelPrint (Printer.hDC)
End Sub
```

3. Locate the Click event procedure for the menu item named **mnuFilePrintProcedure**, then enter the following statement:

```
Private Sub mnuFilePrintProcedure_Click( )
    PrintProcedure
End Sub
```

These statements cause the contents of the rich text box to be sent to the default printer. You now should test the code that you just wrote to be sure the information is being printed.

To print the contents of the rich text box:

1. Save the project then start it.

2. Click **File** then **Print** then **Procedure**. The procedure should be sent to the printer.

3. End the program.

The next step in the program is to write the code to change the formatting of the text displayed in the rich text box depending on the status of the format buttons on the toolbar.

Formatting a Rich Text Box

To format text using the RichTextBox control, you select text to format, just like you select text in other programs like Microsoft Word, then apply the desired formatting by setting a property. The RichTextBox control supports several properties to change the formatting of selected text. You can use the **SelBold**, **SelItalic**, **SelStrikethru**, or **SelUnderline** method to change the font style. These properties can have one of three values:

- If set to **Null**, the selected text contains characters that have a mix of the appropriate font styles. To determine if the value is Null, you can use the IsNull classification function.

- If set to **True**, all the characters in the selection or the character following the insertion point have the appropriate font style.

- If set to **False**, the default, none of the characters in the selection or the character following the insertion point have the appropriate font style.

The program you are creating for Power Parts will allow the user to apply these formats by selecting text in a rich text box, then clicking the Bold, Italic, or Underline buttons on the toolbar.

Like the TextBox control, the RichTextBox control can respond to events like Change, GotFocus, LostFocus, and so on.

The program you are creating for Power Parts requires that the user be able to add, change, and delete text from the rich text box as installation procedures are updated. Also, the user must be able to change the formatting. That is, the user must be able to bold, italicize, or underline text, or remove the formatting. When the cursor is moved in the rich text box, or text is highlighted, the buttons on the toolbar need to be updated to reflect the formatting characteristics of the currently selected text.

You need a way to determine when either the selected text has changed or the insertion point has changed, so you can update the buttons on the toolbar and the menu bar accordingly. For example, if the selected text is bold, the Bold button on the toolbar should display recessed. If the selected text is not bold, the button should display raised. The RichTextBox control supports an event called **SelChange**. This event occurs whenever the selected text changes or the insertion point is moved.

The menus you have worked with to this point have been used to simply execute a set of commands in an event procedure when clicked. Like a toolbar button, however, you need a way to represent a menu item the same way so it can have two values. That is, the Bold menu item either should be checked or unchecked and should be synchronized with the corresponding toolbar button. To create a menu item that can be checked or unchecked, you set the Checked property to True in the Menu Editor at design time. Then, you can read and write the property as needed, just as you can set the state of a button on the toolbar as needed.

To set the value of the Checked property to True or False at run time, you can use the following two statements:

```
mnuFormatBold.Checked = True
mnuFormatBold.Checked = False
```

When the user selects text or changes the insertion point of text, you need to update the state of the Bold, Italic, and Underline menu items and buttons. To accomplish this, you need to write code to determine the state of the text for each formatting characteristic. Based on this information, you need to set the state of the corresponding button and menu item to recessed or raised, checked or not checked.

To program the SelChange event:

1. Activate the Code window for the **SelChange** event procedure for the RichTextBox control **rtfPartProcedure**.

2. Enter the following statements into the Code window:

```
Private Sub rtfPartProcedure_SelChange( )
    If rtfPartProcedure.SelBold = True Then
        tbrPower.Buttons("Bold").Value = tbrPressed
        mnuFormatBold.Checked = True
    Else
        tbrPower.Buttons("Bold").Value = tbrUnpressed
        mnuFormatBold.Checked = False
    End If

    If rtfPartProcedure.SelItalic = True Then
        tbrPower.Buttons("Italic").Value = tbrPressed
        mnuFormatItalic.Checked = True
    Else
        tbrPower.Buttons("Italic").Value = tbrUnpressed
        mnuFormatItalic.Checked = False
    End If

    If rtfPartProcedure.SelUnderline = True Then
```

```
            tbrPower.Buttons("Underline").Value = tbrPressed
            mnuFormatUnderline.Checked = True
        Else
            tbrPower.Buttons("Underline").Value = tbrUnpressed
            mnuFormatUnderline.Checked = False
        End If
    End Sub
```

These statements use the SelBold, SelItalic, and SelUnderline properties to determine the formatting characteristics of either the currently selected text or the insertion point if no text is selected. Depending on the formatting characteristics, the status of the corresponding buttons and menu items are updated accordingly. Note that you determine the correct button by using the string key of the Buttons collection to locate a specific button.

```
If rtfPartProcedure.SelBold = True Then
    tbrPower.Buttons("Bold").Value = tbrPressed
    mnuFormatBold.Checked = True
Else
    tbrPower.Buttons("Bold").Value = tbrUnpressed
    mnuFormatBold.Checked = False
End If
```

These statements test the SelBold property of the RichTextBox control. If the selected text is bold, then the Bold button on the toolbar is pressed, otherwise it is not. This is accomplished using the Buttons collection stored in the toolbar. Remember, a button in the collection can be referenced using a string key or a numeric index. In this case you used the string key used when you created the button. Using this, you set the value to pressed or unpressed depending on the current status of the selected text. In addition to updating the status of the button, you updated the status of the menu item named mnuFormatBold.

```
If rtfPartProcedure.SelItalic = True Then
    tbrPower.Buttons("Italic").Value = tbrPressed
    mnuFormatItalic.Checked = True
Else
    tbrPower.Buttons("Italic").Value = tbrUnpressed
    mnuFormatItalic.Checked = False
End If
```

This If statement works the same way as the other If statement. Instead of checking the SelBold property, however, the SelItalic property is tested. Then based on the value of the selected text, the corresponding button is pressed or not pressed and the menu item is checked or not checked.

```
If rtfPartProcedure.SelUnderline = True Then
    tbrPower.Buttons("Underline").Value = tbrPressed
    mnuFormatUnderline.Checked = True
Else
    tbrPower.Buttons("Underline").Value = tbrUnpressed
    mnuFormatUnderline.Checked = False
End If
```

This final If statement performs the same task as the previous two If statements but with underline this time. You should again test the program to be sure that the button correctly indicates the status of either the selected text or the insertion point.

To test the formatting buttons:

1. Save the project then start it.

2. Click any text that is bolded, then italicized, then underlined. The buttons should display pressed or raised depending on the text format.

3. Make sure to verify that a check box displays next to the corresponding menu item on the Format menu.

4. End the program.

The next step in writing the program is to allow the user to change the formatting of existing text. Thus, when the user selects text in the rich text box, then clicks the Bold, Italic, or Underline buttons, the formatting should be applied or removed depending on the state of the button. The same should occur when a corresponding menu item is clicked.

Programming a Toolbar

When you added the buttons to the toolbar using the Property Pages dialog box, the Button objects were created for you. Of course, you can create them using code by creating instances of Button objects, setting the properties, then adding each object to the collection. You then can write code to determine which button was clicked, or change the state of the button as necessary.

In the program you are writing for Power Parts, when a button is clicked, you need to first determine which button was clicked. Each Button object supports a Key property. This is the value of a button's string key. Thus, each button has a Key value of Procedure, Print, Bold, Italic, and Underline. Because you need to perform these tasks when a button or corresponding menu item is clicked, you must write the general procedures to perform the three formatting tasks.

These procedures need to check the format of either the selected text or the insertion point, then apply or remove the formatting. Then the state of the corresponding button and menu item must be updated.

To create the general procedures to change the formatting of selected text:

1. Insert a general procedure named **Bold**. Set the type to **Sub** then the scope to **Private**.

2. Insert two more general procedures named **Italic** and **Underline** of the same types and scope.

3. Enter the following statements in the **Bold** procedure:

```
Private Sub Bold( )
    If rtfPartProcedure.SelBold = True Or _
        IsNull(rtfPartProcedure.SelBold) Then
        rtfPartProcedure.SelBold = False
        tbrPower.Buttons("Bold").Value = tbrUnpressed
        mnuFormatBold.Checked = False
    Else
        rtfPartProcedure.SelBold = True
        tbrPower.Buttons("Bold").Value = tbrPressed
        mnuFormatBold.Checked = True
    End If
End Sub
```

4. Enter the following statements in the **Italic** procedure:

```
Private Sub Italic( )
    If rtfPartProcedure.SelItalic = True Or _
```

```
            IsNull(rtfPartProcedure.SelItalic) Then
            rtfPartProcedure.SelItalic = False
            tbrPower.Buttons("Italic").Value = tbrUnpressed
            mnuFormatItalic.Checked = False
        Else
            rtfPartProcedure.SelItalic = True
            tbrPower.Buttons("Italic").Value = tbrPressed
            mnuFormatItalic.Checked = True
        End If
    End Sub
```

5. Enter the following statements in the **Underline** procedure:

```
Private Sub Underline( )
    If rtfPartProcedure.SelUnderline = True Or _
        IsNull(rtfPartProcedure.SelUnderline) Then
        rtfPartProcedure.SelUnderline = False
        tbrPower.Buttons("Underline").Value = tbrUnpressed
        mnuFormatUnderline.Checked = False
    Else
        rtfPartProcedure.SelUnderline = True
        tbrPower.Buttons("Underline").Value = tbrPressed
        mnuFormatUnderline.Checked = True
    End If
End Sub
```

There is one procedure to test for bold text, one for italicized text, and one for underlined text. In each case if the selected text is of the specified format, then the formatting is removed, otherwise it is applied. In cases where some of the text is of the selected format, the format is removed.

```
If rtfPartProcedure.SelBold = True Or _
    IsNull(rtfPartProcedure.SelBold) Then
```

This If statement determines the status of the SelBold property of the rich text box. If the selected text is bold or if some of the text is bold, the following statements are executed:

```
    rtfPartProcedure.SelBold = False
    tbrPower.Buttons("Bold").Value = tbrUnpressed
    mnuFormatBold.Checked = False
```

The previous three statements execute when the If statement is True. The first statement removes the bold formatting from the text. The second unpresses the Bold button on the toolbar, and the last statement unchecks the corresponding menu item.

```
    rtfPartProcedure.SelBold = True
    tbrPower.Buttons("Bold").Value = tbrPressed
    mnuFormatBold.Checked = True
```

These statements execute only when the If condition is False. That is, all the selected text is not bold. They bold the selected text, press the button on the toolbar, and check the corresponding menu item. You now need to call each of these event procedures when the corresponding menu item is clicked.

To call the Bold, Italic, and Underline general procedures:

1. Open the Code window for the Click event for the menu item named **mnuFormatBold** and enter the following statement shown in bold:

```
Private Sub mnuFormatBold_Click( )
    Bold
End Sub
```

2. Repeat Step 1 for the event procedures **mnuFormatItalic_Click** and **mnuFormatUnderline_Click.** Replace the **Bold** statement with **Italic** and **Underline** in the corresponding event procedures, respectively.

These statements call the Bold, Italic, and Underline general procedures from the corresponding Format menu item. You now should test the program to verify the menu items are working correctly.

To test the format menu items:

1. Save the project then start it.

2. Select a line of text in the installation procedure.

3. Click **Format** then **Bold** to apply a bold format to the text.

4. Click the menu item again to be sure the item is removed. Also, make sure the corresponding toolbar button is being set correctly.

5. Repeat Steps 2 through 4 to test the **Italic** and **Underline** menu items.

6. End the program.

You still need to program the toolbar so when a button is clicked, it will print or format the selected text as necessary. Unlike a command button, neither the toolbar nor each button responds to a Click event. Rather, when a button on the toolbar is clicked a **ButtonClick** event occurs for the toolbar. One argument is passed to the ButtonClick event procedure—a Button object indicating which button was clicked. This is a Button object from the Buttons collection. To program the toolbar, you need to write the code for the toolbar's ButtonClick event procedure. This event procedure has one argument. The Button object that was clicked. The Key property of the Button object contains the unique string key for the button. You can use this string key in a Select Case statement to call the correct general procedure when a button is clicked.

To change the formatting of selected text by clicking a toolbar button:

1. Activate the Code window for the **ButtonClick** event procedure for the toolbar **tbrPower.**

2. Enter the following statements into the event procedure:

```
Select Case Button.Key
    Case "Procedure"
        PrintProcedure
    Case "Print"
        PrintInventory
    Case "Bold"
        Bold
    Case "Italic"
        Italic
    Case "Underline"
        Underline
End Select
```

These statements determine which button is clicked. Depending on the button, the procedure is printed or the formatting is applied, and the state of both the menu item and button are updated, if necessary. Ted suggests you now test your program to make sure the text is being formatted and the buttons updated.

To test the formatting:

1. Save the project then start it.

2. Select some text from the rich text box, then apply and remove formatting to the text. Repeat this for each of the three formatting buttons.

3. Click the **Procedure** button to make sure the procedure is being printed.

4. End the program.

You have completed the user interface for the program. It uses different types of text boxes to interact with the data in a database table. Using the RichTextBox control, you can format text using both menu items and a toolbar.

 **Quick Check**

1. What is the purpose of the ImageList control and how is it used with a toolbar?

2. How are the buttons in a toolbar related to the images stored in an ImageList control?

3. What is the difference between the MaskEdBox control and an ordinary text box?

4. What is the purpose of an input mask?

5. What is an RTF file and how does it relate to the RichTextBox control?

6. When does the SelChange event occur for a rich text box?

7. How do you create a checked or unchecked menu item?

You have completed this session. You now can take a break or continue to the next session.

SESSION 9.2

In this session you will create reports using a program called Crystal Reports. In your reports you will display each record from a recordset, then count and tally the values of different fields without writing any code.

Introduction to Crystal Reports

To create printed reports, you have written Visual Basic statements to print headings, detail lines, and totals, using the Printer object. The information for these reports generally was gathered from a Recordset object.

Visual Basic supplies a program, called Crystal Reports, to simplify the task of creating and printing different reports. Using Crystal Reports, you can create a report by drawing objects on a form, in much the same way you have used controls on forms. As a result, a report can be created with writing little or no code.

Crystal Reports will create a Recordset object, and display the fields in each record on a report. You do not need to create a Do loop or write any code to print each record. Crystal Reports does this for you. In addition, it can tally the values in columns of numbers and perform several other mathematical functions.

Crystal Reports actually is not part of Visual Basic. Rather, it is a stand-alone product that you can use with Visual Basic or other programming languages. Crystal Reports consists of the following two parts:

- **Crystal Reports** is a stand-alone program that runs independently of Visual Basic. Using the Crystal Reports program, you can design, test, and run reports based on the information contained in an Access database as well as other types of databases. Note that it is not necessary to have Visual Basic running to use the Crystal Reports program. In fact Visual Basic does not even need to be on the system.

- The **CrystalReport** control is an ActiveX control that must be added to your project before you can print a report created by Crystal Reports in Visual Basic. The CrystalReport control establishes a connection between your program and Crystal Reports. The connection is established by setting properties of the CrystalReport control either at design time or run time.

Before using the CrystalReport control, you need to create a report with Crystal Reports. Ted wants a report to list each part number and its corresponding sales amount. This information is stored in the database you used in Session 9.1. In Session 9.2 you will create two reports. Only the second report will be used with the CrystalReport control. The completed report is shown in Figure 9-16.

Figure 9-16 ◀
Completed
report

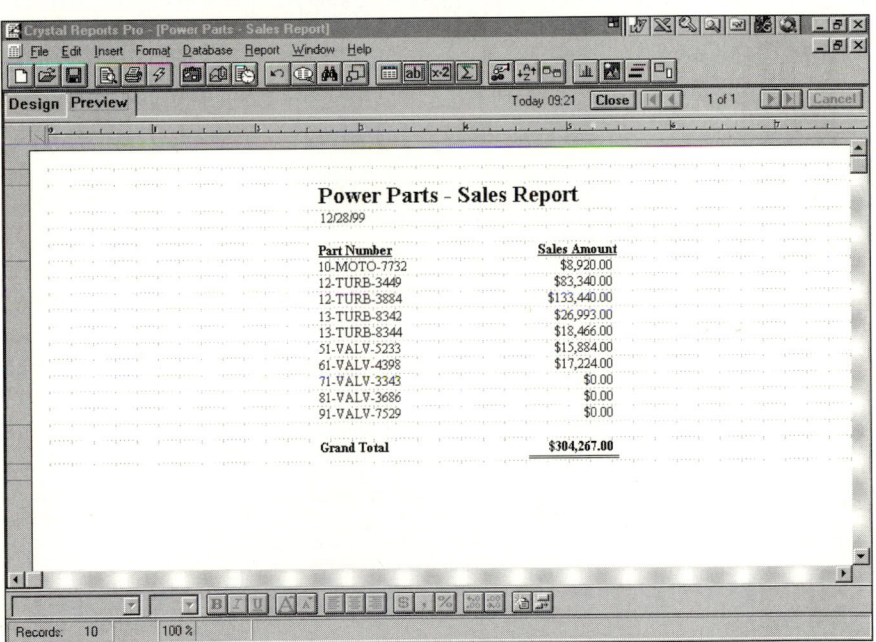

Remember, you added the CrystalReport control in Session 9.1 when you added the other ActiveX controls so it is available for use.

To start Crystal Reports:

1. Click **Start** on the taskbar.

2. Select **Programs** then **Microsoft Visual Basic 5.0** then **Crystal Reports**. Crystal Reports should display on the screen as shown in Figure 9-17. Note that a registration screen may display when you start Crystal Reports. Click **Done** to exit this screen.

3. Maximize the window.

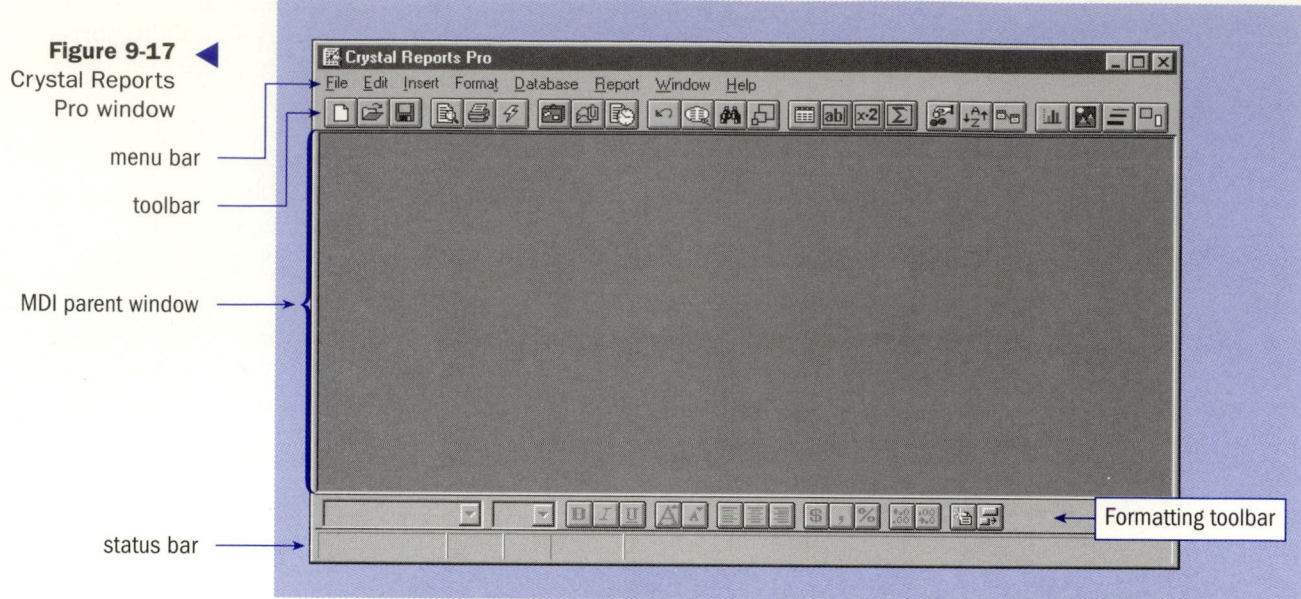

Figure 9-17 ◄
Crystal Reports
Pro window

menu bar

toolbar

MDI parent window

Formatting toolbar

status bar

As you can see from Figure 9-17, Crystal Reports is an MDI program with menus and a toolbar allowing you to create and test reports. There also is a formatting toolbar that allows you to set the formatting characteristics of different fields on a report. Finally, there is a status bar that displays current information about selected text and database files. There are two ways to create a report:

- You can use an expert. An **expert**, which functions like a wizard, leads you through the process of creating a report by allowing you to complete a series of dialog boxes.

- You can create a custom report from scratch. When you create a **custom report**, you draw objects on the report to define the column titles, the database fields you want to display, and any totals. Note that you also can modify a report created by an expert. This process is much like creating text boxes and other objects on a form.

Ted has a simple report he wants you to create that will list each part number in inventory and the corresponding annual sales of the parts. The report should have page titles and column titles like the reports you have created previously. You can use an expert to create the entire report.

Using an Expert to Create a Report

Crystal Reports supports several experts to help you create different types of reports. Each of these experts is listed in the Create New Report dialog box. The Create New Report dialog box is shown in Figure 9-18.

Figure 9-18 ◄
Create New
Report
dialog box

click Standard

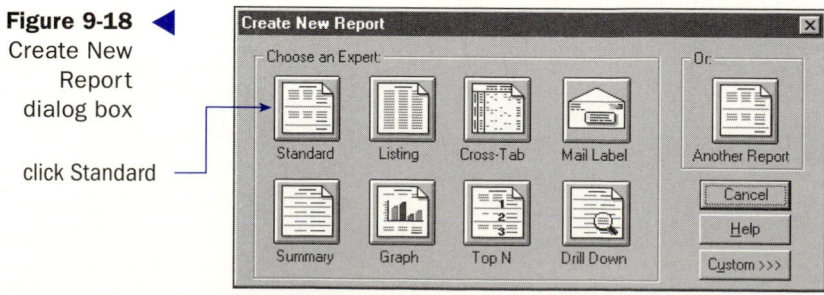

As you can see, there are eight different experts to create eight different types of reports. In this session you will create a standard report. This type of report has characteristics similar to the previous reports you have created.

To select the type of report:

1. Click **File** then click **New** on the menu bar to create a new report. The Create New Report dialog box will display as shown in Figure 9-18.

2. Click **Standard**.

3. The Create Report Expert dialog box displays as shown in Figure 9-19.

Figure 9-19 ◀
Create Report
Expert
dialog box

select to use an
Access database

select to use an
ODBC database

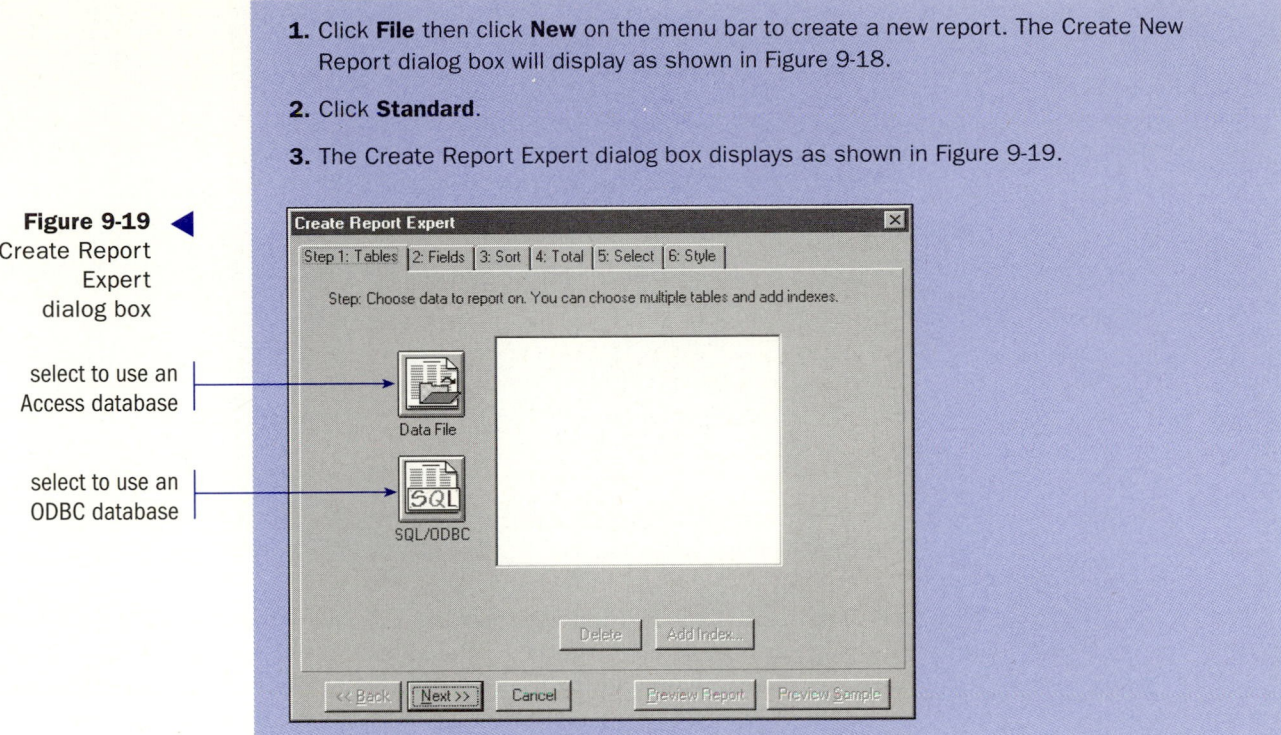

As you can see from Figure 9-19, there are two different sources for your data:

- You can retrieve data from an Access database by clicking the **Data File** button. Crystal Reports will establish a connection with the Microsoft Jet database engine, allowing you to select the fields and tables you want to use.

- You also can use a technology called **Open Database Connectivity (ODBC)**, to establish a connection with Access or other databases that support ODBC technology. ODBC is a technology that allows a single program to communicate with multiple types of databases. Each database vendor that supports ODBC supplies a set of programs that allow another program to access the database using a standard set of functions.

Because you are communicating with an Access database, you can select the Data File option then select the desired database file.

To select the data file:

1. Click the **Data File** button. The **Choose Database File** dialog box should display.

2. Select the file **Power.mdb** in the **Tutorial.09** folder on your Student Disk, then click the **Add** button.

3. Click the **Done** button in the Choose Database File dialog box. The **Links** tab on the expert should be highlighted as shown in Figure 9-20.

Figure 9-20 ◀
Links tab in
Create Report
Expert dialog
box

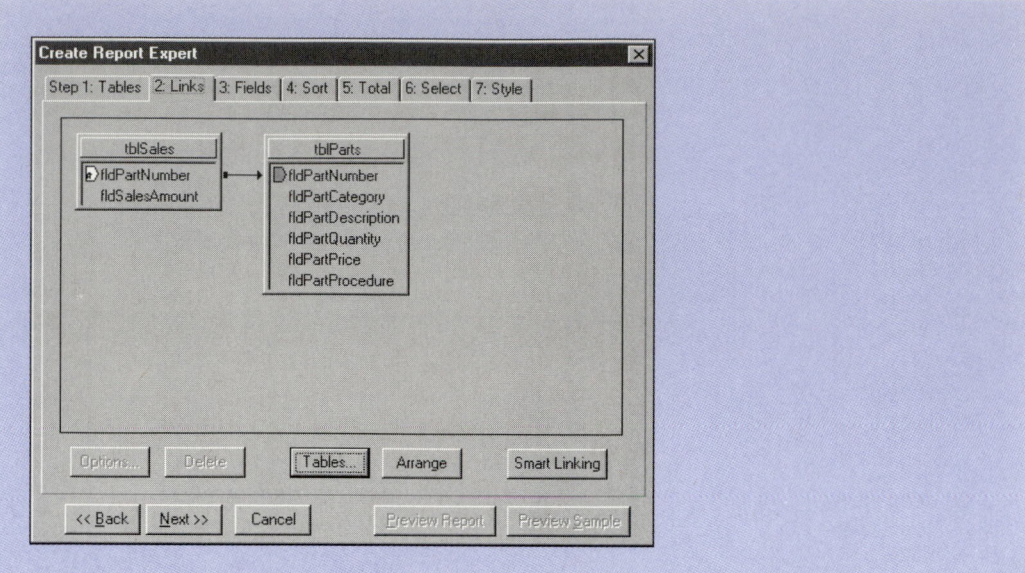

The Links tab displays the relationships between the tables and queries in the selected database. Its purpose is much the same as the Relationships window in Access.

After selecting the database and the tables or queries to use, you can select the fields you want printed on the report. You select the fields you want by using the Fields tab in the dialog box. The Fields tab is shown in Figure 9-21.

Figure 9-21 ◀
Fields tab in
Create Report
Expert dialog
box

available database
fields dispay here

create formula

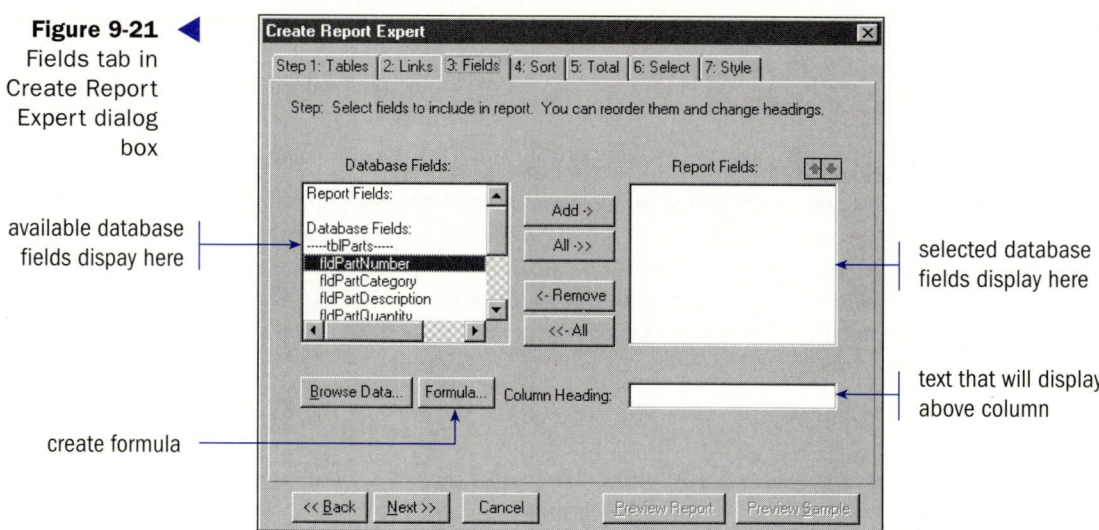

selected database
fields display here

text that will display
above column

Using the list boxes, text boxes, and command buttons on the Fields tab, you can select the fields you want to use on the report, and define the column heading that displays above the columns. You also can look at the actual data in a field and create formulas. The boxes and buttons are as follows:

- The **Database Fields** list box contains a list of the tables and fields in the database. Only those tables selected on the Tables tab are displayed.

- The **Report Fields** list box contains the fields that currently are selected. These fields will be displayed on the report.

- The **Column Heading** text box defines the text that will display above the column on each report field.

- It is possible to display information that is based on computations on columns. To create formulas, you use the **Formula** command button. You will learn how to create formulas later in the session.

- The **Browse Data** command button will display rows from the selected field. This information is the actual data from the database.

Ted suggests you now add the fields. Ted wants the part number and the sales amount displayed on the report. This information is stored in the fields fldPartNumber and fldSalesAmount. He also would like the column heading changed from the default value to a name more descriptive for the user.

To add the fields to the report:

1. Make sure the Fields tab is active, click the field named **fldPartNumber**, then click **Add**. The field is added to the Report Fields section.

2. Set the column heading to **Part Number**. This string will display just above the column of part numbers.

3. Add the field named **fldSalesAmount** and set the column heading to **Sales Amount,** respectively. You will need to use the scroll bars to locate the field. The **Fields** dialog box should look like Figure 9-22.

Figure 9-22
Fields tab in Create Report Expert dialog box

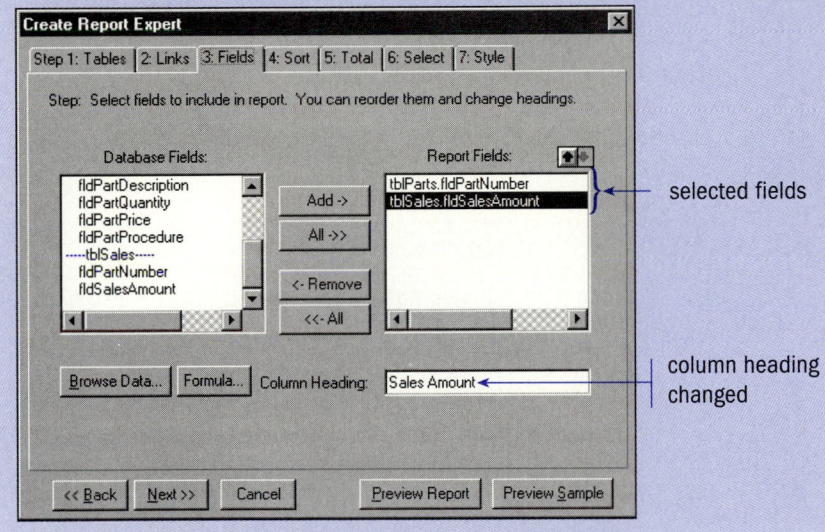

After specifying the fields to be printed, you should specify how the data should be sorted. You can sort data by one or more columns using the Sort tab on the expert. The process of selecting the fields to sort is much like selecting the fields themselves. You select the field to sort, then click the Add command button. Ted wants the report sorted by the part number.

To sort the report:

1. Make sure the **Sort** tab is active.

2. Click the field named **tblParts.fldPartNumber**, then click the **Add** button. Note the order is in ascending order, as shown in Figure 9-23.

Figure 9-23 ◀
Sort tab in
Create Report
Expert dialog
box

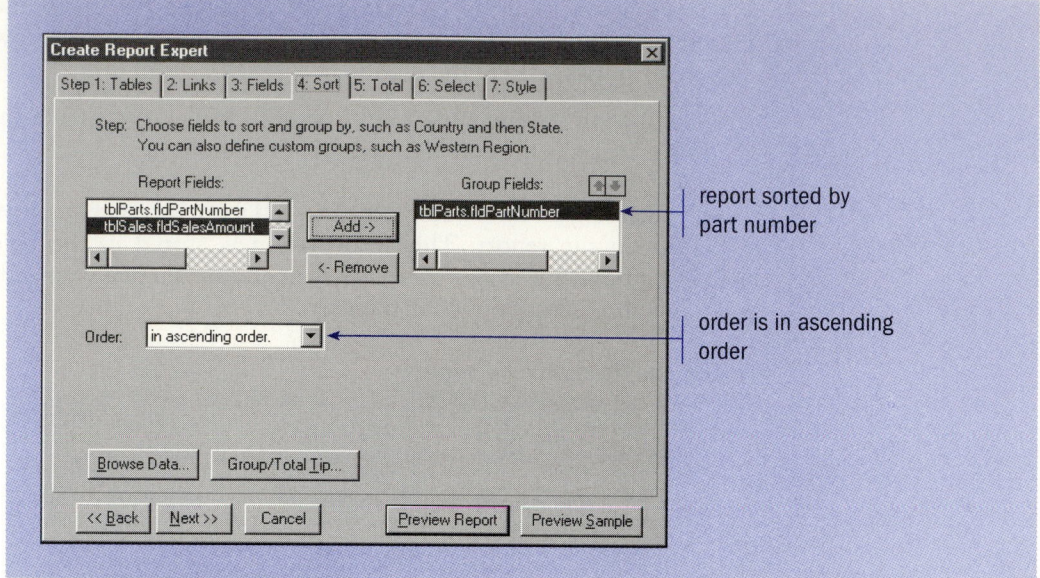

report sorted by
part number

order is in ascending
order

In addition to sorting the fields, you can tally columns of numbers in the same way as you have used counters and accumulators previously. You do not need to write code to add the values to an accumulator with code.

To add columns of numbers, you use the Total tab. By default, the expert will create a subtotal for each part number. Because the part number is unique, a part number subtotal does not make sense. You can remove the subtotal by clicking the item, then clicking the Remove button.

To remove the subtotal:

1. Make sure the **Total** tab is active.

2. Click the field **tblSales.fldSalesAmount** to activate it, if necessary.

3. Click the **Remove** button.

4. Make sure the **Add Grand Totals** check box is checked. The expert should look like Figure 9-24.

Figure 9-24 ◀
Total tab in
Create Report
Expert dialog
box

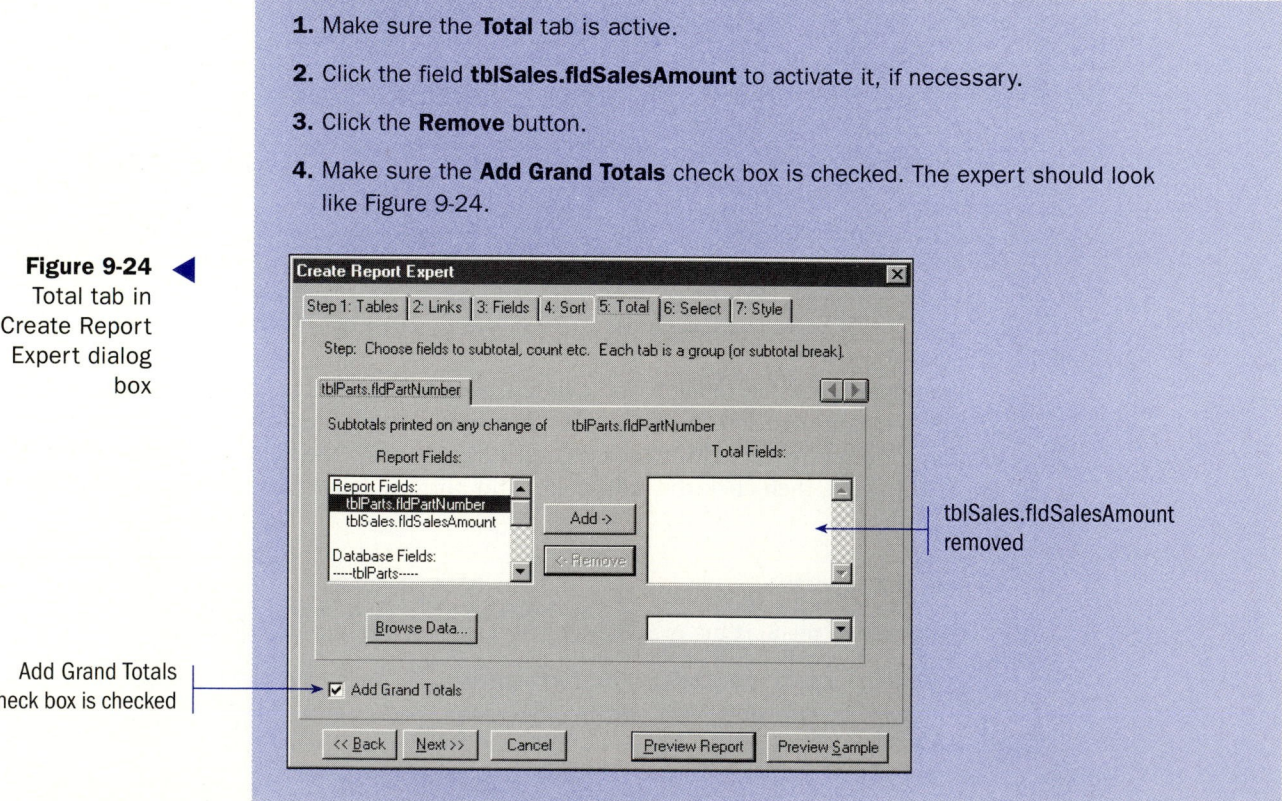

tblSales.fldSalesAmount
removed

Add Grand Totals
check box is checked

You can use the Style tab to refine the formatting of your report. The Report Expert has several defined styles that you can use to improve the appearance of the report. The Style tab, shown in Figure 9-25, contains:

Figure 9-25
Style tab in
Create Report
Expert dialog
box

select style in Style
list box

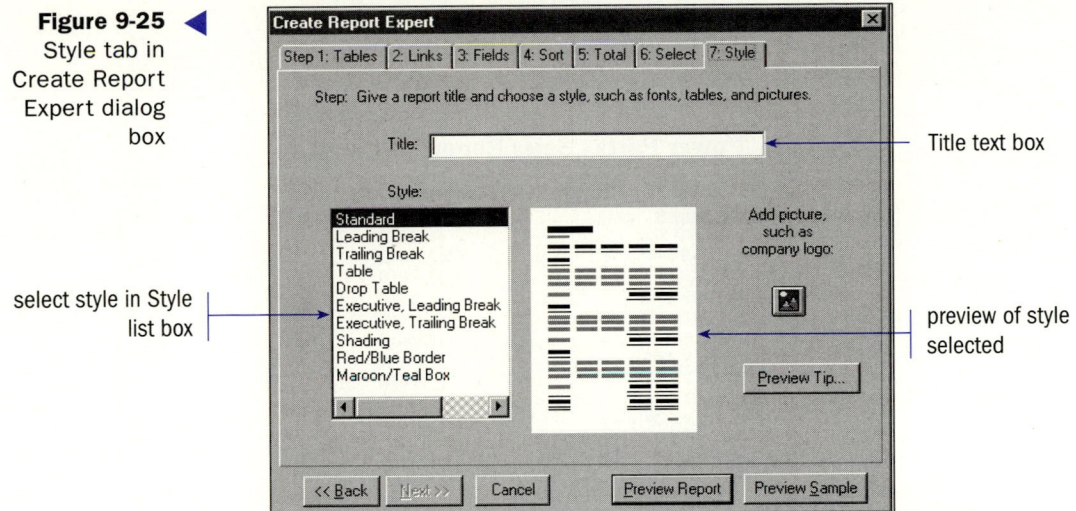

Title text box

preview of style
selected

- You can place a title on the report by placing text in the **Title** text box.

- The Style tab contains a list of predefined styles in the **Style** list box.

- When you select a style in the Style list box, a prototype of the style is displayed to the right of the list box.

Ted wants the title of the report to say Power Parts – Sales Report. Also, he suggests that you look at the different styles you can use for the report.

To view some of the different supported styles:

1. Click the **Style** tab in the Create Report Expert dialog box.

2. Using the **Style** list box, click different styles and preview the appearance of each style selected.

3. Select the **Standard** style.

4. Enter the title **Power Parts – Sales Report.**

You have completed all the definitions for the Create Report Expert to create the report. You now can preview the report and save it on the disk. Reports are saved with the extension "rpt". When you save a report on the disk, it can be saved with the current report data or without the data. If you save the data with the report and the data later changes, you can reload the data by clicking Report then Refresh Report Data on the menu bar.

To preview the report and save it:

1. Click the **Preview Report** command button on the Style tab in the Create Report Expert dialog box.

2. If the data on the report is too small to see, click **Report** then **Zoom** on the menu bar. Your report should look like Figure 9-26.

Figure 9-26 ◀
Completed
sales report

Preview mode —

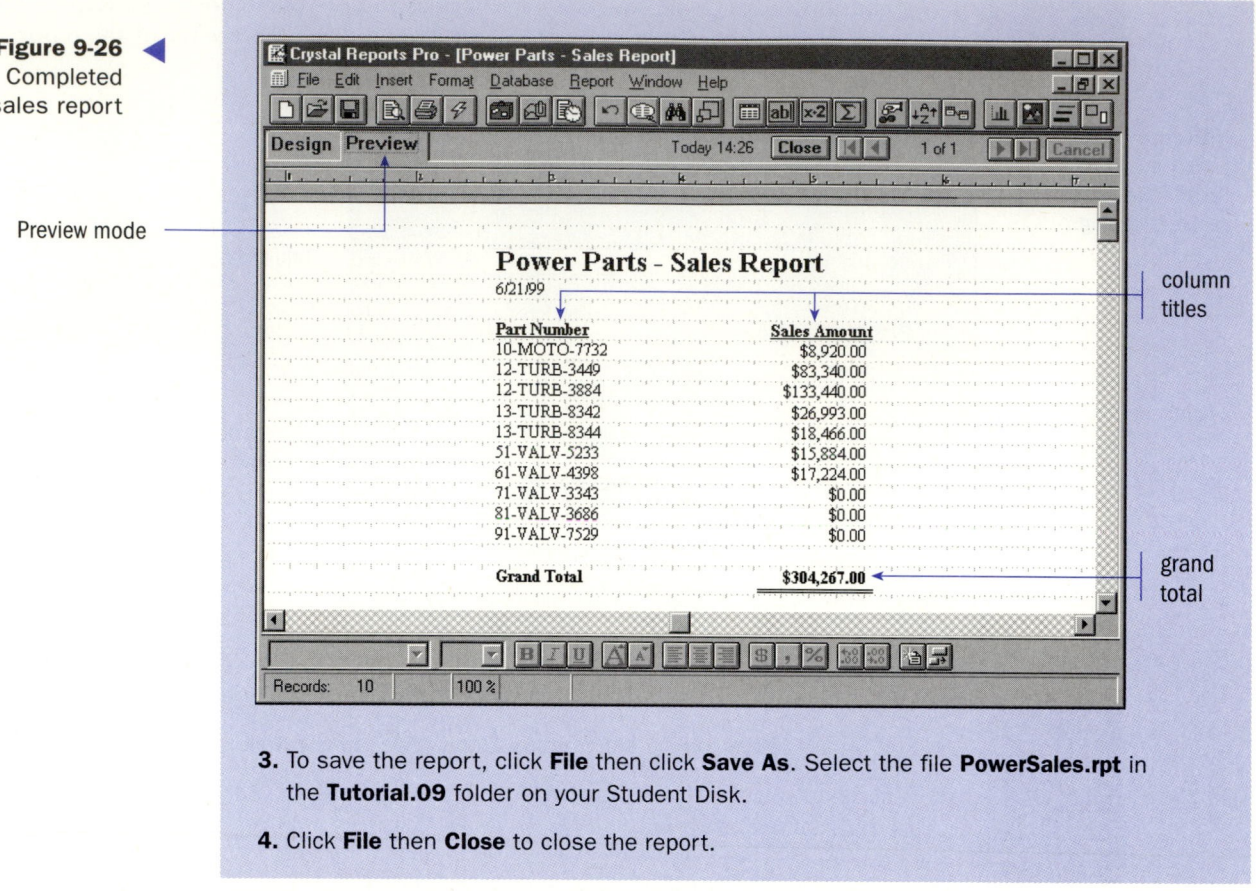

column titles

grand total

3. To save the report, click **File** then click **Save As**. Select the file **PowerSales.rpt** in the **Tutorial.09** folder on your Student Disk.

4. Click **File** then **Close** to close the report.

Any report you create with an expert can be modified later to fit a particular purpose. For example, you can change the formatting and add or remove fields after creating a report with an expert. Ted would like to print another report to determine the dollar amount of the parts in inventory.

Creating and Modifying a Report without the Expert

In addition to using an expert to create a report, you also either can modify reports created by an expert or create reports from scratch.

Creating a report without an expert is much like drawing and moving controls on a form. That is, you create objects on the form to display information. When you modify or create a report without an expert, Crystal Reports operates in either Design mode or Preview mode. Using Design mode, you can change the layout and contents of a report. In Preview mode, you can look at the report as it will display on a printed page. Figure 9-27 shows the completed inventory report in Design mode.

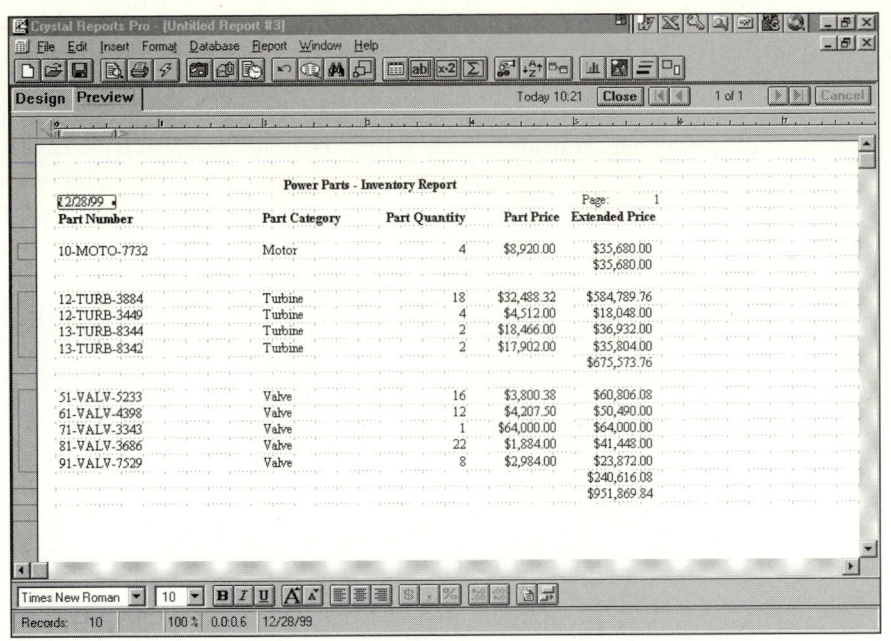

As shown in Figure 9-27 a report is divided into sections. Recall that when you have printed reports in the previous tutorials, you created general procedures to identify the report titles, detail lines, and report totals. Crystal Reports defines sections to perform these functions. The following list describes the different default sections:

- The **Title** section contains the report title. It displays only once on the first page of the report.

- The **Page header** section displays at the top of every page.

- The **Details** section contains one or more lines for each individual record selected from a database table or query.

- The **Page footer** section displays at the bottom of every page.

- The **Summary** section displays at the end of the report.

There is a section named #1: fldPartCategory. This is not a default section. Rather it is a section called a control break. A **control break** is used to create a subtotal whenever the value of the part category changes. Thus, if there were three different part categories, there would be three subtotals.

In each of these sections, you add fields to the report, much in the same way as you draw controls on a form. You can change the font, alignment, and other characteristics of the information in each field. There also are special predefined fields to store dates and page numbers. This is much like the Page property for the Printer object.

There are several types of fields you can insert on a report:

- A **database** field is similar to a bound text box. It displays the data from a database field into a region on the report.

- A **text** field is not bound to a field in a database. Rather it works like a label. A text field has a name. You store a string in a text field that functions like a label's caption. You can use text fields for page and column headers.

- A **formula** field is made up of a name and a formula. You use formulas to perform arithmetic operations on different fields. You would use a formula field to multiply two database fields together. The formula is stored in the field. When the report is run, the formula is evaluated and the result of the multiplication would be stored in the formula field.

- A **summary** field is used to analyze the values of multiple database records. For example, you can count the number of records in a recordset, or add their values. You use a summary field like a counter or accumulator. In addition you can perform statistical functions on a summary field.

■ There are **special** fields to perform common operations like displaying the current date or page number. There also are special fields to add up columns of numbers.

The inventory report you are creating for Power Parts requires that you create a report with different types of fields in each of these sections. You also will need to add other sections to the report. To create a custom report, you must select the type of report and the source of the data. This process is similar to the one you used when you created a report with an expert.

To create a custom report:

1. Click **File** then click **New**.

2. Click the **Custom** command button. The dialog box should look like Figure 9-28.

Figure 9-28 ◄
Create New
Report dialog
box

Custom command
button

select Data File

Custom Report
selected

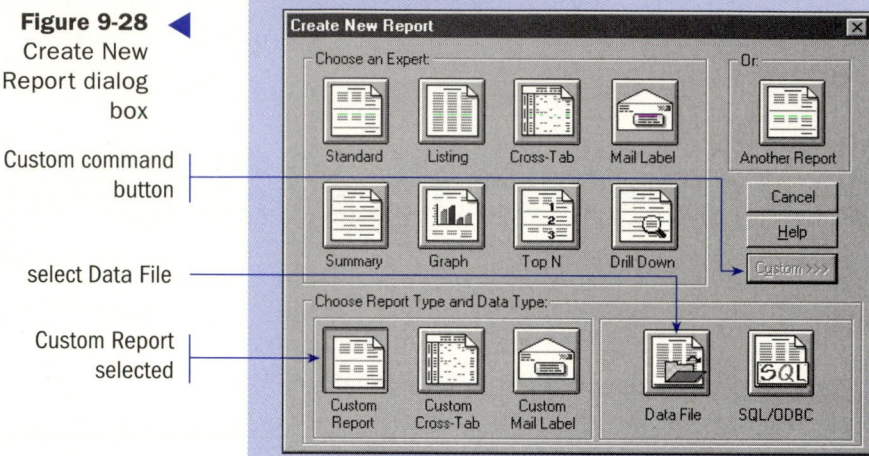

3. Make sure the **Custom Report** button is highlighted. Click the **Data File** button to activate the Choose Database File dialog box.

4. Select the file **Power.mdb** in the **Tutorial.09** folder on your Student Disk, then click **OK**. The report will display in Design mode along with the Insert Database Field dialog box as shown in Figure 9-29.

Figure 9-29 ◄
New report in
Design mode

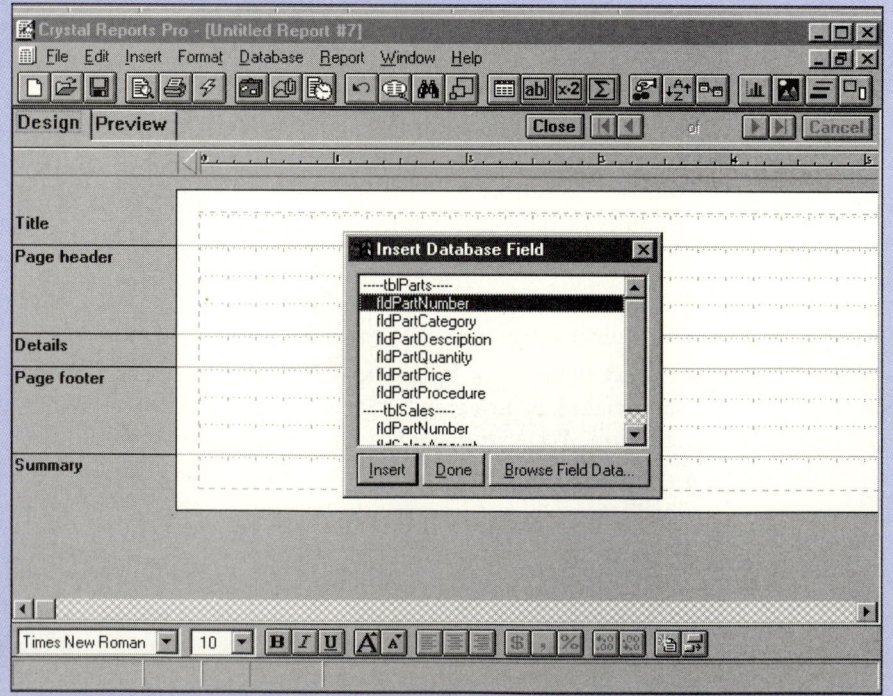

You can click back and forth between the Design and Preview tabs to design the report, then look at the report as it will display on the printed page.

Inserting and Formatting Fields on a Report

Once the blank report has been created, you can insert the fields to be displayed. You insert fields by clicking a field in the Insert Database Field dialog box, clicking the Insert button, then moving the cursor in the desired section, then clicking the mouse button again. By default, two fields are inserted. A text field is inserted to describe the contents of the second field, which is a database type field.

> **REFERENCE window**
>
> ### INSERTING A DATABASE FIELD ON A REPORT
>
> - Click Insert then Database Field to open the Insert Database Field dialog box.
> - Select the desired field then click the Insert command button.
> - Position the field on the form as desired.

Ted wants a report summarizing the different parts in inventory and the sales amount of each. The first step in this process is to select the fields you need to use in the report. These fields include the part number, part category, quantity in stock, and the price.

To select the fields for the report:

1. Make sure the Insert Database Field dialog box is active. If it is not, click **Insert** then **Database Field** on the menu bar.

2. Click the field named **fldPartNumber,** then click the **Insert** command button in the dialog box. Move the cursor to the Details section of the report as shown in Figure 9-30 and click. The database and text fields should display.

Figure 9-30 ◀
Adding fields
to report

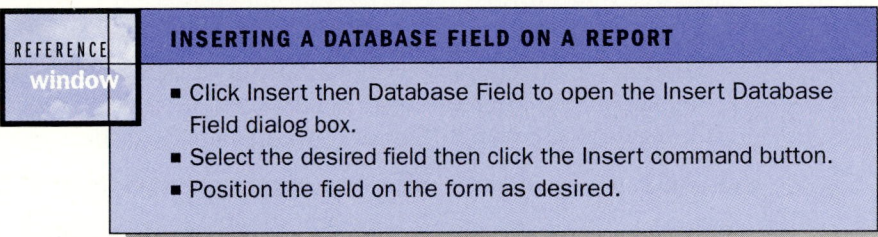

3. Repeat Step 2 for the fields named **fldPartCategory**, **fldPartQuantity**, and **fldPartPrice**.

4. Click the **Done** button in the Insert Database Field dialog box to close it. Your form should look like Figure 9-30.

After placing fields on a report, you can format those fields. Crystal Reports gives you considerable flexibility in formatting the data in a report. You change the formatting characteristics of a field much like you do with a Visual Basic control. You also can select multiple fields and apply formatting settings to them all at once. The following list illustrates some of the formatting you can apply to a report and its fields:

- You can change the font of each field by clicking Format then Font, or activating an object then using the buttons on the Formatting toolbar.

- You can draw borders around fields and create graphical objects, like lines and boxes, by clicking Insert Line or Insert Box on the menu bar. Note in Figure 9-30, a section line is drawn under each text field that represents a column heading.

- The distance between the section lines dividing the section determines the space allocated to a section. You can increase or decrease the height of a section by moving the cursor over the section line, holding the left mouse button down, then dragging the section line up or down to increase or decrease the size of a section.

- You can place multiple fields in a single section on multiple lines.

- You also can resize an object in the same way you do a control drawn on a form. Click the field to activate it, then move the cursor to the highlighted border you want to move. When the cursor changes, hold down the left mouse button, then drag the field.

> *Tip:* In most cases you can apply formatting to a field by clicking the field to activate it, then clicking the desired button on the Formatting toolbar. You also can select multiple objects, then click a button on the Formatting toolbar to apply the same style to them all at once.

Ted would like the report to have a title to display at the top of each page, the column headings to have more descriptive names than the field names, and the column titles to display in bold.

To add the page title and format the column titles:

1. Click **Insert** then **Text Field** on the menu bar. The Edit Text Field dialog box opens.

2. Enter the text **Power Parts – Inventory Report,** then click **Accept**.

3. Position the text field in the center of the Page header section, then click the left mouse button.

4. Click the right mouse button on the text field named **fldPartNumber** and select **Edit Text Field**. Change the text in the field to **Part Number,** then click **Accept**.

5. Change the text in the remaining fields to **Part Category**, **Part Quantity**, and **Part Price**.

6. Hold down the **Shift** key, then click each of the text boxes in the Page header section. Click the **Bold** button on the Formatting toolbar.

Now that your report can display the information from each row in the table, you need to create a formula that multiplies the part quantity by the price to determine the dollar amount of each part currently in inventory.

Creating Formulas

In addition to printing data directly from fields in the database, you can perform computations on the fields for each row. In this case you need to compute the dollar amount of an inventory item by multiplying the quantity in stock by the price of the item. This value must be displayed on the report.

To accomplish this task you must create a formula field. A formula field contains a statement that will manipulate data. The syntax of a formula field is similar to expressions in Visual Basic with some minor differences as follows:

- A formula has a name beginning with an at (@) sign. Crystal Reports adds the @ sign for you.

- Database field names are enclosed in braces { }. You use the table name, followed by a period (.), followed by the field name.

- You can use fields and constant values to make expressions. Expressions can contain arithmetic operators and functions.

- Any text must be enclosed in quotation marks.

For example, if you were using a table named tblParts with the fields fldPartQuantity and fldPartPrice, the following formulas would be valid:

```
{tblParts.fldPartQuantity} * {tblParts.fldPartPrice}
{tblParts.fldPartPrice} * 1.05
```

To create a formula field, you use the Insert Formula dialog box to create a new formula. Then use the Edit Formula dialog box to define the contents of the formula. Ted suggests you begin creating the formula to compute the extended price of each inventory item.

To compute the extended price:

1. Click **Insert** then **Formula Field** to open the Insert Formula Field dialog box.

2. Enter the value **ExtendedPrice** in the Formula Name text box then click the **OK** button. The Edit Formula dialog box will display as shown in Figure 9-31.

Figure 9-31 ◀
Edit Formula
dialog box

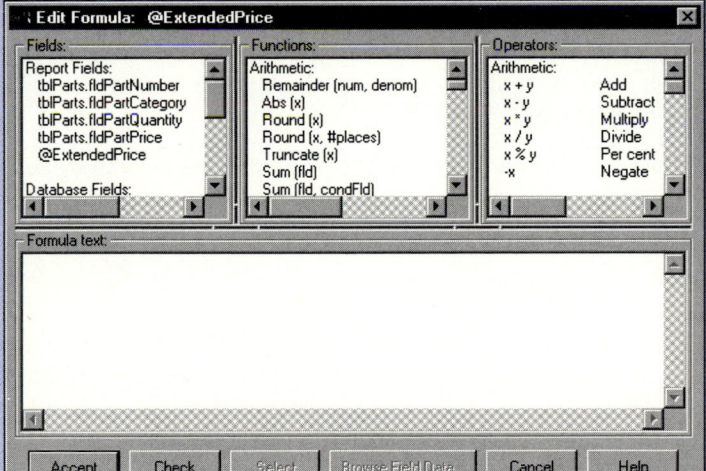

The Edit Formula dialog box contains four sections. You can enter a formula by typing the formula into the Formula text section. You can use the other three sections to help you create the formula. The Fields section lists all the fields defined for the report. The Functions section lists all the functions supported by Crystal Reports. You can use functions to round numbers and perform other mathematical operations. The Operators section contains all the arithmetic operators you can use. You can click the values in one of these windows, then click the Select command button to copy the selected item to the Formula text section.

In this session you need to create a formula that will compute the dollar value total for each item in inventory. This can be achieved by multiplying the quantity in stock by the price of the item.

To create a formula:

1. Click the field named **tblParts.fldPartQuantity,** then click the **Select** command button. The field should be copied to the Formula text section.

2. Click the operator **x*y** in the Operators section, then click the **Select** command button. The * should be copied to the Formula text section.

3. Click the field named **tblParts.fldPartPrice,** then click the **Select** command button. The field should be copied to the Formula text section. Your formula should look like the one in Figure 9-32.

Figure 9-32 ◀
Creating a
formula

formula

check formula syntax

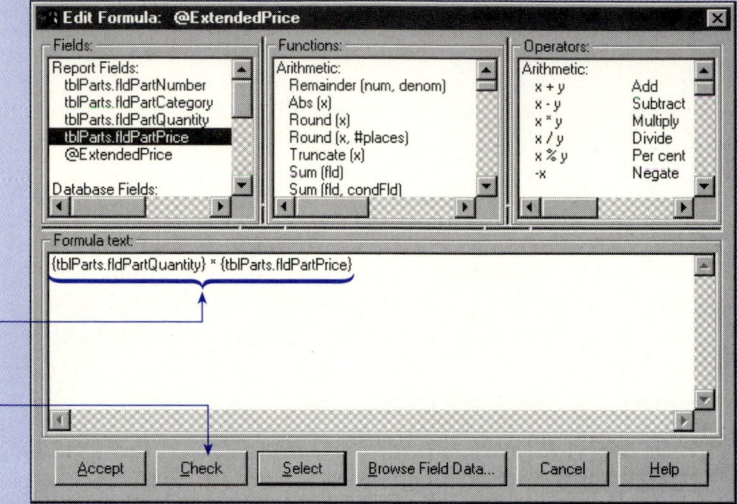

4. Click the **Check** command button to verify the syntax of the formula. A message box should display indicating that there were no errors found. Click **OK** in the dialog box.

5. Click **Accept**. The Edit Formula dialog box will close, and you will be able to position the newly created formula on the report just like you placed database fields on the report.

6. Position the cursor to the right of the **fldPartPrice** database field in the Details section, then click the **left mouse** button to position the field on the form.

7. Set the text in the text field to **Extended Price** and format the text as **bold**.

In addition to the field types you already have used, Crystal Reports supports special fields to handle page numbers and dates. You can create these fields by clicking Insert then Special Field on the menu bar. Ted wants the current date and the page number printed at the top of every page, so you need to insert the fields in the Page header section.

To print the date and page numbers:

1. Click **Insert** then **Special Field** then **Print Date Field**.

2. Position the date in the Page header section of the report as shown in Figure 9-33.

3. Click **Insert** then **Special Field** then **Page Number Field**.

4. Position the page number as shown in Figure 9-33.

5. Click **Insert** then **Text Field** to open the Edit Text Field dialog box. Enter the text **Page:** then click **Accept**.

6. Position the field as shown in Figure 9-33.

Figure 9-33
Adding special
fields

text field
date field
page number field

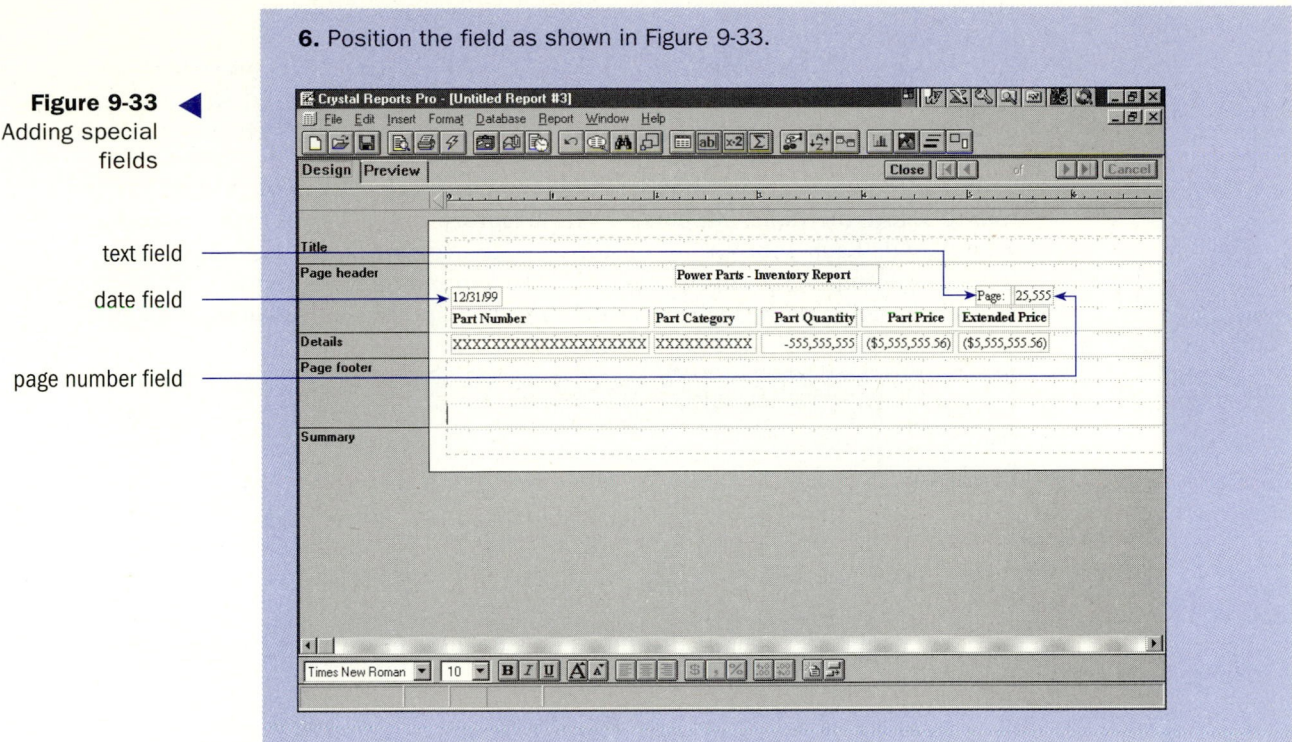

Figure 9-33
Adding special
fields

You now have designed the Details and Page header sections of the report. This is a good time to preview the report to make sure it is correct.

To preview the report:

1. Click the **Preview** tab in the Crystal Reports Pro dialog box.

2. Click the **Report** then **Zoom** if the data on the report is too small to read.

In addition to printing information for each record, Ted wants the total value of the inventory in stock printed at the end of the report. To do this, you need to accumulate the extended price of each inventory item, and print the result after all the items have been printed. Instead of creating an accumulator and manually adding the value of each extended price to the accumulator, Crystal Reports will let you insert a grand total in the report. When you insert a grand total in the report, a new report section, called the Grand Total section, is created. You can create a grand total for a field by clicking the field, clicking Insert then Grand Total on the menu bar.

To insert the grand total:

1. Click the **Design** tab in the Crystal Reports Pro dialog box.

2. Click the **Extended Price** field. A different color border should display around the field indicating it is active.

3. Click **Insert** then **Grand Total** on the menu bar. The Insert Grand Total dialog box should display as shown in Figure 9-34.

Figure 9-34
Insert Grand
Total dialog box

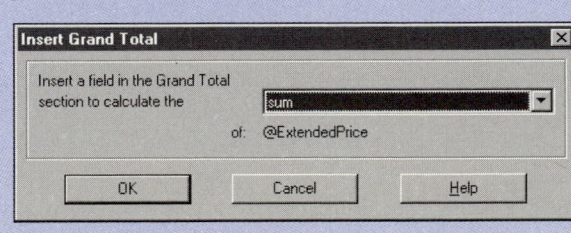

> 4. Select the **sum** function then click **OK**. The Grand Total section should display and the new field should display in the section. Note Crystal Reports automatically positioned the field under the correct column.

In addition to a grand total, you also can create subtotals. For this report, Ted would like to know the dollar amount of the inventory for each part type, in addition to the grand total. Each subtotal is considered a control break. To accomplish this, you can insert a subtotal field. This works much like a grand total but the values are summarized and a subtotal is printed whenever the value of a specific field changes.

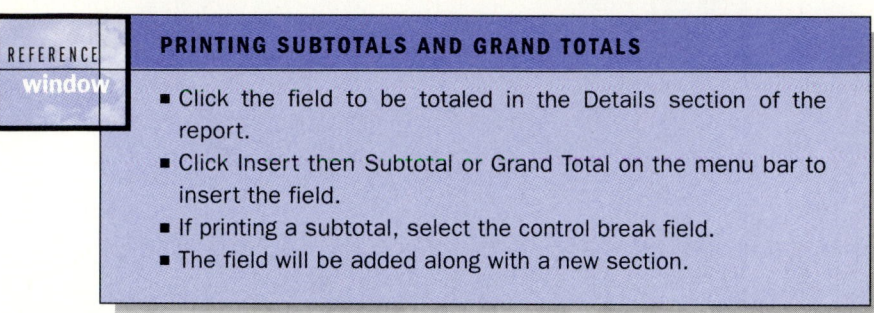

REFERENCE window

PRINTING SUBTOTALS AND GRAND TOTALS

- Click the field to be totaled in the Details section of the report.
- Click Insert then Subtotal or Grand Total on the menu bar to insert the field.
- If printing a subtotal, select the control break field.
- The field will be added along with a new section.

In this case you want to print the total for each part type whenever the part category changes.

To print the part category subtotal:

1. Click the **Extended Price** field in the Details section to activate it.

2. Click **Insert** then **Subtotal** on the menu bar.

3. Select **tblParts.fldPartCategory** in the list box, then click the **OK** button.

4. A new section is added to the report as shown in Figure 9-35.

Figure 9-35 ◄
Creating a subtotal

subtotal section

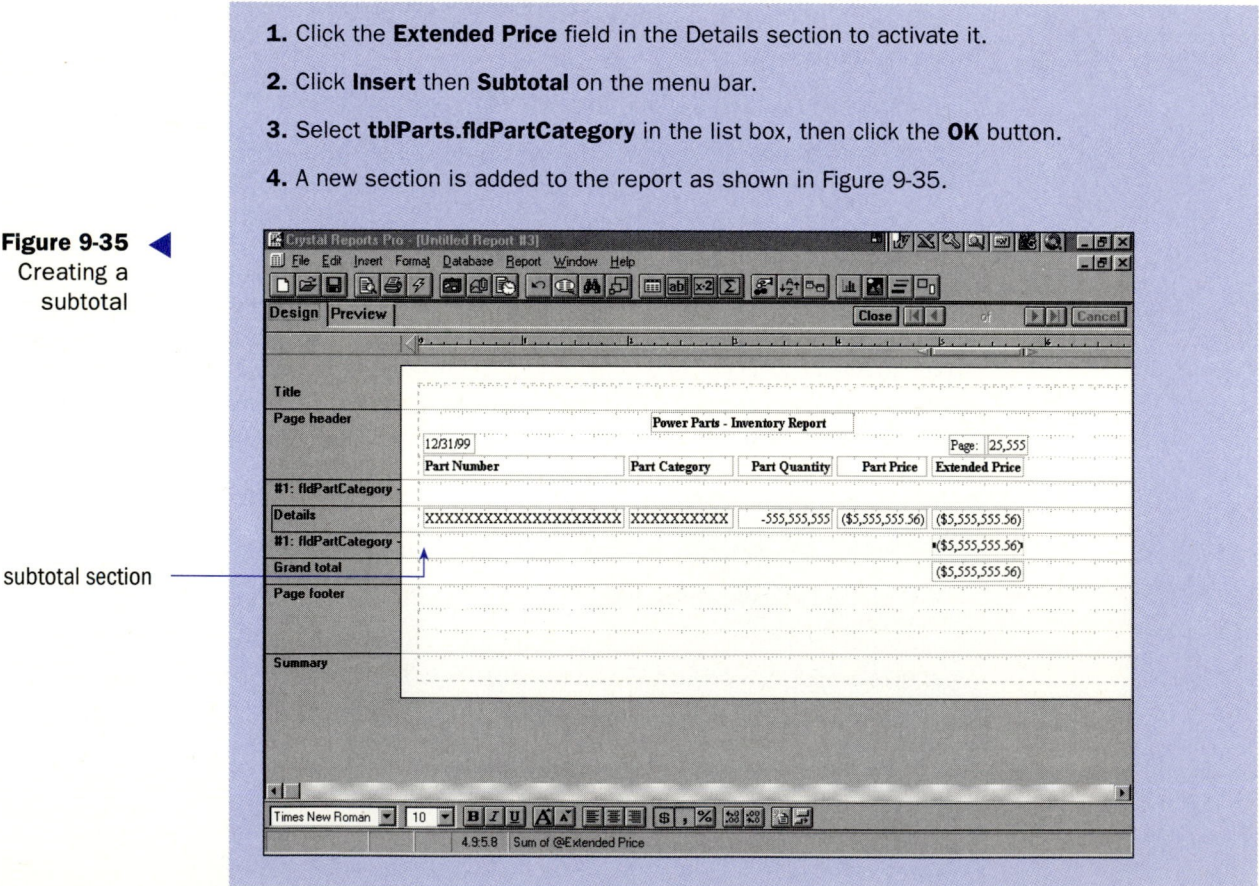

The report now is complete. Before exiting Crystal Reports, you should save the report on your Student Disk and preview it to make sure the information is correct.

To save and preview the report:

1. Click **File** then **Save** on the menu bar.

2. Use the file named **PowerInventory.rpt** in the **A:\Tutorial.09** folder.

3. Click **OK** to save the report.

4. Click the **Preview** tab to view the report. Your report should look like Figure 9-36.

Figure 9-36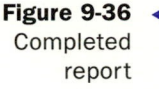
Completed
report

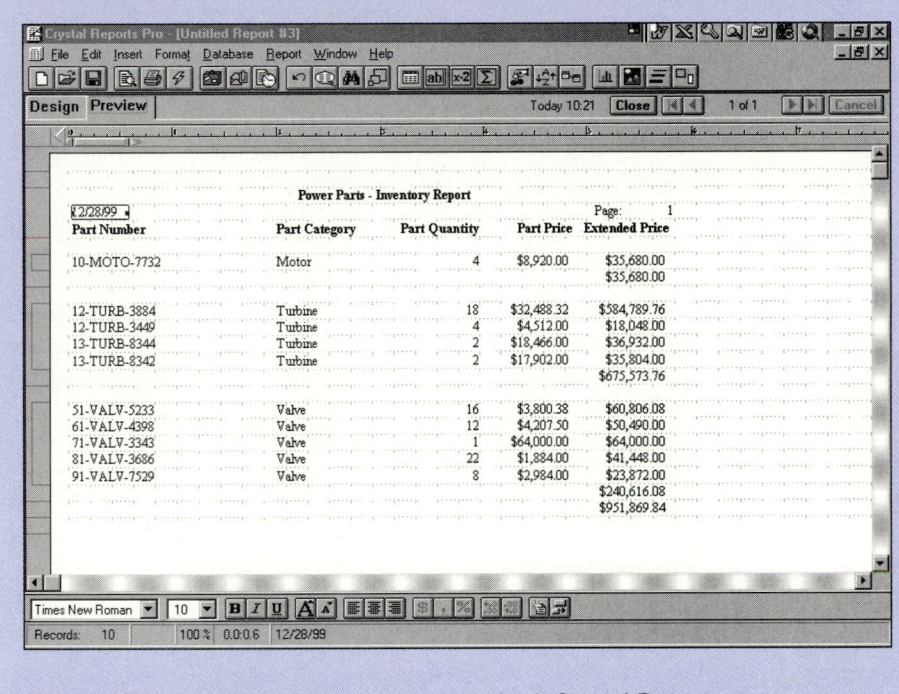

5. Click **File** then **Exit** to close the report and exit Crystal Reports.

Now that you have completed the report, you need to be able to print it from the Visual Basic program you just wrote.

Using the CrystalReport Control

The CrystalReport control is an ActiveX control meaning that you first must add the control to your project before it can be used in a program. The CrystalReport control is used to establish a connection with Crystal Reports to print a report. You either can use the Property Pages of the CrystalReport control at design time to set the properties of the control or set the properties at run time. The standard prefix for the CrystalReport control is "cry".

Ted suggests you now add the CrystalReport control to your project and create an instance of it on the form.

To create an instance of the CrystalReport control:

1. Start **Visual Basic,** if necessary, then load the project named **Power Procedure.vbp**. Make sure the form named **frmPowerProcedure** is active.

2. Click the **CrystalReport** control 🖳 on the toolbar and draw an instance of the control on the form. Like the CommonDialog control, the CrystalReport control is not visible at run time so it does not matter where you place the control.

3. Set the Name property of the control to **cryPower**.

The CrystalReport control has several properties you use to identify the report to be printed and to print the report:

- The **ReportFileName** property contains the filename of the report to be printed. This filename should be the same as the report filename you saved in Crystal Reports.

- The **Destination** property determines where the report is printed. You can use one of three constants to control the report's destination. If set to **0 - crptToWindow** then the report is printed to a window on the screen. You can use the window to look at the different records in the report. If set to **1 - crptToPrinter** the report is sent to the printer. If set to **2 - crptToFile** then the report is printed to a file on the disk. When you use the **crptToFile** destination, you must set the **PrintFileName** to the name of the file where the report will be saved.

- You also should set the **PrintFileType** property to the type of file you want to print. Crystal Reports can print data to files that can be read by several other programs.

- The **Action** property is a run-time property that causes the report to be printed. When you set the Action property to 1 at run time, the report is printed based on the information you specified in the previous properties.

Note that the help for the CrystalReport control is located in Crystal Reports rather than Visual Basic. Ted suggests you now set the properties to print the report you just created to the printer.

To print the report:

1. Insert a general procedure named **PrintInventory** and add the following statements to the procedure:x

```
Private Sub PrintInventory( )
      cryPower.ReportFileName = "A:\Tutorial.09\Power.rpt"
      cryPower.Destination = crptToPrinter
      cryPower.Action = 1
End Sub
```

2. Enter the following statement into the mnuFilePrintInventoryReport_Click( ) event procedure:

```
PrintInventory
```

3. Save and run the program and test the report. Be sure to test both the toolbar button and the menu item.

You have completed the programming for this session. Your program now will print the inventory report you created with Crystal Reports using the CrystalReport control. You now can exit Visual Basic.

Quick Check

1. What is the purpose of an expert?
2. List and describe the different types of fields in Crystal Reports.
3. What is a report section?
4. How do you create a formula in Crystal Reports?
5. How do you create subtotals and grand totals?
6. How do you use Crystal Reports with Visual Basic?

Figure 9-37 lists and defines the new terms presented in this tutorial.

Figure 9-37 ◀
New terms

Term	Definition
Control break	A control break is used to create a subtotal whenever the value of a field changes.
Custom report	Creating a custom report is the second way to create a report. When you create a custom report, you draw objects on the report to define the column titles, the database fields you want to display, and any totals.
Expert	An expert, which functions like a wizard, leads you through the process of creating a report by allowing you to complete a series of dialog boxes. Using an expert is the first way to create a report.
Open Database Connectivity (ODBC)	Open Database Connectivity (ODBC) is a technology that allows different programs to communicate with different types of databases.
Rich Text Format (RTF)	Rich Text Format (RTF) is a standardized file format supported by many programs. It contains special characters to format data.

Tutorial Assignments

In addition to the report that prints inventory information, Ted wants a report to print the part number, type, and description. The report also should count the number of inventory items. This information is stored in the same database. The part description report should include the part number, part type, and part description. Figure 9-38 shows the completed report.

Figure 9-38 ◀

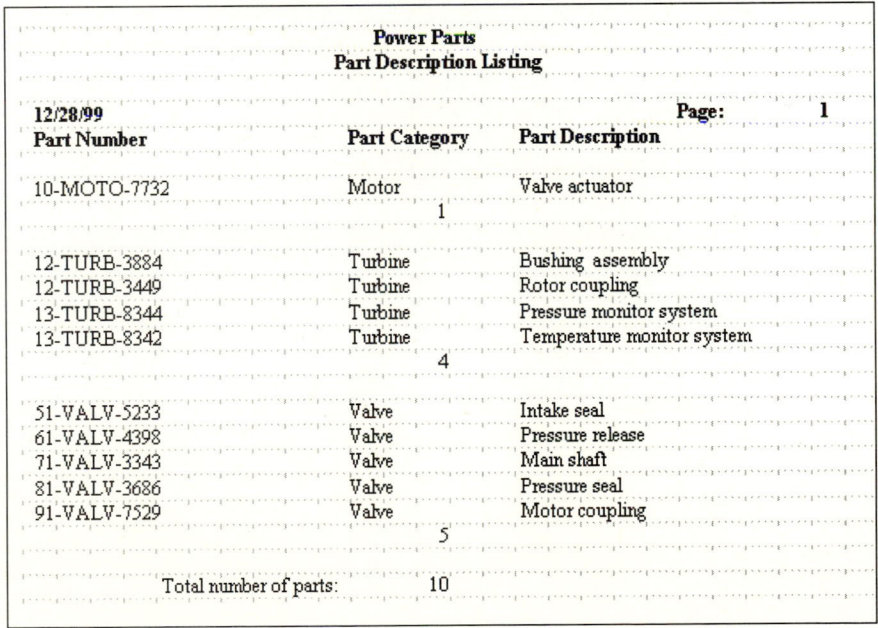

1. Make sure your Student Disk is in the appropriate disk drive, then start Crystal Reports.

2. Create a new report without an expert. The reports should be based on the data file **Power.mdb** located in the **TAssign** folder on your Student Disk.

3. Add the fields **fldPartNumber**, **fldPartCategory**, and **fldPartDescription** to the Details section of the report. Change the text fields in the Page header section to the names as shown in Figure 9-38. Set the font to bold.

4. Add a report title to the Title section as shown in Figure 9-38. You will need to increase the size of the Title section and create two text fields to display two lines.

5. Add the page number and current date to the report. The font also should be bold.

6. Add a grand total to the report. The grand total should count the number of parts listed. Increase the size of the Grand Total section so as to increase the space between the grand total and the field data.

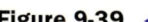

7. Preview the report to verify that it is the same as Figure 9-38.

8. Save the report using the filename **PowerDescription.rpt**.

9. Print the report then exit Crystal Reports.

10. Start Visual Basic, if necessary.

11. Set the form name to **frmPowerDescription** and the caption to **Power Parts.**

12. Save the form using the default name and the project using the filename **Power Description.vbp**.

13. Add the CrystalReport control to the project file and create an instance of the control.

14. Create a command button on the form to print the report you created in the previous steps. You need to set properties of the CrystalReport control.

15. Save the project, test the program, then exit Visual Basic.

Case Problems

1. Davidson Support Davidson Support provides technical support for different computer manufacturers. The organization is broken down into divisions. Each division provides support for a single manufacturer. Inside each division there are departments. Each department provides technical support for the different product lines. They would like you to create a report to print an employee listing by division and department. For each employee, the employee name and year-to-date pay needs to be displayed. You need to create subtotals for each department and division and a grand total of the payroll. Figure 9-39 shows the top of the completed report.

Figure 9-39 ◄

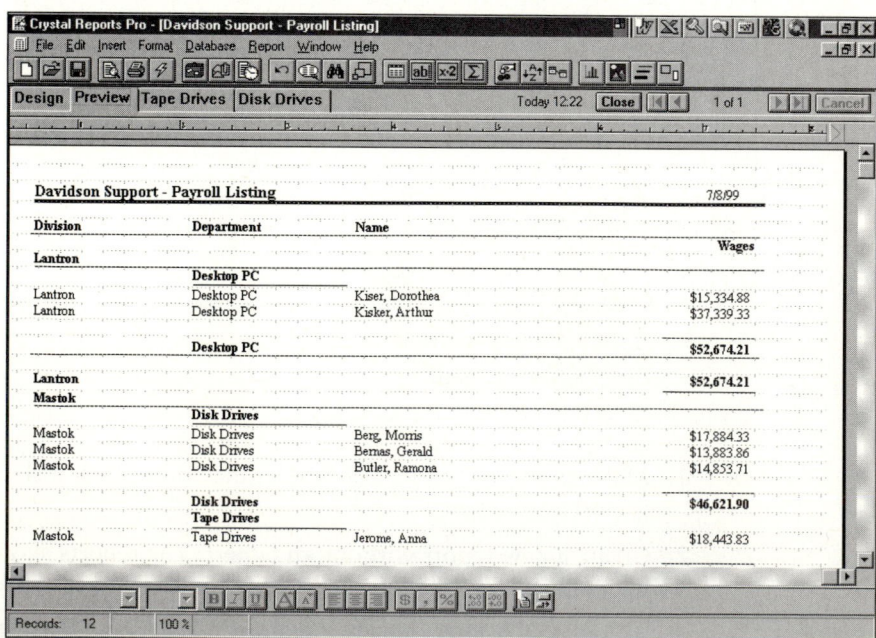

1. Make sure your Student Disk is in the appropriate disk drive, then start Crystal Reports and create a new custom report without an expert.

2. Use the Access database named **Davidson.mdb** as the data file.

3. Create the fields and column titles in the Details section of the report as shown in Figure 9-39.

4. Create a page title with the name of the report and the date.

5. Sort the data by division and department.

6. Create a control break when the division or department changes and compute a subtotal as shown in Figure 9-39.

7. Create a grand total for the total wages.

8. Create lines as necessary to separate the data in the different sections.

9. Save the report using the filename **Davidson.rpt** in the **Cases** folder in the **Tutorial.09** folder on your Student Disk.

10. Exit Crystal Reports.

11. Start Visual Basic. Add the CrystalReports control to the project, and write the necessary statements to print the report you just created. Save the form using the name **frmDavidson.frm** and the project using the name **Davidson.vbp**.

2. Accurate Data Entry Accurate Data Entry performs data entry for a number of different clients. They want a program to help validate fields like telephone numbers, customer numbers, zip codes, and names. They would like you to create the user interface for this program. You do not need to write any code for the program. You only need to create the input masks for several text boxes to conform to the fields shown in Figure 9-40.

Figure 9-40 ◀

First Name	15 characters long
Last Name	20 characters long
Customer Number	111-AAA-111
Address	20 characters long
State	2 characters long
Zip Code	99999-9999
Telephone Number	(999) 999-9999

When complete, the form for this program should look like Figure 9-41.

Figure 9-41 ◀

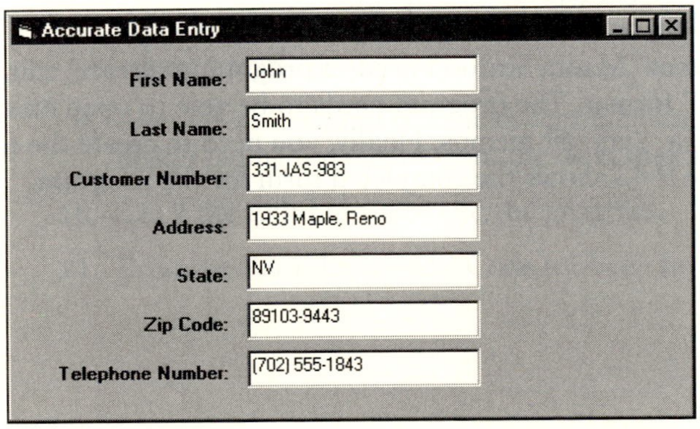

1. Start Visual Basic then create a new project.

2. Add the MaskEdBox control to the project.

3. Name and save the form as **frmAccurateDataEntry** and save the project as **Accurate Data Entry.vbp** in the **Cases** folder in the **Tutorial.09** folder on your Student Disk.

Creating a Multiple Document Application

Creating the User Interface for ABC Concrete

In this tutorial you will:

- Create multiple instances of a form

- Create a user interface that operates with several instances of the same form, called a multiple document application

- Create enumerated data types

- Create your own data type, called a user-defined type, made up of other data types

- Change the size of an array at run time

- Understand the events pertinent to an MDI program

CASE

ABC Concrete

Clive Bornstein is the plant manager for ABC Concrete. ABC Concrete has about 230 cement trucks supplying concrete to construction sites in Cleveland, Ohio. ABC Concrete is in the process of automating the plant where they load their cement trucks. The batch plant, as it is called, consists of 10 batch machines. Each batch machine consists of large hoppers filled with cement, three types of sand, three types of gravel, and water.

Each day, ABC Concrete receives orders for different types of concrete from the ongoing construction projects in the area. When an order is received, Clive wants the operator of the batch plant to be able to fill out a form by specifying the type of sand and gravel, and the amount of each. The operator also needs to specify the amount of cement and water needed in the mix.

When an order is recorded, it is sent to the batch machine for processing. Clive wants the program to keep track of the number of cubic yards of each material used by each batch machine during the day. In addition he wants to know the amount of each material used by all the batch machines each day.

Because some days are busier than others, it is possible for only some of the batch machines to be operational at any given time. Thus, the operator must be able to start and shut down each batch machine depending on the volume of business that day.

As part of the automation project, Clive and the senior programmer, Nancy Wilson, are responsible for creating the program in Visual Basic allowing an operator to specify how much sand, gravel, cement, and water to load on each truck. Each batch machine is equipped with automated controls that will interface with a personal computer and Visual Basic. While another company is performing the task of installing the controls on the batch plant and adding the necessary hardware to the PC, you have been assigned the task of helping Clive complete the user interface in Visual Basic.

> **SESSION**
> **10.1**
>
> *In this session, you will create an MDI program, explicitly create object references, and change the size of an array at run time. You will also create a data type called an enumerated type.*

Understanding the Program's Design

Nancy already has completed the NEADT documentation for the program. As you complete the program, refer to the documentation to help you understand the different tasks and the program's organization.

To view and print the NEADT charts for the program:

1. Using Microsoft Word, open the file named **ABC.doc** in the **Tutorial.10** folder on your Student Disk. If you do not have Word, open the file **ABC.txt** using WordPad.

2. Print the file and exit the word processing program.

As you can see from the NEADT charts, the program consists of three Form modules, and one standard module. One of the forms acts as a container for the form representing a batch machine. The form representing the batch machine allows the user to record an order for concrete. Because there are several batch machines and each form represents a single batch machine, there may be several copies of this form displayed inside the first form when the program is running. Each form will represent an active batch machine. The third form will be used to display the total material usage for all the batch machines. The standard module contains variables and general procedures used by the forms.

Creating a Multiple Document Application

All the programs previously created have used one or more forms called **standard forms**. A standard form is a form that can be displayed anywhere on the visible screen and minimized independently of any other form. In all of these previous programs, you only have used a single instance of a form. Just as you can create multiple instances of controls like command buttons or labels, you can create multiple instances of a form.

You also can create programs that display all their non-modal forms inside the region of another form. These are called **Multiple Document Interface (MDI)** programs. Programs like Microsoft Word and Microsoft Excel are both MDI programs. In Microsoft Word, for example, you can open several documents at once. Each document you open is considered an instance of a form. The region of each document (form) is displayed inside another window. When you create an MDI program, there are three different types of forms that you can use:

- There must be one and only one MDI parent form. An **MDI parent form** acts as a container for other forms. Other forms in the program are displayed inside the region of the MDI parent form. An MDI parent form cannot be displayed as a modal form.

- An **MDI child form** always is displayed inside the region of the MDI parent form. An MDI child form cannot be displayed as a modal form.

- You can continue to use standard forms in an MDI program. **Standard forms** can be displayed anywhere on the screen and are not contained in the MDI parent window. You can use both MDI child forms and standard forms in an MDI program. Standard forms can be displayed as modal forms.

Figure 10-1 shows an MDI parent form with two instances of an MDI child form displayed inside the region of the MDI parent form.

Figure 10-1
Sample MDI
program

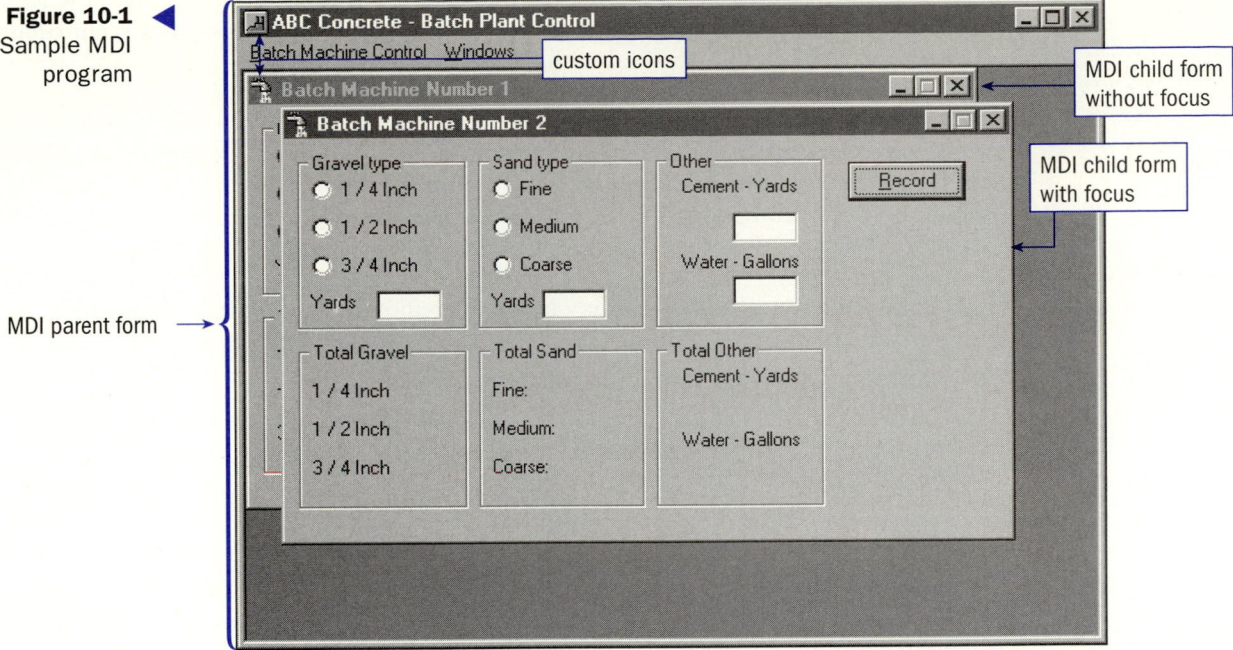

As you can see from Figure 10-1, there is one MDI parent form. Inside the region of the MDI parent form, there are two copies of the MDI child form representing two active batch machines. Notice that each can have a title bar with a caption. Also, only one MDI child form in a program can have focus at a time. In Figure 10-1 Batch Machine Number 2 has focus. Each type of form has a different icon in the Project Explorer. Figure 10-2 shows the Project Explorer with the three different form icons.

Figure 10-2
Project
Explorer with
form icons

MDI child form

standard form

MDI parent form

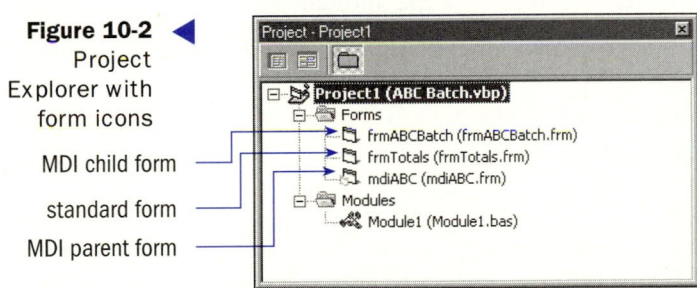

Like other forms, an MDI parent form has properties and methods and can respond to events. In previous tutorials you have used the Initialize, Load, Activate, and GotFocus events with a standard form. When working with MDI programs, however, these events occur both to the MDI parent form and MDI child forms as follows:

- When you run a program with an instance of an MDI parent form, the **Initialize** event occurs first. You can place any startup code in this event.

- After the Initialize event, the **Load** event for the MDI parent form occurs. The Load event has the same effect as it does for a standard form.

- After the Initialize event, the **Activate** event for the MDI parent form may occur, depending on the status of the MDI child forms and standard forms. When the focus changes between two MDI child forms in a program, the Activate event occurs for the MDI child forms rather than the MDI parent form. When the focus changes between an MDI child form and a standard form, the MDI parent form receives the Activate event.

- After the Activate event occurs, the **GotFocus** event occurs. Again, when the focus changes between two MDI child forms in a program, the GotFocus event occurs for the MDI child forms rather than the MDI parent form.

Because an MDI parent form acts as a container for MDI child forms, you do not draw objects like text boxes and command buttons on the MDI parent form. In fact, MDI parent forms can contain only menus and PictureBox controls. You can draw objects inside a PictureBox control but the practice is uncommon. An MDI child form is similar to the standard forms you have used in the past with a few exceptions:

- MDI child forms always display inside the region of the MDI parent form.
- When MDI child forms are minimized at run time, their icons will display at the bottom of the MDI form rather than on the desktop.
- Menus for MDI child forms do not display on the menu bar of the MDI child form. Rather they display on the menu bar of the MDI parent form.
- When an MDI child form is maximized, its title displays in brackets on the MDI parent form.

To create an MDI program, you must add an MDI parent form to your project, then set its properties. To add an MDI parent form to a project, you use the Add MDI Form menu item on the Project menu. Because there can be only one MDI parent form in a project, this menu item is disabled once the MDI parent form has been added. If you want the MDI parent form to be the startup object, you need to change the startup object. The standard prefix for an MDI form is "mdi". The following list describes some of the properties supported by an MDI parent form:

- The **AutoShowChildren** property can be set to True or False. If set to True, any MDI child forms will be displayed when loaded. If set to False, MDI child forms will remain hidden until explicitly displayed with the Show method.
- The **BackColor** property defines the background color of the MDI parent form. The standard background color for an MDI parent form is dark gray.
- The **Caption** property defines the text displayed in the title bar of the MDI parent form.
- Like other forms, the **StartUpPosition** property controls where the form initially is displayed on the screen.

Nancy already has created the form that will be used to control a batch machine. She has not yet created the MDI parent form, however. The first step in creating the user interface is to create the MDI parent form and set its properties. Nancy wants you to set the caption in the title bar, and change the startup position so the form will display in the center of the screen at run time. In addition she would like to change the icon displayed in the upper-left corner of the form.

All form types support the **Icon** property. By default, the icon displayed on a form is controlled by Visual Basic and depends on whether the form is an MDI parent, MDI child, or standard form. You can change the icon by setting the Icon property to any icon file. Icon files typically have the extension ".ico".

To create the MDI form for ABC Concrete's batch system:

1. Start Visual Basic and open the project named **ABC.vbp** in the **Tutorial.10** folder on your Student Disk.

2. Save the form named frmABCBatch as **frmABCBatch.frm** and save the project as **ABC Batch.vbp**.

3. Click **Project** then click **Add MDI Form**. The new form will be added to the project. Because there only can be one MDI parent form in a project, this option on the menu bar is disabled once the MDI parent form has been added.

TROUBLE? If the Add MDI Form dialog box opens, click the Don't show this dialog box in the future check box, make sure MDI Form is selected in the New tab, and click Open.

4. Open the **Properties** window for the MDI parent form you just created.

5. Set the Caption property to **ABC Concrete - Batch Plant Control.**

6. Set the Height property to **6165** and the Width property to **8145**, so the MDI child forms will fit in the region of the MDI parent form.

7. Set the Name property to **mdiABC.**

8. Click the value column of the **Icon** property. Click the **Properties** button [...] to open the Load Icon dialog box.

9. Click the **Look in** list box and locate the **Tutorial.10** folder on your Student Disk.

10. Click the file named **ABC.ico**, then click **Open**. Note the icon is displayed in the upper left corner of the MDI parent form.

11. Click **Project** then **Project1 Properties** to open the Project Properties dialog box.

12. Make sure the **General** tab is active.

13. Select **mdiABC** in the Startup Object list box, then click **OK.**

14. Save the form as **mdiABC.frm.**

Now that you have created the MDI parent form, you can create the menu system for it. Each standard form in a program can have its own menu system, and MDI programs are no exception. The behavior of the menu system in an MDI program, however, works somewhat differently. The differences are as follows:

- Only one menu bar is displayed for both MDI parent and child forms. The menu bar always displays just under the title bar of the MDI parent form.

- When there are no MDI child forms open, the menu bar contains the menu for the MDI parent form.

- When MDI child forms are open, the menu bar contains the menu for the MDI child form. If multiple types of MDI child forms are active, the menu bar for the active MDI child form is displayed.

The menu system for the MDI parent form needs to have functions that will create a new form instance when a batch machine is started and another menu item to exit the program. The MDI parent form and MDI child forms will each have their own separate menus. The menu for the MDI parent form only will be displayed when there are no batch machines active.

To create the menu system for the MDI parent form:

1. Make sure the MDI parent form is active. Use the Tools menu to activate the Menu Editor for the MDI parent form named **mdiABC.**

2. Create a menu title named **mnuBatch** with the caption **&Batch Machine Control.**

3. Create a menu item named **mnuBatchStart** with the caption **&Start Batch Machine**. Make sure to indent the menu item so it will display under the menu title.

4. Create another menu item named **mnuBatchExit** with the caption **E&xit**. The Menu Editor should look like Figure 10-3. Make sure to indent the menu item so it will display under the menu title.

Your program now will display an instance of the MDI child form inside the region of the MDI parent form and it will not be possible to resize the MDI child form. Nancy suggests you now test the program to be sure the forms are being displayed correctly.

To test the MDI child form:

1. Save the project then start it. The MDI child form should display inside the region of the MDI parent as shown in Figure 10-4.

Figure 10-4 ◀
MDI parent and
MDI child forms

MDI child form →

MDI parent form →

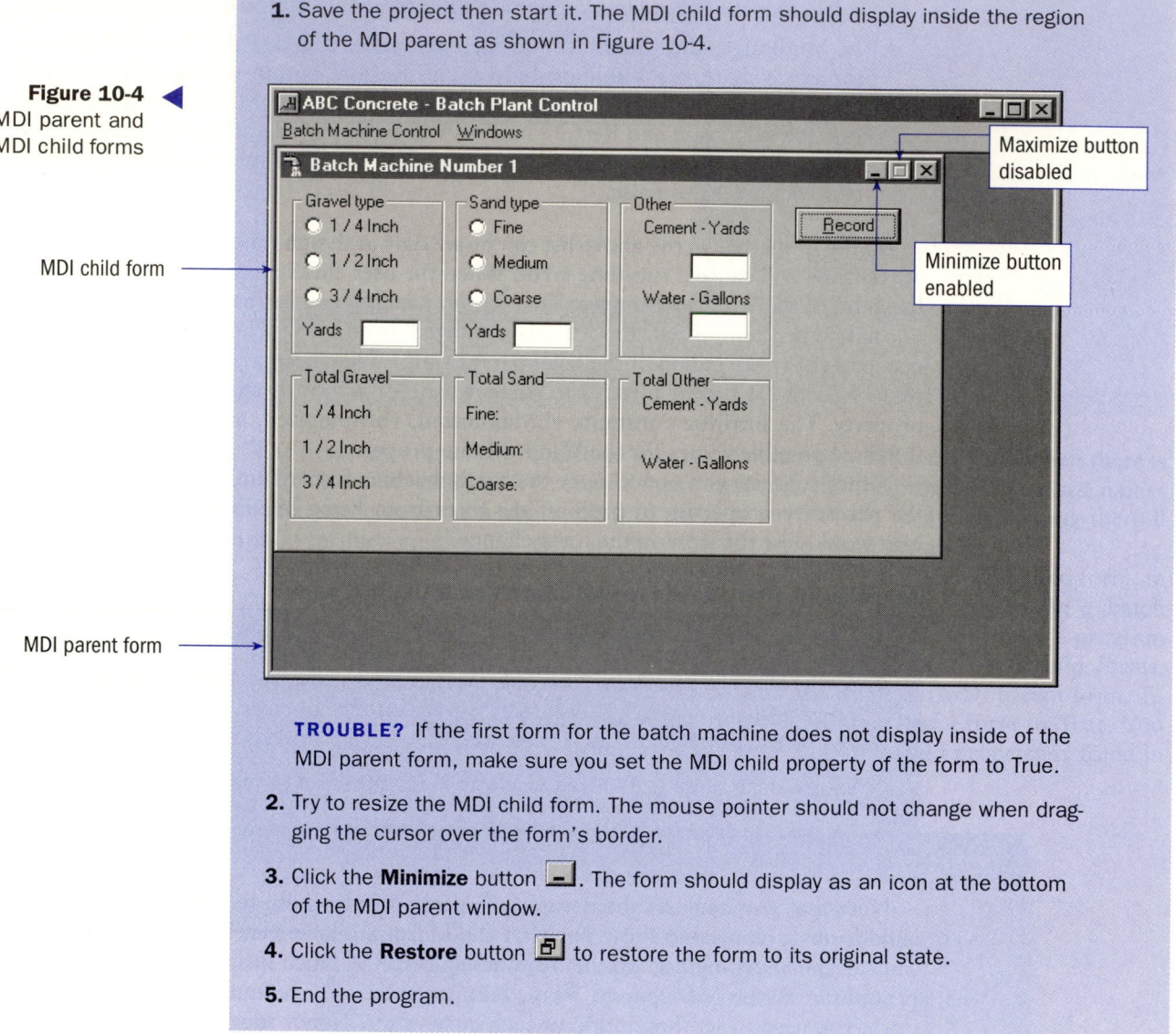

TROUBLE? If the first form for the batch machine does not display inside of the MDI parent form, make sure you set the MDI child property of the form to True.

2. Try to resize the MDI child form. The mouse pointer should not change when dragging the cursor over the form's border.

3. Click the **Minimize** button ⬛. The form should display as an icon at the bottom of the MDI parent window.

4. Click the **Restore** button 🗗 to restore the form to its original state.

5. End the program.

While the code you have written will display an instance of an MDI child form inside the region of an MDI parent form, you need a way to display multiple copies of the same MDI child form at once.

Understanding Object References

The term *class* has been used several times throughout this book. A class is like a template or blueprint for an object. When you create an instance of a class, you create an object. That is, when you draw a command button and text box on a form, you are creating an instance of the command button and text box from the respective class. In addition to controls like command buttons and text boxes, each form in a project also is considered a class. The name of the class is the same as the value stored in the form's Name property. In the project you are creating for ABC Concrete, there are three form classes named mdiABC, frmABCBatch, and frmTotals.

When a form is loaded, or the Show method is called, an instance of the class is created. In the programs you have created so far, you only have created one instance of a form at a time. That is, there is one copy of the form displayed on the screen or hidden, but only one copy of a form loaded. Remember that a hidden form is active, and you can access its objects programmatically even though the form is not displayed on the screen. There are times, however, when it is desirable to create multiple instances or copies of the same form and display them on the screen at the same time.

Consider the program you are writing for ABC Concrete. Clive wants a program to send orders to several batch machines, some of which may not be operating. Each batch machine accepts the same information. That is, each machine uses three types of gravel, three types of sand, cement, and water. One way to implement this user interface is to create one form class, then create an instance of the same form for each batch machine that currently is operating. Thus, if there were three batch machines operating, you would need three instances of the same form. At run time, there will be one instance of the MDI parent form (mdiABC) and zero or more instances of the MDI child form (frmABCBatch).

When a form is the startup form, or you call the Show method on a form in a procedure like Sub Main, Visual Basic automatically creates an instance of the form from the corresponding class, causing a form object to be created. As part of creating the object, Visual Basic creates an object variable so you can reference the form in code. That is, if you have a form named frmABCBatch, an instance of the form is created at run time along with an object variable of the same name. You then can set or retrieve properties and call the methods of the form object using statements like:

```
frmABCBatch.Visible = True
frmABCBatch.SetFocus
```

You do not have to create explicitly the object variable. Rather, for each form in a project, Visual Basic automatically creates an object variable of the same name as the form's class. When you reference the object variable for the first time, Visual Basic creates an instance of the form class, so you can reference the variable.

While you have created object variables to store Database objects, you always have set them to reference an existing object, but you have not created an object explicitly. Consider the following statement:

```
Dim dbCurrent As Database
```

When you create an object variable using a statement like this, an object is not created. Instead, an object variable is created that can reference an object of the specified type, but it does not yet reference an object. Thus, you cannot reference any properties or call methods using this object variable until it references an active Database object. To use the variable, you have called the OpenDatabase method. The code in the OpenDatabase method creates the object for you and a reference to the object is stored in the object variable dbCurrent, as shown in the following statement:

```
Set dbCurrent = OpenDatabase("A:\MyDatabase.mdb")
```

It also is possible to create multiple references to an object. That is, multiple object variables that all point to the same object. Consider the following statements:

```
Dim db1 As Database
Dim db2 As Database
Dim db3 As Database
Set db1 = OpenDatabase("A:\MyDatabase.mdb")
Set db2 = db1
Set db3 = db1
```

The OpenDatabase method creates a Database object and stores a reference to the object in the variable db1. The second and third Set statements create two more references to the same Database object. Note that a new object is not created. Figure 10-5 illustrates this process.

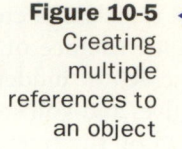

Figure 10-5
Creating
multiple
references to
an object

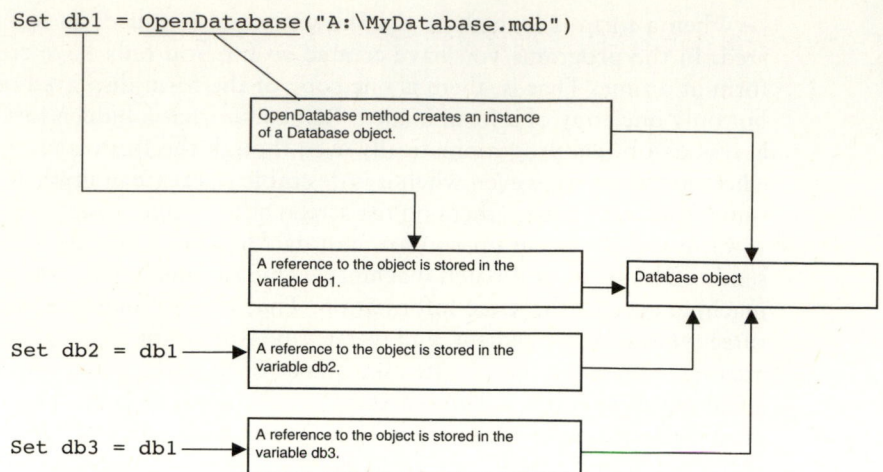

In addition to declaring object variables of a specific type, you also can create generic object variables capable of storing different types of objects. You can use two different data types to store multiple types of objects as follows:

- The **Object** data type is a generic object data type and can hold a reference to any type of object.

- The **Variant** data type can store a reference to any type of object or standard variable.

For example, if the object cmdRecord is a valid instance of a command button, and lblPrompt is a valid instance of a Label object, the following statements would be legal:

```
Dim objGeneric As Object
Set objGeneric = lblPrompt
Set objGeneric = cmdRecord
```

The first statement declares a generic object variable named objGeneric. The second statement causes the object variable to reference the label, and the third statement causes the object variable to reference the command button. These statements do not create a new object. Rather, they create an additional reference to an existing object. You then can use the object variable to call the methods and set the properties of the underlying object using the object variable named objGeneric.

Using generic object variables can degrade significantly the performance of your program. This is due to a process called binding. **Binding** is the process of preparing to call a method or to set or read a property. The amount of time it takes to prepare to call the method or property is called overhead and depends on the type of binding. There are two types of binding:

- When you use a generic object variable of type Variant or Object, Visual Basic cannot determine actual data type until run time. Thus, when you use a generic object variable to call a method or reference a property, Visual Basic must determine the actual object type at run time, before calling a method or referencing a property. This is called **late binding.**

- When you declare an object variable of a specific class like a command button or frmABCBatch, Visual Basic can determine the type of object before run time. Thus, at run time, the overhead to determine an object's type is eliminated. This is called **early binding.**

> *Tip:* Use object variables of a specific class whenever possible so Visual Basic can use early binding. Early binding of object variables will improve significantly the performance of your program. In addition to variables of type Object and Variant, objects of type Form and Control also are late bound.

Explicitly Creating Objects

When you need to create a new object variable from a form's class, you do not use a method like Show as you have done previously to create the object. Rather you must create explicitly the object. You can create a new object variable and a corresponding object with the Dim, Public, Private, or Static statements, using the New keyword. The syntax is identical to the syntax for the Dim, Public, Private, or Static statements you already have used, except the New keyword has been added. The New keyword has the following syntax:

{**Dim|Public|Private|Static**} *varname* [([*subscripts*])] [**As** [**New**] *type*]

The optional **New** keyword when used with the Public, Private, Dim, or Static statements causes a new object variable of *type* to be created. Note that until the object is referenced in code for the first time, the object does not actually exist. You cannot use the New keyword to declare variables of any intrinsic data type like Integer or Single. It only can be used for objects.

Thus, if you wanted to create a Public variable that references a new instance of the form class frmABCBatch, named frmInstance1, you could write the following statement:

```
Public frmInstance1 As New frmABCBatch
```

The first time you reference the object named frmInstance1, either by setting a property or calling a method, the instance is created automatically. In addition to using the Public, Dim, and Private statements to create an instance of an object and store a reference to it in an object variable, you also can use a variation of the Set statement. You have used the Set statement in the past to assign an object reference to an object variable. You also can use the Set statement to create a new instance of an object from its class using the following syntax:

Set *objectvar* = {[**New**] *objectexpression*|**Nothing**}

- The required *objectvar* argument contains the name of the object variable or property to be created.

- The optional **New** keyword will create a new instance of the object form class stored in *objectexpression*. If the variable *objectvar* already references an existing object, that reference will no longer exist, and the new object and reference is created. Just as you cannot use the New keyword in a Dim, Public, or Private statement to create objects of Intrinsic data types like Integer or Single, you cannot use the New keyword with the Set statement to create an object having an Intrinsic data type.

- The required *objectexpression* can contain an object variable or object type.

- The optional **Nothing** keyword is used to remove the association of *objectvar* from an object. When you assign Nothing to an object variable, all the system and memory resources associated with the previously referenced object are released.

Consider the following two statements:

```
Public frmInstance1 As frmABCBatch
Set frmInstance1 = New frmABCBatch
```

These two statements have the same effect as the Public statement with the As New keyword shown in the previous syntax. The first statement creates a variable of type frmABCBatch and the second statement actually creates an instance of the variable.

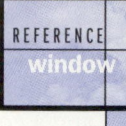

CREATING AN OBJECT VARIABLE EXPLICITLY

- Create an object variable with the Dim, Public, Private, or Static statement.
- Use the New keyword with the above statement to create a new instance of the object
  or
  Use the New keyword with the Set statement to create a new instance of the object.

Remember that for every form in your program, Visual Basic creates a variable with the same name as the form's class. This roughly is equivalent to Visual Basic adding the following declaration to a module in your project:

```
Public frmABCBatch As New frmABCBatch
```

Hidden Variables

A **hidden variable** is a variable declared for you although the declaration of the variable does not appear in the project. The reason this declaration is hidden is because it changes each time you change the Name property of the form. That is, if you changed the name of the form, the declaration discussed above also would change.

This statement creates an object variable named frmABCBatch from the class named frmABCBatch. If you wanted to create two instances of the form named frmABCBatch, you could create two object variables. The following statements create two object variables named frmABCBatch1 and frmABCBatch2 of type frmABCBatch:

```
Public frmABCBatch1 As New frmABCBatch
Public frmABCBatch2 As New frmABCBatch
```

These statements create two separate instances of a form from the class named frmABCBatch. The first instance is named frmABCBatch1 and the second instance is named frmABCBatch2. These are separate objects rather than multiple references to the same object. Consider the following statements:

```
Public frmABCBatch1 As New frmABCBatch
Public frmABCBatch2 As New frmABCBatch
Public frmABCBatchRef1 As frmABCBatch
Public frmABCBatchRef2 As frmABCBatch
```

The first two statements create two instances named frmABCBatch1 and frmABCBatch2 from the form class frmABCBatch. The second two statements create two more object variables. Because the New keyword is not used, an object is not created. Rather the variable contains Nothing until a Set statement is used to cause them to reference an existing object.

```
Set frmABCBatchRef1 = frmABCBatch1
Set frmABCBatchRef2 = frmABCBatch2
```

These two statements create an additional reference to the objects frmABCBatch1 and frmABCBatch2. In other words you can use the object variables frmABCBatchRef1 and frmABCBatch1 to reference the first form object. The objects frmABCBatchRef2 and frmABCBatch2 can be used to reference the second object. Figure 10-6 illustrates this process.

Figure 10-6 ◄
Creating
multiple
instances of a
form and
multiple
references

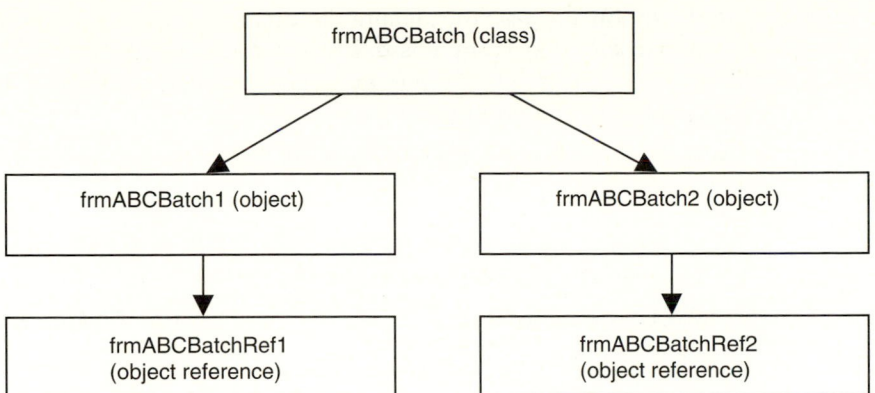

Although a form is considered a class, a standard module is not. That is, you do not create an instance of a standard module to use its variables and procedures. In fact, you cannot create an instance of a standard module.

Standard modules and class modules do not store their data the same way. Each instance of a form has its own copy of the data stored in its properties. If you extend this concept to the controls on a form, each control drawn on a form (an instance of the control's class) has its own copy of its data stored in its properties. For example, the following statements would change the caption of each form:

```
frmABCBatch1.Caption = "First form instance"
frmABCBatch2.Caption = "Second form instance"
```

Each form object has its own copy of the Caption property. Setting the value of one caption will not affect the caption of the other form. Only one copy of the variables in a standard module exists, however. As you know, Public and Private variables declared in the general declarations section of a standard module exist for the life of the program.

Changing the Lower Bound of an Array

Because the program will have multiple instances of the form named frmABCBatch, you need an object variable to hold each individual form instance. One way to do this is to create an object variable of type frmABCBatch for each of the batch machines. Each object variable then would store an instance of the form. Because you do not know how many active machines there will be at any given time, and one of the program requirements is to be able to activate any number of batch machines, using multiple object variables will not solve the problem. You have created arrays to store data types like Integers and Variants. Visual Basic also will allow you to create arrays of object variables. You can create an array, then store each form instance into the array. Clive would like the title bar for each batch machine to display the machine number. Because the batch machines are numbered starting from one, it will make the programming task easier if the elements of each array corresponding to a form had the same number. That is, the first batch machine (machine number 1) had an index of 1 in the array. To dimension an array with a lower bound of one, you could write the following statement:

```
Public gfrmABCBatchArray(1 to 10) As frmABCBatch
```

When it is more intuitive for all or most arrays in a program to have a lower bound of one, you can use the **Option Base** statement, which has the following syntax:

Option Base {0|1}

- The **Option Base** statement must be used at the module level to declare the default lower bound for arrays declared in the module. If used, it must appear before any procedure declarations in the module.

- If Option Base 0, the default, is used, the default lower bound for all arrays declared in that module is **0**. If no Option Base is declared or if the Option Base statement is used without an argument, 0 is the lower bound for all arrays declared in that module.

- If Option Base 1 is used, the default lower bound for all arrays declared in that module is **1**.

- When necessary, you can declare explicitly the lower bound of an array to override the value of the Option Base, for example,

```
Public gfrmABCBatchArray(2 To 11) As frmABCBatch
```

Be aware that setting the Option Base in one module does not change the Option Base in another module. Because each batch machine is numbered from one, Nancy suggests you change the default lower bound for the arrays to one in each form and standard module.

To change the default lower bound for all the arrays in the program:

1. Activate the Code window to the general declarations section for the standard module named **ABC.bas**.

2. Enter the following statement as the first statement in the module after Option Explicit:

   ```
   Option Base 1
   ```

3. Activate the Code window to the general declarations section for the form named **mdiABC** and **frmABCBatch**, respectively, then enter the Option Base statement from Step 2.

Because the array needs to be accessible from each instance of the batch machine form and the MDI parent form, the array needs to be declared as a Public variable in the standard module ABC.bas that Nancy already has created. So an instance of the form class will be created when the object is referenced, you need to use the New keyword when the array is created. One way to create the array is to create an object variable for each of the 10 machines. Thus, you could use the following statement:

```
Dim gfrmABCBatchArray(10) As New frmABCBatch
```

To save memory, however, it is possible to create an array with no elements, then change the size of the array at run time as necessary. This process is called redimensioning an array. Visual Basic will allow you to change the size of any array at run time using the ReDim statement. The ReDim statement has the following syntax:

ReDim [**Preserve**] *varname(subscripts)* [**As** *type*]

- The **ReDim** statement is used to size or resize a dynamic array that already has been declared using a Private, Public, or Dim statement with empty parentheses (without dimension subscripts). You can use the ReDim statement repeatedly to change the number of elements and dimensions in an array. You cannot declare an array of one data type and later use ReDim to change the array to another data type, however, unless the array is a Variant.

- If the optional **Preserve** keyword is used, any data stored in the array will be saved when the size of the last dimension is changed. If omitted, the contents of each element will be destroyed.

- The required *varname* argument must contain the name of the variable. This variable should have been declared using the Dim, Private, Public, or Static statements. The required *subscripts* argument contains the new dimensions of the array and has the same syntax as you have used before.

- The optional *type* may be any of the following data types: Byte, Boolean, Integer, Long, Currency, Single, Double, Date, String, Object, Variant, a user-defined type, or an object type.

In this program you will create an array with no elements, then increase the size of the array and store a reference to the frmABCBatch object into the array each time a batch machine is started (instance of the form created). The array will contain objects of the form class named frmABCBatch.

To create the array to hold the form objects:

1. Open the Code window for the standard module named **ABC.bas**.

2. Enter the following statement into the general declarations section of the standard module just after the Option Base statement:

```
Public gfrmABCBatchArray( ) As New frmABCBatch
```

This statement creates an array named gfrmABCBatchArray to hold objects from the class frmABCBatch. Note the components of the name. Because the variable is global, you used the "g" prefix, followed by the object's type frmABCBatch, followed by the suffix "Array". Each element in the array will be used to store an instance of the form. Initially the array contains no elements. You will redimension the array later in this tutorial when you create the form instances.

Note that there are restrictions on the valid data types for Public variables declared in a Form module. Constants, fixed-length strings, and arrays cannot be declared as Public variables in a Form module.

When the MDI form is loaded, you can write the code to change the size of the array, then create and display the first instance of the form representing the first batch machine started. In addition, you need to know which batch machine the form represents. To accomplish this, you can use the Tag property, which has the following syntax:

object.**Tag** = [*expression*]

- The **Tag** property is used to store an identification string into a form or control. This string is not used in any way by Visual Basic. It can be used by your program to store information about the object that cannot be stored in an existing property.

- The *object* can be any control or form instance.

- The *expression* can be any string.

Because the array currently is empty, it has a size of zero. To create the first object, you need to change the size of the array to one using the ReDim statement. You also will store the numerical value of the current batch machine into the Tag property. You will use this value later in the tutorial as a way to identify the current batch machine.

To create the first instance of the form for the batch machine:

1. Open the Code window for the MDI parent form, then activate the **Load** event procedure.

2. Remove the existing statements from the event procedure. Then enter the following statements.

```
Private Sub MDIForm_Load( )
    ReDim gfrmABCBatchArray(1)
    gfrmABCBatchArray(1).Tag = 1
    gfrmABCBatchArray(1).Caption = _
        "Batch Machine Number 1"
```

```
            gfrmABCBatchArray(1).Show
End Sub
```

The first statement changes the number of elements in the array from zero to one, and the second statement stores the value one into the Tag property. You will use this value later in the session. Note that the Tag is just a string of characters and is not used by Visual Basic. Rather, it gives the program a way to store information about a form. The third statement sets the Caption for the new form instance. The final statement displays the MDI child form inside the region of the MDI parent form.

Now that you have written the statements to display the first instance of the MDI child form, you should test your program to be sure it is working correctly.

To test that the first instance of the batch machine is being displayed:

1. Save the project then start it. Your form should look like Figure 10-7.

Figure 10-7 ◀
MDI parent and
child forms

output section

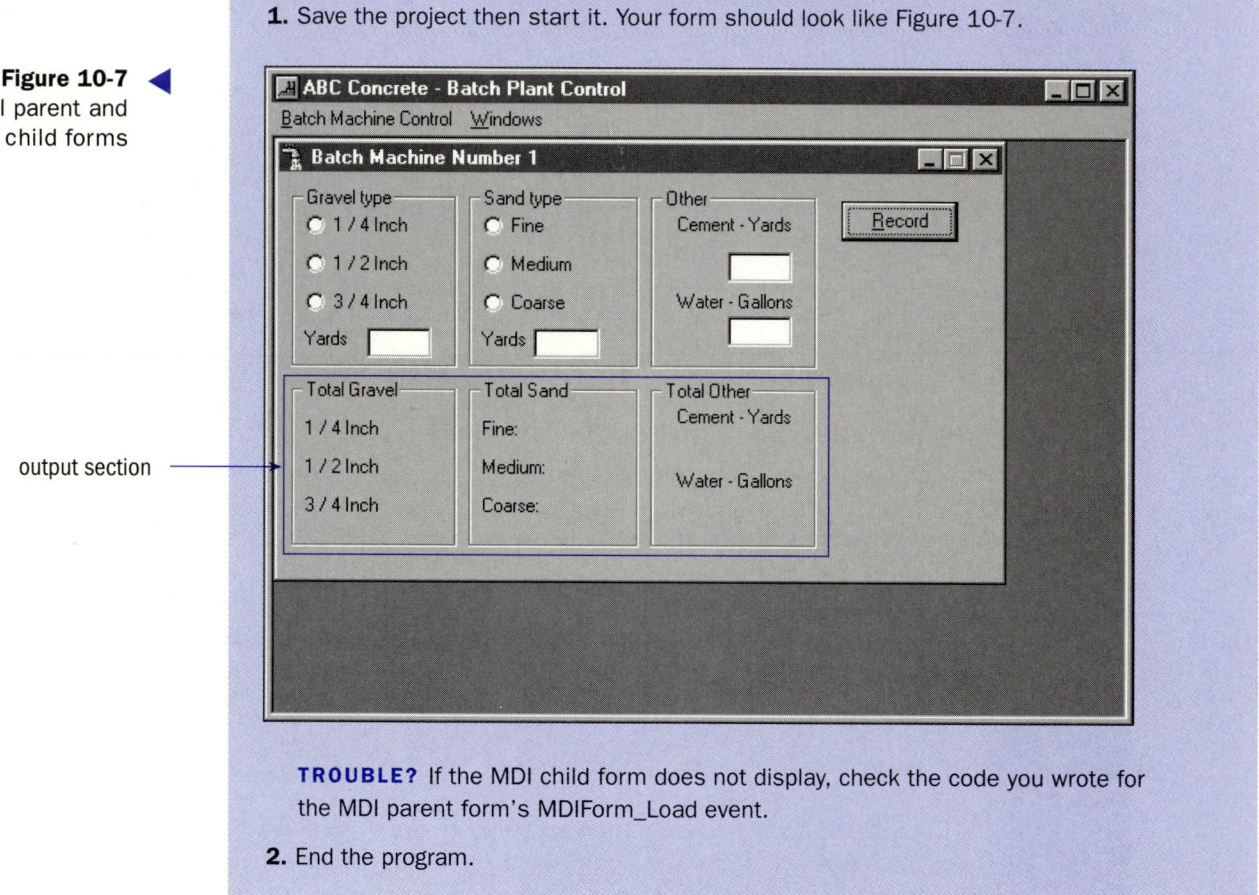

TROUBLE? If the MDI child form does not display, check the code you wrote for the MDI parent form's MDIForm_Load event.

2. End the program.

Notice the form in Figure 10-7 has an output section containing three frames. The first frame contains objects to display the amount of the three different types of gravel used, while the second frame contains objects to display the amount of the three different types of sand used. The third frame displays the amount of cement and water used.

Each time the operator clicks the Record command button, the program should add the amount of each material used to an accumulator, and display the current value of each accumulator in the output section of the form. You need to create accumulators to store this information. Additionally, you need a set of the same accumulators for each form because you must keep track of the materials used for each machine. While you could create arrays in the standard module to store this information, you can store the information inside the form, and reference it from other forms and modules.

Creating Form Properties

Remember that a form is a class and when a form is displayed, an instance of the form is created from the class. When you add a control to a form, you are adding a property to the form class. The property has the same name as the Name property of the object you are adding. This property is a read-only property you use to reference the object. In addition to adding properties to a form using existing controls, you also can create your own properties.

It is possible to store the data inside of the form and reference it from other modules by creating Public variables in a Form module. When you create a Public variable in a Form module, the variable behaves much differently than it does in a standard module. Public variables declared in a Form module do not exist for the life of the program. Rather they exist only while the specific instance of the form exists. Once the instance of the form is unloaded, the variables and their values no longer exist. Furthermore, each instance of a form has its own copy of the Public variable. In fact, Public variables declared in a Form module are treated as properties of the form itself.

One of the important concepts in object-oriented programming is that of encapsulation. **Encapsulation**, simply put, means putting an object's code and data in the same module. In this program you will encapsulate the form's data (the accumulators to determine the total amount of each type of sand, gravel, water, and concrete used) inside the form itself.

Consider an object like a text box. The control itself is a class. When you draw multiple text boxes on a form, you are creating multiple instances of the TextBox class. Each instance of the text box has its own copy of the object's properties. Thus, each text box has a Text property, but the Text property of each text box is a separate value. All the data related to a specific instance of a text box, and the procedures that act on that data, are encapsulated into the text box.

Public variables in Form modules work exactly the same way. When you declare a Public variable in a Form module, it becomes a property of the form. You reference the property using the variable's name. For example, assume you declared the following variable in the general declarations section for a Form module:

```
Public YardsSandFine As Single
```

Notice this variable name may seem to violate the naming conventions for a variable. This variable, however, is a property because it is declared as Public inside of a Form module. Property names should be made up of words, with the first letter of each word capitalized. You should abbreviate words only when the name of the property exceeds 20 to 30 characters.

If there were a valid instance of the Form module named frmABCBatch1, you would write the following statement to reference the property:

```
frmABCBatch1.YardsSandFine
```

The program you are writing for ABC Concrete requires that you maintain an accumulator for each of the three types of sand and gravel. Two more accumulators are necessary to store the yards of cement and the gallons of water used. A simple way to accomplish this is to create Public variables in the Form module. This way, you do not need to create an array in the standard module, then redimension the array each time a new batch machine is started. Using this method to store the information, it is encapsulated in the form.

To create the accumulators for a batch machine:

1. Activate the Code window for the form named **frmABCBatch**, then enter the following statements in the general declarations section after the Option Base statement:

```
Public YardsSandFine As Single
Public YardsSandMedium As Single
Public YardsSandCoarse As Single
Public YardsGravelQuarter As Single
Public YardsGravelHalf As Single
```

```
Public YardsGravelThreeQuarter As Single
Public YardsCement As Single
Public GallonsWater As Single
```

These statements create eight Public variables, which are treated as properties of the form. The first three variables will accumulate the yards of each type of sand used. The second three variables will accumulate each type of gravel used. The final two variables accumulate the yards of cement and gallons of water used, respectively.

A unique copy of each variable will exist for each instance of the form. Also, when the form is unloaded, the instance of the form is destroyed. Thus, the variables also are destroyed.

Now that you have declared the variables to store the value of the accumulators, you need to write the statements to update their values when an order is recorded. The first step in the process is to determine which option buttons representing the sand type and the gravel type are selected. To make your program more readable, you can create an enumeration. An **enumeration** allows you to relate a set of constants together and associate the constant values with names.

Using the Enum Statement

You have used several Intrinsic constants in your programs to improve readability. You also have created user-defined constants. Frequently, you have used an Intrinsic constant and assigned the constant value to a property. In these cases there are a fixed number of values that can be assigned to the property. For example, the value of a check box can be represented by the following three constants: vbChecked, vbGrayed, or vbUnchecked. Each of these constants can be represented as a value: vbChecked = 1, vbGrayed = 2, and vbUnchecked = 0. When you use the Object Browser to look at these different constants you can see that they actually are an enumerated type named CheckBoxConstants. Nancy suggests you look at the Object Browser to verify the type name for the check box constants and the valid values for the type.

To look at the enumerated type for the check box constants and their possible values:

1. Click **View** then **Object Browser** on the menu bar to open the Object Browser.

2. Click **CheckBoxConstants** in the Classes section in the Object Browser. Your form should look like Figure 10-8. Note that the Search Results section in the Object Browser may not display, depending on your Visual Basic configuration.

Figure 10-8 ◀
Enumerated type in Object Browser

indicates an enumerated type

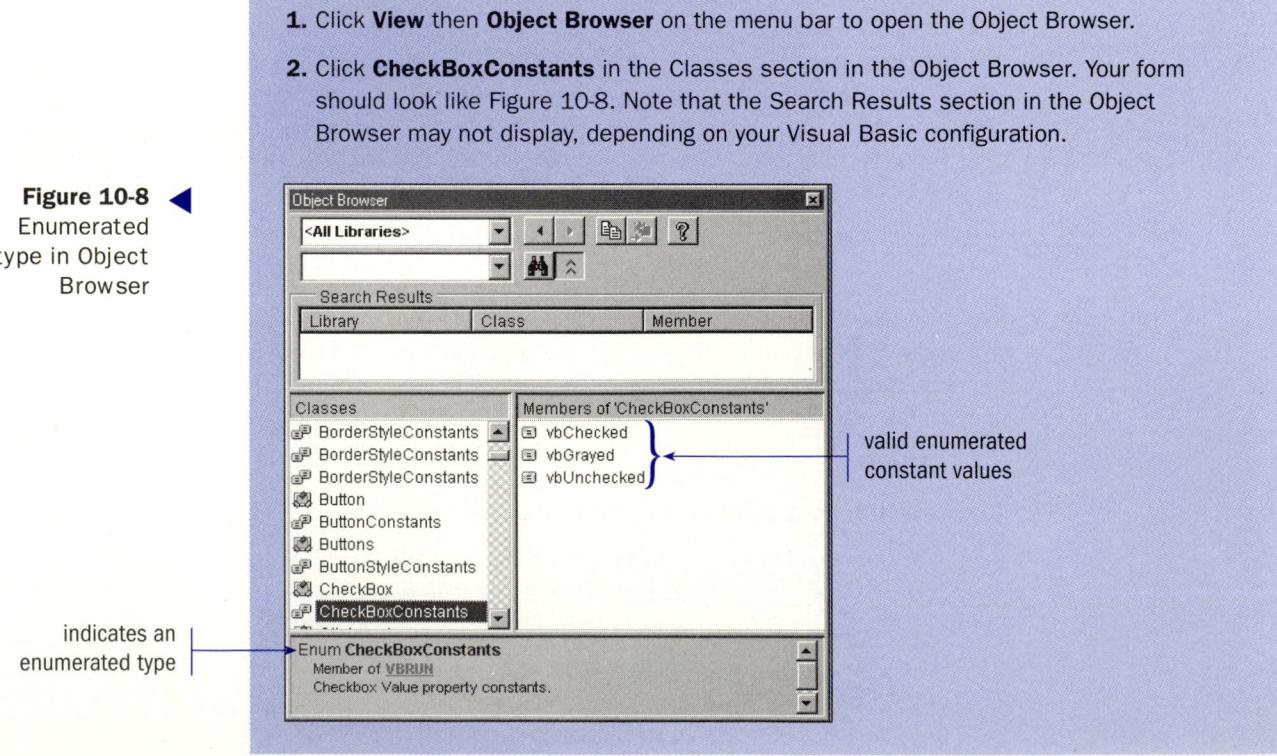

valid enumerated constant values

Notice that CheckBoxConstants is an enumerated type as indicated by the word Enum. Note also that type has three valid values listed in the Members section in the dialog box.

3. Close the Object Browser.

In Visual Basic, you can create your own variables whose values must be one of a defined set of constants. This is called an enumeration. For example, if you wanted to create a variable to represent the days of the week, you can create an enumeration.

To create an enumeration you use the Enum statement, which has the following syntax:

[Public|Private] Enum *name*
    membername [= *constantexpression*]
    membername [= *constantexpression*]
    . . .
End Enum

- The optional **Public** keyword specifies that the enumerated type is visible throughout the project. The optional **Private** keyword specifies that the enumerated type is visible only within the module in which it displays. The Public and Private keywords have the same effect creating enumerated types as they do when creating variables with an Intrinsic type like Integer or Single.

- The **Enum** statement declares the type for an enumeration. An Enum statement can display only at the module level. Once the Enum type is defined, it can be used to declare variables, parameters, or procedures returning its type.

- The *name* represents the name of the enumerated type. The name must adhere to the same rules as variable names.

- The *membername* is an element of an enumerated type. The member of an enumerated type is treated like a constant. When you create variables of an enumerated type, they only can assume member values.

- The *constantexpression* contains the value of the member and is treated as a long integer. This value can be a number or another enumerated type. If you do not specify a *constantexpression*, the first member is assigned the value of zero, the second a value of one, and so on.

- The **End Enum** statement exits the declaration block.

When you create variables of a user-enumerated type, you should use the prefix "e" to indicate an enumerated type. Enumerated types must be Public or Private module-level types. You can create enumerated types in both Form and standard modules. You cannot create an enumerated type inside of an event or general procedure. Once an enumerated type is defined, you can declare variables of that type or procedures that return the type. For example, if you wanted a variable to represent the days of the week, you could create seven constants, representing Sunday through Saturday. Then, you can create a variable to store one of the seven constants, but there is nothing prohibiting the programmer from assigning a value to the variable outside the defined range. To create an enumerated type named eDaysOfTheWeek to store one of the seven constant values representing the days of the week, you would create the following statement:

```
Public Enum eDaysOfTheWeek
    Sunday
    Monday
    Tuesday
    Wednesday
    Thursday
    Friday
```

```
     Saturday
End Enum
```

These statements declare the enumerated type eDaysOfTheWeek. The enumerated type can store seven different values represented by the numbers zero through six. Your code, however, can reference the type using the mnemonic constants Sunday through Saturday. Using enumerated types can improve significantly the readability of your program. Also, if you accidentally assign an invalid constant value to the variable, a run-time error will occur. This can help locate and diagnose possible logic errors.

In the previous statement the name Sunday has a value of zero, Monday a value of one, and so on, because the constant expression was omitted. This is equivalent to the following set of statements:

```
Public Enum eDaysOfTheWeek
    Sunday = 0
    Monday = 1
    Tuesday = 2
    Wednesday = 3
    Thursday = 4
    Friday = 5
    Saturday = 6
End Enum
```

The statements actually do not create a variable. Rather they define an enumerated type. You must create a variable of the enumerated type before the enumerated type can be used. Thus, to create a variable that can store the values of an enumerated type, you can use a Dim, Public, or Private statement as follows:

```
Public eToday As eDaysOfTheWeek
```

This statement creates a Public variable that can be used by all the procedures in your program. The variable has the enumerated data type of eDaysOfTheWeek. The variable can contain the values zero through six, represented by the constant names Sunday through Saturday. Once the variable is created, you can use it in an assignment statement. For example, to set the variable eToday to Monday, you can use the following statement:

```
eToday = Monday
```

> *Tip:* If you try to store a value other than the enumerated constants into the variable eToday, a run-time error will occur. Create enumerated types in your program whenever the value of a variable should only assume a finite set of values, like days of the week or months of the year, to improve the readability of your program.

You can use enumerated types to represent the types of sand and gravel used by the batch machines. For example, ABC Concrete uses: three sizes of gravel—quarter-inch, half-inch, and three-quarter-inch; and three types of sand—fine, medium, and coarse. Thus, you can create an enumerated type for the types of gravel and another for the types of sand. Because all the different modules in your program will use these types, you should declare them in the standard module ABC.bas.

To create the sand and gravel enumerated types:

1. Open the Code window to the general declarations section of the standard module named **ABC.bas**.

2. Enter the following statements into the Code window just after the Option Base statement:

   ```
   Public Enum eGravelType
       GravelQuarter
       GravelHalf
   ```

```
        GravelThreeQuarter
End Enum
Public Enum eSandType
    SandFine
    SandMedium
    SandCoarse
End Enum
```

These statements create two enumerated types named eGravelType and eSandType. The enumerated type eGravelType can be represented by three constant values: GravelQuarter, GravelHalf, and GravelThreeQuarter. The enumerated type eSandType also can be represented by three constant values. Notice each enumerated type begins with an Enum statement and ends with the End Enum statement. This commonly is referred to as an **enumeration block**. Another advantage of using enumerated types is that they display in the Object Browser, and the statement completion feature in the Code window will list the valid constants in the enumeration.

Nancy suggests you now look at the Object Browser to see the enumerated type and the valid constant values.

To view the enumerated type in the Object Browser:

1. Click the **Object Browser** button 🔲 on the menu bar to open the Object Browser.

2. Select **Project1** in the Project/Library list box.

3. In the Classes section, click the type **eGravelType** you just created.

4. Click each constant in the Members of 'eGravelType' section to see the value of each constant. Your screen should look like Figure 10-9. Note that the Search Results section in the Object Browser may not display depending on your Visual Basic configuration.

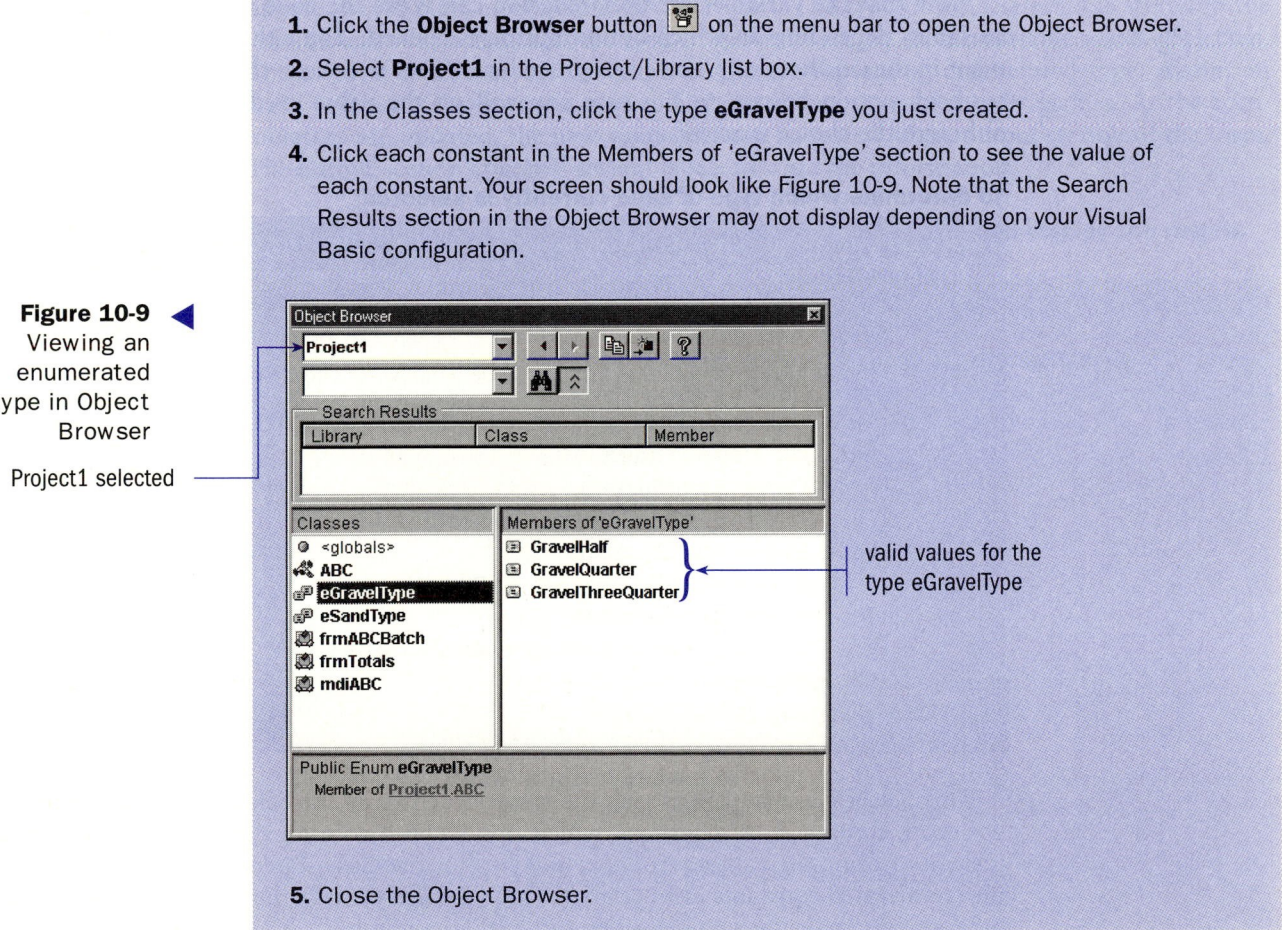

Figure 10-9
Viewing an enumerated type in Object Browser

Project1 selected

Project1 selected

valid values for the type eGravelType

5. Close the Object Browser.

Nancy created two groups of option buttons named optGravelType and optSandType. Each is a member of a control array. When the Record command button is clicked, you need to determine which option button in each option group is active, then update the corresponding accumulator. Instead of using the numeric value representing the index in the control array, you can use the enumerated types you just created. To create a variable of an enumerated type, you can use the Public, Private, or Dim statement as you have with Intrinsic data types.

```
                        YardsGravelHalf = YardsGravelHalf + _
                            Val(txtGravelYards)
                        lblGravelHalf = YardsGravelHalf
                Case GravelThreeQuarter
                        YardsGravelThreeQuarter = _
                            YardsGravelThreeQuarter + _
                            Val(txtGravelYards)
                        lblGravelThreeQuarter = _
                            YardsGravelThreeQuarter
        End Select

        YardsCement = YardsCement + Val(txtCementYards)
        lblCement = YardsCement

        GallonsWater = GallonsWater + Val(txtWaterGallons)
        lblWater = GallonsWater
    End Sub
```

These statements update the values of the accumulators and store the current result in the corresponding output label objects. After the program is performing its basic functions, Nancy will validate the input in the text boxes, so for this tutorial you may assume the user specifies valid input. The first Select Case statement uses the value of the enumerated variable eSandSelected as the test expression.

```
Select Case eSandSelected
    Case SandFine
        YardsSandFine = YardsSandFine + _
            Val(txtSandYards)
        lblSandFine = YardsSandFine
```

Remember that the variable's value must be one of the different valid constant values for the enumerated type. These constant values are used in each individual Case statement. This statement is more readable than using Integer numbers, because it describes the purpose of the Case statement rather than a number with no inherent meaning itself. The statements for each case are very similar. The current number of yards of a specific type of sand is added to the corresponding accumulator. One case is used for each type of sand. For each case, the corresponding accumulator is updated and the updated value is stored in the corresponding output label. Note that the Caption property is the default property for a label, so to improve performance the word Caption is omitted.

```
Select Case eGravelSelected
    Case GravelQuarter
        YardsGravelQuarter = YardsGravelQuarter + _
            Val(txtGravelYards)
        lblGravelQuarter = YardsGravelQuarter
```

The second Select Case statement uses the variable named eGravelSelected for the test expression and updates the appropriate gravel accumulators.

```
YardsCement = YardsCement + Val(txtCementYards)
lblCement = YardsCement

GallonsWater = GallonsWater + Val(txtWaterGallons)
lblWater = GallonsWater
```

These statements update the accumulators representing the amount of cement and water used, then display the result in the corresponding labels.

Now that you have written the statements to update the accumulators, you need to test that they are being updated properly.

To verify the accumulators are being properly updated:

1. Save the project then start it.

2. Click the **1 / 4 Inch** Gravel type option button, then the **Fine** Sand type option button.

3. Enter **3** in the Yards text box in the Gravel type section, then **2** in the Yards text box in the Sand type section. Enter **.5** in the Cement - Yards text box, then **35** in the Water - Gallons text box.

4. Click the **Record** command button. The values in the labels should be updated as shown in Figure 10-10.

Figure 10-10 ◀
Testing
accumulators
(1)

enter these values in
input section

updated values
shown in output
labels

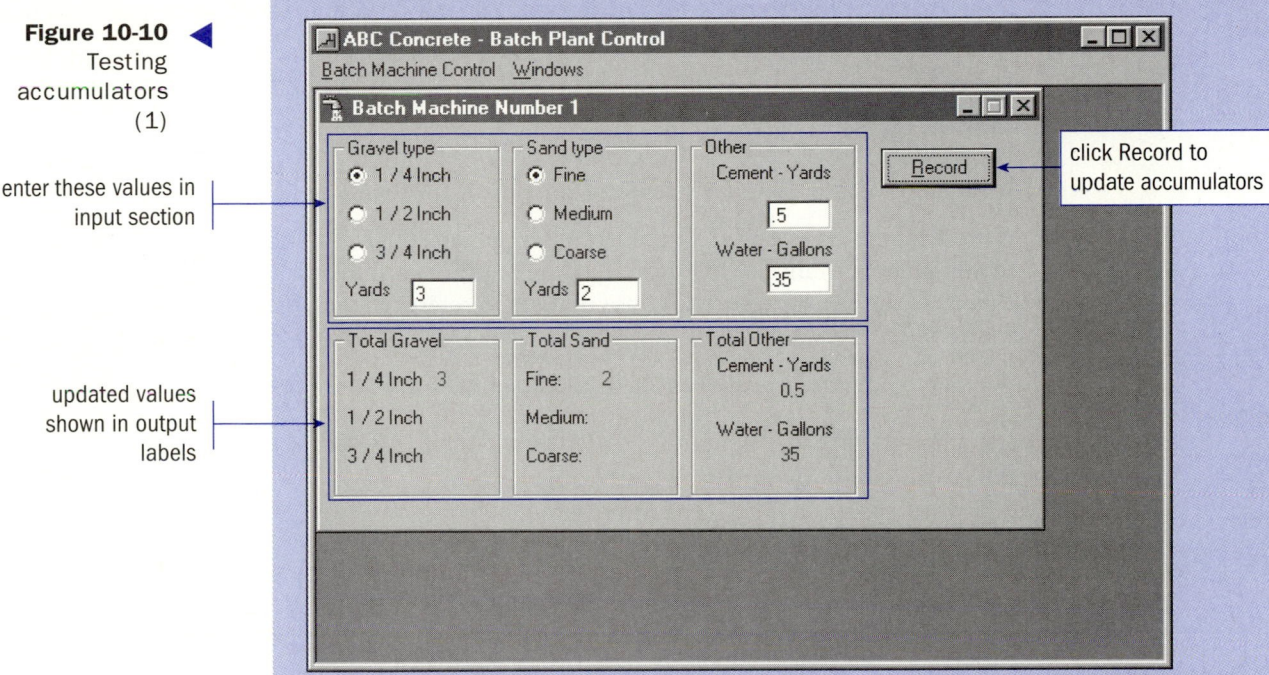

5. Repeat Steps 3 and 4 for the **1 / 2 Inch** Gravel type option button, then the **Medium** Sand type option button. Then repeat Steps 3 and 4 for the **3 / 4 Inch** Gravel type option button, then the **Coarse** Sand type option button. Your form should look like Figure 10-11.

Figure 10-11 ◀
Testing
accumulators
(2)

updated values
shown in output
labels

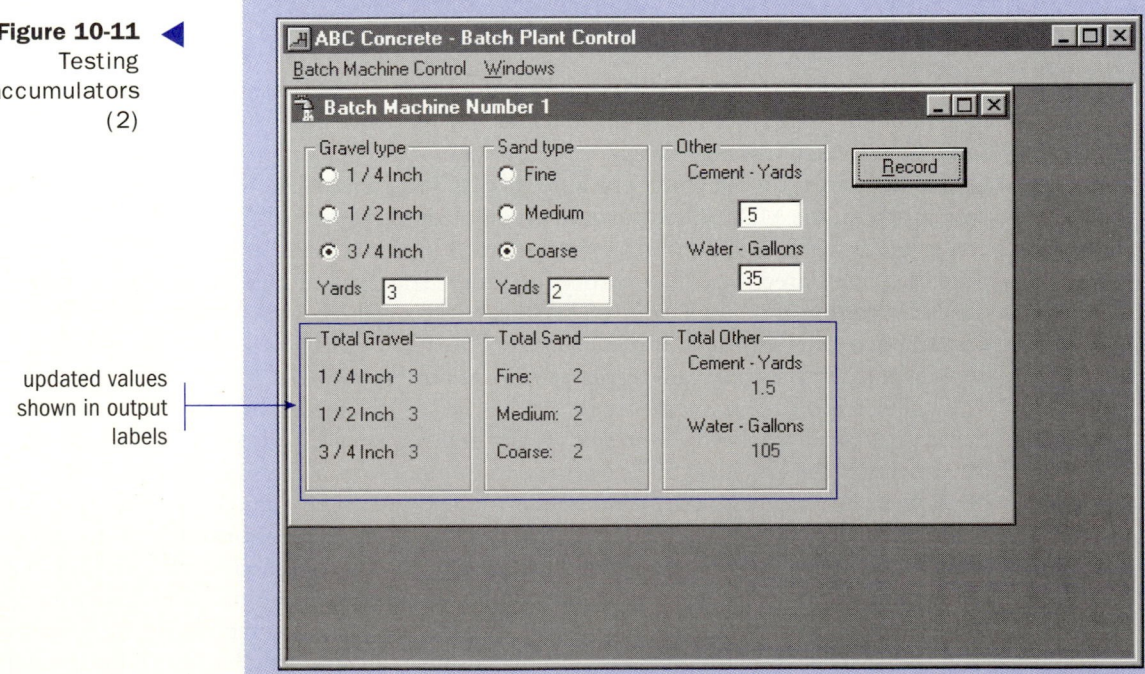

> **TROUBLE?** If the accumulators are not being updated properly, verify the code you wrote for each option button, and that the Record command button is correct. Repeat Steps 1 through 5.
>
> **6.** End the program.

The code you have written so far allows you to start the first batch machine by creating the first instance of the form class frmABCBatch. It also allows you to update the accumulators for each component by updating the Public variables in the form. You have completed the programming for this session. You may continue to the next session or take a break.

Quick Check

1 What are the differences between an MDI parent form and an MDI child form?

2 Write a statement to declare an object variable named frmInstance1 of type Form1 that creates a new instance of the form. Declare another variable named objOne of type Object. Write the statement to cause objOne to reference the object variable frmInstanceOne.

3 What is the difference between early and late binding?

4 What is the purpose of the New keyword and where is it used?

5 What is the purpose of the Option Base statement?

6 What is an enumerated type?

SESSION
10.2

In this session you will create multiple instances of the same form and keep track of each form instance. You also will learn about the events that occur when an MDI program is unloaded.

Creating Multiple Instances of a Form

While the statements you just wrote are useful to start the first batch machine, you need to be able to start multiple batch machines at the same time (multiple instances of the same form). Each instance should represent one of the active batch machines. Nancy created a menu item on the batch machine form to start a new batch machine. You created a menu item on the MDI parent form to accomplish the same task. You need to write a general procedure visible to both forms to start additional batch machines. The procedure needs to be declared as a Public procedure in the standard module to be visible from both the MDI parent and child forms. This procedure needs to increase the size of the array containing a reference to the batch machine form object by one. Then, it must create a new instance of the form and display the form on the screen.

Although you have learned how to use the ReDim statement to change the number of elements in an array from zero (0) to one (1) at run time, you need a way to find out the number of elements in the array so you know the desired size of the array. One way to do this would be to create a variable, then increment the variable each time a batch machine was started. Visual Basic supports two functions to tell you the current dimensions of an array, however, without having to go through the additional steps of declaring and incrementing variables. Using these values, you can compute the number of elements in a dimension of an array, then use the ReDim statement to change its size. The UBound function returns a long integer containing the largest available subscript in a dimension in an array and has the following syntax:

UBound(*arrayname*[, *dimension*])

- The **UBound** function returns a long integer containing the largest available subscript for the indicated dimension of an array.
- The required *arrayname* argument is the name of an array that already has been declared.
- The optional *dimension* argument is a long integer indicating which dimension is being returned. This argument is one-based. That is, the first dimension is one (1), the second two (2), and so on. If you do not specify a dimension, the value one (1) is assumed.

The **LBound** function works like the UBound function and returns a long integer containing the smallest subscript in a dimension in an array and has the following syntax:

LBound(*arrayname*[, *dimension*])

Before calling the UBound or LBound functions, an array must have been assigned some dimension or a run-time error will occur. Thus, you cannot call UBound or LBound on an array that has not been dimensioned. Given the following array declaration, the UBound function will return the values 50, 3, and 4, respectively. The LBound function will return 1, 0, and –3, respectively.

```
Dim ArrayOne(1 To 50, 0 To 3, -3 To 4)
UBound(ArrayOne, 1)
UBound(ArrayOne, 2)
UBound(ArrayOne, 3)
LBound(ArrayOne, 1)
LBound(ArrayOne, 2)
LBound(ArrayOne, 3)
```

By default, the array you are using has a lower bound of one because of the Option Base 1 statement, so the UBound function returns the number of elements in the array. To start an additional batch machine, you can call the UBound function, add one to the value returned by UBound, then use the result as the argument to the ReDim statement to increase the size of the array referencing each form object. In this situation you need to increase the size of the array by one element. Because you do not want the existing objects in the array to be destroyed, the Preserve keyword must be used with the ReDim statement. As each additional batch machine is started, the caption should contain descriptive text followed by the machine number.

To create additional form instances:

1. Activate the Code window for the standard module named **ABC.bas**.
2. Create a Public Sub procedure named **StartBatchMachine**.
3. Enter the following statements into the general procedure:

```
Public Sub StartBatchMachine( )
    Dim pintMachineCount As Integer
    pintMachineCount = UBound(gfrmABCBatchArray)
    pintMachineCount = pintMachineCount + 1
    ReDim Preserve gfrmABCBatchArray(pintMachineCount)
    gfrmABCBatchArray(pintMachineCount).Caption = _
        "Batch Machine Number " & pintMachineCount
    gfrmABCBatchArray(pintMachineCount).Show
End Sub
```

The code you just wrote allows you to create new instances of the form representing an active batch machine. The first statement declares a variable pintMachineCount to determine the number of active batch machines.

```
pintMachineCount = UBound(gfrmABCBatchArray)
pintMachineCount = pintMachineCount + 1
```

These two statements determine the size of the gfrmABCBatchArray array by calling the UBound function. Because the array is of a single dimension, the dimension argument is not necessary. Remember that the first batch machine was activated and the MDI form was loaded so there is at least one batch machine active, then this procedure is called. Because the lower bound of the array is one, the UBound function returns the current number of active batch machines. The next statement increments the local variable by one. This new value will be used to change the size of the array.

```
ReDim Preserve gfrmABCBatchArray(pintMachineCount)
```

The ReDim statement increases the number of elements in the array gfrmABCBatchArray, the value in pintMachineCount, by one. You used the optional Preserve argument so the existing object references would not be destroyed.

```
gfrmABCBatchArray(pintMachineCount).Caption = _
    "Batch Machine Number " & pintMachineCount
gfrmABCBatchArray(pintMachineCount).Show
```

The next statement sets the caption of the form to the constant text "Batch Machine Number", followed by the batch machine number. Finally, the new form instance is displayed when the Show method is called. Note that the object does not exist actually until the Caption property is set.

You must call the general procedure you just wrote before the code will be executed. The procedure must be called when the user wants to start a batch machine. Thus, you will write the code for the Start Batch Machine menu item on the form named frmABCBatch. You also need to call this procedure from the MDI parent form menu.

To write the statements to start the batch machine from the forms mdiABC and frmABCBatch:

1. Activate the Code window for **frmABCBatch**, then locate the **mnuBatchStart_Click** event procedure.

2. Enter the following statement into the event procedure:

```
Private Sub mnuBatchStart_Click( )
    StartBatchMachine
End Sub
```

3. Activate the Code window for **mdiABC**, then locate the **mnuBatchStart_Click** event procedure. Enter the same statement into the event procedure.

The program now is able to start multiple batch machines. Each time the Start Batch Machine menu item is clicked, the number of elements in the array containing each batch machine form instance is increased by one. Then, the new form instance is shown inside the MDI parent form with an appropriate caption. That is, multiple instances of the same form derived from the form class named frmABCBatch will be displayed in the MDI parent form. You now should test your code to be sure the program is working correctly.

To verify the program is creating multiple instances of the batch machine form:

1. Save the project then start it. The first batch machine should display.

2. Click **Batch Machine Control** then **Start Batch Machine** on the form's menu bar to start the second instance of the form.

3. Click **Batch Machine Control** then **Start Batch Machine** on the form's menu bar to start the third instance of the form. Your screen should look like Figure 10-12.

Figure 10-12 ◄
Creating
multiple form
instances

first form instance ⟶

second form instance ⟶

third form instance ⟶

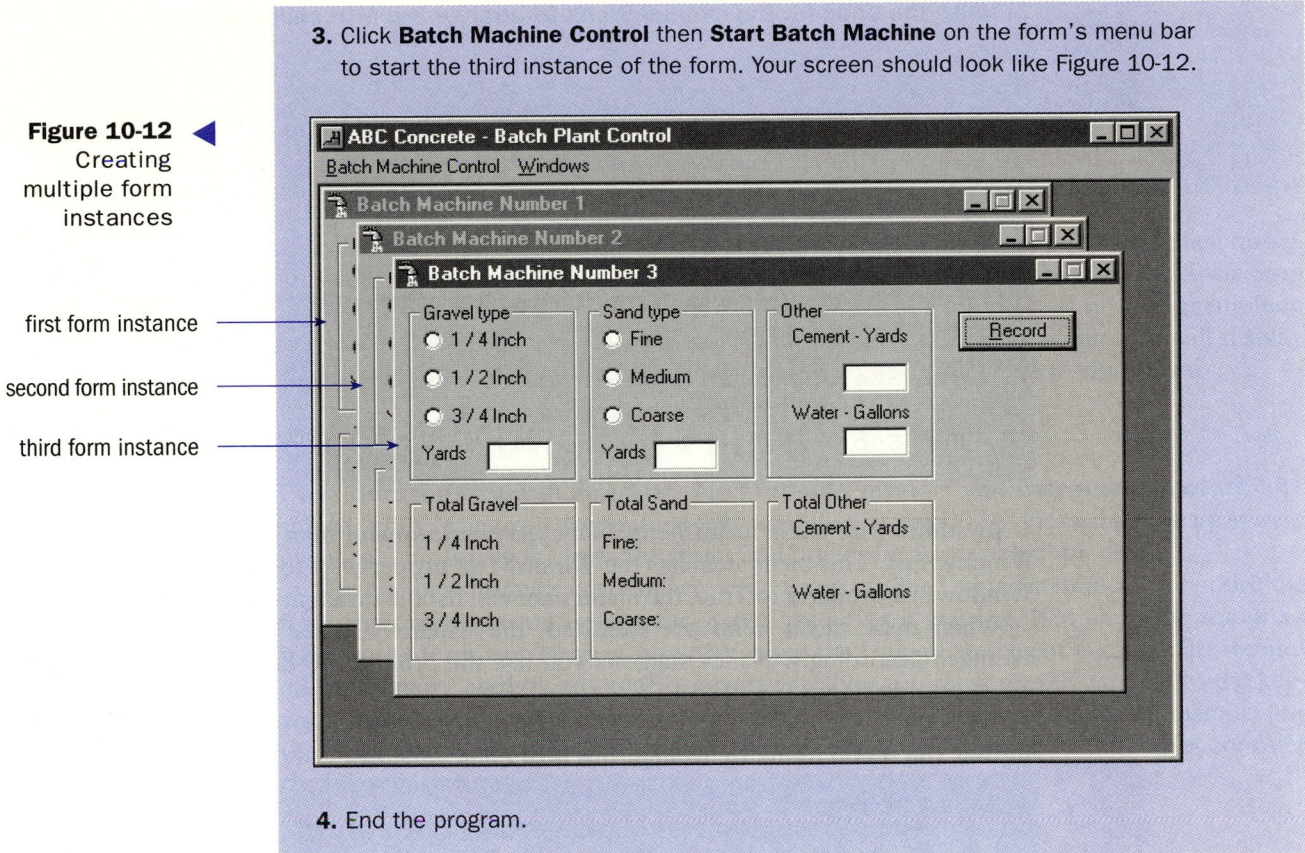

4. End the program.

Now that the user can start multiple batch machines, you must enhance the program so the user can manipulate the different forms.

Arranging MDI Child Forms

Generally, the users of your program will open multiple instances of the same MDI child form much like you may have multiple Microsoft Word documents open at the same time. The MDI parent form supports a method that will resize and modify the position of all open MDI child windows.

Well-written MDI programs should allow the user to rearrange MDI child forms. MDI forms support a method called Arrange that will allow you to cascade, tile, or arrange the icons of MDI child windows. The Arrange method takes one argument—a constant describing how the windows should be arranged. These constants can be one of four values as shown in Figure 10-13.

Figure 10-13 ◄
Constants
supported
by Arrange
method

Constant name	Description
vbCascade	Cascades all nonminimized MDI child forms
vbTileHorizontal	Tiles all nonminimized MDI child forms horizontally
vbTileVertical	Tiles all nonminimized MDI child forms vertically
vbArrangeIcons	Arranges icons for minimized MDI child forms

Clive wants the user to be able to cascade the forms and arrange the icons.

You need a way to unload the active MDI child form when the corresponding menu item or command button is clicked. One reference to the form object is stored in the form's array. There is no information in the array to tell you the active form. The Me keyword, however, can be used to refer to the active form, which is the form being unloaded. You now can write the statement to unload the active instance of the batch machine form, then test it.

To unload the active MDI child form:

1. Make sure the Code window is active for the Form module named **frmABCBatch**.

2. Enter the following statement into the **mnuBatchStop_Click** event procedure:

```
Unload Me
```

3. Save the project then start it.

4. Start a second batch machine.

5. Click **Batch Machine Control** on the menu bar, then click **Stop Batch Machine**. The form should close.

6. End the program.

While the procedures you just wrote create new instances of the form and destroy the existing instances, the program has several deficiencies. First, there is no provision to shut down then restart an existing machine. Instead, the StartBatchMachine general procedure just continues to start a new machine each time it is called. The program needs a way to shut down then restart a batch machine. Additionally, you need a way to keep track of which machines are active and which machines are shut down and ready to be restarted. ABC Concrete always starts the machines in numeric order. That is, Batch Machine Number 1 is started first and Batch Machine Number 2 is started second. If Batch Machine Number 1 were shut down, it would be restarted before Batch Machine Number 3 is started.

You could create multiple arrays to keep track of each item of information pertinent to a form, then redimension the array each time a new form instance is created. Alternatively, you could create a two-dimensional array such that each column would contain one item of information. However, Visual Basic will allow you to create your own data type. That data type will contain different items to keep track of information about the status of each batch machine. This information needs to include the following items:

- A variable to determine if a batch machine is active. That is, if a batch machine has been shut down, it is not active, but if the batch machine is not shut down it is active.

- A variable to determine if an order has been recorded since the batch machine became active.

To accomplish this, you can create a data type to hold this information, then create an array to store the data type you just defined such that there is one element in the array for each batch machine.

Creating a User-Defined Type

As you have worked with different database tables, you have operated on the different fields in a record as a group. It is possible to group together variables so you can pass them to a function or procedure as a single argument and make your program more readable, or simply to help you think of several variables as a group of related items. To accomplish this, you can create your own data type, called a user-defined type, that is made up of different elements. The Type statement has the following syntax:

```
[Public|Private] Type varname
       elementname [([subscripts])] As Type
       [elementname [([subscripts])] As Type]
       ...
End Type
```

- The **Type** statement and **End Type** keywords mark a block containing statements to define each element that makes up a user-defined type.

- A user-defined type can be Public or Private. If the type is **Public**, it is visible from all the modules in your program. If it is **Private**, the type is visible only from the module in which it is declared. User-defined types declared in a standard module are considered Public if the Public or Private keyword is omitted.

- The *varname* is the name of the new user-defined type. It must conform to the standard naming conventions for variables.

- The user-defined type can contain one or more elements identified by *elementname*. These elements can be any of the standard Visual Basic data types or another user-defined type.

- You can create array elements by assigning the *elementname* a *subscript*.

- The **As** *Type* clause is used to specify the data type of the element. It can be any of the standard Visual Basic data types; Object, another user-defined type; or an object type.

There is a limitation on user-defined types. If you create a user-defined type in a standard module, it can be Public or Private. If you create a user-defined type inside of a Form module, the type must be Private. If you try to create a Public user-defined type in a Form module, you will receive a syntax error. Furthermore, the Type statement only can be used in the general declarations section of a Form, class, or standard module. You cannot create a user-defined type inside of a procedure.

A user-defined type contains one or more members. Each member can be a specific type, object, or other user-defined type. The naming convention for user-defined types varies depending on the size of the project. For small projects, it is adequate to give variables of a user-defined type the prefix "t". For large programs, consider a three-character prefix to identify a specific type. This three-character prefix may resemble a three-character object prefix.

In this program you need to keep track of pertinent information about each form. This information includes whether or not a batch machine is active, and whether or not an order has been recorded. Because this status information can be True or False, the variables can be Boolean values as follows:

```
Type tMachineState
     Active As Boolean
     Dirty As Boolean
End Type
```

This user-defined type contains two elements. The first indicates whether or not a form is active. The second indicates whether or not an order has been recorded. If so, the totals in the accumulators will need to be added to additional accumulators to represent the total of each product used for all the batch machines combined. You will create these accumulators in a moment. If, however, no order has been recorded, there is no need to update the accumulators. Once the user-defined type is created, you can create an array of this type.

To declare the user-defined type representing the machine state:

1. Open the Code window to the general declarations section of the module named **ABC.bas**.

2. Enter the following statements in the Code window just after the enumerated types:

```
Public Type tMachineState
```

```
            Active As Boolean
            Dirty As Boolean
      End Type
```

The Type statement merely defines the new data type. It does not declare a variable of that type. This is much like the Enum statement, which does not create a variable, but rather an enumerated type. To declare a variable of a user-defined type, you use the Dim, Public, or Private statements like you have used to declare other variables. But instead of declaring a variable As Integer or As Single, it is declared As *type* where type is the user-defined type you just created.

> *Tip:* The variable named Dirty is a common variable name for a Boolean value indicating that data has changed and some activity needs to occur.

To create a Public variable named MachineState as a tMachineState type, you can use the following syntax:

```
Public MachineState As tMachineState
```

This syntax is identical to the syntax you used to create object variables or variables having one of the Visual Basic Intrinsic data types. Note that you can only create Public variables of a user-defined type in a standard module. If you try to declare a Public variable of a user-defined type inside a Form module, a syntax error will occur.

> *Tip:* Note the variable name MachineState. The name is similar to a property. That is, there is no prefix indicating the data type. Because the syntax to store and retrieve values from a user-defined type is similar to the syntax to reference objects and properties, this naming convention was chosen. Adding a prefix to a user-defined variable also is common. As you write other programs, choose one standard or another and be consistent.

Once a variable of a user-defined type has been declared, you need to know how to store and retrieve information from the individual elements in the type. To reference an element in a variable of a user-defined type, you specify the variable name followed by the member name, separated by a period (.). Thus, to set the value of the member named Active to True in the variable MachineState, you would use the following syntax:

```
MachineState.Active = True
```

You now need to create a variable that will store the state of each batch machine. Because you need a variable to store the information for each batch machine that has been started, you need to create an array. Just as you can create an array of standard data types or objects, you also can create an array of user-defined types. This array will operate in conjunction with the array of form objects you already have created. It will need to work in such a way that when a batch machine is started, and the array containing the form objects is redimensioned, the array containing the MachineState information will need to be redimensioned too. Thus, you will create the array such that it has zero elements when the program is first started—the same number of elements as the array containing the form objects.

To declare a variable of the user-defined type:

1. Activate the Code window for the standard module named **ABC.bas**.

2. Add the following statement to the general declarations section just after the statements declaring the user-defined type:

```
Public MachineState( ) As tMachineState
```

This statement creates an array named MachineState. Each member of the array is of the user-defined type tMachineState. Because you did not specify any dimensions for the array, it initially is empty. You can redimension this array, just as you redimensioned the array that stores a reference to each batch machine instance. Note that this array is declared as a Public variable in the standard module. You cannot declare Public variables of a user-defined type inside a Form module.

When a machine is started, a new instance of the form is created, and the array containing a reference to each form object is redimensioned. Along with this new form instance, you need to redimension the array for the MachineState, and set the Active state to True. You also need to set the Dirty state to False because no information has been recorded yet. This task needs to be performed when the first batch machine is started so you need to add code to the Form_Load event procedure for the MDI parent form.

In addition you need to set the Dirty state to True each time an order is recorded. You will use this information when the machine is shut down. When an order is recorded, you need to find the correct element in the array named MachineState, then set the Dirty flag to True. To do this, you will use the Tag property. This should be the same value as the number of the batch machine. It also is the same value as the index into the corresponding element in the MachineState array. You can use this property with the Me object as an index into the array as shown in the following statement:

```
MachineState(Me.Tag).Dirty = True
```

This statement uses the Tag property of the current form as an index into the MachineState array. The Dirty element of the user-defined type is set to True. You now can set the Dirty flag when the first machine is started and an order is recorded.

To set the Active and Dirty state when the first MDI child form is started:

1. Activate the Code window for the **MDIForm_Load** event procedure for the MDI parent form.

2. Enter the following statements (shown in bold) into the event procedure:

```
ReDim gfrmABCBatchArray(1)
ReDim MachineState(1)
MachineState(1).Active = True
MachineState(1).Dirty = False
```

3. Activate the Code window for **frmABCBatch**.

4. Enter the following statement into the **Click** event procedure for the **cmdRecord** command button just after the Private statement:

```
MachineState(Me.Tag).Dirty = True
```

When a batch machine is started, the size of the MachineState array is increased to one. For the first element, you set the Active flag to True indicating the machine is active, and the Dirty Flag to False because no orders have been recorded. When an order is recorded, the Dirty flag then is set to True.

Just as you have created arrays of Integer, Variant, and object, you can declare arrays of user-defined types and enumerated types.

Nesting User-Defined Types

User-defined types can be nested. That is, a user-defined type can contain a member that is itself a user-defined type. The program you are creating for ABC Concrete needs to keep track of the total amount of the different types of sand and gravel used by all the different batch machines during the day. Most of this information can be stored in two user-defined types. One user-defined type will contain the types of sand and another the types of gravel. Then, you can create a third user-defined type containing two elements. One for the sand type and another for the gravel type.

To declare the user-defined types for the sand and gravel grand totals:

1. Activate the Code window to the general declarations section of the standard module named **ABC.bas**.

2. Enter the following statements into the Code window just after the other Type declaration:

```
End Type
Public Type tGravel
    Quarter As Single
    Half As Single
    ThreeQuarter As Single
End Type
Public Type tSand
    Fine As Single
    Medium As Single
    Coarse As Single
End Type
Public Type tComponent
    Gravel As tGravel
    Sand As tSand
    Cement As Single
    Water As Single
End Type
```

3. Enter the following statement just after the final End Type statement to declare a variable of the tComponent:

```
Public Component As tComponent
```

These statements create three user-defined types. The first describes the three types of sand, and the second, the three types of gravel. The final statement creates a third user-defined type made up of the other two user-defined types, and variables representing the amount of cement and water used. In this example the user-defined type is nested two levels. You can nest user-defined types, however, in as many levels as the program requires.

Now that you can declare user-defined types, you need to know how to reference them. When you reference a member of a user-defined type, you use a syntax that looks identical to the syntax you use to set and read properties. For example, to reference the Active and Dirty members of the first element in the MachineState array, you use the following syntax:

```
MachineState(1).Active
MachineState(1).Dirty
```

Because you used the Option Base 1 statement, the first element of the array is element 1. When using nested types, you add another period (.), followed by the subtype. For example, consider the following statements:

```
Component.Sand.Fine = 1.5
Component.Gravel.Quarter = 1.5
Component.Cement = 1.5
```

Because this variable is not an array, you do not use a subscript. The first statement references the component Sand, which is a user-defined type. Thus, the appropriate member must be selected from the type of Sand. So another period is added followed by the Fine member of the Sand type. The second statement performs the same task on the Quarter member of the Gravel type. Because Cement is an Intrinsic type (Single) rather than a user-defined type, there is no second period.

In addition to assigning values to the members of user-defined types, you can perform operations on all the elements of a user-defined type at once. For example, consider the following statements:

```
Dim Component1 As tComponent
Dim Component2 As tComponent
Dim ComponentSand As tSand
Dim ComponentGravel As tGravel
```

These statements declare the variables Component1 and Component2 of the type tComponent. The variable ComponentSand is of the type tSand and the variable ComponentGravel is of the type tGravel. Remember tSand and tGravel types are both members of tComponent. You can perform assignment statements on variables of a user-defined type, so long as the left-hand side of the expression is of the same type as the right-hand side of the expression. For example, all the following statements are legal:

```
Component1 = Component2
Component1.Sand = ComponentSand
Component2.Gravel = ComponentGravel
```

The following statements will cause a syntax error because the left-hand side and right-hand sides of the expression do not have the same underlying data type. Each of these statements will cause a type mismatch error.

```
Component1 = Component2.Sand
Component1.Gravel = Component2.Sand
ComponentSand = ComponentGravel
```

The program you are writing for ABC Concrete requires that you tally all the materials used by each machine. That information is stored in the properties you defined for the form named frmABCBatch. Because this information will not exist after a form is unloaded, you need to add the quantity used for each component to another set of accumulators that exist after the instance of the batch form has been unloaded.

Now that you have declared the variable to store the grand totals for each material used during the day, you need to write the statements to update those totals. The only time it is necessary to update the grand totals for a batch machine is just before it is shut down. Every form supports a **QueryUnload** event that allows to you update totals, or perform other activities before the form is unloaded.

- The QueryUnload event occurs before a form is unloaded. If you set the Cancel argument to True, the process that triggered the Unload event will be cancelled. The UnloadMode argument contains a constant indicating why the QueryUnload event took place. Refer to the QueryUnload event Help topic for more information about these constants.

- If the QueryUnload event is not cancelled, then the Unload event will occur. This event too can be cancelled by setting the Cancel argument to True.

Just as you have used a With block to write several statements that refer to the same object, you also can use a With statement to refer to the members of a user-defined type. When you use a With statement to refer to a variable of a user-defined type, you specify the variable name, followed by the member name. If a member is a user-defined type, you follow the member name with a period (.), followed by its member name.

The grand total of each component is stored in the variable Component, which is of type tComponent. You can use several variations of a With block to store the values in the Public variables into the members of this variable.

```
With Component
    .Sand.Fine = .Sand.Fine + YardsSandFine
    . . .
    .Gravel.Quarter = .Gravel.Quarter +
        YardsGravelQuarter
    . . .
    .Water = .Water + YardsWater
End With
```

Remember that the Sand and Gravel types are members of the tComponent type. These types in turn have their own members. Thus, the With block has two levels. Because the Water type has no members, there is no period or member name after the member water.

You can decompose further the With block to reduce typing and make the program clearer as shown in the following statements:

```
With Component
    With .Sand
        .Fine = .Fine +YardsSandFine
        . . .
    End With
    With .Gravel
        .Quarter = .Quarter + YardsGravelQuarter
        . . .
    End With
    .Water = .Water + YardsWater
End With
```

These statements have the same effect as the previous statements. Two With blocks, however, have been nested inside the main With Block. This way of writing the code provides a clearer indication of each sub type. It also has the effect of improving the performance of the code slightly.

You now can write the necessary assignment statements inside of a With block to update the value of the variable Component, representing the grand total accumulator. You will update this variable using the Public variables in the batch machine form. These Public variables accumulate the total amount used of each component each time an order is recorded. This task needs to be performed just before the form is unloaded only if an order has been recorded, that is, the Dirty flag is True. If the flag is False, the form should be closed. If True, Clive suggests you display a message box prompting the user for confirmation prior to updating the accumulators and closing the form.

To add the accumulators for a specific batch machine to the grand total accumulators:

1. Activate the Code window for the **Form_QueryUnload** event procedure for the form named **frmABCBatch**.

2. Enter the following statements into the Code window:

```
Dim pintReturn As Integer

If MachineState(Me.Tag).Dirty = False Then
    MachineState(Me.Tag).Active = False
    Exit Sub
End If

pintReturn = _
    MsgBox("Do you want to shut down the machine" & _
    vbCrLf & "and record the material usage?", vbYesNo)

If pintReturn = vbYes Then
    With Component
        With .Sand
            .Fine = .Fine + YardsSandFine
            .Medium = .Medium + YardsSandMedium
            .Coarse = .Coarse + YardsSandCoarse
        End With
        With .Gravel
            .Quarter = .Quarter + YardsGravelQuarter
            .Half = .Half + YardsGravelHalf
```

```
                .ThreeQuarter = .ThreeQuarter + _
                    YardsGravelThreeQuarter
            End With
            .Cement = .Cement + YardsCement
            .Water = .Water + GallonsWater
        End With
        MachineState(Me.Tag).Active = False
        MachineState(Me.Tag).Dirty = False
    Else
        Cancel = True
    End If
```

These statements first determine if an order has been recorded. If not, the form is unloaded automatically and the Active flag for the form is set to False. If an order has been recorded, the next statements first ask the user to confirm that the machine should be shut down. If the user does not want to shut down the machine, the QueryUnload event is cancelled. Otherwise, the accumulators for the specific batch machine are added to the grand total accumulators. Once the machine has been unloaded, MachineState.Active is set to False and the Dirty flag also is set to False.

The code you have written to create new form objects has a deficiency. Presently, the StartBatchMachine general procedure will not restart a batch machine that has been shut down previously. To correct this problem, you need to modify the general procedure to determine if there are any inactive machines before redimensioning the array. To accomplish this, you need to replace the existing statements in the StartBatchMachine general procedure with statements to recycle elements in the batch machine array.

To locate the element in the array in which to place the new form instance:

1. Activate the Code window for the standard module named **ABC.bas**.

2. Locate the general procedure named **StartBatchMachine**.

3. Replace the existing statements with the following statements:

```
Public Sub StartBatchMachine( )
    Dim pblnFoundInactive As Boolean
    Dim pintMachineCount As Integer
    Dim pintElement As Integer
    Dim pintMachine As Integer

    pintMachineCount = UBound(gfrmABCBatchArray)
    For pintMachine = 1 To pintMachineCount
        If MachineState(pintMachine).Active = False Then
            pintElement = pintMachine
            pblnFoundInactive = True
            Exit For
        End If
    Next
    If pblnFoundInactive = False Then
        ReDim Preserve MachineState(pintMachineCount + 1)
        ReDim Preserve _
            gfrmABCBatchArray(pintMachineCount + 1)
        pintElement = pintMachineCount + 1
    End If

    MachineState(pintElement).Active = True
    MachineState(pintElement).Dirty = False
    gfrmABCBatchArray(pintElement).Caption = _
```

```
            "Batch Machine Number " & pintElement
        gfrmABCBatchArray(pintElement).Show
        gfrmABCBatchArray(pintElement).Tag = pintElement
    End Sub
```

These statements create a new instance of the MDI child form named frmABCBatch. If a machine has been shut down and the form closed, there will be an empty element in the array of forms. In this situation the Sub procedure will reallocate the unused array element.

```
Dim pblnFoundInactive As Boolean
Dim pintMachineCount As Integer
Dim pintElement As Integer
Dim pintMachine As Integer
```

These statements declare the local variables used by the Sub procedure. The first, pblnFoundInactive is a Boolean variable to determine if there was a machine that was shut down previously. The variable pintMachine is used in a For loop, and pintElement contains the index of the machine being allocated.

```
pintMachineCount = UBound(gfrmABCBatchArray)
For pintMachine = 1 To pintMachineCount
    If MachineState(pintMachine).Active = False Then
        pintElement = pintMachine
        pblnFoundInactive = True
        Exit For
    End If
Next
```

These statements determine whether or not there is a machine that was shut down by testing the Active flag for each batch machine. If an element in the array is inactive, then the machine can be restarted. Thus, the machine to be used is stored in the variable pintElement, and the flag pblnFoundInactive is set to True indicating that a new array element should not be allocated.

```
If pblnFoundInactive = False Then
    ReDim Preserve MachineState(pintMachineCount + 1)
    ReDim Preserve _
        gfrmABCBatchArray(pintMachineCount + 1)
    pintElement = pintMachineCount + 1
End If
```

These statements inside the If block only execute if an inactive batch machine was not located. In this situation the size of both the MachineState and gfrmABCBatchArray arrays is increased by one. The new element in the array then becomes the active element.

```
MachineState(pintElement).Active = True
gfrmABCBatchArray(pintElement).Caption = _
    "Batch Machine Number " & pintElement
gfrmABCBatchArray(pintElement).Show
gfrmABCBatchArray(pintElement).Tag = pintElement
```

These statements, using the new array element or the recycled array element, set the value of the necessary flags, and the form's caption. Once the properties have been set, the form is displayed. The function will be called when the user clicks the Start machine menu item from the batch machine control menu.

Remember that additional events occur when an MDI form and its MDI child forms are loaded. Additional events occur when an MDI form or its children are unloaded.

If an MDI child form is unloaded because of an Unload statement, or the user closing the form uses the Close button in the form's control box, the following events will occur:

- The QueryUnload event occurs for the MDI child form.

- If the Cancel argument is not set to True in the QueryUnload event, the Unload event occurs on the MDI child form.

If an MDI parent form is unloaded, the following events will occur:

- The QueryUnload event occurs first for the MDI parent form. This event can be cancelled by setting the Cancel argument to True.

- For each MDI child form that is loaded, a QueryUnload event occurs for the MDI child form. If that event is not cancelled, then an Unload event occurs for the MDI child form, which too can be cancelled.

- If none of the MDI child forms cancel the QueryUnload or Unload event, then the Unload event occurs on the MDI parent form. This event also can be cancelled.

Figure 10-16 illustrates this process.

Figure 10-16 ◀
Unloading an
MDI parent
form and MDI
child forms

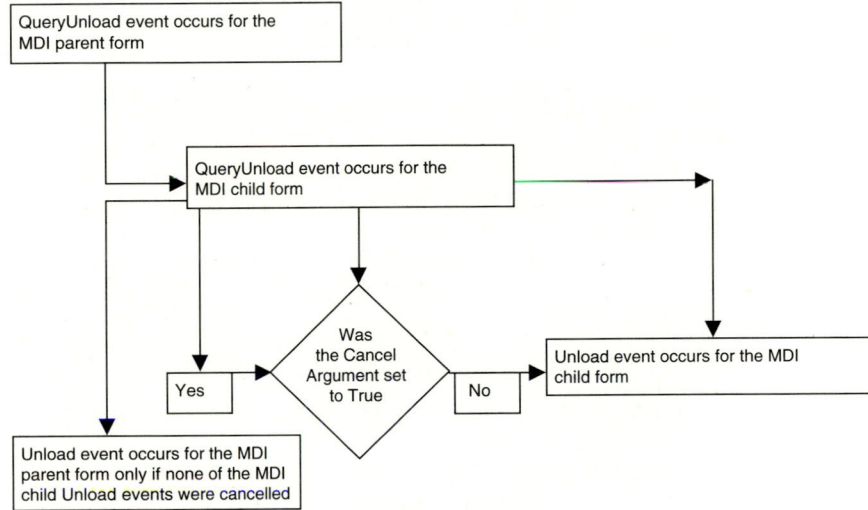

You now should test the program to be sure each form is being loaded and unloaded properly.

To test that the batch machines are being loaded and unloaded:

1. Save the project then start it.

2. Start two additional batch machines.

3. Stop Batch Machine Number 1.

4. Start a batch machine. Note that Batch Machine Number 1 is restarted.

5. End the program.

Remember, when a form is unloaded, the Unload event occurs for a form. When the user wants to shut down a batch machine, the MDI child form representing the batch machine will be unloaded. Because the form instance will no longer exist, you need to add the totals stored in the form's Public variable to the accumulators representing the grand totals for all the batch machines.

Closing an MDI Program

In addition to closing an individual MDI child form, the user may click the Close button on the MDI parent form to exit the program. If there are active batch machines, a QueryUnload event will occur for each batch machine before the MDI parent form is unloaded. Before unloading the MDI parent form, Clive wants you to display another message box requesting confirmation from the user, then display a modal form containing the total quantity used of each component. This form already has been written. You need to display the form on the screen before unloading the MDI parent form, however, and then copy the values of the grand total accumulators into the objects on the form. The Totals form is shown in Figure 10-17.

Figure 10-17 ◀
Totals form

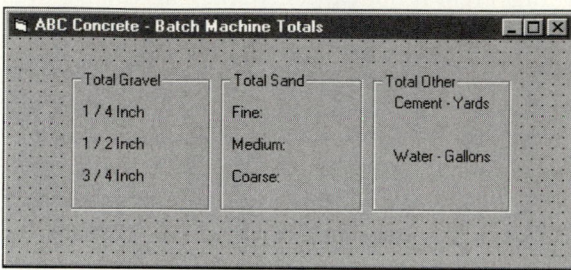

Because you need to store the members of the Components variable, you can again use a With statement.

To store the values of the grand total accumulators into the labels on the form named frmTotals:

1. Activate the Code window for the Form module named **frmTotals** and select the **Form_Load** event.

2. Enter the following statements into the event procedure:

```
Private Sub Form_Load( )
    With Component
        With .Sand
            lblSandFine = .Fine
            lblSandMedium = .Medium
            lblSandCoarse = .Coarse
        End With
        With .Gravel
            lblGravelQuarter = .Quarter
            lblGravelHalf = .Half
            lblGravelThreeQuarter = .ThreeQuarter
        End With
        lblCement = .Cement
        lblWater = .Water
    End With
End Sub
```

When the user exits your program either by clicking the Close menu on the menu bar or by using a menu item to exit the program, you often need to make sure that the MDI form and each of its children have had the opportunity to close any open files and perform any necessary processing before the program exits.

When an MDI form is unloaded, generally because you called the Unload statement on the MDI form, a QueryUnload event is generated first for the MDI forms. Then an Unload event occurs for each of the MDI child forms. If any of these unload events are cancelled, then the Unload event for the MDI parent form also will be cancelled and the MDI parent form will not be unloaded.

You now can write the code for the MDI form's QueryUnload event. This code, when executed, should display a modal form with all the grand totals. When the modal form is closed, you can exit the program. If any of the MDI child forms were not closed, then the QueryUnload event must be cancelled.

To display the grand totals when the MDI parent form is closed:

1. Activate the Code window for the MDI parent Form module named **mdiABC**.

2. Enter the following statements into the **MDIForm_Unload** event procedure:

```
Private Sub MDIForm_Unload(Cancel As Integer)
    Load frmTotals
    frmTotals.Show vbModal
End Sub
```

3. Enter the following statements into the **mnuBatchExit_Click** event procedure for the MDI parent form:

```
Private Sub mnuBatchExit_Click( )
    Unload Me
End Sub
```

You now have completed the program for Clive and should test it to be sure the accumulators are being updated properly.

To test the grand total accumulators:

1. Save the project then start it.

2. Start an additional batch machine.

3. Enter an order for each batch machine, then click **Record**.

4. Stop each batch machine. Answer **Yes** to the message box.

5. Click **Batch Machine Control** then **Exit** on the MDI parent form to exit the program.

    The accumulators should be displayed in the Totals form.

6. Click the **Close** button on the Totals form. Exit Visual Basic.

The program can start and shut down each batch machine and operate with any number of batch machines. Each batch machine supports accumulators to tally the amount of each material used by the machine. When a machine is shut down, the totals for the specific machine are added to the totals for all the machines combined. Just before the program ends, all the totals are printed.

Quick Check

1 What is the purpose of the LBound and UBound functions?

2 What is the purpose of the Arrange method as it pertains to an MDI parent form?

3 Write the statements to create a user-defined type named tEmployee having two members of the String data type named LastName and FirstName.

4 Describe the events that occur when an MDI parent form is unloaded.

Figure 10-18 lists the new terms for this tutorial.

Figure 10-18 ◀
New terms

Term	Definition
Binding	Binding is the process of preparing to call a method or to set or read a property.
Control box	The control box contains the buttons to maximize or minimize, restore, and close a window. The Maximize and Minimize buttons can be disabled. The control box is in the upper-right corner on the form's title bar.
Early binding	Early binding occurs at compile time when an object's type can be determined. It is much faster than late binding.
Encapsulation	Encapsulation means that an object's data and code are stored in the same module. It is a fundamental principle of object-oriented programming.
Enumeration	An enumeration allows you to relate a set of constants together and associate the constant values with names.
Enumeration block	An enumeration block begins with an Enum statement and ends with the End Enum statement, and defines an enumerated type.
Hidden variable	A hidden variable is a variable declared for you although the declaration of the variable does not display in the project.
Late binding	Late binding means that the type of a generic object variable cannot be determined until run time. Late binding is significantly slower than early binding.
MDI child form	An MDI child form is a form with the MDIChild property set to True. MDI child forms are always displayed inside the region of the MDI parent form.
MDI parent form	An MDI parent form acts as a container for the MDI child forms. There can be only one MDI parent form in a project.
Multiple Document Interface (MDI)	A Multiple Document Interface program is a program with an MDI parent form, and one or more MDI child forms. Each MDI child form is displayed inside the region of the MDI parent form.
Standard form	A standard form is a non-MDI form that can be displayed modally.

Tutorial Assignments

At the end of each day, certain repairs must be made to each batch machine. Clive suggests you create a program similar to the one you just completed. The program must contain an MDI parent form. When the program is started, it should receive input from the user indicating how many batch machines exist. Then, it should start an instance of an MDI child form for each batch machine. This MDI child form needs to have a number of objects on it describing the common types of repair. Also, it needs to have a MultiLine text box to contain notes about extraordinary repairs. The MDI parent and child forms for the program are shown in Figure 10-19.

Figure 10-19 ◄

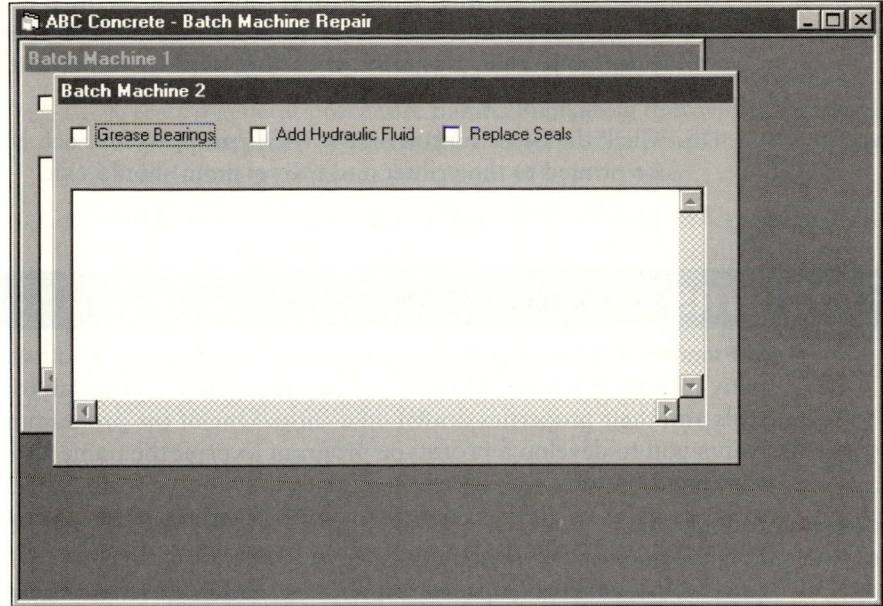

After all the repairs have been listed, a copy of the form must be printed and delivered to the repair crew so the work can be completed that evening.

1. Start Visual Basic and begin a new project.

2. Change the name of the first form to **frmRepair**. Save the form using the default name and the project using **ABC Repair.vbp** in the **TAssign** folder of the **Tutorial.10** folder on the Student Disk.

3. Create an MDI parent form and set the caption of the form to **ABC Concrete - Batch Machine Repair**.

4. Set the Name property to **mdiRepair** and save the form using the default name.

5. Make the mdiRepair form the startup object.

6. Activate the form named frmRepair and change the necessary property to make it an MDI child form.

7. Create the objects on the MDI child form as shown in Figure 10-19.

8. Change the necessary properties so no control box is displayed on the MDI child form.

9. In the Code window for the MDI parent form, enter the statement in the general declarations section to change the lower bound of all arrays to one.

10. Also in the general declarations of the MDI parent form, declare an array named gfrmRepairsArray to hold references to the MDI child form frmRepairs. The array should be empty initially. Make sure to include the New keyword in the Array declaration.

11. When the MDI parent form is loaded, write the necessary statements to display an input box and get from the user the number of batch machines to start. The number of batch machines should be stored in a local variable.

12. In the same procedure, redimension the array you created to store the number of batch machine objects specified by the user using the variable from the previous steps.

13. Create a For loop to change the caption of the MDI child form as shown in Figure 10-19. Inside the same For loop, display the MDI child form.

12. When the MDI parent form is closed, the program must total each accumulator for each coin machine. You need to determine the number of coin machines active, then using a For loop, determine the grand total of pennies, nickels, dimes, and quarters for all the coin machines. Inside the loop, close the form for the current coin machine. When all the coin machines have been examined, print the totals in the Immediate window.

13. Test the program by starting several machines, entering values and recording them. Shut down the program by clicking the Close button on the MDI parent form. The value of the accumulators should be printed in the Immediate window.

14. Save the program then exit Visual Basic.

4. Mentor Customer Tracking Mentor Customer Tracking maintains address information for several companies. This address information is stored in the database named **Mentor.mdb** in the **Cases** folder in the **Tutorial.10** folder on your Student Disk. There is a table named **tblCustomer** with the following fields: **fldCustomerID**, **fldPersonName**, **fldAddress**, **fldCity**, **fldState**, and **fldZipCode**. Each Customer ID number has several names associated with it. Currently there are three different customers, therefore three Customer IDs. You need to create an MDI program that will request input from the user to specify a Customer ID. Then, using that recordset, create an instance of an MDI child form to display all the records for the selected Customer ID. If the user wants to display records for another Customer ID, then another MDI child form and recordset needs to be created to display those additional records. You need to create an MDI parent form and an MDI child form. The MDI child form will have text boxes for each of the six fields above. The user needs to be able to add, change, delete, and scroll through different records on each form independent from the records on the other form. Save the MDI parent form using the name **mdiMentor,** the customer form as **frmMentor,** and the project using the name **Mentor.vbp**.

Programming with Class

Creating an Airport Management System for Airsoft

CASE

Airsoft

Airsoft, headquartered in Seattle, Washington, develops software for airports worldwide. One of the software packages they are developing will allow an airport to charge an airline for the different services provided, including fuel and landing charges. Each time an airplane lands at an airport, a landing fee is incurred. The amount of the fee varies based on the size of the aircraft and how long the airplane is on the ground.

Each airplane has a unique identification number commonly referred to as its "N number," because the identification number always begins with the letter N. This number is followed by a unique four- or five-digit number.

Tina Chang is the senior developer for the project. You have been assigned the task of helping Tina create the program. The program must be able to keep track of the charges for an airplane from its arrival through departure. After an airplane departs the airport, the charges incurred must be appended to a text file. This information will be used later by an airport's billing system to generate individual airline invoices.

SESSION 11.1

In this session you will learn how to create a class module, create properties and methods for the module, and then use the module in a program. You also will learn how to create a collection.

Analyzing the Program

Tina already has created the NEADT charts for the program. These charts identify all the modules in the program and their purpose.

To look at the design specifications for the flight management system:

1. Start Microsoft Word and load the file **Airsoft.doc** in the **Tutorial.11** folder on your Student Disk. Otherwise, open the file **Airsoft.txt** using WordPad.

2. Print the NEADT charts and exit the word processing program.

The form named frmAirport is the main form for the project. It contains buttons to add an airplane when a flight arrives and remove the airplane when the flight departs. Each airplane currently at the airport will be listed in the list box. Whenever an airplane is selected in the list box, the pertinent information about the plane needs to be displayed in the output labels.

Introduction to Class Modules

In addition to creating form classes (Form modules) and using existing classes, you can create classes using a different type of module called a class module. A **class module** is a template for objects you create, as opposed to an object that already is defined for you. A class module contains all the code to implement its properties and methods.

Visual Basic is considered to be an object-oriented programming language. An object attempts to model the real-world behavior of something. For example, you can think of a television's remote control or a telephone as an object. The data and the processes acting on that data are combined together or encapsulated. **Encapsulation** means an object supports a fixed set of data items, processes act on these data items, and all the capabilities of the object are grouped together as a class.

For example, a television's remote control supports data items, like the current channel and volume, and processes to act on these data items, like adjusting the volume or changing the channel. All the capabilities of the remote control are stored in the remote control class. Every class has an interface. The **interface** consists of the properties and methods of the class. It is through the interface that the programmer interacts with the class. The interface for a remote control consists of the buttons on the control. You cannot perform any actions on a remote control without using the interface.

You have seen that objects have properties and methods and may respond to events. Properties are the data that describe an object, and methods are the actions an object can perform. In Visual Basic all objects are created from classes. The description of a class is stored in a type library. A **type library** contains standard descriptions of exposed objects, properties, methods, and collections.

In addition to an object having properties, actions (called methods) are performed on an object. When you call a method, the code in the method may set properties. For example, if you call a method to change the volume on a television, the method would change the value of the Volume property.

While similar to the standard and Form modules you have created earlier, class modules allow you to create your own objects. Class modules can contain variables, functions, and procedures like standard modules. The functions and procedures are used and referenced much differently than standard modules, however. Instead of calling Function and Sub procedures, you read and write properties and call methods.

Class modules also are similar to Form modules but do not appear as visible objects at run time. That is, you do not display a class module on the screen. Rather, an instance of a class module works much like a Recordset object. Once you create an instance of the class you can read and write its properties and call its methods with code.

> *Tip:* When you implement a task that may be performed by several programs, consider implementing it as a class. That way, each program using the class can access it using a well-defined interface.

To create a new type of object, you first need to create a class module. To create a new class module, you add the module to the project, just like you have added Form and standard modules by clicking Project on the menu bar, then Add Class Module on the Project menu. Once the class module has been created, it displays in the Project Explorer just like any other module.

REFERENCE window

TO ADD A CLASS MODULE TO A PROJECT

- Click Project on the menu bar, then Add Class Module on the Project menu, then click Open in the Add Class module dialog box.
- Open the Properties window for the class module, then set the Name property to the name of the class. This name will be used to reference the class.
- Save the class module to the project file by clicking File, then Save *Class1* As, where *Class1* is the name of the class module.

In the program you are creating for Airsoft, you will create a class to represent an airplane. When an airplane arrives at an airport, an instance of the Airplane class will need to be created. Then you will use the properties and methods of each instance of the class to record charges pertinent to each airplane while it is at the airport. When the airplane departs, the information will be recorded to a text file, and the instance of the class terminated. Tina suggests you now create the class module, set its Name property, and save it on the disk. Because the class will represent an airplane, she suggests you set the Name property to Airplane.

To create a class module:

1. Start Visual Basic then open the project named **Airport.vbp** located in the **Tutorial.11** folder on your Student Disk, then open the main form named **frmAirport.frm**.

2. Save the form as **frmAirportManagement.frm** and the project as **Airport Management.vbp** in the **Tutorial.11** folder on your Student Disk.

3. Click **Project** then **Add Class Module**. The Code window opens.

   TROUBLE? If the Add Class Module dialog box displays on the screen, select the Class Module icon then click the Open button. If you want to prevent the dialog box from appearing in the future, check the Don't show this dialog in the future check box.

4. Open the **Project Explorer**.
   Note: A new folder is displayed showing the class modules. This folder contains one module, Class1.

5. Open the **Properties** window for the new class module. There is only one property—Name.

6. Set the Name property to **Airplane**. Your Code window should look like Figure 11-1.

To create the properties for the class module:

1. Make sure the Code window for the class module named **Airplane.cls** is active.

2. Enter the following statements into the general declarations section of the Code window just after the Option Explicit statement. Note that the Option Explicit statement will not appear unless you have turned on the Require Variable Declaration option.

```
Public CarrierName As String
Public AirplaneID As String
Public DepartureDateTime As Date
```

These Public variables will become properties of the class you just created. Thus, they are part of the class's interface. "CarrierName" will store the name of the airplane's carrier. "AirplaneID" will store the identification number. "DepartureDateTime" will store the airplane's departure date and time.

Using the Object Browser to Look at the Class

You have used the Object Browser throughout this book to look at the values of Intrinsic constants supported by a class, like when you looked at the acceptable values of a check box. You also have seen that the enumerated and user-defined types in your project can be viewed in the Object Browser. A class module is no exception. Using the Object Browser, you can look at all the properties and methods of any class. At this time, your class contains just three properties. Tina suggests you use the Object Browser now to look at these different properties.

To view the properties of the class you just created:

1. Click the **Object Browser** button 📇 on the toolbar.

2. Click the **Project/Library** list button, then select the project named **Project1** to view the classes applicable to the project.

3. Click the class named **Airplane** to view the members of the class as shown in Figure 11-3.

Figure 11-3 ◀
Viewing properties of a class module

select Project1 ──

select Airplane class ──

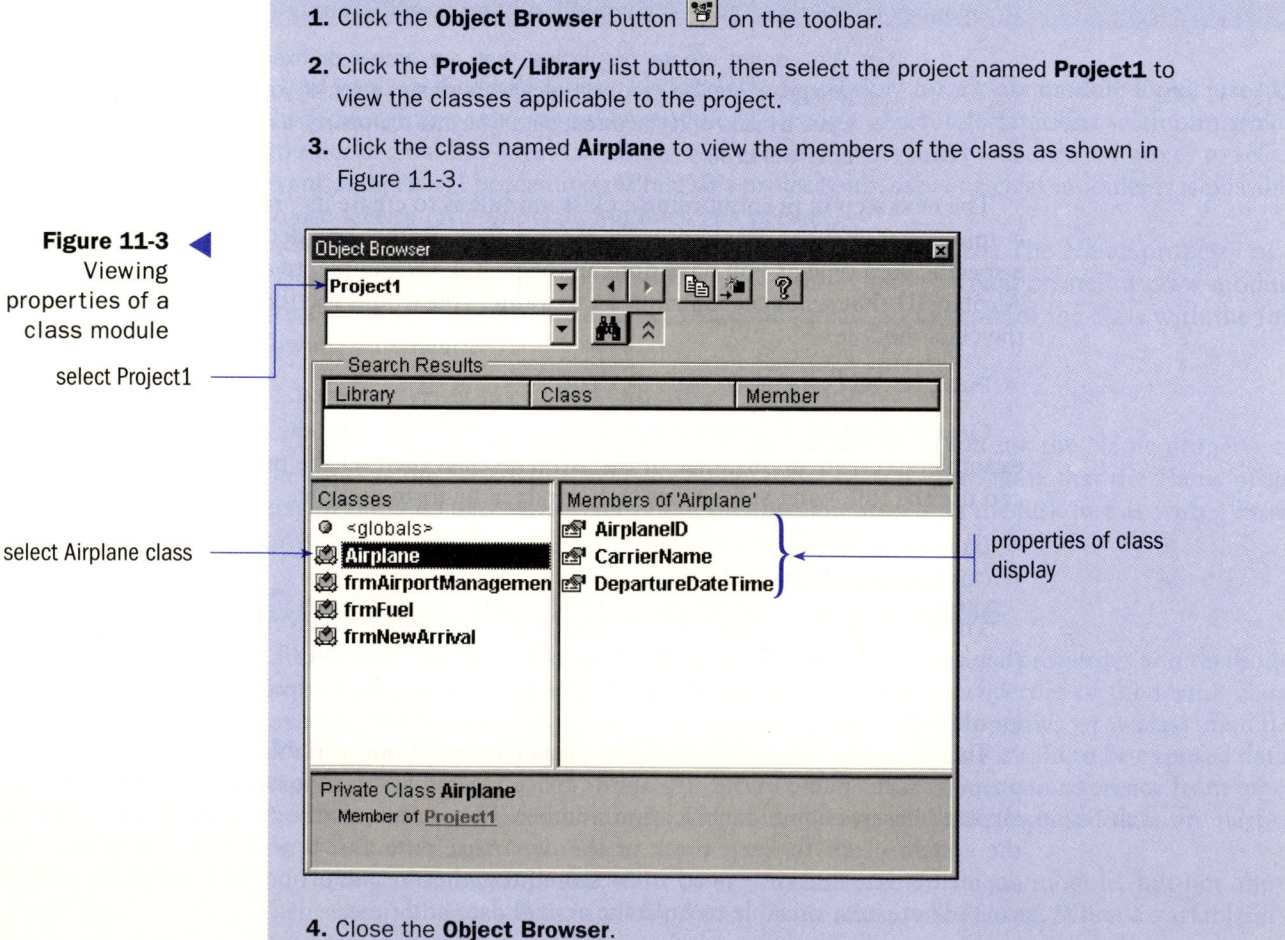

properties of class display

4. Close the **Object Browser**.

Tip: As you create additional properties and methods of the class, you can use the Object Browser to look at them. Also, the code completion features of Visual Basic will display suggestions as ToolTips in the Code window as you set properties and call methods.

Now that you have created the class module itself and the properties for the class module, you can begin to write code for the form that will create an instance of the class, then set its properties. Just as a control or form is a class, and an object does not exist until an instance of the control or form is created, a class object does not exist until an instance of the class has been created.

The program you are creating for Tina will use the class module such that an instance of the class will be created each time an airplane arrives at the airport. When the airplane departs, the information relating to the charges incurred will be saved to a text file, then the instance of the class must be destroyed.

Tina already has created all the objects on the main form to display each airplane currently at the airport. The Arrival and Departure command buttons for this form must create an instance of the airplane class and destroy the instance, respectively. The form is shown in Figure 11-4.

Figure 11-4 ◀
Airsoft - Airport
Management
System main
form

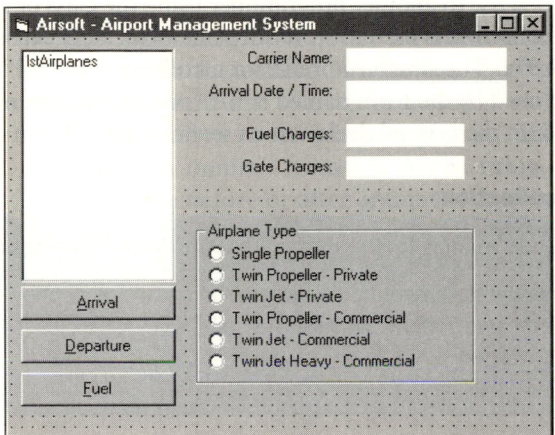

As you can see, the form also contains command buttons to record an aircraft's arrival and departure. There also is a button to record fuel charges. You now need to write the statements, which will record the arrival of an airplane at the airport. When this occurs, you need to create a new instance of the Airplane class, then set the properties describing the Name and Airplane ID. In the previous tutorial, you created an array to store a reference to multiple instances of a form class, and wrote code to add and remove objects from the array. You could use a similar method to manage the Airplane class by including the following statement in the general declarations section of the Form module to create an empty array to store Airplane objects:

```
Private mAirplaneArray( ) As New Airplane
```

Using this method, you would need to redimension the array each time an airplane arrived, and keep track of which element in the array represents which airplane. There is another method to store multiple instances of like objects, however. Just as you used collections to provide a reference to multiple object variables, you can create your own collections then store objects in the collection.

Creating a Collection

Instead of using an array, you can create your own collections using the Visual Basic Collection object. The Visual Basic Collection object works much like the collections you have used in previous tutorials. In previous tutorials the individual objects contained in a collection already have been created for you, either automatically or by calling a method. In this tutorial, however, you must manage the members of the collection yourself.

To add an Airplane object to the collection:

1. Activate the Code window for the Form module named **frmAirportManagement**.

2. Enter the following statements in the **cmdArrival_Click** event procedure:

```
Private Sub cmdArrival_Click( )
     On Error GoTo DuplicateAirplane
     Dim AirplaneNew As New Airplane
     frmNewArrival.Show vbModal
     AirplaneNew.CarrierName = frmNewArrival.txtName
     AirplaneNew.AirplaneID = frmNewArrival.txtID
     mcolAirplanes.Add AirplaneNew, frmNewArrival.txtID
     lstAirplanes.AddItem frmNewArrival.txtID
     Exit Sub
DuplicateAirplane:
     MsgBox "Cannot add. Airplane ID already exists.", _
        vbOKOnly, "Error"
End Sub
```

These statements create a new instance of the Airplane class to store the arriving airplane. Then they display a form to get the information for the airplane that is arriving. Tina already has created this form for you with two text boxes named txtName and txtID, representing the name of the carrier and the AirplaneID number. Once the instance has been created, the airline is stored in the CarrierName property and the Airplane ID number is stored in the AirplaneID property. If the Airplane ID is already in the collection, the error handler is executed and a message box is displayed.

```
On Error GoTo DuplicateAirplane
```

This statement creates the error handler for the procedure. If you try to add an Airplane object to the collection with a duplicate string key, the error handler will be invoked and the object will not be added.

```
AirplaneNew.CarrierName = frmNewArrival.txtName
AirplaneNew.AirplaneID = frmNewArrival.txtID
```

These statements set the CarrierName and AirplaneID properties from the information contained in the corresponding objects on the form frmNewArrival. The object variable was created in the previous Dim statement.

```
mcolAirplanes.Add AirplaneNew, frmNewArrival.txtID
lstAirplanes.AddItem frmNewArrival.txtID
Exit Sub
```

These statements add the new Airplane ID to the list box. This list box will be used to select an individual airplane and update its properties. The final statement adds the object to the collection by calling the Add method. Notice you used two arguments. The first argument is the name of the object you want to add. The second is the string key you will use to look up the object in the collection. After these statements have executed, the Exit Sub statement causes the procedure to exit before executing the error handler.

```
DuplicateAirplane:
    MsgBox "Cannot add. Airplane ID already exists.", _
        vbOKOnly, "Error"
```

If a duplicate string key was detected, the error handler is called. This causes a message box to be displayed advising the user the airplane cannot be added because it already exists.

Using a collection to manage several objects is much easier than using an array because you do not need to change explicitly the size of the collection. Nor do you need to determine exactly where to insert an item. The Collection object keeps track of this information for you.

It is important to note that the variable AirplaneNew is a local variable. When the cmdArrival_Click event procedure ends, this variable is destroyed. Another reference to the object was created when you added the object to the collection, however. Even though the variable AirplaneNew no longer exists when the procedure exits, the object continues to exist because there is a reference to it through the collection. Figure 11-5 illustrates this process.

Figure 11-5 Storing an object in a collection

AirplaneNew
Reference
Airplane object
mcolAirplanes
(1)

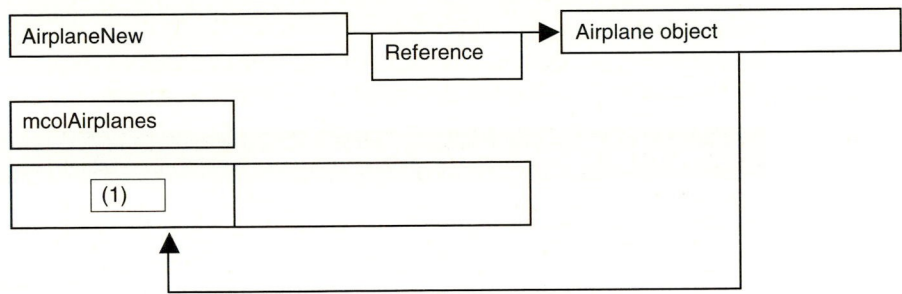

Your program now will create a new instance of the Airplane class when the user clicks the Arrival command button. It also will display the Airplane ID number in the list box. Tina suggests you run the program now to test that the instance of the class is being created and that the list box is being updated properly.

To test the program:

1. Save the project then start it.
2. Click the **Arrival** button to display the arrival form.
3. Enter the information as shown in Figure 11-6.

Figure 11-6 Recording an airplane's arrival

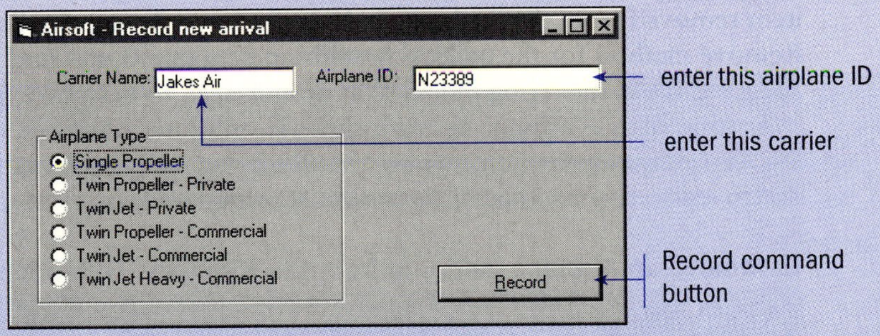

Airsoft - Record new arrival
Carrier Name: Jakes Air
Airplane ID: N23389
enter this airplane ID
enter this carrier
Airplane Type
Single Propeller
Twin Propeller - Private
Twin Jet - Private
Twin Propeller - Commercial
Twin Jet - Commercial
Twin Jet Heavy - Commercial
Record
Record command button

4. Close the form by clicking the **Record** command button.
5. When the form is closed, the Airplane ID number should be displayed in the list box of the main form as shown in Figure 11-7.

Figure 11-7 New airplane shown in main form

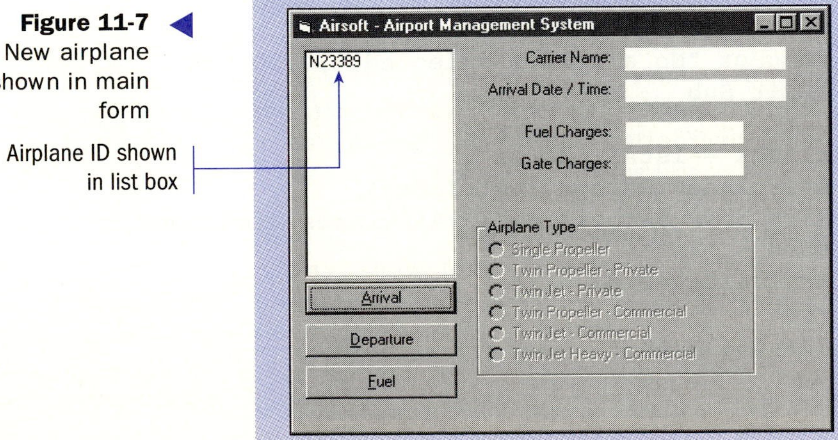

Airplane ID shown in list box
Airsoft - Airport Management System
N23389
Carrier Name:
Arrival Date / Time:
Fuel Charges:
Gate Charges:
Airplane Type
Single Propeller
Twin Propeller - Private
Twin Jet - Private
Twin Propeller - Commercial
Twin Jet - Commercial
Twin Jet Heavy - Commercial
Arrival
Departure
Fuel

Finding an Item in a Collection

To locate an item in a collection, you either can use a numeric index or a string key as you have done previously. For example, to reference a specific airplane in the collection mcolAirplanes, you could use the following statements:

```
Dim CurrentAirplane As Airplane
Set CurrentAirplane = mcolAirplanes(1)
Set CurrentAirplane = mcolAirplanes("N23389")
```

When searching for an item in a collection, you must use a valid numeric index or an existing string key. That is, if there are two objects in the collection, the valid numeric index values are one (1) and two (2). When using a string key, you must use a valid string key enclosed in quotation marks. If an invalid index or string key is specified, a run-time error will occur.

Tina asks you to write the necessary statements to locate a specific airplane in the collection, then display the information pertinent to that airplane. The only information you have recorded so far is the carrier name. Because the value in the list box was recorded at the same time the Airplane object was added to the collection, there is no need to verify the string key is valid. Tina suggests you now write the code for the list box's Click event procedure to locate the Airplane ID, then display the carrier corresponding to that airplane.

To display the current airplane information when an airplane is selected:

1. Activate the Code window for the Form module named **frmAirportManagement**.

2. Enter the following statements in the **lstAirplanes_Click** event procedure:

```
Private Sub lstAirplanes_Click( )
    Dim AirplaneCurrent As Airplane
    Set AirplaneCurrent = mcolAirplanes(lstAirplanes)
    lblName = AirplaneCurrent.CarrierName
End Sub
```

The variable AirplaneCurrent is used to reference an Airplane object in the mcolAirplanes collection. This statement does not create an Airplane object because the New keyword was not used. Rather, the object variable is used to create a reference to an existing object (stored in the collection). The second statement locates the desired object in the collection by using the currently selected item in the list box as the string key. Finally, the caption of the label is set to the CarrierName property of the Airplane object.

Tina suggests you now test the program to verify that you can select different Airplane IDs in the list box and display the corresponding carrier.

To test the Click event procedure for the lstAirplanes list box:

1. Save the project then start it.

2. Click **Arrival** then type **Jakes Air** for the Carrier Name and **N23389** for the Airplane ID number. Click **Record**.

3. Click **Arrival** then type **International** for the Carrier Name and **N18566** for the Airplane ID number. Click **Record**.

4. Click **N23389** in the list box. **Jakes Air** should display in the Carrier Name text box.

5. Click **N18566** in the list box. **International** should display in the Carrier Name text box.

6. End the program.

Your program now can add airplanes to the collection, delete airplanes, and locate airplanes. You now can proceed to compute the charges incurred by an airplane while at an airport.

Hiding Data in a Class Module

There are times when you do not want certain data in a class to be accessible to other modules. That is, you do not want the data to become part of the object's interface. In object-oriented terminology, this is called data hiding. By only exposing certain data as properties, you can change the inner workings of the class module without affecting the programs that use the class. To hide data in the class, you create Private variables. Private variables declared in a class behave the same way as Private variables declared in a Form module. To declare a hidden variable, you use the Private statement. If the variable is declared in the general declarations section of the class module, it can be used by all the procedures in the module. You also can use the Dim statement inside a procedure to create a Private local variable. These variables only can be used by the procedure where they are declared.

You need several Private variables to hold the information in the class. This information includes the charges for fuel, other charges, and the total charges. Also, you need to store the departure date and time.

To declare the hidden variables in the class:

> **1.** Activate the Code window for the class module named **Airplane.cls**.
>
> **2.** Enter the following statements into the general declarations section of the class module just after the Public variables:
>
> ```
> Private msngCharges As Single
> Private msngFuelCharge As Single
> Private mdtmArrivalDateTime As Date
> ```

Notice that each of these hidden variables uses the naming convention for variables rather than for properties. Because these variables are declared with the Private statement, they are not properties nor are they part of the class's interface.

The variable msngCharges will store the accumulated charges accrued for each airplane from the time it arrives until the time it departs. The variable msngFuelCharge will store the charges for fuel. The variable mdtmArrivalDateTime will store the arrival date and time.

> *Tip:* Declare all the properties together and all the Private variables together to improve the readability of the program.

Class Initialization

Just as a form supports an Initialize event that occurs when an instance of the form is first created, a class module also can respond to an Initialize event. Whenever a new class instance is created, an Initialize event occurs. Whenever a new airplane arrives at the airport, a new instance of the Airplane class is created to represent the airplane and add the object to the collection of airplanes. You have not yet recorded, however, the arrival time of the plane in the class instance. While you could create the instance of the class, then explicitly set a property like you did with the CarrierName and AirplaneID properties, you can program the Initialize event to record the arrival date and time in the variable you just created.

To record an airplane's arrival time when the class is initialized:

> **1.** Activate the Code window for the class module named **Airplane.cls**.
>
> **2.** Choose **Class** in the Object list box.

> **REFERENCE window**
>
> ## CREATING A READ-ONLY PROPERTY
>
> - Create a hidden variable inside a class module to store the value of the property.
> - Use the Add Procedure dialog box to create a Property procedure to store the value of the hidden variable in the property.
> - Write the necessary code to read the property in the Property Get procedure, and delete the corresponding Property Let procedure.

Tina suggests you now remove the unnecessary procedure and write the code for the Property Get procedure.

To write the code for the read-only property ArrivalDateTime:

1. Activate the Code window for the class module named **Airplane.cls**.

2. Locate the **Property Let ArrivalDateTime** procedure and remove the entire procedure.

3. Locate the **Property Get ArrivalDateTime** procedure and enter the following code, shown in bold. Note that the Property Get procedure it returns is a Variant by default. Make sure to change the return type to a Date instead of a Variant. Although a Variant will work, it will run slower.

```
Public Property Get ArrivalDateTime( ) As Date
    ArrivalDateTime = mdtmArrivalDateTime
End Property
```

The Property Get procedure stores the hidden variable mdtmArrivalDateTime in the property named ArrivalDateTime. These statements will be executed when the property is read. This Property procedure illustrates the use of hidden variables within a class module. The value of the hidden variable was set by the Class_Initialize event procedure. When the programmer tries to read the ArrivalDateTime property, the corresponding Property Get procedure will be executed, and the value retrieved from the hidden variable. Because there is no corresponding Property Let procedure, the property is read-only. If the programmer tries to write a value to the property, a run-time error will occur.

Now that you have created the Property procedure, you can write the necessary statements to display the arrival date and time on the form by reading the property and storing the value in the corresponding label. This should occur whenever the user selects an airplane from the list box. Thus, you must add statements to the Click event procedure for the list box.

To display the arrival date and time on the form:

1. Activate the Code window for the form named **frmAirportManagement**, and locate the **Click** event procedure for the list box named **lstAirplanes**.

2. Enter the following statement into the event procedure just before the End Sub statement:

```
lblArrivalDateTime = AirplaneCurrent.ArrivalDateTime
```

3. Save the project then start it.

4. Click the **Arrival** command button.

5. Enter **Jakes Air** as the Carrier Name, **N1288** as the Airplane ID number, then click the **Record** command button.

6. Click the **N1288** item in the list box. The information should be displayed as shown in Figure 11-9.

Figure 11-9 ◀
Displaying
arrival time

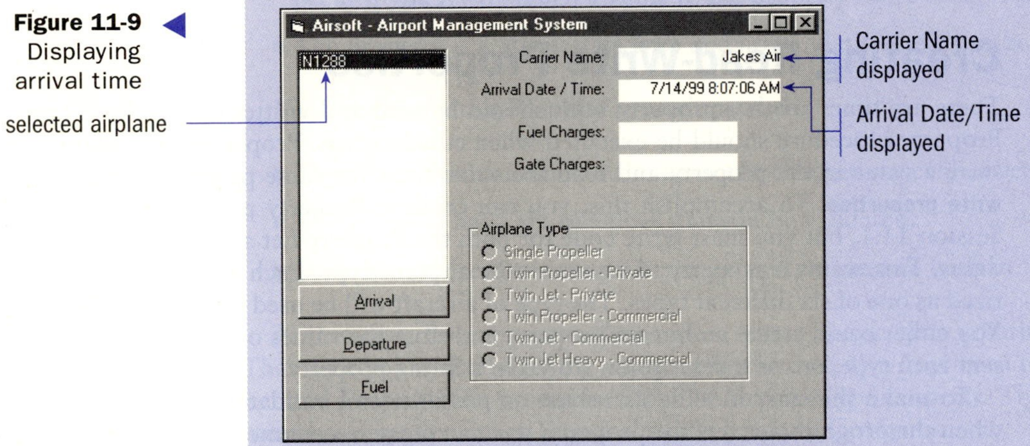

selected airplane

Carrier Name
displayed

Arrival Date/Time
displayed

7. End the program.

You have completed the programming for this session. The program now supports an Airplane class. The class has properties to identify the Carrier Name and the Airplane ID. There also exists a read-only property describing the arrival date and time. You can create instances of the class each time an airplane arrives and terminate those instances when an airplane departs. Also, your program can keep track of each object reference using a collection instead of an array.

Quick Check

1. What is the difference between an exposed variable and a hidden variable in a class module?

2. What types of information can be stored in the Collection object?

3. What are the properties and methods of the Collection object and what is the purpose of those properties?

4. When does the Class_Initialize event occur?

5. What is a Property procedure?

6. How do you create a read-only property?

You have completed the programming for this session. You either may continue to the next session or exit Visual Basic and take a break.

In all cases the Property Let statement takes one argument more than the corresponding Property Get procedure. Also, the final argument in the Property Let procedure must be of the same data type as the return value of the Property Get procedure. That is, the AirplaneType Property Let procedure takes one argument and the corresponding Property Get procedure returns a value. Both procedures are of the same type. Figure 11-10 illustrates this process.

Figure 11-10 ◀
Property Let
and Property
Get procedures

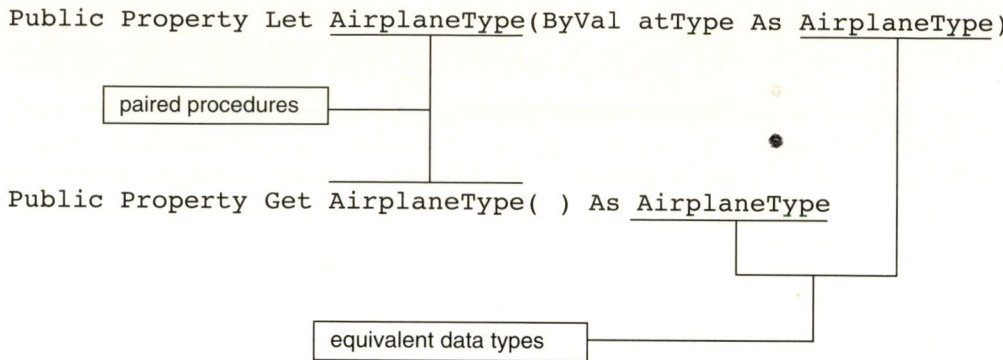

Generating a Run-Time Error

The programs you have written so far have responded to run-time errors caused by conditions like a type mismatch or numeric overflow. In the Airport Management System, you need a way for the Property procedure to communicate to another procedure if it receives invalid data. One way to accomplish this task is for the Property procedure to generate an error if invalid input is received. To do this, you can generate a run-time error that the module using the class then can trap. To generate a run-time error, you use the Err object with the Raise method. This method has the following syntax:

Err.Raise *number*[, *source*][, *description*][, *helpfile*][, *helpcontext*]

- The **Raise** method always is called on the required **Err** object.

- The required *number* argument contains a long integer that identifies the error. Visual Basic errors (both Visual Basic defined and user-defined errors) are in the range 0 – 65535. When setting the Number property to your own error code in a class module, you add your error code number to the vbObjectError constant.

- The optional *source* argument contains a string expression naming the object or application that generated the error. When setting this property for an object, use the form *project.class*. If *source* is not specified, the programmatic ID of the current Visual Basic project is used.

- The optional *description* argument is a string describing the error. If unspecified, the value in number is examined. If it can be mapped to a Visual Basic run-time error code, the string that would be returned by the Error function is used as description. If there is no Visual Basic error corresponding to number, the "Application-defined or object-defined error" message is used.

- The optional *helpfile* and *helpcontext* arguments are used to define the help file where help can be found.

Often you will call a function or method without using all the arguments. You can specify each argument by name by specifying the argument name, followed by the characters := followed by the value. For example, to use the number argument and the description argument to the Err.Raise method, you would use the following statement:

```
Err.Raise Number:=3, Description:="Invalid airplane type"
```

The Property Let procedure that sets the AirplaneType property must validate the value of the argument specified that is passed to it by another module. If it is a valid airplane type, the hidden variable named atAirplaneType needs to be set. Otherwise, the procedure should generate an error. The corresponding Property Get procedure simply sets the property to the value of the hidden variable. Tina suggests you now write the Property Get and Property Let procedures for the AirplaneType property.

To create and write the code for the Property Let and Property Get Procedures:

1. Activate the Code window for the class module named **Airplane.cls**.

2. Click **Tools** then **Add Procedure** to activate the Add Procedure dialog box.

3. Set the Name to **AirplaneType**, the Scope to **Public** and the Type to **Property**. Click **OK**.

4. Enter the following statements into the Property Get procedure:

```
Public Property Get AirplaneType( ) As AirplaneType
    AirplaneType = atAirplaneType
End Property
```

5. Locate the **AirplaneType** Property Let procedure and enter the following statements:

```
Public Property Let AirplaneType(ByVal atType As AirplaneType)
    Select Case atType
        Case atSinglePropeller, atTwinPropellerPrivate, _
            atTwinJetPrivate, atTwinPropellerCommercial, _
            atTwinJetCommercial, atTwinJetHeavyCommercial
        Case Else
            Err.Raise Number:=3, _
                Description:="Invalid airplane type"
    End Select
    atAirplaneType = atType
End Property
```

6. In the general declarations section of the Form module named **frmNewArrival**, enter the following statement:

```
Public SelectAirplaneType As AirplaneType
```

These statements create the Property procedures to read and write the AirplaneType property and validate the argument when the user writes a value to the property.

```
Public Property Let AirplaneType(ByVal atType As AirplaneType)
```

This statement creates the Property Let procedure named AirplaneType. This procedure accepts one argument—the enumerated type AirplaneType.

```
Select Case atType
    Case atSinglePropeller, atTwinPropellerPrivate, _
        atTwinJetPrivate, atTwinPropellerCommercial, _
        atTwinJetCommercial, atTwinJetHeavyCommercial
    Case Else
        Err.Raise Number:=3, _
            Description:="Invalid airplane type"
End Select
```

The Select Case statement validates argument atType. If it has a valid value, then the variable atAirplaneType is set to the type specified by the user. This is a hidden variable that will be used when the property is read by the corresponding Property Get procedure. If invalid data is passed to the Property procedure, the Case Else statement is executed and an error is raised. This error will cause a message to be displayed with the description "Invalid airplane type".

```
atAirplaneType = atType
```

The final statement sets the value of the hidden variable atAirplaneType to the value of the argument specified by the user only if an error is not raised.

```
Public Property Get AirplaneType( ) As AirplaneType
    AirplaneType = atAirplaneType
End Property
```

This procedure is executed when the AirplaneType property is read. The procedure simply stores the airplane type stored in the hidden variable atAirplaneType in the AirplaneType property.

You now need to write the statements to set the airplane type when an airplane arrives and display the current airplane type when an airplane is selected in the list box.

To write the code to read and write the AirplaneType properties:

1. Open the Code window for the form named **frmAirportManagement**.

2. Enter the following statement in the **Click** event procedure for the **cmdArrival** command button:

```
   . . .
   AirplaneNew.CarrierName = frmNewArrival.txtName
   AirplaneNew.AirplaneID = frmNewArrival.txtID
   AirplaneNew.AirplaneType = _
       frmNewArrival.SelectAirplaneType
```

Tina already wrote the code in the frmNewArrival form to set the Public variable SelectAirplaneType to one of the valid airplane types whenever one of the option buttons on the form is clicked. This statement sets the AirplaneType property for the current airplane to the currently selected option button in the frmNewArrival. When this property is set, the AirplaneType Property Let procedure is executed. Note that if you try to store an invalid airplane type into the AirplaneType property, a run-time error will be generated.

3. Activate the **Click** event procedure for the object named **lstAirplanes**.

4. Enter the following statements into the event procedure just before the End Sub statement:

```
   optAirplaneType(AirplaneCurrent.AirplaneType) = _
       True
```

This statement reads the AirplaneType property for the currently selected airplane. Remember this value must be one of the valid values for the enumerated type AirplaneType. This value is used as an argument to set the corresponding option button.

5. Save the project then start it.

6. Record two airplane arrivals with the following information: use the Carrier Name **Jakes Air**, Airplane ID number **N23389**, and Airplane Type **Twin Propeller - Commercial** for the first airplane; and use the Carrier Name **International**, Airplane ID number **N23904**, and Airplane Type **Twin Jet Heavy - Commercial** for the second airplane.

7. Select the second aircraft as shown in Figure 11-11. Your form should look like Figure 11-11.

Figure 11-11 ◀
Testing
AirplaneType
property

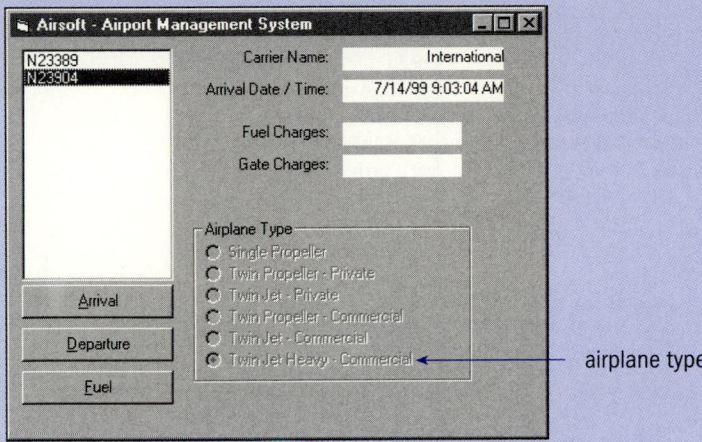

airplane type

TROUBLE? If the airplane type is not displayed as shown in Figure 11-11, make sure the code you wrote in the previous steps is correct.

8. End the program.

Setting the Default Property

Just as objects like text boxes and command buttons can have a default property or method, a class also can have a default property or method. This property or method will be executed whenever the object is referenced without the object or property name. Selecting the Procedure Attributes menu item on the Tools menu or using the Object Browser sets the default property.

Tina believes the AirplaneID property will be used more than any other property so she suggests you set this property to be the default property of the class.

To set the default property to Airplane ID:

1. Open the **Object Browser**.

2. In the Project/Library list box, select the project named **Project1**.

3. In the Classes list box, select the class named **Airplane**.

4. In the Members of 'Airplane' list box, select the member named **AirplaneID**, as shown in Figure 11-12.

Figure 11-12 ◄
Setting a
default
property

Project1 selected

Airplane class
selected

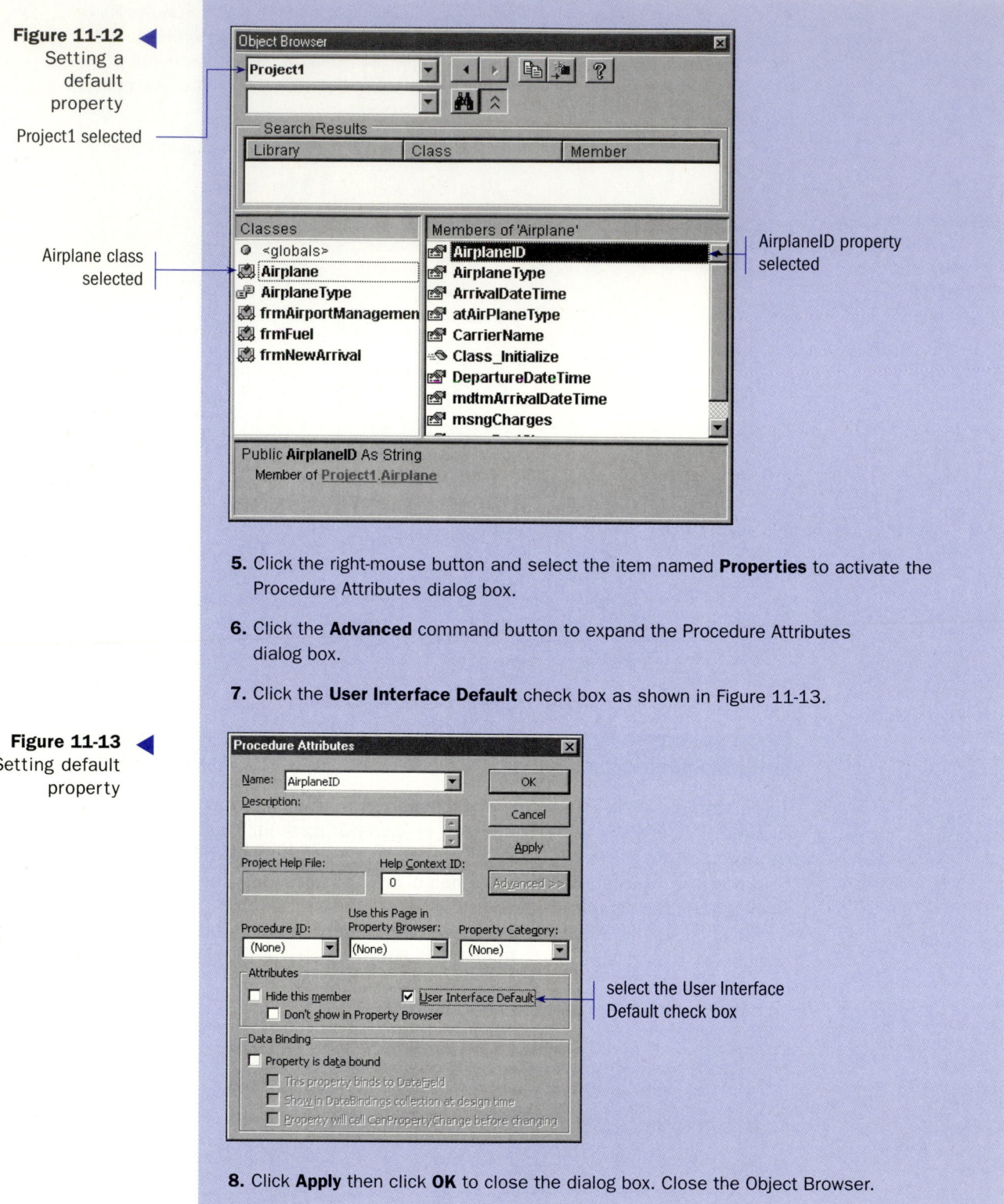

AirplaneID property
selected

5. Click the right-mouse button and select the item named **Properties** to activate the Procedure Attributes dialog box.

6. Click the **Advanced** command button to expand the Procedure Attributes dialog box.

7. Click the **User Interface Default** check box as shown in Figure 11-13.

Figure 11-13 ◄
Setting default
property

select the User Interface
Default check box

8. Click **Apply** then click **OK** to close the dialog box. Close the Object Browser.

These steps cause the AirplaneID property to be the default.

As the program is presently written, the AirplaneID property is a read-write property. Once the property is set, however, it should not be changed. If the programmer accidentally changed the value of this property, the value neither would correspond to the string key in the collection, nor would it correspond to the value in the list box.

Creating a Write-Once Property

When creating a property that will be used as a key, it often is desirable to create the property such that once it is written, it cannot be written again. This is called a **write-once property**. Visual Basic does not support explicitly a write-once property. You can write code to implement a property as a write-once property, however.

Tina suggests you implement the AirplaneID property as a write-once property to be sure the programmer using the class does not accidentally set the property to a different value after the property already has been set. To do this, you need to remove the Public variable named Airplane ID, replace it with a corresponding hidden variable and create Property Let and Property Get procedures.

To implement the AirplaneID property as a write-once property:

1. Activate the Code window for the class named **Airplane.cls**.

2. Remove the following line in the general declarations section:

```
Public AirplaneID As String
```

3. Replace the line with the following declaration statement:

```
Private mstrAirplaneID As String
```

4. Create a Public Property procedure named **AirplaneID.**

5. Enter the following statements into the **Property Get** procedure:

```
Public Property Get AirplaneID( ) As String
    AirplaneID = mstrAirplaneID
End Property
```

6. Enter the following statements into the **AirplaneID** Property Let procedure:

```
Public Property Let AirplaneID(ByVal pstrArg As String)
    If mstrAirplaneID = "" Then
        mstrAirplaneID = pstrArg
    Else
        Err.Raise 1, , _
            "Cannot reset the write-once property AirplaneID."
    End If
End Property
```

These statements implement the Airplane ID as a write-once property instead of a Public property. This improves the class's strength.

Creating a Method

In addition to setting and retrieving properties and/or executing code when those properties are set and retrieved, you also can create methods for the class. There are two types of methods you can create in Visual Basic. You can create:

- Function methods that return a value.

- Sub methods that do not return a value.

Creating a Public, Function, or Sub procedure within a class module creates Function and Sub methods. To call a method, you use method syntax rather than the syntax to call a Function or Sub procedure. Consider the following procedure declaration:

```
Public Sub AddFuel(ByVal Gallons As Single,
    ByVal Price As Single)
```

Function Methods

Function methods work just like Sub methods except Function methods return a value. This is identical to a function in a standard module. In this session you need a Function method to compute the total charges accrued by an airplane. The table shown in Figure 11-14 illustrates the schedule for the charges.

Figure 11-14 ◀
Airplane
Charges

Airplane Type	Charge per Minute
Single Propeller	.25
Twin Propeller - Private	.44
Twin Jet - Private	.92
Twin Propeller - Commercial	1.21
Twin Jet - Commercial	1.84
Twin Jet Heavy - Commercial	2.42

To compute the total charges:

1. Make sure the Code window is active for **Airplane.cls**.

2. Insert a **Function** procedure named **ComputeCharges,** then set the Scope to **Public**.

3. Enter the following statements in the procedure:

```
Public Function ComputeCharges( ) As Single
    Dim psngCharges As Single
    Dim plngElapsedMinutes As Long
    plngElapsedMinutes = DateDiff("n", _
        mdtmArrivalDateTime, Now)
    Select Case atAirplaneType
        Case atSinglePropeller
            psngCharges = plngElapsedMinutes * 0.25
        Case atTwinPropellerPrivate
            psngCharges = plngElapsedMinutes * 0.44
        Case atTwinJetPrivate
            psngCharges = plngElapsedMinutes * 0.92
        Case atTwinPropellerCommercial
            psngCharges = plngElapsedMinutes * 1.21
        Case atTwinJetCommercial
            psngCharges = plngElapsedMinutes * 1.84
        Case atTwinJetHeavyCommercial
            psngCharges = plngElapsedMinutes * 2.42
    End Select
    ComputeCharges = psngCharges
End Function
```

These statements declare a method named ComputeCharges. The method takes no arguments and returns a value of the Single data type.

```
Dim psngCharges As Single
Dim plngElapsedMinutes As Long
```

These statements declare two variables. The first is used to store the dollar amount of the charges, and the second is used to determine the number of minutes the airplane has been at the airport.

```
plngElapsedMinutes = DateDiff("n", _
    mdtmArrivalDateTime, Now)
```

This statement calls the DateDiff function to determine the number of minutes the airplane has been at the airport. The first argument "n" tells the DateDiff function that you want to determine the number of minutes elapsed. The second argument is the hidden variable mdtmArrivalDateTime. This variable contains the arrival date and time of the airplane, and was set in the Class_Initialize event procedure. The final argument is the current date and time. Thus, you are computing the number of elapsed minutes from the time an airplane arrived to the current time.

```
Select Case atAirplaneType
    Case atSinglePropeller
        psngCharges = plngElapsedMinutes * 0.25
    Case atTwinPropellerPrivate
        psngCharges = plngElapsedMinutes * 0.44
    Case atTwinJetPrivate
        psngCharges = plngElapsedMinutes * 0.92
    Case atTwinPropellerCommercial
        psngCharges = plngElapsedMinutes * 1.21
    Case atTwinJetCommercial
        psngCharges = plngElapsedMinutes * 1.84
    Case atTwinJetHeavyCommercial
        psngCharges = plngElapsedMinutes * 2.42
End Select
```

These statements determine the charges by multiplying the number of minutes the airplane was at the airport by the charge per minute.

```
ComputeCharges = psngCharges
```

The final statement sets the return value for the method. This syntax is identical to the syntax you have used with other function procedures.

Now that you have created the method, you need to call the method whenever an airplane is selected. The method should display the value in the corresponding lblCharges label on the form.

To call and test the ComputeCharges method:

1. Activate the Code window for the form named **frmAirportManagement**.

2. Locate the **Click** event procedure for the list box named **lstAirplanes**.

3. Enter the following statement just before the End Sub statement:

   ```
   lblCharges = AirplaneCurrent.ComputeCharges
   ```

4. Save the project then start it.

5. Click the **Arrival** command button and enter the information as shown in Figure 11-15.

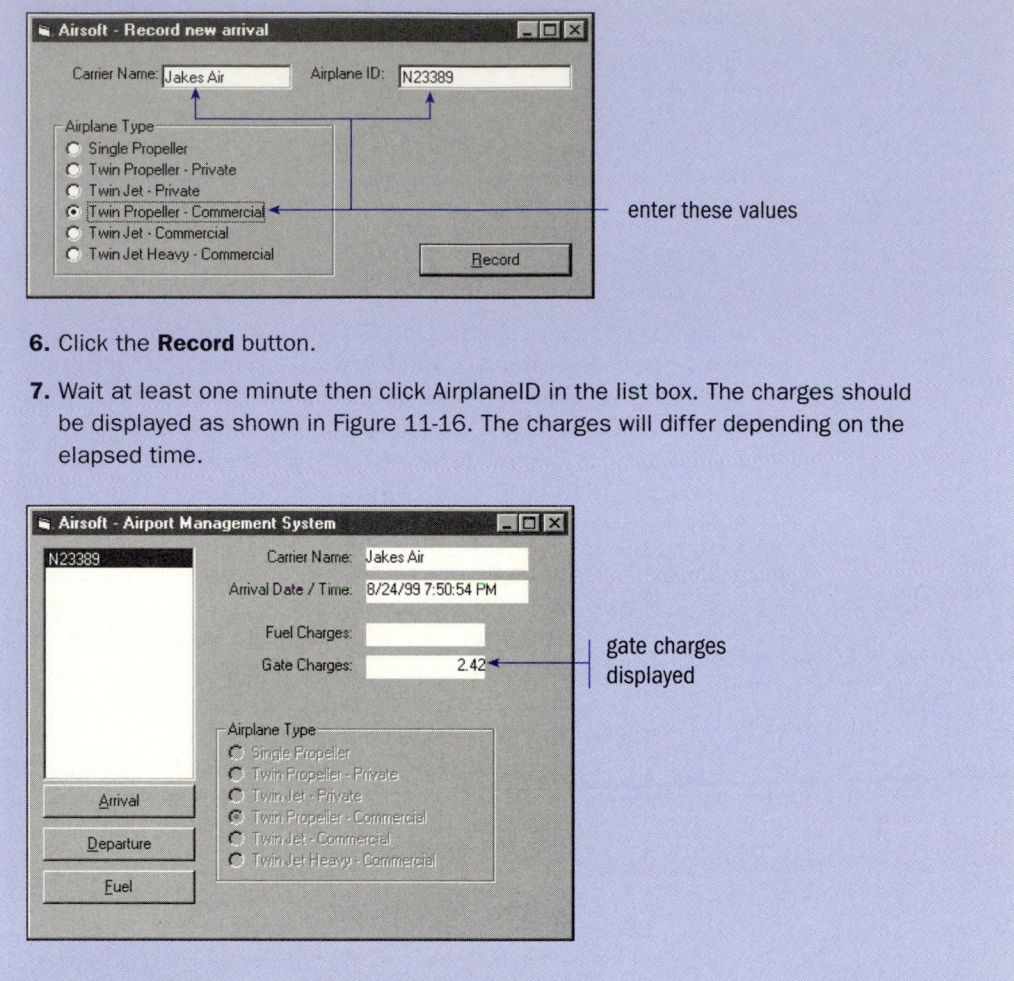

Figure 11-15 ◀
Testing
charges

enter these values

6. Click the **Record** button.

7. Wait at least one minute then click AirplaneID in the list box. The charges should be displayed as shown in Figure 11-16. The charges will differ depending on the elapsed time.

Figure 11-16 ◀
Testing
charges

gate charges
displayed

8. End the program.

Terminating a Class Instance

As the program is presently written, the instance of the Airplane class is terminated when the Departure command button is clicked. Just before the instance of the class is terminated, the information about the current airplane must be recorded so it can be used by another program. Just as the Initialize event occurs before the instance of the class being created, the Terminate event occurs just before the instance is destroyed. Tina would like the information appended to a text file when an airplane leaves the airport. This file will be used by their billing system to produce monthly invoices.

One way to implement this is to create a property containing the filename to be written, and to write the file in the Terminate event. This option would require that the Terminate event verify that the file is valid before it is opened. If not, the event would need to raise an error. You also can call a method with the filename as an argument, and write the file in that method. This implementation would require that you check that the information had been written. If not, an error again would need to be raised. Otherwise, the information would be lost.

In this situation the decision of which implementation to use is subjective. In the Airport Management System you will use the latter approach because it gives the user slightly more control over when the information is written on the disk.

To write the information pertaining to an airplane when the instance is terminated:

1. Activate the Code window for the class module **Airplane.cls**.

2. Enter the following statement into the general declarations section of the class module after the Option Explicit statement:

```
Private mblnRecordWritten As Boolean
```

3. Enter the following statement into the **Class Terminate** event procedure:

```
Private Sub Class_Terminate( )
    If mblnRecordWritten = False Then
        Err.Raise vbObjectError + 1, "Airsoft.Airplane", _
            "Data not written on disk."
    End If
End Sub
```

These statements declare a hidden variable named mblnRecordWritten. This variable needs to be available to the Terminate event and the method you will write in a moment, so you declared it in the general declarations section. It is not part of the class's interface.

The If statement determines if the record has been written. If it has, the instance is terminated. Otherwise, an error is raised. Because you have not yet created a method to write the record and set the variable mblnRecordWritten to True, the Terminate event always will generate an error. You should test your program to make sure the Terminate event is testing the variable mblnRecordWritten correctly.

To test the program and the Terminate event:

1. Save the project then start it.

2. Enter an Airplane arrival.

3. Click the AirplaneID in the list box.

4. Click the **Departure** command button. The Terminate event should generate an error as shown in Figure 11-17.

Figure 11-17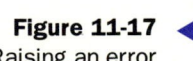
Raising an error

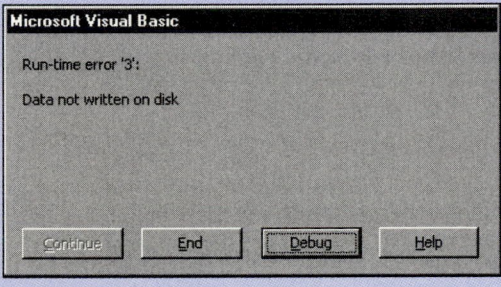

5. End the program.

You now need to write the statements to create the method that will write the text file and call the method when the Departure command button is clicked.

To write the airplane record to a file:

1. Activate the Code window for the **Airplane** class module.

2. Create a **Public Sub** procedure named **WriteAirplane**.

3. Enter the following statements into the Sub procedure:

```
Public Sub WriteAirplane(ByVal pargOutputFile As String)
    Open pargOutputFile For Append As #1
        Write #1, mstrAirplaneID, CarrierName, msngCharges, _
            msngFuelCharge, mdtmArrivalDateTime, _
            DepartureDateTime, atAirplaneType
    Close #1
    mblnRecordWritten = True
End Sub
```

4. Activate the Code window for the form named **frmAirportManagement**.

5. Enter the following statement in the **Click** event procedure for the command button named **cmdDeparture** just before the statement that removes the current airplane from the collection:

```
mcolAirplanes(lstAirplanes).WriteAirplane _
    "A:\Tutorial.11\Airplane.txt"
mcolAirplanes.Remove (pstrIndex)
```

6. Save the project then start it.

7. Record two airplane arrivals and departures.

8. End the program.

9. Start NotePad and verify the contents of the text file.

10. Exit NotePad.

11. Exit Visual Basic.

These statements declare the method to write the information to the text file as specified by the string argument to the WriteRecord method. The last statement calls the method to append the record to the file named Airplane.txt.

You have completed the programming for this tutorial. The program contains a class module and its user interface. The class module can be used by this program or other programs and provides a standardized interface to record the arrivals and departures of airplanes. This standardized interface consists of different properties and methods.

Quick Check

1 How do you create a read-write property using Property procedures?

2 What is the purpose of the Raise method as it pertains to the Err object?

3 How do you set the default property or default method for a class?

4 What is the purpose of a write-once property and what technique can you use to create one?

5 What is the difference between a Sub method and a Function method?

6 What type of processing do you perform in the Class object's Terminate event?

Figure 11-18 lists the new terms presented in this tutorial.

Figure 11-18 ◀
New terms

Term	Definition
Class module	A class module is a template for objects you create. A class module contains all the code to implement its properties and methods.
Data hiding	Data hiding data consists of variables in a class module that are not visible outside the class module.
Encapsulation	Encapsulation is a term meaning the data and the processes acting on that data are combined together into a class.
Exposed data	Exposed data are properties of a class module that are visible to other modules. Exposed data are part of the class's interface.
Interface	The interface consists of the properties and methods of the class. It is through the interface that the programmer interacts with the class.
Read-only property	A read-only property is a property that cannot be written to, but only can return its current setting.
Read-write property	A read-write property allows you to store a value in the property and read the value from the same property.
Type library	A type library contains standard descriptions of exposed objects, properties, methods, and collections.
Write-once property	A write-once property is a property that only can be written once. Future attempts to write the property will generate a run-time error.

Tutorial Assignments

In addition to managing the charges for the airplanes arriving and departing the airport, Tina also would like you to create another program to manage parking charges for the airport. When an automobile arrives at the parking garage, its license number needs to be recorded along with the time the car arrived. Then when the car departs, the parking attendant must be able to look up the license number and compute the parking charges based on the number of hours the automobile has been parked in the garage. The completed form for the program is shown in Figure 11-19.

Figure 11-19 ◀

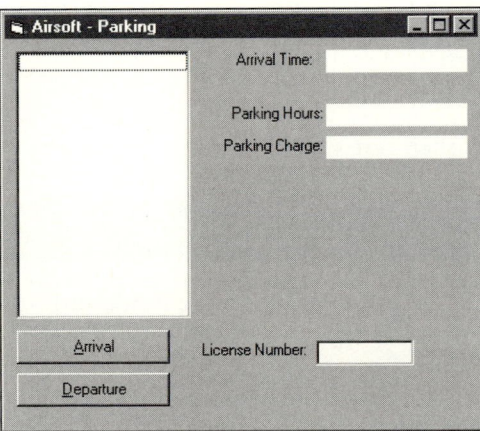

1. Start Visual Basic. Set the form's name to **frmParking**.

2. Add a new class module named **Parking** to the project, and make sure the **Option Explicit** statement is included.

3. Save the form and class using the default names and the project using the name **Parking.vbp** in the **TAssign** folder of the **Tutorial.11** folder on your Student Disk.

4. Create a hidden variable in the class module named **mdtmArrivalTime** to store the arrival time of an automobile.

5. Create a property named **ID** of the String data type that will hold the license number of each car.

6. When a new instance of the class is created, write the code to set the Private variable **mdtmArrivalTime** to the current date and time.

7. Create two read-only properties named **ParkingHours** and **ParkingCharge**. When read, the properties should determine the number of hours the automobile was parked in the garage based on the arrival time stored in **mdtmArrivalTime**. The charge for parking is computed by multiplying the number of hours by $4.00 per hour.

8. Create the necessary objects on the form to use the class as shown in Figure 11-19. Make sure to set the caption of the form.

9. In the general declarations section of the Form module, create a collection named **mcolLicenseNumbers**.

10. For the Arrival command button, create a new instance of the class, and set the **ID** property to the license number of the car.

11. Add the license number to the list box. The list box should be sorted by license number.

12. Add the new object to the collection with a string key. Use the license number as the string key.

13. When the user clicks a license number in the list box, write the necessary statements to read the ParkingCharge property and display the result in the corresponding label. Also display the arrival time and the parking hours.

14. Write the necessary code for the Departure command button to destroy the instance of the class and remove the selected item from the list box and clear the labels.

15. Test the program by adding different license numbers. Then click the list box to verify the parking charges.

16. Print the code for the project.

17. Save the project then exit Visual Basic.

Case Problems

1. Text Processors Text Processors performs word processing and data entry tasks for a number of clients. They want a program that will count the number of characters, words, and lines in a text file. Because several other programs will use this utility program, they would like these functions implemented as a class module. The class module should have one method that will open a text file for input. In the same method the number of characters, words, and lines should be counted and stored in read-only properties. After you create the class module, you will need to create a form to test the program. The form should include a Common Dialog control to open a file as specified by the user. Then, it should call the method in the class module to open the file. Finally, the information in the read-only properties of the class should be displayed in the labels on the form. The completed form is shown in Figure 11-20.

Figure 11-20 ◄

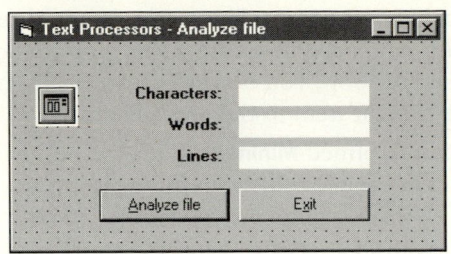

1. Start Visual Basic then create a new project.

2. Create a class module named **StringProcessor.cls**, and make sure to include the **Option Explicit** statement.

3. Create a method named **OpenFile**. This method should accept one argument—the full path of the file to be opened.

4. In the **OpenFile** method, write the necessary statements to count the number of characters, words, and lines.
   Note: A word is a sequence of characters separated by a space. A line is terminated with a new line character. This information needs to be stored in hidden variables.

5. Create three properties named **Characters**, **Words**, and **Lines**. These properties should be read-only properties. Each property should return the number of characters, words, and lines stored in the corresponding hidden variables.
   Note: You need to create Property procedures rather than Public variables.

6. Create a form as shown in Figure 11-20 to test the class module with two command buttons and the necessary labels. You can use the CommonDialog control to get a filename from the user and pass the name to the class module. The first command button should create an instance of the class, then call the method to open and read the file. Finally, it should read the properties and store the information in the corresponding labels. Set the form name to **frmAnalyzeFile** and save it using the default name. Save the project using the name **AnalyzeFile.vbp** in the **Cases** folder of the **Tutorial.11** folder on your Student Disk.

7. Test the program by creating a small text file in NotePad. Then run the program using the text file.

8. Exit Visual Basic.

2. Forte Systems Forte Systems performs statistical analysis and marketing surveys. They want a class module that stores a list of numbers. Once the list of numbers is created, they want to be able to determine the maximum number in the list, the minimum number in the list, and the sum of all numbers in the list. The class needs to contain a private array to store the list of numbers. When the class is initialized, the number of elements in the array should be set to zero. The class will have one method, called AddItem, which will accept one argument—a numeric value to add to the list. There also will be three other methods named Max, Min, and Sum that will return the maximum, minimum, and sum of the list.

1. Start Visual Basic.

2. Insert a class module in the project. Set the name of the class to **Statistical**. Save the class using the name **Statistical.cls.**

3. Declare a hidden array named **msngList** to hold the Single data type. Initially, the array should have zero (0) elements. You will need to redimension the array each time an element is added.

4. Write the statement to set the number of elements in the array to zero when the class is initialized.

5. Create a method named **AddItem**. The method should accept one argument, a Single data type to be added to the list. Write the statement to increase the size of the array by one. Make sure you preserve the existing contents. Store the argument passed in the new array element.

6. Create a method named **Maximum**. The method should return the largest number stored in the list. You need to create a For loop to look at each element in the array. Inside the For loop, you need to create an If statement to determine whether or not the current item in the array is greater than the largest number.

7. Create another method named **Minimum**. This method will work just like the method you created in the previous step but needs to return the smallest number in the list.

8. Create the final method named **Sum**. This method also needs to contain a For loop to look at each item in the list. You will need an accumulator to store the total value of all the elements in the array. After all the elements in the array have been examined, the method should return the total.

9. Write the code to test the methods created in the class module. Create a command button on the main form. The code in the command button should call the AddItem method several times with different numbers. After calling the AddItem method, you need to call the Maximum, Minimum, and Sum methods, and display the results in labels. Verify that the calculations are correct.

10. Save the project using the name **Forte.vbp** in the **Cases** folder of the **Tutorial.11** folder on your Student Disk. Save the main form using the name **frmForte.frm** and exit Visual Basic.

3. MidTex International MidTex International distributes automobile parts across the United States from their central Texas distribution facility. They have a database containing inventory information. They want a program to update prices and delete old parts from a database. They want their programmers to be able to call methods and read and write properties rather than have to learn how to use the SQL programming language. The inventory table (tblInventory) has the following fields:

fldPartNumber	String
fldQuantityInStock	Integer
fldCost	Single
fldSalesPrice	Single

You will need to create the following methods:

- The **Open** method should open a database.

- The **Insert** method should accept four arguments, which are the fields in the table, and insert a part number into the table.

- The **Delete** method should accept one argument, the part number, and remove the part number from the table.

- The **Update** method should accept four arguments, which are the fields in the table. Using the part number, the other three fields should be updated.

Set the name of the class module to **Data**. Set the name of the test form to **frmMidTex.frm**. Save the class and form using the default names. Save the project using the name **MidTex.vbp** in the **Cases** folder of the **Tutorial.II** folder on your Student Disk. When you are finished creating the class module, create a form to test each of the methods.

4. Shuffle Meister Shuffle Meister creates various computer card games. They want you to create a class module that will simulate the shuffling of a deck of cards. The class module, when initialized, should create an array to store a deck of 52 playing cards. You should create a method named **Shuffle** to shuffle the deck of cards. Then you need to create the method to deal the deck of cards. This method, named **DealCard**, should deal the next card off the deck. After creating the class module, you will need to create a form to test the program. The form should contain a list box to display the cards after they have been shuffled. You also will need a command button that, when clicked, will shuffle the deck of cards.

Working with Other Programs from Visual Basic

Creating a Loan Document Processing System for Mid State Bank

OBJECTIVES

In this tutorial you will:

- Use the Windows clipboard to copy data between objects in a Visual Basic program and different applications

- Drag-and-drop objects from within a program

- Use the OLE Container control to access the objects of other programs

- Program an Excel Worksheet object

- Set properties pertinent to the application and set options to determine how a program is compiled

- Create an executable file that can be run outside of the Visual Basic development environment

- Optimize programs for speed

Mid State Bank

CASE

Mid State Bank is a small, regional bank located in Albuquerque, New Mexico. Their customers include individuals and businesses in Albuquerque and the surrounding rural areas. Currently, they have four loan processors working at their main office to create all their loan documents using a word processing program.

Sandra Vincent is the programming manager for the Mid State Bank. You have been assigned to assist her in creating a program that will simplify the preparation of loan documents.

Much of each loan document contains standardized text that is repeated in nearly every document. Some text is unique, however, based on the type of the loan. Some of the textual information exists in files produced by other applications. Some of the textual information, however, is not stored in another program and needs to be stored in the application.

When the loan processor prepares a loan document, he or she should be able to create all the standardized parts of the document without having to type the text. Rather, the standardized text must be inserted by copying it from other objects or programs. After inserting the standardized parts of the document, the user must be able to type the text particular to a specific loan document. Sandra would like a program that will allow the loan processor to create a loan document in a rich text box. This information will come from several sources, as shown in the following list:

- Some information is stored in another text box on the form.

- Some information will be copied to the rich text box by dragging buttons onto the RichTextBox control.

- Some information will be copied to the rich text box by copying the information from other applications, such as Microsoft Word.

In addition to these tasks, Mid State Bank uses complex mathematical computations to compute the current yield on loans and other information. While Visual Basic does not provide intrinsic functions to perform these tasks, Microsoft Excel does. Sandra would like this loan document processing program to start Excel and use it to perform computations. The computations you include in this program will be a prototype for the complex computations loan processors perform on loans.

SESSION

12.1

In this session you will learn how to use the Windows clipboard to copy-and-paste data between objects in your program. You also will learn how to move data between objects using a concept called drag-and-drop.

Analyzing the Program

Sandra already has created the forms for the project and created the objects on each form. These include a splash screen, the main form, and a form to retrieve and display loan payment information. She also has created the NEADT charts for the program, and suggests that you review the design documentation and refer to it as you develop the program. These forms and charts are saved in the Tutorial.12 folder on your Student Disk.

To look at the design specifications for the loan document processing system:

1. Make sure your Student Disk is in the appropriate disk drive. Using Microsoft Word, open the file named **Mid.doc** in the **Tutorial.12** folder on your Student Disk. Otherwise open the file named **Mid.txt** using WordPad.

2. Print the file then exit the word processing program.

As you can see from the NEADT document, the main form contains a rich text box. This object will be used to store the completed loan document. To create the loan document, the loan processor will enter specific information about the client into the rich text box. Then, using the buttons on the form, drag the button into a region of the rich text box causing some predefined text to be placed at the insertion point. The loan processor also will be able to copy and paste text from other sources like Microsoft Word, and other programs.

To open the partially completed loan document processing program:

1. Start Visual Basic and open the project **Mid.vbp** in the **Tutorial.12** folder on your Student Disk.

2. View the form named **frmMidStateBank**. The form should look like Figure 12-1.

Figure 12-1 ◀
Loan
processing
form

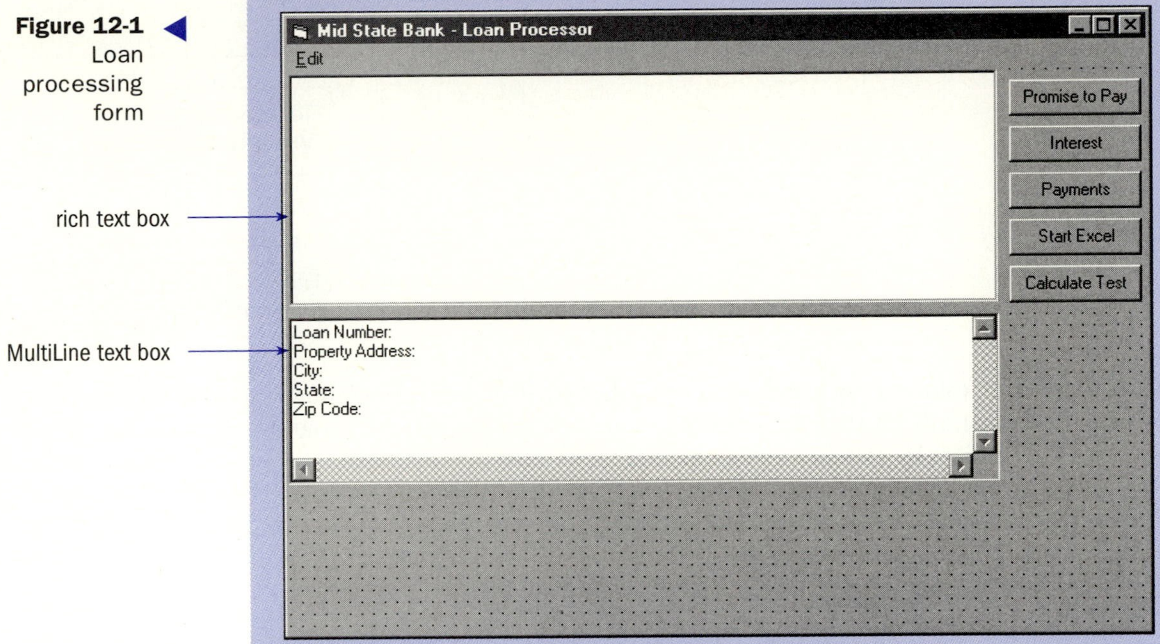

rich text box ———→

MultiLine text box ———→

3. Save a copy of the main form and project using the name **frmMidStateBank.frm** and **Mid State Bank.vbp,** respectively.

As you can see from Figure 12-1, the form contains a rich text box and a text box. The text box at the bottom of the form contains standard text that is used in nearly all the loan documents. Sandra wants the loan processor to be able to select specific text in this text box and copy it to the rich text box without having to type the text again. This is the first task in the project—to write the code that will allow a loan processor to copy text from one text box to another.

Copying and Pasting Data with the Clipboard Object

In addition to providing the loan processor with the capability to cut, copy, and paste data between text boxes on the form, Sandra also wants the program to be able to perform these same functions between different applications. To accomplish this task, you can use the Clipboard object, provided by Visual Basic and Windows 95. One **Clipboard** object is shared by all Windows applications and it allows you to move or copy text and graphics from within an application or between applications. When you copy-and-paste text in programs like Microsoft Word or WordPad, you are using the Windows clipboard. Thus, you can copy text onto the Clipboard object in WordPad, then paste the same text in Microsoft Word or in a text box in your Visual Basic program. You also can supply the same functionality to many different objects in your application including the different types of text boxes. Figure 12-2 illustrates this process.

Figure 12-2 ◀
The Clipboard
object

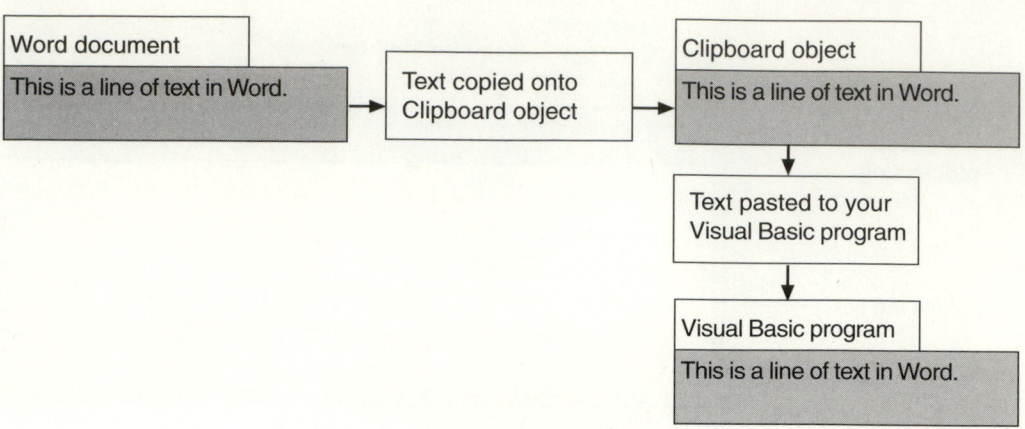

Like the Printer object, the Clipboard object is predefined, so you do not create an instance of the clipboard before it can be used in your program. You use the Clipboard object by calling methods to place text onto the clipboard or remove the existing contents from the clipboard. Before copying any information onto the Clipboard object, you should always remove the existing contents using the Clear method. The Clear method has the following syntax:

Clipboard.Clear

- The **Clear** method removes any text on the Clipboard object.

After calling the Clear method, you can copy selected text onto the clipboard. When the user copies text, he or she does so by highlighting text in an object like a text box or rich text box, then executing a statement that will call the SetText method on the Clipboard object, which has the following syntax:

Clipboard.SetText *data,format*

- The **SetText** method will copy text onto the Clipboard object.

- The required *data* argument contains the string that is copied onto the Clipboard object. You can use selected text from a text box, a variable containing text, or a string literal for this argument.

- Text in the clipboard can be of different formats. For example, you can copy data onto the clipboard using simple text or Rich Text Format. The optional *format* argument contains the format of the text being copied onto the clipboard. If the constant **vbCFRTF** is used, the data is assumed to be in RTF format. If the constant **vbCFText** is used, the data is assumed to be in text format. If no *format* is specified vbCFText is assumed.

Consider the following statements to copy text onto the clipboard:

```
Clipboard.SetText "Text stored on Clipboard"
Clipboard.SetText txtName.Text
Clipboard.SetText txtName.SelText
```

These three statements copy text onto the clipboard. The first stores a literal text string onto the clipboard. The second copies the entire contents of the text box named txtName, and the final statement copies the selected text onto the clipboard. Selected text in a text box is stored in the SelText property of the text box named txtName.

Once text is copied onto the clipboard, it can be inserted or pasted into another object like a text box or rich text box. This is accomplished using the GetText method, which has the following syntax:

Clipboard.GetText (*format*)

- The **GetText** method will return the text string currently stored on the Clipboard object.

- The optional *format* argument contains the format of the text. It can be represented by the same constants used in the SetText method.

When you cut, copy, or paste text in your program, you need to know the control that currently is active (has focus), and the text that currently is selected. To determine the active control, you can use the **Screen** object. The Screen object is used to manipulate forms according to their placement on the screen, and control the mouse pointer outside your application's forms at run time. You can use one of its properties to determine which control currently has focus.

The **ActiveControl** property applies to the Screen object and contains a reference to the control that currently has focus. By using the ActiveControl property of the Screen object, you can access the properties of the underlying control or call its methods. For example, if the active control were a text box, you could read and write the Text property using a string variable and the following statements:

```
pstrTemp = Screen.ActiveControl.Text
Screen.ActiveControl.Text = pstrTemp
```

The first statement reads the text from the active control, and the second statement writes the text to the active control.

> *Tip:* You can use the TypeOf keyword in an If statement to determine the type of the active control. This is useful if you need to perform different actions on different types of controls.

Both the text box and rich text box support properties to determine the text that currently is selected, the first character of the selected text, and the number of characters in the selected text. The SelLength property has the following syntax:

*object.***SelLength** [= *number*]

- The **SelLength** property applies to the text box, masked edit, rich text box, and slider controls. It sets or returns the number of characters selected.

- The *object* can be a text box, masked edit, rich text box, or slider control.

- The *number* argument sets the number of characters selected. The value of *number* must be zero (0) or greater, or a run-time error will occur.

The SelLength property works with the SelStart property. The SelStart property has the following syntax:

object.**SelStart** [= *index*]

- The **SelStart** property is used to identify the first character of the selected text or the insertion point if no text is selected.

- The *object* can be a text box, masked edit, rich text box, or slider control.

- The *index* is a numeric expression that identifies the starting point of the selected text. If you set SelStart to a number greater than the text length, the property is set to the actual text length.

These two properties work in conjunction with the SelText property. The SelText property has the following syntax:

object.**SelText** [= *value*]

- The **SelText** property contains the selected text of the *object*, which can be a text box, masked edit, rich text box, or slider control.

- The *value* is a string expression containing the selected text.

Given a text box named txtExample, you can use the following statements to select text in the text box:

```
txtExample.Text = "Loan Number"
txtExample.SelStart = 0
txtExample.SelLength = 4
Debug.Print txtExample.SelText
```

The first statement sets the Text property of the text box. The second statement marks the first character in the text box as the position of the starting text. Note that the first character has a value of zero (0) and not one (1). The third statement selects four characters. The final statement prints the selected text. Given the above statements, the following text will be printed in the Immediate window:

```
Loan
```

In addition to selecting text with code, the user can mark text by dragging the mouse over specific text. The marked text generally will display in a highlighted color.

Sandra already has created an Edit menu title with three menu items—Cut, Copy, and Paste. These menu items should perform the following functions:

- The Cut menu item should clear the contents of the clipboard, copy the currently selected text to the clipboard, and then remove the selected text from the active control. Removing all the text from the active control can be accomplished by setting the Text property to an empty string. Removing the selected text from the active control can be accomplished by setting the SelText property to an empty string.

- The Copy menu should work just like the Cut menu but the selected text should not be removed from the active control.

- The Paste menu item should copy the text on the clipboard, if any exists, into the active control at the insertion point, if the active control is a text box or rich text box.

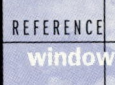

TO CUT OR COPY TEXT ONTO THE CLIPBOARD

- Clear the existing contents of the clipboard using the Clear method.
- Use the SelText property to identify the selected text. Usually, you will use the ActiveControl property of the Screen object to determine the active control.
- Call the SetText method of the Clipboard object to place the selected text onto the Clipboard object.
- If cutting text, set the selected text to an empty string.

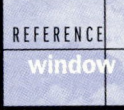

TO PASTE TEXT FROM THE CLIPBOARD

- Call the GetText method of the Clipboard object to retrieve the current text in the clipboard.
- Assign this to the selected text property of the active object using the Screen.ActiveControl property.

Sandra suggests you now write the code to program each of these menu items. You will need to use the ActiveControl property of the Screen object to determine which control has focus. Using the ActiveControl property, you can call the SelText method to reference the selected text in the control. Then you can use the SetText method to copy text onto the clipboard.

To program the Copy, Cut, and Paste menu items:

1. Activate the Code window for the **mnuEditCopy** object's **Click** event procedure for the form named **frmMidStateBank**, and enter the following statements:

```
Private Sub mnuEditCopy_Click( )
    Clipboard.Clear
    Clipboard.SetText Screen.ActiveControl.SelText
End Sub
```

2. Activate the Code window for the **mnuEditCut** object's **Click** event procedure and enter the following statements:

```
Private Sub mnuEditCut_Click( )
    Clipboard.Clear
    Clipboard.SetText Screen.ActiveControl.SelText
    Screen.ActiveControl.SelText = ""
End Sub
```

3. Activate the Code window for the **mnuEditPaste** object's **Click** event procedure and enter the following statements:

```
Private Sub mnuEditPaste_Click( )
    Screen.ActiveControl.SelText = Clipboard.GetText( )
End Sub
```

These three menu items allow the loan processor to cut, copy, and paste text to and from the Windows clipboard:

```
Clipboard.Clear
Clipboard.SetText Screen.ActiveControl.SelText
```

The first statement clears the existing contents of the Windows clipboard. Before copying text onto the clipboard, you always should clear the contents. The second statement uses the ActiveControl property of the Screen object. Remember, this provides a reference to the current control. Then, you used the SelText property to determine the currently selected text. This selected text is copied onto the clipboard using the SetText method.

```
Clipboard.Clear
Clipboard.SetText Screen.ActiveControl.SelText
Screen.ActiveControl.SelText = ""
```

These three statements remove the selected text from the active control and copy it onto the clipboard. First, the contents of the clipboard are cleared. Then the selected text is copied onto the clipboard. Because this is a cut operation, you set the selected text to the null string. This has the effect of removing the selected text from the text box.

```
Screen.ActiveControl.SelText = Clipboard.GetText( )
```

This statement retrieves the current text from the clipboard and pastes it in the currently selected text box. If there is selected text in the active control, it will be replaced by the text on the clipboard. If not, the contents on the clipboard will be pasted into the active control at the insertion point.

> *Tip:* A well-defined standard exists for the shortcut keys pertaining to cut, copy, and paste operations. You always should use Ctrl+X for cut, Ctrl+C for copy, and Ctrl+V for paste. These shortcut keys are common to nearly all Microsoft applications and most others. In this program, however, the paste operation is executed using Ctrl+P. Although this violates the standard, it is necessary because of the built-in characteristics of the rich text box.

The rich text box performs cut, copy, and paste operations for you automatically using the Ctrl+X, Ctrl+C, and Ctrl+V keyboard operations. In other words the functionality is built into the rich text box. Thus, if you select text in another control, copy it onto the clipboard, and paste it onto the rich text box using Ctrl+V, you do not need to write any code in an event procedure. Rather, the paste operation happens automatically. If you used Ctrl+V as the shortcut key for the paste operation in the menu, the contents on the clipboard would be pasted twice—once, when you called the GetText method, and once when the RichTextBox control pasted the contents automatically. To avoid this problem, the shortcut key for the paste operation was set to Ctrl+P in the Menu Editor.

Now that you have programmed these menu items, you should test the program to be sure that the Cut, Copy, and Paste menu items are working correctly. You will test both copying and pasting text from the text box in the application and from Microsoft Word or WordPad.

To test the Cut, Copy, and Paste menu items:

1. Save the project then start it.

2. Click the splash screen to close it and proceed to the main form.

3. Select the text as shown in Figure 12-3.

Figure 12-3 ◀
Testing
clipboard

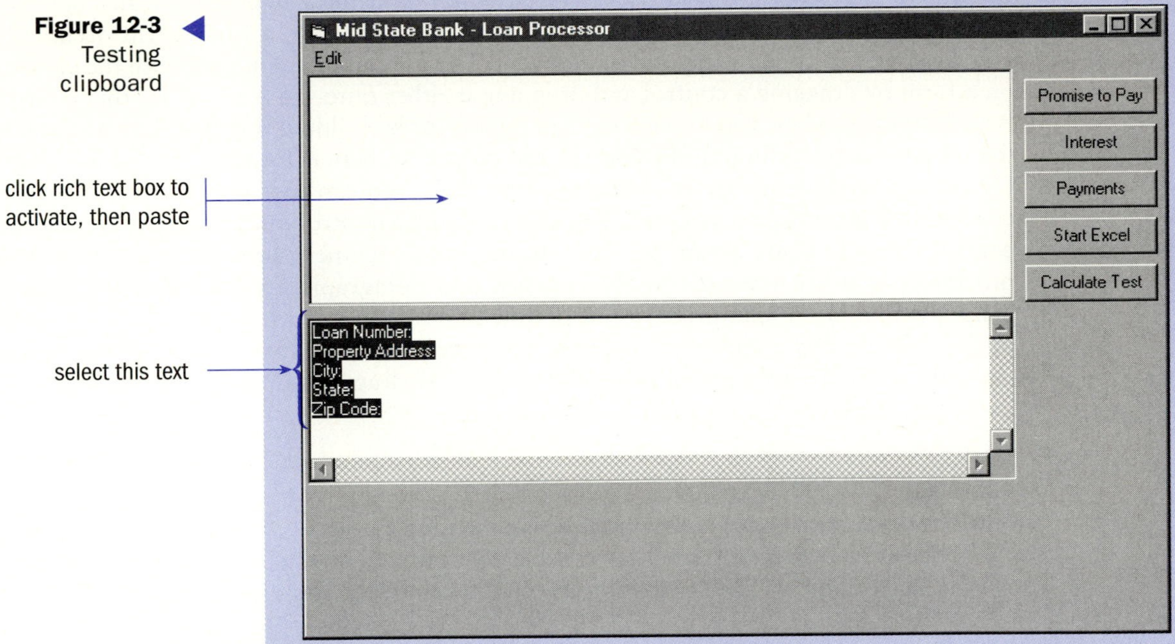

click rich text box to
activate, then paste

select this text

4. Click **Edit** then **Copy** on the form's menu bar.

5. Move the cursor into the rich text box and click the mouse button to activate the object.

6. Click **Edit** then **Paste**. The text should be inserted in the rich text box.

> **TROUBLE?** If the text does not display in the rich text box, make sure the code you wrote for each menu item in the previous steps is correct, then repeat Steps 1 through 6.

7. Start Microsoft Word or WordPad, then enter the following line of text: **Testing the copy and paste operations**.

8. In Word or WordPad select the text then press **Ctrl+C**.

9. Close Word or WordPad without saving the new document.

10. Click the rich text box in your program, then press **Ctrl+V** to paste the text.

The text is inserted in the text box.

11. End the program.

In addition to copying and pasting simple text onto the clipboard, you also can copy and paste pictures onto the clipboard using the SetData and GetData methods. The **SetData** method is used to copy a picture onto the clipboard. The **GetData** method is used to retrieve a picture from the clipboard. These methods support a limited number of graphical image types. You only can store bitmaps, Windows metafiles, device-independent bitmaps, and color palettes.

In addition to copying data between controls using the clipboard, you can use another programming concept called drag-and-drop.

Using Drag-and-Drop

In each of the programs you have written so far, you have interacted with command buttons by clicking them. When you click a command button, a Click event occurs and you have written code to respond to the event. The user also can interact with the controls on a form by dragging a control and dropping it either onto the form or another control. At design time, when you move a control on a form by holding down and then releasing the mouse button, you drag the control and drop it to its new location. It also is possible for the user to drag-and-drop a control at run time. You can drag controls at run time to change their position on the form. You also can drag a control onto the region of another control to cause some action to occur. In the loan document processing program loan processors will use several common phrases and paragraphs in their loan documents. Sandra would like a loan processor to be able to drag a command button onto the region of the rich text box containing the letter, and have predefined text inserted at the current insertion point. To accomplish this task, you can use drag-and-drop. When you use drag-and-drop, there are always two objects involved.

- The **source object** is the object the user drags.

- The **destination object** is the object where the source object is dragged then dropped. The destination object can be any visible object drawn on the form, except for a Line or Shape control. The destination object also can be the form itself.

There are two properties you use to perform drag-and-drop operations on a control. The **DragMode** property controls what happens when the user tries to drag a control.

- When set to **Automatic**, holding down the left mouse button will cause the selected control to be dragged around the screen.

- When set to **Manual**, the default, you must call explicitly the Drag method to begin a drag operation.

When the DragMode property is set to Automatic for objects like command buttons and picture boxes, they do not respond to a Click event. Rather, the user interacts with the control by holding down the left mouse button and dragging the control elsewhere on the form or onto another control.

Sandra suggests you change the DragMode property of the three command buttons labeled Promise to Pay, Interest, and Payments to Automatic and run the program to see the effect of enabling automatic drag-and-drop on these buttons.

To use automatic drag-and-drop for a control:

1. Select the three command buttons named **Promise to Pay**, **Interest**, and **Payments**.

2. Activate the Properties window for the objects. Set the DragMode property to **Automatic**.

3. Save the project then start it.

4. Click the splash screen to close it and proceed to the main form.

5. Hold down the left mouse button on the command button named **Promise to Pay** and drag the control around the form.

An outline of the control displays as you move the control as shown in Figure 12-4.

Figure 12-4
Testing
drag-and-drop

drag this control

outline of control
appears as control
is dragged

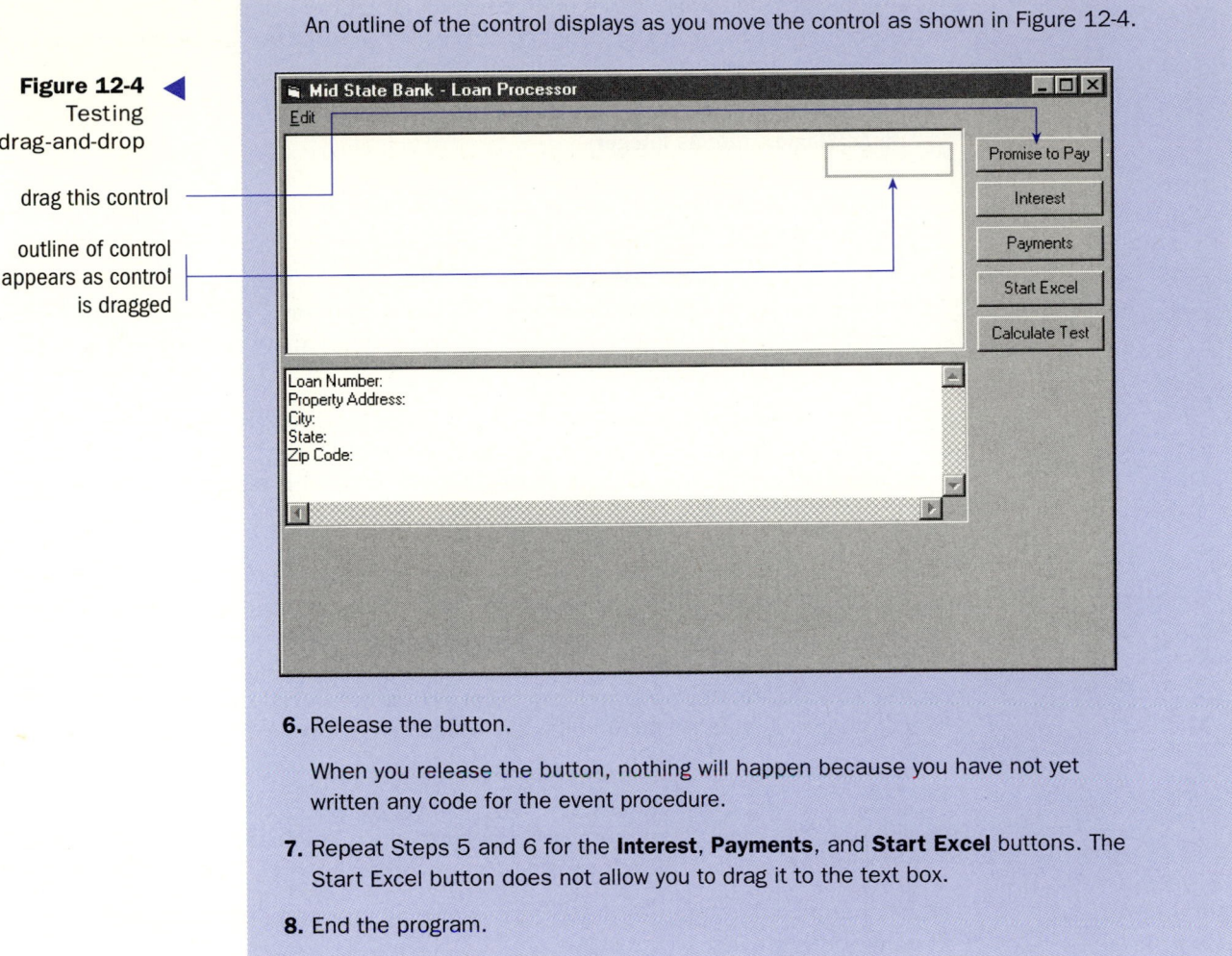

6. Release the button.

   When you release the button, nothing will happen because you have not yet
   written any code for the event procedure.

7. Repeat Steps 5 and 6 for the **Interest**, **Payments**, and **Start Excel** buttons. The
   Start Excel button does not allow you to drag it to the text box.

8. End the program.

The position of the control does not move automatically when you release the mouse
button, nor does any action occur. You must program the events that occur as a button is
dragged and dropped. As a control is dragged across a form or dragged and dropped on a
specific object drawn on the form, two different events occur.

The **DragDrop** event occurs when a control is dragged then dropped over another
object. This event occurs once when the drag-and-drop operation is completed for the target object, that is, when the user releases the mouse button. The syntax differs slightly
depending on whether or not the target object is a form or a control. When the target
object is a form, the event procedure has the following syntax:

Private Sub Form_DragDrop(*source* **As Control**, *x* **As Single**, *y* **As Single**)

- The *source* contains a reference to the control being dragged. You can use this reference to set and read the properties of the source control, and call its methods.

- The *x* and *y* arguments contain a number that specifies the current horizontal (x)
  and vertical (y) position of the mouse pointer on the form, and usually are represented in twips. The upper-left corner of the form has an x coordinate of zero (0),
  and a y coordinate of zero (0).

In addition to the DragDrop event, the DragOver event occurs repeatedly to the destination object as the source object is dragged across the destination object. For example, if
you begin dragging a command button across the form, several DragOver events will
occur for the form as the mouse is moved. When the command button is moved over the

region of another object like a rich text box, then DragOver events occur for the rich text box rather than the form. The DragOver event for a form has a similar syntax as the DragDrop event for a form.

Private Sub Form_DragOver(*source* **As Control**, *x* **As Single**, *y* **As Single**, *state* **As Integer**)

- The *source* contains a reference to the control being dragged. You can use this reference to set and read the properties of the source control, and call its methods.

- The *x* and *y* arguments contain a number that specifies the current horizontal (*x*) and vertical (*y*) position of the mouse pointer on the form, and usually are represented in twips. The upper-left corner of the form has an *x* coordinate of zero (0), and a *y* coordinate of zero (0).

- The *state* argument contains one of three values. If set to zero (0), the source control is being dragged onto the object. If set to one (1), the source control is being dragged off of the object. If set to two (2), the control is being dragged within a region of the object.

Sandra wants the loan processor to be able to customize the form by moving the three drag-and-drop command buttons anywhere on the form where there is no other visible control. Thus, when a command button is dragged to another position on the form, the position of the command button needs to be changed accordingly. To do this, you can write the code for the form's DragDrop event procedure to call the Move method of the selected control. The Move method has the following syntax:

[*object.*]**Move** *left*[, *top*][, *width*][, *height*]

- The optional *object* contains a visible object like a command button that can be repositioned on the screen. If no object is specified, the form with the focus is used.

- The required *left* argument is a Single data type indicating the horizontal coordinate of the left edge of the object.

- The optional *top* argument is a Single data type indicating the vertical coordinate of the top edge of the object.

- The optional *width* argument is used to change the width of the object.

- The optional *height* argument is used to change the height of the object.

To move the command button named cmdInterest when it is dropped on the form, you could use the following statement in the form's DragDrop event procedure:

```
cmdInterest.Move X,Y
```

If you use this statement, the upper-left corner of the control is positioned at the current mouse location as shown in Figure 12-5.

Figure 12-5
Moving a
control (1)

upper-left corner of
control placed at
mouse pointer

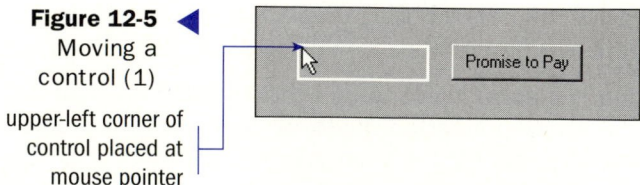

You can solve the problem using the Height and Width properties of the command button to position the control using the following statement:

```
cmdInterest.Move (X — Source.Width / 2), _
    ( Y — Source.Height / 2)
```

This statement centers the button on the cursor. Figure 12-6 shows how this statement works.

Figure 12-6 ◄
Moving a
control (2)

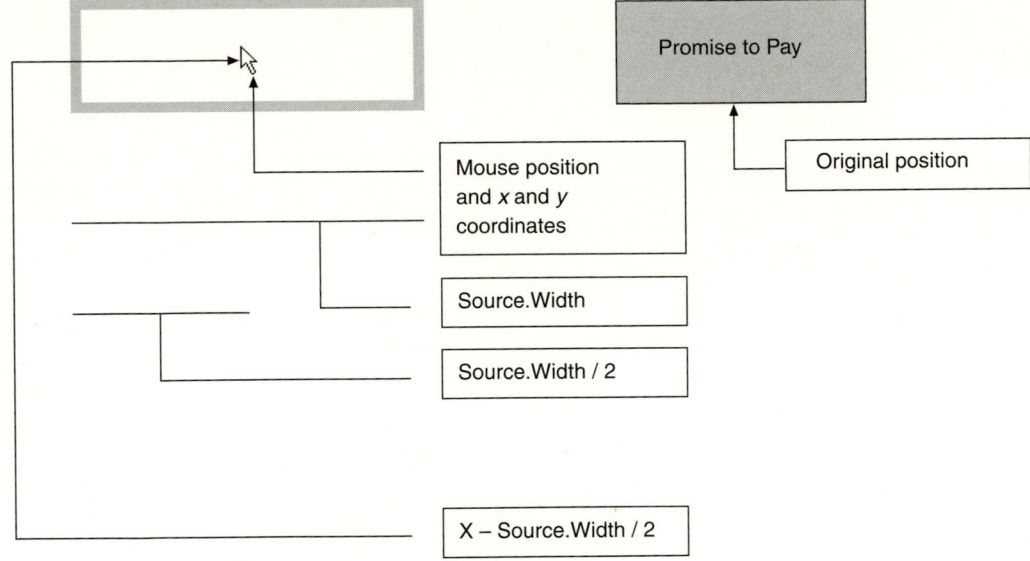

You now can write the statement to move the command buttons to where they are dropped on the form. This statement needs to be executed when a command button is dropped on the form. Thus, you need to write the code in the form's DragDrop event procedure. The statement must change the visible position of the control on the form.

To move a control on a form:

1. Activate the Code window for the form **frmMidStateBank's DragDrop** event procedure.

2. Enter the following statement:

```
Private Sub Form_DragDrop(Source As Control, X As Single,
     Y As Single)
          Source.Move X - Source.Width / 2, Y - Source.Height / 2
End Sub
```

The Private Sub statement in your Code window will display on one line. When the program is run, the DragOver event will occur for the form, as a source object is moved across it. When the user releases the mouse button, the DragDrop event will occur and the selected control will be moved to the new position on the form. Note that if you move the control over another object like the rich text box and release the mouse button, nothing will happen because you have not yet programmed the DragOver or DragDrop event procedures for this object.

Sandra suggests you now test the program to be sure the loan processor can move the applicable controls around on the form.

To test that you can move controls:

1. Save the project then start it. Then click the splash screen to close it and proceed to the main form.

2. Drag the top three command buttons to different locations on the form.

As the mouse is moved, the control visually follows the mouse on the form. When released, the button's position is moved.

3. Drag one of the three command buttons over the rich text box.

The command button does not move to the new location because you have not programmed the rich text box to respond to the DragDrop event.

4. End the program.

In addition to moving controls on a form, Sandra wants loan processors to be able to use these controls to insert standardized text into the rich text box. This will save them considerable typing time. Thus, when a loan processor drags a control over text in the rich text box and releases the mouse, the specified text must be placed into the rich text box at the current insertion point. To accomplish this task, you need to program the DragDrop event for the rich text box to insert the text. The DragOver and DragDrop events for controls have a slightly different syntax than they do for forms. These events have the same arguments as they do for a form except the index argument allows you to program a control array:

Private Sub *object*_**DragOver**([*index* **As Integer,**]*source* **As Control,**

   x **As Single,** *y* **As Single,** *state* **As Integer**)

Private Sub *object*_**DragDrop**([*index* **As Integer,**]*source* **As Control,**

   x **As Single,** *y* **As Single**)

- The *object* is the destination object. It can be any text box, rich text box, image, or other object supporting the DragOver and DragDrop events. Nearly all visible objects support these events.

- If the control is a member of a control array, the *index* argument is used to contain the index of the destination control.

- The *source* control is the control being dragged.

- The *x* and *y* arguments contain a number that specifies the current horizontal (x) and vertical (y) position of the mouse pointer on the form, and usually are represented in twips. The upper-left corner of the form has an *x* coordinate of zero (0), and a *y* coordinate of zero (0).

When the button is dragged into the rich text box, the loan document processing program needs to place the text at the insertion point. You will use the DragDrop event procedure of the rich text box to accomplish this task. Depending on which command button is being dropped, you need to place different text into the rich text box at the insertion point. You can write a Select Case statement in the DragDrop event procedure that will insert different text based on the value of the event's source argument.

Sandra already created a form-level array to store the text for each text box. The array is named mstrParagraphs, is zero-based, and contains three elements—one paragraph of text for each command button used in drag-and-drop operations. Each array element contains standard text corresponding to repayment information, payment of interest, and when payments are to be made. She suggests you write the necessary statements to insert this text into the rich text box depending on which command button is dragged.

To insert the text into the rich text box:

1. Activate the Code window to the **DragDrop** event for the object named **rtbLoan**.

2. Enter the following statements into the event procedure:

```
Select Case source.Name
    Case "cmdRepayment"
        rtbLoan.SelText = mstrParagraphs(0)
    Case "cmdInterest"
        rtbLoan.SelText = mstrParagraphs(1)
    Case "cmdPayments"
        rtbLoan.SelText = mstrParagraphs(2)
End Select
```

The Select Case statement uses the Name property of the source argument. This has the effect of referencing the Name property of the control being dropped on the rich text box. Each Case represents a specific command button. Depending on the command button selected, the text in the corresponding array element is stored in the SelText property. This has the effect of displaying the text in the array at the insertion point in the rich text box.

Your program now will copy text into the rich text box when a command button is dragged into the rich text box. You should test the code you just wrote to be sure that the drag-and-drop operations are working correctly.

To test the drag-and-drop operations for the rich text box:

1. Save the project then start it. Then click the splash screen to close it and proceed to the main form.

2. Drag the **Promise to Pay** command button in the rich text box. The text should display as shown in Figure 12-7.

Figure 12-7 ◀
Drag-and-drop (1)

text dropped from
Promise to Pay
command button

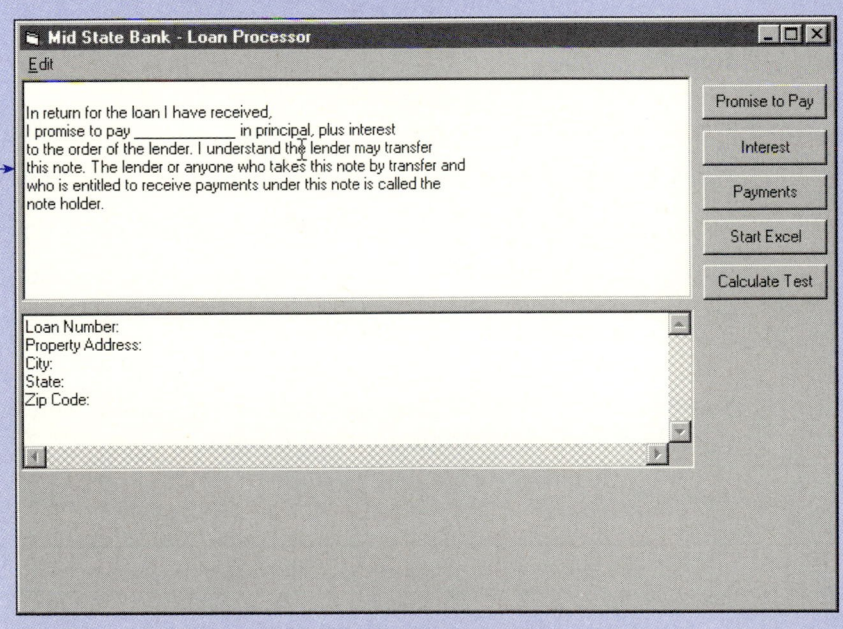

3. Drag the **Interest** command button in the rich text box.

4. Drag the **Payments** command button in the rich text box.

5. Scroll down the rich text box so the third paragraph is visible. Your form should look like Figure 12-8.

Figure 12-8 ◄
Drag-and-
drop (2)

text dropped
from Interest
command button

text dropped
from Payments
command button

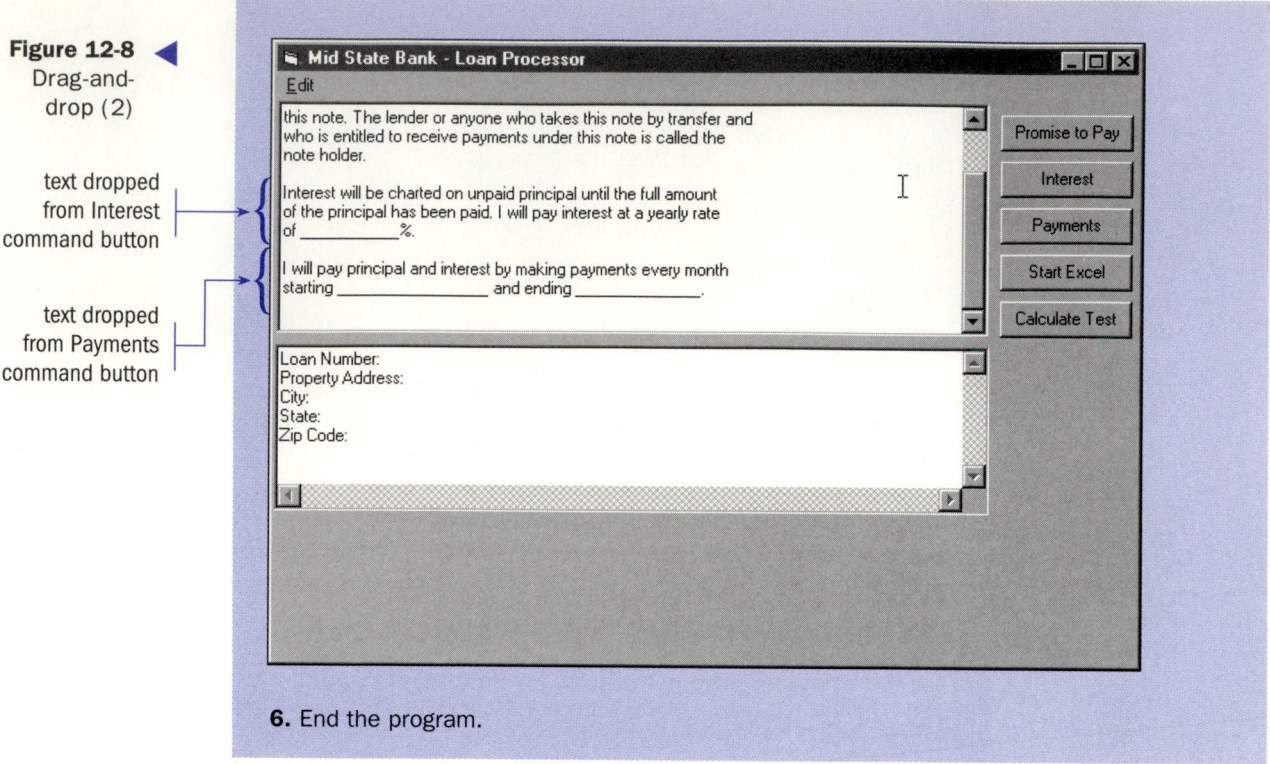

6. End the program.

Your program now can move and copy text using the clipboard. In addition you can paste text from one control to another using drag-and-drop operations.

Quick Check

1. What are the methods you use to copy-and-paste text to and from the Clipboard object?

2. What is the purpose of the ActiveControl property as it pertains to the Screen object?

3. What are the standard shortcut key combinations to cut, copy, and paste text?

4. What is the purpose of the source and destination objects as they pertain to drag-and-drop?

5. What is the difference between the DragOver and DragDrop events?

You have completed the programming for this session. You now may exit Visual Basic and take a break or continue to the next session.

SESSION

12.2

In this session you will make your program communicate with other programs using Object Linking and Embedding technology.

Linking to Objects from Other Programs

Using Windows 95, you are accustomed to programs and their data interacting with each other. This has not always been the case. When you used a personal computer before the advent of Windows, you would run a program and perform one task, like word processing. If you needed to insert some data from a spreadsheet, you would exit the word processing program, start the spreadsheet program, save the information from the spreadsheet in a file format understood by both programs, exit the spreadsheet, restart the word processing program, then insert the new file containing the data.

Programs are no longer islands. You already have seen how Visual Basic can communicate with data stored in an Access database using DAO. Using DAO objects is one method of using Object Linking and Embedding.

Object Linking and Embedding (OLE) is a technology that allows multiple programs to access the data of another program using a standardized interface. Your program can interact with any object that supports a technology called OLE. When you accessed DAO objects, you did so using the DAO object hierarchy. This hierarchy is a standardized interface made up of collections and objects having properties and methods. Using the object hierarchies of other programs, it is possible for your Visual Basic program to interact with a chart or worksheet created in Microsoft Excel or a document from Microsoft Word. Many other programs support similar object hierarchies. There are different ways your program can interact with the objects of another program.

- You can use another Visual Basic control called the OLE Container control and its properties and methods, either at design time or run time, to establish a connection with Word documents and Excel worksheets using the visual interface of Word or Excel.

- Many programs expose themselves as a set of objects, much in the same way as the DAO hierarchy is an exposed set of objects. Both Word and Excel allow you to perform operations on their data using a set of hierarchical exposed objects. You can write code to operate on this data by calling methods and setting properties. For example, you can create a document in Word or a worksheet in Excel by writing code. Your program can choose whether or not to display a visual interface. That is, you can create, edit, print, and perform other operations on these objects without the user seeing an active window on the screen.

First, you will learn how to interact with other programs using the OLE Container control, then learn how to access their objects by writing code. There are two ways to insert another program's data into your program with the OLE Container control.

Creating a Linked Object

You can link another program's data to your program by creating a linked object. A **linked object** is a file that is linked, along with the program that operates on the file, to your program through the OLE Container control. When you create a linked object, you are not inserting the program's data into your application. Rather you store in your program a reference to the data. When you create a linked object, the file also can be linked by other applications. For example, if you created a link to a Word document, other programs could create links to the same document.

Depending on the property settings of the OLE Container control, the user can click or double-click the region of the control to start an instance of the application that contains the linked document. For example, if you create a linked Word document, clicking the OLE Container control at run time will cause Word to be started and the specified document displayed. Thus, if the document is deleted or moved from its specified location on your computer, the link will not function properly. Trying to click the OLE Container control to start the application and load the linked file will cause a run-time error. Figure 12-9 shows the process of linking a Word document to your program.

Figure 12-9 ◀
Creating a
linked object

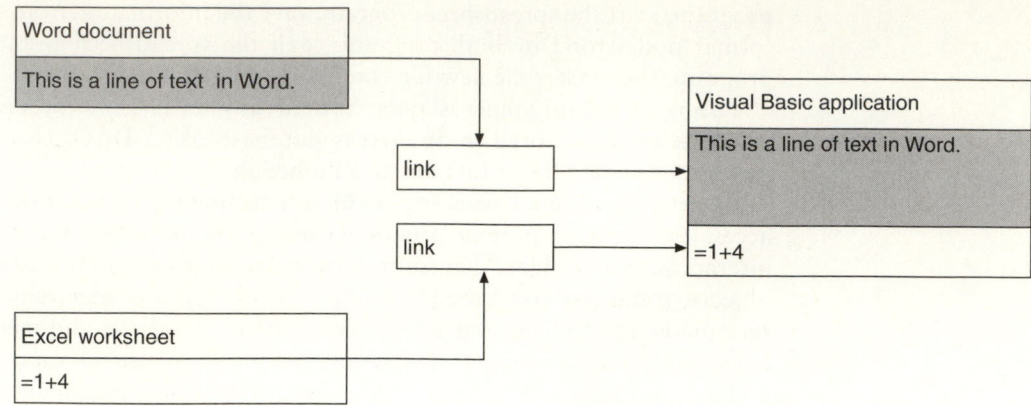

As shown in Figure 12-9, there are two linked objects: one Word document and one Excel worksheet. Each of the linked objects exists as a separate file on the disk.

You also can create embedded objects. An **embedded object** is stored as data in the OLE container rather than in another program. Thus, only the program that created the embedded object can use that object. When you create an embedded object, the data is embedded in the OLE Container control, along with the program that operates on the data. Data embedded in the OLE Container control is saved using the properties and methods of the OLE Container control. Figure 12-10 shows an embedded object.

Figure 12-10 ◀
An embedded
object

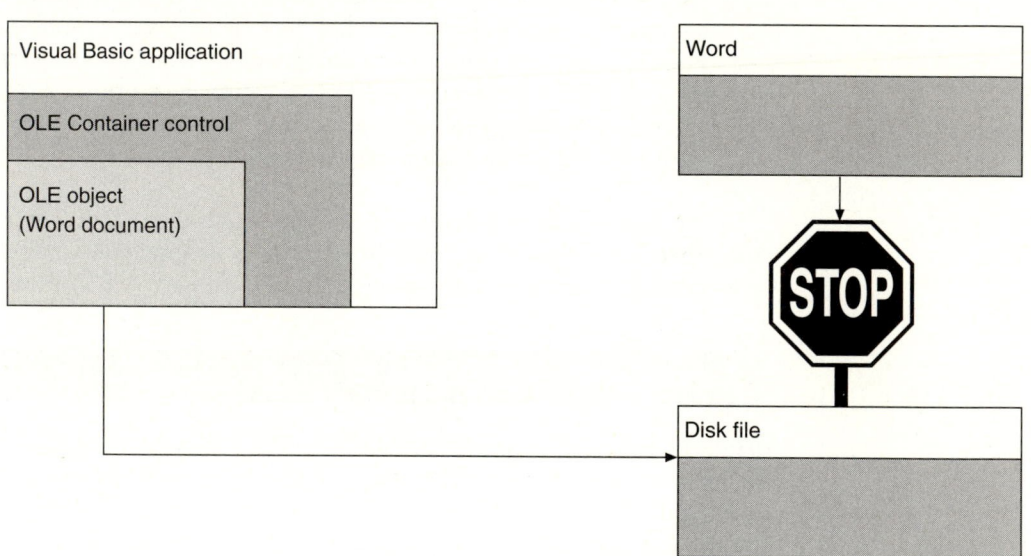

Figure 12-10 shows a Visual Basic application with an OLE Container control. This OLE container has an embedded Word object. Any other programs, including Microsoft Word, cannot use the data in this OLE container.

When you create programs using OLE technology, there exists an OLE client and an OLE server.

- The **OLE server** is a program like Microsoft Word or Microsoft Excel that allows other programs to access its objects. For example, both Word and Excel have an object hierarchy much like the DAO object hierarchy. You can access those objects programmatically just like you can access the objects in the DAO hierarchy.

- The **OLE client** is a program that uses the exposed objects of another program like Word or Excel. When you use the OLE Container control in your program, the control behaves as an OLE client.

Using the OLE Container Control

When you use the OLE Container control, you can link or embed another program's objects either at design time or at run time. The OLE Container control only can display one object from one application at a time. If you need to create a link to multiple objects or multiple applications at the same time, you can create multiple instances of the OLE Container control on the same form or a different form, just like any other control.

When the OLE Container control is drawn on the form, the Insert Object dialog box is displayed automatically, allowing you to create a linked or embedded object at design time.

Sandra has another file containing a list of standardized phrases. She wants the loan processor to be able to display this file using Microsoft Word, then be able to copy-and-paste the contents of the file into the rich text box already drawn on the form. Because this file already exists and needs to be used by other applications, you will create a linked object. You will use the Insert Object dialog box to link the file.

To create a linked object at design time:

1. Click the **OLE** control 🔲 in the toolbox. Draw an instance of the OLE Container control on the form as shown in Figure 12-11.

Figure 12-11 ◄
Creating an
OLE Container
control

new OLE Container
control

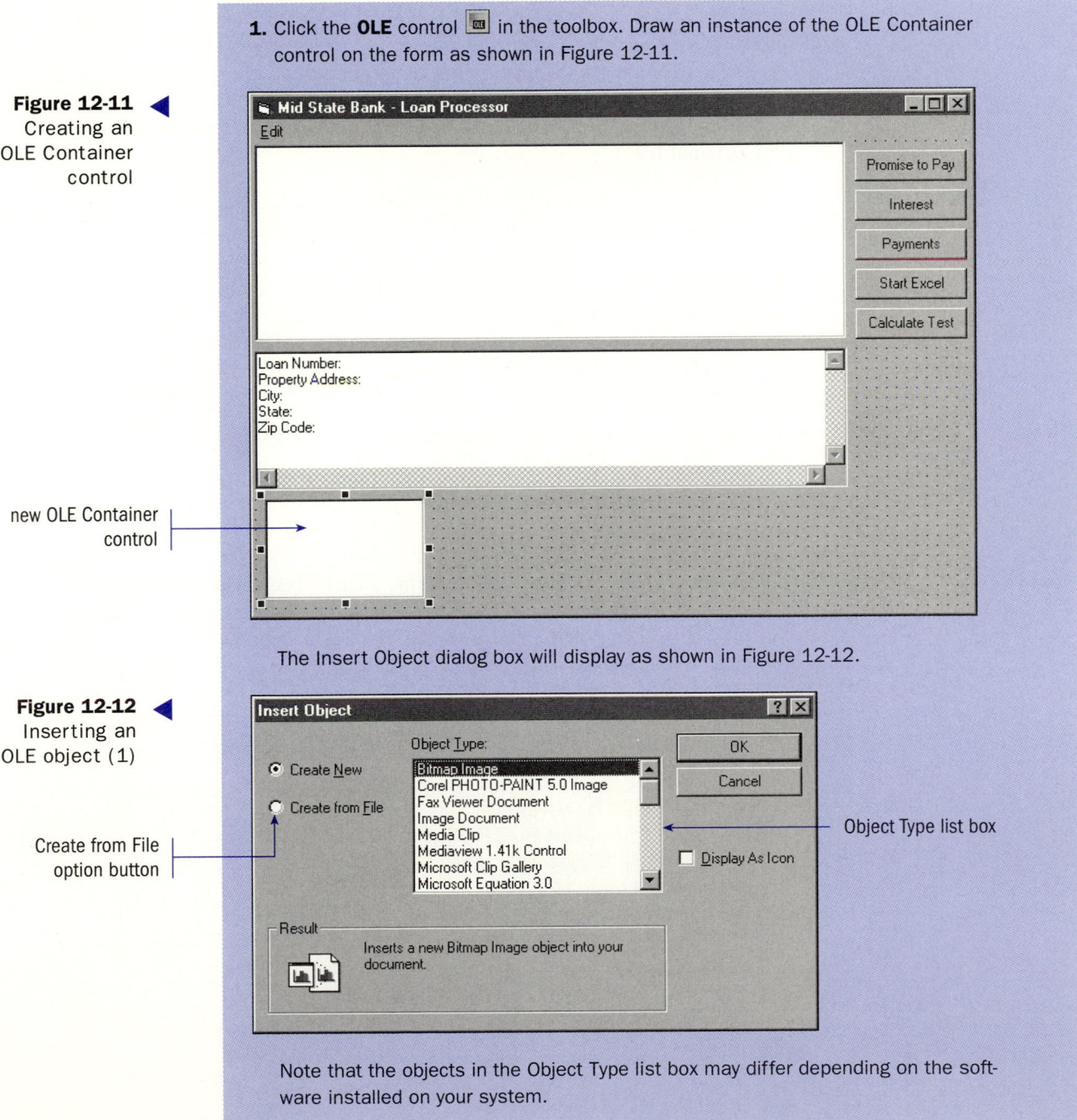

The Insert Object dialog box will display as shown in Figure 12-12.

Figure 12-12 ◄
Inserting an
OLE object (1)

Create from File
option button

Object Type list box

Note that the objects in the Object Type list box may differ depending on the software installed on your system.

As shown in Figure 12-12, the Insert Object dialog box contains the Object Type list box that lists each of the available object types. This list will vary depending on the configuration of your system. Many programs like Corel PHOTO-PAINT and others support OLE. Each program that supports OLE is displayed in this list box. The names in the list box are descriptive names, which correspond to actual class names. For a class to be usable as an OLE object it must be properly registered on the system. This means there must be an entry in the system registry for the class. The system registry is a service maintained by the Windows operating system to keep track of the different programs and devices installed on the system. The object type only is used when you create a new embedded object.

In addition to the Object Type list box, there are two option buttons:

- The **Create New** option button creates an embedded object. You will learn about embedded objects later in the tutorial.

- The **Create from File** option button is used to create a linked or embedded object from an existing file on the disk. For example, you can use the OLE Container control to create a link to a Word document or an Excel worksheet. If you create a linked file, any changes the user makes to the linked file are stored in the file itself. If you create an embedded file, a copy of the existing file is made and stored as an object in the OLE Container control. Changes made to the file will not be reflected in the original file.

Completing the Insert Object dialog box sets several properties for you. You also can set these properties at design time using the Properties window, or at run time using code.

- The **Class** property is used with embedded objects. When you create a new embedded object using the Insert Object dialog box, the Class property is set for you. Each object type you can insert is a member of a class. This is somewhat analogous to the Class module you created in the previous tutorial.

- The **SourceDoc** property is used only when an object is created from a file. It is set to the full path and filename of the data file to be used.

- The **SourceItem** property is used to specify a range of data within the source document. For example, to view only a range of cells in an Excel worksheet, you can set the SourceItem property.

Finally, the Insert Object dialog box contains a check box labeled Display As Icon. By default, when you insert a linked object in the OLE Container control, an image of the data is displayed in the control. You also can display an icon of the program using the data in the OLE Container control. Which to use depends on your application.

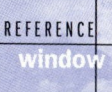

REFERENCE window	**CREATING A LINKED OBJECT AT DESIGN TIME**
	■ Draw an OLE Container control on the form. The Insert Object dialog box is displayed.
	■ Select the Create from File option button.
	■ Click the Browse button and select the file you want in the dialog box.
	■ Click the Link check box.
	■ Click the Display As Icon check box to display an icon of the program in the OLE Container control, if desired.
	■ Click OK to create the linked object.

Sandra would like the linked object to display as an icon on the form at run time. Also, she would like the icon to display on the form such that it does not look to the user like the icon is displayed inside the region of the OLE Container control. To accomplish this, you can set properties using the Properties window to control the appearance of the OLE Container control so you cannot see it.

To set the properties to create and display the linked object:

1. Click the **Create from File** option button to create an object from an existing file saved on the disk. The Insert Object dialog box will change options as shown in Figure 12-13.

Figure 12-13 ◀
Inserting an
OLE object (2)

click Browse to
locate file named
MidLoan.doc

click Link to link file

click Display As Icon
to display an icon in
OLE Container control

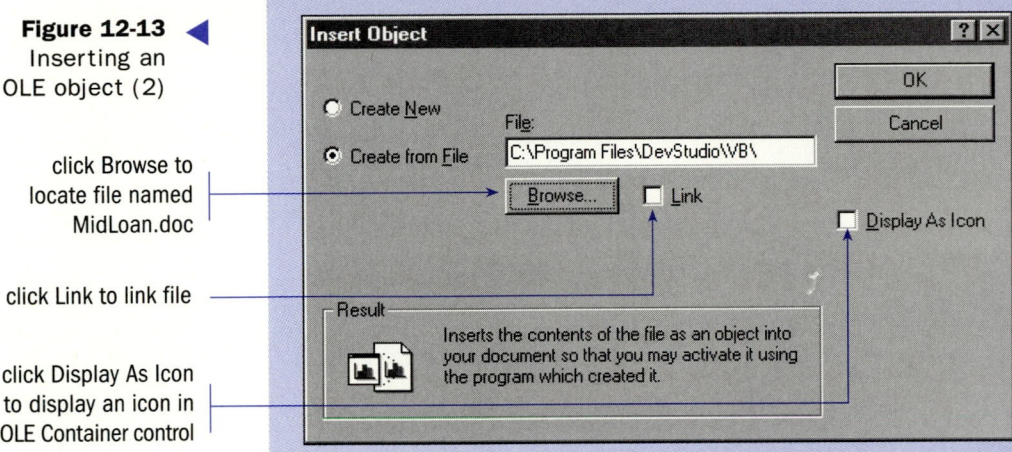

2. Click the **Browse** button to open the Browse dialog box.

3. Locate the file named **MidLoan.doc** in the **Tutorial.12** folder on your Student Disk.

4. Click the **Link** check box to create a linked object.

5. Click the **Display As Icon** check box to display the Microsoft Word icon in the OLE Container control instead of an image of the document.

6. Click **OK** to close the Insert Object dialog box.

7. Open the Properties window for the OLE Container control.

8. Set the BorderStyle property to **0 - None** and the BackStyle property to **0 - Transparent**. Your form should look like Figure 12-14.

Figure 12-14 ◀
Linked OLE
object

icon appears in OLE
Container control

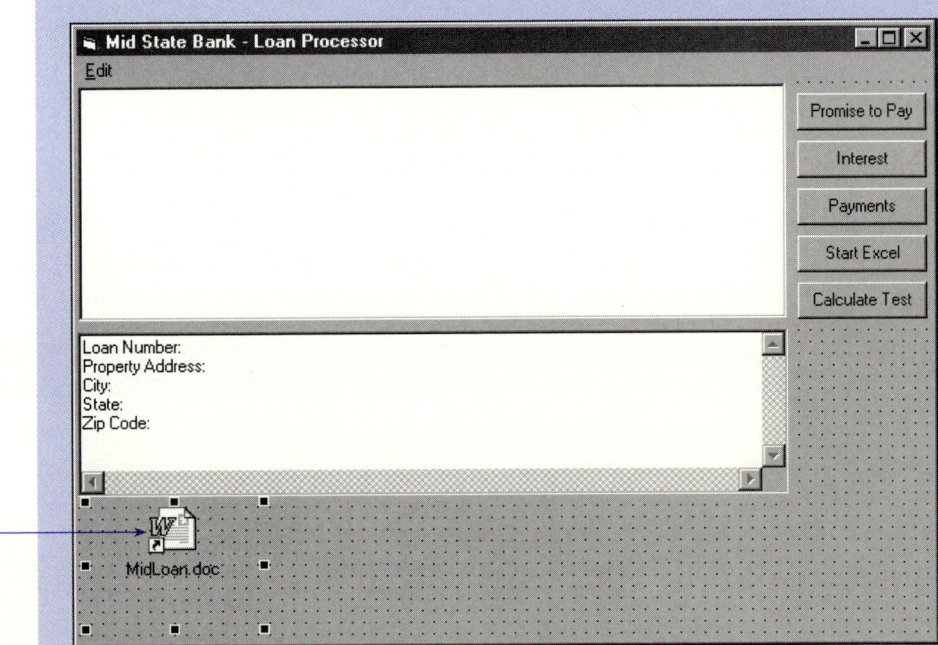

9. Save the project then start it.

10. Click the splash screen to close it and proceed to the main form.

11. Double-click the Microsoft Word icon in the OLE Container control. Word will start and the file will be loaded.

   TROUBLE? If you do not have Microsoft Word on your system, the program will not run, and a run-time error may occur. If another program like WordPad is started, it probably is because either Word does not exist on your system, or because files with a ".doc" extension are bound to a different program like WordPad. If you receive an error message indicating that the component is not registered, contact the administrator of your computer.

12. Click and drag the **mouse** over the first paragraph in the Word document to high-light it, then press **Ctrl+C** to copy the highlighted contents onto the clipboard.

13. Click the rich text box in your program, then click **Edit** then **Paste** on the form's menu bar to paste the contents of the clipboard in the rich text box as shown in Figure 12-15.

Figure 12-15 ◄
Testing linked
object

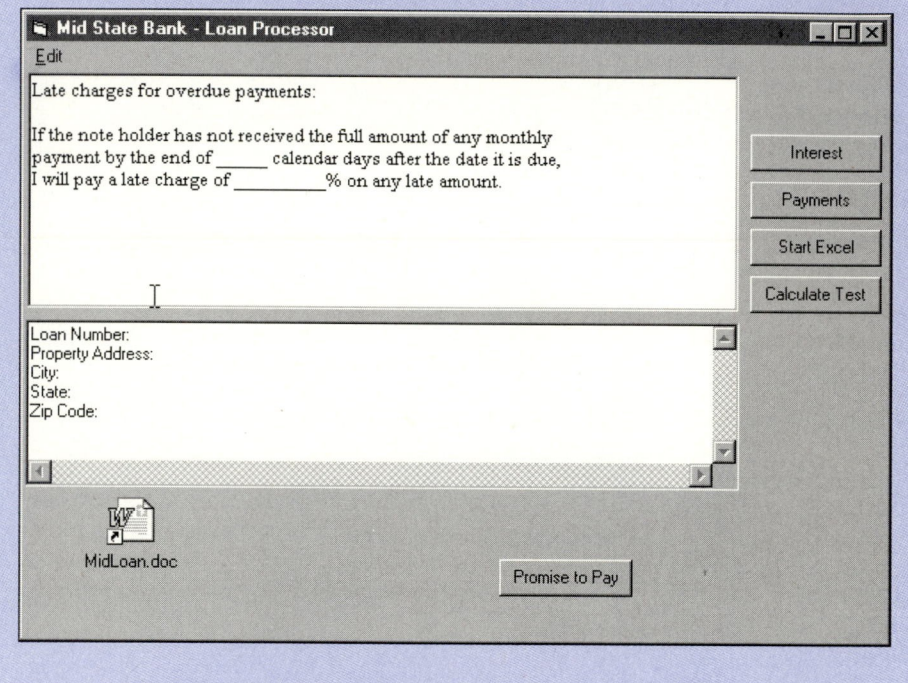

14. End the project then exit Word.

At run time, when the user clicks the OLE Container control, the file will be loaded into a copy of Word running in its own window. Note that if a copy of Word already is running, that copy will be used and the document loaded into a new document window.

Creating Embedded Objects

In addition to creating a linked object, you also can create an embedded object. When you create an embedded object, the data is maintained in the OLE Container control along with the application. When you create an embedded object, which is based on an existing file, a copy of the data is made and stored in the OLE Container control. The control contains a binary image of the data file. All binary data for a control, like the PictureBox, Image, and OLE container is stored in a file with the extension ".frx". When the form is loaded, these contents will be displayed in the OLE Container control.

Any changes you make to the embedded object are not reflected in the original file. If the original file is removed from the system, the file copy will continue to be displayed. You do not save the file using the Save and Save As commands on the File menu of the OLE server application. When you start Word or Excel with an embedded object, their menus are changed such that you can save a copy of the file that Word or other programs can read independently of your program. You cannot use the Save and Save As commands as you usually do, however. To save changes to the embedded object in the OLE Container control, you need to call the SaveToFile and ReadFromFile methods of the OLE Container control.

The OLE Container control can display a shortcut menu at run time. The menu will vary depending on the actions supported by the object. These actions are called verbs. A **verb** is a way of communicating with an OLE object, asking the object to perform an action. Common actions are tasks like opening a file or editing a file.

Whether or not the OLE container will display a list of verbs applicable to the object depends on the setting of the AutoVerbMenu property. The **AutoVerbMenu** property applies to the OLE Container control. It can have the following values:

- If set to **True** then a shortcut menu will display in the control (when activated), and display a list of the verbs applicable to the object when the right mouse button is clicked.

- If set to **False** no shortcut menu is displayed.

Sandra would like the loan processor to be able to start an instance of Microsoft Excel so they can perform calculations by entering numbers into the visual interface. When you use programs like Word and Excel, you either can access their objects with code or use Word and Excel windows. This is referred to as the **visual interface**. The loan processors will not use Excel to save existing files, or create any files at all. Rather it will be used only to perform temporary calculations.

Because there is no file, you cannot create a linked object from a file, rather you need to create a new embedded object. You can accomplish this by drawing another OLE Container control on the form and setting its properties. Again you set the OLE container's properties by completing the Insert Object dialog box.

To create an embedded link to Microsoft Excel:

1. Create an OLE Container control as shown in Figure 12-16.

Figure 12-16 ◀
Embedded OLE
object

new embedded
OLE object

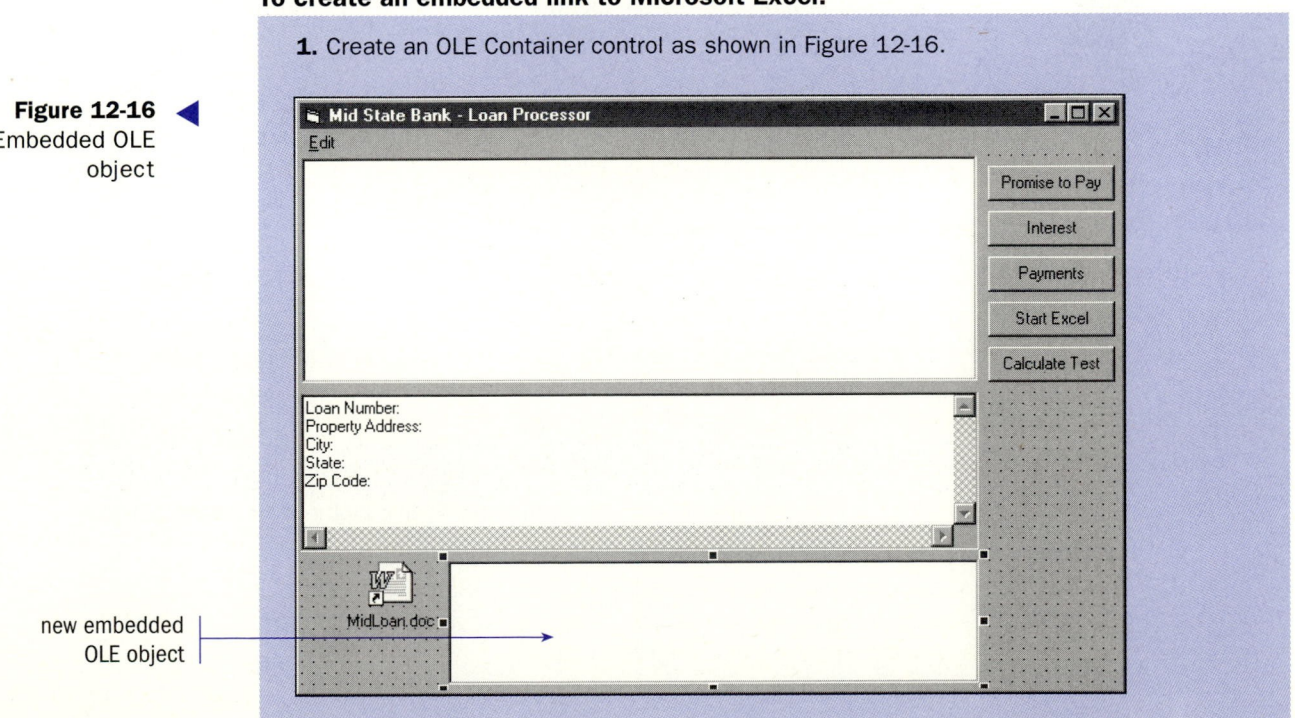

2. When the Insert Object dialog box displays, make sure the **Create New** option button is clicked.

3. Using the scroll bars in the list box, locate the item **Microsoft Excel Worksheet**, then click the **OK** button to insert the object. Note that when the Excel object is drawn inside the OLE Container control, the size may be different than the OLE Container control itself. The menu bar on your form displays several other menus. These are the Excel menus.

4. Activate the **Properties** window for the object. The AutoVerbMenu property is set to **True**. This will allow you to use the OLE object's verbs.

Your program now should start Excel when the control is activated. Because Excel supports different verbs, you will be able to click the right mouse button to determine how the Excel program is activated. Excel supports verbs to open Excel in its own window or inside the region of the OLE Container control.

When you display an embedded object inside the region of an OLE Container control, the behavior of your form's menu system will change slightly. Remember, most applications, including Excel, have a menu bar just like a form in your program. Excel's menu bar must be displayed on the form so the user has access to its menu items. How the OLE server application's menus interact with your menus depend on the setting of the **NegotiatePosition** property in the Menu Editor.

- If set to **0 - None**, the default, the form's menu is not displayed on the menu bar while the OLE Container control is active.

- If set to **1 - Left**, the form's menu is displayed at the left end of the menu bar while the OLE Container control is active. Note that it is possible for a menu title on the form to have the same caption as a menu title application being referenced by the OLE Container control.

- If set to **2 - Middle**, the form's menu is displayed in the middle of the menu bar when the OLE Container control is active.

- If set to **3 - Right**, the form's menu is displayed at the right end of the menu bar when the OLE Container control is active.

Sandra already has set the NegotiatePosition property so the Excel menus will display to the right of the Edit menu title on your form. She suggests you now test the code you just wrote to be sure that Excel is being started correctly.

To test the embedded Excel object:

1. Save the project then start it. Click the splash screen to close it and proceed to the main form.

2. Click the **OLE Container control** for Excel. Then click the **right mouse button** to display the shortcut menu, then click **Edit**. Excel starts. The Excel menus display to the right of your program's menu bar.

3. Click the **rich text box** to deactivate the OLE Container control.

Click the **OLE Container control** for Excel again. Then click the **right mouse button**, then click **Open**. Excel displays in its own window.

4. Click the **File** menu on the Excel title bar. The options on the menu are configured such that you can save a copy of the file, but not the file itself. This is because you are working with an embedded object.

5. Click **Exit** to close the worksheet and exit Excel.

6. End the project.

In addition to creating linked and embedded objects at design time, you also can create them at run time.

Creating Linked and Embedded Objects at Run Time

To create linked and embedded objects at run time, you can call different methods of the OLE Container control. The CreateEmbed and CreateLink methods create embedded and linked objects at run time. The **CreateEmbed** method has the following syntax:

object.**CreateEmbed** *sourcedoc*[, *class*]

- The *object* must be an OLE Container control.

- The required *sourcedoc* argument either can be the filename of a document to be used as a template or if no document is to be specified, the argument must be a zero-length string (" ").

- The optional *class* argument identifies the class name of the embedded object. You can use the Properties window and select the Value column for the Class property to determine the available classes on your computer. The different classes may vary depending on the software installed on your computer.

To create linked objects at run time, you use the **CreateLink** method that has the following syntax:

object.**CreateLink** *sourcedoc*[, *sourceitem*]

- The *object* must be an OLE Container control.

- The required *sourcedoc* argument must contain the filename from which the object is created.

- The optional *sourceitem* argument references specific data within the filename to be linked. The format of this argument varies depending on the application.

Prior to using an embedded object created at run time, you must open it for an operation like editing. This is accomplished by calling the DoVerb method after creating the embedded object with the following syntax:

object.**DoVerb** *verb*

- The **DoVerb** method applies to the OLE Container control. The *object* must be a valid instance of the OLE Container control. The OLE server for the embedded object you create generally supports a number of actions. You can perform these actions by calling the DoVerb method on the OLE Container control.

- The required *verb* argument contains the action to be performed. Each object can support a unique set of verbs. There are, however, several standard verbs that each OLE Container control should support.

There are several constants to represent the different standard verbs that should be supported by all objects. The following list describes the more common constant values:

- If set to the constant **vbOLEOpen**, then the object is opened in its own window rather than inside the region of the OLE Container control. Generally, this window displays with its own title and menu bars.

■ If set to the constant **vbOLEUIActivate**, then the object displays inside the region of the OLE Container control. The menu items applicable to the embedded or linked object will display in the form's menu bar.

Sandra would like you to practice by creating an embedded Excel object at run time rather than at design time. This object, instead of displaying in its own window, should display inside the region of the OLE Container control.

Sandra suggests you remove the existing Excel object and use the second OLE Container control to create an embedded object at run time. The code to create the embedded object will be executed when the corresponding command button is clicked.

To create an embedded Excel object at run time and test it:

1. Click the **right mouse button** on the OLE Container control, then select **Delete Embedded Object** on the shortcut menu to delete the existing Excel object.

2. Activate the Code window for the **Click** event procedure for the command button named **cmdEmbedExcel**.

3. Enter the following statements into the Code window:

```
Private Sub cmdEmbedExcel_Click( )
    OLE2.CreateEmbed "", "Excel.Sheet"
    OLE2.DoVerb vbOLEUIActivate
End Sub
```

The first statement creates an embedded Excel object in the OLE Container control. The object is activated when the DoVerb method is called. The Verb vbOLEUIActivate is the Excel verb to cause Excel to be activated in place.

4. Save the project then start it. Click the splash screen to close it and proceed to the main form.

5. Click the **Start Excel** command button. The menu bar changes to display the Excel menus and the Excel object will display in the OLE Container control as shown in Figure 12-17.

Figure 12-17 ◀
Embedded OLE
Excel object

Excel menu ——

Excel object in OLE
Container control

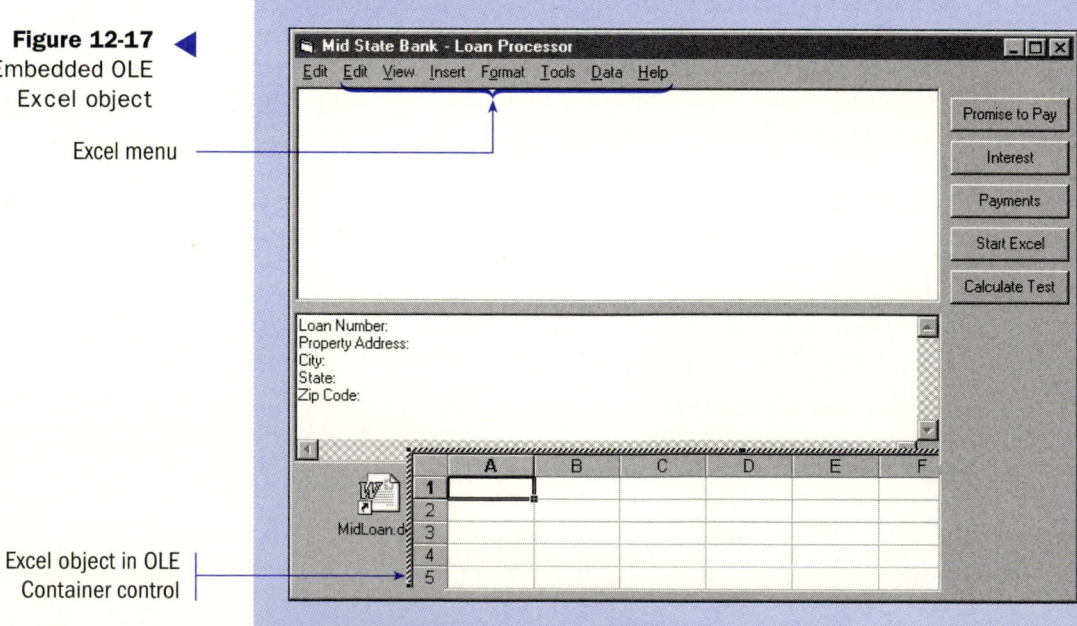

6. Click the rich text box, to deactivate the embedded object. Note the menu on the form returns to its normal appearance.

7. End the project.

In addition to the user interacting directly with an OLE object through its visual interface, you also can write programs that work with OLE objects by writing code.

Programming Another Application's Objects

In addition to interacting with an application using the OLE Container control, your Visual Basic program can interact with the objects of other applications without the user of your program even being aware that the application is running. This process also uses an OLE server. Just as you interact with the Microsoft Jet database engine using a hierarchy of objects, you can interact with Word documents and Excel worksheets using a hierarchy of objects. In this session you will learn how to perform a simple calculation using Microsoft Excel. When you work with another application's objects, you use a concept called OLE Automation. **OLE Automation** is the process by which an application provides an interface to a hierarchy of objects. You actually used OLE Automation when you worked with DAO objects. In fact you reference the objects just like you referenced DAO objects.

> *Tip:* Using Microsoft Word for Windows 95, you can access Word programmatically using Word Basic, which is a form of Visual Basic. Using Office 97, Word and its objects are represented as an object hierarchy like DAO. There also are subtle differences between the object hierarchy using Excel 97 and Excel 95.
>
> You often will hear the term *Automation* to refer to OLE Automation. The term *Automation* is newer and reflects its more general purpose.

Microsoft Excel exposes an Application object that contains a number of different objects and collections. Although the objects and collections perform different tasks, they work the same way. That is, you use For Each loops to iterate through each object in a collection. Furthermore, these objects support properties and methods to store data and perform different tasks. When you work with another application's objects, you can divide them into two types:

- Objects that can be created with the New keyword, like you have done previously, are called externally creatable objects. **Externally creatable objects** are objects that allow you to create an instance of the object without calling the methods of another object. You also can create externally creatable objects using the **CreateObject** function.

- Objects that cannot be created with the New keyword are called dependent objects. **Dependent objects** only can be created using a higher-level object's methods. For example, a Recordset object is a dependent object. You create a recordset using the CreateRecordset method of the Database object, which is the recordset's parent object.

At the top of the Excel object hierarchy is the Application object, just like the DBEngine object is at the top of the DAO hierarchy. The **Application** object represents a running Microsoft Excel application. It is possible to run multiple copies of Excel at the same time, in which case there would be multiple Application objects. Each Application object contains a **Workbooks** collection with zero or more **Workbook** objects. Each Workbook object in turn contains a **Worksheets** collection with one or more **Worksheet** objects. Figure 12-18 shows the relationship between these objects and collections.

Figure 12-18 ◀
Relationships
in Excel object
hierarchy

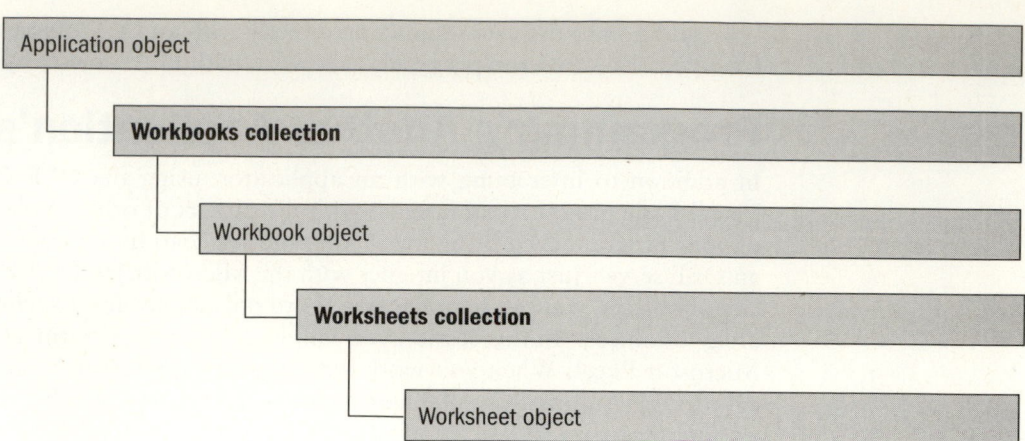

You cannot use an object variable until it references a valid object. This also is true for Excel objects. To create an Excel object at run time using Visual Basic code, you can call the CreateObject function, which has the following syntax:

Set *objectname* **= CreateObject**("*applicationtype.objecttype*")

- The *objectname* can be a generic object variable or a variable of the same type as the object you are creating. Note that when you use a generic object variable, the object is late bound, which reduces performance.

- The *applicationtype* is the name of the application that supplies the object. For Microsoft Excel the *applicationtype* is "Excel." For Word it is "Word." Refer to the Help system for the particular application you are using for the different application types.

- The *objecttype* is the name of the externally creatable object you want to use in your program.

The combination of the application type and the object type references a specific class that must be registered on your computer. If the class is not registered, then a run-time error will occur when the function is called. To start Microsoft Excel, you can write the following statements:

```
Dim objExcel As Object
Set objExcel = CreateObject("Excel.Application")
```

These statements declare an object variable to store a reference to an Excel application. When the CreateObject function is called, Excel is started and you can reference the application using the variable objExcel.

The variable objExcel is late bound because it is a generic object variable. You can improve the performance of the program by using the specific object type as shown in the following statements:

```
Dim xlApp As Excel.Application
Set xlApp = CreateObject("Excel.Application")
```

Even though these statements create an instance of the Excel application, the application does not display as a visible object on the screen. To accomplish this, you need to set a property of the Excel Application object, just like you set other properties. To make the application visible, you use the following statement to set the Visible property of the Excel Application object:

```
xlApp.Visible = True
```

Sandra suggests you now write the necessary statements to start Excel, then make it visible on the screen. Before you can use these objects, you must add the object library to your project using the References dialog box.

To add the Excel object library to your project and start the Excel applications:

1. Click **Project** then **References** to open the References dialog box.

2. Make sure the **Microsoft Excel 8.0 Object Library** check box is selected.

   TROUBLE? If the Microsoft Excel 8.0 Object Library does not display in your References dialog box, Excel may not be installed on your computer, or a different version of Excel may be installed. Microsoft Excel must be installed on your computer to complete this session. If the version of Microsoft Excel you have on your computer is different, click the check box that contains the correct version number of the object library.

3. Click **OK** to close the dialog box.

4. Activate the Code window for the form named **frmCalculate**. Activate the Code window for the **cmdComputePayment** button's **Click** event procedure.

5. Enter the following statements, shown in bold, into the Code window:

```
Private Sub cmdComputePayment_Click( )
    Dim xlApp As Excel.Application
    Set xlApp = CreateObject("Excel.Application")
    xlApp.Visible = True
End Sub
```

Just like adding the DAO object library to your project, adding the Microsoft Office object library that contains the Excel objects to your project, allows you to view the different objects in the Object Browser and makes these objects available to your program.

The first statement declares an object variable to store a reference to the Excel application. The second statement actually starts Excel. Note that the application does not become visible on the screen until the Visible property is set to True for the application in the last statement. Now that you have written the statements to start Excel, you should run the program to verify that Excel is being started.

To test that Excel is being started:

1. Save the project then start it. Click the splash screen to close it and proceed to the main form.

2. Click the **Calculate Test** command button on the main form. The Calculate form should be displayed.

3. Click the **Compute Payment** command button on the form. A copy of Excel should be started in another window. This copy of Excel should exit when the event procedure finishes.

4. End the project then exit Excel, if necessary.

Now that you can start the Excel application, you can begin to program its objects, just like you have programmed DAO objects. That is, you call its methods and set its properties. In Excel you work in a worksheet. Before you can begin to program a Worksheet object, you must create a new Workbook object and add it to the Workbooks collection. This can be accomplished by calling the Add method on the Workbooks collection. The Add method has the same effect as it does for any other collection.

To add a worksheet to the Excel application:

1. Activate the Code window for the form named **frmCalculate**. Activate the Code window for the **cmdComputePayment** button's **Click** event procedure.

2. Enter the following statements, shown in bold, into the Code window:

```
Dim xlApp As Excel.Application
Dim xlBook As Excel.Workbook
Dim xlSheet As Excel.Worksheet
Set xlApp = CreateObject("Excel.Application")
Set xlBook = xlApp.Workbooks.Add
Set xlSheet = xlBook.Worksheets(1)
xlApp.Visible = True
```

These statements declare the other necessary objects to create an Excel workbook and worksheet.

```
Dim xlBook As Excel.Workbook
Dim xlSheet As Excel.Worksheet
```

These two statements declare object variables. The first is an Excel Workbook object and the second is an Excel Worksheet object.

```
Set xlBook = xlApp.Workbooks.Add
Set xlSheet = xlBook.Worksheets(1)
```

The first statement creates a new Excel Workbook object by calling the Add method on the Workbooks collection. When a workbook is added, a default worksheet is added automatically to the Workbook object. Thus, you set the current worksheet to the first worksheet in the workbook.

You now can start the program to be sure the workbook is being created properly.

To test the program:

1. Save the project then start it. Click the splash screen to close it and proceed to the main form.

2. Click the **Calculate Test** command button on the main form. The Calculate form should be displayed.

3. Click the **Compute Payment** command button on the form. Note that Excel is started in another window and a blank worksheet displays as shown in Figure 12-19.

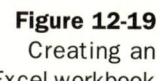 **Figure 12-19**
Creating an
Excel workbook

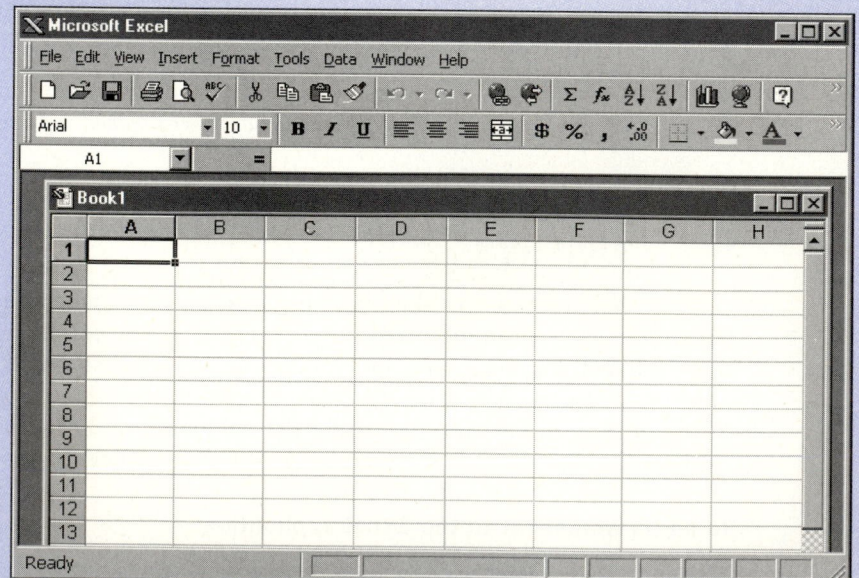

4. Close Excel and end the program.

Now that you have an active workbook and worksheets, you can begin to program these objects to perform computations. You can write statements to store numbers in cells, move numbers from one cell to another, and call different functions. To accomplish this, you need to reference an individual cell in a worksheet using the Cells property, which has the following syntax:

worksheet.**Cells**(*row,column*)

- The *worksheet* is a valid Worksheet object.
- The **Cells** property determines the selected cell or range of cells.
- The required *row* argument is a number, starting at one (1) that references the desired row.
- The required *column* argument is a number, starting at one (1) that references the desired column.

When you use the Cells property, it actually returns another object called a Range object. The **Range** object has several properties and methods to retrieve values from a cell, call functions, and perform other tasks, as shown in the following list:

- The **Formula** property is used to set or retrieve the formula in a range or cell. You can store any Excel formula in the Formula property.
- The **Value** property, when used with a Range object, sets or returns the value of the cell. Note that if the Range object or cell is empty, the Value property returns the value **Empty**. You can use the **IsEmpty** classification function.

Using the Cells property, you could write the following statement to store the constant value 3 into the cell at row (1), column (2):

```
xlSheet.Cells(1, 2).Value = 3
```

Sandra wants to use input from the Calculate form to store information in different cells. Then, you will use the values in these cells to compute some other value and display this information in your program. To accomplish this, you need to store the values stored in the form named frmCalculate into the different cells in the Excel worksheet.

To store the necessary values into the Excel worksheet:

1. Activate the Code window for the form named **frmCalculate**, then select the **cmdComputePayment** button's **Click** event procedure.

2. Enter the following statements into the Code window:

```
xlApp.Visible = True
xlSheet.Cells(1, 1).Value = txtInterestRate
xlSheet.Cells(1, 2).Value = txtTermYears
xlSheet.Cells(1, 3).Value = txtPresentValue
```

These statements store the value of the text box named txtInterestRate into the cell at row 1, column 1. The other two statements store values in cell(1,2) and cell(1,3), respectively.

When you write an Excel formula in Visual Basic, you use the same syntax as you would in Excel. For example, to write a formula that will multiply the value stored in the cell(1,1) by the value stored in cell(1,2) and store the result in cell(1,3), you can write the following statement:

```
xlSheet.Cells(1,3).Formula = "r1c1*r1c2"
```

Sandra wants you to write the necessary statement that will call the Excel PMT function to determine the payment on a loan. To accomplish this, you need to use the Excel PMT function, which has the following syntax:

PMT(*rate,nper,pv,fv,type*)

- The *rate* argument represents the monthly interest rate of the loan.

- The *nper* argument represents the number of payment periods.

- The *pv* argument is the present value of the loan.

- The optional *fv* argument is the future value, or a cash balance after the last payment is made. If *fv* is omitted, the value is zero (0).

- The optional *type* can be zero (0) or one (1). It indicates when payments are due. If payments are due at the end of the period, set the type to zero (0). If payments are due at the beginning of the period, set the type to one (1). If *type* is omitted, the value zero (0) is the default.

Assuming this information is stored in the current Excel worksheet such that the annual rate is stored at row 1, column 1, the number of years at row 1, column 2, and the present value at row 1, column 3, the statement to compute the payment and store the result in row 1, column 4 would be as follows:

```
xlsheet.Cells(1, 4).Formula = "=PMT(r1c1/12,r1c2*12,r1c3)"
```

Sandra suggests you now add the statements to the event procedure to compute the payment of a loan.

To compute the payment of a loan:

1. Activate the Code window for the form named **frmCalculate**, then select the **cmdComputePayment** button's **Click** event procedure.

2. Enter the following statement, shown in bold, into the event procedure:

```
xlSheet.Cells(1, 3).Value = txtPresentValue
xlSheet.Cells(1, 4).Formula = _
    "=PMT(r1c1/12,r1c2*12,r1c3)"
lblPayment = xlSheet.Cells(1, 4).Value
xlApp.DisplayAlerts = False
xlApp.Quit
```

These statements create a formula to compute the payment on a loan, by setting the Formula property to a string containing the intrinsic PMT function. Then, the Cells property is read to obtain the result and store it in the result label. By default, Excel will request confirmation from the user before exiting the program when the contents of a worksheet have not been saved. You can prevent this message from displaying by setting the **DisplayAlerts** property to False.

You now can test the program to be sure the payment is being computed correctly.

To test the Excel PMT function:

1. Save the project then start it. Click the splash screen to close it and proceed to the main form.

2. Click the **Calculate Test** command button on the main form to display the Calculate form.

3. Enter the values in the Interest Rate, Term, and Present Value text boxes on the Calculate form as shown in Figure 12-20.

Figure 12-20 ◀
Calling an
Excel function

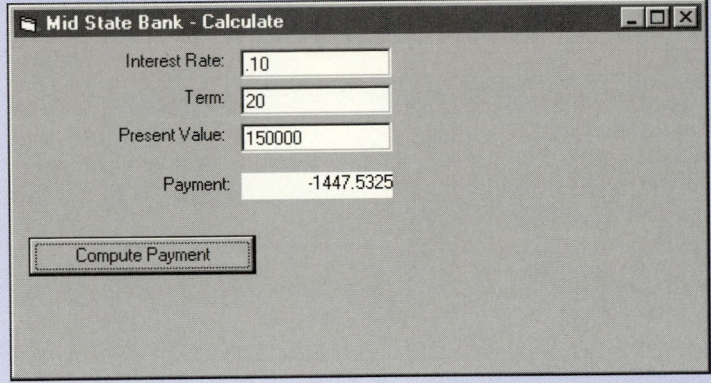

4. Click the **Compute Payment** command button on the form.

The Excel application opens, calculates the payment, and places the value in the Payment text box as shown in Figure 12-20, and quits.

5. End the project.

Quick Check

1. What is the purpose of the OLE Container control?

2. What is the difference between a linked object and an embedded object?

3. What is the difference between an OLE server and an OLE client?

4. What is a verb?

5. What is meant by the term *Automation*?

You have completed the programming for this session. You either may Exit Visual Basic or continue on to the next session.

SESSION

12.3

In this session you will create an executable file that will run outside the Visual Basic development environment. You also will create executable files that are optimized based on different goals. Finally, you will learn techniques that make your programs run faster.

Creating an EXE File

As you have created programs in this book, you have written and tested them in the Visual Basic IDE. This is not how a user generally will use the program, however. In fact you can distribute your programs to other computers that do not have Visual Basic installed. To do this, you compile your program. **Compilation** is a process by which the Visual Basic statements you have written are converted into an executable file. This executable file then can be run directly without the Visual Basic IDE. In fact, Visual Basic does not need to reside on the machine running the program.

When you compile the program, you should set several properties to record information about the program into the executable file, and determine how the program is compiled. All of these options are set from the Project Properties dialog box.

The Make tab of the Project Properties dialog box contains information about the application as shown in Figure 12-21.

Figure 12-21 ◄
Project
Properties
dialog box—
Make tab

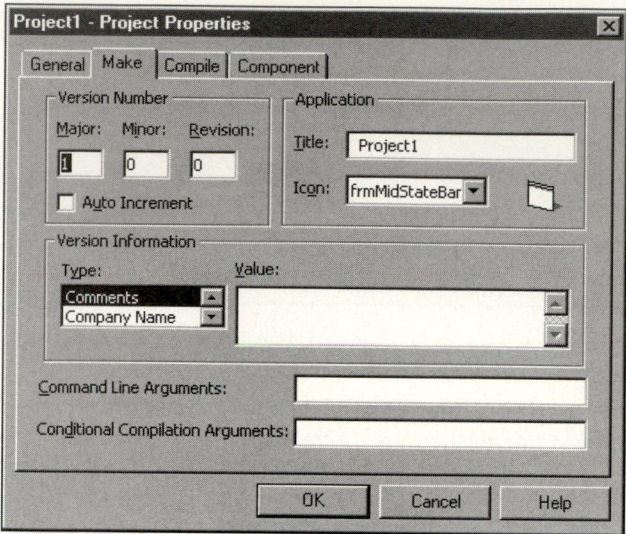

- Most large software programs use version numbers to keep track of revision information. The **Version Number** contains three fields—a Major release number, a Minor release number, and a Revision number. If the Auto Increment check box is checked, the revision number will be incremented by one each time the program is compiled.

- The **Application** contains a Title and an icon. You can select an icon such that when the program is minimized, the icon will be displayed.

- You can include descriptive text in the application by setting the **Version Information** options. Information about the company name, copyright, and legal notices can be included in the executable file.

The Version Information and Version Number information can be used by the App object at run time by reading several different properties. Much of this information commonly is displayed on the program's splash screen or in the About dialog box. The following properties correspond to the Version Number and Version Information options on the Make tab in the Project Properties dialog box:

- The **Major** property is read only at run time.

- The **Minor** property is read only at run time.

- The **Revision** property is read only at run time.

- The **CompanyName** property usually contains the name of the company that created the software.

- The **Comments** property includes any information about the program that does not fit into the other Version Information options.

- The **FileDescription** property should contain information about the program file. This may include the date the executable file was created or the size of the file.

- The **LegalCopyright** property displays copyright information.

- The **LegalTrademarks** property displays trademark information.

- The **ProductName** property should contain the descriptive name of the program, like Microsoft Visual Basic.

Sandra suggests you set this information for the loan document processing program, and display it on a splash screen when the program is run. Because this is the first revision of the program, the version number should be 1.0.1. She also would like the company name and product name included on the splash screen.

To set the Make properties:

1. Click **Project** then **Project1 Properties** to open the Project Properties dialog box. Click the **Make** tab.

2. Set **Major** to **1**, **Minor** to **0**, and **Revision** to **1**.

3. Click **Company Name** in the **Type** list box. Enter **Mid State Bank** in the **Value** text box.

4. Scroll the **Type** list box to select the **Product Name**. Enter **Loan Processor** in the **Value** text box.

5. Click **OK** to close the Project Properties dialog box.

6. Activate the Code window for the splash screen named **frmSplash's** Load event procedure.

7. Enter the following statements, shown in bold, into the event procedure:

```
Private Sub Form_Load( )
    lblVersion.Caption = "Version " & App.Major & _
        "." & App.Minor & "." & App.Revision
    lblProductName.Caption = App.ProductName
    lblCompany = App.CompanyName
End Sub
```

These statements use the properties of the App object and display them on the splash screen.

8. Save the project then start it. The splash screen should display as shown in Figure 12-22.

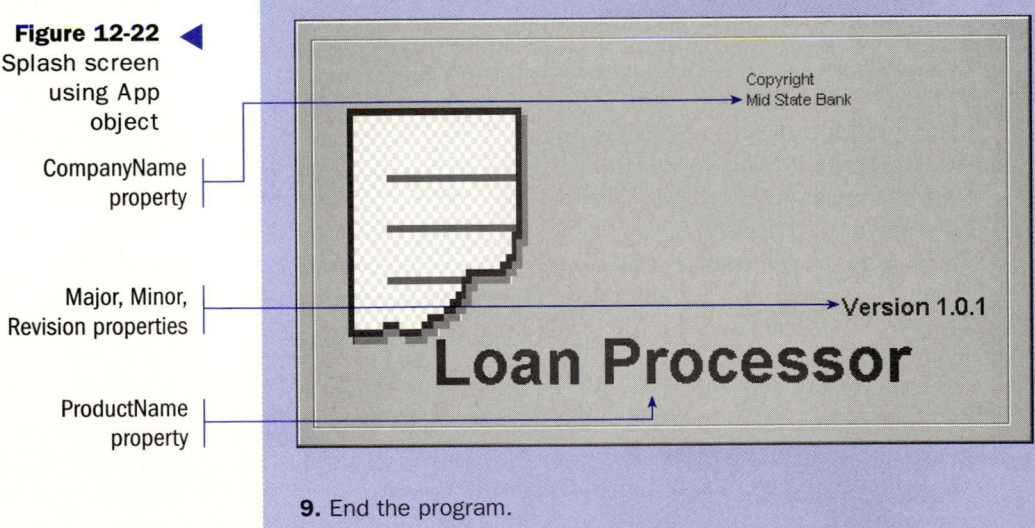

Figure 12-22 ◀
Splash screen
using App
object

CompanyName
property

Major, Minor,
Revision properties

ProductName
property

9. End the program.

Now that you have completed the information for the splash screen, you can proceed to set the pertinent values that determine how your program will be compiled into an executable file.

Compiling the Project

The Compile tab in the Project Properties dialog box allows you to configure how a program will be compiled. The Compile tab in the Project Properties dialog box is shown in Figure 12-23.

Figure 12-23 ◄
Project
Properties
dialog box—
Compile tab

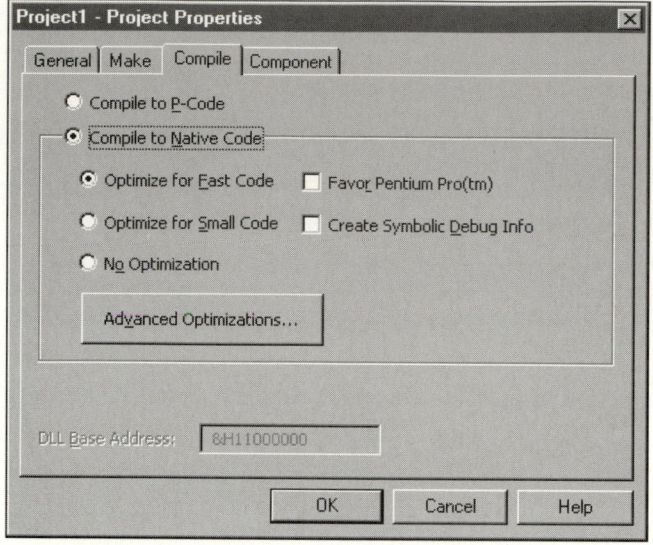

Visual Basic will allow you to create two types of executable files. You can create P-Code or Native Code.

- **Native Code** is executable code that does not require the support of the Visual Basic IDE or any of its run-time libraries. When your program is compiled into Native Code, it will run significantly faster than when it is run in the development environment. Note that any ActiveX controls used by your program must exist on the computer where the program is running.

- **P-Code** is an intermediate step between the Visual Basic statements you write and Native Code. The letter "P" actually stands for Pseudo, although terms P-Code and pseudocode are not synonymous. When you execute P-Code, Visual Basic converts the P-Code representing a statement into Native Code before executing the statement.

When you compile your program into Native Code, there are several options that control how your programs are compiled. These options can significantly impact both the speed of your program and the size of the executable file produced. These options include the following:

- If the **Optimize for Fast Code** option button is selected, the compiler will create an executable file that will run faster at the expense of the size of the executable file. Use this option when disk space is plentiful. Usually, the increase in performance is worth the increased size of the executable file.

- If the **Optimize for Small Code** option button is selected, the size of any executable file produced will be reduced at the expense of program performance. Use this option when disk space is very limited.

- If the **No Optimization** option button is selected, no optimization is performed.

- If the **Favor Pentium Pro(tm)** check box is checked, then the executable file will contain instructions that will improve the program's performance when the program is running on Pentium Pro CPU's. Although the code will run on other CPU's, it will run slower.

- If the **Create Symbolic Debug Info** check box is checked, debugging information will be created so the program can be debugged using Visual C++.

- The **Advanced Optimizations** command button opens the Advanced Optimizations dialog box and provides additional flexibility describing how the program is compiled.

The Advanced Optimizations dialog box contains other options that can improve the performance of your program. The Advanced Optimizations dialog box is shown in Figure 12-24.

Figure 12-24 ◀
Advanced
Optimizations
dialog box

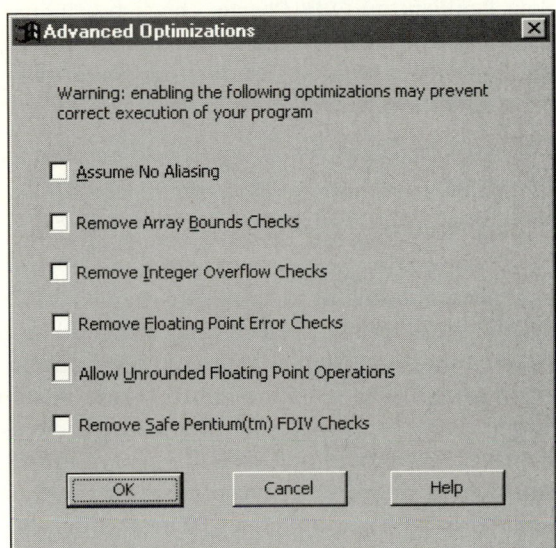

By default, when you run a program, Visual Basic performs several validation checks as you perform arithmetic operations and operations on arrays. For example, if your program tries to reference an invalid array element, or you perform an arithmetic operation that causes numeric overflow, a run-time error will occur. This is because Visual Basic checks the results of these operations. You can use the Advanced tab to remove these validation checks. This will cause your program to run faster. If you remove these checks, no run-time error will occur. Rather, in the case of conditions like numeric overflow, an incorrect result will be stored in a variable. Storing a value into an invalid array element will cause the data to be written to an area of the computer's memory that may be used by another variable. This can cause the program to produce incorrect results again, or to crash unexpectedly.

- The **Assume No Aliasing** check box is used to tell the compiler that the program does not use aliasing. Aliasing occurs when two variable names reference the same memory location. If you check this check box and there are aliases, your program may produce incorrect results.

- The **Remove Array Bounds Checks** check box causes the bounds of an array not to be checked when referenced. By default, whenever you reference an array, the value of the subscript is checked to make sure it is within the array bounds. If it is not, a run-time error will occur that you then can trap with an error handler. If the bounds of an array are not checked, and you set an index to a value outside the array bounds, you will write information to a memory address that may be used by other data. This can cause incorrect results or may cause the program to crash.

- The **Remove Integer Overflow Checks** check box causes the result of Integer arithmetic not to be checked to make sure it is within a valid range. By default, if you store too large a number in an Integer variable, a run-time error will occur. If this box is checked, however, no run-time error will occur and an invalid result will be stored in the result variable.

- The **Remove Floating Point Error Checks** check box causes the results of floating-point (Single and Double data types) arithmetic not to be checked to make sure they are within a valid range. By default, if you store too large a number in a floating-point variable, a run-time error will occur. If this box is checked, however, no run-time error will occur and an invalid result will be stored in the result variable.

- The **Allow Unrounded Floating Point Operations** check box when checked causes floating point operations to be performed more quickly. Significant rounding errors can occur, however.

- The **Remove Safe Pentium(tm) FDIV Checks** check box is used to deal with those Pentium processors with the FDIV bug. Some early Pentium processors had a bug that, on very rare occasions, could cause floating-point division to produce incorrect results. By default, code is checked so correct results will be generated.

> *Tip:* The Advanced Optimizations options should be used with caution. Changing these options can cause the program to produce incorrect results rather than producing run-time errors.

Once you set all the information pertinent to compiling the program, you can build the executable file. This is accomplished by clicking File then Make Project1.exe on the menu bar. Once the executable file is created, you can run it by adding the program to the Start menu, using the Run menu, or double-clicking the program using Windows Explorer.

Sandra suggests you now set the Compile information, create the executable file, and run it. Because the loan document processing program will be used in a large computer with adequate disk space, you should optimize the program for speed. She suggests you do not change any of the Advanced Optimizations options because the program has not been tested thoroughly and any overflow errors or array bounds errors should generate a run-time error so the problem can be identified and repaired.

To set the compile information and create the executable file:

1. Click **Project** then click **Project1 Properties**. Click the **Compile** tab.

2. Make sure the **Compile to Native Code** option button is selected.

3. Click the **Optimize for Fast Code** option button.

4. Click **OK** to close the Project Properties dialog box.

5. Save the project.

6. Click **File** then **Make Project1.exe**.

   The Make Project dialog box displays as shown in Figure 12-25.

Figure 12-25 ◄
Make Project
dialog box

executable filename

folder name

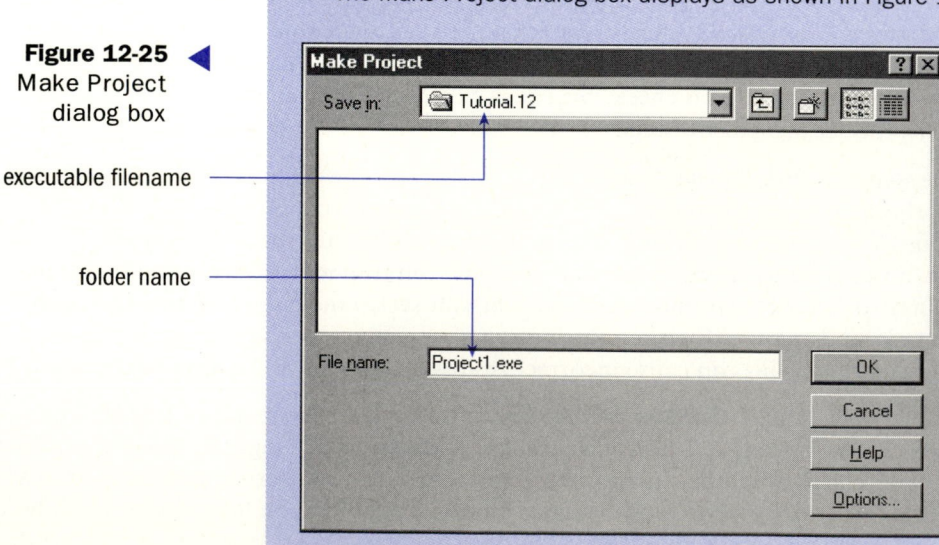

7. Select the **Tutorial.12** folder on your Student Disk and set the name to **MidStateBank**.

8. Click **OK** to compile the project.

   TROUBLE? If you receive a dialog box that says the file already exists, click Yes to replace the existing file.

   Once the executable file has been created you can run it.

9. Click the **Start** button on the task bar.

10. Click **Run**.

11. Enter **A:\Tutorial.12\MidStateBank.exe** in the Run dialog box as shown in Figure 12-26.

Figure 12-26 ◀
Run dialog box

filename

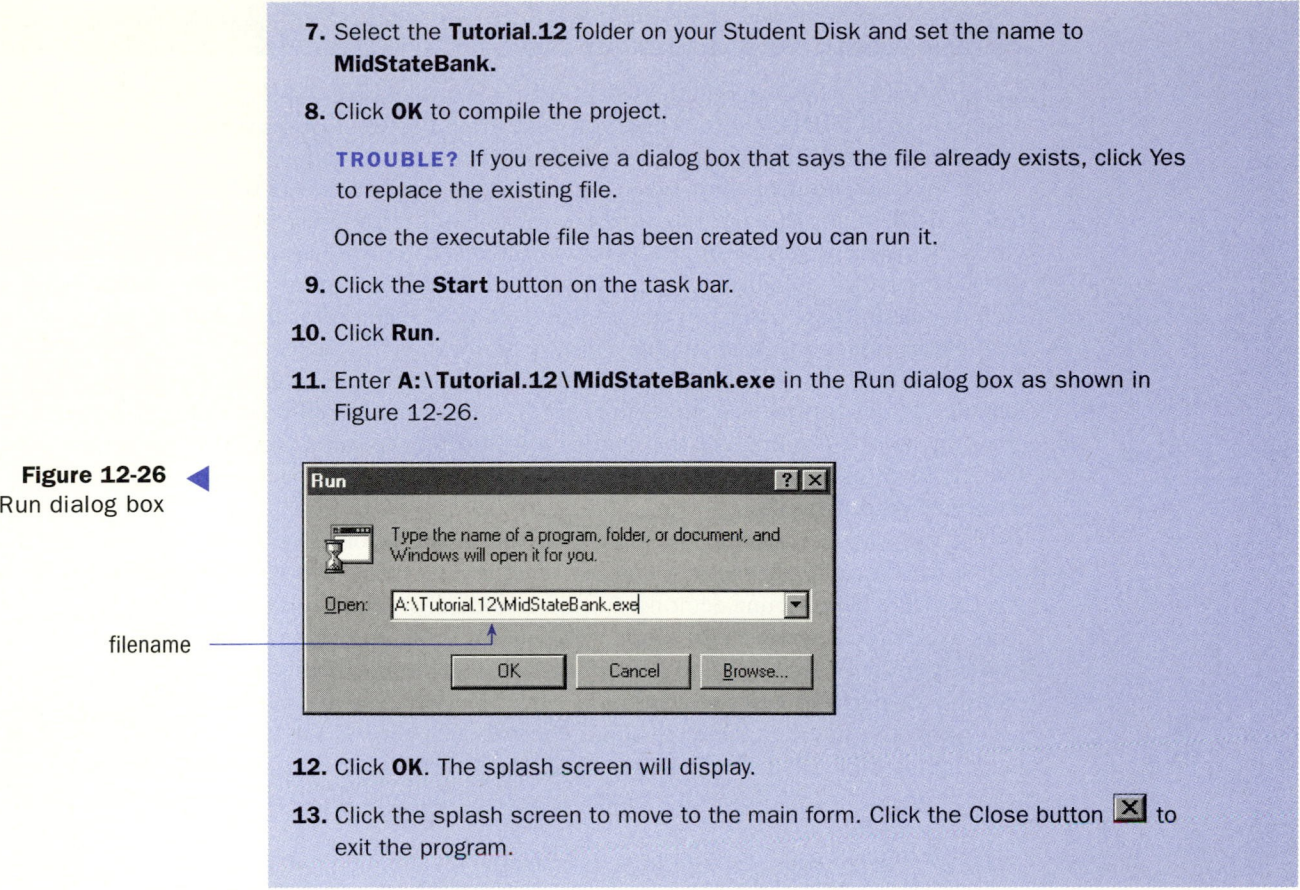

12. Click **OK**. The splash screen will display.

13. Click the splash screen to move to the main form. Click the Close button ⊠ to exit the program.

This tutorial has presented a brief introduction to the concept of OLE. It is possible to change objects at run time and how those objects display on the screen. It also is possible to write more extensive programs using OLE Automation than the one presented in this tutorial.

Optimizing Programs

As you begin to create larger programs, you need to consider carefully the performance of the programs you create. Although a program's performance is not directly part of the user interface, a program that runs slowly will create negative user perceptions. For example, if it takes a long time to move from one form in a program to another, a user may be dissatisfied. The same may occur if it takes minutes to locate a database record. As you create programs you should consider the following carefully:

- Minimize the time it takes to move from one control on the form to another. The user should be able to enter data into one control, tab to another, and begin entering data immediately. Thus, if the user is entering several fields of data, validate the fields all at once, just before a record is recorded to a database to minimize the time it takes to move from field to field.

- Be careful accessing records in a database. In large database tables, make sure that you have created indexes on the appropriate fields. Searching for a record in a table with many records without an index can take several seconds to several minutes. In this case the user may not be dissatisfied, but may think the program or computer has frozen.

- When you cannot prevent an operation from taking more than a few seconds, consider displaying a status message in a form or object on the form, to update the user about the operation's progress and the estimated time of completion.

As a Visual Basic programmer, there are several guidelines you can use to improve the overall performance of your program.

Control Selection and Use

Some controls use more resources than others. For example, labels use far less Windows resources than text boxes do. Thus, you only should use text boxes when input is required from the user. Furthermore, use default properties when possible.

Use ActiveX controls only when their functionality is needed. When an ActiveX control is used in a program, the corresponding ".ocx" file must be loaded into memory when the corresponding form is loaded. While this usually does not pose a problem, using several ActiveX controls on a form can have a negative impact on performance when a form loads. In these cases you can improve the perceived performance of the program by loading necessary forms all at once while a splash screen is displayed.

When using controls, like the CommonDialog control, you often can create only one instance of the control and set its properties at run time for different dialogs, rather than creating several instances of the control and setting the same properties at design time. Each control instance consumes memory and can have an impact on the overall performance of your program.

You have learned how to use many controls in this book. The controls presented offer only a small sample of the total number of controls available today. Included in this book is a CD-ROM containing demonstration versions of several different controls. These controls are ActiveX controls that can be added in your project to supply additional functionality to the Visual Basic programming language. You can purchase additional ActiveX controls to perform tasks like printing bar codes, sending and receiving faxes, and connecting to the Internet. There also are controls that extend the functionality of controls you already have used. For example, there are several controls that work with a database to provide additional flexibility and functionality beyond the capabilities supplied by the DBGrid control.

Using Visual Basic 5.0, it now is possible to create your own ActiveX controls. Creating ActiveX controls is much like creating visible Class modules. In other words they provide you with the capabilities of both a Class module and a Form module. The ActiveX controls you create function much like other ActiveX controls you have used. That is, another programmer using your ActiveX control can use Property Pages to set different properties at design time. Then at run time, the user can interact with the control just like any other control. The programmer also can set properties and call methods at run time.

Data Type Selection

Using the proper data type for different variables both can improve the performance of the program and reduce the amount of memory required by the program.

- Use Integer data types for counters when the value will not exceed 32767.

- Use Integer arithmetic rather than floating-point arithmetic where possible. Arithmetic on integers is significantly faster than arithmetic on floating-point numbers.

- Avoid double-precision arithmetic when possible. Arithmetic on double-precision numbers is significantly slower than arithmetic on single-precision numbers. Double-precision numbers are required only when storing very small or very large numbers.

- Avoid the use of Variant data types. Each Variant variable takes 16 bytes of memory. Excessive use of Variants can increase program size dramatically. Also, because Visual Basic must determine the current data type of a Variant variable when it is used, operations on Variant data are significantly slower.

- Do not use generic object variable types like Object, Form, or Control. These data types are late bound causing increased overhead.

Array Management

In this book, you have created both fixed size arrays and dynamic arrays with the ReDim statement. Each element in an array consumes memory. Thus, if the size of the array will grow and shrink at run time, use dynamic arrays and reduce the size of the array as elements are no longer needed. Again, choose the correct data type for an array.

Module Organization

When you produce an executable file containing several modules, including Form modules, Class modules, and standard modules, the modules are preserved in the executable file. When you run a program made up of several modules, all the modules are not loaded into the computer's memory when the program is started. Rather, modules are loaded "on demand." This means that a module is loaded only when your code calls a procedure in a module. In large programs with several modules, you can organize your procedures to improve performance. For example, you may have a set of procedures that are used frequently in a program. You can store all these procedures in one module so they are loaded only once. If, however, no procedures in a specific module are ever called, then that module will not be loaded into the computer's memory. As a result, you should organize modules such that their procedures perform a set of related tasks. This will improve the performance of the program and also tend to improve the readability.

Storing Data in Programs

Many programs store large amounts of constant data like tax tables, or constant strings. If this data is placed into your application at design time, the amount of memory consumed by the program will be increased. If the data is used frequently, it may be wise to store the data directly into the program. If data is used infrequently, however, consider reading the data on a disk file or database only when needed. This will reduce the total memory needed by the program.

Avoid Dead Code

As programs are developed and modified over a period of time, you may replace general procedures with other procedures. After time, you may find that there are several general procedures and variables that are never used by the program. Even though a variable or general procedure is never used, they continue to consume memory in a program.

Note that unused constants do not display in an executable file. Thus, there is no performance improvement when removing unused constants. Comments are removed from the program when you produce an executable file. Thus, they have no impact on performance.

Quick Check

1. List and describe three properties of the App object.
2. What is the difference between P-Code and Native Code?
3. What is an executable file?
4. What are the possible effects of removing the validation checks from an executable file?

Figure 12-27 lists and defines the new terms presented in this tutorial.

Figure 12-27 ◀
New terms

Term	Definition
Compilation	Compilation is a process by which the Visual Basic statements are converted into an executable file. The executable file can be run directly without the Visual Basic IDE.
Dependent objects	Dependent objects are objects that cannot be created with the New keyword. They only can be created using a higher-level object's methods.
Embedded object	An embedded object is stored as data in the OLE container rather than another program. Thus, only the program that created the embedded object can use that object.
Externally creatable objects	Externally creatable objects are objects that allow you to create an instance of the object without calling the methods of another object.
Linked object	A linked object is a file that is linked, along with the program that operates on the file, to your program through the OLE Container control. When you create a linked object, you are not inserting the program's data into your application. Rather you store in your program a reference to the data.
Native Code	Native Code is executable code that does not require the support of the Visual Basic IDE or any of its run-time libraries. When your program is compiled into Native Code, it will run significantly faster than when it is run inside the development environment.
Object Linking and Embedding (OLE)	Object Linking and Embedding (OLE) is a technology that allows multiple programs to access the data of another program using a standardized interface.
OLE automation	OLE automation is the process by which an application provides an interface to a hierarchy of objects.
OLE client	The OLE client is a program that uses the exposed objects of another program like Word or Excel. When you use the OLE Container control in your program, the control behaves as an OLE client.
OLE server	The OLE server is a program like Microsoft Word or Microsoft Excel that allows other programs to access its objects.
P-Code	P-Code is an intermediate step between the Visual Basic statements you write and Native Code. When you execute P-Code, Visual Basic converts the P-Code representing a statement into Native Code before executing the statement.
Verb	A verb is a way of communicating with an OLE object, asking the object to perform an action. Common actions are tasks like opening a file or editing a file.
Visual interface	The visual interface is one way the user can interact with a program using the window(s) of the program. This can be contrasted with programming an application's objects with code.

Tutorial Assignments

In addition to the loan document processing program you just created, Sandra wants a program that will help her automate the process of writing letters to different customers. The customer information is contained in a database. She wants the user to be able to locate a database record then copy the address information into the letter. Then she will type and print the letter.

To accomplish this, you can use the drag-and-drop facilities described in the chapter to copy the address information from a bound text box into a rich text box. The completed form is shown in Figure 12-28.

Figure 12-28 ◄

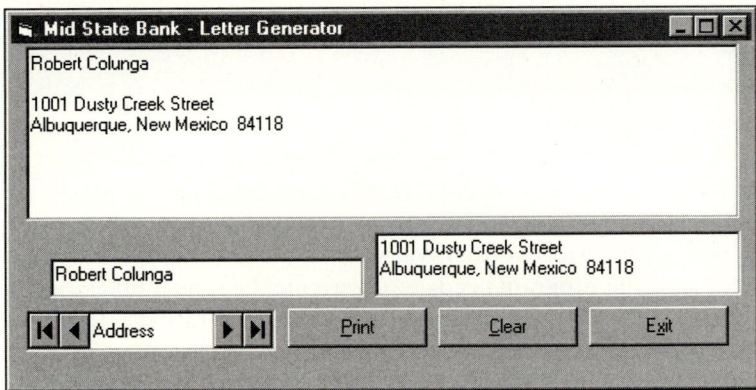

1. Make sure your Student Disk is in the appropriate disk drive, then start Visual Basic.

2. Save the form using the name **frmMidBankLetters** and the project using the name **Mid Bank Letters.vbp** in the **TAssign** folder of the **Tutorial.12** folder on your Student Disk. Set the form's caption as shown in Figure 12-28.

3. Create a Data control to connect to the database **MidState.mdb** stored in the **TAssign** folder of the **Tutorial.12** folder on your Student Disk. The Data control should reference the table named **tblAddress**.

4. Create two bound text boxes as shown in Figure 12-28. Set the name of each to **txtName** and **txtAddress**, respectively. Set the necessary properties so they will display the fields **fldName** and **fldAddress**, respectively, from the Data control created in the previous step.

5. Create a rich text box as shown in Figure 12-28. Remember, this is an ActiveX control so it must be added to the project before it can be used. Set the Name to **rtbLetter** and remove the existing text. Make sure it displays as a MultiLine text box with both vertical and horizontal scroll bars. Note that the scroll bars do not appear in Figure 12-28 because the text will fit in the visible region of the rich text box.

6. Set the necessary properties for the two text boxes to enable automatic drag-and-drop.

7. Write the necessary code so the user can drag the name or address from the text box to the rich text box. You need to code the DragDrop event for the rich text box.

8. Create three command buttons as shown in Figure 12-28. The first should print the contents of the rich text box, the second should clear the contents. The final command button should exit the program.

9. Test the program by selecting different records and copying them to the rich text box control. Make sure to test each of the command buttons.

10. Save the form and project again.

11. Using the Project Properties dialog box, create a comment that reads **Created by Sandra Vincent.**

12. Compile the program and save the executable file in the **TAssign** folder of the **Tutorial.12** folder on your Student Disk.

13. Run the executable file to make sure it is working properly.

14. Print the form as Text and Code, then exit Visual Basic.

Case Problems

1. Color Graphics Tryna Colson is the programming manager for a graphics design firm named Color Graphics. They have several programs that are computationally intensive. That is, it can take considerable time to compute the desired answers. They are getting ready to purchase several new computers. They want you to write a program that will evaluate the performance of various computers to help them make the best purchasing decision. The program needs to determine the time it takes each computer to perform a fixed number of Integer, Single, and Variant operations. This type of program is called a benchmark. In this situation, you will be evaluating the performance of different arithmetic operations in the Visual Basic development environment using an executable file.

They would like you to test the program to determine how long it takes different functions to run. Then, compile the program using different options to determine the impact of the results. The completed form is shown in Figure 12-29.

Figure 12-29

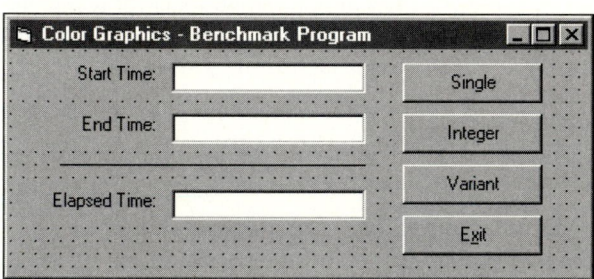

1. Make sure your Student Disk is in the appropriate disk drive, then start Visual Basic.

2. Save the form using the name **frmColorGraphics** and the project using the name **Color Graphics.vbp** in the **Cases** folder of the **Tutorial.12** folder on your Student Disk. Set the form's caption as shown in Figure 12-29.

3. Create the four command buttons on the form as shown in Figure 12-29, and set the Name property appropriately.

4. Write the code for the Exit command button.

5. Create the labels, text boxes, and line as shown in Figure 12-29.

6. Inside the Click event procedure for the Single command button, write the following statements:

```
Private Sub cmdSingle_Click( )
    Dim pintCounter As Long
    Dim psngArg1 As Single
    Dim psngArg2 As Single
    Dim psngArg3 As Single
    psngArg1 = 100
    psngArg2 = 200
    txtStart = ""
    txtEnd = ""
    txtElapsed = ""
    txtStart = Now( )
    For pintCounter = 1 To 100000000
        psngArg3 = psngArg2 * psngArg1
    Next
    txtEnd = Now( )
    txtElapsed = DateDiff("s", txtStart, txtEnd)
    Me.Refresh
End Sub
```

These statements perform a loop 100 million times. Each time through the loop, single precision multiplication takes place. Note that depending on the performance of the computer you are using, you may want to change the number of iterations of the loop. If the number of iterations is too small, however, you may not be able to detect performance differences. If the number is too large, it may take several minutes or hours to obtain the results.

7. Repeat Step 6 and program the command buttons to perform the same multiplication using Integer and Variant data types. Save and run the program. Record the time it takes to perform the operation for each command button by clicking each button. So you get an accurate timing, you should refrain from performing other activities on the computer when the program is running.

8. Save the program again.

9. Compile the program to an executable file.

10. Run the same program again from the executable file and record your results. Note that if you use the Run command on the Start menu, you need to surround the full path and filename in quotes, otherwise the system will not be able to locate the file correctly.

11. Write a report containing a table to explain your results. The table should contain the performance of Single, Integer, and Variant arithmetic both in the Visual Basic IDE and in the executable file.

12. Modify the program so it computes values that generate numeric overflow or divide by zero errors. Then, turn off the validation checks in the Advanced Compiler Options dialog box. Compile the program and run the executable file to see the incorrect results that are generated.

13. Exit Visual Basic.

2. Mail Man Mail Man is a small software company located in Denver, Colorado. They sell a program to send and receive electronic mail. They want you to design a prototype for the user interface.

The user interface for the program must allow the user to select the mail recipient from a combo box containing all the known mail recipients. The user must be able to select an item from the combo box using the mouse. Then, once an item is selected, the user must be able to drag the selected item to one of two different list boxes. When dropped in the list box, the selected name should be added to the list box. The completed form is shown in Figure 12-30.

Figure 12-30 ◀

combo box ——

list boxes ——

OLE container
(embedded
WordPad object) ——

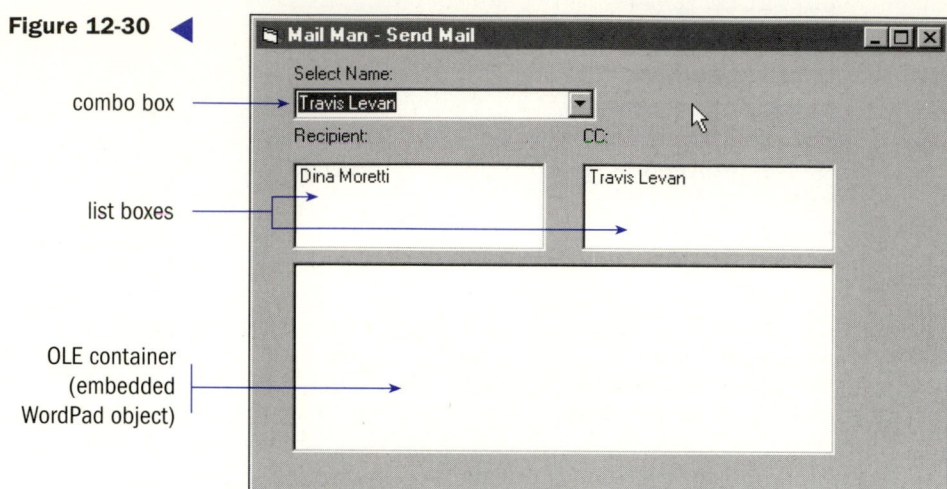

1. Make sure your Student Disk is in the appropriate disk drive, then start Visual Basic.

2. Set the form name to **frmMailMan**, and change the form's caption as shown in Figure 12-30.

3. Save the form using the default name and save the project using the filename **Mail Man.vbp** in the **Cases** folder of the **Tutorial.12** folder on your Student Disk.

4. Create the objects as shown in Figure 12-30 except for the embedded WordPad document shown. This is the large object at the bottom of the form.

5. So the prototype of the program will function, add a list of four names using the AddItem method or by setting the List property of the combo box.

6. Write the necessary code in the Click event procedure for the combo box so when an item is selected, drag-and-drop will be invoked for the object. You need to call the Drag method to initiate this.

7. Write the code in each of the list boxes so when the combo box is dragged into the corresponding list box, the contents of the selected combo box item will be displayed in the list box. You will need to use the AddItem method of the list box in the DragDrop event for each list box to accomplish this.

8. Using the OLE Container control, create an embedded WordPad document to store the mail message.

9. Save the program again.

10. Test the program by dragging the names to the different list boxes to be sure the selected ComboBox item is being added properly to the correct list box.

11. Exit Visual Basic.

3. H2O Engineering H2O Engineering performs numerous calculations in the process of performing ground compaction studies and other tasks. They want you to create a prototype program that will allow the user to enter different Excel formulas. They use Excel because it has some formulas that are not available in Visual Basic. This prototype will compute the standard deviation of a population contained in a list of numbers specified by the user. Figure 12-31 shows the user interface for the program.

Figure 12-31 ◀

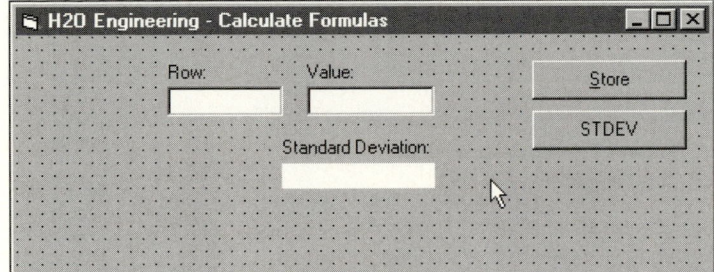

1. Make sure your Student Disk is in the appropriate disk drive, then start Visual Basic.

2. Set the form caption as shown in Figure 12-31. Set the form name to **frmH2OEngineering**. Save the form using the default name and the project using the filename **H2O Engineering** in the **Cases** folder of the **Tutorial.12** folder on your Student Disk.

3. Create the form-level variables to store objects of type Excel.Application, Excel.Workbook, and Excel.Worksheet.

4. Create the objects on the form and change the form's caption as shown in Figure 12-31.

5. Write the code for the **Store** command button that will store the value specified in the Value text box in the selected row. All values should be stored in the first column so you can compute the standard deviation.

6. Write the Code for the STDEV command button to compute the standard deviation of a list of numbers. To compute the standard deviation for the number stored in cells A1 to A7 you would use the following reference:

```
STDEV(A1:A7)
```

7. Save and test the program.

8. Exit Visual Basic.

4. Viper Shipping Viper Shipping is a small trucking company in Mobile, Alabama. Up to seven different trucks can be loaded at the same time at their loading dock. When a truck arrives, the dispatcher must identify and record each of the freight orders for each individual customer that is receiving freight. Figure 12-32 shows the completed form for this program.

Figure 12-32 ◀

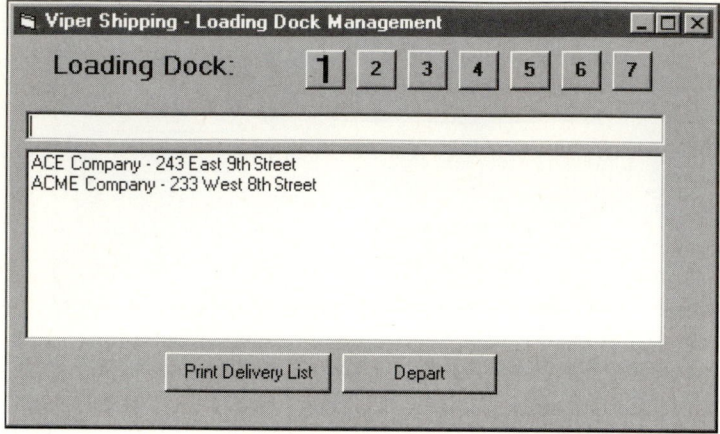

As you can see from Figure 12-32, there are seven buttons to represent each loading dock. There also is a text box for the dispatcher to enter the name and address of the recipient. To record a delivery on a truck, the operator should be able to drag the text box over one of the command buttons with the caption 1 through 7. When this occurs, the contents of the text box should be added to a list box corresponding to the freight on a specific loading dock. Thus, you will need seven list boxes corresponding to the seven loading docks and seven command buttons. When a shipment is recorded, the command button representing the loading dock should be displayed in a large, bold font, and the list box corresponding to the loading box should be made visible. All other list boxes should be invisible.

If the user clicks one of the command buttons to determine if a shipment has been recorded, the list box corresponding to the command button should be made visible and all the other list boxes invisible. Thus, after the first order is recorded, there always will be one visible and active list box, and one command button with large, bold font. Anytime a selection is changed, the previously selected list box and command button should become invisible.

In addition to the command buttons on the top of the form, there should be two more command buttons on the bottom of the form. The user should be able to drag the visible list box onto to either of these command buttons. The first button should print all the items in the list box. The second should depart the list box. You should save the form using the name **frmViper.frm** and the project using the name **Viper.vbp** in the **Cases** folder of the **Tutorial.12** folder on your Student Disk.

Answers to Quick Check Questions

SESSION 7.1

1   Most collections allow their objects to be referenced by an index (starting at zero or one) or by a string key. In each case, the numeric and/or string key must be unique.

2   Collections either begin with an index of zero (0) or one (1), hence the terms zero-based, and one-based, collection. That is, the first element in a collection has an index value of zero (0) or one (1). Older collections are numbered starting at zero (0). At some point, it generally was agreed upon that collections numbered starting at one (1) were more intuitive. Thus, most new collections begin numbering at one (1).

3   Most objects support a default property or method. This allows you to refer to a property or call a method without referring explicitly to the property or method name. Because different code is used when referring to a default property or method, and the code is more efficient, the statement will run up to 25 percent faster.

4   A Database object represents an open database. Each Database object contains a TableDefs collection containing zero (0) or more TableDef objects; one for each table in the database. Note that system tables also are stored as TableDef objects. Each TableDef object, in turn, contains a Fields collection. The Fields collection contains one Field object for each field in the table.

5   A For loop is useful to iterate through elements in an array. When using a collection, however, a For Each loop can be used to iterate through each object in a collection. When iterating through the objects in a collection, the For Each loop generally will perform faster, require less code, and be more readable.

SESSION 7.2

1   DDL and DML make up the statements of the SQL language. DDL statements are used to change the structure of a database. DML statements are used to manipulate the data in the database. In SQL, there are four DML statements: INSERT, UPDATE, DELETE, and SELECT.

2   A DML statement can perform two different actions. One action returns records from a database and stores them into a Recordset object as a result of a SELECT statement. This is referred to as a select query. The other type of statement performs an action on a database table or query but does not return any records. These actions include adding, updating, and removing records. Action statements do not return a recordset. This is referred to as an action query.

3
```
INSERT INTO tblNames FIELDS (fldID,fldLastName,fldDateAdded) _
    VALUES (1,'Ike Smith',#8/12/99#)
```

4   The Execute method of the Database object is used to execute an SQL statement that runs an action query. If the statement returns rows from a database table or query (a select query), you instead open a recordset using the OpenRecordset method of the Database object.

5
```
UPDATE tblPayroll SET fldHoursWorked = 40 WHERE fldID = 123
```

6   The WHERE clause is an expression, much like the expression in an If statement. It is used to restrict the rows returned in a query.

7
```
DELETE * FROM tblPeople WHERE fldDateChanged < #3/23/99#
```

SESSION 7.3

1   An ORDER BY clause is used in a SELECT statement to control how a recordset is sorted. The recordset can be sorted by multiple columns in both ascending and descending order.

2   The Recordsets collection contains zero or more Recordset objects. There is one Recordset object for each active Recordset. Each Recordset object contains some number of rows.

3   The Fields collection of the Recordset object works like the Fields collection of the TableDef object. There is one Field object in the Fields collection for each field in a recordset.

4   To select individual fields from a table or query, the SELECT statement is used followed by the desired field names separated by commas.

SESSION 8.1

1   Intrinsic controls are part of Visual Basic. Intrinsic controls are stored in the executable file produced by Visual Basic. ActiveX controls are not part of Visual Basic itself. Rather the functionality of an ActiveX control is stored in a separate file, typically with the extension ".OCX". For the program using the ActiveX control to run on any computer, the OCX file must exist on that computer. ActiveX controls are built using a standard technology called component object modules or COM.

2   The Components dialog box is used to add ActiveX controls to a project. A reference to each ActiveX control is stored in the project file.

3   The ListField property is used to specify which field in a recordset should be displayed in the DBList or DBCombo box at run time. When an item in the list is selected, the value is stored in the Text property. The Text property is the default property for the DBCombo and DBList controls. The BoundColumn property specifies a column in the source Data control. When a record is selected, the value stored in the corresponding BoundColumn is stored in the BoundText property.

4   The TabAction property is used to change the behavior of the Tab key in the DBGrid control. The value can be set to one of four intrinsic constants.

5   The Columns collection is a zero-based collection and contains zero or more Column objects. Each Column object represents a column in the DBGrid control. There is one Column object for each column in the underlying table or query.

6   The DBGrid control usually is bound to a Data control using the DataSource property. When the DBGrid control is bound to a Data control, the DBGrid is linked to the recordset created by the Data control. Because of this, you can call the methods of the underlying Data control.

SESSION 8.2

1   The Controls collection works like other collections you have used. It is a zero-based collection containing Control objects. For each control drawn on a form, there exists one Control object in the Controls collection. The Controls collection has one property, Count, which specifies the number of Control objects in the collection.

2   The TypeOf keyword is used in an If statement to determine the type of a control or object. Expressions using the TypeOf keyword return either True or False.

3   The CommonDialog control supports 6 methods. The ShowOpen and ShowSave methods allow you to select a file to be opened and saved, respectively. The ShowColor and ShowFont methods allow you to change the fonts and colors of different objects. The ShowPrint method allows you to change printer characteristics like a page range, number of copies, and selected printer. The ShowHelp method displays a Help window.

4   There are two types of fonts—screen and printer. Depending on the fonts installed on the computer, the screen fonts may vary. Also, different printers support different fonts. Thus, the printer fonts also may vary. The Screen object supports the Fonts property, which is a zero-based list describing each of the screen fonts installed on the computer. The Printer object also supports the Fonts property. It serves the same purpose and works the same as the Fonts property for the screen object. The list of fonts are those applicable to the selected printer, however.

SESSION 9.1

1   The ImageList control stores a collection of bitmap or icon images. Each image is stored as a ListImage object in the ListImages collection. The ImageList control should be created before the Toolbar control. The ImageList control is not visible at run time. The icons stored in the ImageList control are displayed in the Toolbar control at run time.

2   The Toolbar control contains a collection of buttons. Each button on the toolbar represents a Button object. The icon displayed in a button comes from a corresponding ListImage object, stored in the ListImages collection in another ImageList object.

3   The MaskEdBox control is a superset of the text box. It supports properties to format input and output text.

4   An input mask is used with the MaskEdBox control to restrict or filter the input of characters into a specific character position. In addition, literal characters also can be used. The user does not enter literal characters. Rather, they are displayed automatically.

5   A Rich Text Format (RTF) file contains printable characters like a text file. Some of the text in the file is not displayed, however. Rather, it is used to apply formatting to selected text. Text can be formatted as Bold, Italic, Underline, and Strikethru. In addition, it is possible to change the font size and type.

6   The SelChange event occurs to the RichTextBox control whenever the selected text changes. Usually one writes code in this event procedure to change the formatting, or to cut, copy, or paste the selected text.

7   It is possible for a menu item to work like a check box. That is, a menu item can be checked or unchecked. By setting the Checked property in the Menu Editor, you create this type of menu item. The Checked property can be tested to determine if it is True or False.

SESSION 9.2

1   An expert is a tool, much like a Wizard, that helps you create standardized reports using the Crystal Reports program. There are several different experts for different types of standardized reports.

2   There are several types of fields in Crystal Reports. A database field is similar to a bound text box. It displays the data from a database field into a region on the report. A text field is not bound to a field in a database. Rather it works like a label. A formula field is made up of a name and a formula. You use formulas to perform arithmetic operations on different fields. A summary field is used to analyze the values of multiple database records. For example, you can count the number of records in a recordset, or add their values. You use a summary field like a counter or accumulator. In addition, you can perform statistical functions on a summary field. There are special fields to perform common operations like displaying the current date or page number. There also are special fields to add up columns of numbers.

3   A report is made up of several sections. The Title section contains the report title. It displays only once on the first page of the report. The Page header section displays at the top of every page. The Details section contains one or more lines for each individual record selected from a database table or query. The Page footer section displays at the bottom of every page. The Summary section displays at the end of the report.

4   To create a formula field, you use the Insert Formula Field dialog box to build the formula. A formula has a name beginning with an at (@) sign. Crystal Reports adds the @ sign for you. Database field names are enclosed in braces { }. You use the table name, followed by a period (.), followed by the field name. You can use fields and constant values to create expressions. Expressions can contain arithmetic operators and functions. Any text must be enclosed in quotation marks.

5 To create a subtotal, you click the field to be totaled in the Details section of the report. Click Insert then Subtotal and select the control break field if printing a subtotal. If printing a grand total, select Grand Total on the menu bar to insert the field.

6 To use Crystal Reports with Visual Basic, you use the CrystalReport control. The CrystalReport control is an ActiveX control that allows a Visual Basic program to print a report already created in Crystal Reports. To print a report you set the ReportFileName property to the name of an existing report; the Destination to the desired printer, screen, or file; and the PrintFileType property to identify the output file type. After setting these properties, the Action property should be set to one (1) to print the report.

SESSION 10.1

1 An MDI program is made up of one, and only one, MDI parent form. This form acts as a container for one or more MDI child forms. Each MDI child form is displayed in the region of the MDI parent form. MDI child forms cannot be displayed as modal forms. When an MDI child form is minimized, its icon appears at the bottom of the MDI parent form, rather than at the bottom of the desktop.

2
```
Dim frmInstance1 As New Form1
Dim objOne As Object
Set objOne = frmInstance1
```

3 Binding is the process of preparing to call a method, or to set or read a property. When you use a generic object variable of type Variant or Object, Visual Basic cannot determine actual data type until run time. This is called late binding. When you declare an object variable of a specific class, like a command button, Visual Basic can determine the type of object before run time. This is called early binding.

4 The New keyword is used to create explicitly a new instance of an object from a class. The New keyword can be used with the Dim, Public, Private, Static, and Set statements.

5 The Option Base statement is used to change the default lower bound for the arrays in the module where the Object Base statement is placed. The Option Base for a module can be zero (0) or one (1). Changing the Option Base in one module does not affect the Option Base for other modules.

6 An enumerated type can be thought of as a constant with a fixed set of values. To create an enumeration you use the Enum statement.

SESSION 10.2

1 The LBound and UBound functions are used to determine the lower and upper bound of an array, respectively. Each function accepts one argument—the dimension of the array to use. When using a one-dimensional array the argument can be omitted.

2 The Arrange method of an MDI parent form is used to modify the appearance of the displayed and minimized MDI child forms. By calling the Arrange method with different arguments it is possible to tile, both vertically and horizontally, the open MDI child windows. The MDI child windows also can be cascaded on top of each other. Finally, the icons displayed in the MDI parent window can be displayed across the bottom of the MDI parent form.

3
```
Type tEmployee
    LastName As String
    FirstName As String
End Type
```

4 When an MDI parent form is unloaded, a QueryUnload event is generated first for the MDI forms. Then an Unload event occurs for each of the MDI child forms. If any of these Unload events are cancelled, then the Unload event for the MDI parent form also will be cancelled and the MDI parent form will not be unloaded.

SESSION 11.1

1　A Class module can contain two different types of variables. Exposed variables are part of the class's interface and are declared using the Public statement. Other modules using the Class module can use exposed variables. A hidden variable only is visible inside the class and is declared using the Private statement. A hidden variable is not part of the class's interface.

2　Any type of object can be stored in a Collection object. You can store Intrinsic data types, user-defined types, and objects in a collection. It also is possible to store different data types in the same collection but it is the responsibility of the programmer to keep track of the data type of specific members of a collection.

3　The Collection object supports the Add and Remove methods to insert and delete an item from a collection, respectively. The Item method is the default method and is used to select an object from a collection. The Count property identifies the number of items in a collection.

4　The ClassInitialize event occurs just before an instance of a class is created. The event is used to perform startup tasks to initialize properties and set hidden variables.

5　A Property procedure is a way of executing code when a property is read or written. Property procedures usually exist in pairs. A Property Let procedure is executed when the value of a property is written and a Property Get procedure is executed when the value of a property is read.

6　It is possible to create read-only properties by creating only a Property Get procedure. By removing the Property Let procedure, attempting to write the value of the property will cause a run-time error to occur.

SESSION 11.2

1　To create a read-write property using property procedures, you create Property Let, and corresponding Property Get, procedures. The Property Let procedure is executed when the property is written, and the Property Get procedure is executed when the property is read. Typically, hidden variables are maintained in the Class module to keep track of the value of the property.

2　The Raise method of the Err object is used to generate explicitly a run-time error. The Raise method takes several arguments. The number argument is a long integer identifying the error. The optional source argument contains a string expression naming the object or application that generated the error. The optional description argument is a string describing the error.

3　To set a default property or default method for a class, select the current project in the Project/Library list box. Then in the Classes list box, select the desired class. After selecting the class, select the desired member (Method or Property) to become the default. Click the right-mouse button and select the item named Properties to activate the Procedure Attributes dialog box, then click the Advanced command button to expand the Procedure Attributes dialog box. Finally, click the User Interface Default check box.

4　The purpose of a write-once property is to create a property that cannot be changed after its value has been set for the first time. It commonly is used with index values so they cannot be changed accidentally. To create a write-once property, you can create a static variable in the Property Let procedure. The first time the procedure is executed, set the value of the static variable to True. In an If statement, test the value of the static variable. If it is True, raise an error indicating that the value of the variable already has been set.

5　Sub and Function methods are two different ways of creating a method in a Class module. Just like in other modules, a Sub method does not return a value while a Function method does. Both Sub and Function methods can accept zero or more arguments.

6　The ClassTerminate event is used to perform housekeeping tasks just before a class instance is destroyed. Commonly, you may want to write information to a database or text file or update accumulators before the class is terminated.

SESSION 12.1

1 The Clear method is used to clear the contents of the Clipboard object before copying data onto the clipboard. The SetText method is used to copy text onto the clipboard. Typically, the text is copied from a text box using the SelText property of the text box. The GetText method is used to copy the contents of the clipboard onto another object.

2 The ActiveControl property of the Screen object is used to determine the control that currently has focus and commonly is used with clipboard and drag-and-drop operations. Using the ActiveControl property, you can call the underlying method and properties of the control.

3 The standard shortcut key for a cut operation is Ctrl+X; for a copy operation it is Ctrl+C; and for a paste operation it is Ctrl+V.

4 Every drag-and-drop operation is made up of a source and destination object. The Source object is the object the user drags. The destination object is the object where the source object is dragged then dropped. The destination object can be any visible object drawn on the form, except for a Line or Shape control. The destination object also can be the form itself.

5 The DragOver event occurs to the destination object repeatedly as the source object is moved across the region of the destination object. When the drag operation is complete, the DragDrop event occurs once to the destination object.

SESSION 12.2

1 The OLE Container control allows you to add the objects of other applications to your program. The OLE Container control only can be used with applications that support Object Linking and Embedding (OLE).

2 The OLE Container control can be used to create two types of objects—linked and embedded. A linked object is a file that is linked, along with the program that operates on the file, to your program through the OLE Container control. When you create a linked object, you are not inserting the program's data into your application. Rather you store, in your program, a reference to the data. An embedded object is stored as data in the OLE container rather than another program. Thus, only the program that created the embedded object can use that object. When you create an embedded object, the data is embedded into the OLE Container control, along with the program that operates on the data.

3 An OLE server is a program like Microsoft Word or Microsoft Excel that allows other programs to access its objects. For example, both Word and Excel have an object hierarchy much like the DAO object hierarchy. An OLE client is a program that uses the exposed objects of another program like Word or Excel. When you use the OLE Container control in your program, the control behaves as an OLE client.

4 A verb is a way of communicating with an OLE object, asking the object to perform an action. Common actions are tasks like opening, or editing, a file. Different OLE servers support different verbs.

5 When you work with another application's objects, you use a concept called OLE automation. OLE automation is the process by which an application provides an interface to a hierarchy of objects. You actually used OLE automation when you worked with DAO objects. In fact you reference the objects just like you referenced DAO objects.

SESSION 12.3

1 The CompanyName property usually contains the name of the company that created the software. Include in the Comments property any information about the program that does not fit into the other Version Information options. The FileDescription property should contain information about the program file. This may include the date the executable file was created or the size of the file. The LegalCopyright property displays copyright information. The LegalTrademarks property displays trademark information. The ProductName property should contain the descriptive name of the program, like Microsoft Visual Basic.

2   Native Code is executable code that does not require the support of the Visual Basic IDE or any of its run-time libraries. A program compiled into Native Code will run significantly faster than when it is run in the development environment. Note that any ActiveX controls used by your program must exist on the computer where the program is running. P-Code is an intermediate step between the Visual Basic statements you write and Native Code. The letter "P" actually stands for Pseudo, although the terms P-Code and pseudocode are not synonymous. When you execute P-Code, Visual Basic converts the P-Code representing a statement into Native Code before executing the statement.

3   An executable file is a file that can be executed from within an operating system. An executable file is not run inside of the Visual Basic IDE.

4   Removing the validation checks from an executable can cause incorrect results to be produced from arithmetic expressions when overflow errors occur, or an array reference is made outside of the array's bounds. If the validation checks are made run time error will occur.

Creating a Calculator

CASE

Utility Solutions

Utility Solutions is a small computer software company located in Rio, Nevada. The company has been in business since 1984. They develop, manufacture, and distribute several different software packages all over the world. The owner of the company, Casey Mudd, has decided to create a set of utility programs to sell to their customers. One of the programs that will comprise this set of utility programs is a calculator. He would like you to create the calculator program. Figure 1 shows the completed form for the calculator.

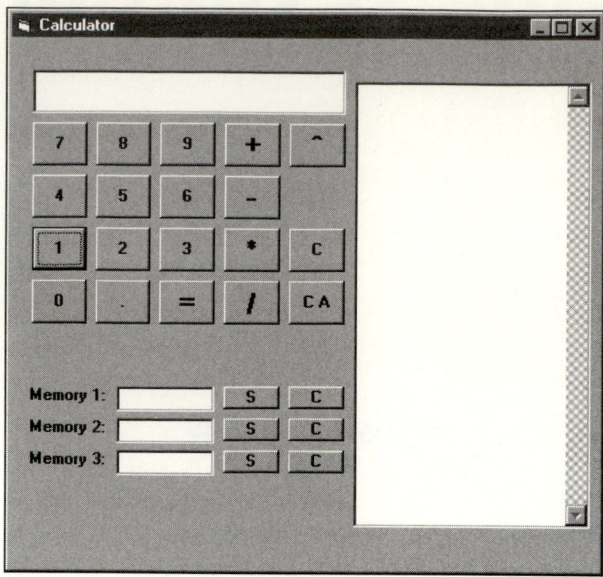

As you can see from Figure 1, the calculator consists of numeric buttons (zero (0) through nine (9) and a decimal point) and operator buttons (+, − *, /, ^). As each numeric button is clicked, the digit corresponding to the button must be displayed in the text box at the top of the form. There is a text box on the right side of the form that must work like the paper tape on an adding machine. When one of the operator buttons is clicked, the contents of the text box at the top of the form must be copied to the tape, and the contents of the text box at the top of the form cleared. Finally, there are three text boxes at the bottom of the form that must work like the memory on the calculator. The command buttons next to these memory text boxes are used to store and clear values to and from each memory location.

The following list describes some of the general characteristics of the calculator:

- The user must be able to enter numbers into the calculator using a numeric keypad (command buttons on the form). As each individual digit is entered, it must be appended to the current number displayed in a text box. For example, clicking the buttons 1 then 2 would cause the value 1 then 12 to be displayed in the text box. If a decimal point is entered, it too must be displayed in the text box. Because a number may contain only one decimal point, however, the button should be disabled once the decimal point is entered. Once an operation is performed on the number, the decimal point button needs to be enabled again.

- The user also should be able to use the keyboard to type numbers directly into the text box, and switch back and forth between using the buttons and the keyboard.

- Once a number is entered, the user should be able to perform an operation on that number. These operations include addition, subtraction, multiplication, division, and exponentiation. Each time an operator button is clicked, the current number stored in the text box at the top of the form should be cleared.

- As each operation is performed, the information should be displayed in another text box much in the same way as an adding machine would display the information on a paper tape. Each time an operation like addition or subtraction is performed, the result also should be displayed on the tape.

- Just as many calculators have a memory to store and retrieve values, your calculator also should support a memory function. Casey wants three memory locations instead of just one. The user should be able to copy the values stored in those locations to the text box containing the current number.

- The user also should be able to copy a number to and from memory using drag-and-drop operations. That is, dragging a number from memory location 1 to the current number text box should cause the contents of the current text box to be replaced by the value in the dragged memory location. Dragging a number from the current number text box to a memory location should cause the contents of the memory location to be replaced by the current number.

- Each memory location should have two associated command buttons. One button should clear the contents of the memory location. The other should store the current value of the tape to the memory location.

- The calculator must have a Clear button and a Clear All button. The Clear button should clear the current number and the contents of the tape, but not the contents of the values stored in memory. The Clear All button should clear the contents of the previous items and all the memory locations.

Consider the following guidelines as you develop the calculator program:

- As you develop the program, test each function as it is developed. This way you can pinpoint the cause of any errors more quickly.

- Logically, you can divide the buttons into three groups. Organize each group as a separate control array. The first group consists of the buttons the user will click to enter the numbers zero (0) through nine (9) and a decimal point. The second group consists of the operators like addition (+), subtraction (−), and so on. The final group represents miscellaneous functions like clear and clear all. These two buttons could be implemented as a separate control array or as an operator.

- Each time a number on the keypad is clicked, you can use the index of the control array to determine the value of the number. Pay attention to the value of the Index property of each element in this control array. You can simplify the code considerably.

- The operators like addition (+) and subtraction (−) and so on, can make up another control array. By placing all the operators into a control array, you can localize the function of the different mathematical operations. Consider the task of adding the numbers 1 and 2. You can think of the task as one operator, addition (+), and two operands, 1 and 2. Your program must be able to deal with the special case where the user is entering the first number in an expression. That is, the user has clicked 1 and + but has not entered the second number. Note that the addition should not be performed until the user has entered the second number. When this occurs, the two numbers should be added together and the result displayed on the tape.

- Because the user must be able to both click buttons and type numbers on the keypad to store values in the current number text box, you cannot use automatic drag-and-drop, because the control would not receive focus. Instead, you need to program the MouseDown and MouseUp events. When the MouseDown event occurs, you can call the Drag method explicitly on the text box, using an appropriate argument to start the drag operation. When the mouse button is released, the drag operation should be terminated.

- Make sure to validate user input. That is, the user should not be able to enter characters into the text box. The only valid characters are the numbers zero (0) through nine (9), and a decimal point. Be sure that your program does not try to divide a number by zero, and displays an error message if numeric overflow occurs.

1. Start Visual Basic.

2. Save the form using the name **frmCalculator.frm** and the project using the name **Calculator.vbp** in the **Problem1** folder of the **AdditionalCases** folder on your Student Disk.

3. Create the objects on the form as shown in Figure 1. To simplify the programming process, make sure to create different control arrays as indicated in the previous list.

4. Write the necessary code to store digits in the current text box number.

5. Write the necessary statements to perform arithmetic operations on the current numbers. If the operation is the first operand in an expression, then just display the operand in tape text box. Otherwise perform the operation and display the result in the tape text box. Each time an operation is performed, the contents of the current number text box should be cleared.

6. Write the necessary statements for the Clear and Clear All buttons.

7. Write the necessary statements to perform drag-and-drop between the current number text box and the three different memory locations.

8. Write the necessary statements for the command buttons to store and clear values from the three memory locations.

9. Test the program by using each number and each operator. Make sure to test that each memory location is working correctly, and that the drag-and-drop operations also are working correctly.

10. Create an executable file named **Calculator.exe**.

11. Exit Visual Basic.

Creating an Order Entry System

OBJECTIVES

In this case you will:

- Use several ActiveX controls

- Interact with a database using both Data controls and programmatically using SQL statements

- Create multiple Form and standard modules including MDI parent, MDI child, and standard forms

CASE

Monarch Roofing

Monarch Roofing manufactures roofing tiles in Midland, Texas. These roofing tiles are sold to construction companies throughout Texas and the surrounding states. Candice Yfantis is the information systems coordinator for Monarch Roofing and has been charged with the task of developing an order entry system for Monarch Roofing. This order entry system must allow the user to process new orders by specifying an existing customer. Once a customer has been specified, a new order needs to be created. Each new order must have an order date and a requested shipping date. Once the order is created, the user needs to be able to select items from inventory, then add those items to the order. Once complete, a report needs to be printed and sent to the customer confirming the order. In addition to entering new orders they also want to be able to edit existing orders, and print several different reports. The information for the order entry system is stored in a Microsoft Access database. The database consists of four tables. The table tblCustomers contains the customer information. The table tblInventory contains the inventory information. The table tblOrderMaster contains the general information about an order, and the table tblOrderDetail contains the different inventory items and quantities pertaining to the order. Figure 1 shows the structure of the table tblCustomers.

Figure 1 tblCustomers table

Column Name	Data Type
fldCustomerID	Number (Long)
fldCompanyName	Text
fldLastName	Text
fldFirstName	Text
fldAddress	Text
fldCity	Text
fldState	Text
fldZipCode	Text
fldPhone	Text
fldFax	Text
fldOrderLimit	Currency

Figure 2 shows the structure of the table tblInventory.

Figure 2 tblInventory table

Column Name	Data Type
fldPartID	Number (Long)
fldDescription	Text
fldCost	Currency
fldSalesPrice	Currency
fldQtyInStock	Number (Long)

Figure 3 shows the structure of the table tblOrderMaster.

Figure 3 ◀
tblOrderMaster
table

Column Name	Data Type
fldOrderID	Number (Long)
fldCustomerID	Number (Long)
fldOrderDate	Date/Time
fldShipDate	Date/Time

Figure 4 shows the structure of the table tblOrderDetail.

Figure 4 ◀
tblOrderDetail
table

Column Name	Data Type
fldOrderID	Number (Long)
fldPartID	Number (Long)
fldQtyOrdered	Number (Long)

The relationships for the database also have been defined as shown in Figure 5.

Figure 5 ◀
Relationships
between
tblCustomers,
tblOrderMaster,
tblOrderDetail,
and tblInventory

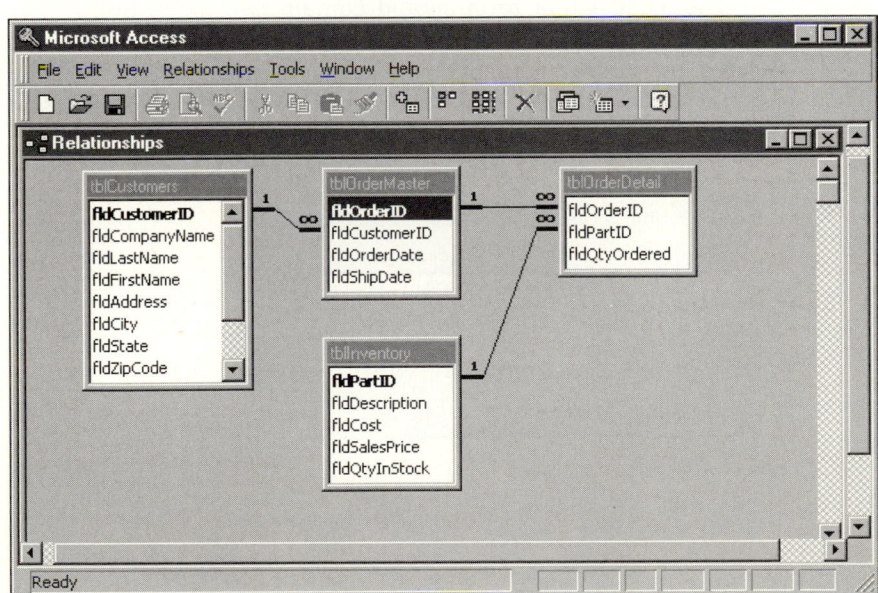

Candice wants the program to be an MDI program consisting of several forms. The following list describes the general purpose of each form:

- A splash screen should be provided displaying the company name and pertinent information about the program.

- The MDI parent form will display each of the different MDI child forms.

- The Find form will be used to locate a customer by selecting a company. This form should be displayed as a modal form. Thus it will not be an MDI child form.

- The New Order form will be used to enter a new order into the system, then print a confirmation of the order. This form should be an MDI child form.

- The Edit Order form will be used to view, and possibly change, the contents of an existing order.

When the program first is started, the Sub Main procedure should execute. This procedure should perform the following tasks:

1. Display the splash screen.

2. Load all the forms in the project.

3. Using a CommonDialog control, it should open the database as specified by the user, the common dialog should be configured such that it looks for the default filename **Monarch.mdb** in the folder named **AdditionalCases** on your Student Disk. Consider creating a Function procedure to open the database.

4. If a database was opened successfully, then continue to display the MDI parent form. Otherwise display a message box asking the user if they want to try again. Depending on user input, either exit the program or try again to open a database.

The MDI parent form should contain two menu titles. The first, File, contains one menu item to exit the program. The second, Orders, contains two menu items—one to add a new order, and another to edit an existing order.

Before adding or editing an order, an existing customer must be located using the Find form. The Find form is shown in Figure 6.

Figure 6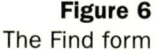
The Find form

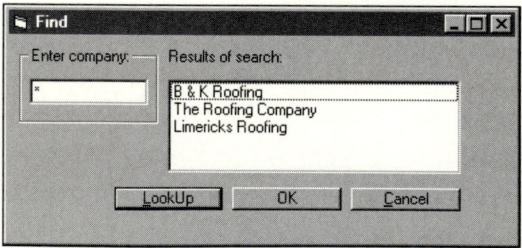

This Find form should give the user considerable flexibility in searching for a company. As shown in Figure 6, the company name specified is an asterisk (*), meaning search for all companies. If the company "B*" was selected, then all the companies with the name starting with the letter "B" should be selected. When the company is selected, and the LookUp command button is clicked, the program should create a corresponding SELECT statement to create a Recordset object containing the companies that match the search criteria. You can use the LIKE clause of the SELECT statement to do this. Then, each record in the recordset needs to be displayed in the list box as shown in Figure 6. The user then will select the company they want by clicking the desired item in the list box then clicking the OK button. If the Cancel button is clicked, then the form should be hidden. The form needs to communicate three items of information to other forms. First, a flag needs to be set indicating whether or not a company was found, another to indicate the current customer ID, and another describing the company name. To improve the user interface for this form, consider resetting the default command button and focus as the user selects a company.

When adding an order, the New Order form should be displayed as shown in Figure 7.

Figure 7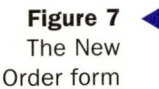
The New
Order form

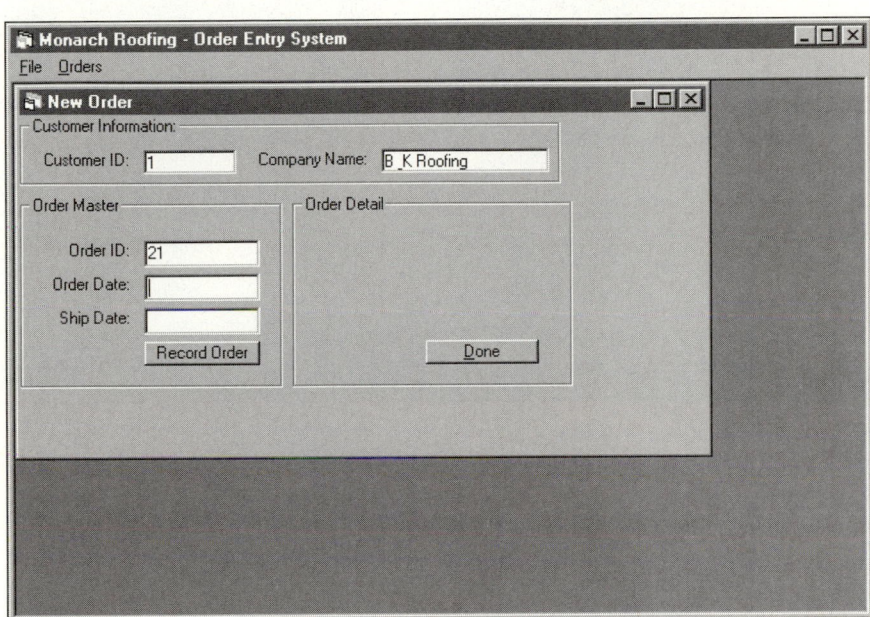

The New Order form consists of three sections. The first section displays the Customer ID and current company. The Customer ID and current company should not be changed from this form. The Customer ID and current company information should have been determined by the Find form.

The second section contains the information pertinent to the table named tblOrderMaster and contains the Order ID, Order Date, and Ship Date. Note from Figure 7 that the Order ID text box is filled in. This field should be filled in automatically by the program. That is, when the form is displayed, a new Order ID should be generated. This can be accomplished by determining the maximum Order ID value in the table named tblOrderMaster and adding one to that value. The user should not be able to change this value. You can accomplish this using a SELECT statement. The default value for the Order Date should be the current date as shown in Figure 8.

Figure 8 ◄
Default value
for Order Date

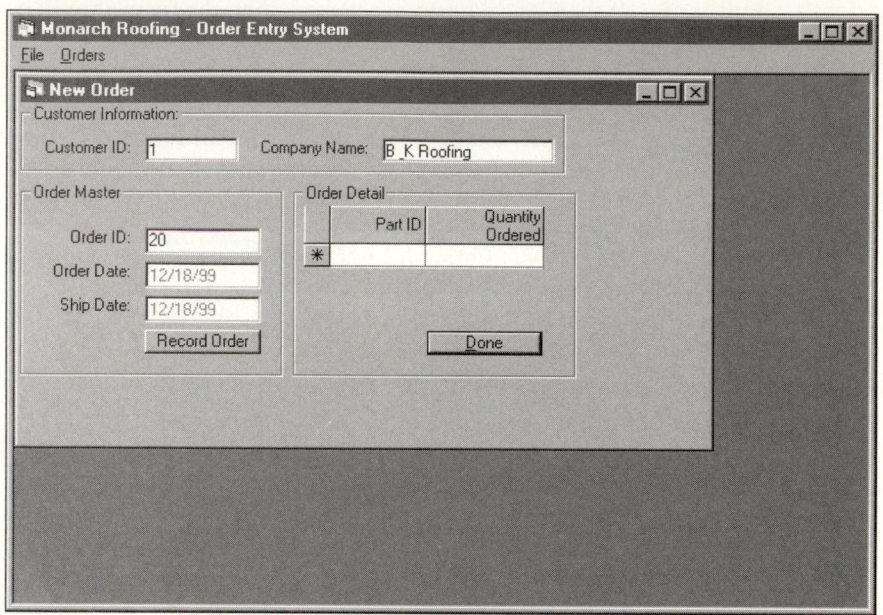

Once the Order Date and Ship Date are entered, the information should be validated to make sure that both are valid dates. When the Record Order command button is clicked, the new order should be added to the table named tblOrderMaster. Again, this can be accomplished using an SQL INSERT statement. Do not use bound controls. After inserting the Order Master table information, a DBGrid control should be displayed so the user can proceed to specify the different inventory items and quantities desired for each item.

The user then can specify the Part ID and Quantity Ordered for each item. When the order is complete, the Done command button should hide the form.

You can think of entering a new order as a series of steps as follows:

1. Locate an existing Customer ID and a Company Name by displaying the Find form.

2. If a customer was found, then display the New Order form. Otherwise do not.

3. Assign a new Order ID by finding the maximum Order ID in the table tblOrderDetail and adding one to that number.

The Edit Order form will be used to view and edit an existing order. This form is shown in Figure 9.

Figure 9 ◀

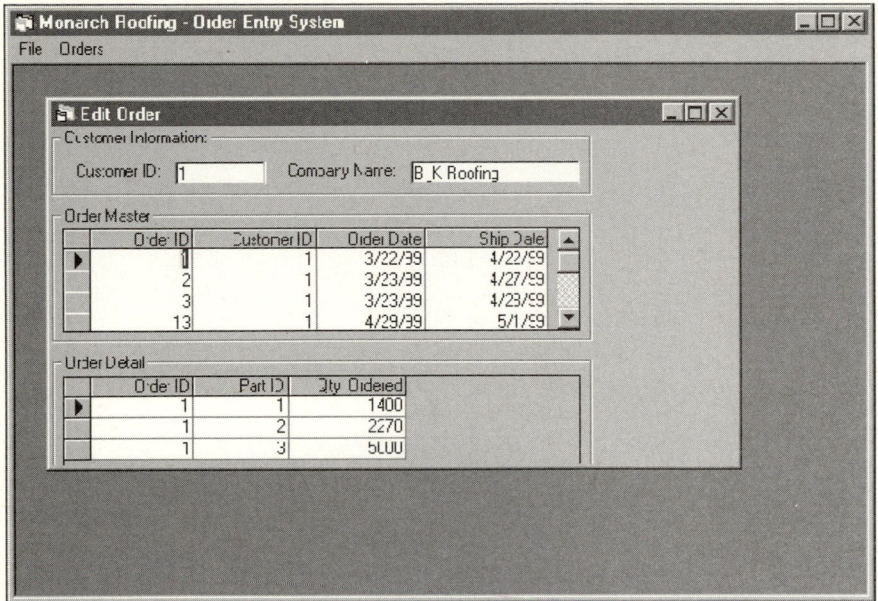

The Edit Order form displays the current customer and company just as the New Order form does. The form also contains two DBGrid controls. The first should display the information from the Order Master table. Note that the records corresponding to the current Customer ID should be displayed. When the user selects an Order ID, then detail information should be displayed in the other DBGrid control. If the user selects a different Order ID, then the records displayed in the second DBGrid should be updated accordingly.

You can think of editing an existing order as a series of steps as follows:

1. Locate an existing Customer ID and a Company Name by displaying the Find form.

2. If a customer was found, then display the Edit Order form. Otherwise do not display the current Customer ID and Company Name on the form.

Creating a Customer Service Program

OBJECTIVES

In this case you will:

- Create MDI parent, MDI child, and standard forms

- Create and use a Class module

- Create a toolbar

- Use arrays and collections

- Create enumerated and user-defined types

- Create multiple instances of a form

Lyons Bank

CASE

Lyons Bank is an issuer of credit cards. Currently, it has about 250,000 credit cards issued. Its customer service center is located in Fort Collins, Colorado. The customer service center employs about 100 people to answer telephone calls from customers. Customers call the customer service center to check on their balances, available credit, and other account information.

Each time a call is received, certain information about the call is recorded in a text file. One text file is produced for each employee during his or her shift. At this time, however, the supervisors and managers do not have a program to analyze the information that is collected. Sabrina Brown is the general manager of the customer service center. She wants a program that will allow her and the supervisors to view and summarize this information so they can better assess employee performance and the types of calls that are being received. She wants to find out the average duration of each type of call for each employee. Also, she wants to be able to compute additional statistics for all employees.

Sabrina has determined that many of the tasks related to processing the log files will be used by other programs they are developing. Therefore, she has suggested that you encapsulate the processing of the text file into a Class module.

The input data for the program is well defined. Each record in the text file has the following format:

Field Description	Data Type
Call Type	Integer
Resolution Code	Integer
Start Time	Date
End Time	Date
Account Number	String

The first two fields have well-defined values. The type of call can be a number between zero (0) and seven (7). Each value has the following meaning:

Lost Card	0
Check Balance	1
Limit Increase	2
Address Change	3
Payment Information	4
Additional Card	5
Cancel Card	6
Stolen Card	7

The resolution of the call is represented by one of three integer values. Each value has the following meaning:

Refer to Supervisor	1
Problem Solved	2
Call Back	3

Sabrina has defined the properties and methods of the Class module. When an instance of the class is created, there should be a method to load an input file into the class. Each record should be stored in a private array of user-defined types. The type should correspond to the format of the input file.

You also need to create an array to hold the summary information. After the log file is read, you need to store summary information in another private array according to the following guidelines:

- The array should have eight elements, corresponding to each call type. You should create another user-defined type with six members for the elements.

- The first member should identify the call type.

- The second member should contain the number of calls having the specified call type.

- The third member should contain the average duration of the calls of that type.

- The fourth, fifth, and sixth members should contain the count of calls referred to a supervisor, problems solved, and calls to be returned.

You will create methods to locate different elements in the arrays and summarize the information. You also will create several properties so the information can be displayed on the form.

Sabrina wants the program to operate as an MDI program. There will be one type of MDI child form. Each MDI child form will display the information corresponding to a single text file stored in an instance of the class. That is, the information represents the call activity for the work shift of a single employee. It should be possible for a supervisor to open any number of MDI child forms. Each MDI child form should call the methods of a class. These methods should open files, load the information into memory, and locate different records.

The class should work much like a recordset. Each line read from the text file can be thought of as a record. You should store each record into an array. You will call methods like FindFirst, FindNext, FindPrevious, and FindLast to navigate through the array. When you read the properties representing an individual field the value should be retrieved from the current record. Thus, your class will implement the concept of a current record pointer.

The following list describes the properties of the class and their behavior:

- The **AccountNumber** property should be a read-only property that returns a string.

- The **StartTime** and **EndTime** properties should be read-only properties of the Date data type corresponding to the call's starting and ending times.

- The **CallType** property should be a read-only property. The valid values are the integers zero (0) through seven (7). You can use an enumerated type to represent these values.

- The **Count** property should be a read-only property containing the number of records in the class instance.

- The **Current** property should be a read-write property identifying the current record. When setting the Current property, the Property procedure should verify that the value is within the acceptable range. That is, it should be between one (1) and the number of records in the array.

- The **CurrentSummary** property should be a read-write property identifying the current summary record. When setting the CurrentSummary property, the Property procedure should verify that the value is within the acceptable range.

- The **Duration** property should be a read-only property. It should compute the duration of the call by subtracting the end time of the call from the start time of the call. The property should return a string. The format of the string should be the elapsed minutes and seconds of the call in the form mm:ss.

- The **LogBOF** property should be a read-only property indicating that beginning of file has been reached. It should be True when the first record is the current record.

- The **LogEOF** property should be a read-only property indicating that end of file has been reached. It should be True when the last record is the current record.

- The **ResolutionCode** property should be a read-only property. The valid values are the integers zero (0) through two (2). You can use an enumerated type to represent these values.

- The **SummaryCallType** property should be a read-only property and return the call type of the currently selected summary record.

- The **SummaryCallCount** property should be a read-only property and return the count of the calls corresponding to the SummaryCallType.

- The **SummaryAverageDuration** property should be a read-only property and return the average time of the call of the currently selected SummaryCallType.

- The **SummaryReferToSupervisor**, **SummaryProblemSolved**, and **SummaryCallBack** properties should return the count of the resolutions for the selected SummaryCallType.

In addition to these properties, the class should have several methods to read the information from a file and locate different records. The following list describes the methods of the class.

- The **FindFirst, FindNext, FindPrevious**, and **FindLast** methods should locate the first, next, previous, and last detail records, respectively.

- The **FindFirstSummary**, **FindNextSummary**, **FindPreviousSummary**, and **FindLastSummary** methods should locate the first, next, previous, and last summary records, respectively.

- The **Load** method should accept one argument—the disk file to load into the class instance. This method should return True if the file was loaded successfully and False otherwise. The information should be stored in a private array. Each time a record is loaded, you will need to redimension the array. After the array is loaded, the information needs to be summarized and recorded in a second array.

The MDI parent form should have one menu title with the caption **File** with two menu items, **Open** and **Exit**. The Open menu item should cause several actions to occur. First, an instance of the class and an instance of the MDI child form needs to be created. You can keep track of each form and class instance using collections. Once the instance of the class is created, you need to allow the user to specify a filename to be loaded. The name of the file is the same as the EmployeeID number.

The MDI child form also should have a menu system. The File menu should be the same as the MDI parent form with the addition of a Close menu item. The Close menu item should unload the instance of the form, and destroy the corresponding instance of the class. Figure 1 shows the MDI child form at run time inside the MDI parent form.

Figure 1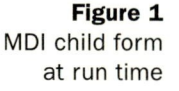
MDI child form
at run time

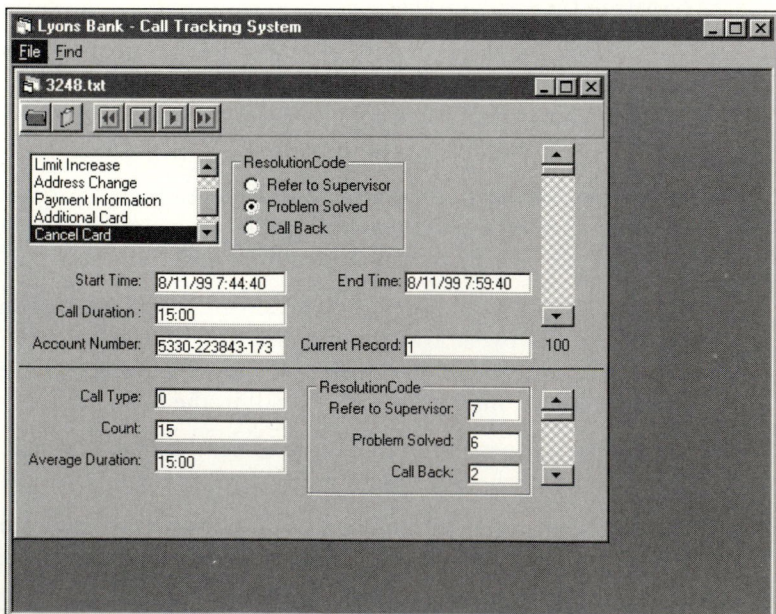

As you can see from Figure 1, the form is divided into two sections separated by a line. The first section displays detail information. The current call type is displayed in a list box, the current resolution code is displayed in an option group, and the start time, end time, and call duration is displayed in labels. In addition, the current record and account number also are displayed. Note that there is a vertical scroll bar on the right side of the form. This scroll bar should display the relative position of the current record pointer in the list of records. If the user moves the scroll bar, the current record should be updated accordingly, and the correct information displayed. Also the user should be able to locate different records on the toolbar using the items on the Find menu and the buttons on the toolbar. The icons and bitmaps for the toolbar are stored in the **AdditionalCases** folder on your Student Disk. They have the following filenames: **First.bmp**, **Next.bmp**, **Last.bmp**, **Previous.bmp**, **Open.bmp**, and **Close.bmp**.

The second section of the form displays summary information. The scroll bar in this section should change the current call type and display the appropriate information, just like the scroll bar in the first section.

In addition to using the scroll bars to locate information, the Find menu should contain menu items to locate the first, next, previous, and last summary and detail records.

Some hints to solving the problem are as follows:

- Use an enumerated type for both the CallType and the ResolutionCode. This will make the program more readable and less error prone. Also create a user-defined type to store the input records.

- Create a collection to store each form instance and another collection to store the class instance corresponding to the form. Use the Tag property of the form to keep track of the current form.

- Make sure that you properly deal with the first and last summary and detail records. A common problem is to miss these records.

- When an input file is read, load the detail array. Then using that array as input, derive the information in the summary array. Note these arrays should be private to the Class module. The form accessing the Class module will retrieve elements using properties and methods.

1. Start Visual Basic.

2. Create a new project with an MDI parent form, an MDI child form, a Class module, and a standard module.

3. Create the menu systems and necessary objects for the MDI parent and child forms as described in the case and shown in Figure 1.

4. Create the properties and methods of the Class module.

5. Save the forms and project.

6. Test the program by using the input files.

7. Exit Visual Basic.

Debugging

In this appendix you will:

- Prepare a Visual Basic program for debugging

- Locate and fix run-time errors

- Trace the execution of your program

- Set breakpoints in code

- Set watch expressions in code

- Inspect the value of variables and objects using the Immediate window

- Look at the active procedures in a program

Types of Programming Errors

Programming errors can occur in your program when you are writing code or when you are running the program. A **programming error** is any error in a program that causes it to end abnormally or produce unexpected results. A programming error commonly is called a **bug**.

Programming errors can be categorized into three different types: syntax errors, run-time errors, and logic errors. **Syntax** is the set of rules that specifies the proper way to use the statements that make up a programming language. A **syntax error** occurs when you write a statement that Visual Basic cannot understand. If you misspell a word such as Dim when declaring a variable, Visual Basic will detect a syntax error. Syntax errors are found either when you enter statements in the Code window or when you compile a program. **Compiling** your program is the process of translating the Visual Basic statements you wrote into statements the computer can understand. When you encounter a syntax error, look closely at the Visual Basic Help window that describes the statement or expression, and make sure you have typed it correctly.

A **run-time error** occurs when your program is running and usually results from the following:

- A statement that attempts an invalid operation caused by an unexpected user action. For example, a user may have entered a letter into a text box and you tried to use it in an arithmetic expression without verifying the validity of the data first. These errors can be fixed by writing code to validate data and creating error handlers for procedures.

- Errors in your program that result from trying to divide a number by zero (0) or trying to store too large a number into an Integer variable.

A **logic error** occurs when the program does not perform as intended and produces incorrect results. You generally notice logic errors at run time. For example, if you intend to compute the area of a rectangle, you would multiply the length by the width. If your program added the numbers rather than multiplying them, the program would not generate the right answer and you would have created a logic error.

The distinction between logic and run-time errors is not always clear. You might have coded an expression incorrectly. For example, a logic error would occur if you intended to add two numbers together but wrote statements to multiply them instead. When the program is run, the multiplication could generate a number that is too big for the system to deal with. In this example the logic error, in turn, causes a run-time error.

To find and fix run-time and logic errors in program code, you go through a process called **debugging**. Visual Basic provides built-in tools that help you debug your programs. Using the debugging tools described in this appendix will help you fix run-time and logic errors.

Preparing a Program for Debugging

Visual Basic checks for syntax errors when a program compiles, or translates, the code you write into executable code. How a program is compiled, and how errors are handled, depend on settings in the Options dialog box. These settings are saved to your environment, so you should verify that they are correct before you begin to debug your program.

> *Tip:* You may find it useful to display the Debug toolbar containing the more frequently used debugging commands. To display the Debug toolbar click View, then Toolbars, then Debug.

To set the Compile and Error Trapping settings in the Options dialog box:

1. Start Visual Basic and make sure your Student Disk is in the appropriate disk drive.

2. Click the **Open Project** button 📂, and then open the project named **RunTime.vbp** located in the **Appendix.A** folder on your Student Disk.

3. Click **Tools** on the menu bar, then click **Options** to open the Options dialog box.

4. Click the **General** tab as shown in Figure A-1.

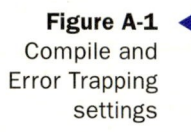

Figure A-1
Compile and
Error Trapping
settings

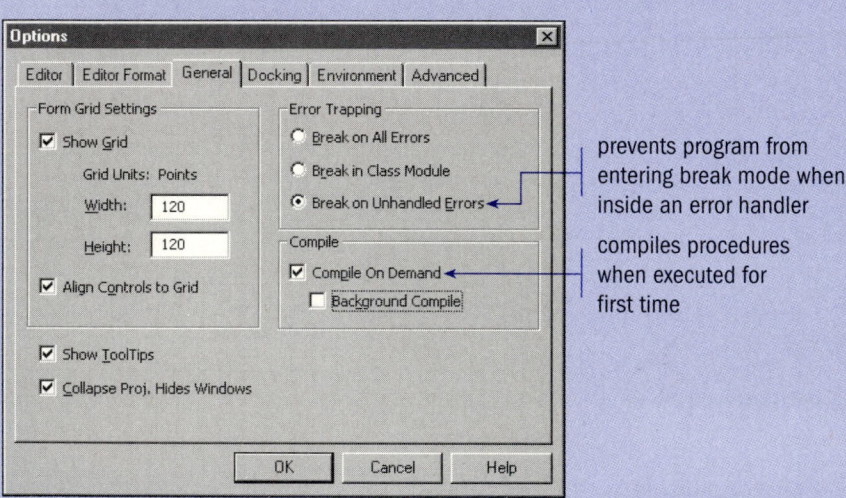

prevents program from entering break mode when inside an error handler

compiles procedures when executed for first time

5. If necessary, change your settings so they are the same as those in Figure A-1.

6. Click the **OK** button to close the Options dialog box and save the settings.

The Compile section of the General tab contains two check boxes:

- If the **Compile On Demand** check box is checked, Visual Basic will compile the current procedure and analyze it for syntax errors as it is run. For example, a procedure will only be compiled when it is called for the first time. When the Compile On Demand option is selected, Visual Basic will not find all the syntax errors until you execute all the procedures in your program. While you are writing and testing programs, checking this box will cause your programs to start much faster. If the Compile On Demand check box is not checked, the syntax of an entire program is checked before the program begins executing. As you write the programs in this book, you can turn off Compile On Demand and then run your program to check for any syntax errors you might have created in different procedures.

- If the **Background Compile** check box is checked, a program will be compiled while the computer is idle during run time. Background Compile can improve run-time execution speed the first time procedures are executed. This option is available only when Compile On Demand is checked. Leaving the Background Compile option off will ensure that you get the same results described in this appendix.

As with syntax errors, how Visual Basic handles run-time errors depends on settings in the Options dialog box. The General tab on the Options dialog box contains a section named Error Trapping. The three options in this section control the behavior of Visual Basic when a run-time error occurs:

- When the **Break on All Errors** option button is selected, any run-time error will cause Visual Basic to enter break mode, open a dialog box allowing you to activate the Code window, and display the line that caused the error.

- When the **Break in Class Module** option button is selected, errors in class modules that are not handled by an On Error statement cause Visual Basic to enter break mode, allowing you to fix the error. Refer to Visual Basic online Help for more information on the Class modules and the On Error statement.

- When the **Break on Unhandled Errors** option button is selected, Visual Basic enters break mode when a run-time error occurs that is not handled by an On Error statement. In this appendix you use this setting so your error handlers will execute without generating a run-time error.

When you debug a program, you might have several windows open at a time, which might cause windows to obscure each other. Consider making the Immediate window and the Code window as small as possible so you can see each window on the screen. Also, try to keep windows from obscuring the toolbar. You will use these toolbar buttons often, and they might be hard to find if obscured by another window.

Visual Basic Debugging Tools

The Visual Basic debugging analysis tools consist of commands that allow you to suspend temporarily the execution of your program by entering break mode, and then follow the execution of statements and procedures. You can execute each statement in the program line by line and have your program stop executing when a specific statement is reached or when the value of a variable or object changes.

Whenever you suspend the execution of your program, you do so to try to identify a particular problem. This involves looking at the values of the variables and object properties in your program to see if they contain correct data. You can look at the contents of variables and objects using three windows called Immediate, Watch, and Locals. You use the debugging commands in conjunction with these windows as tools to help you locate and fix run-time and logic errors in your program.

Locating and Fixing Run-time Errors

Run-time errors can occur for many reasons, but unlike syntax errors, they do not occur when a program is being compiled. Rather, these errors occur while a program is running and are caused by performing an operation such as storing data of the incorrect type into a variable or object property, or performing invalid run-time operations on a database object like a Recordset. Because this information is not known until the program is running, the statements actually will not cause an error until they are executed.

When you write programs, you frequently can prevent run-time errors from occurring by carefully validating the correctness of user input before using that input in other parts of your program. Consider the following guidelines when writing code using input from the user.

- Numeric data entered into objects like text boxes should be checked before being used in computations. Use the **IsNumeric** and **IsDate functions** to check for valid numbers and dates, respectively.

- Input that is required, like a first and last name, often must exist before the statements can execute. Compare the variable or object properties with the null string "" to test for existence.

- Perform range checking to prevent overflow and other errors.

When a run-time error cannot be prevented, consider creating an error handler in a procedure that will execute when the error occurs. An **error handler**, or error handling routine, in your code determines whether or not it is reasonable for the program to continue processing. Refer to the OnError statement if you are not familiar with the process of creating an error handler. Inside the error handler, your code first should determine the cause and seriousness of the error. Based on this information, your program must decide what action to take. For example, a calculator program may operate on user input that would cause a number to be divided by zero (0). In this case the error handler should advise the user of the program what happened, the possible causes, and continue to let the user correct the problem.

When a run-time error occurs, one of two dialog boxes can open. One contains an OK button that, when clicked, activates the Code window and highlights the statement that caused the error. You then can edit your code to fix the error. The other dialog box contains two items of information—an error number and a description. Error numbers typically are used by an error handler in your code. A well-designed program should alert the user to the problem, but continue to run, even when the program encounters an error or the user gives the program erroneous input.

For debugging purposes, always read the description of the error carefully to determine the nature of the error. You can choose from four actions in the second type of dialog box:

- Click the **Continue** button to try to run your program from the point where the error occurred. Depending on the nature of the error, this option sometimes is disabled, indicating that you cannot continue execution until the problem is fixed.

- Click the **End** button to end your program. This will cause Visual Basic to return to design mode.

- Click the **Debug** button to attempt to fix the program. The Code window will be activated and the statement causing the error will be highlighted. After fixing the statement or statements that caused the error, click the Start button on the toolbar to continue execution from the statement that caused the error. If the corrections require that you change variable declarations or add new variables or procedures, however, end and restart the program from the beginning.

- Click the **Help** button to get more information about the nature of the problem if you do not understand the meaning of the run-time error.

Run-time errors come from many sources. They can be caused by using incorrectly typed arguments when calling functions, or by trying to store data of the wrong type into a property or variable. The underlying cause of a run-time error might stem from other statements in your program. So, as you analyze the error, look at the preceding statements to help you identify the problem. When you write statements to perform arithmetic operations, you must be careful to use the correct data type for the operation you are trying to perform. If you use an Integer data type, the variable cannot store a number larger than

32767. If you try to store a number larger than that into an Integer, you will get an **overflow error**. Generally, the solution to an overflow error is to use a data type that can store a larger number or to check the user input to make sure it is within a valid range. You also can write an error handler that will advise users of the problem so they can try to correct their input values.

Another error is caused when you try to store a character string in a numeric data type like Integer or Single. This error is called a **type mismatch error**. A type mismatch error can happen when a user enters invalid data into a text box that you intend to use as a number. To prepare for this kind of invalid data entry, you can call the IsNumeric function or the Val function on the user input. If the input is valid then call the function; otherwise you could display a message box.

To find and fix overflow and type mismatch errors:

1. Click the **Start** button ▶ on the toolbar.

2. Enter **.25** for the Interest Rate, **15000** for the Periods, and **1000000** for the Amount, then click the **Numeric Overflow** button. The Microsoft Visual Basic dialog box opens with a run-time error message, as shown in Figure A-2.

Figure A-2 ◀
Microsoft Visual
Basic dialog box
with Run-time
error message

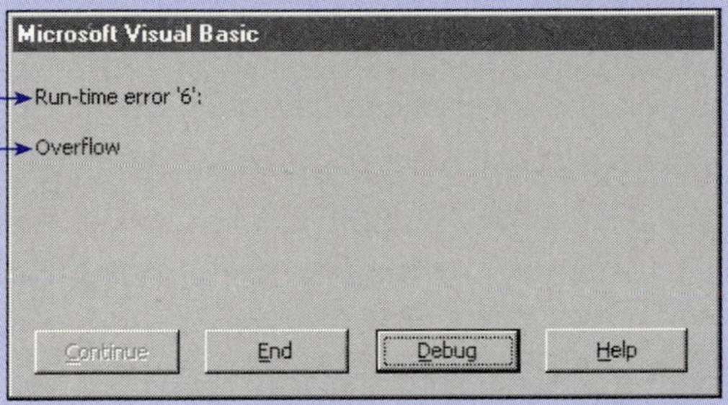

error number ——

error description ——

3. Click the **Debug** button to look at the statement causing the error.

   Note that the line containing the error is the Pmt function. One way to allow the program to continue after it encounters this error is to write an error handler that displays a message box describing the problem to the user. Although the program can continue to run, the results will not be accurate.

4. Read the comments in the event procedure. Follow the instructions in the comments to uncomment the necessary lines that will create an error handler.

5. Click the **End** button on the toolbar to end the program, then repeat Step 2.

   Note that the message box appears and the run-time error is handled by the program rather than causing execution to terminate.

6. Click the **OK** button to return to running the program.

7. Enter the text **abc** in the Interest Rate text box, then click the **Type Mismatch** button. When the run-time error occurs, click the **Debug** button.

   This error is caused by trying to store text into an argument of the Pmt function that can contain only numbers.

8. Read the comments in the command button's Click event procedure and fix the program.

9. End and start the program, then repeat Step 6 to verify that the If statement validates the user input before calling the Pmt function. The error handler detects the type mismatch, prevents any calculations, and nothing changes on the form.

10. End the program.

In some cases the statement that caused the error may be only a symptom of the underlying problem. You found the cause of the previous errors by debugging the statement that caused a run-time error. A program will sometimes produce incorrect results, but will not generate a run-time error, or you may want to look at the statements that led up to the run-time error. For example, if you called the Pmt function and the argument values were incorrect, the function call would generate a run-time error. You would need to first determine the argument that is incorrect, then locate the statement that set the value of the argument.

Tracing Program Execution

Often a program contains logic errors—that is, it produces incorrect results, but does not necessarily generate a run-time error or the actual cause of a run-time error is not apparent. This is when the debugging tools are most useful. When a program is producing incorrect results, but you are not sure why, it often is helpful to step through the statements in a program. There are several commands that allow you to follow the execution of your program.

- The Step Into button allows you to execute one statement at a time. When you use the Step Into button, a single statement is executed then Visual Basic enters break mode. If the statement is a procedure call, the procedure declaration for the procedure that will be executed next is highlighted in the Code window.

- The Step Over button works like the Step Into button. If the statement is a procedure call, however, then all the statements in the procedure are executed, and then Visual Basic will enter break mode just before executing the statement following the procedure call.

- The Step Out button is similar to the Step Over button. When clicked, the Step Out button will execute all the remaining statements in the current procedure.

- You can alter the flow of execution during break mode by clicking a statement in the Code window, then clicking Debug, and then clicking Set Next Statement on the menu bar.

To use the Step Into button to examine statements and procedures:

1. Click the **Start** button ▶ on the toolbar.

2. Click the **Exit** command button on the form. Notice that the word "program" in the message box is misspelled.

3. Click **Yes** in the message box to stop execution and return to design mode.

4. Click **View**, **Toolbars**, **Debug** to display the Debug toolbar, if necessary.

5. Because you are not sure where the MsgBox function is called or where the prompt is being set, click the **Step Into** button 🔲 on the Debug toolbar to begin execution of your program. The first statement to execute is in the Form_Load event procedure, so the Code window becomes the active window and this procedure is highlighted indicating that the procedure will be executed next. The next time you click the Step Into button the first statement in the procedure will be highlighted.

6. Before executing the procedure, correct the spelling for the word **program**. Add a **?** to the end of the prompt.

7. Click the **Step Into** button 🔲 twice to execute the first statement in the procedure.

8. Continue clicking the **Step Into** button 🔲 until the form appears. At this time, no procedure is executing. Rather your program is waiting for the user to generate an event.

9. Click the **Exit** command button to generate the cmdExit_Click event. The Code window is activated.

10. Continue to click the **Step Into** button ⬚ until the message box appears.

11. Click the **Yes** button in the message box and continue to click **Step Into** ⬚ until you exit the program and return to break mode.

12. End the program.

In addition to stepping through every statement in every procedure in a program, you can step through parts of a program or pause the program and continue executing statements one at a time. When you are debugging a procedure that calls other procedures, you do not have to trace through the statements in a procedure when you know it works correctly. You can use the Step Over button to execute all the statements in a procedure and suspend execution from the statement following that procedure. Furthermore, you can suspend execution at any time by clicking the Break button at run time.

To suspend the program and step over a general procedure:

1. Click the **Start** button ⬚ on the toolbar. Your program is in run mode and will execute the statements without displaying them in the Code window.

2. Click the **Break** button ⬚ on the Debug toolbar. The Immediate window opens and Visual Basic enters break mode.

3. Click the **Step Into** button ⬚ to begin stepping through each statement in the program.

   At this time, no statement is executing. The form has been loaded and Visual Basic is waiting for an event to occur. When you generate an event, the Code window again will become active and you can continue to click the Step Into button to trace the execution of your program.

4. Activate the form and click the **Exit** command button. The Click event procedure is activated in the Code window.

5. Click ⬚ again. The ExitProgram general procedure is highlighted.

6. Click the **Step Over** button ⬚ on the Debug toolbar. You already have verified that the ExitProgram general procedure is working correctly. Notice the procedure will execute and the message box will appear.

7. Click the **No** button to continue running the program.

8. When the ExitProgram general procedure is finished, Visual Basic will suspend execution and enter break mode from the statement after ExitProgram. You can continue to examine the code statement by statement.

9. Click the **End** button ⬚ on the toolbar.

As you debug your programs, you will find it useful to pause the program and then step through each statement that you suspect is in error. When general procedures appear to be working correctly, you should step over them.

Setting Breakpoints

When you suspect a problem is occurring in a particular procedure or that a particular statement is not correct, you can suspend execution of your program at any executable statement by setting a breakpoint. A **breakpoint** is a program line you specify where the program will stop execution and enter break mode. Setting a breakpoint can be accomplished by locating a statement in the Code window and clicking the Toggle Breakpoint button or pressing the F9 key. The Toggle Breakpoint button is available only when the Code window is active.

When a breakpoint is set on a line, the line will appear in a highlighted color. To clear a breakpoint, click the line in the program where a breakpoint is set and click the Toggle Breakpoint button. When you run the program and the statement containing the breakpoint is reached, Visual Basic will suspend execution of the program and enter break mode just before executing the statement containing the breakpoint. The line will appear highlighted.

Once in break mode, you can use the Immediate window and the Step Into or Step Over buttons to find problems in your code. You also can look at the values of variables and objects in the Immediate window. For example, if you have determined that a function such as Pmt is producing incorrect results, you might want to set a breakpoint just before the function is called, and then look at the values of the arguments to determine which one is not correct.

To set a breakpoint in your program:

1. Be sure the program is in design mode. Activate the Code window for the **ExitProgram** general procedure. Move the cursor to the beginning of the following line:

   ```
   pintReturnValue = MsgBox(mstrPrompt, mintButtons,
       mstrTitle)
   ```

2. Click the **Toggle Breakpoint** button 🖑 on the Debug toolbar.

   The line appears highlighted in a different color.

3. Click the **Start** button ▶ on the toolbar to run the program.

4. Click the **Exit** command button. The program enters break mode just before executing the MsgBox statement where you set the breakpoint. You now can examine the statement.

5. Click **Debug** then **Clear All Breakpoints** to clear the breakpoint you just set.

After you have set a breakpoint, you often will want to look at the values of variables or the properties of objects. You do this using the Immediate window.

Using the Immediate Window

You use the **Immediate** window to look at the values of variables and object properties and to change those values. There are two ways to use the Immediate window:

- You can use the **Debug.Print** method in a program. When this method is called, the values of its arguments are printed in the Immediate window.

- You also can type Print statements directly in the Immediate window to look at values in the program. You can type statements in the Immediate window only while a program is in break mode or design mode. Most statements are valid only in break mode.

You also can execute a procedure simply by typing its name and arguments into the Immediate window.

To look at program values using the Immediate window:

1. Make sure the Immediate window is active and the program is in break mode. You may want to resize or move the Immediate window and the Form window so they do not obscure each other.

2. Type the statements into the Immediate window as shown in Figure A-3.:

Figure A-3 ◀
The Immediate window

enter these statements to display values

enter this statement to call the Sub ExitProgram general procedure

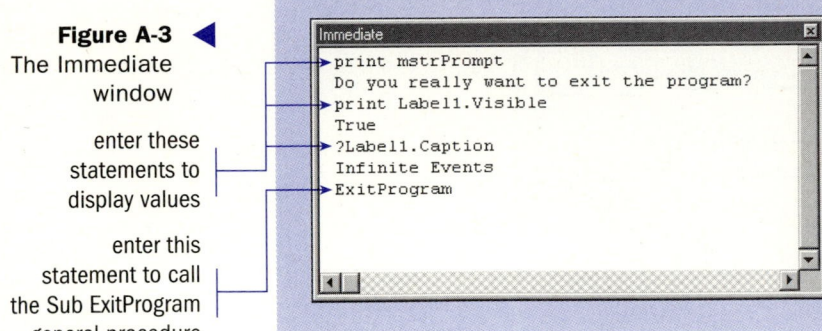

```
Immediate                                          ×
print mstrPrompt
Do you really want to exit the program?
print Label1.Visible
True
?Label1.Caption
Infinite Events
ExitProgram
```

Tip: You can use a question mark "?" in place of the Print statement to save typing. In the Immediate window, the ? has the same meaning as print.

In addition to looking at the values of properties and variables, you can use the Immediate window to set properties and the values of variables. When you change the values of variables using the Immediate window, the changes take effect only while the program is running.

To set properties and values from the Immediate window:

1. Be sure Visual Basic is still in break mode.

2. Enter the following statements in the Immediate window. Be sure to press Enter after each statement.

```
Label1.Caption = "New Caption"
MstrPrompt = "New prompt for the MessageBox"
```

3. Click the **Start** button ▸ on the toolbar to run the program.

Notice that the Infinite Events label at the bottom of the form now says "New Caption".

4. Click the **Exit** command button. The message box displays the new prompt.

5. Click the **Yes** button to exit the program.

You now can set breakpoints explicitly at specific statements in your program. You can set as many breakpoints as you want throughout a program. When you close the project or exit Visual Basic, all breakpoints disappear. The Toggle Breakpoint button works like a switch. If you want to remove an existing breakpoint, click the line containing the breakpoint, and then click the Toggle Breakpoint button.

In addition to setting breakpoints, Visual Basic also allows you to stop a program based on the status or value of an object or variable by watching an expression.

Adding Watch Expressions

Watch expressions are similar to breakpoints, but **watch expressions** allow you to suspend execution when a condition is True or when the value of an object or variable changes. Like breakpoints, watch expressions can be created, changed, or deleted while a program is in design mode or break mode. Watch expressions are not preserved after you close a project or exit Visual Basic. The more watch expressions you define, the longer it will take your program to execute, because Visual Basic must check each watch expression for every statement that is executed. When you debug a program, use watch expressions sparingly.

Visual Basic uses the Add Watch dialog box to add a watch expression to the project. Figure A-4 shows the Add Watch dialog box.

Figure A-4 ◀
Add Watch
dialog box

enter expression
to watch

define where
to watch expression

define what to do
when something
happens to
expression

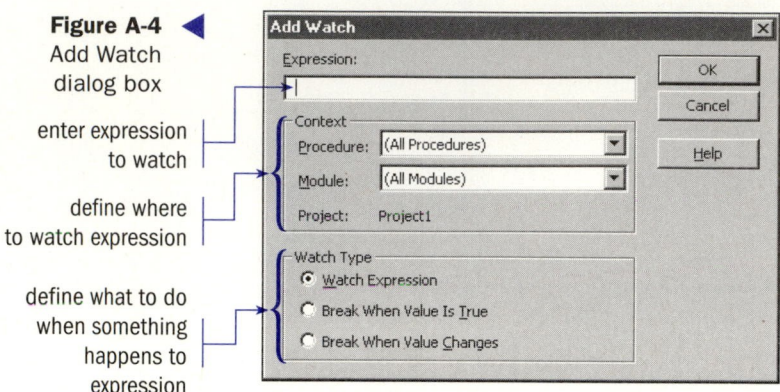

The Add Watch dialog box contains three sections:

- The **Expression** text box is where you enter the expression you want Visual Basic to evaluate. If you want to watch the value of a variable, enter the variable name. You can copy the expression or variable from the Code window to the Add Watch dialog box using the Copy and Paste commands to avoid typographical errors. The watch expression can be a variable, a property, or procedure call.

- The **Context** section sets the scope of the expression to watch. This is useful if you have variables of the same name in different procedures. **Module** refers to the form or standard module in your project that should be watched.

- The **Watch Type** section tells Visual Basic how to respond to the watch expression. If the **Watch Expression** option button is selected, Visual Basic will display the value of the expression in the Watch window but the program will not enter break mode when the expression becomes True or changes. You should consider selecting the Watch Expression option button if you print the value of a variable frequently when you reach a breakpoint. This option also is useful for tracing the value of a variable when you are using the Step Into button to watch the contents of a variable in detail. If the **Break When Value Is True** option button is selected, Visual Basic will enter break mode whenever the expression is True. If the **Break When Value Changes** option button is selected, Visual Basic will enter break mode whenever a statement changes the value of the watch expression.

The watch expressions you create appear in the Watches window. As their values change, the contents of the corresponding variables or expressions also will be shown. Figure A-5 shows the Watches window with the three watch expressions you will create next.

Figure A-5
The Watches window

watch expression but do not suspend execution

break when expression is True

break when expression has changed

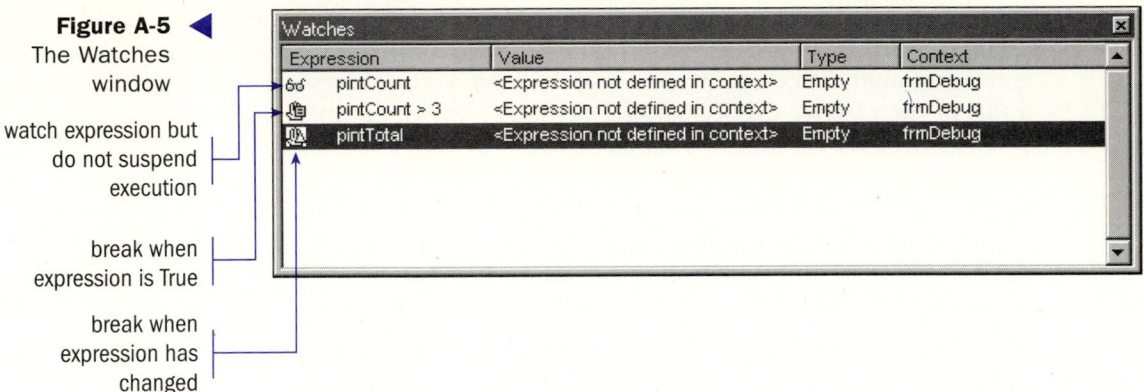

The Watches window contains four columns. The **Expression** column describes the watch expression and its type. The **Value** column displays the current value of the watch expression. Remember that local variables exist only while an event or local procedure is active. When a procedure is not active, the value "Out of context" is displayed. You also will see the Out of context message at design time. The **Type** column identifies the data type of the expression. The **Context** column defines the context of the watch expression—usually, the form name followed by the procedure.

When you create a watch expression, the Add Watch dialog box tries to anticipate the context based on the active procedure in the Code window. If you are watching a variable that is local to a specific procedure on a specific form, activate that procedure before setting the watch expression and Visual Basic will set the context for you.

To set a watch expression:

1. Activate the Code window for the **cmdAddList_Click** event procedure.

2. Click **Debug** on the menu bar, then click **Add Watch**.

3. Type **pintCount** in the Expression box.

4. In the Context section, make sure **frmDebug** is the module and **cmdAddList_Click** is the procedure.

5. In the Watch Type section, make sure the **Watch Expression** option button is selected.

6. Click the **OK** button to add the watch expression.

A more complex expression that causes the program to enter break mode when an expression is True is useful to find why a For loop is not working correctly or an array is exceeding its bounds.

To set a watch expression that will enter break mode when the expression is True:

1. Click **Debug** on the menu bar, then click **Add Watch**.

2. Type **pintCount > 3** in the Expression text box.

3. In the Context section, make sure **frmDebug** is the module and **cmdAddList_Click** is the procedure.

4. In the Watch Type section, click the **Break When Value Is True** option button to select it.

5. Click the **OK** button to add the watch expression.

In some circumstances, you might want to generate a breakpoint when a value changes. For example, if you are working with a payroll program and the gross wages are not being computed correctly, you could write a watch expression to break whenever the value of the variable sngGrossWages changes. This would save time in locating the statement causing the error.

To set a watch expression that will enter break mode when an expression changes:

1. Click **Debug** on the menu bar, then click **Add Watch**.

2. Type **pintTotal** in the Expression text box.

3. Make sure **frmDebug** is the module, and **cmdAddList_Click** is the procedure.

4. In the Watch Type section, click the **Break When Value Changes** option button to select it.

5. Click the **OK** button to add the expression.

Now that you have set the watch expressions, you can look at the values of these expressions as your program runs.

To test the watch expressions:

1. Click the **Start** button ▶ on the toolbar.

2. Click the **Add List** command button. The event procedure begins to execute. Visual Basic enters break mode when one of the watch conditions becomes True. Then the Watches window becomes active and the active watch expression is highlighted. Notice the values of the watch expressions you created.

3. Continue to click ▶ until a run-time error occurs. This error happened because one of the list items contains invalid data. Type the Print statements you used in previous steps in the Immediate window to find the item that contains invalid data. To correct the error you could add the necessary statements to verify the data contains a valid number by using a function like IsNumeric.

4. End the program.

You can edit a watch expression when a program is in design mode or break mode. To edit a watch expression, click an expression in the Watches window, then click Debug, then click Edit watch on the menu bar. This will activate the Edit Watch dialog box, which allows you to change any of the settings in the watch expression.

You can delete a watch expression when a program is in design mode or break mode. To delete a watch expression, click the watch expression in the Watches window, and then press the Delete key.

Tracing the Events in a Program

Another problem with event-driven programs is that improper logic can cause events to trigger each other indefinitely. This problem happens when a statement causes a Change event in one object. That object, in turn, causes a Change event in a second object, and so on. If an object down the line causes a Change event in the first object, this program becomes circular—that is, the events will continue calling themselves indefinitely.

Consider this problem in a simple example with two text boxes. When each text box receives the focus, it sets the focus to the other text box, and focus shifts back and forth between the two text boxes indefinitely. The program seems to lock up, and you cannot click any other object on the form while the text boxes are updating each other. Whenever a program seems to lock up, you should press the Ctrl+Break keys and then check the relationship between the events in your program. Setting breakpoints and watch expressions might be the only way to determine the sequence of events that is happening.

To see events call other events infinitely:

1. Click the **Start** button ▶ on the toolbar.

2. Click the text box containing the text **Text2**. The contents of the text boxes are updated each time a text box receives the focus. You cannot click the End button or the Exit command button to end the program.

3. Press the **Ctrl+Break** keys to stop the program and enter design mode.

4. In the **Text1_GotFocus** and **Text2_GotFocus** events, set a breakpoint in the line that reads **pintTimes = pintTimes + 1**.

5. Click the **Start** button ▶.

6. Click the **Text2** text box. The program breaks and shows you the Code window each time the variable times is updated in the GotFocus events of the text boxes.

7. Continue to click the **Start** button ▶ several times to see the event procedures being called indefinitely.

8. Delete one of the SetFocus statements to end this infinite loop.

9. Click the **End** button ■.

Identifying the exact cause of a problem like this can be difficult. You might need to set breakpoints or use the Step Into button in each event procedure that might be causing the problem, in order to see which events are being called. The best solution to the problem is prevention. Good design and well-written pseudocode and NEADT charts will help avoid such problems.

You should use the Visual Basic debugging tools to diagnose errors interactively in your program. As your programs become larger, be sure to write small pieces of code, and then thoroughly test the code and fix any problems. Then, as you continue developing a program, you can step over those procedures that you know are working.

When you notice that a variable has a value you do not expect it to have, set a watch expression that will cause the program to enter break mode whenever the value of the variable changes. If a procedure seems to be incorrect, set a breakpoint just before the first statement of the procedure executes and then trace each statement in the procedure, if necessary.

Designing Visual Basic Programs

Over the past 30 years, many tools have been developed for planning and documenting both programs and complete applications. One of the first concise development and design tools was NCR's Accurately Defined Systems (ADS) developed in the late 1960s. The more modern common public tools are program flowcharts, data flow diagrams, Gantt charts, Critical Path Method (CPM), Program Evaluation and Review Technique (PERT), structure charts, decision trees, structured walk-throughs, data modeling, query analysis, Computer Aided Software Engineering (CASE), prototyping, and hundreds of proprietary products and methodologies from dozens of vendors. All these tools were, in one way or another, constructed to help the programmer do the following:

■ **Write programs that are correct** — a program that does not accomplish what it is constructed to do functionally is worthless. The program may have some value if it performs most of the things it is required to perform. If a program inadvertently performs unwanted activities like corrupting elements of a database, however, then very serious consequences for both the programmer and the user quickly will appear.

■ **Write programs that are easy to understand** — programs that are impossible for anyone but the original programmer to understand are very dangerous. In any fairly large business, the author of a particular program rarely will be the individual called on to maintain the product. This is true especially in today's Rapid Application Development (RAD) environment where the whole idea is to be able to quickly improve programs and respond quickly to the needs of the users.

■ **Write programs that are easy to change** — programs that can be understood but are impossible or difficult to modify are equally useless. Visual object-oriented languages, especially where the visual interface is concerned, excel at being easy to modify to the demands of the user.

■ **Write programs that are written efficiently** — the language used to construct the program must be powerful enough to remove many of the microtasks that formerly concerned the programmer. Before the advent of object languages, the programmer reinvented the wheel with almost every program. The programmer becomes vastly more productive and efficient by: reusing code; using methods (pre-written named code blocks) that are simple to understand and use, but in reality may be quite complex; and using objects that are provided by the programming language vendor exposed as system objects, or by third parties, that can be configured easily to solve a variety of problems.

- **Write programs that execute efficiently** — even though the typical program user has tremendous computing power on their desktop, new operating systems (running many programs simultaneously) and the sheer amount of program code that new software requires to provide the vast improvement on capabilities while providing simpler user interfaces, make it imperative that today's programs still must coexist happily and not slow down the user's machine.

(Adapted from Philippakis, A.S., and Leonard J. Kazmier. *Program Design Concepts.* New York: McGraw Hill, 1983.)

RAD Environment Tools Today

Surprisingly, few generalized non-vendor tools have been developed for program construction and documentation for today's Rapid Application Development (RAD) environment. The common tools today consist of pseudocode, an interface drawing, and the Task-Object-Event (TOE) chart.

Pseudocode simply is describing the task(s) that the program should accomplish in standard English. By design, pseudocode should not be written towards any specific programming language, but rather should provide a means for the programmer to think or brainstorm while capturing the essence of the program's requirements.

An interface drawing is a sketch of what the user will see when the program is running. The interface drawing allows the programmer to create a model that describes how the user will interact with the program while suggesting the objects that will be used to perform the tasks and their placement on the screen.

A TOE chart is a simple three-column chart that describes the task the program should perform, the object(s) used to accomplish the task, and the event(s) that will cause the objects and any associated code to execute.

These tools are useful in constructing simple programs and applications. They tend to ignore, however, important sections of the design process like how errors are handled in the program, program construction details like object names, and the flow of various user interface forms during the running of the program or application.

Designing Object-oriented/Event-driven Programs Using NEADT

Like most other program design tools, the Newman-Ekedahl Application Development Tool (NEADT) follows a standard set of steps, known as a methodology, for designing and documenting object-oriented, event-driven programs. This methodology consists of steps in one of five levels that the programmer must accomplish before moving on to the next level. Some steps are required while others are optional depending on the application requirements.

In order to address the shortcomings of existing tools while maintaining simplicity, NEADT was developed as an extension to the TOE chart model tool and to provide a consistent documentation and design format. The NEADT design and documentation tool is being used by the authors in *New Perspectives on Visual Basic 5.0 for Windows—Introductory: An Object-oriented Data-driven Approach* because Visual Basic 5 almost fully supports the pure object model, including classing and inheritance, and integrates advanced system object browsing. NEADT helps solve the serious shortcomings of existing design and documentation tools.

Using the NEADT Tool

First, using any design and documentation tool requires the programmer to completely understand the problem and what data is needed to solve it. In Tutorial 2 the Island Financial company required a calculator program to calculate the future value of an investment at various percentage rates. Using the NEADT methodology, NEADT forms have been created to design and document the program.

The Project IPO Pseudocode Abstract

The conceptual Input-Output-Processing (IPO) model often helps the programmer to visualize the true nature of the problem. After this process has taken place the programmer begins the NEADT methodology by breaking the problem down in English to the macro-task(s) that must be accomplished and any subtasks that also can be broken out of the general problem using the **NEADT Level 1 Project IPO Pseudocode Abstract** form as shown in Figure B-1. Tasks can be listed as simple task groups or modeled into the IPO format.

Figure B-1 ◀
NEADT Level 1 Project pseudocode abstract form

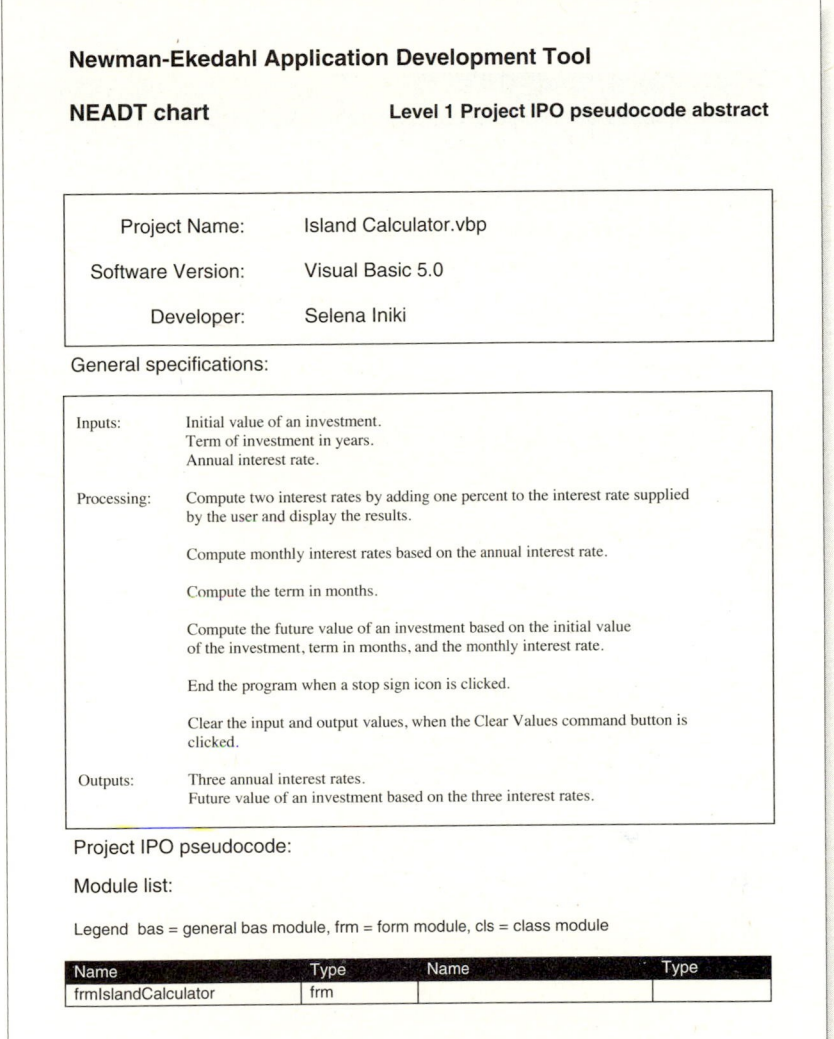

Of all the steps in writing a program, or a complete system for that matter, really understanding what you want to accomplish may be the most difficult. This is because most problems are not structured originally or given in the terms that you need to set them up on a computer. Also, some problems may require that you break them down into multiple programs with multiple tasks for each program. For example, Island Financial would like to make a set of tools to help them simplify the work of managing their clients' financial matters. This is an example of a macro (large) problem that must be investigated further and broken down into the actual tasks that Island Financial employees perform for their day-to-day work. These tasks in turn can be ranked from the most to the least time consuming task and the most to the least repetitive task. Then you must determine what tasks can be accomplished by using a computer program(s). Sometimes you will find that simply redoing the tasks on a computer may not be the best way to accomplish the overall goal. In some cases, a complete change in the activity to use the computer to its best advantage may provide the best solution to the actual problem.

The Island Financial problem is rather simple and the NEADT Level 1 Project IPO Pseudocode Abstract form defines the problem in general terms using the IPO model. The task to be performed is to compute the future value of an investment at different interest rates. For clarity, the user interface should change as the user enters information. The data that is required is the initial value of the loan, the term of the loan, and the rate of interest. When the data has been captured the program will calculate the future value of the loan at the interest rate and display the result to the accountant.

The general specifications block in the NEADT Level 1 IPO Pseudocode Abstract form contains the project name (Island Calculator.vbp), the software version (Visual Basic 5.0), and the developer's name (Selena Iniki). Pseudocode specifications for the project are contained in the Project IPO pseudocode block.

User Interface Design

Using the Project IPO pseudocode, the programmer designs the interface screen(s) depicting how the computer's screen(s) should look to the user. This can be accomplished using the **NEADT Level 2 User Interface Design** form shown in Figure B-2, or using the visual programming environment itself to place various objects on the screen that will be used to accomplish the macrotasks and microtasks of the application. This step requires one interface drawing for each form in the project.

Figure B-2 ◀
NEADT Level 2
User Interface
Design form

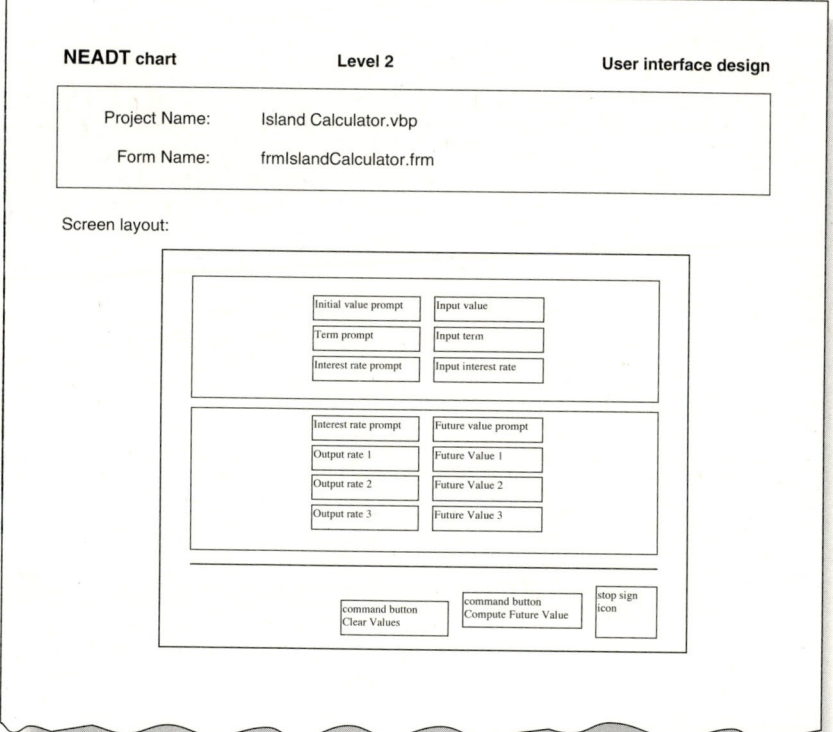

The NEADT Level 2 Interface Design form starts with an identification block noting the project name, particular form name, and form shape. The screen layout for the Island Financial calculator contains 11 labels used to display prompts and values, and three text boxes (Input value, Input term, and Input interest rate) for user input. The form also contains a command button to clear the input values, another command button for calculating the future value, and an image of a stop sign icon to end the program. The form therefore contains 17 objects, not counting the form itself. Additional NEADT Level 2 Interface Design forms would be used for each additional form in the project.

Object Event Analysis

The **NEADT Level 3 Object Event Analysis** form shown in Figure B-3, documents each interface form event in the Island Financial calculator project, task description, and whether any error handling is required. It also details task types like calls to other procedures with references and property settings for the Form object. The Event column includes the actual name of the event procedure to be coded. The interface documentation continues with the same details for all interface objects contained by the form including any exposed objects that are used in the application. There also is a notation for other variables and properties that may be affected by revisions to this code.

Figure B-3 ◀
NEADT Level 3
Object Event
Analysis form

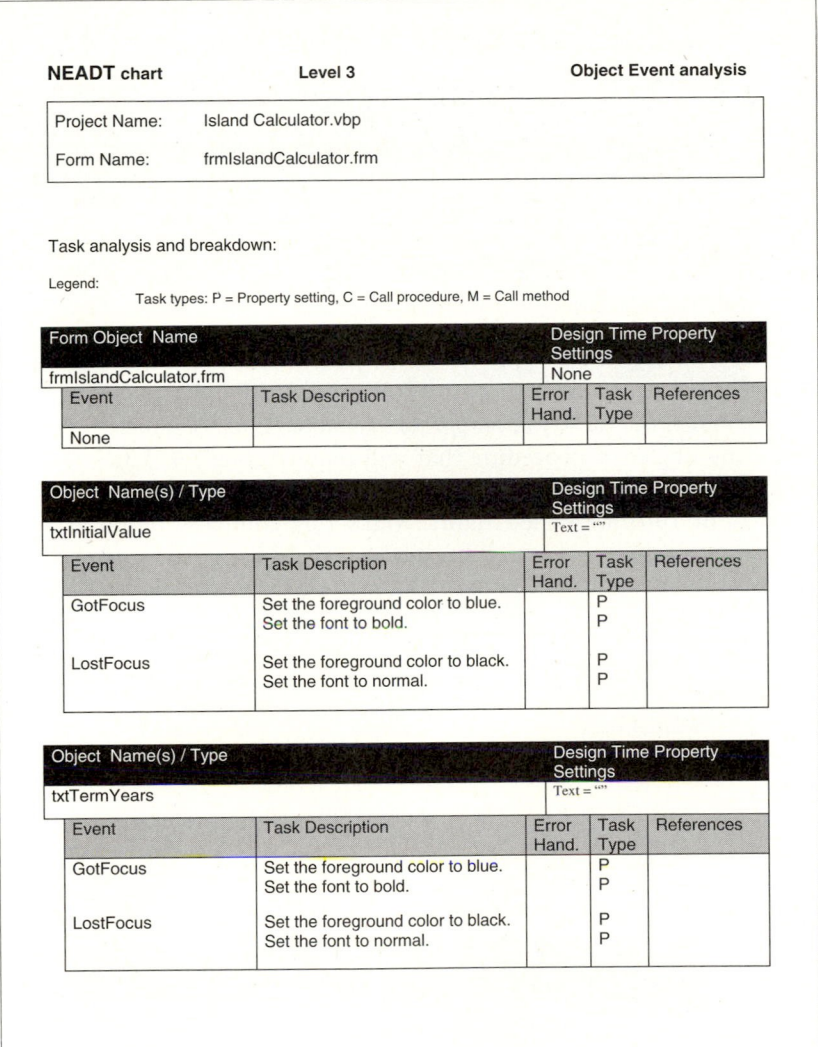

The NEADT Level 3 Object Event Analysis form contains a project identification block. The main block contains the Task analysis and breakdown section. In the Island Financial project there are four tasks that need to be performed on two objects. The first object, txtInitialValue, performs two tasks. When the object gets focus, the appearance of the characters change, and when the object loses focus, the appearance of the characters change again. The second object performs the exact same two tasks. Event code will need to be generated for the LostFocus and GotFocus events for each text box.

Shared Module Analysis

Using the **NEADT Level 4 Shared Module Analysis** form shown in Figure B-4, shared general modules of code are documented as objects and events as they were in Level 3. This form includes the module name, procedure name, and a description of the tasks that should be performed. In addition, there is a reference to the error handler, if any, the task type, and any variables or other objects that are referenced by the task.

Figure B-4 ◄
NEADT Level 4
Shared Module
Analysis form

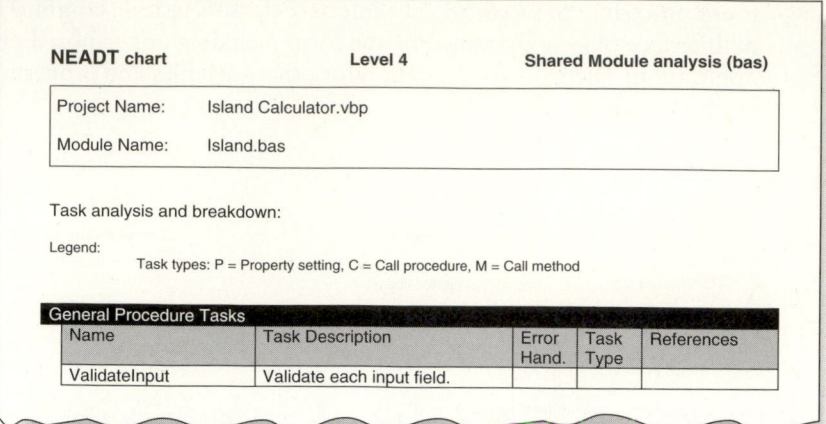

NEADT chart	Level 4	Shared Module analysis (bas)

Project Name: Island Calculator.vbp

Module Name: Island.bas

Task analysis and breakdown:

Legend:
Task types: P = Property setting, C = Call procedure, M = Call method

General Procedure Tasks

Name	Task Description	Error Hand.	Task Type	References
ValidateInput	Validate each input field.			

Data Validation/Error Response

Finally, the **NEADT Level 5 Data Validation/Error Response** form shown in Figure B-5 details any object or procedure that will require code for data validation or error handling, the actual validation requirements, and the response to be generated due to those errors.

In Tutorial 4 the Atlantic Marketing company required a client tracking system with the capability to search for clients and add, change, and delete information pertaining to those clients using the NEADT methodology. As shown in Figure B-5 input must be validated when two different event procedures occur.

Figure B-5 ◄
NEADT Level 5
Data
Validation/
Error Response
form

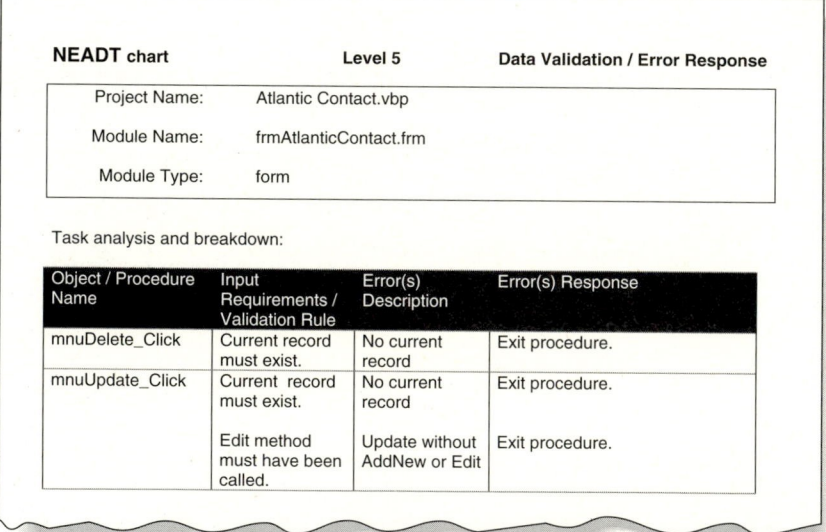

NEADT chart	Level 5	Data Validation / Error Response

Project Name: Atlantic Contact.vbp

Module Name: frmAtlanticContact.frm

Module Type: form

Task analysis and breakdown:

Object / Procedure Name	Input Requirements / Validation Rule	Error(s) Description	Error(s) Response
mnuDelete_Click	Current record must exist.	No current record	Exit procedure.
mnuUpdate_Click	Current record must exist.	No current record	Exit procedure.
	Edit method must have been called.	Update without AddNew or Edit	Exit procedure.

When the mnuDelete_Click event procedure happens, there must be a current record to delete. If there is not, the event procedure should exit. When the mnuUpdate_Click event procedure executes, a current record must exist, and the Edit method already must have been called thereby making the record editable. Otherwise, the event procedure should exit.

As you become a more experienced programmer, you will realize that creating programs involves more than simply sitting down at a computer, designing the interface, and writing the code. To ensure a quality product, you should follow these guidelines, modify them to suit your own work style, and spend an adequate amount of time understanding the problem and finding the best solution before writing the actual program. Adequate time spent in planning will save you many hours of work debugging a program or correcting design flaws. Computer programs look and work better with some forethought to the final product and where that product will fit into other programs.

Database Design

The Purpose of a Database

Before the advent of database technology, programs to manage large amounts of data were more complex to create. These programs used traditional file processing systems. In a **traditional file processing system**, each computer application is designed with its own set of data files. Much of the data contained in these files likely existed in files for other applications as well. Furthermore, computer programmers were forced to sort data manually in several different physical files. If you wanted to create reports based on information in multiple files, your program would have to open each of the different files to obtain the necessary information, then examine and process each record (or entry) manually. The same was true if you wanted to change information in multiple files. The following list illustrates some of the disadvantages of traditional file processing:

■ **Data redundancy** — in a traditional file processing system, each application has its own files. This causes disk space to be wasted.

■ **Inconsistent data** — when the same data is stored in different files, the data can become inconsistent. That is, a person's name may be changed in one application's file but not in another.

■ **Limited data sharing** — when each application uses its own files, there is little opportunity to share data between one application and another.

■ **Low programmer productivity** — in a traditional file processing system programmers had to write statements to define each record and additional statements to control the input and output of data.

By using a database, each of the problems listed above either is minimized or eliminated. As a result, use of a database to manage an organization's data is increasingly common.

Designing a Database

Before you create a database, you must design its structure. The structure of a database is known as the schema. The **schema** of a database describes each of the tables, the fields in those tables, and the relationships between the information contained in each table. The schema is the structure in the database in which the information will be stored. Just as planning is an important step in creating a program, properly designing the database schema also is an important process.

The first step in defining a database is to identify each data item. A **data item** is the smallest unit of data that has meaning to the user. A data item is analogous to a field. In the database for Atlantic Marketing in Tutorial 4, fields like Last Name and First Name are both data items. Figure C-1 describes each data item stored in the Atlantic Marketing database.

Figure C-1 ◀
Atlantic
Marketing
data items

Client ID	Notes
Last Name	Salesperson Last Name
First Name	Salesperson First Name
Telephone Number	Sales Date
Date Added	Sales Amount
Estimated Sales	Sales Description

After the data items have been defined, they should be grouped together such that data is stored only once. That is, the last name and first name of a client should only exist once and only in a single table. Data items are grouped together into data aggregates. A **data aggregate** is a collection of data items stored and referenced as a unit. A data aggregate is represented in a database as a table. Figure C-2 shows the different tables in the Atlantic Marketing database.

Figure C-2 ◀
Atlantic
Marketing
data items

Contact table	Sales table
Client ID	Client ID
Last Name	Salesperson Last Name
First Name	Salesperson First name
Telephone Number	Sales Date
Date Added	Sales Amount
Estimated Sales	Sales Description
Notes	

Each data aggregate or table can have a primary key, if necessary. A **primary key** uniquely identifies each record. In the case of the Atlantic Marketing database, the table named tblContact uses the Client ID field as the primary key. That is, each client ID stored in the table named tblContact uniquely identifies the record. Note that the Last Name field is not a primary key because a last name is not necessarily unique. For example, it is likely that two people could have the last name of Smith. It is possible to use multiple fields as part of the primary key.

After each table is created, associations can be defined. An **association,** or **query,** is a logical, meaningful connection between data items stored in one or more tables. In the database for Atlantic Marketing, sales records can be associated with client records as shown in Figure C-3.

Figure C-3 ◄
Clients/Sales
association

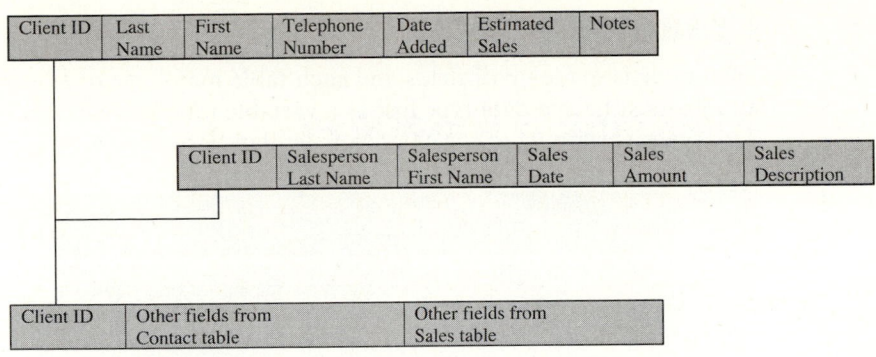

Client ID	Last Name	First Name	Telephone Number	Date Added	Estimated Sales	Notes

	Client ID	Salesperson Last Name	Salesperson First Name	Sales Date	Sales Amount	Sales Description

Client ID	Other fields from Contact table		Other fields from Sales table	

A common type of association is a **one-to-many association**. That is, for each data item stored in one table, there may be zero (0), one (1), or an arbitrary number of data items in another table. When creating an association, there must be a common data item in each table, like the Client ID field.

Creating a Database

To create a new database for use with the Microsoft Jet database engine, you can use Microsoft Access. While there are other ways to create a database that can be manipulated by the Microsoft Jet database engine, using Access is the simplest. All the information for a database is stored in a single file with the extension .mdb. This file contains all the tables, fields, and other objects related to a database. The example in this appendix uses Access 97. If you are using another version of Access, your screens may differ slightly.

To create a new database:

1. Start **Microsoft Access**. The dialog box shown in Figure C-4 will display asking you whether or not you want to create a new database or open an existing database.

Figure C-4 ◄
Creating a
database

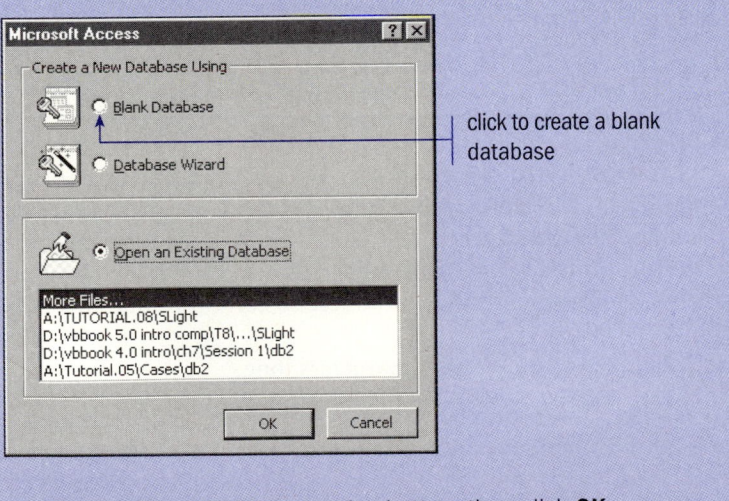

click to create a blank database

2. Click the **Blank Database** option button, then click **OK**.

3. The File New Database dialog box will display asking you the folder and file name of the database.

4. Select the folder named **Appendix.C** on your Student Disk and enter the file name **AM_CMS.mdb**, then click the **Create** button. This will create an empty database.

While you have created an empty database, you have not defined the data items (fields), data aggregates (tables), or the associations (queries) between those data items. The next step in creating the database is to define the tables and the fields in those tables. After the tables are created, the next step is to define how the tables are related to each other, and then define how information in the different tables will be retrieved.

Creating a Table

Each table is made up of fields and each table may have one or more fields. Each field in a table must have a data type just as a variable must have a data type. Figure C-5 lists the data types pertaining to the Microsoft Jet database engine.

Figure C-5 ◀
Data types
supported by
the Microsoft
Jet database
engine

Field type	Description
Text	A Text field is a string containing letters, numbers, spaces, and special characters between 1 and 255 characters in length. Names and addresses, for example, are stored in Text fields.
AutoNumber	An AutoNumber field most commonly is used with primary keys. Microsoft Access will assign a new and unique number to each record created. This can be used as the primary key to identify each record uniquely.
Currency	A Currency field is similar to the Number field in that it stores numeric data. A Currency field, however, eliminates the possibility of rounding errors when performing computations on very large or very small floating point numbers.
Date/Time	A Date/Time field can store either dates, times, or both, and is equivalent to the Date data type in Visual Basic. It is possible to perform calculations on Date fields. For example, you can subtract one date from another to find out how many days have elapsed.
Memo	A Memo field is similar to a Text field in that it stores the same type of data, but Memo fields can store up to 64,000 characters.
Number	A Number field stores numbers like integers and floating point numbers. Fields could be totals, amounts, accumulators, age, distance, weights, and size. As in Visual Basic, there are different types of numbers like integers and single.
OLE Object	An OLE Object is used for other applications that can be linked or embedded in a Microsoft Jet database.
Yes/No	A Yes/No field is equivalent to the Visual Basic Boolean data type. It stores True or False values.

Tables store information that does not repeat. For example, the Contact table for Atlantic Marketing contains fields for the Client ID, Last Name, First Name, Telephone Number, Estimated Sales, and Notes. Each of these fields is unique to a single client and is therefore stored in the same table. Just as variable names must adhere to specific requirements, field names also must adhere to certain requirements like the following:

- They can be up to 64 characters long.

- They can have letters, numbers, spaces, and characters except for the following three characters: an exclamation point (!), brackets ([or]), and an apostrophe (').

- They cannot begin with a space.

In addition each field should begin with the "fld" prefix followed by a descriptive name. Each table name should begin with the "tbl" prefix. Each field you create has properties. The term **properties** is used because fields in Access actually are considered objects.

The properties applicable to each field depend on the data type. The following list describes some of the properties supported by fields:

- You can use the **Required** property to specify whether or not a value is required in a field. If this property is set to Yes, you must enter a value in this field when entering a record.

- You can use the **AllowZeroLength** property to specify whether a zero-length string ("") is a valid entry in a field. This property applies only to Text and Memo fields.

- You can use the **Indexed** property to set a single-field index. An index speeds up queries on the indexed fields as well as sorting and grouping operations. For example, if you search for a specific employee name in a Last Name field, you can create an index for this field to improve significantly the performance of the search.

You now are ready to create the tables and the fields stored in those tables for the Atlantic Marketing database.

To create a table:

1. Click the **Tables** tab in the Database window, then click **New.** The New Table dialog box will appear as shown in Figure C-6.

Figure C-6 ◄
Creating a new table

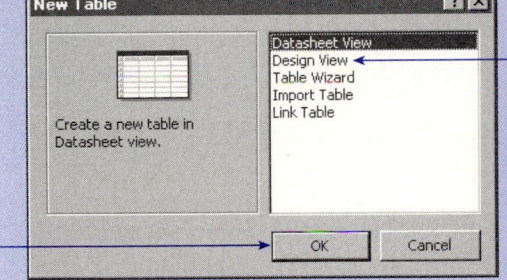

click Design View

click OK to create table

2. Select **Design View** from the list box then click **OK**. The table will open in Design view.

3. Enter the name **fldClientID** in the Field Name column, then press the **Tab** key to move to the Data Type column.

4. Select the **Text** data type from the list box. Because the field may store letters and numbers this is the appropriate selection.

5. Click the **Primary Key** button on the toolbar to make this field a primary key. Thus, each client ID must be unique. Note the Primary Key icon appears to the left of the field name.

6. Press the **Tab** key twice so the cursor appears in the next row of the Field Name column.

7. Create another field named **fldLastName** with a Data Type of **Text**. Set the Required property to **Yes**. Set the FieldSize property to **25**.

8. Click the Value column of the Required property and set the value to **Yes**. By setting the Required property to Yes, the user will be required to enter data into this field.

9. Set the Field Name to **fldFirstName,** then the Data Type to **Text**. Set the FieldSize property to **25**.

10. Create another field named **fldTelephoneNumber** with a Data Type of **Text**. Set the FieldSize property to **14**. Set the Required property to **No**, then the AllowZeroLength property to **Yes**.

11. Create a field named **fldDateAdded** with a Data Type of **Date/Time**. Set the Required property to **No**.

12. Create a field named **fldEstimatedSales** with a Data Type of **Number**. Set the Required property to **No**, then the FieldSize property to **Single**.

13. Create a field named **fldNotes** with a Data Type of **Memo**. Set the Required property to **No**, then the AllowZeroLength property to **Yes**.

Now that you have created each of the fields, you can proceed to save the table. Until the table is saved, the information about the table's characteristics is not saved on the database.

To save the new table:

1. Click **File** on the menu bar, then click **Save**. The Save As dialog box will display as shown in Figure C-7.

Figure C-7 ◄
Saving a table

enter tblContact in
Table Name text box

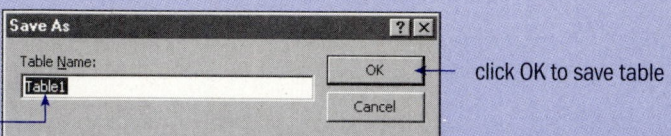

click OK to save table

2. Enter the name **tblContact** then click **OK** to save the table. Click the **Close** box ✕ to close the table. Notice the new table name displays on the Tables tab in the Database window.

In addition to the table for the contact information, a table is needed to store the sales information. To do this you must create a second table named tblSales.

To create the second table named tblSales:

1. Click the **Tables** tab in the Database window, then click **New**.

2. Create the following fields:

Field Name	Data Type	Properties
fldClientID	**Text**	Required=**Yes**
fldSalesLastName	**Text**	FieldSize=**25**
fldSalesFirstName	**Text**	FieldSize=**25**
fldSalesDate	**Date/Time**	Required=**Yes**
fldSalesAmount	**Number**	FieldSize=**Single**, Required=**Yes**
fldSalesDescription	**Memo**	Required=**No**

3. Click **File** then **Save** on the menu bar. Enter the name **tblSales** then click **OK**. Close the table.

Creating a Relationship

Microsoft Access is a **relational database**, which means the data stored in multiple tables can be viewed as if it were stored in a single table. Furthermore Access allows you to establish rules defining the relationships between multiple tables. To define these rules, you create a relationship. A **relationship** is used to match data between two tables using a field(s) from each table. For example, in the database for Atlantic Marketing, it does not make sense to create a sales record for a client ID unless there is a corresponding client ID in the Contact table. All relationships in Microsoft Access are created using the Relationships window.

To create a relationship:

1. Click **Tools** then **Relationships** to open the Relationships window.

2. Click the **Show Table** button ⬚ on the toolbar if necessary to view the tables in the database. The Show Table dialog box is shown in Figure C-8.

Figure C-8 ◀
Adding tables to
a relationship

select tblContact then
click Add

select tblSales then
click Add

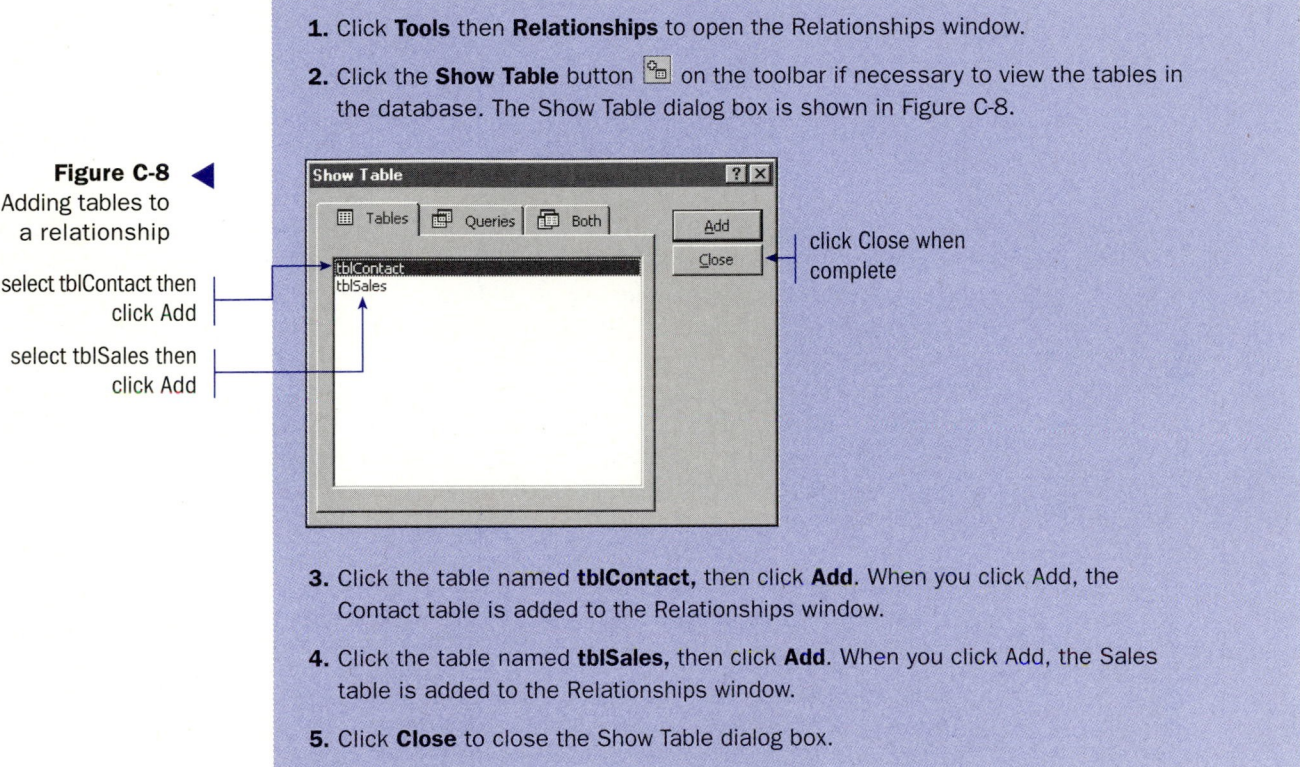

click Close when
complete

3. Click the table named **tblContact,** then click **Add**. When you click Add, the Contact table is added to the Relationships window.

4. Click the table named **tblSales,** then click **Add**. When you click Add, the Sales table is added to the Relationships window.

5. Click **Close** to close the Show Table dialog box.

Once you have added the tables that make up the relationships, you need to create the relationship itself. In this case you need to create a one-to-many relationship between the tblContact and the tblSales tables. That is, for each client ID in tblContact there can be many records with the same client ID in tblSales. A client ID, however, cannot be created in tblSales unless a corresponding client ID exists in tblContact. By creating this relationship, your program does not need to check that these rules are followed. Rather, if you try to add, change, or delete a record that would violate a relationship rule, the Microsoft Jet database engine will generate an error. Your program can trap the error using an error handler. Now that you have defined the two tables in the relationship, you can create the relationship itself.

To create a relationship:

1. Click the field named **fldClientID** in the table named tblContact in the Relationships window.

2. Click and hold down the mouse and drag the cursor to the field named **fldClientID** in the table named tblSales. The Relationships dialog box will display as shown in Figure C-9.

Figure C-9 ◀
Defining a
relationship

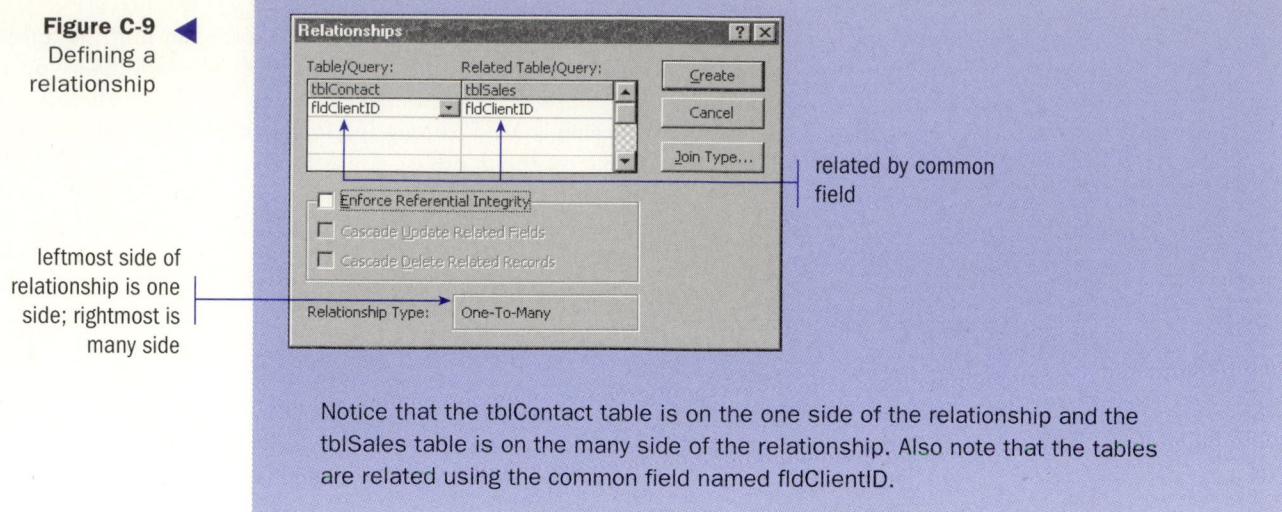

related by common
field

leftmost side of
relationship is one
side; rightmost is
many side

Notice that the tblContact table is on the one side of the relationship and the
tblSales table is on the many side of the relationship. Also note that the tables
are related using the common field named fldClientID.

When a relationship is being created there is a check box that you can select to enforce
referential integrity. **Referential integrity** is the set of rules that are followed to preserve the
defined relationships between tables as you add, change, or delete records. If you enforce
referential integrity, the Microsoft Jet database engine prohibits you from adding records
to a related table when there is no corresponding record in a primary table. It also prohibits
you from deleting a record in a primary table if there are existing records in a related table.

The primary table in this relationship is tblContact and the related table is tblSales.
You want to be sure that a client ID exists in the primary table for each record in the
related table. Thus, you should enforce referential integrity for this relationship.

When referential integrity is enforced on a relationship, two other check boxes are activated.

- If **Cascade Update Related Fields** is checked, then the corresponding field in the
  related table will be changed automatically when an update is performed on the
  primary table.

- If **Cascade Delete Related Records** is checked, then deleting a record from the primary table will cause all the corresponding records in the related table to be deleted.

The relationship for Atlantic Marketing should enforce referential integrity. Also
updates and deletions should be cascaded.

To enforce referential integrity on a relationship:

1. Click the **Enforce Referential Integrity** check box. Notice that the two check
   boxes below it will be enabled.

2. Click the **Cascade Update Related Fields** and **Cascade Delete Related Records**
   check boxes.

3. Click the **Create** button to finish creating the relationship. The Relationships
   window should look like Figure C-10.

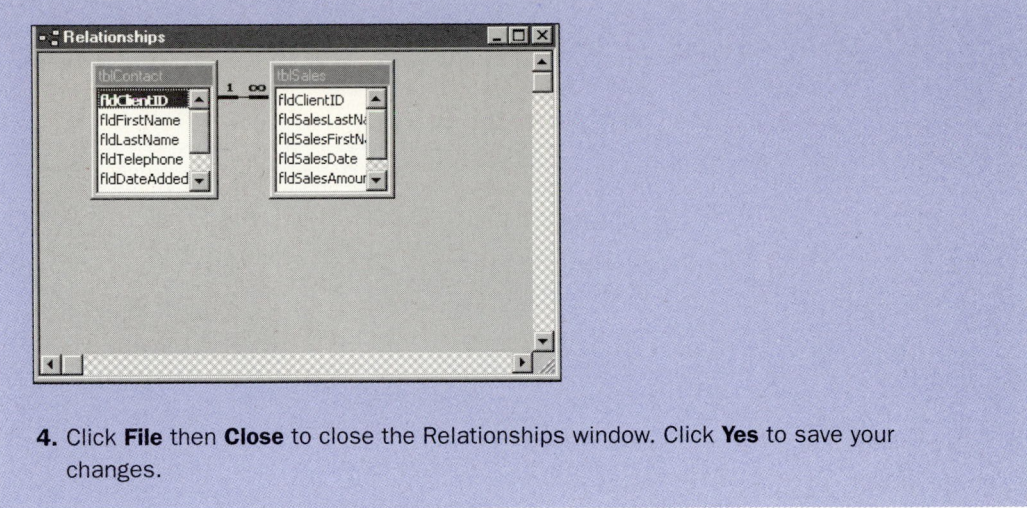

Figure C-10 ◀
Relationships
window

4. Click **File** then **Close** to close the Relationships window. Click **Yes** to save your changes.

The database for Atlantic Marketing has a single relationship. As you create databases with many tables, you most likely will have several relationships.

Creating a Query

Once you have created the relationships, the next step is to define the query. A **query** is a formalized set of instructions to a database either to return a set of records from one or more tables or to perform an action on a set of records. In other words a query is how you ask a question about the data in your database.

The database for Atlantic Marketing needs the following query.

■ One query will view the list of clients so it appears sorted by last name.

In Microsoft Access the most common way to create a query is to use **Query by Example (QBE)**. QBE is a user interface that allows you to select: the tables used in the query; the fields that are to be used; and how the records are to be sorted. You create a query using a procedure similar to the one you used to create a table. First you need to activate the Queries tab in the Database window, and then click New to create a new query. Then you define the characteristics of the query, and finally save it.

To create a new query:

1. Click the **Queries** tab in the Database window, then click **New**. The New Query dialog box will display as shown in Figure C-11.

Figure C-11 ◀
Creating a
query

click Design View —

click OK to open |
QBE window |

New Query   ? ✕

Create a new query without using a wizard.

Design View
Simple Query Wizard
Crosstab Query Wizard
Find Duplicates Query Wizard
Find Unmatched Query Wizard

OK   Cancel

2. Click **Design View** then click **OK** to open the QBE window.

The next step in creating the query is to define which tables and fields are used in the query. The query you are creating will display each client record and any corresponding sales records so you need to select both tblContact and tblSales.

To add the tables to the query:

1. Click **tblContact** in the Show Table dialog box, then click **Add**.

2. Click **tblSales** in the Show Table dialog box, then click **Add**.

3. Click **Close**. The two tables you added display in the Query1 : Select Query window as shown in Figure C-12.

Figure C-12 ◀
Creating a
query

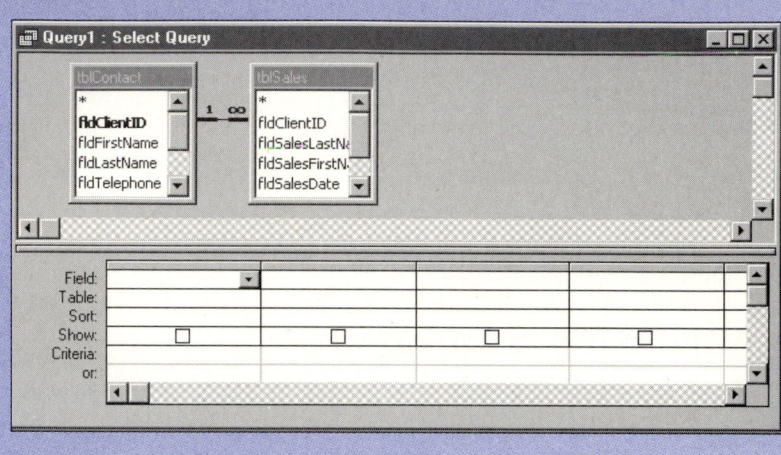

Now that you have chosen the tables you must select the fields to include in the query. QBE will allow you to select all the fields or just the fields required by the query. The query you will create to join the clients with their corresponding sales data will use all the fields from both tables.

To add the fields to the query:

1. Double-click the field **fldClientID** in the tblContact table. The field will appear in the Query Design grid.

2. Repeat Step 1 for each field in the tblContact table. You may need to use the scroll bars to locate each field.

3. Double-click the field **fldSalesLastName** in the tblSales table.

4. Repeat Step 3 for each field in tblSales. You may need to use the scroll bars to locate each field.

By default, each record in a query will display in a random order. It usually is desirable to sort each record by a field like Last Name. The Sort row in the Query Design grid allows you to control the order of each record. This query for Atlantic Marketing should be sorted by last name. If two records have the same last name then each record with the same last name should be further sorted by first name. You can sort records either in ascending or descending order.

To sort the records in the query:

1. Click the **Sort** row in the fldLastName column in the Query Design grid.

2. Select **Ascending** using the list arrow.

3. Repeat Steps 1 and 2 for the field **fldFirstName**.

The query now is complete. You have selected the fields that make up the query and how the records will be sorted. Now you must save the query.

To save the query:

1. Click **File** then **Save** on the menu bar. The Save As dialog box will display.

2. Enter the name **qryContactSales**, then click **OK**.

This appendix has presented only an introduction to creating a database, its tables, and queries. Most databases you create will have many more tables and relationships but the concepts presented here provide a template for creating more complex databases. It also is possible to create more complex queries that can restrict which records are selected. It also is possible to create queries that create other tables and update data in existing tables.

Microsoft Visual Basic 5.0 Index

If you are using this text as part of our Custom Edition Program, you will find entries in the Index and Task Reference that do not apply to your custom tutorials.

Microsoft Visual Basic 5.0 **Task Reference**

TASK	PAGE #	RECOMMENDED METHOD	NOTES
Accumulators, using	VB 5.33	Declare a variable to be used as an accumulator and set the initial value to zero (0). Add to the accumulator each time through a Do loop or For loop.	
Arrays, changing the lower bound of	VB 10.13	Set the Option Base to one (1) to change the default lower bound of an array from zero (0) to one (1).	**Option Base {0|1}**
Arrays, changing the size of	VB 10.14	Use the ReDim statement to change the number of elements in an array. Use the Preserve keyword to preserve the array's existing contents.	**ReDim [Preserve]** *varname(subscripts)* **[As** *type*]
Arrays, creating	VB 6.13	Use the Dim, Private, or Public statements followed by the array name. Enclose the subscript(s) in parentheses. Use the As clause followed by the data type.	**[Dim|Public|Private]** *array-name(lower-bound* **To** *upperbound)* **As** *datatype*
Arrays, finding the upper and lower bound	VB 10.27	Use the UBound and LBound statements to find the largest and smallest subscript for *arrayname*. If an array has only one dimension, omit the *dimension* argument. Otherwise specify the desired dimension.	**UBound**(*arrayname[, dimension]*) **LBound**(*arrayname[, dimension]*)
Arrays, referencing	VB 6.13	Use the array name followed by an Integer subscript enclosed in parentheses.	Use two subscripts with a two-dimensional array.
CheckBox control, creating	VB 3.3	Set the Caption property to display a prompt for the object. Use the Value property at run time to determine if the box is checked or not.	See Reference Window, "Adding a CheckBox Control to a Form."
Class module, creating	VB 11.3	Click Project then Add Class Module on the menu bar. Set the Name property to define the name of the class.	See Reference Window, "To Add a Class Module to a Project."
Class module, creating methods	VB 11.27	Create a Public Function or Sub procedure in a Class module. Use Function procedures when the method should return a value. Otherwise use a Sub procedure.	Note that a method can accept zero or more arguments.
Class module, creating properties	VB 11.4	In a class module, declare a public variable of an intrinsic, enumerated, or object type.	Note that you cannot create properties of a user-defined type.
Class module, creating read-only property procedures	VB 11.17	Create a read-only property when the interface of the class dictates that the user should not be able to change explicitly the value of the property. Create only a Property Get procedure and remove the Property Let procedure or raise an error.	**[Public | Private][Static]** **Property Get** *name* [(*argumentlist*)] **[As** *type*] [*statements*] [*name =* *expression*] **[Exit Property]** [*statements*] [*name =* *expression*] **End Property**

Microsoft Visual Basic 5.0 **Task Reference**

TASK	PAGE #	RECOMMENDED METHOD	NOTES
Class module, creating read-write properties	VB 11.20	Create a property procedure, when you want to hide data in the class or execute code when a property is read or written.	**[Public|Private]** **[Static]** **Property Let** *name* [(*arglist*)] [*statements*] **[Exit Property]** [*statements*] **End Property**
Class module, creating write-once properties	VB 11.27	Create a hidden variable in the class module. In the Property Let procedure create an If statement to determine if the property already has a value. If it does, raise an error. Otherwise set the value of the hidden variable.	
Class module, hiding data	VB 11.15	In a Class module, declare a private variable of an intrinsic, enumerated, or object type.	Note that you can create hidden variables of a user-defined type.
Class module, initializing and terminating	VB 11.15	Write code for the ClassInitialize event to perform startup activities, and the ClassTerminate event to perform shutdown activities.	These are the only events for a Class module.
Class module, setting the default method or property	VB 11.25	Open the Object Browser. In the Project/Library list box, select the project you are working on. In the Classes list box, select the desired class. In the Members list box, select the desired property or method.	
Clipboard, copying data	VB 12.7	Clear the existing contents of the Clipboard object with the Clear method. Use the SetText method to place the selected text onto the clipboard.	See Reference Window, "To Cut or Copy Text to the Clipboard."
Clipboard, cutting data	VB 12.7	Use the same steps as copying, but clear the selected text of the source object.	
Clipboard, pasting data	VB 12.7	Call the GetText method of the Clipboard object. The result usually is assigned to the SelText property of the current object as referenced by Screen.ActiveControl.	See Reference Window, "To Paste Text from the Clipboard."
Code window, inserting a general procedure	VB 3.30	Verify that the Code window is active for the desired module. Click Tools then click Add Procedure on the menu bar to activate the dialog box. Specify the procedure name. If the procedure returns a value, select the type Function. Otherwise select Sub. If the procedure will be used by multiple modules, set the Scope to Public. Otherwise make the procedure Private.	When using multiple Form or standard modules, make sure the Code window is set to the correct module.
Code window, setting the active procedure	VB 1.38	Click the desired module in the Project Explorer, then click the View Code button ⬚. Select the desired object then the desired event or general procedure from the Object and Procedure list boxes at the top of the Code window.	

Microsoft Visual Basic 5.0 **Task Reference**

TASK	PAGE #	RECOMMENDED METHOD	NOTES
Code, printing	VB 2.44	Click File then click Print. Click Code. Use the Range section in the dialog box to print the current module or the Project.	
Collection, creating from the Collection class	VB 11.7	Use the Dim, Public, or Private statement with the New option to create a new Collection object. You can store multiple different objects in the collection. The Count property contains a long integer representing the number of objects in the collection. Use the Add and Remove methods to add and delete objects from a collection.	Note the Collection object is one-based, and supports both a numeric index and a string key. You cannot create a collection of user-defined types.
Collection, programming the Controls collection	VB 8.35	A Controls collection exists for each form, and contains a reference to each control on the form, including invisible controls. Use a numeric index or string key (the same as a control's Name property), to reference a specific control. Use a For Each loop to iterate through all the controls in the collection.	*object.***Controls**(*index*)
Collection, referencing an object in	VB 7.4	Use the collection name, followed by either the numeric index or string key if supported by the collection.	The Item property of most collections is the default property and need not be referenced explicitly.
ComboBox control, creating and programming	VB 6.3	Set the Style property to control the appearance of the object. Set the List property at design time, or call the AddItem method at run time to fill the list with the desired items.	*object.***AddItem** *"Text"*
CommandButton control, creating and programming	VB 2.12	Set the Caption property to display text on the button. Write statements for the Click event procedure that are executed when the button is clicked at run time.	See Reference Window, "Creating a Command Button Object."
Comments, creating	VB 2.22	Begin a comment with the apostrophe character ('). All characters on a line after the apostrophe are ignored by Visual Basic.	
CommonDialog control, programming the OpenFile dialog box	VB 8.33	Set the DialogTitle property to the desired window title. Set the FileName and InitDir properties to the default filename and initial folder displayed. Set the Filter property to select files with a particular extension. Set the CancelError property to generate a run-time error if the user clicks the Cancel button. After setting the properties, call the ShowOpen method to display the dialog box.	*object.***Filter** [= *description1\filter1 \description2 \filter2...*] See Reference Window, "Creating an Open CommonDialog Control."

Microsoft Visual Basic 5.0 Task Reference

TASK	PAGE #	RECOMMENDED METHOD	NOTES
CommonDialog control, creating and programming	VB 8.30	Use the Property Pages dialog box to set the design-time properties. Note there is a Property Page for each dialog box. Call a method at run time to display the desired dialog box.	Create only one instance of the CommonDialog control to reduce memory usage. Note the CommonDialog control is an ActiveX control.
Constants, intrinsic	VB 3.17	Use intrinsic constants to improve program readability. Use Help and the Object Browser to find out the constant names that pertain to specific intrinsic functions and object properties.	
Constants, user-defined	VB 3.21	Create user-defined constants to store information that will not change at run time.	[**Public|Private**] **Const** *constantname* [**As** *type*] = *expression*
Control array, creating	VB 3.11	Activate a control instance. Copy and Paste the object. Respond Yes to the Create a control array dialog box. Position the object on the form. Use the Index argument for the event procedure to reference the specific object in a control array.	See Reference Window, "Creating a Control Array of Objects."
Control Box, modifying	VB 10.6	Set the ControlBox, MinButton, and MaxButton properties to True or False to cause a control box and its buttons to appear or not. Note that if the BorderStyle property is set to none, a control box will not appear.	Use the WindowState property to determine the current state of a window.
Controls, binding to a Data control	VB 4.18	Set the DataSource property to an existing Data control, then set the DataField property to a field in the table.	Make sure to create the Data control and set its properties before binding other controls like text boxes.
Controls, deleting	VB 1.35	Select the object(s) and press the Delete key.	You can use the Edit Undo menu command to undo accidental deletions.
Controls, determining the type of	VB 8.36	Use the TypeOf keyword in an If statement. The type of each control is the same as the control's class name.	**If TypeOf** *objectname* **Is** *objecttype* **Then** [*statements*] **End If**
Controls, moving	VB 1.33	Select the object(s) to move. With the cursor in one of the selected objects, drag the objects to their new position.	
Controls, resizing	VB 1.34	Activate the object to move. Drag one of the sizing handles to resize.	
Controls, selecting a group of	VB 3.14	Hold down the Shift key and click the controls to select them, or use the mouse and draw a rectangle around the objects you want to select.	Selected controls appear with grayed handles

Microsoft Visual Basic 5.0 **Task Reference**

TASK	PAGE #	RECOMMENDED METHOD	NOTES
Counter, using	VB 5.33	Declare a variable to be used as a counter and set the initial value to zero (0). Add one (1) to the counter each time through a Do loop. A For loop will increment a counter automatically.	
CrystalReports control, creating and programming	VB 9.42	Set the ReportFileName property to the report's filename already created with Crystal Reports. Set the Destination property to control where the report will be printed. Set the Action property to one (1) to print the report.	Note that the CrystalReport control is an ActiveX control.
Data control, creating and programming	VB 4.13	Set the DatabaseName property to database file, then set the RecordSource property to the name of the Table or Query you want to use. The database and table already must exist.	See Reference Window, "Using a Data Control to Connect to an Existing Database."
Data types, choosing	VB 2.30	Create an Integer or long variable for numbers without a decimal point. Use a Single variable for numbers with a decimal point. Use the Currency data type when performing mathematical operations on data representing dollars and cents. Use Double only for very large or very small numbers. Character strings should have the String data type.	
Database, opening programmatically	VB 7.6	Call the OpenDatabase method with the database name as an argument. The method applies to the Workspace object and returns a Database object.	**Set** *database* = *workspace.* **OpenDatabase** (*dbname, options, read-only, connect*)
DBCombo and DBList controls, creating and programming	VB 8.6	Set the RowSource to the name of an existing Data control. Set the ListField property to the fields that will be displayed in the DBList or DBCombo control. Use the BoundColumn and BoundText properties to return values from another column in the table.	See Reference Window, "Using a DBList or DBCombo Object to Display Information from a Database." Note the DBCombo and DBList controls are ActiveX controls.
DBGrid control, adding records to	VB 8.22	Set the AllowAddNew property at run time or design time to allow the adding of records. Respond to the BeforeInsert, BeforeUpdate, AfterUpdate, and AfterInsert events as needed to perform data validation and error checking.	Note the DBGrid control is an ActiveX control.
DBGrid control, creating	VB 8.9	Set the DataSource property to the name of an existing Data control.	
DBGrid control, deleting records from	VB 8.28	Set the AllowDelete property to allow record deletion. Respond to the BeforeDelete and AfterDelete events as necessary to request user confirmation and handle errors.	

Microsoft Visual Basic 5.0 **Task Reference**

TASK	PAGE #	RECOMMENDED METHOD	NOTES
DBGrid control, referencing a cell	VB 8.11	The Row and Column properties can be read and written to refer to the active cell.	
DBGrid control, updating records	VB 8.22	Set the AllowUpdate property to allow record updates.	
Debugging, creating watch expressions	VB A.10	Click Debug then click Add Watch to open the Add Watch dialog box. Enter the expression and the context. Depending on the action you want to take when something happens to the expression, set the Watch Type.	Use watch expressions sparingly in large or long running programs. They can slow down your program significantly.
Debugging, examining each statement	VB A.10	Click the Step Into button ⬚. The Code window will display each statement with a different color just before it is executed.	
Debugging, looking at variables in break mode	VB A.9	Activate the Immediate window. Type a Print statement followed by the variable or object property you want to look at. You also can move the cursor over a variable or property to display a ToolTip containing the value of a variable or property.	Set watch expressions for variables you look at frequently.
Debugging, setting breakpoints	VB A.7	Activate the Code window and locate the statement where you want to set a breakpoint. Click the Toggle Breakpoint button ⬚, or click the left margin of the Code window. The line will appear in a different color.	To remove the breakpoint, click the line in the Code window and click the Toggle Breakpoint button ⬚ again.
Debugging, stepping over procedures	VB A.6	Click the Step Over button ⬚. If the statement is a procedure call, the entire procedure and any procedures it calls will execute, then Visual Basic will return to break mode.	Visual Basic will enter break mode if it reaches a breakpoint or watchpoint in the code.

Decision making, using a Select Case statement	VB 3.26	Use Select Case statements with control arrays to determine which object is active and execute the correct statements. When a Select Case statement is used, the *testexpression* is evaluated only once.	**Select Case** *testexpression*
			  Case *expressionlist1*
			      block1-statements
			  Case *expressionlist2*
			      block2-statements
			  Case *expressionlist3*
			      block3-statements
			  [**Case Else**
			      [*else-block-*
			          statements]]
			End Select

Decision making, using an If statement	VB 3.15	Write an If statement to execute one set of statements when one set of circumstances is True, and other statements when another set of circumstances is True. Use the ElseIf statement when the decision has three or more options.	**If** *condition1* **Then**
			    statement-block1
			ElseIf *condition2* **Then**
			    statement-block2
			ElseIf *condition-n* **Then**
			    statement-block-n
			[**Else**
			    [*statements*]]
			End If

Microsoft Visual Basic 5.0 **Task Reference**

TASK	PAGE #	RECOMMENDED METHOD	NOTES
Drag-and-drop events, writing code for	VB 12.4	The DragDrop event occurs to the destination object once when the source object is dragged onto the destination object. The DragOver event occurs repeatedly as the source object is dragged over the destination object.	**Private Sub Form_DragDrop** (*source* **As Control**, *x* **As Single**, *y* **As Single**) **End Sub Private Sub Form_DragOver** (*source* **As Control**, *x* **As Single**, *y* **As Single**, *state* **As Integer**) **End Sub**
Drag-and-drop events, using automatic	VB 12.10	Set the DragMode property of a control to Automatic. Clicking the object will start a drag-and-drop operation rather than generating a Click event.	
Error handler, creating an	VB 4.37	Prevent run-time errors from causing your program to abort by creating error handlers in an event or general procedure. You can define one error handler per procedure.	**On Error GoTo** *ErrorHandler* *statements* **Exit Sub** *ErrorHandler:* *statements* [**Resume Next**] **End Sub**
Errors, generating run-time	VB 11.22	Use the number argument to assign a numeric value to the error. Specify a *description* to assign a meaningful error message to the error. Use the *source* argument to assign a name to the application that generated the error.	**Err.Raise** *number*, *source*, *description*, *helpfile*, *helpcontext*
Errors, locating run-time	VB A.3	Click OK or Debug in the RunTime dialog box when displayed. Pay careful attention to the description of the error. Enter Print statements in the Debug window to look at the object and variables involved and correct the statements as necessary. Click the Start button ▶ to continue or end and run the program again.	If necessary, set watch expressions and search through program statements to locate the cause of the error.
Executable file, creating	VB 12.33	Use the Compile tab on the Project Properties dialog box to configure how a program will be compiled. Then click File then Make EXE to create the executable file.	
Executable file, working with the App object	VB 12.34	Set the VersionNumber, Application, and Version Information properties to embed information about your program into the executable file. This information can be accessed by the App object.	

Microsoft Visual Basic 5.0 **Task Reference**

TASK	PAGE #	RECOMMENDED METHOD	NOTES
Fonts, using printer and screen	VB 8.37	Use the FontCount property of each object to determine the number of fonts on the system. Use the Fonts property with an index to obtain the name of a specific font.	Note the Fonts property is not a collection. It is a a list that is referenced with an index like an array is referenced with a subscript. The first font in the list is font (0).
Form image, printing	VB 3.39	Call the PrintForm method on a form object.	*form*.**PrintForm**
Form, activating	VB 5.11	Call the Show method of the form object to display a form and give it focus. Use the vbModal constant to create a modal form.	*form*.**Show** [**vbModal**] No other form in the application can receive focus until a modal form is hidden or unloaded.
Form, adding	VB 5.2	Click Project then Add Form to insert a new or existing form into the project. Set the Name and Caption properties as needed.	
Form, creating properties	VB 10.17	Create a Public variable in a Form module to create a form property. Note you cannot create Public variables of a user-defined type.	
Form, repainting	VB 5.10	Use the Refresh method on a form or control to force the object to be redrawn.	*object*.**Refresh**
Form, tags	VB 10.15	Use the Tag property to store an identification string into a form or control. The string is ignored by Visual Basic.	*object*.**Tag** = [*expression*]
Form, unloading	VB 5.11	Use the Unload statement followed by the object to unload. Any properties set at run time for the object are lost when the object is reloaded.	**Unload** *FormName*
Format function, using	VB 2.37	Use the Fixed format to display data with two decimal places. Use the Currency format to display with a leading dollar sign.	**Format**(*expression*[, *format*])
Frame control, creating	VB 3.9	Set the Caption property to display a prompt in the frame. Draw option buttons in the frame so they will work as an option group.	See Reference Window, "Adding a Frame Control to a Form."
HScrollBar control, creating	VB 3.5	Set the Max, Min, LargeChange, and SmallChange properties to define how the object will behave at run time. Use the Change event to check the Value property at run time.	See Reference Window, "Adding a Scroll Bar Control to a Form."
Image control, using	VB 1.37	Set the Stretch property to True to size the picture to the size of the object. Set the Picture property to the filename containing the picture. The image can respond to a Click event.	See Reference Window, "Adding an Image Control to a Form."

Microsoft Visual Basic 5.0 **Task Reference**

TASK	PAGE #	RECOMMENDED METHOD	NOTES
ImageList control, creating and programming	VB 9.4	The ImageList control stores a collection of bitmap and/or icon images in the ListImages property. Each bitmap/icon is stored as a ListImage object in the ListImages collection. Use the Property Pages dialog box to add the images to the collection. Set the Index and Key properties so you can reference each object in the collection.	See Reference Window, "Creating an ImageList Object and Adding Images." Note the ImageList control is an ActiveX control.
InputBox function, using	VB 4.31	Set the prompt to display a *prompt* in the box, and set the *title* to display information in the title bar. Set the *default* to define which is the default button. If the user presses the Cancel button in the input box, then a null string is returned.	**InputBox**(*prompt*[, *title*] [, *default*])
Label control, creating	VB 1.31	Set the Caption property to display text on the label. Set other properties to justify and change the appearance of the text.	See Reference Window, "Adding a Label Control to a Form."
Line control, creating	VB 2.19	Set the BorderWidth property to change the thickness of the line or the ForeColor property to change the color.	See Reference Window, "Creating a Line Object."
ListBox control, filling with data	VB 6.11	Set the List property at design time, or call the AddItem method at run time, to fill the list with the items you want.	
ListBox control, referencing items	VB 6.15	Use the List property with an index as an argument to reference the contents of an item in the list. Use the ListCount property to determine the number of items in a list, and the ListIndex property to identify the active item.	The ListIndex property begins at zero (0) for the first item in the list. If there is no active item this property is set to minus one (–1).
ListBox, clearing the contents of	VB 6.24	Use the Clear method on a ListBox object to remove all the items in the object.	The ListIndex property is set to minus one (–1) after this method is called because there is no active item.
ListBox, removing a single item from	VB 6.26	Use the RemoveItem method on a ListBox object to remove an item. The method takes one argument—an index representing the item to remove.	*object*.**RemoveItem** *index*
Looping, fixed number of times	VB 6.19	The *counter* will be initialized to *start*. If it is less than or equal to *end*, the statements in the loop will execute, otherwise the statement after Next will be executed. Each time through the loop, *counter* is incremented by *increment*.	**For** *counter* = *start* **To** *end* [**Step** *increment*] [*statement-block*] [**Exit For**] [*statement-block*] **Next** [*counter*]

Microsoft Visual Basic 5.0 **Task Reference**

TASK	PAGE #	RECOMMENDED METHOD	NOTES
Looping, objects in a collection	VB 7.10	The *element* will be initialized to the first object in *group*. Each time through the loop, *element* will reference the next object.	**For Each** *element* **In** *group* [*statements*] [**Exit For**] [statements] **Next** [*element*] See Reference Window, "Iterating through the Object in a Collection with a For Each Loop.
Looping, until a condition is True	VB 5.26	Create a Do While loop to execute statements while a condition is False or a Do Until loop until a condition is True.	**Do** [[**While|Until**] *condition*] *Statements* **Loop**
MaskEdBox control, creating	VB 9.12	Use the MaskEdBox control like a text box to format input and output. Set the Mask property to define an input mask and the Format property to the output mask.	
MDI program, arranging child forms	VB 10.29	Call the Arrange method on an MDI parent form to arrange the child forms or the icons.	
MDI program, creating	VB 10.2	Add an MDI parent form to the project. Set the MDI child property of other forms as necessary.	Note that a program can have only one MDI parent form, and MDI child forms cannot be displayed modally. See Reference Window, "Creating an MDI Program."
MDI program, unloading	VB 10.41	The QueryUnload event occurs for the MDI parent form. Then the same event occurs for each open MDI child form. If any events are cancelled, the corresponding Unload event also will be cancelled.	
Menu item, creating a shortcut key for	VB 4.8	For a menu item, select the desired shortcut key from the Menu Editor.	You cannot define a shortcut key for a menu title.
Menu, creating	VB 4.5	Open the Menu Editor for a form. Set the Name and Caption properties. The caption is displayed on the menu. The name is used to reference the Menu Item event procedure. Indent the menu to the desired level.	See Reference Window, "Creating a Menu System."
Menu, creating an access key for	VB 4.4	Place an & character before the character to be used as an access key.	Be careful not to use the same access key on a menu or menu title.

Microsoft Visual Basic 5.0 **Task Reference**

TASK	PAGE #	RECOMMENDED METHOD	NOTES
MsgBox function, using	VB 3.42	Set the *prompt* to display a prompt in the box, the *title* to display information in the title bar, and the *buttons* to specify the number and caption of the buttons in the message box. The MsgBox function returns a value indicating which button was clicked. This value can be represented by intrinsic constants. The value can be stored in a *variable*.	*Variable* = **MsgBox**(*prompt*[, *buttons*][, *title*])
Object properties, printing	VB 2.44	Click File then click Print. Click Form As Text. The nondefault properties of an object are printed.	
Object references, creating explicitly	VB 10.11	Use the New keyword with a Dim, Public, Private, or Static statement to create an object instance. Omit the New keyword to create an object variable to reference an existing object.	{**Dim**|**Public**|**Private** |**Static**} *varname* [([*subscripts*])] [**As** [**New**] *type*]
Object, defining startup	VB 5.7	Click Project then click Properties. Click the General tab then select the desired startup object from the list box.	
Objects, referencing	VB 10.8	Use the Set statement to cause an object variable to reference an existing object. Use the New keyword to create a new instance. Note that setting an object variable to Nothing destroys the reference to the object.	**Set** *objectvar* = {[**New**] *objectexpression* |**Nothing**} See Reference Window, "Creating an Object Variable Explicitly."
OLE Automation, creating an instance of another application	VB 12.27	The *objectname* is the name of an object variable to store a reference to the application. Use the *applicationname* to identify the class name of the application. Once the application is running and a reference is stored, you can call the methods and set properties of the object.	**Set** *objectname* = **CreateObject** ("*applicationtype. objecttype*")
OLE object, creating embedded at design time	VB 12.22	Create an instance of the OLE Container control. When the Insert Object dialog box appears, click Create New. Using the scroll bars, select the type of object you want to embed.	
OLE object, creating embedded at run time	VB 12.25	Call the CreateEmbed method on an OLE Container control. The *class* argument is the name of the class from which to create the object.	*object*.**CreateEmbed** *sourcedoc*[, *class*]
OLE object, creating linked at design time	VB 12.20	Create an instance of the OLE Container control. When the Insert Object dialog box displays, click Create From File then select a filename. Click the Link check box.	See Reference Window, "Creating a Linked Object at Design Time."
OLE object, creating linked at run time	VB 12.25	Call the CreateEmbed method on an OLE Container control. The *sourcedoc* argument is the name of an existing file to link.	*object*.**CreateLink** *sourcedoc*[, *source item*]

Microsoft Visual Basic 5.0 **Task Reference**

TASK	PAGE #	RECOMMENDED METHOD	NOTES
OptionButton control, creating	VB 3.10	Set the Caption property to display a prompt on the option button. Draw buttons inside a Frame so they will work as an option group.	See Reference Window, "Adding an Option Button Control to a Frame."
Program, ending	VB 1.21	Click the End button ■.	The program will be in design mode after clicking the button.
Program, entering break mode	VB 1.21	Click the Break button ❚❚ on the toolbar.	Program will be in break mode. You can type statements in the Immediate window.
Program, starting	VB 1.21	Click the Start button ▶.	Program will be in run mode after the button is clicked.
Project, adding an ActiveX control to	VB 8.4	Click Project then click Components on the menu bar. Select the controls or group of controls you want to add. The controls will display in the toolbox.	See Reference Window, "Making ActiveX Controls Available to a Project."
Project, adding an Object Library to	VB 7.3	Click Project then click References. Select the library to add then click OK.	
Project, opening	VB 2.5	Click the Open Project button 🖰 and select the name of the project in the dialog box.	Project filenames have the extension ".vbp". See Reference Window, "Opening an Existing Project."
Project, saving	VB 1.17	Click the Save Project button 🖫 on the toolbar. If you have not saved the project before, the Save File As dialog box will prompt you for the form(s) names and the Save Project dialog box will prompt you for the project name.	The project file contains the name of the form and other modules in your program.
Properties window, opening	VB 1.21	Click the Properties Window button 🖆.	
Properties, selecting the active object	VB 1.26	Click the object to activate it. Click the right mouse button, then click Properties.	
Recordset, adding records	VB 4.26	Call the AddNew method on an existing Recordset object at run time, change the contents of each field, then call the Update method.	*object*.**AddNew** You cannot call the AddNew method on a query joining multiple tables.
Recordset, deleting records from	VB 4.29	Call the Delete method on an existing Recordset object at run time. After deleting, call the MoveNext method of the recordset so the user will not see the record on the screen.	*object*.**Delete** You cannot call the Delete method on a query joining multiple tables.

Microsoft Visual Basic 5.0 **Task Reference**

TASK	PAGE #	RECOMMENDED METHOD	NOTES
Recordset, finding records in	VB 4.31	Call the FindFirst method on an existing Recordset object using the necessary criteria to find the first record matching the criteria. Call the FindNext method to locate subsequent matches. Use the NoMatch property to determine if a record was found.	*object*.**FindFirst** *criteria* *object*.**FindNext** *criteria* *object*.**NoMatch**
Recordset, referencing fields in	VB 5.29	Use the name of an existing Recordset object followed by an ! character followed by the field name. If the field contains spaces, put the field name in brackets ([ ]).	*Recordset-name*! *field-name*
Recordset, updating records	VB 4.27	Call the Update method on an existing recordset, after calling the AddNew or Edit method to save the contents of the edit buffer to the database table.	*object*.**Update** You cannot call the Update method on a query joining multiple tables.
Reports, printing	VB 5.23	Use the Printer object to send information to the printer. The Print method will write output. The EndDoc method will send any output in the print buffer to the printer. Use the Tab and Spc arguments of the Print method to format the report. Use the NewPage method to advance to the next page. Use the Page property to determine the current page.	**Printer.Page** **Printer.Print** **Printer.NewPage** **Printer.EndDoc**
RichTextBox control, creating	VB 9.15	Use the RichTextBox control like a text box to display information in Rich Text Format. RTF formatted data can accept different fonts and font attributes. Use the LoadFile and SaveFile methods to read and write RTF files to and from the RichTextBox control.	*object*.**LoadFile|SaveFile** *pathname*, *filetype*
RichTextBox control, formatting the contents of	VB 9.18	Read the SelBold, SelItalic, SelStrikethru, and SelUnderline properties to determine if the selected text is of the specified format. If Null, then there is a mix of characters having the format. If True, all the characters have the selected format. If no characters have the selected format, the value is False. Set these properties to change the format of the selected text.	When the selected text is changed, the SelChange event occurs.
RichTextBox control, printing the contents of	VB 9.17	Call the SelPrint method to print the selected text or, if no text is selected, the contents of the object. Use the hDC property of the Printer object as the device contents.	*object*.**SelPrint**(*hDC*)

Microsoft Visual Basic 5.0 **Task Reference**

TASK	PAGE #	RECOMMENDED METHOD	NOTES
Shape control, creating	VB 2.17	Set the BorderWidth property to change the thickness of the line around the shape. Set the BackColor and BackStyle properties to control the background of the Shape. Set the FillStyle and FillColor properties to control the foreground of the Shape.	See Reference Window, "Adding a Shape Object to a Form."
SQL, deleting rows	VB 7.26	Set the *tableexpression* to the name of the table from which to delete records. Set the *criteria* to an expression indicating which records to delete.	**DELETE** * **FROM** *tableexpression* **WHERE** *criteria* See Reference Window, "Creating a DELETE Statement."
SQL, inserting rows	VB 7.17	Set the *target* to indicate the name of the destination table. Set *field* to the name of the field. Each field corresponds to a *value*. Enclose date values in pound signs (#), and text fields in quotation marks ("").	**INSERT INTO** *target* [(*field1* [, *field2*[, ...]])] **VALUES** (*value1* [, *value2*[, ...]]) See Reference Window, "Creating an INSERT Statement."
SQL, selecting rows	VB 7.28	Select one or more fields from *table*. Restrict the number of rows by specifying a WHERE clause. Modify the order in which records are returned with an ORDER BY clause.	**SELECT** [*table.*]*field1* [**AS** *alias1*] [, [*table.*] *field2*[**AS** *alias2*] [, ...]] **FROM** *tableexpression* [**WHERE**...] [**ORDER BY**] *field1* [**ASC|DESC**][, *field2* [**ASC|DESC**][, ...]]
SQL, updating rows	VB 7.21	Set the *tablename* to the name of the table to be updated. Set the *fieldname* to the *newvalue* for each field to be updated. *Fieldname* must exist in *tablename*. *Newvalue* can be a literal, or expression.	**UPDATE** *tablename* **SET** *fieldname* = *newvalue* [,*fieldname* = *newvalue*] ... See Reference Window, "Creating an UPDATE Statement."
Standard module, adding	VB 5.4	Click Project then Add Module on the menu bar. The Code window will be opened and set to the new module.	
String, right justifying a fixed length	VB 5.30	Use the RSet statement to right justify *string* and store the information in the fixed-length string *stringvar*.	**RSet** *stringvar = string*
Tab order, setting	VB 2.16	Change the TabIndex property of objects that receive focus. The first object to receive focus has a TabIndex of zero (0), and the second a TabIndex of one (1).	

Microsoft Visual Basic 5.0 **Task Reference**

TASK	PAGE #	RECOMMENDED METHOD	NOTES
Text file, closing	VB 6.9	Use the Close statement followed by the filenumber(s) to close. Filenumbers should be separated by commas. If you do not specify a filenumber, all open files will be closed.	**Close** [*filenumberlist*]
Text file, opening	VB 6.7	Use the Open statement followed by the name of the file. Add the For Input, For Output, or For Append clause depending on whether you are reading or writing the file. Add an As clause followed by an unassigned filenumber.	**Open** *pathname* **For {Input|Output |Append} As** #*filenumber* See Reference Window, "Opening a Text File."
Text file, reading	VB 6.8	Use the Input statement followed by the file-number of a file opened with the Open statement. Append variable names separated by commas that correspond to the fields in the input file.	**Input** #*filenumber*, *variablelist* See Reference Window, "Reading a Text File."
Text file, writing	VB 6.35	Use the Write statement followed by the filenumber of a file opened with the Open statement. Append variable names separated by commas as necessary.	**Write** #*filenumber*, *variablelist* See Reference Window, "Writing a Text File."
TextBox control, creating	VB 2.10	Set the Text property to display text in the text box. Set other properties to justify and change the appearance of the text.	See Reference Window, "Creating a TextBox object."
TextBox control, specifying multiple lines in	VB 4.21	Set the MultiLine property to True. Set the MaxLength property to the maximum number of characters that will be stored in the object. Set the ScrollBars property to display vertical and/or horizontal scroll bars in the object.	The MultiLine property must be set to True to display scroll bars.
Toolbar control, designing	VB 9.8	Create an ImageList control to hold the different images used by the toolbar. For each button on the toolbar, set the Image to the key or index of the button in the ImageList control. Set the Align, Appearance, and BorderStyle properties to change the appearance of the toolbar. Set the Style property of each button to change its behavior.	See Reference Window, "Creating a Toolbar." Note the toolbar is an ActiveX control.
Types, creating enumerated	VB 10.19	The *name* specifies the name of the enumerated type. After the enumerated type is declared, you can declare variables of that type. Each enumerated type can contain one or more *membernames*. By default, the value of the first membername is zero (0), the second one (1), and so on, unless a *constantexpression* is specified.	**[Public|Private] Enum** *name* *membername* [= *constant-expression*] [*membername* [= *constant-expression*]] . . . **End Enum**

TASK	PAGE #	RECOMMENDED METHOD	NOTES

Types, creating user-defined	VB 10.32	The *name* specifies the name of the user-defined type. After the user-defined type is declared, you can declare variables of that type. Each user-defined type can contain one or more *elementnames*. Each elementname can be an intrinsic, object, or user-defined type. Note that user-defined types can be nested.	**[Public|Private] Type** *varname*
			 elementname
			 [([subscripts])]
			   As *Type*
			 [*elementname*
			 [([subscripts])]
			   As *Type*]
			 …
			 End Type

Validating input	VB 4.34	Use the classification functions IsDate and IsNumeric to verify input is correct. When impossible to classify, write an error handler to prevent run-time errors.	**IsDate**(*string*) **IsNumeric**(*string*)
Variables, declaring local	VB 2.32	Write a Dim statement in a general or event procedure and specify the data or object type. Local variables are declared in a procedure. Module-level variables are declared in the general declarations section of a module.	**Dim** [*Varname* [**As** *Type*]] See Figure 2-26 on page VB 2.30 for the valid data types.
Variables, declaring module level	VB 2.31	In the general declarations section declare a variable using the Private statement. Variables will be visible anywhere in the Form or standard module in which they are declared.	**Private** [*Varname* [**As** *Type*]]
VScrollBar control, using	VB 3.5	Set the Max, Min, LargeChange, and SmallChange properties to define how the object will behave at run time. Use the Change event to check the Value property at run time.	See Reference Window, "Adding a Scroll Bar Control to a Form."
With statements, using	VB 8.39	Use a With statement to refer to an object without specifying the name of the object. The With statement also can be used with user-defined types.	**With** *object* [*statements*] **End With**

What's on the **Student Developer's Kit** CD-ROM?

Discover more about Visual Basic's capabilities with the New Perspectives *Student Developer's Kit* CD-ROM. Part of Visual Basic's tremendous success as a programming language can be attributed to the many controls supplied by third-party vendors that can be used in Visual Basic programs. These controls perform tasks such as sending faxes, printing bar codes, and performing statistical analysis. The *Student Developer's Kit* CD-ROM gives you the opportunity to explore several of these third-party controls. Look in the Controls folder on the CD-ROM for folders containing controls from the following vendors.

Vendor	Folder Name	Control Description
AddSoft	AddSoft	Gantt chart and project scheduler
BeCubed Software	BeCubed	OLE tools
Dart Communications	Dart	Internet tools
Evergreen Software Tools, Inc.	Visible	Database support tools
Great Lakes Business Solutions	glbs	Installation and software patch software
Larcom and Young	Lyoung	Resize control that will resize forms to fit any monitor
Pegasus Imaging	Pegasus	Graphical and imaging controls
ProtoView Development Corp.	ProtoView	Enhanced bound data controls and development tools
Progress Software	Crescent	Internet and communications controls
Sheridan	Sheridan	Data widgets, calendar widgets, and various enhanced 3D controls

Microsoft Visual Basic Control Creation Edition The *Student Developer's Kit* CD-ROM also contains the Visual Basic Control Creation Edition, a complete standalone edition of Visual Basic that allows you to create ActiveX controls that can be used by other programs and on the Internet. The Visual Basic Control Creation Edition is in the VBCCE folder on the CD-ROM.

Developer's Reference A complete reference chart of the standard Visual Basic naming conventions for objects and controls used in this book is in the Naming Conventions folder on the CD-ROM. Templates for the NEADT charts used for design and documentation are included in the NEADT folder. All of these files can be viewed and printed from WordPad.

Student Disk files All of the Student Disk files needed to complete the tutorials in this book are in the Student files folder on the CD-ROM.

New Perspectives Course Lab The Visual Programming Course Lab is an interactive tutorial designed to get new programmers started with visual programming. The Course Lab is required for the Lab Assignment at the end of Tutorial 1. Complete installation instructions are included in the Course Lab folder on the CD-ROM.

How to Use the CD-ROM Refer to the Readme file on the CD-ROM for a complete listing of the contents of each folder on the CD-ROM. Each third-party control and the Visual Programming Course Lab has its own Readme file with installation instructions. You can view the Readme files using WordPad. To use the Student Disk files on the CD-ROM with the tutorials in this book, refer to the "Read This Before You Begin" pages preceding Tutorials 1 and 7.